The Royal Air Force

An Encyclopedia of the Inter-war Years

Volume I

The Royal Air Force

An Encyclopedia of the Inter-war Years

Volume I

The Trenchard Years
1918 to 1929

Wing Commander Ian M. Philpott (RAF Retd)

First published in
Great Britain in 2005
By Pen and Sword Aviation
An imprint of
Pen and Sword Books Ltd
47 Church Street
Barnsley
South Yorkshire
S70 2AS

ISBN 1 84415 154 9

Typeset by Mac Style Ltd, Scarborough
Printed and bound by CPI Bath

Pen and Sword Books Ltd incorporates the imprints of Pen and Sword Aviation, Pen
and Sword Maritime, Pen and Sword Military, Wharncliffe Local History, Pen and Sword
Select, Pen and Sword Military Classics and Leo Cooper.

For a complete list of Pen and Sword titles please contact
Pen and Sword Books Limited
47 Church Street, Barnsley, South Yorkshire, S70 2AS, England
E-mail: enquiries@pen-and-sword.co.uk
Website: www.pen-and-sword.co.uk

Major-General Sir David Henderson, as Director-General of Military Aviation, wrote the Charter for the RFC in 1912, and in 1917 prompted Smuts to take it over for the first constitution of the RAF.

Major-General Hugh Trenchard, the future Chief of the Air Staff of the Royal Air Force, to be for ever remembered as 'the Father of the RAF'.

Contents

Author's Foreword

My own service experience is rooted in units that were in action during the inter-war years. I served for twenty years in the RAF Regiment, a ground mobile force formed in 1942 to protect RAF airfields and installations against attack from ground forces (field squadrons) and low-level air attack (light anti-aircraft squadrons). My longest spell of service with one RAF Regiment squadron was on No. 2 (Field) Squadron.

No. 2 (Field) Squadron predated 1942 by twenty years. In fact my squadron was and still is the direct descendant of No. 2 Armoured Car Company, Royal Air Force. Armoured car companies served in Mesopotamia (Iraq) and later in Transjordan and Palestine. They operated in support of flying squadrons that had replaced the large Army formations which had previously maintained order threatened by dissident tribesmen. This was known as 'Air Control', and features in the chapters of this book. Perhaps the proudest moment of my service career came in November 1959, when I was privileged to receive the Battle Standard on behalf of N.2 (Field) Squadron on a presentation parade at RAF Ta Kali, Malta. The presenting officer was Air Chief Marshal Sir Hubert Patch, who had been a young officer in No. 2 Armoured Car Company in Transjordan during 1928 (see p. (xvi)).

I have always found the inter-war years fascinating, from a political, a military and a historical point of view. These years witnessed the first real attempt to bring potential and actual conflict before a world forum, the League of Nations. Yet sadly the one country that needed to be there was not. The Senate of the United States of America refused to ratify the Covenant of the League, and the country slipped back into isolationism, not formally to re-emerge until the Japanese attack on Pearl Harbor in December 1941. This meant that the victorious European Allied Powers, notably Britain and France, had to extort reparations for death and war damage from the defeated Central Powers, which included Germany and Austria-Hungary. At first the faltering steps of the League met with some success, as long as conflicts or disputes did not affect the national interest of the major powers. But once Italy and Germany became dictatorships and Japan became an expansionist country in the Far East, the League failed and the continent of Europe became embroiled in a world war for the second time in the half century. The reasons for this I go into in Part I of Volume II. The unfolding international political situation forms a back-drop to the development of British air power between the wars.

And so I decided to put together under one cover a comprehensive account of all aspects of the progress of British air power between the wars. Times have moved on from the inter-war years, and it was always my intention to sit back and look at them objectively. While researching this book I learned of accounts that are sycophantic, but there are also those works, often written by non-service academics, which are over-critical of the RAF. I make no secret of my intense pride in having served in the RAF, but on the other hand a university education taught me to look at evidence and weigh it carefully when it conflicts. I hope very much that I have bridged the gap between empathy with the RAF and an objective analysis of the events of the time. While serving in Cyprus in the mid-1960s I wrote to the *RAF News* during Battle of Britain Week and naively suggested that the existence of the Royal Navy in home waters played a significant part in defeating Hitler's plans for invasion. It should come as no surprise that I received outright condemnation from retired senior RAF officers in the next issue for ever having suggested it. This time round I hope that my readers will be more reflective.

So extensive are the areas covered that I decided that two volumes would be necessary. Volume I takes the reader from 1919 to 1929, and Volume II from 1930 to 1939. Some of the detail in the Appendices covers the entire inter-war period, to enable the reader to look forward or backwards as the case may be. The treatment varies, and the reader will find that in some parts there is a purely historically descriptive narrative of events. But when the occasion demands, particularly in telling the story of the RAF in the Middle East and on the North-West Frontier of India, or social life in the RAF, then the treatment is sometimes anecdotal. And there is argument, too, in the chapters dealing with air control, command at Air Ministry/Air Staff level and the interface between the senior airmen and their political masters. There are lots of maps, pictures and tables, with 115 pages of aircraft information alone.

There is a detailed Index at the rear, but I don't want my readers to have to look things up at the back of the book unless it is absolutely necessary. Every chapter begins with a description of the chapter content, and paragraphs are headed in bold type to make things easy to find. Another departure from the normal layout of books of this kind is that I have not used footnotes. All references to other publications are made in the text. I have used a great deal of source material found both in the National Archives and at the RAF Museum, but beyond publishing a list of books or documents that are recommended reading in the Bibliography, it was always my firm intention from the outset that this book would be a comprehensive account with the utmost ease of reference.

And what will you find? The list, which is not exhaustive, covers the postwar run-down of the RAF in Volume I to its expansion in the late 1930s in Volume II, the growth of the aircraft industry and civil aviation, which go hand-in-hand with the development of military aircraft, airships, testing of aircraft prototypes, aircraft engine development, high-speed and high-altitude flight, long-distance flight, officer, aircrew and technical training, promotions, careers, postings, operations and training. I could go on. If I have succeeded – and my readers will be the judge of that – this compendium will be a handy work of reference, which, if it doesn't provide all the answers, will point the way for the student of air power.

I hope you derive as much interest and pleasure from reading this work as I have had in writing it.

Wing Commander I.M. Philpott MSocSc, BSc(Econ.), MCMI, RAF Retd

Acknowledgements

To John James and publishers Macdonald and Co. for *The Paladins*, a social history of the RAF up to the outbreak of the Second World War II, which was the inspiration for undertaking the compilation of this encyclopaedia.

To the staff of the National Archives, Kew, for their help in providing source material covering a range of issues related to the development of British airpower in the inter-war years.

To Mr Peter Elliott and his research staff at the RAF Museum, Hendon, for their patient delving into matters relating to the RAF during the period 1918 to 1939.

To Group Captain Larkin at RAF Halton who provided expert knowledge of the Boy Apprentice scheme put into place by Air Marshal Trenchard in the early 1920s.

To Mr Claude Whistler CBE of Eastry, Nr Sandwich, Kent, who provided pictures and personal history of his father, who fought with distinction during the Great War and during operations on the North-West Frontier in India.

To Wing Commander C.G. Jefford MBE RAF (Retd), who gave advice, and for the use of material from his book on RAF squadrons that lists the whereabouts of RAF units for the period 1912 to the 1970s.

To Mr Gibbings of Agusta Westland, who helped with photographs.

To the author John W.R. Taylor and publishers Ian Allen for *A Pictorial History of the RAF 1918–1939*, Vol. I. This book provided a wealth of useful photographs of the period.

To the Putnam Press and HMSO for the most useful accounts of the development of the aircraft industry from 1918 to 1939 as seen through the eyes of Harald Penrose, the chief test pilot of Westland during the period. (see bibliography).

To Karl Hayes and his history of the Royal Air Force and the United States Naval Air Service in Ireland 1913–1923, Irish Air Letter 1988.

To the authors and publishers of books listed in the bibliography not already mentioned.

Preface

British Air Policy from 1918 to 1939

With the memory of the 1999 Balkan air campaign fresh in the mind, it is fair to conclude that airpower alone forced President Milosevic of Serbia to withdraw his forces from Kosovo to let in the NATO-led troops. On the other hand it may be argued that it was the threat of a land invasion that tipped the scales in NATO's favour. Whichever view is taken, it cannot be denied that NATO aircraft inflicted unacceptable damage to Serbian military, industrial, communications and transport targets. Moreover, in spite of the Serbs having a sizeable air force, little or no attempt was made to defend the country against NATO bombardment. Can it therefore now be claimed that, with the sophistication of modern strike-aircraft armed with laser-guided weapons, the employment of airpower alone can result in a belligerent nation suing for peace without even putting up a fight? This question is very relevant to this history since the the Air Staff's argument in the early 1920s in fighting for the survival of the RAF as an independent service was based upon the doctrine of the offensive use of airpower independent of the other two services. Chapter 10 critically examines the RAF's bombing doctrine, or lack of it, in the inter-war years.

In 1918, the year the Great War ended, the Independent Bomber Force (IBF) of the Royal Air Force was formed. It was to operate independently of the battlefield, unlike the many Allied squadrons operating in direct support of the land and naval forces, i.e. the strategic rather than the tactical use of airpower. The IBF was tasked with attacking industrial targets and so weaken the enemy's will and ability to continue with the war. The Germans for their part had employed Zeppelin airships and Gotha bombers to attack targets in England. Strategic bombing became a possibility when bomber aircraft and airships had the range and bomb-carrying capacity to take the war to the enemy's homeland. As the war ended there was already speculation that the employment of airpower alone had the potential to bring victory. It was said that the bomber would always get through, and that the effect on the morale of the civil population at the prospect of air bombardment could itself be decisive. Among exponents of the offensive use of airpower were Major-General Hugh Trenchard, later appointed to the post of Chief of the Air Staff, of the RAF, the American Colonel Billy Mitchell and the Italian Douhet. Trenchard was quite clear about the importance of maintaining a strong offensive bomber force. Even after his retirement from the RAF in 1930, he continued to press the case for bombers, seeing little need for fighters if the war was taken to the enemy. In retrospect, claims made for the effectiveness of the bombers were perhaps premature. Strategic bombing in the Great War was in its infancy. Some of the units of heavy bombers, such as the HP V/1500, were only working up as the war ended, and Berlin was not bombed. The claims made for the effectiveness of bombing were based more on its perceived potential to bring an enemy to sue for peace than experience gained in war. For all the talk of heavy bombing, small two-man biplane bombers, almost indistinguishable from the fighters, continued in service until the mid-1930s.

In the event, the formulation of air policy in 1919 and the years that followed was not so straightforward. In general terms air policy is determined by a mix of factors. Firstly, there is the foreign policy stance of a nation, i.e. does it stand alone, is it neutral like Switzerland or Sweden, or is it a partner in a military alliance when friendly countries may be expected to provide military support in the event of an attack by a country or countries outside the alliance? Countries in an alliance may also be able to reduce the burden of defence expenditure through collaborative efforts in weapon design, development and procurement, contingency planning and joint exercises. Secondly, there is the willingness of governments, and indirectly electorates, to spend money on defence rather than on hospitals and schools. Thirdly, there is the industrial capacity of a nation to produce aircraft and weapons at home. The alternative is to import, but countries then run the risk that foreign sources of supply might dry up in the event of war. Finally, and perhaps most importantly, is the need to maintain national security. By this is not meant the use of aircraft against the civilian populations, which is internal security, but defence against attack by a belligerent nation. This can extend to the oceans, since the protection of maritime trade can be vital to a country such as Britain.

The First World War, or the Great War, as it was then known, ended on 11 November 1918. In order to understand how British air policy was formulated on cessation of hostilities, and how it developed in succeeding years, one has to consider the situation faced by the British government of the day and the British people. To begin with there were the memories of the slaughter of millions of men in the bloody trench warfare in Flanders and beyond, which created war weariness. This had to be the war to end all wars, and Britain was to be 'a land fit for heroes'. Then there was the League of Nations, which would be a world forum to which nations could appeal if a dispute looked likely to lead to conflict, and naturally hopes were pinned on the League to avert war. Finally there was the 'Ten-Year Rule'. This was national defence policy framed in the belief that Britain would not be involved in a major conflict for at least ten years. For all these reasons defence expenditure would be low on a list of priorities for public expenditure.

In these circumstances there was no need for 184 operational squadrons backed by training units at home and abroad, and a period of rapid disbandment followed, so that the number of operational squadrons was reduced, by March 1921, to a mere twenty-eight fully formed squadrons; and of these, twenty-one were abroad and three in Ireland. The RAF also gave up 149 airfields, 122 landing grounds and 2,240 hirings (land and buildings). Of the four remaining squadrons three were with the Royal Navy. This left one RAF squadron in England, giving refresher training to pilots. To make matters worse, the Admirals and Generals saw little reason for the maintenance of a separate air force, and argued for the return of squadrons to their respective services whence they had come on 1 April 1918, the day the RAF was officially formed from units of the Royal Naval Air Service and the Royal Flying Corps. It was argued that the expense of maintaining an Air Ministry alone was unacceptable in the prevailing financial climate.

On 11 January 1919 Hugh Trenchard was reappointed to the post of Chief of the Air Staff (CAS) in succession to Major-General Sykes. Trenchard had resigned as the RAF's first CAS following differences with Lord Rothermere over policy. For his part Sykes sought to secure the future of the RAF as an independent force by advocating an imperial service involving the Dominions of Canada, Australia and New Zealand, the Union of South Africa and India. At that time neither the Westminster Parliament nor the Dominions were ready for such a grandiose plan of expansion. Trenchard, on the other hand, it was said, 'was prepared to make do with a little and would not have to be carried'. This made him much more appealing to a cost-conscious government. And so it fell to Trenchard to fight the battle for survival. He was fortunate in having the sympathetic ear of Winston Churchill, who was Secretary of State for War and the Air. Churchill had no intention of returning the RAF to the Royal Navy or the Army, and, instead, asked Trenchard to put in writing his own ideas for the new service. This was to be the Trenchard Memorandum, which laid down the foundations of the independent air force. Its publication was followed by the granting of new RAF rank titles, which served to emphasize a separate identity. Once the Memorandum was accepted, the RAF moved forward, even though attempts by the Royal Navy and Army to reclaim what they regarded as their air components continued for some years to come. It was not until 1937 that the Royal Navy took complete control of the Fleet Air Arm, but by that time the RAF was firmly established as the third armed service. Another factor that helped to sustain the RAF in the face of inter-service rivalry and government cut-backs was air control. At the Cairo Conference in March 1921 it was accepted that the RAF should replace the Army as the primary force in maintaining order in the Middle East. Trenchard had shown that it was

possible for a few aircraft, with a minimum of air-transportable land forces, to suppress revolts by dissident tribesmen when the 'Mad Mullah' was defeated in the protectorate of British Somaliland in 1920. Formerly large Army garrisons had been necessary to maintain order. Aircraft were much quicker in nipping incipient trouble in the bud. By the time Army troops arrived on the scene it was more likely that the trouble would have escalated, resulting in heavier casualties on both sides. As a consequence air control was much more economical in money and lives than in those operations where only land forces were used. This was bound to be attractive to a government seeking economies. Air control, then, gave the RAF an operational *raison d'être*, and was used in Mesopotamia (Iraq) and India, followed later by Transjordan and Palestine.

The next development in air policy was for the Conservative government to recognize the need for the RAF to contribute to national security. By now the nation realized that the Royal Navy could no longer guarantee that the territory of the British Isles would not be violated by an enemy. It was agreed that the RAF could expand to fifty-two squadrons, seventeen fighter and thirty-five bomber, but that in the prevailing economic climate this would not happen immediately. It would be phased in over a minimum of five years. Add to this the Ten-Year Rule, the hope that the League of Nations would prove effective in preventing conflict on a large scale and the declared pacifism of a number of MPs, and it may be understood that the Westminster Parliament would not wish to be seen sending signals to the rest of the world that it was rearming Britain. Strange then that the preponderance of squadrons from the fifty-two would be bomber, but this was the very essence of Air Staff thinking at the time, i.e. offensive defence. The number of squadrons needed to defend Britain would be that necessary to defeat an aerial assault by any power within striking distance of its shores. It may seem bizarre to have seen France as a potential aggressor in the early 1920s, but this was not the intention. It was that France had, at that time, the largest air force in Europe. This was to be the yardstick. Therefore, by the end of 1923, British air policy provided for the continued existence of the RAF as a separate service, air control in India and the Middle East and the gradual expansion in an unspecified number of years to fifty-two squadrons for national defence, plus a continuation of the Ten-Year Rule.

It would seem strange today if civil aviation comprising commercial airlines came under the control of a ministry of defence. But this was the situation after the Great War. Even the Air Estimates, the money voted annually by Parliament for expenditure on the RAF, contained an element for civil aviation. This might seem all the more perplexing since the government's attitude was that the airlines should 'sink or swim', so to speak, in the market place. The explanation for public expenditure on civil aviation lies in the overlap between the development of military and civil flying, and the great reliance that the struggling firms in the aircraft and aero-engine manufacturing industry placed on aircraft orders. The aircraft industry badly needed contracts for both civil and military types to survive, and there was little to choose between the design of both. Indeed, a civil airliner could always be adapted for military use. Therefore the larger the civil air fleet, the larger the nation's war potential. Both civil and military aircraft prototypes went to the RAF's experimental establishment at Martlesham Heath in Suffolk for airworthiness tests and evaluation, if land-planes, and to the Marine Experimental Establishment, Felixstowe, if they were flying-boats or floatplanes. If found satisfactory by the RAF test pilots, they could then enter service or receive modifications. To have required the nascent aircraft industry to set up its own parallel organization would have been too costly. As it was, the French were prepared to subsidize their airlines, and for a while in 1921 only foreign aircraft touched down at Croydon. In the end the British government relented and granted a modest subsidy of £60,000 to help the airlines. And because the costs of civil aircraft development were met in part from public funds, the airline and aircraft industries were given time to get on their feet, if one will forgive the malapropism. Indeed, at a time when the RAF was unable to place orders for new military aircraft, Trenchard sensibly awarded contracts for prototypes so that firms manufacturing aircraft could at least keep their core staff of designers and builders in employment until better days came along. Each year's specifications for military aircraft were sent out to aircraft manufacturers numbered sequentially throughout the year, e.g. Specification 16/22 called for a long-distance coastal-defence biplane. Finally, it should be remembered that most of the pilots of both civil aircraft and airships were ex-service pilots who flew in their retired ranks, thus emphasizing the parallel development of military and civil flying.

The development of airships was very prominent during the inter-war years. Owing to their low speed and poor manoeuvrability relative to aircraft, however, airships were not considered a serious rival in combat, although they were admirably suited to reconnaissance, particularly maritime reconnaissance. Where the airship could score over the aircraft of the day was in long-distance flying, and the idea of linking the far-flung Dominions of Canada and Australia with the Mother country was appealing. Indeed, the necessary airship sheds and mooring masts for berthing airships were built in such places as India in preparation for Imperial air routes. But the inter-war years are best, if sadly remembered, for the catastrophes befalling airships, although British enthusiasts like Commander Burney remained undaunted. It was not until the tragic loss of the R101 at Beauvais in northern France on a flight to

India in 1930 that the policy was virtually to abandon further airship development. Only a small staff was kept on at Cardington in Bedfordshire for work on balloons, and the latter were to feature as part of aerial defence during the Second World War. Until the loss of the R101, governments had been equivocal in giving support to airship development. On the one hand there was the feeling that since airships were to be used commercially then the private sector should bear the cost of development, but on the other hand the government had a part to play to give British airships a fighting chance in the developing international airline market. After all, the Germans were successfully using airships on long-haul civil flights. The result was that two large airships were built in the late 1920s. One, the so-called 'capitalist' airship, was a private venture titled R100, and the other, the so-called 'socialist' airship, was state funded and titled the R101. As has been said, the loss of the R101 spelled the end of serious airship development in Britain, but in Germany too the end was not far off. The tragic loss of the German airship Hindenburg at Lakehurst, New Jersey in 1937 sealed the fate of lighter-than-air machines for all practical purposes.

In the early 1930s successive British governments saw the need to strengthen the RAF in an uncertain world, at the same time wishing to be seen to play their full part in general disarmament. The League of Nations had been successful in averting conflict involving smaller countries, but was unable to prevent a determined major power from acting aggressively. First it was Japanese expansionism in the Far East, when, in 1932, Manchuria became Manchukuo. This was followed by the Nazis coming to power in Germany to create the Third Reich in 1933, and lastly there was the Italian aggression against Abyssinia in 1935. When the League sought to admonish Mussolini it only threw the latter into the arms of the German dictator, Adolf Hitler, so creating the Rome–Berlin Axis. Since neither leader ran a democracy they could spend money on armaments pretty well at will. As the Disarmament Talks at Geneva got bogged down in endless bickering over the details of disarmament, they eventually ran into the sands. Hitler could conveniently see no reason why the the major powers should not come down to the arms limits imposed upon his country at Versailles in 1919. Of course Hitler would be happy not to see arms limitations adopted that might limit his own freedom to act. When he withdrew Germany from membership of the League of Nations, the time had come for Britain to look to its defences. No longer would she look at France's air capability, but at that of the Third Reich.

So began the policy of rearmament and expansion. More squadrons with up-to-date aircraft and new airfields were going to be needed. Now it was not the funds made available by the Treasury that was to be the constraint, but the ability of the RAF and the aircraft industry to cope with the demands made upon them.

Trenchard had built 'his cottage'. He had built an air force that placed quality before quantity, and his successors were initially loath to water down a highly professional force through too fast an expansion. Fortunately the opening of reserve and auxiliary squadrons from 1925 onwards, and the introduction of short-service commissions in 1923 meant that there was a pool of reserve and ex-service pilots in civilian jobs who could be called on to serve. For the aircraft industry the answer lay in the contracting-out of work to 'shadow' factories. Motor car firms were involved in building engines and airframes to designs and specifications put out by the aircraft industry.

As the inevitability of a second world war became clear for all to see, the fear grew that Britain was dropping behind Germany in the production of military aircraft and the forming of air units, and so criticism fell on His Majesty's Government that not enough was being done. Winston Churchill, then on the back-benches of the House of Commons, and thus out of government, was loudest in voicing his discontent. The British Prime Minister in 1938, Mr Neville Chamberlain, did not succeed in persuading Hitler to abandon his territorial

ambitions. Having already absorbed Austria into the Third Reich and brought about the dismemberment of Czechoslovakia, Hitler had eyes on Poland, and there was added fear that Britain would not be ready if war came in 1938. If not successful in bringing 'peace in our time', which Chamberlain had declared on his return from the Munich Conference, having signed away Czechoslovakian independence, he did at least give the RAF and the aircraft industry a breathing space, so that when war did come in 1939, there was an effective radar-based fighter control system in place, and Spitfires and Hurricanes were coming off the production lines to provide defence. But except for the Battle light bombers sent to France with the Advanced Air-Striking Force in September 1939, the heavy bombers needed to carry the war to the enemy were still to come.

This book goes into detail to explain how air policy was applied in the years between 1919 and 1929 by dealing with all the major events in this context. It tells of the famous and the not-so-famous, the successes and the failures and the advances made in aircraft and air weapon design over the first ten years in this volume, Volume I, and between 1930 and 1939 in Volume II.

Ranks and Responsibilities of Officers, NCOs and Aircraftmen of the RAF

AIR OFFICERS applicable between the wars (with abbreviations)

Marshal of the RAF (MRAF)

This is the highest rank in the RAF, but is not the most senior serving member of the service. An MRAF will have left active service but is not actually retired. It is in that sense an honorary rank, which the officer holds for life thereafter. Lord Trenchard was promoted to MRAF shortly before his retirement in 1930.

Air Chief Marshal (ACM)

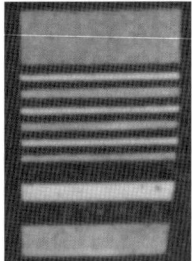

This is the rank of the most senior serving officer of the RAF who is also Chief of the Air Staff, with a seat on the Air Council. He is the senior service adviser to the Secretary of State for Air.

Air Marshal (AM)

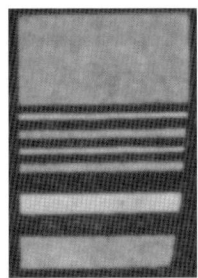

An air marshal commanded an operational or training command or an overseas command. A command comprised a number of groups or stations.

Air Vice-Marshal (AVM)

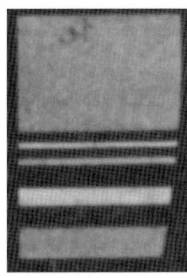

An air vice-marshal commanded an operational or training group. It should be remembered that for much of the inter-war period Halton and Cranwell had command status, but were commanded initially by air commodores later promoted to AVM.

Air Commodore (Air Cdre)

An air commodore was mainly found in the staff of a command or group, but could also, on occasion, be designated a force commander or station commander of large stations, e.g. RAF Cranwell and Halton.

SENIOR OFFICERS

Group Captain (Gp Capt)

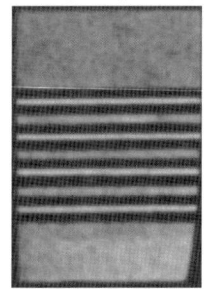

Another rank like the air commodore, in having a status that was not easy to define. This came to be the rank of an RAF station commander. A station would house a number of RAF squadrons. Group captains were also force commanders, and did command groups in the early days. They also served on staff appointments.

Wing Commander (Wg Cdr)

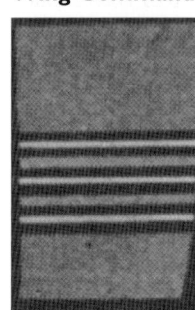

A wing commander would normally command a wing comprising two or more squadrons, but might also be posted to command a small station. Additionally a wing commander could be found on the staff of a command or a group. Exceptionally a wing commander could command a squadron. (In 2005 this is the norm).

Squadron Leader (Sqn Ldr)

A squadron leader would normally command an RAF squadron comprising three flights of four aircraft, although this number varied. Additionally, a squadron leader could be found on the staff of a command or group, and might command a small RAF station/unit.

JUNIOR OFFICERS

Flight Lieutenant (Flt Lt)

A flight lieutenant would normally command a flight of four aircraft on a squadron, although this varied with individual units, or he might be a squadron or unit adjutant. Flight lieutenants could also be found in junior staff positions.

Flying Officer (Flg Off)

A flying officer was normally a squadron pilot or observer with at least two years' commissioned service.

Pilot Officer (Plt Off)

A pilot officer is the most junior officer in a unit. On flying squadrons during the inter-war years he would be a junior squadron pilot initially just out of training. In the RAF of 2005 a pilot will have reached the rank of flying officer by the time he has completed a much longer period of flying training before being posted to a squadron.

Note: It has been made clear that the above designations of duties and responsibilities of all the ranks mentioned is a rough guide. No allowance is made for non-flying units or officers in ground branches. For example, a pilot officer is not always a pilot. He may be a junior stores or accounts officer.

AIR OFFICERS

GROUP CAPTAINS

OTHER OFFICERS

NON-COMMISSIONED OFFICERS

Warrant Officer (WO)

A warrant officer is the most senior rank not holding the King's or Queen's commission. WOs held a variety of positions on a station, from the station warrant officer responsible to the station commander for discipline on the station to WOs holding senior positions in workshops or stores akin to a civilian foreman of trades.

Flight Sergeant (Flt Sgt)

Flight sergeants filled a variety of posts on an RAF unit. They were in a supervisory capacity on ground duties in discipline, administration, technical and other trades. They were also trained as pilots or observers.

Sergeants (Sgt)

The description of a sergeant's responsibilities is broadly the same as for a flight sergeant, but at a lower level. Again, sergeants were trained as aircrew. All the above ranks are senior non-commissioned officers, and to this day live in a sergeants' mess.

Corporals (Cpl)

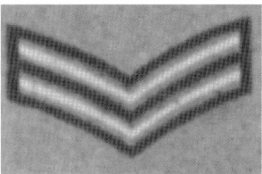

Corporals were to be found at the lowest supervisory level in the variety of trades in the RAF. Corporals were known as Junior NCOs and had their own corporals' club on a station.

Note: The above ranks were all non-commissioned officers and lived in their own separate messes or had their own clubs distinct from aircraftmen.

AIRCRAFTMEN

Leading Aircraftmen (LAC)

These were trained airmen in the variety of trades in the RAF, i.e. they would have been qualified in their various trades after passing the appropriate trade tests. Aircraftmen passing out from the RAF Apprentice School at Halton could expect to leave as LACs.

Aircraftmen

Aircraftmen wore no badge of rank. This badge would be found on their caps. Recruits to the service would join as aircraftmen. After basic recruit training they would undergo trade training.

Service Dress Caps worn by SNCOs, JNCOs and aircraftmen

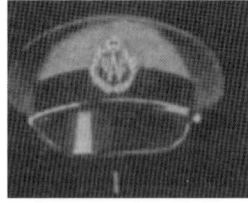

Forage Caps worn by non commissioned ranks

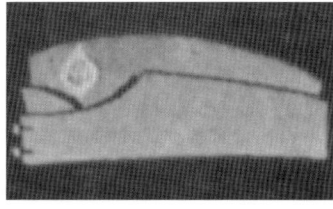

Note: JNCOs and LACs could also be employed as gunners on aircraft, and they were so used in air-control operations in India and the Middle East and in multi-engined or dual-seat aircraft at home. Tradesmen also carried badges distinguishing them as signallers, bandsmen, physical training instructors, bomb disposal personnel, drum majors and apprentices.

No. 2 Squadron RAF Regiment is the direct successor of No. 2 Armoured Car Company that was formed in the inter-war years to assist the flying squadrons to maintain internal security in the Middle East. Here we see the author receiving the battle standard of No. 2 (Field) Squadron from Air Chief Marshal Sir Hubert Patch at the standard presentation parade, Ta Kali airfield, Malta, in November 1959.

Presentation of the Squadron Standard at RAF Ta Kali, Malta.

PART I

Operations and Training

Chapter 1
Order of Battle – 11th November 1918

Air Council and Air Ministry – UK Commands including Ireland, France and Belgium, Middle East and India – Wing and squadron formations – Roles of squadrons bringing them to 11 November 1918 locations

THE AIR COUNCIL AND AIR MINISTRY

Following the formation of the Royal Air Force on 1 April 1918, the Air Council and the Air Ministry were established bodies at the cessation of hostilities on 11 November that year. The new service was formed from units and personnel of the Royal Naval Air Service (RNAS) and the Royal Flying Corps (RFC). The most senior officers in the service all commenced their careers in the Royal Navy or the Army, many of them having learned to fly immediately before the First World War or during the war itself. As the year ended they still bore their Army/Navy ranks, and there was a mixture of uniforms.

It is appropriate briefly to trace the developments that brought about the formation of the RAF in 1918. Dominion soldiers, sailors and airmen fought alongside British forces in the Great War. And so it was appropriate to bring a South African into the War Cabinet, and General Jan Smuts was available to the Prime Minister, Lloyd George, as an adviser without any government departmental responsibilities. When the German Gotha bombers flew from their Belgian airfields to attack London in 1917, the air defences were found wanting. The anti-aircraft guns were manned by the Army and the fighter aircraft were from either the RNAS or RFC. The means of giving a warning to take cover were almost non-existent, and the fighters had such a poor rate of climb and speed that they could hardly catch the Gothas, even if they were airborne at the time. Smuts was given the task of investigating and reporting back to the War Cabinet. As a direct result of his report, the defences of London were brought under one unified command. But this did not solve the problem of inter-service rivalry in procuring the latest aircraft types or in allocating priorities in combat. Naturally the Navy would put defence of the fleet before defence of the capital, and the Army would put reinforcement of the air units on the Western Front (Belgium and France) before reinforcement of fighter defences around London. Smuts therefore went on to look into these matters, and he came up with the idea that only a single integrated flying service would stop the squabbling over resources and the allocation of flying units to the various theatres of operations. Hence the Royal Air Force came into being.

The Air Council

The Air Council in 1918 was the supreme governing body of the Royal Air Force, and it brought together the most senior officers of the service with their political masters. The Air Minister was appointed by the prime minister of the day, and his most senior service adviser was the Chief of the Air Staff. The Air Council met as required, but the Air Minister left the day-to-day running of the service to the Chief of the Air Staff and the service heads of the various departments. While governments came and went, the senior members of the RAF stayed until retirement, resignation or death, thus providing continuity of policy and direction. On the other hand, governments were formed from different political parties, and during the inter-war years Britain had, for the first time in its history, Labour governments. The Conservative and Liberal parties also formed governments, and because of the economic crises that hit Britain in the period 1930–35 it was necessary to form national governments from more than one political party. The changes of government, as will be seen in Chapter 16, would bring with them changes in air policy.

At the cessation of hostilities in 1918 there had been a coalition government headed by the Liberal party leader, David Lloyd George. Sir William Weir had been appointed as Secretary of State for the Royal Air Force on 27 April 1918, and he remained in that post until 14 January 1919. He was then succeeded by Winston Churchill, whose title was Secretary of State for War and the Royal Air Force. In March 1919 this was abbreviated to Secretary of State for War and Air; Churchill holding that post until 5 April 1921. In other words, Lloyd George did not want the Air to be a separate department of state. But Churchill had no intention of absorbing the

Lloyd George.

RAF into the Army. Indeed, in a letter to Walter Long, the First Lord of the Admiralty, Churchill made it clear that he intended giving new ranks and titles to members of the Royal Air Force as if to emphasize its existence as a separate arm of the British services, ranking with the Royal Navy and the Army. The Chief of the Air Staff on the Air Council at the cessation of hostilities was Major-General F.H. Sykes CMG, although he was not the first incumbent, as Major-General Sir Hugh M. Trenchard had resigned the post over a policy disagreement with Lord Rothermere. Trenchard, being so senior a member of the service and one of its founder members, could not be allowed to do nothing, and he was placed in command of the Independent Bombing Force on the Western Front. This was his opportunity to employ the bomber in a strictly strategic manner, i.e. to bomb targets removed from the battlefield, targets behind the enemy lines and industrial targets in Germany itself, with the intention of reducing the enemy's ability to wage war.

The other members of the Air Council provided direction and policy in matters of personnel, aircraft construction, supply and organization, with a Permanent Under-Secretary as the senior civil servant. Standards throughout the service would be maintained by the office of Inspector-General, although the latter was dropped from the Air Council on 6 February 1919 and the post was abolished on 1 April 1920, not to be reintroduced until 1 September 1937.

THE AIR COUNCIL, 11 NOVEMBER 1918
SECRETARY OF STATE FOR THE ROYAL AIR FORCE
The Lord Weir of Eastwood PC

PARLIAMENTARY UNDER-SECRETARY OF STATE FOR AIR
Major J.L. Baird CMG, DSO, MP

PERMANENT UNDER-SECRETARY OF STATE FOR AIR
W.A. Robinson Esq. CB, CBE

CHIEF OF THE AIR STAFF
Major-General F.H. Sykes CMG

MASTER-GENERAL OF PERSONNEL
(Later entitled Air Member for Personnel)
Major-General W.S. Brancker AFC

CONTROLLER-GENERAL OF EQUIPMENT
(Later entitled Air Member for Supply and Organization)
Major-General E.L. Ellington CMG

DIRECTOR-GENERAL OF AIRCRAFT PRODUCTION
(MINISTRY OF MUNITIONS)
Sir Arthur Duckham KCB

ADMINISTRATOR OF WORKS AND BUILDINGS
Sir John Hunter KBE

INSPECTOR-GENERAL OF THE ROYAL AIR FORCE
Major-General Sir Godfrey M. Paine KCB, MVO
(ex-RNAS officer)

Major-General Frederick H. Sykes CMG.

The Air Ministry

The Air Ministry was divided into departments concerned with different aspects of policy. The titles are mostly self-explanatory and go to show how complex a military organization is at staff level. Indeed many of these staff posts are replicated, albeit with a reduced scope of responsibility, at lower levels of command, in November 1918, areas and groups.

1. **Department of the Chief of Air Staff** Coming directly under the Chief of the Air Staff, Major-General Sykes, were the staff officers responsible for the conduct of air operations, organization and air intelligence. This included the deployment of wings and squadrons between home and overseas commands and the acquisition of intelligence necessary for the prosecution of effective air operations, together with the organization necessary to give effect to them.

2. **Master-General of Personnel** Major-General Brancker's department was responsible for all aspects of personnel, such as promotions and postings to ensure that stations and squadrons were manned to meet operational and training tasks to agreed establishments. Training, so vital to ensure that personnel were fitted to take their place on operational units, came under this department. Finally the department administered the medical services of the RAF. Its head was later titled Air Member for Personnel.

3. **Controller-General of Equipment** Major-General Ellington oversaw the provision of aircraft storage parks and repair depots. The Air Quartermaster's department was responsible for the provision of aircraft spares and equipment, together with technical and domestic supplies and the supply depots that stocked them. Other sub-departments provided for Kite balloons, marine, wireless and photographic equipment. The head of this department was later titled Air Member for Supply and Organization.

4. **Director-General of Aircraft Production** Sir Arthur Duckham was responsible for the procurement of aircraft by awarding aircraft contracts for prototypes and the production of approved designs for operational and training units.
5. **Administrator of Works and Buildings** Sir John Hunter's department oversaw works and buildings, including such items as airfield construction, airfield drainage, water, heating and work at marine establishments.

THE OPERATIONAL AND TRAINING COMMANDS AT HOME AND OVERSEAS, NOVEMBER 1918

The organizational charts and maps that follow show squadron deployments and therefore the Order of Battle on Armistice Day 1918, together with a brief description of the circumstances that brought the various squadrons to those locations. The roles of the squadrons – for example, fighter, bomber or anti-submarine – are shown on the theatre maps. The specifications of aircraft in service on Armistice Day, and those that were introduced into squadron service by the end of 1929, are shown in Appendix A. The locations of all operational units on Armistice Day, and their movements between the wars and at the outbreak of hostilities in 1939, are in Appendix B.

Home Commands
Transition from Admiralty/War Office to Air Ministry Organization
On 1 April 1918 the command structures for the RAF were those that had been passed on by the older services, the Royal Naval Air Service and the Royal Flying Corps. The flying units of the RNAS came under the command of naval flag officers for fleets at sea, e.g. Flag Officer Grand Fleet, for ship- or carrier-borne aircraft, and home port establishments, e.g. Plymouth, Devonport, Chatham or Rosythe, for shore-based squadrons. Those of the RFC were organized into training divisions, both operational and training, broken down further into brigades, wings and squadrons. In order to avoid confusion with Navy and Army command structures it was decided at a meeting of the Air Council on 19 February 1918 to use Areas, numbered 1 to 6, rather than Commands, used by both the older services, or Divisions, used by the Army. The areas were subdivided into Groups, which would not clash with either of the two sister services, and being indeterminate in size, they allowed the RAF to decide in time how many wings and squadrons should make up a group. This in turn gave rise to an interesting anomaly when the new RAF ranks were introduced in 1919. Initially group captains did command groups, wing commanders wings and squadron leaders squadrons. Often, if a force was set up for a particular operation, a group captain could well

command. The Indian Group on the North-West Frontier was commanded by a group captain. But these were the days before RAF stations were the established norm. Wings and squadrons could well be situated on an airfield that also housed other minor units, and a squadron might be commanded by a wing commander who doubled up as OC squadron and OC minor units, as at Kohat and Basra, for example. Later, RAF stations became the norm, and squadrons or wings could come and go, but the piece of real estate that was the RAF station stayed put. It was therefore necessary to appoint group captains to be the commanding officers of stations superior in rank to the commanders of wings and squadrons that had taken up residence on a station. A number of stations would then comprise a group, which had to be commanded by an officer of superior rank to a group captain. Strangely enough, this was not to be an air commodore but an air vice-marshal. The air commodore was mostly found on the headquarters staff or as the commanding officer of a station with group status, such as Halton and Cranwell.

Later, large RAF stations, particularly flying stations, commanded by a group captain, had three wing commanders under command. These would be the Wing Commander Flying, who had the operational squadrons, the Wing Commander Technical, who presided over the engineering, armament, signals, safety equipment, photographic and motor transport sections, and finally the Wing Commander Administrative, who looked after equipment, accounts, personnel, married quarters, padres and other miscellaneous sections.

The numbering of areas did not last long, and on 8 May 1918 the numbered areas became geographical areas. These are shown below, with reference notes following. The RAF Commands introduced in the 1930s were functionally organized, e.g. Fighter, Bomber, Coastal, Training, but the RAF Areas of 1918 were multifunctional. Thus Major-General F.C. Heath-Caldwell CB, based at the Covent Garden Hotel, London, commanded all units in the south-eastern counties. These included Home Defence fighter squadrons based at such stations as Detling and Biggin Hill, as well as the anti-submarine squadron based at Dover and the maritime reconnaissance squadron based at Manston. But some units for logistical or organizational reasons did not come under the command of the General Officer Commanding of their areas. So Newhaven, the home of No. 242 Squadron, with its Short 184s, DH6s and Campanias employed on anti-submarine duties, was part of No. 10 (Operations) Group, which came under the command of Major-General M.E.F. Kerr CB, MVO, based in Salisbury, commander of South-Western Area. These areas were to undergo several modifications in the years that followed, mainly to reflect the peacetime organization of the forces, bearing in mind that the RAF was to designate aircraft for cooperation with the Army and to man, alongside naval airmen, carrier-borne aircraft of the various fleets. All the shore-based squadrons that used to belong to the RNAS had a 200 prefix, so that No. 1 Squadron became No. 201 Squadron.

The sixth geographical area, which was unnumbered, was the Irish Area. Since all thirty-two counties of Ireland came under the Crown, RAF squadrons were based in what is now Ulster, as well as in the southern

ORDER OF BATTLE, UK AREAS, 11 NOVEMBER 1918

AIR COUNCIL

AIR MINISTRY

SOUTH-EASTERN AREA
Covent Garden Hotel, London WC 2

All units in London, Middlesex, Kent, Sussex, Surrey, Henlow/Beds, Buckingham, Berkshire, Essex, Oxford, Hertford and Martlesham Heath and Orford in Suffolk (see Note 1)

SOUTH-WESTERN AREA
Chafyn Grove, Salisbury

All units in Wiltshire, Glamorgan, Dorset, Devon, Hampshire, Somerset, Cornwall, Monmouth, Scilly Isles and Gloucester (see Note 2)

MIDLAND AREA
Somerset House, Clarendon Place, Leamington Spa

All units in Leicester, Stafford, Anglesey, Pembroke, Rutland, Warwick, Flint, Merioneth, Carmarthen, Nottingham, Worcester, Montgomery, Bedford, Lincoln, Shropshire, Cardigan, Northampton, Lancashire, Huntingdon, Cheshire, Denbigh, Hereford, Cambridge, Brecknock, Carnarvon, Radnor, Norfolk, Suffolk and Derby (see Note 3)

NORTH-EASTERN AREA
Racecourse Buildings, York

All units in York, Durham, Northumberland, Westmoreland and Cumberland, and those portions of Nottinghamshire and Lincolnshire north of the line Worksop–Lincoln (exclusive)–Horncastle–Ingoldmelts

NORTH-WESTERN AREA
Adelphi Hotel, Argyle Street, Glasgow

All counties in Scotland except units under C-in-C, Grand Fleet

Note 1. The Sussex units did not include the airship station at Polegate and the seaplane station at Newhaven, which came under the command of No. 10 (Operations) Group.

Note 2. The South-Western Area incorporated Polegate and Newhaven. The Gloucester units did not include Rendcombe, which came under South-Eastern Area, No. 2 (Training) Group.

Note 3. The Nottingham/Lincoln units did not include No. 8 Balloon Base at Immingham, which was under No. 18 (Operations) Group in North-Eastern Area, and those portions of Nottinghamshire and Lincolnshire north of a line Worksop–Lincoln (exclusive) –Horncastle–Ingoldmelts, which were in No. 16 (Training) Group, North-Eastern Area. The Bedford units did not include Henlow, which was in South-Eastern Area. The Norfolk and Suffolk units did not include those in No. 4 (Operations) Group, South-Eastern Area, and Experimental Group, South-Eastern Area.

counties. This area or command later took on group status, becoming No. 11 (Irish) Group.

Finally, references to General Officers Commanding of RAF areas persisted until the new RAF titles were introduced on 27 August 1919, when GOC became AOC, or Air Officer Commanding, the term air officer referring to officers of the highest rank, from Air Commodore to Marshal of the Royal Air Force. It must be borne in mind that the order of battle for units at home and overseas as depicted in this chapter had to undergo major changes following the rapid rundown from 188 operational squadrons to fewer than thirty. That is why this chapter concentrates on the circumstances that brought the units to the airfields, landing grounds and RAF stations of November 1918. Most of the stations were relinquished, only to be resurrected in the 1930s with the expansion programmes.

Units under Command, Geographical Areas in November 1918

These were as follows:

1. Air defence squadrons
2. Bomber/torpedo squadrons
3. Maritime reconnaissance squadrons
4. Squadrons aiding the civil power in Ireland

Air-Defence Squadrons

The deployment of air-defence squadrons on Armistice Day 1918 was not dissimilar to the deployment of squadrons of fighter command in 1940, but with three major differences. Firstly, the range of enemy aircraft was not as great as it is today, and since German bomber units could get no closer to Britain than their airfields in Belgium there was no threat of attack to the south-west of England, the west Midlands, Wales, the north-west and Scotland. Admittedly the Zeppelins had the range and had penetrated UK air defences on a number of occasions in the First World War, but airships were vulnerable, being slow and presenting far too large a target to fighters. By 1917 the threat of Zeppelin attacks had receded and was superseded by raids from Gotha bombers, which had to be fitted with extra fuel tanks to give them the range to reach London with a margin for bad weather or dispersion should formations be attacked.

Secondly, the bomb load was not as great as it was in 1940, nor was the sophistication of bombsights. Although 1,000 lb and 500 lb bombs were common in the Second World War, a typical bomb load of an entire formation of Gothas dropped on London in 1917, for example on Friday 25 May, was 163 bombs weighing 4,550 lb in total. This was from twenty-one aircraft that crossed the coast, out of twenty-three that set out from Belgium. And that raid did not cause the greatest monetary loss to Britain, being £19,405, compared with £205,622 lost on Saturday 7 July, when only 3,149 lb were dropped, i.e. luck played a major part.

Thirdly, in the First World War there was no radar-controlled fighter defence system, with sector operations rooms directing fighters to attack incoming enemy bombers, as there was in 1940. When the Gotha raids began in 1917 the air defences were so uncoordinated that the Gothas could bomb almost with impunity. They would have London as the primary target, but secondary targets were planned in case of bad weather or diversion because of fighter interception. When Folkestone came under heavy attack there was great pressure from the civilian population to provide adequate air defence. Three things had to happen in 1917. Firstly, the combined defences of the capital had to be brought under one command, that is heavy ack-ack batteries, as well as defending fighters of the RFC and RNAS. Secondly, there had to be an effective means of giving air raid warnings. And thirdly there was a dire need for modern fighter aircraft that had the rate of climb and speed to catch the enemy. This meant diverting aircraft from the Western Front and also stopping the wrangling between the Army and the Navy over the acquisition of aircraft from the factories. This wrangling ceased when the RFC and the RNAS were merged into the RAF the following year.

The map shows that the faster, more agile aircraft, e.g. Camels, Snipes and SE5As, were situated round the capital. The slower Avro 504Ks were relegated to the more northerly stations, which only the Zeppelins could reach. A typical Gotha attack pattern, which explains the positioning of fighter units, is shown below.

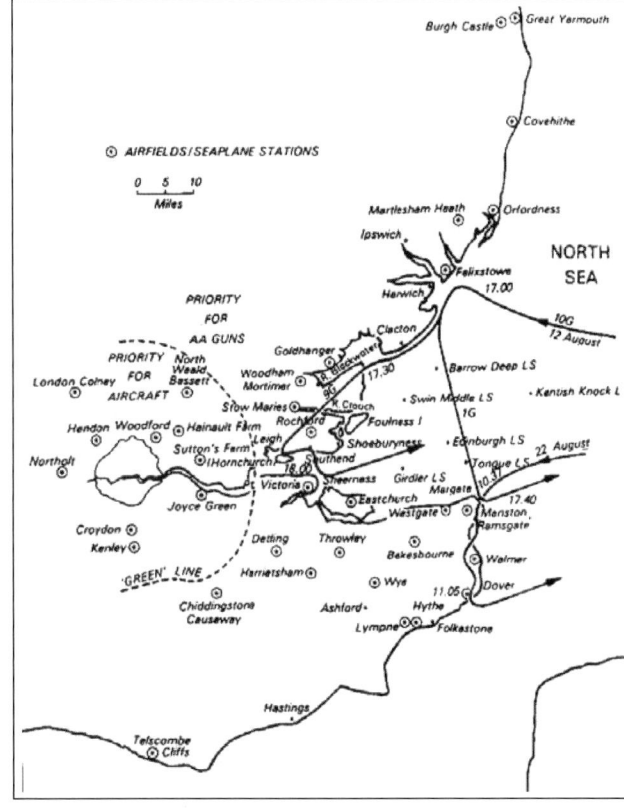

AIR DEFENCE SQUADRONS BASED IN THE UNITED KINGDOM 11th NOVEMBER 1918

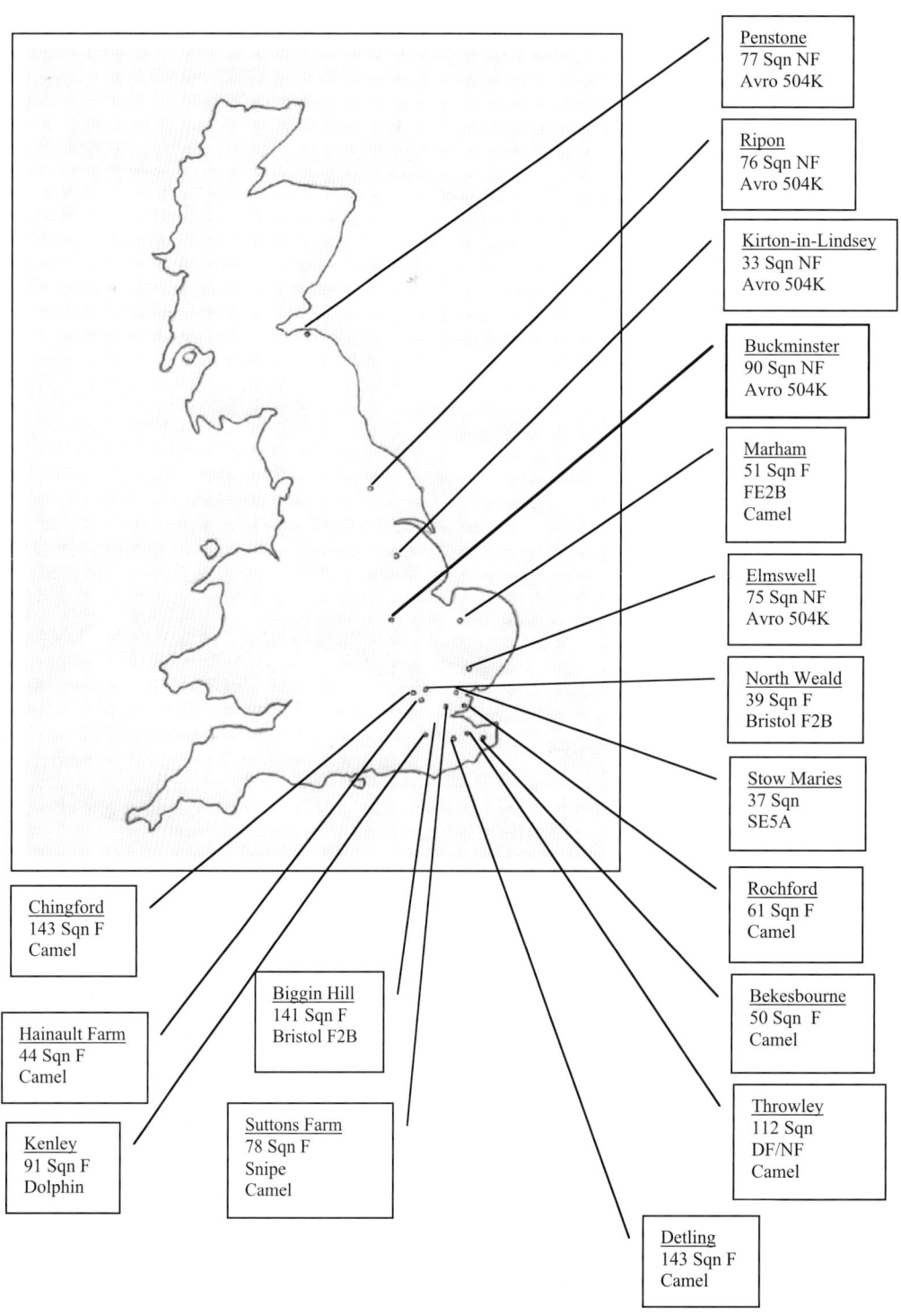

Penstone
77 Sqn NF
Avro 504K

Ripon
76 Sqn NF
Avro 504K

Kirton-in-Lindsey
33 Sqn NF
Avro 504K

Buckminster
90 Sqn NF
Avro 504K

Marham
51 Sqn F
FE2B
Camel

Elmswell
75 Sqn NF
Avro 504K

North Weald
39 Sqn F
Bristol F2B

Stow Maries
37 Sqn
SE5A

Rochford
61 Sqn F
Camel

Bekesbourne
50 Sqn F
Camel

Throwley
112 Sqn
DF/NF
Camel

Chingford
143 Sqn F
Camel

Biggin Hill
141 Sqn F
Bristol F2B

Hainault Farm
44 Sqn F
Camel

Kenley
91 Sqn F
Dolphin

Suttons Farm
78 Sqn F
Snipe
Camel

Detling
143 Sqn F
Camel

LEGEND
F – Fighter
DF – Day-fighter
NF – Night-fighter

Bomber/Torpedo-Bomber Squadrons

A close inspection of the map on the next page shows that there were virtually no operational bomber units on the British mainland in November 1918. The reason for this is simple. Almost the entire strategic bomber force, 8 Brigade, was in France, commanded at the cessation of hostilities by Major-General Trenchard. Those units that were in the UK were working up to operational readiness in November 1918, and a few units were actually in the act of disbanding. These were squadrons with the DH9, 9A or Salamanders, all aircraft that would need to be much closer to the enemy to be effective. The only units of significance in this context were the squadrons equipped with the HP 0/400 and HP V/1500

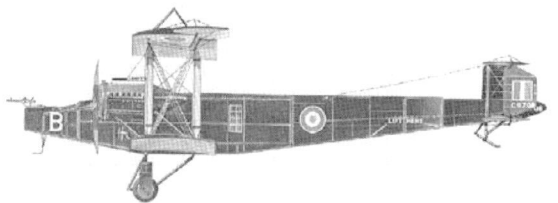

HP 0/100.

HP 0/400.

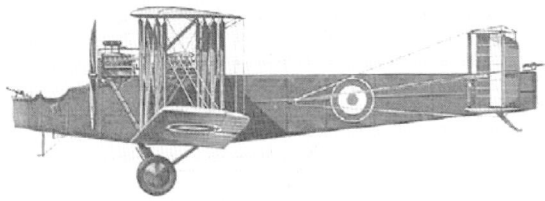

HP V/1500.

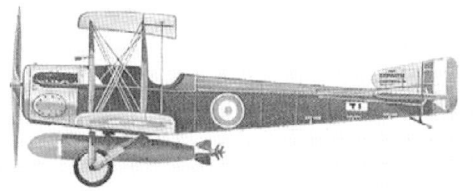

Sopwith Cuckoo.

aircraft, which could operate from the United Kingdom. In the case of the HP V/1500, bombing attacks from the UK base on Berlin were planned, and No. 117 Squadron, based at Norwich, was part of the Independent Bomber Force (IBF). Nos 166 and 167 Squadrons at Bircham Newton were designated night-bomber squadrons.

RAF First World War bombers   It was to be the Royal Navy that first entered into strategic bombing, just as it is the Navy today that deploys the strategic deterrent. It was the Admiralty in 1914 that asked the aircraft industry for a 'bloody paralyser' for the bombing of Germany. This was to be the Handley Page 0/100, which went into service with the RNAS in November 1916 and bombed U-boat bases, railway stations and industrial centres. Its successor was the HP 0/400, of which nearly 800 were ordered during the war and approximately 550 were built in the UK. There were 258 HP 0/400s on charge to the RAF at the Armistice, and they could carry a bomb up to 1,650 lb in weight. It was used as a day- and night-bomber by both the RFC and the RAF in the IBF. This type remained in RAF service until 1920. The HP V/1500 was too late for the First World War and was of no use in the 'whittled-down' peacetime RAF. Since it did go into production and did equip three RAF squadrons in the UK, the V/1500 does have a place in history. It was the first four-engined bomber in service and was the largest aircraft built by a British aircraft company in the First World War. The Air Ministry required an aircraft that had a combat radius of 600 miles, i.e. so that it could bomb Berlin from Bircham Newton. The first prototype flew in May 1918, powered by two tandem pairs of 375 hp Rolls-Royce Eagle VIII engines.

Anti-shipping   The only anti-shipping unit was No. 185 Squadron based in East Fortune, Scotland. Armed with torpedoes, the Sopwith Cuckoos could attack surface craft in the North Sea. The Cuckoo was not delivered until July 1918, and met the need for a single-seater, land-based aircraft carrying one or two 1,000 lb torpedoes and having an endurance of four hours. A total of 350 Cuckoos were ordered, but contracts were curtailed with the coming of the Armistice, and in the event only 150 were built.

Maritime Reconnaissance and Anti-Submarine Squadrons

The map on page 12 shows the disposition of maritime reconnaissance and anti-submarine squadrons. Seaplane stations abounded to cover not only the English Channel but also the Western Approaches for sea traffic coming into the Bristol Channel, as well as the Irish Sea approaches to Liverpool and the approaches to the Clyde. The units in eastern and north-eastern England patrolled the North Sea. When one considers that today there is just one maritime reconnaissance and strike base

OPERATIONAL AND NON OPERATIONAL BOMBER UNITS AND TORPEDO UNIT BOMBER UNITS – 11 NOVEMBER 1918

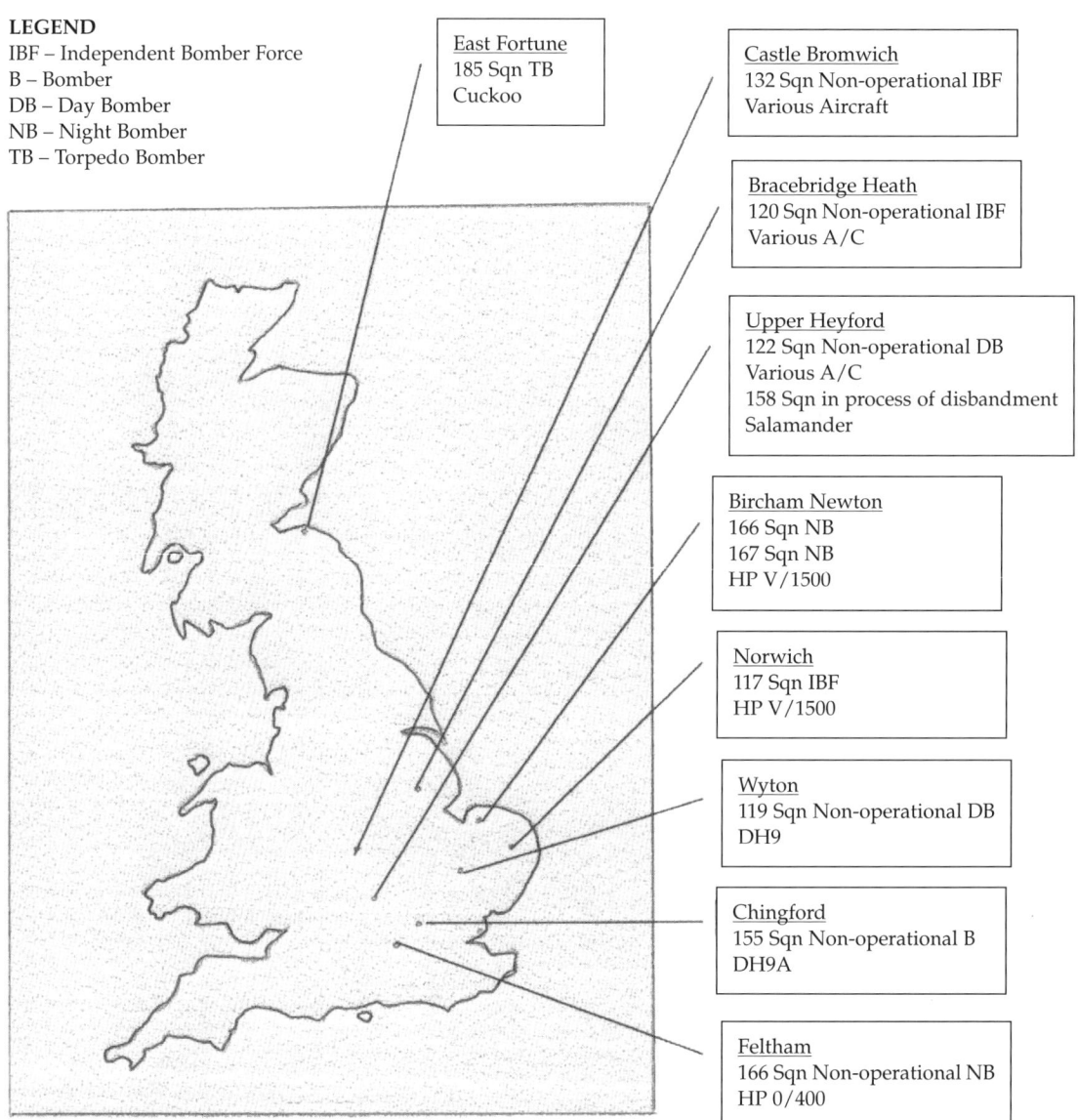

LEGEND
IBF – Independent Bomber Force
B – Bomber
DB – Day Bomber
NB – Night Bomber
TB – Torpedo Bomber

East Fortune
185 Sqn TB
Cuckoo

Castle Bromwich
132 Sqn Non-operational IBF
Various Aircraft

Bracebridge Heath
120 Sqn Non-operational IBF
Various A/C

Upper Heyford
122 Sqn Non-operational DB
Various A/C
158 Sqn in process of disbandment
Salamander

Bircham Newton
166 Sqn NB
167 Sqn NB
HP V/1500

Norwich
117 Sqn IBF
HP V/1500

Wyton
119 Sqn Non-operational DB
DH9

Chingford
155 Sqn Non-operational B
DH9A

Feltham
166 Sqn Non-operational NB
HP 0/400

in the UK, at Kinloss, to cover all approaches to the United Kingdom, together with flights of No. 22 Squadron dispersed at various stations around our shores for air-sea rescue, it is a far cry from the twenty-six airfields and flying-boat stations of 1918. The range and speed of these relatively fragile machines meant providing dense coverage of the sea areas around the United Kingdom to ensure interception of submarines. The same would apply to reconnaissance if the approach of hostile vessels was to be known.

A number of squadrons, notably No. 230 Squadron, were equipped with a variety of aircraft, but this does not seem to have posed a maintenance problem. Of interest is the equipment of No. 241 Squadron at Portland, which had the handful of Wight Converted seaplanes bought by the Admiralty from J. Samuel Wight & Co., East Cowes, Isle of Wight. Another rare aircraft, the Kangaroo, equipped just No. 246 Squadron at Seaton Carew. These were sold after the war to be used for commercial flights. The Felixstowe family of flying-boats made at Felixstowe not unsurprisingly equipped all of the four squadrons based there. With regard to maritime operations at the close of hostilities in November 1918, the patrol of the waters off the coasts of

FOUR AIRCRAFT TYPICAL OF THOSE USED IN MARITIME OPERATIONS IN 1918

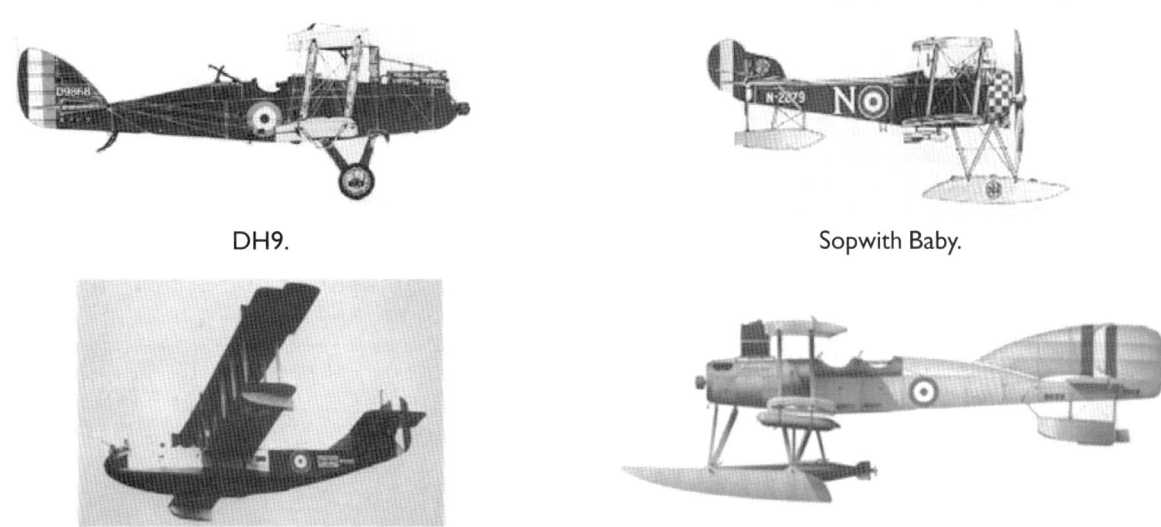

DH9.

Sopwith Baby.

Felixstowe F2A.

Short 184.

The map below graphically illustrates the necessity for the dense anti-submarine defence capability and the formation of No. 10 (Operations) Group RAF.

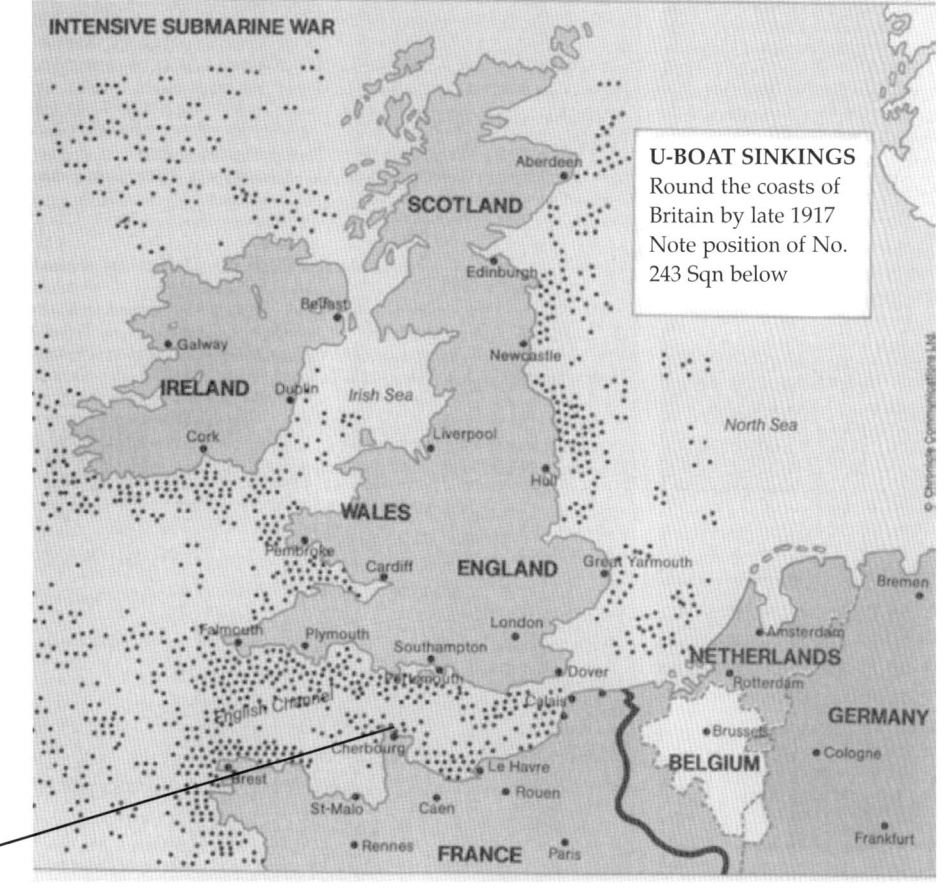

Cherbourg
No. 243 Sqn
Wight
Converted

MARITIME RECONNAISSANCE/ANTI-SUBMARINE SQUADRONS BASED IN THE UNITED KINGDOM – 11 NOVEMBER 1918

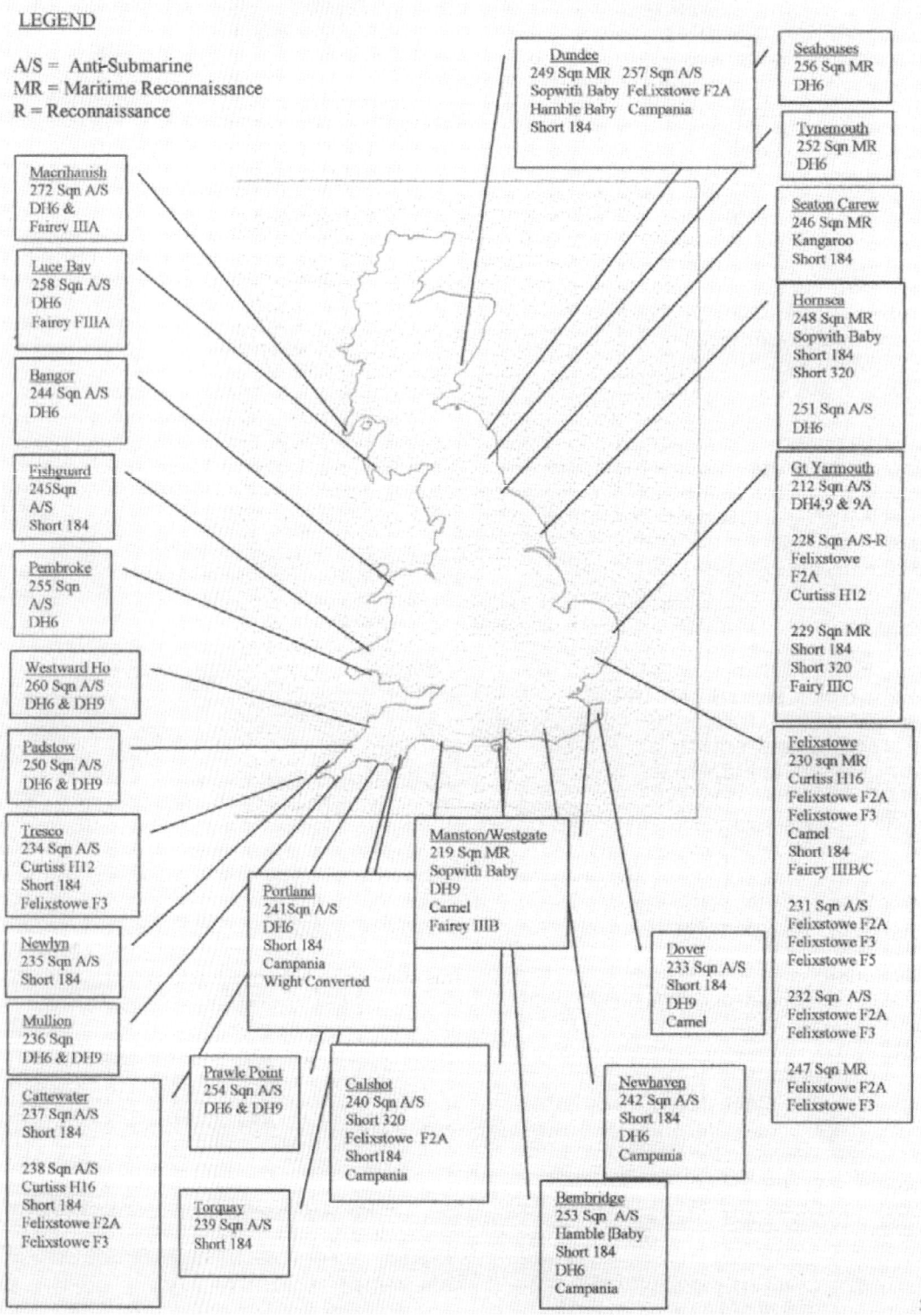

Airfields and flying boat stations - Squadron Nos. with aircraft

LEGEND

A/S = Anti-Submarine
MR = Maritime Reconnaissance
R = Reconnaissance

Macrihanish
272 Sqn A/S
DH6 &
Fairey IIIA

Luce Bay
258 Sqn A/S
DH6
Fairey FIIIA

Bangor
244 Sqn A/S
DH6

Fishguard
245Sqn
A/S
Short 184

Pembroke
255 Sqn
A/S
DH6

Westward Ho
260 Sqn A/S
DH6 & DH9

Padstow
250 Sqn A/S
DH6 & DH9

Tresco
234 Sqn A/S
Curtiss H12
Short 184
Felixstowe F3

Newlyn
235 Sqn A/S
Short 184

Mullion
236 Sqn
DH6 & DH9

Cattewater
237 Sqn A/S
Short 184

238 Sqn A/S
Curtiss H16
Short 184
Felixstowe F2A
Felixstowe F3

Torquay
239 Sqn A/S
Short 184

Prawle Point
254 Sqn A/S
DH6 & DH9

Portland
241Sqn A/S
DH6
Short 184
Campania
Wight Converted

Calshot
240 Sqn A/S
Short 320
Felixstowe F2A
Short184
Campania

Manston/Westgate
219 Sqn MR
Sopwith Baby
DH9
Camel
Fairey IIIB

Bembridge
253 Sqn A/S
Hamble [Baby
Short 184
DH6
Campania

Newhaven
242 Sqn A/S
Short 184
DH6
Campania

Dover
233 Sqn A/S
Short 184
DH9
Camel

Dundee
249 Sqn MR   257 Sqn A/S
Sopwith Baby FelLixstowe F2A
Hamble Baby   Campania
Short 184

Seahouses
256 Sqn MR
DH6

Tynemouth
252 Sqn MR
DH6

Seaton Carew
246 Sqn MR
Kangaroo
Short 184

Hornsea
248 Sqn MR
Sopwith Baby
Short 184
Short 320

251 Sqn A/S
DH6

Gt Yarmouth
212 Sqn A/S
DH4,9 & 9A

228 Sqn A/S-R
Felixstowe
F2A
Curtiss H12

229 Sqn MR
Short 184
Short 320
Fairy IIIC

Felixstowe
230 sqn MR
Curtiss H16
Felixstowe F2A
Felixstowe F3
Camel
Short 184
Fairey IIIB/C

231 Sqn A/S
Felixstowe F2A
Felixstowe F3
Felixstowe F5

232 Sqn A/S
Felixstowe F2A
Felixstowe F3

247 Sqn MR
Felixstowe F2A
Felixstowe F3

the British Isles remained a high priority. The RNAS had started to do this in September 1914, and by the time of the declaration of the Armistice the RAF maritime squadrons were employed on searching for enemy submarines, escorting convoys, assisting surface vessels to hunt down enemy submarines and locating and destroying mines laid by the enemy off the coasts of Britain, particularly in the entrance to the major ports. By July 1918 no fewer than thirty balloons were being taken to sea by the Grand Fleet on all occasions. They aided materially in the anti-submarine campaign, and were towed from drifters, trawlers and motor launches in large numbers for reconnaissance purposes.

Air defence of the English Channel grew from a single seaplane station at Calshot when, in early 1915, Bembridge on the Isle of Wight was added. When U-boat sinkings rose in 1916, Portland was opened as a seaplane base, and when cross-Channel traffic of men and supplies in and out of Newhaven attracted the attention of U-boat commanders, that station also was added. To cover the northern half of the Channel was an airship base at Polegate, and when it was seen that there was insufficient capacity to provide adequate maritime reconnaissance, two mooring-out stations were added. Protection of shipping in the southern half of the Channel was catered for by the establishment of a seaplane base at Cherbourg, where traffic had increased. To coordinate the air defences of this vital sea area it was decided to establish No. 10 (Operations) Group with a senior air officer and staff situated at Warsash. Seaplane training was moved from the operational base at Calshot to a training establishment at Lee-on-Solent.

RAF Squadrons and training establishments in Ireland

The map on Page 14 is different from the others in that it shows training establishments in Ireland. Far away from the fighting in Flanders, there were four training depot stations there, and flying training could safely take place. Additionally there were two operational squadrons and an attached flight from the mainland.

Operational duties

In April 1918 the military situation in France caused the British government to extend conscription into the armed forces to Ireland. This was deeply unpopular, added to which the matter of Irish Home Rule still remained unresolved. Fearful that trouble might be caused by Irish Republicans, the Lord Lieutenant of Ireland, Field Marshal Viscount French, drew up plans to police Ireland using airpower. He told the Prime Minister, Lloyd George, of his plans to establish strongly defended air camps from which aircraft could patrol with bombs and machine-guns.

Accordingly two squadrons were dispatched in May 1918 – No. 105 Squadron to Omagh and No. 106

The approach to the mooring – Malahide Castle, Ireland.

Squadron to Fermoy. Both units had been formed at Andover in September 1917. Flying RE8s, they were both corps reconnaissance units, and that is what they remained, i.e. they were not used in an offensive role, in spite of French's original intent. These aircraft also proved useful in a communications role. A pilot joining No. 106 Squadron told of his approach to Fermoy in County Cork. He had been led to believe that the airfield was a racecourse just on the outskirts of town. He was shocked to find that the airfield was surrounded with barbed-wire entanglements and sand-bagged gun emplacements, almost as if it was on the front line in France.

Anti-submarine duties were also important. To cover the Irish Sea were units at Fishguard, Pembroke and Bangor. No. 244 Squadron, equipped with DH6 aircraft at Bangor, detached a flight to Tallaght, south-west of Dublin, to cover the sea approaches to that port. When the United States of America came into the war in 1917, it sent not only airships to augment those operated by the RNAS in the fight against the U-boat, but battleships in case the enemy should decide to use surface forces against Allied convoys and coastal shipping. The vital importance of anti-submarine forces was brought home to all concerned when the Royal Mail Steamer *Leinster* was sunk *en route* from Kingstown to Holyhead on 10 October 1918. More than 500 persons were either killed or injured. The day before the sinking, the airship that should have been covering the sea approaches to Kingstown was caught in the trees and wrecked as it approached its mooring at Malahide Castle, near Dublin. Five RAF passengers were buried in the military cemetery beside the Phoenix Park in Dublin.

Flying Training in Ireland

On 6 July 1918 plans were finalized to establish four training depot stations in Ireland. No. 22 TDS Gormanston, Co. Meath, was to become operational on 4 October, No. 23 TDS Baldonnel, Co. Dublin, on

RAF SQUADRONS AND TRAINING ESTABLISHMENTS IN IRELAND, NOVEMBER 1918

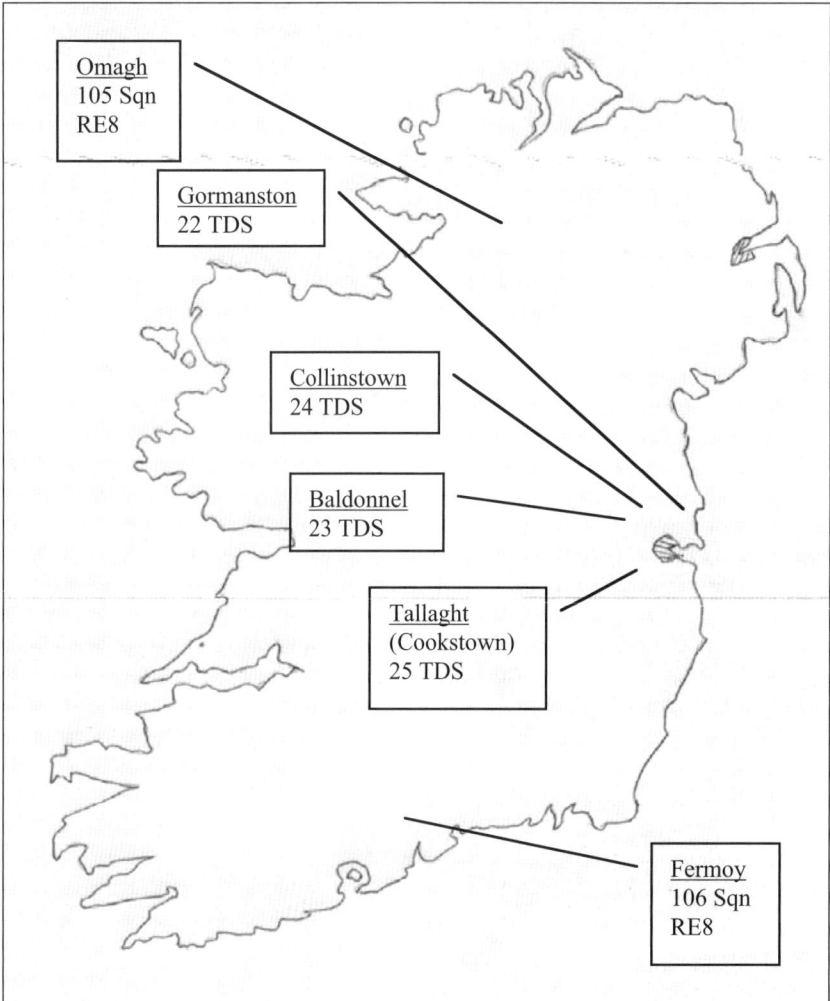

Omagh
105 Sqn
RE8

Gormanston
22 TDS

Collinstown
24 TDS

Baldonnel
23 TDS

Tallaght
(Cookstown)
25 TDS

Fermoy
106 Sqn
RE8

ORDER OF BATTLE: RAF IN THE FIELD, 11 NOVEMBER 1918

RAF in France and Belgium

The Final Allied Offensive The final offensive began on 8 August with the Battle of Amiens, and by 27 September the notorious Hindenburg Line was being assaulted. The RAF had 800 aircraft to support the armies, together with some 1,100 French aircraft. Confronting them were only 365 German aircraft, of which forty were fighters. Although 23,000 German prisoners had been taken, the enemy put up a tenacious defence, as the Americans found out. More than a thousand aircraft supported the attack on the enemy-held line. Seven hundred tons of bombs were dropped and 26,000 machine-gun bullets fired from the air. The map overleaf shows the concentration of operational squadrons in the Cambrai area. By nightfall on the 27th, a further 10,000 prisoners had been taken, together with two hundred guns, i.e. 33,000 prisoners in one day. Throughout October the offensive continued, and by 18 October the Belgian Army had reached Bruges and Zeebrugge and the British were holding a line along the River Lys. As they went the Germans carried out delaying demolitions. The warfare, which had been stuck in the trenches for well-nigh four years, was now fluid, and the cavalry could at last come into its own. By 1 November, the British forces had reached the Scheldt and the Oise, and Valenciennes was captured. German prisoners were now being taken in their thousands, and on 9 November British troops crossed the Scheldt. Two days later the Armistice was signed.

Fighter/Bomber Tactics in late 1918 As the war neared its end, the RAF had the strength and superiority that permitted the use of formations in wing strength. 10 Brigade's No. 80 Wing, for example, was operating fighter sweeps in layers. The Snipes of No. 4 Australian Squadron would form a top layer at 7,000–8,000 ft. Lower down would be the Bristol Fighters of No. 88 Squadron at 6,000 ft, the Camels of No. 46 Squadron at

9 October, and No 24 TDS Collinstown, Co. Dublin, and 25 TDS Cookstown, Co. Dublin, on 25 October. But the Armistice intervened before these stations could make any real contribution to the war effort. The main period of training activity at the four Irish TDSs was brief, lasting only from August until December. The plan was then to move the training units back to the mainland, but the rapid rundown in 1919 saw most training units disbanded. It is interesting to recite that American service personnel were posted to the TDSs to repair US naval aircraft.

RAF Strength in Ireland

RAF operational and training aircraft, together with the US Curtiss flying-boats, numbered more than 300 at the Armistice. There were 184 Avro 504s and 41 DH9s, together with the RE8s of the two squadrons at Omagh and Fermoy.

4,000 ft, the SE5As of No. 2 Australian Squadron at 3,000 ft, and finally the DH9s of No. 103 Squadron would be at 2,000 ft. The DH9 bombers would have the immediate protection of the SE5As, which themselves had three layers of fighters above. This left the Germans with no choice but to attack only the top layer of fighters if they were not themselves to come under attack. No. 80 Wing operated between Ypres and Arras and could penetrate some fifteen to twenty miles into enemy territory. While the German fighters were not destroyed in the air, they were driven from the skies. The wing therefore attacked the enemy's airfields, and the Germans risked either losing their aircraft on the ground or taking to the air to be engaged by the British forces. Indeed, during the last year of the war a great number of dogfights took place, the last major one taking place on the morning of 4 November. The Germans may have been outnumbered, but they were defeated not so much in the air as through the lack of fuel.

The Independent Bomber Force This comprised squadrons of 8 Brigade and units based in East Anglia. The squadrons of 8 Brigade were equipped with DH4s and DH9s of No. 41 Wing at Azelot, the Camels and DH9As of No. 88 Wing at Bettoncourt and the HP 0/400s of No. 83 Wing at St Inglevert, Xaffevillers in Belgium and Rovilles-aux-Chenes. In May 1918 the government decided that 8 Brigade had proved so successful in attacking targets divorced from the battlefield that it should be expanded into an Independent Bombing Force, the first of its kind to operate entirely independently of the Army. Its commander was Trenchard, who had resigned from the post of Chief of the Air Staff following

a disagreement with Lord Rothermere. Trenchard's command of 8 Brigade taught him the importance of the bomber offensive. Its primary targets would be German munitions factories, poison-gas plants, and aeroplane and aero-engine factories, with secondary targets in railways and blast furnaces if the primary targets could not be reached. The Camels of the IBF were there to provide fighter protection to the day-bombers, for the Germans were determined to stop the onslaught. But even when a formation lost most of its bombers other bombers would return to the same target. In addition, single aircraft of the force carried out photo-reconnaissance missions at great height. In this way the most economical use was made of the bomber effort. Altogether 550 tons of bombs were dropped in five months, 160 tons by day and 390 tons by night. Of the total, 220 tons were dropped on enemy aerodromes. As for attacks on British aerodromes, not a single aircraft was destroyed by enemy bombing during the lifetime of the IBF. The Handley Page V/1500s of the IBF were intended to bomb Berlin directly from their bases in the UK, but the Armistice intervened.

Deployments in France and Belgium The following pages list the units of the RAF in Brigades, Wings and Squadrons. These are shown in Appendix B as at their locations on 11 November 1918. It should be remembered, however, that the war was very fluid by this time, and unit locations would be changing to meet the needs of Army formations. The map on Page 16 only shows RAF squadrons. There were French and American units also taking part in the air offensive.

DEPLOYMENT OF RAF WINGS/SQUADRONS IN FRANCE AND BELGIUM, 11 NOVEMBER 1918

See map below

1. St Inglevert	115 Squadron	HP 0/400	
2. Calais (Marcke)	29 Squadron	SE5A	
3. Bergues	213 Squadron	Camel	
	202 Squadron	DH4	
4. Ste Marguerite	149 Squadron	FE2B	
5. Linselles	4 Squadron	RE8	
6. Menin	7 Squadron	RE8	
	70 Squadron	Camel	
	82 Squadron	AW FK8	
7. Halluin	41 Squadron	SE5A	
8. Reckem	48 Squadron	Bristol F2B	
	79 Squadron	Dolphin	
9. Bisseghem	24 Squadron	SE5A	
	108 Squadron	DH9	
10. Heule	204 Squadron	Camel	
11. Cuerne	74 Squadron	SE5A	
12. Harlebeke	38 Squadron	FE2B	
13. Staceghem	10 Squadron	AW FK8	
14. Sweveghem	53 Squadron	RE8	
15. Ascq	42 Squadron	RE8	
16. Lille (Ronchin)	103 Squadron	DH9	
17. Merchin	54 Squadron	Camel	
18. Gondercourt	6 Squadron	RE8	
19. Chemy	214 Squadron	HP 0/400	
20. Provin	58 Squadron	HP 0/400	
21. Carvin	152 Squadron	Camel	
22. Bersee	88 Squadron	Bristol F2B	
23. Auchy	16 Squadron	RE8	
24. Genech	2 Squadron	AW FK8	
25. Froidmont	21 Squadron	RE8	
26. Beavois	57 Squadron	DH4	
27. La Brayelle	18 Squadron	DH9A	
	25 Squadron	DH9A	
	32 Squadron	SE5A	
28. Bruille	203 Squadron	Camel	
	209 Squadron	Camel	
29. Erre	148 Squadron	FE2B	
30. Aniche	22 Squadron	Bristol F2B	
	40 Squadron	SE5A	
	64 Squadron	SE5A	

31. Abscon	19 Squadron	Dolphin	Iris Farm	20 Squadron	Bristol F2B
	98 Squadron	DH9		211 Squadron	DH9
32.. Villers-les-			Bertry East	23 Squadron	Dolphin
Cagnicourt	27 Squadron	DH9		92 Squadron	SE5A
	49 Squadron	DH9	Maretz	208 Squadron	Camel
	62 Squadron	Bristol F2B	Reumont	218 Squadron	DH9
33. Cambrai clutch of			Busigny	46 Squadron	Camel
airfields			Escaufort	85 Squadron	SE5A
Boussières	87 Squadron	Dolphin	34. Senlis-le-Sec	94 Squadron	SE5A
	210 Squadron	Camel	35. Bancourt	151 Squadron	Camel
Carnières	13 Squadron	RE8	36. Grand Fayt	35 Squadron	Bristol F2B
Estourmel	12 Squadron	RE8	37. Flaumont	80 Squadron	Camel
Inchy	3 Squadron	Camel	38. Aulnoy	5 Squadron	RE8
La Targette	56 Squadon	SE5A		52 Squadron	RE8
	201 Squadron	Camel	39. Tarcienne	9 Squadron	RE8
Quievy	60 Squadron	SE5A	40. Moislains	107 Squadron	DH9
Bevilliers	102 Squadron	FE2B		205 Squadron	DH9A
Selvigny	15 Squadron	RE8	41. Estrées-en-		
Malincourt	8 Squadron	AW FK8	Chausée	83 Squadron	FE2B
	73 Squadron	Camel		207 Squadron	HP 0/400
Caudry	59 Squadron	Bristol F2B	42. Bouvincourt	1 Squadron	SE5A
Bethencourt	11 Squadron	Bristol F2B		3 Squadron	Snipe
Bertry West	84 Squadron	SE5A	43. Hancourt	101 Squadron	FE2B

Note: Squadron locations not shown on the map below. Four airfields just south of Nancy hosted the following units:

Azelot – 55 Squadron DH4
          99 Squadron DH9/9A
          104 Squadron DH9
Bettoncourt – 45 Squadron Camel
          110 Squadron DH9A
Rovilles-aux-Chenes – 216 Squadron
Xaffevilliers – 97 Squadron HP 0/400
          100 Squadron HP 0/400

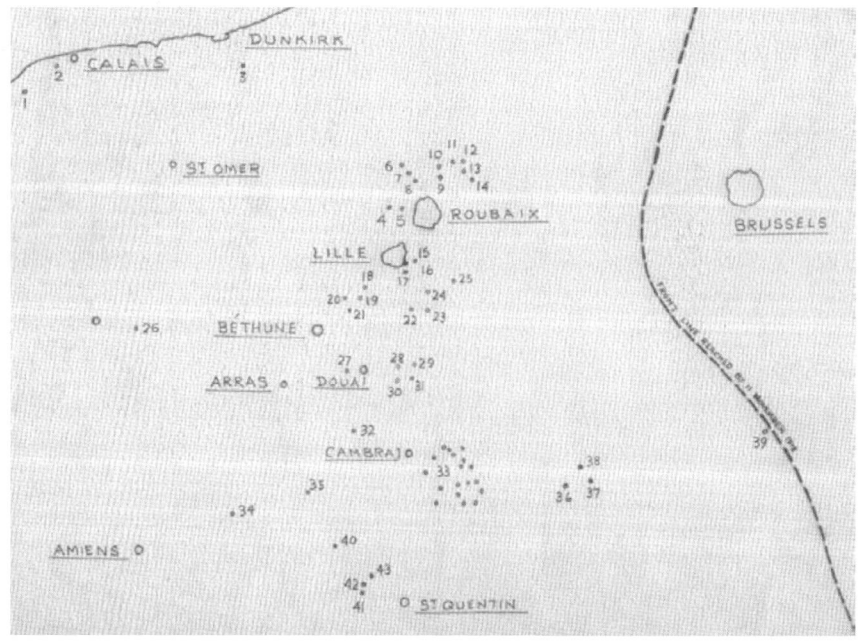

BRIGADES, WINGS, SQUADRONS AND MISCELLANEOUS UNITS

RAF in France and Belgium

HQ RAF
HQ Communications Squadron
No. 1 Aircraft Depot (includes No. 1 Port Depot)
No. 1 Aircraft Depot (D)
No. 1 Aircraft Depot (M)
No. 1 Aeroplane Supply Depot
No. 2 Aircraft Depot (includes No. 1 Port Depot)
No. 2 Aeroplane Supply Depot
Engine Repair Shops
British Aeronautical Supplies Depot

9 BRIGADE RAF **attached to GHQ**

No. 9 Wing comprising:
No.18 Sqn – DH9A (La Brayelle)
No.25 Sqn – DH9A (La Brayelle)
No.27 Sqn – DH 9 (Villers-les-Cagnicourt)
No.32 Sqn – SE5A (La Brayelle)
No.49 Sqn – DH9 (Villers-les-Cagnicourt)
No.62 Sqn – Bristol F2B (Villers-les-Cagnicourt)

No. 51 Wing comprising:
No. 1 Sqn – SE5A (Bouvincourt)
No. 43 Sqn – Snipe (Bouvincourt)
No. 94 Sqn – SE5A (Senlis le Sec)
No. 107 Sqn – DH9 (Moislains)
No. 205 Sqn – DH9A (Moislains

       9th Aircraft Park
5th Air Ammunition Column
9th Air Ammunition Column

   6th Reserve Lorry Park
20th Reserve Lorry Park

1 BRIGADE RAF **attached to 1st Army**

No. 1 Wing comprising:
No. 5 Sqn – RE8 (Aulnoy)
No. 16 Sqn – RE8 (Auchey)
No. 52 Sqn – RE8 (Aulnoy)

L Flight

1st Balloon Wing
4, 10 & 12 Balloon Companies

1st Aircraft Park
1st Air Ammunition Park

10th Wing comprising:
No. 19 Sqn – Dolphin (Abscon)
No. 22 Sqn – Bristol F2B (Aniche)
No. 40 Sqn – SE5A (Aniche)
No. 64 Sqn – SE5A (Aniche)
No. 98 Sqn – DH9 (Abscon)
No. 148 Sqn – FE2B (Erre)
No. 203 Sqn – Camel (Bruille)
No. 209 Sqn – Camel (Bruille)
I Flight
1st Reserve Lorry Park
11th Reserve Lorry Park

2 BRIGADE RAF **attached to 2nd Army**

No. 2 Wing comprising:
No. 4 Sqn – RE8 (Linselles)
No. 7 Sqn – RE8 (Menin)
No. 10 Sqn – AW FK8 (Staceghem)
No. 53 Sqn – RE8 (Sweveghem)
No. 82 Sqn – AW FK8 (Menin)

M Flight

No. 11 Wing comprising:
No. 29 Sqn – SE5A (Marcke)
No. 41 Sqn – SE5A (Halluin)
No. 48 Sqn – Bristol F2B (Reckham)
No. 70 Sqn – Camel (Menin)
No. 74 Sqn – SE5A (Cuerne)
No. 79 Sqn – Dolphin (Reckham)
No. 149 Sqn – FE2B (Ste-Marguerite)
No. 206 Sqn – DH9 (Linselles)

2 BRIGADE RAF

2nd Balloon Wing
Nos 5, 6, 7, 8 & 17 Balloon Companies

2nd Reserve Lorry Park
7th Reserve Lorry park
No. 8 Salvage Section

2nd Air Ammunition Column
7th Air Ammunition Column

3 BRIGADE RAF attached to 3rd Army

12th Wing comprising:
No. 12 Sqn – RE8 (Estourmel)
No. 13 Sqn – RE8 (Carnieres)
No. 15 Sqn – RE8 (Selvigny)
No. 59 Sqn – Bristol F2B (Caudry)
N Flight

13th Wing comprising:
No. 56 Sqn – SE5A (La Targette)
No. 60 Sqn – SE5A (Quievy)
No. 87 Sqn – Dolphin (Boussières)
No. 210 Sqn – DH9 (Iris Farm)

No. 3 Balloon Wing
Nos 12, 16, 18 & 19 Balloon Companies

3rd Aircraft Park
3rd Air Ammunition Column
3rd Reserve Lorry Park

19th Reserve Lorry Park
No. 6 Salvage Section
No. 9 Salvage Section

5 BRIGADE RAF attached to 4th Army

No. 15 Wing
No. 6 Sqn – RE8 (Gondecourt)
No. 8 Sqn – AW FK8 (Malincourt)
No. 9 Sqn – RE8 (Tarcienne)
No. 35 Sqn – Bristol F2B (Grand Fayt)
No. 73 Sqn – Camel (Malincourt)
No. 3 Sqn (Australian Flying Corps)

No. 22 Wing
No. 24 Sqn – SE5A (to Bisseghem)
No. 46 Sqn – Camel (Busigny)
No. 80 Sqn – Camel (Flaumont)
No. 84 Sqn – SE5A (Bertry West)
No. 85 Sqn – SE5A (Phallempin)
No. 208 Sqn – Camel (Maretz)

No. 89 Wing comprising:
No. 20 Sqn – Bristol F2B (Iris Farm)
No. 23 Sqn – Dolphin (Bertry East)
No. 92 Sqn – SE5A (Bertry East)
No. 101 Sqn – FE2B (Hancourt)
No. 211 Sqn – DH9 (Iris Farm)
No. 218 Sqn – DH9 (Reumont)

No. 5 Balloon Wing
Nos. 13, 14 & 15 Balloon Companies

4th Aircraft Park
4th Aircraft Ammunition Depot
No. 7 Salvage Section

4th Reserve Lorry Park
12th Reserve Lorry Park

10 BRIGADE RAF attached to 5th Army

No. 80 Wing comprising:
No. 54 Sqn – Camel (Merchin)
No. 88 Sqn – Bristol F2B (Bersée)

No. 81 Wing comprising:
No. 2 Sqn – AW FK8 (Genech)
No. 21 Sqn – RE8 (Froidmont)

No. 103 Sqn – DH9 (Ronchin)
(Australian Flying Corps)
No. 2 Sqn – SE5A
No. 4 Sqn – Snipe

No. 42 Sqn – RE8 (Ascq)

P Flight

No. 8 Balloon Wing
Nos. 3, 11 and 20 Balloon Companies

10th Aircraft Park
10th Air Ammunition Column
9th Reserve Lorry Park

8 BRIGADE (INDEPENDENT BOMBER FORCE)

41st Wing comprising:
No. 55 Sqn – DH4 (Azelot)
No. 99 Sqn – DH9 (Azelot)
No. 104 Sqn – DH9 (Azelot)

No. 83 Wing comprising:
No. 97 Sqn – HP 0/400 (Xaffevillers)
No. 100 Sqn – HP 0/400 (Xaffevillers)
No. 115 Sqn – HP 0400 (St Inglevert)
No. 215 Sqn – HP 0/400 (Xaffevillers)
No. 216 Sqn – HP 0/400 (Rovilles-aux-Chenes)

No. 88 Wing comprising:
No. 45 Sqn – Camel (Bettoncourt)
No. 110 Sqn – DH9A (Bettoncourt)

3rd Aircraft Depot
6th Aircraft Park
12th Aircraft Park
8th Air Ammunition Column

5th Reserve Lorry Park
10th Reserve Lorry Park
3rd Aeroplane Supply Depot

(Source document: National Archives, AIR/1/2129)

Aircraft Repair Depot near Rang-du-Fliers. Damaged aircraft were rebuilt at these depots and reissued to the mobile supply parks nearer the front line.

RAF padre takes a Sunday-morning service at No. 2 Aeroplane Supply Depot in 1918.

The pilot of an SE5A holding 85 Squadron's score-board for 14 days in June 1918.

THE ITALIAN THEATRES OF OPERATIONS

The British Air Service did not operate on the Italian Front until November 1917, after the Italian retreat from Isonzo, when the Italian Brigade was formed and dispatched. With the intervention of the Allies, the Austrians retreated and this was then turned into a rout. Cooperation with the Russians in this theatre commenced in the latter part of 1916. The Italian theatre of operations in 1918 was divided between northern and southern Italy. The RAF squadrons in the north supported the Italian armies facing the Austro-Hungarian forces. The air tasks were shared by British, French and Italian units. The RAF squadrons in the south were concerned principally with the containment of the enemy naval threat posed by Austro-Hungarian

and German surface vessels and submarines operating from ports in the Adriatic. The protection of Britain's trade and reinforcement routes through the Mediterranean Sea meant stationing naval units in Gibraltar, Malta and Alexandria in Egypt. Land operations in Albania had also to be supported, and the deployment of RAF squadrons in Italy and Malta reflected these operational requirements. Although all the deployments in this chapter are given for 11 November 1918, it is worth remembering that the Allies negotiated a separate peace with Austria-Hungary on 4 November.

Northern Italy

The Piave offensive by the Austro-Hungarian forces in June 1918 was meant to defeat the Italian armies facing them across the River Piave. After initial successes, the Italians finally drove them back across the river, and the front was again stabilized. The RAF's contribution to the land operations comprised ground attack, artillery observation, reconnaissance and air fighting. The ground-attack squadrons were No. 66, based at San Pietru, in Gu, and No. 28 at Sarcedo, equipped with Camels. The RE8s of No. 34 Squadron based at San Luca carried out artillery observation reconnaissance. This was often a very hazardous task since the observer would have his eyes down for most of the time and could easily miss enemy fighters swooping down from above. The Bristol fighters of No. 139 Squadron based at Arcade provided fighter and escort patrols. Major W.G. Barker VC, DSO, MC, who was the commanding officer of No. 139 Squadron during 1918, brought down fifty-three German aircraft and ranked seventh among the air aces. The aircrews who fought in direct support of the land forces were called 'corps' pilots, whereas the fighter pilots were called 'Army' pilots. To gain awards for valour was much more difficult for the 'corps' pilots since success was not measured in numbers of aircraft shot down.

Southern Italy

The RAF squadrons based in southern Italy, as has been said, were principally involved in containing the threat posed by enemy naval forces. Not surprisingly, all the RAF units involved were ex-RNAS squadrons, which all

DH9s of No. 226 Sqn at Taranto/Pizzone.

THE ITALIAN THEATRES AND MALTA – 11 NOVEMBER 1918

LEGEND
Anti-submarine   A/S
Bomber   B
Fighter   F
Fighter/Ground
  Attack   F/Ga
Fighter Escort   E
Artillery
  Observation   A/O
Reconnaissance   R

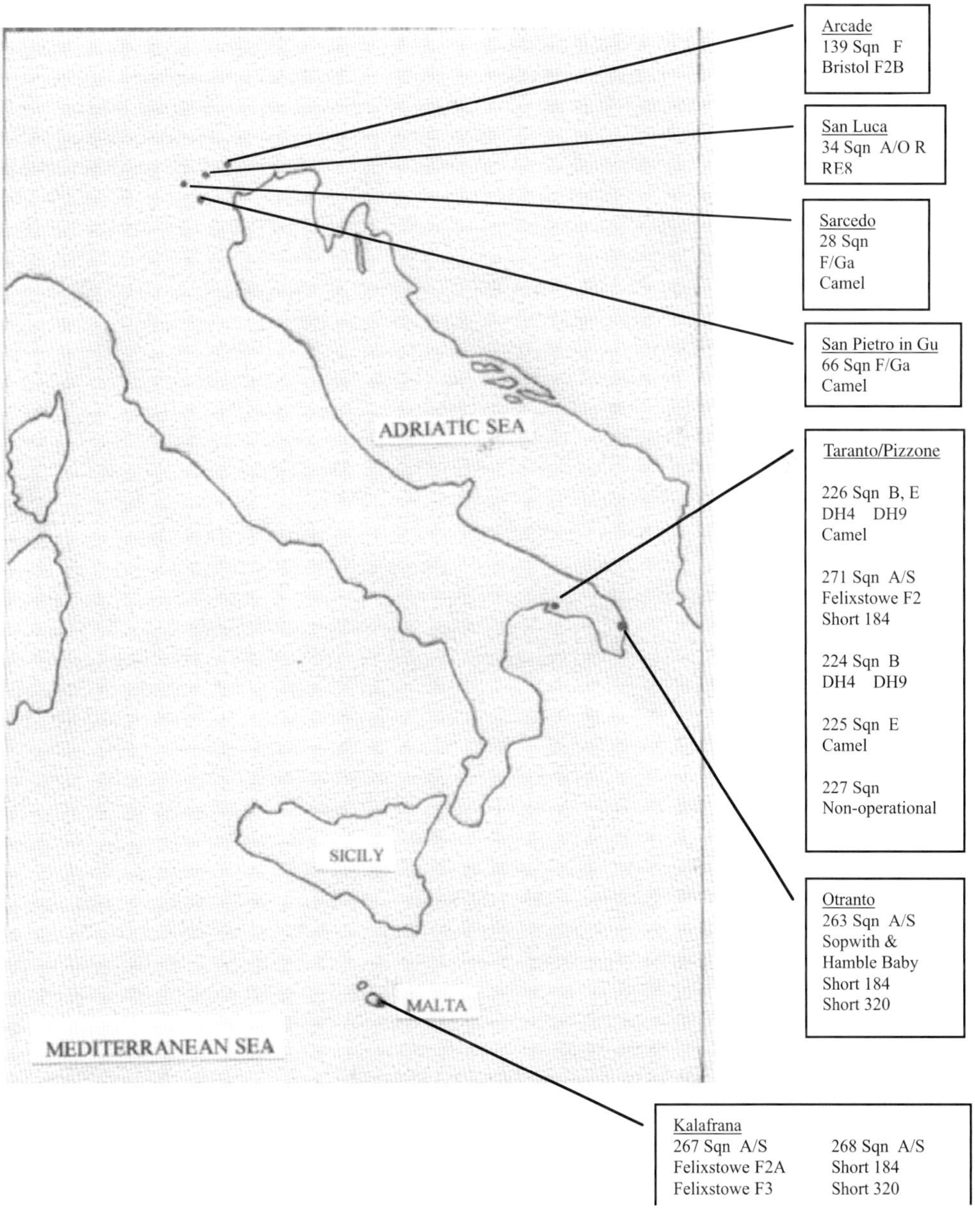

ADRIATIC SEA

SICILY

MEDITERRANEAN SEA

MALTA

Arcade
139 Sqn   F
Bristol F2B

San Luca
34 Sqn A/O R
RE8

Sarcedo
28 Sqn
F/Ga
Camel

San Pietro in Gu
66 Sqn F/Ga
Camel

Taranto/Pizzone

226 Sqn B, E
DH4   DH9
Camel

271 Sqn A/S
Felixstowe F2
Short 184

224 Sqn B
DH4   DH9

225 Sqn E
Camel

227 Sqn
Non-operational

Otranto
263 Sqn A/S
Sopwith &
Hamble Baby
Short 184
Short 320

Kalafrana
267 Sqn A/S   268 Sqn A/S
Felixstowe F2A   Short 184
Felixstowe F3   Short 320

had the old numbers prefixed with 200 when the RAF took them over in April 1918. In view of the activities of enemy submarines in the Mediterranean and Adriatic, the work of the aircraft engaged in anti-submarine duties was of a most important character. In the early part of 1917 a wing was formed in southern Italy to assist the Otranto barrage in closing the southern end of the Adriatic to enemy submarines, and in bombing the Austrian naval ports in the Adriatic. These units also assisted materially in protecting convoys and in harassing submarines in all parts of the Mediterranean. Other functions were the bombing of lines of communication and places of military importance in Turkey and Albania, and the defence of Allied territory from enemy aerial attack.

MIDDLE-EASTERN THEATRES – EGYPT, PALESTINE AND IRAQ

Egypt

The RFC had forces protecting the Suez Canal and its sea approaches as soon as it was known that the Turks intended attacking the canal early in 1915. With the build-up of a training organization in 1916, the RFC was able to provide units for Mesopotamia (Iraq) and Salonica in Greece. The RFC organization became a brigade based on Egypt, then, in 1917, a major-general's command. By October 1918 in Egypt, there was one training brigade of eight squadrons, three schools of special flying, one cadet wing and a school of military aeronautics. It was then possible to support one brigade of seven squadrons in Palestine, one wing of three squadrons in Mesopotamia and one wing of three squadrons in Macedonia.

Palestine

The final Allied offensive of the war against the Turks in Palestine began on 17 September 1918. Air power played a very important part in the offensive, and units of the RAF and RAAF (Royal Australian Air Force) were in action against German and Turkish telephone exchanges, and telegraph offices at Tulkarm, Nablus and Afula were bombed. Thus all contact between General von Liman and his subordinate commanders was severed and the main German airfield at Jenin was put out of action. During the ensuing seven days roads, railways and troop concentrations were bombed. On 20 September Allenby's troops entered the Jezreel Valley. As the Turks retreated from Tulkarm and Nablus, the RAF and RAAF harried the retreating forces, creating such carnage that some pilots asked to be spared any future missions. The Turks had been overwhelmed by British airpower.

Mesopotamia (Iraq)

The RFC in Mesopotamia in 1915 consisted of a composite unit of aircraft sent from Egypt. The air force personnel in 1915 were titled 'air unit personnel' gazetted to the RFC as A Flight. On 4 November 1915 a reinforcement draft arrived at Basra comprising a flying squadron headquarters and B Flight to be added to the existing unit (A Flight), which was then titled No. 30 Squadron. This unit was severely handicapped through lack of machines, climatic conditions and inadequate personnel. So in 1917 an extra unit, No. 63 Squadron, was sent out to form a wing. This came under the command of the Middle-East Brigade. In March 1918 No. 72 Squadron arrived at Basra, and the wing rapidly gained air ascendancy. Air supremacy was maintained for the remainder of the war. At the cessation of hostilities all three squadrons were equipped with Martinsyde 'Elephants' and were deployed as shown on the map opposite.

A scene photographed on 20 September 1918 on the Nablus–Beisan Road.

RE8 of 142 Sqn, Palestine.

SE5As of 111 Sqn, also in Palestine.

MIDDLE-EASTERN THEATRES – PALESTINE, EGYPT AND IRAQ, 11 NOVEMBER 1918

LEGEND
F = Fighter
G/Ga = Ground Attack
TR = Tactical Reconnaissance
AO = Artillery Observation

B = Bomber
A/S = Anti-submarine
Co-Op = Army Co-operation
E = Escort

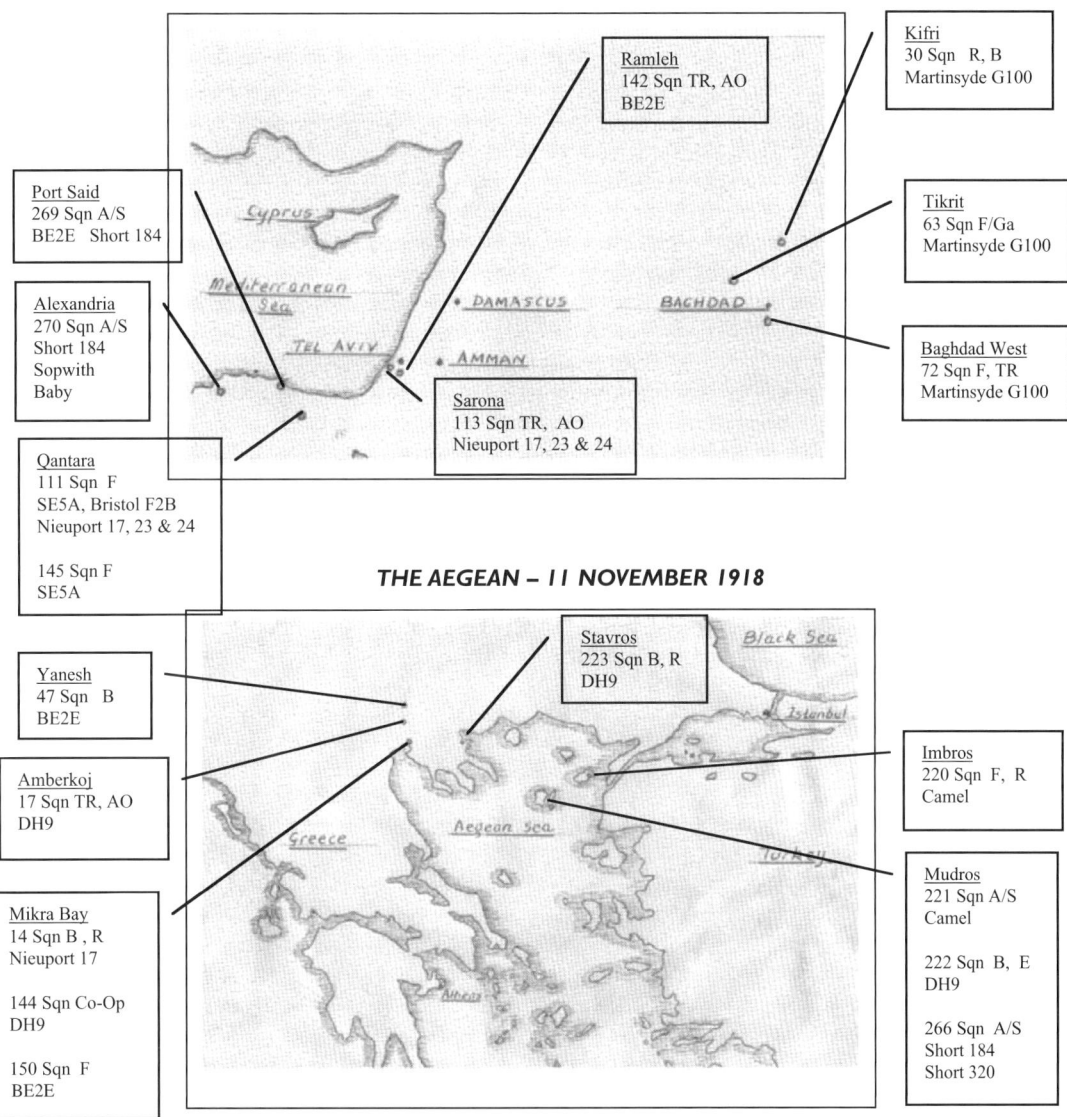

Kifri
30 Sqn R, B
Martinsyde G100

Ramleh
142 Sqn TR, AO
BE2E

Port Said
269 Sqn A/S
BE2E   Short 184

Tikrit
63 Sqn F/Ga
Martinsyde G100

Alexandria
270 Sqn A/S
Short 184
Sopwith
Baby

Baghdad West
72 Sqn F, TR
Martinsyde G100

Sarona
113 Sqn TR, AO
Nieuport 17, 23 & 24

Qantara
111 Sqn F
SE5A, Bristol F2B
Nieuport 17, 23 & 24

145 Sqn F
SE5A

THE AEGEAN – 11 NOVEMBER 1918

Stavros
223 Sqn B, R
DH9

Yanesh
47 Sqn B
BE2E

Imbros
220 Sqn F, R
Camel

Amberkoj
17 Sqn TR, AO
DH9

Mudros
221 Sqn A/S
Camel

222 Sqn B, E
DH9

Mikra Bay
14 Sqn B, R
Nieuport 17

144 Sqn Co-Op
DH9

266 Sqn A/S
Short 184
Short 320

150 Sqn F
BE2E

The assets of No. 221 Squadron were absorbed by No. 222 Squadron in October 1918, but since 221 Squadron was reconstituted with DH9s in December it has been left as a Mudros unit.

THE AEGEAN THEATRE

Group Origins The origins of the Aegean Group RAF, composed largely of ex-RNAS units, did not follow the European pattern of simply adding the Number 200 to the RNAS squadron number. Air Organization Memorandum 800 provided that, on 1 April 1918 ,the numbering of ex-RNAS units remote from the European theatre would be Nos 220 to 227 Squadrons inclusive. Of these, the ex-RNAS units in the Aegean were lettered A, B, C & D Squadrons, and these, according to best evidence, became Nos 222, 223, 220 and 221 Squadrons RAF respectively. The map above shows the location of these and the other units in the Aegean theatre on 11 November 1918. The units belonged to Nos 62 and 63 Wings of No. 15 (Aegean) Group.

Operations   On 14 September the Allies launched their offensive on the Salonika front. On that day the Austrians asked the Allied Powers, together with the USA and the neutrals, to agree to a 'confidential and non-committal exchange of views' on neutral soil with a view to seeing if peace might be possible. Some 36,000 Serb, Italian and French forces were in action against German and Bulgarian forces. On 16 September two Bulgarian regiments mutinied and the Germans had to act to prevent a rout. No German forces were available for reinforcement, the nearest being a brigade in the Crimea. The Bulgarian defeats in Macedonia led to unrest in the Bulgarian capital, Sofia, and on 25 September British forces entered that country. With the Germans in retreat, all hope of holding the Balkans was gone, and the southern approaches of the heartland were open to Allied advance. The squadrons based in the northern Aegean were employed in bombing, artillery observation, reconnaissance and Army cooperation in support of the land campaign against the Central Powers. Only at Mudros were there units employed in maritime reconnaissance and anti-submarine work. Below is the report from the RAF Aegean Group based at Mudros, dated 27 October 1918:

> Five DH machines of No. 226 Squadron left Marsh aerodrome at 09.15 hrs on the 25th October. And landed at Imbros to refuel. They left again at 10.50 hrs to carry out a photo reconnaissance of Constantinople. Attacked by German machines … a Fokker and an Albatross shot down … anti-aircraft fire accurate. All aircraft landed safely at Imbros then returned to their base at Lemnos.

It is clear from reports at this time that San Stefano airfield was frequently reconnoitred, as was Hardar Pasha railway station. Shipping was also observed. No. 220 Squadron at Imbros was also actively engaged in reconnoitring railway stations for evidence of troop and materiel movement.

INDIA AND ADEN, 11 NOVEMBER 1918

Operations in India

In 1917 two squadrons of the RFC were provided for India, where they played an important part in quelling trans-frontier risings. As early as 1916 a flight of aircraft had been dispatched from Egypt to play a useful part in an expedition against Darfur. At the Armistice only two RAF squadrons were stationed in India – No. 114 Squadron at Lahore and No. 31 Squadron at Risalpur. These were engaged in sporadic activity in support of

the Waziristan Field Force. Extracts from squadron records show that these units were engaged almost exclusively on training. The greatest threat to life was cholera, which claimed some lives, and influenza outbreaks could reduce squadron manpower availability to less than 50 per cent.

No. 31 Squadron (HQ and three flights) – Risalpur **for week ending 9 November 1918**

Sunday	Four Lewis gun practices for training pilots and observers.
Monday	Two practice recces including recce to Tarbala.
Tuesday	Four bomb-dropping practices. Twenty 20 lb bombs dropped. Training of pilots and observers.
Wednesday	Practice flight over Camera Obscura. Training of pilots and observers.
Thursday	One photo-recce where 48 plates were exposed. Training of pilots and observers.
Friday	Two cross-country flights. Lahore to Risalpur, delivery of a machine by air.
Saturday	Test flying for officer joining the RAF, practice flights, engine rigging and tests.

General   The average sick and unavailable for duty is 22% of strength. Influenza epidemics still causing considerable loss of efficiency in the work of the squadron but is now apparently decreasing in severity.

Total flying times: By Pilots – 19 h 27 min
By Observers – 7 h 7 min

No. 114 Squadron (HQ and B Flight) – Quetta   [Records do not show on which days during the week ending 9 November the following activities took place.]

Day 1   Five machines flew across country from Quetta to Lahore (about 700 miles). Formation flight Quetta to Jacobabad, Reti, Lodran, Multan, Montgomery and Lahore. En route photographs were taken of landing grounds etc., fourteen exposures being made. The flight was completely successful and the five machines arrived simultaneously at Lahore in excellent formation. The times were as follows:

Quetta to Jacobabad	3 h 50 min
Jacobabad to Reti	2 h 25 min
Reti to Multan	3 h 32 min
Multan to Montgomery	1 h 47 min
Montgomery to Lahore	<u>1 h 43 min</u>
	13 h 17 min

Day 2   36 photographs taken for mosaic of Lahore.

Day 3   Test flight for officers joining the RAF.
Day 4   Engine and rigging tests.

General   HQ and B Flight moved from Quetta to Lahore. The average sick and unavailable for duty is 13% of strength.

Total flying hours: By Pilots – 129 h 44 mins By Observers – Nil

No. 114 Squadron (A Flight) – Lahore
Day 1   Seventeen contact patrol practices over aerodrome for purpose of training special class of infantry officers, NCOs and men.
Day 2   Test flights for officers joining the RAF.
Day 3   Engine and rigging tests.

General   The average sick and unavailable for duty is 13% of strength.

Total flying hours By pilots – 7 h 26 min
By Observers – Nil

Operations in Aden

Aden Flight   Operations for the week ending 12 November 1918

Operations   Active operations ceased on 31 October owing to the Armistice with Turkey and by orders of HQ Aden Field Force flying ceased on that date.

General   During the week all engines fitted to machines have been top overhauled. The four machines erected have been thoroughly examined and overhauled. Two engines have also been completely overhauled in workshops. All engines on charge are now serviceable. In spite of the influenza epidemic the <u>death</u> of the flight remains satisfactory.

There have so far been no cases of influenza in the unit. There have been two admissions to hospital since the last report, with minor ailments.

[Note: the word 'death' has been underlined in the text above and a question mark was placed against it in the original records due to this amusing typographical error.]

Total flying hours: 1 h 19 min

Signed Major SOII for Director of Aeronautics in India

THE NORTH-WEST FRONTIER OF INDIA, 11 NOVEMBER 1918

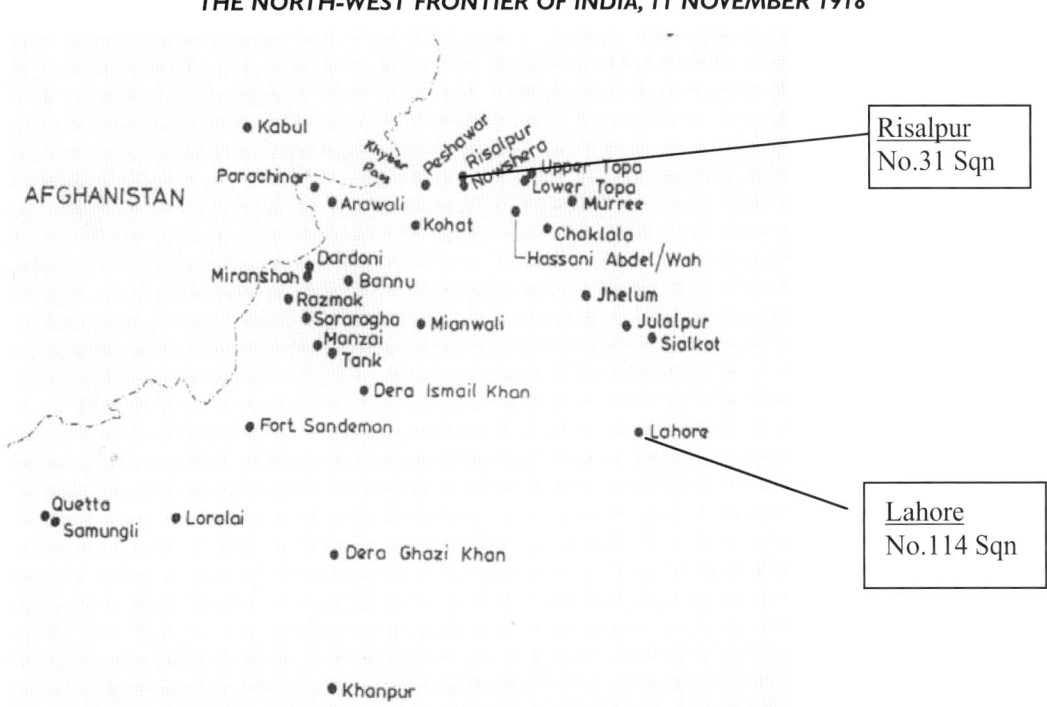

A Bristol Fighter 2B of No. 31 Squadron in India. These aircraft replaced the BE2Es in June 1919, and remained in service in India until 1931.

A BE2E at Tank on the North-West Frontier during operations against the Mahsuds.

State of the Royal Air Force at the cessation of hostilities. Source: National Archives AIR/1/718

Service Squadrons maintained A comparison between the active operational squadrons on strength in August 1914 and 31 October 1918 shows how massively the RAF (RFC and RNAS) grew over the war years:

Theatre of Operations	August 1914	October 1918
Western Front	4 (RFC)	84 + 5 flights
Independent Force	–	10
5 Group	–	3
India	–	2
Italy	–	4
Middle East	–	13
Russia	–	1/2
Home Defence	–	18
Naval Units	1 (RNAS)	64
	5	200 + 5 flights

Expansion of Motor Transport (RFC only)

	August 1914	August 1915	August 1916	August 1917	31 October 1918 (RAF)
On charge	320	2,469	5,282	8,584	23,260

The statistics below show the enormous increase in aerial photography, an aspect of reconnaissance that not only informed Army commanders of enemy troop positions but helped air commanders to assess the effectiveness of bombing raids.

Results of Operations in the Air

	Enemy A/C accounted for	Our machines missing	Bombs dropped (tons)	Rounds fired at ground targets
Western Front – July 1916 to 11 November 1918	6,904	2,484	6,402	10,238,182
1 January to 11 November 1918				
Independent Force	150	111	540	353,237
Home Forces	8	Nil	Nil	Nil
5th Group & Naval Units	470	114	662	Nil
Italy	405	44	59	222,704
Egypt	25	9	43	50,937
Mesopotamia	6	13	25	107,563
Salonika	59	8	130	193,354
Palestine	81	24	74	735,550
India (Aden)	Nil	Nil	30	7,527

Other Statistics (all theatres)
Enemy Balloons Brought Down (Western Front only) – 258
Hours flown – 1,016,846
Photographs taken – 501,116

The Qualities of Aircraft and Aircrews

Before moving on to describe the fortunes of the RAF in the 1920s, a little thought is given to the quality of aircraft and aircrews at the cessation of hostilities in 1918.

Quality of Aircraft The aircraft of the RFC/RNAS were developed from the flimsy Blériot-like aeroplanes that took to the air in 1914 to the much more powerful machines with longer range, armament and bombs that

were on strength in November 1918. Starting out as a reconnaissance vehicle, during the war the aeroplane had also become a reconnaissance seaplane, a torpedo-bomber, a land bomber, a ground-attack aircraft and a fighter. By 1918 a four-engined bomber, the HP V/1500, flying from Norfolk, had the range and bomb-carrying capacity to reach and cause serious bomb damage to Berlin. The reliability of engines had also increased to the point where, within a year of the war's ending, a Vimy bomber was able to fly the Atlantic Ocean, only ten years after Blériot's crossing of the English Channel. The Camel, Snipe, SE5A and the Pup were all fighters with enhanced service ceilings and the speed to outclimb adversaries. Although the Camel could be very tricky in a turn, once a pilot had mastered this aircraft he had a formidable weapon, and the Camel accounted for over 2,800 enemy aircraft. The SE5A was easy to fly and was strong. Both aircraft had a similar service ceiling of some 22,000 feet and an endurance of two and a half hours, although the SE5A was faster, with a top speed of 138 mph. Two aircraft that were to survive the war and go on to serve the RAF into the 1930s were the Bristol F2B and the Airco DH9A. The DH9A could carry a larger bomb load than the Bristol Fighter, 250 lb as against 112 lb, but both were used as general-purpose aircraft in Ireland, India and Mesopotamia during the inter-war years. Their rugged construction meant that they could operate in hostile environments. The biplane, and even more so the triplane, was very manoeuvrable, and because there were two wings to share the aircraft's load, they were not so highly stressed. Manoeuvrability, rate of climb, good top speeds and sturdy and simple construction

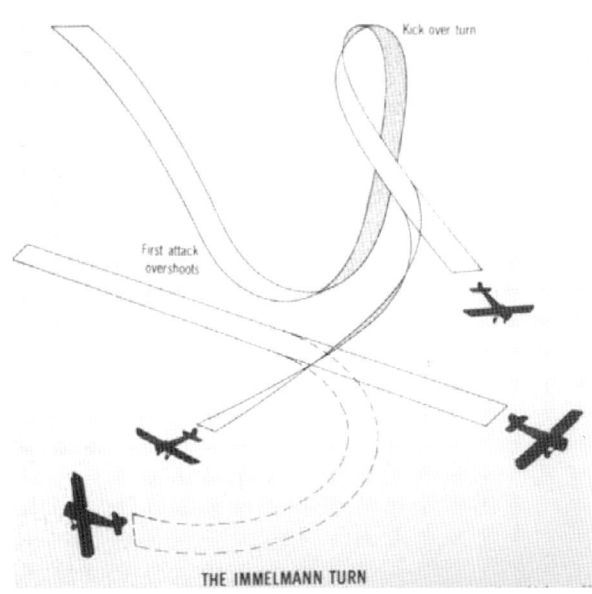

Kick over turn

First attack overshoots

THE IMMELMANN TURN

were the hallmark of the RAF's best fighter aircraft in 1918. Finally there was the Avro 504, of which variants A to L were built. Although used as a home-defence fighter and by the RNAS as a bomber, its most outstanding role was as an *ab initio* trainer. Altogether over 10,000 of these aircraft were built, yet when it was first conceived by Alliot Verdon Roe he expected only a handful to be ordered.

Quality of Aircrews As has been pointed out, the First World War began with the aeroplane intended simply as a reconnaissance vehicle. When air fighting began, both sides developed tactics in an attempt to gain an advantage, but this was always temporary since the other side would seek to redress the balance. The 'Lufbery Circle' and the 'Immelman Turn', attributed to the pilots named, provide examples of how tactics were developed, given the performance of adversarial aircraft.

What made these 'Knights of the Air' was a recognition of general rules of survival in combat. There were no self-sealing fuel tanks, no protective armour and no parachutes. A fighter pilot survived long enough to become a veteran if he overcame the initial desire to open fire at very long range instead of waiting until he got in close. By 1917 the lone pilot had been replaced by the patrol leader, who would need to see the enemy first and lead his patrol to effect surprise and bring the maximum number of guns to bear on the enemy. Most air battles lasted only a matter of minutes, and the leader needed to keep calm and use sun and cloud to his

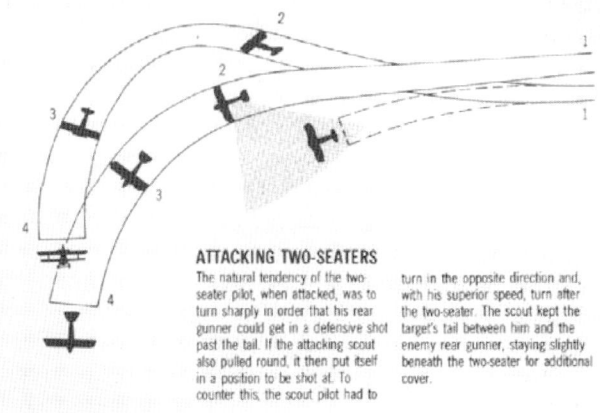

ATTACKING TWO-SEATERS
The natural tendency of the two-seater pilot, when attacked, was to turn sharply in order that his rear gunner could get in a defensive shot past the tail. If the attacking scout also pulled round, it then put itself in a position to be shot at. To counter this, the scout pilot had to turn in the opposite direction and, with his superior speed, turn after the two-seater. The scout kept the target's tail between him and the enemy rear gunner, staying slightly beneath the two-seater for additional cover.

Camel Tactics

advantage. During the war, air fighting schools and night bombing schools proliferated to keep pace with the needs of squadrons at home, on the Western Front and further afield.

When the war ended the RAF had only the experience of the one conflict upon which to build an air force for the future. The service was left with the biplane, canvas and wood construction, the open cockpit, the Lewis and Vickers gun. It was to be almost twenty years before stressed skin, closed cockpit, eight-gun Browning- or cannon-armed, all-metal monoplane fighters took their place on RAF squadrons.

Chapter 2
The Lean Years, 1919 to 1924

The Trenchard Memorandum – Airships – Civil aviation – RAF operations in Russia, Ireland, Germany, the Middle East, India and the Chanak crisis – RAF air policy – State of the RAF – Demobilization – RAF v. Navy and Army – the Salisbury Committee and RAF expansion – New defence orders – Hendon Air Pageants – RAF training

The Trenchard Memorandum

A Role for the RAF? While RAF volunteers were fighting in Russia, of which more later in the chapter, the parent arm was being run down from a wartime strength of 188 operational squadrons and fifteen flights, with a complement of 291,170 officers and men and 22,647 aircraft. Within months only thirty-three squadrons remained, of which eight were in the process of formation. There was still an RAF presence in Ireland and India, just two squadrons in each location, and in the Middle East. The strategic bomber force had been disbanded, which, apart from the colonial deployments already mentioned, left only cooperation with the Army and aircraft for the Navy. A *raison d'être* for an independent air force seemed to some almost extinct, and the Chief of the Imperial General Staff (CIGS), Sir Henry Wilson, and the First Lord of the Admiralty, Walter Long, saw no good reason why members of the RAF should not be returned to their respective services where they belonged before 1 April 1918. The Prime Minster, David Lloyd George, did not, at that time, wish to see Air as a separate ministry, and Churchill, the War Minister, was titled Minster for War and the Air. Churchill, however, did not intend allowing the RAF to be absorbed back into the Army, and in a letter to Walter Long he made it clear that he was giving new ranks and titles to the RAF, thus sending a clear message to both sister services that the RAF was to remain an independent air force.

Trenchard replaces Sykes When Trenchard resigned as Chief of the Air Staff (CAS) in April 1918 over differences between himself and Lord Rothermere, the Air Secretary, his place was taken by Major-General Sykes. The Secretary of State for Air had been Lord Weir, and on leaving his post, he pressed Churchill to reappoint Trenchard to the post of CAS. He felt that Trenchard had a mind of his own, but Trenchard and Sykes had very different ideas about the future of the RAF. Sykes had a plan that was too grandiose, given the political and financial climate of 1919. His was a plan for an Imperial Air Force, including the Dominions, and while Canada and Australia supported the idea, offering to provide some aircraft, the cost of Sykes's proposals amounted to £21 million. In contrast , as Lord Weir put it to Churchill, Trenchard 'can make do with a little and won't have to be carried'. This swung opinion in Trenchard's favour.

His plan was to simply build the foundations for a future expanded service, keeping only the barest number of squadrons to meet the requirements of the Royal Navy, the Army and defence of the outposts of the Empire. Trenchard described it as 'building the foundations for a castle which may be built at some later date but in the meantime building a cottage upon those foundations'. The problem of what to do with Sykes was solved by appointing him as Controller of Civil Aviation, with a CBE to match. On Trenchard's reappointment as CAS on 11 January 1919, Churchill asked him to put his ideas for a future independent air force on paper; he, Churchill, would do the same, and then they would compare notes. Churchill accepted Trenchard's proposals but got his own way on the new RAF titles, upon which the CIGS, Field Marshal Sir Henry Wilson, had predictably poured scorn. The result was the Trenchard Memorandum.

White Paper Cmd 467: The Permanent Organization of the Royal Air Force

This was the official title of the Trenchard Memorandum, which ran to 7,000 words and cost 1d from His Majesty's Stationery Office, and is reproduced in Appendix C. The Air Ministry was to be divided into:

a. A service department
b. A civil department
c. A supply and research department
d. A clerical department

As has been said, Trenchard had to make do with a little. The Air Estimates for the year 1919/20 amounted to £21,471,000. From that sum an element had to go to civil aviation, which came under the Air Ministry. From these meagre resources he had to maintain the squadrons remaining in service and the bases on which they were situated. In India, however, the funds for maintaining RAF units came from the Indian government, but this was to give rise to friction later because the RAF Command was subordinated to the Army, and the money came from the Army vote. Later RAF inspecting officers were to report on the sad material state of squadrons in India.

Where new expenditure would be required it was for training and support facilities for the RAF. While grudgingly accepting that the RAF would, at least for the time being, remain independent, the Army and the

Royal Navy saw no reason why the new service should not use existing colleges, training depots and supply and medical services. But Trenchard took literally the meaning of the word independent. He wanted above all to create an 'air force spirit'. Air operations were not simply to be an adjunct to land or sea operations, but ones that could be carried out independently. He did not want RAF pilots simply to be at the beck and call of Army commanders, acting as taxi drivers. An RAF spirit could only be engendered if RAF aircrews were taught the business of air operations and aircraft handling from the beginning. If the Army wanted RAF support, squadrons would be assigned on an Army cooperation basis. Similarly the Navy would be assigned RAF units to work on aircraft-carriers. Maritime operations by land-based aircraft would be provided by the RAF squadrons. It might be more expensive to create the new training organization, but Trenchard believed that financial sacrifices would have to be made if he was to create a truly independent service.

Operational Aspects of the Memorandum

Deployments Trenchard recommended that eight squadrons should go to India and three to Mesopotamia (Iraq), with the necessary facilities for repair. Seven squadrons would go to Egypt and there would be a seaplane unit in Malta and a further one in the eastern Mediterranean, probably at Alexandria. Egypt was important, being regarded as the 'Clapham Junction' between East and West and therefore in easy reach of areas of potential unrest. The number of squadrons would also provide a small reserve. At home there would be four squadrons apart from those earmarked for Army cooperation and deployment on aircraft-carriers (see Chapter 6). Trenchard aimed at two Army Cooperation Squadrons, based at Farnborough and Stonehenge; those for the Navy going to the Firth of Forth and Gosport.

Army and Navy v. RAF These proposals inevitably brought Trenchard into conflict with Admiral Beatty, the First Sea Lord, and Sir Henry Wilson CIGS. The Memorandum allowed that those elements working with the Army and Navy might, at some time in the future, become an arm of the older services. It has been suggested that Trenchard afterwards regretted making that concession, but did so as a sop to the two men. As it was, the Navy was to wait until 1937 before it regained ownership of its ship-borne aircraft belonging to the Fleet Air Arm. Eventually the Army was to have its own air component in the form of the Army Air Corps, and in the same way the RAF, unable to rely on the Army to defend its airfields in the heat of a fluid land battle during the Second World War, formed its own soldiery in the shape of the RAF Regiment. But in 1919 Trenchard knew that if Beatty and Wilson were determined to

smother the infant RAF at birth there was little he could do to stop them. So Trenchard pleaded for at least a year to get the RAF established, during which time he would do his best to provide the units both men wanted. At least Beatty was prepared to be conciliatory, whereas Wilson was not. Beatty agreed to leave the RAF alone for a year on condition that the RAF met the Navy's requirements. These were the provision of three squadrons (reconnaissance, torpedo and fighter), plus two seaplane squadrons for cooperation with the Fleet. Beatty wrote to Trenchard on 9 December 1919, saying, 'I hope you understand that I am in no way out to wreck the Air Ministry . . . I will do all I can to assist in making the accepted policy a working one.' But Trenchard had already made clear to him that the Air Ministry could not meet those requirements, at least within the year of grace given to him. So it must be assumed that Beatty was at least prepared to give Trenchard a sporting chance to get the RAF established. (These matters are developed further in Chapter 6.) As regards the Army, Wilson would promise nothing, and there, for the time being, the matter rested. Both men would return to the fray later, for with the coming and going of governments of different political parties there was always the possibility that an incoming prime minister and cabinet could be persuaded to change the policy.

Aircraft Chapter 5 deals comprehensively with the RAF aircraft that existed in 1918 and those that were developed during the inter-war years. Suffice here to note that some 10,000 war-surplus aircraft were then on the market for sale, both at home and overseas, by the Aircraft Disposal Company Ltd. With limited funds at his disposal, Trenchard knew that he could equip his squadrons with refurbished First World War aircraft at much less expense than purchasing new designs. Indeed, the DH9A, or 'Ninak', and the Bristol Fighter continued in service throughout the decade. At the same time he knew that without orders for new aircraft the struggling aircraft industry could founder and his service would be left with obsolete aircraft unable to counter any threat from a potential enemy with more modern aircraft. This was his dilemma, and sensibly he chose to offer the competing companies contracts for prototypes, the latter being paid by the Air Ministry as soon as a prototype was handed over to the RAF pilots at the experimental establishment at Martlesham Heath in Suffolk.

Airships Lighter-than-air craft had been useful during the First World War. Balloons had been used for battlefield and maritime reconnaissance, and airships for maritime reconnaissance, but unlike Germany, Britain had not used them for offensive operations. The disasters that were to befall airships lay in the future. In 1919 Trenchard had to weigh the future military and commercial use of airships against the prohibitive cost of a lighter-than-air service. It was proposed that one airship section be maintained at Howden, where there was sufficient accommodation for two rigid and a few smaller ships. This would permit continued research and development.

Training Aspects of the Memorandum

It was the training of RAF personnel that was the vital ingredient of the Memorandum, for Trenchard was determined to build that 'air force spirit'. He wanted officers and NCO aircrews skilled in the arts of flying and the use of associated weaponry, guns, bombs, depth-charges and torpedoes. There would be a need for a college to train cadets from universities and schools for permanent careers in the RAF. And for officers aspiring to the higher ranks of the service, staff training would be needed to create a body of competent staff officers skilled in the arts of air warfare. As things stood, his senior officers, like Trenchard himself, had started life in the Army or Royal Navy. Finally, he needed a body of competent technical tradesmen, skilled, not simply to avoid accidents through mechanical failure, but to meet the needs of RAF squadrons operating in a hostile environment and in testing climates. To meet these needs he proposed opening new, or maintaining existing, establishments.

The RAF College, Cranwell

RAF Cranwell was to be the home of the college for training officers who would receive permanent commissions in the RAF, i.e. a full career in the service. The site chosen was originally HMS *Daedalus*, opened in April 1916 as a training establishment for the Royal Naval Air Service. It is twelve miles south of Lincoln, far enough from the London fleshpots to give the young men a fairly Spartan existence. It is renowned for its stylistic college building designed by James West along the lines of the Royal Hospital, Chelsea. Entrants were recruited from the universities and secondary schools, and some who showed promise in the non-commissioned ranks were also admitted. Besides classroom instruction, field sports, gymnastics and the inevitable but essential parade-ground drill, cadets at Cranwell began flying training in Avro 504Ks from the outset. On leaving Cranwell after the three-year course, the young pilots would go to Andover on a course of cross-country flying before being posted to a service squadron. After a period of five years, pilots were expected to undertake specialist study such as navigation, engines, armament or wireless. In this way squadron officers could be expected to oversee those aspects of squadron work. It was not until later that specialist ground branches were formed. In a flying service officers were expected to fly. Readers may remember a scene from ITV's production entitled 'A

Piece of Cake', about an RAF fighter squadron in the Phoney War of 1939/40. Whatever the shortcomings of this production with regard to historical accuracy, and the portrayal of the behaviour of RAF officers of the period, the author did enjoy the exchanges between the squadron adjutant, who had been in the service since the First World War and the squadron intelligence officer who was an ex-Cambridge don hastily recruited following the proclamation of a state of emergency. In an opening scene the adjutant turns to the squadron intelligence officer. On hearing that the IO does not find flying to his liking, the adjutant says, 'You really ought to fly. The chaps expect it!' This matter also features in John James's excellent social history of the RAF entitled *The Paladins*, and in Chapter 9.

There was a paucity of vacancies for promotion to the higher ranks of the service, and not every cadet could expect to get to Air rank. However, those leaving Cranwell stood a better chance, since 40 per cent of the officer intake were on short-service commissions, which had just been introduced. A further 10 per cent of officers were seconded from the Army or Royal Navy, which aided inter-service cooperation. The RAF was, and remains, a service with a high complement of officers, the more so since senior NCO (SNCO) pilots were phased out after the Second World War. Unlike a unit of comparable size to an RAF station in the Army, say a battalion, the RAF needs a much larger mess to house all its officers.

RAF Staff College

To cater for the training of officers heading for higher rank who would fill command and staff positions, and needed to be skilled in the arts of air warfare, the RAF Staff College at Andover was opened for students on 3 April 1922. In the many battles fought between the Army and the RAF in the early 1920s over the RAF's existence as a separate service, some on the Army side were happy to pour scorn on the quality of RAF staff officers. Given that all of them at that time had started life as Army or Royal Naval officers it would take some time before RAF officers would emerge as fully competent in their sphere. Be that as it may, officers like Portal, Harris and Newall, who were to be RAF leaders in the Second World War, were not found wanting.

Technical training of ground tradesmen

The RAF needed a body of highly trained technical personnel, not simply to prevent air accidents through mechanical failure, but to service aircraft and equipment in hostile environments and in testing climates away from home. A site was chosen on Alfred de Rothschild's estate outside Wendover in Buckinghamshire. The wealthy banker had let both the Army and the RFC use his estate for training, and some of Kitchener's Army were held there under canvas before being shipped out to Flanders and the trenches. When Rothschild died in January 1918, the estate was loaned to the Crown at Trenchard's insistence. Later it was sold to the Crown, and RAF Halton, so named after the nearby village, came into being. This was now the home of the RAF Apprentices, or 'Brats', as they were affectionately known. After three years' training as fitters, carpenters and carpenter-riggers, coppersmiths and turners, the apprentices would pass into the ranks of the regular service as leading aircraftmen (LACs). Further training would be carried out to reach the rank of corporal. Some were selected for training as officers, and in later years Halton Brats were to reach Air rank. Apart from the experience of service life, a further attraction was the enhanced prospect of a well-paid job on leaving the service, when their skills would be in demand. Airmen of the electrical and wireless trades were to be trained at Cranwell and Flowerdown. Non-technical training for cooks, supply tradesmen, etc. was to be carried out at Uxbridge, and the school of gunners was to be at Eastchurch. Chapter 7 deals with these matters in greater detail.

With the contents of the Memorandum agreed, Trenchard could hopefully move on to establish his new service, but always in the knowledge that any failure on his part to deliver what the government or his sister services were demanding would be seized upon. He had already resigned once over policy differences with his Minister, and he could hardly afford the luxury of threatening resignation a second time if he did not get his way.

The Avro 504K in which many a Cranwell cadet began his flying career.

the unit at Howden, but the impetus for development was to come from civilian instructors and enthusiasts. Some German Zeppelins had been handed over as part of the peace treaty ending the First World War. Zeppelins L64 and L71 had been acquired by Vickers, the firm working on designs suitable for Empire air services. The Vickers R80, for example, had a total lift of 38.5 tons and a disposable load of 17.5 tons, with a maximum speed of 65 mph and a cruising radius of 6,500 miles. In addition to passengers, such aircraft could take international mail. Barnes Wallis was to be responsible for designing the Vickers Wellington bomber and the 'dam-busting' bombs dropped by Lancasters of No. 617 Squadron in 1943 against targets in the Ruhr. In 1919 he was in receipt of a retaining fee of £250 p.a. because there was no work at Vickers' Barrow plant at that time.

But airship policy was in doubt, and matters were not helped when the R34 hit a hillside in Yorkshire in 1921 because three out of four engines were out of action. It was eventually moored but was damaged in the wind. This was a bad omen for the slightly larger R36, with a passenger saloon, built by Beardmore, which was ready for flight. And then there was the R37, built by Short Brothers at the National Airship Factory, Cardington, Bedfordshire. Britain's collection of airships was growing, but to what purpose? Even the loss of the

The Royal Air Force College at Cranwell. The main college building seen here was designed by James West and was completed in 1933.

Dr Barnes Wallis.

AIRSHIPS

The memorandum did allow for a very small commitment to lighter-than-air craft development with

The *Dixmude.*

R38 in July of that year seemed only to act as a temporary check on airship development. The attractions were obvious. Airships held the prospect of luxury, long-distance travel connecting Britain to her Dominions overseas at a speed not that much slower than contemporary aircraft, and without having to land to refuel at regular intervals. This was something that fixed-wing airliners of the day could not do. The French, too, had acquired Zeppelins as part of war reparations, but the L72, renamed the *Dixmude*, was lost on 27 December 1924 over Italy. The airship had been destroyed by fire, and the commission of enquiry confirmed the cause as lightning. The Americans, however, used helium to eliminate the fire risk, although it was much more expensive than hydrogen, and their *Shenandoah* ZR1 airship was helium filled. But this could not prevent a near-disaster at Lakehurst, New Jersey, where the German airship *Hindenburg* was to crash in flames while mooring in 1937. On 16 January 1925, after four days at the mooring mast, the *Shenandoah* was ripped from her anchorage by a violent gale and disappeared into the rain-swept darkness. The ex-German Zeppelin pilot, Captain Heinen, did eventually bring her back under control, but it took until the early

hours of the following morning before he could bring her back, with a severely damaged bow. The litany of woes is completed by the loss of the Italian semi-rigid airship *Roma*, which crashed because of structural failure, and only emphasized the insufficiency of knowledge about the aerodynamic forces on airships and the methods of calculating stress. Seemingly blind to these risks, the British government was considering a plan for an Imperial airship service prepared by one of the airship enthusiasts of the day, Commander Berney. Chapter 3 continues the story of airship development up to the rivalry between the R100 and R101.

CIVIL AVIATION

The funds for civil aviation came from the air force vote (Air Estimates), and one of the first considerations for Sykes was the granting of subsidies to the industry. French airlines received subsidies and threatened to undercut their British counterparts. In the hope of stimulating interest in civil aviation in 1922 the government held a conference at the Guildhall in London. At Croydon every type of airliner was on display in the buildings of the Aircraft Disposal Company, whose aircraft were stood on their noses to make room. But flights and demonstrations only served to show that no real progress had been made since the previous year. Municipal airports for internal services were largely non-existent and much of the trade was cross-Channel. Airliners had only basic instruments, there were no landing aids, no air corridors where aircraft were required to fly at designated intervals, heights and bearings, no diversion airfields in the event of bad weather, no radar and little in the way of radio communications. As an illustration the following is a commercial airline pilot's account of a typical flight from Paris to London in the early 1920s.

At Le Bourget the clouds are at 800 feet; rain and drizzle is coming down on and off; visibility is 2,000 yards; a 20 mph wind is blowing from the west and is stronger higher up. I will have to take a chance on the weather in the Channel, for Lympne aerodrome, high on its hill, also reports low cloud, but the crossing

The R34.

seems passable. While taxiing out to take off I am getting wet and uncomfortable because of the open cockpit. Once airborne, though still comparatively close to the ground we are just below cloud. I start on the usual compass course with a mentally calculated allowance for drift which I shall correct on a known landmark ten miles hence; but after six miles there are tree-covered hills shrouded in wisps of cloud. It is now obvious that that a compass course is impossible so I turn left and pick up the main road from Paris to Boulogne. I follow it for some time, but the ground is gradually rising to the hills south of Beauvais and the clouds become slightly lower owing to the wind on the hills. Visibility has decreased to some 500 yards, a distance I am covering in 10 seconds, so I fly about 150 feet off the ground, which feels a mere 50 feet, and I am compelled to stick to this road as completely as a motor car, for if I lose sight of it I am to all intents lost. Flying so low in such bad visibility keeps me so busy looking for obstructions, and the compass is doubly useless, for I cannot fly straight long enough to settle to a correct heading, and in any case I am literally unable to take my eyes from looking ahead. After some minutes of this uncomfortable flying we pass the hills, and with lower ground comes comparative peace for a while, but I must stick to that road for the ground gradually slopes up and up towards Poix. I get lower and lower until I cannot pass; I am right on the tree tops and wisps of cloud increasingly blind me. I must turn back. It is unbelievably tricky to turn a heavily loaded machine under such circumstances. I am tempted to leave the road and take a short cut to lower ground near Amiens, thence along low ground by the Somme to the coast. The next part is easy enough, for though the clouds are low on the sand dunes, I can fly skimming those flats. I intend to leave the coast at Boulogne, but the high waves show that the wind across the Channel is much stronger than over the land. So to lessen the risk of drifting off-course in such bad visibility I follow the coast of Cap Gris Nez and then start across the Channel, flying at 150 to 200 feet with 500 yards visibility and patches of drizzle. It is easy flying, though disconcerting that a patch of nil visibility might occur at any moment, but at last the white cliffs loom ahead with cloud all over them. I am not sure whether they are Dover or Folkestone cliffs but it does not matter for I follow them round until I can see across the low ground of Dungeness. A straight line to Croydon is impossible as there are too many cloud-covered hills to pass so I select a known low-ground course and, in continuing bad visibility, keep a steady look-out. I traverse a considerable detour hopefully to arrive at Croydon. Completion of the journey has depended entirely on the risks the pilot is prepared to take. In such bad weather the avoidance of a collision with a machine coming in the other

direction is frequently a matter of luck. One sees that there is little hope for regular commercial night-flying; lighting the air routes and other assistances appear to me to be useless for the great problem is to fly and navigate in weather when these lights cannot be seen. We must find a method of flying in no visibility at all.

It is a wonder that, under these circumstances, anyone would wish to risk a passenger flight in an airliner in the early 1920s. This pilot goes on to talk about the lack of reliable instrumentation and the need for constant practice, particularly in flying in cloud. The above passage encapsulates the hazards of flying in bad weather, and shows the enormous strides that were going to have to be made before commercial flying would be both reasonably safe and a serious rival to rail and boat passenger/freight services.

Transatlantic Flight by Alcock and Brown

The newspapers were often do to their bit to promote flying during the inter-war years, and the Daily Mail offered a prize of £10,000 for the first non-stop transatlantic flight. US flyers had done this, but in a series of hops that therefore did not qualify. The importance of such a flight is that it might pave the way for non-stop transatlantic commercial flying. In Britain it was left to private enterprise. Sopwith had tried with a biplane, but had failed. Then Vickers offered a Vimy bomber powered with two Rolls-Royce Eagle engines and put its aircraft at the disposal of Captain John Alcock, who had been a naval air pilot in the RAF. His navigator was Lieutenant Arthur Brown. Extra fuel tanks were fitted to carry 855 gallons of fuel and 50 gallons of oil, to give an estimated range of 2,500 miles. The aircraft was shipped to Newfoundland for test flying, and the two men eventually took off from St Johns at 5.28 p.m. BST on Sunday 15 June 1919. The flight took 15 hours 57 minutes at an average speed of 116 mph. It was less than ten years since Blériot's historic cross-Channel flight, and both men were knighted for their feat.

Major-General Sykes as Controller-General of Civil Aviation

Sykes set about developing a network of domestic air services, and local authorities were asked to purchase land for airfields, for there was little public money for development of civil aviation generally. As important as the building of airports was the building and development of airliners. This was limited since only £500,000 was available for civil aircraft research from a total budget of £2 million for research purposes overall. On the positive side Sykes reported that over 500,000 air miles had been flown and 52,000 passengers carried in the six months since the inauguration of civil flying. A total of 240 civil aircraft had been certified as airworthy and 374 pilots had been granted certificates of proficiency. In that time there had been only two fatal accidents.

Necessity for route planning to avoid collisions

These were the days before air corridors, when aircraft captains were not required to submit flight plans to the air traffic control authority before departure. Today aircraft in air corridors must stick to a prearranged altitude, with a horizontal separation between aircraft travelling in the same direction along the corridor. In 1922, with the growth in air traffic, it was felt that meetings of pilots should take place to plot definite routes, all marked by easily distinguishable landmarks, and that all aircraft must keep to the right of them. Wirelesses should also be carried. The French pilots agreed, for the problem was that each pilot had his own landmarks on certain parts of the route, and agreement should be sought to cater for every kind of weather.

The Weir Committee – Imperial air routes

Lord Weir chaired a committee to look at the establishment of an Imperial air route to Australia. A 'demonstration route' was selected involving both fixed-wing aircraft and airships. England to Egypt would be the first leg , then Egypt to India. The committee thought that airships could be used for these long-haul flights, and an airfield in Malta was considered. Aircraft could fly the Egypt–India leg

Vickers Vimy Commercial.

with fuel stops every 250 miles, and after 500 miles passengers could be transferred to another aircraft. There would have to be emergency landing grounds every fifty miles, and the aircraft used could be adapted Vickers Vimy bombers, the Vimy Commercial, This is a far cry from today's non-stop thirteen-hour flight of some 5,500 miles at 35,000 feet in a Boeing 747.

Subsidies

It was felt that Imperial air routes should be state-aided private enterprise. The French were doing it, so why not Britain? But to what end? Subsidies or not, was there a market? Air travel was not then considered as a serious alternative to sea and rail travel, but more of a stunt to be exploited for publicity purposes. Mr Frederick Handley Page felt that a more serious approach to civil aviation was required. He felt that too many ex-RAF pilots were flying civil aircraft, but this is hardly surprising, given the thousands made redundant from military flying. Commercial pilots should be recruited and trained as such, but trained initially as mechanics. Lord Weir agreed that too many ex-RAF pilots were employed as civil airline pilots, and Air Transport and Travel Ltd was advised to follow Handley Page's advice.

By 11 March 1920 the Weir Committee concluded that civil aviation needed aid on a limited number of demonstration routes. The government took a contrary view, believing that civil aviation must fly by itself, but Weir persevered and proposed that 'approved' routes should receive direct assistance amounting to 25 per cent of their gross revenue, the total sum available amounting to £250,000 spread over two years. Trenchard, on the other hand, objected, believing that subsidies should be limited to the provision of landing grounds, free meteorological information, wireless services and the marking out of air routes. In spite of Trenchard's objections, Weir got Churchill to endorse his draft report. Trenchard then wrote a minority report saying that civil aviation was a question that did not appear to have been adequately examined, bearing in mind the need for the utmost economy. Furthermore he did not accept the justification put forward in some quarters for the nation's possession of airliners, that they provided a reserve for national defence if converted for military use.

Trenchard's recommendations for civil aviation subsidies

1. It is not advisable to give direct subsidies to aerial transport companies for work done nor do I think that the necessity has yet been shown for doing so.
2. It would be preferable to allot all the money suggested for subsidies to design and research by

placing orders for experimental machines with certain approved companies.

Minority reports are rendered if a member or members of a committee fundamentally disagree with the consensus that the chairman is trying to achieve. Trenchard did, however, concede that if subsidies were to be approved they should be given in the manner suggested in the Weir majority report.

Events leading to Sykes's resignation

The Treasury considered both the Weir Committee's majority report and the minority reports, and accepted the latter on the ground that civil aviation must 'fly by itself'. Then in 1920 several companies got into difficulties. Handley Page shut down its London–Paris passenger run, needing £2 12s 6d per passenger to be viable. Air Transport and Travel Ltd closed down and went into liquidation. In spite of this, the Cabinet postponed indefinitely the implementation of the majority Weir report. In October 1920 Sykes returned to the justification for possessing civil aircraft referred to earlier. He said, 'The nation which is strongest in air traffic will be the strongest in the aerial warfare of the future.' Early in 1921 all British commercial air services ceased in the face of subsidized foreign competition, and for a while only foreign airliners used Croydon, getting their services free. Fear was again expressed that the industry would go to pieces, and so Churchill announced that a grant of £60,000 for British companies on 'approved routes' as per the Weir recommendations would come into effect on 19 March 1921. Handley Page and Instone Airlines took off again. The maximum liability to the Air Ministry would be £88,200, this sum to come from the total vote for civil aviation of £880,000, from a total RAF vote of £18,410,000. Then Churchill was moved to the Colonial Office, to be replaced by Captain F.E. (Freddie) Guest, but by that time Sykes felt that he could no longer remain as Controller-General of Civil Aviation, given the scaling down of his department, leaving him little scope, as he saw it, for his position. He resigned on 1 April 1922, on the expiration of the term for which he had been originally appointed.

Sir Sefton Brancker takes over as Director of Civil Aviation

Sykes was replaced by the monocled Sir Sefton Brancker. In the Air Estimates for the year 1922/3 the funds for his department were reduced to £364,000, but the subsidy to the airlines, based on the Weir Committee proposals, was made permanent. This was 25 per cent of gross earnings. Sefton Brancker only reported to the Air Council, whereas Sykes had been a member of it. The Australian airline, the Queensland and New Territories Air Service (QANTAS), had been formed, with its government providing a subsidy. At home the Hambling

DH34 Airliner.

Committee was formed to consider the working of the scheme of cross-Channel subsidies and to advise on the best method of subsidizing air transport in the future. Regular services between Paris and London were in place using the DH34 airliner. The Lympne–Ostend return flight was £3 per head in 1922, but it was uneconomic to subsidize airlines competing with each other. The Hambling Committee reported quickly. Up to that time four routes had been allocated to the four companies participating in the scheme: Handley Page Transport, the Daimler Airway, the Instone Airline and British Marine Air Navigation. The committee recommended the formation of a single company to replace the four existing airlines, with government nominees on the board of directors. The new company would take over existing services and go on to expand civil air transport. The committee further recommended that the government should guarantee a subsidy of no less than £1 million spread over ten years, while a similar sum should be subscribed by the public for the purposes of research, development and supply. Thus the recommendation that a single monopoly company in which the interests of the older companies should be safeguarded was accepted by the Cabinet and incorporated into the Air Estimates for 1923/4.

Formation of Imperial Airways Ltd

On 31 March 1924 the formation of the new airline was announced. Sir Eric Geddes was appointed chairman and Sir Herbert Hambling, who had chaired the

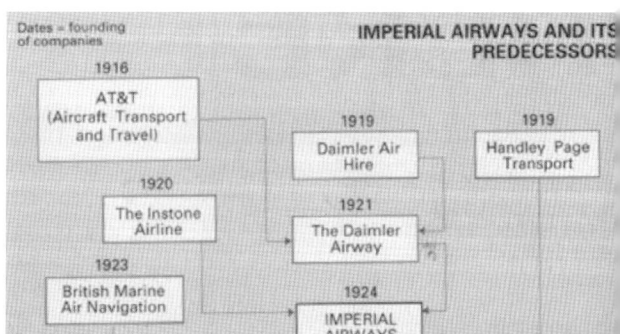

committee on subsidies, together with Major J.W. Hills, were the two government directors. Mr S. Dismore of Handley Page became secretary. But immediately there was trouble with the pilots, who would be required to fly an average of two hours per day. Geddes said that records showed that the average earning of pilots during the preceding twenty months had been in the neighbourhood of £680 per annum. The pilots of the constituent airlines disagreed with Geddes' figures, and the result was a strike, which meant that Imperial did not commence operations until 26 April 1924. Once the dispute was settled, Imperial went on to fly 18,000 route-miles, an increase of some 12,000 miles covered by all British airlines since 1920. In the event, both France (Air France) and Germany (Lufthansa) were to follow Britain's example.

RAF OPERATIONS, 1918 TO 1924

Although dubbed the 'peace years', the inter-war years were, for the RAF, years of non-stop operational activity. During the period 1918–24 the RAF was required, for a brief period, to help police Germany pending a peace settlement, to join in the Russian civil war on the side of the White (anti-Bolshevik) forces, to help maintain internal security in Ireland, to intervene during the Chanak crisis to prevent possible Turkish aggression, and to implement a policy of 'air control' in British Somaliland, Mesopotamia, India and in other minor disputes.

RAF Operations in Russia

The operations in the Middle East and India have been well chronicled, but what are less well known are the operations in northern and southern Russia during the period 1918–20. Units of the RAF fought alongside and against Russians in the civil war between the Bolshevik Red armies under Trotsky's command and the counter-revolutionary White armies.

The Pact of London signed by Britain, France and Russia on 5 September 1914 committed the signatories not to negotiate a separate peace with the Central Powers, principally Germany, Austria-Hungary and Turkey. When the First World War began, Russia was ruled by Tsar Nicholas II, but when the Bolsheviks seized power in November 1917, Lenin, the Soviet leader, felt under no obligation to respect the Pact of London. His immediate concern was to extricate Russian soldiers from the bloody trench warfare on Germany's Eastern Front. There had already been mass desertions by Russian soldiers, and in December 1917 hostilities between the German and Russian forces were suspended pending negotiations. This state of affairs suited both sides. Germany was able to redeploy forces from the Eastern to the Western Front, and the Soviets had extricated their troops from the conflict. On 15 December an armistice between the Central Powers and the Bolshevik government was confirmed at Brest Litovsk. Initially a cessation of hostilities was to last from 17 December until 14 January 1918 while peace terms were hammered out, but in the event hostilities were over, and Lenin, ably assisted by his Red Army commander Trotsky, wished to devote all his efforts to consolidate the gains of the Communist revolution, i.e. to ensure that there was no return to Tsarist or Social Democratic rule. Inside Russia there was considerable resistance to the Communist take-over in the form of the 'White' armies assisted by a variety of non-Russian forces, among which were units of the Royal Air Force.

The RAF became embroiled in both northern and southern Russia. Firstly, in northern Russia a mixed expeditionary force was dispatched to Murmansk. It included a flight of DH4 bombers aboard HMS *Elope*. In July a further five Fairey Campanias, two Sopwith Babies and one Sopwith Camel arrived in the carrier *Nairana*. Archangel was occupied on 2 August, and RAF aircraft carried out strafing and bombing attacks so that Allied infantry could reach Obozerskaya, about one hundred miles south. Later the RAF was established at bases in Archangel and Murmansk. In the south the defeat of Turkey led to the need to provide 'protection' for the territories surrendered by the Turks. Major J.O. Andrews DSO, MC, commanding No. 221 Squadron, equipped with a mixture of DH4s, DH9s and 9As, with some Camels as fighter escorts, was ordered to take his unit to Batum on the Black Sea. From Batum the unit moved to Petrovsk, a port on the Caspian, arriving there on 12 January 1919, where the aircraft were unloaded.

Operations in Southern Russia

The assembling of the DH9s and 9As began on 14 January in temperatures below zero, the aircraft being assembled in the open behind protective screens to shield the riggers from the appalling weather. Before the aircraft could be test flown, sometimes in gale and blizzard conditions, water and oil had to be heated before radiators and sumps were filled. Operations were in support of General Denikin's White Army, but it was not always easy for the squadron pilots to identify the enemy, and in February a squadron of White cavalry came under air attack. In March 1919 No. 266 Squadron, equipped with Short 184 floatplanes, was transferred from Malta to Petrovsk to join 221 Squadron. Both squadrons remained operational at that location until they were disbanded on 1 September.

The War Minister, Winston Churchill, had to face Parliamentary objections to foreign entanglements. He therefore replaced the operational squadrons with an advisory force to train White Russian pilots, entitled innocuously the RAF Training Mission, which arrived at Taganrog on the Sea of Azov in May 1919. The mission, under the command of Lieutenant-Colonel A.C. Maund, was to train the White Russian pilots on RE8s, 130 of

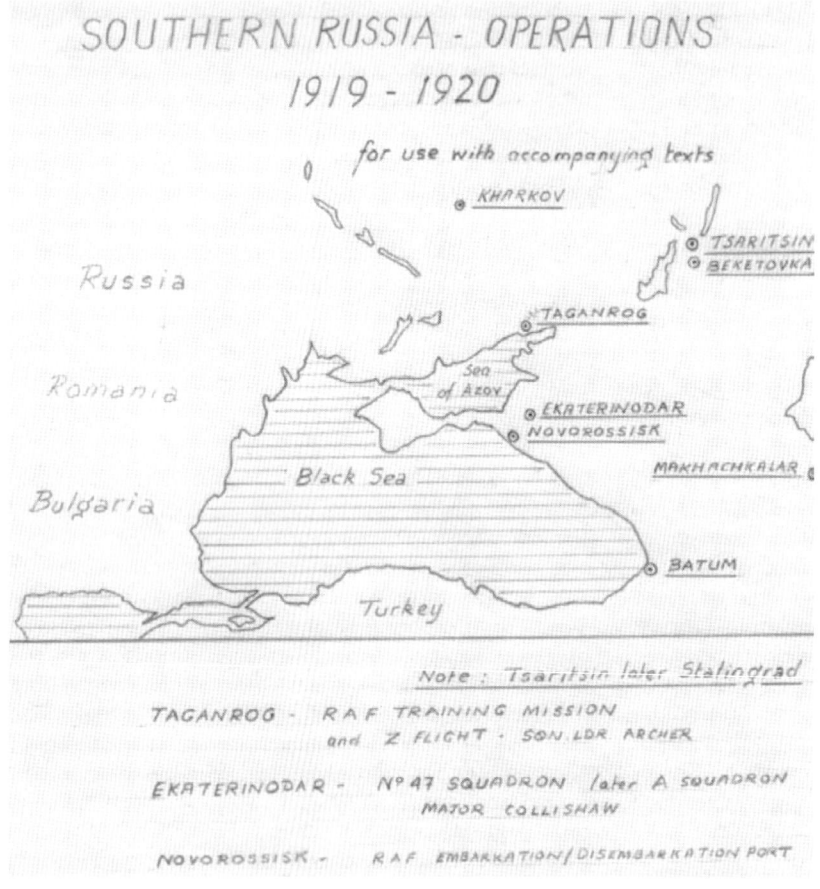

SOUTHERN RUSSIA - OPERATIONS
1919 - 1920

for use with accompanying texts

Note: Tsaritsin later Stalingrad

TAGANROG - RAF TRAINING MISSION
and Z FLIGHT - SQN.LDR ARCHER

EKATERINODAR - No 47 SQUADRON later A SQUADRON
MAJOR COLLISHAW

NOVOROSSISK - RAF EMBARKATION/DISEMBARKATION PORT

Tsaritsin, and this required C Flight to move up to Beketovka. C Flight maintained its pace of operations throughout August, using DH9s, while, back at the squadron base, A Flight was being re-equipped with DH9As. Railway stations, Red airfields and Red cavalry were attacked.

One particular mission deserves mention, and serves to show the courage of No. 47 Squadron's aircrews. On 30 July Captain W.F. Anderson and Lieutenant J. Mitchell in a DH9 were photographing the results of a squadron attack on Tcherni-Yar when enemy ground fire hit the starboard fuel tank, which began to leak petrol. Mitchell promptly climbed out onto the wing to plug the hole with his fingers. Captain W. Elliott and Lieutenant H.S. Laidlaw in their DH9 had acted as cover in the event of air attack when they too were victims of ground fire, which hit the engine, and Elliott was forced to land close to a large force of Red cavalry. When the latter began to move towards the stricken machine he set fire to his aircraft to prevent it falling into enemy hands. Meanwhile Anderson landed close by with Mitchell still out on the starboard wing, and both Elliott and Laidlaw clambered aboard. Still under fire, Anderson managed to get his heavily laden aircraft airborne for the 110-mile trip back to base, with Mitchell still plugging the hole in the starboard fuel tank. This he did in spite of being burned by the exhaust pipe, and the aircraft was landed successfully. Captain Elliott survived this action to rise to the rank of air chief marshal.

The RAF Mission to Russia thus masked the RAF's continued involvement in the civil war. But in October 1919 No. 47 Squadron ceased to exist in name when it was simply retitled A Squadron. Pressure had been brought to bear on the government by various factions to end British involvement in the Russian civil war. Not unsurprisingly, one of these factions was the embryo Communist party of Great Britain. A Squadron had officially to be part of the training mission. All members of what was No. 47 Squadron were then asked to sign a form volunteering to fight in support of General Denikin and Wrangel's White Russian army. Needless to say, A Squadron simply carried on where No. 47 Squadron left off.

In October the Red armies attempted to recapture Tsaritsin. Armoured trains, vessels on the Volga river

which had been given to them by Britain. Once trained, they were to fight in support of General Denikin's forces. But while Britain had officially disengaged from all operational involvement in Russia's civil war, No. 47 Squadron, which had been stationed in Macedonia since September 1916, was ordered to move to the port of Novorossick on the Black Sea from its base in Salonika. From Novorossick the squadron reassembled at Ekaterinodar to the north-east with an assortment of aircraft, including DH9 bombers.

When No. 47 Squadron became operational in May 1919, it was under the temporary command of Captain S.G. Frogley, but a Canadian fighter ace, Major Ray Collishaw DSO, DSC, DFC, was meanwhile busy in the United Kingdom recruiting volunteers to fight in south Russia. He had aleady been appointed as OC No. 47 Squadron, and he had no difficulty in recruiting ten officers and 255 non-commissioned airmen to fight against the Red Russian forces. The party arrived at the port of Novorossick on 8 June, having travelled through France and Italy by train. By the time Collishaw arrived at the squadron base on 11 July, operations had already begun. These operations, against a variety of targets, centred around actions in support of Baron Wrangel's White Russian forces. These had occupied the town of

Major Ray Collishaw DSO, DSC, DFC, OC No. 47 Sqn and ex-First World War fighter ace.

and aircraft were used by the Red forces, and A Squadron was active in operations designed to stem this advance. The Red cavalry force under Dumenko was halted by a combination of air attacks and White cavalry. B Flight was engaged in operations against Red cavalry, while A and C Flights attacked Red ships in the Caspian. Just as Denikin's army was reaching the peak of success, Collishaw fell ill with typhus, of which there was a lot at this time. By the time he had returned to duty the White armies were in retreat. By 11 December A and B Flights had been withdrawn to the HQ of the training mission, leaving only C Flight in contact with the enemy on the Volga river. But the advance of the Red forces was so rapid that A Squadron was ordered to evacuate south Russia from Novorossick. The squadron retreated, step by step, still harassing the Red forces as it went.

Retreating with Collishaw's squadron was Squadron Leader Joe Archer's Z Flight, another operational RAF unit in the area. This had been formed from volunteers of the training mission and was equipped with RE8s. Although Archer had hoped to launch a bombing raid

on Moscow, permission was refused and he had to join Collishaw in having his unit evacuated. Collishaw himself took part in the last of the bombing and strafing attacks on 29 March 1920. Before his unit had left Russian soil, the 47 Squadron numberplate had already been given to a DH9 bomber unit , formerly No. 206 Squadron at Helwan in Egypt, on 1 February.

Operations in Northern Russia

The RAF bases in Murmansk and Archangel secured extra reinforcements in the early summer of 1919. As with Collishaw's squadron in the south, the northern contingent was made up almost entirely of RAF volunteers. Some had actually enlisted to serve in Russia following a public poster campaign, and some officers were recruited personally in the RAF Club in London. A number had won the Victoria Cross during the First World War. Indeed, for many this was a way of avoiding the tedium of peacetime service, as T.E. Lawrence's accounts of life at Uxbridge will bear witness.

This 'relief force' was shipped to Russia in early June. The RAF at Archangel base then established an airfield at Bereznik, some 140 miles distant. Aircraft included a motley collection of DH4s, DH9s, Camels, Snipes and 1½ Strutters. Units formed were the No. 1 Slavo-British Squadron and a White Russian unit commanded by Staff Captain Alexander Kazakov, the leading Russian fighter ace of the First World War. The purely British units were identified simply as Nos 2 and 3 Squadrons, but had no connection with the regular RAF units of the same numbers.

Operations against Bolshevik forces on the Dvina and Vega fronts began in July. The RAF nicknamed the Bolsheviks the 'Bolos', and Bolo air units in this sector had a collection of ex-British, French and German types. Initially the RAF attacks consisted of bombing and strafing, but while there was little air opposition, enemy ground fire was effective. The greatest fear that aircrews might have in this war was not to engage the enemy but to be captured if shot down in enemy territory. They were advised to carry a pistol and shoot themselves rather than risk capture, for the enemy was known to show barbarity towards its attackers. For example, on 11 August seven DH bombers of No. 2 Squadron were sent to attack Red forces in the village of Gorodok. Flying into fog, the aircrews lost direction and only two returned to base. One of the aircraft that force-landed in enemy territory was crewed by Lieutenants D'Arcy Levy and Bugg. D'Arcy Levy made the mistake of asking an enemy soldier where he was, and then, on realizing that he was in enemy territory, he sprinted back to his aircraft but choked the engine so that it would not start. He climbed out and attempted to swing the propeller, but by this time enemy soldiers had arrived in force and he was bayoneted to death. Fortunately for Bugg, he had a mechanic's overalls over his officer's uniform and he was

Captain S.M. Kinkead DSO, DSC, DFC in front of his Camel fighter of B Flight, No. 47 Squadron, South Russia, 1919.

Two DH9As and a Snipe at Bereznik airfield in August 1919.

not recognized as such. He was sent to a prison camp.

By the end of August things were not going well for the White Russian forces, and evacuation of the RAF relief force was imminent. The aircrews continued flying until the first week in September, when they were ordered back to Archangel for embarkation and return to England. The White Russian aircrews were obviously depressed, but turned down pleas by their RAF allies to accompany them to England. The loss of their hero, Kazakov, in a flying accident on 3 August only added to the gloom. Apparently he climbed into his Sopwith

fighter and took off, but pulled up into a looping manoeuvre when only twenty feet off the ground, whereupon his aircraft stalled and dived vertically into the ground. He was buried the following day with full military honours.

The entire Russian operation could be regarded as a costly failure. There is evidence of arms and equipment being used ineffectively. In any event failure of the White Russian armies on the battlefield meant that the RAF would have to withdraw, for there was no intention to mount a strategic bombing offensive against Red Russia. For Churchill it was another failure to add to the Dardanelles campaign. He had no love for a Bolshevik-run Russia, but given feelings at home towards Britain's involvement in the Russian civil war, he was left with no choice.

RAF OPERATIONS IN IRELAND, 1920 TO 1924

Throughout 1920 the political situation in Ireland worsened, with Irish Republican Army (IRA) attacks being stepped up. There was popular resentment towards His Majesty's Government over conscription being applied to Irish citizens, the harsh treatment meted out to those who took part in the 1916 uprising against the Crown and the perceived tardiness on the part of HMG to implement Home Rule for Ireland. The RAF had had two operational squadrons, Nos 105 and 106, equipped with RE8s in Ireland at the Armistice, but although Field Marshal French had intended that these units would patrol with bombs and machine-guns, RAF activity had been confined to reconnaissance, communications and running the mail. With demobilization came a reduction of British Army and Air Force personnel in Ireland, but when Sinn Fein won a landslide victory in the General Election of 1918 the new Members of Parliament refused to take their seats at Westminster, established an independent legislative assembly and issued a Declaration of Independence. Serious violence followed in 1919, and the IRA campaign against the British forces began in earnest.

Initial Deployments   In response to the deterioration in the internal security situation, Nos 105 and 106 Squadrons changed to the Bristol Fighter and were joined by 141 Squadron in March 1919, also with the Bristol Fighter. In that month No. 149

Squadron arrived at Tallaght, having been operational in France during the closing stages of the war. No. 117 Squadron joined No. 149 Squadron at Tallaght, also in March, but then moved on to Gormanston. Formed in January 1918 in Hampshire, 117 Squadron had never become operational as its pilots were constantly being posted to France, and when all its personnel had been posted away in October the squadron had been disbanded, its assets being absorbed by No. 141 Squadron on the 6th of that month. No. 141 Squadron had been a Home Defence fighter unit. Hence the RAF contingent was a mixed bag. Nos 105, 106 and 141 Squadrons were up to strength, 149 squadron was below strength and 117 Squadron had only four pilots and two observers before absorption.

1919 Reorganization   In July 1919 the British forces in Ireland numbered 59,529 officers and men in the Army and 1,789 with the RAF. In August two cadre units, i.e. skeleton staff only, of Nos 2 and 100 Squadrons arrived in Ireland. The assets of all five squadrons listed in the foregoing paragraph were run down and either absorbed by Nos 2 and 100 Squadrons or returned to England. No. 2 Squadron was equipped with Bristol Fighters and 100 Squadron with the same, plus DH9As, eighteen of which had been flown over from England. Under the 'Defence of Ireland Scheme' the two squadrons were deployed as shown on the map below. The flight at Oranmore was to patrol the Limerick area. The two flights at Fermoy would patrol Fermoy itself. The 100 Squadron flight at Castlebar would patrol the Athlone area, while Dublin, the Curragh and Ulster would be patrolled from the three flights at the Curragh.

DEFENCE OF IRELAND SCHEME – NOS 2 & 100 SQUADRON DEPLOYMENTS

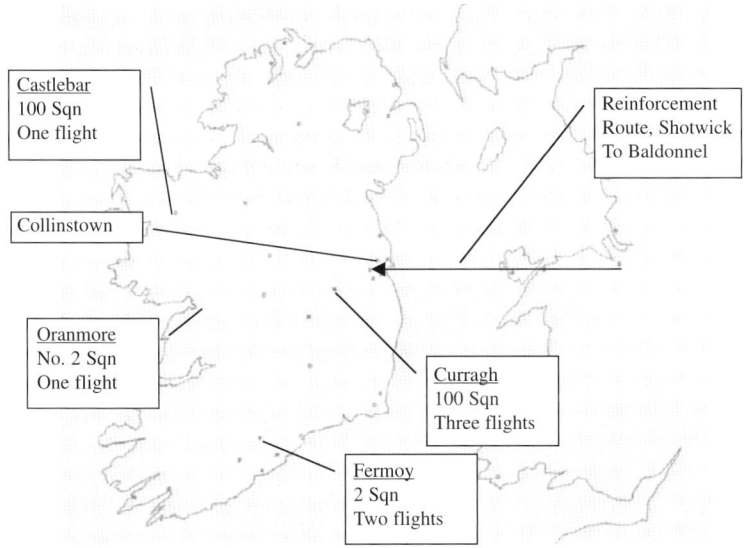

Castlebar
100 Sqn
One flight

Collinstown

Oranmore
No. 2 Sqn
One flight

Curragh
100 Sqn
Three flights

Fermoy
2 Sqn
Two flights

Reinforcement
Route, Shotwick
To Baldonnel

The two squadrons became operational on 1 February 1920.

Reinforcement Route   Before moving on to the operations carried out by the RAF in Ireland, the method of reinforcing units in Ireland will be considered. Whereas previously aircraft had been taken aboard ship, by 1919 aircraft had more reliable engines and more experienced pilots, with war experience of flying over water. So permission was granted for aircraft to fly from Shotwick, near Chester, to Baldonnel, the headquarters of the RAF in Ireland. There were sixty-eight nautical miles of sea to cross, bad weather or engine failure could make things difficult, and crews might have to ditch in the sea. This happened on 17 December 1920 to an HP 0/400 bomber, Serial No. J2259, attached to the School of Aerial Navigation and Bomb Dropping at Andover. The aircraft was on a training flight and had to ditch in the sea fifteen miles from Holyhead, in Anglesey. The rescue ship found the two crewmen sitting on the wing, and shortly after their rescue the aircraft disappeared beneath the waves. When whole squadrons were crossing, only six aircraft at a time were permitted to be airborne over the Irish Sea, and the remainder waited until word arrived of the first echelon's safe arrival. If an aircraft failed to arrive, a sea search was mounted. Sometimes a pilot would fly out from Baldonnel to meet the incoming crews and escort them in. CW (Morse) radios were carried, and Baldonnel and Shotwick maintained a listening watch, together with the naval W/T station at Kingstown. On 1 May 1919, with the ban on civil flying into Ireland lifted, air routes linking the major cities brought aircraft into Baldonnel like their service counterparts. These would be for passengers bound for Dublin.

Attacks on RAF Aerodromes and Personnel   Aerodromes were ideal targets for the IRA, having large perimeters that were all but impossible to secure without employing a large number of troops and wire fortifications with manned strongpoints. On 19 March 1919 the IRA launched an attack on Collinstown aerodrome. Soldiers on guard were overpowered at 2.30 a.m. by a raiding party of more than fifty men, and a large quantity of rifles, bayonets and ammunition was stolen. Vehicles were disabled to prevent pursuit. After this audacious attack there was a lull, and with the long period of inactivity that followed, No. 141 Squadron took to painting its Bristol fighters in bright colours. Baldonnel was raided on 28 August 1920, when intruders gained entry without a guard being alerted. On this occasion a safe was rifled and Army codes and ciphers were stolen, together with arms and equipment. On 19 November 1920 a soldier on guard duty was shot dead and another injured when a gang of raiders attempted to obtain arms and ammunition. On another occasion aviation fuel *en route* for Oranmore was also intercepted. RAF personnel also came under attack. Vehicles travelling between bases were frequently shot at, and it was not safe for RAF personnel to go out of camp alone. On 26 March 1921 an RAF tender and a car were fired at in Dublin and RAF personnel were injured. Aircrews were equipped with pistols, and if required to make a forced landing they were ordered to stay with their aircraft. If approached by a hostile crowd they were to fire over their heads, and if that failed to stop them they were to fire at the crowd.

Operations

The RAF's role The RAF's role in Ireland had been unclear in the past. Assisting the Army by engaging in internal security duties could mean anything. As it happened, the RAF was never put on an offensive footing during the troubles in Ireland, that is to say bombs and bullets were not used against known ground targets or targets of opportunity. The usefulness of aircraft to the Army was nevertheless not in doubt. Aircraft could be used for communications, particularly the carrying of mails, for general reconnaissance, the prevention of demonstrations by a show of force and the spotting of IRA training and drilling in remote locations, particularly at weekends.

Communications Communicating with Army units in the field, in the absence of ground-to-air radio, was rudimentary by modern standards. Weighted bags with streamers attached were dropped into a 15 ft diameter circle marked out on the ground near an Army unit headquarters, but as the reader may learn in Chapter 4, it did not take long for the enemy to deceive RAF pilots as tribesmen had done during air control in the Middle East. On 14 September 1920 a band of IRA members, dressed in Army uniforms, got an RAF pilot to drop official mail bound for the military in Bantry. To retrieve messages an aircraft had to trail a hook, then fly at 50 ft above the ground between two masts to 'snatch' the bag, which was then reeled in through a hatch on the underside of the fuselage.

Patrolling and Convoy Protection Since the RAF never went on the offensive in Ireland, in the sense of using their machine-guns and bombs, politicians and others began to question their effectiveness. Although Brigade Major Montgomery, a later field marshal of renown, opined that 'the RAF knew nothing about the war or the conditions under which it was being fought', the patrolling presence of aircraft, particularly in remote

areas, performed a valuable service to the Army in deterring open displays of hostility and quasi-military presence and intelligence gathering. Patrolling routes taken by convoys acted as a deterrent, as the author knows from personal experience, having spent many hours seated in the rear seat of a Chipmunk while an RAF convoy below wound its weary way up into the Troodos Mountains to resupply the radar unit during the Cyprus emergency. One convoy proceeding from Fermoy to Oranmore was attacked by rebels at Bruff, County Limerick. Although the raiders were driven away, Flying Officer Whatling, the convoy commander, suffered a serious shotgun wound in the head. A bomb hurled at the lead vehicle was picked up by AC2 Hill and then thrown back at the assailants, for which he was commended for a bravery award. It is significant that no attacks or obstructions were experienced after air cover was provided. The General Officer Commanding 16 Infantry Brigade also requested air reconnaissance to attempt to discover ambush preparations, such as the digging of trenches close to or overlooking a road where vehicular traffic had to slow to a crawl, or where vehicles could not be turned round in the road and thus were most likely to be ambushed, e.g. in mountain passes or on sharp bends. Leaflet dropping may be added to this list of operational duties, when towns or villages would be targeted to ask the public for information about wanted men.

One incident deserves mention before closing on this phase of Irish operations, for it gave rise to questions in Parliament at Westminster. Following the killing of fourteen British Army intelligence officers in a carefully planned IRA operation on the morning of Sunday 21 November 1920, the internal security force known as the Black and Tans (they wore black berets with their khaki uniform) drove their armoured cars into Croke Park football ground, allegedly to see if they could catch any armed men who might be suspects, but once in the ground they turned their guns on the footballers and the crowd, killing fourteen and injuring over sixty persons. An RAF aircraft circling overhead was thought to be

A Bristol Fighter of No. 141 Squadron during 1919 (written off by the IRA on 10 February 1921).

A Bristol Fighter of No. 105 Squadron,
Oranmore, in 1920.

involved, but it was reported that its gun was partially dismantled. Whatever the veracity of that report, there is no evidence linking the pilot to the events taking place below other than to say that patrols over the Dublin area were not unusual at this time.

A sample of daily squadron activity from the records of No. 11 Irish Wing, signed by their Commanding Officer, Group Captain A.V. Bettington, can be found in Appendix D.

RAF Withdrawal from Ireland

Creation of the Irish Free State   RAF withdrawal from Ireland followed the creation of an Irish Free State with Dominion status on the signing of 'The Articles of Agreement for a Treaty between Great Britain and Ireland' on 6 December 1921. Ireland had already been effectively partitioned following the passing of the Ireland Act in 1920. The six predominantly Protestant 'Orange' counties of Ulster wished to remain loyal to the Crown, leaving the twenty-six counties of the South to form a separate state, although this was not the British government's intention. It was always hoped that the North and South could get together under Home Rule, and as a temporary measure a parliament for Ulster was established at Stormont Castle on the outskirts of Belfast to govern the six counties. In the meantime a Council of Ireland was set up in the hope that it would act as a forum for discussion and compromise. The Council never met, and what was meant to be a temporary arrangement became permanent, as the Orangemen dominated the Ulster Assembly. The Protestants were quite determined that they were not going to be ruled by a Catholic South. In the South there were those who supported Collins and the 26-county Ireland and those who supported De Valera and the aim of getting Britain out of the island of Ireland altogether, to leave a 32-county state. The Collins faction felt that twenty-six counties were better than nothing, and since compromise was not in the air, civil war threatened, which would endanger British forces and prevent an

orderly withdrawal. The Treaty was ratified by the Irish Parliament on 7 January 1922 by 64 votes to 57, which only emphasized the split. Michael Collins was going to die for his signature on the Treaty, as Republicans ambushed and killed him. Civil war was only months away.

Retaining British facilities   Since the Irish Free State had Dominion status, it was to remain, theoretically at least, loyal to the Crown, and the Treaty made provision for British garrisons at certain ports for the purposes of naval defence so that, in time of war or strained international relations with a foreign power, the sea areas around Ireland might be secured. These 'Treaty Ports', namely Queenstown, Berehaven Dockyard, Lough Swilly and Belfast, were to have attendant aviation facilities, and there were to be fuel stocks on Haulbowline Island. Belfast was to be a Treaty Port because, as has been explained, it was then hoped that all thirty-two counties of Ireland would eventually be the Irish Free State. As it was, the six counties of Ulster, which were predominantly Unionist and Protestant, were to be governed separately under the Crown, and any military facilities maintained in Ulster would have the support of the Stormont parliament in Belfast. In the twenty-six counties of the Irish Free State the Treaty provided that the British Army and the government would withdraw.

RAF withdrawal begins   The withdrawal programme called for all RAF aircraft to be flown initially to Shotwick, near Chester, and then for No. 2 Squadron to go to Digby, while 100 Squadron would relocate at Spittlegate, both stations in Lincolnshire. The Irish Stores and Repair Unit would then complete the closing down of all RAF stations in Ireland. Having disposed of all equipment and engines, spares, etc., the unit would disband, with HQ 11 Irish Wing moving to Spittlegate. No. 2 Squadron left at the end of January 1922. The detached flight of No. 4 Squadron rejoined its parent unit at Farnborough, and 100 Squadron withdrew in its entirety during late January and early February. All administrative and technical personnel and stores had to return by sea since no transport aircraft existed at that time.

Formation of the Irish Flight   Group Captain Bonham Carter, by then Officer Commanding No. 11 Irish Wing, urged the retention of some aircraft in Ireland to cover the final British withdrawal. There was growing probability of strife between the pro- and anti-Treaty factions that would threaten an orderly withdrawal. He therefore proposed the formation of an Irish Flight, an independent unit not belonging to or detached from any squadron, composed of sufficient pilots and observers, technical and administrative personnel to be based at Baldonnel. He

Bristol Fighter J6696 comes to grief by a haystack, flattening a hay cart in the process. This aircraft belonged to No. 2 Squadron.

A DH9A of No. 100 Sqn on a mail run, Baldonnel to Fermoy, in 1921. (Note the mail sack by the port wheel.)

A Hucks starter being used in a DH9A of 100 Squadron at Baldonnel.

pointed out that there were Bristol Fighters undergoing repair that could be assigned to this unit. The ground personnel could come from the Irish Stores and Repair Unit, and there were three pilots of No. 5 FTS and three from No. 4 Squadron attached for ferry duties. He further proposed that Squadron Leader Wynne Eaton plus three pilots be retained for this flight. After some thought about the political implications of retaining flying units in Ireland after withdrawal HMG decided that in view of the deteriorating internal security situation the Irish Flight could be formed.

Reinforcement of the RAF in Ireland The Irish Flight became operational in the April of 1922, and was to have a six-month existence. There was always a 'bolt-hole' in Ulster if the military situation in Ireland suddenly worsened, as the population in the North was largely sympathetic to operations being undertaken by British forces. The difficulty in guarding Baldonnel, however, meant that both the HQ RAF Forces in Ireland and the Irish Flight, together with ancillary units, would have to move. The former moved, first to General Headquarters in Parkgate and then to Island Bridge Army barracks, the latter to Collinstown airfield. Irish Flight operations began with the escorting of troop trains evacuating the Army from Ireland, covering the lines from the Curragh and Dundalk to Dublin. But approval having been given for the forming of the Irish Flight, this was not then considered adequate should the military situation deteriorate. No. 2 Squadron, so recently retired to Digby, was ordered back to Ireland and to Aldergrove. The squadron's aircraft could not make the sea crossing from Shotwick to Collinstown without first being fitted with wireless, but there was not time to have the aircraft crated for transportation by boat. The order went out on 31 May, and the unit was on the move the next day. Technical and administrative personnel and remaining aircrews caught the ferry from Fleetwood. On arrival, No. 2 Squadron was to carry the mails and patrol the Ulster border in support of Army units. Initially there was a shortage of petrol, and troops of 17 Brigade had to be found to guard the airfield.

Outbreak of the Civil War On Wednesday 28 June 1922, Irish government forces moved to evict Republicans who had taken over the Four Courts in Dublin and other public buildings. At 04.15 hrs that day the Republicans resisted, and firing broke out, heralding the commencement of the civil war. The following day, 29 June, Bonham Carter decided to reinforce Collinstown, and No. 2 Squadron aircraft from Aldergrove were flown in. Now the RAF would equip its aircraft with munitions. Two DH9As arrived at Collinstown armed with 250 lb bombs, which were too heavy for the Bristol Fighters. Bonham Carter could then report from his Island Bridge HQ that aircraft under his command were in a position to carry out offensive operations, the DH9As with 250 lb bombs and the Bristol Fighters with 112 lb bombs. The Irish Flight continued operations from Collinstown throughout August and September and into October 1922. The most important task was the daily mail run, which the flight shared with the Bristol Fighters of No. 2 Squadron. Convoy escorts also continued to be an important task as the withdrawal progressed. During the summer some of the Irish Flight's aircraft were transferred to the provisional government for use with its new air service, which had taken over Baldonnel. de Havilland also provided civil flights into Collinstown to collect photographs and news items for publication in London, such was the interest on the mainland on the course of the civil war.

Final withdrawal The necessity for offensive action did not, in the event, materialize. The Irish Flight ceased flying on 14 October 1922, and on the 21st of that month a convoy arrived at Collinstown from Aldergrove to collect bombs, ammunition and other stores, which aircraft of No. 2 Squadron escorted back to Aldergrove on 28 October. The next day the Bristol Fighters of the Irish Flight, which had been held up by bad weather, flew to Aldergrove, ending RAF movements at Collinstown, and the airfield was handed over to the Royal Engineers. Once the remaining personnel and stores had been shipped out, the Irish Flight was disbanded on 1 November, and Collinstown was handed over to the government of the Irish Free State. On Sunday 17 December 1922 the final British withdrawal from the Irish Free State took place.

OCCUPATION OF GERMANY

RAF Deployment in Germany Following the ending of hostilities in November 1918 and pending the signing of a peace treaty between the belligerents, it was decided that RAF squadrons should be deployed to German airfields. A clutch of stations between Cologne and Bonn, and two further airfields between Bonn and Aachen, were chosen. The occupation lasted from 6 December 1918, with the arrival of No. 7 Squadron at Elsenhorn, until the same squadron departed on 21 September 1919 from Heumar. In all, twenty squadrons were involved between these dates, the majority being based at Bickendorf, in the north-western outskirts of Cologne. As in Ireland, mail runs were all-important, and a fair mixture of aircraft types were involved. The deployment of squadrons was as follows:

Squadron	Aircraft	Deployment
7	RE8	Elsenborn, Bickendorf, Spich, Bucheim and Heumar
9	BF2B	Ludendorf
11	BF2B	Spich
12	BF2B	Duren
18	DH9A	Bickendorf and Merheim
22	BF2B	Spich
25	DH9A	Bickendorf and Merheim
29	SE5A	Bickendorf
43	Snipe	Bickendorf and Eil
48	BF2B	Bickendorf
49	DH9	Bickendorf
59	BF2B	Bickendorf and Duren
62	BF2B	Spich
70	Camel	Bickendorf and Elsenborn
79	Dolphin	Bickendorf
84	SE5A	Bickendorf and Eil
149	FE2B	Bickendorf
206	DH9	Bickendorf
207	HP 0/400	Merheim and Hangelar
208	Snipe	Heumar and Eil

VULNERABILITY OF CAPITAL SHIPS

Both in the UK and in the USA bombing trials were carried out to test the vulnerability of capital ships (battleships and battle cruisers) to aerial bombing. In the USA two obsolete battleships, the *Virginia* and the *New Jersey*, were sunk by a twin-engined bomber. The *Virginia* went down in twenty-six minutes and the *New Jersey* in seven. But of more interest to British armament specialists was the defensive armament carried by the bomber, for the five Lewis guns were deemed to be important for aerial defence of bombers in the UK in 1922. A bombing trial was conducted that year against two targets representing the size of the battle cruiser HMS *Hood*. The purpose of the trial was to determine the accuracy with which bombs could be placed on or near a warship from various heights, and to compare the results obtained at different altitudes and with two different methods of attack. Dummy bombs were dropped from 2,000 ft and 8,000 ft while the targets were moving and changing course. It was observed that the results from individual bombers were superior to those achieved by formation bombing, and the accuracy achieved at 8,000 ft was broadly similar to that at 2,000 ft, i.e. at both heights there was a 7 per cent chance of scoring a direct hit and a 27 per cent chance of bombing within 50 ft of the target.

In the Second World War capital ships like the *Bismarck*, *Prince of Wales* and *Repulse* were to be sunk as a direct result of aerial attack, and when that war ended the aircraft-carrier was to replace the battleship as the capital ship of the fleet. But in 1922 the Royal Navy predictably played down the vulnerability of its capital ships because, as their Lordships saw it, the radius of action of anti-ship aircraft was very limited. Sir Percy Scott, who had been responsible for the wartime defence of London, took a contrary view in believing that battleships in war were so menaced by bombing and torpedo attacks that their best place was in a home port. This view might have been a little extreme in 1922, if prophetic.

RAF OPERATIONS IN THE MIDDLE EAST AND INDIA FROM 1920 TO 1924
Source: National Archives, AIR10/1367

Although operations against dissident tribesmen in India had been conducted during the First World War, the policy of air control, i.e. the use of airpower to maintain internal security, was not officially sanctioned until after the Cairo Conference of March 1921. This conference in turn resulted from the success gained by the RAF in British Somaliland against the forces of the 'Mad Mullah'. Not only were the money and lives saved following the implementation of air control welcome in times of financial stringency, but it also helped towards the survival of the Royal Air Force as a separate third arm at a time when the two older sister services wished to see it disbanded. Air-control operations during the period 1920–24 continued throughout the entire inter-war period, and are described in this and the following chapter, as well as in Volume II.

Air Operations in British Somaliland 1920 The 'Mad Mullah' was a source of repeated trouble to the colonial authorities for some twenty years. During 1903/4 he had tied down a force of over 5,000 regular soldiers and 1,000 irregulars under the command of a major-general. During the period 1910–12 the interior of the territory had to be evacuated, it was necessary to deploy forces to further restrict his activities during the period 1914/15, and pressure on him was maintained for the four years up to 1919. Trenchard had been approached by the Colonial Secretary, Lord Milner, to see what the RAF might be able to do. Trenchard characteristically said, 'Why not leave the whole thing to us?' A force was then assembled, comprising a naval contingent, half a battalion of Indian infantry, a composite battalion of King's African Rifles, the Somaliland Camel Corps and six RAF aircraft. The RAF element was commanded by Group Captain R. Gordon. Combined operations lasted for twenty-three days, and the Dervishes were completely defeated and dispersed. From then on the Mad Mullah was a fugitive. The Dervishes were normally good fighting men, but the use of aircraft had an immediate and demoralizing effect on them. Imperial casualties were only three native troops killed and eight wounded, and one officer of the Camel Corps was slightly wounded. At a cost of £70,000, compared with an estimated £6,000,000 had only ground troops been used, the whole operation was most successful.

Zeyla 1920 The effects that even the threat of the use of airpower had at this time is illustrated in the Zeyla incident in 1920. Four years after the district officer had been attacked and wounded, the tribesman involved had still not been surrendered by his tribe. The latter was therefore informed that aircraft would be used to enforce obedience if the assailant was not surrendered. The very act of starting work on the aerodrome at Zeyla was sufficient to achieve the desired result.

The Cairo Conference, March 1921 Air control as a means of maintaining internal security was shown to be feasible and economic in the operations to counter the Mad Mullah in British Somaliland. Winston Churchill had moved from the post of Secretary of State for War and Air to be the Colonial Secretary, and in 1921 he knew Trenchard's capabilities well. In response to major problems of law and order in Iraq during the summer of 1920, Churchill called upon Trenchard on 29 February 1921 to submit a scheme for the maintenance of internal security in Mesopotamia (Iraq), i.e. not the defence of that country against external aggression. In the event, the Turkish army was to enter the country, for Turkey had not then recognized the state of Iraq. He saw the need for the control of Iraq to be transferred from the War Office to the Air Ministry, and proposed the establishment of secure air bases from which operations could be mounted, including bombing, strafing and the conveyance of small parties of troops by air. Trenchard was also asked to consider the use of chemical bombs that did not kill but inflicted various degrees of annoyance, e.g. tear gas. Trenchard produced a draft scheme in a fortnight. He would need an aeroplane to convey stores to outlying posts and a troop-carrying aircraft capable of carrying small bodies of troops. He already had the DH9A bomber and the Bristol Fighter to carry out the offensive operations, and these aircraft had been tested in the First World War. Upon receipt of Trenchard's proposals, Churchill convened a conference of his service chiefs in Cairo in March 1921. The traditional methods of control had been tried, i.e. the use of punitive Army columns sent to trouble spots in response to outbreaks of unrest, but these operations were very costly, too costly in terms of money during a period of financial stringency, and also of lives. After much heartsearching it was decided to place Iraq under RAF command. This entirely novel arrangement meant that, for the first time in service history, Army troops would come under the command of a Royal Air Force Air Officer Commanding (AOC). Trenchard admitted that a certain amount of risk was involved, and predictably the Chief of the General Staff, Sir Henry Wilson, poured scorn on the decision, describing the go-ahead for the RAF to police Iraq as 'hot air, aeroplanes and Arabs'. The RAF force that was to give effect to the policy of air control consisted of eight squadrons of DH9As, Bristol Fighters, Vickers Vernon transports and RAF armoured car companies.

Burao 1922 In Burao a British officer was murdered by tribesmen in February 1922. The Governor applied for aircraft from Aden to carry out a demonstration of air power over the territory where the incident took place, for there were other small troop detachments up country that could also be threatened, and the Somali companies of the Camel Corps were not wholly reliable. The Governor had also asked for British troops to be held in readiness in Aden in case the situation deteriorated. He later reported that, in the event, neither the King's African Rifles nor other troops on stand-by would be required. The mere sight of aircraft patrolling the affected area was sufficient, not only to give heart to the small troop detachments, but to secure the payment of the fine of 3,000 camels by the recalcitrant sections of the tribe, in full and without delay. This contrasted with a similar incident in Jubaland, when the Ogaden tribe refused to pay a fine of 10,000 camels either voluntarily or under compulsion.

Air Operations in Iraq, 1920 to 1924

Events in Iraq, 1920–22 In 1920 an insurrection broke out in Iraq when the whole of the lower Euphrates rose in arms and there was a complete breakdown of order outside the perimeter of the Baghdad garrison. There were 60,000 troops in Iraq at the time, together with four armoured car companies and two RAF squadrons of aircraft. Large reinforcements had to be brought in from India, and active operations continued from July to October 1920. During that period the security forces suffered 2,269 casualties against 8,450 suffered by the Arabs. It had not been possible to check the insurrection in its early stages owing to the lack of means of transport, the long distances involved and the need to protect the long lines of communication, and throughout 1921 and 1922 the condition of Iraq remained disturbed.

Situation at the end of August 1922 The situation by August 1922 was at least as serious as it had been in 1920.The Baghdad Wilayat and the Euphrates tribes were on the verge of rebellion, the latter being particularly defiant, and some of the tribes had embarked on a plan to overthrow the government. Administration in the Rumaithah area was intermittent and precarious, for this is where the insurrection had broken out. The power and pretensions of Ibn Saud and raids by the Akhwan tribe made the desert tribes restless, resulting in the whole of Kurdistan being abandoned early in September. The High Commissioner reported that he would not risk the lives of British officials and other non-Muslim employees in Sulaimania, and had them evacuated by air on 5 September, the RAF conveying sixty-seven persons to Kirkuk. This left Kurdistan exposed, as the administrative boundary was moved down to the plain of Iraq. Kurdish towns and military posts were then occupied by Turkish irregular forces, and a Turkish local governor was installed to administer an area fifty miles inside the Iraqi frontier. The Turks also let it be known

that they intended to recover Mosul. During this time the Imperial forces consisted of nine battalions of infantry, two batteries of artillery, four armoured car companies and (from May) eight RAF squadrons. It was considered that nine battalions of infantry were insufficient to maintain order, particularly in the distant foothills of Kurdistan, when troops could be cut off from reinforcement from Baghdad.

The Assumption of Air Control in Iraq The following were the Air Staff's recommendations for troop levels necessary to maintain internal security under Army command, assuming no external aggression and no serious internal uprising:

- 2 British battalions
- 10 Indian battalions
- 2 Indian pack batteries (artillery)
- 6 RAF squadrons + armoured car companies
- 1 cavalry regiment
- 1 RFA battery (artillery)
- 2 sapper and miner companies
  Local forces (mainly Levies)

In contrast the force level required if the RAF assumed responsibility for internal security in Iraq would be:

- 8 RAF squadrons + armoured cars
- 1 British battalion
- 3 Indian battalions
- 1 Indian pack battery (artillery)
  Local forces (mainly Levies)

It may seem surprising that the RAF, so young a service in the early 1920s, should presume to know what forces the Army might need in these circumstances, but one should remember that all RAF officers of staff rank at this time had probably spent more time in the Army than in the RAF, and would therefore have had basic all-arms training, if not Army staff training. And so it was that His Majesty's Britannic Government decided, after much soul searching, to substitute Air for Army command and control in Iraq as recommended by the Cairo Conference on security in the Middle East. The handover was in August 1921, and the first Air Officer Commanding was Air Marshal Sir John Salmond.

Air Marshal
Salmond.

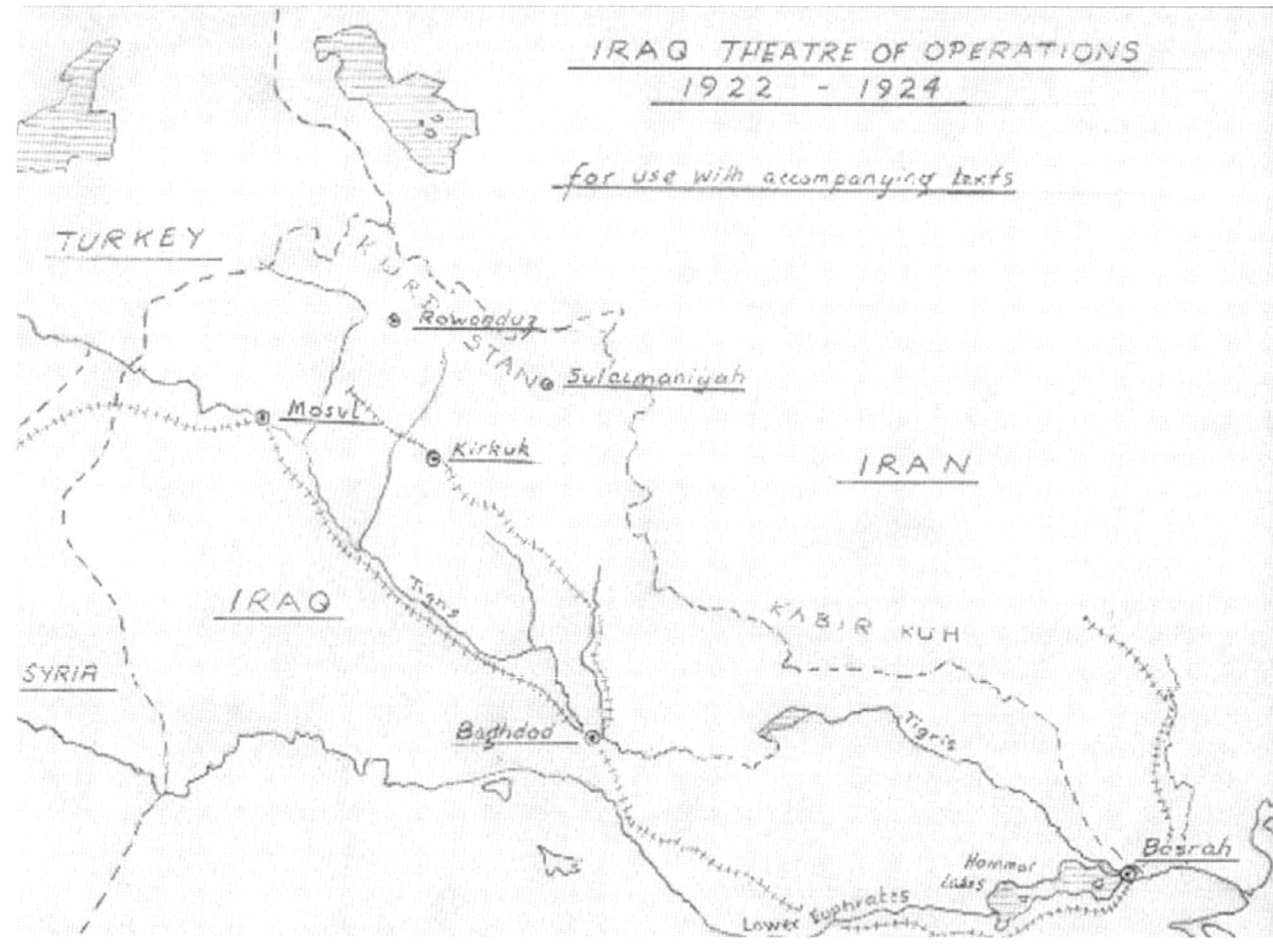

IRAQ THEATRE OF OPERATIONS
1922 - 1924

for use with accompanying texts

TURKEY

KURDISTAN

Rowanduz

Sulaimaniyah

Mosul

Kirkuk

IRAN

IRAQ

Tigris

KABIR KUH

SYRIA

Baghdad

Tigris

Hammar Lakes

Basrah

Lower Euphrates

Effects of Air Action The effects of vigorous air action both in the lower Euphrates and in Kurdistan were as follows:

Lower Euphrates A group of insurgent sheikhs were actually in the process of throwing off the authority of the government, but by the end of the month they had surrendered and the Euphrates divisions were able to embark upon a period of reconstruction.

Kurdistan Air action was taken against the Turks and their adherents wherever they showed their faces, and they were eventually forced to withdraw from the Rania district to concentrate in Rowanduz.

The High Commissioner in his report on these operations applauded the RAF for their audacious actions, being largely responsible for the successful outcome.

The Threat to Mosul, *1923* Since it was considered a strong possibility that the Turks would try to take Mosul, most of the Imperial forces in Iraq, both RAF squadrons

and Army troops, had to be moved north and several hundred miles from the sea where reinforcments might come aboard ship. But the air units could always move back very quickly if the need arose. The occupation of Mosul by the British thus denied it to the Turks. In the event there were four minor outbreaks of disorder among tribesmen, but these were dealt with by air units without having to call away the squadrons concentrated in the north.

The Chanak Crisis, October 1922 to April 1923 In 1922 the Turkish leader Kemal Ataturk had repudiated the Treaty of Sèvres, the treaty between Turkey and the Allied Powers at the end of the First World War. One of the terms of the Armistice was that the Allies might enter the Dardanelles, the Bosphorus and the Black Sea and occupy any strategic points in Turkey that they might desire and have the immediate control of the wireless and other telegraphic systems. Observation posts were established to keep watch on the narrow sea passages to ensure that navigation in and out of the Black Sea was not hindered. Turkey had then inflicted a defeat on Greece during its recent war, and its advance had brought Turks right up to the barbed wire of the British positions at Chanak. If the Turks were to take these positions they could place guns on them that could threaten ships passing through the Straits. Lloyd George decided that the British must stand firm, and it was decided to reinforce the air strength in the region by one bomber and one fighter squadron, which arrived in Constantinople aboard HMS *Argus*. However, Lloyd George's brinkmanship in this crisis cost him the general election, and his place as prime minister passed to Bonar Law, whose declared policy at the election was to bring stability and tranquillity to the area. He would reach an agreement with Turkey; but it was not so straightforward. The Turkish leader also coveted the Mosul region of Northern Iraq, and he would not accept League of Nations mediation – only a plebiscite in Mosul.

Operations in Northern Iraq   In Kurdistan there were anti-British outbreaks, which King Faisal either could not or would not check. The Kurdish rebel leader, Sheikh Mahmud, disputed British occupation rights in the frontier region in the neighbourhood of Rowanduz, a small town in the Kurdistan Hills some forty miles from Kirkuk. Mahmud had taken possession of the town when the British forces had been evacuated, following unrest in the Lower Euphrates, and the administrative boundary had been redrawn further south in the plain of Iraq. Kurdistan had therefore been virtually abandoned. It has already been stated that vigorous air action helped to evict Turkish and irregular forces from southern Kurdistan, resulting in the withdrawal of Turkish forces to Rowanduz. It was at this point that differences of opinion emerged between Trenchard and the local air commander, AVM Salmond. Trenchard felt that Salmond should use airpower from the centre outwards, it being the soundest, safest and cheapest method of expelling an invader without air cover of his own. He questioned whether Rowanduz mattered or if a small area was turbulent and under the control of the Turks. What mattered more to Trenchard was the security of Iraq, Rowanduz could wait! But Salmond was not prepared to give up the town without a fight, and his answer was his 'Forward Plan'. In this he had been swayed by the views of Sir Percy Cox, the retiring High Commissioner. The latter was certain that Kemal had set his heart on the Mosul region and would seize the territory unless forcibly forestalled. The Forward Plan meant moving substantial forces into the Mosul region, but the Cabinet of Bonar Law was hesitant to act in case of a breach with Turkey. The *Daily Express* thundered that Britain should not go to war over Mosul and that the mandate should be handed over to the League of Nations. Salmond, however, was not prepared to wait, and he put his Forward Plan into action with the utmost secrecy. When word did get to

the Cabinet there was great alarm. Trenchard had to cable Salmond that if his forces encountered Turkish resistance he should withdraw, knowing, perhaps, that Salmond might turn a Nelsonian blind eye. As it turned out, it was not the Turks who acted, but Sheikh Mahmud, who attacked Kirkuk with a force of Kurds and hill Arabs. After two months of vigorous action by Imperial forces Kirkuk was reoccupied, and with air support Rowanduz was also taken with few casualties. In fact there was a greater threat to life from the dysentery that afflicted the troop columns, causing 200 casualties who were evacuated by air, thereby saving lives. Turkey's bluff had been called, and Kemal withdrew Turkish columns from the mountainous frontier region. The whole operation had been carried out at a cost of £100,000 and Salmond was rewarded with a promotion to the rank of air marshal.

Consolidation of Authority of Government in the Remainder of Iraq   There were many areas of Iraq where government authority was either non-existent or ineffective. The southern portion of Kurdistan remained very disturbed, and a local religious leader, Sheikh Mahmud, was behaving like the Mad Mullah of Somaliland, escaping to Persia (Iran) when the security forces closed in on him, and it took four years to subdue him. The area flanking the railway into Baghdad, where it passes through the lower Euphrates, was inaccessible and thus ripe for unrest, and dissident tribesmen again threatened to tear up the railway tracks. When attempts to achieve a settlement without resort to force failed, two days and two nights of air action secured the submission of all the tribes in the area. As a result enforcement of government authority in the whole of the Euphrates basin was achieved. Finally the marsh area in the region of the Hammar Lakes was also inaccessible to government ground forces, and when the local sheikh became openly defiant his fort and guest house was singled out for air attack after he and the townsfolk had been given time to evacuate. Both these buildings were destroyed, and the sheikh surrendered unconditionally.

Use of air transport to ferry troops   One of the problems in using ground forces to deal with unrest was the response time. In 2005 it is taken for granted that troops will be airlifted into world trouble spots by jet-powered troop carriers and helicopters. In 1923 it was still something of a novelty to convey troops by air. The Vickers Vernons used for evacuating the troops sick with dysentery, as mentioned above, could also be used to convey troops of platoon strength to a trouble spot. When a serious dispute occurred between Assyrian (Christian) local forces and Muslim townsfolk in May 1924, two platoons of infantry (sixty men) were flown from Baghdad to Kirkuk the same day and the situation was quickly restored. Aircraft could also be used where roads were impassable.

Turkish Aggression, 1924 Aggression began on the northern border of Iraq with Turkey in September 1924 involving Turkish regular and irregular forces. Formations of the Turkish VII Corps were concentrated on the Iraqi border, and two cavalry formations crossed into Iraq on the 13th of the month. They were promptly engaged by patrolling RAF aircraft and routed. While the Turks were supposed to be mounting a punitive expedition against Assyrians and Kurds they were undoubtedly testing the defences of the Mosul Wilayat. During this air action RAF armoured cars and a force of Indian troops, Iraqi soldiers and Iraq Levies were on hand, but were used on only one occasion. For one month air action against the Turks was maintained until their forces were compelled to withdraw behind the frontier. These operations finally checked any further Turkish aggression into Iraq and Kurdistan, but the AOC could not turn his full attention to internal security within Iraq until a treaty with Turkey was signed in 1926 following a report by the Boundary Commission of the League of Nations. In the report by His Britannic Majesty's Government on the Administration of Iraq during 1923/4 it was stated:

Work of the Royal Air Force

During the whole period under review, a main factor in the pacification of the country has been the Royal Air Force. By prompt demonstrations on the first sign of trouble carried out over any area affected, however distant, tribal insubordination has been calmed before it could grow dangerous, and there has been an immense saving of blood and treasure to the British and Iraq Governments. In earlier times punitive columns would have had to struggle towards their objectives across deserts or through difficult defiles, compelled by the necessities of their preparations and marches to give time for their opponents to gain strength. But now almost before the would-be rebel has formulated his plans, the droning of the aeroplanes is heard overhead, and in the majority of cases their mere appearance is enough.

In the report of the High Commissioner on the Development of Iraq, 1920–25, he states:

Forces of Order and Public Security

I need not recall at length the obligations of Iraq to the Royal Air Force, upon which former reports have insisted. The power and efficiency of that force overshadows the whole country, and must be realised as backing up all other instruments of security.

Reductions in the Military Garrison in Iraq, 1921 to 1924 The table below shows the steady reduction in the strength of the British Military Garrison in Iraq between March 1921 and October 1924. British military expenditure in Iraq fell as a direct result of air control from £7 million in 1922/3 to under £2 million in 1929/30. In Appendix E may be found an extract from a report on Iraq Administration by the High Commissioner dated April 1922 to March 1923.

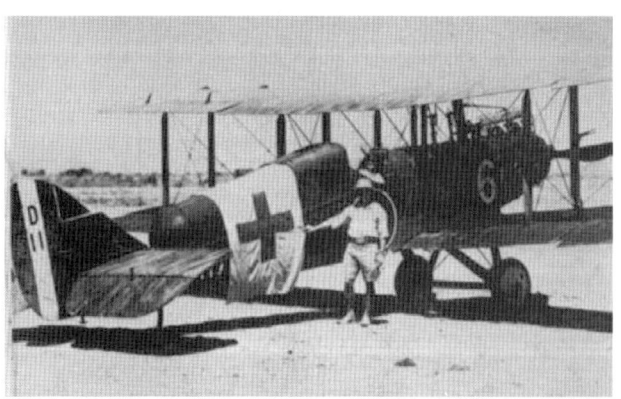

A DH9 converted to the air ambulance role during operations in British Somaliland in 1920 against the 'Mad Mullah'.

A Vickers Vernon troop-carrying aircraft vital to the success of air-control operations in being able to carry troops and supplies to remote locations.

REDUCTIONS IN MILITARY GARRISON IN IRAQ (COMBATANT UNITS ONLY)

Date	British and Indian Army	RAF	Iraq Levies
March 1921	33 battalions 6 cavalry regiments 16 batteries 6 S & M coys 4 armoured car coys	4 squadrons	
October 1921	17 battalions 13 batteries 4 S & M coys 3 armoured car coys	6 squadrons became 7 sqns in Feb 1922 and 8 sqns in May 1922	4 cavalry regts 1 pack battery 2 battalions 3 machine-gun coys
October 1922	9 battalions 2 batteries 1 S & M coy 2 armoured car coys	8 squadrons 2 armoured car coys	4 cavalry regts 4 battalions 1 pack battery
October 1923	6 battalions 1 battery RFA 1 pack battery 1 S & M coy	8 squadrons 4 armoured car coys	4 battalions 2 cavalry regts 1 battery
October 1924	4 battalions 1 pack battery 1 S & M coy	8 squadrons 4 armoured car coys	Ditto

A Nieuport Fighter of No. 203 Squadron being repaired near Constantinople during the Chanak Crisis of 1922.

RAF armoured cars during operations against Sheikh Mahmud in Iraq.

AIR OPERATIONS IN INDIA, 1919 TO 1924

Difficulties encountered in the early years   The RAF aircraft in India in 1919 were few in number, mostly primitive and of low offensive power. For example, in air operations in Waziristan in 1919 only two tons of bombs a day was the total striking power. Precision bombing was not possible and the aircraft were unreliable. Owing to unserviceability aircraft were fit to fly less than one-third of the hours possible by aircraft in 1935. Moreover air attacks were carried out spasmodically over too wide an area. Finally financial stringency in the immediate postwar years meant that the supply situation of technical stores had become very serious.

Air Staff Proposals   In 1921 the Air Staff made proposals for the increased use of air power both for frontier control and for external operations. Essentially, as the Air Staff saw it, this meant transferring the frontier region from

Army to RAF control. While the Viceroy's Council unanimously supported the idea, the funds for its implementation were not forthcoming and the project came to nothing. At that time (1921) air control had not been initiated in Iraq and Transjordan that showed that enormous financial savings could be achieved by substituting RAF squadrons for Army battalions. Had the government of India had that knowledge things might have been different. In the event air operations on the North-West Frontier against dissident tribesmen were to prove economical in money and lives. Whatever the cost, however, this was borne by the Indian government and did not therefore have to come from the very limited funds available to Trenchard at the Air Ministry. By 1924 action had been taken to remedy the sad state of affairs, and from then onwards RAF squadrons were able and were permitted to undertake and initiate air operations, i.e. those not in direct support of land forces.

Operations in Waziristan between 1922 and 1924
Operations against the Guri Khels in September and October 1923 Sections of the Mahsud tribe, notably the Guri Khels, were responsible for sniping, raiding and thefts. As was usual in such cases, warnings of impending air operations were given if political pressure failed to have any effect on the perpetrators. On 16 September 1923

such a warning gave seven days' notice of air action if government terms were not accepted. The Garrari section of the tribe was also named in the warning, and since they had had experience of air bombing they accepted, but the Guri Khels held out. Bristol fighters and two bombing aircraft from Risalpur commenced operations on 23 September and continued until 28 October. During this period bombing was resorted to on only eight days, but this was sufficient to persuade the Guri Khels to come to terms. No casualties were sustained by RAF personnel, but no information was available regarding casualties among the tribesmen. RAF headquarters staff were of the opinion that information about the tribesmen was scanty before operations commenced, and better intelligence would have resulted in the use of continuous patrols and delayed-action bombs, with a consequent shortening of operations.

Operations against certain Mahsud sections. 16 May to 2 June 1924 Operations were carried out against four sections of the Mahsud tribe during the above period in Spli Toi and Dre Algad. After the usual warnings had been given, two flights of DH9As were sent to Dardoni to reinforce the Bristol Fighters there. The tribal sections had until 23.59 hrs on 24 May to comply. By 23 May political pressure and air

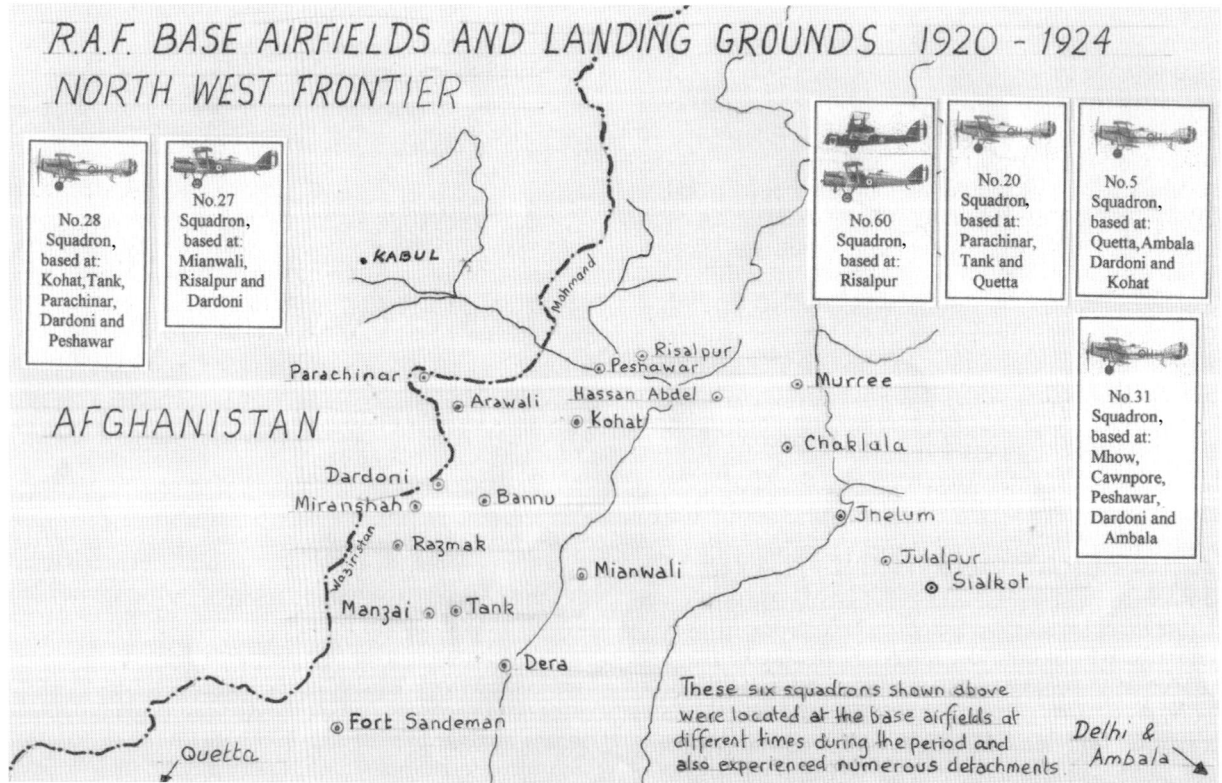

R.A.F. BASE AIRFIELDS AND LANDING GROUNDS 1920 - 1924
NORTH WEST FRONTIER

No.28 Squadron, based at: Kohat, Tank, Parachinar, Dardoni and Peshawar

No.27 Squadron, based at: Mianwali, Risalpur and Dardoni

No.60 Squadron, based at: Risalpur

No.20 Squadron, based at: Parachinar, Tank and Quetta

No.5 Squadron, based at: Quetta, Ambala Dardoni and Kohat

No.31 Squadron, based at: Mhow, Cawnpore, Peshawar, Dardoni and Ambala

These six squadrons shown above were located at the base airfields at different times during the period and also experienced numerous detachments

AFGHANISTAN

KABUL

Parachinar
Arawali
Risalpur
Peshawar
Hassan Abdel
Kohat
Murree
Chaklala

Dardoni
Miranshah
Bannu
Razmak
Jhelum

Manjai
Tank
Mianwali
Julalpur
Sialkot

Dera

Fort Sandeman

Quetta

Delhi & Ambala

demonstrations succeeded in securing the compliance of the Maresai and Guri Khel sections, but operations had to commence against the Faridai and Abdur Rahman Khel sections on 25 May. Both bombing and reconnaissance ensued before the GOC Waziristan District suggested that there were insufficient targets to justify bombing, and further bombing was postponed to permit the inhabitants of the villages to come out of their caves. The GOC intervened again when bombing was supposed to have resumed on 1 June. He stopped the attack since he maintained that all hostiles had left the area for Afghanistan. In the event it was the Abdur Rahman Khels who had left; the Faridai section complied with terms on 2 June and all operations ceased. In assessing the effectiveness of these air-control operations the Air Staff made the following points: firstly, the threat of air action was sufficient to bring only two of the tribal sections to terms, i.e. the surrender of all captives and pending the handing over of hostages. This may be put down to the fact that air demonstrations were not made in force but by only a flight of aircraft at a time; secondly, the first attacks were not delivered in force; thirdly, air action was suspended immediately the enemy took to the caves, which would suggest a difference of opinion between the GOC and air commanders. Finally, the Air Staff reported that the cost of seventeen days' operations was £5,103 1s 0d and that no RAF casualties were sustained.

Operations against the Mahsuds – Shabi Khels – 26–30 July 1924   This was yet another defiance of government authority by the Mahsuds, this time by the Shabi Khels section of the tribe. They were held responsible for several cases of sniping, kidnapping and raiding, and on 11 and 19 July demonstration flights were carried out over their territory and photographs taken of possible targets. Following the usual warning, which failed to gain compliance, bombing was commenced on 26 July. One squadron of Bristol Fighters, plus an additional flight, together with two flights of DH9As, were involved on the 26th, 27th and 28th of the month. On the 28th heavy clouds and mist descended over the hills, and two aircraft crashed, killing their crews. Meanwhile a third aircraft made a forced landing, but right among those being attacked, and the crew were taken prisoner. Operations were then suspended pending negotiations for their release. When the Shabi Khels did not immediately surrender them, bombing was resumed later in the day and continued on 29 July with a warning that the whole tribe would be held responsible and intensive action would ensue if they did not comply. At 14.00 hrs on 30 July, the head of the Shabi Khels is reported to have brought in the RAF officer they were holding and the fine demanded was paid in full. The official report then goes on to talk about two Air Force

prisoners, which conflicts with the previous statement. Actually the officer captured was the OC No. 5 Squadron. The second prisoner was his passenger, who was returned to the RAF via Razmak the day after his capture. Because of the crashes and losses of aircraft the cost of the action was £18,087, with four aircrew casualties.

Postscript on operations   It is worth noting that during the period 1920–24 ground troops were used in conjunction with RAF units, for apart from any other consideration, the tribesmen would need someone on the ground with whom they could negotiate and to whom they could hand over prisoners or fines. Operations involving only RAF units were on occasion possible when the RAF armoured car companies were used. These units, referred to in the Foreword, were the antecedents of a number of RAF Regiment squadrons, e.g. Nos 1, 2 and 3 Armoured Car Companies, which are Nos 1, 2 & 3 Squadrons RAF Regiment today.

STATE OF THE ROYAL AIR FORCE

Rapid Rundown of the RAF
Personnel and Real Estate   By the beginning of 1920 the RAF had demobilized more than 23,000 officers, 21,500 cadets (prospective pilots) and 227,000 other ranks, and on 31 March 1920 the Women's Royal Air Force was disbanded (see Chapter 9). There then remained only 3,280 officers and 25,000 men. The RAF also surrendered 149 aerodromes and 122 landing grounds, and auctioned or sold 2,240 hirings, land and buildings (see Chapter 7).

Squadron Disbandments and Deployments   Even before the Armistice was signed there was a slowing down in the pace of the formation and equipment of squadrons. During 1919 and into 1920 this was replaced by rapid disbandments (details of which can be found in Appendix F), and some 10,000 aircraft became surplus to requirements. These, together with engines and spares, were sold off to the Aircraft Disposal Company for £5,700,000 (see Chapter 5). The RAF strength had fallen from a total of 188 squadrons and five flights to twenty-nine squadrons on 1 March 1920, the lowest point that the service was to reach in the inter-war years, and of these seven were only of cadre strength. On page 54 is the squadron strength of the RAF on 1 March 1920. Trenchard then decided which squadron numberplates were going to survive the rundown, and some surviving squadrons were renumbered on 1 April – namely those squadrons that had a distinguished service record.

RAF SQUADRON DEPLOYMENT AND AIRCRAFT, 1 MARCH 1920

Unit	Location	Aircraft/Remarks
United Kingdom (including Ireland)		
No. 2 Squadron	Oranmore	Bristol F2B
No. 4 Squadron	Uxbridge	Cadre strength
No. 24 Squadron	Kenley	Bristol F2B
No. 39 Squadron	Uxbridge	Cadre strength
No. 100 Squadron	Baldonnel	DH9A, Bristol Fighter
No. 203 Squadron	Leuchars	Sopwith Camel
No. 207 Squadron	Bircham Newton	Cadre
No. 210 Squadron	Gosport	Sopwith Cuckoo
No. 230 Squadron	Felixstowe	Fairey IIIC, Felixstowe F2A, F3 and F5
No. 238 Squadron	Cattewater	Cadre – disbanded 20/3/22
Germany		
No. 12 Squadron	Bickendorf	Bristol F2B – disbanded July 1922
Malta		
No. 267 Squadron	Kalafrana	Short 184, Felixstowe F2A and F3 Redesignated No. 481 Flight on 1/8/23
Palestine		
No. 14 Squadron	Ramleh	Bristol F2B
Iraq		
No. 6 Squadron	Baghdad West	Cadre – until July, when equipped with Bristol F2B
No. 30 Squadron	Baghdad West	RE8
Egypt		
No. 47 Squadron	Helwan	Airco DH9
No. 55 Squadron	Suez	Airco DH9
No. 56 Squadron	Aboukir	Sopwith Snipe
No. 70 Squadron	Heliopolis	HP 0/400, Vickers Vimy
No. 208 Squadron	Ismailia	RACFy RE8
No. 216 Squadron	Qantara	HP 0/400
India		
No. 1 Squadron	Risalpur	Sopwith Snipe
No. 3 Squadron	Ambala	Cadre – until June, when equipped with Sopwith Snipes
No. 20 Squadron	Bannu	Bristol F2B
No. 31 Squadron	Risalpur	Bristol F2B
No. 48 Squadron	Quetta	Bristol F2B – renumbered 5 Sqn on 1/4/20
No. 97 Squadron	Lahore	DH10 – renumbered 60 Sqn on 1/4/20
No. 99 Squadron	Mianwali	DH9A – renumbered 27 Sqn on 1/4/20
No. 114 Squadron	Ambala	Bristol F2B – renumbered 28 Sqn on 1/4/20

RAF Strength on 1 March 1921 One year after the RAF had reached its lowest point, there were now only twenty-eight squadrons, but since these were now fully formed the actual RAF strength had increased:

6 squadrons – Egypt/Palestine
5 squadrons – Iraq
8 squadrons – India
1 squadron – Germany

1 squadron – Malta
3 squadrons – Ireland
3 squadrons – with the Navy
1 squadron – in the United Kingdom giving refresher courses

The total number of personnel at this time, both on squadrons and in training establishments, was 2,900 officers and 25,000 men.

Squadron Deployments/Formations in 1921 In the summer of 1921 the first three of the contemplated four UK-based squadrons were formed, i.e. two bomber and one fighter, joined in 1922 by a bomber squadron withdrawn from Ireland after the establishment of the Irish Free State. But in November 1922 the fighter squadron and two of the bomber squadrons went to the Middle East in response to the Chanak crisis. Two flights of a fighter squadron returned to the United Kingdom in December from Egypt. At the close of 1922, therefore, the RAF at home comprised:

2 fighter flights
4 naval cooperation squadrons in the Coastal Area
2 bomber squadrons
1 Army Cooperation squadron
1 communications squadron

Note: Only the two fighter flights and a bomber squadron could be regarded as available for home defence.

Aircraft Strengths, 1922 The number of aircraft possessed or on order by the RAF is shown below. In the current estimates for that financial year it was proposed to order ninety-two new aircraft, of which sixty-five were to be converted. Of the existing stocks of aircraft, 361 were to be reconditioned by contractors and a further 184 were to be reconditioned in repair depots. The figures given opposite include thirty-six Vernons, six IIIDs and twenty-two Walrus aircraft not then received. It is significant that the inventory of the RAF in 1922 was virtually of a First World War vintage. The new designs like the Fawn, Siskin and Aldershot were still to make their appearance. The Bristol Fighter and the DH9A constituted the backbone of the service.

Reconditioning and Conversions The number of machines on order by the RAF in the immediate postwar years was such that the survival of sixteen airframe manufacturers could not be possible without reconditioning and conversion contracts. For example, a DH9A had been converted to the same specification as the Westland Walrus and was known as the Tadpole. A number of Avro 504Ks were converted to Type L seaplanes. For reconditioning, Bristols had a few fighters at a time, Blackburn some Cuckoos, Hawkers some Snipes, Boulton & Paul and Handley Page a few DH9As, and so on. The result was most often the emergence of a reconditioned aircraft that looked as good as new. Apart from that, as is explained in Chapter 5, the design teams were kept busy producing prototypes for which they were paid by the Air Ministry whether or not they went into RAF service. By these and other means, therefore, the aircraft industry survived the 'lean years'.

THE NUMBER OF AIRCRAFT POSSESSED OR ON ORDER BY THE RAF IN 1922

Land-planes	Active Service	Training	Stored	Total
Snipe	96	39	397	532
Avro 504K	14	395	514	923
Bristol Fighter	360	227	503	1,090
DH9A	271	124	268	663
DH10	60	7	12	79
Vickers Vimy	–	14	71	85
Vickers Ambulance	3	–	–	3
Vickers Vernon	36	–	–	36
	840	806	1,765	3,411

Marine Aircraft				
F2A & F5	45	24	40	109
Fairey IIIC	12	–	10	22
Fairey IIID	42	12	–	54
Sopwith Cuckoo	24	6	15	45
Westland Walrus	24	24	–	48
Parnall Panther	36	3	51	90
Sopwith 2F1 Camel	36	–	43	79
	219	69	159	447
GRAND TOTAL	1,059	875	1,924	3,858

New Home Defence Areas and Command Ranks Further changes in the command structure of the RAF in the United Kingdom took place on 21 August 1919, when the Air Council proposed to reduce the number of areas from five to four, i.e. Northern, Southern, Naval (or Coastal) and Army (Inland). During September/October of 1919, Northern, Southern and Coastal Areas came into being. Another change occurred in 1920 when Northern and Southern Areas became, simply, Inland Area. Together with Coastal Area, this left the RAF at home with just two main commands and an independent group in Ireland that was later reduced to a wing status. The word 'main' is used because there were at the time and until July 1936 two others, namely RAF Cranwell and RAF Halton, two stations accorded command status. In 1936 there was a major reorganization of the command structure following the huge expansion of the number of squadrons, and both Halton and Cranwell were absorbed into one of the new commands. Nos 5 and 29 (Operations) Groups formed to fight the war in the Channel lost their command status in 1919. The status of an RAF command is important in determining the rank of the commander. It became the practice for areas/commands to be commanded by an air marshal, groups to be commanded by an air vice-marshal and large RAF stations to be commanded by group captains. The one rank that mostly got left out of it, unlike its Army equivalent of brigadier, was an air commodore. In the Army a brigadier plainly commanded a brigade, but the poor old air commodore often seems to have been relegated to staff positions, to re-emerge into the world of leading men in battle as air vice-marshals commanding groups. But of course nothing is fixed in stone, and the rank applied to a number of command positions in the RAF could vary to suit local circumstances.

The Future of the Royal Air Force?

A question mark is posited alongside the heading because of the wrangling that went on between Trenchard and the other two service heads, the latter wishing to see the RAF disbanded and the relevant air units returned whence they came on 1 April 1918. The detail of the battles between the Admiralty and the Air Ministry is reserved for Chapter 6, which deals with the RAF at sea. For the sake of completeness and to assess the weight of argument that Trenchard had to face from both the First Sea Lord and the Chief of the Imperial General Staff, the outline of the Navy's argument is included here. The various government committees that met to consider the future of the RAF and the effects of the famous 'Geddes Axe' is further discussed in this chapter.

The wrangling between the Royal Navy and the RAF
The beginning of this chapter dealt with the Trenchard Memorandum, which was the blueprint for the future RAF. On 9 December 1919, in a letter to Trenchard, Admiral Earl Beatty at the Admiralty had agreed to grant him a year's grace to get his air force established. At the end of that period he would be looking to Trenchard to meet the Navy's requirements in shore-based squadrons – that is, five squadrons: one fighter, one reconnaissance, one torpedo-bomber and two seaplane. The airpower needs of the Navy were twofold. Firstly, there was

Admiral Earl Beatty.

the protection of the fleet in harbour and in home waters, including ships of the Merchant Navy. By home waters is meant the Western Approaches to the British Isles, the Irish Sea, the English Channel and North Sea and the waters off the north coast of Scotland, particularly the Scapa Flow base in the Orkneys. Abroad this meant the security of waters off such bases as Malta, Alexandria and Gibraltar. For this, shore-based squadrons of land- or seaplanes would be needed. Secondly, there was the need to provide aircraft to operate with the various fleets sailing outside home waters, where aircraft would either be catapulted from the decks of warships or merchant ships or flown off the decks of aircraft-carriers. In 1918 all the RNAS flights were amalgamated into RAF squadrons that came into RAF ownership and under RAF control, serviced and flown by RAF ground- and aircrews. But things were not so straightforward afloat. Who would provide the aircraft, ground- and aircrews for the naval flights on warships, merchant ships and aircraft-carriers? If the Navy had wrested the ownership and control of all its air units in 1922 to return to the pre-1918 situation, it would have left the RAF as a hardly viable rump. Add to this the possibility that General Wilson would have got back all those squadrons working with the Army, and it would have rung the death knell of the RAF. Trenchard, with Churchill's support, had his Air Staff Paper, 'The Role of the Air Force in the System of Imperial Defence', circulated as a Cabinet Paper. This, together with Mr Balfour's report on that paper, issued on 26 July 1921, is shown at Appendix G.

Wrangling between the Army and the RAF   The Chief of the Imperial General Staff, General Sir Henry Wilson, was not prepared to be as generous as Earl Beatty. On several occasions he let it clearly be known that he wished to see an end to the RAF, it being an expensive luxury at a time of such financial stringency. Wilson and Trenchard disagreed over fundamentals. To the Army mind wars were won and lost on the battlefield. Aircraft were only useful in so far as they helped to achieve victory on the battlefield. Wilson did not deny their usefulness in the reconnaissance role nor in the vital task of denying the battlefield to the enemy's aircraft, but in both those roles it was sensible to keep all air units firmly under Army control. Finally, only ground troops could occupy enemy territory, proving that it was the Army that should be in control of air forces to make that possible. Trenchard's belief was that air forces could operate strategically, that is to say entirely independently of any land battles. They could bomb enemy industrial and military targets to the point where an enemy would sue for peace. Even supposing long-range bombing aircraft could inflict such damage on an enemy, Trenchard was not satisfied, taking the view that if such aircraft came under Army command and there was a conflict between the needs of the land

General Sir Henry Wilson.

forces and the needs of strategic bombing units, the latter would suffer. Trenchard did not want pilots to be mere taxi drivers for Army commanders. He wanted to create an 'air force spirit' by training his men for a career that was essentially a flying career, where they would be trained in the necessary skills of military aviators. Since Wilson was not prepared to give any ground, Trenchard had repeatedly to present cogent arguments for the retention of an independent air force during this period. Sadly, Sir Henry Wilson was to die near his home in Belgravia, London on 22 June 1922 at the hands of two Irishmen who had served as British soldiers in the war. Perhaps because he was an Ulsterman, the Irish troubles, recounted in the earlier part of this chapter, had claimed another victim.

Report by the Standing Defence Sub-Committee of the Committee of Imperial Defence, April 1922

In deciding the future strength of the RAF at home, the government used as a yardstick the strength of the largest continental power at that time, France. The Chiefs of Staff did not share the politicians' concern. The Air Staff took the view that the government should agree to fourteen home-based squadrons, of which five could be auxiliary units, akin to the Army's auxiliary Army units, with the power to expand to twenty squadrons in the event of war. After a few years, permitting these squadrons to bed in, the number of home-based squadrons could then be increased to twenty, with the power to increase to fifty squadrons in the event of war. Trenchard believed that it was unrealistic to seek parity with the French. Germany was the more likely enemy and Germany did not then possess an air force. If, however, parity with France was required then Trenchard advised the addition of twenty squadrons to the existing three at home earmarked for home defence. Fifteen squadrons would be regular units and five auxiliary. The twenty-three squadrons would then have 501 machines to France's 596, although the French had the potential to produce many more aircraft.

In 1922, Britain had built 300 machines, both civil and military,and the French had built 3,300 machines, of which only 300 were civil. And so the Cabinet approved the CID's (Committee of Imperial Defence) recommendations on 3 August 1922 to spend an increase of £2 million per annum. The Air Ministry was thus empowered to place orders for aircraft, engines and spares and at once with private firms, the bulk to be delivered in 1923. But then the government fell, and Mr Bonar Law, the new Conservative Prime Minister, was contemplating the disbandment of the RAF. With this prospect Earl Beatty could not resist the demand for full control of his naval airmen, threatening resignation if his demand was not met. And so Trenchard was summoned to Downing Street. When he learned of Beatty's threat he too threatened resignation if any attempt was made to 'carve up' the RAF. The PM's answer was usual for British governments. If in doubt set up an inquiry. On 9 March 1923 a sub-committee of the CID met under the chairmanship of Lord Salisbury.

The Salisbury Main Committee, March to October 1923

The Committee began its meetings on 15 March 1923, and continued until October. The chairman was required to inquire into the cooperation and correlation between the Navy, Army and Air Force from the point of view of national and imperial defence generally, including the question of establishing some coordinating authority, whether by a Ministry of Defence or otherwise. (It is of interest to note that such a ministry was not considered vital to the successful prosecution of the Second World War and that a Ministry of Defence was not set up until 1964.)

In particular the committee was to consider three questions:

1. The relations of the Navy and Air Force as regards the control of fleet air work

2. The corresponding relations between the Army and the Air Force

3. The standard to be aimed at for defining the strength of the Air Force for purposes of home and Imperial defence

At the first meeting the Air Minister, Sir Samuel Hoare, did not tell Trenchard that the Prime Minister had plans to withdraw the RAF from the Middle East. Trenchard reportedly laughed when he was told, thinking of the attitude of Turkey, in whose side the RAF had been a thorn, or the effect that this would have on security in Iraq, where the employment of airpower had been conspicuously successful.

The committee found it desirable to make some immediate recommendations, which the Cabinet felt obliged to accept on 20 June 1923. It was accepted that in addition to the RAF's commitment to provide the Navy and the Army with air units, and to maintain squadrons overseas, there must be a Home Defence Air Force of sufficient strength to protect the British Isles from air attack by the strongest air force within striking distance of this country. This brings the discussion back to the 'yardstick' principle, in which France was the yardstick without actually being branded a potential aggressor. This may sound bizarre in the days of collective defence when countries in an alliance, like NATO, sum their forces for the purposes of arriving at a total alliance force strength to face a potential aggressor. If Trenchard had regarded Germany as being the only possible potential aggressor at that time, one might have expected the air forces of Britain and France to be aggregated. In France's case, in 1922, that country had the potential markedly to increase its strength of military aircraft, while Germany under the terms of the Versailles Treaty was not permitted to have an air force. Therefore the parity had to be with France. Yet the British aircraft industry had been reduced to such a state that it would have been well-nigh impossible to meet the demands of a rapidly expanding air force. Those aircraft could have been supplied by the Aircraft Disposal Company, which held vast war-surplus stocks, but that would have meant equipping the RAF with obsolete aircraft. The committee therefore proposed that the Air Ministry be instructed to draw up detailed proposals for the creation of such a home-defence force, to be organized in part on a regular permanent military basis. 'In part' meant that the fullest use would be made of civilian labour and facilities. It was accepted that the first stage in the creation of such a force would absorb the entire capacity for aerial expansion in the immediate future but should provide a strength of 600 first-line machines to give parity with France. Further expansion should be considered but in the light of the air strength of foreign powers.

The committee recommended the approval of expenditure in the then current financial year of a sum not exceeding £500,000, apart from any savings the Air Ministry might be able to make on the RAF's approved Estimates for the year. The preliminary expenditure should go on the purchase of land for aerodromes, immediate increases in the number of officers and other ranks, increases in the recruiting machinery, an increase in the Air Ministry staff and additional research.

Finally, and perhaps incongruously, the Cabinet was being asked to approve the expenditure on a home-defence force while also acknowledging the government's commitment to reduce aerial and other armaments through international agreement. Then there was the 'Ten-Year Rule', which was supposed to underline defence policy at the time, that is that no major war could be expected within that period. The government could be in danger of sending to the world conflicting signals, i.e. that Britain was rearming, not disarming. On the other hand, defence of the nation against external attack could hardly be construed as a threat to world security. Of course, in Britain's case, with its Imperial and League of Nations responsibilities, such defence was necessary beyond the shores of the British Isles.

The Expansion Plan
New Home Defence squadrons The expansion plan provided for fifty-two metropolitan squadrons, but for various reasons this scheme was never to be fully implemented between the wars. The previous paragraph made clear that the government was torn between air parity with a potential continental aggressor and keeping to the spirit of disarmament under the League of Nations. This dichotomy was to persist right into the early 1930s, when Japanese aggression in Manchuria and the coming to power of Adolf Hitler in Germany, together with the League's failure to bring about international agreement on disarmament, turned rearmament into a national priority. Be that as it may, the expansion plan was understandably welcomed by Trenchard. With a substantial increase in Home Defence squadrons and the commitment to air control, the new service was becoming much more firmly established and could more easily fight off any threat from the sister services.

Air Staff Doctrine Trenchard dominated the implementation of the plan, keeping all administrative details under his control, and he personally presided over a number of staff meetings in the planning stages. For him it was the mix of squadrons that was important. Another CAS might have simply provided for fifty-two fighter squadrons, but Trenchard believed in offensive defence.

The best way, as he saw it, to defend the nation was to bomb an enemy's means of attacking the British Isles. Targets would therefore include munitions and aircraft-production factories as well as enemy airfields. Fighters would be necessary to intercept any enemy aircraft that did succeed in penetrating British air space, but the bomber was the key to successful defence. (The implementation of this doctrine is critically examined in Chapter 10, where the Air Staff's arrangements for providing, training and exercising a strategic bomber force are called into question.) The fighters then would be short-range. Trenchard did not envisage long-range fighter protection of the bombers. He put his faith in a force that was large enough to cause an enemy to sue for peace before Britain. The nation that could stand the punishment the longest would win in the end. He expressed his views in an Air Staff Memorandum dated 19 July 1923 and sent to the AOCs Central and Inland Areas. In this document, in which he spelt out the strategic air doctrine, the following words may be found:

It must be clearly realised that home defence does not mean only keeping attacking aircraft from flying over this country. In its broadest sense it means the winning of an air war against any Power which may decide to attack us. To win this war it will be necessary to pursue a relentless offensive by bombing the enemy's country, destroying his sources of supply of aircraft and engines and breaking the morale of his people.

In a briefing to his staff he said that it was better to attack the source of supply of bombs than to intercept an aircraft carrying ten bombs.

The mix of squadrons And so it was that the plan provided for seventeen fighter squadrons equipped with 204 aircraft, and thirty-five bomber squadrons with 394 aircraft. All the fighter squadrons and twenty two of the bomber squadrons would be regular. The remaining thirteen bomber squadrons would be seven Special Reserve squadrons and six Auxiliary squadrons. This would correspond to the Army militia and Territorial units.

Attitude of the Army It is at this point that Trenchard clearly distinguished between the role of the Army and that of an independent Air Force. He took the view that the policy of the Army was to defeat the enemy's army. The role of the RAF was to defeat the enemy nation. This was an important signal to send to the politicians and the other service chiefs who might still be harbouring thoughts of dismantling the RAF. Where the late Sir Henry Wilson left off, the War Minister, Lord Derby, took up the fight. He wrote privately to the Prime Minister, expressing disquiet over the decision to go ahead with the expansion plan. While he acknowledged the quality of Trenchard's leadership, he doubted that those in staff positions in the Air Ministry had the experience to run an enlarged independent air force. He asserted that there was a lack of suitable officers for staff appointments. He was prepared to lend staff officers to the RAF but doubted that they would wish to serve under senior RAF officers. But senior officers like the Salmond brothers, Robert Brooke-Popham, R.M. Groves and Philip Game did not need to prove themselves, indeed Edward Ellington had, by 1923, spent most of his career as a staff officer. Furthermore it certainly overlooked the talent among the younger officers on the staff and in the field, such as Cyril Newall, Arthur 'Bomber' Harris, Hugh Dowding, Charles Portal, Arthur Tedder, John Slessor and others who were to become household names in the years to come. Not all of them became Chief of the Air Staff, but they certainly reached Air rank. It seems that the only other ground that Lord Derby could think of on which to question the independence of the air force was the diseconomies in running separate medical, dental and chaplaincy services, but a Cabinet sub-committee had already looked into the matter of placing these services under Army control and concluded that no substantial economies could be effected by so doing. The Cabinet agreed, and Trenchard wrote a letter to Philip Game in India, expressing his belief that the war with the Army was at last over but that the war with the Navy was still intense.

The attitude of the Navy While it was then clear for all to see that it was not just the Army that could carry the war to the enemy, it was also clear that it was not just the Navy that could prevent an enemy from invading or attacking the country. The German Zeppelin and Gotha bomber raids had shown that to be true. The Admiralty continued to press its case for a separate air arm. The Salisbury Main Committee did not agree to this. Having a separate naval air arm meant distinguishing between shore-based and fleet-based units. With a single air arm whereby the RAF provided air forces for both the Army and the Navy, it meant that it did not matter whether or not an action was shore based or fleet based. Apart from that, there would be unnecessary duplication of training schools, airfields, equipment and technical support. However, it was conceded that naval officers and ratings might be attached or seconded to the RAF to gain experience in air operations.

It was recommended that the proportion of naval officers seconded, or attached, to the RAF should be increased from 20 per cent to a maximum of 30 per cent of the Naval Air Wing. They would be permitted to retain their naval uniforms and wear a special badge denoting the Air Branch, but this arrangement did not answer the question about the career structure of naval officers. To what extent would flying training and time spent on naval air units be counted as a prerequisite for staff training and eventual command of a warship? Those who became too involved with flying might lose their place on the promotion ladder to senior rank. The arrangements for putting RAF aircrews on board ships and for the progressive training of naval personnel were, none the less, put in place, although the First Lord of the Admiralty doubted whether the proposals were workable and he would not regard them as a final settlement. Several newspapers, also, were against the Main Committee's report, parts of which had clearly been leaked by the Admiralty. Beatty and the Sea Lords had to be persuaded not to resign as a body, and for the time being the Navy accepted what they regarded as a 'stop gap'. The Fleet Air Arm of the RAF was formed on 1 April 1924, and a Fleet Order 1058/24 called for volunteers from Navy officers to join the new arm. On 16 June 1924 the first course of thirty-five naval officers assembled at Netheravon in Wiltshire. Each officer on the course was given a 'shadow' RAF rank for administrative and disciplinary purposes. Meanwhile the RAF had directed that a small number of crews and technical tradesmen be assigned for duties with the FAA. And this is how it was to be managed, although there were later discussions about the proportion of naval to RAF officers assigned to these duties. By the time the Navy did get control of the Fleet Air Arm in 1937, the RAF was so well established, and was in any case rapidly rearming, that the loss of the naval component was no longer of any great significance. These events and the management of the FAA arrangements are described in Chapter 6, 'The RAF at Sea'.

The 'Geddes Axe' Before moving on to the implementation of the air expansion plan it is right to consider another threat to the RAF's existence, but one that did not materialize. The Committee on National Expenditure had been established under the chairmanship of Sir Eric Geddes to make recommendations to the Chancellor of the Exchequer for effecting all possible reductions in the government's expenditure, having regard to the present and prospective position on revenue, principally from direct taxes on income and indirect taxes on expenditure. This involved cuts in the Annual Estimates on expenditure by each of the armed forces. Overall government expenditure for the year 1922/3 had to be reduced from £603,000,000 to £490,000,000. As part of the economies that the services could make, the Geddes Committee had recommended the reduction in RAF strength in Egypt and Palestine to save £2,500,000. Winston Churchill, in a statement to Parliament on 9 March 1922, had countered by pointing out the great savings that had been effected using aircraft instead of ground troops in maintaining internal security in the Middle East, and that the squadrons in Iraq had been raised to eight in number. This was before the implementation of air control under Sir John Salmond. The debate that followed showed how the policy of air control was a much better way of reducing public expenditure than anything proposed by the Geddes Committee.

The Air Estimates, 1923/4, and implementation of the Expansion Plan Sir Samuel Hoare, the Air Minster, presented the Air Estimates to Parliament for the financial year 1923/4, which showed a net increase of £1,000,000. He referred to the difference in size of the air forces of France and Britain, and while emphasizing that it was inconceivable that the two great allies could ever enter into hostilities, that the RAF was only one-quarter the size of its French equivalent and the RAF now had the responsibility for Iraq and home defence. This was the year when the Navy Estimates were £58 million and those for the Army £52 million, yet the RAF had to make do with £12 million. It would, he said, require an immediate increase of £5 million, followed by a further increase of £17 million to keep pace with the progress of other great powers. With that latter sum the RAF could be increased fourfold, with expenditure little more than double the present cost. He did point out, however, the need to avoid an arms race. He commended to the House the work being done by the Committee of Imperial Defence looking into the whole problem of Imperial and national defence in relation to the three services, and spoke of the need to have an air force that, if not large, was of good quality. Fifteen new squadrons would be formed for home defence by April 1925, of

which initial expenditure for eight squadrons would arise in the coming financial year. Three squadrons would also be added to the Navy. Significant further expansion was in the new Auxiliary Air Force and Reserve, for which £238,000 was earmarked. Indeed the creation of an air force of part-timers and reservists meant that the paper strength of the RAF grew without the increases in expenditure that would result from an all-regular air force. Whether or not the British aircraft industry could produce the required new aircraft when it employed only 2,500 people, compared with 9,250 persons in France, was of course another matter.

RESERVE AND AUXILIARY FORCES
Source: National Archives, AIR/32/15

It was the key to Trenchard's plan for rapid expansion that there should be a reserve in the event of a sudden emergency or a general war. He had built a 'cottage on the foundations of a castle so that a castle may be built in time of need'. In his Memorandum of 1919 he had said, 'The present need is first and foremost the making of a sound framework on which to build a service which, while giving us now the few essential service squadrons, will be capable of producing whatever time may show to be necessary in the future.' The RAF was made up of layers representing various degrees of commitment to the service as follows:

1. Full-time regular service – the RAF as a career
2. Short full-time service + a number of years on the Reserve
3. The Auxiliary Air Force
4. The Royal Air Force Reserve
5. The Royal Air Force Volunteer Reserve
6. The Civil Air Guard

Note: The last two listed above did not materialize until the 1930s, and are dealt with in Volume II. The Civil Air Guard was in fact disbanded on the outbreak of the Second World War. The Auxiliary Air Force roughly corresponded to the Territorial Army, intended to merge with the regulars on embodiment. It was a fusing of the above elements that went into battle with the *Luftwaffe* in 1939.

Encouraging a spirit of air mindedness We return yet again to a theme that runs throughout Trenchard's new service, and that is the necessity to create an 'air force spirit'. Trenchard wanted to attract young men into the RAF from universities and schools and educate them uniquely to become airmen. Two ways of doing this were:

1. *The University Air Squadrons* These were to be staffed by the Royal Air Force with members recruited from the universities. They had no liability to serve with

the RAF, though, of course, every encouragement was given to them to do so. Flying facilities were provided by the RAF and an annual camp was arranged.

2. *Officer Training Corps*   The other force was in schools, and corresponded to the Army Cadet Force. This was the Officer Training Corps and was the forerunner of the Air Training Corps. Corresponding to the Air Defence Cadet Corps there were, in schools, the Air Section of the OTC.

Note: As a matter of interest the three separate service cadet elements in schools were amalgamated into the Combined Cadet Force in 1948 (the author spent twelve years with the CCF).

Short-Service Commissions   The real expansion of reserve training did not begin until the 1930s. At the beginning, however, there was a large pool of ex-service pilots that could be drawn upon. The problem was not in finding ex-service pilots who would be prepared to serve in the Reserve but in finding the flying training capacity. This is dealt with in detail in the following section, and consisted of contracting civilian firms to carry out the ground and air training required. Such firms would have to have aircraft repair facilities adjoining their aerodromes. As has been pointed out, the organization of the RAF envisaged a small nucleus of regular personnel supported by a large reserve. Only the full-time regulars were offered a full career in the RAF, but casualties in air warfare can be high and squadron wastage could only be met by bringing in reservists. This was the idea behind the Short-Service Commission scheme. The Army had personnel on short-service engagements, but the RAF was the first to apply it to officers. Since short-service commissioned officers served as regulars for a number of years followed by a period on the reserve, these officers filled the lower ranks on squadrons, and then went on to join the pool of trained pilots available in case of war or emergency. Indeed the large majority of pilots entered the RAF under this system in peacetime. The terms of service were originally for six years on the active list followed by four years on the reserve. Unlike its sister services, the RAF was essentially a short-service force and its flyers were birds of passage.

The formation of the Reserve   In 1922 a comprehensive scheme for reserve training was drawn up. Once the Short-Service Commission scheme had settled down, the Air Ministry was ready to introduce the Auxiliary and Special Reserve squadrons. Since the short-service officers would pass into the reserve on completion of their regular service, the RAF Reserve had been in place since 1919, at that time limited to 200 pilots. In 1923 it was decided to expand the Reserve to 700 officers and 12,000 men, divided into two sections, the Reserve of Air

Force Officers and the Men of the Royal Air Force Reserve. This was split into the following classes:

1. *Class A –*   Officers with short-service commissions who would pass into the Reserve on completion of their engagement
2. Class AA   Officers entered direct to the Reserve, either from the class of pilots who served in the 1914–18 war or from suitable civil pilots
3. Class B   Officers with previous service experience for technical duties requiring up-to-date knowledge of aircraft
4. Class BB   Officers without previous service experience for technical duties requiring up-to-date knowledge of aircraft
5. Class C   Officers with previous service experience for technical, accountant and other duties not requiring an up-to-date knowledge of aircraft
6. Class D   Medical officers
7. Class E   Men of the Reserve with previous air force experience
8. Class F   Men of the Reserve without any previous air force experience

Note: There were also plans to form an airman pilot reserve, but this did not mature for some years. It eventually became known as Class E.

During the first year of operation it was proposed to enter the following members or personnel into the Reserve:

1. Class A –   74 short-service commissions
2. Class AA -   280 to undertake requalifying courses
   20 to undertake an instructor's course at the Central Flying School and become instructors at the civil schools
   20 with sufficient recent experience to pass direct to annual refresher training
   50 employed on civil aviation and therefore needing no training
   444 total

The Auxiliary Air Force and Air Force Reserve Act of 1924 brought into being the Auxiliary and Special Reserve squadrons in 1925.

FLYING TRAINING

Introduction   Flying training during the First World War was carried out at a number of flying training schools for *ab initio* training, advanced flying training, night flying, fighter and bomber schools. Most of these were disbanded as surplus to requirements following the 1918 Armistice. Details of these schools and their locations can be found in Chapter 7, dealing with airfields. With the formation of the Cadet College at Cranwell, the *ab initio* flying training for the permanent career officers was carried out as part of the two-year course at the college, after which these officers went on an air pilotage course before being posted to a squadron. The short-service officers were trained at flying training schools in the United Kingdom and at No. 4 FTS Abu Sueir, Egypt. But these schools simply did not have the capacity to take on the task of training the large numbers of reservists as described in the last section, and so it was decided to utilize civil firms that had aircraft repair facilities adjoining their aerodromes. The primary object was to secure good economic training by using the simple and compact organization of these firms.

The Opening of Civilian Flying Training Schools The scheme received Treasury approval in January 1923, and it was decided to open five civilian operated schools, each with an allotment of seventy pupils:

1. *Stag Lane School* opened on 1 May 1923, operated by the de Havilland Aircraft Company Ltd, with three Avros for elementary training and three DH9s for service training, and a capacity for forty on annual training and seventy on requalifying courses.
2. *Filton School* opened on 28 May 1923 and was operated by the Bristol Aeroplane Co Ltd, with three PTMs for elementary training and three Bristol Fighters for service training, and a capacity for forty on annual training and seventy on requalifying courses.
3. *Coventry School* opened on 31 July 1923 by Armstrong Whitworth Aircraft Ltd, with three Avros for elementary training and three DH9s for service training, and a capacity for forty on annual training and seventy on requalifying courses.
4. *Brough School* opened on 21 May 1924, operated by the North Sea Aerial and General Transport Ltd, with three Avros for elementary training and three Kangaroos for service training, and a capacity for forty on annual training and seventy on requalifying courses.
5. *Renfrew School* opened on 24 July 1923, operated by William Beardmore & Co. Ltd, with three Avros for elementary training and three DH9s for service training, and a capacity for forty on annual training and seventy on requalifying courses.

The requalifying course for ex wartime pilots in their first year was not specifically defined but could obviously vary according to circumstances and the individual's past flying experience. It consisted of flying on an elementary machine such as an Avro or similar type as required, together with five hours solo and appropriate dual flying on a service type such as a DH9 or Bristol Fighter.

Progress in the first year By 31st December 1923 a total of 205 pilots had passed through the civil schools. The training period was roughly six weeks, and as a guide a minimum of fifteen and a maximum of twenty-five hours was laid down for elementary flying. Later it was found possible to accept an average of about fourteen hours' flying, and the minimum then laid down was twelve hours. Annual training courses consisted of twelve hours solo flown on a service type (e.g. Bristol Fighter), with appropriate dual flying. This was carried out in four periods, each of two to six days' duration. In 1924 it was laid down that the aircraft in use at the civil schools should have a common minimum performance. The speed was to be 100 mph at 6,000 ft, and although the types of aircraft to be used were not specified, the types of engine to be used were the Lion, the Condor, the Jupiter and the Jaguar. The aircraft in general use at this time were the DH9s and Bristol Fighters. The school at Brough that was equipped with twin-engined aircraft was not affected by this order.

Courses and Fees For the next ten years very little progress was made in the training of these reserve forces, and the size of the RAF Reserve remained fairly static. The financial arrangements with these civil companies, however, required constant revision. After the schools had been in operation for a year it was found that they were operating at a loss, and new contracts had to be drawn up. These new agreements laid down the quarterly periods of refresher training as two to six days, and a maximum period of sixty-one days for the requalifying courses. The standard aircraft establishment was three elementary and three service aircraft per school. The original fees were as follows:

Annual Course SE – £150
Annual Course TE – £180 (TE = twin-engined)
Requalifying – £200
Requalifying – £240 (SE = single-engined)

For broken courses the rate was £10 per hour, up to a maximum of £50. In 1925 the revised rates were:

Annual Course SE – £300
Annual Course TE – £280
Requalifying – £200
Requalifying – Nothing quoted

A premium for broken time was charged at £8 per hour for elementary types and £22 for new service types. The upper limit of £50 was abolished.

THE AEROPLANE AND ARMAMENT EXPERIMENTAL ESTABLISHMENT

Brief History During the period 1919–24 the RAF station at Martlesham Heath in Suffolk continued the experimental work on aircraft, mostly prototypes coming from the aircraft manufacturers to see if they were fit for operational service in the RAF. The Experimental Aircraft Flight had been transferred from Upavon in January 1917. Armament experiments that had been carried out at Orfordness then came under Martlesham. In the autumn of 1917 the unit's name was changed to Aeroplane Experimental Unit RFC, and when hostilities ceased in November 1918 the tempo of the unit slowed as aircraft prototypes were not being rushed into operational service. The test aircraft present at the time became almost resident. There were some notable events, however, during the immediate post-war period. The HP V/1500, which just missed operational service, was represented at Martlesham by Serial J1936, named 'Old Carthusian', and this flew from the station to Lahore in December 1919. And on 21 March 1920 the station was the venue for a successful attempt on the world's airspeed record. A Martinsyde Semiquaver – G-EAPX, flown by Mr F.P. Raynham – set up a new record of 161.434 mph over one kilometre, and it was a Martlesham pilot, Flying Officer C.E. Horrox, who won the handicap race at the RAF Pageant, Hendon, in an Aldershot bomber, J.6852.

Formation of the A & AEE The Aeroplane and Armament Experimental Establishment was formed on 20 March 1924 at Martlesham when it absorbed the Armament Experimental Flight previously situated on the Isle of Grain. Thus armament testing was to be added to aircraft testing, and the personnel were formed into two squadrons, Nos 15 and 22.

No. 15 Squadron No. 15 Squadron's duties included the testing of guns and gunsights, bombs, bomb release gear and bombsights. The guns and bombs were tested at the nearby Orfordness ranges previously acquired, and a number of 'hack' aircraft were kept, upon which various guns and bombs were attached.

No. 22 Squadron No. 22 Squadron tested and reported on all new civil and military prototypes, for it will be remembered that civil aviation came under the Air Ministry at that time, and it was the Air Ministry that issued Certificates of Airworthiness. Some older types were also presented for testing, e.g. those that had been re-engined or rearmed Thus it was necessary for No. 22 Squadron to carry out all aspects of flight testing and acceptance trials. To do this the squadron was divided into three flights:

A Flight – tested fighters and light civil aircraft
B Flight – tested bombers and large civil aircraft
C Flight – tested all aircraft that did not fit neatly into the
        above categories, such as Army cooperation or
        naval aircraft

Aircraft Testing The performance testing included almost every characteristic of the aircraft. The test pilots

had to find out the exact speeds of aircraft up to the ceiling (the absolute attainable height), the rate of climb, length of take-off and landing runs and general handling qualities. Engine behaviour under all conditions, engine cooling, instruments, landing gear, construction and ease of maintenance were all reported upon. A complete list of all aircraft tested at Martlesham between 1919 and 1929 is shown at Appendix H, in which references are made, for example, to the failed Dragonfly engine, the crashes that occurred and the scrapping of aircraft after flight.

Indeed, the reader will get a much better idea of what is meant by performance testing than ploughing through a narrated catalogue of the daily tasks performed by the test pilots. On occasion an aircraft in competition with others for an Air Ministry production contract had an inferior performance to its rivals but won favour because of the ease of maintenance. In the photograph below is one of the aircraft that came to Martlesham and achieved a new British speed record of 194.6 mph on 19 December 1921, a Mars Bamel I, Registration No. G-EAXZ. From 1924 new RAF fighters were expected to be able to survive test dives at the maximum speeds of which they were capable. The first aircraft to display its ability to do this was the single-seater Gloster Grebe. A speed of 240 mph was achieved before the pilot pulled out of the dive, but further testing revealed a tendency to wing flutter, and Vee bracing struts had to be fitted to the top wing extensions. And this before the wearing of parachutes became compulsory for RAF aircrews, which happened in 1925. New military aircraft usually returned to have armament fitted and tested. Such aircraft were flown in by the firm's test pilot and handed over to the RAF test team. Sometimes the former was not satisfied that his aircraft was ready to hand over to the RAF for evaluation, but in the early 1920s aircraft production firms, struggling to survive, knew that the Air Ministry would pay them on the delivery of a prototype to Martlesham. But when one considers that the majority of company test pilots were ex-RAF officers, in many cases ex-Martlesham, there was a considerable degree of understanding between all concerned.

Mars Bamel I.

C Flight hangar ablaze at 05.00 hrs on 6 October 1922. The picture below shows the smoking debris later that morning. The engine and wire-spoked wheels of a burned-out machine can be seen, probably one of the captured German aircraft.

Hangar Fire, 6 October 1922   The fire that engulfed C Flight's hangar on 6 October 1922 was potentially a disaster, for it was the middle hangar of three alongside the road running through the camp. This was one of those built by prisoners-of-war, and contained many stores as well as a collection of captured enemy aircraft. The station fire section prevented the fire from spreading, assisted by a horse-drawn engine from the Woodbridge Fire Brigade. Apparently the Fire Chief gave his orders using a bugle. The cause of the fire was not known.

THE MARINE AIRCRAFT EXPERIMENTAL ESTABLISHMENT

Felixstowe was home to four seaplane and flying-boat squadrons during the First World War, and was selected to remain open after the Armistice. Its role was to test-fly all seaplanes and flying-boats, both civilian and military,

and to declare them airworthy before entering service. This work had been carried out at Grain on the peninsula overlooking Sheerness, but on 17 March 1924 all experimental work was carried out at Felixstowe when Grain/Port Victoria closed. The following are examples of the work of the MAEE during the period 1919–24:

Felixstowe Report F/A/10 – Experiments in Staining the Surface of the Sea with Aluminium Powder
Source: National Archives, AVIA19/256

Description of Trials   The experiments were carried out with a view to ascertaining the value of discharging fine aluminium powder from a surface marine craft as a mark for aircraft. Two boxes, each containing two pounds of aluminium powder, were to be discharged into the water from the stern of a motor boat travelling into wind at a water speed of approximately 12 knots. The first test was carried out inside Harwich harbour, where the water was smooth, and with a wind speed of approximately ten knots. The second box was discharged at the mouth of the harbour, where there was a slight swell and the surface of the sea was broken. Two aircraft were employed to make observations, one flying at a height of 1,200 ft in order that photographs could be taken, the other at a height of 4,000 ft. The second aircraft was not able to observe at a greater height owing to the presence of clouds. The sun was appearing at frequent intervals through the clouds, so that the effect of the powder on the water was observed both with the sun shining on the surface and when it was shaded by clouds.

Discharging powder from motor boat   The motor boat proceeded at 12 knots and then its engine was shut off. Two pounds of powder were then discharged from the stern of the boat at a height of approximately two or three feet above the surface of the water. The time taken to discharge the powder was approximately five seconds, and it was estimated that at least 20 per cent of the powder was blown away in a cloud when reaching the surface of the water in the vicinity of the motor boat. After the discharge of the powder, the cloud drifted away in the air astern of the patch of powder resting on the surface of the water. The cloud of powder rose approximately thirty feet above the surface. The patch discharged in calm water remained intact for a period of approximately twenty minutes after it had been discharged, but it was finally broken up through being carried away by the tide onto a mud bank. It was easily visible with the reflecting sun from a range of approximately five miles and at a height of 3,000 ft, and it could be spotted at this height up to a distance of ten miles, or up to a distance of approximately eight miles when the sun was obscured by the clouds or was not reflected in the patch. A patch discharged in broken water did not last more than four minutes, but during this time it was as easily discernible as a patch discharged in calm water. The patches had a very distinctive appearance and were not easily mistaken for any normal sea effect or sand bank. The maximum area to which patches extended before they disintegrated was estimated at approximately 600 square feet. If the powder could be more efficiently discharged by means of a special container that eliminated the waste of powder, under certain circumstances this might prove of considerable use as marks for aircraft flying over the sea.

Ditching Tests with a DH19 in May 1924
Source: National Archives, AVIA/249

The trials were carried out with a DH19 Civilian Registration No. G-EAWW powered by a Lion engine on 2 May 1924. The weather conditions were: surface wind, SW 14 mph; wind at 1,500 feet, SSW 17–20 mph; sea moderate with moderate swell.

Preparation
The aircraft, piloted by an experienced pilot of this unit, was a standing commercial aircraft used on civilian air routes. There were no special arrangements of any kind provided for the machine to alight satisfactorily or float after 'ditching' except that the openings for the controls in the cabin were made watertight. Rubber was fitted round the cabin door as in later aircraft of this type. The pilot's cockpit was to the rear of the cabin space. A usual load of 900 lb was carried, including the pilot and fuel. This was increased to 1,500 lb by the addition of ballast, and the aircraft floated satisfactorily. For this purpose the twelve sandbags, each weighing 50 lb for easy handling, were prepared, six being placed in a dinghy, the other six being retained in a motor boat, ready to be added when the aircraft was moored up, if still sufficiently afloat.

The test
The aircraft arrived over Felixstowe dock at approximately 11.12 hrs and headed straight into wind. The pilot flew at about 100 feet above the water, and it was at once obvious that the tail was not sufficiently down to make a very flat or partially tail-down landing in spite of the fact that the elevator control was being held fully back. Consequently a three-point landing was not effected. The aircraft pitched on its nose and took up an almost vertical position.

From the pilot's report it is observed that the aircraft was flying well below stalling speed when striking the water. The depth of the water at the point of impact was 36 feet. The water pressure on top of the lower plane forced the aircraft slightly under. The reserve of buoyancy in the wings, etc. caused the aircraft to rise again, and the tail fell back. In this position, about two minutes after touching, the six bags of ballast were handed over to the pilot, who dropped them into his cockpit before leaving the aircraft. This lowered the tail slightly more, but the aircraft remained in this position for a considerable time with most of the cabin submerged. By the time the ballast was placed on board the officer in charge of the motor boat N972 secured a line to the engine bearers of the aircraft, and proceeded to tow her slowly towards a flying-boat mooring buoy. This was necessary owing to the desirability of salving the aircraft as soon as possible for examination and to prevent her drifting with the ebb-tide. The tide was still flooding with the strong SW wind. This operation took approximately twenty minutes, and then, with the turn of the tide, the aircraft swung to the opposite side of the buoy and completely sank, dragging the buoy under the water also.

Effects of staining the sea with aluminium powder in Harwich Harbour, 1924.

4. As many airbags as possible should be fitted inside the unwanted parts of the fuselage. This would not add any appreciable weight to the aircraft and the airbags could always be kept inflated.
5. Handrails should be provided for the emergency hatch, etc.
6. Metal aerostructures of the lower planes should be made completely watertight. This is quite possible.
7. It is thought that as the pilot would be the only member of the crew capable of making a wireless signal in the event of a forced landing, adjustable and quickly detachable windscreens should be fitted to minimise the risk in case of a heavy landing, thus causing injury to the pilot.

5 May 1924
MAEE Felixstowe.

Salvage and Inspection
For some time it was not certain if the aircraft and buoy had broken loose and drifted out to sea, and a search was immediately made by marine craft. During the afternoon it was discovered lying in a fathom or two of water. Salvage operations during Saturday 3 May enabled the aircraft to be successfully beached and the engine removed. This had now been stripped and cleaned and was being reassembled for transfer. On examination of the fuselage it appears that water entered through the forward emergency hatch when she assumed the vertical position, probably owing to the fabric of the windows giving way to the pressure of water through impact, thereby flooding the cabin. No water appears to have entered the fuselage in any other place in any volume with the exception of a slow leak through the undercarriage bracing, which was fabricked over but did not hold on the left side. The fuselage was intact.

Conclusion and Recommendations
From the above experiment it is obvious that a DH19 commercial aircraft as at present equipped stands little chance of affording safety to the pilot and passengers in the event of a forced landing on water, however calm the weather and the sea may be. The following modifications are suggested:

1. The weight can be afforded but it is desirable to fit an arrangement whereby the undercarriage can be jettisoned.
2. It should be possible to jettison the petrol in the tanks.
3. Hydrovanes could be fitted to the wheel axles but it is doubtful whether this could be afforded from the point of view of wind resistance and weight.

Changes in Organization of the Royal Air Force
Source: Air Ministry Weekly Orders 1923. Order No. 201

Before leaving Chapter 2 it is of interest to note that concrete changes were occurring as a result of the expansion scheme.

1. Formations. The undermentioned group headquarters and squadrons were re-formed on 1 April 1923:

No. 3 Group Headquarters ....Spittlegate
No. 19 Squadron (1 flight) ....Duxford *
No. 29 Squadron (1 flight)................................Duxford
No. 32 Squadron (HQ + 1 flight) ....Kenley
No. 12 Squadron (HQ + 1 flight) ....Northolt
No. 41 Squadron (HQ + 1 flight) ....Northolt

* No. 19 Squadron was to be the first unit to be equipped with the Supermarine Spitfire in 1938, and was still then a Duxford squadron.

HENDON AIR PAGEANTS
Trenchard lost no opportunity to show off the RAF to the public. If he could get them on his side he stood a much better chance of fighting off demands for the RAF's absorption in to the other two services. Beginning in the summer of 1920, the Hendon Air Pageant (later titled the Display) was an annual event. Encouraged by the press and newsreel reports they continued almost up to the outbreak of the Second World War. Not only were these events an opportunity to thrill the public with daring deeds of aerobatics and parachuting, but the RAF could show off its latest aircraft and so keep the public informed of aviation progress. It also became part of the

Aircraft on display at the very first RAF Pageant, 1920.

Visitors' cars, but only a fraction of any RAF Open Day of today.

annual training programme of the RAF, and the first display attracted over 60,000 people, with attendances growing year by year. Being so close to the centre of London, it was easy for spectators from all over the metropolis to get to Hendon, and part of the gate money went to RAF charities. Even King George V, who was said to dislike noisy aeroplanes and the reckless pilots who flew them, attended regularly.

Even the weather could not dampen the public enthusiasm for the RAF Pageant. On 24 June 1922, for example, the enclosures became a sea of umbrellas, yet the rain could not spoil a great display with spectacular aerobatics, races, formation and crazy flying. Then there was a mock battle between a DH10 and two SE5As. In the 1923 display the bright sky turned to overcast but the quality of the performances was unimpaired. Featuring in the pageant was the Blackburn Dart, the Cub-powered Avro Aldershot, Westland Weasel and Walrus, the Blackburn Blackburn four-seater Fleet spotter, Avro

Bison, Supermarine Seagull, Fairey Flycatcher and its rival the Parnall Plover, the Handley Page Hanley, Fairey Fawn and the new Gloster Grebe. In spite of the low cloud ceiling the aerobatic displays were excellent. Mock battles took place between Nieuport Nighthawks and the Boulton Paul Bourges, and a mock Army garrison was reinforced by troops landed in three Vickers Vernons. But some of the latest aircraft were absent, namely the Armstrong Whitworth Siskin III and Awana and the Vickers Victoria and Vanguard. And still First World War aircraft, the SE5As, Bristol Fighters, DH9As and Vickers Vimys, were the mainstay of the show. The 1924 Pageant attracted a crowd of 80,000, but still the formation team of DH9As were stars of the show. They were by then yesterday's aircraft.

King George V and Queen Mary at the 1923 Display.

Chapter 3
The Locarno Honeymoon, 1925 to 1930

The Locarno Treaty – State of the RAF – Special Reserve and Auxiliary Squadrons – University Air Squadrons – Air Operations: the Middle East and India – the Schneider Trophy Races – the RAF Display – A & AEE Martlesham – MAEE Felixstowe – Parachutes and pilotless bomber – Airships – Civil Aviation – Training and Air Exercises – Trenchard's Farewell

The Locarno Honeymoon

During his brief period in office as the first Labour prime minister in history, Ramsay MacDonald set in motion in 1924 a series of events designed to strengthen the League of Nations. In the context of RAF expansion and the climate of hope engendered by the new League in finding ways to bring about lasting world peace, successive British governments had to balance the needs of home defence and defence of Imperial outposts with the need to demonstrate to the world community that Britain was serious about international disarmament. The period from 1925 to the end of the decade has been described as the Locarno honeymoon. The Kellogg–Briand Pact, which was to follow in 1928, further strengthened the determination of the major powers for peace. In spite of reparations that Germany had to pay to the Allied Powers resulting from the 'war guilt' clause in the Versailles Treaty for damage and casualties inflicted in the First World War, that country under Stresemann's leadership was doing well economically. But all that was to come to nought with the 'Wall Street Crash' of 1929, which was followed by a severe economic depression that threw thousands out of work in the USA and Western Europe. The rise of the Fascist dictators and Japanese aggression in Manchuria (Manchukuo) in 1932 led to the failure, in Geneva, of the entire disarmament process. But these events are dealt with in Volume II. In 1925 Trenchard had his imperial policing role to fulfil and a modest re-equipment programme to implement as part of the expansion plan.

The Locarno Treaties, 1925/6 One of these treaties was the Rhineland Pact, which confirmed the sanctity of the borders of Belgium, France and Germany. It also confirmed the demilitarized zone of Germany west of the Rhine in which Germany was not permitted to station troops. Another treaty, the Treaty of Arbitration, bound Germany and France to accept mediation in disputes, and Germany made similar arrangements with Belgium, Poland and Czechoslovakia, with France guaranteeing to protect them in the event of German aggression. To satisfy Russian fears Germany renewed the Treaty of Rapallo. Finally, later in 1926, Germany was admitted to the League of Nations, with a seat on the Council of the League.

The Kellogg–Briand Pact The French minister Briand produced a plan for collective security under the League. France and the USA would sign a pact to renounce war, and this was enthusiastically received by Kellogg, the American Secretary of State, who suggested that more countries be invited to join the declaration. In 1928 sixty-five League members signed the Pact. But this left open the vital question of what to do if any country that had solemnly signed the Pact subsequently committed an act of aggression against another member of the League, or any other country. There was no international force under the League's control that could intervene to prevent or curtail conflict. Sanctions were always one method of bringing pressure to bear on an aggressor. Indeed sanctions were later used against Mussolini over Italy's aggression against Abyssinia, but they had the perverse effect of throwing Mussolini into an alliance with Hitler to form the Rome–Berlin Axis. In the mid- to late 1920s Hitler had still to become a threat to world peace following the failure of his attempted coup in 1923 and his spell in prison. Mussolini, although heading a Fascist regime, was not at that time a threat to any other state. And so in the heady days of peace in the mid-1920s these thoughts were at the back of statesmen's minds.

The State of the RAF

The RAF was continuing with its policy of Imperial policing, and at home was carrying out a modest expansion towards the eventual target of fifty-two Home Defence squadrons. Trenchard had begun the slow process of modernizing the inventory of RAF aircraft, with aircrews wedded to the biplane and open cockpits. A start, however, had been made to move towards all-metal aircraft construction and greater streamlining.

1925

Air Estimates, 1925/6 On 19 February 1925, Sir Samuel Hoare addressed Parliament on the debate on the Air Estimates for 1925/6. Parliament was being asked to authorize an expenditure of £15,513,000, compared to £14,720,000 for 1924/5. The cost of air-control operations and RAF activities afloat meant an additional income from the Colonial Office for Iraq (£2,744,100) and Palestine/Transjordan (£372,600), and from the Admiralty a vote of £1,320,000 for the Fleet Air Arm.

RAF strength, 1925
Sir Samuel Hoare then went on to inform the House of the strength of the RAF. Apart from training units and establishments there was an equivalence of fifty-four squadrons. Of these, forty-three squadrons and two flights were RAF squadrons, and there were twenty-one flights, each of six aircraft, for the Fleet Air Arm. Of the established squadrons their deployment was as follows:

United Kingdom	– 25 squadrons + 1 flight
Iraq	– 8 squadrons
India	– 6 squadrons
Egypt/Palestine	– 4 squadrons + 1 flight

Of the twenty-five squadrons in the United Kingdom, eighteen were regular Home Defence squadrons. During the financial year a further two regular squadrons were to be added, togther with one Special Reserve squadron and four Auxiliary squadrons, about which more later. It may be recalled, from Chapter 2, that there were to be fifty-two Home Defence squadrons in the expansion plan, but that no completion date for this plan had been specified. The Air Minister's presentation to Parliament on 19 February 1925 prompted *The Times* to warn that Parliament had hardly erred on the side of extravagance. Given that only two extra regular squadrons were to be formed that year, the paper observed that it would take until 1936 to raise the strength to just forty squadrons. Sir Frederick Sykes, the former Chief of the Air Staff, asked about wastage, and Hoare reported that, for the twelve months ended 31 October 1924, 339 aircraft had been written off charge following accidents and that eighty-one aircraft had been lost through fair wear and tear, service terminology for simply wearing out. The average age of aircraft, he said, was about five years, and the average flying life about 130 hours.

1926

Changes in Organization
Source: Air Ministry Weekly Order 354/1926
This Air Ministry Weekly Order laid down the changes to areas and groups, and the allocation of stations to groups. The units listed in the following texts will give the reader some idea of how complex the organization of the Royal Air Force had become by 1926, and all for £15.5 million, less than the price of one Tornado MRCA today (2004). The Home Defence Force, comprising the Wessex Bombing and the Fighting Areas, were the manifestation of the expansion plan, which provided for fifty-two bomber and fighter squadrons to defend the United Kingdom. The Inland Area comprised all those stations involved in flying, technical and recruit training and for the provision of a host of support services. It also included stations on which Army Cooperation squadrons were based.

Inland Area On 1 June 1926, Headquarters of the Inland Area moved to Bentley Priory, Stanmore. The Inland Area was then organized into three groups. Owing to the changes made to the organization of groups at home, some units were based temporarily at a station not in that group, so see the notes below.

No. 21 Group Formed on 12 April at West Drayton. The No. 21 Group stations were Altrincham, Ascot, Henlow, Ickenham, Kidbrooke, Martlesham, Milton, Orfordness, Ruislip, Shrewsbury, West Drayton and Uxbridge. The following units came under Group command:

Reception Depot, West Drayton
No. 1 Stores Depot, Kidbrooke
Port detachment, No. 1 Stores depot, South Dock, West India Dock, London E14
School of Store Accounting and Storekeeping, Kidbrooke
Medical Stores Depot, Kidbrooke
No. 2 Stores Depot, Altrincham
No. 3 Stores Deport, Milton
No. 4 Stores Depot, Ickenham
The Packing Depot, Ascot
Record Office, Ruislip
RAF MT Depot, Shrewsbury
Home Aircraft Depot, Henlow
Aeroplane and Armament Experimental Establishment, Martlesham
Detachment, Orfordness
RAF Depot (including School of Physical Training), Uxbridge
Superintendent, RAF Reserve, Northolt
Headquarters Air Defence Great Britain (administration only), Uxbridge
RAF Officers' Hospital (administration only), Uxbridge

Note: Nos 23 and 43 (Fighter) Squadrons belonging to Fighting Area were temporarily based at Henlow, a 21 Group station.

No. 22 Group Formed on 12 April at Farnborough. The No. 22 Group Stations were Farnborough, Larkhill and Old Sarum. The following units came under Group command:

School of Photography, Farnborough
Experimental Section, Royal Aircraft Establishment, Farnborough
No. 4 (Army Cooperation) Squadron, Farnborough
School of Army Cooperation, Old Sarum
No. 16 (Army Cooperation) Squadron, Old Sarum
School of Balloon Training, Larkhill
No. 13 (Army Cooperation) Squadron, Andover
No. 2 (Army Cooperation) Squadron, Manston
Detachment of Electrical and Wireless School accommodated at Worthy Down

No. 23 Group   Formed on 12 April at Spittlegate. No. 23 Group Stations were Digby, Eastchurch, Flower Down, Manston and Sealand. The following units came under Group Command:

No. 1 Flying Training School, Netheravon
No. 2 Flying Training School, Digby
No. 5 Flying Training School, Sealand
Armament and Gunnery School, Eastchurch
School of Technical Training (Airmen), Manston
Central Flying School, Upavon
Electrical and Wireless School, Flower Down

Notes: There was no No. 3 FTS, and No. 4 FTS was at Abu Sueir, Egypt. Temporarily the following squadrons belonging to Wessex Bombing Area and No. 22 Group were located at No. 23 Group stations: from Wessex Bombing Area, No. 207 (Bombing) Squadron at Eastchurch, No. 9 (Bombing) Squadron at Manston and from No. 22 Group, No. 2 (Army Cooperation) Squadron at Manston.

Home Defence Force, Air Defence of Great Britain (ADGB), formed 1.1.25

Wessex Bombing Area   The Wessex Bombing Area comprised the following units:

No. 12 (Bombing) Squadron, Andover
Staff College Andover (administration only)
No. 58 (Bombing) Squadron, Worthy Down
No. 11 (Bombing) Squadron, Netheravon
No. 100 (Bombing) Squadron, Spittlegate
No. 39 (Bombing) Squadron, Spittlegate
No. 7 (Bombing) Squadron, Bircham Newton
No. 99 (Bombing) Squadron, Bircham Newton
No. 9 (Bombing) Squadron, Manston
No. 207 (Bombing) Squadron, Eastchurch

Note: Temporarily the following units of Inland Area were located at stations of the Wessex Bombing Area: from No. 22 Group, No. 13 Squadron at Andover and the Electrical and Wireless School Flight at Worthy Down, and from No. 23 Group, Group HQ at Spittlegate and No. 1 Flying Training School at Netheravon.

Fighting Area   Fighting Area comprised the following units:

No. 32 (Fighter) Squadron, Kenley
No. 24 (Communications) Squadron, Kenley
No. 56 (Fighter) Squadron, Biggin Hill
Night-Flying Flight, Biggin Hill
No. 41 (Fighter) Squadron, Northolt
Communications Flight, Northolt
No. 25 (Fighter) Squadron, Hawkinge
No. 17 (Fighter) Squadron, Hawkinge

No. 19 (Fighter) Squadron, Duxford
No. 29 (Fighter) Squadron, Duxford
No. 111 (Fighter) Squadron, Duxford
No. 3 (Fighter) Squadron, Upavon
No. 23 (Fighter) Squadron, Henlow
No. 43 (Fighter) Squadron, Henlow

Note: Temporarily the following units were located at stations of the Fighting Area: No. 600 Auxiliary Air Force Squadron and No. 601 Auxiliary Air Force Squadron at Northolt, Central Flying School (No. 23 Group) at Upavon and Superintendent of RAF Reserve (HQ Inland Area), also at Northolt.

Special Reserve and Auxiliary Command   These were the new Special Reserve and Auxiliary squadrons that had just been formed manned by reservists, sometimes called the 'weekend' flyers:

No. 502 Special Reserve (Ulster) Bombing Squadron, Aldergrove
No. 600 (City of London) Bombing Squadron, Northolt
No. 601 (County of London) Bombing Squadron, Northolt
No. 602 (City of Glasgow) Bombing Squadron, Renfrew
No. 603 (City of Edinburgh) Bombing Squadron, Turnhouse

The Organization of Stations   Paragraph 4 of this AMWO laid down the responsibility for administration and discipline. For example, a 'Commanding Officer' as opposed to an 'officer commanding' is an officer with specified disciplinary powers to award punishments and the authority to hold public and non-public funds. It was explained in Chapter 1 that the Royal Air Force had pieces of real estate, in the case of airfields large pieces of real estate, called RAF stations, and these were most often commanded by a group captain. As John James explains in Chapter 5 of his most excellent book *The Paladins*, the RAF had to decide whether it was going to copy the Army and have its officers spend much of their service with a regiment and be specialized in infantry, artillery and cavalry. That is to say, should RAF officers serve on a bomber, fighter, coastal or Army Cooperation wing, such wings comprising numbered squadrons that would stay together and move as titled wings? This was not to happen. The basic unit was to be an RAF squadron, which might serve as part of a numbered wing for a specific operation, such as the wings in India, but usually squadrons were allotted to groups. An officer would normally serve one tour with a squadron. He would therefore be posted to a squadron on a station. His immediate superior would be his 'officer commanding' the squadron, but his 'commanding officer' would be the Station Commander. When the squadron went to war the commanding officer stayed put in command of his piece of real estate. The RAF would appoint another officer to exercise overall operational command of squadrons that left their parent stations. That is not to say that individual officers did not specialize on, say, coastal or fighter aircraft, but any pilot could undertake operational conversion training to fit him to change role, for example from fighter to bomber. Technical and administrative personnel could be posted to a squadron and move with that squadron if it left its parent airfield on operations. Other technical and administrative personnel were simply posted to an RAF station to remain there to serve the needs of squadrons based there. Hence para. 4 states that where two or more units are located at a station then an officer will be appointed as Station Commander. If only one unit was located at a station the officer commanding the squadron could be given the powers of a commanding officer and serve in that dual purpose. Thus, when a station was established for a Station Headquarters, a station commander would be appointed. The station commander would be responsible for training, discipline and administration on his station, and his immediate superior would be the Air Officer Commanding the group to which his station belonged. If any female reader wonders why no reference is made to 'his or her' station, she is advised that from 1920 until 1938 the RAF was a male-only service.

1927

Air Estimates, 1927/8   The Air Estimates for the year 1927/8 were published on 5 March. Parliament was asked to vote for £15,550,000, which was a reduction of £450,000 on the previous year. Savings were made on personnel, works and buildings, but an increase was allowed for in spending on technical equipment, which included two new types of aircraft. The Air Minister made the point that, 'This was the policy of replacing aeroplanes and engines of war-time design by modern types. Steady progress was being made and it was the intention that in future no more aircraft or engines of war-time designs should be bought.' Sir Samuel Hoare made an allocation of £137,000 to subsidize Imperial Airways for its European services, and £93,600 for the Cairo–Karachi route. A further £111,000 would go to work at Croydon airport, which was due for completion in 1928. There would be £10,000 for a new wireless telegraphy station and £8,000 for meteorological services. The vote for the RAF was little changed.

1928

The Tenth Anniversary of the RAF   On 1 April 1928, on the occasion of the tenth anniversary of the RAF, Lord Weir, the former Air Minister, and closely identified

with its inception, sent a cable to Trenchard with these words:

> I regard it as incomparably the most efficient Air Force in existence, creditable alike to British organization and British character. It is a welcome portent to the Empire that this new fighting Service affords opportunity not only to British qualities of courage, determination and enterprise, but also to the spirit of true scientific progress.

These were welcome words to someone who had worked so hard to fashion the RAF, always sacrificing quantity for quality and managing on a shoestring budget, all the time being buffeted by the predictable claims on the nascent RAF by the Royal Navy and the Army for the return of their air units. Even so, the ten years had not witnessed as great a change as might have been expected, partly owing to the lack of money. Was the Siskin, for example, such an advance on the Bristol Fighter? Did not the lumbering Vickers Virginia still not have the same ungainly appearance of the HP V/1500? The twin Vickers gun and the Scarff-mounted Lewis gun still remained supreme, together with open cockpits and biplane construction. Air-cooled radials were half the price of water-cooled engines and easier to install and service. Moving the radiators to the wings did mean that aircraft with water-cooled engines, like the Fairey Fox, could have a more streamlined appearance. Although engines were more powerful and reliable, speeds would not increase substantially until the monoplane was the norm.

1929

The Air Estimates, 1929/30   The figure announced was £16,200,000 net. In spite of the fact that the annual figure was reduced from the £16,563,000 of the previous year, seven squadrons would be added to the seventy-five then in existence. The annual figure does not tell the whole story. The Estimates were broken down into Votes. Two of these votes were of significance in determining how much was spent on men and machines. Vote 1 was for pay and allowances, and that rose from £3,401,000 the previous year to £6,585,000. Vote 3 was for warlike stores, i.e. aircraft and weapons, not barrack furniture and uniforms. Vote 3 rose from £6,567,000 to £6,585,000. The small rise for Vote 3, although marginal, can be misleading. Pay is for services rendered by the week or the month. Money spent on aircraft is spread over many years, given the time from drawing board to prototype, and from there to squadron service. More squadrons meant more personnel, but not necessarily more RAF stations. Permanently commissioned officers would be needed in such numbers as would be needed to provide for full career posts and to ensure that there was a sufficiency of permanent officers to provide a nucleus in the event of sudden expansion. The remainder would be on short-service engagements followed by a number of years in the RAF Reserve of Officers, when the RAF would try to ensure that such officers were educationally prepared for jobs outside the service. In the event, during the rapid expansion of 1938, and using Bomber Command as an example, there were insufficient permanent officers to provide middle management. There were only twelve wing commanders against 325 pilot officers.

Location of Units The number of squadrons in the table below gives the picture for the whole decade. It is clear that the number of squadrons overseas remained remarkably static and that only one new theatre of operations emerged, namely the Far East. As was to be expected, the expansion programme saw the number of home-based units grow. Interestingly the latest types of aircraft did not go into operational service overseas. There was no need for fighters. The two fighter squadrons of Snipes were disbanded for that reason, and there was certainly no need for heavy bombers. What was needed was a rugged general-purpose aircraft for air control, and that is exactly what the DH9As and the Bristol Fighters were.

Overseas

Theatre	Malta	Egypt	Iraq Aden	Transjordan Palestine	India	Africa	Far East
1922	1	3	8	1	6		
1925		3	8	1	6		
1927		3	6	1	6	1	
1929	1	3	6	2	8	1	1

United Kingdom

Type	Fighter	Bomber	Army Co-op	Torpedo-Bomber	Fighter-Bomber	Comms
1921	2	2	2	2	3	
1925	9	9	4		1	
1927	12	9	4		1	1
1929	12	10	6	1	2	1

Note: two of the bomber squadrons listed above were notional, being those at Martlesham Heath, the experimental wing comprising Nos 15 and 22 Squadrons.

RAF SQUADRON DEPLOYMENT AND AIRCRAFT, 31 DECEMBER 1929

Unit	Location	Aircraft/Remarks	

United Kingdom

Regular Squadrons

No. 1 Squadron	Tangmere	Siskin IIIA	Fighter
No. 2 Squadron	Manston	Atlas	Army Cooperation
No. 3 Squadron	Upavon	Bulldog II	Fighter
No. 4 Squadron	Farnborough	Atlas	Army Cooperation
No. 7 Squadron	Worthy Down	Virginia X	Bomber
No. 9 Squadron	Manston	Virginia X	Bomber
No. 10 Squadron	Upper Heyford	Hyderabad	Bomber
No. 12 Squadron	Andover	Fox	Bomber
No. 13 Squadron	Netheravon	Atlas	Army Cooperation
No. 15 Squadron	Martlesham	Various	A & AEE

No. 16 Squadron	Old Sarum	Bristol F2B	Army Cooperation
No. 17 Squadron	Upavon	Bulldog II/IIA	Fighter
No. 19 Squadron	Duxford	Siskin IIIA	Fighter
No. 22 Squadron	Martlesham	Various	A & AEE
No. 23 Squadron	Kenley	Gamecock	Fighter
No. 24 Squadron	Kenley	Various	Air Min/Communications
No. 25 Squadron	Hawkinge	Siskin IIIA	Fighter
No. 26 Squadron	Catterick	Atlas	Army Cooperation
No. 29 Squadron	North Weald	Siskin IIIA	Fighter
No. 32 Squadron	Kenley	Siskin IIIA	Fighter
No. 33 Squadron	Eastchurch	Horsley	Torpedo-Bomber
No. 35 Squadron	Bircham Newton	DH9A/Fairey IIIF	Bomber
No. 41 Squadron	Northolt	Siskin IIIA	Fighter
No. 43 Squadron	Tangmere	Siskin IIIA	Fighter
No. 56 Squadron	North Weald	Siskin IIIA	Fighter
No. 58 Squadron	Worthy Down	Virginia VI, IX & X	Bomber
No. 99 Squadron	Upper Heyford	Hinaidi	Bomber
No. 100 Squadron	Bicester	Horsley	Torpedo-Bomber
No. 101 Squadron	Andover	Sidestrand	Bomber
No. 111 Squadron	Hornchurch	Siskin IIIA	Fighter
No. 201 Squadron	Calshot	Southampton II	Maritime Reconnaissance
No. 204 Squadron	Mountbatten	Southampton II	Maritime Reconnaissance
No. 207 Squadron	Bircham Newton	Fairey IIIF	Maritime Reconnaissance

Special Reserve Squadrons

No. 501 Squadron	Filton	DH9A	Bomber
No. 502 Squadron	Aldergrove	Hyderabad	Bomber
No. 503 Squadron	Waddington	Hyderabad	Bomber
No. 504 Squadron	Hucknall	Horsley	Bomber

Auxiliary Squadrons

No. 600 Squadron	Hendon	Wapiti	City of London
No. 601 Squadron	Hendon	Wapiti	County of London
No. 602 Squadron	Renfrew	Wapiti	City of Glasgow
No. 603 Squadron	Turnhouse	DH9A	City of Edinburgh
No. 605 Squadron	Castle Bromwich	DH9A	County of Warwick

Squadrons Overseas

Palestine

No. 6 Squadron	Ismailia	Bristol F2B	General-Purpose
No. 14 Squadron	Amman	Fairey IIIF	General-Purpose

Iraq and Aden

No. 8 Squadron	Khormaksar	Fairey IIIF	General-Purpose
No. 30 Squadron	Mosul	Wapiti	General-Purpose
No. 55 Squadron	Hinaidi	DH9A	General-Purpose
No. 70 Squadron	Hinaidi	Victoria III & IV	Transport
No. 84 Squadron	Shaibah	Wapiti	General-Purpose
No. 203 Squadron	Basra	Southampton II	Maritime Reconnaissance

Egypt

No. 45 Squadron	Helwan	Fairey IIIF	General-Purpose
No. 208 Squadron	Heliopolis	Bristol F2B	General-Purpose
No. 216 Squadron	Heliopolis	Victoria I, IV & V	Transport

India

No. 5 Squadron	Quetta	Bristol F2B	General-Purpose
No. 11 Squadron	Risalpur	Wapiti	General-Purpose
No. 20 Squadron	Peshawar	Bristol F2B	General-Purpose
No. 27 Squadron	Kohat	DH9A	General-Purpose
No. 28 Squadron	Ambala	Bristol F2B	General-Purpose
No. 31 Squadron	Quetta	Bristol F2B	General-Purpose
No. 39 Squadron	Risalpur	Wapiti	General-Purpose
No. 60 Squadron	Kohat	DH9A	General-Purpose

Africa

No. 47 Squadron	Khartoum	Fairey IIIF	General-Purpose

Malta

No. 202 Squadron	Kalafrana	Fairey IIID	Maritime Reconnaissance

Far East

No. 205 Squadron	Seletar	Southampton II	Maritime Reconnaissance

Special Reserve and Auxiliary Squadrons

Formation The purpose of the expansion plan was to provide Britain with an air force capable of meeting the threat from the air from the largest continental power within striking distance of the shores of the United Kingdom, using both purely defensive and offensive air units. To this end the number of regular air force squadrons, both fighter and bomber, was to be increased, but it was also envisaged that trained reservists could be added to the strength, giving a proportionate mix of regular to reserve squadrons that would be available in a state of emergency. Accordingly in 1925 the Air Ministry made the following announcement:

> For various reasons the main part of the Home Defence Air Force must necessarily be established on a regular basis, but it has been decided that part of the new organization should consist of non-regular units. These will be divided into two classes: Special Reserve Squadrons and Auxiliary Air Force Squadrons, together forming a quarter of the total strength as at present.

There were to be seven Special Reserve squadrons and six Auxiliary squadrons. These squadrons would be akin to the Territorial units of the British Army, and were to be either city or county based. In the event only five Special Reserve squadrons were to be formed, and these were absorbed into the Auxiliary Air Force during 1936 and 1937, for over the years the number of units was to rise proportionately to the number of regular squadrons. By the outbreak of the Second World War there were to be twenty-one Auxiliary squadrons. The full strength would eventually rise to 360 officers and 2,400 airmen. A start was made in 1925, when the first HQ for two Auxiliary squadrons was formed at RAF Hendon. These

were No. 600 City of London and No. 601 County of London Squadrons. The same year two Auxiliary squadrons were formed in Scotland, No. 602 City of Glasgow Squadron at Renfrew and No. 603 City of Edinburgh Squadron at Turnhouse. The first Special Reserve unit was to be No. 502 (Ulster) Squadron, formed at Aldergrove. By 1929 there were four Special Reserve squadrons and five Auxiliary Air Force squadrons in existence (see Appendix B). Of interest, perhaps, to numerologists, No. 500 (County of Kent) Squadron was not to be formed at RAF Manston until 16 March 1931.

Equipment and Personnel The equipment of these units varied. Initially they would be aircraft of First World War vintage. At its formation No. 502 (Ulster) Squadron got just two Vimy bombers, later updated to the Hyderabad. All four of the Auxiliary Air Force squadrons were initially equipped with the DH9A (Ninak), but by the end of 1929 Wapitis had replaced Ninaks in three of these units. The Horsley bomber was also pressed into service. Even though the Special Reserve squadrons were given titles suggesting local affiliation, they were commanded by a regular air force officer who was given a nucleus of regular SNCOs. The remainder of the unit strength of officers and men would come from reservists living nearby. The Auxiliary squadron, on the other hand, was raised and maintained by a county Territorial association, and manned by local personnel, with only a small cadre of regulars on strength. The squadron commander was also a reservist. These reserve units had little difficulty in attracting recruits. Flying was an enormously popular pastime, and it enabled those who had a civilian career also to indulge in it without personal cost. For the Westland senior test pilot of the 1930s, Harald Penrose, learning to fly was achieved as a reservist. Many squadrons, apart from undertaking a programme of training, had a social focus taking on the characteristics of a club. No. 601 Squadron personnel claimed, for example, that their unit was formed, not at RAF Northolt, but at White's Club in St James, and their first commanding officer was Lord Edmond Grosvenor. Others of high social status who flew with these reserve units included Viscount Runciman, the Marquess of Clydesdale and Sir Philip Sassoon. This involvement of the famous and not-so-famous in the activities of the RAF only heightened interest in the service. Social activities aside, these units trained for war. The routine was to fly at weekends, which required a considerable degree of commitment and sacrifice among those affected, since they were already away from their families during the working week. Then there were summer camps held on major RAF airfields, with these reserve units taking part in the national Air Exercises.

University Air Squadrons

Trenchard's Speech to the Cambridge Union   On 29 April 1924 Trenchard gave a speech to the Cambridge Union. As ever, he would seize upon any chance to raise the profile of the RAF. The Annual Display was the opportunity to reach out to Royalty, Parliament, the press and the general public. Speaking to the undergraduates of Cambridge gave him the opportunity, not only to involve the brains of the nation in aviation, but hopefully to enlist officers who would be imbued with the air force spirit even before they joined. Among other things he spoke of the wastage of aircraft in peace, which was about 30 per cent per annum compared with 80 per cent per month in war. So the side that could keep re-equipping with pilots and machines would probably win. But there was no need, he said, to locate squadrons all over the Empire – as long as there were operational facilities available, units could be very mobile. He said, somewhat surprisingly, given the recent accident with the R33, which had its nose torn off in a mooring accident, that airships would be the great aircraft-carriers of the future. He then announced to his audience the creation of university air squadrons, starting with Oxford and Cambridge.

Inauguration of the University Air Squadrons   he idea of university air squadrons had originated at Cambridge, where a number of wartime RAF officers had gone to university to take up courses in engineering. Sir Samuel Hoare's Personal Private Secretary was Sir Geoffrey Butler, the MP for Cambridge University in the days when there were two university seats in Parliament for Oxford and Cambridge. Trenchard enthusiastically backed the scheme, and on 1 October 1925 Cambridge University Air Unit was officially inaugurated, to be followed by Oxford. These units were to be formed in other universities, and ex-UAS pilots were to be given seniority if they subsequently joined. On the outbreak of the Second World War the Oxford squadron alone was able to provide nearly 500 officers for the RAF. These units remain, today, as a valuable source of air-minded men and women for both the RAF and the nation.

An Avro 504N of Cambridge University Air Squadron.

RAF OPERATIONS

Having established air control in Iraq, Sir John Salmond continued with his task of maintaining internal security. During this period air control was exercised in Aden, Transjordan and Palestine. In India operations designed to contain the activities of certain tribes also continued, the main difference being that in India overall control remained with the Army. What follows in this section of Chapter 3 is a narrative of events. These operations are more closely scrutinized in the next chapter.

The R33 with its nose torn off!!!

Operations in India
Source: Air Staff Memorandum No. 48

Operations against the Abdur Rahman Khels – March to May 1925   No complete settlement had been arrived at with the Abdur Rahman Khel section of the Mahsud tribe. In December 1924 this tribal section made absurd demands, which were dismissed. This and other sub-sections of the tribe committed further offences and had to be warned that air action would be taken against them if they had not met government demands by 7 March. When no reply was received, air action commenced on 9 March. The C-in-C India had agreed that on this occasion the situation could be dealt with by the RAF alone, since the political officers had not the resources to deal with the unrest. These then were the operations that became known as 'Pink's War', named after Wing Commander Pink, Officer Commanding No. 2 (India) Wing. The aircraft committed were the Bristol fighters of No. 5 Squadron, Tank, and DH9As of No. 60 Squadron, Miranshah, a total of twenty-six aircraft, forty-seven officers and 214 airmen. As operations progressed, two further flights of Bristol Fighters from No. 20 Squadron were added. The essence of the air operations was not to act routinely, so that the tribesmen never knew when aircraft might fly overhead, and they were subjected to a mixture of an air blockade, night bombing and intensive air attack. Air operations continued for a period of fifty-four days, of which forty-two were spent bombing. Altogether 2,700 hours were flown, with only one fatality. The total cost of the air operations was £75,000. All the tribes involved in the air action subsequently paid outstanding fines, and the subsequent decisions of the political officers were carried out promptly. The GOC Waziristan admitted that he could not have accomplished what the RAF had done with troops even if they had been available. At the time of these operations the weather was severe and the terrain could not have easily been traversed by ground forces.

Operations against the Mohmands, 6 to 8 June 1927   On 4 June 1927 a tribal leader in the Mohmand country had collected a large body of men and was prepared to attack blockade posts on the Mohmand border. Political reports showed a concentration of between 1,000 and 2,000 men. In response a column of infantry, cavalry and armoured cars was dispatched from Peshawar to Shabkadar to attack the enemy if they should attempt to come down into the plains. In the event the tribesmen did not proceed beyond the blockade line, and for a while only a watch was maintained, but on 5 June the blockades were attacked. Bombing operations therefore commenced at 18.00 hrs on 6 June, and were maintained until 09.30 hrs on 8 June, sixty attacks having been carried out by day and night. As a result the hostile tribesmen were dispersed. RAF operations involved four squadrons less one flight per squadron. The official report states that neither officers nor men were required to be recalled from leave to carry out these operations, which took less than forty hours to achieve the objective. This may be compared with an Army operation in 1908 against the Mohmands that took one month of marching and fighting to contain a similiar situation. The report went on to say that the entire territory could be covered by aircraft in just under two hours' flying. No casualties were sustained on either personnel or aircraft, but the enemy lost between thirty and forty killed. The total cost of the operations was put at £1,703.

Operations against the Giga and Neksan Khel, November 1928   Two sub-sections of the Mahsud tribe had committed various offences, and their defiant attitude was having an unsettling effect on the other sections of the tribe. At the beginning of November 1928 the Giga and Neksan Khels decided to stay, for the winter, in their summer quarters, some 8,000 feet above sea level, inaccessible to the supervision of the political officers. The approach of Army troops would alert the tribesmen, who could be expected to decamp into Afghanistan. No reply was received to an ultimatum, and air operations began on 15 November 1928. One squadron was involved, flying from Kohat and from a detached location at Miranshah. The small targets and the nature of the terrain precluded the use of large bomber formations and low-flying attacks. Furthermore friendly tribesmen were living in close proximity to the target locations, so accurate bombing was required. Later it was confirmed that 49 per cent of the total bombs dropped were direct hits. By 20 November the tribes concerned had accepted the full terms of the political authorities. Because of the surprise of the attack they had made no preparations to remove their property. The report claims that the operations were brought to a rapid conclusion owing to the accuracy of the bombing, which also localized the damage to houses and property of the insurgent tribesmen. The Chief Commissioner of the North-West Frontier Province made clear that the houses and property of those tribesmen who were well disposed to the government were not affected. The cost of the operations was £3,037.

Operations in Aden
The hinterland of the Aden Protectorate resembled parts of the North-West Frontier of India. The leader of the adjoining territory, the Imam of Yemen, was steadily encroaching on the Protectorate in an area of roadless country some 100 miles from the British garrison outposts. In this hinterland were sheikhs under British protection whom the Imam had evicted, installing Zeidi garrisons in their place. In 1926 the military authorities considered using troops to restore government authority over the region. This would mean occupying Dhala,

seventy miles north of the port of Aden, but it would be impossible to go beyond Dhala because of the nature of the terrain. Not only would it be necessary to use Dhala as a firm base, it would be vital to keep open lines of communications and have enough extra troops in the event of a sudden reverse. A division of troops no less, minus some artillery, was deemed necessary for this operation. Moreover operations would be restricted to the period between November and March if sickness and a lack of water was not to be experienced. The cost of these operations would have to include getting the troops in and out of Aden, and the figure was put at anything between £6 million and £10 million. The upper

figure should be set against the annual air estimates for maintaining the entire Royal Air Force in 1926, which was £16 million. The Air Staff suggested sending a squadron to Aden to prevent any further encroachments by the Imam's forces. Accordingly No. 8 Squadron became operational at Khormaksar on 27 February 1927, equipped with DH9As. In January the following year these aircraft were replaced by Fairey IIIFs.

Operations against the Zeidi Imam of Yemen, 1928 In February 1928 the territory of two sheikhs in the Aden hinterland was invaded by a Zeidi military force. Under British protection at that time were the Alawi Sheikh and

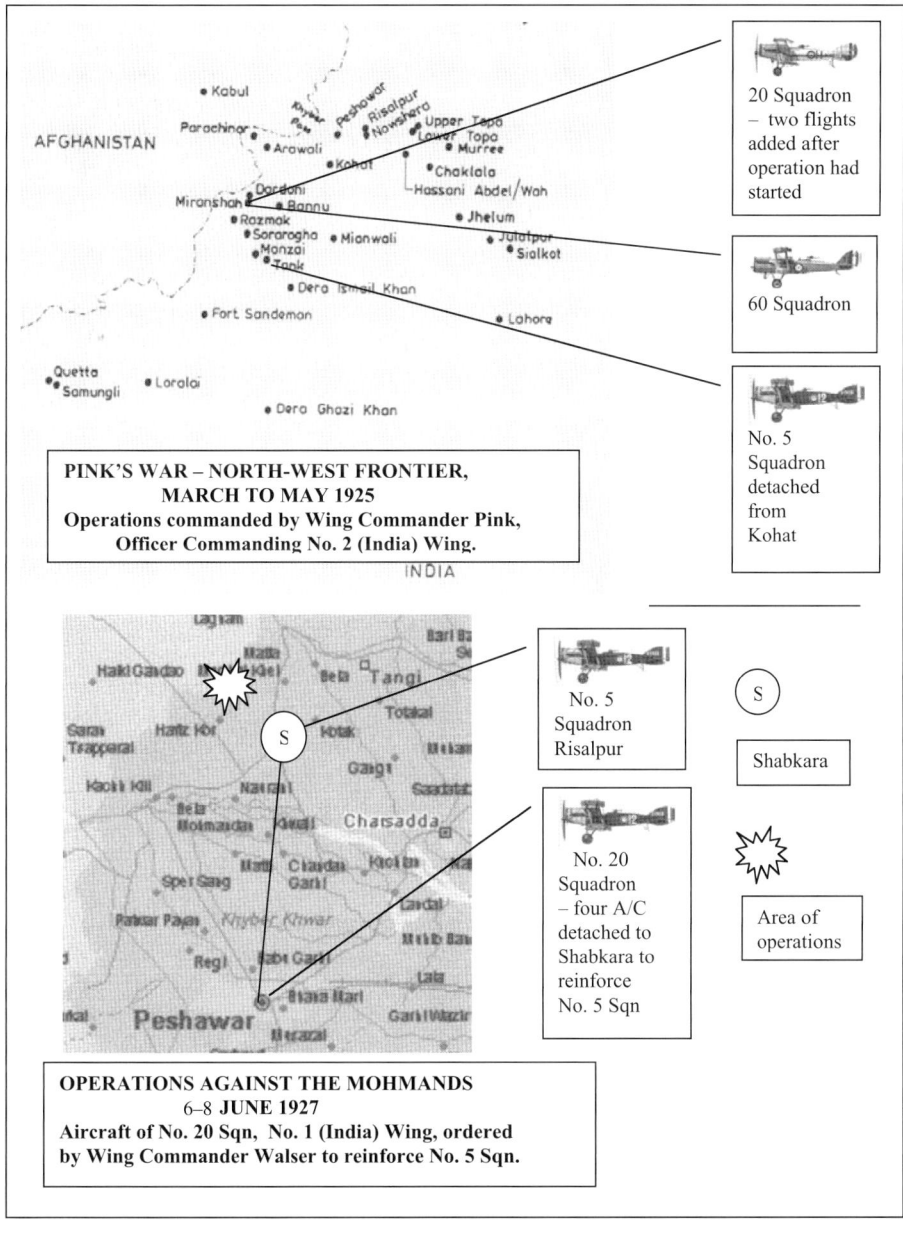

20 Squadron – two flights added after operation had started

60 Squadron

No. 5 Squadron detached from Kohat

PINK'S WAR – NORTH-WEST FRONTIER, MARCH TO MAY 1925
Operations commanded by Wing Commander Pink, Officer Commanding No. 2 (India) Wing.

No. 5 Squadron Risalpur

S

Shabkara

No. 20 Squadron – four A/C detached to Shabkara to reinforce No. 5 Sqn

Area of operations

OPERATIONS AGAINST THE MOHMANDS
6–8 JUNE 1927
Aircraft of No. 20 Sqn, No. 1 (India) Wing, ordered by Wing Commander Walser to reinforce No. 5 Sqn.

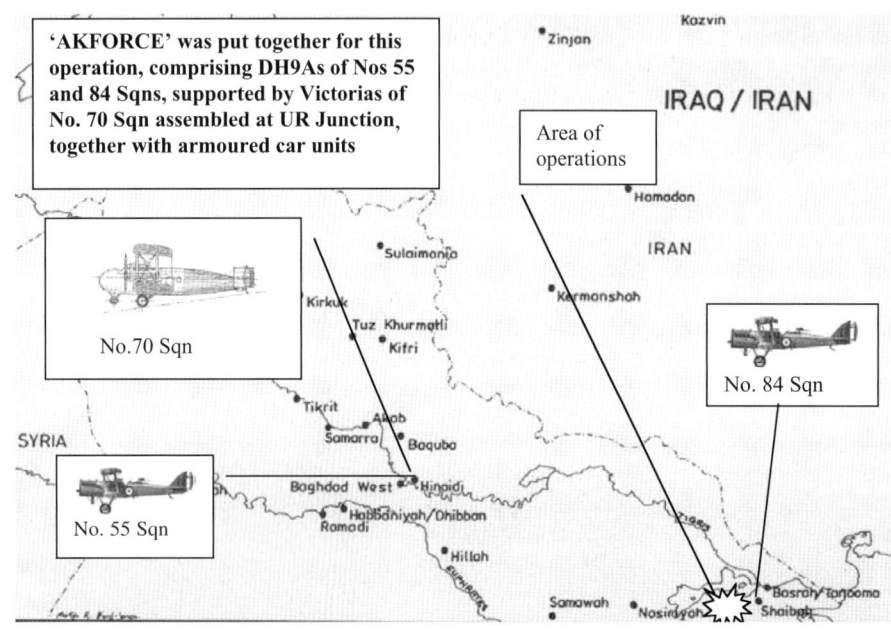

'AKFORCE' was put together for this operation, comprising DH9As of Nos 55 and 84 Sqns, supported by Victorias of No. 70 Sqn assembled at UR Junction, together with armoured car units

No.70 Sqn

No. 55 Sqn

No. 84 Sqn

Anti-Nejd Operations – Iraqi Theatre of Operations, November 1927.

the uncle of the Sheikh of Koteibi. Both of these men were captured, in spite of warnings issued to the Imam not to encroach on territory of people who had treaty relations with the British government. A decision was therefore made to bomb Qataba, the HQ of the Zeidi forces in the Dhala/Radfan area, and other Yemen towns. Forty-eight hours were given after warning notices had been dropped before air action commenced on 21 February, when No. 8 Squadron commenced operations against Qataba. During the bombing runs the

ADEN THEATRE OF OPERATIONS.

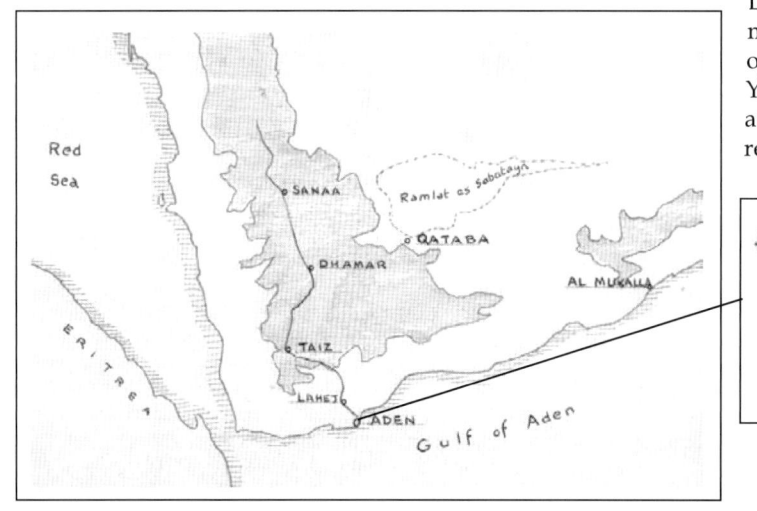

No. 8 Sqn
Khormaksar

aircraft came under heavy rifle fire. Operations continued on the 22nd and 23rd, after which they were suspended to give the Imam the opportunity to surrender the captured sheikhs. This did not produce the desired result, but it was not until 10 March that operations were resumed, when Maflis and troop concentrations were targeted. However, because of low cloud on the mountains, flying sorties were intermittent. Then the Governor of Taiz, no doubt with prompting from the Imam, asked the Sultan of Lahej for his principal sheikh in the Protectorate to assist in opening negotiations between the government and the Imam. The latter had agreed to the immediate release of the captured sheikhs and had asked for a truce of thirty days in order to arrive at a peaceful settlement. This would mean suspending bombing until 23 April.

Owing to the protracted nature of these discussions the truce was extended to 17 July. HM Government wished to see Zeidi forces being withdrawn from all areas in the hinterland that they had occupied. Dhala, the principal town, was to be evacuated by 20 June 1929 as a sign of the Imam's good faith. Failure to comply would be met by the resumption of air operations. But instead of evacuating Dhala the garrison was reinforced. Moreover it transpired that during the period that the truce had been in place there had been active recruitment to the Imam's cause throughout the southern Yemen. The Imam's intention was to attack Lahej, then the Protectorate itself. And so warning messages were dropped on 21 June, and air operations resumed on the 25th. A number of Yemen towns, including Taiz and Qataba, were attacked, together with the fort of Dhala. The renewed bombing raised the morale of the Protectorate tribes, and those from Lahej, who had sought safety in Aden, felt able to return. Under air cover members of the Koteibi first thwarted the Zeidi advance then progressively forced them back on Dhala, which was recaptured on 14 July with the assistance of forces raised by the local Amir. With the Amir settled in Dhala, the local tribes settled down, when, on 1 and then 5 August, Zeidi attacks on border villages were resumed. On the approach of aircraft the Zeidi withdrew, and the Protectorate tribes were able to reoccupy the affected villages in the area on 15 August, without opposition. All the territory of the sheikhs in treaty with Britain was restored to them. Normally a permanent Army garrison could be expected to have been put in place to prevent any further encroachments, but the Zeidi knew that the Fairey IIIFs at Khormaksar could respond rapidly to any moves on their part. The cost of one RAF squadron over a five-month period was put at £8,500. It was reliably reported that the inhabitants of the Yemen capital of Sanaa, 185 miles distant from Khormaksar, had never seen or heard an aircraft, but the mere threat of bombing emptied the Bazaar and brought trade to a standstill for over a month.

Operations against the Subaihi, 1929   In the south-west corner of the Aden Protectorate certain sections of the Subaihi tribe were carrying out raids on villages and caravans in the region. These sections were warned that they must make restitution for these raids if air action was not be taken against them. When the warning was ignored, the villages occupied by the guilty tribe were bombed on 30 January 1929, and this action continued at intervals until 11 March, when the tribesmen asked to negotiate. Restitution was made in accordance with the demands of the British Resident, who reported a successful outcome on 27 March.

Operations in Iraq

Appointment of AOC Iraq, Air Vice-Marshal Sir Edward Ellington   Air Vice-Marshal Sir Edward Ellington was appointed Air Officer Commanding Iraq on 19 November 1926. He had previously been AOC Middle East and AOC India. Sir Edward had had a most unusual career, having spent it almost entirely as a staff officer. He started life in the artillery before going into aeronautics in 1913, then back to the cavalry in 1915, before returning finally to the air service in 1917. His only active operational period of air force command was not as a junior or senior officer, but as an Air officer.

Operations against Mahmud   Sheikh Mahmud, the self-proclaimed 'King of Kurdistan', had retreated to

Persia (Iran) following combined action by RAF aircraft and Levy troops, and his forces had remained inactive throughout the winter of 1925 and 1926. But in the spring of 1926 he had his men infiltrate some tribal villages. During March and April the weather was against British attempts to expel the rebels, and it was not until June that intensive air action became possible. RAF units that went into action were Nos 1 and 30 Squadrons. No. 1 Squadron had Sopwith Snipes detached to Sulaimania, and these aircraft were successful in dispersing Mahmud's forces. A detachment of these aircraft was left at Sulaimania to prevent any recurrence of trouble, but in September 1927 the parent squadron was disbanded and re-formed as a fighter squadron in the United Kingdom. Aircraft of the disbanded squadron were disposed of locally and the personnel posted to other RAF units in Iraq to complete their overseas tours. There simply was not a need for fighters to act in an escort role since there was no air opposition in the Middle East at this time. The DH9As of No. 30 Squadron, Kirkuk, were used in the same operation. When one of these Ninaks was forced down with engine trouble on 14 June, the crew was captured and the retreating rebels took them to their usual refuge. However, not only was the sheikh persuaded to surrender his captives in October, he also agreed to the terms of the political officer and caused no further trouble for three years.

Operations against Sheikh Ahmad   With Mahmud quiescent for a while, the government took the opportunity to reinforce another area of possible unrest in Central Kurdistan. This time it was Sheikh Ahmad, who had fought against foreign administrative control since the end of the First World War. In 1926 the territory, which he regarded as his area of influence, came under the nominal control of the Iraqi government. In 1927 punitive action taken by a force of Iraq Levies, which occupied Barzan, and Ahmad and his immediate entourage took to the hills. The Bristol Fighters of No. 6 Squadron and one flight of No. 55 Squadron, with its Ninaks, ensured government success in expelling Ahmad.

The Anti-Nejd Operations, 1927   At this time troubles repeatedly arose when tribes competed for supremacy over other tribes. Prominent among Arab leaders was Ibn Saud from the territory bordering Kuwait known as the Nejd. There had been inter-tribal conflict since the immediate post-war period, but when these troubles involved the authorities action had to be taken. On the night of 5/6 November 1927 a party of Mutair tribesmen attacked a post of the newly created Iraqi Camel Corps. Having killed all but one policeman, the assailants fled into the Nejd, leaving the injured survivor to raise the alarm. When attacks across the border continued, it

Sopwith Snipe.

A Ninak of No. 84 Squadron, the unit that attacked the island of Gubbah on the Hammar Lake.

became clear that Ibn Saud was either unwilling or unable to control his men. Since he had displayed personal hostility to King Feisal, it was probable that he was not prepared to stop the incursions. Accordingly he was given six weeks to restrain his men if he was to avoid a blockade of the Nejd and Hasa coasts and air attacks. The use of force was authorized on 3 January 1928. While awaiting the reaction of Ibn Saud the authorities took the precaution of forming an advanced headquarters known as 'Akforce'. On 8 February, elements of Nos 55, 84 and 70 Squadrons assembled at Ur Junction, together with armoured car units. At Akforce HQ the Victoria IIIs of No. 70 Squadron were on hand for reinforcement and supply. Meanwhile advanced operational bases were established at Busaiya and Sulman. Warning notices went out on 11 January to the effect that any rebel tribesmen found in the proscribed area would be bombed without warning. At first these warnings seemed to be having the desired effect, but when it became evident that there was not compliance, warning bombs were dropped around the tribesmen's encampments to avoid casualties. Then, on 27 January, an Akwhan force of 300 men mounted raids on Kuwait tribes seventy miles south-west of Basra. The next day RAF aircraft joined in the pursuit of the raiders,

making contact with a large party fifteen miles north-east of Hafar. Accurate rifle fire succeeded in bringing down one aircraft, and it was usual in these circumstances for a friendly crew to attempt to retrieve the crew of an aircraft that had been forced down and rescue them. The following day another party of tribesmen was attacked eight miles west of Hafar. Again one aircraft was forced down by rounds that penetrated the radiator. The Ninak was flown by a lone pilot who was only 400 yards from the tribesmen when his aircraft came to a halt. In spite of intense rifle fire that was directed at the Ninak, Flight Lieutenant J.F.T. Barrett DFC, piloting another DH9A, landed close by and rescued his colleague. By February the number of rebel tribesmen involved was estimated to be in excess of 50,000, but individual raiding parties usually comprised only 4,000 men, and permission was given to use bases in Kuwait to repel the incursions. Akforce was reinforced by a flight of No. 30 Squadron and a section of armoured cars from Hinaidi. At Heliopolis in Egypt one flight of No. 216 Squadron (Victorias) was put on stand-by. Patrolling continued throughout March and April, but air action declined as the tribesmen progressively retreated inland. By 3 June Akforce could be stood down, and all air units were returned to their normal bases and duties. Just before the stand-down an attack was made on the remote island of Gubbah on the Hammar Lake, the stronghold of one rebel sheikh. The Ninaks of No. 84 Squadron bombed the banking that surrounded the island, and breached it, which caused flooding, and the rebels were forced out of their refuge. Ibn Saud then gave a formal written undertaking to restrain his tribes thereafter.

Reduction in the Iraqi Garrison Continued success on the part of government forces in Iraq made possible further reductions in the military garrison, aircraft replacing ground troops, which had always been the intention. The figures were:

REDUCTIONS IN MILITARY GARRISON IN IRAQ (COMBATANT UNITS ONLY)

Date	British and Indian Army	RAF	Iraq Levies

This shows the situation at the beginning of the decade. The table below shows further reductions.

Date	British and Indian Army	RAF	Iraq Levies
March 1921	33 battalions 6 cavalry regiments 16 batteries 6 S & M coys 4 armoured car coys	4 squadrons	

Date	British and Indian Army	RAF	Iraq Levies
October 1925	4 battalions 1 S & M coy	8 squadrons 3 armoured car coys	4 battalions 2 cavalry regts 1 battery
October 1926	do.	do.	do.
October 1927	2 battalions 1 S & M coy	5 squadrons 4 sections armoured cars	3 battalions 1 cavalry regiment
October 1928	1 battalion 1 S & M coy	5 squadrons 6 sections armoured cars	2 battalions
October 1929	Nil	4 squadrons 6 sections armoured cars	2 battalions

British Somaliland

In the opinion of the Air Staff, the Mijjertein Incident of 1927 is an illustration of how the morale effect of air power can gain an objective without casualties to either side. The Italian government had ordered military operations to be taken against the Mijjertein tribe inhabiting the border region between Italian and British Somaliland, resulting in this tribe crossing the border to escape the attentions of the Italians. When bombs were carried forward to an advanced landing ground by the RAF, the word got through to the sultan of the tribe, who was persuaded to surrender rather than face air action.

The Kabul Rescue

(See the history of No. 60 Squadron in Chapter 4 for a detailed account of this operation.)

At the end of 1928 a force of 1,000 rebels, led by an insurgent named Habibullah, captured forts to the north-west of the capital of Afghanistan, Kabul. His men captured stocks of rifles and ammunition and went on to engage King Amanullah's attacking troops. The problem for Britain was that this action threatened the British Legation, which was then cut off from the capital, and the British Commissioner radioed for help. Air Vice-Marshal Sir Geoffrey Salmond, the AOC India, decided to attempt an evacuation of the Legation by air. This was by 1928 standards a hazardous operation that would involve flying from Peshawar over 10,000 ft mountains covered in cloud. Salmond first sent in unarmed DH9As with leaflets to warn of the airlift. Then, on 23 December, a Wapiti with a radio went as a pathfinder through the Khyber Pass to check that Victoria transports could land at Sherpur aerodrome. Subsequently a Victoria of No. 70 Squadron flew in to bring out twenty-three women and children, their baggage being collected by DH9As. On Christmas Day a Victoria, a Wapiti and eleven DH9As took out another twenty-eight persons. By New Year's Day 586 people had been rescued, including the Afghan Royal Family, together with 24,193 lb of luggage. More than 28,000 miles were flown in some of the worst weather on record.

The Kabul Rescue, December 1928.

Shanghai Defence Force

The Chanak crisis had shown how a distant theatre of operations could be reinforced with RAF squadrons using aircraft- or seaplane-carriers. In early 1927 the RAF was again called upon, this time in China, as part of a tri-service force. The city of Shanghai had been threatened with invasion and occupation by Cantonese Chinese revolutionaries led by Dr Sun Yat Sen. Hankow, some 400 miles up the Yangtze river, had been overrun, and attacks upon Nanking had taken place. HMG now feared that British lives and property in Shanghai would come under threat. The air element in the newly created 'Shanghai Defence Force' was titled 'Royal Air Force China', and was commanded by Group Captain E.D.M. Robertson DFC. Originally Robertson had air sections that were aboard HMS *Hermes* based in China and the ex-UK seaplane-carriers *Argus*, *Vindictive*, *Enterprise* and *Tamar*. To these ship-borne aircraft would be added the Bristol F2Bs of No. 2 Squadron, RAF Manston, commanded by Squadron Leader W. Sowrey DFC, AFC. No. 2 Squadron was shipped aboard SS *Neuralia* on 20 April 1927, and arrived in Shanghai on 30 May.

The problem confronting the air commander was the lack of any suitable landing ground, but there was a possibility of finding one on the Kowloon peninsula. A recreation ground alongside the Shanghai racecourse provided a 400 yd landing run parallel to the racecourse grandstands, and bamboo hangars were hastily erected by local Chinese contractors. (This was eventually to become RAF Kai Tak.) By the time the aircraft had arrived, Shanghai was already being threatened with mob violence from its Chinese population of more than two million. The RAF strength was equivalent to five squadrons, and they maintained regular air patrols around the settlement until Nationalist Chinese forces assumed control of the Shanghai area, permitting the return of No. 2 Squadron to Manston in October. It was believed that the presence of RAF aircraft in the Settlement prevented the outrages that had occurred in Nanking and Hankow. One positive outcome was the preparation of the site at Kai Tak by an RAF rear party, for a permanent airfield, which was to become an RAF station.

Singapore

The Threat Another theatre of operations that had exercised the minds of Trenchard and the Air Staff was Singapore. The staff at the Admiralty were intent upon converting the base into a 'Gibraltar' of the Far East, and proposed siting 15 in. naval guns to protect the port from the sea. It was reasoned that the dense jungle of the hinterland would make an attack from the landward side, that is down the Malay peninsula, inconceivable. Japan, potentially the largest naval power in the Far East, could be expected to attack from the sea. The lessons of Aqaba during the First World War seemed not to be have been learned. There the Turkish garrison had its main armament facing out to sea in the belief that no attacking force could come out of an impassable desert, which is precisely what T.E. Lawrence did at the head of a force of Arab tribesmen. He did what the enemy least suspected, which gave him the element of surprise. When the Japanese took Singapore in 1942 they attacked from the landward side.

Guns v. Aircraft

In considering how best to defend Singapore, His Majesty's Government was preoccupied with managing the General Strike, and left it to the services to sort out the matter between them. Eight 15 in. coastal guns were favoured by the Navy and Army staffs, while Trenchard proposed a force of torpedo-bombers supported by fighters and reconnaissance aircraft. With an operational radius of 150 miles, torpedo-bombers could intercept battleships way beyond the twenty-mile range of coastal artillery. Beatty was on his sick bed at the time, and conceded that as a first stage only three guns would be installed, pending an investigation into the relative merits of guns and aircraft. The balance of five guns might be set aside in favour of aircraft. The downside for the RAF, so to speak, would be the need for a chain of aerodromes/landing grounds from Calcutta to Singapore for reinforcement, and the development of torpedo-bombers capable of filling a dual role of coastal defence and frontier warfare. Subject to these provisos it was agreed to delay implementation of the second stage, and on 3 August 1926 the Cabinet accepted this compromise. But a long delay ensued. Firstly, the War Office could not decide on the type and mounting of the 15 in. guns, and secondly, Sir Laming Worthington-Evans, the War Minister in 1928, admitted that trials with heavy guns at Portsmouth and in Malta gave cause for 'reasonable doubt', and so installation was delayed for a year. Trenchard seized the opportunity to suggest that aircraft might fill the gap until the problems with the guns were sorted out. The Committee of Imperial Defence agreed.

THE SCHNEIDER TROPHY RACES

The RAF's involvement in the Schneider Trophy races during the inter-war years is well documented, and it is certain that the development of airframes and engines to meet the needs of this contest contributed to the introduction of the Merlin-powered Spitfire in 1936. The Trophy was the idea of the armaments magnate Jacques Schneider, and was awarded to the winner of an international competition between seaplanes, based on speed and endurance. Should any national team win on three successive occasions that country would win the trophy outright. The French were the first winners in 1913 with a Derpudussin that flew at 45 mph over a distance of 172.5 miles near Monaco. In 1914 the British won with a Sopwith seaplane at a speed of 86.78 mph.

The races were suspended during the hostilities of the First World War, and when they were resumed the distance was extended to more than 200 miles. The winners in succeeding years were Italy in 1920, 1921 and 1926, Great Britain in 1922 and the USA in 1923 and 1925.

The RAFs involvement in the races   The 1926 race was won by Major Mario de Bernadi at an average speed of 246.5 mph. This Italian success could be put down to official government backing, and there was a growing recognition that the competition was not something for private sporting individuals, if only because of the expense involved, and the British had not entered a team that year. Those interested in the Schneider competition who were present at a meeting on 19 March included the Air Ministry, the Royal Aero Club and the Society of British Aircraft Constructors. There was unanimous agreement that there should not be a British team entered in 1926, but since there had not been a competition in 1924 and the USA had won in 1923 and 1925 the Americans could win the trophy outright. Although the Italian success in 1926 effectively scuppered the USA, it jolted Britain into the realization that a more positive approach to these races was essential if the trophy was not to be lost to another country by default. The British Air Minister, Sir Samuel Hoare, took the view that the British government should defray the cost of the machines and that the RAF might take over the training of pilots to fly them. The Air Estimates for the year 1926/7 accordingly included the sum of £100,000 with Treasury approval.

The 1927 Contest
The RAF team went off to Venice for the 1927 competition with two Supermarine S5s and three Gloster biplanes. The race was to take place over the Lido, the long island forming a barrier between the Lagoon of Venice and the Adriatic. At the mid-point of the Lagoon was the Excelsior Palace Hotel, headquarters of the British team. The contest was to be along the 13.5 nautical miles of the Lido bathing beaches. The US Navy Department had to withdraw its entrant, Lieutenant Alford, holder of the 1923 world record of 266.6 mph, since he could not complete the tests necessary to qualify for entry; and this left only Britain and Italy in the race. Having arrived earlier than expected, the British seaplanes had been erected and were ready for test. The Crusader was slower than the other machines and the engine was susceptible to cutting out, so it was designated the test aircraft. On 11 September Flying Officer H.M. Schofield took the Crusader out and made a long take-off run, but his aircraft was no sooner clear of the water than it half-rolled and dived into the lagoon upside-down, tearing off a float and holing the fuselage, so that water rushed in with such force that Schofield was ejected. When he was rescued it was found that

virtually all his clothes had been ripped from his body. When the aircraft was recovered a week later from the bed of the lagoon, it was discovered that the control wires to the ailerons had been crossed so that they had the opposite movement to that intended. One of the essential pre-flight checks carried out by a pilot is to observe the movements of all flying surfaces in response to movements of the controls, so clearly this had been forgotten in the excitement. But the workmen responsible for assembling the aircraft had not done their job, nor had those responsible for checking the work prior to the flight, with nearly fatal consequences.

On Friday 23 June there were the navigation and mooring tests. The race, due to take place on the Sunday, was postponed because of bad weather, and it was not until 12.30 hrs on Monday 26 September that the three British machines, followed by the three Italian racers, moved down the canal. Flight Lieutenant Kinkead was at the controls of the Gloster IVB biplane racer, and Flight Lieutenants Webster and Worsley flew the Supermarine S5s. The Italian team was led by the previous world record holder, Major de Bernadi, in a Macchi M.52, with team mates Lieutenants Guazzetti and Ferrarin. The Italians suffered bad luck throughout the contest. Initially de Bernadi drew roars of applause from the crowd as he pulled out of a dive with a zooming turn, but he was seen shortly afterwards rolling in the swell, as his engine had failed with a broken piston. The last of the Italians to start was Ferrarin, but his aircraft also suffered engine failure, through a broken piston. The last surviving Italian, Guazzetti, was meanwhile being lapped by Webster with a first-lap average speed of 280 mph. Kinkead in the Gloster had also to abandon the race when his seaplane suffered a spinner failure and a strip of metal wrapped itself round one of the propellers, which set up tremendous vibration. Then, on his fifth lap, Guazzetti was nearly blinded by leaking petrol and had to alight on the lagoon. When the spectators could see that it was left to the two S5s to battle it out the crowd began to melt away. Webster's seaplane had a 900 hp geared Napier Lion engine. The original engine had been a 450 hp unit, which had been uprated for racing, and it gave Webster the edge over Worsley with his fixed-drive engine. Webster attained an average speed of 281.65 mph, beating the existing world speed record by a mere 3 mph.

The 1929 Contest
The aircraft and the team   There being no contest in 1928, the 11th Schneider Trophy Competition was staged at Calshot in September 1929, it being the custom that the venue for each contest would be determined by the winner of the previous one, i.e. Britain in Venice in 1927. It was in 1928, also, that the race's promoter, Jacques Schneider, died. He too was a pilot, having been taught

Supermarine S6 No. 247, one of two entered for the 1929 Schneider Trophy Competition.

by no less than Louis Blériot. On 12 August the press were invited down to Calshot to view the British entry. The Gloster IVB and Supermarine 5s of the 1927 competition were designated training aircraft, and could be compared with the two S6s and the Gloster VI of the 1929 entry. The Gloster VI was painted in gold, and the Supermarine S6s in blue and silver. It was plain to see the improvements that Mitchell of Supermarine and Folland of Gloster had made to their seaplanes. The S6s had Rolls-Royce engines and the radiators were built into the wings, flush with the wing surfaces. The RAF had formed a High Speed Flight, commanded since January 1929 by 35-year-old Squadron Leader A.H. Orlebar AFC. His team comprised Flight Lieutenant D. D'Arcy Greig DFC, AFC, Flight Lieutenant H. Stainforth and Flying Officers Atcherly and Waghorn. The 30-year-old

Stainforth, with Atcherly and Waghorn, both 25 years old, were Wittering-based pilots. The two younger men had both been members of the 1927 Hendon Aerobatic Display team commanded by D'Arcy Greig. The latter had become famous for baling out of a Grebe fighter that was in an uncontrollable spin and for leading inverted Genet Moths in formation during the 1927 Display.

Pre-Race problems
On 22 August Italy suffered a setback with the death of Lieutenant Motta at his training base in Italy when he crashed in the tandem-engined Savoia Marchetti low-wing tail-boom seaplane. The team also lost the Fiat C.29, but without killing the pilot. So the Italians asked for a postponement, but according to the rules, this could only be granted on account of bad weather. The

The Gloster VI entered for the 1929 Schneider Trophy Competition.

Italians believed that there was a precedent when the Americans had postponed the race in 1926 because the Italians had not arrived in the USA in time for the preliminaries. The race did not start until November, and then the Italians won. Should Britain show the same generosity? France had withdrawn and the USA was having trouble with its Mercury monoplane. The RAF team was also not without its problems. The liner *Mauritania* almost swamped one of the Supermarine S6s as it steamed up Southampton Water. Strong winds prevented practice flights with the training machines, and Squadron Leader Orlebar had to be towed in when there was a petrol feed problem with the Gloster VI. On 28 August General Balbo let the world's press know that Italy would enter the race as a gesture of chivalrous sportsmanship. The death of Lieutenant Motta had not only deprived Italy of its best pilot, claimed Balbo, but also the machine and engine perfected for the race. One of the two Italian seaplanes that had arrived in London had not even been in the water, and when General Balbo arrived in England he was worried about the amount of casual shipping that crossed the Spithead race course. By the time that the five Italian machines had arrived, there was still trouble with the Supermarine S6s, which had water getting into the floats. When the practice flying did commence with a vengeance, it was clear that the Italians were relying on two scarlet Macchis. The British team, meanwhile, was still having trouble with fuel starvation, and although Stainforth and D'Arcy Greig agreed that the Gloster VI handled well, during a last test-flight on Thursday before the race the sound of the machine misfiring over Calshot meant only one thing. There would not be a Gloster VI in the competition.

The Race

On Friday 6 September the qualifying trials took place. The competitors had to take off, fly a short course, alight, taxi between two buoys, take off again to fly the short course and alight a second time. Each aircraft had then to be moored for six hours without sinking. All the aircraft passed, and on the morning of Saturday 7 September the machines were taken to the start line. Privileged guests watched from the lawns of the Royal Yacht Squadron, crowds were gathering on the Cowes waterfront and RAF patrol boats were busy keeping small craft out of the contest area. At exactly 2 p.m. the starting gun fired, and Waghorn was away in the S6. On return to Cowes there was speculation about the speed on the first lap, and this proved to be 324 mph, 6 mph above the world speed record and 43 mph faster than the S5 in 1927. As Warrant Officer Dal Molin took off in the Macchi M52 bis, Waghorn overtook him on the Cowes–Ryde leg. Then D'Arcy Greig followed in the S5. Lieutenant Cadringher in one of the new Macchi M67s was next, but flew wide at Cowes, blinded by fumes that restricted his view through the small windshield. As he passed Southsea,

witnesses saw a streaming exhaust. The Italian then crossed the mouth of Southampton Water, barely cleared the hill above Castle Point, then dived out of view to land safely. Meanwhile Waghorn was completing succeeding laps without difficulty, followed by Warrant Officer Dal Molin and D'Arcy Greig in the S5. The swell had increased when the gun went for Atcherley, causing his S6 to porpoise, but he then took off smoothly. Waghorn had been briefed to nurse his engine to complete the distance. Atcherley's first lap was at a speed of only 302 mph, and when he lost his goggles he missed his turning point, resulting in his disqualification. The last to take off was Tenente Monte, but having achieved a first-lap speed of 301 mph, he was forced down off Hayling Island with a broken oil pipe, which caused bad scalds to his arms and legs. Waghorn lost count of the number of laps that he had completed, and shortly after flashing past the winning post he ran out of fuel. It was not until the RAF tender reached him that he was relieved to learn that he had been attempting to fly an extra lap. He was the winner, followed by D'Arcy Greig in the S5 and WO Dal Molin flying the slowest of the Italian machines. Thus Britain had won the Trophy on two consecutive occasions. Everything depended upon a third win for Britain to retain the Trophy in perpetuity.

Other Matters

The King, the Prime Minister and other members of the government had every reason to be pleased with the RAF's second win in the Schneider contest. When the news of the 1927 win came through, Sir Samuel Hoare, the Air Minister, happened to be Minister-in-Attendance on the King at Balmoral. 'The King realized that his Air Force had gained considerable prestige by the result', Hoare recalled. He wanted to know whether or not the training and the high-speed flight had affected the pilots' health, and was interested to hear that they had given up alcohol and tobacco. The Prime Minister, who had to justify all public expenditure on the part of his government, was pleased. Mr Ramsay MacDonald was present with his Air Minister, Lord Thomson, and a ship had been chartered for the 1929 race from which the distinguished guests could watch. At an after-dinner speech he pledged that Britain would enter a team in the next race, but this was not due until 1931, and the economic situation at that time would mean that pledges made in 1929 could not be honoured by the government. Another famous man who was present at the 1929 race, who had achieved fame but later sought anonymity, was Aircraftman Shaw (Lawrence of Arabia), who was closely concerned with the safety of the race course, through his work in developing high-speed launches at Calshot.

Postscript

The detailed arrangements made for RAF personnel to view the Schneider Trophy race of 1929 make interesting

Supermarine S.5

The Supermarine S5 of the 1927 Schneider Trophy Competition, Venice.

Grebe.

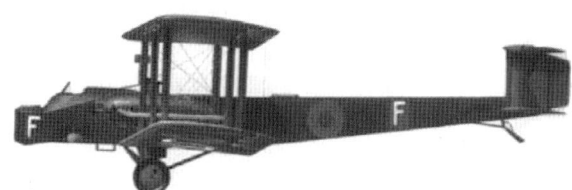

Virginia.

Gamecock.

DH9A.

reading, and can be found at Appendix J. RAF Gosport was going to bulge at the seams, being prepared to accept 500 officers and airmen as spectators, not to mention a maximum of 170 aircraft parked on the airfield for those travelling to the event by air. Throw in an Army fort that would act as a viewing vantage point for the race, a local golf course for the relaxation of visiting officers and arrangements for car parking at the princely fee of 10s (50p), and the reader will see that great care was taken to see that the home team would be well supported.

THE RAF DISPLAY

The RAF Pageant, or Display, as it had been retitled, continued to attract huge crowds each July, come rain or shine. The display could be divided into the following elements:

1. The flying displays, including aerobatic performances
2. A means of introducing new types to the public
3. The provision of a ground display to permit the public to take a close look
4. The focus of annual training by aircrews

The 1926 Display
The 1926 Display was held on Saturday 3 July. It was a hot day with brilliant sunshine and some cumulus cloud. In spite of this being the last day of the Henley Regatta, the Display still attracted a crowd of 120,000, and the ladies were turned out in their finery. The events were longer and fewer than in the previous year. The flying

Bristol Fighter.

Avro Avenger.

Fairey Firefly.

Fairey Fox.

Gloster Gorcock.

Hawker Hornbill.

Hawker Heron.

displays featured not only some of the latest aircraft but the names of pilots who were to succeed to Air rank – Atcherly, Slessor, Harris and Longmore – as well as those who had already made a name for themselves, such as Squadron Leader Collishaw, the fighter ace who had commanded No. 47 Squadron in South Russia during the Russian Civil War. Some of the aircraft that featured in this display were the Bristol F2B Fighter, the Gamecock and Grebe, Virginia and DH9A. The Gloster Grebes had R/T, which permitted Squadron Leader Peck to announce the various manoeuvres to his pilots.

But where the display was different from its predecessors was in the preponderance of aircraft designed and built since 1918 in the Experimental Aircraft Park. These are shown on this page, and the more aerodynamic qualities stand out and can be contrasted with the unorthodox appearance of the Westland Pterodactyl, which did not enter RAF service, and the Cierva Autogyro. The Hawker Heron was still undergoing trials at Martlesham Heath and had to be flown to Hendon specially for the Display.

In the flying display the Armstrong Whitworth Atlas, Army Cooperation aircraft, was shown off for the first time. The Fairey Fox, with its American Curtiss engine, thrilled the crowd by screaming like a banshee as it pulled out of a dive. This was a beautifully clean aeroplane, the radiators being buried in the wings. These aircraft were all faster than the Bristol Fighter, yet the improvement in performance was not spectacular. The new Hawker Horsley was also present. It was designed by Sydney Camm, Hawker's new designer, who was to go on to design the famous Hurricane.

The 1927 Display

In stark contrast to 1926, the Display of 1927 was a day of drizzle and a gusty north-west wind. But this annual event had become so firmly established in the public's mind that the crowds still turned up in their thousands to fill the newly erected 3,000-seat grandstand and the car parks. At 3 p.m. the King and Queen arrived, accompanied by the King of Spain, the Duke of York and the exiled King and Queen of Greece, together with the Air Minister, Sir Samuel Hoare, Sir Hugh Trenchard and

Sir Philip Sassoon. In addition to the usual flying display, six parachutists dropped from three Vickers Vimys, a Kite balloon was destroyed, though not before a stuffed dummy, who went by the name of 'Major Sandbag', descended from it by parachute, and there was always a 'set-piece' battle as the grand finale, involving a fort or some other structure that could be demolished in a blaze of pyrotechnics. In 1927 a fort was attacked with bombs and machine-gun fire, and Fairey Foxes beat off the attacking forces while troop carriers flew in to rescue the defenders. A close-formation aerobatics display was led by Flight Lieutenant D'Arcy Greig, the chief instructor of the Central Flying School, Wittering, and also a member of the British team in the Schneider Trophy races. His formation of scarlet-topped Genet-powered de Havilland Moths, flown by his assistant instructors, performed formation-flying inverted. Apart from the difference in speeds then and now, very little has been added to the quality of aerobatic displays over the years. As the photograph on page 87 shows, the practice of two aircraft flying towards each other on a collision course only to miss by feet was there in the Hendon display as it is with the Red Arrows today.

PLAN OF HENDON RAF DISPLAY, 1928

The 1928 Display

Notice the space reserved for royal visitors, Members of Parliament and the public schools in the plan below. The latter would provide the recruits to long-term commissioned service in the RAF via, in some cases, the university air squadrons. One must not forget the importance attached to this annual event as a public relations exercise. Members of Parliament needed impressing that the legislature was voting sums on a service that would be well spent. A public aware of the efficiency of the peacetime air force would support it and recruits would be forthcoming. By 1928, however, the threat of extinction posed by her sister services having receded, Trenchard could concentrate on his quest for quality. The RAF Display was his way of proving that quality.

The 1929 Display

Owing to the imminence of the Olympia Air Show, there was no parade of prototypes at Hendon, for this would have dented the impact of the former. But the 1929 Display did show off the 'new look' of the RAF, featuring the Siskin and Bulldog fighters and the Sidestrand bomber. One of the pilots who flew inverted in the Genet Moths was Flying Officer Dermot Boyle, later to become Chief of the Air Staff. The classic beauty of the Fairey Fox made it probably the most pleasing-looking aircraft of its time, and it

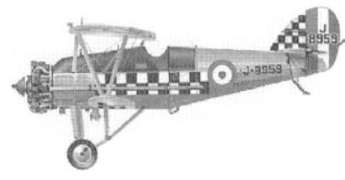

Siskin.

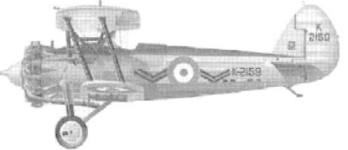

Bulldog.

Sidestrand.

was held that the banshee-like scream would have put the fear of God into many a hill tribesman in the Middle East or on the North-West Frontier. In fact the Fox was never used in air-control operations. It was the Wapiti that would replace the old DH9As and Bristol Fighters in those theatres.

The Aircraft and Armament Experimental Establishment, Martlesham

By 1926 the work of the A & AEE was respected not only in the RAF but in the aircraft industry and civil aviation. Although the work involved a considerable degree of risk, the test pilots knew that they were at the cutting edge of technology. The firm's test pilots who brought the aircraft to Martlesham also shared the dangers of test flying, but it was left to the RAF pilots to test an aircraft to the limit to be sure that it would survive in combat. Harald Penrose, who became the chief test pilot of Westland

Gloster Goldfinch.

Boulton Paul Partridge.

Vickers 141.

Aircraft, described how he came to deliver the prototype Widgeon to Martlesham in February 1928. Remember these were the days when there were none of the formalities of flying today, such as flight planning and radio contact. He left Yeovil to fly eastwards, keeping a look-out for aircraft using airfields in his path, such as Old Sarum and Andover. He skirted London and droned eastwards across East Anglia to Ipswich before picking up the pine-fringed airfield that was his destination. There were no red or green Very lights. If the field and approach was clear, he said, one landed. Once there, he saw a wealth of new types in the hangars, such as the Gloster Goldfinch, Boulton Paul Partridge and the Rolls-Royce-powered Vickers 141, which caused him to reflect how far aviation had progressed in the few years since the epic flight of the Wright brothers. Test-pilot reports were readily accepted by manufacturers, who would often incorporate modifications into the basic design. At the annual Display the latest aircraft were on show and were flown by Martlesham pilots, those being the only ones with enough experience to fly new types. Accordingly the aircraft companies tried to ensure that they would have a prototype on trial at the time of the Display.

Martlesham Airfield The airfield at Martlesham, in common with other airfields of the day, was unsurfaced and consisted of a large field of turf and close-cropped heather. This meant that aircraft could take off in pretty well any direction, according to the wind, but the prevailing one was south-westerly, and so the majority of take-offs were in the direction of the Dobb's Lane corner of the airfield and the approaches were made over Martlesham village. Left-hand circuits of the airfield were usual, and since all landings were visual, the aircraft in circuit remained, for the most part, within the airfield perimeter. Until the introduction of tail-wheels, taxiing aircraft meant picking up quantities of turf and heather in the metal tail-skid.

Death of Flying Officer G.V. Wheatley To emphasize the danger of test flying, Flying Officer G.V. Wheatley was carrying out a terminal velocity dive in a Gloster Gamecock, from which he did not survive. The station

That's test flying for you!! But at least this pilot crawled out uninjured.

experienced a lively social life and was a close-knit community. The loss of a test pilot, therefore, had a profound effect on those who knew him. A special memorial service was held in the men's dining hall, attended by officers from Martlesham's sister establishment, the Marine Aircraft Experimental Establishment, and Shotley Royal Naval Training Establishment – in all some 450 officers and men. No. 22 Squadron personnel headed the cortège, and all three service padres officiated. Flying Officer Wheatley was buried amid a mass of floral tributes, his coffin draped with the Union Flag, and a firing squad fired the three volleys.

Other Hazards There were other flying hazards in the 1920s that are unheard of today. Nowadays fuel can be dumped if an aircraft gets into difficulty, this being particularly important just after take-off when the tanks are full. On 18 June 1927 Flight Lieutenant C.R. Carr and Flight Lieutenant P.H. Hackworth were flying a Hawker Horsley II, Serial No. J.8608, on a long-distance flight. They had on board 1,000 gallons of fuel when a sudden oil leak meant a forced landing. It was a considerable feat of airmanship to land without mishap. Their flight was from Cranwell to the Persian Gulf when the oil leak happened. Cranwell was the station from which long-distance flights took off, since it had a sufficiently large grassed area for a take-off run with a heavily loaded aircraft.

The Fairey Postal Martlesham pilots were also involved in the long-distance flights of the Fairey Postal. Squadron Leader Jack Noakes was selected to be the test pilot of the Postal MkI, Serial No. J.9479, in November 1928, but he was injured when the Parnall Plover that he was testing crashed. His replacement was Squadron Leader A.G. Jones-Williams. This officer, together with Flight Lieutenant N.H. Jenkins, had already made a long-distance flight of 4,130 miles from Cranwell to Karachi. Unhappily both officers were killed instantaneously during a non-stop attempt to fly from Cranwell to Cape Town, when their aircraft flew into a mountain-side while crossing the Atlas mountain range.

Changes in Organisation and Typical Flying Hours

During the decade 1920 to 1929 the following dates chart the organizational changes affecting the station:

January	1920	Station in No. 3 Group, Spittlegate, Lincolnshire
1 April	1920	Station establishment, 17 officers and 284 men
June	1921	Armament Experimental Section, Orfordness, closed
August	1921	Station in No. 1 Group, Kenley
July	1922	To Coastal Area
September	1922	Establishment of two Home Defence squadrons
May	1923	Station changed back to No. 3 Group No. 22 Squadron formed
March	1924	Headquarters and No. 1 Flight, No. 15 Squadron
May	1924	2nd Flight, No. 15 Squadron, formed. Orfordness reopened, armament ranges
April	1925	Rebuilding of station begun
July	1926	Station moves to No. 2 Group, Inland Area

Typical Flying hours –	No. 15 Squadron –	1927	481 hours
		1928	782 hours
		1929	570 hours
	No. 22 Squadron –	1927	1,670 hours
		1928	1,967 hours
		1929	1,799 hours

The Marine Aircraft Experimental Establishment, Felixstowe

Three experiments/investigations carried out at Felixstowe during the late 1920s have been selected for inclusion in this chapter. The first is because it concerns one of the Schneider Trophy aircraft, the second because it gives a detailed account of experiments with the forerunner of the wet suit. Now that wet suits are commonplace, the account of experiments with the 1920s version is almost hilarious yet represents a serious attempt to improve the survival time of aircrews brought down in the sea. The third was selected because it is an investigation of a flying-boat accident when a Southampton actually got airborne at its moorings. Such was the wind strength that she rose up from the sea and turned turtle to sink and break up.

Speed Course Test of Supermarine S5

Source: National Archives, MAEE Report F/2/51a, dated 26 July 1927

Speed runs were carried out on the above aircraft over the 3 km speed course at Calshot. Timing was done by means of cinema camera guns. The arrangements and timing operations were carried out entirely by personnel of the MAEE Felixstowe. The results were as follows:

Date: 24/7/27
Time: 05.52–06.01 hrs
Wind: Approx. 2 mph
Engine: Ungeared Napier Lion
Airscrew: Fairey-Reed with medium-width blades
Markings: Unknown
Mean rpm during trials: 3,050
Mean measured ground speed: 284 mph

Run No. 1 Calshot to Southampton: 23.7 seconds at a
    ground speed of 283 mph
Run No. 2 Southampton to Calshot: 23.8 seconds at a
    ground speed of 281 mph
Run No. 3 Calshot to Southampton: 23.9 seconds at a
    ground speed of 280 mph
Run No. 4 Southampton to Calshot: 23.1 seconds at a
    ground speed of 290 mph

The accuracy of the individual readings, neglecting
errors in laying out the course, windage and piloting
(maintenance of direction and constant height) is
estimated to be 2 mph. The mean speed is estimated to
be accurate to 1 mph.

The 'Everwarm' Safety Suit
Source: National Archives, MAEE Report F/A/17

The safety suit has been under test at Felixstowe for four
months. The suit is a combination overall garment
covering the occupant with the sole exception of head
and hands. The material is a fairly thin rubberised fabric.
Round the neck and the wrists the fabric is replaced by a
tight-fitting collar and cuffs. The soles of the feet are
reinforced by thin crepe rubber soles. Straps are
provided externally at the ankles and internally at the
shoulders. There is no front or rear fastening to the body
of the garment. Entry is obtained through a large
opening as if getting into a sack. The legs are then drawn
on and the neck and wrists are passed through the collar
and cuffs respectively. The slack or mouth of the sack
then hangs loosely in front of the chest and is wound up
tightly into a flat tube on the vertical axis and secured by
two straps. Internal to the suit and secured to it by
buttons are chest and back pads. These are quilted and

stuffed with kapok. The
weight of the suit
complete is 9 lb and can
be stowed in a space
approximately 2 ft × 1
ft 8 in. The suit has been
tested as: (a) a flying
suit, (b) an emergency
flotation device and (c)
a garment for waders.

Use as a flying suit The
suit is adequately warm
at normal seaplane
flying altitudes except
that the hands become
cold owing to the
circulation of blood
being impeded by the
tight-fitting cuffs. The
warmth is contingent
upon the occupant being warm on entering the suit, the
point of which is not helped by the necessity for
removing the boots prior to putting on the suit. The suit
is not comfortable, it being cumbersome, and hinders
movement. As far as, for instance, getting in or out of the
aircraft, starting up engines on the water, attending to
moorings, etc. To get in or out of the suit whilst on board
an aircraft is also difficult to manoeuvre even in the
relatively large space of a boat seaplane hull. The
material is not elastic hence the only method of
obtaining room to move is by making the suit 'baggy'.
This contributes to the cumbersomeness. Some
improvement might be obtained in this respect. Also, as
regards the necessity for removing the boots, if slack
were intentionally provided this could be taken up by
some form of ripcord or puttees. The rubber collar is
uncomfortable and chafes the neck. More slack might be
provided to allow the turning of the head. The bulky pad
produced by lashing the mouth of the sack down on to
the chest is inconvenient. It tends to catch in the controls,
instruments and cockpit fittings. It also obstructs the
view within the cockpit. It is considered that this trouble
might be reduced by folding the material horizontally
and bringing the ends away to straps under the arms. It
is pointed out that the build of the pilot in question
influences the comfort of the suit, in other words the use
of the stock size of the garment is contra indicated. It is
suggested that the garment, being airtight, is not
hygienic. Heat is obtained, not by encouraging
circulation, but by impeding bodily ventilation. If used
on long flights other allied considerations will come into
play.

Use as an emergency flotation device Two floating
positions can be obtained, horizontal with no ballasting of
the suit or vertical with the legs of the suit lashed close to
the occupant's calves and the ankles weighted. A weight
of 25 lb was found to be suitable with the water level
neck-high. When floating in the horizontal position water
enters at the neck area. Even when the occupant remains
still except in a flat calm the head tends to go underwater
if any movement is made. It is difficult to get out from a
prone position on the back over on to the chest or the side
owing to the air in the suit providing buoyancy which
resists motion. The legs are too buoyant to allow the leg
movements for swimming but the arms can be used. But
if an attempt is made to swim with the arms the cuffs
stretch and allow water to enter. When ballasted and
floating vertically the above remarks apply with the
following exceptions. Firstly the ballast, instead of the leg
buoyancy, prevent swimming. Secondly the neck leakage
does not occur until the water is slightly rougher though
a slight lop is quite sufficient. The neck leakage is due to
the collar not fitting the cross-section of the neck
especially at the back. It is not seen how a close fit can be
obtained without throttling the occupant. Temporary

expedients in the form of scarf, soft rubber padding or otherwise might keep the water out for a while but will probably make the suit more uncomfortable in the air. The wrist leakage and the leg buoyancy are allied difficulties given the fact that ease of movement can only be obtained by 'bagginess'. The legs are 'baggy' but the arms are not, hence the legs are over-buoyant while the arms pull on the cuffs and cause leakage. Improvement might be obtained by providing leg and arm puttees so that after getting into the suit the slack might be taken up except at the joints. Also at the wrists independent rubber bands might be used leaving the wrists reasonably free in the air and making them even tighter in the water. Slight leakage occurs through the front flap unless it is closed with great care also through any adventitious holes after the suit has become stretched by use. The total leakage was sufficient to give waterlogging of the legs in five minutes on a fairly calm day.

Use of the garment for waders If used with weighted boots the suit would form a useful garment for waders especially when working in rough waters with trolleys drawing much water. It would need to be made of much more robust material or the expense of maintenance or frequency of replacement would be excessive.

Conclusion The suit, as designed and made, makes getting in and out of aircraft very difficult. There would need to be wholesale redesign of cockpits with resiting of instruments and the material from which it is made renders it perishable in stores. The suit would have to be worn before an accident occurred for there would not be time afterwards if an aircraft ditched or the pilot was trying to free himself from the wreckage. Even if the pilot got free into clear water he would probably drown in attempting to swim.

Loss of a Southampton flying boat at its moorings
Source: National Archives, MAEE Report F/A/148, dated 6 December 1928

Summary Southampton flying-boat No. S1248 was wrecked at its moorings during the recent gales. This report discusses those aspects of the occurrence which are of technical interest. Prior to the gale it was found possible to photograph the attitude of the aircraft pitching in the water. The minimum angle was observed [see photo bottom left] and the maximum [see photo below]. The conclusions that are drawn that some method of reducing the lift of a seaplane at moorings is essential and that investigations into the loads produced on the mooring gear is also required.

Description of the accident The flying-boat was lying at No. 1 Mooring on Thursday 15 November when a gale sprang up which gradually veered to the West, and during the day attained an average speed of 35 mph with gusts up to 42 mph which was the wind velocity when both the accompanying photographs were taken. There was a heavy swell running and during the following day the gale gradually increased in volume until about 18.00 hrs on Friday 16 November with recorded gusts reaching 60 mph and even exceeding that figure. This will be seen from the photographed portion of the wind velocity chart. In this connection it should be pointed out that the intensity of the gusts experienced by the flying-boat was probably greater than that recorded on the chart. At about 18.00 hrs, during the dark, the Southampton was

Maximum angle photographed.

Southampton S1248 riding on No. 1 mooring with the minimum of pitch observed.

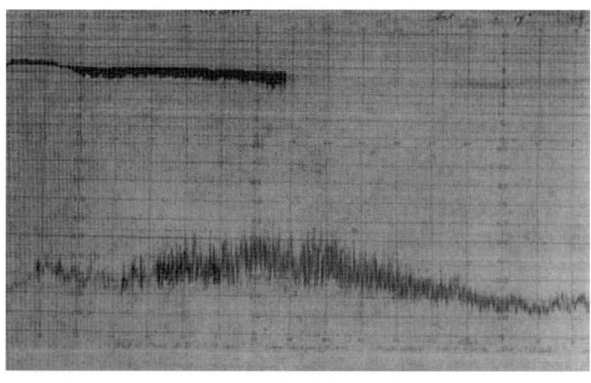

Wind velocity chart.

lifted off the water by the wind, turned over in the air on to her back and struck the water again in that attitude. The aircraft was submerged and broken up and the wreckage could not be recovered until the following day.

Mooring gear used   The Southampton moorings weighed approximately 14,000 lb and all the aircraft's controls were locked in the normal manner. The mooring gear used on this occasion consisted of $1^1/2$ in. cable carried straight from the lower keel fitting on the flying-boat to the buoy through the intermediary of a ring. Another cable ran from the ring to the bow fitting and a third cable from the buoy to the bollards but it should be clear that the flying-boat was riding solely on the first direct cable. The other two cables constituted purely safety factors and did not take any normal stress. It is interesting to note that the mooring gear was found to be intact after the accident. During the Thursday afternoon it was possible to secure photographs of the Southampton pitching at her moorings [see page 92]. The greatest upward angle of pitch actually photographed was 15.5 deg. The greatest downward angle was 2.5 deg. But there is no doubt that both angles were considerably exceeded on the following day of which, unfortunately, there are no photographs. During the Thursday and especially on Friday afternoon it was observed that the flying-boat, when caught with the wind in the act of pitching to a swell, was lifting clean off the water by the wind force and was actually flying at the mooring.

Conclusion   It is evident, therefore, that in leaving boat seaplanes moored out, steps will have to be taken to spill the lift of the wings to the point where take-off becomes impossible. This method had obvious advantages if it is practicable and experiments in this direction have been initiated. It is also clear that in calculating the stresses exerted on a seaplane at its moorings care will have to be taken of wind forces experienced at angles some 15 deg in excess of normal i.e. 5.5 deg. Whilst the aircraft was riding at moorings there was a noticeable absence of snatch on the mooring line and this coupled with the fact the mooring gear was found intact after the accident points to the efficacy of the system of mooring gear consisting essentially of mooring by a single line attached to the lower keel fitting. This point will be dealt with in a comprehensive report on mooring gear generally which is in the course of preparation.

Considerable difficulty was experienced in salving the wreckage which had fouled the channel bed but when it was retrieved it was found that the hull, which was forward of the tail structure, snapped clean in half. This damage was sustained during the accident and not subsequently. The Southampton, however, is designed throughout on a flexible principle except on this one point, where a heavy hoop is introduced to take the tail attachments.

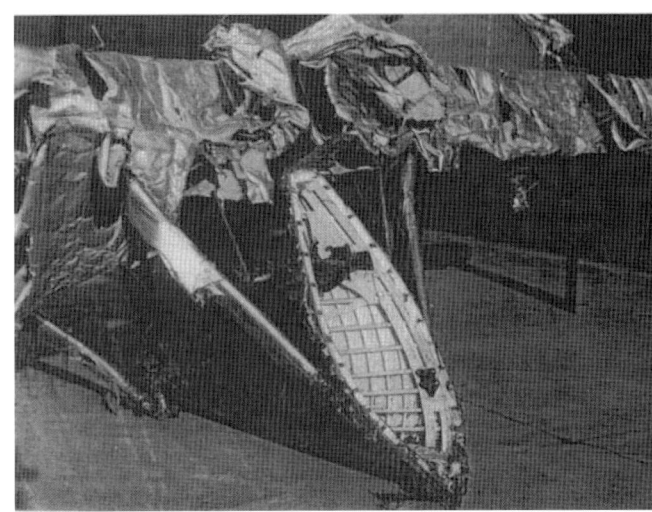

Some of the aircraft damage.

Recommendation   It is recommended that in the future designs of hulls sudden changes in section should be avoided and tail attachment points distributed over a wider area.

TRAINING

Annual Air Exercises

Not only did the RAF Display provide a focus or end point to annual training in the inter-war years, so too did the Annual Air Exercises, which were introduced in 1927. Even though the full air-defence organization was not completed until 1935, the stated objective of these exercises was to test the defensive measures to be adopted in a future air war. The prevailing air doctrine did not envisage just searchlights, anti-aircraft guns and fighters, but a strike force of bombers that could bomb those military and industrial targets that made the attacks on Britain possible, i.e. offensive defence. In 1927 the exercises were designed to pit a force of day- and night-bombers against a force comprising fighters, AA guns and searchlights. The only experience that the armed forces had at that time consisted of the Zeppelin and Gotha raids on Britain during the First World War. Then, fighter interception, the system of air raid warning and the integration of tri-service air-defence forces was still in its infancy. By the end of that war there was an unchallenged assumption that the bomber would so frighten populations that with the awful prospect of death and destruction an enemy could be expected to sue for peace in the early stages of a conflict. Air Staff policy was to give rise to contradictions, inconsistencies and criticism that are further explored in Chapter 10.

The 1927 Air Exercises

Eastland had at its disposal eight bomber squadrons of the Wessex Bombing Area under command of Air Vice-Marshal Steel. *Westland*'s force consisted of eleven squadrons of the Fighting Area commanded by Air Vice-Marshal Brooke-Popham, who also had at his disposal units of the Observer Corps, anti-aircraft batteries of the Royal Artillery and searchlights. The capital of *Westland* was London, which would be subjected to heavy bombardment by the forces of *Eastland*, forcing the government to flee the capital. While London continued to be bombarded, other targets outside the capital would be hit. One object of the exercise was to see whether or not the *Westland* forces could meet all these attacks. To this end, rules had to be devised to permit the umpires to declare who had won each encounter. Firstly, it was necessary to establish the casualty rate between fighters and single-engined bombers. In a straight encounter it would be the size of the formations that would form the basis of establishing casualty rates, so that half the difference in strength would be awarded against the smaller formation. In any engagement between fighters, like the Siskin, and twin-engined bombers, like the Vimy,

the strength of bomber formations was doubled and half the difference in strength awarded against the smaller formation. Applied to an engagement between three fighters and four twin-engined bombers, for example, this formula would result in two and a half fighters being destroyed; yet the experience in the First World War showed that fighters had at least an equal chance of knocking out bombers in an interception. It seemed to observers, therefore, that the results were being 'skewed' in favour of bombers by giving a bomber arbitrarily twice the killing power of a fighter. Since the fighters had only a 1 in 2 chance of making a successful interception, the bombers would sustain only 25 per cent casualties. As for the potential damage inflicted by the bombing force when it was impossible to use live bombs, the umpires had to anticipate the accuracy of the raid. The method used to check the accuracy of bombing lay in a wireless installation and a camera obscura at each target zone. The camera was able to record the aircraft position at the time of the bomb release, which was radioed down by an airborne umpire. Yet it was one thing to drop a bomb on the target, and quite another to be sure how much damage each bomb would cause.

Date 1927	Total raids	Raids scrubbed	Raids not intercepted	Raids intercepted	Intercept rate (%)
25 July	8	1	5	2	29
26 July	6	2	2	2	50
27 July	12	1	6	5	42
28 July	22	0	8	14	64
29 July	6	1	3	2	40
Totals	54	5	24	25	51

Comments on the 1927 exercise results Given the then current 'RAF Air Doctrine' of offensive defence, as much importance had to be given to the interception of incoming enemy bombers as the damage inflicted on enemy industrial targets. If one accepts that the bomber will always get through, then defence against bombing attacks become of critical importance when one is on the receiving end. In 1927 the British day-bomber outperformed the fighter. Success was more likely if slower, less manoeuvrable twin-engined bombers were intercepted. Of course radar interception was still to come.

1928 Air Exercises

The 1928 air exercises took more or less the same form as before. Again it was Steel v. Brooke-Popham, and battle commenced on 13th August. The defence of London and the efficiency of individual units were tested. By day the capital was attacked by DH9As, Fairey Fawns, IIIFs and

Foxes, and by night by Virginias and Hyderabads. Opposing them was a force of Gamecocks, Siskins and Woodcocks. There was one actual casualty during these exercises, and that was a Siskin that crashed into Kew Gardens, its pilot parachuting to safety. The statistics are given below:

Miles flown	250,000
Weight of imaginary bombs dropped by aircraft that reached their targets	202 tons
Raids made by day-bombers	57
Raids made by night-bombers	not given
Daylight raids attacked on run in to target	39
Daylight raids attacked on leaving target	37
Daylight raids not intercepted	9
Adjudication– Day-bombers shot down by fighters	151
– Day-bombers shot down by Ack-Ack	20
Number of fighters lost	139

It was held that by day the clouds and strong winds favoured the bombers but by night the weather favoured the fighters. The interception of bombers was said to have improved since 1927, but air pilotage by bomber crews has also improved. Praise was also bestowed on the Auxiliary squadrons, the Observer Corps and searchlight crews, and thanks were extended to those who accepted searchlight batteries onto their property and to the civilians who looked after the flares on emergency landing-grounds.

Comments on the 1928 air exercises   The high level of interception meant that few bombers got through to their targets at night. Could it therefore be assumed that the risk from bombers was not as great as originally feared unless the bombers flew higher and faster, then what? Then again, London was much closer to the coast than many continental capitals and was therefore particularly vulnerable. On the basis of these exercise results could the Air Staff planners guarantee that RAF bombers would deliver such devastating attacks on an enemy's industrial and military targets that the problems for the defence would be progressively reduced, if not eliminated? If after the commencement of hostilities enemy bombers continued to attack in large numbers, the exercises had shown that the cost to the defence would be anything between thirty and fifty fighters a day. Could the Air Staff be sure that an offensive that was meant to deliver the knockout blow did not become a war of attrition, in which case how long would such fighter losses be sustainable? The following year Trenchard was to remain unswerving in his commitment to offensive defence. These matters are discussed in greater detail in Chapter 10.

Flying Practices

The following examples of flying practices in the late 1920s show how they were still quite rudimentary, certainly by today's standards. It reminds us that R/T communications between aircraft in flight were not the norm and that Second World War bombing equipment had still to be adopted.

The dropping of flour bags from aircraft to simulate bombing
Source: Air Ministry Weekly Orders (AMWO) 122/1929, dated 28 February 1929

This order relates to the system whereby paper bags containing flour could be used to represent bombing from the air. Authority was granted for expenditure on flour, cotton wool and grocers' white bags, and the total weight of the practice bomb was not to exceed 4 oz. The pilot of a single-seat fighter was instructed to drop his 'bombs' from bomb containers of either the smoke or incendiary variety. Pilots were not permitted to drop their 'bombs' by hand, but air gunners of multi-seater aircraft could if they so wished. Presumably having one hand on the control column and the other on the 'bomb' would be to risk hitting the ground at a point that would have embarrassing consequences, for the order warns that flour bags must not be dropped into gardens in the immediate neighbourhood of lands temporarily hired for training purposes, nor near public roads or private houses. Training exercises over military training areas posed no such problems, providing the ordinary limits of flight safety regulations were observed.

Visual Signals between Aircraft
Source: AMWO 738/1928, dated 1 November 1928

This order accepts that visual signals for use between aircraft in flight that had been laid down in the Flying Training Manual were unnecessarily complicated. A revised code of signals was therefore promulgated in this Order on a trial basis in lieu of the provisions of Air Publication 928. Air or other officers commanding were requested to forward to the Air Ministry a report on the suitability of these signals not later than 1 October 1929. Air Ministry Publication 928 would not be amended until the new code of signals had proved to be satisfactory. These signals with explanatory texts are shown overleaf:

VISUAL SIGNALS BETWEEN AIRCRAFT

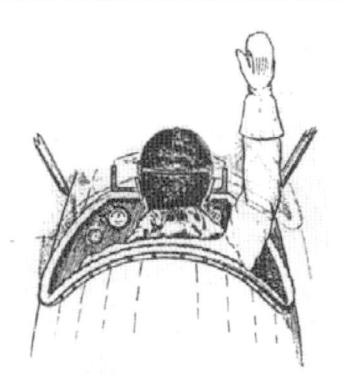

Arm raised vertically:

a. **'Prepare to take off'**
   (in formation)

b. **'Open formation'**
   (from squadron
   formation)

**Arm extended and brought
down in the desired direction:**

'Change direction'

when in 'squadron
formation' only

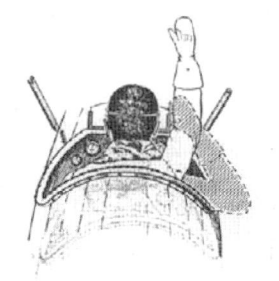

**Arm raised vertically
above the head three or
more times and then
dropped:**

**'Prepare to release
bombs'**

for formation bombing

Note: Bombs will be released when the leader's bombs are seen to leave the aircraft.

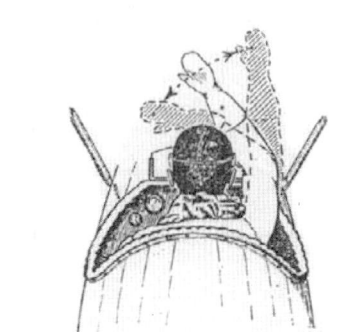

**Arm or arms waved from side
to side above the head:**

'Break formation' (when given by
formation leader, means 'break into sub-
formations'. When given by sub-formation
leader, means 'proceed independently'.

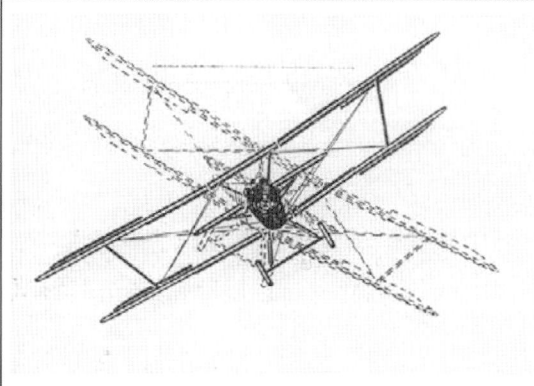

**Rock aeroplane laterally and slowly several
times:**

a. **'Enemy in sight'**, or when given by leader,
b. **'Close up'**

Leader rocks aeroplane fore-and-aft:

'About to attack' signals given by
leaders must be repeated by leaders
of sub-formations.

COURSES OF INSTRUCTION
Source: RAF Museum, AMWO 85/1927

The following courses of instruction provide an example of the nature of training during the late 1920s. The courses were for officers and air gunners:

Venue	Course	Duration	Comments
RAF Cranwell	Accounting Officers' Course	6 weeks	
RAF Cranwell/Henlow	Stores Course	23 weeks	13 Weeks at Cranwell 10 Weeks at Henlow
Armament and Gunnery School	Air Gunnery and Course (Continuation Course)	8 weeks 8 weeks	for pilots and observers
	Air Gunners	6 weeks	
RN College Greenwich	Advanced Armament Course	under consideration	
School of Photography	Air Photography Course	13 weeks	for pilots and observers
	Long Photography Course	8 months	
RAF Base Calshot	Air Pilotage Course	13 weeks	One officer selected yearly for a long course of air navigation of 7 months' duration
	Coastal Reconnaissance Pilots' Course	5 months	
	Seaplane Flying Course	as requisite to enable pupils each to receive 5 hours' flying training	
Chemical Warfare Dept. Porton	Regimental Instructors' Course	4 weeks	in addition 1 NCO on each course
	Staff Officers' Course	1 week	
School of Army Co-operation	Army Co-operation Course for RAF Officers for Army Officers	12 weeks 4 weeks	
Henlow	Engineering Course	2 years	
Cambridge University	Course A – Electrical and Wireless Engineering	2 years	
Imperial College of Science and Technology	Course B – Aeronautical Engineering	1 year	
	Course C - Aeronautical Research	1 year	
	Meteorology	1 year	
Any recognized university in the UK	Course D – Maths, Physics and kindred subjects	3–4 terms	
School Of Naval Co-operation	Naval Observers' Course	18 weeks	
Electrical and Wireless School	Short Signals Course	12 weeks	
	Long Signals Course	8 months	
Staff College Andover	RAF Staff Officers' Course	15 months	to include: 2 Navy officers 1 Army officer 1 Indian Army officer 4 Dominion officers
London Imperial Defence College	Imperial Defence Course	1 year	

Flying Training Courses

No. 1 Flying Training School	Ab initio	6 months	Usual officers on a syllabus for Fleet Air Arm
		11 months	RAF officers and airman pilots

Nos 2, 4 & 5 Flying Training Schools	*Ab initio*	11 months	RAF officers and airman pilots
The Cadet College (Cranwell)	*Ab initio*	2 years	
Certain Home-Defence Squadrons	*Ab initio*	11 months	
Central Flying School	Flying Instructors' Course	11 weeks	

Ground Training

The Electrical and Wireless School The 1928 Air Estimates announced that the Electrical and Wireless School, where officers and airmen were trained in signals duties and where aircraft apprentices entered training in the electrical and wireless trades on a three-year course, was moving from Flowerdown to Cranwell. The Cranwell command then included the Royal Air Force College (previously designated the Royal Air Force Cadet College) and the Electrical and Wireless School. At RAF Cranwell between 1926 and 1929 there were no apprentices until the closure of Flowerdown and the move of the trainees as previously described.

Apprentice Service and Airmen Pilots The pass-out of the 6th Entry from Halton in 1927 brought the total of ex-apprentices trained at either Cranwell or Halton to 4,000. The 1927 Air Estimates refer to apprentice training and show how increasing reliance was placed on that system of training ground engineers. In 1926 provision was made for the training of 208 airmen pilots, many of whom were ex-apprentices. By 1927 the established number of airmen pilots had been increased to 242, and these men, in addition to undertaking flying duties, would be eligible to carry out certain technical duties that had previously been performed by officers. After five years' flying service they were to return to their normal ground trades but remain in flying practice and be liable for flying duties in the event of war. The Reserve of Short-Service Officers was correspondingly reduced by this substitution of airmen pilots for officers. The 1927 Air Estimates also called for ninety-six boys to begin training as apprentice clerks at Ruislip, the home of the RAF Record Office (there had been an experimental entry of boy clerks in 1921). The apprentice clerks who had come into existence in 1925, again thanks to Trenchard's foresight, continued until the last entry, No. 61 Entry, passed out in 1942. By that date a total of 2,080 apprentice clerks had been trained, of whom a high proportion were either commissioned or became aircrew. According to the 1929 Estimates, technical and clerk apprentices who entered service at about the age of 16 years, to fill technical and clerical trades respectively, would continue to be recruited for twelve years' active service, counting from the age of 18, with no reserve liability. At the beginning of 1927, according to recruiting announcements, 3,500 apprentices had already entered the Royal Air Force, and that figure was to reach 5,000 one year later. At this juncture a new grouping with wings was introduced, so that an entire entry was attached to one specific Apprentice Wing.

Flying Training
Source: National Archives, AIR/32/15

Seaplane training When the Reserve was formed it was intended that seaplane training should also be carried out for reservist personnel. It did not actually commence, however, until April 1925. The firm selected was the North Sea Aerial and General Transport Ltd (a subsidiary of Blackburn Aircraft Ltd), which was already carrying out twin-engined training at Brough. Prior to this an investigation had been carried out with a view to carrying out floatplane training at Calshot. The estimate was too expensive, however, and the Calshot scheme was dropped. Training at Brough commenced on 1 April 1925. Both annual refresher and requalifying courses were carried out, and a total of twenty pupils per year were to be rate trained at a cost of £425. In 1926 the fee was raised to £800 because the first estimate proved to be far too low. The aircraft used were the Dart-Lion floatplanes. In 1927 the capacity was raised to thirty pupils per year, and these aircraft were provided, the contract lasting for two years.

Expansion of capacity The size of the Royal Air Force Reserve under Treasury authority was to be 700 pilots. In order to deal with these personnel it had originally been planned to open more schools, each training seventy pupils as the personnel became available. After the first year of operation, however, it was decided to expand four of the schools to a capacity of 100 pupils per year instead. This gave a total training capacity of 490 pupils (including twenty doing seaplane training). The contractual arrangements for the four schools for the four years 1925–9 were as follows:

Stag Lane/Filton/Coventry/Renfrew – 400 pupils over 4 years
Brough – 280 pupils over 4 years

The remaining 210 members of the Reserve were to be made up of instructors at civil schools and personnel engaged in civil aviation. The strength of the Reserve, however, in 1925 was considerably below 700 pilots.

Introduction of Ab Initio Training   As time went on, the number of ex-service pilots joining the RAF Reserve dwindled and the supply of reservists from the Short-Service Commission scheme was insufficient to make up for the loss. Consequently a scheme was drawn up in order to increase the number of pilots in the Reserve by accepting direct-entry personnel with no previous air force experience and giving them a course of *ab initio* training. This scheme was submitted to the Treasury and approved as an experiment in May 1925. Two courses totalling fifty pupils commenced training at two of the civil schools, Filton and Stag Lane, towards the end of the year. The course was continuous and lasted three months, and the syllabus provided thirty hours' flying on elementary types of aircraft, which included both dual and solo, followed by five hours solo to go with the appropriate dual on a service type. Ground instruction was also included in the course. These pupils then carried out the normal annual refresher training. The next two years saw little development in this direct-entry *ab initio* scheme. The first courses passed out in early 1926. Fifty more pupils were trained in 1927 and a further sixty in 1928. To summarize, the *ab initio* courses were as follows:

	1926	*1927*	*1928*
Stag Lane	25	20	30
Filton	25	20	30
Renfrew	–	10	–

Coventry and Brough were not used for *ab initio* training. At the former the aerodrome was unsuitable, and at Brough twin-engined aircraft and seaplanes were in use.

Further developments   The Treasury was asked to approve the scheme permanently on 7 December 1926, but instead gave its sanction to a further four years on the basis of sixty pupils a year (fifty in 1927). A further request for permanency led to approval for an annual intake of sixty pupils up to 31 March 1933. In 1928 the Beardmore School in Renfrew was closed down owing to financial loss incurred by the school while carrying out reservist training. The school actually closed on 3 November 1928. In 1929, when the contracts were about to be renewed (they had been established on a four-year basis in 1925), the annual refresher training consideration was given to the performance of the aircraft in use at the schools. So far as single-engined types were concerned, it was considered unnecessary to call for a higher standard of performance, and so its existing equipment continued to be used. The school at Brough, however, equipped with twin-engined Kangaroos, was considered out of date, and they were replaced by Darts with the object, *inter alia*, of providing training on a Fleet Air Arm type. Seaplane training had been carried out for Reserve personnel at this school since 1925 with Dart aircraft, and it was thought that a smaller aircraft establishment would serve the sea- and land-plane sides of the school better than if two types were in use, since land and float undercarriages could readily be interchanged. Twin-engined training was not continued owing to the high operating cost involved using modern twin-engined types. When in 1929 the new contracts were drawn up for training at the civil schools, they catered for a total of 2,080 training courses to be carried out in a four-year period. Of these 120 were annual refresher seaplane courses, 1,720 were annual land-plane refresher courses and 240 were *ab initio* land-plane courses for direct-entry reservists. The requalifying courses for ex-wartime pilots were, by this time, unnecessary.

Airships

Airship Development   On 19 October 1923, Sir Samuel Hoare had announced to the Imperial Economic Conference being held in London that the Air Ministry had been authorized to proceed with an airship programme based on a plan put forward by Commander Dennistoun Burney. Burney, with the support of Vickers-Armstrongs, had proposed the construction of six airships, each of 5 million cubic feet, to be built by private enterprise over a period of years with a view to providing an Imperial service to Egypt, thence to India, twice weekly with passengers and mails. A regular UK–USA service was also envisaged. In order to get a government subsidy it had been necessary to persuade Parliament that airships were the most economical means of getting mails to the Middle East, India, the Far East and Australia, and for this purpose the Airship Guarantee Company was proposed. Unfortunately for Burney, the Labour government of Ramsay MacDonald rejected his plan on 7 May 1924 because of the complicated finance involved. But Lord Thompson, the Air Minister, cleverly proposed that airship development should be in the hands of the government since military considerations could be kept in view at all times. This scheme, dating from February 1924, was approved by the Cabinet.

Plans for the R100 and R101   With the government, and not private enterprise, in charge of airship development, the Air Ministry went ahead with the reconditioning of two existing airships, the R33 and R36, which would undertake full-scale experimental flights fitted with special recording instruments. The plan was for a large airship, the R101, to be built by the Cardington team with facilities to enable it to operate to Egypt and India. Since the Burney team at Howden was still in place, it was decided that private enterprise could simultaneously build a second airship, the R100, at a cost not exceeding £350,000, to be spread over three years on condition that, on completion, it was handed over to the Air Ministry with an option to repurchase the airship for £150,000. The military justification for its being built lay in the provision that the government could lease it back if required for defence purposes. The choice of the number 101 for the Cardington-built ship was that it was held to be the first of a new design, whereas the R100 was the last of the old. This was regarded by some as a snub to Burney and Barnes Wallis, the designer of the R100, and his team at Howden.

Air Ministry/Admiralty rivalry over the R101 The Cabinet paper referring to the construction of the R101 had used the phrase, 'the primary function should be naval reconnaissance'. This had the effect of reviving the hostility between the Admiralty and the Air Ministry over air matters. On 18 July 1924 the First Lord of the Admiralty wrote to the Secretary of the CID, 'As it has been decided that the Cardington ship (R101) is to be built primarily for naval reconnaissance, the task must be carried out with naval personnel under the direction of the Admiralty.' But it was not as clear cut as it may have appeared. The clear waters were muddied by reference to its possible use as an aircraft and troop carrier, and this was a matter for the Air Minister. Owing to the rising bitterness between the two service ministries, the Prime Minister requested Lord Haldane to try to resolve the dispute. The First Lord of the Admiralty, Lord Chelmsford, asserted that the Navy would not have complete confidence in any airship developed or manned by another service. The demand that naval duties must be carried out by naval personnel under naval command was all too familiar. When the new Conservative government came in at the end of the year, Mr W.C. Bridgean became the new First Lord, and he urged a return to the Burney proposals. However, the

Cabinet decided that the Labour decision should stand for the sake of continuity in airship policy, and there, for the moment, the matter rested.

Construction of the airships An Open Day was held at the Royal Airship Works to publicize the R101 and to let the pressmen see that the huge airship structure was almost complete. For those who had also seen the R100, it was interesting to note the different ways in which the rival constructors solved similar problems. The 'capitalist' ship, the R100, used a standard system of screwed collars to connect the helically seamed tubular framed girders at all junctions, while the R101 used Boulton and Paul patented girders of high-tensile steel strip, rolled and drawn into tubes. Machine stampings bolted together at junction points were used and braced by diagonal wires in the bays. There were more than 25 miles of steel or duralumin in both airships, but the two constructors used different methods for transferring the lift from the gas bags to the airship's structure. It was very important that unacceptable loads should not be placed upon the structure when the ship was out of level or if one of the gas bags deflated. There was also a difference in motive power. The R101 was to operate in hot climates, and the increased risk of fire persuaded the builders to go for diesel fuel rather than petrol, and five Beardmore compression-ignition engines with a combined power of 3,250 hp were fitted. The cost of diesel fuel was £5 per ton compared with £25 per ton for petrol used in the Rolls-Royce Condor engines of the R100. These engines had a combined power of 4,200 hp. However, the fuel economy and reduced fire hazard in the R101 was offset by the weight of the power cars, each of which was more than twice the weight of its rival. Moreover, the R101 had a long crankshaft in the eight-cylinder in-line engines, which produced such torsional resonance that torque variations twenty times the normal had been measured at 950 rpm. This resonance in turn caused the failure of the hollow steel blades of the reversible-pitch propellers, and solid alloy blades had to be developed in lieu.

German and American Rivals Meanwhile the Luftschiffban Zeppelin GmbH had produced a longer airship than the two British ones. Called the *Graf Zeppelin*, it left Friedrichshafen on 11 October 1928 for a flight to Lakehurst, New Jersey, piloted by Dr Hugo Eckener. It arrived safely on the 15th, although there were some problems with the weather during the flight, causing a diversionary route down the Rhone Valley and thence by Gibraltar and Bermuda. A squall tore the fabric from the airship's 60-ft-long horizontal fin, and the commander idled

The R101 over Bedford in October 1929.

the engines while crew members, including his son, went outside to effect repairs. Be that as it may, the Germans had stolen the limelight from the R100 and R101. They had had much commercial success with airships between the wars, whereas Britain with an Empire to serve still had not inaugurated a scheduled passenger and mail service. The Americans too were able to display success with their airships when, in January 1928, the USS *Los Angeles* showed off its manoeuvrability by landing on the aircraft-carrier USS *Saratoga* without the aid of a mooring mast. The airship was moored to the stern of the carrier while passengers, fuel and supplies were transferred, demonstrating that in future airships might be able to accompany the US fleet. But neither British constructor would be drawn as to a date for completion of its airship, and it was not until October 1929 that the R101 was ready for flight testing, followed by the R100 in the December. The story of these two airships is taken up in Volume II, 1930 to 1939.

Civil Aviation

Future development of civil aviation In 1928 the argument used in giving state-financed aid to support civil aviation was that it strengthened the potential reserve for war. Civil aircraft could be adapted for military use, as Sykes had pointed out when he was Controller-General of Civil Aviation back in the early 1920s. A sum of £415,000 was proposed to defray the cost of civil aviation for the year ending 31 March 1929. Squadron Leader the Hon. F.E. Guest made this proposal in Parliament, but Lieutenant-Colonel Moore-Brabazon took the contrary view, arguing that training for war should be divorced from civil aviation. Sir Samuel Hoare, in winding up the debate for the government, said that the consolidation of Imperial Airways had resulted in a remarkable record of reliability and was the envy of every other country.

Future development of civil aircraft In the report of the Aeronautical Research Committee for the year 1927/8, there was an indication of the envisaged technical trend in aircraft development. Sir Sefton Brancker, the Director of Civil Aviation, had been consulted to learn of his research requirements in the immediate future. These were stated as:

1. A high power heavy-oil engine to secure low fuel bills
2. Use of geared engines
3. Pusher propellers to reduce noise
4. Development of all-metal structures

As a further step, following a crucial report, a special sub-committee was formed to examine the problems of reducing air resistance in 'practical aircraft', an aspect largely neglected during the years 1926 and 1927 in favour of research into safety and reliability. But the monoplane was still some way from common acceptance, and biplanes still featured large in both military and civil inventories. The one exception was the Fairey Postal, the long-range monoplane that was ready for flight testing in the late summer of 1928.

Trenchard's Farewell

Farewell Message The following is the text of the farewell message from Marshal of the Royal Air Force Sir Hugh M. Trenchard published in Air Ministry Weekly Order No. 802 dated 31 December 1929:

> On leaving the Air Service after 17 years' work in the Royal Flying Corps and the Royal Air Force, and on ceasing to be Chief of the Air Staff after 11 years' service in that post, I wish to bid good-bye to all ranks of the Royal Air Force and to thank them all for the hard work and keenness which has been shown in the building of this new Service and in raising it to the position which it now occupies. I am certain that the future will add still further to the reputation of the Air Force and to its importance in the defence of the British Empire.

Trenchard's record and his successor Trenchard, who was succeeded by Air Chief Marshal Sir John M. Salmond KCB, CMG, DSO as Chief of the Air Staff, was given a peerage, to become Baron Trenchard of Wolfeton in the County of Dorset. His command of the RAF is dealt with in some detail in Chapter 10, and it is sufficient at this point to pick out his most notable achievements from the many for which he will be remembered. He fought off a determined attempt by the Army and Royal Navy in the early 1920s to take back their air components, which would have resulted in the demise of the RAF. He then went on to establish an independent air force on a shoestring budget. He did not sacrifice quality for quantity, and was determined to build the foundations for a greatly enlarged service at a later date. The essential elements of his peacetime service were a cadet college to train the permanently commissioned officers of the future, a school for apprentices where boys could be trained to become a future highly skilled technical work force, the creation of a staff college to prepare officers for positions of high command, the establishment of air control in the Middle East and India and encouragement to the aircraft industry to produce prototypes that would put the RAF ahead of its rivals in other countries. Building airfields and accommodation had to wait, but the expansion plan of 1923 allowed Trenchard to be creative and to develop new aircraft and create a reserve air force and short-service commissions. He stuck to his conviction that an air force should go onto the offence as the best means of defending the nation, even if he did overstate the power of an air force to defeat an enemy through air power alone. Above all he was determined to create an 'air force spirit'. There can be no question that in this he succeeded, and he may rightly be called the Father of the Royal Air Force.

Chapter 4
Air Control in the Middle East, India and Ireland

The nature of air control – Background to air-control operations – RAF participation by squadrons – Consideration of air control –
Air substitution – Limits of air substitution – Attitude and response of tribesmen and racial groups to air control – Conclusion

The Nature of Air Control Air control by the RAF during the inter-war years meant, quite simply, the maintenance of internal security in a territory primarily through the use of aircraft. Primarily means that aircraft were almost always supported by ground forces. Before aircraft came into military use Britain maintained internal order and security in her dependent territories overseas through the use of ground forces. These would act on the request of the civil power, often in the shape of local political officers who were responsible to the government or colonial governors for the administration of the areas under their control. In internal security jargon this is known as 'aid to the civil power'. This is most important, for the military were never to act except that the authorities requested the help of the Army or RAF. Troops would be used to suppress rebellion or contain disorder typically among tribes or sections of tribes that inhabited the region. The problem was that once the military authorities had been alerted and troops dispatched, the situation on the ground could deteriorate, requiring even more troops to be sent. Such troops were always at risk from ambush and could become battle or medical casualties. Evacuation of such casualties only added to the difficulties facing troop-column commanders: the more remote the region, the more expensive the expedition. The military aeroplane transformed the situation. RAF squadrons could deploy aircraft to forward landing grounds within a matter of hours, and these aircraft could be in action shortly afterwards and at a much lower cost. In 1920s money this could mean the difference between millions and thousands of pounds. The speed and flexibility of aircraft operations meant that trouble was often 'nipped in the bud'. Moreover the punitive element of air, as opposed to purely ground operations, was quite often avoided. The mere threat of the use of bombing aircraft could result in a favourable outcome for the authorities, and if this was not enough, the sight of aircraft circling overhead could bring tribesmen to meet the government's demands. Only after warnings were given and these demands remained unheeded did RAF aircraft bomb. Since disruption to economic life, and not death or injury to tribesmen or their families, was the aim, the tribes would be given time to evacuate the site to be bombed. But one must not imagine that the RAF had it all its own way. Tribesmen learned to retaliate; indeed, if such operations were carried out today, retaliation could include surface-to-air missiles.

The Background to Air-Control Operations
Territories involved in air-control operations, 1919 to 1929 Air-control operations were described in Chapter 2. This chapter looks closely at the squadrons involved and discusses air control under various headings. The territories involved comprised six operational theatres:

1. The United Kingdom including Ireland
2. India
3. Aden
4. Iraq
5. The Sudan
6. The Mandated territories of Palestine and Transjordan

The United Kingdom Aircraft were used during the General Strike of 1926, but the main theatre of operations within the UK was southern Ireland. When air-control operations began during the First World War the twenty-six counties of what is now the Republic of Eire were under the British Crown. Following partition of northern from southern Ireland in 1920, the RAF continued to operate in the south until final British withdrawal in 1922 from what was by then the Irish Free State.

India India had the largest garrison in the British Empire, and its North-West Frontier Province was the land border in the Empire over which invasion was most feared, whether by Afghan or Soviet troops. There was also a threat to internal security from mountain tribes, as well as nationalist agitation in the cities and on the plains. For some time aircraft had been used in support of operations carried out in support of land operations in Waziristan, and at the cessation of hostilities in November 1918 there were just two RAF squadrons in India, No. 31 Squadron at Risalpur and No. 114 Squadron at Lahore. Unlike Iraq, however, the government of India was not prepared to transfer overall operational control from the Army to the RAF, although it was conceded that aircraft had a useful part to play, particularly on the Frontier, where their use would be more economical than the employment of ground forces alone. But as the experience of Palestine was to show, the use of aircraft was inappropriate in dealing with urban unrest. In June 1922 the Sub-Committee on Indian Military Requirements noted the economies that could be achieved by the use of aircraft, and Air Vice-Marshal John Salmond toured RAF units in India to prepare a report on their role, organization and administration. He found the aircraft in India in a sad state owing to government economies, and he advised that there should be better buildings and maintenance facilities, and a separate budget so that the RAF would not have to go cap in hand for funds. He also advised a definite role in the security of the Frontier, which would require two more squadrons, but as things stood, the RAF's pilots were losing confidence in their aircraft. The Army C-in-C, Lord Rawlinson, accepted most of these proposals, but, as has been said, was unwilling to hand over operational control to the RAF, at all events not before air policing was seen to be effective. In 1925, however, the Army General Staff did agree that the RAF could run its own campaign. Unrest far from an Army garrison in that year was the signal for independent air-control operations. Between March and May operations were carried out against the Mahsuds, and the RAF flew 2,000 flying hours and dropped 150 tons of bombs. As a result of the 1925 campaign a scheme for air control on the Frontier was drawn up and the number of squadrons was increased from six to eight. Operations against the Mohmand Laskar in June 1927 was a further feather in the RAF's cap, but when Trenchard proposed replacing twenty-five to thirty Army battalions by a further five to six squadrons the government of India drew the line. Such a proposal, had it been carried into effect, would have resulted in widespread redundancies in military and support personnel. In any case the retention of military personnel was essential for other reasons.

Aden   The British had governed the city of Aden from 1839. It was valued as a naval anchorage and fuelling station for major warships and a wireless telegraph station. To the north of the port of Aden the fertile land was controlled by the Imam, head of the Zeidi Sect, who had effectively gained independence after a long struggle with the Turks. He disputed the boundary drawn by the Ottomans and the British in 1905 and claimed the entire protectorate as his domain. It was usual in air-control operations to reduce the military garrison once aircraft were substituted for ground troops, but encroachments by Zeidi troops into the Protectorate occurred at a considerable distance from Khormaksar, the RAF airfield and base. This would put targets out of the range of Bristol Fighters unless they were provided with forward landing grounds equipped with fuel, armament and aircraft spares, and these would then need the protection of ground troops. Day-bombers were therefore recommended, and the British Resident believed that an attack on the Yemeni capital, Sana, would show that the British meant business. A diplomatic mission to Sana in January 1926 failed, by which time Zeidi encroachments had taken place. In keeping with the policy of air control, No. 8 Squadron was transferred from Iraq to Khormaksar equipped with DH9As, and the squadron became operational in March

1927. Two British battalions were to be withdrawn, leaving three armoured car units and the Aden Protectorate Levies in defence of Aden. In January 1928 the Air Ministry took over control of defensive operations.

Iraq   It was in Iraq that the policy of air control was born and developed. In response to a major rebellion in the country, Winston Churchill, by then moved from Air Minister to Colonial Secretary, called a conference of his service chiefs and colonial officials in Cairo in March 1921. Traditional methods of control were ruled out because of their high cost, and with the success in British Somaliland still fresh in the mind it was proposed that Iraq should be placed under overall RAF command, an Air Officer Commanding replacing the General Officer Commanding. Since it had never been tried before, there were considerable misgivings, but economy won the day. A force of eight squadrons of DH9As, Bristol Fighters and Vickers Vernon transports, together with a brigade of British and Indian troops and four companies of RAF-manned armoured cars, took over the defence and internal security of Iraq.

In this sense the Indian situation was the same as that in Iraq, i.e. there was a threat from across the border as well as an internal security problem. In Iraq there was unrest with tribes, some as far south as the Hammar Lakes. The external threat was from Turkish incursions into Kurdistan or from local puppets with Turkish backing, for the Turks still regarded that part of Iraq as rightfully theirs. On 1 October 1922 Air Marshal Sir John Salmond assumed command as AOC Iraq.

The Sudan   The use of aircraft in the Sudan had begun in 1916 when the Royal Flying Corps had helped to suppress the rebellion of Ali Dinar, the Sultan of Darfur. Again, in 1920, aircraft were dispatched from Egypt to make punitive raids on the Garjack NUR of the Sobat District. In August 1924 a flight of four aircraft was established at Khartoum, arising from the political crisis in the Sudan at that time, and Sir Samuel Hoare, the British Air Minister, believed that the country was eminently suited to the use of aircraft in policing. There were frequent military operations in the southern Sudan, but the increase of air strength from a flight of four aircraft to an entire squadron could only be justified if the Sudanese garrison was reduced by one British battalion. At a conference in Cairo in March 1925 Trenchard's proposal for the stationing of a squadron in the Sudan was accepted, but since neither the Sudanese government nor the British Treasury came up with the funds, the idea was temporarily put on the 'back burner'. Differences of opinion as to the best means of maintaining internal security between the Army and the RAF persisted. Trenchard believed that a squadron of bombers based at Khartoum and good landing grounds up country was the best way of maintaining a visible British presence, with reinforcement from Egypt if required. But the Army wanted one battalion to garrison Khartoum and part of another to protect lines of communication. And because they did not like splitting units that meant two battalions. In the end, compromise was effected. The Cabinet decided that an RAF squadron should be based at Khartoum for one year to allow a 'fair and thorough trial', after which the matter would be considered further. An interest-free loan was granted to the Sudanese government to defray the difference in cost between the maintenance of a squadron at home and in the Sudan. No. 47 Squadron moved from Helwan to Khartoum on 21 October 1927.

Palestine After the First World War Palestine was placed under military rule of OETA (Occupied Enemy Territories Administration). Following the Balfour Declaration of 1917, Zionist hopes were raised with the promise of a Jewish home in Palestine and the expulsion of the Turks. Jewish immigration followed, to the extent that, in March 1921, a Congress of Palestinian Arabs met in Haifa to consider a petition to end Jewish immigration and British support for the Jewish 'national home'. The Congress also petitioned for the creation of a representative government. In the summer a civil administration replaced military rule. Riots had already occurred in Jerusalem in April, and in May 1921 ninety-five people were killed in disturbances in Jaffa, and bombs were dropped to protect Jewish settlements from Arab raiders. In November 1921 there were 7,670 Imperial troops in Palestine, which included three battalions of infantry and three regiments of cavalry, at an annual cost of £3.5 million. Churchill proposed replacing the Army garrison with an RAF squadron backed by armoured cars and a local gendarmerie. Since the War Office did not regard Palestine as strategically important, an RAF Air Officer Commanding assumed command in May 1922, and by 1925 the garrison had been progressively reduced to a single cavalry regiment, a company of RAF armoured cars and No. 14 Squadron. Military expenditure had been cut by a half.

Transjordan The future shape of the administration of Transjordan was settled early in 1921. Churchill originally recommended a military occupation to prevent raids on Palestine and to stop intrigue against the French in Syria, but the Cabinet was unwilling to commit an entire battalion. It was at this time that the Cairo Conference was in session, which paved the way for air control in Iraq, and separate discussions took place in Jerusalem with Amir Abdullah, the bother of Faisal. It was agreed that Abdullah should govern in Transjordan for at least the next six months. He asked for the help of British officers, funds and bombers, and in April, His Majesty's Government agreed to this request. Three aerodromes were to be built in

Transjordan, and the Air Force squadrons were to mark out a desert route across country to link Palestine and Iraq. The decision to underwrite Abdullah with aircraft mirrored the creation of an Arab kingdom under Faisal in Mesopotamia, and Abdullah came to depend more and more upon the RAF for his survival.

RAF Participation in Air-Control Operations, 1919 to 1929

This chapter continues with an account from service records and other sources of the operations of squadrons involved in air-control operations except in Ireland, which is amply dealt with in Chapter 2. Most of the squadrons in question served almost entirely in one theatre, but where squadrons did move, their changed deployments are recorded. They are:

INDIA

No. 1 Sqn	Snipe
No. 3 Sqn	Snipe
No. 5 Sqn	Bristol F2B
No. 11 Sqn	Wapiti
No. 20 Sqn	Bristol F2B
No. 27 Sqn	DH9A
No. 28 Sqn	Bristol F2B
No. 31 Sqn	Bristol F2B
No. 39 Sqn	Wapiti
No. 60 Sqn	DH10/10A & DH9A

EGYPT

No. 8 Sqn	DH9A
No. 45 Sqn	DH9A, Vimy & Vernon
No. 47 Sqn	DH9A
No. 56 Sqn	Snipe
No. 70 Sqn	HP 04/00 & Vimy
No. 202 Sqn	Short 184
No. 208 Sqn	RE8 & Bristol F2B
No. 216 Sqn	DH10, Vimy & Victoria II, III, IV & V

IRAQ and ADEN

No. 1 Sqn	Snip
No. 6 Sqn	Bristol Fighter
No. 8 Sqn	DH9A and Fairey IIIF
No. 30 Sqn	RE8, DH9A & Wapiti
No. 45 Sqn	Vernon
No. 55 Sqn	DH9A
No. 70 Sqn	Vimy, Vernon & Victoria I, III & IV
No. 84 Sqn	DH9A & Wapiti
No. 203 Sqn	Fairey IIIF

THE SUDAN

No. 47 Sqn	DH9A & Fairey IIIF

PALESTINE AND TRANSJORDAN

No. 6 Sqn	Bristol F2B
No. 14 Sqn	Bristol F2B, DH9A & Fairey IIIF

The Three Major Players in Air Control Operations

'Brisfit'.

One 275 hp Falcon III engine
Maximum speed: 125 mph at sea level
Duration: 3 hours
Ceiling: 20,000 feet
Armament: 1 fixed Vickers + 1 Lewis gun

'Ninak'.

One 400 hp Liberty 12 in-line engine
Maximum speed: 123 mph at sea level
Range: 620 miles
Ceiling: 16,750 feet
Armament: 1 fixed Vickers + 1 or 2 Lewis guns

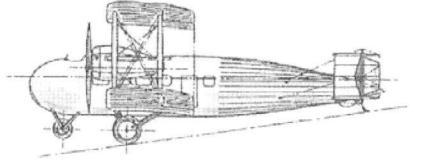

Vickers Vernon.

Two 450 hp Napier Lion II engines
Maximum speed: 118 mph
Cruising speed: 80 mph
Range: 320 miles
(All the above aircraft could be fitted with bombs)

Before reading the extracts from squadron diaries or squadron histories the following points may be of interest:

1. The squadron adjutant generally maintained squadron diaries in the days before squadron operational record books. There is great variety in the way these diaries were kept, some recounting events after they had taken place, others maintaining them on an almost daily basis, while others often left gaps. The texts have been taken from microfilms held in the National Archives, Kew, and have only been edited in minor ways, e.g. when the sense of what is being reported is lost through grammatical errors. Where the author has felt the need to clarify what is being reported his comments are in square brackets.

2. In some cases there are large gaps in the records or they were not kept or are not traceable, as in the case of No. 60 Squadron, where records in the National Archives start in 1935. No. 60 Squadron's history has been used instead, and is the most complete record in this chapter.

3. The details maintained vary enormously. Some units kept detailed records of operations, while others, such as No. 47 Squadron, placed operational records in separate appendices. As many personnel movements, promotions and honours, etc. as possible have been included, but where there are months of only routine administration to report these have been passed over. The aim has been to provide a wide and detailed picture of activity during the 1920s for squadrons employed on air-control operations, but for the sake of completeness, all squadrons that were stationed abroad during the period 1919–29 have been included, whether or not they were so employed.

4. Among items of particular interest one may note the months of UK leave granted to officers serving abroad, the deaths due to flying accidents and sickness, the training of RAF personnel on camel riding, the fact that officers flew, no matter what their specialist responsibility on the squadron, and the paraphernalia carried aboard the aircraft so that emergency repairs could be carried out if a forced landing took place.

5. Area maps, large and small scale, are provided so that the reader may locate places mentioned in the texts.

6. The different aircraft types with which squadrons were equipped during the 1920s are shown alongside the appropriate squadron crests.

No. 1 Squadron
In Omnibus princeps (First in all things)

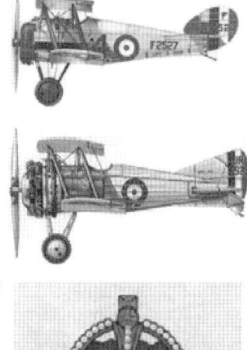

This squadron was only briefly employed on air-control operations. It served with distinction during the First World War and was re-formed at Risalpur, India, on 21 January 1920, equipped with Sopwith Snipes, but there was no requirement for fighters in India in the 1920s since no air opposition was expected or materialized. Having moved to Bangalore on 11 May 1920, the squadron moved again to Hinaidi in Mesopotamia on 20 April 1921. The squadron did see brief operational service while in Iraq when the Snipes were detached to Sulaimania. Together with No. 30 Squadron's Ninaks, the Snipes were successful in dispersing

the forces of the self-proclaimed 'King of Kurdistan', Sheikh Mahmud, in June 1926 after tribal villages had been infiltrated by his men. To prevent a recurrence of trouble, No. 1 Squadron's Snipes were left at Sulaimania until the squadron's disbandment. It was in Iraq that Nos 1 and 8 Squadrons were chosen to undertake service trials, under tropical conditions, with the Nighthawk fighter, and since there was no requirement here, either, for fighters, the unit disbanded on 1 November 1926 on completion of the trials, to re-form with the Siskin fighter at RAF Tangmere in February 1927.

No. 3 Squadron
Tertius primus erit (The third shall be first)

No. 3 Squadron also did not operate as a fighter squadron during its short time in India. Having served in the First World War, the unit was disbanded at Uxbridge on 27 October 1919 and was re-

established at Ambala, India, on 21 January 1920. But since air opposition was neither expected nor experienced, after a short spell at Bangalore the squadron returned to Ambala on 1 April 1920 where it was disbanded on 30 September 1921. The squadron re-formed at RAF Leuchars, Scotland, on 1 October 1921, equipped with three-seater DH9As.

No. 5 Squadron
Frangas non Flectas (Thou mayest break but shall not bend me)

In April 1920 the squadron was under canvas at Miranshah. Equipped with Bristol Fighters, the unit, under the command of Squadron Leader P.C. Maltby DSO, AFC, was part of No. 3 (Indian) Wing. In May 1924 No. 5 Squadron then became known as No. 5 (Army Cooperation) Squadron. The total hours flown between April 1924 and March 1925 were 2,995.

1924

Squadron Move On 31 December 1923 Squadron Leader A.J. Capel arrived to take command of the squadron, which was then based at Ambala and came directly under HQ RAF India. During January and February, A Flight was deployed to Futwa and C Flight to Dhana, and then, on 10 March, the squadron was moved to Dardoni in Waziristan to take over from No. 31 Squadron, which moved to Ambala. Squadron ground personnel moved by troop train and the aircraft all arrived safely at the new base. No. 5 Squadron then came under No. 1 (Indian) Wing.

Operations Fortnightly patrols were instituted to ensure that the forts of Wana and Tenai were not falling into disrepair, together with the reconnaissance of tribal areas where trouble might be expected and the carriage of Army and political officers. On 16 May orders were given to search for the gang involved in murdering police officers at Manjhi, and searches were carried out to the south and south-west of Jandola. No gangs were spotted but the terrain offered great scope for anyone wanting to take cover. Between 25 and 28 May operations were carried out against the Abdur Rahman Khel tribe in the Spli Toi valley. Twenty-two raids were carried out using 20 lb bombs and Baby incendiaries. Targets were mostly small encampments and a few towers, but the area was plentifully supplied with caves to which tribesmen could go during RAF raids. When it was reported on 28 May that tribal sections were on the move towards Afghanistan, it was evident that they were undertaking their annual summer migration.

Between 26 and 31 July 1924, No. 5 Squadron, plus a flight from No. 28 Squadron at Peshawar and one flight each from Nos 27 and 60 Squadrons at Risalpur, came under the command of Wing Commander A.A. Walser MC, DFC. The targets allotted consisted of two areas, one in the Zairian Alghed, north of Piazhe, where there were two small villages, both with towers, and the other was a single Arab Kot near the mouth of the Shaktu river, where it flowed into the Bannu Plain. Raids were carried out between the 26th and 31st, thirty-eight raids being carried out by No. 5 Squadron alone, using 112 lb bombs. On the 27th a very bad storm hindered operations and few pilots got through to their objectives. However, all returned safely from operations that day. On the morning of 28 July, the last formation of the first series of raids were over Zadrana when very thick clouds came up suddenly, stretching from ground level to a great height and accompanied by a thunderstorm, with extremely bumpy conditions. The last three machines were caught over the target, and in attempting a turn all three crashed. Two of them were 28 Squadron machines and the four occupants were all killed, two near Razmak aerodrome and two near Duncan's Piquet on Razmak Marai, through flying into the ground. The third machine was flown by Squadron Leader Capel and LAC Bell of 5 Squadron. After getting out of control in clouds, they came down in a narrow dip in the hills near the Sham Plain and just got out of the clouds in time to get the aircraft under control, landing on a patch of ground, but the aircraft turned over, without injuring the occupants. A section of the Wazirs captured both pilot and passenger at once, and after much haggling with many of the Arap's followers of the Mahsud's tribe, who quickly arrived on the scene, Squadron Leader Capel was handed over to them. LAC Bell was returned via Razmak by the Wazirs on the morning of the next day. Squadron leader Capel was kept as a prisoner of the Arap until the 31st, when they decided to accept the terms of the political authorities and returned Squadron Leader Capel under escort to Soraragh. In spite of the bombing continuing until 31 July, Squadron Leader Capel had been well treated by his captors.

On 1 November 1924 the Air Officer Commanding, Sir Edward Ellington, inspected the squadron at Dardoni. Flight Lieutenant A.F. Quinlan, who had recently joined the squadron, was killed in a flying accident on that day. His passenger, LAC Jones, escaped with only a shaking and minor injuries. No. 5 Squadron went on to win the Waziristan British Football Cup open to all units in the military district serving at Dardoni during 1924. By the end of the year No. 5 Squadron had flown 2,615 hours 40 minutes.

1925

In January the squadron received orders to evacuate Dardoni, which was to be given up as a military and air force station, to move to Kohat, where new buildings and quarters had been erected for one squadron. Again operations were in the Spli Toi valley against the Mahsuds. The squadron moved up to Tank for operations, thereafter under the command of Wing Commander R.C.M. Pink CBE. The tribesmen would take to the caves when under air attack and missions were made against those villages that offered the best targets, the Ninaks dropping 230 lb and 112 lb bombs and the Bristols dropping 112 lb bombs, 20 lb Cooper bombs and Baby incendiaries. At first machine-guns were used as well, but later, restrictions were imposed as to height, and the discontinuance of low flying made the use of machine-guns of little effect. After the phase of intensive bombing, which had imposed considerable strain on personnel, machines and engines, a system of air blockades was next used. Pilots usually worked in pairs, being distributed at uncertain times of the day over the whole area in order to keep the tribesmen in a continual state of apprehension. Night-flying by a flight of No. 31 Squadron, operating from Tank, did further increase the strain. However, the continued bombing had so interrupted the normal economic life of the tribes that they gave up and agreed to the political terms.

On 5 October No. 5 Squadron received orders to proceed to Risalpur to join No. 2 (Indian) Wing. The move-around of the squadrons on the frontier was due to the new policy that Nos 1 and 2 (Indian) Wings should each have an Army Cooperation squadron and a bombing squadron and so be self-sufficient for their minor operations. Until then No. 1 Wing had been the Army Cooperation Wing, and No. 2 Wing the Bombing Wing. No. 2 Wing was at this time commanded by Wing Commander Pink. However, shortly after the arrival of No. 5 Squadron he handed the wing over to Wing Commander W.C. Hicks AFC. The work of the squadron at Risalpur consisted of much more real Army cooperation than had been undertaken during the previous eighteen months, and the squadron was working directly with the following units:

1. First Cavalry Brigade at Risalpur
2. Nowshere Infantry Brigade
3. HQ Rawalpindi District
4. Abbotabad Infantry Brigade
5. Rawalpindi Infantry Brigade
6. Jhelum Infantry Brigade

1926

In the hot weather of 1926 it was decided to try a new scheme, to send one flight from each Army Cooperation squadron at Ambala, Risalpur and Peshawar to Quetta for two months at a time, complete with personnel, instead of closing down the flights and sending the personnel to the RAF Hill Depot, which for the first time was located at Lower Tope, Darian now having been given up. In pursuance of this policy, C Flight went to Quetta on 1 April, the aeroplanes going by air via Fort Sandeman, and the remainder of the personnel by train. At the end of May, they returned and A Flight took their place for the next two months. This scheme of rotating the men had the following disadvantages:

1. The risk of sending parties of men through the Sind Desert during the worst of the hot weather.
2. The difficulty of the officers getting any leave when the flights were kept at work continuously throughout the twelve months of the year.
3. The fact that the airmen got no rest throughout the year from their actual work on aeroplanes and engines, and the consequent risk of their going stale.

Headquarters personnel of the squadrons went to the Hill Depot as before. This only accounted for a small proportion of the squadron, as the flight for Quetta was made up to full working strength by the attachment of various headquarters personnel, such as photographers, armourers, W/T personnel, etc. During June, C Flight, on return from Quetta, was stationed at Miranshah, as the station was now permanently occupied by a detached flight taken in turns from each of the four squadrons in the North-West Frontier Province. In addition to its normal training, this flight carried out cooperation with troops stationed in Waziristan, and carried out the Wana and Tanai patrols fortnightly. This scheme also had the advantage of teaching all pilots, in turn, the job of being in Waziristan, which could be the most useful in the event of operations in that district.

October 1926 The squadrons now working in cooperation with the Army in artillery shoots.

During 1926 No. 5 Squadron flew 3,149 hours 5 minutes.

1927
March 1927 In March 1927 the Peshawar Royal Air Force Sports Week was resuscitated, and No. 5 Squadron took part, winning the Football Cup and the Officers' Boxing Cup. This was the last time that this Sports Week was held, and in 1927 it was decided not to hold it owing to the Royal Air Force Display at Delhi taking place at approximately the same time as the Sports Week would have been held. Subsequently Headquarters decided that Sports Week should not be held again. Operations against the Lashkar tribe early in 1927 were successful since a considerable number of casualties were caused among that tribe. For the first time in the squadron, wireless telephony was used at three practice camps. Although little practical work was

accomplished, an enormous number of lessons were learned. Practical experience was gained both in the use of R/T Tender and the Pack Set and the many difficulties to be overcome, causes of failure, best method of moving over bad country, speed over the ground that could be expected and so on. Both the tender, the ordinary Crossley, and the pack set were largely experimental, and numerous minor adjustments and alterations were made from time to time, and by the end of the season most of the faults seemed to have been located and were on their way to being rectified. [The apparent contradiction in the above passage taken from the squadron ORB concerning the lack of accomplishment of practical work must relate to the use of the wireless sets in actually communicating – not practical work with the sets in the vehicles and practical use of the vehicles.]

Atlas trials During 1927 the Armstrong Whitworth Atlas, with a supercharged Jaguar engine, was received in the squadron for erection and subsequent test as a suitable machine for Army cooperation work with the Army in India. Flying began on this machine in April 1928, and various tests of climb, speed, take-offs and landing runs and climbs with load were carried out, when it was found that in the hot weather the Jaguar engine got too hot; the oil temperature rose quickly above the maximum allowed and it was impossible to get the machine up into the cooler altitudes quickly enough to avoid a long period at too hot a temperature, nor was it possible to fly the machine for any length of time at low altitudes as the oil temperature stayed too high. In August the two non-supercharged engines that had been flown in the Siskins were received back in the squadron, and after the various modifications necessary for fitting these engines to the Atlas had been carried out one was fitted and tests were resumed, the non-supercharged engines standing up to the heat successfully.

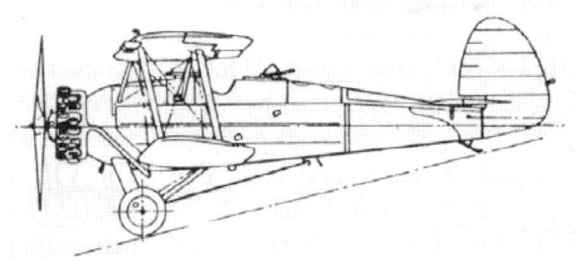

The Atlas

1928
Change of Command Command of the squadron changed from Squadron Leader Capel to Squadron Leader Bryson MC, DFC, AM. The roll of officers and

A rare picture of No. 5 Squadron with her sister squadrons Nos. 20, 28 and 39 at Peshawar at the end of the 1920s.

other ranks who were killed or had died during service with No. 5 Squadron between 1 January 1924 and 1 November 1928 were, in date order:

285000 AC.1 McManus – died 8 June 1924 – drowned while bathing

Flight Lieutenant A.F. Quinlan – died 1 November 1924 – killed in a flying accident

327725 AC.1 Sutcliffe H – died 5 October 1925 – natural causes

Flying Officer E.L.W.H. Alms – died 1 March 1926 – accidentally killed

Flying Officer C.C. Harris – died 6 July 1926 – killed while flying

330954 LAC Avery C.R. – died 6 July 1926 – killed while flying

344719 AC.1 Jones P – died 22 September 1926 – drowned as a result of a flying accident

362519 AC.1 Bumpstead E.H. – died 17 July 1927 – natural causes

During the same period there were mentions and honours:

Squadron Leader Capel – DFC , DSO and Mentioned in Dispatches
Flight Lieutenant Somerville – AFC

NORTH WEST FRONTIER OPERATIONS – GENERAL REFERENCE MAP

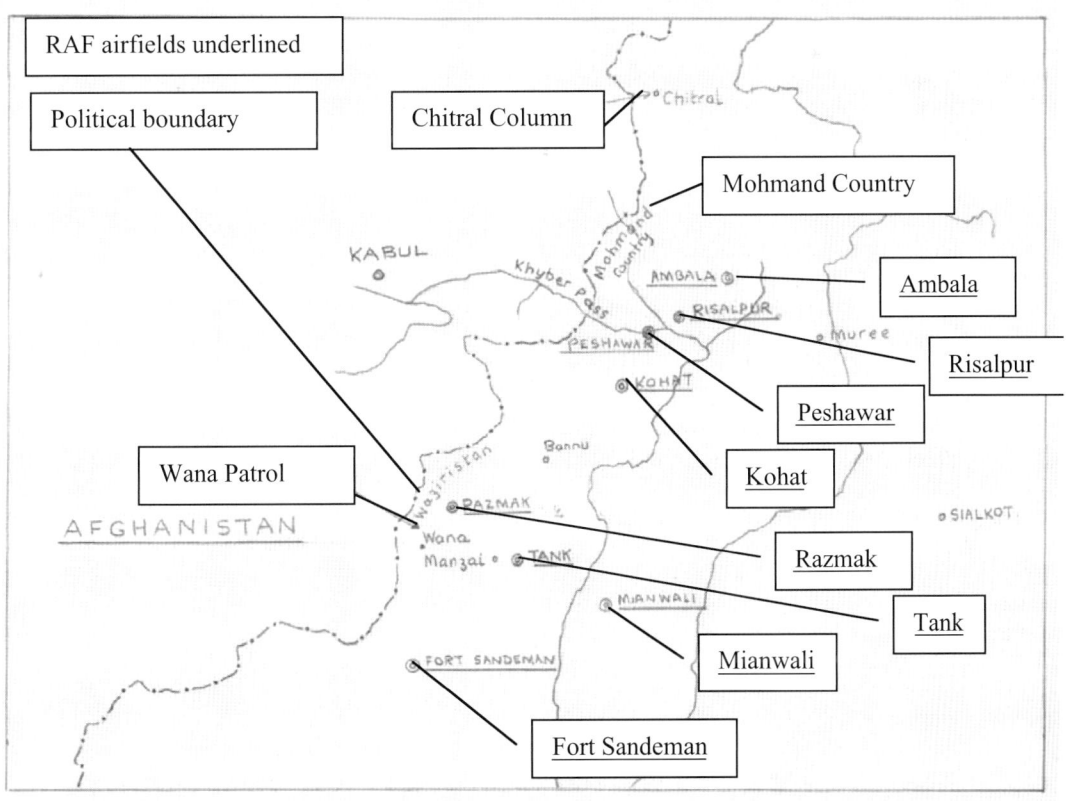

Flight Lieutenant Haslam – MC , DFC and Mentioned in Dispatches
Flying Officer R.W.M. Hall – Mentioned in Dispatches
Corporal Small – Mentioned in Dispatches
Corporal Robins – DFM
LAC Wright – AFM

The squadron, less C Flight, departed Quetta on 15 December 1928 to carry out cooperation with Northern Command.

No. 6 Squadron
Oculi exercitus (The eyes of the Army)

The extracts from the history of No. 6 Squadron have been chosen because they give an insight into the role of the unit and take a retrospective view of the year 1928. The source for this material may be found in AIR27/78 at the National Archives.

1924
September This month saw the squadron again in action when several punitive bombing and machine-gun attacks were made on tribesmen and Turkish regulars who were attempting to cross the frontier into Iraq. Several of the squadron personnel were injured in these operations by machine-gun peppered bullets. Lord Thompson, the Secretary of State for Air, made a visit to the squadron on the 28th and personally congratulated Flight Lieutenant Roberts MC, DCM on his action when the Turks first crossed the frontier. He expressed his great appreciation for the services of all ranks concerned in these operations.

1925
February No. 6 Squadron had the distinction of flying five members of the League of Nations Commission on the Turko-Iraqi border on a reconnaissance of that border. On the 14th Colonel Commandant H. Dobbin DSO, commanding the Mosul garrison, paid a ceremonial visit to the squadron and invested Sergeant Dicks, squadron armament sergeant, with the DFM, earned for gallant and distinguished service in the air while employed as an aerial gunner and observer during operations in Kurdistan between October 1922 and August 1923.

April During operations against recalcitrant tribesmen at Mir-Khan, one machine was observed flying too low at

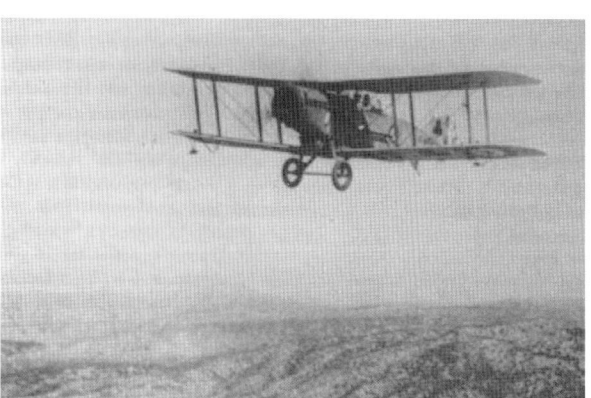

A Bristol Fighter of No. 6 Squadron over Iraq in the early 1920s.

the target. The pilot, Flying Officer Pontifex, dropped his first bomb, which fell in the middle of the village. Immediately afterwards petrol was seen streaming from the machine. This was followed by a burst of flames and the machine took a sudden turn and spun into the ground enveloped in flames. The death of the two occupants, Flying Officer Pontifex and AC2 Barber, must have been instantaneous. A personal message of condolence was received from the Secretary of State for Air, Sir Samuel Hoare, expressing his grief on hearing of the casualties.

1926/7
The routine orders for No. 6 Squadron for the two years 1926/7 consisted of frontier and police post reconnaissances, armed demonstration flights over affected territory and cooperation with armoured cars and Iraq Levies in addition to the normal training programme of a bombing squadron.

1928
[The squadron records contain an appendix, which is a report on several aspects of the squadron's work for the year and is reproduced below.]

1. *The Role of the Squadron* The role of the squadron at the beginning of 1928 remained the same, that is to provide air forces in support of military operations in Northern Iraq and to undertake duties, within the capacity of its aircraft, of independent air control. The primary necessity for the fulfilment of this role is that flying personnel be trained to the standard required in the following items:

   a. Knowledge of all landing grounds in the locality.
   b. Knowledge of engines and aircraft and behaviour of both under various seasonal conditions.
   c. Attainment of the standard of skill in air firing, bombing, picking up of messages, flying by compass, airmanship and Army cooperation.

To this end the majority of flying is carried out in connection with training flying personnel both as laid down in the annual training syllabus for this type of squadron and to fit the personnel for possible operations. For the latter purpose regular frontier patrols are flown each week throughout the year. Whenever practicable, cooperation exercises are arranged with the local military forces. The squadron also carries out considerable communication duties, transport of personnel, pay, mail and stores and is responsible for the production of any aerial photography required within the area of Northern Iraq.

2. *Organization* Mosul station is organized as a self-contained unit within its own wired perimeter, being equipped with every requisite department and carrying stocks of stores and commissariat for six months. The OC No. 6 Squadron also fills the appointment of Station Commander and has disciplinary control over No. 5 Armoured Car Section and the Mosul RAF Supply Depot, both units being stationed within the station perimeter and for all other purposes coming under the Armoured Car Wing, Hinaidi, and the Assistant Director of Supply and Transport (A D of S & T), Hinaidi, respectively. Owing to its isolated position, that is 100 miles from a railhead at Baiji, the squadron establishment is augmented as regards MT vehicles and drivers, workshop fitters and wireless personnel. Within the squadron area are situated four petrol dumps at Zakho, Arbil and Shergat landing grounds for the aircraft and the armoured cars and at Ain Gazelle Police Post for armoured cars only. The supplies are maintained by A D of S & T upon request of the squadron. The petrol dump was withdrawn from Zakho during the spring. Wireless outstations are maintained by the Squadron at Diana and Billeh for Iraqi Levy camps at these places. The Iraqi Army camps at Arbil have recently [beginning of 1928] been withdrawn, at Zakho during the late spring and Bebadi during the summer. The area is divided into three sectors by the Tigris north of Mosul and a line from Mosul to Amadia and a line from Mosul to Diana, being renamed the 'desert', 'eastern' and 'western'; one flight's base and landing ground being maintained in each sector which are as follows:

a. Desert (B Flight)   – A Class – Shergat and Arbil
                        – B Class – Quaiyara, Tel-awailat and Tel-as-shor
b. Eastern (A Flight) – A Class – Diana, Billeh, Mosul
                        – B Class – Khaniuthman and Batas
c. Western (C Flight) – A Class – Zakho
                        – B Class – Semmel, Faish Khabur, Aqra and Bebadi

Sectors are allocated to flights for a monthly period and the flight concerned carries out all that is required within its sector for that month. One day each week is allocated to each flight for night-flying and endeavour is made to give each pilot a night flight each month.

Officer/Personnel retrospect for 1928
On 10 January Squadron Leader C.H. Keith was posted from No. 70 Squadron to command and took over from Flight Lieutenant J.S.T. Ford DSC, DFC, who was acting CO in the absence of Squadron Leader G.C.M. Lowe MC, DFC. Flight Lieutenant Ford left Mosul on leave to England pending posting on 23 January. At this time the Flight Commanders were:

A Flight – Flight Lieutenant P.J. Clayson MC, DFC
B Flight – Flying Officer C.F. Steventon
C Flight – Flight Lieutenant G.S. Oddie DFC, AFC

On 9 March Flight Lieutenant G.H. Russell DFC was posted in and took over B Flight, Flight Lieutenant Steventon proceeding to England pending posting. On 9 April Flight Lieutenant Clayson was invalided to England and, thereupon, Flight Lieutenant C.H.L. Evans took over command of A Flight for the rest of the year. Flying Officer F.C. Farrington MC was station adjutant but proceeded on leave to England pending posting on 13 August, having been promoted on 1 July. He was relieved by Flying Officer F.S. Hodder who had joined the squadron for flying duties from No. 13 Squadron on 30 March. On 9 July Flight Lieutenant W.E.G. Mann DFC proceeded on leave to England pending posting, and he was relieved as Signals Officer by Flying Officer M.C.W.C. Flint MC posted from No. 30 Squadron with effect from 23 July. Flying Officer F.C. Chalmers, Accountant Officer, was posted to the UK and left on 7 November, being relieved by Flying Officer R.T. Carter posted from Armoured car Wing. Flying Officer Chalmers was promoted on 1 July.

Flying in Retrospect
During the year a total of 3,800 hours was carried out, made up as follows:

Operations – 522 hours
Transport – 1,664 hours
Training – 1,490 hours
Flying practice – 124 hours

Establishment of workshops – Capacity to service 24 engines per annum + 6 engines supplied from the depot at Hinaidi.

This budgets for 300 hours' flying per month irrespective of premature engine failures or early replacements due to crashes. During the year nine aircraft were returned to Depot time expired for a rebuild, and three were returned struck-off after damage in crashes for rebuilds. Eighteen newly rebuilt aircraft were received from the Depot. No aircraft were built within the squadron. On 28 March the IE establishment was increased to thirteen by one Bristol Fighter for photographic duties. This was allocated to B Flight to be under Flight Lieutenant Russell, which qualified him for the letters Ph, temporarily filling the post of photographic officer. The average serviceability of aircraft throughout the year was 12.1 (93%).

The following crashes occurred throughout the year:

1. 9 January – Flying Officer Fisher and Lieutenant Haserick – both killed – machine and engine written off. [This means written off the stock ledger, which records all equipment held.]
2. 27 February – Flight Lieutenant Perry-Keene and LAC Organ – both injured.
3. 9 March – Flying Officer Evans with AC Fitch – neither injured – machine a write-off.
4. 25 April – Flying Officer Parkin – no passenger – uninjured – machine a write-off.
5. 8 June – Sergeant Garner and Sergeant Futcher – both killed – machine and engine a write-off.
6. 4 July – Flying Officer Kay and LAC Bolton – both died of injuries – machine and engine a write-off.
7. 27 August – Squadron Leader Keith and Lieutenant Gibbs – neither injured- repaired at Billeh.
8. 26 November – Flight Lieutenant Russell and Flying Officer Anderson – neither injured – aircraft in for repairs.
9. 27 December – Flying Officer Anderson and AC Collins – neither injured – depot for repairs. [Assuming these last two crashes involved the same officer, he certainly was accident prone, but happily remained unhurt.]

Training in Retrospect

Training was carried out as laid down for an Army Cooperation Squadron in AP [Air Publication] 874. Advantage of the necessity of sending a party to Ba'aj to collect a crash was taken to establish an air firing practice camp at this place. The camp operated from 5 to 7 March, all pilots and air gunners firing at standard 10 ft × 10 ft targets. Early in the year negotiations started for the establishment of a permanent air firing and bombing range near the aerodrome. This was finally completed and brought into use on 18 June.

1929

March On 22nd Squadron Leader Keith with Flying Officer McWeeney made a non-stop flight from Hinaidi to Shaibah.

October Sir Aurel Stein, the world-famous archaeologist of the Indian Government, was taken over the Western Desert to search for Roman ruins and was

landed at Parthan in the city of Hatra. This was Sir Aurel's first experience of flying. Major Harman, US Army Air Corps, was flown on a reconnaissance over the eastern frontier by Squadron Leader Keith. Sir Gilbert Clayton KCB, High Commissioner for Iraq, was flown along the north-western frontier and landed at Tele Rumellan to inspect the areas of recent tribal disturbances with the French. On 28th the squadron moved to Ismailia. The move was made without incident and the following telegram was received from the Chief of the Air Staff:

I have heard from the AOC Iraq that No. 6 Squadron's move to Moascar was most successful. Will you please congratulate OC No. 6 Squadron and all ranks on the most successful move and say that it will be of great value to the Air Force as a whole. I hope that, in due course, I shall get a report from the Officer Commanding.

From this date the squadron ceased to operate as an Army Cooperation squadron. The three flights of No. 6 Squadron were detached to Ramleh under Squadron Leader Keith for operations during the Palestine emergency. They carried out regular reconnaissances and cooperated with the Palestine Police and with the Transjordan Frontier Force during the disturbances.

No. 8 Squadron
Uspiam et passim (Everywhere unbounded)

ADEN 1927
March On 16 March a general reconnaissance was carried out to see if there is any trouble – one fire was burning in a village and a look-out was made to see if there were any ground stripes laid out by ground forces. Squadron Leader McClaughly was leading the formation on 18 March and left Khormaksar at 07.05 hrs. On this occasion a signal stripe was seen laid out by the lake. The aircraft glided down and dropped a message bag by the lake containing a message from Major Fowle. Squadron Leader McClaughly had used W/T on this flight which had worked satisfactorily. On 19 March

again went to reconnoitre Sheikh Abdullah. Everything quiet and normal. No ground stripes observed.

Interestingly as they passed over Shukara several people were observed walking about the town but took to shelter when machines passed over at low altitude. Two tents observed just outside the town in a north-east direction but no ground stripes or smoke signals observed. The rest of March seems quite uneventful, patrolling from Khormaksar, particularly Sheikh Abdullah. On 30 March a formation led by Squadron Leader McClaughly left Khormaksar and one machine was forced to land in the desert at 10.00 hrs between Jmonis and Lahej and a second machine landed alongside it. This was standard practice and both machines landed intact back at Khormaksar at 10.30 hrs.

September   In September Squadron Leader McClaughly says that dropped messages were observed to be read by the natives and no one appeared to be firing at them.

October   On 6 October Squadron Leader McClaughly notes that Zeidis had just evacuated a village which had just been reoccupied by Protectorate tribesmen. On 7 October Flying Officer Knox had just force-landed his aircraft and certain stores were dropped to him. A car with a new engine had reached him and the work on changing the engine was in progress.

1928
May   On 22 May, on a bombing run to Qataba four 230 lb bombs were dropped. One 230 lb bomb hit the walls

of a barracks about 1,000 yards north-west of the town. Three 122 lb bombs were dropped at Qataba and one container of BIB [Incendiary]. These bombs nearly all fell a little short and brought firing activity on the part of the enemy in the town, the barracks and the surrounding country. The camera vertical on one aeroplane was hit by a bullet, the wing of another and third machine was hit. They returned to Khormaksar at 15.05 hrs.

June/July   It is June 1928 and the bombing of Qataba is still going on. In July the attacks are on the barracks at Taiz and between 15.30 and 16.30 hrs on 9 July the objective was the Zeidi garrisons in the villages in Qataba, when the formation had to turn back through poor visibility. On a raid on 13 July the objectives were Qataba and Nadira – 112 lb bombs were dropped on Qataba before aircraft proceeded to Nadira in which there were only three men. The Fort at Dhali was machine-gunned in which there were four people. 100 rounds were fired then the gun jammed. Slight enemy fire was observed.

August   Through August the objective seemed to be Awabil.

1929
February   On 3 February the establishment and strength of the unit was:

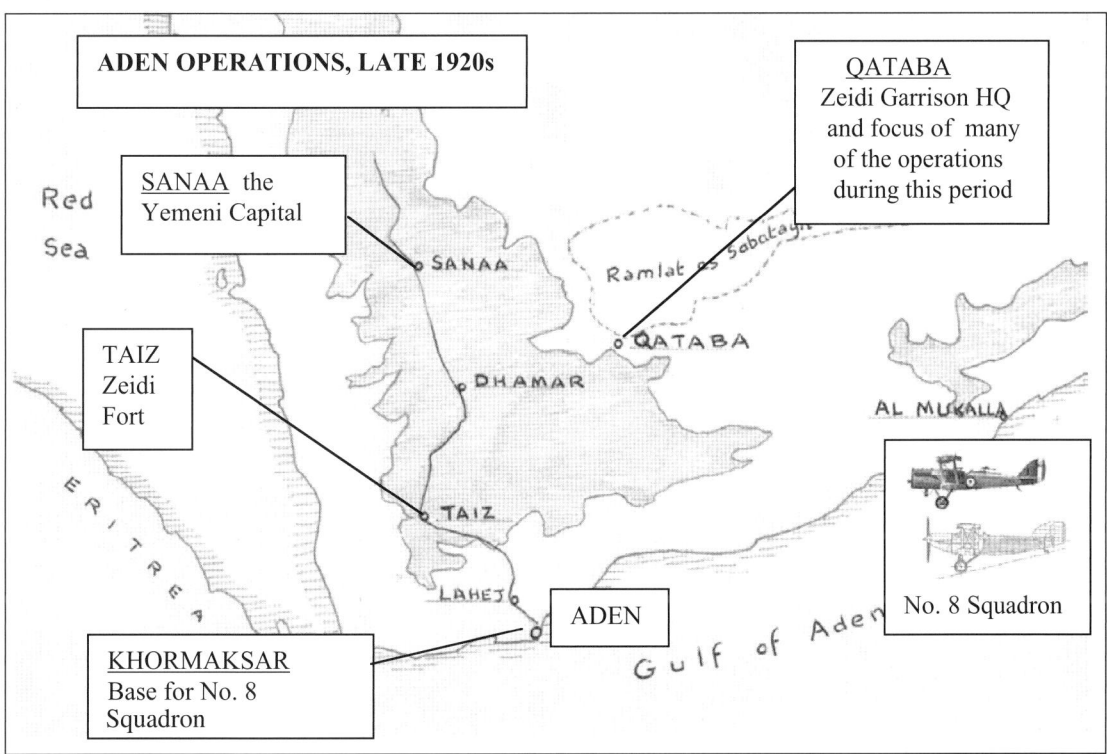

Establishment of Pilots Officers 14   *Strength* 10
SNCOs 6   2
Establishment of Air Gunners and Special Duty
12 Airmen   *Strength* 10
Establishment of Aircraft 12   Strength 10 serviceable
2 U/S [unserviceable]

March   On 5 March legitimate targets were bombed at Amtawar and two direct hits were obtained but aircraft failed to fire the objectives with incendiaries. Machine-gunned Wali Tukar and inflicted casualties on cattle. Cattle were economic targets. Certainly throughout this period the number of officers and airmen available were pretty good considering the climatic conditions. On 7 March 12 officers were on establishment of which 9 were available. For airmen 3 out of 6 were available. Confirmation of Orders bestowed on members of the squadron for operations in Aden in 1928 were:

Flight Lieutenant A. Maxwell-Richards – an OBE
Flying Officer(Now Flight Lieutenant) George Norman Patrick Stringer – a DFC
Corporal Berber – a DFM
Several Mentioned in Dispatches

The pilots had continuously to look out for forced-landing sites for their aircraft, and some of these potential ones were visited by officers travelling by vehicle.

A line-up of No. 8 Squadron DH9As at Hinaidi, c. 1925, before moving to Aden.

No. 11 Squadron

Ociores acrioresque aquilis
(Swifter and keener than eagles)

1928

December   The   squadron
sailed from Southampton in HMD *Nevassa*.

1929

January   On 22nd arrived at Risalpur. The squadron strength consisted of the following officers and 65 airmen:

Officer Commanding	– Squadron Leader P.H. Cummings DFC
OC A Flight	– Flight Lieutenant F.G. Robinson
OC B Flight	– Flight Lieutenant B. Ankers DCM
OC C Flight	– Flight Lieutenant B.W.T. Hare
Armament Officer	– Flying Officer P.W. Lowe-Holmes
Photographic Officer	– Flying Officer L.S.T. Brown
Air Pilotage Officer	– Flying Officer W.L. Freebody
Signals Officer	– Flying Officer H. Broadhurst
Workshops Officers	– Pilot Officer M.G. Bircham
	– Pilot Officer F.G. Ferrier
	– Pilot Officer R.W.A Stroud

29 January – Pilot Officer Bircham remained in Karachi to superintend the assembly of aircraft. The following airmen pilots also included in the squadron strength were Sergeants G.W.T. Thomas, E. Mayne, D. Grout, R. Jarred and O.C. Clarke.

February   On 6th, Squadron Leader Cummings and Flying Officer Brown proceeded to Karachi by rail and flew the first two Wapitis back to Risalpur.

March   On the 8th, Flying Officer Stroud (promoted) to Karachi to relieve Pilot Officer Bircham of his duties at the Aircraft Park. On 13th, Pilot Officer P.G.J. Atkinson posted to the squadron from No. 4 Flying Training School as wastage establishment.

April   By the 1st the squadron had received its full complement of machines and individual training programme was started. On 8th Flying Officer Stroud returned to Risalpur on completion of his duties at Karachi. On 22nd Flying Officer Freebody and Sergeant Clarke proceeded to Belgaum on a Gas course, returning on 12th May.

June   At Muree, Flight Lieutenant Ankers attended the Northern Command Intelligence Course and passed out with distinction.

July   On 26th at Lower Topa, Squadron Leader Cummings is appointed to command the RAF Hill Depot until the end of the last Hill party.

October   Flying Officer Bircham transferred to the Reserve with effect from 3/10/29 to fulfil a civilian appointment. On 13th, Flight Lieutenant Ankers is posted to No. 2 (Indian) Wing for photographic duties.

December   On 30th C Flight is to take over detached flight duties at Miranshah under command of Flight Lieutenant Hare. The flight will consist of four machines. The pilots proceeding with the flight are Flying Officers Lowe-Holmes and Stroud and Sergeants Mayne and Clarke.

No. 14 Squadron
I spread my wings and keep my promise

1919
October   In October 1919 it is interesting to note the changes in ranks, e.g. Lieutenant Grant-Doulton resumed command of the squadron on 7 October and on 6 January 1920 was relieved by Wing Commander C.S. Burnett CB, DSO.

1920
January to March   The formation was known at this time as 'Arbitive Almagamated Headquarters', but in March 1920 it was redesignated 'The Palestine Group'. On 20 March Wing Commander Burnett vacated that command on proceeding to Iraq and Wing Commander Grant-Doulton again took over the formation.

April   In April the squadron was commanded by Squadron Leader W.L. Welsh. The aircraft in Palestine, which were Bristol Fighters, were engaged in minor operations against the Arabs. On 23 April a goods' train was held up and fired on by a large party of Arabs between Semakhand and Jasir Mejamie. These Arabs were engaged that evening and the next morning by Indian cavalry. But at 07.30 hrs on the morning of 24 April the Arabs attacked in great strength. They were

subjected to concentrated machine-gun fire and bombing attacks of aircraft and were eventually dispersed. In the words of the War Office report of the affray, 'The RAF were largely responsible for the withdrawal of the enemy.' The casualties consisted of seven British and Indian wounded while the Arab losses were estimated at 200 killed and wounded. The pilot of one of the aircraft was wounded and forced to land.

November   There was a further change in command in 1920 when, on 26 November, Group Captain M.J.D. Board assumed command of the group.

1921
Spring   In the spring of 1921 martial law had to be proclaimed in Jaffa. A labour meeting was disturbed by a group of Jewish Communists. The latter were driven back into the Jewish/Muslim quarters of the town and riots broke out. Aircraft also assisted the police by dispersing crowds through low flying. Casualties during the disturbances numbered 85 dead and 350 wounded. Meanwhile in early 1921 the sphere of air control was extended to Transjordan.

Air control in Transjordan   In the middle of April it was decided that operations in Transjordan were to be an Air Force responsibility, but their future action was to have the approval of the High Commissioner for Palestine; it being understood that offensive action required by the Emir Abdullah would not be undertaken without the sanction of the High Commissioner and approval by the Air Ministry. When Emir Abdullah required help in 1921, with the trouble in Palestine, four cars and three tenders were supposed to be put at the disposal of the RAF under Wing Commander G.R. Carmichael, but they were not forthcoming and so No. 14 (Bomber) Squadron had to undertake operations alone, but these nevertheless had the desired effect.

December   On 1 December Squadron Leader J.S.D Bradley took over No. 14 (Bomber) Squadron.

1922
Changes in the command structure in the Middle East   There was a change of command of the Palestine Group in 1922. On 1 January Group Captain R.P.F.M. Fellowes DSO assumed command, and on 1 April reorganization took place in the Middle East Command. An RAF command was established in Transjordan with an HQ at Amman under the command of Group Captain R. Gordon CB, CMG, DSO, with the control of RAF units in Palestine. The Palestine Group HQ became the Palestine Wing HQ under the command of Wing Commander G.I. Carmichael DSO, AFC. On 19 July Palestine Wing HQ closed down at Ismailia and reopened on 25 July at Bir Saku. The Palestine Wing was transferred from the

control of the Air Officer Commanding RAF Middle East to the control of the General Officer Commanding Palestine and Transjordan. The former continued to be responsible for the maintenance of personnel, technical equipment and stores for the Palestine Wing, but for all other purposes the wing was under the administrative control of the GOC.

September   On 21 September Squadron Leader W.H. Dolphin assumed command of No. 14 (Bomber) Squadron.

November   When trouble was imminent in the autumn of 1922, the GOC Palestine visited Amman by air to see the situation for himself, and on the 15th agreed that if operations became necessary the RAF should cooperate with the Arab Legion. This was when relations between the government of Transjordan and the Sultan Adwhan had become very very strained. It got to almost breaking point, and an ultimatum was put from the Emir to the Sultan stating that he must come to Amman by 09.00 hrs on 17 November, failing which all forces, RAF and Arab Legion, would be employed against him. RAF action succeeded in dispersing the Sultan's forces, and he and his sons escaped to Syria. The only RAF casualty during the operation was one airman slightly wounded in an armoured car section.

1924

February/April   The Palestine Wing HQ was abolished from 1 February 1924 and two months later on 1 April the military and Air Force in Palestine were placed under command of the Air Officer Commanding, Air Commodore E.L. Gerrard CMG, DSO, who was designated Air Officer Commanding Palestine Command.

June   On 6 June command of No. 14 (Bomber)Squadron changed when Squadron Leader A.N. Gallehawk assumed command from Squadron Leader Dolphin.

August   On 23 August operations were initiated against the Wahabis. The enemy forces consisted of between 4000 and 5000 men mounted on dromedaries except that about 200 were horsemen. Enemy casualties were estimated at about 500 killed, and a number of prisoners and camels were taken. The armoured cars fired some 600 rounds and a captured banner hangs in the squadron mess today.

1925

January   Reports during the period 17–29 January showed that a flight of aircraft of No. 14 Squadron cooperated with a composite force of Palestine Gendarmerie and Arab Legion in the country south-west of Beersheba. The object of the operation was threefold:

1. Reconnaissance
2. The arrest of certain definite offenders
3. A demonstration

August   The squadron was composed of three flights of DH9A aircraft:

Squadron Commander – Squadron Leader Gallehawk
Flight Commanders – Flight Lieutenants Wigglesworth DSC, Crow MC and Thornton
Flying Officers – Castaleini, Falconer, Stevens, Brickman, Anderson, Pallin, Evan-Evans, Cook, Pallon
Pilot Officers – Beattle, Moritz, Silcock and Bailey
Stores Branch Officers – Flight Lieutenant R.G. Gore and Flying Officer Charleson
Accounts Officer – Flying Officer Freeman
Medical Officer – Flight Lieutenant White

1928

January   On 1 January Squadron Leader Hopcroft is in command with Flight Lieutenants Wigglesworth and Crow still as Flight Commanders. Flight Lieutenant Cormack is the new flight commander.

The adjutant is Flying Officer Falconer and the stores officers and medical officer as before. On 21 January 14 Squadron sent three aircraft on a liaison to the French Air Force in Syria. Between 21 and 24 January the team visited Damascus, Ryak and Derra. The French returned the compliment by sending three of their aircraft, one of which crashed on landing, but the occupants were not hurt.

March   The squadron completed 630 hours of flying. On 28 March Flight Lieutenant McCormack and LAC Kimberly were killed in a DH9A on a mail flight to Ramleh. They were buried on 29 March in the British Cemetery in Ramleh.

April   During April the squadron engaged in three reconnaissances daily in northern, southern and eastern Transjordan, a precaution adopted owing to the Wahabi tribes threatening to attack the country. More credence was given to this than usual. The threat did not materialise. On 7 April at Amman the squadron was visited by the Crown Prince of Italy. The RAF provided a guard of honour and the Transjordan Frontier Force gave a display. On the 23rd twelve aircraft started out on the Lloyd Reliability Trial, but with combined engine trouble, mostly defective water jackets, six aircraft fell out before completion of the test on 26 April.

August   On the 31st Sergeant Pilot Saunders and LAC Fletcher were killed in an aeroplane accident. While taking off the aircraft stalled and hit the ground, bursting into flames. They were buried at Ramleh on 1 September.

Of interest is this BE2C. which equipped No. 14 Squadron when it first arrived in Egypt. In these earlier machines the pilot sat in the rear cockpit with the air gunner/observer in the front.

The Under-Secretary of State for Air, accompanied by Air Commodore Longmore, visited the station by Wapiti aircraft from Heliopolis, *en route* for Iraq. Sir Philip Sassoon remained for about two hours before flying on.

October   On the 31st was the first rain of the winter.

December   Personnel of the squadron on the 31st were as follows:

> Squadron Commander – Squadron Leader Hopcroft
> Flight Commanders – Flight Lieutenants Sutherland, Lester and Waite
> Squadron Adjutant – Flight Lieutenant Hurley
> Stores Officer – Flight Lieutenant Burridge
> Medical Officer – Flight Lieutenant Jenkins
>
> The squadron also had an Armament, Signals and Photographic Officer, and seven Sergeant Pilots

Cups won by the squadron between 1928 and 1929 were:

1. The Proficiency Cup
2. The Lloyd Cup for Lloyd Reliability Flying Competition
3. The Command Cup for musketry and pistol shooting
4. The Middle East Staff Cup for proficiency and bombing

1929

August   On 23 August began the operations, afterwards known as the 'Palestine Disturbances of 1929', being the outbreak of intense inter-racial fighting between the Jewish and Arab elements in Palestine, characterised by scenes of murder, looting, pillage and the burning of Jewish settlements. It was the culmination of the bitterest religious and racial feeling brought to a sudden head by occurrences at the 'Wailing Wall' in Jerusalem and the stabbing of a Jewish youth. Scenes at his funeral and the general feeling amongst the Arabs that their country, with government assistance, was being exploited for the benefit of the Jewish colonists. At this particular time of the year the Armed Forces of the Crown were so located in the usual summer dispositions as to be the least easily available to deal with any trouble in Palestine itself. The Arab movement in Palestine of course could expect support from Syria and Sinai so they had to watch out for reinforcements from those areas, and patrols were sent out and in some instances were called upon to act independently, using their guns to prevent the concentration of advance of Arab gatherings and to deal with looters caught in the act. Vickers Victorias of No. 216 Squadron brought in troops, and so aircraft of Nos 208 and 45 Squadrons were brought in to help, and aircraft from the carrier *Courageous* arrived at Jaffa from Malta. Further infantry reinforcements came in by train from Egypt and by naval vessels from Malta. RAF armoured car companies rapidly brought into Palestine from their various dispositions in Transjordan were eventually augmented by armoured cars sent from the Egyptian Command. It was in this situation that aircraft were of limited use in crowd dispersal. They could fire on looters, which they did, but this is where ground forces were more important. All the aircraft could do was to fly low overhead in the hope that if the aircraft opened fire the crowd would disperse to their homes.

September   On 1 and 2 September 1929 the squadron noted concentrations of Arabs and Arab tents which were of course a threat if they moved in to support the Arabs in Palestine, and the Green Howards had to round up some 1,000 Arabs in the Nebiyusha District.

November It was decided that No. 14 Squadron would carry out the Cape–Cairo Flight in 1930. The Fairey IIIF aircraft, by which type the flight would be undertaken, were supplied to the squadron in November in order that the pilots selected should have an opportunity of becoming acquainted with their characteristics. These pilots were Flight Lieutenant Greet, Flying Officers Hutchinson and Wayte and Sergeant Richardson. Flying Officer Gibbon of No. 216 Squadron was chosen to act as the navigator.

December Squadron Leader Soden DFC took over from Squadron Leader Hopcroft as CO. In fact Squadron Leader Soden had flown all the way from the United Kingdom in his private Moth.

No. 20 Squadron
Facta non verba (Deeds not words)

No. 20 Squadron's Operations Record Book is full of action for the first quarter of 1920. The adjutants of the various squadrons differ greatly in what they enter in the respective logs. The adjutant of 47 Squadron, for example, placed all details of operations in separate appendices. The details of action in January 1920 for No. 20 Squadron, although a little repetitive, do illustrate the amount of hostile activity that could go on for several months, i.e. there was no single punitive operation that had a clear beginning and an end when fines were paid by recalcitrant tribes on conclusion. Clearly the Mahsuds regarded air force action as one of the hazards of everyday life to be endured, and they were not backward in retaliating. Be that as it may, the records of this and other squadrons show that RAF fatalities often occurred, not directly through enemy action, but during take-off or landing or forced landing following engine failure.

1920
January On the 2nd, twelve Cooper bombs dropped. About 100 enemy observed on north slope of the hill. Eight Coopers and 100 rounds of SAA (small arms ammunition) fired at these men with good results. Reconnaissance of the area Inzartangi and Marraghzai and NNW of Kotkai. Seven Coopers and 600 rounds SAA fired at small parties of Mahsuds with good results. Four Coopers direct hits on Dutarri Kot. Four Coopers 200 yards west of Galli Kot, one 112 lb bomb plus two Coopers + 300 rounds SAA fired into Dutarri Kot and surrounding villages with 232483good results. Four Coopers – two OK on Dutarri Kot and three Coopers + 100 rounds west of Galli Kot. 50 rounds SAA fired on persons observed to be firing at machines. On 3 January reconnaissance west of Taki-Zan between Ahnai Tangi and area 2 miles NW of Kotkai. Movement normal. 8 Coopers and 200 rounds SAA fired into nullahs – good results. On the 4th at Bannu 8 Coopers + 400 rounds SAA scoring direct hits on villages. Aircraft heavily fired on. A further 8 Coopers, six direct hits on village line of piquets one mile north of Kotkai. 8 Coopers in nullahs in

advance of line to assist in covering withdrawal. Fired at from caves near Ziriwan, twelve tribesmen seen. 8 Coopers, one direct hit on cave. 150 rounds SAA fired into caves. Covered retirement of our troops from Sandy Ridge to Kotkai. No enemy observed. 8 Coopers dropped, 3 dud no enemy movement observed. Our troops retiring rapidly to Kotkai. 7 Coopers dropped in nullahs on tribesmen. 1 Cooper in Inzai Tangi river one half mile west of Kotkai. 8 Coopers and 600 rounds of SAA on hills and river bed between Zariwan and Kotkai. About 100 enemy observed in river bed and on hill, some were holding a sangar [defensible earthwork]. Machine heavily fired on. Parties of tribes observed in caves, 8 Coopers and 350 rounds SAA fired on caves to good effect in vicinity 2 miles north of Kotkai. Troops to withdraw to Tank Zan – no enemy movement observed. 8 Coopers and 250 rounds of SAA fired on dugouts and nullahs while troops withdraw.

The rest of January is very much of the same intensity of operations. On the 27th fired on heavily while escorting the Chief Commissioner 4 miles north of Khajuri. 7 Coopers dropped on enemy. On the 28th 16 Coopers dropped and 1,000 rounds SAA fired on enemy dugouts. Machine heavily fired on.

March Parties of enemy were bombed and fired on. Machine was fired at and bombs dropped in a number of areas. On the 5th machine fired at and bullet went through tailplane. On the 8th machine again heavily fired at from village in vicinity of Land-Sar. 8 Coopers dropped. Villages in area displayed white flags but machine occasionally fired on. On the 10th observed that new building was in progress at Makin. Machine fired at by men with catapults.

Throughout 1920 these operations continued.

1921
January On the 19th, Flying Officers Irving-Bell and Smythe left Tank at 09.00 hours to fly to Wana with mails and stores. Last seen flying over Wana at about 6,000 feet in a WNW direction at 09.45 hours. No further news of whereabouts or fate of occupants or machine. On the 23rd, Flying Officers Kiddament and Kirby left in response to a call to carry out a reconnaissance north of Sarwekai. Engine cut out dead when two and a half miles north of Sarwekai and machine crashed in river bed. Pilot and observer OK. 1st and 4th Gurkhas guarded machine and held off parties of tribesmen totalling about 100. Instruments, etc. stolen during the night.

March/April Bombing raids were carried out in the general area.

1922
March On the 3rd, machines numbers BF 1548 flown by Flight Lieutenant Fox and BF 2442 flown by Flying

Officer Buckley collided in mid-air over Atari. Both machines were totally wrecked and all occupants killed. Sergeant Hemmings and Aircraftman Richardson were passengers. Flying Officer Ware in BF5058 flew back to Lahore to report crash.

April On the 7th, J6594 crashed at about 09.10 hours near Kach. Pilot and observer, Flying Officer Loch and Flying Officer Stringer, were both killed. Cause of crash unknown.

August On the 29th, practices releasing pigeons from machines in flight. Four birds released successfully. All birds returned.

September As above on the 11th. On the 16th pigeons released at various heights and distances. Those from 8 miles and released at ten feet returned to loft safely.

October On the 24th the squadron moved to Quetta to do some training. Training was carried out until the end of the year.

1923
August On the 26th the following personnel and machines were detached to Fort Sandeman:

D8039 Pilots: Flight Lieutenant Chamberlaine; Observer AC Stevens
Flying Officer Usher-Somers; Observer AC Goodwin*
* second aircraft unspecified. All personnel returned from Fort Sandeman same day.

1924
January On the 25th Aircraft D8039 crashed. Flying Officer Jacques slightly injured. LAC Stevens killed. [Note: This is the same Bristol Fighter mentioned above. The deceased airman had been this aircraft's observer in August and had been promoted LAC before his death.]

There are no records for the period 25 January 1924 to 3 June 1927

1925
January On the 5th the squadron moved to Peshawar.

1927
June The commencement of the Mohmand War. The circumstances of the squadron are:

Aircraft – Establishment: 15 Serviceable: 8
                                              Unserviceable: 4
Pilots – Establishment: 22   Available: 10
Gunners – Establishment: 12 Available: 5

Note: The aircraft establishment included dual and 2 reserve.

The unit was stationed at Peshawar under the command of Flight Lieutenant F.H. Lawrence and equipped with Bristol Fighters. The small number of pilots and air gunners is accounted for by the fact that:

1. The war took place in midsummer and the hot-weather programme was in force. [This would mean some men at the Hill Depot, Lower Topa.]
2. A certain number of officers were on leave, one in the UK.
3. One officer was on a course in Muree.
4. Two officers and airmen were returning and ferrying machines to and from Karachi.
   [The detailed orders for the units involved in the Mohmand war may be found in Appendix K.]

On the 6th, orders were received from No. 1 (India) Wing that two aeroplanes were to stand by ready to carry out a reconnaissance at half an hour's notice from 08.00 to 10.30 hrs. Orders were received that Shabkadar could be evacuated at any time convenient after 12.00 hrs. Flying Officer Booth left for Shabkadar with two heavy tenders at 11.30 hrs to withdraw the remainder of 20 Squadron stores. Shabkadar was evacuated at 16.00 hrs, arriving back at Peshawar at 18.00 hrs. A congratulatory signal was received from AOC RAF Simla at 11.00 hrs.

A narrative for the operations carried out on 6 June 1927 An extract from the war diary of No. 20 Squadron:
Five aircraft (FH1428, F4908, FH6893, J6621 and H1601) armed with 8 × 20 lb bombs and rear guns with four pans of SAA left Peshawar for Shabkadar at 05.15 hrs. Four aircraft landed at Shabkadar at 05.40 hrs, aircraft H1601 having to return to Peshawar owing to oil pressure trouble. This trouble was rectified and the aeroplane left for Shabkadar at 08.55 hrs, arriving there at 09.25 hrs. Three of these aircraft returned to Peshawar at 12.30 hrs without carrying out any active operations. Flying Officer Smith's aircraft was found to have developed an internal water leak and had to be left at Shabkadar. Four aircraft left Peshawar at 18.00 hrs to carry out an offensive bombing reconnaissance over the area: Hafiz Kor, Karappa, Kandao and Halki Pandiali. This raid was carried out in conjunction with No. 5 Squadron. The flight arrived over the target at 18.20 hrs. Flying Officer Pilling observed a party of men approximately 30 strong in the vicinity of Hafiz Kor and dropped 6 × 20 lb bombs on them. The results obtained could not be observed. Flight Lieutenant Paynter, Flight Lieutenant Spittle and Pilot Officer Smith dropped no bombs as they saw no favourable targets. The flight then returned to Peshawar and landed at 19.30 hrs. A convoy consisting of one light tender and two heavy tenders left Peshawar for Shabkadar at 05.15 hrs carrying 3 NCOs and 7 Airmen and the following stores:

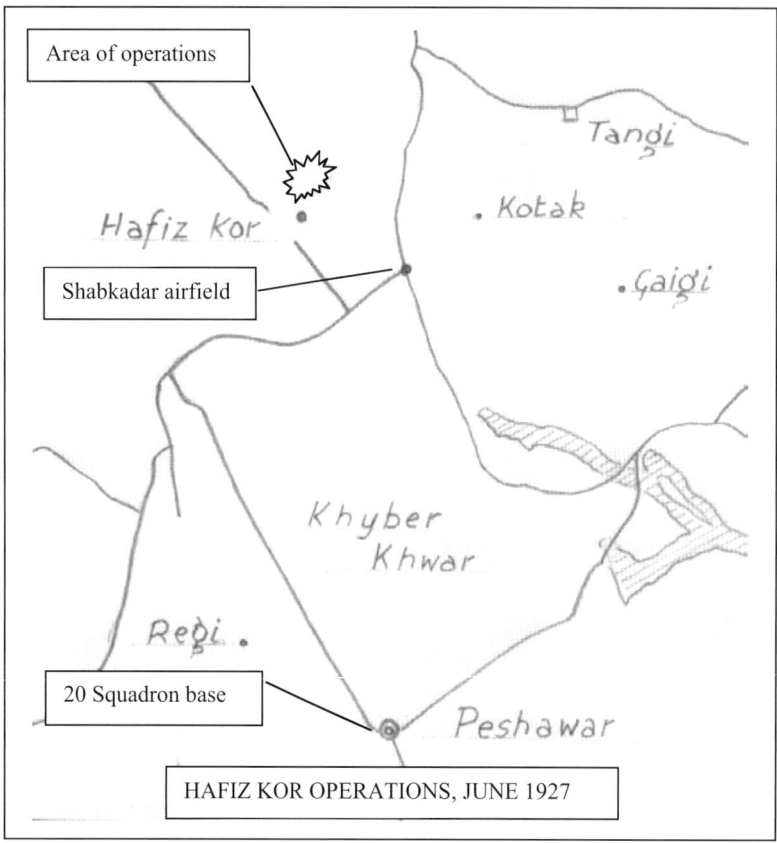

Area of operations

Shabkadar airfield

20 Squadron base

HAFIZ KOR OPERATIONS, JUNE 1927

(map labels: Tandi, Kotak, Hafiz Kor, Gaigi, Khyber Khwar, Regi, Peshawar)

200 × 20 lb bombs 20 spare detonators 2,000 rounds
of SAA

150 gallons   1 day's rations for
aviation petrol   15 airmen
10 gallons of oil Flight spares

As the flight did not remain at Shabkadar, the convoy returned to Peshawar at 14.10 hrs. Pilot Officer Smith and one fitter returned with the convoy.

On the 7th Flying Officer King-Lewis and Corporal Walstow took off at 18.40 hrs and landed at 20.00 hrs This was one of a formation of two aircraft on a bombing raid and reconnaissance in an area Matta Mughal Khel, Laghan, Karappa, Kandao to Hafiz Kor. 2 × 20 lb bombs

A full line-up of 20 Squadron's 'Brisfits' in 1929.

were dropped in the nullah two miles NW of Matta Mughal Khel. Two drums of SAA fired in this area. Three bombs dropped and one drum of SAA fired in nullah three miles west of Matta Mughal Khel. One bomb dropped and one drum fired at fire in river bed one mile NW of Hafiz Kor. Returned to Peshawar. On the 8th J6650 was flown by Flying Officer Smith with LAC Clarke as air gunner/observer. 05.05 hrs take-off. 07.00 hrs time down. Three grass huts, 30 goats and 12 cattle observed. 2 × 20 lb bombs dropped which fell a few yards from the goats which were driven by about ten men towards the nullah. About fifteen to twenty men were then observed to enter the nullah and two bombs were dropped, one fell in the nullah and one on the edge. Four more bombs were dropped, three fell in the nullah and one 300 yards away. No further activity seen and aircraft returned to Peshawar. On the 10th the casualties inflicted on the Mohmands are being collected and sifted by Intelligence. Last night the Political Officer stated that 40 were definitely killed and further reports will tend to increase this figure. Report that night raids by No. 5 Squadron were successful, six men being killed by one bomb. The results were far in excess of expectations. Jehads [holy wars] in Mohmand country will be an unpopular form of amusement. [This squadron adjutant displays some wit.]

[No further records were maintained for the 1920s.]

No. 27 Squadron
Quam celerrime ad astra
(With all speed to the stars)

1924
January On the 24th at 08.00 hrs a special flight was made to collect Major Erskine of the Tochi Scouts. One machine on flight to Dardoni returned Risalpur after duty. On the 29th at 14.35 hrs Flying Officer Hugh-Jones was carrying out practice landings after a recent posting to the squadron. His machine crashed and burst into flames. He was

killed and his passenger, Corporal Hall, was slightly injured.

February   On the 21st a special flight flying the Miang-Gul of Swat over his country. Route taken was Risalpur–Mardan–Hustan–Nawaga–Daggar–Kababsorran–Chaksar–Jmbele–Khwaji–Kila–Khoro–Thujee–east bank of Swat river–Manglaor–Manaora–Saida–Thanu–Chakdara–Malakand–Mardan–Risalpur. Total distance covered 25 miles!!!!! [This was a grand tour in a pocket-sized country!]

March   On the 28th a special reconnaissance of the frontier for Air Vice-Marshal Sir Edward Ellington. Aircraft escorted by a wireless machine.

April   On the 7th a special flight conveyed the Judge Advocate-General from Rawalpindi to Risalpur. Return flight after. Also special flight to Chitral.

May   Dardoni on the 21st – demonstration flight of four machines. Movement observed of personnel and cattle in the area Ahmadwan and Kariguram. On the 22nd survey made of area – bombing, villages and a number of houses off prepared map. Vertical photography – 27 plates exposed of Dre-Deped and Walna – machines fired at from some villages. On the 24th demonstration flight over Ahmadwan, a height of 7,000 feet being maintained. Reconnaissance report handed to OC Y Force stationed at Dardoni. On the 25th demonstration flight of four machines over Ahmadwan and Spli-Toi areas. Sketch maps made by pilots. No movements observed from the hostile area which had been raided by No. 5 Squadron.

May/June   Through rest of May and June similar routine activities continued.

July   Risalpur and Dardoni – photographic surveys carried out. On the 26th a bomb raid of three machines on objective Zadraka village – six 230 lb bombs dropped as follows: one 50 yards NE of village, one on outbuildings on edge of village, one near graveyard in village and two in graveyard. Weather very overcast. Clouds at 7,000 feet. Bombing raids continued. Weather remained overcast. On the 27th raid at 17.40 hrs, overcast and thick cloud between 5,000 and 8,000 feet. On the 28th bomb raid – three machines – three dropped OK on village, two 20 yards from tower inside village, one failed to explode. Bomb raids continued on that day. Three machines with objective Arap Kot – five 230 lb bombs dropped, one in compound, one failed to explode, two fifty yards to the east of the target, one hit wall of village and one bomb failed to release. Weather now fine. On the 29th operational flight Dardoni to Tank had to return owing to Tank aerodrome being unserviceable due to heavy rain.

September   On the 24th Risalpur – cooperation with the Chitral relief column – one machine, WT carried, mails dropped on column.

1925
March   On the 9th bomb raids at 09.50 hrs, 10.15 hrs, 10.30 hrs, 12.40 hrs, 12.55 hrs and 13.10 hrs, all involving between four and six 230 lb bombs being dropped in the Spli Toi area. [The ORB then records only the bombs dropped on the 17th, 18th, 20th and 21st.]

April   [ORB only records bombs dropped on the raids throughout the month.]

August   On the 15th two machines went on bomb raid at 16.10 hrs but mission not accomplished due to one machine being unable to climb to 500 feet and returned to aerodrome. Machine due for Depot overhaul.

December   On the 22nd long-distance flight Risalpur to Calcutta with three machines. Formation all told was six machines, the other three coming from No. 60 Squadron at Kohat.

1927
October   On the 5th at 09.55 hrs experimental flight with the Atlas (Army Cooperation aircraft). After erection engine OK – rigging – swinging slightly to the right,

The 'Flying Elephants' – the officers of No. 27 Sqn in the later 1920s. Back row – ?; Martin; Butcher; Mangles; ? ; McKee; Seated: Fressanges; Brodie; Sqn. Ldr L.M. Bailey AFC (OC); Prendergast; ?

otherwise OK. On the 7th and 11th experimental flights continued. All done prior to taking on a full war load, finishing with a practice landing on the 12th. All at Risalpur. On the 13th at Miranshar – active operations with the Razmak and Daghai columns. Pinpointed positions of columns. Messages dropped to both columns and DHQs Manzai. Reconnaissance of Nillkuch and Sheranni with one machine. Active operations with the Razmak and Daghai columns on the 14th, 16th and 17th. Operations with the Manzai and Razmak columns on the 19th and to the end of the month. On the 21st the Atlas crashed on take-off due to engine cutting out.

December The 6th to 17th, escorts to tour of HM King of Afghanistan.

1928
January Demonstration flights and active operations with the Wana Patrol. [This adjutant's writing is extremely small and the diary is exceedingly difficult to read.]

September On the 9th at 10.15 hrs. Active operations with Chitral Column. Liaison with column and dropping messages throughout the entire month. On the 21st a machine crashed while diving to drop mail. Very strong down current in valley at the time of the accident. The machine was burned after all the equipment had been salvaged. Engine and other equipment returned by pack mule to Risalpur.

October On the 9th active operations with the Chitral Relief Column. Also taking photographs and dropping messages. At Risalpur on the 11th the Under-Secretary of State for Air visited all stations on the North-West Frontier in order to ascertain the use of aircraft as a sole administrator. Aircraft returned to Risalpur.

November Northern Command manoeuvres using formations of three machines and taking photographs. Ditto December.

December On the 18th at Kohat. Reconnaissance over Kabul. One machine locating force-landed machine and a message panel was dropped on the British Legation at Kabul. On the 22nd a further reconnaissance over Kabul. All-clear signal displayed at legation. On the 23rd a reconnaissance over Kabul during evacuation of women and children. One machine landed at Jeheppur aerodrome, Kabul. On the 24th evacuation of women and children. On the 25th stand-by for evacuation duties. On the 29th returned to operations with the Wana patrol.

1929
January to May Active operations, reconnaissance and demonstrations. On 17 May active operations with one

machine – vertical exposures of tribal territory. Exposures made of Marmora range and Goganai Village.

June On the 29th demonstration flight with six machines of 27 Squadron and six machines of 60 Squadron carried out over Strakel owing to unrest being exported in that district. [This would have been a considerable show of force.] Vertical photography exposed in this area for future reference. W/T was carried and constant communications established.

September On the 19th at Miranshah. Reconnaissance with two machines over northern Waziristan. This was carried out as a gathering had been reported between Tochi and Central Waziristan Road as far as Razina. No movements were observed. W/T was carried and communications established both ways.

No. 28 Squadron
Quicquid agas age (Whatsoever you may do, do)

1920
June On the 7th Nos 28 and 31 Squadrons ceased to come under the command of HQ RAF India, and were placed under HQ 4th Wing at Ambala, under Wing Commander C.L. Courtney CBE, DSO.

July On the 10th the 4th Wing became No. 2 (Indian) Wing.

October On the 25th HQ RAF India was moved from Simla to a permanent location at Ambala.

1923
April On the 19th a letter received by the squadron commander said:

Will you please convey to the Officers of No. 28 Squadron the very grateful thanks of the 9th Brigade for the excellent work done by them in connection with the Wana operations. We attribute our immunity from attack largely to the work of the RAF. The enemy were still there all right on several occasions but the work of the machines was so good they decided not to show themselves.

1924
January/February No. 28 Squadron flew 262 hours in January and 150 hours in February. In all these times the

aircrews were cooperating with various regiments in Army cooperation. Indeed they took part in a tactical exercise with 131st Indian Cavalry Brigade.

March/April/May The flying hours for each month respectively were 197,183 and 156.

May On the 19th support was given to No. 5 Squadron in the Spli Toi operation and in the Zadrana Alghed areas.

July On the 26th there were fatal accidents. Six aircraft of Nos 28 & 5 Squadrons ran into fog during operations. Flying Officer I.P. Anderson and AC1 K.H. Taylor of No. 28 Squadron crashed on landing at Razmak and were killed. Flying Officer Bell of No. 28 Squadron crashed at Duncan's Piquet and was killed. His passenger AC1 Slack died from his injuries on the 30th. Squadron Leader Capel and his passenger of No. 5 Squadron landed in enemy territory and were taken prisoner. One other aircraft of No. 5 Squadron also crashed. Typical of flying operations at this time showed 17 × 112 lb bombs dropped, 69 × 20 lb bombs dropped and 440 incendiaries. Total flying time for the month – 48 hours 45 minutes.

August On the 4th another fatal accident. Flying Officer D.M. Murphy crashed at Peshawar owing to engine failure and died from multiple injuries. He was flying solo. [The Diary entries end in 1926. There was no trace of any records for the period 1926–31.]

No. 30 Squadron
Ventre a terre (All out)

1926
November On the 5th of the month the squadron was commanded by Squadron Leader F.H. Coleman. Initial equipment was DH9 aircraft. Ten aircraft were located with the forward detachment at Kirkuk, and two aircraft were at Hinaidi with the Base Section. The aircraft at Kirkuk were cooperating with two columns, Gocol and

Bencol [codenames of military columns], which were shepherding the Jaf migratory tribes during their annual return to Iraq to take up their winter quarters. On the 27th the aircraft at Kirkuk carried out further cooperation with Paicol, which left Sulaimania to assist in bringing the areas on the right bank of the Tiala southwest of Qaradagh under administrative control.

December On the 7th Gocol, Bencol and Paicol have all returned to Sulaimania and air cooperation with these columns therefore ceased. Six of the ten aircraft at Kirkuk returned to Hinaidi, making the squadron organization – two flights + HQ at Hinaidi. One flight comprising forward detachment at Kirkuk.

31 December – Hours flown during 1926 – 3,767 hrs
            Present % serviceability of aircraft in 1926
            – 87.2%
            No. of pilots effective – 14.9 (average)

1927
April Squadron organization was amended ready to commence operations as follows:

Hinaidi – Base Section with stores, Accounts Section, workshops and reserve aircraft.
Kirkuk – Squadron Headquarters and two Flights.
Sulaimania – A detachment of four aircraft with necessary ancillary, medical and sanitary services under Flight Lieutenant R. Harrison DFC.

On the 22nd operations were commenced, consisting of operations with columns, bombing of villages and pursuit of marauding bands of recalcitrant tribesmen.

May Operations officially terminated. Note: these operations have been dealt with in C051 Ops connected with the operations in Penjwin. The following awards were subsequently made to squadron personnel:

Squadron Leader Coleman DSO – Mentioned in Dispatches (MID)
Flight Lieutenant Harrison DFC   – MID
Sergeant Pilot Newman   – MID
Corporal Reeves   – MID
Corporal Beauchamp   – Military Medal

June On the 26th Sulaimania was evacuated by the squadron detachment, the flight moving to Kirkuk.

July On the 23rd Squadron Leader F.H. Coleman left on leave to the UK and the squadron was commanded in his absence by Flight Lieutenant K. Harrison DFC.

October On the 27th evacuated Kirkuk and returned to join its Base Section at Hinaidi. This marked the first occasion in the history of this squadron when it had been located in its entirety on the same station. On the 29th Squadron Leader Coleman returned to resume command.

December The Accounts Section was absorbed into the newly formed Station Accounts Hinaidi. On the 31st the following figures were given for the year 1927:

Hours flown during the year   – 4,158
Percentage serviceability   – 81.7%
Number of Pilots effective in 1927 – 15.1

1928
January On the 7th Squadron Leader H.P. Hale DSO, DFC took over command of the Squadron. On the 9th Flight Lieutenant Harrison, Flight Lieutenant Barlow and Flying Officer Riggs were attached to AKFORCE.

February One flight under command Flying Officer Garvie also attached to AKFORCE.

March On the 28th the above-mentioned officers and Flying Officer Garvie's flight returned from detachment to AKFORCE.

April On 2nd one Flight under Flight Lieutenant Harrison DFC left for Shaibah on attachment to AKFORCE. One aircraft force landed and one aircraft crashed near Hillah. Pilot Officer J. W. Wood and the passenger (LAC Waugh??) were both killed. The Flight was reinforced by two further aircraft from Hinaidi.

July On the 15th three aircraft left for Egypt to collect the AOC. On the 21st these three aircraft returned with the AOC.

December Hours flown in 1928   – 4,766
Percentage serviceability – 82.3%
Number of pilots effective – 13.7

The squadron was awarded the Sassoon Bombing Cup, being the squadron which had carried out its bombing most effectively.

1929
January On the 7th one flight left for Kerbala for operations in the Western Desert.

February On the 16th one flight left for Nukhaib on Western Desert operations.

March On the 22nd one flight left for Rutbah to assist the civil authorities to settle the dispute between the Rowalah and the Amarat sections of the Anaizah Confederation of tribes. On the 25th the flight returned from Rutbah.

April On the 12th flight returned from Nukhaib. Between Western Desert operations numerous reconnaissances were carried out, photographs taken and surveys made. On the 19th the squadron received its first Wapiti MkIIA aircraft, the type with which the squadron was to be re-equipped. On the 25th Flight Lieutenant P. Murgatroyd flew the AOC to Egypt in a Fairey IIIF, returning on the 27th!!!

June On the 5th and 6th was the annual AOC's inspection. On the 29th two Wapitis escorted three visiting French Potez aircraft to Shaibah. One Wapiti escorting French aircraft crashed at Loqait. The pilot, Flight Lieutenant Halliday, was killed.

September On the 15th the equipment of the squadron with Wapiti Mk IIAs was complete. Four aircraft with Wing Commander J.A.G. De Courcey MC as Senior RAF Officer carried out a liaison tour of Syria.

October From the 7th to the 12th the AOC and two aircraft carried out a liaison tour of French air stations in Syria. On the 23rd Squadron Leader H.P. Hale DSO, DFC took over command of RAF Station Mosul, vice Squadron Leader C.H. Keith. On the 25th the squadron completed the move to Mosul.

December The squadron performance figures for the year 1929 are given as:

Airfields of Iraq.

Hours flown   – 5,429
Percentage serviceability   – 91.6%
Number of pilots effective   – 13.9

Loading a stretcher into a Vickers Vernon ambulance in the Middle East during the 1920s.

No. 31 Squadron

In caelum indicum primus (First into Indian skies)

There is no record prior to 3 September 1928

1928

September Quetta – 3 September 11.45 hours. A composite flight of the squadron proceeded to Bostan to cooperate with the 14th Field Brigade RA [Royal Artillery] and the 2nd Mounted Brigade under the command of Flight Lieutenant Akerman. The following officers composed the flight:

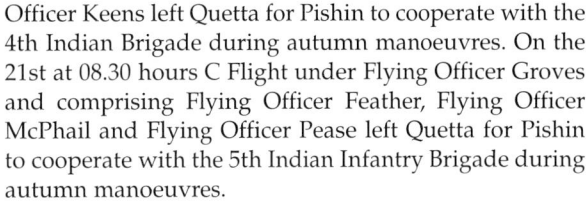

Flying Officer Opie
Flying Officer McPhail
Flying Officer Nancarrow
Flying Officer Hughes.

Twelve shoots were carried out, 10 of which were successful and 2 unsuccessful owing to W/T failure. The flight returned to Quetta at 10.00 hours on the 9th. On the 11th Flight Lieutenant Nicolls RAFMS and Flight Lieutenant Cross returned to the squadron after a year at the Aircraft Depot. On the 14th at 10.30 hours A Flight under Flying Officer Roberts and comprising Flying Officer Ommanrey, Flying Officer Hughes and Flying

Officer Keens left Quetta for Pishin to cooperate with the 4th Indian Brigade during autumn manoeuvres. On the 21st at 08.30 hours C Flight under Flying Officer Groves and comprising Flying Officer Feather, Flying Officer McPhail and Flying Officer Pease left Quetta for Pishin to cooperate with the 5th Indian Infantry Brigade during autumn manoeuvres.

October On the 1st Flight Lieutenant Akerman and Flying Officer Holmes proceeded to Fort Sandeman in cooperation with the Royal Artillery. On the 2nd Wing Commander Patison arrived at Quetta to settle the training programme for the coming year. On the 3rd Flight Lieutenant C.G. Lucas left the squadron on posting to Home Establishment following medical recommendation. On the 5th B Flight returned from Fort Sandeman after successful cooperation. Squadron Leader Gordon was back in command of the squadron on the return of Wing Commander Archer [Squadron Leader Gordon had been acting wing commander]. Flight Lieutenant Stevens from HQ RAF India visited the station and remained until the 9th. On the 10th Flight Lieutenant Strudwick again assumed command of the squadron when Squadron Leader Gordon proceeded to England on leave until March 1929. On the 11th Flying Officer Roberts brought A Flight back from Pishin. He received his order at 07.00 hours to move his detachment immediately and in 50 minutes was on the move. In 1 hour 23 minutes his aircraft were on Quetta aerodrome. On the 9th Flying Officer Nancarrow left the squadron for Home Establishment on medical recommendation. On the 10th Flying Officer K.S. Blacke was promoted to flight lieutenant. Flight Lieutenant Strudwick proceeded to Pishin to command C Flight for the Divisional Exercises and Western Command manoeuvres. Flight Lieutenant Akerman assumed command of a composite Flight A and B, this composite flight operating from Quetta. On the 22nd Sir Philip Sassoon, the Under-Secretary of State for Air, visited Quetta and remained for one night. He was accompanied by Air Commodore Longmore and Group Captain Mills and was flown from Peshawar in a Handley Page Hinaidi piloted by Flight Lieutenant Anderson. On the 23rd the whole party departed at 07.30 hours *en route* for Karachi. Two escorting DH9As were flown by Squadron Leader Bailey and Flight Lieutenant Fressanges of No. 27 Squadron. On the 24th Flight Lieutenant Akerman and Flight Lieutenant Blacke proceeded to Surab by air, then to Wadh and returned on the 25th.

1929

January On the 7th Flying Officer Keens admitted to British Military Hospital with typhoid fever. Flight Lieutenants Strudwick and Opie proceeded to Karachi on a General Court Martial (as members).

February   On the 21st flying was carried out for the first time since the 5th due to the airfield only just being made serviceable after heavy rain and snow. Flight Lieutenant Opie returned from a tactical ride and court martial duty at Karachi.

April   On the 10th five Wapiti aeroplanes arrived from No. 39 Squadron piloted by Squadron Leader De Crespigny, one flying officer and three NCO pilots. Duty air pilotage and W/T aeroplanes left for Risalpur on the 12th, the same day that Flight Lieutenant Opie married. On the 13th Flight Lieutenant Opie was posted to the UK on a long engineering course at Henlow. He took his bride with him. On the 29th Flying Officer Pease was admitted to British Military Hospital, Quetta, and Flying Officer Keens was discharged to be attached to the RAF Hill Depot, Lower Topa, for convalescence. He was evacuated to Rawalpindi by air.

June/July   [This was entirely devoted to administrative matters, e.g. admissions to hospital, leave, etc. There were no references to training.] On the 26th July Flying Officer Merrett was granted 158 days leave and proceeded to England.

August   On the 2nd Flying Officer Groves was posted to No. 27 Squadron. On the 12th Flight Lieutenant D.F. Anderson DFC of No. 2 (India) Wing carried out extensive experiments with parachute-dropping apparatus to find out effective height and rate of fall.

September   On the 30th Flight Lieutenant Akerman and Flying Officer Ommanrey conveyed mails from Quetta to Karachi by air owing to floods in the Sind Desert causing cessation of rail traffic.

October   On the 1st the above-mentioned officers returned, carrying mails from Karachi. Letter of appreciation received form postal authorities. On the 24th the squadron returned to Quetta after cooperation exercises with 2nd Indian Division. On the 29th Squadron Leader Gordon had again to take command of No. 3 (India) Wing, vice Wing Commander Archer. Flight Lieutenant Akerman assumed command of the squadron.

November/December   [The remainder of the year is taken up with pure administrative routine.]

No. 39 Squadron
Die noctuque
(By day and night)

No. 39 Squadron did not arrive in India until January 1929, the Squadron's aircraft not arriving until March.

No. 39 was to remain in India throughout the 1930s, and features mainly in Volume II. During 1929 the squadron spent most of its time settling in.

Risalpur   The cantonment of Risalpur lay some twenty-five miles east of Peshawar in the North-West-Frontier Province. Risalpur means literally 'Place of Cavalry', and was indeed home to the 15th/19th Hussars and the 21st Indian Lancers. Sometimes the cavalry officers would complain to the aircrews that the aeroplanes frightened the horses, but on the whole Army/RAF relations were good. No. 39 Squadron was part of No. 2 (Indian) Wing and shared Risalpur with No. 11 (B) Squadron. The accommodation was pre-Indian-Mutiny bungalows, and electrically driven 'punkahs' provided the cooling in the hot dry summers, though these were not needed in the winter, when the temperature fell to around 45 deg F and the men changed from khaki drill to RAF blue uniform. The dry conditions were not good for airfield operations, and a special grass was imported from Australia, which had to be watered by pumping from the Kabul river. Diverting water to the polo pitch once a week also helped inter-service relations.

Training in 1929   With twelve Wapitis on strength the aircraft were allocated four each to A, B and C Flights. The squadron commander was Squadron Leader De Crespigny, who was particularly keen on good formation flying. He had a spare aircraft to take pictures of his pilots in formation, and would have the photographs rushed to him after landing so that he could use them for debriefing the pilots. Financial constraints were imposed on the RAF in India, and the Indian government placed limits on the amount of fuel and spares purchased. This obliged unit commanders to include as many exercises as possible in one training session, and a typical sortie could include a height test with full war load, mosaic photography, wireless training, navigational and meteorological flight. This could result in some unexpected and one might say amusing outcomes. Remember, the aircraft were carrying a full war load, and the squadron records tell of a Sergeant Pilot Whitwell and AC1 Roe (armourer/air gunner) who began their sortie with a meteorological flight. This involved Roe keeping an aneroid barometer strapped to his knees to note the pressure in millibars during ascent and descent every 1,000 feet. Meanwhile a thermometer that read the ambient temperature was strapped to one of the wing struts and this could only be read from the cockpit by raising a magnifying glass over the face of the thermometer so that Roe could read the

A 39 Squadron formation of Wapitis. Squadron Leader De Crespigny had a spare aircraft fly around the formation taking photographs for a squadron debrief.

scale. This, believe it or not, was achieved by a system of cords from the cockpit. At 15,000 feet the photographic part of the sortie began by covering an area around the Khyber Pass. By the time the photography had been completed, both crewmen were so cold that they agreed to descend as rapidly as possible, and the quickest way down for a Wapiti was to spin it. This Whitwell did, forgetting that the two 230 lb bombs under the wings would hinder spin recovery. He could not release the bombs, since they were wired to prevent accidental release, and so he was stuck with them. Fortunately for both men, Whitwell recovered the aircraft at 1,000 feet, and they agreed to keep 'mum'. The aircraft riggers nevertheless suspected something amiss when they had to re-rig the entire aircraft.

Operations Owing to the arrival in India of No. 39 Squadron so late in the decade, its exploits are more closely followed in Volume II. However, two missions carried out in 1929 are of interest because of their unusual nature. One was a mercy flight from Risalpur to Bangkok carrying drugs needed to save the life of the heir to the Siamese throne. Squadron Leader De Crespigny and Sergeant Lockhead undertook this flight on 24 July 1929, but after a night stop at Ambala a message was received to the effect that the drugs were no longer required. Also in that year, all the frontier squadrons, including No. 39, were involved in a mercy

mission following flooding of villages in the Peshawar basin. Medical equipment, food and blankets were dropped to isolated villages. Supply dropping, like so many other techniques used in air operations and training at this time, were in the early stages of development. The station Parachute Officer at Risalpur, Flight Lieutenant D.F. Anderson, devised a way of dropping these supplies so that they would not be damaged on impact. Sacks of corn were suspended from the bomb carriers with a static line parachute attached to the sacks, which were stiffened with battens. A static line is attached to an aircraft so that when a person or container falls from that aircraft the parachute is opened as the line reaches its extremity. A weak link is sufficient to develop the canopy before the link is broken. The squadron was not to engage in its first active air-control operations until May 1930, and these continued throughout the decade. They are described in Volume II.

No. 45 Squadron
Per ardua surgo (Through difficulties I arise)

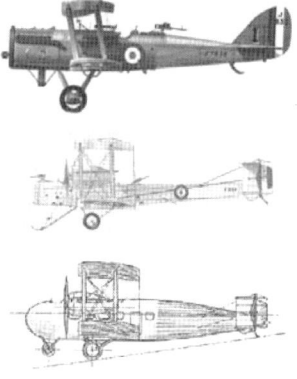

When reductions throughout the RAF took place following the Armistice, No. 45 Squadron was disbanded and existed in name only until re-formed at Helwan, Egypt, in 1920, remaining there only a few weeks. During this time the pilots obtained a little practice on DH9As of No. 47 Squadron, their own aircraft having not arrived. The principal administrative work having been carried out, the squadron moved to Al Masah and was equipped with Vickers Vimys. On these aircraft, training was carried out in preparation for the move to Iraq, for duty on the Cairo–Baghdad airmail. Early in 1922 the squadron was re-equipped with Vickers Vernons, powered by two Rolls-Royce Eagle III engines. The squadron then moved immediately to Iraq and was stationed at the new aerodrome of Hinaidi.

1922
April to September The Cairo–Baghdad airmail and local duties in Iraq were shared between No. 45 Squadron and No. 70 Squadron.

October Having been re-equipped with Vickers Vernons (Napier Lion engines), No. 70 Squadron took over the Cairo mail run while No. 45 Squadron took over most of the local duties in Iraq. Operations in Kurdistan saw No. 45 squadron bombing the enemy out of their villages to enable the ground forces to advance without serious opposition, and afterwards in carrying equipment to the advancing columns and evacuating their sick.

1922 to 1923

December to April Operations of a minor nature took place in the region of Tiwaniyah and Samawa. The very accurate bombing of No. 45 Squadron by day and night was instrumental in bringing quickly to an end what might have developed into serious trouble.

1924

May A serious disturbance broke out in Kirkuk and fighting took place between the local inhabitants and the Assyrian Levies [locally raised troops]. These Christians had at first refused to obey their officers, and British troops were carried 150 miles to Kirkuk from Hinaidi by aircraft of Nos 45 and 70 Squadrons, arriving there a few hours after the disturbance first started. This was quelled without difficulty after the arrival of these troops. On the 27th and 28th Sulaimania, the HQ of Sheikh Mahmud, was heavily bombed. That portion of the operation that was based on Kingervan was commanded by Squadron Leader A.T. Harris AFC, OC No. 45 Squadron. In addition to No. 45 Squadron he had under his command detachments of Nos 55 and 70 Squadrons. The bombing resulted in the flight of the Sheikh, who lost most of his influence with the surrounding tribes.

July Sulaimania was occupied by Arab armies supported by No. 6 Armoured Car Company, Nos 1 and 30 Squadrons. Detachments of the Arab army were conveyed to Sulaimania by No. 45 Squadron assisted by No. 70 Squadron.

October The squadron's re-equipment with Napier Lion Vernons was completed. No. 45 (B) Squadron took over the Cairo airmail and continued with this duty until February 1926 when No. 70 Squadron again took over. During this period two Secretaries of State for Air, Lord Thompson and Sir Samuel Hoare, were carried from Cairo to Baghdad and back again and King Faisal was carried from Amman to Baghdad. On the 26th operations took place against raiders, the chief centre of operations being at Rutbah, 180 miles west of Ramadi and 250 miles from Baghdad. One flight of 55 (B) Squadron with DH9As and one section of armoured cars

were stationed at Rutbah and were entirely maintained by one flight of No. 45 Squadron with Vickers Vernons. In 15 days over 230 hours were flown and 30 tons of stores and passengers were carried. On the 16th, Vernon 7545, pilots Flying Officer J.V. Kelly and Sergeant Dingwell, completed 10 hours 20 minutes, and on the 21st, Vernon 7539, pilots Flying Officer K.W. Burnett and Sergeant Bennett, completed 9 hours 20 minutes.

November Owing to the reduction in the Army garrison No. 45 Squadron was to be withdrawn from Iraq and on the 1st the squadron was reduced to one flight in preparation for that withdrawal.

1927

January On the 17th No. 45(B) Squadron was withdrawn from Iraq. On withdrawal the squadron was reduced to 4 officers and 4 airmen. This cadre was transferred to Egypt and posted to No. 47 (B) Squadron, Helwan, at which unit personnel for re-forming the squadron were collected, thus repeating the history of 1920.

April The squadron re-formed at Heliopolis under the command of Squadron Leader J.K. Summers MC, the personnel moving over from Helwan. There being insufficient personnel available for a whole squadron, only HQ and A Flight were formed. The squadron re-formed as a single-engined bombing squadron and was equipped with DH9As.

October On the 1st a large draft arrived from Iraq bringing the squadron up to strength. Included in this draft was a large number of airmen who had been with the squadron in Iraq. On the 21st the squadron moved as a complete unit to Helwan. The following letter was sent by the OC No. 70 (B) Squadron to OC (45) Squadron in appreciation of the work carried out by the squadron at Rutbah:

> To OC 45 (B) Squadron. With reference to the work carried out by 45 (B) Squadron in October in conveying rations, stores and petrol to the detachment of 55 (B) Squadron at Rutbah I am instructed to convey the appreciation of the AOC to Squadron Leader Summers and officers and other ranks who were engaged in this work.
> (signed) H.R. Nicholl, Wing Commander

1928

March On the 15th two flights proceeded to Ramleh and stood by to assist No. 14 Squadron in the event of their commencing operations against Ibn Saud and the Wahabis. On the 25th when these operations seemed imminent, one flight moved to Amman to assist No. 14

Squadron in their reconnaissance flights, leaving one flight in reserve at Ramleh.

April   On the 10th both flights returned to Helwan.

May   On the 9th No. 45 Squadron won the Lloyd Cup presented by H.E. Lord Lloyd to the squadron which obtained the greatest number of points awarded for a pre-arranged endurance flight amongst all the squadrons in the Middle East Command.

October   On the 3rd Sir Philip Sassoon inspected No. 45 Squadron during his tour of the Middle East. On the 15th No. 45 Squadron again flew in the Lloyd Cup Reliability Trial but failed to repeat the previous performances, and the Cup was eventually won by No. 14 Squadron.

November   On the 15th Squadron Leader F.J. Vincent took over command of No. 45 (B) Squadron.

December   Total hours flown during 1928 were 4,017.

1929
March   On the 19th the AOC, Air Vice-Marshal Ince Webb-Bowen CB, CMG, held his annual inspection of the squadron. On the 25th a further endurance flight of 7 hours 10 minutes was carried out by squadron aircraft. The course taken was Helwan–Cairo–Abu Sueir–Deversoir–Suez–Cairo–Abu Sueir–Deversoir–Suez–Cairo–Helwan.

March to May   [The rest of the entries for this period were purely administrative, involving postings, comings and goings.]

June   A new record in hours flown – 539 hours and 15 minutes.

July   Record for July – 547 hours 55 minutes.

August   On the 24th at 13.25 hours two aircraft left for Gaza to protect Imperial Airways aeroplane landing to refuel. Landed at Gaza to await the arrival of the Hercules. At 14.45 hours four aircraft left for Zuheron Jacab. Arabs reported attacking orphanage containing 100 children half-way between Jaffa and Haifa. Flight leader, Flying Officer Stanley Turner reported, 'Orphanage OK but several houses burning a few miles north. Action taken and about 30 Arabs killed.' At 16.20 hours two aircraft, Squadron Leader Vincent and Flight Lieutenant Riccard of No. 14 Squadron, left for Gaza and Wadi Ghuzze to locate 5,000 Arabs. Reported nothing of that nature seen. All aircraft returned safely, the last four landing at dusk. On the 28th two aircraft, Flight Lieutenant Carter (leader), left for Gaza and district to drop leaflets and to attack, if necessary, a party of 5,000 Arabs reported marching northwards. This activity continued throughout the rest of August, dropping leaflets and watching for movements of Arabs. On the 29th at 09.15 hours Squadron Leader F.J. Vincent and three Ninaks left Ramleh to patrol the Nazareth and Tiberius districts and to get in touch with HMS *Courageous*. On the 30th Flight Lieutenant R.H. Carter with two Ninaks left with a flight of Fairey Flycatchers [from HMS *Courageous*] to reconnoitre a large body of people who had crossed the Syrian border coming south on Safad, north of Tiberias.

[There then follows in the diary a proclamation by the High Commissioner and C-in-C Palestine, which is printed in its entirety on page 130.]

A Vickers Vernon, probably belonging to No. 45 Squadron, comes to grief in the 1920s.

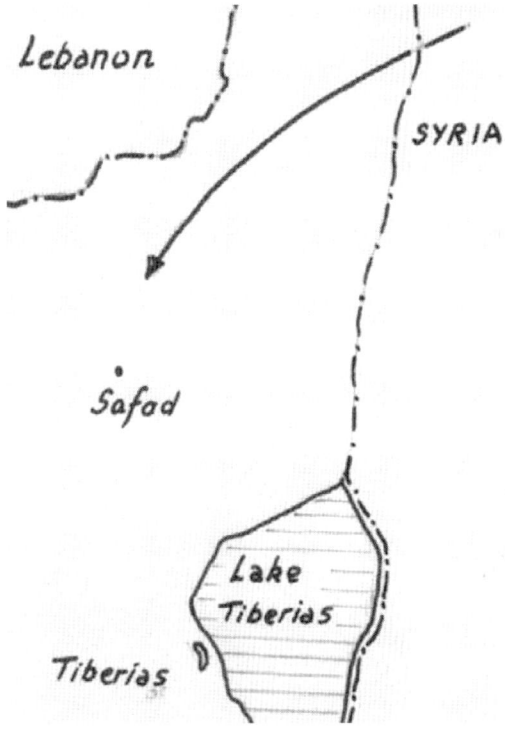

PROCLAMATION

I have returned from the United Kingdom to find to my distress a country in a state of disorder and a prey to unlawful violence. I have learned with horror of the atrocious acts committed by bodies of ruthless and bloodthirsty evil-doers, of savage murders perpetrated upon defenceless members of the Jewish population regardless of age or sex, accompanied as at Hebron by acts of unspeakable savagery, of the burning of farms and houses in town and country with the looting and destruction of property. These crimes have brought upon their authors the execration of all civilised peoples throughout the world. My first duties are to restore order in the country and to inflict stern punishment upon those found guilty of acts of violence. All necessary measures will be taken to achieve these ends and I charge all inhabitants of Palestine to assist me in discharging these duties.

In accordance with an undertaking I have given to the Committee of the Arab Executive before I left Palestine in June, I initiated discussions with the Secretary of State when in England on the subject of constitutional changes in Palestine. In view of recent events I shall suspend these discussions with His Majesty's Government. In order to put a stop to mendacious statements that have recently been circulating on the subject of the 'Wailing Wall' I hereby, with the concurrence of His Majesty's Government, make it known that I intend to give effect to the principles laid down in the White Paper of 19th November 1928 after methods of applying them have been determined.

J.R. Chancellor
High Commissioner
and C-in-C
Palestine

September On the 3rd Patrol No. 34 returned reporting 300 Arabs and 200 horses one mile north of Khalasa, and on the return journey these had dispersed. Informed by W/T that it was market day at this place so no action was taken. Large camp, 200 tents observed 5 miles east of Khalasa. Other camps in some places as reported in previous recces.

October/November No active operations only reconnaissances. On the 18th Pilot Officer Hunter posted from No. 4 Flying Training School.

December On the 14th Lord Lloyd Reliability Cup – Autumn Trial, the course being from Helwan to Khartoum and return. The squadron completed the trial, giving 100% to the aircraft completing the course.

No. 47 Squadron
Nili nomen roboris omen
(The name of the Nile is an omen of our strength)

1927
August Air Ministry Order No. 1696 dated 23 August 1927 was received today and reads as follows:

Helwan – It is notified for information that No. 47(Bombing) Squadron, HQ and two flights will move from Helwan to Khartoum early in October 1927. [The third flight had been detached to Khartoum ever since February 1920 and was thus already in situ.] The accommodation presently used in the Said Pasha Barracks by the flight detached from No. 47 Squadron will continue to be used by the RAF and such additional accommodation as might be considered necessary will be provided by means of canvas. The aircraft will be accommodated in Bessoneau hangars. On the arrival of the Headquarters the detached flight will be reabsorbed into the squadron and the squadron will then be placed on Establishment. ME711 dated 25 April 1927.

Signed Air Ministry. Group Captain A.B. Burdett

September On the 16th Hockey was played against 45 Squadron on the squadron ground. We lost 3–1. On the 18th weather was too hot and no church parade was held. On the 21st Squadron Leader C.R. Cox AFC arrived from Home Establishment [the United Kingdom] to take over command of the squadron. A conference was held at HQ RAF Middle East, Cairo, to arrange the details of the move of the squadron to Khartoum. The following officers have been provisionally selected for duty at Khartoum:

Squadron Leader Flying and Officer Commanding 47 Squadron – Squadron Leader C.R. Cox

Flight Commanders – Flight Lieutenants Gayford, Harrison and Rowe

Armament – Pilot Officer A.W.A. Rix

Photographic – Flying Officer J.A.P. Harrison

Air Pilotage and parachutes – Flying Officer C.K.J. Coggall

Adjutant (Flying Officer/Pilot Officer) – Flying Officer F.S. Homersham

Accounts (Flying Officer/Pilot Officer) – Flying Officer J.J. Caiger

Stores (Flying Officer/Pilot Officer) – Flying Officer L.L. Bray

Medical Officer (from Palestine General Hospital) – Flight Lieutenant A. Harvey

Flight pilots – Flying Officers Gray and Gee, Pilot Officer Timmins and Sergeant pilots Baker, Bowen, Pickard and Humphrey due to arrive from Home Establishment on about 30 September 1927 for the move to Khartoum.

On the 22nd HQ Middle East have decided, provisionally, that the squadron, less aircraft, will move to Khartoum on 15 October. In the meantime preparations had to be made for the move of the squadron aircraft by air and personnel and baggage by rail and road and boat. As No. 45 (B) Squadron were taking over all station and unit equipment less aircraft, the RAF Depot, Middle East, was instructed to dispatch, direct to Khartoum, complete equipment stores for a DH9A squadron. On the 24th the squadron suffered many changes in personnel in view of the new establishment for this unit, ME711, and also on account of the postings due to the trooping season.

October   On the 1st Flight Lieutenants K.L. Harrison and H.G. Rowe reported from Home Establishment for duty. On the 11th at 05.30 hours two DH9As left for Khartoum piloted by Flying Officer Bett and Sgt Humphrey. Passengers were LAC Boulton and AC1 Mortimer. Flight Lieutenant A. Harvey arrived from No. 4 FTS on being posted to the squadron as medical officer. On the 12th Squadron Leader C.R. Cox assumed command of the squadron. The two DH9As which left on the 11th arrived safely at Khartoum. All ranks were grieved to hear of the death of 335619 LAC Hirschberg from malaria in the British Military Hospital, Khartoum. From the 16th to the 21st the squadron moved by road, rail and boat. During the journey the airmen suffered considerable hardship. There were no sanitary arrangements in the airmen's coach and no fans nor light. Railway officials did not carry out the arrangements made for the supply of drinking water and, at intermediate stations, it was not possible to replenish water bottles until arrival on the train at Luxor

at 07.45 hours on the 17th. The boat was adequate and accommodation clean. The river journeys were without incident. The behaviour of the airmen was excellent. Health and spirits were good in spite of the privations they had to undergo so far on the rail journey and it was possible to arrange for the airmen to have a bath while they were on the steamer. The Sudanese government railway officials were very helpful (unlike the Egyptians previously mentioned) in getting them on their way to their new station. Six aircraft and personnel were flown out on the 24th crewed as follows:

Squadron Leader Cox and LAC Hall, Flight Lieutenant Rowe and Flight Sergeant Johnson, Flying Officer Gray and LAC Downey, Flying Officer Homersham and LAC Wyatt, Flying Officer Adams and Corporal Hart and finally Flight Lieutenant Buxton and LAC Baird

November   In view of the fact that the squadron is made up for the most part of pilots and personnel new to the Sudan, it was decided to commence training at once. Although the possibility of many disturbances in this country are at present remote, minor operations may take place in January or before. It was therefore decided to train the crews of aircraft to fit them for minor operations. For this purpose formation flying was carried out and the surrounding country visited. Pilots and air gunners started ground training in the use of bomb sights, Vickers and Lewis guns. As it was considered necessary to carry out cooperation with mounted infantry and Political Officers, the construction of the necessary W/T and message picking-up apparatus was commenced. Two RAF W/T sets were put together and all aircraft were wired for wireless work. At 05.30 hours on the 2nd, General Huddleston, who was GOC Sudan Defence Force, was flown down the Nile to Renk 260 miles south of Khartoum. At the same time two other aeroplanes proceeded to Malakal on inspection of aerodromes. Squadron Leader Cox flew with General Huddleston as his passenger, returning the same day to arrive at 14.00 hours. 30 November – preparations are going ahead for the move south in connection with Patrol S8 and also for the Annual Inspection of the AOC which is taking place on 9 December. Stores are still being unpacked and binned. The Accounting Branch has closed the stores and the accounting ledgers of the detached flight [the one that had been in the Sudan since 1920] and opened new inventories for the squadron [that had just arrived]. It was readily admitted that the forced training undertaken for possible operations and the AOC's inspection had thrown a considerable amount of work on all ranks just at a time when the squadron should now be settling down in its new surroundings and opening up new accounts and ledgers. The average temperature at midday for the month of November was 96 degrees Fahrenheit.

December An unprovoked attack was made on the District Commissioner of Yirrol at Lake Jorr, 25 miles north [That should read south] of Shambe by a section of the Garluark Nuers under Chief Juarlark. El Kaimakam Fergusson Bey, District Commissioner, and a Greek merchant were killed. Operation orders have been issued by HQ Sudan Defence Force though no definite objectives could be given to the RAF detached flight now at Malakal and it was thought better not to take any air action. The GOC was also of the opinion that the RAF could not be usefully used in such wooded country and large swampy areas. Here in the squadron it is thought that air action could be usefully employed, however we take our orders from Headquarters. Temperature 96 deg. F.

1928

January On the 2nd flying of the Fairey IIIFs was commenced and dual instruction was started. Only two IIIFs and the Nigerian Flight IIIF that had landed at El Obeid was allotted to the squadron for training purposes. ME [Middle East Command] stated that as

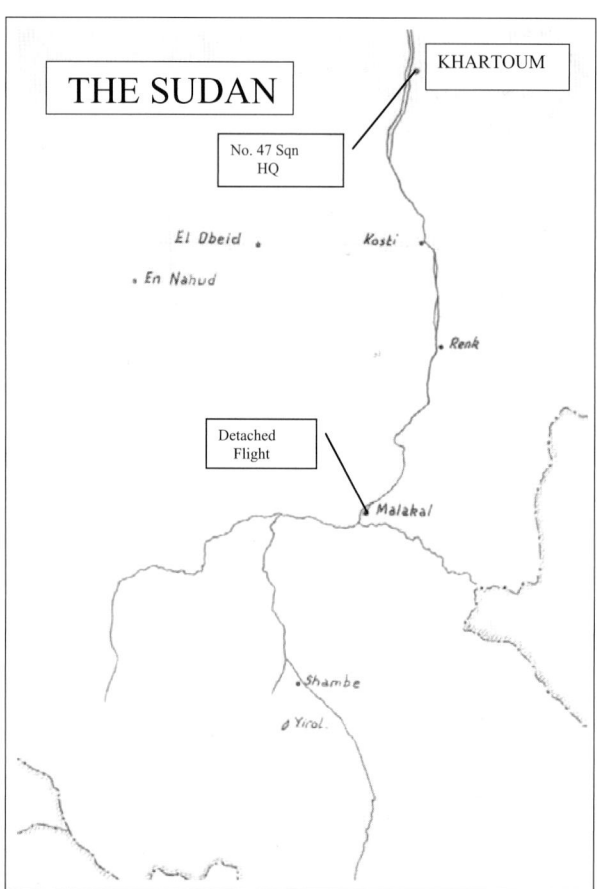

soon as flying personnel became efficient more IIIFs would be allocated. On the 20th organized resistance is at an end in Patrol S8 area. Chiefs are coming in bringing young men in. [Presumably the perpetrators of crimes.] Two Fairey IIIFs arrived from Cairo with Sir Philip Sassoon as a passenger.

December On the 22nd three aircraft left Khartoum for the south of Sudan to carry out a combined reconnaissance/wireless/demonstration flight and landing ground inspection. At Kapoeta most of the young Kaposa chiefs and headmen came in and took a lively interest in the flight. They expressed a desire to go up in the air and were taken up for short flights. They were very frightened! On the 26th a tragic accident occurred when two aircraft were returning from inspection duties. Flying Officer Rix crashed and the aircraft caught fire. Both passengers, Captain Doyle AID and Sergeant Long, were killed, as was Flying Officer Rix. A memorial service was held at Khartoum Cathedral by the Right Reverend Llewellyn Gwynne with the Reverend M.C. Jones, Army chaplain, in attendance. His Excellency the Governor-General of the Sudan Sir John Maffey and the GOC British Troops in the Sudan and all government officials attended. The two British regiments in the Sudan Defence Force also sent representatives. The squadron attended this service. The Frontier military intelligence officer was flown over the country east of Kaliau towards Moruakeppi. The courses of rivers not marked on the map were traced and also a considerable amount of water, the existence of which was not previously known. It was also discovered that it is possible to build a road in this previous uncharted area.

1929

February On the 13th a B Flight aircraft was fitted with floats and launched and satisfactorily tested. The 1929 Cape Flight, comprising Squadron Leader Cox, Flight Lieutenant Rowe and Flying Officers Burnett, Coggall and Harrison, arrived from Wadi Halfa. Three aircraft, one from each flight, left on reconnaissance duties south of Malakal. On the 23rd a squadron formation of nine aircraft led by a floatplane escorted the steamer carrying His Excellency the High Commissioner for Egypt and the Sudan, Lord Lloyd, on his official arrival in Khartoum during his tour of inspection of the Sudan.

April On the 1st three groups of aircraft arrived in Khartoum, the combined flights of the squadron, the 1929 Cape Flight and a South African Air Force flight comprising Lieutenant-Colonel Van der Spee, Lieutenant J.B. Donald and others.

June During the month night flying was carried out locally. On the 29th a Fairey IIF was converted to float undercarriage and was successfully launched from Moghren Quay.

July On the 10th the floatplane was damaged in hoisting out of the water at Moghren Quay. The force of the current submerged the starboard float and the tail, and the floatplane sank. Later the same day another floatplane was successfully launched from the Quay.

September During the month aircraft were employed on an anti-locust campaign. Districts were visited and poison carried to the affected areas. The use of aircraft was in the nature of an experiment and proved of value, and it is the intention to draw up a comprehensive programme for the use of aircraft in 1930, that is conveying personnel quickly from place to place to collect the information from outstations where there is no telegraph, etc. On the 24th three aircraft were used to carry out a reconnaissance of the railway line damaged by floods. The temperature is 117 deg. F.

November On the 27th the West African Flight, on their return journey, left for Heliopolis on the 28th. Extensive night-flying practice was carried out in preparation for the Lloyd Reliability Trials.

December On the 2nd the Lloyd Reliability Trial commenced. Twelve aircraft started for Atbars and Aswan. The next day Assuit was visited, the aircraft staying at Aswan again. The third day the squadron carried out a night flight from Atbara to Shendi, 90 miles distant. Two aircraft crashed on landing. Ten aircraft successfully completed the test, arriving home on 5 December. On the 24th, air operations against the Nubas, Patrol S10, were undertaken at the request of HQ Sudan Defence Force. By the 31st there were decided signs of the enemy giving in.

No. 55 Squadron
Nil nos tremefacit
(Nothing shakes us)

1921
March The situation on the 19th of the month is that the squadron is based at Mosul, equipped with DH9As under command of Squadron Leader Vivian Gaskell-Blackburn DFC, AFC. The squadron formed part of the Mesopotamian

Wing commanded by Group Captain A.E. Porton CMG, DSO, AFC, and was attached to the Army Command in Mesopotamia. In 1921 the squadron was employed in minor operations to the west and south-west of Mosul against Arab tribesmen who were inclined to indulge in their ancient occupation of brigandage. The squadron's principal activity soon became to counter Turkish encroachment and influence in the Kurdistan area of Iraq.

September The action was still against the Turks and the squadron was busily engaged in close cooperation with the ground forces to clear Dasht-i-Harir of a party of Turks and to suppress the rebellion they had stirred up amongst the Kurds inhabiting the area.

December One aircraft was disabled by rifle fire and its pilot compelled to land on bad ground in his burning aircraft. He was severely burned by petrol from the bursting tanks. Within a few hours he was flown back to Mosul where he died from shock a few days later.

1925
October Squadron Leader Eric Digby Johnson AFC assumed command of the squadron, vice Squadron Leader E.R.L. Corballis DSO, OBE.

1927
February Flight Lieutenant Harry Augustus Smith MC assumed command of the squadron temporarily, vice Squadron Leader Johnson AFC.

July Squadron Leader H.A. Whistler DSO, DFC assumed command of the squadron, vice Flight Lieutenant H.A. Smith.

1928
February On the 20th Flying Officer R.B.H. Jackson was shot down in the vicinity of a party of raiders and was shot dead after landing. His body was brought in by Flight Lieutenant Barrett of No. 84 (Bombing) Squadron later in the day. Flying Officer Jackson was flying solo as reserve aircraft in formation.

February On the 27th the squadron returned to Shaibah leaving one flight at Busaiyah from whence frequent reconnaissance flights were made.

April On the 25th Squadron Leader Arthur Hicks Peck assumed command of the squadron, vice Squadron Leader H.A. Whistler DSO, DFC.

1929
January 07.00 hrs on the 2nd at Hinaidi. There was considerable indication of a renewal of raiding into Iraq by Najd Bedawin as occurred during the winter of 1927–1928. A Flight left Hinaidi for a detached duty at

Kerbala. Air Headquarters confirmed the awards given to members of the squadron, officers and airmen, in respect of operations against the Najd Bedawin or the Akhwan in the Southern Desert during the winter of 1927–1928.

Squadron Leader Whistler DSO, DFC – a second bar to his DFC
Flight Lieutenant Parker – a DFC
Squadron Leader Peck – Mentioned in Dispatches
The late Flying Officer Jackson – Mentioned in Dispatches
Flight Sergeant Gardener – a DFM

No. 56 Squadron

Quid si coelum ruat
(What if heaven falls)

After having operated on the Western Front as a Camel squadron from January 1918, it was partially equipped with Sopwith Snipes and later was selected for duty in Egypt. The remaining Camels were then replaced by Snipes and the squadron left France for Egypt at the end of May 1919.

1920

February On the 1st the identity of No. 56 Squadron was established by renumbering No. 80 Squadron in Egypt. This squadron had been serving in Egypt since June 1919 and operated in the Western Desert.

1922

September The squadron remained in Egypt until the 23rd when it was disbanded, but owing to the Chanak crisis, the detachment of the squadron still remaining was attached to No. 208 Squadron and sent to Constantinople. The detachment retained the identity of No. 56 Squadron on duty with the Constantinople Wing.

November The squadron, less one flight, was reformed at Hawkinge, Kent and equipped with Sopwith Snipes.

No. 60 Squadron

Per ardua ad aethera tendo
(I strive through difficulties to the sky)

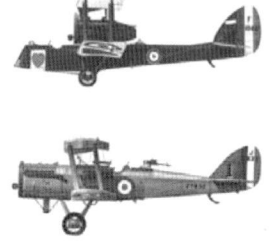

The account of No. 60 Squadron's history is the most complete of all those that feature in this chapter, and therefore provides a very detailed account of military life and air-control operations on the North-West Frontier of India in the 1920s. One aspect stands out, and that is the appalling state of the RAF in India at the beginning of the decade. This is attributed to the RAF coming under overall Army command and control, subject to funding by the Government of India.

Note: All references to No. 97 Squadron refer also to No. 60 Squadron, which it became when it was renumbered.

1919

September On the 16th the squadron was established at Lahore. Flight Lieutenant Graham air tested DH10 E5453. On the 17th he beat all previous altitude tests in India, climbing to 17,600 ft with two passengers. The DH10 was not, however, a successful aeroplane, being difficult to fly.

October During the first week in October Flight Lieutenant Graham left with three of the four troublesome aircraft plus 40 men to establish a detachment at Mianwali, Punjab province, on the east bank of the River Indus, to come under command of 52 Corps (Wing HQ) to join No. 99 Squadron with DH9As. This was for operations of six months' duration. The outcome of the Third Afghan War of 1919, when British and Indian forces had to retire from forward frontier areas, gave the military authorities the problem of regaining control over the tribes of the North-West Frontier. Squadron operations were in support of the Army [Tochi] column which had arrived at Makin and Kaniguram, the two most important centres of the Mahsud tribe. Active operations continued against Shah Daula when No. 97 Squadron arrived at Mianwali, and at once the squadron went into action to bomb Wana and Makin. On these raids the DH10 carried both 112 lb and

20 lb bombs slung below the wings, whilst some Cooper bombs were carried in the front observer's cockpit.

November   The Army advanced on Datta Khel with little trouble and then withdrew leaving a garrison at Dardoni with the main concentration at Bannu, supported by Nos 20 (AC) Squadron, 99 (B) Squadron and No. 97 (B) Squadron. Day and night raids carried out on tribes causing damage.

December   Early in the month the Army [Derajat] column had concentrated and arrived at Jandola on the 17th. Flying Officer Webster had flown from Dera Ismail to bring Wing Commander Minchin OC No. 52 (Corps) Wing to Mianwali. Only three operational DH10s of the squadron's detachment gave close support to the Derajat column flying over new, very rough country and with poor maps. On the 18th low-flying aircraft pursued a large body of Mahsuds in open country, harassing them with bombs and Lewis gunfire. On the 19th the Army advanced up the Tank Zam valley, encountering severe opposition by some 900 armed tribesmen when attacking Mandanna Hill. On the 20th six DH9As of 99 Squadron, four Bristol Fighters of No. 20 Squadron and three DH10s of No. 97 Squadron maintained a constant patrol over the Hill, bombing and machine-gunning the reverse slopes during 27 sorties. Over three days up to the 21st the Army suffered 179 killed, including five British officers and 456 wounded amongst the tribesmen. There was bad weather on the 22nd but on the 25th the Hill was retaken with close air support, including three DH10s of No. 97 Squadron.

1920

January   On the 7th the Derajat column met some 3,500 Mahsuds in an attack upon Ahnai Tanji. On the 9th a second attack was mounted but there was a shortage of aircraft. It took until the 14th to secure the passage over the gorge after fierce fighting. Two aircraft of No. 20 Squadron were shot down and another force-landed but the crew escaped. On the 18th the Derajat column reached Sorarogha where a landing ground was established and used constantly by No. 20 Squadron. No. 97 Squadron raided Bada Toi, the Spin Plain, Kaniguram and Makin. On the 29th Flying Officer Webster reported that excellent results were obtained bombing ponies laden with ammunition.

February to May   On the 16th the Derajat column reached Makin, and Kaniguram eighteen days later, but operations continued throughout March and April, coming to an end officially on 7 May, and a road suitable for motor vehicles was built from Kaniguram to Ladha, where a South Waziristan Scout Post was constructed. This became of much importance until the Wana Fort

was retaken and occupied. The Official Historian made the following comments on the air action:

> For the first time in the history of the North-West Frontier, aeroplanes were employed extensively against the tribes. The aeroplanes used were the DH9As, Bristol Fighters and DH10s. It is impossible to overestimate the value of aircraft in tactical cooperation with other arms. Their presence alone greatly raised the morale of our troops while correspondingly decreasing that of the enemy … Aeroplanes when thus employed in tactical cooperation did considerable damage and helped in no small measure towards the success of many of the actions. The information from air photos, both vertical and oblique, was of great tactical and topographic value, and officers of the land forces would find their labour well repaid if they undertook the study of this important auxiliary to the art of tactics.

At the beginning of February No. 97 Squadron was beginning to be referred to as No. 60 Squadron. The No. 60 Squadron Cadre which had been at Narborough [later RAF Marham] was moved to Bircham Newton, finally disbanding on 22 January 1920. At the same time No. 97 Squadron was renumbered No. 60 Squadron. No. 99 Squadron was renumbered No. 27 Squadron, which then joined 60 Squadron at Risalpur, both squadrons coming under command No. 1 (India) Wing at Peshawar, commanded by Wing Commander G.S. Mitchell DSO, MC, AFC. The RAF in India was, at this time, reorganized onto a 'Group' basis. In May the squadron was then formed into flights, still flying the dangerous DH10s. Flying Officer Ashmore crashed on a test flight with Flying Officers F.D.C. Gaiger and F.S. Stokes.

June   On the 28th Flying Officer J.R. Swanston DFC and AC F.C. Oliver were both killed while taking off on a reconnaissance flight. Due to crashes and serviceability problems the squadron received its first DH10A (Amiens MkIIIA) as replacement. This was a modified DH10 built by Mann-Egerton Ltd with the Liberty engines mounted on the lower planes and heavy-duty wheels. The DH10A had a much improved performance and a top speed of nearly 130 mph, but the squadron had only one or two of these new aircraft.

July   During hot weather little flying was done although some photographic work was carried out. There was continuous trouble with the aircraft and Flying Officer Webster had to make two forced landings on the airfield. One was due to a burst petrol pipe on a DH10 and the other to a jammed throttle on a DH10A. Squadron Leader Quinnel left for the United Kingdom and Flight Lieutenant Champion de Crespigny assumed temporary command until 15 September. Operationally, mostly due to the hot weather, 1920 was a quiet period for the squadron. In wider fields some semblance of order was appearing in Waziristan, the Army conducting minor operations in July against Makin. The only roads suitable for motor transport in Waziristan led from Tank, via Jandola to Ladha Post; and in the north from Bannu via Dardoni to Datta Khel Post. From these two roads heads forward all transport, as by camel and mule. Late in the summer an Afghan group under Shah Daula, with tribesmen led by Haji Abdur Razak, supported by Afghanistan, had become active in South Waziristan. It was decided to undertake punitive operations against the Wazirs of the Wana Plain for their part in the Afghan War, subsequent raiding in 1919 and to reoccupy Wana Fort. For this purpose the 'Wana Column' was formed and ultimately reached Wana in December 1920, as a result of which the Jandola–Shahur–Sarwekai MT road was built. However, Wana went through many difficulties through the years and it was not permanently occupied until November 1929.

September No. 60 Squadron was back in action again. The Yusufzai Pathans were causing trouble in the Black Mountain area of the Hazara District, situated on the east bank of the River Indus about 50 miles north-east of Attock. These tribes had given trouble only four times since 1850, the last occasion resulting in the Second Hazara Expedition of 1891. The Black Mountain range was some 40 miles long with ground rising to 8,000 ft. Flight Lieutenant Graham, who had been seriously wounded at Mianwali, was the Forward Ground Liaison Officer at Abbotabad during these operations. Flying Officer Ivelaw-Chapman, with his two observers, Flying Officers C.H.F. Nesbit and G.R. Terry, had force-landed when his engine cut out returning from a raid on Seri. Squadron Leader Sherren sent two fitters in a car to repair the engine. On their journey to the spot where the aircraft had gone down the two fitters were surprised to see the three officers on horseback riding towards them in the light of their headlights. It took several days to repair the engine before the DH10 could be flown back to Risalpur. During the month the squadron supported the Chitral column, which was going to relieve the garrison at Chitral, high in the Himalayas. An engine failure whilst flying amongst the very precipitous landscape would almost certainly have resulted in a crash.

October The advent of the colder weather saw the beginning of the trooping season. Following an invitation from the Air Ministry to officers who had previously served on an RAF squadron to apply to rejoin those units. This policy had resulted in the arrival of Flying Officer Hammersley, who had been with the squadron in 1917.

1921

January to December No. 60 Squadron was not greatly affected by the tribal raids and consequent minor operations during 1921. Instead the squadron was engaged on normal training for most of the year. In July, Flying Officer Webster made yet another forced landing and he went to Drigh Road to collect a new DH10. He left Karachi on 11 July but his port engine caught fire on the first leg to Sukkur and he had to force-land at Hyderabad. After an engine change he had to return to the airfield with loose engine pins. This was followed by another delay at Multan due to bad weather. A flight from Karachi to Risalpur with a night stop at Multan normally took 8½ hours' flying time. It took Flying Officer Webster ten days to make the delivery flight.

1922

January At the beginning of the month Flying Officer Webster was awarded the AFC and he was later to win the Schneider Trophy Race at Venice in 1927. By the beginning of November 1921 no replacements could be obtained following the many crashes with the DH10s, and only four aircraft could be mustered on the 12th for a bombing raid on Datta Khel, north of Dardoni. This raid followed an ambush of an Army column, and the tribesmen responsible had taken refuge in a hollow surrounded by 5,000 ft hills. Nos 27 and 60 Squadrons flew in formation, but it is an indication of the parlous state of the RAF in India at that time that Flying Officers Waters in a DH9A and Chick in a DH10 had to return to Risalpur immediately after take-off with ignition trouble. This was followed by Flying Officer Hammersley, whose DH10 developed an oil leak. Flight Lieutenant Grenfell then suffered engine trouble with his Ninak and he had to turn back to Bannu after jettisoning his bombs. With fifty miles still to go there were only three Ninaks and one DH10 left in the formation, now led by Flying Officer Oliver. On reaching the target at 15.45 hrs few tribesmen were seen but there was a lot of cattle. The aircraft descended to 1,500 ft for bombing to commence. Although Oliver succeeded in hitting the target with a 112 lb and a 20 lb bomb, his two 230 lb bombs failed to explode. In fact only two 230 lb bombs exploded out of all those that were dropped. At that time Kohat was a landing ground and after the raid Flight Lieutenant Scott landed there with his 230 lb bomb 'hung up' and he had to land with great care. Meanwhile Flying Officer Lewin crashed on the airfield, leaving Oliver as the only 27 Squadron pilot to complete the raid and return to Risalpur.

February Squadron Leader Sherren was posted at the end of the month. He was sadly to be killed in the King's Cup Air Race in 1937.

March On the 27th Flight Lieutenant de Crespigny MC, DFC was promoted to Squadron Leader and assumed command of No. 60 Squadron.

May Air Headquarters which had been moved to Ambala became HQ RAF India, the old title of RAF Indian Group being abolished.

August Out of an establishment of 70 aircraft on the North-West Frontier only 7 were serviceable. Aircraft were in such a lamentable state that some took off without tyres on their wheels. The DH10s of the squadron had constantly to be cannibalised for spares, and many of the squadron's aircraft wrere sold for scrap at an auction in the autumn. Sir John Salmond is sent to India to see the situation for himself and report back to the government of India.

December The 'Razmak Force' made an advance at the beginning of the month to construct the Dardoni–Razmak road. This followed the decision to construct the Central Waziristan road to occupy Razmak, which was opposed by local tribesmen. The normal garrison at Dardoni was an infantry battalion and one Army Cooperation squadron accommodated in portable hangars and mud huts. On the 12th of the month Lieutenant Dickson, the Royal Engineer officer supervising the work on the road, was murdered by Mahsuds, and on the 17th Nos 27 and 28 Squadrons bombed the tribe. During the attack two aircraft force-landed in tribal territory, which was unadministered territory north of the Tochi river, i.e. there would not be a resident Political Officer. British forces constructing the Tochi–Razmak section of the road were also shot at by the Abdullah section of the Mahsuds from Makin, and over the following fortnight the squadron carried out operations against this section of the tribe using four DH10s and one or two DH10As.

1923

January On the 23rd Razmak was occupied but operations continued through to March.

February The squadron had ceased to take part in the Waziristan operations because only two DH10s remained at the end of the month. Of the three machines at Dardoni one was being used as a transport, one had returned to Risalpur for overhaul and one had crashed. At the end of the month Flying Officer H.E. Greenbury arrived from No. 207 Squadron, a DH9A unit. He was to train Flying Officer Webster who in turn would train other squadron pilots on this aircraft with which the unit was to be re-equipped. At Lahore the first DH9A was converted to dual control for this purpose. Flying Officer Greenbury went to Karachi to test fly the newly arrived squadron DH9As. On two of the delivery flights Greenbury was marooned in the Sind desert after forced landings. The squadron none the less found the Ninaks more reliable than the DH10s. On the 5th Flight Lieutenant Dearlove was posted to No. 60 Squadron,

Flying Officer Gardner and Pilot Officer Grace being posted in at the end of the month.

April On the 14th five Afridi outlaws raided the Kohat Cantonment and entered a bungalow and murdered the wife of Major R.J. Ellis DSO of the Border Regiment who was away on tour at the time. They also kidnapped Molly Ellis aged 17 and escaped with her to Tirah, north-west of Kohat, in inaccessible mountainous country. On the 15th the squadron carried out deep searches of the area and subsequently bombed Khanki Bazaar. Molly Ellis was later recovered unharmed, but thereafter nightly patrols were mounted, comprising local armed personnel commanded by an RAF officer. On the 19th Flying Officer Graham-Nicholls was posted in as adjutant. During the Afridi punitive operations Squadron Leader Capel of No. 5 Army Cooperation Squadron crashed on the target village when it was being bombed. It was advised to keep up the bombing in spite of the risk to the lives of the downed RAF aircrew. Both the squadron leader and the air gunner had 'blood chits', and they were later released in return for a reward.

May to October 1923 was the first year of the comprehensive occupation of Waziristan. Control was based on Political Officers, backed by Scouts and Khassadars or local tribe levies who provided road protection, inter-clan security and police duties. Waziristan was bisected from north to south by the Dardoni–Spinwam–Thal road, and the RAF 'Wana Patrol', instituted that summer, kept contact with the Wazir Khassadars isolated in the Wana fort. The Datta Khel Tochi Scout Post was completed and occupied that summer.

November The new AOC India was Air Vice-Marshal Sir Edward Ellington KCB,CMG,CBE.

December Wing Commander R.C.M. Pink assumed command of No. 2 (Indian) Wing, and on the 2nd Squadron Leader James took over command of the squadron.

1924

January The command posts in the squadron were:

Officer Commanding – Squadron Leader A.H.W. James MC
OC 'A' Flight – Flight Lieutenant J.W. Baker MC *
OC 'B' Flight – Flight Lieutenant C.W. Busk MC
OC 'C' Flight – Flight Lieutenant R.C. Savery DFC

* later Air Chief Marshal Sir John Baker GBE, KCB, MC, DFC

Sergeant pilots had just been introduced into the RAF and three came to No. 60 Squadron – Sergeants Munro, Hawkins and Smalley.

During the year the new split-axle undercarriage was received and wastage due to minor crashes was thus reduced, whilst the last camouflaged aircraft were withdrawn and the whole squadron had silver-doped machines painted with squadron markings. At first these consisted of a white figure in a black rectangle on the engine cowling, a small black triangle pointing forward being painted in front of this. Initially figures were used to differentiate between No. 60 Squadron's Ninaks and those of No. 27 Squadron, which used the letters A–K, although the squadron later used the letters L–Z, and kept them up to 1939. The squadron also painted the radiator shutters alternately in black and yellow.

March The squadron had no badge and so Squadron Leader James chose the head of a Kabuli markhor (Capra Falconer), which was found at this time in all the hill ranges of the North-West Frontier bordering Pakistan. The badge was first drawn by Flight Lieutenant Savery, and the original is held by the squadron. Soon after its adoption, the head of the markhor was painted on the tail fins of the squadron's aircraft. It was Lord Hugh Cecil, one of the first recording officers of the squadron, who suggested the squadron motto. Up to the 31st of the month Waziristan was still under military command, the situation that had prevailed ever since the Third Afghan War, then a Political Officer took over. The spares situation was getting better and there was an all-round improvement in morale and material efficiency. This meant that the periodic cessation of training was reduced and a revised training programme could be launched. Under Wing Commander Pink's energetic command the previous confinement of the Ninaks to only the largest landing grounds was relaxed, and Mianwali, Kushab and Thal were frequently used. This permitted training exercises to be undertaken worked out with great ingenuity by Flight Lieutenant Savery.

April At the end of the month a programme of flights to Quetta had been prepared for both 27 and 60 Squadrons, a flight of five hours' flying at 12,000 ft made hazardous by heat and dust haze which made map reading with poor maps all the more difficult.. The first of these was scheduled for A Flight on the 29th but was postponed when one aircraft crashed on take-off. When flights were resumed there were crashes, tyres bursting in the heat and engine trouble.

May Nos 27 and 60 Squadrons commenced flight detachments to Dardoni, and this was to continue for a number of years. During the middle of the month Flight Lieutenant Savery commanded Y Force. Monthly climbs to the service ceiling were instituted, and this proved to

be 13,500 ft with four 112 lb bombs, 500 rounds of Vickers ammunition and four drums of Lewis gun ammunition. The bombs were jettisoned before landing since it was deemed to be dangerous to do so on the old type of undercarriage, i.e. before the introduction of the split axle.

July In the middle of the month operations were resumed and the squadron moved to Dardoni. The raid near Razmak saw two Bristol fighters crash, killing the crews of both aircraft. Cloud had settled on the mountains as they were attacking down a valley, and various other aircraft crashed in nearby locations, all aircraft being wrecked. These incidents highlighted the extent to which climatic conditions could influence operations on the Frontier. This was the combined effect of height and heat on the performance of aircraft.

October With the onset of autumn the hot weather eased. The squadron made daily reconnaissance flights over the Chitral relief column. The AOC was escorted from Hassan Abdul to Risalpur on the 28th during his tour of the Frontier. This was his usual practice during autumn and spring moves of Air Headquarters between Delhi and Simla. Flying Officer C.B.R. Pelly joined the squadron from No. 39 Squadron at Spitalgate. He was amongst the first of the regular officers then leaving the RAF College Cranwell and he would retire as an Air Chief Marshal.

November/December Between 17 November and 3 December the squadron, together with No. 27 Squadron, went on the first practice Mobilisation Camp held at Arawali where there was a considerable underground bomb store. This was a large natural landing ground on a rock plateau about 4,000 ft above sea level, situated in the Kurram Valley near the Afghan frontier. It was sited as being the nearest possible aerodrome in a direct line between British India and Kabul, from which bomb-laden aircraft could climb the intervening ridges without detours. The heights to be crossed, however, were up to 12,000 ft, and they were much higher than those on the Khyber route. It seems doubtful, therefore, whether formations could have used the Kurram Valley route safely in all seasons to a sufficient extent to justify such an exposed base. For the purpose of these practice camps, the squadrons moved on a genuine mobilisation basis over a hundred miles from their peace stations, which enabled a severe test to be made of the transport and supply organisation. On this occasion the aircraft followed up the advance party on 21 November. All seems to have gone well during the war-load tests over the next two weeks, but then a minor incident occurred. One of 60's pilots had an engine failure when returning to Risalpur and crash-landed without casualties near Thal. An officer flew as a passenger to find him, subsequently returning to Risalpur in a staff car. On the way back he was sniped by an Afridi tribesman between Kohat and Peshawar. The road from Arawali ran down the Hangu valley, which was Administered Territory; but on leaving Kohat it climbed up the hill to the north known as the Kohat Pass, through the salient of Afridi tribal territory to Peshawar. To snipe at British cars on this road was considered by tribesmen, who had a distorted sense of humour, to be a fair and natural sport.

1925

January   At the instigation of Wing Commander Pink, Nos 27 and 60 Squadrons made history by providing the aircraft and crews which carried out the first long-distance formation flight. On the 14th the six flight commanders of the two squadrons set off. One of 27 Squadron's aircraft carried Wing Commander Pink who flew as a passenger. The other two 27 Squadron aircraft were piloted by Flight Lieutenants J.L.M. Hughes-Chamberlain and S. Graham carrying between them a wireless operator and a fitter. The 60 Squadron pilots were Flight Lieutenants R.S. Savery, J.W. Baker and C.W. Busk, carrying between them, respectively, Flight Lieutenant Laurence ,the wing adjutant, who navigated, a corporal rigger and sergeant fitter. The purpose was not only to test the capabilities of aircraft and crews to operate away from equipped bases but to 'show the flag' across Northern India. From the latter point of view this flight was a pronounced success, especially at Patna and Calcutta, where service aircraft were practically unknown. From the former aspect the results were not quite so good; in fact the gradual elimination of aircraft, for one reason or another, from further participation in flight, reads rather like the 'ten little nigger boys'.

The first outward stage from Risalpur to Ambala was uneventful. The following morning, however, Savery's machine would not start so Laurence transferred to Baker's machine and the sergeant fitter remained behind to attempt to rectify the fault. Over Delhi, Hughes-Chamberlain's machine left the formation to force-land. His generator was unserviceable and he subsequently broke a flying wire; but after repairs he followed the flight down to Calcutta a stage behind, and he reached there a day after the others. The four remaining aircraft reached Cawnpore safely, stayed the night with the Durham Light Infantry, and proceeded without incident the next day to Patna. In the meantime Savery at last got away from Ambala, but at Aligarh, south of Delhi, he force-landed with a seized engine. A local rajah took charge of him and immediately sent the sergeant fitter off on a horse to catch a train, which enabled him to rejoin the flight and Baker's machine at Cawnpore, whence Laurence went on to Calcutta by train. Savery very gallantly remained with his aircraft, dismantled it unaided and ultimately conveyed it by elephant transport to the railway and returned with it to Risalpur

by train. The four remaining machines, having reached Patna uneventfully, remained there over the 17th as the hospitality was so good and it gave the mechanics a chance to look over the machines and engines.

For the last stage to Calcutta, it was fortunate that immediately ahead of the flight Sir Alan Cobham had just completed one of the first of his pioneer flights with Sir Sefton Brancker. Cobham landed on the racecourse at Calcutta but, appreciating that the area available would be too small for DH9As, he arranged for a long stretch of the Ellenborough Maidan (which corresponds to Hyde Park) to be cleared, a ditch to be filled in and for the ground to be marked and policed. The four machines of the flight landed safely on the 18th, Hughes-Chamberlain arriving the following day. The flight of 1,330 miles had been completed in $14\frac{1}{2}$ hours' flying time. An immense crowd greeted the flight, and some 400 police were on duty guarding the landing area. The officers were accommodated by the garrison in Fort William, made honorary members of the messes, guests of the Bengal and United Services Clubs and entertained whole-heartedly by a society which ran one of the gayest winter seasons in the world. The press also gave considerable space to the flight.

After a five-day visit the aircraft took off again on the 23rd on the return flight to Risalpur, led by Hughes-Chamberlain, but the aircraft were only in the air for an hour before Harris had to turn back to Dum-Dum with his ammeter showing a discharge. Fortunately he was able to catch the ground party before their departure by train, and he caught up with the others at Patna after a new generator had been fitted. It was Graham's turn to be left behind the next day, and when he finally took off he crashed on landing at Cawnpore, for his wheel buckled when his aircraft ran into a hole on the airfield. The remaining aircraft reached Cawnpore safely, from where three went on to Delhi to remain an extra day, which enabled Harris to make a detour to Agra with Wing Commander Pink. On the 27th the flight got to Ambala for lunch and refuelled at Lahore in the afternoon. It was on this stage that Busk went down with a broken inclined drive. He landed safely but heavy rain that night made the cultivated ground boggy and there was no alternative but to dismantle the aircraft and bring it into Lahore by train. By coincidence he met Graham, who was accompanying his machine that had crashed at Cawnpore, and they returned together to Risalpur.

Only three machines were left to make the last stage from Lahore to Risalpur on the 28th. Hughes-Chamberlain and Baker got off all right but Harris's machine had a dirty filter which caused fuel starvation to his engine. Hughes-Chamberlain decided to return to find out what the trouble was but he misjudged his landing and crashed just as Harris was taking off to join him. The two remaining aircraft then continued, but over Jhelum, Harris with Wing Commander Pink had to go down again. Baker landed to offer assistance, and it was filter trouble again. Once this was remedied the two aircraft finally reached Risalpur. And so ended this spectacular if troubled flight.

February Following the closure of Dardoni the Indian government decided that a permanent Air Force garrison should occupy Miranshah, home of the Tochi Scouts, which could be extended to accommodate Nos 27 and 60 Squadrons, with overall operational command being exercised by Wing Commander Pink from Tank, which housed ten Bristol Fighters of No. 5 Squadron. On the 25th a warning of bombing attacks had been issued to the Abdur Rahman Khel, but as usual was disregarded.

March A further warning was given to the tribe on the 5th, and when this was again disregarded operations began according to the tactical plan. This involved:

Air attacks on villages after they had been evacuated
Air blockade of certain areas
Night bombing

Routine was avoided, to 'wrong foot' the tribesmen, who could never be sure when they were about to be attacked and so could not know if it was safe to commence grazing. The target area was between 3,000 and 6,000 ft above sea level. Fuel capacity had to be cut down to 60 per cent to enable the aircraft with a full bomb load to reach the required altitude. The bombing attacks were mounted some 3,000 ft above the targets to keep the aircraft out of the range of rifle fire and to enable the aircraft that got into difficulties to get to a safe landing ground, save, that is, in the case of complete engine failure. The air attacks on villages were usually made in flight formation so that the bombs could be dropped in a salvo on a signal from the formation leader or individually with the aircraft flying a circuit over the village. Bombing by the DH9As was usually followed by the Bristol Fighters firing into the caves and dugouts. It was found that the best arrangement of bombs under the DH9As was eight 20 lb bombs under the wing and two 112 lb bombs under the centre section. Carrying this bomb load reduced the endurance to three hours, but the aircraft could still remain over the target for one and a half hours. If necessary W/T patrols could report back to the base airfield to dispatch stand-by aircraft if any important enemy activity arose. Night-bombing could further disrupt the economic life of tribesmen, not to mention their chances of sleep. The night-bombing was carried out by Brisfits of No. 5 Squadron. This then was an air blockade activity.

April A night-flying attack was carried out by a single Brisfit on 30 March, and this was so successful that a

further two more night fliers were brought up to Tank on the 6th, where reinforcement by a further flight of these Army Cooperation aircraft had taken place on 18 March. The trooping season had just passed, and new arrivals in India had had to be trained to prepare them for operations. There was a shortage of aircraft, and rigid economies were being applied, so that there was a risk that operations would have to be carried out on a dwindling scale. The squadrons on the North-West Frontier were a long way from a base supply, so keeping nine out of twelve aircraft serviceable on a daily basis became a real problem. The operations continued throughout the month, but with the advent of hot weather, Flight Lieutenant Busk's flight left for the Hill Depot with the commencement of the hot-weather routine. Squadron Leader Hazell had had to force-land on his first raid but managed to jettison his bombs and avoid injury to himself and his air gunner. On the 9th an afternoon patrol sighted and attacked a large lashkar of Faridai tribesmen. Miranshah was called on to supply supporting aircraft, but the weather closed in and they were unable to take off. Meanwhile Flight Lieutenant Savery had force-landed at Sorarogah, and on the 15th another of the squadron's aircraft force-landed.

May On the 1st the Abdur Rahman Khel and all their supporters agreed to the Political Officer's terms and operations came to an end on the 9th. The remainder of the squadron returned to Miranshah. The first independent RAF operations just described were adjudged a great success. The morale effect, particularly at night, had been very great, and Wing Commander Pink had been singled out for praise. It was said that he had shown a fine example to his men in taking part personally in a number of raids, and he had shown resource, determination and energy. The operations had lasted for 54 days, and on 42 of the first 45 days bombing was carried out on the area proclaimed with some 2,070 hours of war flying and 650 hours of flying by squadrons supporting the main operation. The Aircraft Depot worked overtime to keep the squadrons supplied with replacement aircraft and engines. There was, however, some criticism of the operation. Firstly, that the operations were unduly prolonged by the exclusion of the Army, who could be forgiven that they might be excluded from future operations of this kind. Secondly, the government sanction for military operations had been delayed through cold weather, implying that the discomfort brought to the tribesmen were not as great as it might have been. Thirdly that there were inadequate coordination of political intelligence systems within the RAF. Finally that tribal disrespect for political control was encouraged on this occasion by a Political Officer paying a fine of rifles for a tribe from his own stock and a general remitting the ordered fine of one of them. As a result of the success of these operations, the AOC and his staff put forward detailed plans for complete control of the Frontier tribes by the RAF to the GOC-in-C India. It should be noted, in this respect, that RAF operations described did involve ground units, i.e. Frontier Scout units. It should not, therefore, be thought that these operations were carried out exclusively by aircraft. The GOC-in-C did not approve these plans, for the following reasons:

The solution of the tribal problem basically depended upon the civilizing influences which required good and safe ground communications.
Frontier Scout units required Regular Army support.
Public opinion at home, with its aversion to bombing tribesmen and villages, believed credulous or irresponsible stories.

Nevertheless, the Air Force had been given the opportunity to show the Army what they could do, and they had done so most successfully. It was a turning point in the history of the RAF in India. The squadron's achievements and total of flying hours were the highest of any squadrons taking part in these operations, as a result of which Flight Lieutenant Baker was awarded the

DFC, Sergeant Pilot Hawkins the DFM and Flight Lieutenant Savery 'Mentioned in Dispatches'. Squadron Leader Capel of No. 5 Squadron, who had crashed on the Afridi target village in the 1923 operations, was awarded the DSO, whilst the commendation of Wing Commander Pink resulted in his accelerated promotion to group captain. A little later the squadron lost Flying Officer L.W. Aiken, who died of enteric fever, and Flying Officer W. Wynter-Morgan took over adjutant duties. Towards the end of May the aircraft of Nos 27 and 60 Squadrons moved from Risalpur to Peshawar to allow the aerodrome at Risalpur to be regrassed. To make room No. 20 joined No. 5 Squadron, both of them temporarily occupying Kohat, which by now had been built as a single-squadron station. At the same time , the fourth flight of either 27 or 60 Squadrons went to Quetta and a change-round was instituted every six weeks.

October   After the return of Flight Lieutenant Busk's Persian Gulf flight, now that Kohat was ready for permanent occupation, a general reorganization of the Frontier squadrons took place and 60 Squadron moved from Peshawar to Kohat in September 1925. By 15th October these moves had been completed as follows:

No. 1 Wing	No. 20 (AC) Squadron	Bristol Fighters	Peshawar
	No. 60 (B) Squadron	DH9As	Kohat
No. 2 Wing	No.5 (AC) Squadron	Bristol Fighters	Risalpur
	No. 27 (B) Squadron	DH9As	Risalpur
No. 3 Wing	No. 28 (AC) Squadron	Bristol Fighters	Quetta
	No. 31 (AC) Squadron	Bristol Fighters	Ambala

The squadron settled down quickly at Kohat. Squadron Leader Hazell was OC No. 60 Squadron and Station Commander.

November   Six days after the AOC had inspected the squadron between the 18th and 20th the unit moved to Risalpur for the four-day Northern Command manoeuvres to the Campbellpore area. On conclusion of these exercises Wing Commander R.C.M. Pink was posted back to the UK on completion of his Indian tour.

December   In the middle of the month it was decided to repeat the flight to Calcutta to assess further the techniques required in such long-distance formation flights and again to 'show the flag', particularly in Bengal, where service aircraft were practically unknown. Squadron Leader L.M. Bailey AFC, OC No. 27 Squadron, was to lead the formation of six aircraft, with Flight Lieutenant Baker as deputy leader, together with Flying Officer D.L. Thomson and Sergeant Pilot Munro from 60 Squadron. After last year's experiences it was arranged that duplicate ground parties from each squadron would leap-frog each other to alternate landing grounds during

flight. Ultimately Squadron Leader Bailey could not go and Flight Lieutenant Baker led the flight.

1926

January   Flight Lieutenant Baker carried out an air test in a DH9A fitted with a metal propeller, which was perhaps the first occasion where it had been tried out in India.

March   During the early part of the month, individual and formation live bombing-classification flights took place over the new range at Kohat, leading up to the Ellington Trophy competition. The latest instruction required that the squadrons should compete on local bombing ranges supervised by independent judges. The Squadron won the Trophy by a big margin. At that time Pilot Officer Beamish was posted to the squadron, and he was destined to become one of the leading Battle of Britain pilots. Sadly he was killed in March 1942, having been awarded the DSO and Bar, DFC and AFC.

April–October   There were no active operations, although the Mahsuds and Wazirs had an inter-tribal boundary dispute. The Viceroy of India, Lord Irwin, made an extensive tour of the Frontier, and on 19 October 1926 he travelled by road from Bannu to Miranshah, where he inspected A Flight, which was on detachment there until 30 November.

1927

January Air Vice-Marshal Sir Geoffrey Salmond KCB, KCMG, DSO took over as AOC India, relieving Sir Edward Ellington, who went to command the RAF in Iraq.

March Two Fairey IIIFs were flown up to Kohat from the aircraft park at Lahore by Flying Officer Rigg and one of the ferry pilots to go through evaluation trials. It was evolved from the Fairey IIID GP reconnaissance aircraft of 1922. Extensive tests were made and the more experienced pilots took the opportunity of flying both machines. On the 7th one was flown to Miranshah for Flight Lieutenant Busk and his flight to try out. Unfortunately the trials were tragically interrupted on the 12th when Rigg, who had taken the other Fairey to Peshawar to demonstrate it, crashed and was killed with his mechanic, the machine bursting into flames and being completely destroyed. After this crash the remaining Fairey was handed over to Flight Lieutenant Baker to complete a series of climb tests with varying loads laid down by Air HQ Delhi, during which he reached 20,000 ft with two 230 lb bombs, and favourable reports on these and the hot-weather tests were submitted.

April Flight Lieutenant Busk's flight returned from Miranshah early in the month. Flight Lieutenant Savery left the squadron on return to the Home Establishment to retire from the service in 1937, only to be called up for active service in 1939. At the beginning of the hot season Squadron Leader Hazell was adversely affected by the conditions and climate of India, which aggravated the head wounds he had sustained as a Scout pilot during the First World War. He was posted home and retired at his own request, for he had been categorised as 'Fit Home Service Only' and he had enjoyed overseas life so much. He was a good CO and sportsman and was sadly missed by the squadron and his many friends in Northern India.

May/June During the early months of 1927 the Haji of Turangzai (Fazel-i-Wahid) stirred up trouble against the Upper Mohmands, leading them on to a tribal feud against the Lower Mohmands. This led to the first active operations in this area since the First World War. The Haji had three sons, Badshah I, II and III, who were to become notorious outlaws. During the course of these operations another minor leader emerged, and this was Faqir of Ipi (Mirza Ali Khan), aged about thirty years. In May the Haji was joined by the Faqir of Alingar (Faqir

Shah), another notorious hostile who had strong influence in Bajaur, and their aim became to declare a Jehad, or Holy War, against the British. On 1 June lashkars up to 1,500 strong advanced on the Mohmand blockade line of forts surrounding the Peshawar Plain to the north. On the 4th the blockade line was reinforced, and the squadrons at Peshawar, Risalpur and Kohat came under the orders of the GOC-in-C Northern Command. The two available flights of the squadron, now commanded by Flight Lieutenant Baker (one flight being at the Hill Depot on summer routine), joined No. 27 Squadron at Risalpur, and on 6 June they went into action., together with Nos 5 and 20 Squadrons, the latter from Peshawar. During the afternoon, nineteen aircraft from these squadrons bombed two hundred tribesmen near Shabkadar Fort during a dust storm, Nos 5 and 20 Squadrons carrying out low-flying attacks. On the 7th fifteen aircraft of Nos 20, 27 and 60 Squadrons carried out reconnaissance and bombing of villages in the Gandab and Pindiali Valleys, whilst that night No. 5 Squadron carried out night-bombing with flares. Dawn on the 8th quickly brought about the submission of the tribesmen; for their leaders, having promised that the bombs would not explode, were at once discredited. Tribal casualties were few, being fifteen killed and sixteen seriously wounded among the lashkar of twelve to fifteen hundred, whilst government casualties were nil. The very rapid success of the operations was attributed to the timely bombing in adequate strength and especially to the night-bombing. The use of flares by night was something spectacularly new to the tribes and it destroyed their morale. This short and successful operation, in which no Army column was employed, was a typical example of the efficiency of independent air action when applied, immediately and in adequate strength, against a focus of insurrection.

July During the summer the only notable event was the establishment of a new air firing range against the foothills north-east of Kohat. This permitted front-gun shooting, although the approach had to be made over undulating country.

September Flight Lieutenant Baker returned to India in the SS *Ranpura* with his wife, who chaperoned Flight Lieutenant Busk's fiancée on the voyage. Flight Lieutenant Busk met them in Bombay and the Bakers were the sole witnesses at their wedding in the cathedral on the 24th. Thus two flight commanders broke a squadron tradition of all officers except the adjutant being batchelors. The new Squadron CO, Squadron Leader Neville, had, by coincidence, travelled out on the same ship.

October On the 1st Squadron Leader R.G.H. Neville assumed command of the squadron. He had come from the command of No. 29 Squadron at Duxford, flying Gloster Grebes, and felt that he had taken a step backwards in time. His first impression of the RAF in India was reported as follows:

> Having left an up-to-date fighter squadron he watched the ancient DH9As, their pilots still without parachutes, waffling off the ground at landing strips high above sea level and having to be lifted over the mountains with a glider up-current technique. This filled him with horror. They seemed to him to be as manoeuvrable as a Leyland lorry, and of about the same performance. The bulk of the Liberty engine in front of the pilot made the view forward very poor, nor was the Ninak responsive to the side-slip approach in the rarefied Indian air, as he soon discovered by removing the undercarriage sideways at the first attempt. Flying the old Ninaks on the North-West Frontier was obviously an art rather than a technique, but he could not think of it as an art with much of a future. The reliability of the Liberty engines was, however, admirable and a, literally, saving grace. These famous engines were, none the less, just as prehistoric as the rest of the Air Force equipment in Europe.

There was some unrest amongst the Orakzai Afridis in the tribal salient north of Kohat, owing to fierce dissensions between the Shiah and Sunni Sects of the Muslim faith. To prevent an extension of the trouble the squadron made a number of demonstration flights over the area. The District Commissioner, Major Thomson-Glover, made several personal flights over the area with the squadron, dropping pamphlets relating to negotiations between the opposing parties. The trouble eventually petered out. On the 17th Flight Lieutenant Baker carried out a test flight with oxygen equipment. This was probably the first time that oxygen had been used by the RAF in India. Soon after Squadron Leader Neville assumed command, an end was put to the practice which had resulted in the comparative early unreliability of the Liberty engine in the DH9A. It took some time to warm up the water-cooled Liberty engine properly in the Ninak, and the mechanics in most squadrons had the 'stupid' habit of warming them up at slow revolutions. There was thus a consequent lack of proper oil pressure and circulation. It was possible with the coil dual-type ignition to tune the engine to tick over at such a slow speed that one could slowly count each individual exhaust from each cylinder. The mechanics used to compete between flights to see whose engine would run the slowest! One could see them all over the airfield ticking over like grandfather clocks! Directly this practice was forbidden in the squadron the engines gave far better service, the wear on the moving parts of the engine being reduced by the proper flow of oil. When 27 Squadron continued to have trouble with their engines,

Air HQ set up an inquiry to find out why 60 Squadron's engines gave so much better service. As a result of this inquiry 27 Squadron was ordered to adopt the squadron's practice. Very few forced landings resulted from complete engine failures. One notable experience befell a Ninak which was dismantled in tribal territory and the Liberty was brought back to the nearest road on the back of a camel!

December   On the 7th Flight Lieutenant Busk flew with Squadron Leader Neville as passenger, as the latter still had insufficient knowledge of the landscape of the Frontier. Busk led B Flight to Quetta via Miranshah, overflying Fort Sandeman with A and C Flights following. Flying Officer Bardon of A Flight and Flying Officer Blomfield of B Flight both force-landed in a valley, north of Takatu, near Quetta. Bardon had crashed his aircraft but Blomfield rectified his problem whilst on the ground and moved on to Quetta. On the 10th a machine of C Flight force-landed in a dry river bed. On the 8th the squadron flew escort to the train of King Amanullah of Afghanistan. On the afternoon of the 11th the wing flew in formation over the King's train as it approached Karachi, and when the King sailed to Bombay from Karachi the following day, flying-boats took over the escort, once out to sea. At the same time as King Amanullah was passing through Karachi, Wing Commander H.M. Cave-Brown-Cave came in, leading four Southampton flying-boats which were taking part in the Plymouth–Singapore 23,000-mile flight which had left Plymouth on 17 October. The CO and seven officers of the squadron were invited to take part in a trial flight. On the 15th the squadron returned to Kohat to find Colonel A.V. Holt DSO at Multan. Colonel Holt commanded the Black Watch at Multan and had been CO of No. 35 Squadron RFC in France in 1917. Squadron Leader Neville had been one of his flight commanders. In the latter half of the month the squadron competed in and won the Ellington Trophy for the third successive year.

1928

January   On the 21st a squadron formation demonstration was made over the Orakzai Afredis, which seemed to quell any further possibility of trouble. Flight Lieutenant Baker suddenly became ill and had to be invalided home. He received a telegram from Air Vice-Marshal Sir Geoffrey Salmond thanking him for his services to No. 60 Squadron.

May   On the 22nd a Russian equivalent of a DH9A crashed at Parachinar after the crew lost their way on a flight from Termuz to Kabul. The crew and aircraft were brought to Kohat the same day. The crew were reportedly civilians, although they were rough and had poor table manners. The following day an Afghan officer arrived from Kabul and, after being entertained in the

Mess, returned the same day with the aircraft and crew, by road through Peshawar and the Khyber Pass. During the hot weather Flying Officer E.C. de V. Lart carried out an extensive reconnaissance in the Gilgit Area for a landing ground. This was a dangerous flight to make in anything but the finest weather, flying through high passes and down valleys flanked by soaring mountains on either hand rising to some 16,000 ft above sea level. Gilgit was some 160 miles by air from Srinagar, which is at an altitude of 5,200 ft. But immediately after leaving Srinagar he had to weave between mountains up to 13,000 ft high to the Burzil river and then follow this valley upstream until he crossed the Burzil Pass at 13,775 ft. Thence he followed the valleys to Gilgit at 4,770 ft, which was dominated to the north by Rakaposhi at 25,550 ft. Flying Officer Lart, who flew this sortie, could be expected to return from sorties with the branches of trees and telegraph wires trailing from his undercarriage. He was very popular, a keen pilot and a formidable polo player. He was also a linguist and a graduate with a BSc. He spoke Urdu and Pushtu and later qualified as an interpreter in German.

August Night-flying training commenced on the DH9As. The exhaust manifolds had first to be modified to prevent glare. The original exhaust stubs were almost like a firework display in front of the pilot's eyes, especially when the engine was throttled down. At first the squadron had to do its night-flying at Risalpur, as Air HQ considered the proximity of the mountains at Kohat to make night-flying practices there too hazardous. This was later permitted at Kohat when the moon was full. On the commencement of training, pilots would carry out landings on the flare path with the aid of wing-tip flares, fired electrically as the pilot made his approach. When the pilot was more experienced he would dispense with the wing-tip flares. This feature of training generally had moments of excitement, particularly for the officer in charge of the flare path. Gooseneck paraffin flares were laid out on the airfield in the form of a letter 'T', the tail consisting of four flares over a distance of about 250 yards, whilst the arms terminated by flares 100 yards from the head of the 'T'. Number One flare was at the tail, fifty yards from the next one. Here was stationed the officer in charge of the flare path, known in some

squadrons as 'Paraffin Pete', with an airman holding an Aldis lamp. This was a chilly duty in the cold weather, and warm clothes, flying boots, gauntlets and overcoat collar turned up was the order of the day. The officer kept strict control of all air movements. A pilot would request permission to leave the tarmac by flashing his aircraft letter on his recognition light. This was granted or declined by flashing the same letter in green or red from Number One flare. If granted the pilot then taxied out to the right-hand side of the flare and took off down the flare path. The left-hand side was kept for emergency landings. To get down the pilot circled the field and flashed his recognition light again, requesting permission to land. Once it was granted the pilot would bring his aircraft to touch down on the right of and in the light of Number One flare. Since the light cast on the ground by these flares was not very widespread, it was necessary to bring the aircraft down as close to the flares as possible. On occasion the approach made by a novice pilot could cause 'Paraffin Pete' to have to make a run for it!

October On the 21st the squadron was inspected by the Under-Secretary of State for Air, the Rt Hon. Sir Philip Sassoon, Bart GBE, CMG, MP, accompanied by the AOC. In preparation for the arrival of Nos 11 and 39 Squadrons in India to add to the total of squadrons, there was a further reorganization. The No. 1 (Indian) Group was formed at Peshawar with two subordinate wings, Nos 1 and 2 (Indian) Wings. Group Captain R.P. Mills MC, AFC was placed in command of the group. Squadron Leader H.V. Champion de Crespigny MC, DFC, who brought No. 39 Squadron from RAF Spitalgate, was promoted to the rank of wing commander and placed in command of No. 2 Wing for the following five years. No. 1 (Indian) Wing was commanded by Wing Commander Murlis-Green DSO (Bar), MC (2 Bars), Karageorge [the latter was a Serbian Order]. Murlis-Green was a distinguished First World War pilot with twenty victories to his credit. No. 3 (Indian) Wing was commanded by Wing Commander J.C. Slessor MC, later to become Chief of the Air Staff. The exciting thing about the arrival of Nos 11 and 39 Squadrons was that they were both equipped with a new aircraft, the Westland Wapiti. The new organization was as follows:

Group HQ	No. 20 (AC) Squadron	Bristol Fighters	Peshawar
No. 1 Wing	No. 20 (B) Squadron	DH9As	Kohat
	No. 60 (B) Squadron	DH9As	Kohat
No. 2 Wing	No. 11 (B) Squadron	Wapitis	Risalpur
	No. 39 (B) Squadron	Wapitis	Risalpur
No. 3 Wing	No. 5 (AC) Squadron	Bristol Fighters	Quetta
	No. 31 (AC) Squadron	Bristol Fighters	Quetta
Under Air HQ	No. 28 (AC) Squadron	Bristol Fighters	Ambala
	Aircraft Park		Lahore
	Aircraft Park		Karachi

Westland Wapiti J.9719 of No. 60 Squadron on a bombing mission over the North West Frontier.

December Many postings took effect on the squadron during the year, so that by the end of the year the three flight commanders were Flight Lieutenant S.J. Smetham (A Flight), Flight Lieutenant J. MacBain DFC (B Flight) and Flight Lieutenant C.B.R. Pelly (C Flight). Some of the new officers were specialists. Smetham and Flying Officer Worsley were 'photographic', Flying Officer A.H. Cocks was 'signals'. Flying Officer H.G. Wisher was ' air pilotage' and Flying Officer H.D. Spreckley was 'armament'. In mid-December the first issue of parachutes was made to pilots and air gunners. Surprisingly some pilots resisted wearing them, claiming that their weight reduced the war load of the aircraft, i.e. bombs and ammunition. Pilots had not worn parachutes from the earliest days of the RFC. Regulations soon came in making their wear compulsory.

The Kabul Rescue

After King Amanullah returned from his European Tour, which had impressed him greatly, he realized how backward his country was. He carried out a number of sweeping reforms, determined to improve conditions amid mounting resentment among his Kabuli subjects. He attempted, for example, to abolish the use of the purdah veil by women. This was too much for strict Muslims to accept, and a revolt against his reforms ensued in November, led by Bacha-i-Saqao, an unknown water carrier's son. He led a large army, aided by a lashkar of 2,500 Wazirs and Mahsuds, and sacked Kabul.

The news very quickly got through to Peshawar, and the British minister, Sir Francis Humphrys, who had been in the RAF in 1918, remained in contact with Peshawar using W/T communications, the telegraph wires having been cut. The British Legation was situated outside Kabul and away from the other foreign embassies, and Sir Francis, his wife and some forty Europeans found themselves in a war zone and surrounded. Communications through the Afghan W/T station ceased on 17 December in the middle of a request for a reconnaissance of the area and the evacuation of all the women and children in the Legation.

The RAF in India was therefore faced with the prospect of having to undertake an air evacuation over some of the most forbidding mountainous terrain on the planet. The Bristol Fighters did not have the range to get to Kabul, unlike the DH9As of Nos 27 and 60 Squadrons and one Hinaidi flown by Flight Lieutenant D.F. Anderson, recalled from Iraq. No. 70 (B) Squadron, equipped with Victorias, was also available, if needed, in Iraq.

The first step was for the DH9As to be stripped of military equipment, and on 18 December Flying Officer C.W.L. Trusk flew the 150 miles from Kohat to Kabul, taking with him a Popham Panel to be dropped on the Legation, so enabling messages to be sent to aircraft circling overhead. Trusk's aircraft was hit by rifle fire as it flew low over the Legation, and a hit was sustained in the radiator and the oil pump, but the radio operator, LAC G. Donaldson, managed to get off a message before Trusk force-landed his aircraft at Sherpur airfield, some 6,000 ft above sea level and from where the Popham Panel could be delivered by road. Trusk and Donaldson did not themselves get to the Legation. During the afternoon Flight Lieutenant A.R. Prendergast of No. 27 Squadron delivered another panel. He was warned to fly high and not to attempt a landing. On the 19th the squadron became involved when Flight Lieutenant Smetham and Corporal Ottey dropped an Aldis lamp in the grounds, being hit by nine bullets in the process. One of these hits broke a flying wire, but the aircraft got back to Kohat. On the 21st Flying Officer H.G. Wisher and Flight Sergeant Sheers, in two of the squadron's aircraft, flew to Kabul. Wisher intended landing but was warned not to do so. On the 20th Prendergast and LAC Locke of 27 Squadron flew over the Legation. W/T signals were again being received by the Legation on an emergency set, and the Afghan W/T station had been reopened when royalist forces drove the rebel forces away.

On the 23rd one Victoria (Squadron Leader Maxwell), twenty-four DH9As and two Westland Wapitis were available for operations, and two more Victorias were requested from Iraq. Squadron Leader Nicholas's radio-equipped Wapiti was flown to Kabul, and the squadron leader reported that all was well, which meant that the Victoria and three DH9As could be flown to Kabul with Army signals personnel equipped with a short-wave W/T set to be set up in the Legation. Meanwhile other European embassies and legations requested that their women and children be evacuated by air. During the day Squadron Leader Maxwell and the three DH9As returned to Risalpur with twenty-one women and girls and 590 lb of baggage.

On the 24th Flying Officer E.G.H. Russell-Stracey flew the W/T Wapiti ahead of the Victoria and eleven DH9As. This enabled the Wapiti to radio the Legation and have the evacuees, twenty-one French and German women, ready for instant evacuation. On Christmas Day no evacuation took place. A further twenty-six women and children plus 730 lb of baggage were lifted on Boxing Day, but snow prevented any flights for the next two days. Then, with two Victorias available, theDH9As were held in reserve. The evacuation continued, and a spare engine and two fitters were flown up to get Trusk's DH9A serviceable.

1929

January There was a surprise change at the top when Group Captain H. le M. Brock DSO was posted in from Hinaidi, Iraq, to command No. 1 (Indian) Group at Peshawar. On the 1st the last of the 134 women and children, together with the two fitters, were evacuated from Kabul. On the 9th King Amanullah approved a weekly airmail service, but the next day the rebels advanced on Kabul and King Amanullah abdicated in favour of his brother Inayatulla, who reluctantly became Amir. He then flew to Kandahar. On the 18th Squadron Leader Maxwell and Flight Lieutenant Ivelaw-Chapman flew to Kabul in two Victorias and landed at Sherpur airfield, which was surrounded by the rebel army. Ivelaw-Chapman evacuated Inayatulla, and Maxwell flew out the harem of ten wives. Bachi-i-Saqao at once seized the throne, taking the name of Habibullah II. The same day Sir Francis Humphrys decided to close the Legation, resulting in all the other embassies and legations to decide to evacuate Kabul completely. Habibullah permitted two aircraft to land daily and one airmail aircraft to land on Wednesdays. Accordingly five more Victorias were ordered from Iraq and Egypt, and these had reached Risalpur by 15 February. The operation was carried out in the worst weather conditions ever experienced on the Frontier. The temperature was down to –20 deg C. The pilots of the squadron in their open cockpits escorted fifteen evacuation flights. Crews took off at dawn to reach 6,000 ft under full throttle, the lowest possible height to fly between the snow-covered peaks, which rose to 10,000 ft or more. Intermittent bad weather grounded the aircraft, and air and ground crews faced very severe conditions. Further evacuation commenced at 10.00 hrs on the 29th, when Ivelaw-Chapman, accompanied by Flying Officer A.R.S. Davies in a Victoria, took off from Risalpur, together with Flight Lieutenant Anderson in the Hinaidi equipped with W/T. Anderson reached Kabul but Ivelaw-Chapman did not. En route the Napier Lion engines of the Victoria gradually faded, and he crash-landed on the only piece of flat land near the junction of the Kabul and Kunar rivers. The land on which the Victoria had been brought down was only some sixty

yards square, falling steeply on three sides for 200 ft and rising on the fourth. It was found that the petrol filters had one and a half inches of ice on them.

February For three days Ivelaw-Chapman and Davies were missing, until Squadron Leader Maxwell and Flying Officer L.H. Anness spotted their Victoria. The two men reached Jalalabad on the 4th and stayed at Charbagh Fort. A suitable landing ground was found at Sultanpur three miles distant, and Peshawar was notified. On the 10th Flying Officer Hancock of No. 20 Squadron landed at Sultanpur in a Brisfit escorted by two other aircraft, damaging the aircraft in the process. While repairs were carried out rebels could be seen and Jalalabad arsenal was blown up. On the 12th Hancock took off, taking Davies, who had a knee injury, with him. Meanwhile, over the next five days Ivelaw-Chapman had enlisted help in clearing the landing ground, surrounded by rebels fighting over loot. On the 18th he was flown out by Hancock, escorted by Flying Officer McKee in a W/T-equipped DH9A. Subsequently Ivelaw-Chapman was awarded the AFC. In the meantime the evacuation of Kabul continued under appalling weather conditions, with seventeen inches of snow at Sherpur airfield and temperatures as low as –18 deg C. Sir Francis had to get the Afghans to trample a runway 1,000 yards long and 120 yards wide, but on the 25th the evacuation was successfully completed.

March Wing Commander Murlis-Green was posted home to command the Armament and Gunnery School, Eastchurch. He was replaced as OC 1 Wing by Wing Commander C.C. Darley AM, who came from the P Staff (Personnel) at Air Headquarters, Delhi. Flight Lieutenant W.F. Dickson arrived to join the staff of No. 1 Wing. He was later to come Chief of the Air Staff, and he did a great deal towards furthering the good relations between the RAF and the Indian Army in Kohat and between the wings and squadrons.

April Squadron Leader Neville was detached to the Hill Depot, Lower Topa, to command until July. An illustration of how local tribesmen could try to wangle a few rupees from the British is to be found in one particular bombing practice, when a bomb was dropped outside the range area to explode on the edge of a small village. Later in the day a group of hostile tribesmen arrived at the entrance to the RAF station with a blood-stained casualty on a stretcher claiming compensation for the injuries caused by the bomb. The Medical Officer was called and he confirmed that the man was suffering from knife wounds, not bomb fragments. Obviously the man had been in a fight or the injuries might have been self inflicted, but it was a good try!

October The Viceroy of India visited the Frontier. On the 16th Flying Officer Morison flew Sir Denis Bray, the

Foreign Secretary, for an urgent appointment with the Viceroy, later flying him back to Risalpur via Manzai. Flight Lieutenant Pelly was posted home after five years with the squadron, his place being taken by Flight Lieutenant E.C. de V. Lart.

No. 70 Squadron
Usquam (Anywhere)

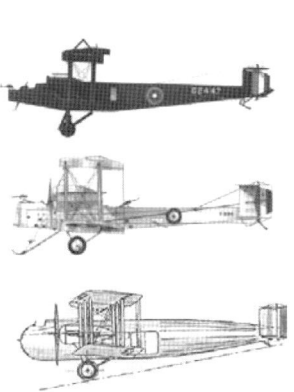

1926

September Wing Commander Nicholl assumed command of the squadron, which was at this time carrying out a fortnightly airmail service from Baghdad to Cairo. The equipment of the squadron was four Vickers Victorias and six Vickers Vernons. The mail work was continued to the end of 1926, when it was taken over by Imperial Airways, a civilian subsidized service. The first Imperial Airways aircraft arrived at Hinaidi on 31 December 1926.

1927

January On the 1st two Vickers Victorias of No. 70 Squadron proceeded to Shaibah and thence to India as escorts to the Air Secretary, Sir Samuel Hoare, accompanied by Lady Hoare. These machines were:

Serial No. 7922 – Pilots – Wing Commander Nicholl
  and Flying Officer Richardson
Serial No. 7926 – Pilots – Flight Lieutenant King and
  Flying Officer Stuart

Both aircraft proceeded from Hinaidi to Karachi, after which a tour of the RAF stations on the North-West Frontier of India was carried out. This tour included Jodhpur, Delhi, Ambala, Lahore, Risalpur, Peshawar, Kohat, Multan and back to Karachi. Meanwhile Nicholl followed the Secretary of State back to Baghdad. Flight Lieutenant King returned to Delhi and took part in the first display of the RAF in India. During the absence of Wing Commander Nicholl, the squadron was commanded by Squadron Leader Keith. The residue of No. 45 Squadron was attached to No. 70 Squadron, the former's Vernons being taken over by the latter. (No. 45

Squadron moved to Helwan without aircraft in cadre form on 17 January and was not established at Heliopolis until the 25th. This considerably retarded the recovering of the Victorias.

LXX SQUADRON

February to March Hinaidi – the squadron trained as a night-bombing squadron. This was followed by an exercise in troop carrying carried out with the 14th Hyderabads. Training flights to Cairo were inaugurated in place of the former airmail service to keep pilots conversant with the Cairo–Baghdad route. The squadron maintained a detachment of wireless telegraphy stations at Ramadi. And training for the year was completed with the following average errors:

At 10,000 ft – day-bombing – 65.9 yards
  – night-bombing – 54.8 yards

November Troop-carrying exercises were carried out, 240 troops being given a flight of about 30 minutes. It was found possible to dispatch aircraft at one-minute intervals to deplane troops at the same rate, provided three machines could deplane simultaneously. Between 27 November and January 1928 the squadron was visited by parties of officers from HMS *Enterprise*, *Emerald* and *Triad*, the numbers being conveyed to and from Shaibah by air in Victorias.

December During 1927 there were only two flying accidents, each resulting in the write-off of a Vernon. There were no casualties to personnel and there were no losses of men due to sickness, except one airman invalided to the United Kingdom.

1928

January At Hinaidi on the 6th the squadron proceeded by air to join AKFORCE. The constituent list of pilots and other personnel, and details of work carried out, is contained in INPOL reports dated 31 March 1928 to 3 May 1928. During this period the squadron carried out air transport to advanced bases on a larger scale than had hitherto been tried. The summary is as follows:

Total weight carried from airhead to ground columns
  – 517.39 lb
Total passengers carried – 1,192
Total number of hours flown on operations – 2,074
  hours, equal to 50 hours per aircraft for the month.

The squadron also took part with three Victorias in the raid on Al Safa.

November On the 26th Wing Commander J.A.G. De Courcey assumed command of the squadron, his vice being Wing Commander Nicholl. Air Vice-Marshal Ellington was carried to Ramadi on posting to Home Establishment.

December From the 28th until March 1929 – operations in connection with the evacuation from Kabul. Victorias of No. 216 Squadron, Egypt, were loaned to No. 70 Squadron as replacements during this period.

1929
October to December Journeys between Iraq and Egypt in connection with the move of No. 5 Squadron . Total flying hours for the year – 4,190 hours, of which 3,498 hours were operational flying. Total persons carried was 15,862.

Troops emplaning in a Vickers Victoria.

No. 84 Squadron
Scorpiones pungunt
(Scorpions sting)

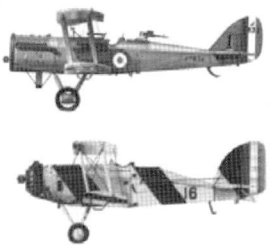

1927
October On the 21st nine aircraft left with the SSO as passenger to carry out a bombing raid on Salman-al-Fadhal and Jabbar. Both villages were heavily bombed and fired by incendiaries and petrol to eliminate all cover such as ditches, with the result that a few horses and cattle were discovered and destroyed. A Flight returned to base to refuel and stand by. C Flight returned at 07.00 hrs for a similar purpose, leaving Squadron Leader Vincent with B Flight to cooperate with the police. At a given signal from the CO, the police advanced unhesitatingly, to gain their objective in a few

minutes, and completed the destruction of the property, grain, tents, etc. This operation was completed successfully at 08.15 hrs GMT under the direction of Captain Gorry. On receiving a signal from the police, the aircraft returned to Nasiriyah, arriving at 08.45 hrs GMT. The SSO was deplaned near the police on the ground at approximately 07.00 hrs, and returned to Shattrah on foot with a police column. A Vernon pilot, Flying Officer Switzer, was allotted to the squadron by No. 70 (Bombing) Squadron for the purpose of carrying supplies from Shaibah. This aircraft arrived at 08.00. The two aircraft pilots were Squadron Leader Vincent and Flight Lieutenant Ridgway. With the Admintor and a mechanic as passengers they left for Shaibah at 11.50 hrs GMT to confer with the Mutassarif and Inspector of Police. The tribal leaders were seen and informed of the fine imposed upon them and their tribe by the Admintor and the Mutassarif, which was 150 modern rifles with 50 rounds of SAA [small-arms ammunition] each, 10 lira per rifle and one rupee to be paid for all shortages – a 300,000-rupee fine in all, to be paid within 48 hours, which was to expire at 08.00 hrs local on 24 October 1927. The Admintor was also flown over the scene of the operations and afterwards expressed himself completely satisfied with the action taken by police and the squadron. The aircraft returned to Nasiriyah at 14.00 hrs GMT.

1928
January On the 27th Flight Lieutenant Sayward with three Rolls-Royce armoured cars went out to Potter's force-landing (at Hadaniy) but could not reach the aircraft owing to surrounding cliffs. Flying Officer Sandiford went out to the force-landing in the afternoon and collected certain items. The aircraft required a new engine. Two companies of the Arab army arrived at about 14.00 hours local. Flying Officer Sandiford, Flying Officer de Burgh, Flying Officer Kellett and Sergeant Hale returned after 4½ hours' reconnaissance over Al Shasas. They were unable to find Ibn Sharain so continued reconnaissance up to the north of Al Lauqah. They reported that Shamar Abdur was located about 15 miles south of Al Ghasas and he would therefore appear to be returning to the Nejd. Sergeant Hale crashed on landing, writing off Serial No. 7797. Flight Lieutenant Ridgway, Flying Officer de Burgh, Flying Officer Tomkins and Sergeant White returned after 4¾ hours over the city of Birkat-al-Askat and had nothing to report as they were flying over sand most of the time. Flight Lieutenant King and Sergeant Hill to Shaibah to undergo dual instruction. Flight Lieutenant Barrett, Flight Lieutenant Barlow, Flying Officer Tomkins and Sergeant White left on a reconnaissance and to drop messages on the Dhahamshah and Lauqah tribes telling them they need not move, but the reconnaissance flight returned as Tomkins had engine trouble. The

reconnaissance resumed as soon as the trouble was rectified but was recalled by Flight Lieutenant Ridgway when they had just passed Takhadid. On arriving there was a message from AKFORCE giving orders for all aircraft to proceed to Busaiyah. One flight of No. 55 Squadron was shot up. Flight Lieutenants Barrett and Ridgway and Flying Officers Sandiford, de Burgh and Kellett and Sergeant White left for Busaiyah at 19.00 hours, arriving there two hours later. On the 30th Flight Lieutenant Barrett and six aircraft left for Buscol at 07.00 hours to cooperate with other aircraft. Aircraft returned to Rukhaimiyah owing to low clouds. Left again on reconnaissance at 11.15 hours except Sandiford whose engine would not start. At 13.05 hours six aircraft located 100 camels and approximately 40 men eight miles from Hafar. Aircraft fired on raiders, bombed and machine-gunned them – 24 bombs and 150 rounds altogether. Flying Officer Kellett landed with complete engine failure $1/4$ mile from the raiders, who were hiding in the wadi. At 15.30 hours Flight Lieutenant Barrett landed and his and Kellett's aircraft came under fire. Aircraft from Buscol were summoned by W/T. Owing to raiders hiding in wadi it was very difficult to inflict heavy casualties. Flying Officer Kellett succeeded in salving guns, block and bolt, also ammunition, before abandoning aircraft, although still under fire. Both the other flights of No. 55 Squadron received our message re raiders and attacked them. On the 31st Flight Lieutenants Barrett and Ridgway and Flying Officers Kellett and Tomkins left Busaiyah and returned to Salman. An evening reconnaissance was carried out but there was nothing of importance to report. Flying hours for the month totalled 683 hours.

February   On the 1st Flight Lieutenant Barrett with three aircraft and the SSO as passenger returned from a reconnaissance to Ansab, Umm-ar-Rudhumma and Matriba. Approximately 800 camels and a few flocks of sheep were located, all proceeding northwards. The majority of camels appeared to be loaded or grazing, indicating tribesmen on the move. Aircraft were not fired on. One warning bomb was dropped on 28 black tents approximately 4 miles north of Umm-ar-Rudhumma and on 80 tents approximately near Matriba, mostly black, one white. This confirms reports that Habbas-Ibn-Habbas was moving southwards. No Iraqi tribes in the city of Takh Adid. A majority of tents at Umm-ar-Rhudhumma appear to be of the Dhafir type but with small brown Akhwan types among them. The camels on the move might conceal raiders and therefore require watching. On the 2nd Flight Lieutenant Barrett and three aircraft returned from a reconnaissance of Umm-ar-Rhudhumma at 10.45 hours and reported that, five miles south of Ansab, 70 camels and five flocks of sheep were moving north-east. Ten miles south of Ansab 24 tents were located *en bloc* nearby. At Matriba 23 tents

in four groups, 200 camels grazing and 15 sheep located. Three bombs dropped. Ten miles west of Matriba were 11 tents in two groups, one bomb dropped near each group. Shamar Abdur had moved slightly further south. On the 3rd Squadron Leader Vincent DFC and three aircraft returned at about 11.15 hours GMT from a reconnaissance and reported that a landing was made on the camp of Arsi-Ibn-Sharain at Al Aida. Arsi reported the intention of moving, rising gradually towards Takh Adid, during a brief interview by the SSO, Flight Lieutenant Hindle. He expressed friendliness towards Iraq and a desire to cooperate against Dawish. A landing was made 15 miles east of Aqubbah camp of Al Saijah, sub-section of the Dhahamshah of Mohammed, Turkey. Tents of the Mahailat, sub-section of the Dhahamshah, located at the base of Batin Ridge, west of Aqubbah. The camp of Jazzi-Ibn-Mizlad was located near Khusmat-al-Dhafari, 60 miles west of Aqubbah. White flags were waved and landings were made in the proximity of Jazza's tents. Jazza was absent but his Wakil states that Jazza wishes to meet the SSO as soon as possible to discuss his return to Iraq. Revised orders regarding Jazza have been dropped as he had moved towards Iraq. Arrangements made to send personnel to Shaibah for one week's rest to be continued until all personnel have had a rest. Four aircraft only to remain at Nugrat Salman. On the 4th aircraft were unable to leave on reconnaissance owing to sand in the air from yesterday's gale. On the 5th Flight Lieutenant Barlow and three aircraft, the SSO as passenger, left for Al Ghasas to pick up SSO's agent, then proceeded to Jazza's camp, west of Aqubbah. The weather is considerably improved. The reconnaissance reports – 'Located Ibn Sharain moving north-east over ridge at Al Aida.' The SSO interviewed Arsi-Ibn-Sharain who repeated his intention to remain in Iraq. According to instructions. the SSO also interviewed Nutlaq-Ibn-Ali privately. He reports losing 2,000 camels, 35 tents and 5 men killed including his nephew Hammad in the Jilbabi raid. These losses included 10 tents of Dhafir Anslab camped with him. Nutlaq states that he has received promise of full protection from Ibn Saud which has so far not been carried out. Mohammed, brother of Hammad, has proceeded to Riyadh to lodge a complaint. Nutlaq interviewed Dawish at Linah after the raid but was threatened with death if he did not leave immediately. Dawish also expressed definite intentions of further raids into Iraq including raids against government posts being considered. Ibn Saud at present unable to suppress Dawish. The SSO landed at Khashlate-al-Dhanari in Camp Jazza. He denies having paid 'Zikkat' to Agent officials but the state's fresh demands had just reached him. He has agreed to move tomorrow to the Almiya area. He appears to have sent messengers to Ibn Saud asking permission to enter Iraq temporarily and is likely to be delayed unless carefully watched by aircraft. Jazza reports presence of Abdullah-

Ibn-Bayudh. Officials of Ibn Mussaad at Al Qawa Ajitim on Darbzubadiah for his demanding 'Zikkat'. Time did not permit verification of this. Ibn Sharain requests permission to supply caravan to visit Samah via Salman. Ibn-Bayudh reported to have collected list of losses on Sahammar Dhafir and Dhahamshah dispatched to Ibn Saud. Friction between Dhahamshah and Ibn Hadhal not really probable but this needs watching.

October Squadron leader J.J. Breen arrived by air to take over command of the squadron, vice Squadron Leader F.J. Vincent, who proceeds to No. 45 Squadron direct from leave. Between the 23rd and 31st the position of aircraft on the squadron is now two flights of Wapitis and one flight of DH9As, with three Wapitis and one DH9A in reserve.

November On the 1st there was nothing to report. From the 6th to 10th the squadron carried out the annual classification practice. The results were good in view of the fact that this was the first time bombing had been carried out with the new aircraft. An Armistice Day parade was held in the morning of the 11th, observing two minutes silence. On the 12th an incoming draft from the UK arrived on board HMT *Nirvana*, our strength being 5 officers and 54 other ranks. The officers were Flight Lieutenant Bussel who relieves Flight Lieutenant Barrett, Flight Lieutenant Drummond who takes over full signals duties from Flying Officer Kellett, Flying Officer Pleasance, Flying Officer Harris and Flying Officer Richards who is to take over as Accounting Officer, vice Flying Officer Goodall. The strength of the draft of airmen is 54, which included 5 attachments from AID and 5 airman pilots.

December On the 29th a flight left Sulman at 09.40 hours local and reconnoitred Al A'an-Shibrun where large flocks were observed grazing to the East of Aqubbah. Then proceeded to a point approximately 29 deg 39' Lat. and 45 deg 37' East. Reference Map – White and Black Basra Map. 1-1. Discovered approximately 130 camels which were halted on south side of high cliffs. In this position it would have been impossible to locate them from the ground approaching from the north to the south until the base of the cliff was reached. The aircraft then circled the camel men several times and men could be seen running about amongst the camels and throwing themselves prone to the ground. Captain Glubb requested that we try to ascertain whether or not aircraft were being fired on. The aircraft was throttled back and held on its automatic slots. [Slots are dealt with in detail in Chapter 5. They enable aircraft to fly very slowly almost at the point of stall.] This enabled the position to be held without difficulty. Rifle fire was distinctly heard and building up in fire power. General movement was now afoot and it was obvious that preparations were

being made to scatter. Captain Glubb informed Flight Lieutenant Lock that he was satisfied that the camel men were raiders and instructed that they were to be bombed. The first 'sighter' bomb was OK. Two camels with riders fell. Bombs were dropped with good effect and aircraft engaged the raiders with machine-gun fire. On the 30th nothing to report. On the 31st the flight on reconnaissance went to Shaibah. The total flying time for the month was 570 hours and for the complete year was 5,286 hours, which was considered very good taking into consideration time lost while the unit was being re-equipped with a new type of aircraft [the Wapiti].

1929

May, June and July Unit training was carried out.

August Air Marshal Sir Geoffrey Salmond, en route for India, accompanied by Air Commodore Burnett, arrived at Shaibah and proceeded to No. 203 Squadron at Basra. Air Commodore Burnett then departed by air. On the 16th Flying Officer Fogarty proceeded to Bahrain in an Imperial Airways machine to make a report on Bahrain landing ground.

September On the 18th, the AOC carried out his annual inspection of the unit. On the 27th Building No. 1, the old MT shed, blew down during the night in a gale.

October From the 14th to 21st the squadron carried out annual airfiring and bombing classification. On the 25th reconnaissance by A Flight carried out. No air action was taken. On the 27th reconnaissance was carried out by a composite flight. On the 30th HMT *Nirvana* arrived at Basra. The incoming draft comprised Squadron Leader H. Stewart, who takes over command, Flying Officer Stowell and 22 airmen. They disembarked at 14.00 hrs and arrived at Shaibah at 17.00 hours by trolley [*sic*]. The outgoing draft left on 1 November.

[For the remainder of the year the entry on the microfilm has been double-typed, making reading impossible.]

No. 202 Squadron
Semper vigilate
(*Be always vigilant*)

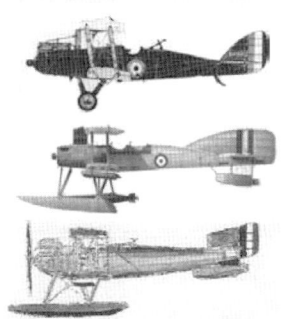

A Fairey IIID seaplane over Malta.

1920

January Squadron equipped with DH9s at Spittlegate and disbanded on the 22nd.

April On the 9th, squadron reformed at Alexandria from a flight of No. 267 Squadron and equipped with Short 184.

1921

May On the 16th squadron disbanded.

1929

January On the 1st, squadron reformed at Kalafrana, Malta equipped with Fairey IIIDs, No. 481 Flight renumbered.

No. 203 Squadron

Occidens oriensque
(West and East)

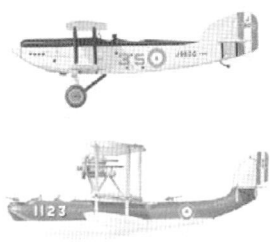

The following extracts from the operations record book of No. 203 (Flying-Boat) Squadron show the organization required to transfer a squadron from the United Kingdom to Basra, Iraq. The Southamptons were a new aircraft and their arrival was preceded by the setting up of a Seaplane Flight, which would reconnoitre the Persian Gulf for possible seaplane bases or landing areas. It is also of interest that a squadron was commanded by a wing commander who would have a number of ancillary units under his command, such as the Provost (police), sick quarters and stores depot.

1928

June The formation of a temporary seaplane flight at Basra, together with a flying-boat/seaplane base with adjoining aerodrome, was first considered during the winter of 1927/1928. The stores depot at Mareil was reduced to Care and Maintenance (C & M) during the second quarter of 1928, leaving a section of its stores, MV pool and small marine section. In June a temporary seaplane flight was formed under the command of Squadron Leader C.B. Dilson AFC who was also in command of the C & M party. Two Fairey IIIF floatplanes were allotted with the addition of one motorboat and the necessary flight personnel to C & M establishment. The aircraft were based in a temporary hangar at Mareil and they were hoisted by crane on to the jetty.

August Squadron Leader Dilson left the country, and command of the seaplane flight devolved to Flying Officer F.E. Fairhead, Squadron Leader W.C. Clark being in command of the C & M party.

November Squadron Leader Woodhouse DSO, MC, in command of the Armoured Car Reserve at Basra, was detailed to supervise the affairs of the seaplane flight in November 1928. The seaplane flight was formed in order to start flights in the Gulf as soon as the political situation permitted and to prepare the way for the Southampton flying-boats. It was not until the end of November that flights could be made in the Gulf, and it was emphasized that the initial stages to Kuwait and Bahrain were to be thoroughly consolidated before extending further eastwards.

December On the 5th Flight Lieutenant A.P. Revington arrived at Basra having been sent out to carry out operations with the seaplane flight and to prepare the ground for No. 203 (Flying-Boat) Squadron, Flying Officer Fairhead remaining in command of the flight however. On the 10th the first flight over the Gulf to Kuwait was carried out by Squadron Leader Woodhouse and Flight Lieutenant Revington.

1929

January On the 4th a second reconnaissance flight was made to Kuwait to a point 25 miles to the southwards.

February At Basra on the 4th the Sheikh of Kuwait and the Political Agent were given a flight in a Fairey IIIF by Flight Lieutenant Revington. Owing to the imminent arrival of the flying-boats from England it was decided not to extend the seaplane flights to Bahrain as this would have involved a sloop [light naval craft] standing by in an intermediate position as a precaution and also for W/T purposes. Flight Lieutenant Revington was detailed to visit and report on sites for seaplane bases in the Persian Gulf, and left Basra on the 10th aboard a

Royal Naval vessel. He proceeded to the Trucial coast, visiting Dubai, Sharjah and Ras-al-Khaimah, returning to Hanjam via Basidev on the 18th where he embarked on SS *Barretta* and proceeded to Bahrain, where 24 hours were spent before returning to Basra. On the 24th No. 203 Squadron personnel arrived from the UK. Instructions had been received from Air Headquarters during his absence that Flight Lieutenant Revington was to take over command of No. 203 Squadron, to which the seaplane flight was now attached. And the C & M party, Basra, under Flight Lieutenant A.T. Shaw (Stores Branch) being in command of the latter was now placed in charge of the Stores Disposal Section only.

February Handing over was completed by the 6th, and preparations could now go ahead more rapidly. [The following passage describes the redeployment of 203 Squadron from Cattewater (RAF Mount Batten), Plymouth, to Basra, Iraq, to join the seaplane flight equipped with Fairey IIIF floatplanes.] On the 28th the flight of (Southampton) aircraft left Cattewater and went as follows:

Cattewater–Bordeaux–Marseilles–Naples–Kalafrana (Malta)–Benghazi–Aboukir (Egypt)–Alexandria–Hinaidi–Basra

Spares were put down *en route*, a spare engine, radiator and wing tip float at Malta together with a tail dolly [a wheel which dollies like the swivelling wheels under a sofa], a spare engine and radiator at Aboukir and other spares. On the 29th a temporary W/T station was erected and in operation by the end of the month. Three moorings were laid between Coal Island and the right bank of the Shatt-al-Arab. The situation lies two miles above the stores depot at Mareil. It was the only available site that was sufficiently far from river traffic to ensure the safety of the boats on moorings.

March When the flying-boats arrived on the 14th there were only two general-duties officers at the unit, Flight Lieutenant Revington in command and Flying Officer Baird. Wing Commander T.E.B. Howe then took over command of No. 203 (Flying-Boat) Squadron at Basra. The following were included in his command:

The Base Supply Depot
Station Sick Quarters
The Provost Marshal

The strength of the C & M party had been 25 airmen and 20 attached to the seaplane flight during the fortnight succeeding the arrival of squadron personnel on 24 January. Twenty-five airmen were posted away leaving a total strength of 73 and a surplus of 6 airmen. The establishment of the RAF Station Service Police was included in No. 203 (FB) Squadron establishment.

3 × Southampton flying-boats (the two Fairey IIIF seaplanes left the unit on 13 April)
3 × Motor launches
2 × Brooke motor boats
11 × MT vehicles
3 × Dinghies fitted with outboard motors

[The remainder of the records for 1929 are almost unreadable and concern the settling in of the flying-boat squadron at Basra.]

No. 208 Squadron
Vigilant

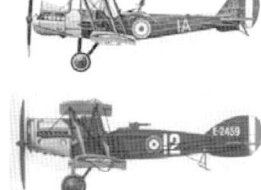

1920
October The squadron was re-equipped with Bristol Fighters.

1922
Squadron Leader A.P. Ellis assumed command in 1922.

September Orders issued for the squadron to mobilise. On the 25th the unit embarked at Alexandria in SS *Podesta* for operations in Turkey.

1923

September The unit returned to Alexandria and the aircraft were railed to Aboukir where they were assembled, tested and flown to Ismailia.

October Squadron Leader A.C. Winter assumed command.

1924

January On the 1st Squadron Leader Probyn DSO assumed command.

1925

November Squadron Leader MacLaren OBE, MC, DFC, AFC took over command.

1926

November Squadron Leader MacLaren was invalided to the United Kingdom. Flight Lieutenant Green assumed temporary command. Until February 1927.

1927

February/March On 26 February Squadron Leader Lindsay was posted from Home Establishment to command No. 208 Squadron, arriving in Egypt on 12 March to take over command from Flight Lieutenant Green on 14 March. On 31 March four aircraft flew to Heliopolis for an aerial demonstration which included a low bombing attack on a tank on Heliopolis race course on the occasion of the Command Military Police Sports Day.

May From the 11th to 14th a searchlight army tattoo.

June On the 14th on the occasion of the passage through the Suez Canal of Group Captain HRH. Duke of York KG, KT, GCMG, KCB. Five aeroplanes of the squadron provided a display. Formation dive in salute and circled twice before returning to Ismailia.

October On the 27th the move took place from Ismailia to Heliopolis. The move was carried out by road and by air as follows: By Air – On the 26th 5 officers and 5 airmen; on the 27th 7 officers and 7 airmen. By road – 5 officers and 83 airmen. Total 17 officers and 95 airmen. The officers were accommodated in the Mess at No. 216 (B) Squadron and the airmen took over the huts recently evacuated by No. 45 (B) Squadron.

1928

February On the 16th a display by the RAF in Egypt was held at Heliopolis and officers and aircraft of the squadron took part. Messages were picked up, there was the low bombing of a tank and a set-piece attack. The squadron was re-equipped with Morris 6-wheeled tenders to replace the heavy Leyland 3-ton lorries and the light Crossley 30 cwt tenders. Re-equipment commenced during the last week of February when eight Morris tenders were received.

May On the 11th was the Annual Inspection by the AOC, Air Vice-Marshal Webb-Bowen CB, CMG and officers of the HQ staff. The following are extracts from the AOC's report:

> The turnout of No. 208 Squadron was excellent, the drill seen was up to standard and the handling of arms was very good. The hangars are very old and dilapidated but clean and well kept. The barracks are clean and in good order. The Corporal's Room is clean and well run. The Airmen's Institute is well patronised and properly run. No. 208 Squadron is in very good order and has earned high praise from the General Officer Commanding British Troops in Egypt this training season. The move from Moascar to Heliopolis had had most excellent results and very close liaison between Army units at Abbassid and No. 208 Squadron now exists.

September On the 14th a Royal escort was provided by the squadron for the Prince of Wales and the Duke of Gloucester coming through Suez. On the 29th a search was instituted for a shooting party lost in the Western Desert. Information was received on the evening of the 29th that a shooting party, which included an official of the King's Household, the Chief of the Association of International d'Assistance d'Egypt, a chauffeur and an Arab guide have been lost in the Western Desert for 24 hours. The party had intended returning the same day and carried no food or water. At dawn on the 30th a 7-hour search of an area 70 miles west of the Pyramids was carried out by a Vickers Victoria of No. 216 Squadron without success.

October On the 1st the search was continued over an extended area in conjunction with an aircraft of No. 208 Squadron. The search was continued on the 2nd, 3rd and 4th but no trace of the party could be found. On the morning of the 5th Vickers Victoria pilots Flying Officer Sofiano and Sergeant Melville searched the district around Fayoum. Whilst over Quartet-al-Gatgehannah a man was observed waving what appeared to be a flag. The pilot immediately landed and two men, both semi-nude and in a state of collapse, were then observed walking towards the aircraft. After finding the third member of the party (which must exclude the one seen waving the flag) in a nearby cave, the whole party was conveyed to Heliopolis by air where they received medical attention.

1928/1929

November to March There was Army cooperation. The hours flown during the last training season were a great increase on the hours flown the previous year. At the summing up at the final conference on the last day of the Command Manoeuvres, the GOC British Troops, Egypt, Lieutenant-General Sir Peter Strickland KCB expressed himself highly pleased with the work of the squadron. The summary of hours flown was:

Unit Training	– 427 hours 40 minutes
Royal Artillery	– 45 hours 50 minutes
Brigade Training	– 167 hours 45 minutes
Command Manoeuvres	– 111 hours 30 minutes
	752 hours 45 minutes

These figures compared very favourably with 331 hours 35 minutes for 1928.

September As a result of serious fighting between Jews and Arabs a composite flight of the squadron was dispatched to Ramleh as reinforcements. The flight was commanded by Flight Lieutenant Lloyd Williams MC and included Flying Officers Noble, Ckoch and Dudgeon. The four aircraft left Heliopolis at 13.30 hours on the 7th and the remainder of the flight personnel consisting of 18 airmen and two Morris 6-wheelers, complete with one month's stores, left by 18.00 hours for Ramleh.

October The flight was detached at Ramleh until 11 October, when it returned to Heliopolis, being relieved by B Flight of this unit. During its time at Ramleh from 7 September until 11 October 162 flights were made involving 208 hours 25 minutes flying. Work consisted of daily reconnaissances over the disturbed areas and taking air action against those seen burning or plundering villages.

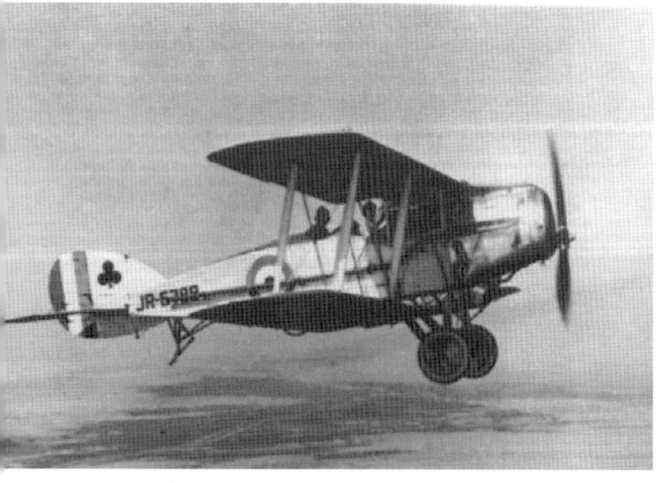

A Bristol Fighter of No. 208 Squadron flying over Heliopolis.

No. 216 Squadron
CCXVI dona ferens
(216 bearing gifts)

The move from France to Egypt began in August 1919 with the arrival of Major W.R. Read MC, who landed at Qantara aerodrome on 12 August 1919. The move was not complete until 16 October, due to one aircraft having to be fitted with a replacement engine at Viennes, near Lyons.

Lieutenant Sawyer was in the last of three aircraft to leave France on 21 July, but he had a particularly successful flight, reaching Qantara on the same day as Major Read, having covered the distance in three weeks. Thus by the middle of October the squadron consisted of six Handley Pages, and, stationed at Qantara, it was utilized in carrying passengers and mail between Egypt, Palestine and Iraq. In order to facilitate demobilization in November 1919, No. 216 Squadron was reduced to an establishment of one flight of five machines.

Between 1921 and 1922 the OC Squadron was Major Henderson followed by Squadron Leader Modin DSC.

1925
April On the 1st, Heliopolis station was formed and No. 216 Squadron was formed at the station. During the year the mileage covered by the squadron was 23,333 miles. Flying hours were 365 and the number of passengers carried was 32.

1926
January On the 1st the squadron was re-equipped with Vickers Victorias in place of the Vimys. [It appears that the adjutant is trying to remember what has happened over the years and jotted it down in the diary, which then jumps to 1927.]

1927/1928
The squadron came top of all TE bombing squadrons in RAF bombing.

1929

February Owing to the absence of aircraft from No. 70 Squadron in India, one flight of No. 216 Squadron was attached to No. 70 (B) Squadron at Hinaidi in Iraq for duty in that country and completed 270 hours flying in one month.

August/September Palestine disturbances but no account of operations maintained.

November Wing Commander E.H.B. Rise MC assumed command.

A CONSIDERATION OF AIR CONTROL

Thus far air control has been described using Air Ministry reports and RAF squadron records and histories as source material. They show that most often the immediate operational objectives were realized, but that after a period of relative calm trouble could break out again, sometimes involving the sections of tribes that had previously been in trouble. These records also show that the threat to the lives of RAF aircrews did not come just from hostile action. There was the ever-present threat of mechanical breakdown, resulting either in a forced landing, sometimes in contact with the enemy, or a fatal crash. The fact that tribesmen did retaliate is acknowledged, but things are not seen from the 'enemy's' point of view nor do they consider the lengths that tribesmen would go to, to deceive and confuse RAF aircrews. David Omissi's book, *Air Power and Colonial Control*, does give a refreshing insight into air control from both points of view, and at times he does paint a rather dark picture of the attitude of RAF commanders in carrying out their task. He does not confine his work to India and the Middle East, and rightly discusses the use of aircraft during the 1926 General Strike in Britain and the Irish troubles. Finally the air operations in relation to the inter-communal fighting between Arab and Jew in Palestine are considered, particularly since they raise the question as to whether or not they were appropriate in the circumstances.

Air Substitution

In the context of air operations carried out by RAF squadrons between the wars, air substitution meant the replacement of ground forces or naval units by RAF units (aircraft and armoured cars). What air substitution did not mean was the total replacement of ground and naval forces by RAF squadrons. With respect to ground operations, aircraft in the past had always acted in support of operations by ground forces. Under air control the roles were reversed, so that ground units would act in support of air forces. The important point is that air substitution was justified because the number of ground units required to provide effective air policing was, in many instances, drastically reduced. The

narrative in Chapters 2 and 3, for example, show the regular year-on-year reductions of ground forces in Iraq. In other words the attraction to politicians in government was the greatly reduced cost of garrisoning the Empire between the wars compared to what it had been before the advent of military aircraft. For Trenchard, as we have seen, this was a heaven-sent opportunity for his new service to prove itself and to fight off attempts by the Army and Navy to have the RAF disbanded. Perhaps, then, Trenchard may be forgiven for, as one would say these days, 'going over the top' by proposing air control whenever and wherever the opportunity presented itself. One such example is the suggestion that floatplanes could take over the policing of the slave trade in the Red Sea from the Royal Navy. But the problem for the RAF was that aircraft cannot hold ground or areas of oceans or seas. To do that ground troops and naval vessels are necessary. What air power provided, on the other hand, was flexibility and speed of response.

The Limits of Air Substitution

Air substitution could be limited in a number of ways. Geography and climate, technical difficulties, political attitudes and the attitude and response of those on the receiving end of air action could singly or severally determine the effectiveness and advisability of using air power.

Geography and Climate

Geography is an obvious limitation. Since ground forces acted in support of the RAF squadrons, aircraft could not bring about a permanent state of affairs on the ground without the presence of ground forces. Political officers had to be able to reach tribal areas to receive fines of money or weapons and to be able to negotiate the handover of hostages if these were not brought in. During the early 1920s the most suitable vehicle for use by ground forces was the armoured car. It had a reasonable cross-country capability and provided protection for the crew from small-arms fire, the most that was likely to be thrown at them by hostile tribesmen. Since the Army was not prepared to make these available for air-control operations, Trenchard formed his own companies. These were the days before the formation of the RAF Regiment, which did not come about until 1942, and so these RAF armoured car companies were manned by RAF aircrew officers and ground tradesmen. Six-wheeled Crossley tenders were tried out, but not until 1929. The problem was that if it rained the armoured cars could be confined to metalled roads in the rainy season, and the armoured car company's vehicles at Basra were unable to leave the roads between December 1923 and February 1924. Where aircraft had suitable landing grounds close to the area of operations, they could be used for resupply of food, ammunition and other supplies, evacuation of patients, transportation of troops, the carriage of political officers and Army officers and reconnaissance. But air-policing operations could so easily be prevented or hindered by the descent of low cloud or mist (these were the days before all-weather flying), high winds or sandstorms. Locust swarms and bird strikes were an added hazard. The heat could exhaust ground crews, cause rapid deterioration of aircraft and evaporate petrol.

There were also limitations on the use of seaplanes. The only serious proposal made during the inter-war years to replace ships with aircraft was in policing the slave trade in the Red Sea. The RAF had the Short 184 at Alexandria, but No. 202 Squadron was disbanded in May 1921, and it was not until 1929 that floatplanes reappeared in the form of the Fairey IIID at Kalafrana, Malta. During the 1920s there were no RAF flying-boats in the area of the Suez Canal or Red Sea. The flying-boat has the hull of a ship and is designed to carry substantial armament, and also has a longer operational range than a floatplane. A floatplane is simply a land-plane fitted with floats instead of an undercarriage. Once again the idea of using aircraft was enormously appealing because intelligence could be acted upon swiftly and no surface vessel could outrun an aeroplane. In the heavy swell experienced at the southern end of the Red Sea, a flying-boat might fare better than a floatplane, but both suffered the limitation that once on the water they were more vulnerable to an armed Arab dhow in which slaves were carried. Since policing the slave trade meant warning a dhow suspected of carrying slaves that the aircraft was to land to carry out an on-board inspection, the dhow could open fire once the aircraft had alighted, and whether or not this occurred the aircraft could still be damaged if it came into contact with a vessel when one of the crew was trying to transfer to the boat. In the event, air substitution was a non-starter.

Technical Limitations

Maintaining aircraft in the Empire, often in remote locations, presented the Air Ministry with considerable logistical problems, not helped by the financial stringency imposed by the Government of India, cited by No. 39 Squadron in its history. In October 1926, squadrons were grouped at the centres of air-control activity, ie. Iraq – eight squadrons; India – six squadrons; Egypt – three squadrons; and Palestine – one squadron. A movement of just one squadron, particularly from the United Kingdom, involved the crating of cumbersome stores, the crating and shipping of aircraft and the loading of nearly four dozen vehicles, together with 800 tons of other equipment. In 1920 the estimated time required to get a squadron operational in Mesopotamia was between six and nine months.

Everything but the kitchen sink!

Once in position and operational, a squadron had to contend with an environment that was trying for both technical personnel and aircrews. Tail-skid fractures, stones, ruts and thorns that damaged tyres, and fuel capacity that was too low for the distances to be covered were features of desert operations. Low-pressure tyres helped, but larger fuel tanks made the Fairey IIIF slow on take-off and too fast in landing, not to mention sluggishness of the controls. The Wapiti mounted two underwing 60 gal tanks that helped in this respect.

It was not uncommon for aircraft to be force-landed in remote locations when survival was at stake. Added to the risk of being taken prisoner by a hostile tribe, squadron commanders ran the risk of losing both pilot and aircraft if some essential spares were not carried. Some units tended to go to extremes, and the DH9As of No. 84 Squadron were festooned with clutter. They carried two auxiliary fuel tanks under the top wing, an extra wheel fastened to the side of the fuselage, a 5 gal drum of emergency drinking water suspended from the bomb rack, a spare radiator under the belly, screw pickets with rope to tether the aircraft in a high wind, blankets, rations and, believe it or not, spares for the armoured cars. Finally a chargul of water was tied to the wing tip to provide a cold drink immediately on landing. Since all these stores had to be carried externally, the increased drag can be imagined. This put extra strain on the Ninak's engine, which could be unreliable, and squadrons ended up in a vicious circle. The greater the load of spares, the greater the chance of engine failure, resulting in a forced landing. Eventually the Air Ministry had to issue guidelines to squadrons operating in desert conditions to the effect that desert equipment carried by aircraft was to be for emergency use only and not to permit the aircraft to be maintained away from its base. The AOC (Iraq), Sir Brooke-Popham, did propose using multi-engined aircraft, but these did not materialize until the arrival of the Blenheim in 1939.

Even when aircraft were operating from their base airfields, high states of serviceability were rare. In 1922, on a tour of inspection of India, Sir John Salmond found that the squadron at Quetta had only five of its twelve aircraft serviceable. At Risalpur he found that the two squadrons between them could only muster two aircraft fit to fly, and in the Sudan in 1920 a fire destroyed all the aircraft spares in the country. Salmond estimated that, even when spares were plentiful, the depots could not carry out the repairs and overhauls fast enough in 1924 to keep all the aircraft of a squadron fully serviceable for even one month. Having twelve serviceable aircraft for prolonged operations by one squadron was virtually unachievable.

For all these reasons the Air Ministry required, not a fighter or a bomber for policing the Empire, but a general-purpose aircraft of rugged construction and simple design. Whatever the Bristol F2B and the DH9A may have been during the First World War, they became general-purpose aircraft between the wars, as did the Wapiti and the Fairey IIIF that replaced them.

Political Limitations

General Limitations   The willingness of His Majesty's Government and the Air Ministry to use airpower to maintain order at home and abroad depended upon the theatre. Within mainland Britain the use of bombs and machine-guns to maintain internal security would be unthinkable. During the General Strike of 1926, when normal communications were likely to be paralysed, RAF aircraft were used to carry vital mails, as well as newspapers to inform the population. By 13 May the Virginias of Nos 9 and 58 Squadrons had carried 1,377,000 copies of the *British Gazette*, and in the so-called 'Red' towns where communists were perceived to have influence, papers were dropped in bundles from light bombers. In Ireland it was Field Marshal French's intention that aeroplanes could be used offensively, using machine-guns and bombs if the situation demanded, but as Chapter 2 revealed, this was not, in the event, to happen. The squadrons that operated in the south of Ireland between 1920 and 1922 were not employed on air-control operations as generally understood when ground troops operate in support of air operations. Rather it was the other way round. RAF aircraft provided valuable communications between Army units and formations, dropped supplies and gathered intelligence by attempting to spot illegal gatherings of the IRA in remote locations where the latter were training. In particular they would attempt to keep the roads open for Army convoys by spotting potential or prepared ambush positions and reporting these to Army units or convoy commanders. Overall, therefore, there was an understandable reluctance to use air power against Europeans. There was not the same political sensitivity when it came to operations involving hostile tribesmen in Africa, the Middle East or India, and this may be seen as Britain employing double standards. These different theatres are now considered in the context of political correctness.

Ireland   Trenchard consistently opposed the violent use of aircraft in Ireland. Some would argue that he could conveniently do so because, as has already been said, there was no prospect of air control in the province. His reason was that it was more difficult to distinguish friend from foe and that leaflets warning of impending air action, if dropped, could fall into the wrong hands. He also feared reprisals against aircrews forced to land, yet this was a strong possibility abroad. Again, to stress the RAF's subordinate role in Ireland, the Cabinet sanctioned the arming of aircraft only after action had been requested by commanders of brigades or higher formations. Aircraft were to attack bodies of men actually fighting government troops, those who had just fought them as in an ambush, or were clearly preparing to do so. The nearest the RAF might have come to taking offensive action was during the final withdrawal from Ireland in 1922. Extricating British troops could have been messy, but RAF Ireland was disbanded in early 1923 without incident.

Palestine   Limitations in the use of air power in Palestine were considerable. Confrontation between Arab and Jew meant that the tried and tested methods of air control were often inappropriate to the needs of the situation on the ground. In May 1922 an Air officer assumed command in Palestine, and by 1925 the garrison had been reduced progressively to:

A single cavalry regiment
A company of armoured cars
No. 14 Squadron RAF

Military expenditure had been cut to a half, and the aircraft were being employed mainly on the border to prevent Bedouin incursions. Lord Plumer, the British High Commissioner, was confident that the risk of serious communal disturbance had receded to the point where he felt it safe to disband the gendarmerie. The last remaining regular troops were removed to serve in the new Frontier Force in Jordan. The defence of Palestine then rested on the police, the RAF armoured cars and No. 14 Squadron. So far so good! This was air control, and the fruits of air control were economy and speed and flexibility of response. As long as the Arab community could not be reinforced, so to speak, they were more likely to accept that they would have to live peaceably alongside the Jews. But in 1928 the decline in Jewish immigration was reversed, and in the summer of 1929 there were widespread attacks by Arabs on Jewish settlements. To meet this new threat to internal security ground troops were vital to be interposed between the two communities. Three British foot battalions had to be rushed to Palestine, and a brigadier-general assumed temporary command of all ground forces. Air operations had to be limited to patrolling and the protection of outlying Jewish settlements, the machine-gunning of looters, patrolling the frontier to prevent Arab incursions and the ferrying in of Army reinforcements from Egypt. The question then was whether the Army or the RAF should be in overall control. The Cabinet met to consider it, and decided that the Air Ministry should remain answerable for defence but that the Senior British Army Officer should have the right of direct access to the High Commissioner on all internal security matters, and that there should be a minimum Army presence in the country at all times. This compromise situation remained in force until 1936.

Africa and Egypt The RAF never dominated the defence of British colonial Africa to the extent that it dominated the defence of the Mandated Territories of the Middle East, and Trenchard denied that air substitution was practical in Egypt since much of the Egyptian population was concentrated in towns. Although aircraft were involved in the disturbances of December 1921 and January 1922, activity was limited to providing patrols overhead in an attempt to deter the crowds from acts of violence or sabotage. The Air Ministry did recognize that the role of the RAF would remain subordinate to that of the Army. Egypt remained as Trenchard foresaw it in his famous Memorandum of 1919, the 'Clapham Junction' of the Middle East, providing a reserve in the area and flying training for RAF or Army personnel who wished to become aircrew.

The Slave Trade in the Red Sea This matter has already been discussed under the heading of geographical/climatic limitations. Politically too there were objections to air substitution, which seemed good at the time, for in early 1928 the Air Ministry took control of Aden and the Admiralty suggested one or two aircraft from Khormaksar be earmarked to work with the Navy. Of course Trenchard was interested, but inwardly he had air substitution in mind, and he revealed his plan in a paper on Air Power in 1929. In it he proposed two flying-boats equipped with searchlights and a small gun. But there were problems. To begin with a seaplane could not legitimately take action against a dhow unless there was clear proof that there were slaves on board. Since the slaves were shipped across the Red Sea from the port of Jadjira in French Somaliland, and then marched up the coast for sale, for aerial patrols to be effective aircraft would have to search the African coast and land in French, Yemeni or Hijazi territory. The diplomatic objections to air policing in the Red Sea were too strong to be overcome by technical agreement, and the Foreign Office concluded that the difficulties were too great for air substitution.

Tactical Limitations
The effectiveness of aircraft It was not until the end of the decade that the Wapiti and the Fairey IIIF entered

RAF service, so it fell to the DH9A (Ninak) and the Bristol F2B (Brisfit) to carry out the air-control operations. Sopwith Snipe fighters had been withdrawn since no air opposition was ever likely to be encountered. The Ninak and the Brisfit were both First World War aircraft. There is no doubt that in its day the Brisfit was a formidable fighter, but for air-control operations its range was too short and it could not be fitted with a bombsight, which meant using bombs with short-delay fuses. Nor could the aircraft simultaneously carry extra fuel and a wireless set. Since the bombs were a vital part of an offensive mission, radios could not be carried, thus reducing the chance of an early rescue if downed in a remote location. The Ninak fared little better. Too many emergency stores were carried externally (witness the aircraft of No. 84 Squadron), which together with the bomb load placed too great a strain on an already unreliable engine. Given her age by the late 1920s, the Ninak required all too frequent attention. Nevertheless, it may be concluded that, in spite of all that was asked of them by the aircrews and what was thrown at them by the enemy and the elements, these two aircraft filled the gap until more-up-to-date aircraft arrived on the scene. Given the war surplus of these two aircraft and the financial stringency faced by the RAF after the First World War, it is hardly surprising that they should be pressed into use.

The Attitude and Response of those subjected to Air-Control Operations
David Omissi has some unkind things to say about the attitude of RAF officers to tribesmen and their perception of the attitude of tribesmen to air policing. He cites Wing Commander Bottomley, who, on giving a speech to the boys of Marlborough School, gave his opinion that the more primitive the race the more it respects sheer power. On the other hand, since tribesmen were so primitive and illiterate, who recorded their feelings, attitudes and responses to air attack? Omissi concludes that Trenchard was too shrewd to overplay his hand when it came to claims made for the effectiveness of air-control operations.

The bomber and the bombed Was it the uniqueness of bombing operations or, as Bottomley suggests, the ignorance and superstition of tribal populations that resulted in the desired outcome of air-policing operations? In June 1928 the Governor-General of the Sudan, J.L. Maffrey, suggested that the provinces of the Upper Nile were 'a morass of ignorance', and that he had detected strongholds of superstition and witchcraft. This conjures up a picture of tribesmen who would be so overawed by the mere sight of an aeroplane that they would fall prostrate in abject fear. Others emphasized the unique qualities of the bomber – not those at the receiving end of bombing. At the Quetta Conference of

1922 John Salmond declared his belief that 'humanity is the same the whole world over'. He went on to state three phases of reaction by peoples to bombing everywhere:

1. Initial attacks might induce a sudden panic, particularly if not bombed before.
2. Once it was realized that bombing did not produce extensive material damage, panic would give way to indifference or even contempt for the air attacks.
3. After a sustained bombing offensive the continued disruption of everyday life would create intensive weariness and a longing for peace.

As regards Phase 3, the economic life of nomadic tribes relied crucially upon their animals. Since RAF pilots targeted the animal herds, it was possible to destroy almost completely the vital economic underpinning of their very existence, in which case they were bound to capitulate in weeks, if not days. In complex modern economies this was not possible in anything but the very long term, and even then, as in the cases of Cologne, Dresden and Berlin in the Second World War, it was still necessary for ground troops to fight their way into Berlin for Germany to capitulate. Be that as it may, the Salmond doctrine was all embracing, and that made it most acceptable to Trenchard, whose claims for the power of air were thus endorsed by a probable successor.

Vulnerability of aircraft to attack from the ground
During the inter-war years there was no threat to aircraft operating in the air-policing role from the air, and so the Snipe fighter squadrons in India and Iraq were disbanded. As for the threat from the ground, the preceding squadron histories record instances of aircraft being hit by rifle fire from the ground. Yet in December 1923 Wing Commander Edmonds publicly claimed that the chance of hitting an aircraft with a rifle shot was so small that tribesmen would not waste valuable ammunition in an attempt. If rifle fire was not a threat it does not explain why RAF bombers on the North-West Frontier employed gliding tactics or approached their targets by night in a shallow dive with engines throttled back to minimize the risk of premature detection. But even then some tribesmen would set up a primitive 'observer corps': signals or warning fires of the approach of aircraft were used, and this could result in aircraft switching targets at the last moment. A second point is that aircraft at this time did not carry protective armour, so that even well-placed stones could cause damage or injury. In some aircraft the control wires were fed through to the gunner's cockpit to give a small chance of survival should the pilot be incapacitated. Thirdly, some tribes had modern weapons, including repeating rifles, and defeated tribes would be required to hand over some, if not all, of them as part of the fine imposed upon

them. By 4 February 1921 more than 63,000 rifles and nearly three million rounds of ammunition had been collected by the security forces. In the Sudan in 1927 pilots were told never to fly below 500 feet and to climb to 1,000 feet if fired upon. During the Waziristan operations of 1925 bombers were stripped of their machine-guns to save weight. Basil Embry, later to achieve Air rank, paid tribute to the effectiveness of tribal rifle fire when he acknowledged their marksmanship, tactical skill and use of terrain on the North-West Frontier.

Development of the tactics of Resistance
Use of darkness and terrain Some tribesmen soon learned to move in darkness if they wanted to reduce the risk of detection, although parachute flares were sometimes used to illuminate targets. There was ample cover for persons moving over the ground in the Aden Protectorate, and Zeidi soldiers were particularly adept at exploiting caves and caverns, which were put to good use in avoiding detection. When it was discovered that a single bomb dropped into the middle of a mass of men could inflict heavy losses, tribesmen adopted looser formations that made concealment easier. The Ikhwan raiders in Iraq had, by 1928, adopted loose formations for movement and combat, and RAF pilots were urged not to delay in attacking in force once a suitable target had been identified. If the enemy could be engaged before they had had a chance to scatter, the pilot could most usefully aim his aircraft at his target using his fixed forward-firing machine-guns, but if they had dispersed then the trainable rear gun was of more use. Man-made defences such as strong towers and forts were put to use. The smaller towers could be difficult to detect from the air, and strong towers and forts could prove resistant to bombing. The tiny 20 lb Cooper bombs could only be used as markers, for it needed a well-placed 230 lb bomb to cause decisive structural damage, and it would take a 500 lb bomb to shatter the masonry of a large fort. Indeed, in 1928, at least eight tons of bombs were dropped on the fort of Dhala, yet the walls and towers remained undamaged; and this at a time when Trenchard was proclaiming the 'power of the Air' and the ability of bombing aircraft to inflict unacceptable damage upon an enemy.

Deception When aircraft were operating in conjunction with ground forces, large strips of white cloth could be laid out on the ground in prearranged patterns to give instructions to over-flying aircraft. They could be used to point the direction and distance to enemy forces or to instruct pilots not to bomb in an area occupied by friendly forces. But tribesmen learned the purpose of the ground strips, and in 1925 Zeidi tribesmen in the Aden Protectorate managed to capture some of these cloths. In October they mounted a successful counter-attack when they laid out strips to instruct RAF pilots to stop bombing in their operating area, but this tactic appears to have been used only once. In Ireland, Republican elements would dress in British Army uniforms and deceive RAF pilots, who were persuaded to drop confidential documents intended for Army formations.

Use of ack-ack, rifle fire and aircraft As has been said above, many tribesmen had modern weapons. The ability of tribal marksmen to damage or destroy RAF aircraft could not prevent, but could impede, RAF operations. Some of the less-disciplined tribesmen would take a 'pot shot' against any aircraft, but this would give away their position. Pilot Officer Carr of No. 55 Squadron claimed to feel vulnerable to small-arms ground fire, and with seventy-five bullet holes in his aircraft, including one in his parachute pack, he had good reason. Ack-ack guns were installed in the forts at Qataba, Taiz and Mafalis by the summer of 1928, but these appear to have been less effective than rifles because of the inadequacy of sighting instruments. Aircraft were also made available to the Imam in Aden by the Italians, but the former had no trained Yemenis to fly them.

Threat against downed aircrews There was always a possibility that aircrews could be forced down and captured by tribesmen who might kill or mutilate them. For this reason aircrew 'ghooly chits' might be carried, which offered a reward for good treatment of those who might otherwise face castration. Air gunners were issued with a revolver and twenty rounds to defend themselves against hostile Nuer tribesmen. Lewis gun parts could be thrown overboard if capture was unavoidable, and aircraft could be set on fire. But although Flying Officer Jackson was killed by the Wahabis, who were renowned for their cruelty, there is no record of aircrews being killed in this way between 1925 and 1930. Sheikh Mahmud, on the other hand, regarded captured RAF aircrews as bargaining counters to extract concessions.

The Attitude of RAF Commanders

Limited and unlimited use of force Internal security operations have characteristically always been seen as the limited use of military force in support of the civil power. The guiding principle is the 'use of minimum force', that is to say that if the firing of one shot in quelling incipient civil unrest achieves the desired outcome a second shot will not be fired. If it takes 1,000 shots then 1,001 will not be fired. But if individual battles are won in this way, the war may not necessarily be won. Thirty years of military involvement in Ulster since 1969 has not seen an end to the war. Then as now the problem for politicians is that their military commanders may persuade them that a military solution is the only way to achieve a final political one. There is therefore an underlying tension between the

political need to use minimum force necessary, if only to avoid lasting resentments, and the desire of some military commanders to use the maximum violence at their disposal. In the 1920s a bomb dropped by an aircraft was hardly a precision weapon, in spite of the claims made by some RAF commanders, and mistakes were made. Churchill's original idea to use asphyxiating gas against tribesmen was dropped, for the use of gas had connotations. RAF commanders could always claim that, since warnings were given to tribal people before air action was ordered, the use of force was a last resort. But intelligence had to be good to be sure of hitting the right target, and tribes needed to be given precise terms for capitulation. If warnings went unheeded then bombing had logically to continue until the desired outcome was achieved. The quickest way was to kill the cattle, but this could cause lasting resentment among some tribes, particularly the Nuer of Sudan. We are back to square one! In the event, dilemmas regarding the level of force to be used were resolved more by the operational limits of the aeroplane than by any classification of the relationship between political aims and the appropriate level of force.

RAF command in practice Omissi believes that there were hawks and doves among senior and middle ranks of the RAF. On the hawkish side were Philip Game, the AOC India, and predictably Arthur 'Bomber' Harris, the then future C-in-C of Bomber Command in the Second World War who ordered the bombing of Cologne, Hamburg and Dresden. He feels that Harris displayed a distasteful relish in his attitude to the bombing of tribesmen. The latter would soon find that they could stand the noise of bombing but would also find that within forty-five minutes a full-sized village could be practically wiped out and a third of its inhabitants either killed or injured. And to add insult to injury the aircraft offered no real target, no real opportunity for glory as warriors. Omissi says that the Air Ministry underlined some of the more unpleasant passages in reports emanating from Harris. On the other hand McClaughly and Portal were less brutal in Aden. Differences between Portal and Harris over the efficacy of bombing resurfaced during the Second World War, but no one pretended that bombing tribesmen was remotely akin to bombing Germany. Experience gained by senior and middle-rank RAF officers in the inter-war years would not fit them for a European war, and strategic doctrine was not framed from any lessons learned in the Sudan, Aden, Palestine, Iraq or India, particularly since no air opposition was encountered. Even so, Edward Ellington was fond of drawing parallels between air policing and a European war. Finally, it is worth remembering that the RAF did not always get its own way. It may appear that air policing presented tribesmen with an unequal contest, but RAF commanders in the field lost their men, not infrequently, to air accident, dysentery, malaria, typhoid and gastro-enteritis.

PART II

The Anatomy

THE CONTENT OF THESE FACING PAGES IS INTENDED FOR THOSE UNFAMILIAR WITH THE PARTS OF AN AIRCRAFT OR AIRCRAFT TYPES DESCRIBED IN CHAPTER 5

THE CONSTRUCTION AND ARMAMENT OF A TYPICAL BIPLANE OF THE GREAT WAR/ EARLY INTER-WAR YEARS

A BIPLANE FIGHTER WITH ONE FIXED AND ONE TRAINABLE MACHINE-GUN

Aileron

Lewis gun on Scarff ring, but limited in its arc of fire by the fuselage and wings

Fuselage

Rudder

Fin

Tail skid

Lower wing attached by struts

Tailplane

Fixed-pitch propellor

SPARS

WING

MONOCOQUE FUSELAGE

RIB

LIGHT BOMBER AND TORPEDO BOMBER

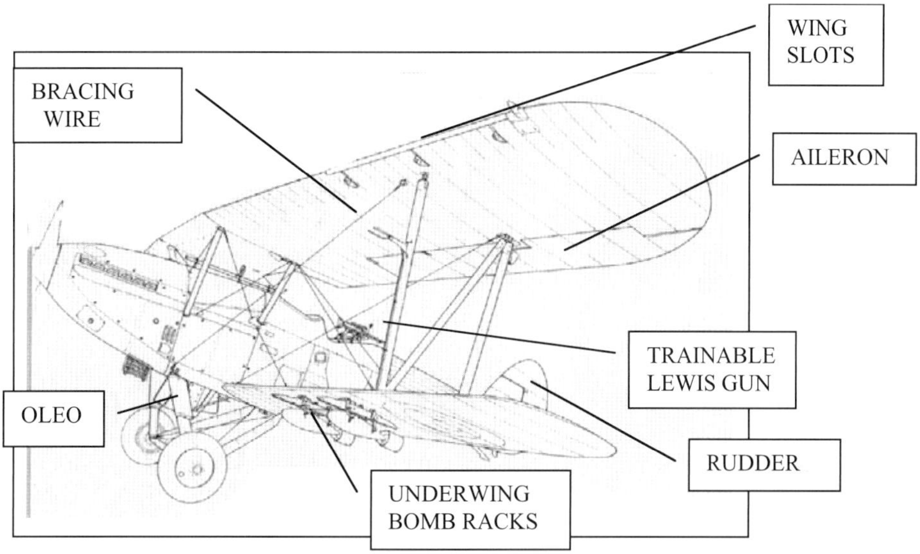

WING
SLOTS

BRACING
WIRE

AILERON

TRAINABLE
LEWIS GUN

OLEO

RUDDER

UNDERWING
BOMB RACKS

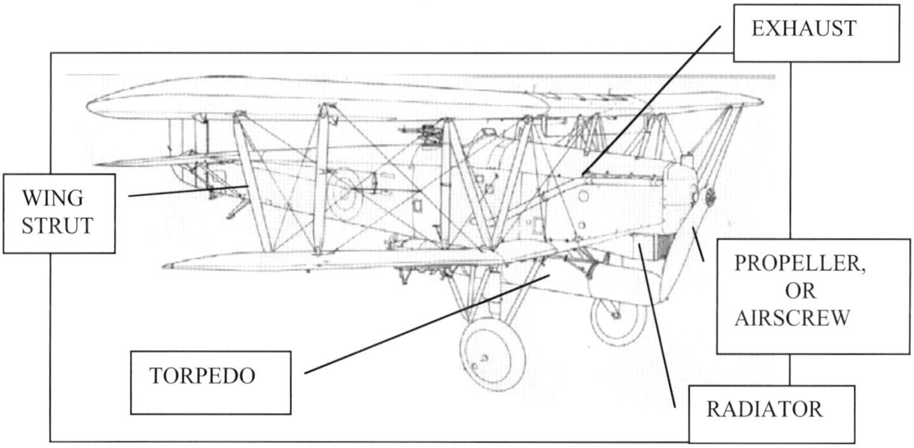

EXHAUST

WING
STRUT

PROPELLER,
OR
AIRSCREW

TORPEDO

RADIATOR

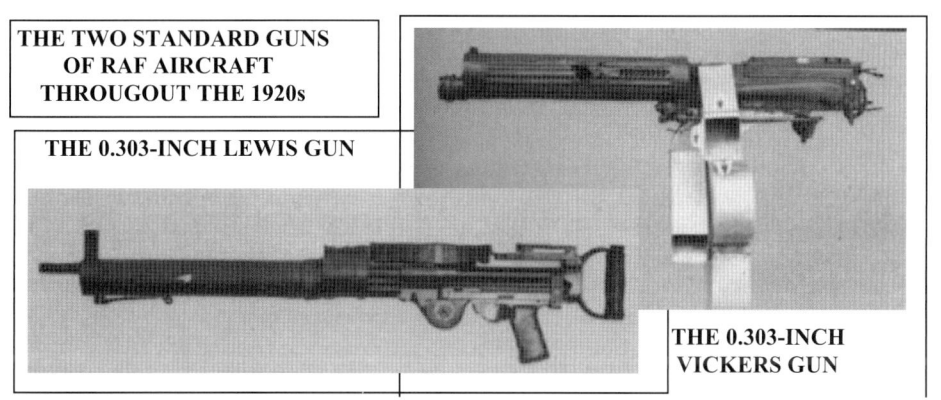

**THE TWO STANDARD GUNS
OF RAF AIRCRAFT
THROUGOUT THE 1920s**

THE 0.303-INCH LEWIS GUN

**THE 0.303-INCH
VICKERS GUN**

Chapter 5
Aircraft, Weapons and Defence Systems – Procurement and Development

The aircraft industry – Survival, growth, consolidations – Owners and designers – Biplane v. monoplane – Wood v. metal construction – Open and closed cockpits – Test flying at Martlesham, Felixstowe and RAE Farnborough – Some notable flights of prototypes – Aircraft weapons – Bombing techniques – Aero engine development

This chapter traces the development of the aircraft industry in Britain year by year over the period 1920–29. There are three outstanding themes that recur in the narratives that follow that may seem strange in an era of fast jet travel and supersonic all-metal aircraft. Firstly, there was the debate over whether aircraft should be made largely of wood, covered in fabric. The quality of wood as a raw material, its ease of working and relative cheapness made it attractive to people like old Dick Fairey of Fairey Aviation or to firms struggling to make a profit. Yet there were other firms, like Shorts of Rochester, that were determined to press ahead with all-metal construction. Secondly, there was the debate over biplane or monoplane. The attraction of the biplane was that, having two pairs of wings, the weight of the aircraft was spread over a larger wing area. This meant that wing loading was lighter, hence stresses were not as great. When the early monoplane designs like the Westland Dreadnought came to grief it is easy to see why biplanes remained in common use both commercially and in military service well into the 1930s. Thirdly there was the closed cockpit versus open cockpit debate. Again it seems unthinkable in the days of fast jet travel that any pilot would want to be exposed to the elements, but in the 1920s that was very much the case, and there was great resistance to the idea of closed cockpits. This may be partly explained by the desire to exit an aircraft quickly in an emergency, since, without parachutes in the early days, aircraft in trouble would be brought down for an attempted landing.

Weapons development does not feature greatly in Volume I since most advances were made in the 1930s and therefore mostly relate to Volume II. Aero engine development is very important and features in both volumes, and in this context the debate over air-cooled versus water-cooled, radial versus in-line, engines is of interest. Finally when it comes to defence systems some scientists are alleged to have worked on a 'death ray', but the only system of note and the one that was vital to the air defence of Great Britain in 1940 was radar.

1920
Aircraft Disposal
The British aircraft industry that provided aircraft for the Royal Flying Corps (RFC) and the Royal Naval Air Service (RNAS) in the Great War, which began in August 1914, comprised such companies as Handley Page, Airco, Fairey, Sopwith, Avro, Bristol, Nieuport, Armstrong Whitworth, Wight, Vickers, Short and the Royal Aircraft Factory. These companies grew to meet the needs of the RFC and RNAS, which later merged to become the Royal Air Force in April 1918, and even as the war ended in the following November new types were entering squadron service, aircraft such as the V/1500 four-engined strategic bomber. But with peace came a rapid rundown, leaving a huge surplus of some 10,000 warplanes (see page 165). These aircraft were held, on the government's behalf, by the Aircraft Disposal Board, but a syndicate registered as the Aircraft Disposal Company Ltd purchased these aircraft from the Ministry of Munitions. The aircraft company Handley Page Ltd acted as technical adviser and sole selling agent. Handley Page had already sent missions to overseas countries with the aim of exporting these war-surplus aircraft. It was the policy that all machines would be refurbished prior to sale. This involved stripping the aircraft down and replacing nuts and bolts, worn moving parts and engines if required. The result was an as-good-as-new product. Refurbished aircraft could also equip RAF units requiring replacement aircraft, aircraft like the Bristol fighter and the DH9A, nicknamed the Ninak, which saw service into the early 1930s.

Such was the more rudimentary design of aircraft in 1919 that service aircraft could quite easily be adapted for civilian use and vice-versa. Indeed, with the advent of peace the size of the civil air fleet of a potential enemy was deemed to constitute a threat if its civil aircraft could be converted to the bombing role. Given, then, that the war-surplus aircraft could be exported, used for domestic civilian purposes or used to re-equip RAF squadrons, the Aircraft Disposal Company Ltd posed a threat to the survival of the nascent aircraft industry. Indeed, if Britain was to remain in the forefront of aircraft design and development in the postwar years, if only to produce military aircraft superior to those of any potential aggressor, it was vital for these companies to retain their design staff and at the very least a nucleus of production staff.

WAR-SURPLUS AIRCRAFT PURCHASED BY THE AIRCRAFT DISPOSAL COMPANY LTD

Some 10,000 aircraft which included:

DH6

DH9

DH9A

DH10

SOPWITH CAMEL

SOPWITH PUP

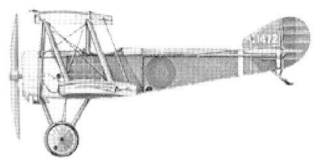

R A/C FACTORY FE2B

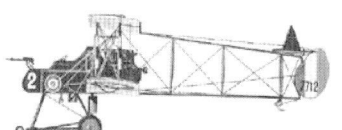

R A/C FACTORY BE2E

R A/C FACTORY SE5A

BRISTOL FIGHTER

VICKERS VIMY

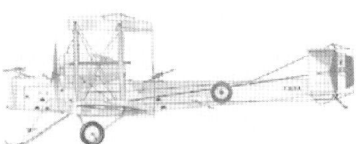

AVRO 504K

SOPWITH SNIPE

MARTINSYDE ELEPHANT

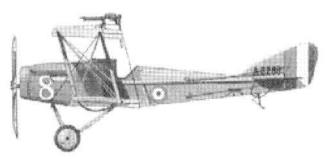

SOPWITH DOLPHIN

Survival

This, then, is a story, firstly, of survival in the immediate postwar years. The Bristol Aircraft shops were almost empty of aircraft, for all contracts had been cancelled, so work went over to tram-car bodywork and the construction of saloon bodies for Armstrong Siddeley cars. Indeed every aircraft company was seizing on any kind of work to keep going. Avro was into cars, Short into bus bodies and marine craft, and Sopwith and Martinsyde into motor cycles. But things were going from bad to worse. At the flying school in Cambridge aircraft were being sold at auction at rock bottom prices. DH6 trainers, for example, were going for just £2 5s (£2.25). Manufacturers who had aircraft ready for the Schneider Trophy international seaplane races found that they could not afford to send them. Nieuport and General Aircraft Company Ltd had to close their works when the slump hit the aircraft and motor industries, and on 11 September the Sopwith Aviation and Engineering Co. Ltd went into voluntary liquidation. When firms went into the hands of the Receiver the Treasury seized the works to realize excess profits' duties payable as a result of wartime contracts. Banks and other creditors received nothing. Also hit was the Air Ministry Competition at the Aircraft and Armament Experimental Establishment, Martlesham Heath, in Suffolk. Airco, maker of the DH6 and DH9, had to scratch because of the company's liquidation. Neither the Beardmore nor Saunders aircraft were ready for the competition, and so only Handley Page or Westland could be winners.

Both military and civil aviation came under the control of the Air Ministry, and a portion of the Air Estimates voted annually by Parliament was earmarked for civil flying. As has been pointed out, the aircraft industry relied upon civil aircraft orders as well as export and RAF orders. Since the latter needed a strong and confident aircraft industry, the state of civil aviation is relevant in this context. The link between civil and military aviation is further emphasized by a view expressed by the Controller-General of Civil Aviation at an air conference in October 1920, when he said, 'The nation which is strongest in air traffic will be the strongest in aerial warfare of the future.' Fear was expressed that the aircraft industry would crumble to pieces. Of the £2 million in the Air Estimates for research and supply, only £500,000 went to civil aviation, the rest to the RAF. It was the sheer financial risk of building aeroplanes on speculation for the RAF when orders might not be forthcoming that troubled the pioneers of aviation. Herbert Smith, Sopwith's designer, said that, in his opinion, 'The day of the large aeroplane has not yet come and much remains to be investigated and determined concerning multiple-engined machines. The Sopwith Company are at present pinning their faith on single-engined aeroplanes of moderately high speed. They are constantly receiving enquiries but orders are not exactly plentiful as they desire and the Air Ministry does not provide the help and encouragement expected of them.'

ENGINES AND SPARES PURCHASED BY THE AIRCRAFT DISPOSAL COMPANY LTD

The 35,000 engines included: Other engines were produced by:

Rolls-Royce Eagles	Fiat
Rolls-Royce Falcons	Anzani
Napier Lions	Renault
Siddeley Pumas	ABC
Wolsley Vipers	Le Rhône
Wolsley Adders	Clerget
Hispano-Suizas	Monosoupape

Avro 504Ks overhauled at the Aircraft Disposal Company outside the company works at Croydon for sale to overseas military and civil buyers.

Avro 504K fuselages stacked inside the Croydon works, stripped and rebuilt to emerge as good as new.

Spares held:

> Between 500 and 1,000 tons of ball-bearings, 350,000 spark plugs, 100,000 magnetos, and a vast store of nuts and bolts.

Additionally the syndicate held some large and small flying-boats, such as the Blackburn Baby, and a few Handley Page 0/400 two-engined bombers below:

VALUE OF ENTIRE STOCK OF AIRCRAFT, ENGINES, EQUIPMENT AND SPARES:
£5,700,000

THE SYNDICATE PAID:
£1,000,000 on condition that half the profits of the sales would be repaid to the government.

State of civil airlines The regular services between international and domestic airports that we take for granted today were unknown. There were few domestic airports, although local authorities were asked to purchase land for airfields to create a network for civil airlines. There were no air corridors where aircraft travelled at an agreed height with vertical and horizontal separation between aircraft in flight, and no blind-flying aids. Transatlantic and other long-distance commercial flights lay in the future. Air taxi work was popular, as was joy-riding, and this was the foundation in Australia for the Queensland and Northern Territories Aerial Services (now the famous QANTAS), which began these services in Western Queensland on 16 November 1920, albeit with a subsidy from the Australian government. But within Britain too joy-riding was an immensely popular pastime, and there were plenty of old service aircraft and ex-RAF pilots to do just that. Because distances between destinations in western Europe were relatively short, and with nearly all the intended airline flights taking place over populated areas where help was on hand, regular passenger and freight services were a distinct possibility. A typical return fare to Paris in 1920 was 18 guineas (£18.90) and the single fare 10 guineas (£10.50). Freight charges were 2s (10p) per pound, and less for larger consignments. Civil air transport companies had to persuade London businesses to send their freight by air rather than rail and boat. But as 1920 drew to a close, winter weather caused flight cancellations and thus reduced incomes. Businessmen could not therefore rely upon aircraft to meet deadlines. Scores of forced landings had to be

made because of bad weather and engine failure. Putting down in a field today would be unheard of, but in the inter-war years it was quite common for civil aircraft for the reasons given and RAF aircraft on training flights to put down in a field, if only to allow the instructor to pick mushrooms for dinner!

Not unsurprisingly the London–Paris air services were not prospering. The *Daily Mail*'s Paris correspondent reported on 6 December that Air Transport & Travel Ltd was bankrupt and the Instone Airline had laid up its aircraft for the winter. Handley Page Transport was not running a regular service, flying only when there were passengers or freight to warrant it. To make matters worse, Robert Bager, HP's chief pilot, was killed when his aircraft hit a tree and burst into flames after taking off in mist from Cricklewood.

Aircraft company intentions At A.V. Roe Ltd the convalescent Roy Chadwick was intent upon a single-engined heavy bomber. This was to be the Aldershot. Vickers was invited to tender for a long-distance twin-engined bomber with flat top wing and dihedral on the lower wing.

The cost seemed remarkably low, and an initial order was placed for two airframes, each at £13,250. The Vickers Viking, which had a retractable undercarriage, was test-flown at Brooklands by Captains Cockerell and Broome. Armstrong Siddeley offered a similar product. At Short Brothers, Oswald Short was intent upon his all-metal Swallow, later to be called the Silver Streak, even though the Air Ministry metallurgists were backing high-tensile, thin-walled, steel girder frames with conventional fabric covering for fuselage and flying surfaces. There was a setback for the development of super-large aircraft when Felixstowe lost its Fury triplane flying-boat, which stalled and crashed on take-off, drowning its pilot, Squadron Leader 'Rolly' Moon. Armstrong Whitworth felt that there was still a place for a fighter aircraft in spite of the economies forced on the Air Ministry and the surplus of machines held by the Aircraft Disposal Company, and was pushing the Siskin, an aircraft not unlike the SE5.

Investigations into aircraft handling At RAE Farnborough the chief test pilot, only 26 years old, was Squadron Leader R. M. Hill MC, AFC. He was making the first-ever detailed investigation into the flying characteristics of aircraft. For example, it needed to be explained why a very stable aircraft in straight and level flight, with a trimming tail to compensate for variations in the disposition of weight in an aircraft, e.g. pilot, bomb load, stores or passengers, could almost fly by itself at most speeds, but was less manoeuvrable, stiff and unresponsive in a dive, and was generally more unwieldy. The Sopwith Camel and SE5 fell into this category. Squadron Leader Hill described the DH9A as excellent because of its general handiness and straightforward control. The HP 0/400, on the other hand, would only feel nose heavy in a dive if badly out of trim. The Vickers Vimy felt very nose heavy as it always diverged from its stable trimming speed, and at 120 mph the force was so considerable that the pilot had difficulty in pulling up the nose. The DH10 was satisfactory in flight but was tricky during take-off. When it came to lateral and directional stability the SE5A was excellent, but the Bristol Fighter was so poor that it was difficult to keep an accurate compass course when in cloud. Hill warned that more powerful aircraft of future design might have characteristics that would render even simple manoeuvres such as landing fraught with difficulty, or a medium-sized, under-powered, lightly loaded aircraft could be difficult to get off the ground. Such then were the problems to which Squadron Leader Hill had to put his mind.

Aircraft engines Things were a little better for British aircraft engines that were displayed at Olympia in 1920. They showed that great strides had been made in the five years since pre-war days. The Jupiter engine display secured for Bristol a contract from the Air Ministry for ten experimental engines. The company's biggest rival was Siddeley, with its 300 hp 14-cylinder Jaguar. Although Rolls-Royce was the most firmly established in the aero engine field, the company was at this time more interested in car production, and the aero engine department was confined to overhauls of existing engines. Napier was developing a double V 1,000 hp engine, that is to say an engine that was X shaped in end view. The Air Ministry had ordered this engine in 1919 at a price of £10,000 per unit. Other firms at Olympia were Beardmore, Gwynne and Sunbeam. Finally the Aircraft Disposal Company had a stand, and could undercut the engine makers for spares, instruments and magnetos.

1921

Air Ministry orders Early 1921 saw the RAF, ever mindful of the need to help the ailing aircraft industry, awarding contracts to Avro for its Aldershot bomber, to Vickers for its Vimy bomber, to Bristol for its shaft-driven powered biplane, to Boulton Paul for a similar aircraft and to Fairey and Parnall for their two-seat amphibians. The Westland Company at Yeovil was completing an Air Ministry order for extensive modifications to the DH9A, converting it to a three-seater for naval use with a Napier Lion instead of the usual Liberty engine. Supermarine had received an order for the development of a single-engined commercial amphibian flying-boat named the Seal. Some companies used to develop their own aircraft to prototype stage called private-venture projects. So it was that the Air Ministry purchased the private-venture Swift from Blackburn, which then bore the Serial No. N139 instead of the civilian designation G-EAVN, but tests at Martlesham showed the rudder to be too small.

Engine orders Development contracts had also gone out for engines, notably to Bristol for its Jupiter and to Armstrong Siddeley for its radial engines, for the Napier 1000 hp Cub, and for the 600 hp Rolls-Royce Condor to go in the scaled-up version of the DH9A, the DH14.

The DH14.

The DH14 The DH14 had been ordered in 1918 as a replacement for the DH9A, but in spite of its good performance, all the urgency had gone once hostilities ended, and although the prototype J1939 was delivered to Martlesham for testing and evaluation, a contract for production was not awarded and it did not, therefore, enter RAF service. Although Britain had only two aircraft on display at the Paris Air Show, the Bristol Jupiter made up for it. The Jupiter was the first to pass the 100-hour running test, and attained 450 hp. This was followed by a British government order for forty-two Jupiter engines with 100 per cent backing of spare parts.

The Aircraft Companies in 1921

de Havilland To assist matters financially, contracts were issued for the repair of aircraft and engines. Indeed, for the next ten years the RAF, operationally in its air-policing role, was to stagger on with repaired and refurbished Bristol Fighters and DH9As. In a period of austerity it was all that could be expected. DH9s and DH9As were being rebuilt at de Havilland's Stag Lane works. The aircraft would be stripped down and all small parts on the fuselage and aircraft could be passed off as new. The DH29 monoplane was causing de Havilland concern over the machine's behaviour, and so a biplane replacement was being designed. The DH32 was set to replace the DH29, and was to be powered by the Rolls-Royce Eagle engine at a price of £1,000.

The DH29s were needed for the Daimler Airways new cross-channel service in the spring of 1922, and so de Havilland was offering the DH32 instead.

DH29 Airliner.

The Bristol Aircraft Company Bristol, on the other hand, had had an order for three of its Bullfinch fighter. Its designer, Captain Frank Barnwell, was disheartened that this and his other military projects had been turned down. His single-engined monoplane could be converted to a two-seat reconnaissance biplane by adding a small lower wing, but to no avail. So he resigned from Bristol and accepted a commission in the Royal Australian Air Force, to be posted to its Aircraft Experimental Department at Randwick. The experience of de Havilland and Bristol is of considerable interest in the debate that kept resurfacing during the inter-war years, namely biplane versus monoplane and enclosed cockpits versus open cockpits. As with the DH29, so also with the Bristol prototype, the concern was about the stability of monoplanes. Aircraft with two wings meant that the aircraft's weight was shared between two wings rather than a single one with the resultant low wing loading. As for enclosed cockpits, they were simply not favoured by aircrews.

Bristol Bullfinch.

Short Brothers One of the most famous and long-standing test pilots of the period was John Lankester Parker, whose name will crop up several times in this chapter. In early 1921 he was test-flying the Short Silver Streak. It should be remembered that aircraft, having been test-flown by the manufacturer's test pilot, were handed over to the RAF team of test pilots at Martlesham in Suffolk, for evaluation as either a military or a civil aircraft. Civil aviation came under the Air Ministry at this time, and civil prototypes would therefore be tested. Obviously military aircraft would be placed under greater stress in dives and spins, rolls or loops. Remembering the financial plight of most aircraft companies at this time, company managers were eager to hand over prototypes to Martlesham, for which they received payment from the Air Ministry. There were times when Lankester Parker was not entirely happy with a prototype, but had, reluctantly, to deliver it to Martlesham. The Silver Streak had been built with an aluminium skin, but this rippled in flight and was replaced with duralumin. The RAF test team, Squadron Leader Roderic Hill, Flight Lieutenants Noakes and Scholefield, flew the aircraft up to 10,000 ft. With a top speed of 125 mph, ease of control and excellent manoeuvrability, it was agreed that the performance was astonishingly good, yet no further test flights were authorized. Priority by the Air Ministry at this time was given to steel-girder fuselage construction rather than streamlined monocoque. Unlike civil aircraft, military types would be placed under more severe stress to simulate combat conditions. The Silver Streak was not accepted.

Paris Air Show The Paris Air Show opened on Saturday 14 November 1921, but such was the state of the British aircraft industry with its lack of confidence in international sales that only two aircraft were on display. One was a torpedo-bomber with a 370 hp Lorraine engine, and the other was a Vickers Vimy Commercial powered by two Napier Lions.

Life for civilian pilots at Croydon in 1921 An insight into the development of flying in those early pioneering days can be gained by looking at the life of pilots, most of whom were in their mid-twenties, who worked out of Croydon in 1921. These young men often arranged a weekend race meeting, using joy-riding aircraft such as SE5As. The pay was not great and they might supplement their incomes by production-testing aircraft of the Aircraft Disposal Company for a fee of £1. If an aircraft was delivered to the continent, a pilot's return fare would be deducted from his fee. Whereas most airline pilots wore a motley variety of civilian attire, Instone Airline introduced uniforms based on the naval reefer jacket. Refuelling was improved when a battery of pumps appeared in the Customs enclosure provided by the rival companies. Previously aircraft had had to be refuelled by hand-operated bowser and petrol cans, and as an aid to navigation for pilots using Croydon and

Lympne airports aerial lighthouses were erected to help in conditions of poor light. These lights could be seen for some thirty miles.

1922

Wood v. Metal Construction

Wooden construction   To add to the continuing debate on the merits of biplanes versus monoplanes and open versus closed cockpits was that of wood versus metal aircraft construction. Geoffrey de Havilland, for example, did not believe that all-metal construction was practicable at that time. He believed that the life of a wooden machine was longer than generally believed and was cheaper to construct. But manufacturing firms found it difficult to assess how well their products performed in respect of durability since aircraft were taken away by Martlesham for testing and evaluation by the RAF team of test pilots. De Havilland pleaded for government support to enable manufacturing firms to carry out more full-scale flying tests. The case of the DH34 was cited. It underwent airworthiness tests in one day at Martlesham before being delivered to Daimler Airways at Croydon on 31 March 1922. Only very obvious faults would be detected and no dive was attempted. Tom Sopwith, with his wartime experience, added his voice. He emphasized how quickly new designs constructed with wood could be built, tested and abandoned, if need be, like the semi-cantilever parasol monoplane built to Air Ministry Specification 7/22 and named the Duiker. This was abandoned after test.

All-metal construction   Others argued that using metal was rather more a science than an art. It was held that all-metal machines could be built 10 per cent lighter than wooden structures of the same dimensions. During 1922 more work on all-metal aircraft was evident and tubular-steel structured-girder fuselages were favoured. Westland was using metal construction but restricted it to wing spars.

Aircraft Companies

Avro and Westland   Bert Hinckler became the chief test pilot for A.V. Roe Ltd in 1922, and flew its first postwar service prototype, the fleet-spotter Type 5SS Bison. The

Avro Bison.

pilot sat up high in front of the top centre section of the wing, with a steeply sloping cowling for maximum deck-landing view. But the first flight revealed similar problems to those experienced with the de Havilland monoplane through interference between wing and fuselage exacerbated by the leading edge of the cockpit opening. This caused directional instability, and the elevators and full-span ailerons required too much strength to operate. The Walrus, produced by Westland, had suffered many crashes and was thus regarded as a stop-gap aircraft. Avro and Blackburn were aiming to replace it.

Vickers Victoria, Virginia and Vixen   Up to now the RAF had the Vimy as a bomber and the Vickers Vernon as an air ambulance, both of which provided satisfactory in service, and so the Air Ministry had no immediate need to replace them. Work on their replacements had therefore been slow. The Victoria transport capable of carrying twenty-three troops and a crew of two had been trialled at Vickers and was at Martlesham for testing. On 24 November 1922 the Vickers test pilot, Captain Cockerell, had made the maiden flight of the prototype of the Virginia bomber, Serial No. J6856. The Victoria was a very similar machine to the Virginia except for its bulky fuselage. Since Cockerell considered the Virginia's rudders were too small, the prototype with larger rudders went to Martlesham on 11 December for full load trials. Although there was trouble with vibration in the starboard engine, it was a popular aircraft with the

Westland Walrus.

Vickers Victoria.

Vickers Virginia prototype (J6856). Later modified to a MkVIII with 'fighting tops', seen above.

test pilots. The private-venture Vixen two-seat biplane was almost ready, but with the 'Geddes Axe' falling on the RAF it was unlikely that there could be more than token orders for what Vickers hoped would be a replacement for the Bristol Fighter and DH9A. The latter were to remain in service abroad into the 1930s.

Handley Page W8b and HP21   The Handley Page W8b civil airliner is an example of where a civil prototype could, with modification, become a military type. At Martlesham tests showed that the aircraft could be flown straight on one engine but would lose height with an all-up weight (AUW) of 12,500 lb. A reduction of 1,000 lb, the equivalent of a third of the fare-paying passengers or all the fuel load, meant that the aircraft could remain aloft on one engine. It had a low landing speed of 40–42 mph but a poor climb with a full load. The design was being modified to become a heavy bomber, the Hyderabad. Richards, the Handley Page designer, was also working on wing slots to give high lift with a smaller wing. The US Navy was interested for future fighters, space being at a premium in an aircraft-carrier. What was ingenious was the mechanism that controlled the leading-edge slot and trailing-edge flap, which was the length of the wing. The mechanism incorporated differential for lateral control, i.e.lateral control could be maintained in whichever position the flap was lowered. Flaps and slots together make possible low landing speeds without the risk of stalling, in this case 44 mph with slots and flaps at maximum lift. Richards had put the new slots and flaps into the HP21, of which three had been ordered by the US Navy, with an option on a further twenty-seven, but the Air Ministry had doubts about Richards's design, regarding it as too complicated.

Handley Page Hyderabad.

Aircraft safety – parachutes and fuel tanks   The staff officers at the Air Ministry were more concerned, in 1922, with fire risk than the safety afforded by parachutes, and a competition, which attracted twenty-six entries, was for a fuel tank that could withstand machine-gun and shell fire and would not burst open or leak following a crash. The first prize went to the India Rubber Gutta-Percha & Telegraph Works Company Ltd. But there would be the problem of extra weight. The RAF, as has been noted, were not showing an interest in the Calthrop parachute, the 'Guardian Angel', which was designed to lift a man from an aircraft falling out of control. A small parachute deployed, to pull out a second then the third man-carrying chute. A demonstration using an Avro 504 K, piloted by Captain Muir at Croydon in early May, was successful, but the parachute was deemed too clumsy and heavy. This was inevitable since the design had to ensure that the parachute would stream whatever the attitude of the aircraft. This meant loose folding with a circular diaphragm spring inserted across the mouth of each parachute.

1923

State of the aircraft industry   By 1923 the aircraft industry was reduced to such a state that only 2,500 men and women were employed in it, and of the few firms engaged in the manufacture of aircraft and engines some were on the verge of closing down. Following the announcement of an expansion plan to take the RAF up to fifty-two squadrons (seventeen fighter and thirty-five bomber) for home defence in an unspecified number of years, the Air Ministry was then faced, not only with having to buy back airfields against much local opposition, but with having to equip these squadrons either with obsolete types from the Aircraft Disposal Company or from an aircraft industry that was in the state described. In order that the aircraft manufacturing firms could hold on to their core design staff and builders, the Chief of the Air Staff, Air Marshal Trenchard, saw to it that, if nothing else, firms got contracts for prototypes. Developing aircraft to the prototype stage in 1923 was nothing like as protracted as it is today, when it takes several nations, not companies, to collaborate to build a fighter or bomber such as the Tornado or European Fighter aircraft. Indeed this was part of the case for constructing aircraft out of wood. A prototype could be quickly and cheaply constructed, and even if no production contracts followed, a company at least received payment for the prototype.

Wood v. metal construction   This is a cue to return to the continuing debate. The question now was, should aircraft be constructed in duralumin or thin steel sheets? Duralumin, favoured by the French, was cheaper and thicker (weight for weight), and it had intrinsic stability – therefore a simple method of making spars that ran through the wings and tailplane was to draw duralumin tube to rectangular section, which was much cheaper than the riveted steel used by British firms. Professor Junkers was an advocate of duralumin, but Handley Page contested the statement that the material does not deteriorate. The duralumin floats of Junkers seaplanes leaked at the joints and had to be replaced by wooden ones. The Air Ministry forbade the use of duralumin for highly stressed aircraft parts, preferring instead high-tensile steel, arguing that most of an aircraft is highly stressed. Avro and Blackburn were cautiously introducing metal components, whereas Fairey and Parnall preferred wood as the immediate economic material. Typical aircraft components of mixed wood and metal included, from left to right below, the tail skid for an SE5, a combined oil and fuel cock with fuel equalizer box and wing root fillings.

Avro 561 Andover.

used in the passenger/transport and ambulance roles would attract a production order. The Aldershot was eventually to equip No. 99 Squadron at Bircham Newton, Norfolk. The variant was to be the Avro 561, later named the Andover. It was to replace the DH10s on the Cairo–Baghdad route.

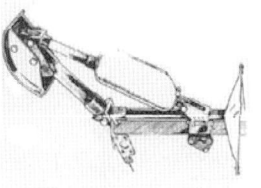 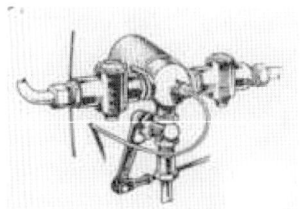

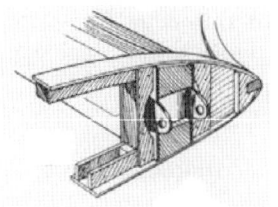

The Fairey Fawn The Fairey Fawn Mark I prototype was built to Air Ministry Specification 5/21 and had a short fuselage. The Fawn II, built with a longer fuselage, was more stable in flight, but the eventual production model built to Air Ministry Specification 20/23 was the Fawn III, powered by a 470 hp Lion II engine. Notice the 'Hucks Starter', which was in common use in starting an aircraft in the 1920s.

Prototypes – Aldershot and Andover It is difficult to imagine a so-called heavy bomber today being driven by one engine, but this was the case with the Aldershot. It was a large machine and did look imposing with its large four-bladed propeller and double undercarriage. Roy Chadwick at Avro compromised with regard to the use of wood and metal in the Aldershot. The fuselage was metal-tube framed with wooden wings, fin and tail, and the aircraft was powered with a Napier Cub X 1,000 hp engine. The prototype, Serial No. J6852, was flown for the first time at Hamble in October 1921 with Bert Hinkler at the controls. Sir Geoffrey Salmond with Air Ministry officials were present to witness the maiden flight, and they saw Hinkler take off in just 200 yards. Press reporters were told afterwards that it was 'nice on the controls and easy to manage'. In January it was delivered to RAE Farnborough, where its stability in flight made it a suitable candidate for night flying. It was hinted that a variant fitted with the Condor engine to be

Weapon development Nothing so far has been said about aircraft weapons development. For the whole of the 1920s little was done in this field. The real advances were made during the rearmament of the mid- to late 1930s. The two guns used in nearly all RAF aircraft were the Vickers or Lewis gun. These could be mounted in one of several positions in the aircraft and were either fixed or trainable. Fixed meant that the aircraft and not

Fairey Fawn of No. 100 Sqn.

Avro Aldershot.

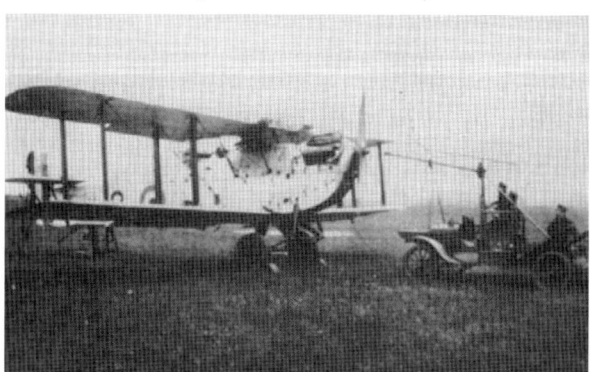

the gun had to be pointed at the target, and sights were fitted in front of the pilot's line of vision. If fixed guns were mounted on the fuselage to fire within the arc of the propellers, they had to be synchronized with the movement of the propeller blades, so as not to hit them when fired. Interrupter gears had been fitted to aircraft during the First World War. Before the interrupter gear was introduced, angular blocks of metal were fitted to the propeller blades so that if a bullet struck them it would, hopefully, glance off and not hit the aircraft or any member of its crew. A trainable gun was one which could be aimed by a gunner, who might be the pilot or another crew member, at a target and did not rely on the aircraft being pointed at the target. These trainable guns could either be fitted on the upper wing of a biplane to be fired by the pilot, or in a cockpit, mounted on a Scarff ring, and in multi-engined aircraft such as bombers in a gun position in the nose, amidships or in the tail. These were called the nose, tail, ventral or dorsal positions. Work carried out at the Aircraft and Armament Experimental Establishment included the improvement

of gunsights; the introduction of a slimmer 0.303 in. round for RAF use, because standard Army ammunition did not perform well in the airflow, when bullets lost velocity in flight; investigations into the effects of cordite burning in machine-gun barrels; and the fouling of the rifling of gun barrels by a composition of carbon and metal from the cartridge rim. When it came to bombing, advances had been made since the days when bombs were simply dropped over the side of the fuselage. It was the bombsight and not the bomb-release gear that was vital to get right. Captain Henry Tizard, while at Martlesham, tested a high-altitude drift sight for use up to 17,500 ft, but this had limitations since it was only effective either directly up or down wind. What was needed was a sight that could place a bomb on a target regardless of wind direction. In 1924 the Course Setting Sight, which allowed for a wind vector, was introduced (see below). Apart from that there were some *ad hoc* arrangements made by resourceful unit commanders in the Middle East when carrying out air-control operations against dissident tribesmen.

The Drift bombsight

The Course Setting Sight

The aircraft approaches the target either directly, up or down wind, and thus allowance has to be made only for a tail or head wind.

The wind is blowing from the west, so the aircraft's nose is pointed to the west (the heading) of the course actually desired, and when the bomb is released it, like the aircraft, will be taken downwind.

The 1924 Prototypes and Design Development
Prototype contract for a day-bomber Westland, Bristol and Handley Page all secured a prototype contract for a single-engined day-bomber capable of carrying a 1,500 lb bomb, Air Ministry Specification 26/23. The Aldershot has already been described, and this did see service with No. 99 Squadron at Bircham Newton, but only fifteen had been ordered from Avro since it was considered too big and unwieldy.

Westland Dreadnought The Dreadnought provides another example of the industry trying to move towards monoplane construction, and this prototype was expected to establish a new generation of fighter and transport aircraft. With the Westland's test pilot Stuart Keep at the controls, the maiden flight was made at Yeovil on 9 May 1924. He made several runs across the airfield without leaving the ground. When he did finally attempt a take-off run, the climb was far too steep, and

Westland Dreadnought.

even with the engines at full throttle he was unable to keep her in the air. The right wing dropped and the aircraft struck the ground with the nose and right wing. As a result of the accident Keep had sadly to have both legs amputated, but he remained with the firm in a managerial capacity. The Dreadnought episode only highlights the perils facing test pilots in those days, for there were no emergency medical facilities on hand, if one excepts the office medical box, and no crash-fire facilities.

Aircraft design Air Ministry staff decided what was required in terms of materials used, structural integrity, weaponry and performance, and air specifications were issued to competing firms. There follows an aircraft specification typical of the inter-war years. Sending prototypes to Martlesham, if a land plane, or Felixstowe, if a seaplane, for evaluation and testing was by 1924 standard practice. Performance checking was the responsibility of Captain R.N. 'Loopy' Liptrot and his small Air Ministry staff at Kingsway in London. Structural integrity was the responsibility of Frank Cowlin, Head of Airworthiness at RAE Farnborough. At this time there were only a few books of reference to guide aircraft designers, such as Bairstowe's *Aerodynamics* and Pippard & Pritchard's *Aircraft Structures*. Apart from books such as these there were only standard engineering textbooks. There were no special instruments, no strain gauges and no electronics. A hand-held spring balance was the usual instrumentation by which a pilot brought back confirmation that the controls were too heavy, and the phases of instability were measured by a stopwatch. Although wind-tunnel testing was to be developed during the inter-war years, most firms would have to use the one at the National Physical Laboratory. But because aircraft were of a simpler design and manufacturers' design teams were small, they could work much faster. Only eleven months, on average, was necessary from inception to the first flight of the prototype. The more determined manufacturers, who were convinced of the worth of their designs, like Fairey, would undertake private ventures in an attempt to

prove that the Air Ministry specification was outmoded. To give an indication of the performance qualities of an aircraft that had to be ascertained during test flying, the following are extracts from a typical Air Ministry specification for a bomber aircraft between the wars:

Contractor's flight trials

1. *Diving* These must include the following diving tests – the aircraft must be dived to an indicated air speed 50% in excess of that attained in level flight at maximum rpm at rated height, or to the speed that can be reached without the engine exceeding that which is allowable. The diving tests are to be made under the following conditions:

   a) Full service load which gives the aftermost CG [centre of gravity] position at full load.
   b) Reduced load with CG at the aft limit of the basic range extended aft by 10% of that range.
   c) The dives are to be made with throttle settings as follows:
       i) One dive with loading as per sub-paragraph a. with throttle setting corresponding to full power.
       ii) Dives with loads as per sub paragraphs a. and b. with throttle setting corresponding to one-third power.

Each dive is to be commenced with the aeroplane flying horizontally at its maximum speed and trimmed to fly elevators free at that speed. The throttle is then to be set to the desired position and the aircraft dived until the limiting speed as defined above is attained. The tail setting is to be maintained in the dive unless the force required on the control column becomes excessive. During the dive at the maximum speed each control organ is to be moved through small angles to test its effectiveness and to detect any tendency to excessive oscillation.

2. *Performance, stability and control*
   a) The maximum speeds at altitudes of 5,000 feet and 15,000 feet are to be not less than 195 mph and 205 mph respectively.
   b) The time taken to reach 15,000 feet is not to exceed 20 minutes.
   c) The service ceiling is to be not less than 25,000 feet.
   d) The aircraft shall be able to keep at a height not less than 10,000 feet with one engine out of action.

The Grebe and Gamecock In 1923 a replacement for the Snipe on fighter squadrons was being actively considered. Larry Carter had flown the prototype Grebe that year in the King's Cup Air Race. The Grebe had a Jaguar III engine and could carry four 20 lb bombs under

Gloster Grebe.

Gloster Gamecock.

Fairey Fox.

each wing. It was deemed both a day- and a night-fighter, and 132 were bought for the service. Its outstanding characteristic was its manoeuvrability, having 'harmonized' controls, and was a great favourite with pilots. For the Gloster Aircraft Company the Grebe contracts were the first real evidence of the new policy of expansion to provide new squadrons for home defence. Yet again the Air Ministry was mindful of the need to keep feeding work to firms other than the one that might be successful in the competitive bid. In securing the contract to build the Grebe, Gloster was required to sub-contract the production of wings and tail units to de Havilland, Avro and Hawker. Bristol, under the direction of Mr Roy Fedden, had developed a new radial engine, and induced Gloster to incorporate it into a modified Grebe: this became the Gamecock. With an extra 100 hp, the RAF was pleased to order ninety of these aircraft.

Radial or water-cooled engines   Contemporary aircraft of the day had either radial or water-cooled engines. The radial engines could be cowled, but were often open, leaving the cylinder pots exposed to the air, and were thus air cooled. The water-cooled engines required a large, bulky radiator. The result was either the exposed frontal bulk of the DH9A radiator, or, if the radiator was enclosed in metal, the unstreamlined appearance of an

Aldershot or Fawn. The chairman and managing director of Fairey Aviation Ltd, Mr G.W. Hall FRAeS, was so impressed with the performance of the Curtiss D12 racers in the 1923 Schneider Trophy seaplane races that he proposed to the Air Ministry a two-seater bomber that was faster than any single-seater fighter of the day. Given Trenchard's view that success in war lay in offence, not defence, this should have been appealing, but his proposal was rejected. So Mr Hall embarked upon a private venture, sailed to the USA and came back with the rights to the Curtiss engine, the Read propeller, wing surface radiators and various other design features. Fairey could now build a light bomber with a small frontal area, giving an elegant streamlined appearance. This was to be the Fairey Fox.

Armstrong Whitworth Siskin   The Siskin continued the trend towards all-metal construction. Although marginally inferior in speed and range, it was regarded

Armstrong Whitworth Siskin.

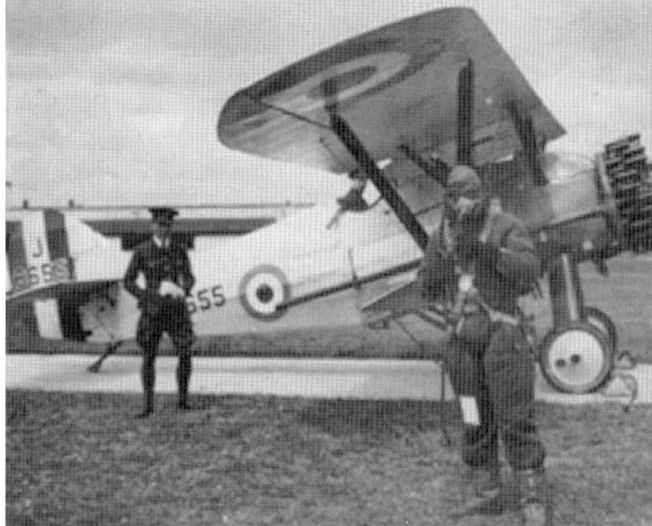

as a safer aircraft than contemporary ones of its type. The conversion from composite wood/metal structures to all-metal ones was gathering pace. Gloster obtained shares in the Steel Wing Company, a firm dedicated to all-metal construction since 1919.

Inadvertent stalling One of the major problems confronting designers and pilots in 1924 was inadvertent stalling. Normally this occurs when the pilot raises the nose of his aircraft, as in a climb, but with insufficient power to maintain that climb. Eventually the aircraft suddenly loses lift and the nose drops abruptly, so that the aircraft is put into a dive. If an aircraft has sufficient height the pilot can pull out of the dive, but in some cases this can be dangerous, if not fatal. If the stall occurs close to the ground the aircraft may crash before the pilot can recover from the dive. Even if the stall occurs at a safe height the aircraft may go into a spin. Since some fifty lives were being lost in the RAF each year through spinning accidents, the matter was a principal concern of RAE Farnborough, and the pilots there were making spins with different aircraft types to assess the factors involved. One answer was to incorporate Handley Page slots into the wing of an aircraft, but the variations of slot were complicated and difficult to adopt.

1924 developments in design Before the year's end several interesting developments in design had taken place. Bristol had tested the all-metal cantilever wing. Hawker proved that strict weight control paid dividends and Short showed that shapely and strong fuselages could be fairly simply made using duralumin monocoque. Finally Westland's use of full-span combined aileron and flap meant complications in attaining full lateral control.

1925

The year 1925 was one of considerable activity in the development of aviation in general and military aviation in particular. With the RAF expansion plan in place, albeit spread over an indeterminate number of years, Trenchard and his staff at the Air Ministry could begin to replace outdated types and place orders to equip the new squadrons. This included significantly the Special Reserve and auxiliary squadrons, the introduction of which was described in Chapter 3. The new types were to go to the home-based squadrons. Paradoxically the RAF squadrons employed operationally during the 1920s in India and the Middle East were equipped with the Bristol F2B and the DH9A, both First World War aircraft. But these two aircraft, previously a fighter and a bomber, were of simple design and able to withstand the rugged terrain, the intense heat and, in India, the paucity of spare parts, some of which had to be manufactured locally. Their employment in air policing resulted in their being classified 'general-purpose' aircraft, as were those that were to follow, like the Wapiti.

Further company developments With the demands placed upon the aircraft industry increased because of the RAF expansion plan, companies sought increases in manufacturing capacity. With the rise from eighteen to fifty-two Home Defence squadrons, design teams were busy. A.V. Roe kept his design and experimental staff at Hamble but purchased 163 acres of land at Woodford for a new airfield from where he could operate aircraft away from the industrial haze of Manchester. The large hangars taken from the vacated airfield at Alexandra Park were reassembled at Woodford. In them aircraft were reassembled after manufacture in Manchester. Similarly, Armstrong Whitworth had separated design and testing facilities. The design staff remained at the original office in the Parkside works, Coventry. A flying school was established at Whitley with facilities for testing experimental aircraft. The company's aircraft production shops were also moved there. One of the aircraft being work on at that time was the Atlas, a two-seater Army Cooperation machine that was then still on the secret list.

Aircraft Disposal Company The Aircraft Disposal Company (ADC) still represented a threat to the struggling firms in the industry that could have sold spares to the purchasers of war-surplus machines. By 1925 the ADC had disposed of millions of pounds' worth of stocks, thereby repaying the government £1.25 million exclusive of taxation, and their premises at Croydon were larger than those of any other aircraft manufacturer. Sales included Scarff rings, bombsights, machine-guns, reconditioned engines and other spares. This service was particularly useful to countries that could not afford expensive armaments. Significantly the Air Ministry ordered one hundred DH9As with the Liberty engine in 1925. Their rugged qualities made them particularly suitable as general-purpose aircraft in Mesopotamia and India.

More Prototypes

A wealth of types from a wide range of companies came on the scene in 1925. Before naming the individual aircraft, the biplane versus monoplane debate is further considered. *Flight* Magazine in 1925 published an article saying, 'We do not think that the marked superiority of the monoplane over the biplane in such large machines has yet been conclusively established and we believe that the future will show room for both.' The fate of the Westland Dreadnought certainly showed that there was much work to be done, and so it was that most of the new aircraft coming on stream were biplanes.

Fairey Fox The prototype Fairey Fox was first flown by Norman McMillan at Hendon on 3 January 1925. Although a two-seater day-bomber, it was 50 mph faster than the Fairey Fawn. This was the fruit of importing design features from the USA, resulting in a streamlined appearance. The aircraft was demonstrated at Northolt in October 1925 in front of Trenchard and Geoffrey Salmond. Speed and the aerodynamically clean appearance appealed to Trenchard with his view about offensive defence. Fairey was also building a single-seater version called the Firefly. But orders for the Fox meant importing £60,000 of American engines, since no British engine was available at this time. Accordingly only one squadron was equipped with this aircraft.

Gloster Grebe, Gamecock and Gloster II In February Larry Carter flew the Gloster Gamecock fighter to Martlesham for test and evaluation. It was a Grebe with a Bristol Jupiter engine. He also flew the Gloster II at Cranwell with a Napier Lion engine uprated to 700 hp at 2,700 rpm. The intention was to make comparative tests on several metal propellers, radiators and so on. Carter fractured his skull and broke a leg when he had to make an emergency landing at 200 mph that carried away the undercarriage. Tail flutter had developed while he was flying at 40 feet above the speed course, but as the cause and the cure seemed apparent, work on the Gloster IIIA and the Supermarine S4 seaplanes was pressed forward, and Hubert Broad and Bert Hinckler were selected to fly them.

Gloster II.

Armstrong Whitworth Atlas The Atlas was flown for the first time in May 1925. It was designed as a replacement for the Army Cooperation Bristol Fighter and was a two-

Armstrong Whitworth Atlas.

seater, single-bay aircraft. Although smaller and stockier than the Bristol Fighter, its all-up weight was greater. Powered with a geared Armstrong Siddeley Jaguar engine the, prototype J8765 achieved over 140 mph. The test pilot, Frank Courtney, found that it had a tendency to stall sharply and the ailerons were too heavy. Moreover it had a tendency to drop a wing on landing. Nevertheless, production between 1926 and 1933 totalled 450, including trainers.

The Westland Bomber This aircraft was test-flown and found to be satisfactory on its maiden flight. Frank Courtney was brought in to test-fly the bomber for a fee of £100. Although Westland's new test pilot, Major Lawrence Openshaw, was available, his services were not used on this occasion, as he had been absent from test work for some time.

Westland Bomber.

The Bristol Berkeley and Bloodhound The Bristol Berkeley arrived at Martlesham on 5 March 1925. This had a nose cockpit, affording the pilot an excellent view forward, but the Martlesham pilots preferred the aft

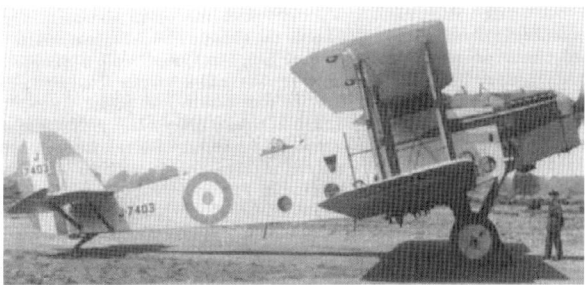

Bristol Berkeley.

Bristol Bloodhound.

cockpit of the rival Westland Bomber and the Handley Page Horsley. Bristol had little better luck with its Bloodhound, as the constructional system of fabricated steel was considered impractical.

Supermarine Southampton The prototype N218, built to Air Ministry Specification 18/24, was well received by the RAF test pilots and showed the trust which the Air Ministry had in the work of R.J. Mitchell, the designer of the Spitfire. Such was the trust that six were ordered by the RAF from the drawing board. The prototype Southampton was first flown on 14 March 1925. Since no modifications were deemed necessary, the seaplane was handed over to the MAEE (Marine Aircraft Experimental Establishment), the seaplane equivalent of Martlesham, on 15 March 1925. The Southampton was a significant advance on the wartime-designed Felixstowe F5. The uncowled engines and gravity-feed tanks were good from a mechanic's point of view, with the tanks located under the top wing to reduce the fire hazard The height of the propellers above sea level matters in high seas, and the only criticism that could be levelled at the design was that the propellers could have been higher.

Supermarine Southampton.

Short Singapore Oswald Short did not get the contract for the seaplane to Air Ministry Specification 13/24 with his all-metal Condor-powered flying-boat, and so he telephoned Sir Geoffrey Salmond to say that he was going to build the aircraft even if it made him bankrupt. Thereupon Salmond went the next day to see the seaplane for himself. Oswald Short got the contract, and this was to be the Short Singapore.

Short Singapore.

Hawker Horsley The Horsley was a rival to the Westland Bomber, but the test flight by George Bulman was disappointing, for the aircraft was longitudinally unstable and the cooling system with radiators each side of the fuselage just ahead of the pilot was useless. This was remedied by fitting a single radiator below the nose, but the instability was intrinsic in the modified Gottingen thick aerofoil chosen because of its high-lift coefficient and to enclose the fuel tanks within the contours of the aircraft. By repositioning the radiator the centre of gravity was brought forward, which improved matters, but ultimately sweep-back had to be incorporated into the wings. Eventually this aircraft was accepted as a day-bomber by the RAF.

Hawker Horsley.

de Havilland Moth de Havilland's Moth was an important addition to the list of inter-war prototypes. A dual-control trainer, it was a 'must' for the country's flying clubs and could provide valuable experience for

de Havilland Moth.

those air-minded men who would eventually join the RAF. The prototype G-EBKT was first test-flown on the afternoon of Sunday 22 February 1925 at de Havilland's Stag Lane aerodrome. Geoffrey himself flew the aircraft, which was airborne in just 100 yards. When he landed Hubert Broad joined him for a second flight and to try the dual controls. The aircraft performed well and both men were well pleased. Even in the waterlogged state of the airfield the Moth took off quickly and climbed well. It had enough stability to fly hands off. Initially the prototype's rudder had no balance, and foot pressure was necessary to hold directional trim, but this was remedied. Production machines were to sell at £900.

Wood construction again   The debate about wooden construction was revived by old Dick Fairey of Fairey Aviation, insisting still that aircraft should be constructed of wood, even though the Air Ministry wanted his Fairey IIID to be of metal construction, for the termites simply loved the wood and fabric of Fairey seaplanes abroad. While Dick Fairey was away in France convalescing from an illness, Colonel Nicholl signed a works order for a metal version. In the event a great deal of the aircraft's construction was changed – it was not simply a conversion of wooden to metal parts.

Aero engine development   Napier was doing well and turned in the highest profit in the firm's history. The figure for the financial year 1924/5 was £237,542. Montague Napier was none the less concerned that the Cub engine, which was set to replace the Lion, would only have a limited future. He felt that the firm should branch out into air-cooled engines but knew that Armstrong Siddeley and Bristol already had a five-year lead. Radials were air-cooled, and since the engines were externally mounted, they were easier to service, and Trenchard favoured their practical merits and simplicity for fighters. On the page below are the silhouettes of three contemporary aircraft showing that the bulk of radiators inside the contours of an aircraft, such as the unstreamlined Fairey Fawn, compared unfavourably with the Fairey Fox with its streamlined appearance. The aircraft with radial engines combined ease of access and the simplicity of design that obviates the need for radiators with an element of streamlining. Then there was the question of engine reliability. The Aldershot was designed as a single-engined heavy bomber and fitted with a Rolls-Royce Condor. The larger the aircraft the more difficult it would be to put down in a field in the event of engine failure. In future all heavy bombers were to be multi-engined, and for this reason the Blackburn Cubaroo was rejected.

THE EFFECTS OF AIR AND WATER COOLING OF AERO ENGINES UPON STREAMLINING

The unstreamlined appearance of this aircraft which has to incorporate a radiator for the water-cooled engine.

A more streamlined appearance with the cylinder pots protruding into the airstream. Ease of access means faster servicing turnaround.

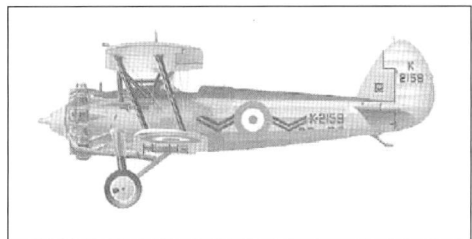

The Fox combines a streamlined appearance with water-cooling, the radiators being mounted in the wings.

1926

Air Ministry Orders and Specifications In 1926 the government still backed the biplane. This caution was in part explained by the unfortunate post-war experience with monoplanes. Hawker, the firm that was to produce the Hurricane in the mid-1930s, had the Jupiter turned down for this reason. The Air Ministry policy of placing competitive orders with two or more firms for aircraft had become firmly established. The Atlas was in competition at Martlesham with the DH56 Hyena, the Bristol Boarhound, which had been at Martlesham since the summer of 1925, and the private-venture Vickers Vespa, which had first flown in September 1925 and was delivered to Martlesham in civil guise. To obtain the requisite low landing speed these prototypes would all, save the Atlas, have wings approaching 45 ft span. The Hyena was a redesign of the all-metal DH42B Dingo III to overcome the deficiencies of the pilot's view, so his cockpit was now in line with the trailing edge of the wing and not under it. But this meant rebalancing the weight distribution, so the top wing was moved rearwards by raking the rear interplane struts back and swinging the front ones into the vertical. Finally the nose was extended to bring the weight of the 385 hp Jaguar forward. But better performance did not result, and a 422 hp Jaguar IV engine had to be fitted.

1926 Prototypes

The RAF in 2005 has just the Harrier, Tornado and Jaguar as strike aircraft, and the Tornado as a fighter, with only the European Fighter Aircraft on the horizon. When it comes to long-haul airliners the Boeing 747 is getting long in the tooth, and the Concorde has passed from service with nothing to replace it in supersonic service. In stark contrast, the 1920s saw the prototypes coming thick and fast. Although only a few actually reached RAF service, it is from the experience gained from all prototypes presented for RAF acceptance that the reader can follow the wood versus metal, air-cooled versus water-cooled, biplane versus monoplane debate. Indeed, several of the aircraft taking part in the 1926 Hendon Air Pageant did not see operational RAF service.

Bristol Bagshot and Westland Westbury These were two aircraft that were built to Air Ministry Specification 4/24. Since the Air Ministry was unsure about the

Bristol Bagshot.

aerodynamics of the monoplane Bristol Bagshot, a competitive tender was put out to Westland for a twin-engined biplane fighter. The expert predicted that a monoplane would be much heavier than a biplane equivalent, but this was not to be the case. The Bagshot was only 350 lb heavier than the Westbury, at 7,875 lb.

Fairey IIID The Fairey IIID had been built both as a land-plane and a floatplane. It was solid and the RAF employed it for maritime duties. It was easy to fly although it had poor lateral control when the ailerons cum flaps were lowered. It was powered with various marks of the Napier Lion engine. The reliability of this engine was proved when four IIID land-planes, led by Wing Commander Pulford, flew from Cairo on 1 March 1926 to reach Cape Town on the 12th.

Fairey IIID floatplane.

Fairey IIID land-plane.

Westland Westbury.

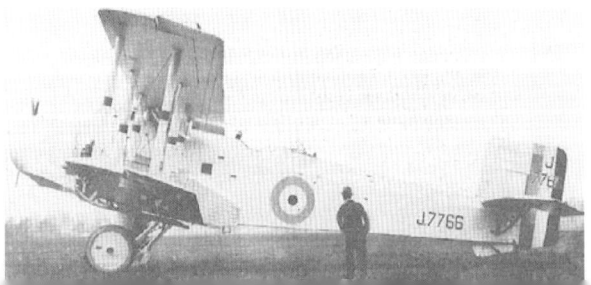

Note: The photographs illustrate clearly that a floatplane, such as the Fairey IIID floatplane above, has basically the same fuselage as a land-plane, with the addition of floats that keep the fuselage clear of the water. (The four Fairey IIIDs mentioned above started their return flight to England as land-planes, but had floats fitted at Aboukir.) A flying-boat, however, has the hull of a boat and sits in the water, as illustrated at the bottom of page 180.

Other prototypes These included the Vickers Vendace, which was recommended as a deck-landing trainer after naval trials, the Firefly I of composite construction, which failed to get the RAF's blessing or orders, the Avro Avenger, which was turned down by the RAF because it was felt that equipment stored in the fuselage would not be readily accessible, and the Vickers Type 121, which was that company's first attempt at all-metal construction. When the latter was test-flown, Flight Lieutenant E.R.C 'Tiny' Scholfield, a giant of a man, was fortunately issued with the first Irvine parachute for civilian use. When the Type 121 got into an uncontrollable inverted spin, Tiny baled out under 2,000 ft, the aircraft crashing into the Vickers Sports Club grounds. Tiny had to walk back to Brooklands with his parachute tucked under his arm. The Blackburn Iris and the Saunders Roe Valkyrie were contenders for the Air Ministry Specification R14/24. The Iris took more than two years to build but had a metal hull. Short had shown that water-soaking wooden hulls were obsolete. The Valkyrie was equally seaworthy and was somewhat cleaner in appearance, but did not win the RAF's favour. It seems that considerations of maintenance, such as the removal of engines and mountings, outweighed performance. Most French aircraft of the period were aerodynamically cleaner than their British counterparts. The French were more concerned with speed for both fighters and bombers, and multi-guns to drive off attacking fighters, coupled with small bomb loads to aid speed. It is interesting that the Valkyrie was test-flown by the 'ubiquitous' Mr Frank Courtney, who had been paid £100 to test-fly the Westland Bomber.

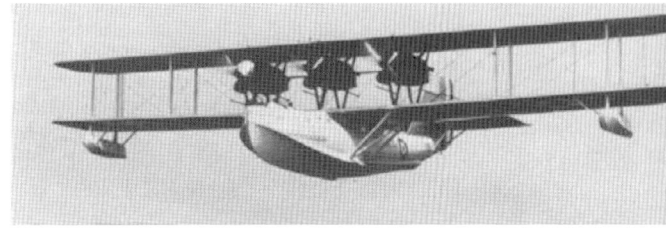

Saunders Roe Valkyrie.

Test flight of the Short Singapore This aircraft was mentioned for the year 1925. On 17 August 1926 the new flying-boat took to the water at Rochester. Lankester Parker, chief test pilot of Shorts, was at the controls, with Eustace Short as observer for this maiden flight, and all the employees came out to watch. But only a two-minute hop was possible that day, owing to the loss of an engine cowling, to be followed two days later by water leaking into the bilges, and the aircraft had to be returned to the shops for rectification.

RAF Accidents and Aircraft Safety

Compared with the accident record of civil aviation, that of the RAF can only be described as disastrous. Every type of RAF aircraft had been involved, and fifty-one fatal accidents had occurred since the beginning of the year. Fifteen of them involved Bristol Fighters and eleven DH9As. One wing commander, two squadron leaders and three flight lieutenants lost their lives, but most fatalities occurred among the ranks of flying officers who had the least flying experience. Concern over these deaths reached Parliament. Following investigations by the *Daily Express*, Mr Hoare Belisha, Liberal MP for Devonport, asked the Prime Minister if he would allot one day of parliamentary business to discuss the cause of these fatalities. Since most accidents involved spinning, RAE Farnborough had been working on the problem. Tests had shown that a bigger rudder on the Bristol Fighter would give immediate recovery from a spin, yet none was ordered. Handley Page Ltd had demonstrated its special wing with interlinked wing-tip slots and ailerons, but this necessitated a redesign of the wing structure. But it was cheaper to leave the Bristol

Blackburn Iris.

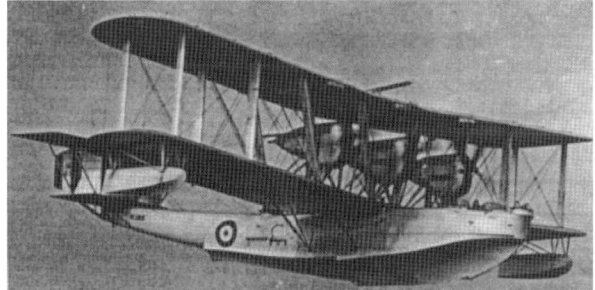

Fighter as it was, for the aircraft was soon to be replaced by the Armstrong Whitworth Atlas. Be that as it may, Mr Handley Page was able to announce at his company's AGM that the Air Ministry had directed that all MkIII Bristol Fighters in service were to be fitted with the automatic slots. The question of the effectiveness of wing and flap slots has been discussed before in this chapter. Pictured on page 181 is a Handley Page Hendon flying very slowly past the camera with its nose well up. The leading-edge slots can clearly be seen.

Under normal circumstances this aircraft would have stalled, and the technical experts at the Air Ministry were blamed for the deaths of their pilots in spinning accidents following a stall because these slots were not adopted. While the aircraft industry's test pilots had flown the Hendon there was no rush to adopt them. Indeed, RAF pilots found that the interlinked slots and lift flaps were cumbersome to operate and caused big changes in trim. Ailerons interconnected with wing-tip slots were also stiff. All one could say was that a crash from a rapidly sinking aircraft was preferable to one that resulted from an aircraft spinning into the ground.

Other work in pursuance of aircraft safety centred on stress. In a lecture to the Royal Aeronautical Society Professor H.B. Howard, head of RAE's airworthiness department, said, 'The maximum loads which the structure [of an aircraft] will be called on to carry cannot be stated with certainty as they depend primarily on how the pilot manipulates his controls. The maximum he can impose is calculable but it is greatly in excess of those he uses. It is neither practicable nor necessary to make the aeroplane absolutely unbreakable at all speeds.' One area that received particular attention was in tapered-wing monoplanes. Because of the greater simplicity of biplanes, this problem had not been given sufficient serious thought. Another problem centred on the oleo strut that attached the wheels to the wing spar. On landing the force of impact has to be transferred from the wheels to the spar. Bristol had been worried that putting twin spars in its Bagshot monoplane would cause the aircraft to be overweight.

The COW gun The retention of the well-tried and tested Vickers and Lewis guns after the First World War has already been mentioned. Cannon with greater hitting power were to come. What makes the COW (Coventry Ordnance Works) gun so interesting is that it was to fire a 37 mm shell, the gun being six feet long. The rate of fire was only 100 shells per minute, which was much slower than machine-guns of 0.303 in. calibre. Moreover, the recoil of some 2,000 lb had to be allowed for in its effects on aircraft handling during firing, not to mention the problem of mounting it in an aircraft. The COW gun did not become standard armament equipment for the RAF.

The General Strike In closing the narrative on 1926, the strides being made by the aircraft industry are seen against the backdrop of industrial unrest. Men who had served an apprenticeship to become skilled workers could earn, in 1926, only £3 per week, compared with, say, a railway porter, who could earn £4 plus tips. But aircraft workers were employed in work of an exciting nature at the cutting edge of technology. With high job satisfaction, most of those who did not join the General Strike were non-unionized, and London district aircraft firms Fairey and Hawker had 50 per cent and 60 per cent respectively who stayed at work. The strike had been brought about by the Triple Alliance of miners, dockers and railway workers, and the strike at national level lasted only nine days, the TUC calling it off on 12 May. The miners held out for another six months, losing a further £60 million in wages, a sum, collectively, that they would never make up.

1927

State of the aircraft industry The General Strike had not touched the aircraft industry as much as the older traditional ones such as mining, the railways and ports. Job satisfaction in working with aircraft certainly contributed to the lack of involvement in industrial strife, but industrial patterns were changing. Workers were migrating from the industrial and depressed areas of the north of England to the London area. London, on the periphery, was growing with heavy industries, including petroleum refining, chemicals and textiles, and Ford at Dagenham in the Thames estuary, as well as light industrial firms like Hoover in north London. With the expansion came council housing estates and 'ribbon' development along the roads leading out of the capital. But the aircraft industry served a much smaller market. Only the rich could afford to purchase aircraft, and relatively few could afford to travel by air. These were the days before package holidays when, as now, the mass public flies all over world. Add to this the very meagre expansion of the RAF and one can imagine that it made little sense to have sixteen major airframe builders and four engine makers. From the RAF's point of view, however, a change in the international situation could require the industry to expand production with little warning, as indeed happened in the mid-1930s. Then it was necessary to bring in the car makers to assemble airframes and engines to meet the surge in demand. For the single-minded pioneers of flying this was not a problem. They were involved in producing designs to meet Air Ministry specifications, followed by yet more designs, more prototypes and more test flying. Hence the large number of aircraft that fill these pages. One hundred and fifteen separate aircraft of all types equipped RAF squadrons between the two world wars. The French aircraft industry had even more capacity, with thirty-six aircraft manufacturers and ten aero-engine makers. They too needed an annual appropriation of state funds spread thinly over the whole industry, and this was used mainly to fund experimental aircraft.

Developments in aircraft component design Squadron Leader G.H. Reid DFC, inventor of the aircraft turn indicator, had formed the Reid Manufacturing and Construction Company Ltd to market this and other devices on his retirement from the RAF. There were also developments in the design of aircraft superchargers. Experimental work on superchargers began during the latter stages of the First World War, but no great advances had been made. Folland was cooperating in trials of a Bristol turbo-supercharged Jupiter engine, but the system proved to be too unreliable. In France and the USA work on exhaust-driven turbo-compressors had been undertaken, while in Germany and Switzerland research had centred on gear-driven multi-stage superchargers. The problems associated with systems driven by exhaust gases were explained by Roy Fedden on 1 February 1927 to a meeting of the RAeS and Institution of Automobile Engineers. Turbine wheels and casings with rotors running at 27,000–30,000 rpm in exhaust gases at 650–700 degrees C had to be manufactured. The problems that arose involved exhaust joints that were not gas tight, the effect of blowers on crankshaft, synchronous speed, the reduction of thermal efficiency and the difficulty of engine and gas cooling. There were also snags with lubrication. Fedden's prognosis was that ground-boosted gear-driven blower engines of a smaller capacity should replace the naturally aspirated engines currently used in fighter aircraft. For larger, general-purpose machines he pointed the way to supercharged engines throttled on the ground but opened up to full power at some predetermined altitude. Exhaust-driven turbo-compressors were more suitable for high-altitude, long-distance bombers where fuel consumption was vital. But Farnborough's 'Jimmy' Eltor was convinced that supercharging would become practicable much sooner if designed around the principle, instead of trying to accommodate the principle to a design intended for naturally aspirated engines.

1927 prototypes

The Wapiti The Westland Wapiti, a general-service aircraft destined to take over as the work horse in the imperial policing role, made its initial flight, piloted by Openshaw. The Wapiti was a derivative of the tried and tested DH9A, using its standard wings and control surfaces. After the maiden flight on an early Sunday morning, Openshaw reported that there was little response from the rudder. Clearly a deep fuselage can have a major effect by shielding the rudder from the airflow, so extra plywood was added, which, however, did not produce the desired effect. A very large rectangular rudder was fitted, but this was disproportionate to the fin. The aircraft was nevertheless favourably received by the Martlesham test pilots.

Westland Wapiti.

The Fairey Postal The RAF planned to take the record for a long-distance flight, and Fairey learned of this project through Squadron Leader Carr, a friend of Air Marshal Sir John Higgins, who decided that a special aeroplane must be built to establish a prestige lead over the French, Italians and Americans. Fairey set out to build a high-wing monoplane with a fixed undercarriage, named the Postal. The idea was to provide the best possible lift and drag component and fly at the most economical cruising speed using a special Napier Lion engine. Fuel consumption was promised at .52 pints/bhp/hour, but the cruising speed was only 25 per cent above the stall. It was presumed that high 'g' would be avoided with low-strength factors to give a light structure. Add to this a hoped-for tail wind, and it was felt that the record could be broken.

New orders for the aircraft industry   As a result of the accidents previously mentioned involving Bristol Fighters, Handley Page was to profit from an Air Ministry order to fit automatic slots to the wings of these aircraft to lessen the likelihood of stalling. The value of the related patents was put at £75,000. By this time Handley Page had become a well-established company. During 1927 all loans had been discharged; assets totally unencumbered and trading profits maintained. Likewise Supermarine had done well from profitable orders, and early in 1927 was registered as Supermarine Aviation Works Ltd, with capital of £300,000. The work in hand meant that its original sheds were too small, and since the Southampton flying-boat was being constructed, the wartime assembly shops on Southampton Water belonging to May, Harden and May were taken over.

Aircraft Production Orders

On the whole the aircraft industry was busy in 1927, although there were some firms that were struggling. The situation for the Bristol Aeroplane Company was becoming critical, as it only had overhaul contracts for the obsolete Bristol Fighter. A production order was badly needed, and the Bulldog fighter was a strong possibility. Beardmore, Parnall, Saunders and Short were all short of production orders, but the design staffs of these companies were not idle. Bill Shackleton at Beardmore was busy on a 140 ft wing-span all-metal aircraft, Knowles at Saunders was designing a fighter and a simplified flat-sided metal hull for a standard Southampton superstructure, and Short had in mind a four-engined version of its Singapore flying-boat. Armstrong Whitworth had full production lines with its Siskin fighter and Atlas Army Cooperation aircraft. Avro, believe it or not, was still building 504Ns at its Manchester, factory while Blackburn was working on an experimental contract for three Iris flying-boats to Air Ministry Specification 31/27, Boulton Paul had six Sidestrand bombers on the go and de Havilland was turning out its Moths. Fairey was busy producing the IIIF, which differed from the prototype in having rounded fins that shielded a balanced rudder. Gloster was producing Gamecock fighters, Handley Page its Hyderabad bomber, Hawker the Horsley and Supermarine the metal-hulled Southampton. Finally, Vickers was busy with Victorias and Virginias, while Westland was building Wapitis.

Air Ministry Specification F9/26 called for a fighter, and both Blackburn and Westland had produced prototypes. The Blackburn machine was designed by B.A. Duncan. It was deemed capable of 200 mph at 15,000 ft using a supercharged Mercury engine. Since the Air Ministry performance estimator could not accept these figures, the tender was not accepted, yet Blackburn's private-venture Turcock, powered with a supercharged Jaguar VI, was tested on 14 November and achieved a speed of 176 mph.

Since Armstrong Whitworth was appointing Alan Campbell-Orde as its chief test pilot, it is well to reflect upon the precarious life of test pilots at this time. It has already been mentioned, for example, that Westland's Stuart Keep lost his legs when test-flying the Dreadnought prototype at Yeovil when only the office medical kit was available for injury. Now the famous Frank Courtney was out of a job, and because he wore glasses, he could not get a 'B' Licence for commercial flying. And as for Macmillan, test flying for Dick Fairey, he was not insured by his company for the risks that he took. He later wrote that he had broached the matter with Dick Fairey only once. The latter's reply was that Macmillan could insure himself out of his own salary if he wished, but when the insurance companies were asked about it they considered that the risks associated with test flying were unacceptable. At no time in his civil flying career was Macmillan covered, for when they did accept the risks at a very high premium, the aircraft manufacturers seemed to regard their test pilots as 'disposable'. Both the pay and the insurance cover then was poor recognition for the vital part that test pilots played in aircraft development.

Commercial Airline Services

Internal UK air services   No internal UK air services were marketed at this time, even though cross-Channel ones had been provided for a number of years. Clearly it was much quicker to go to Paris by air than take the train and ferry, but for purely inland journeys the trains could provide a fast, reliable service not likely to be interrupted by adverse weather conditions. Indeed, seven years on and the London and North Eastern Railway could provide a profitable, fast, day-return service from Newcastle to King's Cross tailored for businessmen. This was the streamlined express, Silver Jubilee.

International civil aviation   There was no doubt that air travel could compete with ocean liners to the Middle and Far East, if not the North Atlantic. It was hoped that airships would provide economic long-distance travel, but the disaster that was to befall the Airship R101 over France on a proving flight to the Middle East and India in 1930 was to spell the end of the airship as a serious competitive rival to sea travel. In contrast, Imperial Airways was doing well. Profits between 1927 and 1928 rose from £11,000 to £72,500. But then Imperial did receive government help in the form of subsidies. Provided services to the Middle East and Europe were maintained over a ten-year period, almost £2 million of subsidy could be earned. The government in 1927 had extended existing agreements for European destinations for a further five years and those for the Middle East to seven years. Passenger numbers had risen for the existing agreements from 11,395 in the first year to 26,479 in the fourth. The Imperial fleet comprised two Short Calcuttas, one Supermarine Sea Eagle, two de Havilland 50s, two HP W8bs, one W8f Hamilton, one W9 Hampstead, three W10s, five de Havilland Hercules and three Armstrong Whitworth Argosys, with a further three on order. Imperial's chairman , Sir Eric Geddes, visualized an extension of routes to take in the Cape and Singapore, and eventually Australia, and hoped for future government subsidy once these routes were organized. He saw the airline concentrating its activities on these main imperial routes, with other airlines and air taxi firms providing feeder services.

1928
Work on Croydon Airport
Waddon and Wellington aerodromes were combined to become Croydon, and the new airport could boast a terminal building, a hotel and aircraft sheds. There were facilities for customs, emigration and immigration. A concrete apron for embarkation and disembarkation had replaced a muddy field, but when the ground was waterlogged, tailskids were broken as aircraft were moved off the grass area onto the concrete. To counter this a chalk platform had to be constructed. A control tower afforded unobstructed views of the airfield, and a wireless operator was employed to transmit and receive wireless messages. Telephone and Morse communications with aircraft were carried out on 9,000 metres using Marconi equipment. Inter-aerodrome communications, which formerly had been conducted by the Air Ministry and transmitted to Croydon by GPO telephone, was replaced by a Marconi set working on 1,400 metres using aerials sited on the edge of Mitcham Common.

The amount of traffic using the airport at that time was insufficient to give a commercial return on the capital employed in building the new facilities, and high rents were deemed necessary by HM Treasury in spite of complaints by the users. Commercial aviation was to become big business, but it would take time. The hotel was particularly popular as a social meeting place for pilots after a long cold flight battered by the winds, for it

must be remembered that they still flew in open cockpits exposed to the elements, and to unwind at the bar after a flight was welcome.

Future development of civil aircraft In the USA or Australia today, domestic air services are important because of the enormous distances to be covered, but in the United Kingdom the rail and motorway networks can compete on equal terms. However, in 1928 the suggestion that the four major rail companies (LNER, SR, LMS and GWR) should operate their own air services was seen as a threat to Imperial Airways. The growth of manufacturing had increased the demand for fast, efficient, freight services. LNER operated its daily 'Scots Goods' from London to the North to guarantee next-day delivery, but aircraft seemed to provide the answer for mails, newspapers and low-bulk/high-value goods such as electricals, and Imperial won Air Ministry approval for the provision of these services. When the railway companies applied to Parliament for private legislation, permitting them to operate their own air services, this was seen as an intention on the part of combined railway interests to put Imperial out of business. GWR's general manager had seen that the canals had gone out of business following the growth of a railway system in Britain, and he did not want to see the same fate befall the railways. GWR was soon to operate its own air service, but with the benefit of hindsight, the railway companies need not have worried.

Happenings in the Aircraft Industry
Handley Page Handley Page Ltd was able to pay a 10 per cent dividend to its shareholders in 1928, and this was after £15,000 had been allocated to the reserve and £3,239 had been written off for depreciation, leaving a credit balance of £31,638. One of the reasons for Handley Page's success was undoubtedly the use of its slotted wing-slot patents, but Mr S.R. Worley, HPs chairman, pointed out that HM Government had a right to any patent without reference to the patentee, in which case compensation was to be determined by the Royal Commission on Awards to Inventors, and it was impossible to forecast the extent of any such award.

Vickers Ltd Vickers was a rival to Handley Page for large aircraft, but it was also into shipbuilding, armaments and engineering. In 1928 Vickers showed a gross profit of £1,275,995. Within the Group, aircraft construction had been profitable, and an announcement was made that it would be floated as a limited company and separate subsidiary to be known as Vickers Aviation Ltd. On the Board of Directors were Sir Robert McLean as chairman, with special directorships going to Captain Acland and Maxwell Muller. Sadly the linchpin between the company and the RAF at Martlesham, Oliver Vickers, died a few weeks later from pneumonia.

A.V. Roe & Co. Ltd and Armstrong Siddeley Crossley Motors Ltd was the chief shareholder of A.V. Roe Ltd, but in 1928 its losses amounted to £65,518 owing to the cost of developing a new 20.9 hp six-cylinder car. However the aircraft section of Avro had accumulated reserve profits in excess of £37,000. Crossley's manager sold the whole of its shareholding in Avro to Armstrong Siddeley Development Company Ltd. Thus Crossley realized a sum of £270,000 in cash for the sale, a profit of more than £200,000 after deduction of its losses. Alliot Verdon Roe, an early aviator and still only 51 years of age, was expected to rest on his laurels and sit back and enjoy his riches, but he had other ideas. With Armstrong Siddeley now the major shareholder, John Siddeley decided to run Avro and Armstrong Siddeley as complementary firms. Lloyd would design Armstrong Siddeley aircraft and Hiscock would produce them. Chadwick was to continue as Avro's chief designer, with Parrott managing the Hamble factory and Roy Dobson in charge at Manchester.

1928 Prototypes and other aircraft developments

The Fairey Postal – maiden and development flights In September the 82 ft wing-span monoplane was taken by road to Northolt for erection and first flight by Norman Macmillan. Dick Fairey was anxious that the RAF should succeed in its bid for the long-distance record, but favoured a biplane rather than the monoplane that his designer Hollis Williams had worked on. Then there was the Fairey-Reed fixed-pitch propeller. The pitch of a propeller blade is important in various stages of a flight. For take-off with a full load the propeller had to give maximum thrust, whereas at cruising speed only 57 per cent efficiency was called for. The French Ratier propeller had an ingenious system whereby it could be 'pumped up' for take-off, whereupon the system would leak until the blades were turned for cruising after about five minutes of flight. But Dick Fairey would have none of it. His aircraft was going to be all British. A retractable undercarriage, flaps and slots were considered by the experts at Farnborough, and the Air Ministry all but agreed that the extra weight and complication involved did not warrant their inclusion, and that went for a variable-pitch propeller. The single huge wing presented torsional problems, and Hollis Williams had devised a pyramid structure whereby the big wooden spars took all the bending and the pyramid all the torsion, apart from the lower flanges of the spars that formed the base of the pyramid.

Dick Fairey's Postal had a competitor in the Bristol Type 109, which had a 51 ft wing span, a supercharged Jupiter XIF engine and enclosed cockpit, but when this was unsuccessfully tendered the directors decided to build the aircraft as a private venture to gain publicity for the engine. The Type 109 pictured opposite had a crew of two, dual controls and an estimated range of

5,400 miles. Since it was of simpler construction than the Postal it was completed more quickly and was ready in July. Then it was engined with a Jupiter VIII, but there were problems with the fuel system. Only after limiting fuel to the gravity tanks could Bristol's test pilot, Uwins, undertake the first flight on 7 September, but there were then problems with longitudinal and directional stability. Modifications were put in hand, including moving the engine forward, but by that time the Postal was being assembled at Northolt. The Type 109 was thereafter used for air endurance-testing of prototype engines.

On 30 October the Postal was cleared for flight. Macmillan made some fast taxiing runs with a ground engineer aboard, then two straight hops when the aircraft cleared the ground. There was then a delay before the maiden flight was made in mid-November, and for the ensuing three weeks Macmillan continued with preliminary test evaluation. On 7 November the Postal was taken up to 10,700 ft, and on the 8th it went to RAF Cranwell. There the RAF's test pilot for this venture, Squadron Leader A.G. Jones-Williams MC, with Macmillan, undertook a programme of flight trials lasting several months. On hand was Flight Lieutenant Major, the second pilot, and Fairey technicians.

The RAF's quest for the long-distance record was not confined to 'one-upmanship', as Dick Fairey explained in justifying long-range potential. In referring to contemporary designs he saw that the maximum range of fighters at that time did not exceed 400 miles, two-seater light bombers or reconnaissance aircraft could go to 600 miles and the longest range of troop carriers and bombers did not exceed 1,200 miles. He therefore reasoned that a 600-mile band of ocean was all that was necessary to protect one country against another when operating from its own territory. If radii of action were to be increased then the effective load would become smaller. Coincidentally the greater would then become the chance of early warning of an enemy's approach. Using the Postal as an example, the range could be increased from an estimated 5,500 miles to 6,700 miles by reducing fuel consumption with a given payload. On the

Fairey Postal.

Bristol Type 109.

other hand, if the range was reduced to 2,000 miles a useful load of 5,000 lb could be carried. Increasing range without sacrificing payload depended crucially upon engine development. He spoke of installing a 1,800 hp engine in an 'ideal' aeroplane that could have a range of 10,000 miles, or if the range was dropped to 2,000 miles, then a load of 20,000 lb might be carried.

Vickers Virginia X   The Virginia had been repeatedly modified. The Mark X had twin 580 hp Lion VB engines that doubled the service ceiling and raised the speed from 97 to 108 mph. At Martlesham tests were in hand of a Mark VII with metal wings, but there were problems with aileron overbalance and flying one wing low. The metal-structured tail eliminated the standard fins and had all-moving balanced rudders. To give further improvements a trial was being undertaken at Brooklands using Jupiter engines, installed because of the eloquent salesmanship of Roy Fedden. The Mark IX Virginia introduced a tail gunner's position, nicknamed 'tail-end Charlie', but this meant moving the centre of gravity forward to compensate for the gunner's weight. This was achieved by lengthening the nose. It is significant that this ungainly biplane remained the mainstay of Bomber Command until 1937.

and if one engine failed trim was impossible unless flown with sideslip, so that yawing the aircraft from side to side only amplified the rudder. One answer was to use servo Fletners, like those on the Singapore. Nevertheless *Flight* Magazine declared that it was the best light bomber of the decade, given its climb, service ceiling and a speed of 130 mph.

Bulldog II   The Bristol Bulldog II won the Air Ministry Specification F9/26 for the prototype, followed by a contract for Specification 17/28, twenty-five production aircraft. It seems that RAF pilots still preferred biplanes, as was evident with Specification 12/26, which follows.

Air Ministry Specification 12/26   There were three prototypes in the contest for this requirement for a light bomber. The specification called for a two-seater metal-framed biplane day-bomber. The prototype Hawker Hart, J9052, was flown by George Bulman in June. Fairey also put up its Fox IIM, J9834, and the third contestant was the Avro Antelope. The latter had flat sides and a 'chinned' radiator similar to the Horsley, whereas the other two aircraft had pointed noses. Structurally the Antelope was ahead of the Hart, but, though it handled well, RAF maintenance crews preferred space-frame construction. All three contenders had special balanced gun rings to facilitate movement of the Lewis guns at

Hawker Hart.

Boulton Paul Sidestrand   The Sidestrand day-bomber had problems. Test pilot Harald Penrose was allowed to try the controls when it was being flown by the RAF's oldest flight lieutenant, Bill Markham. So great was the stability and so heavy the controls that Penrose remarked that it was like a 'train on the rails'. To apply rudder without bank required the full strength of the leg,

Fairey Fox IIM.

AVRO Antelope.

acute angles of fire, for greater speeds had made Scarff rings unusable. The Hart had a wooden propeller, whereas the Fox IIM and the Antelope featured the Fairey-Reed propeller of twisted duralumin. The Hart and Fox were equally matched at a maximum speed of over 180 mph, but the Antelope, not unsurprisingly, was 10 mph slower. At this time these machines were the most secret in the country.

Beardmore Inflexible Once described as the most impressive and useless aeroplane of 1928, the Beardmore Inflexible had to be moored in the open at Martlesham, where it went for evaluation. It had triple Rolls-Royce Condor engines, a 157.5 ft wing span and was painted in khaki. It had to be taken by sea to Felixstowe, then transported to Martlesham for reassembly. Its construction was more like that of a bridge or a ship than an aeroplane, and made as it was of dural plates, it was

The Beardmore Inflexible.

so overweight that it had little room for any payload. The load on the cantilever wing was such that a 6-inch circumference funk-wire hawser had been added either side of the fuselage to relieve the upload, although the strength of the box-spar was sufficient for downloads. It had to have wheels of more than 6 ft diameter specially built by Dunlop. It was nicknamed 'the impossible', and so it was, for it failed to gain RAF acceptance.

Other prototypes In Hawker's drawing office a top-secret design was a single-seater fighter powered by a Rolls-Royce XIS engine, based on the Hart but lighter by 130 lb and with 6 ft less wing span. This was the Hornet. At Bristol, test pilot Uwins was flying the Bullpup powered temporarily with a Jupiter VI engine, but since Bristol's Bulldog II had just won the Air Ministry competition for Specification F9/26 it seemed unlikely that the company would get yet another fighter contract at this time. Westland, on the other hand, was working on a monoplane, a low-wing interceptor powered with a Jupiter engine, pending development of the Mercury. The 38 ft wing-span interceptor was light on the controls, delightfully easy to fly, gave a perfect pilot's view from the cockpit and was the first of current designs to feature wheel brakes. But pilots objected to the bracing wires that went from the longitudinal stringers inside the fuselage and the underside of both wings to mounting points behind the landing wheels. They felt that if the

Westland Interceptor's bracing wires.......
and with enlarged tail plane

undercarriage was damaged the wings would collapse. There was also a problem of 'corkscrewing' in a 'g' stall, but when a larger tail plane was fitted, as illustrated on page 188, the problem was not solved. There was, in any event, still a prejudice in favour of biplanes in spite of the splendid all-round view afforded by the single pair of wings.

Stalling and wing slots   Stalling was still a problem in 1928. Flight Lieutenant S.M. Kinkead DSO, DSC, DFC was killed while flying off the Isle of Wight, probably because of a stall. Major J.P.C. Cooper, the Inspector of Accidents, concluded that Kinkead's death was due to his misjudging his height in the sun-filled haze of the afternoon and flying into the water or stalled. The day after Kinkead's death, Flight Lieutenant I.E. McIntyre CBE, AFC was involved in a fatal stalling accident in Melbourne. So even the most experienced pilots could succumb. The danger could be ameliorated, if not removed, by using Handley Page's automatic slots. Geoffrey de Havilland demonstrated the effectiveness of slots with his prototype Moth by pulling up violently at 200 ft, and it did not spin. But he had foreseen that although the slots stabilized the aircraft laterally the rate of descent was increased, so that a conventional straight axle could not withstand the impact on landing. So he substituted this with a split-axle type of wider tread, giving one-third extra shock absorption. It might be added that on his third demonstration to journalists and club representatives de Havilland succeeded in spread-eagling the undercarriage and snapping off the fuselage at the front cockpit. But he could console himself in the knowledge that things might have been much worse without the slots.

In concluding the year 1928, it is a sobering thought that racing cars were then faster than the fastest fighter aircraft. Malcolm Campbell had set a new world record in Bluebird at Daytona beach in Florida with a speed of 206.96 mph, beating Major Seagrave's racer by just 5 mph.

1929

Monoplane v. Biplane

The debate on the matter of the superiority of the biplane over the monoplane continued unabated. Opponents of the monoplane considered that the necessity for bracing wires, the decreased payload and higher landing speeds of such aircraft could not compete with the more lightly stressed, lighter structures of biplanes. It must be remembered that aircraft, even at airports, still landed on the grass. Heavy aircraft would sink into soggy ground and landing strips would need to be much larger to accommodate aircraft with high landing speeds. Biplanes were more economical in carrying passengers or freight than monoplanes of a similar size. At the Air Ministry, senior officers, brought up on biplanes, saw no reason to pave runways to accommodate heavier aircraft. Indeed both civil and military aircraft could still put down in a field if there was engine failure. The reason why the Air Ministry had built no more single-engined heavy bombers after the Aldershot was precisely because, in the event of single-engine failure, the aircraft would have to put down in a field and would then have to be dismantled to effect recovery.

The debate was taken up by academics speaking from both points of view. Professor Melville Jones MA, FRS delivered a lecture entitled 'The Streamlined Aeroplane', while W.S. Farren MA lectured on the Monoplane v. Biplane. Professor Melville Jones compared the air resistance of current aircraft with those theoretically possible. Based upon experimental work, he contended that greater streamlining was the future of aircraft design. This would result in lower fuel consumption and higher speeds, and streamlining would be applied to all external surfaces. In this he was supported by Geoffrey Hill, who foresaw the drag of military and commercial aircraft being halved. With the aid of aerodynamic knowledge then available the ability to set standards for streamlining aircraft for drag was a major factor.

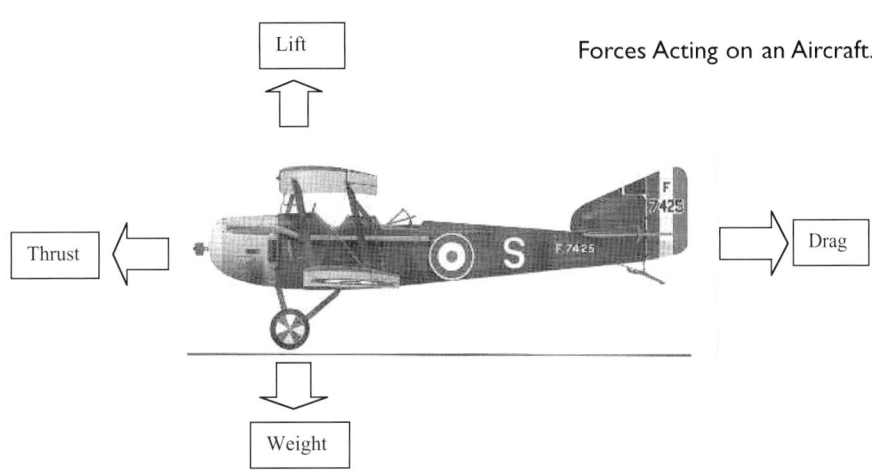

Forces Acting on an Aircraft.

W.S. Farren hit back with hard figures. While admitting that the biplane suffered from the parasitic resistance of the wing structure, turning a biplane into a monoplane reduced payload by 20 per cent. Thus, if a commercial airline wanted to increase the cruising speed of monoplane airliners it would be very costly. He did not visualize biplane aircraft ever weighing more than 40,000 lb.

The debate was joined by others. Geoffrey Hill attacked Farren for basing his arguments on a bad monoplane, in which case he must not be surprised if he came up with the wrong figures. Charles Walker maintained that the question of monoplane versus biplane depended on the practical consideration of the aircraft's intended use. He argued that monoplanes were of simple design but in practice were not always as efficient as the biplane. Others thought that British airworthiness requirements placed monoplanes at a disadvantage in demanding too large a tail area. Handley Page, with an eye on publicity, declared that monoplane design implied heavy loads and higher landing speeds unless his slots were used. He nevertheless felt safer with the rigid wings of a biplane rather than watching a monoplane's wings flex in turbulence. He cited Junkers aircraft whose wings flexed up and down several feet in bumps. Mr Trost of Junkers retorted that, of the sixty-eight world records recognized by the FAI, thirty-eight were held by monoplanes. Even the pilots differed in their views, some favouring biplanes because of easier handling and others monoplanes if flown from good surfaces that would permit higher landing speeds. Clearly it was only a matter of time before paved runways were introduced.

Airships – the R100 and R101

On 29 July 1929 a week-long inflation of the R100 began at Howden, supervised by Lieutenant-Commander Burney. Vickers had grown anxious about the delay through cost overrun, and it was hoped to get the airship airborne within two months. The R100 was built by the Airship Guarantee Company, a subsidiary of Vickers, at the same time as a rival airship, the R101, was being built at Cardington with public funds. The contract for the R100 had been accepted in 1924, but unlike its state-financed rival, Vickers had to foot the bill for losses caused by cost overruns. Vickers's chairman, the Hon. Sir Herbert A. Lawrence, pointed out at the Annual General Meeting that owing to it being work of national importance and of an experimental nature the Group did accept work on which losses might be incurred. There was an added urgency in that the *Graf Zeppelin* was stealing the limelight, even though a flight to New York had to be abandoned over Spain in May because of engine failure. But in August a successful flight to Lakehurst, New Jersey, was completed.

The 'Socialist' Airship, R101.

The press were invited to Cardington on 2 October to view R101 in its shed before the launch programmed for the 7th, but when that day arrived a 10 mph wind was too strong to get it out of its hangar, for it was calculated this would crash the airship against the hangar wall with a force of 4 tons. It was not until 12 October that conditions were right to take her out. It took six minutes to reach the mooring mast, after which she had to be raised so that the coupling in the nose could be connected to the masthead. It is difficult to see how, on these grounds alone, profitably run timetabled commercial airship services might have been achieved, but since the catastrophic loss of this airship in the following year put an end to any hopes of marketing airship services, we shall never know.

It was not until 10.30 hrs on 14 October 1929 that the airship was ready for flight. On board the R101 were Major R.B.B. Colmore, the Director of Airship Development, Lieutenant-Colonel V.C. Richmond, her designer, Major Scott, the commander, and a hand-picked crew. Forty minutes later the engines were started, the mooring cables were slipped and she made her way under power to 1,500 ft as she left the airfield and was then turned towards London several years later than anticipated. She later flew to Edinburgh and Belfast and over Sandringham for the King to see. Lord Thomson, Secretary of State for Air, was also carried as a passenger. On 11 November she rode at her mooring mast at Cardington in winds averaging 70 mph, gusting to 83 mph, when the maximum load on the coupling rose to over a third of its breaking load of 30 tons.

The Vickers team at Howden also invited the press to inspect R100. In the early morning of 16 December she was taken out. Squadron Leader Booth, her commander, was at the controls, but Major Scott was in overall charge. After handling trials she went to Cardington, and on arrival it was noticed that the fabric covering the

The 'Capitalist' Airship, R100.

aft part of the hull and the bottom fin pulsated in the slipstream. The outer fabric covering was pressing in on the frames, unlike the R101, where air pressure kept her fabric taut. The second flight, on 17 December, was made to investigate the tautness of the fabric. On the 18th she went to the second airship shed for adjustment.

Loss of the seaplane, 'City of Rome'   The hazards of commercial flying-boat services are in evidence in the loss of the Short Calcutta 'City of Rome' on 26 October on the London–India airmail route. She ran into a gale after leaving Naples. With a wind speed of 70 mph, Captain L.S. Birt was forced to alight on the sea ten miles south of Spezia. An SOS was picked up by the Italian steamer *Famiglia*, and since the flying-boat was riding the seas quite well, a 250 yd line was thrown and secured to the nose of the aircraft. Progress was made towards land with the help of the seaplane's engines, but fifteen

A Short Calcutta similar to the 'City of Rome' that foundered in the seas off Naples.

minutes later the cable snapped. The 'City of Rome' was seen for a few minutes and her engine noises were heard, but when her navigation lights disappeared it was no longer possible to fix her position. Although three circuits were made of her last known position there was no trace of the seaplane. The crew and four passengers had drowned. The lesson learned from this episode was that, no matter how sound the hull of a flying-boat may be, the wings are fragile. Once the lower wings nearest the water were buckled by the heavy seas, the entire biplane structure collapsed. Cantilever monoplanes might be safer, but their wing-tip floats were also vulnerable. Even though the Italians had produced a twin-hulled flying-boat that would be stable even with damaged wings, the Air Ministry boffins had turned down proposals by Sir Oswald Short to build such a craft.

Note: The Calcutta pictured above is moored in the Thames. In the 1920s there was no bar to waterway operations by flying-boats.

More accidents involving test and other pilots   The theme of the hazards of test flying in the inter-war years is again taken up. Avro almost lost its chief test pilot, H.A. Brown, when the first Avocet crashed through engine failure at Woodford aerodrome. At Westland, its interceptor, referred to on p. 189, was being flown by Louis Paget. This, it may be remembered, had had a larger tail plane fitted to correct corkscrewing in a 'g' stall. Having dived the aircraft, he discovered on landing that the fuselage fittings of the tailplane front struts had failed. Another dive would almost certainly have resulted in the collapse of the structure. At Bristol, C.R.L. Shaw was diving the wooden Bristol 101 when the centre section suddenly swung back over his head. With the strength one can only muster in an emergency he succeeded in pushing it back to allow him to escape. He baled out, his canopy opening at a mere 1,000 ft. But other equally experienced pilots were not immune. Flight Lieutenant A.S. White, a seasoned de Havilland instructor, was flying with a potential customer in a Gypsy Moth. On turning to land, his aircraft was struck by a single-seater Moth flown by Captain G.F. Boyle. The left wings became interlocked and both aircraft burst into flames on hitting the ground. Finally two RAF aerobatic pilots were killed in separate incidents. Flying Officer C.H. Jones stalled his aircraft when he pulled round too steeply after take-off, and Flying Officer J. Clarke flew into the downdraught above the Blackburn factory. He crashed onto the concrete apron, where his machine caught fire.

Test flight of the Blackburn Iris III   Blackburn launched its Iris III flying-boat on 21 November at Brough. This aircraft differed from the prototype in having duralumin-structured wings. Since Dasher Blake, the

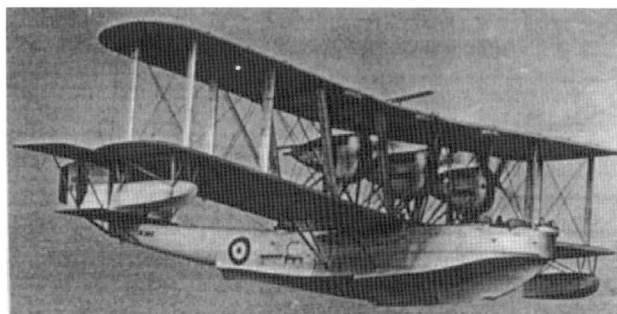

Blackburn Iris III.

test pilot, had not flown flying-boats, he was accompanied for the acceptance flight by Squadron Leader Rea, an experienced marine pilot. Also on board was N.H. Woodhead as second pilot and Major Rennie as observer. A thirty-minute test flight was provided for in the contract, after which the RAF pilots took Iris III to Felixstowe for performance trials. Felixstowe was the Martlesham equivalent for flying-boats and floatplanes.

Reflections on the Decade 1919–29

This volume has been titled 'The Trenchard Years', for at the close of 1929 Sir Hugh Trenchard retired from his post as Chief of the Air Staff, to be succeeded by Air Chief Marshal Sir John Salmond. His unique place in the history of the RAF is dealt with in Chapter 3. In this chapter it is the contribution he made to the development of aircraft and engines that is considered. From the outset Trenchard had to make do with meagre resources. He knew that the RAF could not afford wholesale replacements of squadrons of new aircraft. The huge war surplus of machines such as the DH9A and Bristol Fighter could, when refurbished, give good service for years to come, and they did. At the same time he knew that the survival of the aircraft industry was vital if Britain was to remain in the forefront of design and development to provide the latest in technology when his aircraft, which were designed in the First World War, were finally retired from active service. Of course, in the peace that followed the war it might have been expected that commercial flying would provide the stimulus required, but readers will recall that civil aviation came under the Air Ministry and its annual vote of money from Parliament, and civil aviation's share was very small. This is why commercial aviation has been included in this history of the RAF between the wars.

And so Trenchard had the foresight to issue contracts to competing firms for prototypes, which permitted the companies to retain at least a nucleus of design and production staff. And when production contracts were awarded they were sometimes subject to the condition that some of the work be sub-contracted to other companies. Although a number of companies did go into liquidation during the period 1919–29, the majority

survived the 'lean years'. But it was not simply business from the RAF and civil aviation that kept the companies going. This chapter has recounted a number of private ventures that were undertaken to prove a point to the Air Ministry when there was insufficient interest in a prototype. Remember Oswald Short's threat to go bankrupt rather than see his Short Singapore flying-boat fail after being found unacceptable to the Air Ministry. He succeeded in getting Sir Geoffrey Salmond down to Rochester the next day. The aircraft and aero-engine companies were led by enthusiasts and true entrepreneurs, aided by test pilots and design and production staff who were dedicated to the work in hand. Geoffrey de Havilland, Frederick Handley Page, Roy Chadwick, Dick Fairey, Roy Fedden are but a few, for they were typical of the men who pioneered the development of aircraft and engines during this period. And people like Stuart Keep, Dasher Blake, Frank Courtney and Lankester Parker are just a few names among the many who risked their lives to test these early prototypes. There were also the RAF test pilots who took over these aircraft to assess their suitability for the RAF and the airlines.

The continuing debate during the decade about biplanes versus monoplanes, wood versus metal construction and open versus closed cockpits is of enormous interest, but it was only a passing phase. It was always inevitable that, as engine power was increased and streamlining introduced, both flying and landing speeds would be increased. The wooden, fabric-covered biplane landing and taking off from grass airfields had had its day. Volume II of this work will take the reader forward to the years leading to the outbreak of the Second World War. Then only a handful of biplane designs remained in service, and by the time that that war ended, aircraft were jet powered and bordering on the speed of sound.

As for airships, their bulk and slow speed relative to fixed-wing aircraft made them unsuitable for military use except for maritime reconnaissance, and perhaps the carriage of troops and freight. As with the development of fixed-wing aircraft, the design and development of airships was in the hands of enthusiasts and dedicated pilots. Where the airship could score over civil airliners of the decade was in having the range and payload potential. Although steps were taken to establish airship stations between Britain and the Middle and Far East, Canada and the USA, there were technical problems to be overcome, not least the use of highly inflammable gas. Even though the airship was not to survive the 1930s as a serious commercial rival to the aeroplane or the ocean liner, its place in this history is important because it was used operationally by Britain and offensively by the Germans. Indeed, the Zeppelins went on to be a viable commercial alternative to fixed- wing airliners and flying-boats. By the outbreak of the Second World War the RAF had no further use for lighter-than-air craft beyond the barrage balloon, which gave a measure of defence against low-flying aircraft attempting to attack populated areas and industrial targets.

Finally, little mention is made of aircraft armament and the development of air-defence systems. That is because there is little to report. While there was talk of a 'death ray' to bring down enemy aircraft, nothing was done .Where the RAF continued to be operational, in the Middle East and India, improvements in bombing were largely the result of improvisation. RAF aircraft continued to use the tried and tested Vickers and Lewis guns, either mounted on a Scarff ring or fixed to the airframe, for the COW gun was not accepted for service use. It was to be the 1930s that witnessed the considerable advances that were to take the RAF into the Second World War.

As a postscript, the locations of the firms that had survived the lean years after the First World War and made up the British air industry are shown below.

Locations of the Major Players in the Aircraft Industry, 1929.

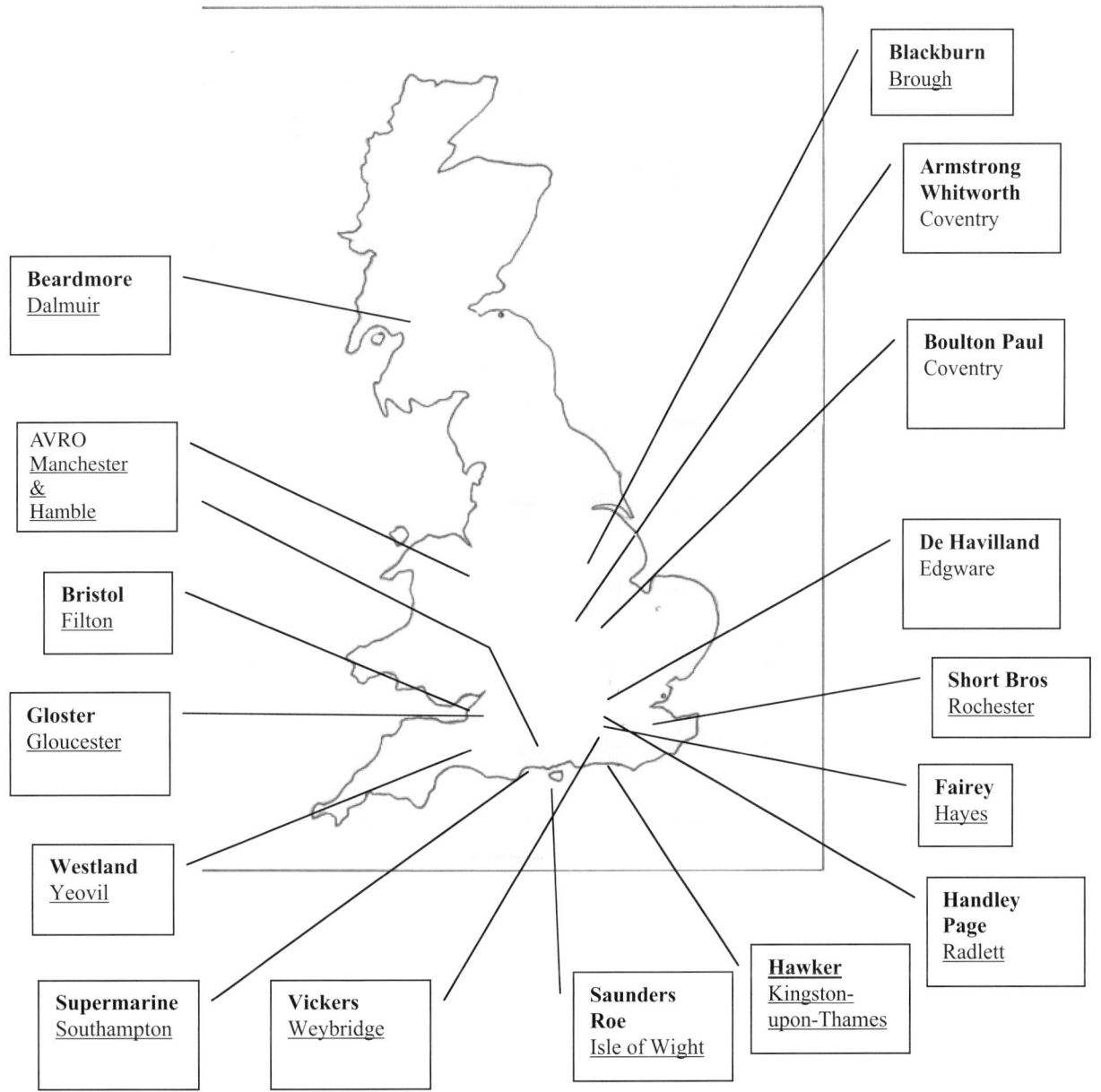

Chapter 6
The RAF at Sea

The RAF v. Royal Navy battles – RAF operations from a carrier or warship – Manning of RAF units afloat – Naval aircraft – Introduction and development – Discussion of the operations of various air units afloat, 1919–29

Chapter 2 makes a brief reference to the battles during the immediate postwar years between Trenchard, on the one hand, and the Chief of the Imperial General Staff, Sir Henry Wilson and Admiral Earl Beatty, the First Sea Lord, on the other. The battles were over the survival of the RAF as an independent third service and Wilson's and Beatty's determination to wrest back the ex-RFC and RNAS units to their respective services whence they came to form the RAF in April 1918. Wilson regarded the RAF as an extravagant luxury that the nation could not afford at a time of economic cut-backs, and would have had the RAF disbanded there and then. Beatty, on the other hand, was prepared at least to give Trenchard a year to see if the air units necessary to satisfy naval requirements could be provided by the RAF.

In his Memorandum on the Permanent Organization of the RAF in 1919, Trenchard had acknowledged that he could not simply limit the RAF to offensive defence, using bombers together with fighters, to protect the UK base. He had earmarked Army Cooperation squadrons to work closely with the Army, and these units would be equipped with the appropriate aircraft and train with the Army in peacetime. But whatever Trenchard would do to satisfy Wilson, it made no difference to the latter's attitude. The provision of naval air units was complicated by the fact that some RAF units would be land based and some sea based. One could say that a land-based unit would be RAF manned, serviced, equipped and operationally commanded and controlled by the RAF. The squadron or wing commander would simply take his orders from HQ Coastal Area, the RAF's home-based formation, comprising all land-based aircraft employed on maritime reconnaissance, anti-submarine patrols and attacks on enemy shipping. But naval air units at sea were located in aircraft-carriers and aboard warships. A fleet commander with naval air units at his disposal must have operational command and control of them. Were, then, RAF personnel to be seconded to the Royal Navy or attached, perhaps taking their orders from a senior RAF officer ashore? And what of naval personnel who might wish to be pilots, observers or mechanics? Could they serve under or alongside RAF personnel?

The government, for its part, had accepted that the newly formed RAF should be the service to provide all the aeroplanes, otherwise what would be the point of its existence? But the Navy had already shown that it could carry the war to the enemy's homeland with its 'bloody

paralyser', so was an independent air force really necessary? (Even today it is not the RAF but the Royal Navy with its Trident submarines that carries the strategic deterrent.) Be that as it may, in 1919 the government had accepted that the RAF should provide the aeroplanes, and apart from any other consideration there was always the likelihood of duplicating the aircraft and spares procurement organizations in two or even three services if each service had its own aeroplanes, and this the government was keen to avoid. On the other hand, there was always the possibility that an incoming government could be persuaded to review the whole business of a independent RAF. Both Wilson and Beatty would exploit such a situation, and Trenchard knew that he would have to be ready with arguments to defend his position. This should be borne in mind in reading the following paragraphs.

The Battles with the Army and the Royal Navy
The future of aircraft-carriers and battleships   In 1920 Rear Admiral Sir Reginald Hall MP had a series of articles published in *The Times*. His claim that the battleship's days were numbered and that Britain's naval supremacy could be adequately and economically served by light aircraft, submarines and aeroplanes must have been music to Trenchard's ears. For good measure Trenchard expressed doubts about the future of the aircraft-carrier too, it being too expensive and vulnerable. As it turns out, it was Sir Reginald who was prophetic, not Trenchard. One has only to think of the fate of German, British and Japanese battleships in the Second World War, and remember that it was aircraft from the *Ark Royal* that damaged the steering of the *Bismarck*, which led ultimately to its sinking. As so often in the 1920s, Trenchard went over the top with his claims for the efficacy of airpower, and he did not see the need for naval air units when a string of aerodromes could be built to cover the main routes of the British Empire. Many squadrons of torpedo and bombing aircraft could be provided for the cost of one battleship. However, their Lordships at the Admiralty were not about to give up either the battleship or the aircraft-carrier. Perhaps the more telling point, and one which did strike a raw nerve at the Admiralty, was Trenchard's claim that in any future conflict the threat would not be invasion of these islands, for which the Royal Navy had for centuries been the gate guardian: the threat would come from the air, in the form of bombing, and Trenchard was therefore

suggesting that a leading role of the Royal Navy had been assumed by the RAF.

The role of the Air Force in the system of aerial defence
This was the title of an Air Staff draft paper shown to Winston Churchill when he returned from the Middle East in March 1920. Although no longer the Secretary of State for Air, Churchill could still be relied upon by Trenchard to support him in air matters in the corridors of power, and sure enough, Winston persuaded Austen Chamberlain, the Leader of the House of Commons, to circulate the document as a Cabinet Paper. The claims made by the RAF at this time may be stated as follows:

1. The primary function of the Air Force in the future would be the defence of the British Isles from invasion by air from the continent of Europe. This defence would largely take the form of a counter-offensive from the air, assisted by a ground organization coordinated by the Air Ministry. (This was Trenchard's offensive defence.)
2. Certain responsibilities at present assigned to the Navy and the Army could be more economically and just as adequately carried out by air units, notably the maintenance of order in certain areas of unrest in the Middle East, the protection of the British Isles from overseas invasion, coastal defence and the protection of merchant shipping in certain areas.
3. Under present conditions the strength of the RAF at home was absorbed by its functions as an auxiliary to the Navy and Army, and while the proper discharge of these functions was of vital importance, there should be more use made of the Air Force as an independent arm, used, not as an auxiliary, but as a substitute for naval and military forces.

Of course, contents of this Paper meant that Trenchard would face renewed hostility from Wilson and Beatty. This was not the first, nor would it be the last, time that HM Government became entangled in the continuing inter-service rivalries of the early 1920s. Mr Balfour, the Prime Minister, could not get the Standing Defence Sub-Committee to reconcile the differences, so he produced an independent report stating his own views. He felt that the Army and the Navy had discounted the effects that large-scale bombing might have in any future war. He came down on the side of the RAF while trying to understand the Admiralty's anxiety that operational accountability and chains of command would be unacceptable unless the Navy had full control of its own naval air force. The system that Balfour was prepared to agree to was as follows:

1. The Admiralty to ask for what they required for their fleet, and the Air Ministry to provide it.
2. The Admiralty to pay to the Air Ministry a grant-in-aid to cover the expenditure.

3. The Air Ministry to keep all units up to strength in personnel and material, and all personnel should remain with the Navy for a period of three years. In return the Navy must offer every facility to naval officers to become airmen and encourage a few to go for general service in the Air Force to gain wide experience.
4. The training of personnel, prior to their allocation to the fleet, to be an Air Ministry responsibility.
5. All personnel, both of naval and Air Force origin, should remain and be paid as airmen, but should be at all times and in all respects under the absolute orders of the Admiralty to do all that was required as airmen.
6. All personnel when ashore to be accommodated at Air Force stations, which would be administered and paid for by the Air Ministry but would remain under naval control for all practices and exercise designed to maintain their efficiency for fleet work.
7. A senior Air officer, with a small staff of permanent Air Force officers, to be on the staffs of all admirals commanding independent fleets.

At best these arrangements were untidy but necessary if there was to be split responsibility for the maintenance of naval air units. Trenchard discussed Balfour's paper with Churchill and added three provisions of his own:

1. The Admiralty, as in supreme command of all fleets and naval operations, to keep in the closest touch with the RAF Coastal Area, and to enable such close touch it was desirable that the Coastal Area Headquarters should be housed in the Admiralty or close by. (RAF Coastal Area was formed in December 1919, and controlled all units working with the Navy, including airships under naval control and units afloat in aircraft-carriers.)
2. The Admiralty to be responsible for the number of units required for embarkation with the Navy afloat, and for the payment for the same, and to be responsible for all air work by these units both when embarked and while at shore stations when the work was for the Navy afloat.
3. The Air Ministry to be responsible for all operations from shore bases, not only in its independent capacity in carrying out the air defence of Great Britain and other work allotted to it, but also for those aerial operations carried out in cooperation with the Navy to assist the fleet in operations afloat.

The document embodying these principles was sent by Mr Churchill to the First Sea Lord at the beginning of July 1922. In the atmosphere of economic stringency following the 'Geddes Axe', the Army and the Navy continued to attack the idea of an independent RAF.

Memorandum by the Secretary of State for Air – Reply to Admiralty Memorandum on Relations between the Navy and the Air Force

Source: National Archives P.3736 – Air Ministry, 11 February 1922

In February 1922 the Secretary of State for Air, Captain F.E. Guest, felt obliged to respond to yet another attack by the Admiralty on the continued existence of a separate air arm, which had followed an assault by the Army. He rebutted the fresh arguments put forward by citing Lord Curzon's Air Board Report, the Report of War Cabinet Committee on Air Organization, August 1917 (the Smuts Report) and Conclusions of War Cabinet on establishment of a separate air force, August 1917, proposing and supporting the idea of a separate air arm. He also cited Mr Balfour's Defence Sub-Committee (See p. 195) and the Geddes Committee, which looked into the ways of effecting economies and found no extravagance in the Air Ministry's spending, and furthermore concluded that no substantial savings would be achieved by disbanding the RAF. Captain Guest also made light of the Admiralty citing the French Admiral Le Bon, since France did not have a separate air arm, and French naval aviation, he said, was still in an undeveloped state. He rather cited the United States Aviation Mission that had visited Europe after the First World War and had strongly supported Britain's separate air force, and he put the failure of America to form a separate air force down to the strengths of vested interests rather than the merits of the case.

Cabinet Paper – The relations between the Royal Air Force and the Navy

Source: National Archives document – 1922 undated

This paper asked members of the Cabinet to consider the Admiralty's demand for a separate Naval Air Service. The paper was submitted by Captain F.E. Guest, Secretary of State for Air, and it accused the Admiralty of obscuring the argument in camouflage and technical detail. He began by suggesting that the question should be considered from a political viewpoint, not a technical one, since all fighting services would use every endeavour to protect their corners, whereas the politicians could take a wider look. Secondly, he stressed the importance of a correct solution of the air problem to the well-being of the Empire, whether in peace or war. The Secretary of State suggested that a widely scattered Empire could be reached more quickly by air than by sea, but he could not say at the time whether airpower would supplement or supplant seapower, given the potential of airpower and unforeseeable ways in which airpower might develop. Of course such an assertion was hardly likely to smooth ruffled naval feathers. A

premature decision about the formation of a separate Naval Air Service, he said, should be avoided since the aircraft was still in the early stages of development and the whole system of defence could be jeopardised if a wrong decision was made. 'The foresight of earlier generations gave us mastery of the seas, it is now ours to ensure for our successors the mastery of the air', he added. It had taken five years to create a unified air service, and all that work would go to waste if the RAF were then dismembered. On the other hand, the maintenance of three separate air services was out of the question, adding only confusion and rendering the solution to air problems impossible. In para. 6 of the paper the Secretary of State accused the Admiralty of avoiding concrete criticisms for abstract ones. He refuted their Lordships' argument that command of the seas, depending as it did on the efficiency of the fleet, could not be guaranteed unless it had control over all its components, including its air arm. He countered this argument by saying, to use the Admiralty's logic, that an air force which had to fight an air war over land and sea could not successfully prosecute such a war unless it had entire and absolute control of all air units, including Army cooperation and naval air units. Logically the RAF would have to have its own aircraft-carriers to fight an air war over the sea, which was plainly ridiculous when the Navy could cooperate and provide and man the carriers as a base for RAF air units.

Captain Guest was only trotting out the by then familiar RAF arguments to counter those of the Royal Navy. He could not envisage a Navy with an air arm, which would be isolated and a service without roots. He added the factors of duplication in training and aircraft procurement/development, which was what led to the Smuts Report of 1917 and the formation of a unified air force in the first place. In para. 7 he declared that the present system had not been shown to be defective, and that some Members of Parliament had tried to show that the Navy had been starved of machines (aircraft). In para. 8 he concluded by urging the government to give the RAF more time to develop its cooperation and support for both the Army and the Navy, saying that the Navy had nothing to lose by sticking to the existing arrangements. If the Admiralty was to have complete control of its air arm (in 1922) it would not have the expertise to run it. Given time, the Navy could have some of its personnel trained so that, if a future government decided to meet the Navy's wishes, it would at some later date be better equipped to take it over. This is, of course, what eventually happened.

In the mean time Churchill felt that the RAF should be the parent service of all airmen in their capacity as airmen, while Beatty continued to state his preparedness to accept an independent air force while still wanting his own naval air arm. On 27 July 1922 the Admiralty circulated a paper reinforcing this point. The Air

Minister's reply was that aircraft working with the fleet could not be regarded as distinct from those working as part of the fleet. He believed that the Admiralty was fearful that the Navy would not have full control of the former. He did concede that the Navy did not have all the naval air units it needed, but then neither did the Army, for there was simply a lack of funds. The Navy was therefore asked to give the RAF a further two years to try out the system explained in the foregoing paragraphs. The Navy was also invited to second to the RAF officers of appropriate rank to be trained in flying and air organization.

The Salisbury Main Committee
When the coalition government fell in early 1923, Bonar Law became the new Conservative Prime Minister, and he was contemplating the disbandment of the RAF. The point has already been made that the heads of the other two services would be very likely to exploit such a situation, and Beatty threatened to resign if he could not get control of his naval airmen. Trenchard found himself being summoned to Downing Street, where he too threatened to resign if any attempt was made to carve up the RAF. Faced with the possible resignation of his two service chiefs, the Prime Minister did what British prime ministers do best. If in doubt, set up an inquiry! And so on 9 March 1923 he ordered the setting up of yet another committee of inquiry. This would be a sub-committee, under the chairmanship of the Marquess of Salisbury, of the Committee of Imperial Defence (hereafter known as the Main Committee). The sub-committee would inquire into the cooperation and correlation between the Navy, Army and Air Force from the point of view of national and Imperial defence generally, including the establishment of some coordinating authority, whether by a Ministry of Defence or otherwise. Three points in particular were to be considered, only one of which is pertinent to this chapter, namely the relationship between the Navy and the Air Force as regards control of fleet air work.

The committee began its series of meetings on 15 March 1923, and it continued into the autumn. It did not feel that a Ministry of Defence was necessary to coordinate the work of the three services, but that the present CID (Main Committee) could be enlarged to include the three service chiefs. The committee felt that when two services were working together on the same military operation, one service should be selected as the predominant partner. The committee rejected the proposal that the Army should take over the RAF. When the sub-committee reported back, the Main Committee did not agree to a separate Fleet Air Arm, believing that a single service was necessary because all involved were airmen. A line should not therefore be drawn between what was a shore-based naval air action and one that was fleet based. Furthermore there should not be

duplication in equipment supply, the procurement of aircraft, the establishment of airfields and training schools etc. It was conceded, however, that where naval officers were seconded or attached to the Fleet Air Arm they should retain their naval uniforms and wear a special badge denoting the Air Branch.

The Main Committee report was approved by the Cabinet on 31 July 1923, but the First Lord and the Admiralty doubted whether the proposals were workable, and they were not regarded as a final settlement. Further concessions followed in order to bring the Admiralty 'on side'. It was recommended that the proportion of naval officers should be increased from 20 to a maximum of 30 per cent of the strength of the naval air wing, though neither Beatty nor the Sea Lords were happy, and they had to be persuaded not to resign *en masse*. And so on 1 April 1924 the Fleet Air Arm came into existence.

The RAF officer component of the Fleet Air Arm (FAA) was to be 70 per cent as against 30 per cent for naval officers. Beatty felt that RAF Coastal Area should be regarded as FAA for the purposes of deciding the 70 per cent figure, i.e. there would be more naval officers to be trained for service afloat. He also felt that the other ranks on board aircraft-carriers should be naval personnel. Trenchard was instructed to get agreement with the Navy on the interpretation and implementation of the Balfour recommendations. This was done, and the main points of agreement are listed below. The only point upon which agreement was not forthcoming was over the incidence of the cost of maintaining the FAA as between the Admiralty and the Air Ministry, and so this matter was passed to the Treasury for a decision.

Agreement between the Royal Navy and the RAF on the management and operation of the Fleet Air Arm The following five points of agreement, which were approved by the CID on 15 July 1924, laid down the basis for the running of the FAA in the years ahead, although the Admiralty never stopped trying to gain total control, which did not occur until 1937:

1. As regards design of aircraft for whose construction the Air Ministry was responsible, the Admiralty would list the numbers of aircraft required, together with the performances desired. The Air Ministry would then prepare detailed specifications incorporating these and any subsequent amendments by the naval staff.
2. When FAA units were to be landed ashore the Navy would tell the RAF Commander, Coastal Area, the nature of the training, and the RAF would then carry it out.
3. Naval ratings would gradually replace airmen on board aircraft-carriers in various duties and trades such as cooks, carpenters and the like.

4. Up to 70 per cent of officers in the FAA could be provided by the Navy and Royal Marines, and such officers could be attached temporarily for specific periods, during which they would be granted Air Force rank and would be eligible for promotion in the RAF irrespective of their naval rank.
5. All air observation duties with the fleet, including gunnery spotting and reconnaissance, would be carried out by naval officers who would not be attached to the RAF.

RAF Operations from an Aircraft-Carrier or Warship

EARLY DEVELOPMENTS

Almost all the basic techniques of modern carrier design and deck flying were developed during the 1920s. First World War carriers like HMS *Furious* had primitive deck-landing facilities. Arrester wires were stretched across the flat deck of the carrier to bring the aircraft to a halt. The fore-and-aft arrester wires on the *Furious* were a few inches apart, supported six inches above the deck, which measured 284 feet by 70 feet. The carrier's aircraft had skids, not wheels, and the horns of the skids engaged the arrester wires. If the aircraft overran there was a rope crash barrier as a last means to stop the aircraft tipping over into the sea. But this barrier famously buckled wings and broke propellers. Then there was the turbulence set up by the midships funnel and superstructure. Dangerous air currents over the rear of the deck only added to the hazards of landing.

As a result, the Navy and the Air Force did some research with the carrier HMS *Argus*, which had been rebuilt. The flight deck measured 550 feet by 68 feet, and it was completely unobstructed, with the exhaust from the funnels being fed out astern. In the course of 500 landings there were forty crashes, with light damage in ninety other touchdowns. The aircraft having skids instead of wheels meant that if the horns of one skid became engaged in the fore-and-aft arrester wires the pilot had no hope of taking off for a second attempt: both skids had to be made to engage the arrester wires for a successful landing. By lowering the aircraft lift nine inches below deck level it was hoped that the pilot could

HMS *Argus*.

land in 'the pit' and run up a ramp, gradually narrowing the gap between the horns on the skids and the arrester wires. When HMS *Eagle* entered service there was a recessed pit right across the flight deck, together with hinged wooden flaps at intervals. The aircraft would then be slowed down by progressively knocking down the flaps. The problem with this arrangement was that aircraft often lost their undercarriages.

From 1926 until 1931 the arrester gear was abandoned and aircraft landed on a plain deck. The completely successful apparatus for deck landing came in with the aircraft-carriers, HMS *Glorious* and HMS *Courageous*. The aircraft now had wheels, not skids, and trailed a hook that engaged spring-loaded transverse arrester wires. Instead of the fore-and-aft arrester wires there were palisades to prevent the aircraft from drifting over the side into the sea. The first aircraft to use it was a Fairey IIIF. The transverse arrester wires had friction brake drums and were reset electrically, and in 1933 hydraulically, which is still the system in use today. The major changes made to carriers in later years have been the angled deck and the ramp for use with the VSTOL Harriers. Unlike on the *Argus*, there was a bridge superstructure, but one that did not cause dangerous wind currents. This island bridge was essential for all-round observation, and since the carrier sailed into the wind when launching or receiving aircraft, pilots would turn to port if aborting a landing, thus minimizing the risk of a collision with the bridge, which was sited on the starboard side of the vessel.

Other means of launching aircraft from naval vessels such as battleships and, believe it or not, submarines were tried. During the First World War platforms were erected over the gun turrets to permit the launching of

Gun platform for launching aircraft.

The M2 submarine launching the Parnall Peto. The first
two pilots of this aircraft were Lieutenants
C. Keighley-Peach and C. W. Byas, both of whom
received flying pay and submarine pay!

reconnaissance planes. These were replaced by powerful
steam catapults. Experiments with steam catapults were
carried out as early as 1917–18 using a Fairey N.9
seaplane. In October 1925 Wing Commander Burling
was successfully catapulted from HMS *Vindictive* in a
Fairey IIID. After this it was possible to use light
reconnaissance aircraft from cruisers and battleships.
Experiments were also carried out using a submarine.
This was the M2, which had a hangar in front of the
conning tower, and it housed a Parnall Peto light
reconnaissance biplane. The small size of this aircraft did
limit its usefulness. When the M2 sank, sadly with all
hands, off Weymouth in 1932, the project was
abandoned. It is possible that the hangar doors were
open and let in water when the craft submerged.

Finally there was the experiment involving the 'S'
Class destroyer HMS *Stronghold*. This warship had a
simple counter-weight catapult in her bows. There were
two aircraft, one on a launching platform aft of the launch
rails, and the other in place of No. 1 Gun immediately
before the bridge. The photograph, probably taken in
1925, actually shows a radio-controlled flying bomb.

HMS *Stronghold* with bow launcher.

Flight operations on aircraft carriers

Aircraft-carriers were not only expensive to
build, they were also very expensive to
operate. Even during times when fuel
economies were in force these could not apply
to carriers flying-off or landing-on aircraft. The
engines had to be run up to full speed and
turned into wind, which tended to put a strain
on the hull and wear the engines out. This
meant more frequent refits. When flying was in
progress it was not what airmen were used to
on aerodromes back on land, for aircraft could
only land one at a time. The ground crews
crouched in nets at the side of the flight deck, and as
soon as the aircraft had landed on the deck they had to
fold the wings before the aircraft could descend on the
lift. The ground crew had six minutes to be back up on
deck for the next aircraft on approach. Once down
below, the aircraft had to be tethered to ring bolts on the
hangar floor by wire strops with turnbuckles, and if the
sea became rough the crew would have to stand by to
tighten the lashings.

Typical of the sort of work of an RAF ground crew
aboard a carrier in the 1920s was the arming of an
aircraft like the Blackburn Dart with a torpedo. The 'tin
fish', as the torpedo was known, was secured to the
aircraft by a couple of wire strops with turnbuckle
screws at the end. The torpedo had to be wheeled under
the aircraft for winching up by hand, and once in
position there was very little room to move. A torpedo
mechanic would prepare the torpedo for running, which
relied upon a gyroscope and the correct adjustment of
valves. For his part the pilot had to drop the torpedo at
the correct height above the sea, which would ensure
that it entered the water at not too steep an angle.
Shallow running was essential if the torpedo was not to
pass beneath the keel of the target ship.

When it came to meal times the food had to be
collected by the duty mess man, but the galleys were so
far from the mess decks that the food could be nearly
cold by the time he returned. Nevertheless, although
work could be hard and the hours long, most RAF
airmen enjoyed their time on carriers.

One interesting Air Ministry Weekly Order, No.
55/1929, pertains to the operation of aircraft from an
aircraft-carrier at the end of the decade. The reference to
disembarked flights in the AMWO mean that the ship's
aircraft are flown to a Fleet Air Arm airfield, where among
other things the aircraft can receive more detailed attention
than is possible with the limited facilities aboard ship.

55. – Fleet Air Arm – Training of pilots in Deck-landing Afloat (883043/28)

1. As a result of experience to date, the following
instructions are issued as a guide to the procedure which

should be adopted in an aircraft-carrier when pilots are being trained in their initial deck landings.

i. No difficulty should occur as regards pilots posted to embarked flights from the RAF Training Base, Leuchars, or the RAF Base, Gosport. When pilots have been posted to disembarked flights, however, care must be taken that they are given adequate flying practice until the opportunity to train them in deck-landing afloat arises.

ii. It should first be determined whether the pilot to be trained is conversant with all deck-landing signals and their significance.

iii. The method of approach, the approximate distance and height and distance from which to approach before a landing, the necessity of opening his throttle to go round again in plenty of time if he is not straight before landing, and the absolute necessity, once he has landed and finds himself running towards the palisades, of switching off, must be explained.

iv. (a) In multi-seaters, the pilot should always be given one or two landings as passenger in order that he may grasp the correct height from which to approach, the amount of rudder and bank necessary to a steady approach, the correct height to come in over the stern, and finally, the right moment to shut off his throttle before landing.

  (b) In single-seaters he should watch one or two demonstration landings by experienced pilots before attempting it himself.

v Before actually landing, a pilot should do two or three dummy runs over the deck so as to get his eye in. When he waves his hand to signify he is quite confident of landing-on, the affirmative can then be put out.

vi. The number of landings that a pilot makes at any one time during his training is left entirely to the discretion of the CO of the carrier. Six landings, however, in one day are considered sufficient for anybody. On the other hand, some pilots in only four landings can demonstrate their ability to land-on. If the CO considers that a pilot is able to land consistently after four landings, he should have no hesitation in passing him out.

vii. The speed of the relative wind over the deck should be adjusted, as far as possible to what is considered the easiest speed for landing-on for any particular type of aircraft. If possible, training should not be carried out on days when the wind is gusty.

viii. Training should always be carried out in sight of land and, whenever possible, with an aerodrome at hand.

ix. In the event of a pilot making a series of indifferent dummy runs and wild approaches, he should on no account be allowed to attempt a landing, but be sent back to the base aerodrome for further flying practice.

2. When an officer completes his deck landing afloat and qualifies or fails as a deck-landing pilot, the fact is to be reported on RAF Form 292 [note: RAF, not RN, form].

Manning of RAF units afloat

When the FAA was formed in April 1924, RAF units working with the fleet moved from the control of HQ Coastal Area to the new Air Arm. Air and ground crews were posted to the FAA for a tour roughly equivalent to an overseas posting. The problem for the FAA was that when RAF personnel with fleet experience returned to land based duties there was a lack of continuity and therefore a lack of efficiency.

Life afloat Life afloat was a naval existence for RAF airmen. In HMS *Furious*, for example, some airmen found discipline strict. They were detailed to first or second port or starboard watches and received the time-honoured rum ration. One RAF squadron leader controlled the flying, and the servicing personnel were RAF except for the naval telegraphists employed on wireless duties and a few deckhands. Training and employment ashore would prepare an airmen for his work aboard a carrier. One airman working as a torpedo fitter on No. 210 Squadron at Gosport was warned to stand by for the same work on No. 460 Torpedo Flight, HMS *Eagle*, to which he was posted in 1924. He had worked with Sopwith Cuckoos, Blackburn Darts, Avro 504Ks, DH9As and Bristol Fighters. The RAF men got on well enough with their naval colleagues, who nicknamed them the 'crabfat soldiers', after the paint used on the outside of the carrier, which resembled the colour of the RAF uniform.

Establishment of RAF ground crews The establishment of NCOs and airmen of a fleet torpedo flight in 1925 was as follows:

1 flight sergeant fitter or carpenter
1 sergeant or corporal rigger or carpenter
1 sergeant or corporal aero engine fitter
1 corporal or airman wireless operator mechanic
5 aircraftmen aero engine fitters
5 aircraftmen carpenters or riggers
3 aircraftmen aircraft hands [batmen]

Careers for Naval Aircrew The problem for the Navy was to have a body of ship handlers or seaman officers who understoon naval aviation. Successful naval operations involving carriers require admirals and ships' captains who understand the demands of aircraft flying off and landing on a carrier. The best example of this maxim is to be found in World War II during the Battle of Midway when both the Japanese and American carrier forces played cat and mouse in the Pacific. It was of crucial importance that the reconnaissance pilots on both sides did not, on sighting the enemy carrier force, confuse the actual heading of carriers with the course being sailed by the fleet course. This episode also demonstrated the vulnerability of carriers to air attack in the middle of rearming and refuelling their own aircraft.

In 1924 the naval airmen were supplied mostly by the RAF, so where was the Navy to get its career officers who were seamen as well as aviators? The agreement the Navy had with the RAF was that the Navy was to allot a number of officers a year, up to 70 per cent of pilot vacancies with the Fleet Air Arm. The time spent away from seaman duties had to include a period of training spent with the RAF, together with at least one commission spent with the FAA. But the way to promotion and command of a ship, and hopefully a fleet, was to serve on a variety of ships in a variety of seaman capacities until one was deemed fit for command. Taking time off to learn to fly was seen as an unnecessary deviation from the chosen career path, and therefore a 'dead-end' job. Trenchard, of course, was always willing to supply RAF pilots, including SNCOs, but if ever the Navy was going to have complete control over its Air Arm this problem was going to have to be faced. Appendix L gives details of the arrangements for attachments from the Navy to the RAF, showng that the Navy is anxious to ensure that volunteers have a balanced career between general naval service and air service.

Officer manning of the FAA in the 1920s It has been explained that, of the pilots serving with the fleet in 1924, a number were naval officers. Part of the complement of an aircraft-carrier was a unit akin to a miniature RAF station, normally commanded by a squadron leader, and assisted by three flight lieutenants, although the RAF Lists show strengths both over and under establishment. The four men would, between them, have the accepted specialist qualifications of officers on RAF squadrons at that time, i.e. armament, photography, signals and navigation. In addition there would be an officer of the RAF Stores Branch. When the carrier was in port the pilots and aircraft were held at a land station, but the 'station headquarters' unit aboard remained manned. It was these posts that the Navy needed to have manned by naval officers, yet even after the formation of an independent Fleet Air Arm in 1937/8 there were still RAF officers aboard carriers on the eve of the Second World War. Carrier pilot manning figures for 1923 show

that the *Pegasus* and *Ark Royal* serving in the Mediterranean had twenty-six pilots between them. HMS *Argus* had a wing commander and four flying officers on the ship's strength, which would indicate that this was the manning of the headquarters unit and that the carrier was waiting for the aircraft with its pilots to be flown on. The base airfield for the Argus was Gosport, where the Navy List showed the names of the aircrew for that commission. Of approximately 700 pilots serving on RAF squadrons at the time, only some fifty were required for fleet duties. The following extracts from RAF Lists covering three different years of the 1920s name the RAF officers posted for duty with the headquarters units on the various carriers. The pilots on the strength of the various fighter, fleet spotter or reconnaissance flights may be found at Appendix M.

April 1922
HMS *Argus*
Wing Commander D.A. Oliver DSO, OBE
Flight Lieutenant W.R.D. Acland DFC
Flying Officers   C.C.K. Dagg AFC
                      G.M. Bryer AFC
                      T.J.E. Thornton
                      F.H. Davis
Stores Officer – Flying Officer H. Parker

HMS *Pegasus*
Squadron Leader R.M. Field
Flight Lieutenant A.R.T. Pipon DSC
Flying Officer/Observer Officers
   W.V. Simmons   R.E. Dean AFC
   J.W. Young MBE   E.S. Ades
   G.S. Shaw   L. Martin
   W.E. James   W. Wheatley
   J.F.H. Stevens   S.A. Conway
   G.R.B. Smythe   V.H. Clift
Pilot Officer J.G. Peck
Stores Officer – Flying Officer C.J. Elliott

January 1924
HMS *Argus*
Wing Commander C.F. Kilner DSO
Flight Lieutenant R.F.S. Leslie DSC, DFC, AFC
Flying Officers/Observer Officers: J.W.Turton Jones, F. Jezzard MBE, F.H. Davis
Stores Officer – Flying Officer E.S.Bullen

HMS *Eagle*, HMS *Hermes*
Both these carriers in January have Coastal Area listed instead of crews. This indicates that these two carriers were not commissioned at the time. The crews and aircraft will have been flown off to an RAF Base, either Gosport or Leuchars.

May 1924
HMS *Argus*
Group Captain C.F. Kilner DSO
Wing Commander A.J. Miley
Squadron Leader R.F.S. Leslie DSC, DFC, AFC
Flying Officer/Observer Officers: J.W. Turton Jones, F. Jezzard MBE, F.H. Davis
Stores Officer – Flying Officer E.S. Bullen

HMS *Eagle*
Wing Commander W.L. Welsh DSC, AFC
Squadron Leader E.R. Pretyman AFC
Flight Lieutenant D.K. Cameron
Flying Officers: B.I. Carter, H.W. Beck
Stores Officer – Flying Officer J.G. Smithson

HMS *Hermes*
Wing Commander J.T. Cull DSO
Flight Lieutenant P.C. Wood
Flying Officers: S.H. Reynolds, W.H. Jinman
Stores Officer – Flying Officer W.C. Farley

HMS *Pegasus*
Squadron Leader E.L. Tomkinson DSO, AFC
Flight Lieutenant G.E. Livock DFC
Flying Officers: E.P.M. Davis AFC, AM, F.H.Isaac DFC, L. Martin, A.R. Wardle, A.J. Rankin, H.A. Dinnage, L.D. Stewart
Stores Officer – Flying Officer A.J. Redman

February 1928
HMS *Argus*
Wing Commander C.E. Maude
Squadron Leader R.B. Munday DSC, AFC
Flying Officers: J.W. Hutchins, P. Jones
Stores Officer – Flight Lieutenant T.A.G. Hawley

HMS *Eagle*
Wing Commander E. Osmond CBE
Squadron Leader C.O.F. Modin DFC
Flight Lieutenant B.A. Malet DFC
Flying Officer J.A.B. Hutson (Lt (E)RN)*
Stores Officer – Flight Lieutenant H.J. Barnham

*(Note: Flying Officer Hutson on board HMS *Eagle* has both a naval and RAF rank. For an explanation see Appendix L, para. 5.)

HMS *Furious*
Wing Commanders W.H. Pulford OBE, AFC, psa
T.E.B. Howe AFC, psa
Squadron Leader T.W. Elsdon
Flight Lieutenant H.W. St.John DFC
Flying Officers: J.J. Teasdale, H.T. Herring (Hon. Flight Lieutenant)
Stores Officer – Flight Lieutenant S.D. Dennis

HMS *Hermes*
Wing Commander H.J.F. Hunter MC
Squadron Leader L.C. Keeble
Flying Officers: S.F. Cole, A.L.Macmillan
Stores Officer – Flying Officer A.G. Stratford-Tuke

Aircraft and Carriers of the Fleet Air Arm

The aircraft listed in this chapter are those that served almost exclusively with the fleet. Those that also equipped RAF squadrons, such as the Parnall Panther and the Nightjar, are listed in Appendix A. Aircraft required by the Admiralty for service with the fleet were procured by the Air Ministry using specifications based on naval requirements for each type. The difference between a land-plane and one which was carrier-borne was that the latter had to be much more robust in its construction. This in turn meant a heavier aircraft with reduced performance and a more limited range that its land-based counterpart. Landing on a heaving deck would mean that the shock to the undercarriage was transferred to the airframe. The wings had constantly to be folded and unfolded alternately for stowage and flight, and they needed a lot more manhandling to get them into a precise position in a very limited space. For this reason fleet aircraft, with the exception of the two mentioned above, were designed for the Navy.

In the year following the Armistice the economic situation demanded the reduction of naval aviation to one spotter/reconnaissance squadron, one fighter flight and half a torpedo squadron. There was also a seaplane flight and a flying-boat flight. Strength in aircraft grew painfully slowly during the inter-war years. Following the modest expansion of the RAF at home to fifty-two squadrons, the Fleet Air Arm also saw an increase in aircraft strength. In January 1924 there were seventy-eight naval aircraft in thirteen flights. By October that year a further five flights had been added, taking the total to 128 aircraft. By the end of the decade a total of 144 aircraft equipped twenty-four flights.

The growth in aircraft flights was matched by the building of new carriers. *Furious* and *Argus* were of First World War vintage. To these two, five new carriers were added: HMS *Eagle* entered service in 1922, *Hermes* in 1923, *Glorious* and *Courageous* in 1928 and *Ark Royal* in 1938. *Courageous* was the result of the major reconstruction of a light battle cruiser that was commissioned as a fleet carrier on 14 February 1928. The aircraft capacity was forty-eight, and bulges had to be added to improve stability to counter the increased top weight. There were cranes for aircraft handling at both ends of the hangar, and palisades and wires aft of the island were fitted to prevent aircraft without arrester gear from going over the side. There was a lower sloping flight deck, or slip deck, from which fighters could take off directly from the hangar.

HMS *Courageous*.

The photograph below shows a Flycatcher leaving its hangar on board the carrier HMS Glorious. Aboard the Navy's carriers during the inter-war years was a succession of biplanes. These are described below in the order in which they were introduced into fleet service.

Avro Bison

Like the Blackburn Blackburn that follows, the Avro Bison was an extremely ugly aircraft. The reason for this is that both were designed to give priority to the needs of the crew. The very large cabin with its equally large windows housed the observer and wireless operator, the maps' plotting table and wireless sets. This resulted in a fuselage of such large cross-section that the pilot found himself sitting high above the line of the propeller. An aiming rod had to be fitted parallel to the line of flight to assist the pilot in landing and taking off. The first prototype was Bison I (N153), which came out in 1921. The second prototype (N154) was exhibited in the 'new types' park at the Hendon Display in 1923. Fifty-three aircraft of this type were built for the FAA – twelve MkIs and forty-one MkIIs. The two marks differed in that the MkI had the top wing attached to the top of the fuselage whereas the MkII had the top wing raised on centre-

A Flycatcher fighter leaving its hangar on board HMS *Glorious*.

section struts and had a long dorsal fin extension. The first Bisons equipped No. 423 Fleet Spotter Flight at Gosport in 1923, and they served until 1929, when they were replaced by the Fairey IIIF. The allocation to units was:

No. 421 Flight – Gosport and HMS *Furious*
No. 421A Flight – HMS *Furious*
No. 421B Flight – HMS *Eagle*
No. 423 Flight – Gosport and HMS *Eagle*
No. 447 Flight – HMS *Furious*
No. 448 Flight – Hal Far, Malta and HMS *Eagle*

Technical Specifications:
Span: 46 ft
Length: 36 ft
Wing area: 630 sq. ft
Weights: Empty, 4,116 lb
 Loaded, 6,132 lb
Power plant: One 480 hp
Napier Lion II

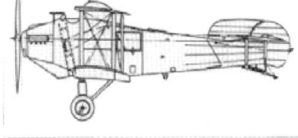

Avro Bison.

Performance:
Maximum speed: 110 mph
Cruising : 90 mph
Climb: 24 minutes to 10,000 ft
Range: 360 miles
Service ceiling: 12,000 ft

Armament:
One free-mounted Lewis gun on a Scarff ring amidships and a single, fixed, forward-firing Vickers machine-gun.

Blackburn Blackburn
The photographs of the Bison and Blackburn show that there was little to choose between the ugliness of the two aircraft. The Blackburn was designed for spotting and reconnaissance duties to work in close cooperation with naval gunnery. Like the Bison, there is the large cabin for the observer, but again this was at the expense of performance. The first of three prototypes (N.150, 151 and 152) appeared in 1922. It is remarkable that two aircraft made by two different companies should share

the same features. The Blackburn even aped the Bison by having both wings attached to the fuselage in the MkI. No. 422 Fleet Spotter Flight on HMS *Eagle* with the Mediterranean Fleet was the first unit to receive this aircraft, followed by HMS *Argus* on the China Station. In 1926 the Blackburn Blackburn replaced the Westland Walrus. In May 1929 the Blackburn flights were redesignated Nos 450 and 449, part of the reorganization of fleet spotter reconnaissance flights. During this aircraft's service, which ended in 1931, a total of thirty-three Blackburn MkIs and twenty-nine MkIIs were delivered to the FAA. The allocation to units was:

No. 420 Flight – Gosport and HMS *Furious*
No. 422 Flight – HMS *Eagle* with Mediterranean Flight and HMS *Argus*, China Station
No. 449 Flight – HMS *Furious* and HMS *Courageous*
No. 450 Flight – HMS *Argus* and HMS *Courageous*

Technical Specifications:
Span: 45 ft 6½ in.
Length: 36 ft 2 in.
Wing area: 650 sq. ft
Weights: Empty, 3,929 lb
Loaded, 5,962 lb
Power plant: One 450 hp Napier Lion IIB or V

Performance:
Maximum speed: 122 mph at 3,000 ft
Climb: 690 ft/min
Range: 440 miles
Service ceiling: 12,950 ft

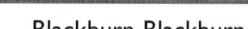
Blackburn Blackburn.

Armament: One Lewis machine-gun on Scarff ring in rear cockpit and one fixed Vickers machine-gun forward.

Fairey Flycatcher

The Fairey Flycatcher was the most successful naval fighter of the period. It was comfortable to fly and excellent for aerobatics. When the throttle was opened spectators would always be thrilled by the roar of the engine. Its appearance was unmistakable, having no dihedral on the lower wing but marked in the upper wing. The flaps extended the full length of the wing, the outer sections of which served as ailerons. This made it ideally suited to carrier operations, for the flaps steepened the glide path and shortened both take-off and landings. The Flycatcher was the only type of fleet fighter, and served from 1923 until 1934, when it was replaced by the Hawker Nimrod. It could be launched from a platform mounted on the turret of a warship and had interchangeable undercarriage and floats. Indeed, some of the Flycatchers had floats that incorporated wheels, making it an amphibian.

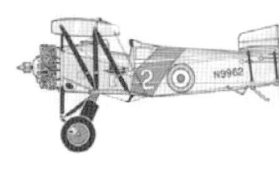

The prototype Flycatcher (N163) was built to Spec. 6/22 and was first flown on 28 November 1922 at Hamble. Service trials were conducted at Martlesham Heath, and the prototype then went to HMS *Argus* for deck trials. Since, at this time, the arrester gear consisted of fore-and-aft wires, two steel jaws had to be fitted to the undercarriage spreader bar. When the fore-and-aft arrester wires were abandoned in 1926, the Flycatcher could still land without them, for its hydraulic wheel-brakes could bring the aircraft to a halt in fifty yards.

Flycatchers of No.405 Flight, HMS *Glorious*.

These brakes were not standard, however, until 1933 with the Fairey Seal. The first prototype was fitted with a Jaguar engine, being later re-engined with a Jupiter, but the production aircraft had the Jaguar. It was the third prototype, N165, that was the amphibian. Interestingly the Flycatchers did not have folding wings but could be dismantled in such a way that no section exceeded 13 ft 6 in. in length. Production Flycatchers were issued from 1923, and Fairey was busy into the 1930s. The first service aircraft joined No. 402 Flight. The other fleet fighters at this time were the Nieuport Nightjars and the Parnall Plovers, but the Flycatcher soon took their place. The allocation to Units was:

No. 401 Flight – (1924–33) Leuchars, Hong Kong, *Argus*, *Courageous* and *Furious*
No. 402 Flight – (1923–32) Malta, *Eagle* and *Courageous*
No. 403 Flight – (1924–34) Leuchars, *Hermes* and Catapult Flight, 5th Cruiser Squadron, China
No. 404 Flight – (1924–33) Leuchars, Donibristle, *Argus* and *Courageous*
No. 405 Flight – (1924–33) Leuchars, Donibristle, *Furious* and *Glorious*
No. 406 Flight – (1924–34) Leuchars, Donibristle, *Glorious* and East Indies Catapult Squadron
No. 407 Flight – (1928–32) *Glorious* and *Courageous*
No. 408 Flight – (1929–32) Donibristle, *Glorious* and *Courageous*
No. 409 Flight – (1932) No. 801 Sqn, (1933–4) *Furious*; Base training squadrons at Leuchars and Gosport until March 1932. Also from capital ships as turret-platform fighter.

Technical Specifications:
Span: 29 ft
Length: 23 ft
Wing area: 288 sq. ft
Weights: Empty, 2,039lb
Loaded, 3,028 lb
(3,531 lb with floats)

Performance:
Maximum speed: 133 mph at 5,000 ft
126 mph as a seaplane
Climb: 9½ minutes to 10,000 ft
Power plant: One 400 hp Armstrong Siddeley Jaguar III or IV
Range: 263 miles at maximum speed at 10,000 ft
Service ceiling: 19,000 ft or 14,000 ft as a seaplane

Flycatcher Seaplane.

Armament: Twin synchronised Vickers machine-guns. Provision for four 20 lb bombs below the wings.

Blackburn Dart
The Blackburn Dart was a torpedo-carrying aircraft that served with the FAA from 1923 until 1933. The Dart prototypes, N140, 141 and 142, appeared in 1921, and the production aircraft entered service with Nos 460 and 461 Flights in 1923. It had a split-leg undercarriage so that it did not have to be jettisoned on releasing its torpedo as was the case with the Blackbird.

Darts flew with No. 423 Fleet Spotter Flight at Gosport in 1923, and they served until 1929, when they were replaced by the Fairey IIIF. The allocation to units was:

No. 460 Flight – (1923–31) *Eagle*, Mediterranean Fleet)
No. 461 Flight – (1923–9) Gosport and *Furious*, Home Fleet)
No. 462 Flight – (1924–9) Gosport and *Furious*, Home Fleet)
No. 463 Flight – (1928–33) *Courageous*, Mediterranean Fleet)
No. 464 Flight – (1928–33) *Courageous*, Mediterranean Fleet)
No. 465 Flight

The Dart also served briefly with No. 810 Squadron before converting to Ripons after its formation out of Nos 463 and 464 Flights in April 1933.

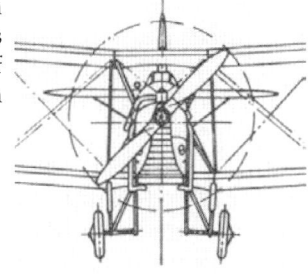

Dart undercarriage.

Technical Specifications:
Span: 45 ft 6 in.
Length: 35 ft 4½ in.
Wing area: 654 sq. ft
Weights: Empty, 3,599 lb
Loaded, 6,383 lb
Power plant: One 450 hp Napier Lion IIB or V

Performance:
Maximum speed: 107 mph at 3,000 ft
Climb: 600 ft/min
Range: 285 miles
Service ceiling: 12,700 ft

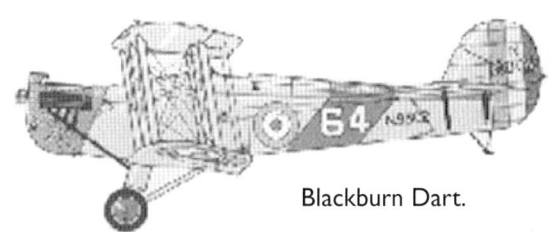

Blackburn Dart.

Armament: Provision for one 18 in. torpedo beneath the fuselage or equivalent bomb-load comprising two 520 lb bombs.

Blackburn Darts of No. 460 Flight aboard HMS *Eagle* in the Mediterranean in 1928. The fuselage bands are in black, which was *Eagle*'s colour, upon which the fleet numbers are marked. Their torpedoes can be seen underslung each aircraft.

Parnall Plover
The Plover was produced by George Parnall & Co. Ltd of Bristol in 1922, the company already having established itself as a designer of naval aircraft. The Plover was built to Air Ministry Specification 6/22, which called for a deck-landing fighter, capable of superseding the Nieuport Nightjar with either an Armstrong Siddeley Jaguar radial engine or a Bristol Jupiter. Unfortunately for Parnall, it never outclassed the Flycatcher, which had been designed to the same Air Specification. Henry Bolas

designed both the Parnall Panther and the Plover, and three prototypes were built of the latter, numbered N.160, 161 and 162, the first and second with the Jupiter engine, the third having the Jaguar. Like its rival the Flycatcher, the Plover also appeared as an amphibian (N.161), and the aircraft was displayed in the New Types park

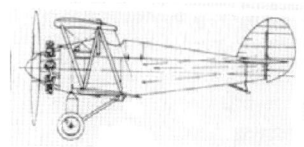

Parnall Plover.

at the Hendon Display in 1923. Six Jupiter-engined Plovers entered service with Nos 403 and 404 Flights alongside Nightjars of No. 401 Flight and the Flycatchers of No. 402 Flight. The Plover exhibited some structural weakness, which may account for its short time with the FAA, for when one of these aircraft was on test at RAF Leuchars in 1924 the centre-section collapsed during aerobatics, and the pilot, who did not have a parachute, was fortunate to get the aircraft down on a moor near the mouth of the River Eden. Later that year Plovers were superseded by the Flycatcher. Only ten Plovers were built, in two batches, for the FAA. The allocation to units was:

Nos 403 and 404 Fleet Fighter Flights

Technical Specifications:
Span: 29 ft.
Length: 23 ft
Wing Area: 306 sq.ft
Weights: Empty, 2,035 lb
Loaded, 2,984 lb
Power plant: One 436 hp Bristol Jupiter IV

Performance:
Maximum speed: 142 mph
Climb: 25 min 13 sec to 20,000 ft
Service ceiling: 23,000 ft

Armament: Twin, synchronized Vickers machine-guns

Fleet Air Arm Operations and Training in the 1920s

The details of air operations involving aircraft-carriers may be found in Chapters 2, 3 and 4. The following descriptions are given, carrier by carrier, for the 1920s. For those unfamiliar with naval matters it should be noted that HM ships were commissioned for specific periods of time. John James in his book of the social life of the RAF between the wars called *The Paladins* describes it beautifully when he says that commissioning is akin to

taking a ship, filling it up with men, food and supplies, screwing on the cap and putting it into the water until it is at the end of the commission.

HMS *Argus*

Argus was laid down in June 1914 and launched on 2 December 1917. It was the first flush-deck carrier capable of operating wheeled aircraft in any navy. She was commissioned on 14 September 1918 and carried out her flying trials in the Firth of Forth. *Argus* did not have an island bridge. Following original proposals put forward by Flight Commander H.A. Williamson, a pilot serving in the Air Department, the idea of a bridge structure was adopted. Accordingly, during October 1918 *Argus* carried a wood-and-canvas island to provide data for HMS *Eagle*'s final design, and the trials were successful. On the 10th of that month No. 185 Squadron RAF embarked on *Argus*. The torpedo-bombers worked up for operations and were due to attack the German High Seas Fleet at Wilhelmshaven, but the Armistice intervened. On 23 December the prototype fore-and-aft arrester wires were fitted, and a series of flying trials were carried out during March 1919. The following week the Grand Fleet was dispersed, and *Argus* was attached to the Atlantic Fleet. In June Fairey IIIC floatplanes were ferried to Archangel for the north Russian operations (see Chapter 2).

At the end of January 1920 *Argus* took part in the Atlantic Fleet's spring cruise to Gibraltar and the western Mediterranean. On this occasion she carried 1½ Strutters, Camels, DH9As and Fairey floatplanes. Most of the flying was slow and experimental, and forty minutes to launch two aircraft was not satisfactory. The rotary engines could not be kept idled and the ship had therefore to be faced into wind before the engines were started up. In July *Argus* returned to Devonport dockyard for improved arrester gear to be fitted. The next year saw the ship back with the Atlantic Fleet in UK waters, and the Mediterranean. Pilots under training at Gosport used the opportunity of her being in home waters to practise flying out to the carrier.

During the Chanak crisis in 1922, *Argus* was stationed near the Dardenelles, and twelve Bristol F2Bs landed ashore to operate with the Anglo-French forces (see Chapter 2). On 1 November 1925 the carrier was paid off prior to a major refit at Chatham. This took two years, and she was not recommissioned until 19 January 1927. The following month she joined the China Station, embarking No. 441 Flight with Fairey IIIDs at Malta, and arrived in Hong Kong. On her return from the Far East *Argus* rejoined the Atlantic Fleet in August 1928.

HMS *Furious*

Furious was laid down on 8 June 1915 and was launched on 15 August 1916. She had a forward flying-off deck that was intended to enable fighters to be launched directly off it out of the upper hangar when the main

flight deck was not available (as shown in the accompanying photograph), but this proved unsuccessful and was abandoned in the 1930s. In front of the aircraft can be seen a lateral protective windscreen, that on the upper flight deck being seen in the lowered position.

After her completion, *Furious* joined the Grand Fleet at Scapa Flow in July 1917, where flying trials were carried out. Squadron Commander Dunning was sadly killed on 7 August, having successfully landed a Sopwith Pup on the flying-off deck on the 2nd. In November 1917 *Furious* was returned to the builders to have the aft 18 in. gun replaced with a landing-on deck before recommissioning in Rosyth to accept a flying squadron and fly the flag of the Admiral Commanding Aircraft. Further flying trials followed in April 1918 with Sopwith Pups, but only three out of thirteen landings attempted were successful. The $1^1/2$ Strutters and Camels could take off but not land. However, seven Camels were successful in attacking the Tondern airship base to destroy Zeppelins L54 and L60 on 19 July. In the following December *Furious* joined the Atlantic Fleet before proceeding to the Baltic to give support to the White Russian forces fighting the Bolsheviks. With the drastic rundown after the First World War, *Furious* was placed on the Reserve and laid up in Rosyth, but in July 1920 the Admiralty gave approval for the carrier to be rebuilt as a flush-deck carrier, the work being carried out at the Devonport dockyard. When the work was completed in August 1925 *Furious* joined the Atlantic Fleet with a considerable complement of aircraft. Nos 404A, 405 and 406 Fighter Flights (Flycatchers), No. 420 Flight (Blackburns) and No. 421 Spotter Reconnaissance Flight (Bisons), No. 443 Reconnaissance Flight (Fairey IIIDs) and both Nos 461 and 462 Torpedo Flights (Darts) were embarked and took part in every major exercise during the late 1920s.

HMS *Glorious*

Glorious was laid down on 1 May 1915 and launched on 20 April 1916. She was the sister ship to *Courageous*. Originally these two ships were built as large cruisers, and to reconstruct them as carriers their 15 in. guns were removed, eventually to find themselves on the battleship *Vanguard*, which entered service at the end of the Second World War. As was common in the First World War, flying-off platforms were placed above the gun turrets, and these were fitted in February 1918. In 1919 *Glorious* was paid off into the Reserve, and in January 1921 she was used as a turret drill ship for the Plymouth Gunnery School. On 1 February 1924 she arrived at Rosyth to be converted from a cruiser to an aircraft-carrier. The work was completed at Devonport, where she was recommissioned on 7 January 1930.

HMS *Eagle*

Eagle was laid down as a battleship for the Chilean Navy, named the *Almirante Cochrane*, but when war was declared in 1914 the ship was completed as a warship for the Royal Navy. Laid down on 20 February 1913, she was not launched until June 1918. Flight trials were carried out in 1920 to validate the starboard-side island design. This was in May, when a specially formed 'Eagle' Flight was based at Gosport for the trials in the English Channel. These had proceeded to the point when, on 1 June, the first deck landing was made by a Sopwith Camel. Other aircraft that took part in the trials were Parnall Panthers, DH9As, Bristol Fighters and Sopwith Cuckoos. The trials were then moved up to the Pentland Firth in the hope of finding bad weather. In stormier conditions 143 landings were carried out. There were no casualties and only twelve minor accidents, and as a result the Admiralty agreed to complete the vessel as an aircraft-carrier on 24 September 1920. In February 1921 *Eagle* was transferred to Portsmouth for completion, but it was not until February 1924 that she was commissioned with the Mediterranean Fleet. A work-up was initiated that permitted her to relieve *Ark Royal* with an air group comprising No. 402 Flight (Flycatchers), No. 422 Flight (Blackburns), No. 460 Flight (Darts) and No. 440 Flight (Seagull IIIs). On 1 January the following year Fairey IIIDs replaced the Seagulls.

In 1926 *Eagle* was refitted at Devonport, when the fore-and-aft arrester gear was removed. (The reader may recall that naval carriers landed aircraft without arrester gear throughout the late 1920s until the transverse wires were fitted in 1930s.) In 1927 the ship rejoined the Mediterranean Fleet, but she had to go back into the dockyard the following year for fitting of a hangar spray system before again rejoining the fleet.

HMS *Hermes*

Hermes was laid down on 15 January 1918 and launched on 11 September the following year. She was the first

ship in the world to be designed, ordered and built as an aircraft-carrier, and after launching she went to Devonport Dockyard from Elswick for fitting out. Steaming trials in Plymouth Sound followed, and, when she was considered fit for sea, landing-on trials were commenced with No. 403 Flight (Flycatchers) and Parnall Panther spotter aircraft. The accompanying photo of *Hermes* was taken while she was lying at anchor off Malta in 1924 before she was commissioned for operational service. The exaggerated flare of the forward flight deck was designed to provide the greatest possible width for take-off. This vessel was small by the standards of later postwar carriers.

Commissioned for operations on 3 June 1925, *Hermes* proceeded via Portland and Gibraltar to join the Mediterranean Fleet with an air group comprising Nos 440 and 442 Flights (Fairey IIIDs) and No. 403 Flight (Flycatchers). She was soon deployed to the China Station, based on Hong Kong. On 13 December 1927 she was paid off at Devonport, having been relieved by HMS *Eagle*. She was then refitted at Chatham before rejoining the China Station with the same air group, but with Fairey IIIFs having replaced the IIIDs.

Chapter 7

RAF Stations, Airfields and other Establishments

Airfield types, layout and facilities – progressive development of airfields/seaplane bases and other establishments – Closing and opening of RAF stations/airfields/establishments during the 1920s – Airfields at home (by region) and abroad

This chapter will include the histories of RAF airfields and landing grounds in existence on 11 November 1918, both at home and overseas. It will chart the rapid rundown after the First World War to those that survived, and the opening of airfields in the 1920s. During the post-war rundown many airfields were returned to agriculture. In these days, before paved runways, only the disposal of buildings presented a problem, whereas post-Second-World-War counties like Norfolk and Suffolk were littered with decaying paved runways, as well as Nissen huts and control towers. Maps will show the myriad of airfields and landing grounds in 1918 and the situation eleven years later after the rundown. For the purpose of describing airfield history and development, the United Kingdom is divided into regions, with a further section on some airfields overseas. A general description of airfields is followed by a brief description of each airfield/landing ground or seaplane base in alphabetical order by region.

The need for airfields during the First World War The need for airfields and landing grounds during the First World War was not dissimilar to that in the Second. The parts of the UK facing the continent, namely the South-East, East Anglia, Lincolnshire, Yorkshire and East Scotland, witnessed the growth of fighter stations with attendant landing grounds. Racecourses made ideal airfields because of the large expanse of mown grass, and familiar names will crop up in the lists that follow. The bomber airfields were nearly all in France. Only in maritime defence were there major differences. During the First World War aircraft like the DH6 and Short 184 did not have the range to go far out to sea. Consequently it was necessary to ring the United Kingdom with airfields and seaplane bases, and seaside resorts like Torquay and ports such as Dover, Newhaven and Felixstowe were pressed into use. In contrast, in the Second World War long-range aircraft like the Short Sunderland could operate far into the Atlantic and Western Approaches from a few bases in west Wales, Northern Ireland and Scotland.

The need for landing grounds One of the most pressing needs in the days of fragile aircraft with unreliable engines was for landing grounds. Fighter aircraft like the Avro 504 operating from a base airfield needed somewhere where they could put down in an emergency, as well as having somewhere to which the

aircraft could be dispersed. In the days before radar, and therefore with little in the way of early warning, it was essential that fighter aircraft should either be aloft in their patrol areas or ready for instant flight. There were only primitive facilities at these landing grounds. All that was needed was a hut, a telephone, a levelled field and, where possible, no nearby obstructions such as tall buildings, chimneys or power lines. Low landing speeds meant only a relatively small grassed area compared with today's airfields. Forced landings in fields were quite commonplace through to the 1920s. The following is the text of an Air Ministry Weekly Order concerning compensation in the event of a forced landing:

AMWO 266 In the event of a forced landing the officer or pilot in charge of a machine must not in any way discuss with the farmer or local landowner concerned the question of compensation.

These landing grounds, no matter how small or humble, have been included. Readers may find this interesting if one of these fields is close to where they live. The author lives within walking distance of Walmer airfield near Dover, overlooking the Goodwin Sands, and it is difficult to imagine that the site once buzzed with busy biplanes in 1917/18.

Layout of airfields Today many airfields have just one paved runway, and pilots are required to land at either end, ie. approach to landing is made on only two compass directions. In 1918 grass airfields sported a windsock, which was a large cylindrical envelope that filled with air and swung on a post to show the pilot the wind direction. The pilot would then land into the wind. The wind not only gave the aircraft lift at low speeds, it also acted as a brake. Unless there was a limiting factor, pilots could choose the approach direction for landing. A description of landing at Martlesham Heath in Chapter 2 shows how pilots had a preferred approach determined by the prevailing wind. Once down, an aircraft would be taxied over the grass fitted with a tail skid, not a tail wheel, and in the early days without brakes. Diagram A on page 210 is an illustration of the airfield layout that characterized the inter-war years. Obviously for airfields housing two or three squadrons the number of hangars, technical and other buildings would be greater. For the sake of comparison an airfield of the 1940s and 1950s in shown in

Diagram B, and those in the jet age in Diagram C. It has all to do with all-up weight, lift, drag and engine power. Heavier aircraft with powerful engines and brakes were less dependent on wind to get airborne or to land. That is to say, it was no longer essential for an aircraft to be pointed directly into the wind to land safely or to get airborne before reaching the airfield boundary. In the inter-war years this was very important, with, for example, the Fairey Postal beginning a long-distance flight abroad when Cranwell was singled out as having a sufficiently large grassed airfield to get airborne with full petrol tanks.

Airfield facilities In the First World War and after, airfields were either bases for squadrons or simply landing grounds for emergency or operational use. If they were bases they needed, not only hangars for storing or servicing aircraft, but workshops, armouries, stores, living accommodation, catering facilities, etc. on sites fringing the airfield itself; and as far away as possible from living or working areas were the bomb dumps and fuel storage tanks. In the early post-war days aircraft W/T (wireless telephony) was in its infancy and there were no control towers with air traffic controllers

DEVELOPMENT OVER THE YEARS FROM GRASS AIRFIELDS TO PAVED RUNWAYS.

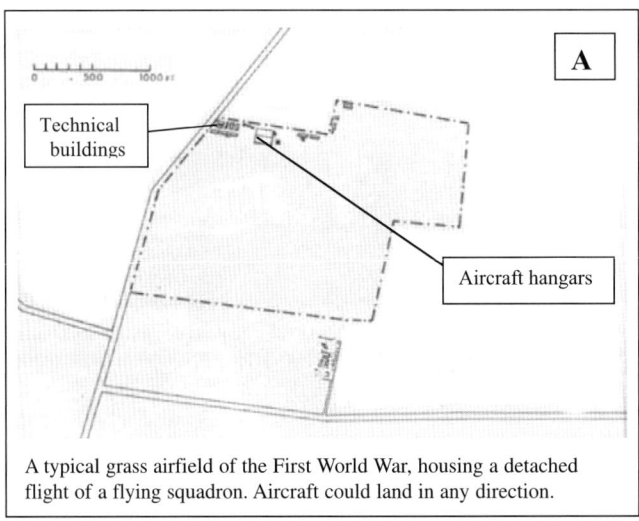

A typical grass airfield of the First World War, housing a detached flight of a flying squadron. Aircraft could land in any direction.

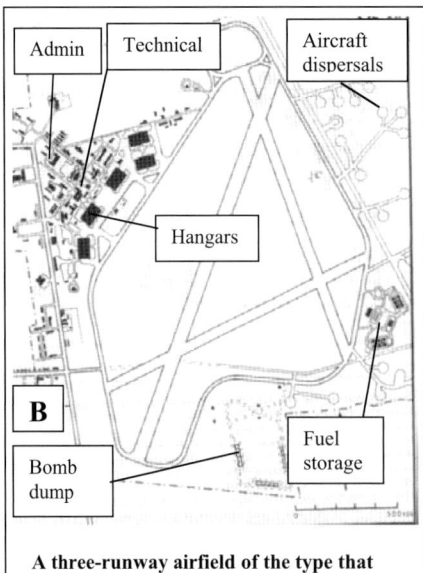

A three-runway airfield of the type that appeared in the 1940s and permitted an approach in any one of six compass headings, depending upon wind direction.

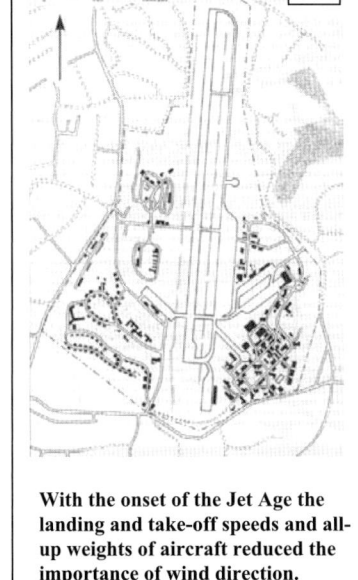

With the onset of the Jet Age the landing and take-off speeds and all-up weights of aircraft reduced the importance of wind direction.

Bessoneau hangars.

Belfast hangar exterior.

Belfast hangar interior.

talking aircraft down to a safe landing. There was only a watch office with a duty officer to whom pilots could report. If a visiting aircraft, the pilot would need to know where he was required to park his aircraft and where he might refuel. Rudimentary lighting was available, but by and large each pilot had to manage his own landing, keeping a watchful eye out for other aircraft in the vicinity.

Once on the ground, aircraft were either parked in the open or inside hangars, particularly if servicing was required. Originally these were of simple wooden construction, but during the First World War the Bessoneau hangar came into use. Since this could be erected and taken down rather like a large circus tent, it was transportable, which was ideal since airfields were often not permanent. But a more permanent hangar, which incorporated offices and stores, came into use, and this was the Belfast. Unlike the Bessoneau, the Belfast was a permanent structure and was a common feature of the inter-war stations. It was not until 1937 that the C-Type Hangar, a larger hangar, came into use.

Then, as now, aircraft could receive simple maintenance, known as first-line servicing, in hangars on the airfield to fit them for daily flight. This could extend to engine changes and, in the early 1920s, fabric and other structural repairs. To conclude, a base airfield required aircraft hangars, a watch office, first-line servicing facilities, workshops, arms/bomb dump, fuel storage, sleeping and messing quarters and social facilities. Once these base airfields became established after the First World War, much temporary accommodation, such as tents for airmen, gave way to brick buildings. These became RAF stations with a station commander in overall command, and they might house one, two or three squadrons of aircraft, usually of the same type, e.g. fighter or bomber.

Floatplane or flying-boat stations The main difference between an airfield and a seaplane/flying-boat station was that the aircraft hangars were bordered by a large

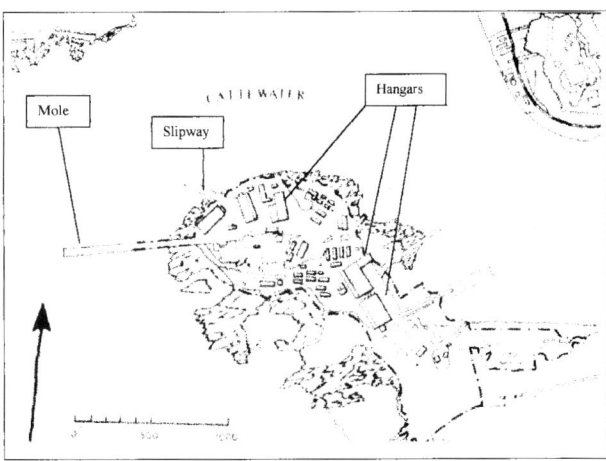

concrete apron from which ran a slipway into the water. In this way aircraft could be launched before take-off from a sheltered stretch of water, although it was not uncommon for seaplanes to be hoisted into the water from a mole. In all other respects the seaplane base had requirements for facilities similar to that of an airfield. The diagram on page 211 shows the layout of a typical seaplane/flying-boat station of the period.

Airship and mooring-out stations Airship stations abounded around the coasts of Britain during the First World War. Associated with the airship station, which was the home base for an airship unit, was the mooring-out station. Its purpose was very similar to the landing ground for fixed-wing aircraft, i.e. it was for airships detached from their main base to provide dispersal in the event of attack and to put them closer to the area of operations, which involved convoy protection and maritime reconnaissance. In both cases the sites would have airship sheds where airships could be stored, repaired and inflated. These were not a feature of the 1920s, as all airship stations were closed, except those like Howarden and Cardington, where research was carried out into lighter-than-air craft.

Non-flying stations Many non-airfield sites were requisitioned for use by the RFC/RNAS/RAF fromd 1914 into the 1920s. These included stores depots, aircraft acceptance parks, aircraft repair depots, headquarters that might be stately homes, hospitals and maintenance units. Aircraft acceptance parks received aircraft from the manufacturers, and these units, together with aircraft repair depots, although non-flying establishments, would for obvious reasons have an airfield close by. All such units, in common with flying stations, needed domestic and technical accommodation.

Naming of stations The names of stations in wartime can become household words. Places like Scampton, of 'Dambuster' fame, Biggin Hill, in the Battle of Britain, or Manston. Without this attachment to famous squadron missions or periods in history, these villages or even hamlets would not be known much beyond the local communities. Since most RAF stations were sited well away from built-up areas, the name given to them depended on the villages around the airfield perimeter. Since the latter could be several miles long, there might be three or four villages that could give their name to an RAF station. Usually it was the one closest to the main entrance to the station, but this was by no means a 'hard and fast' rule. If two stations sounded alike to the ear, that could be a reason to change to avoid confusion. Scopwick and Shotwick fell into this category, and so the former was renamed RAF Digby, the latter RAF Sealand. An airfield name might also be derived from a farm that had been taken over. The most famous of these is probably Sutton's Farm, later RAF Hornchurch.

The immediate post-war rundown

Most RAF squadrons in the UK at the end of 1918 were 'put on hold', and it was not long before RAF stations were relinquished, and landing grounds closed down and then relinquished when squadrons and training units were disbanded. The following is an extract from AMWO Nos 79 and 80 of 1919:

79. Relinquishment of RAF Stations (A.17137)

The land and disposal of buildings at the under-mentioned stations have been handed over to the Disposals Board for disposal:

Catterick Aerodrome
Hucknall Aerodrome

The land and buildings at Gullane Aerodrome were handed over to the War Office with effect from 1 December 1919.

80. Landing Grounds, &c., not to be used. (A.36806)

With reference to Weekly Order 1217 of 1919, the following landing grounds, &c., are not to be used owing to their having been closed down or in the process of closing down:

A – Aerodromes relinquished:

Ashington	Hadleigh	North Coates Fitties	Whitburn
Atwick	Haggerston	Owthorpe	Wyton
Buckminster	Harpswell	Penston	
Butley	Helperby	Redcar	
Catterick	Hornsea	Ripon	
Copmanthorpe	Hull	Seahouses	
Cramlington	Kirton Lindsey	Seaton Carew	
Cullercoats	Leadenham	Sedgeford	
Easton-on-Hill	Lilbourne	Southport	

RAF HAWKINGE, Kent
One of the survivors of the massive run down of the post-war years. Notice the Belfast hangars and the airfield name picked out in white.

Edzell	Lincoln (Racecourse)	Turnberry
Elmswell	Marham	Tydd St Mary
Elsham	Mattishall	Upwood
Greenland Top	Narborough	Usworth
Gullane	Newmarket	West Ayton

B. – Aerodromes in the process of closing down:

Castle Bromwich	Crail	Tadcaster
Coal Aston	Newcastle (Town Moor)	Whitby Abbey
Coventry	Sherburn-in-Elmet	

It will be seen that land and buildings were to be handed over to the War Office. The Disposals Board would take care of the surrender of War Office land to former occupiers and the auctioning of buildings. It was not until 1930 that the Air Ministry took responsibility for its own land acquisitions and relinquishments. Of interest is the case of military land that was not returned to former landowners by the civil servants at the Ministry of Agriculture after the Second World War. The Crichel Down affair later became standard teaching for all students of Government and Politics as to the responsibility of Ministers for the actions of their civil servants, when Sir Thomas Dugdale, the Agriculture Minister, was obliged to resign. It has already been mentioned that there were a large number of landing grounds used by Home Defence squadrons during the First World War, and the following AMWO, again published in 1919, relinquishes them:

343. Landing Grounds – Relinquishment (B.7395)

The following grounds will be relinquished, and the necessary arrangements are being made to return the land to the former occupiers and to recover the huts and telephones.

Scalford	Eccles Tofts	West Rudham
Runwell	Fyfield	Wigsley
Thurgarton	Frinstead	Moorby
Tynehead	Guilton	North Benfleet
Harty	Gosberton	Plough Corner
Swinstead	Gilling	Ripon Racecourse

Thorne	Kelstern	Rennington
Bancroft	Longhorsley	Rye
Burton-on-Wolds	Murton	Sible Hedingham
Braceby	Market Deeping	Sheerness LG
Carlton	Edgware (Stag Lane)	Stutton
Catley Hill	Leigh Green	Snipe House
Coldham	Easington	Southfields
Cottenham	Freethorpe	Sadeberge
Earsham	Frettenham	Sole Street
Anwick	Gifford	Swingfield
Arlington	Gooderstone Warren	Sawbridgeworth
Barmby	Horseheath	Spennymoor
Bedfield	Little Downham	South Otterington
Bucknall	Orton	South Belton
Binsoe	Shipton	Thaxted
Cockthorns	Saxthorpe	Waterloo Sands
Cuxwold	Sporle	Willian
Cliff End	Tottenhill	Wormingford
Easthorpe	Tibenham	

REGIONS OF THE UNITED KINGDOM

The pages that follow have maps showing the number of RAF airfields/landing grounds/seaplane bases at the Armistice in November 1918 and a second map to show the situation at the end of 1929. After the immediate post-war rundown there was a very gradual increase in the number of RAF stations, and land had again to be requisitioned for this purpose. This reflected the expansion scheme that allowed for fifty-two Home Defence squadrons. The real expansion, which did not occur until the 1930s, is dealt with in Volume II. The breakdown is as follows:

1. Greater London
2. Central-South and South-East England
3. East Anglia
4. Lincolnshire and the East Midlands
5. The South-West
6. The Cotswolds and the Central Midlands
7. Yorkshire
8. Wales and the North-West
9. Scotland, North-East England and Northern Ireland
10. Overseas.

READING THE MAPS AND AIRFIELD DESCRIPTIONS
The regional airfield and seaplane base maps which follow show Airfields, Landing grounds and Seaplane bases in the United Kingdom during the period 1918 to 1928. The place names are either underlined or ordinary type:– *Stations/landing grounds/seaplane bases underlined.* They are the ones which were open on 11 November 1918 and were still open on 31 December 1929. These opened after the end of the First World War have the date of opening inserted. *Stations/landing grounds/seaplane bases in Nornal Type* They are the ones which were open on 11 November 1918 but were closed before December 31 1929. This will illustrate the enormous rundown in real estate during the period 1919–22. Only a handful of stations were opened up during the 1920s, and some of those, like Henlow, had lain dormant under Care and Maintenance (C & M), which means that the essential services were provided and steps taken to ensure that the premises were safeguarded. A number of airfields shown as closing in the period 1919–22 were reopened or were opened for the first time during the 1920s. In such cases the year of opening is placed in brackets against the name of the establishment.

Landing grounds are simply airfields or grass strips where aircraft may set down or from which aircraft may take off to engage in combat. They will not be RAF stations. Mooring-out stations are the airship equivalent of landing grounds designed to put the airship closest to the scene of anticipated operations and/or to ensure that sub-units were suitably dispersed, not only to avoid 'having all the eggs in one basket' during enemy attack, but also to prevent fog or high winds at a single station impeding airship operations.

The RNAS organized its operational flying units into flights. These were absorbed into the RAF in April 1918, but it was not until August that these became part of numbered RAF squadrons, all in the 200 series, e.g. No. 219 Squadron at Westgate.

Important abbreviations in this chapter are:

TDSs – Training Depot Stations, which housed a number of Training Squadrons (TS)
HD – Home Defence (fighter defence of the UK)
AAP – Aircraft Acceptance Park
FTS – Flying Training School
RS – Reserve School

Airfields in Greater London
Acton W of London, south side of A40
Acton was opened as an aerodrome in 1910 and known as the London Aviation Ground. It was used by a variety of aircraft until taken over by the National Guard on the outbreak of the First World War. It was used initially as a civilian flying school to train service personnel, but it was not up to standard in either machines or instructors, and the temporary hangars were taken down and the other buildings were taken over by the newly formed Alliance Aeroplane Company. Flying did take place after the war, but when the Alliance Aeroplane Company was wound up Acton was closed in early 1920.

All Hallows NE of Chatham
Third-class landing ground used by 143 Squadron as a relief landing ground during the First World War. Closed postwar.

Bentley Priory
Purchased by the Air Ministry in 1926 for approximately £25,000. It was the HQ of Inland Area RAF from 26 May 1926, before becoming HQ Fighter Command.

Biggin Hill N of Biggin Hill and Westerham
Biggin was opened on 14 February 1917 as an RFC radio signals unit and used for wireless experiments. In February the following year No. 141 Squadron arrived and remained there until the end of the war. It was one of Biggin's Bristol Fighters that shot down a Gotha bomber over Harrietsham aerodrome, Kent. When No. 141 Squadron moved out on 1 March 1919, it was replaced by No. 37 Squadron, then No. 39 Squadron as a cadre unit, which then went to Kenley in 1922. The following year No. 56 Squadron and the Night-Flying Flight moved in, but when these units left – No. 56 Squadron to North Weald in October 1927, and the Night-Flying Flight in 1929 – the empty station underwent an extensive building programme.

Brooklands SW of Weybridge
Brooklands was used by A.V. Roe in 1908, and Short joined A.V. Roe to build aircraft from 1910, as also did Martinsyde (Martin and Hanasyde). The airfield was taken over by the Royal Flying Club as a training station for *ab initio* pilots. In 1915 the station was also home to Nos 1, 8 and 10 Squadrons. Firms such as Sopwith also began to build aircraft at Brooklands, the total built by all firms exceeding 4,600, including SE5s and the Vickers Gunbus. No. 10 Aircraft Acceptance Park at Brooklands stored SE5s and Snipes. On 31 January 1917, No. 2 Reserve School left for Northolt. The airfield itself was situated inside the motor racing circuit and was bounded on three sides by high-tension cables. In spite

GREATER LONDON AIRFIELDS 11 NOVEMBER 1918 AND 31 DECEMBER 1929

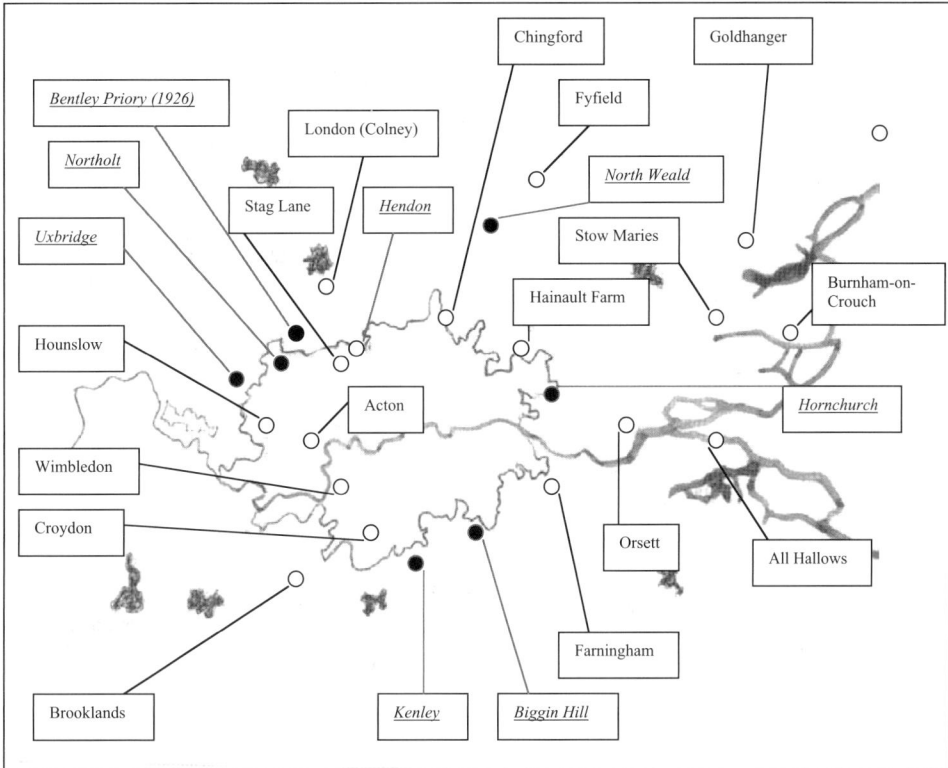

of this, the airfield continued to be used after the war, but it did not remain in RAF use.

Burnham-on-Crouch   E of Burnham-on-Crouch

This was a 1st-class landing ground sited on the north bank of the River Crouch, and came under No. 50 Wing throughout the First World War. It was used briefly in the war by No. 37 Squadron, but it was too low lying and marshy, and so it was abandoned.

Chingford   just N of London, between Enfield and Chingford

Opened in 1915 as a 2nd-class landing ground, it came under No. 49 Wing and was used by No. 44 Squadron on HD duties. Chingford was also a depot and main training station for the RNAS. Eventually No. 207 TDS was housed there, and the station remained in the training role for the remainder of the war. It closed in 1919.

Croydon   SW of Croydon

Throughout 1916 and 1917 No. 17 Reserve (Training) Squadron was based at Croydon, to be replaced during 1917 by No. 40 TS, which then moved to Tangmere in 1918. Croydon was used by No. 141 Squadron as a landing ground, and by No. 29 Squadron, with whom Prince Albert (later King George VI) gained his 'wings' in 1919. In July of that year the airfield was used by an

Air Council Inspection Squadron as No. 1 Group Headquarters. In October Nos 207, 32 and 41 Squadrons came to the station, but all without aircraft. No. 207 Squadron moved out on 16 January 1920, and the other two squadrons were disbanded. When the RAF left in February 1920 the airfield returned to civil flying.

Farningham   S of Dartford

Farningham was taken over in 1915 as one of a number of landing grounds encircling London, and was an auxiliary to Joyce Green. This small site was never developed and was abandoned after the war.

Fyfield   Close to Chipping Ongar

Sited 1$\frac{1}{2}$ miles from Chipping Ongar station, this landing ground came under No. 49 Wing, and No. 39 Squadron used it for HD duties. It closed immediately after the First World War.

Hainault Farm   (Fairlop) W of Romford

Hainault Farm was taken over for service use in 1915 and soon housed a flight of No. 39(HD) Squadron giving air-defence cover to the east of London. Hainault aircraft were successful in tackling the Zeppelins when L32 was shot down by Lieutenant Sowrey and L33 was hit by Lieutenant Brandon. On 24 July 1917 No. 44 Squadron was formed at Hainault, remaining there to the end of the war. In May 1918 No. 207 TDS began to use Hainault as a substation, and No. 151 Squadron formed there on 12 June, moving to France within the week. There then followed No. 153 Squadron, not formed until November, by which time the Armistice had been signed. When Nos 44 and 153 Squadrons had disbanded the airfield was returned to agriculture.

Hendon Between Edgware and Hendon

This airfield had the very earliest connections with flying, well before the First World War, but the military use of Hendon did not arise until 4 August 1914, when the aerodrome was requisitioned under the Defence of the Realm Act. There were, at the time, five flying schools at Hendon, including the famous Grahame-White's school, contracted to train pilots for the RFC, including such famous names as Mannock, Ball and Warneford. The RNAS established a delivery centre for aircraft at Hendon, which became No. 2 Aircraft Acceptance Park. Hendon was becoming a centre for aircraft production, being responsible for some 7,800 aircraft produced during the war years, including DH2s, 4s, 5s, 6s, 9 and 9As, BE2cs and 504Ks. When the war ended the newly formed No. 1 (Communications) Squadron began ferrying officials and documents to Paris for the Peace Conference. When this unit moved to Kenley in May 1919, only civilian concerns operated from the airfield, though it was still in service hands. Grahame-White could hardly sell his aircraft into a market saturated with war-surplus machines, and he began producing car bodies and furniture. In 1920 the RAF Tournament, later known as the 'Pageant', and then the 'Display', was initiated, to become an annual event each summer until the late 1930s. By 1925 most of the civil concerns , such as de Havilland and Handley Page, had moved, and the airfield was sold to the RAF. In 1927 the two London auxiliary squadrons, No. 600 and 601, moved in from Northolt.

The aircraft sheds at Hendon in 1923.

Hornchurch (ex Sutton's Farm) Between Hornchurch and Rainham

During 1915 some land round Sutton's Farm was requisitioned by the government. By 1916 the airfield was part of No. 18 Wing and was the base for No. 39 (HD) Squadron. Since 18 Wing was responsible for the defence of London it was important to give Sutton's Farm permanent wooden hangars as well as messes and workshops. The airfield became famous when Second Lieutenant Brandon shot down Zeppelin L.15. This was followed by another victory over the Zeppelins when Lieutenant W. Leefe-Robinson shot down SL.11. With the Zeppelin and Gotha threat to London, No. 46 Squadron was withdrawn from France in July 1917 to join the resident flight of No. 39 Squadron. When these two squadrons moved elsewhere, No. 78 Squadron moved in on 20 September, together with No. 189 Night-Training Squadron from Ripon. When both these units were disbanded in 1919 the buildings were demolished and the land restored to its original state. By 1921 there was virtually nothing left of the old station when a reluctant farmer, Mr Crawford, was told that the site was again wanted under the new home-defence expansion plan. Mr Crawford was obliged to give some land back for the building of a new, permanent, peacetime RAF station, but he was allowed to keep some farmland north of the landing ground. When the new station was opened on 1 April 1928, it was renamed Hornchurch. (Retaining the old name would doubtless have brought back painful memories for Mr Crawford in his battle with the War Office.)

Hounslow SE of the site of the present London Airport

Hounslow was taken over in August 1914 for RFC training. Operational squadrons also came and went, including Nos 10, 15, 24, 27, 39, 52, 85 and 87, some of which had formed at Hounslow. When No. 18 Wing Aeroplane Repair Section came it remained until August 1919. When Nos 85 and 87 Squadrons moved to France in mid-1918, No. 42 TDS moved in and, in March 1919 No. 107 Squadron came home to disband. Once No. 42 TDS disbanded the site returned to civil use.

Kenley S of Croydon on the A22

Kenley was opened in the summer of 1917 as No. 7 Aircraft Acceptance Park. From the summer of 1918 several squadrons were in residence, but by November 1918 all but No. 91 Squadron had moved out. When this unit moved out on 3 July 1919 it left only No. 1 (Communications) Squadron, which had come from Hendon in the April. On 1 April 1920 No. 24 (Communications) Squadron formed at Kenley. Eventually selected for retention as a permanent RAF station in the early 1920s, it was home for fighter squadrons, including Nos 13 and 32. In January 1927 No. 24 Squadron moved to Northolt, to be replaced by No. 23 Squadron with its Gamecocks on 6 February that year. (This was to be the squadron which Douglas Bader joined in 1930. Shortly afterwards he lost his legs in a flying accident at Woodley Aerodrome, near Reading)

London (Colney) 5 miles SW of Hatfield

London (Colney) was established as a 2nd-class landing ground during the First World War and came under SE Area. It was used by No. 44 Squadron during the early part of the war, and in the spring of 1916 a training aerodrome was established, the first resident squadron being No. 56, which came from Gosport on 4 July, the first squadron to receive SE5 fighters. The fighter ace Captain Albert Ball was one of the squadron pilots when it flew off to France on 7 April 1917. No. 56 Squadron was replaced at the station by No. 56 TS. On 10 July No. 74 Squadron came to the airfield with 504Ks and SE5As, but it moved to Goldhanger in March 1918. Under RAF administration No. 56 TS became No. 41 TDS, flying 504Ks and Snipes. When the training role of the station came to an end after the Armistice, Nos 1 and 24 Squadrons arrived, but only in cadre form, and it was decided not to retain the airfield in the peacetime RAF. It closed in December 1919.

Northolt W of London on the A40

Construction began in early 1915, and the aerodrome officially opened on 1 March with the arrival of No. 4 Reserve Aeroplane Squadron. It was also a night landing ground, having primitive airfield lighting. From No. 4 Reserve Squadron No. 18 Squadron was formed, which later went to France. A number of units passed through, and meanwhile the airfield was used for flight-testing aircraft constructed by the nearby Fairey works. Only one contact was made with the enemy during the First World War by Northolt-based aircraft, when Gothas were intercepted over Ilford, Essex. Both Americans and Russians came to Northolt for flying training, indeed Northolt as a training aerodrome witnessed many accidents, some fatal. In 1917 there were three fatal crashes killing sixteen persons in all. In February 1918 the three training squadrons, Nos 2 and 4 TS and 86 Squadron, became No. 30 TDS. After the Armistice and following the disbandment of its units, Northolt ceased to be a fighter-training station, and in June 1919 it was home to South-Eastern Communications Flight, which provided refresher courses for officers. By then Northolt had become a joint RAF/civil airfield, and the Central Aircraft Company moved in to operate a flying school. In 1923 the resident flight became the Inland Area Communications Flight, and on 1 April No. 12 Squadron re-formed with DH9As, to be followed in 1924 by No. 41 Squadron with Snipes. There were problems with the drainage, and a proper drainage system was installed in 1925. That year saw the formation of the first auxiliary squadrons, with both No. 600 (City of London) and No. 601 (County of London) Squadrons forming on 14 October. When both these squadrons moved to Hendon on 18 January 1927, No. 24 Communications Squadron moved in to provide continuation training for RAF pilots on the staff of the Air Ministry, and to fly Air officers on

their visits around the United Kingdom. Fairey also maintained its use of the airfield throughout the 1920s, testing, among other prototypes, the long-range Fairey Postal.

North Weald W of Chipping Ongar

The aerodrome was constructed in 1916, and in August No. 39 Squadron had a detached flight there. It was from North Weald that Second Lieutenant W.J. Tempest shot down Zeppelin L.31 over Potter's Bar on 1 October 1916. When the Gotha threat replaced that of the Zeppelins No. 39 Squadron put two more detached flights into the airfield so that the squadron was complete at that airfield. On 22 May 1918 No. 75 Squadron joined No. 39, and in October the latter left for France. After the Armistice No. 75 Squadron was disbanded, and although No. 44 Squadron moved in for a short time, when it too was disbanded North Weald had no resident squadron. It lay dormant for a few years but was reopened on 27 September 1927 after a year of building reconstruction. On 11 October 1927 the Siskins of No. 56 Squadron flew in from Biggin Hill, to be followed on 1 April 1928 by No. 29 Squadron from Duxford. Both units were equipped with Siskin IIIAs.

Orsett (Essex) NE of Grays

From 1917 until 1919 Orsett was used by No. 49 Wing, being a 1st-class landing ground. The airfield had only tented accommodation and was closed after the war.

Penshurst (Kent) 4 miles NW of Tunbridge Wells

During the First World War Penshurst housed No. 2 Wireless School, formed on 8 November 1917. Equipped with DH6s, the school provided a one week's course for Scout pilots and one week for wireless personnel. Penshurst was also a depot for wireless stores and repair and testing of wireless apparatus. When the school closed on 23 March 1919 the airfield closed and the buildings were dismantled.

Stag Lane Edgware, to the N of London

This was a 2nd-class landing ground in the South-Eastern Area under No. 49 Wing. It was used during the First World War by No. 44 Squadron, and was closed after the Armistice. It later became famous for de Havilland aircraft production.

Stow Maries 9 miles SE of Chelmsford

Stow Maries started life in 1916 as home to a No. 37 Squadron detachment . It was the policy in the First World War to spread an HD squadron over three landing grounds, with up to eight aircraft at each. The squadron headquarters could well be at another location, in this case Woodham Mortimer, with two other detachments at Goldhanger and Southend (Rochford). In June 1918 the squadron headquarters moved to Stow Maries, and 37

Squadron became a night-fighter squadron with Camels. When the detached flight at Goldhanger withdrew to Stow Maries on 20 February 1919, the unit was at last all together at one airfield, but when it moved to Biggin Hill on 17 March that year the airfield was abandoned and returned to agriculture.

Uxbridge SE of Uxbridge

Acquired by the government in early 1915, it was intended originally as a prisoner-of-war camp, but became a convalescent hospital for Canadian soldiers, and then the RAF Armament School in 1918. One of the first tasks undertaken by the school was to give armament training to cadets prior to flying training, but this was threatened with closure after the Armistice. In August a detachment of the RAF Depot moved from Halton, which, together with the Recruits' Training Depot, was to train recruits and to be called the Uxbridge Depot. In September 1919 the Armament School left, and in the same month the School of Music arrived from Hampstead. Other units included HQ No. 2 Group, HQ Southern Area, Southern Area Medical HQ and Southern Area Barrack Stores. There then followed Southern Area HQ of the Air Construction Service and the South-Eastern Group HQ of the same service, and just to fill the place up, the cadres of Nos 4 and 39 Squadrons arrived, followed by those of 3 and 207 Squadrons, although it was not long before these squadrons were on the move again on re-formation. Later in 1920 the Discharge Centre moved from Halton and a detachment of the Records Office moved from Blandford. In April the School of Music became the Royal Air Force Central Band. In May the School of Physical Training and Drill was established, and if the reader is worried that Uxbridge must have been close to bursting they would be wrong. In June the Officers' Invaliding Board arrived from Hampstead, and the station was also a major centre for demobilization. With the Royal Air Force band and the home of RAF drill, Uxbridge took part in many ceremonial functions, including tattoos. Life at Uxbridge is described by T.E. Lawrence (of Arabia) in his book *The Mint*, extracts of which appear in the chapter on personnel. During the 1920s there were some unit movements in and out of the station. With the rundown of the RAF to its peacetime establishment, the Discharge Centre and Inland Area Invaliding Medical Board ceased to function in 1921, followed by the Inland Area Medical HQ in 1922. In 1925 the RAF Officers' Hospital moved from Finchley. In June 1926 the HQ Inland Area moved to Bentley Priory, to be replaced in Hillingdon House by the HQ Air Defence Great Britain (ADGB). This was followed by HQ Fighting Area. Finally, in the 1920s, short-service commissioned officers came to Uxbridge, doing a month's drill and being fitted with uniforms before going on to Nos 2, 3, 4 and 5 FTS.

Wimbledon

A 3rd-class landing ground that came under No. 49 Wing during the First World War and was used mainly by 141 Squadron. It was dismantled soon after the Armistice.

What the London home-defence squadrons were up against. This is the wreckage of a Zeppelin shot down during the First World War.

Airfields and Seaplane Bases of Central and South-East England

Andover 2½ miles W of Andover

Opened in August 1917, the first task of the new aerodrome was with the work-up of RFC bomber squadrons, starting with Nos 104, 105 and 106, followed by No. 148 Squadron in February 1918. When these units departed for operations, Nos 207 and 215 Squadrons returned from operations to convert from the HP 0/100 to the 0/400. On 1 May 1918 No. 2 School of Navigation and Bomb Dropping was formed here. Following the Armistice training continued into 1919. The No. 2 School of Navigation and Bomb Dropping was absorbed into the station in September, and the combined unit was renamed the Air Pilotage School, but it did not survive the post-war axe. It was reduced to a cadre on 1 April 1920 and disbanded during December 1922. No. 7 Group formed at Andover on 1 April 1920 to administer Army Cooperation squadrons, and the Staff College opened there on 3 April 1922. In January 1923 No. 11 Squadron re-formed at Andover, and this was followed by a variety of units and aircraft, including Bristol Fighters, Fairey Fawns and Foxes and Boulton & Paul Sidestrands. A station headquarters was established on 1 April 1925.

Bekesbourne 4 miles SE of Canterbury

Requisitioned as an emergency landing ground in 1916, its first use was by B Flight of No. 50 (HD)

AIRFIELDS AND SEAPLANE BASES OF CENTRAL, SOUTH AND SOUTH-EAST ENGLAND – 11 NOVEMBER 1918 AND 31 DECEMBER 1929

Reading (Colney Pk.

Grain

Rochford

Sheerness

Leysdown

Eastchurch

Manston

Andover

Farnborough

Throwley

Odiham

Detling

Godmersham Park

Hythe

Chattis Hill

Telscombe Cliffs

Eastleigh

Hamble

Gosport

Slindon

Wye

Lee- on-Solent

Kingsnorth

Lympne

Somerton

Dymchurch

Bembridge

Goring-by-sea

Hawkinge

Foreland

Shoreham

New Romney

Capel

Rustington

Tipnor

Dover Harbour/Swingate And Guston Road

Southbourne

Tangmere

Ford

Polegate

Bekesbourne

Newhaven

Eastbourne

Walmer

Westgate

Squadron, accepting FK3s, FK8s, BE2s and BE12 variants. No. 50 Squadron was reinforced by squadrons from France following the Gotha raids on London in 1917. Ironically there were no raids while the SE5As of No. 56 Squadron were detached to Bekesbourne, since two days after the SE5As returned to France London was bombed again. Following an upgrading of Bekesbourne in 1918, the whole of No. 50 Squadron moved in. At the time of the Armistice the squadron was run down and disbanded in June 1919. The aerodrome was relinquished in 1920.

Bembridge (Isle of Wight) 3½ miles SE of Ryde
Opened as a substation of Calshot in 1915, this seaplane station was part of the Solent Defence Scheme. Short 184s operated sixty miles out from the Isle of Wight, and in January 1917 Bembridge joined the reorganized Portsmouth Group. There was little action for the unit, although a Bembridge-based 184 had a probable U-boat kill on 18 October 1917. On 1 April 1918 the Portsmouth

Group became No. 10 Group based at Warsash. Nos 412 and 413 Flights RNAS became No. 253 Squadron RAF, which was disbanded in May 1919. The station was closed in September and disposed of in 1920.

Capel 2 miles NE of Folkestone
A site between Dover and Folkestone was cleared during April 1915, and sheds were erected for airships. RNAS Capel was commissioned on 8 May 1915. Unfortunately the sheds were not big enough for the SS airships for which they were intended. Four of these craft were on convoy protection duties by the end of June. After this initial hiccup, Capel became the main assembly shed for the SS-type airship. In April 1918 the Capel station became part of No. 5 Group, which embraced the whole of the Dover Area. There were then five SSZ ships on strength, in addition to others under construction or repair. After the Armistice Capel/Folkestone was closed in 1919, and the land and buildings were passed to the Disposals Board in August 1920.

Chattis Hill 2¹/₂ miles W of Stockbridge

The site was prepared during the summer of 1917. Nos 91 and 93 Squadrons formed on 1 September 1917, to be joined later by No. 92 Squadron from London (Colney). No. 91 squadron undertook wireless training, while Nos 92 and 93 Squadrons were to be fighter training units. The site did suffer from muddy conditions, requiring an American construction unit to build a more permanent station. From April 1918 the School of Wireless Telegraphy was opened at Chattis Hill, as was No. 43 TDS with 504s and Camels. After Christmas 1918 some aircraft were flown to storage, but many were used until unserviceable and then broken up. Chattis Hill was still open in June 1919, but was abandoned either late that year or early in 1920.

Detling 4 miles NE of Maidstone

Early in 1915 the Directorate of Works was surveying landing grounds on the North Downs, and Detling was settled on. Aircraft operated from the field until March 1916, but then went on to C & M. At this time it was a RNAS field, and then it was transferred to the RFC on 3 April 1917, and No. 50 HD Squadron moved in, flying BE2cs and B.12s, which achieved no success in intercepting German airships or aircraft. No. 143 Squadron with Camels moved to Detling from Throwley on 14 February 1918, and this unit was active against a Gotha raid on 18 May. When the unit re-equipped with SE5As, which had water-cooled engines, it was found that they took too long to warm up to be sure of an interception, and so in August the squadron reverted to Camels. No. 50 Squadron had meanwhile redeployed to Bekesbourne. Before No. 143 Squadron disbanded on 31 October 1919 it was equipped with Snipes. Detling was abandoned in December of that year.

Dover (St Margarets/Swingate Down) 2 miles NE of Dover

Swingate Down, above Dover, had been used by aviators making a Channel crossing, and the RFC chose the site as its jumping-off point for squadrons going to France. At the beginning of the First World War the RFC had only a handful of squadrons, and when these left for France only one flight of No. 4 Squadron was left *in situ.* for patrol work. By the end of August 1914 the landing ground was left deserted. In May 1915 it was converted into a proper aerodrome and was to host a flying school, a machine-gun school and Nos 12 and 13 Reserve Squadrons, the latter becoming Dover's training unit. Other units came and went, and when training depot stations were introduced by the RAF in 1918 Dover was home to No. 53 TDS from 15 July of that year. The Marine Operations Pilots' School gave specialized instruction on anti-submarine and convoy-escort work. Both units were closed during 1919, and the airfield was closed to all but aircraft in distress. In 1920 the airfield was derequisitioned, although the sheds were retained longer for storage purposes.

Dover (Guston Road) 1¹/₂ miles NE of Dover

Like the RFC, the Navy wished to provide a jumping-off point for RNAS aircraft crossing the Channel, as well as having an airfield to protect the Dover naval base. With the outbreak of war in 1914, completion of the airfield was hastened on a site between the old Fort Burgoyne and the Duke of York's Military School. No. 2 Squadron RNAS arrived in December 1914, soon to be replaced by No. 1 Squadron, combining training with an air-defence task shared with Dunkirk-based aircraft. In 1915 the Dover Defence Flight was the resident unit, but from 25 March the unit was developed into a training base. Various other units formed and re-formed at Guston Road until the RAF took over in April 1918, when No. 218 Squadron was formed here on 24 April. In August 1918 the aircraft and crews of the former Dover and Walmer stations were reorganized as No. 233 Squadron, where the aircraft of No. 491 Flight at Guston Road helped to virtually close the Dover Straits to U-boats. When No. 491 Flight moved to Walmer in January 1919, Guston Road was abandoned, and it was finally closed in 1920.

Dover (Marine Parade) on Dover sea front.

On 18 November 1914 a skating rink on the Marine Parade, Dover, was requisitioned to provide a shed for seaplanes. A slipway was built to enable the seaplanes to be manhandled across the road to the beach. But an overcrowded harbour meant that take-offs and landings could not take place inside the breakwater. Following the heavy sinkings of May 1915, most of the operational flying was transferred to Dunkirk, and Dover assumed a training and repair role. With the formation of the RAF in 1918, Dover-based seaplanes joined No. 5 Group, and because of the effectiveness of their patrols few U-boats passed down the Channel after May 1918. With No. 233 Squadron having flights at Guston Road and Walmer, the four 184s at Dover Harbour became No. 407 Flight. Squadron Headquarters was on the Marine Parade, Dover. No. 407 Flight probably vacated the harbour on 26 March 1919, and No. 233 Squadron disbanded on 15 May. Although the site was given up in 1920, Dover Harbour remained an official flying-boat alighting area during the 1920s and 1930s, and was occasionally visited by current operational types.

Dymchurch (Hythe/Palmarsh) 2¹/₂ miles SW of Hythe

The RFC Machine-Gun School moved from Dover to Hythe/Palmarsh on 27 November 1915 to take advantage of the better facilities available on the gunnery ranges near the town. The unit became the School of Aerial Gunnery on 3 September 1916, and the Kite balloons were moved to sheds on a site near the

Dymchurch Redoubt because of the increased activity at Hythe. In January 1917 the unit was renamed No. 1 (Auxiliary) School of Aerial Gunnery, providing, among other things, two-week courses for observers. Another name change in March 1918 was to the No. 1(Observer) School of Aerial Gunnery. When this unit moved to a much better location just before the Armistice at New Romney, Dymchurch became an emergency landing ground for aircraft using the Hythe ranges. Land and buildings were disposed of and the site cleared during 1920.

Eastbourne   2 miles N of Eastbourne

On declaration of war in 1914 the Admiralty took over the existing airfield as a training school, and it became RNAS Eastbourne, a premier *ab initio* training base with a large range of aircraft types. Despite continuous drainage problems with the ditches, flying operations were continued throughout the war. When the RAF took over in April 1918, No. 50 TDS was moved from Castle Bromwich to Eastbourne on 6 July 1918. Although still active in July 1919, the airfield was empty and in 1920 was handed back to Frederick Fowler, the prime mover behind the flying school, originally at Eastbourne. But when the financial support from the Air Ministry for civil flying at the airfield ran out, Fowler was bound to let it go and return it to agriculture.

Eastchurch   1¹/₂ miles SE of Eastchurch village

The very first four naval airmen, E.L. Gerrard, R. Gregory, A.M. Longmore and C.R. Samson, all learned to fly at Eastchurch, which started life as an airfield in 1909. Although low-lying and close to marshland it was well drained. In 1911 the Admiralty was persuaded to take an interest, and in April 1912 the Naval Wing of the RFC set up its headquarters there. Samson's enthusiasm and energy saw the Navy's presence increase to cover development in several fields of naval aviation, and the establishment was titled HMS *Pembroke*, parented by Chatham Naval Barracks. On 1 July 1914 the RNAS was formed and the naval land-planes went to Eastchurch for mobilization. The airfield was used for trials with the HP 0/100, the so-called 'Bloody Paralyser', home-defence patrols against Zeppelins and training. From February 1917, flying training of pilots and observers also took place. Enlargement took place in 1916 and again in 1917, and following the death of Horace Short (Short Bros) the aircraft works was sold to the government. On the amalgamation of the RFC and RNAS into the RAF, No. 58 Wing was formed on 1 April 1918. The naval flying school became No. 204 TDS. After the Armistice Eastchurch became the Armament School and was retitled the Armament and Gunnery School on 1 April 1922, when the airfield was used by aircraft of the squadrons on courses and for courses flying on the Leysdown ranges. In October 1923 bombing trials were conducted here using W/T, and tests were carried out on aircraft engine silencers. On 1 April 1926 Eastchurch was transferred to No. 23 Group and was home to the Fairey IIIFs of No. 207 Squadron, which arrived on 3 October 1923, to be followed by the Horsleys of No. 33 Squadron on 14 September 1929, when No. 207 Squadron went to Bircham Newton.

Eastleigh   1¹/₂ miles S of Eastleigh town

In 1917 the War Office decided to expand the RFC Depot in Leigh Road into an aircraft acceptance park, and North Stonham Farm was requisitioned. Four large hangars and five storage sheds were built along the Eastleigh–Southampton railway line. The Americans then approached the British government for an assembly base for American-built aircraft of their Northern Bombing Group, a flood of which were expected during the summer of 1918. These would come in through the port of Southampton for assembly at Base B, as the US aviation service called Eastleigh. Assembly work ceased four days after the Armistice, and Eastleigh was handed back to the RAF on 10 April 1919, when the hangars were used for RAF demobilization. This continued until 20 January 1920, when the rundown was accelerated, and after auctioning stores and buildings the station closed in May 1920.

Farnborough   2 miles NW of Aldershot

The use of Farnborough for air-related activities dates back to 1905 and the Royal Engineers (RE), when a balloon-erecting shed was built in May of that year. On 28 February 1911 the Air Battalion of the RE was formed with No. 1 (Airship) Company at the site. With the coming of the RFC on 13 May 1912, that unit became No. 1 Squadron. The Royal Aircraft Factory was also established at Farnborough, and while a variety of RFC units came and went the station settled down to build aircraft and undertake research and development. It was War Office policy at the time for its aircraft to be designed and built at Farnborough, whereas the Admiralty was disposed to try aircraft built by private companies, notably Short Brothers, A.V. Roe and Sopwith. Since the War Office requirement was at that time to build aircraft for reconnaissance, it wanted aircraft that were stable in flight, not ones that were highly manoeuvrable as fighters needed to be. In July 1918 the Royal Aircraft Factory was renamed the Royal Aircraft Establishment. At the end of the war aircraft design and construction were discontinued and the Wireless School moved to Flowerdown. Farnborough was part of South-Western Area in November 1918, but became a No. 7 Group station in Southern Area on 20 September 1919. On the research side experiments had concentrated on armaments and aerodynamics, and two wind tunnels were built during 1916/17, when trials were conducted on aircraft spinning. By June 1920 personnel had been reduced in numbers from 5,000 to 1,380, commensurate with peacetime commitments. In 1921 the RAE absorbed the Instrument Design Establishment, which moved from Biggin Hill, and the Airworthiness Department moved from the Air Ministry. On 12 April 1926 Farnborough was placed under No. 22 Group, Inland Area, with responsibility for the School of Photography, the Experimental Section RAE, No. 4 Army Cooperation Squadron and units at Andover, Larkhill and Old Sarum.

Ford 2³/4 miles W of Littlehampton

Officially known as Ford Junction, this airfield was one of a large number of training stations authorized in 1917. Work started in 1918 with German POWs building most of the camp, and it was earmarked for the US Air Service as a training aerodrome to train crews for the US-built HP 0/400 bombers expected to arrive in large numbers during the summer of 1918. But the RAF were in first with No. 148 Squadron on 1 March 1918 and No. 149 Squadron on 3 March. When these units left for France on 2 June 1918, the airfield was free for the Americans to move in, which they did on 15 August. A Night Bombardment Training School, intended to teach night navigators about radio interception, opened on 15 September. As for the Americans, there were snags in receiving the 0/400s, and the Armistice was signed before one machine was assembled or one training course completed. On 17 November 1918 the Americans moved out and Ford was then used to demobilize RAF squadrons. Reference to Appendix B shows which squadrons came to Ford for this purpose. Only one squadron, No. 97, was turned round at Ford, and this one left for India in July 1919 equipped with DH10 bombers. The station closed in January 1920.

Foreland (Isle of Wight) 5 miles S of Bembridge

Foreland was used by aircraft on anti-submarine duties. When the RAF took over in April 1918 No. 253 Squadron operated DH6s from the station, which contributed to the significant reduction in shipping losses to U-boats. Nos 511 and 512 Flights of the squadron were disbanded on 21 January 1919, and the airfield site was relinquished early in 1920.

Godmersham Park 2¹/2 miles N of Wye

This was a mooring-out station for Capel Le Ferne, protected from the prevailing wind by Kings Wood, and it was usual to moor-out one SSZ airship at Godmersham Park from the late spring of 1918. The base was abandoned after the Armistice.

Gosport 4 miles W of Portsmouth.

Work on the airfield began early in 1914, and No. 5 Squadron moved in from Netheravon on 6 July. When that unit left for France the RFC had neither the aircraft

nor personnel to man the airfield. When these later became available, a succession of units came and went, and in December 1916 Major R.R. Smith-Barry was given command of No. 1 Reserve Squadron at the station. He had been appalled at the quality of pilots arriving for operational duties on the Western Front, and was determined to bring in proper instructor courses. One of his ideas was for a speaking tube between instructor and pupil, and this became the 'Gosport Tube', which came into use all over the world. In May 1917 he wrote a set of training notes, and General Salmond then sanctioned the formation of a Special School of Flying at Gosport, Nos 1, 25 and 55 Training Squadrons being amalgamated for this purpose in August 1917. By early 1918 all training schools were instructed to adopt Gosport training methods. On 31 January 1918 Gosport became home to the School of Aerial Cooperation with Coast Defence Batteries. With the formation of the RAF, Gosport was placed in No. 2 Area, No. 8 Group still housing No. 1 Special School of Flying, but in July each RAF Area was given its own training organization, and the former was renamed South-West Area Flying Instructors' School. HQ Gosport was formed on 28 October 1918 to deal with an unwieldy collection of units, but with the Armistice Gosport's future was uncertain. However, in June 1919 it was confirmed that the RAF's torpedo school was to be sited there, and in September it was formally listed as a permanent No. 10 Group station in Coastal Area. During the 1920s Gosport fulfilled a variety of roles, including observer training, coastal battery cooperation and night landing on aircraft-carriers.

Grain 1¹/2 miles S of Grain Village

Grain was commissioned by the Admiralty on 30 December 1912 to carry out development work on seaplanes. Following further development of the air station, Grain succeeded Eastchurch as the HQ Sheerness Naval District. During 1914 all available seaplanes were concentrated on Felixstowe, Yarmouth and Grain to control the approaches to the Thames Estuary. Early in 1915 the emphasis moved from operations to repair. Adjoining rough grazing fields were levelled, and Grain became a land-plane and seaplane base, to be commissioned as the Royal Naval Aeroplane Repair Depot. At the end of the year, the Experimental Armament Section was established alongside the repair depot. When an experimental construction section was proposed, the Admiralty agreed to the combined unit becoming the Marine Experimental Aircraft Depot, and simulated aircraft-landing trials were conducted at Grain – indeed the construction section produced several naval aircraft types. Equally the Experimental Armament and Test Depot was busy evaluating such weapons as the anti-Zeppelin Rankin darts and the Davis recoilless gun. After the war work on the station proceeded at a more relaxed pace, but when Orfordness closed in 1921 the Armament Experimental Squadron moved in, testing such aircraft as the Short Cromarty and the Fairey Atalanta. But on 17 March 1924 the Marine Aircraft Experimental Unit moved to Felixstowe and Grain/Port Victoria was closed.

Hamble 4 miles SE of Southampton
Although used for seaplane construction during the First World War, the construction sheds at Hamble were demolished in 1919. Hamble is best known for its association with Fairey Aviation and A.V. Roe Co. Ltd during the decade after the war.

Hawkinge 2 miles N of Folkestone
The War Office acquired the land for an airfield in 1915, and it was initially used by squadrons transiting to France. By the autumn of 1915 Folkestone (Hawkinge) had Bessoneau hangars and tents. Since compasses were so inaccurate at the time, pilots were literally pointed at St Omer in northern France by having two circles cut in the turf so that, when lined up, the aircraft was pointed in the right direction. In January 1917 HQ 21st Wing RFC changed the name from Folkestone (Hawkinge) to simply Hawkinge to avoid confusion with Folkestone (Capel), the airship station. The unit then became the Aeroplane Dispatch Centre, later developed into No. 12 Aircraft Acceptance Park (South-East Area). Work on the park was almost complete by the time of the Armistice, and squadrons awaiting demobilization were held there. Early in 1919, with chronic shortages of food and clothing in Belgium, Hawkinge was used by the Air Travel and Transport Ltd to ferry these items across the Channel, using DH9As with service pilots. Mail was also flown from the station to the occupation forces. HP V/1500 bombers were stored at Hawkinge, along with other smaller types awaiting scrapping. The Aircraft Acceptance Park was disbanded in July 1919, along with No. 120 Squadron in October, which by that time had gone to Lympne. During 1920 the station was taken over by the Inter-Allied Commission of Control. On 20 April 1920 No. 25 Squadron re-formed at Hawkinge, making it nominally a fighter base. At that time it was the only fighter squadron in the United Kingdom, and it took charge of 127 Sopwith Snipes, fourteen HP 0/400s, twenty-one HP V/1500s, a Bristol F2B and two Avro 504Ks, although the squadron had only sufficient personnel to fly the two 504Ks. No. 25 Squadron was deployed in the Chanak Crisis of 1922, but returned to Hawkinge in October 1923. From 1923 onwards Hawkinge remained a fighter station through to the Second World War.

Kingsnorth 5 miles NE of Rochester
Kingsnorth started as an Admiralty establishment providing airship cover close to the Chatham naval base. In October 1913 it was agreed that the Admiralty should

have the sole responsibility for powered lighter-than-air craft, and so that the Navy took over the airship facilities at Farnborough also. Kingsnorth was commissioned in January 1914, and on 1 July the Naval Airship Branch was absorbed into the RNAS. In March 1915 the remaining design staff and equipment were transferred from Farnborough, and a training school was opened to train air and ground crews to operate the new non-rigid airships. Experimentation with new types and the building of established types was undertaken, but with the end of the First World War the programme was rapidly cut. When it was decided that aircraft were more effective than airships, airship stations were closed down during 1919. Kingsnorth was dismantled during early 1920.

Lee-on-Solent 2¹/₂ miles NW of Gosport
With the heavy shipping losses of the spring of 1917, the seaplane training unit at Calshot could not cope with increased training requirement for aircrews. A brand-new school was planned on Holy Island, off the Northumbrian coast, and in the meantime a temporary substation was established at Lee-on-Solent. Work started in July 1917, and the Naval Seaplane Training Unit was opened on 30 July. In November the plan to move to Holy Island was scrapped, and so Lee-on-Solent became permanent. On 1 April 1918 the station was transferred to the Air Ministry, and the training unit became No. 109 TDS, No. 10 Group. Personnel numbers peaked in December 1918, but all training ceased in January 1919. It was then decided that the station was to be retained in the much reduced peacetime air force, and on 16 June 1919 the RAF Seaplane School was established. Although there was a brief training commitment for crews going to Russia, budgetary cuts forced Lee-on-Solent onto a C & M basis in December 1919. This was only a brief spell, for the HQ of No. 10 Group was moved from Warsash in July 1920 and the seaplane school was retitled School of Naval Cooperation and Air Navigation. With the services' love of frequent name changes at this time, this was simplified to be the RAF Seaplane Training School in April 1921, running courses for pilots who could double as fleet observers. But back went the name in May 1923 to the School of Naval Cooperation when RAF and RN observer courses were combined. In January 1924 the school devoted itself entirely to fleet observer training. Trials with W/T-controlled Fairey IIIDs and Flycatcher floatplanes were also conducted, and in January 1925, No. 444 Flight was formed for fleet spotter duties using three Fairey IIIDs stressed for catapult work.

Leysdown (Shellbeach) 1¹/₂ miles SE of Leysdown-on-Sea
Leysdown is recognized as the first flying field in Kent, and was associated with J.T.C. Moore Brabazon and

Short Brothers. With the expansion of the naval flying school at Eastchurch, the Leysdown landing ground was used for emergency forced landings until 1917, when bombing and gunnery ranges were established offshore. The airfield became the Pilots'and Observers' Aerial Gunnery and Aerial Fighting School (South-East Area) on 1 April 1918. After the Armistice the school was closed in 1919, but the station remained open to administer the ranges used by aircraft from Eastchurch, and this situation continued throughout the inter-war years and the Second World War.

Lydd 2¹/₂ miles NW of Lydd

In 1916 sixty acres of Dering Farm were requisitioned as a landing ground, which was then used by aircraft of an artillery-cooperation flight working with guns on a local range, and was in full operation by January 1917. It was then graded as a 3rd-class landing ground to be used by No. 112 (HD) Squadron. No. 2 Balloon School was also situated just north of Lydd, and this was closed in September 1918, followed shortly by the Artillery Cooperation Flight. No. 53 (HD) Wing. Lydd was then relinquished as a landing ground and returned to farmland.

Lympne 2¹/₂ miles W of Hythe

The aerodrome originated as a flying field for the Machine-Gun School, Hythe. The original site was found to suffer from water-logging, and a new site was chosen nearby in March 1916. Lympne was then an emergency landing ground for home defence, and by October 1916 the aerodrome was well advanced. In 1917 work on storage accommodation began for No. 8 Aircraft Acceptance Park, but on 25 May 1917 Lympne received the attention of Gothas of *Kagohl* 3, whose crews were prevented from attacking London because of the weather and chose Lympne as a secondary target. No. 8 AAP was involved in ferrying aircraft to France, and since the airfield was designated as a 1st-class landing ground in 1918 it was used by Home Defence squadrons. After the Armistice the presence of the AAP prevented an immediate closure, and extensions to the airfield were being negotiated in April 1919. Lympne was used for military aircraft engaged in ferrying mail to the continent, as well as disbanding squadrons, but as the mail commitment dwindled the Air Ministry did not need both Hawkinge and Lympne, and the latter was turned over to civil aviation.

Manston 2 miles W of Ramsgate

It was the RNAS that looked for a safe night-landing ground and selected a large field near Ramsgate. The field known as Manston LG was improved in 1916. A variety of operational units used the airfield during 1916/17, notably No. 3 Wing, and in the spring of 1917 part of the Pilot Training School at Eastchurch was

transferred to Manston and formed the nucleus of the War School to provide advanced instruction on aircraft that pilots would be flying operationally. Again in 1917, the Admiralty selected Manston and Cranwell for the training of air mechanics, of whom there was an acute shortage. With the training came the necessity to construct buildings so that Manston could become a permanent station. With the formation of the RAF in April 1918 came the establishment of a three-squadron day-bomber unit. No. 203 TDS and the War School became a pilots' pool. The former was then renumbered No. 55 TDS, and the War School was absorbed by the newly formed No. 219 Squadron, which operated landplanes at Manston and seaplanes at nearby Westgate. Next was the formation of No. 2 School of Observers, and No. 55 TDS moved to Narborough (Marham). At the end of September 1918 the station was virtually complete. With the Armistice came the usual rundown in activity, but Manston was one of the few stations that was to avoid closure. Indeed it remained an active station until its closure in March 1999. In October 1919 it was decided that the School of Technical Training (Men) would move from Halton to Manston, and after some refurbishment of accommodation training courses commenced in May 1920. In May 1921 a cadre of No. 6 Flying Training School (FTS) arrived from Spittlegate to give refresher flying for pilots proceeding overseas. The station was also used for mobilization during the rail strike of 1921, but the 'Geddes Axe' of 1922 saw the disbandment of No. 6 FTS in April of that year, the dismantling of the wireless station and the reduction in size of courses of instruction attending the School. On 31 March 1924 the Bristol Fighters of No. 2 (Army Cooperation (AC)) Squadron arrived, and No. 3 Squadron was meant to come to Manston but went instead to Upavon. The reason was that the Vimys of No. 9 (B) Squadron would not fit into Upavon's narrow hangars, so the Vimys came to Manston instead. On 1 April 1926 Manston was transferred to No. 23 Group from No. 1 Group. Again the station was involved in a national industrial dispute, this time the General Strike, when No. 9 Squadron delivered newspapers, and personnel from Manston were detailed for guard duties at stores depots. During the 1920s the station was also used for summer camps for units of the newly raised Auxiliary Air Force. Finally, from April to October 1927 Manston's Bristol Fighters were deployed to the Far East (see Chapter 3).

Newhaven ¹/₂ mile SE of Newhaven town

Selected as a seaplane base in 1917, following the upsurge of U-boat activity, RNAS Newhaven opened in May 1917 as an offshoot of the main base at Calshot, housing four Short 184 floatplanes. Owing to the unprotected nature of the base, there being no sea wall, the improved Dover-type 184s, with strengthened floats, were later used that could cope with the swell. By the end of 1917 there were six aircraft in all, numbered 408 Flight. When the RAF took over in 1918 No. 408 Flight was joined by No. 409 Flight, becoming No. 242 Squadron RAF in the August. Campanias and Fairey IIIBs joined the 184s as the resident aircraft. During 1919 activity wound down, and when No. 242 Squadron was disbanded on 15 May the station closed, and the buildings were auctioned early in 1920.

New Romney 2 miles N of New Romney
The aerodrome was opened on 1 August 1917 when No. 3 (Auxiliary) School of Aerial Gunnery was formed at Littleton/New Romney to increase training facilities for observer pupils. Amazingly three public roads crossed the aerodrome, and so it was not a convenient place from which aircraft could operate. On 9 March 1918 the unit became No. 1 (Observers) School of Aerial Gunnery, and aerial activity was conducted at Dymchurch/Pelmarsh. After the Armistice it was decided to close New Romney, and in September 1919 the School of Aerial Gunnery moved to RAF Manston. In November pilots flying in the vicinity were ordered to avoid landing except in an emergency. Shortly afterwards the airfield passed into the hands of the Government Surplus Property Disposal Board.

Odiham 6½ miles ESE of Basingstoke
Odiham came into use when the Air Ministry purchased the land south-west of Odiham town as a summer camp landing ground during exercises with the Army. From 1926 onwards the Bristol Fighters of Nos 4 and 13 Squadrons used the airfield, to be followed later by the Armstrong Whitworth Atlas. Odiham was particularly favoured because it was within easy travelling distance of Aldershot and the Farnborough R/T range where communication experiments were being made.

Polegate 3½ miles NW of Eastbourne
Polegate was officially opened as an airship station on 6 July 1915. It was sheltered and had good access by road, which was ideal for airship operation, but in spite of all the efforts the sheds remained waterlogged for most of the year. An SS40 airship operated from Polegate over enemy territory and was supposed to be used for clandestine operations, e.g. dropping agents – hence the black colour. Instead it was used on night reconnaissance duties. Parachute trials were also conducted at Polegate, and these were successful, leading to the introduction of parachutes for airship crews and, later, aircraft. In 1917 Polegate was transferred to Portsmouth Command and the SS Zero airship came to the station. When the RAF took over Polegate in 1918 the airships remained on Admiralty charge. In October 1918 No. 10 Group at Warsash took control of the station and its substations at Slindon and Upton. Polegate was closed in 1919.

Reading (Coley Park) ¾ mile S of Reading town centre
With the urgent need to increase training facilities following the expansion of the RFC in 1915, the buildings of the University College Reading were taken over and the School of Instruction established. Providing initial training for prospective pilots and observers, it was renamed No. 1 School of Military Aeronautics on 27 October 1916, with the main classroom in Wantage Hall, accommodation being requisitioned in various parts of the town. A small airfield was later established at nearby Coley for student pilots, and it was also used as a landing ground for visitors. The training facilities at Reading and Coley closed after the Armistice.

Rochford 2 miles N of Southend
Following the Zeppelin raids on London in the spring of 1915 there was a recognition that landing grounds were a necessity for aircraft employed on HD duties, and the Admiralty established eight forward landing grounds to counter the Zeppelins that were attempting a landfall in East Anglia. But naval priority was given to the defence of the fleet, and aircrews with little or no night-flying experience were allotted to HD duties. In February 1916 home defence became a War Office responsibility. Rochford was transferred to the RFC on 4 June 1916, No. 37 and then No. 11 (Reserve) Squadrons took up residence, the latter becoming the Home Defence training unit, being renamed No. 98 (Depot) Squadron. Soon pupils from the School of Military Aeronautics came to Rochford and undertook night defence training in Avro 504s and Sopwith Pups. When No. 99 Depot Squadron moved in to take care of the increasing numbers of trainees, No. 98 Squadron was retitled No. 198 (Depot) Squadron. No. 99 Squadron then moved to East Retford and No. 37 Squadron to Stow Maries. In its place No. 61 (HD) Squadron was formed on 2 August 1917. Rochford aircraft were soon in action against the Gothas mounting daylight attacks, and the station was bombed. When No. 190 (Depot) Squadron was formed at Rochford in October 1917 the new unit concentrated on primary training, allowing No. 198 (Depot) Squadron to concentrate on the advanced phases of the course. Both squadrons were designated night training squadrons on 21 December 1917, and in March the following year 190 Squadron moved to Newmarket. By September 1918 the station was virtually complete, but once the Armistice was signed it began to run down. No. 61 Squadron was disbanded on 13 June 1919, followed by No. 198 Squadron in September. Apart from some joy-riding immediatly post-war, no other flying was taking place, and the station closed in 1920, the land being released for agriculture.

Rustington 2 miles E of Littlehampton
In 1918 Rustington was accepted as one of a string of training depot stations built along the south coast for the

US Air Service capable of operating HP 0/400s. The Armistice intervened while construction was still in progress, and in October 1919 instructions were issued for the buildings to be disposed of and the land relinquished.

Sheerness the Port of Sheerness
It was not until 1917 that the town was again directly involved with flying. One site was developed to the south of the dockyard for Kite balloon training under Admiralty control. There was an RFC establishment one mile to the east of the town. The balloon training base trained observers for sea reconnaissance and was titled No. 1 Balloon Training Base (South-East Area). The RFC at its establishment provided an emergency landing ground for Home Defence aircraft, notably No. 37 Squadron at Rochford. During 1918 Sheerness was also used as a landing ground for artillery-cooperation aircraft. Both units closed down after the Armistice, although the balloon base was not transferred to the Admiralty for naval use until September 1919.

Shoreham 1 mile NW of Shoreham-by-Sea
This established aerodrome was acquired by the War Office in August 1914, and immediately became a training base, but at the beginning there was a lack of instructors and aircraft that left Shoreham practically deserted. On 21 January 1915 the nucleus of No. 3 Reserve Aeroplane Squadron moved in, but no sooner was it set on the business of training than No. 14 Squadron was formed using No. 3 RAS personnel. At the beginning of the war there was always the problem of competing operational and training requirements. With the decentralization of Training Brigade on 10 January 1917, No. 3 Reserve Squadron, as it now was, came under Eastern Group Command, the reserve squadrons now becoming training squadrons. No. 3 TS was employed training pilots from scratch on a six-week course, including a minimum of three hours' dual and three hours' solo. In July 1918 the South-Eastern Area Flying Instructors' School replaced No. 3 TS, and the former was disbanded early in 1919. In April 1919 No. 1 Wing Canadian Air Force moved into Shoreham, but in 1920, when the Canadians returned home, it left only a packing section. When this unit had completed its work in December 1921 the aerodrome was closed and the airfield returned to grazing.

Slindon 6½ miles NE of Chichester
Slindon was activated on 28 April 1918 as a mooring-out station for Polegate, where two SSZ airships operated. Mooring-out stations proliferated during the First World War, so that with the dispersal of airships fog or high winds would be less likely to impede airship operations, and Slindon had the reputation of being the best mooring-out station in the Group. The site was abandoned soon after the Armistice.

Somerton 1 mile S of Cowes
Somerton was opened initially by J. Samuel White and Co. Ltd for development flight trials of its products. In 1918 the School of Aerial Cooperation with Coastal Artillery started to use Somerton as a day landing ground. The Armistice brought an end to Samuel White production on 21 January 1919, but the Coastal Battery Cooperation unit, as it was now called, was still operating there that August, when it was decided to close and dispose of the air station.

Southbourne 6 miles W of Chichester
Southbourne was intended as a training depot station for a 0/400 unit of the US Air Service, and construction was well under way in August 1918, but following the Armistice the buildings were auctioned off and the land returned to agriculture.

Swingfield 6 miles N of Folkestone
Swingfield was used as a 2nd-class landing ground for HD squadrons but was promptly returned to agriculture in 1919.

Tangmere 3 miles E of Chichester
Tangmere was not requisitioned under the Defence of the Realm Act until 25 September 1917, and German POWs assisted in clearing the site, so that the aerodrome was well advanced in February 1918. The War Office offered the station to the US Air Service and the Americans decided to have it as a Handley Page training depot station, which meant modifying the hangars to take the larger aircraft. This delayed the planned June take-over. Between March and July No. 92 Squadron RFC used Tangmere for training on its SE5As, and No. 61 TDS was formed here with 504s and F2Bs. It was further used by the aircraft from Somerton (see above), until the Americans finally took over in September. No sooner had they done so than they were leaving, following the Armistice, and Tangmere was left in the hands of No. 61 TDS. Training continued at a reduced rate into 1919, with the unit redesignated No. 61 Training School. Squadrons returning from France were held at Tangmere awaiting disbandment, and in December 1919, with demobilization largely complete, Tangmere was declared surplus to requirement and the airfield closed in 1920. The Air Ministry retained the land and buildings, and on 1 June 1925 Tangmere reopened as the Coastal Area Storage Unit and on 23 November 1926 the airfield was reactivated. When a station headquarters was formed No. 43 Squadron with Gamecocks moved in from Henlow on 12 December, to be followed in February 1927 by No. 1 Squadron when it was re-formed, having recently been disbanded in Iraq. No. 1 Squadron was equipped with the new Siskin fighter, as was No. 43 Squadron. Tangmere was then the premier fighter station in the UK. Of considerable interest is the

fact that Tangmere operated a 'tropical' routine in the late 1920s by starting work at 07.30 hrs and standing down at 13.00 hrs. In this Tangmere was unique. Although criticized by other stations, Nos 1 and 43 Squadrons managed to fly more hours than other units. At the end of the decade the station underwent a face-lift with the building of permanent barrack blocks, messes and married quarters.

Telscombe Cliffs 2¹/₂ miles W of Newhaven
This airfield was first used by detached flights of No. 78 Squadron in the war against the U-boats. With the formation of the RAF in 1918, A Flight of No. 253 Squadron came to the airfield, and then 514 Flight of No. 242 Squadron, which had its headquarters at Newhaven. With the disbandment of 514 Flight on 20 January 1919, the landing ground was relinquished and the site reverted to farmland.

Throwley 5 miles S of Faversham
Throwley was opened as an HD aerodrome in October 1916 to house No. 50 Squadron, which had its HQ at nearby Harrietsham. No. 112 Squadron was formed at the airfield on 30 July 1917 from B Flight of No. 50 Squadron. On 20 December, No. 188 Training Squadron with 504s came to the station, and when No. 143 Squadron formed there in February 1918 the place was really crowded. Accommodation was at a premium until 143 Squadron went off to Detling. Throwley squadrons were active in defending London against the Gothas in May 1918. The German attack of 19 May was so soundly rebuffed that the raids were not repeated. At least No. 112 Squadron scored its first, if only, success of the war. No. 188 TS, now a night training unit, received some Camels in July to provide advanced training. With the Armistice came the usual rundown as Throwley's resident units were disbanded, No. 112 Squadron being the last to go on 13 June 1919. The airfield site was subsequently cleared and the land returned to agriculture.

Tipnor 2¹/₂ miles N of Portsmouth city
Tipnor was opened in 1917 as an operational Kite balloon station, and provided balloons for the ships of Portsmouth Command. With the formation of the RAF this unit became No. 15 Kite Balloon Base in No. 10 Group. In August 1919 the RAF handed the base over to the Admiralty, and it was later developed as a range.

Walmer 2 miles S of Deal
Walmer was established in May 1917 as a satellite of RNAS Dover to provide cover for merchant ships anchored in the Downs off Deal, the unit being known as the Walmer Defence Flight. But the title belies the fact that home-defence operations were also carried out. In August 1918, the resident 471 Flight became part of No.

233 Squadron, Dover, under the operational control of No. 5 Group. In January 1919 No. 491 Flight moved to Walmer, followed by 233 Squadron headquarters in March. On 15 May 1919 No. 233 Squadron was disbanded and the aerodrome was abandoned soon afterwards.

Westgate 1¹/₂ miles W of Margate
Westgate opened on 1 August 1914 when the Admiralty became increasingly concerned about the vulnerability of the naval bases in the Thames Estuary. Once the British Expeditionary Force was safely in France there was no longer any need to provide anti-submarine cover, and Westgate was then simply a stand-by base. By 1915 Zeppelin commanders were becoming more confident, and visits were paid to Margate and Ramsgate. But Westgate-based aircraft did not score their first victory until 20 March 1916, when five German seaplanes were intercepted over the Goodwin Sands and one was shot down. The use of Westgate aerodrome ceased when accidents occurred in high winds or when aircraft made take-offs or landings into the cliff, but the seaplane base continued in operation with Short 184s. When Westgate became an RAF station in August 1918, No. 219 Squadron took over the squadron's aircraft, at both Westgate and Manston. Even after the Armistice there was a need to maintain anti-submarine patrols until the whereabouts of all enemy submarines had been established. After these operations had ceased in the late summer of 1919, the station was closed on 7 February 1920, the installations and hangars being dismantled and sold by auction.

Worthy Down 3 miles N of Winchester
The Wireless and Observers' School had been obliged to leave Brooklands owing to the expansion of aircraft construction, and in August 1917 the racecourse was acquired for use by the school. The construction of hangars and accommodation continued, and the station was opened in 1918. In August the school was retitled the RAF and Army Cooperation School, acting as a finishing school for corps reconnaissance pilots. This was joined by a detached flight of the Artillery Cooperation School, Lydd. After the Armistice, Worthy Down was used for the flying phases of courses at No. 1 (T) Wireless School, Flowerdown. In December 1920 the retitled RAF/Army Cooperation School moved to Old Sarum. During the period 1921–4 Worthy Down was little more than Flowerdown's flying wing, but then, on 1 April 1924, No. 58 Squadron was re-formed at the station, to be followed by No. 7 Squadron in 1927. Heavy snowfalls at the end of 1927 cut the station off except by rail, and the Commanding Officer, the Hon. J.D. Boyle CBE, DSO, took to his skis. An eighteen-month building programme saw the construction of barrack blocks by the end of the decade.

Wye *4 miles NNE of Ashford*

During the First World War, Wye was used for pilot training and housed a variety of RFC units, to be joined by the Americans in mid-1918. At its height there were Avro 504Ks, Sopwith Camels, 1½ Strutters and Bristol M1Cs on the airfield. After the Armistice the Americans departed and No. 42 TS was disbanded on 1 February 1919. For a while No. 3 Squadron personnel from the continent came to Wye, sans aircraft, but when they departed for Dover in June Wye was surplus to requirements, and following disposal the site was returned to agriculture.

Airfields and Seaplane Bases of East Anglia

Bircham Newton *11 miles NE of Kings Lynn*

Bircham Newton was built in 1916 and became the home of No. 3 Fighter School. Fighter pilots were also trained at nearby Seighford up to 1917, when Bircham Newton, being the larger airfield, took over from Seighford. Towards the end of the First World War the station was then chosen to be the mobilization unit of No. 27 Group, which was tasked to prepare for long-range bombing attacks on Germany, and on 13 June 1918 No. 166 Squadron was formed to take over the new four-engined bomber, the HP V/1500, with the range to reach Berlin. But the Armistice had been signed when the unit had only three aircraft and had not become fully operational. No operations were flown and No. 166 Squadron disbanded on 31 May 1919. The same fate befell its sister squadron, No. 274. But this seems to have marked Bircham Newton as a bomber station, and it survived the post-war closures. On 1 June 1923 No. 7 Squadron was formed with Vickers Vimys, to be followed in May 1924 by No. 99 Squadron. On 12 September 1924 Bircham Newton was established as an RAF station. No. 7 Squadron moved on to Worthy Down on 7 April 1927, and in the same month No. 99 Squadron went to Upper Heyford. On 21 March the following year No. 101 Squadron formed and was equipped with the new Sidestrand bomber in April 1929, but it left for Andover on 12 October that year. No. 101 Squadron was replaced at Bircham by No. 35 Squadron equipped with DH9As and Fairey IIIFs.

Burgh Castle *3½ miles SW of Great Yarmouth*

No. 273 Squadron was formed at Burgh Castle in August 1918 from Nos 470, 485, 486 and 534 Flights RNAS with DH4s, DH9s and Camels. This unit was to disband at nearby Great Yarmouth in July the following year. Burgh Castle also received detachments from the Westgate-based No. 219 Squadron in mid to late 1918. The airfield did not remain open after the Great War.

Duxford *9 miles S of Cambridge*

Duxford was quite the exception. While the majority of the wartime airfields and landing grounds of the RAF were either being abandoned or auctioned off in 1919, Duxford was being opened. In 1920 No. 2 FTS took up residence flying Avro 504s, Bristol F2Bs, DH9As and RE8s. In July 1924 No. 2 FTS moved to Digby, and following a review of air-defence requirements of the UK, Duxford became a fighter station charged with the responsibility to defend East Anglia and the East Midlands. Nos 19 and 29 Squadrons were earmarked for this task and were re-formed on 1 April 1923 equipped with Sopwith Snipes, which were soon to be replaced by Gloster Grebes. Again in 1923 a third squadron, No. 111, re-formed at the station with Grebes, but these were replaced with Siskin IIIs, and in 1926 'Treble-One' as it was called, became the High-Altitude Squadron tasked with developing equipment for high-altitude flying. The other two squadrons were also equipped with Siskin IIIAs. On 1 April 1928 both Nos 29 and 111 Squadrons left, leaving No. 19 Squadron the sole resident squadron. From 1926 Duxford was also home to the Cambridge University Air Squadron, which had formed on 1 October 1925 to encourage interest in an RAF career among the undergraduates.

Elmswell *5 miles NW of Stowmarket*

Elmswell was home to No. 75 Squadron from 8 September 1917 until 22 August 1919, with detached flights at Harling Road and Hadleigh. During this period the squadron operated BE12s, BE12Bs, FE2Bs and Avro 504K night-fighters. Elmswell was not retained after the Armistice.

Felixstowe *Felixstowe Dock*

Felixstowe had been home to eleven RNAS flights when the RAF took control of naval aircraft in April 1918. It was in August that year that naval flights around the country were formed into RAF squadrons in the 200 series. In common with nearby Great Yarmouth, this occurred on 20 August, and Nos 230, 231, 232 and 247 Squadrons were the resident squadrons. Between then and the end of the war a great variety of aircraft types had to be maintained by the technical personnel on the base. These were the Felixstowe F2A, F3 and F5, the Curtiss H.16, the Camel, Short 184 and Fairey IIIB/C. After the Armistice only No. 230 Squadron survived, being sent to Calshot on 7 May 1922 with its Felixstowe F5s. No. 231 Squadron was disbanded on 7 July 1919. No. 232 Squadron was disbanded on 5 January 1919, being redesignated No. 4 (Communications) Squadron, and No. 247 Squadron was disbanded on 22 January 1919. Felixstowe was not closed. On 17 March 1924 it took on the very important role from Grain of experimenting and testing marine aircraft, the maritime opposite number of Martlesham Heath just up the road, and was titled the Marine Aircraft Experimental Establishment (MAEE). Not only were military and civilian seaplane and floatplane prototypes tested, but other experiments were carried out on such things as lighting for night landing and the colouring of the surface

AIRFIELDS AND SEAPLANE BASES OF EAST ANGLIA ON 11 NOVEMBER 1918 AND 31 DECEMBER 1929

See London Map for Goldhanger

of the sea to facilitate search and rescue (see Chapters 2 and 3).

Fowlmere   8 miles S of Cambridge
Fowlmere was first opened as a training establishment in 1918. Post-war the airfield was used to store HP 0/400s. The hangars were demolished in 1923.

Goldhanger   4 miles ENE of Maldon
Goldhanger was used by only two squadrons during the First World War. No. 37 Squadron had detached flights on the airfield from September 1916 until the Armistice. No. 74 Squadron was there for only five days in March 1918, when it was equipped with the SE5A before proceeding to St-Omer on the 30th.

Great Yarmouth
Great Yarmouth came into use as an airfield and seaplane base in the war against the U-boats, and had

been the home of ten RNAS flights. When the ex-RNAS flights were combined into RAF squadrons in August 1918, the flights at Great Yarmouth became Nos 212, 228 and 229 Squadrons on the 20th of that month. Between them these squadrons had DH4s, DH9s, DH9As, Felixstowe F2As, Curtiss H12/16s, Sopwith and Hamble Babies, Short 184s and Short 320s. After the Armistice No. 229 Squadron left for Killinghome on 3 March 1919, and No. 212 squadron left on the 7th for Swingate, Dover. Four days later No. 273 Squadron arrived from Burgh Castle, but only in cadre strength. On 30 April No. 228 Squadron left for Brough, leaving just the cadre of No. 273 Squadron, which disbanded on 5 July. Great Yarmouth was not selected for retention in the post-war RAF.

Hadleigh   8 miles W of Ipswich
This was a landing ground used by No. 75 Squadron between September 1917 and the Armistice.

Harling Road 8 miles ENE of Thetford

Harling Road housed Nos 88, 89 and 94 Squadrons during August 1917, and received detachments from Nos 51 and 75 Squadrons.

Hingham 5 miles W of Wymondham

No. 100 Squadron was formed from the nucleus of No. 51 Squadron on 11 February 1917 with BE2cs, only to move on to Farnborough on the 22nd of that month. No. 102 Squadron formed on 9 August 1917 with FE2Bs, and moved on to André-aux-Bois on 24 September. No. 51 Squadron was a Home Defence squadron with detachments at Harling Road, Narborough and Mattishal between 23 September 1916 until 7 August 1917, when the squadron left Hingham for Marham. Originally equipped with BE12s, No. 51 Squadron was later equipped with FE2Bs and BE2Es.

Marham (opened as Narborough)

Marham, opened in August 1915, was then named Narborough (an adjacent field) to provide night landing for aircraft employed on anti-Zeppelin raids. In 1916 stewardship passed to the Army, and the RFC used the airfield for training fighter pilots. FE2Bs and Vickers fighters arrived from Thetford in June 1916. Then No. 59 Squadron formed with RE7s and BEs, and Narborough became a TDS preparing squadrons for France. After the war squadrons came to the airfield to disband. Closure followed and the RAF station did not open at Marham until 1 April 1937.

Martlesham Heath 6 miles ENE of Ipswich

The airfield was officially opened in January 1917, and for the next twenty-two years was used for testing civilian aircraft and military aircraft and weapons. In 1924 Martlesham was given the title Aircraft and Armament Experimental Establishment (A & AEE). The armament unit became No. 15 Squadron and the aircraft unit became No. 22 Squadron. Both units had aircraft notionally allotted to meet any possible mobilization, but they tested whatever aircraft were delivered to them for testing and evaluation. There was also a parachute section. Chapters 2 and 3 give more detailed accounts of the activities of the A & AEE, and Appendix H gives a complete listing of all aircraft, both civilian and military, tested by the A & AEE in the 1920s.

Mattishal 4 miles E of East Dereham

This landing ground received detachments of No. 51 Squadron from 7 August 1917 until the Armistice. There is no recorded post-war use.

Norwich (Mousehould Heath) Eastern outskirts of Norwich

Mousehould Heath was used during the First World War as a transit airfield. For example, No. 18 Squadron came from Northolt on 16 August 1915 and was equipped with Vickers FB5s before heading off for St-Omer on 18 November. No. 37 Squadron formed at the airfield from a nucleus of No. 9 Reserve Squadron and left the following day for Orfordness. No. 85 Squadron moved from Upavon on 10 August, only nine days after its formation, and on 27[h] November moved on to Hounslow. Finally No. 117 Squadron moved from Hucknall on 15 July 1918 and left for Wyton in November. There is no recorded post-war use of this airfield.

Sedgeford 4 miles SE of Hunstanton

Sedgeford was a busy airfield during the First World War, used as it was by six squadrons between 1916 and 1919. No. 45 Squadron came from Thetford with Henry Farman F20s on 21 May 1916. $1^1/_2$ Strutters were also added to the squadron inventory before it moved on to St-Omer, the reception airfield in France for ex-UK squadrons, on 12 October. No. 64 Squadron was next and was formed at the airfield on 1 August 1916 from a nucleus of No. 45 Squadron, and was equipped with Henry Farman F20s, to be followed by BE2Cs, Pups and 504s before moving on to St-Omer on 14 October. No. 72 Squadron came from Netheravon on 1 November 1917 with Pups and 504s, but a little over a month later was *en route* for the Persian Gulf. No. 87 Squadron, which flew in from Upavon on 15 September 1917 with various aircraft, moved on to Hounslow on 19 December. From Dover (Swingate) on 26 November 1917 came No. 110 Squadron with various aircraft, which moved on to Kenley on 15 June 1918. No. 122 Squadron was formed at the airfield on 1 January 1918, but was disbanded before the war's end. Finally No. 13 Squadron came from St-Omer on 27 March 1919, but was not disbanded until 31 December that year. There is no recorded post-war use of Sedgeford.

Therfield 2 miles SSE of Royston

The only recorded use of this landing ground during the First World War was for detachments of No. 75 Squadron, Goldhangar, between 12 October 1916 and 8 September 1917 . The field was abandoned after the war.

Thetford 3 miles SE of Thetford

Thetford was a busy airfield during the First World War. Nos 35, 38 and 77 Squadrons were formed here in 1916, No. 80 Squadron in 1917 and No. 128 Squadron in 1918. Nos 25, 51 and 119 Squadrons were based here between 1915 and 1918.

Tydd St Mary 6 miles NNE of Wisbech

No. 51 Squadron detached its aircraft from Marham between 7 August 1917 and the Armistice. There is no recorded post-war use.

Wyton NE of Huntingdon

The site was opened in 1916 for reserve and training squadrons, but closed after the First World War. Wyton was reopened during the 1930s expansion and remains an active RAF station to this day.

Yelling 6 miles ENE of St Neots

No. 75 Squadron detached its BE2cs to Yelling between 12 October 1916 and 8 September 1917. There is no recorded postwar use.

A barrack block built at Bircham Newton in 1929.

Barclays Bank seemed to have taken a liking to what was once Bircham Newton's guardroom built to Pattern 166 of 1923.

Mullion Airship Station – Cornwall.

Netheravon Camp in 1918.

Airfields and Seaplane Bases of Lincolnshire and East Midlands

Bracebridge Heath *S of Lincoln, E of A15*
Bracebridge Heath was opened in late 1917 and became the home of No. 4 Acceptance Park. The airfield was closed in 1920 following the rundown of the RAF.

Buckminster *1 mile E of Buckminster*
Buckminster was opened in 1916 and housed C Flight of No. 38 (HD) Squadron, which had its headquarters at Melton Mowbray. Equipped with FE2Bs, C Flight was employed on anti-Zeppelin patrols. In May 1918 this unit left, to be replaced in August 1918 by No. 90 (HD) Squadron with Camels and Avro 504s used as night-fighters. A further use of the airfield was as an aircraft acceptance park. No. 90 Squadron was disbanded in June 1919, and when the acceptance park closed the airfield was returned to agriculture.

Cranwell *12 miles S of Grantham*
Work began on the RNAS shore station *Daedalus* on 28 December 1915. There were two airfields, one south of the B1429 with wooden hangars and two flight sheds, and a second to the north of the road with several balloon sheds on its northern edge. The station was opened on 1 April 1916 as the RNAS Training Establishment, tasked with training officers and ratings of the Royal Navy on aeroplanes, Kite balloons and dirigibles, and in July 1916 the station received a visit from the King. In April 1919 HMS *Daedalus* became RAF Cranwell. Originally the station was home to Nos 201, 202 and 213 TDS, later renamed 56, 57 and 58 TDS respectively. Constituent units included the Airship Training Wing, Boys' Training Wing, Aeroplane Repair Section, PT School and Wireless Operators' School. When the First World War ended, the future of Cranwell was in doubt, but Trenchard, backed by Winston Churchill, wanted the station for his Cadet College, far enough away from the 'fleshpots' of London. And so it became, the first course for officer cadets commencing on 5 February 1920. A wide variety of aircraft operated from the two airfields. The 504Ks, which had wheels painted to denote the cadet flight to which they belonged, were replaced by 504Ns in 1927. In 1921 Snipes came to Cranwell and remained there until September 1927, to be replaced by Siskins for those cadets going on to fighters. The station was also associated with long-distance flights, such as the Horsley flight to the Persian Gulf by Flight Lieutenant Carr in May 1927 and the Fairey long-range monoplane flight to Karachi. These flights came under the RAF Long-Range Development Flight formed in 1927.

Digby (Scopwick) *W of B1191 from Scopwick village*
Work began on the site in 1917, and hangars and accommodation were to be provided to take the overflow from HMS *Daedalus*. When further buildings, such as messes and barrack blocks, were built in 1918 it was possible for Scopwick, as it was then called, to operate as a separate station. In March 1918 it was ready to receive Handley Page bombers, and the airfield was administered by No. 12 Group. In November 1918 No. 59 TDS was formed, but the Armistice came before it was fully established. It seems that early in 1919 this unit became No. 59 TS, tasked with the training of bomber and fighter pilots. During the Irish troubles Shotwick airfield near Chester became the jumping-off point for aircraft crossing the Irish Sea to Dublin, and confusion arose in correspondence and signals. So Scopwick became RAF Digby and Shotwick became RAF Sealand. In April 1920 No. 3 Flying Training School formed at the station to come under No. 23 Group. However, with the rundown of the postwar RAF No. 3 FTS was disbanded and the station was placed on C & M. It was not dormant for long, and in June 1924 No. 2 FTS moved in from Duxford with Avro 504s, Snipes and 'Brisfits'. Development and expansion took place, with married quarters being added, and in 1926 Vimys joined the other aircraft on the inventory. Three very famous names are associated with Digby. The OC in 1918 was Squadron Leader D'Albiac DSO, later Air Marshal Sir John D'Albiac KCVO, KBE, CB, DSO. Then in April 1921, Squadron Leader A.T. Harris AFC became OC No. 3 FTS, and was later to become 'Bomber' Harris, the AOC-in-C Bomber Command during the Second World War. Finally there was Wing Commander A.W. Tedder, who came to Digby in 1924 as OC No. 2 FTS, and later became MRAF Lord Tedder GCB, DCL, LLD.

Doncaster *SW of racecourse on A638*
This racecourse turned First World War airfield housed No. 15 RAS from January 1916, followed by No. 47 Squadron from June of that year. Then No. 46 RS formed there in the October but moved out shortly afterwards. In 1917 it was the turn of the Canadians, when No. 80 TS formed, but it moved to Canada shortly thereafter. On 15 March No. 90 TS formed at Doncaster and moved on in the April. So the airfield saw many comings and goings. From February to November 1917 No. 82 Squadron with AWFK8s was the resident unit until it moved to France. No. 49 RS also left, to be followed by No. 47 TDS comprising Nos 41 and 49 TSs with Avro 504s and SE5s. The depot station and the airfield closed in 1919.

Elsham Wolds *approx. 7 miles NE of A15*
Elsham Wolds became a landing ground for HD duties, and a detached flight of No. 33 Squadron used this field from December 1916 until after the Armistice, when the field was abandoned. This was C Flight, equipped with FE2Bs.

**AIRFIELDS AND SEAPLANE BASES OF LINCONSHIRE AND THE EAST
THE EAST MIDLANDS ON 11 NOVEMBER 1918 AND 31 DECEMBER 1929**

Elsham Wolds

Doncaster

Gainsborough

SHEFFIELD

SCUNTHORPE

Kirton-in-Lindsey

Helmswell

Immingham

GRIMSBY

Kelstern

North Killinghome

Greenland Top

North Coates

South Carlton

Waddington

LINCOLN

Scampton

Bracebridge Heath

Papplewick Moor

Hucknall

NOTTINGHAM

DERBY

Cranwell

Digby

BOSTON

Freiston

Harlaxton

Buckminster

Spittlegate

Grimsthorpe

*Holbeach
(1928)*

*Sutton Bridge
(1926)*

LEICESTER

STAMFORD

Freiston E of Boston on Wash mud flats

Freiston was opened in September 1917 as an RNAS station under the control of HMS *Daedalus*, sited on the mud flats and marshes of the Wash, because it was ideal for live firing and bombing. Freiston thus became an armament training school. With the coming of the RAF in April 1918, No. 4 Aerial School of Fighting was formed at the airfield with DH5s and SE5As, only to be renamed No. 4 Fighting School, training scout pilots in gunnery. When this unit was disbanded in March 1920, Freiston closed.

Gainsborough Lincolnshire

It has already been explained that HD squadrons during the First World War usually had a squadron headquarters in one location with three detached flights at airfields close by, although one of the flights might be collocated with squadron HQ. The German Zeppelin L.13 had dropped bombs on Gainsborough, and even though little damage was caused, the War Office deemed dispersal of squadron flights necessary. (On Second World War airfields squadrons were based on one airfield, but with paved runways and perimeter tracks it was possible to site aircraft well away from the main station buildings on dispersal pans yet get them to the runway quickly for take-off. Refer to the airfield diagram at the beginning of the chapter.) No. 33 Squadron had its headquarters at Gainsborough, and a small landing ground was opened in December 1916. The squadron's detached FE2Bs and FE2Ds were elsewhere, but could be flown in to the HQ airfield for maintenance or repair. In June 1918 the squadron HQ moved to Kirton-in-Lindsey, and after the Armistice Gainsborough was abandoned.

Greenland Top W of Grimsby and NE of Keelby
Opened in 1918 and housed 251 Squadron, 505 Flight, with DH6s on A/S duties. The airfield closed in 1919.

Grimsthorpe 4 miles NW of Bourne
This was an Emergency Landing Ground only during the First World War, but was not retained afterwards.

Harlaxton 2 miles S of Grantham
Harlaxton was built by the RFC in 1916 as a training aerodrome. In November that year No. 44 RS moved in, equipped with 504s, BE2s and RE7s. Renamed No. 44 TS, the unit remained there until November 1917. A succession of training units used Harlaxton, and following the reorganization of flying training establishments in 1918 the airfield became home to No. 40 TDS in the summer of 1918. When this unit disbanded the airfield closed in 1919.

Hemswell (formerly Harpswell) approx. 13 miles N of Lincoln
This airfield bore the name of Harpswell during the First World War. In common with other sites selected along the Lincoln Cliff, it was an ideal site for a training station. The airfield was a late starter, not being opened until June 1918, to house No. 199 TS, tasked with training pilots and observers for night operations, but when the unit disbanded in June 1919 the airfield became redundant and was closed.

Holbeach on mud flats of the Wash
Holbeach was sited on the mud flats of the Wash near Holbeach St Matthew and was opened as a bombing and gunnery range in 1928. Still in use.

Hucknall On the outskirts of Hucknall
The site was purchased from the Duke of Portland, and the airfield was opened as a training ground. It remained in this role throughout the war, training the Americans as well as RFC/RAF personnel. It went out of use after the Armistice, and the buildings were sold off.

Immingham On the S bank of the Humber
From April 1918 it was home to No. 8 Balloon Station RAF, but closed with the disbandment of the unit in 1919.

Kelstern NW of Louth
Used as an emergency landing ground by Home Defence squadrons during the First World War, and the site was discarded on cessation of hostilities.

Kirton-in-Lindsey N of Lincoln
Opened when B Flight of No. 33 Squadron moved in during December 1916 using Avro 504 night-fighters.

The airfield was abandoned in June 1919.

North Coates S of Grimsby
Opened in 1918 to house 404 Flight of No. 248 Squadron employed on coastal patrols. The unit was disbanded in March 1919 and the airfield closed.

North Killinghome NW of Grimsby
North Killinghome was opened as a seaplane base in August 1914 at the northern end of the Killinghome Marshes on the Lincolnshire side of the Humber. There was also an airfield, so that coastal patrols could be carried out by both seaplanes and land-planes. During the latter part of 1917 Redcar and other Yorkshire-based squadrons used the airfield. In July 1918 North Killinghome was taken over by the US Navy, to be returned to the RAF in January 1919. In October of that year the base closed completely.

Papplewick Moor approx. 7 miles N of Nottingham
In 1918 Papplewick Moor served as a relief landing ground for No. 15 Training Depot Station, but when this unit was disbanded in 1919 the landing ground was abandoned.

Scampton (Brattlebury) N of Lincoln
Brattlebury opened in November 1916 and initially housed No. 49 RS, which then moved to Grantham, to be replaced by No. 37 RS the same month. In December No. 33 (HD) Squadron detached one of its flights to the airfield with FE2/FE2Bs. A typical anti-Zeppelin patrol would be from Spurn Head to just south of Lincoln, but since the Zeppelins came over at 18,000 ft and the FE2Bs had a service ceiling of 12,000 ft, there was no hope of catching them. The 504s and RE8s of No. 60 RS arrived in April 1917, to be renamed No. 60 TS. This was followed in July by the formation of No. 81 Squadron, a fighter unit, strangely also classified as a training squadron. On 15 September 1917 No. 11 TS moved in from Grantham, and in July the following year all three of the aforementioned units were merged into No. 34 TDS, flying, among other types, Dolphins and Camels. After the Armistice the remaining machines and personnel were transferred to No. 46 TDS at South Carlton and the station closed. By 1920 no trace was left of what was to become one of the most famous stations of the RAF in the Second World War and afterwards, RAF Scampton.

South Carlton just N of Lincoln
South Carlton opened in November 1916 and housed a variety of training units. The airfield also acted as a demobilization base. When the last unit left in April 1920 the airfield closed.

Spittlegate E of Grantham

First constructed in 1916, Spittlegate started as and remained a training airfield throughout the First World War. Used immediately post-war by a variety of operational units, and during 1920 No. 6 FTS was formed here. In April 1922 No. 3 FTS moved in. In June 1928, when Nos 39 and 100 Squadrons left, it was solely a training station.

Sutton Bridge E of Kings Lynn

Sutton Bridge was first used in 1926 as a temporary armament practice camp for use by fighter squadrons or advanced flying training units of the RAF. It was not established as a full-time permanent RAF station until 1936.

Waddington S of Lincoln

The station opened in November 1916 as a flying training station. The station was closed in 1919 but it was one of the few First World War stations to retain its buildings and airfield during the rundown immediately after the war. The station reopened in October 1926 as the base for the newly formed No. 503 Special Reserve Squadron. This was a bombing unit initially equipped with Fairey Fawns. In February 1929 these were replaced by Hyderabads (see airfield layout below).

Spittlegate, A First World War airfield which survived the post-war rundown.

Waddington during the 1920s. This is a typical layout of the period. Waddington was given a major face-lift in the 1930s in conformity with the changed airfield layouts of the major expansion period.

Waddington in 1918, home to Nos, 47 and 48 Training Squadrons.

Airfields and Seaplane Bases of the South-West

Beaulieu
Beaulieu was used by RFC/RAF during the First World War but was put up for sale by the Aerodrome Disposal Board in July1919. The site was sold by auction in 1920.

Boscombe Down Wiltshire
The building of the aerodrome was about 50 per cent complete by the end of 1918. Despite the ending of the war, construction of six GS sheds and a similar-sized repair shed (180 ft × 100 ft) was continued, which, when completed in 1919, was used for storage. The station closed in 1920.

Brockworth nr Hucclecote, Gloucestershire
At least one operational squadron, No. 90, briefly dwelt at Brockworth, leaving Shotwick on 15 July 1918 newly equipped with Sopwith Dolphins, but the squadron was disbanded on the 29th of that month. Brockworth was also an aircraft acceptance park for Gloster aircraft during the First World War. In 1919 the AAP was disbanded and the RAF withdrew, though the Air Board retained ownership of the assembly sheds and used them for storage. Gloster purchased the airfield, hangars and offices in November 1926. Before that Gloster had rented the hangar space.

Bude Cornwall
Bude was a mooring-out site for Coastal-type airships for RNAS Mullion. Operational patrols of St George's Channel and the Bristol Channel areas were the day-to-day task of the Bude detachment, which had become part of No. 9 Group RAF by October 1918. When a decision was made in early 1919 to cease non-rigid airship operations, the Bude substation was soon abandoned.

Calshot SE of Fawley
Calshot was used by the RNAS during the First World War for Channel patrols using floatplanes and then flying-boats. When the RAF was formed in April 1918, Calshot became HQ No. 10 Group, and was the base for No. 240 Squadron. Post-war it became the School of Naval Cooperation and Aerial Navigation, but was retitled RAF Base Calshot on 5 February 1922. Southamptons followed the Felixstowe flying-boats, and the station was used by the High-Speed Flight training for the Schneider Trophy races between 1927 and 1931. From 1 January 1929 until March 1937 201 Squadron was the only operational unit based at Calshot.

Chickerell NW of Weymouth
Chickerell was originally established in 1918 as one of a series of small aerodromes strategically positioned around the coastline of Britain for use by short-range anti-submarine aircraft. D Flight of No. 253 Squadron with DH6s was detached from Bembridge in June 1918, and aircraft of No. 241 Squadron came from Portland in August. But post-war it was planned to be part of a chain of civil aerodromes, and civil aviation came under the Air Ministry at that time. And so Chickerell was retained during the 1920s. From 1927 to 1930 the airfield was used as a temporary base for Fleet Air Arm units exercising with ships off Portland.

Falmouth Cornwall, N of town in outer harbour
Falmouth was used occasionally by small detachments of seaplanes during the First World War, and moorings between Trefusis Point and the village of Flushing were used by squadron cruises during the inter-war years.

Filton 4 miles N of Bristol
This was the base of the British and Colonial Aeroplane Co. Ltd from February 1910. Expansion took place on the outbreak of the First World War, and at the Armistice 3,000 persons were on the payroll. From December 1915 the RFC made use of the airfield to work up new squadrons before they left for France. The South-West Aircraft Acceptance Park was formed at Filton to process aircraft completed by the factories in the area. Post-war the company was awarded a contract to run a Reserve School for the RAF, which opened on 15 May 1923 using Bristol aircraft types. On 14 June 1929 No. 501 (County of Gloucester) Squadron was formed as a Special Reserve squadron flying Avro 504s.

Laira Devon, old Plymouth
Laira was a mooring-out station for RNAS Mullion. Commissioned in May 1918 for two SS or Coastal-type airships, Laira came under No. 9 Group RAF, but was closed in 1919 along with Bude.

Lake Down Wiltshire, 7 miles NNW of Salisbury
Otherwise known as Druid's Lodge, Lake Down was requisitioned early in 1917 as a flying training station. No. 2 TDS formed here on 15 August 1917 with BE2Cs, RE8s and DH4s, but moved to Stonehenge in December. This unit was replaced by Nos 107 and 108 Squadrons, which were day-bomber units 'working up' for operations. No. 136 Squadron also formed here on 1 April 1917, and then No. 14 TDS formed on 6 June 1917. To make way for the TDS No. 107 Squadron went to France and No. 108 Squadron to Kenley. Then No. 136 Squadron was disbanded. Construction of the station was almost complete by early August 1918, but No. 14 TDS was reduced to a cadre by the end of the year. No. 201 Squadron moved in briefly before it too was disbanded at Eastleigh. Accordingly the buildings were removed and the site was auctioned. Lake Down was completely abandoned by 1920.

AIRFIELDS AND SEAPLANE BASES OF THE SOUTH-WEST ON 11 NOVEMBER 1918 AND 31 DECEMBER 1929.

Larkhill 4 miles NW of Amesbury

Old Larkhill is one of the oldest military airfields in British aviation history, preceding even the formation of the RFC. In the spring of 1911 No. 2 (Aeroplane) Company was formed here, becoming No. 3 Squadron on formation of the RFC in April 1912, but with the coming of war in 1914 the airfield site became covered with corrugated-iron huts as the barracks expanded. Aircraft were by then operating from such nearby airfields as Old Sarum, Upavon and Netheravon. The site was maintained for use by aircraft taking part in the annual Army exercises on Salisbury Plain during the inter-war years, the participating aircraft usually taking off from Sarum.

Leighterton Gloucestershire

Leighterton was built in 1917 for the Australians, and was opened in February 1918 as No. 2 Station of the 1st Wing, Australian Flying Corps, housing No. 8 (Training) Squadron equipped with Sopwith Pups and Camels to provide embryo fighter pilots. This unit was followed by No. 7 (Training) Squadron to train pilots and observers on Avro 504s, BE2Es and RE8s for reconnaissance duties over France. By October 1918 an aircraft repair section had been formed at Leighterton capable of dealing with all types except the Snipe, which had to go to Yate for

crash repair. There was a rapid rundown after the First World War, and although building work continued until early 1919, Australian personnel started to leave from the February. Nos 28 and 66 Squadrons came to the airfield awaiting disbandment, and the government auctioned the assets in 1919.

Lopcombe Corner Wiltshire, 8¹/₂ miles NE of Salisbury

Lopcombe Corner was opened in September 1917 as No. 3 TDS, a single-seater fighter pilot training school. The tail skids cut the thin turf to stir up the chalk, forming dust clouds in fine weather. Following the formation of the RAF, the unit operated as part of No. 34 Wing, No. 8 Group, using 504Ks and Camels. Following the Armistice Lopcombe gradually wound down during 1919. Nos 74 and 85 Squadrons were housed there on their return from the continent in February, but the remnants of these units were dispersed in July. In November 1919 the aerodrome officially closed to aircraft except in an emergency. A series of auctions was completed in 1920 and the disposal of the airfield completed.

Merifield Cornwall, 2¹/₂ miles WNW of Devonport

Merifield commenced operations in 1918 with No. 16 Balloon Base, No. 72 Wing, No. 9 Group. From here Kite balloons were deployed for convoy protection duties. Merifield was closed after the Armistice.

Minchinhampton Gloucestershire, 1¹/₂ miles SE of Chalford

Minchinhampton was opened for the 1st Wing Australian Flying Corps, No. 6 (Training) Squadron, which arrived form Ternhill on 25 February 1918 and was joined by No. 5 (Training) Squadron on 2 April. By August 1918 the establishment was twelve Camels, twelve SE5As and twenty-four Avro 504s, although many more machines, including Pups, were actually on the strength. Flying ceased at the Armistice and the two training squadrons were disbanded. When the Australians went home the station was all but deserted. The buildings were auctioned in 1920 and the site was cleared for agriculture.

Moreton Dorset, 4¹/₂ miles E of Dorchester

Moreton was intended to plug the gap in the chain of airship stations providing convoy coverage off the south coast of England. The land was requisitioned early in 1918, but the Armistice intervened before work on the airship sheds and a gas plant was completed. The work was terminated and the site cleared.

Mountbatten (Cattewater) 1 mile S of Plymouth across the Sound

Cattewater was recognized as a natural seaplane base early in the First World war, and it became RNAS Cattewater in February 1917. After the formation of the RAF in April 1918, two large hangars were built alongside the Cattewater. During August 1918 No. 237 Squadron with Short 184s and No. 238 Squadron with Felixstowe F2As formed here. Most building work was completed as the war ended, but patrols continued up to the end of 1918 (in case any U-boat commanders had not heard that the war had ended). No. 237 Squadron disbanded in May 1919 and No. 238 Squadron remained in cadre strength as a storage unit for spare flying-boats until it was closed down in March 1922. RAF Cattewater was put into reserve until 1925, when an Act of Parliament secured the land for the Crown to become a permanent base. Be that as it may, it remained dormant until No. 482 Flight formed with Southamptons in September 1928, becoming No. 203 Squadron on 1 January 1929. No. 204 Squadron also took up residence there and was the sole unit based at Cattewater when No. 203 Squadron left for the Middle East in March 1929. But when Cattewater became RAF Mountbatten on 1 October 1929, No. 209 Squadron was formed there shortly afterwards with Iris flying-boats.

Mullion Cornwall, 2 miles NW of Mullion village

The RNAS Mullion was commissioned in June 1916 This airship station on the Lizard peninsula was intended to cover the Western Approaches. On 3 April 1917 Mullion became part of South-Western Group. Early in 1918 DH4s joined the airships at Mullion to provide inshore patrols. In August 1918 ex-naval squadrons became part of the RAF, with No. 236 Squadron at Mullion with DH6s and DH9s. At the Armistice the airships were deflated and the land-planes were flown occasionally until No. 236 Squadron was disbanded on 15 May 1919. Mullion was soon cleared and abandoned.

Netheravon 6 miles N of Amesbury

On 16 June 1913 No. 3 Squadron RFC moved from Larkhill, and two days later No. 4 Squadron moved from Farnborough to take up residence. In 1914 the whole military wing of the RFC assembled here to test the use of aircraft in war. Nos 3 and 4 Squadrons then left for France as part of the Expeditionary Force, to be replaced by No. 1 Squadron in November, and this unit acted as a training school until March 1915. Since Netheravon was thus being used to build up new squadrons, it soon began operating reserve and school squadrons, which became No. 4 Reserve Wing in 1917. During 1918 Netheravon housed both Nos 8 and 12 Training Depot Stations, flying types as diverse as Avro 504Ks And HP 0/400s. After the First World War Netheravon was used to disband operational units, e.g. 35, 42, 52 and 208 Squadrons. No. 12 TDS was disbanded in April 1919 but was replaced by Netheravon Flying Training School in July 1919, to be renamed No. 1 Flying Training School (No. 1 FTS) in the December. In 1924 a gradual expansion started with a commitment to train Fleet Air Arm pilots. A number of operational squadrons were based at Netheravon until No. 23 Group took over the station in April 1935.

Newlyn Cornwall, 2 miles S of Penzance

Newlyn was a seaplane base with Short 184s. These aircraft cooperated with the airships out of Mullion and the flying-boats at Tresco in the Scilly Isles to provide continuous cover for the convoys. In August 1918 No. 235 Squadron was formed at Newlyn, and a number of Short 320s arrived to supplement the Short 184s. Following the Armistice No. 235 Squadron was disbanded on 22 February 1919. Although the station was closed it remained on the Air Ministry's emergency base list and was visited by the Seaplane Development Flight in August 1922. But the site was not favoured and finally went out of use in the late 1920s.

Okehampton (Folly Gate) 1¹/₂ miles NW of Okehampton

At Folly Gate in 1928 this airfield was opened up for Army Cooperation exercises, i.e. a landing ground for aircraft flying on artillery observation practices from May to September. Bristol F2Bs of 13 and 16 Squadrons were involved and the personnel lived in tents on the airfield. These detachments continued up to 1939. There were no facilities at the landing ground.

Old Sarum (Ford Farm) 2 miles N of Salisbury

The site was acquired by the War Department in 1917, and huts and hangars were built in the August to house Nos 98, 99 and 103 Squadrons. They were day-bomber squadrons and trained there before moving to France in the spring of 1918. By the time Ford Farm had been renamed Old Sarum, No. 11 TDS moved in, remaining there until the end of the war with Avro DH4s and DH6s. Old Sarum was retained after the war, and the School of Army Cooperation was formed there in 1920, running courses for Army officers and the RAF pilots and observers of the Army Cooperation squadrons to learn artillery observation and tactical reconnaissance. From April 1924, Nos 13, 16 and 59 Squadrons were all attached to the school.

Padstow Cornwall, 1½ miles NW of Padstow

To increase inshore patrol capability in the SW peninsula, Padstow airfield was chosen more for its position than its suitability as an airfield. By removing the Cornish drystone walls a 1,500 ft landing run for lightly loaded biplanes was provided. The RNAS airfield became operational by March 1918. The DH4 and DH9 aircraft became No. 250 Squadron RAF, and this airfield was the most difficult one from which to operate. It remained open until March 1919, but when No. 250 Squadron was disbanded the site was returned to agriculture.

Portland 3 miles S of Weymouth

The harbour at Portland was a natural choice for a seaplane base, given the number of U-boat attacks in the English Channel, and Short floatplanes were based there from 28 September 1916. With the formation of the RAF in 1918 the base was taken over by the Air Ministry, and in the August No. 241 Squadron was formed as part of No. 10 (Operations) Group until it was disbanded in June 1919. Portland then reverted to naval use and was the main anti-submarine base for the Royal Navy after the war.

Porton Down Wiltshire, 5 miles NE of Salisbury

The site was opened in 1920 as a bombing range, but became increasingly associated with the Chemical Defence Establishment. A landing ground was laid alongside the bombing range for use by Army Cooperation aircraft during exercises.

Prawle Point Devon, 3 miles SE of Salcombe

Prawle Point landing ground was opened in April 1917 with nominal facilities to support four aircraft with personnel under canvas, but demands made by the forces on the Western Front resulted in the withdrawal of these aircraft in August that year. However, following the resurrection of the Coastal Patrol Scheme in 1918, Prawle Point was reactivated with DH6 and DH9 aircraft, and the RNAS flights became No. 254 Squadron

RAF. More substantial accommodation was being built at the time of the Armistice, but all flying then ceased and No. 254 Squadron disbanded on 22 February 1919. The airfield remained open a little longer for use by an artillery-cooperation squadron, but when that was withdrawn in August, Prawle Point was closed the following year.

Rollestone 1 mile E of Shrewton village

The War Office site had been in existence since No. 1 Balloon School was formed in July 1916 to train personnel in the use of observation balloons. The unit survived the wholesale cuts in the services during the period 1919–22, and the unit at Rollestone was renamed the RAF School of Balloon Training and continued in operation throughout the 1920s and much of the 1930s. The balloons were housed in large Bessoneau hangars, which were easily damaged in high winds. The balloons were usually Type R of 35,000 ft capacity.

Tilshead Wiltshire, 1 mile W of Tilshead village

Used from 1925 as a landing ground for aircraft in Army Cooperation duties during annual Army manoeuvres on Salisbury Plain.

Toller Somerset, 6 miles NE of Bridport

This airship station was constructed in the spring of 1918 and later that year was commissioned in No. 9 Group, from which Zero non-rigid airships were operated. Toller was deactivated in December 1918 and abandoned early in 1919.

Torquay Devon, close to town centre

Torquay was opened early in 1918 with Short 184 floatplanes. Although a slipway was constructed it remained the usual practice to hoist the aircraft into the water using a crane. Space was at a premium and in the event only six 184s could be accommodated. No. 239 Squadron was formed in August, taking over No. 418 Flight, and the squadron was disbanded on 15 May 1919. The site was handed over to the Government Surplus Property Board in August, when the buildings were auctioned.

Tresco Isles of Scilly, ½ mile S of New Grimsby

Nearby Port Mellen had been considered as a base for the Curtiss H12 flying-boats, but the stretch of water needed for taking off was considered too 'open'. So Flight Commander R.B. Maycock RN surveyed the islands and recommended a site on the almost land-locked New Grimsby Harbour. Tresco provided an excellent take-off and landing area for the six-boat detachment. Felixstowe F2As and F3s followed, but on 1 July 1918 only one F3 and a Short 184 were available to mount attacks on U-boats. In August the detached flight became No. 234 Squadron, and by the end of September eleven boats were on strength. Following the Armistice No. 234 Squadron was disbanded in May 1919, and the air station was closed soon afterwards.

Upavon Wiltshire, 1½ miles SE of Upavon village

Upavon is one of the earliest known military airfields in Britain and began life as an aerodrome in 1912. When buildings were completed in June it became the Central Flying School (CFS) of the newly formed RFC. When the country went to war it differed little in its role from other advanced training units apart from the Experimental Flight, which formed in November 1914 to evaluate new equipment. This became the Aircraft and Armament Experimental Flight, which moved to Martlesham Heath in January 1917. From then until the end of the First World War Upavon turned out a steady stream of pilots for the squadrons in France. There was confusion about Upavon's future when the Armistice was signed, but the station regained its role as CFS for the RAF, starting operations in March 1920, turning out flying instructors. The Avro 504K was the standard trainer, with the Snipe for advanced work. On 30 April 1924 No. 3 Squadron came to Upavon from Manston with its Snipes, and later the station was placed under No. 3 Group. As the CFS moved to Wittering in October 1924, No. 17 Squadron arrived from Hawkinge with its Woodcock IIs, and for three years Nos 3 And 17 Squadrons were the only night-fighter squadrons in the RAF.

Upton Dorset, 2 miles NW of Poole

Upton was commissioned in 1918 as a mooring-out base for SS Zero non-rigid airships detached from Mullion. The site was quickly abandoned after the Armistice.

Watchet Somerset, 1 mile E of Watchet

During the 1920s the Army established an anti-aircraft gunnery range near Watchet, using it throughout each summer for training camps. Targets were towed by aircraft operating from Weston Zoyland, and to facilitate liaison a piece of flattish ground was cleared alongside Watchet Camp. Aircraft up to the size of Horsleys used it on occasion.

Weston Zoyland Somerset, 4 miles SE of Bridgwater

Weston Zoyland was first used by the RAF when Horsleys of No. 100 Squadron spent a summer camp there in 1926 to cooperate with the gunners at nearby Watchet. In 1929 the Night-Flying Flight, Biggin Hill, took over and was renamed the Army Cooperations Flight, which then took over the summer camps at Weston Zoyland. They had become an annual event when the landing ground was opened up.

Westward Ho Devon, 2½ miles N of Bideford

Westward Ho was established early in 1918 to operate ex-trainer DH6s on coastal patrol work, and Nos 502 and

503 (Special Duty) Flights became operational in June 1918, both being absorbed by No. 260 Squadron, which was disbanded on 22 February 1919. The golf links were restored to their former glory.

Yate Gloucestershire, 10 miles NE of Bristol

The airfield was built during 1916/17 to provide test and delivery facilities for No. 3(Western) Aircraft Repair Depot. After the First World War Yate was abandoned by the Air Ministry and the buildings remained empty until taken over by George Parnell & Co. in 1925.

First World War hangar, Helperby, Yorkshire.

Old Sarum Airfield, Wiltshire, a typical grass airfield layout.

Yatesbury Wiltshire, 4 miles E of Calne

Yatesbury was opened in 1916 as a training station and was home to several units, including Nos 36 and 37 Training Depot Stations, using a variety of aircraft, including the ubiquitous Avro 504K. After the Armistice the TDSs ceased to operate and the airfield closed in 1919.

Airfields in the Cotswolds and Central Midlands

Bicester 1½ miles NE of Bicester town

The airfield came into use in late 1917, and from January the following year No. 118 Squadron mobilized here, remaining until November. In October 1918 No. 44 Training Depot Station arrived, to be followed by No. 2 Squadron, the latter remaining until 19 September 1919, to be replaced by No. 5 Squadron with Bristol Fighters. When this unit was disbanded on 20 January 1920, Bicester closed in the March, but was not to remain unused for long. In 1925 the station was reactivated when the Air Ministry decided to station bomber squadrons in the Oxford Area. The new station was officially opened in January 1928 to accept the Hawker Horsleys of No. 100 Squadron from Spittlegate. They remained there until it was decided to redeploy the torpedo squadron to Donibristle in November 1930.

Cardington 3 miles SE of Bedford

Cardington first came into use when Short Brothers became involved in airship construction in 1915. The site was chosen for its scope for development and communication links, and the firm built a housing estate for the workers, naming it 'Shortstown'. When the Admiralty planned to take over Cardington, Short was meant to run the station and build airships there, but the firm did not agree to the terms for the take-over and the site was nationalized. With the departure of Short in April 1919, the Royal Airship Works came into being, and the R31, R37 and R38 were all associated with Cardington during this period. However, the R38 ran into numerous problems, finally breaking into two on 24 August 1921. With work on airships suspended for the time being, Cardington was placed under Care and Maintenance between 1921 and 1924. With the decision to build two airships for use on long-haul civil international routes, Cardington came back into use. The state funding for the R101 was justified on the grounds that the airship could also be used by the Royal Navy in time of war. It was to be built and test-flown from Cardington. Additionally the R33 was reconditioned at the station, indeed it was the success gained with the R33 that swung government opinion behind building the R100, the privately built airship, and the R101.

Castle Bromwich 4 miles ENE of Birmingham

The War Office requisitioned the site in 1914 for flying schools, which included No. 5 Training Squadron. Nos 19 and 55 Squadrons also formed here. Others units came and went, and an aircraft acceptance park was established in April 1918 to test locally built HP 0/400s and SE5As. Castle Bromwich was acquired by the Air Board in August 1919, but it was initially used for civil aviation. On 15 October 1926 No. 605 Auxiliary Air Force Squadron (County of Warwick) formed here equipped with DH9As.

Henlow 5 miles NNW of Hitchin

Construction on the site began in April 1918, and the first unit to be established was No. 5 Eastern Aircraft Depot. Although the Americans came to Henlow they soon left after the Armistice and aircraft repair stopped. Aircraft held in store were auctioned at prices even lower than those that are quoted in Chapter 5 at the Cambridge flying school. A small aircraft cost the princely sum of 10 shillings (50p), while a bomber cost just twice that. On 1 April 1919 Henlow hit the headlines when airmen awaiting demobilization mutinied over increased working hours, and fifty six were tried by court martial. The Air Ministry planned to keep Henlow as a post-war station, and an airfield for flight testing was added. On 16 March 1920 the Inland Area Aircraft Depot was opened, where aircraft and engine repair, overhaul and reconditioning was to be undertaken. A further unit was added to the station in April 1924 in the shape of the Officers' Engineering School, which moved from Farnborough. By this time Henlow was a hive of activity, with a wide variety of aircraft and engines being worked upon. As if that wasn't enough, Henlow was chosen to house two fighter squadrons. Reference to the airfield maps in this chapter may impress the reader with the great number of airfields, seaplane bases and landing grounds surrendered just after the First World War. With the modest expansion of the home air force in the mid-1920s, the Air Ministry had to cut back or requisition new airfield sites. Until then existing bases had to be used. On 1 July 1925 Nos 23 and 43 (Fighter) Squadrons were formed at Henlow equipped with Snipes. New airfields were soon found, and both squadrons were equipped with the new Gamecock fighter before departing, 23 Squadron to Kenley and 43 Squadron to Tangmere. On 4 April 1926 Henlow was retitled the Home Aircraft Repair Depot, part of No. 21 Group. The Parachute Test Unit was then added in October 1926, an amalgam of the Parachute Test Section and the Northolt Parachute Training Section. Using Vimys, parachutists would hang on the wing struts of these aircraft while the parachute deployed, allowing the chute to open to pull them off the wing.

Rendcombe 1½ miles NE of North Cerney

It was at Rendcombe that No. 48 Squadron was first to equip with the Bristol Fighter. The airfield opened in

AIRFIELDS IN THE COTSWOLDS AND THE CENTRAL MIDLANDS ON 11 NOVEMBER 1918 AND 31 DECEMBER 1929

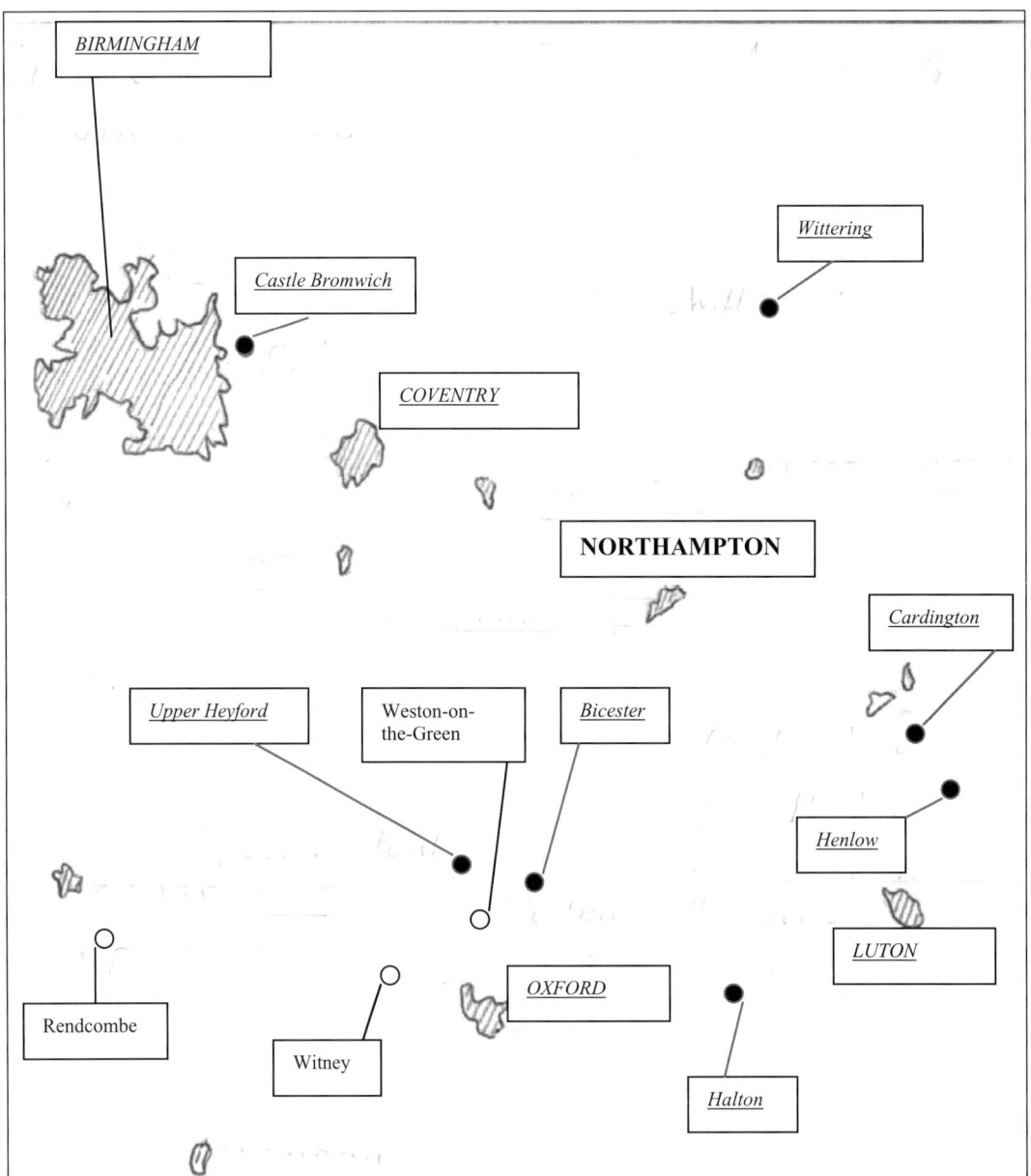

1916, and by mid-1918 housed No. 45 Training Depot Station, with elementary, advanced and operational squadrons. This meant a variety of aircraft, including BE2Cs, F2Bs and RE8s, and when the Armistice came squadrons that were disbanding came to Rendcombe. When this had taken place the station closed in late 1919 and was abandoned in early 1920.

Upper Heyford 5 miles NW of Bicester
Upper Heyford was first home to the Canadians, who formed there on 20 January 1918 as No. 123 Squadron,

later renamed No. 2 Squadron Canadian Air Force, and equipped with Sopwith Dolphins. When this squadron left it was replaced by No. 1 Squadron Canadian Air Force, the latter moving to Shoreham in March 1919. Upper Heyford was closed in 1920, but with the modest expansion scheme of the 1920s it was selected as a bomber station and reopened on 12 October 1927. No. 99 Bomber Squadron moved in from Bircham Newton, commencing the move on 12 December 1927, to be equipped with Hyderabads in the January of 1928. That same month No. 10 Squadron formed here, also with

Hyderabads. During 1929 No. 99 Squadron's aircraft were replaced with Hinaidis, very similar in appearance but powered with Bristol Jupiter engines. A lodger unit which moved into Upper Heyford during the late 1920s was the Oxford University Flight, equipped with 504Ns.

Weston-on-the-Green   3¹/₂ miles SW of Bicester
The site was acquired for military use in 1916. By July 1918 No. 28 Training Depot Station had taken up residence, using Sopwith Camels and 504s. By the time the TDS had closed in 1919 the Camels had been replaced by the ground-attack Sopwith Salamanders. Nos 2 and 18 Squadrons came to Weston prior to their disbandment, and by 1921 all activity had ceased and the site returned to grazing land.

Witney   1 mile W of Witney
During the First World War the airfield was used for training in fighter tactics. In 1918 Nos 7 and 8 Training Squadrons arrived with their 504Ks, F2Bs and DH5s. These units combined on 5 August 1918 to become No. 33 Training Depot Station, which was disbanded in 1919, whereupon Witney closed.

Wittering   3 miles S of Stamford
During the First World War the site was simply known as Stamford. Between 1916 and 1917 the airfield was home to the FE2Bs of No. 38 HD Squadron. Between August 1917 and May 1919 No. 1 Training Depot Station was at Stamford, together with C Flight of No. 90 Squadron. At the cessation of hostilities it became a storage depot and was eventually placed on C & M in January 1920. Following the defence review, the airfield was resurrected and renamed Wittering, after the nearby village, and the Central Flying School moved in, the advance party arriving on 21 July 1926. The transfer was completed on 17 October. CFS turned out flying instructors, and the school's E Flight introduced the Standard Refresher Course. Blind flying, using instruments only, was also developed by the school.

Airfields and Seaplane Bases in Yorkshire

Appleton-Wiske   SE of Darlington
A 2nd-class landing ground used by No. 76 Squadron on home-defence duties, and promptly abandoned after the First World War.

Atwick   N of Hornsea
A 2nd-class landing ground also used by No. 76 Squadron, and in regular use from May 1918 by No. 504 Flight of the RNAS, which operated DH6s on anti-submarine patrols. The ground was closed immediately after the First World War.

Barlow   S of Selby near the River Ouse
In 1917 the War Office leased the airfield to Armstrong Whitworth for construction of airships, which included the R29 and the R33. With the end of the airship era the airfield was abandoned.

Bellsize   E of Howden
This was a 1st-class landing ground, and yet another to be used by No. 76 Squadron, but being near the River Ouse the airfield was subject to flooding and was little used. It was closed after the First World War.

Beverley   N of Kingston-upon-Hull
Beverley was used by No. 90 Training Squadron from April 1917, and although flying ceased at the end of the First World War the site remained with the RAF and was used by a radio section in the 1930s.

Binsoe   NW of Ripon
This was a 3rd-class landing ground, and yet another used by the 504s of No. 76 Squadron. There were no permanent buildings and little use was made of the site. It was returned to its former use at the Armistice.

Brancroft   SE of Doncaster
This site was retained by the farmer, but A Flight of No. 33 Squadron had use of this landing ground with its 504s until 1918 in the defence of Leeds and Sheffield (munitions-producing areas). The field was abandoned at the Armistice but a site nearby later became RAF Finningley.

Carlton   W of Goole
Used as a landing ground by No. 33 Squadron but abandoned after the Armistice.

Catterick   S of Catterick village
Catterick was opened in 1914 by the RFC for pilot training and for HD units. On 1 April 1918 it became RAF Catterick, and when No. 49 TDS was disbanded at the end of the First World war, the station was retained by the Air Ministry. Permanent buildings and married quarters were added, and on 11 October 1927 No. 26 Army Cooperation Squadron was formed and Army Cooperation Command controlled the station until 1939.

Copmanthorpe   3 miles S of York
Used by A Flight of No. 76 Squadron operating 504Ks until March 1919, when the airfield was closed.

Cullingworth   W of Bradford
This grass landing strip used by Nos 33 and 76 HD Squadrons between 1916 and 1919 was abandoned after the First World War.

AIRFIELDS AND SEAPLANE BASES OF YORKSHIRE ON 11 NOVEMBER 1918 AND 31 DECEMBER 1929

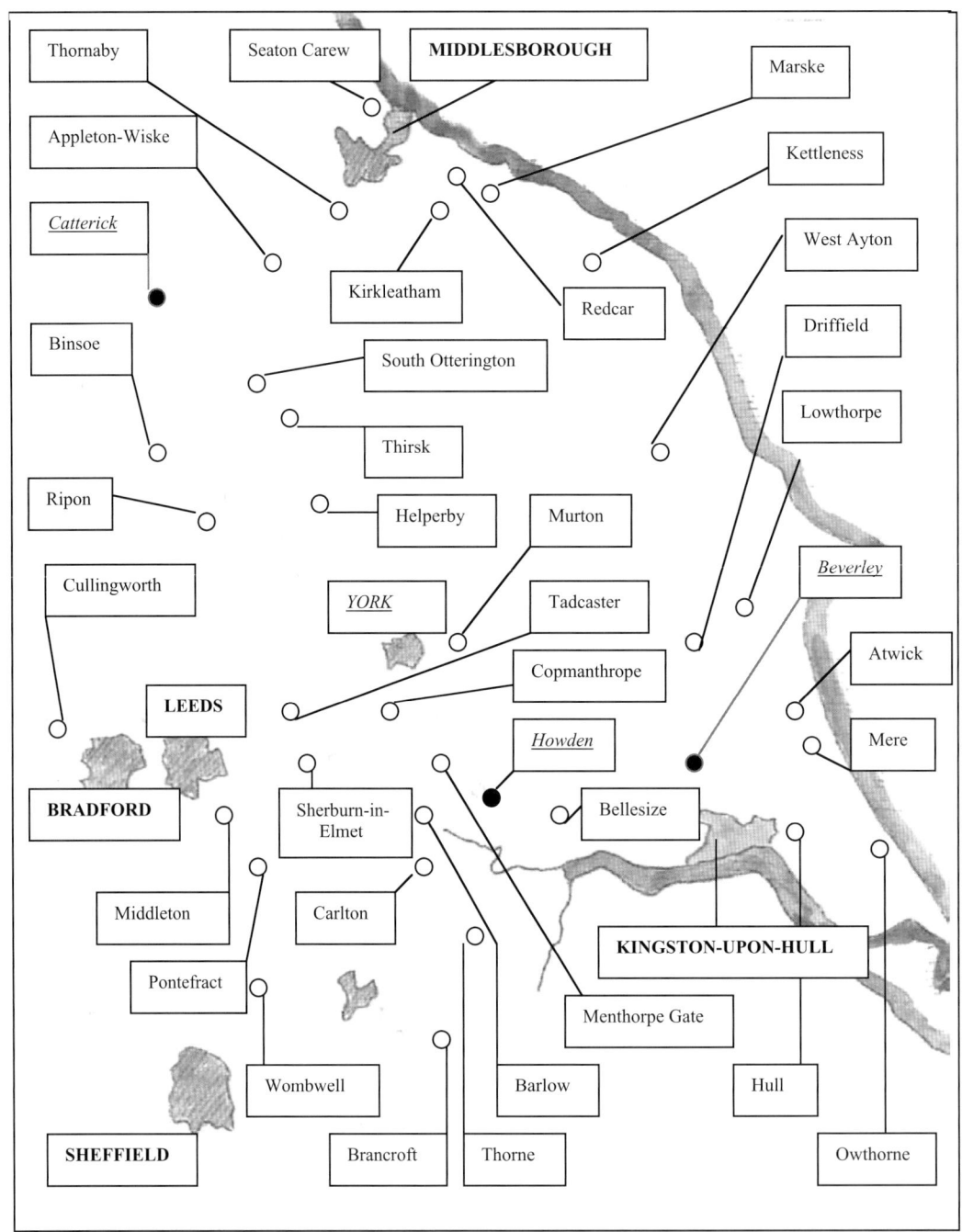

Driffield

Driffield was not developed as a permanent airfield until 1918, when it opened as Eastburn aerodrome, and on 15 July No. 21 TDS was formed here. In February 1919 construction work was finally completed, but when No. 21 TDS was disbanded the station was put under Care and Maintenance, not to be reactivated until the late 1930s.

Helperby S of Thirsk

Used by B Flight of No. 76 Squadron's 504s until March 1919. When the 504s moved to Tadcaster the airfield closed.

Hornsea Mere on W side of Hornsea

Hornsea Mere was used by the Short 184s of 404 and 405 Flights RNAS. Then Nos 504, 505, 506 and 510 Flights with DH6s became No. 251 Squadron RAF. When this unit was disbanded the site was closed.

Howden N of Goole

Howden opened in March 1916 and became one of the most important operational airship stations housing the newest non-rigid SSZ class in early 1918. In April 1918 Howden became part RN, part RAF, and at the Armistice, the airship fleet was run down but the airfield was saved from closure, as it was Trenchard's plan to maintain a nucleus of craft and personnel for airship development. However, with the tragic loss of the R38 in 1921 the programme was halted, and the last flight from Howden was on 20 September 1921. The station was closed and fell into disrepair, but in 1924 the Airship Guarantee was formed and leased Howden from the Air Ministry. Work on the R100 took place until November 1929, but then the loss of the R101 at Beauvais in France brought an end to the airship programme and the dispersal of Howden's staff. Howden's huge hangar was dismantled and sold for scrap.

Hull E of Kingston-upon-Hull

During the Great War Hull was listed as a 2nd-class landing ground and used by BE2Cs of C Flight, No. 33 Squadron, and aircraft of No. 76 Squadron. The field was closed after the Armistice.

Kettleness NW of Whitby

Kettleness was used as an RNAS landing ground during the First World War, and an inshore reconnaissance station. It was of no further use after the war but was retained as a coastguard station.

Kirkleathem W of Redcar

This mooring-out station was opened in May 1918 for airships from Howden, and used during August, September and October. It was closed immediately after the Armistice.

Lowthorpe SW of Bridlington

This was also a mooring-out station for Howden, which opened in April 1918. Between then and the end of the war an adjoining field was used by A Flight of No. 251 Squadron carrying out anti-submarine patrols. It was not selected for retention after the war, and Lowthorpe mooring-out station and airfield closed.

Marske SE of Redcar

Marske opened on 1 November 1917 for No. 4 Auxiliary School of Aerial Gunnery, using DH9s and Dolphins. On 6 May 1918, No. 2 School replaced No. 4 School as No. 2 School of Aerial Fighting and Gunnery. On 29 May 1918 this was redesignated No. 2 Fighting School, with Bristol 1Cs, Camels, DH4s and 9s. With the Armistice there was rundown and closure as No. 2 Fighting School was closed in 1919.

Middleton S of Leeds

This night landing ground was used from March to October 1916 by B Flight of No. 33 Squadron employed on home-defence duties. After that period there was little activity and the field was abandoned after the First World war.

Murton E of York

A grassed landing area used by the 504s of No. 76 Squadron. The site was abandoned after the First World War.

Owthorne immediately E of Withernsea

This was an open grass field that came into use as a landing ground in 1917. During 1918 it was used by 506 Flight's DH6s on anti-submarine patrols. The site was abandoned after the Armistice.

Pontefract between Castleford and Pontefract

This was a racecourse that became a ready-made airfield. The BE2Cs of B Flight, No. 33 Squadron, operated from here during 1916, to be followed by No. 76 Squadron. The airfield was abandoned after the Armistice.

Redcar on the outskirts of Redcar

This was another racecourse turned airfield, and used by the RNAS for training. The DH4s, BE2Cs and Bristol Scouts of No. 273 Squadron operated from Redcar on anti-submarine patrols. No. 7 (Naval) Squadron and HP 0/100s also operated on anti-submarine patrols. During 1918 C Flight of 252 Squadron with DH6s was employed on convoy escort duties. In 1918 the North Eastern Flying Instructors' School formed at Redcar, and on 5 October No. 63 Training Squadron came from Joyce Green. Both these units disbanded after the First World war and the airfield closed.

Ripon SE of Ripon

Ripon Racecourse was pressed into service, and No. 76 Squadron was formed here on 15 September 1916, using many of the local landing grounds already listed in this section. On 20 December 1917 No. 189 Training Squadron formed here as a night training unit, which moved to Sutton's Farm on 1 April 1918. In March 1919 No. 76 Squadron moved to Tadcaster and the land was returned to the racing fraternity.

Seaton Carew S of Hartlepool

Seaton Carew was, in fact, two separate stations. In the First World War this was Seaton Carew Flight Station, 6th Brigade and Seaton Carew (II) Marine Operations (Seaplane) Station. It was occupied by C Flight of No. 36 Squadron on home-defence duties flying BE2Cs from the spring of 1916. The Seaton Carew area was attacked by German airships L30 and L34. The only Blackburn Kangaroos in RAF service were based here on No. 246

Squadron. The seaplane station occupied seven acres on the northern foreshore of the Tees estuary. No. 246 Squadron and 402/3 Flights were employed on anti-submarine patrols. Work to complete the station was scheduled to be completed by 31 December 1918, but all work stopped at the Armistice and both sites were quickly abandoned.

Sherburn-in-Elmet 12 miles E of Leeds

Sherburn-in-Elmet was used during the First World War as an RFC/RAF aircraft acceptance park. By 1918 there were eight hangars and storage sheds. The production of the Sopwith Cuckoo was centred here. The airfield was not retained after the war, although it was the home of the Yorkshire Aeroplane Club, which opened in January 1926.

Tadcaster SW of York

The airfield opened in the spring of 1916 with the arrival of B Flight of No. 33 Squadron, using BE2Cs for the defence of Leeds and Sheffield. In December 1916 No. 46 (Reserve) Squadron arrived from Doncaster, and in April 1917 this was joined by No. 68 (Reserve) Squadron, to be followed by No. 69 in October. No. 46 RS moved to Catterick, and on 15 July 1918 No. 38 Training Depot Station was formed. In November 1918 No. 94 Squadron arrived from Senlis, France, to be followed by No. 76 Squadron in March 1919. When both these squadrons and the TDS were disbanded the airfield closed.

Thirsk on W side of Thirsk

This was yet another racecourse pressed into service during the First World War, and was used by No. 76 Squadron during 1916, flying their 504Ks. The site reverted to agriculture after the war.

Thornaby W of Middlesborough

Thornaby was used as a 2nd-class landing ground by No. 36 Squadron during the First World War and abandoned thereafter.

West Ayton W of Scarborough

This was Scarborough Racecourse, turned into an airfield, and was first used in 1916 by the RNAS, using BE2Cs on anti-Zeppelin patrols. During the latter part of 1918 No. 251 Squadron operated DH6s on convoy-protection duties and inshore reconnaissance patrols. When 251 Squadron left, the site was not retained by the RAF.

Airfields and Seaplane Bases in Wales and North-West England

Hooton Park Cheshire, 1 mile SE of Eastham

During the First World War Hooton Park was a racecourse that was requisitioned by the Army for training purposes. Belfast hangars were built in 1917 on the area once occupied by the horse paddock, to house

American-built aircraft shipped to Liverpool. But instead of these aircraft arriving, No. 4 Training Depot Station moved from Tern Hill in September 1917, and there was also an aircraft repair section. In 1919 the TDS was disbanded and the site was left unused until 1927, when it was used for civil aviation.

Sealand (Shotwick) 1 mile NE of Queensferry

In 1917 the station, then known as Shotwick, housed a variety of aircraft where aircrews worked up to operational standards. When the operational squadrons moved to France it was intended that training squadrons should move in, but changes of policy resulted in further operational units being posted in. On 15 July 1918 No. 51 TDS was absorbed into No. 5 Flying Training School using 504s. On 23 May 1929 the RAF Packing Depot arrived from Ascot and was responsible for the crating of all aircraft being sent overseas.

AIRFIELDS AND SEAPLANE BASES OF WALES AND NORTH WEST ENGLAND ON 11 NOVEMBER 1918 AND 31 DECEMBER 1929.

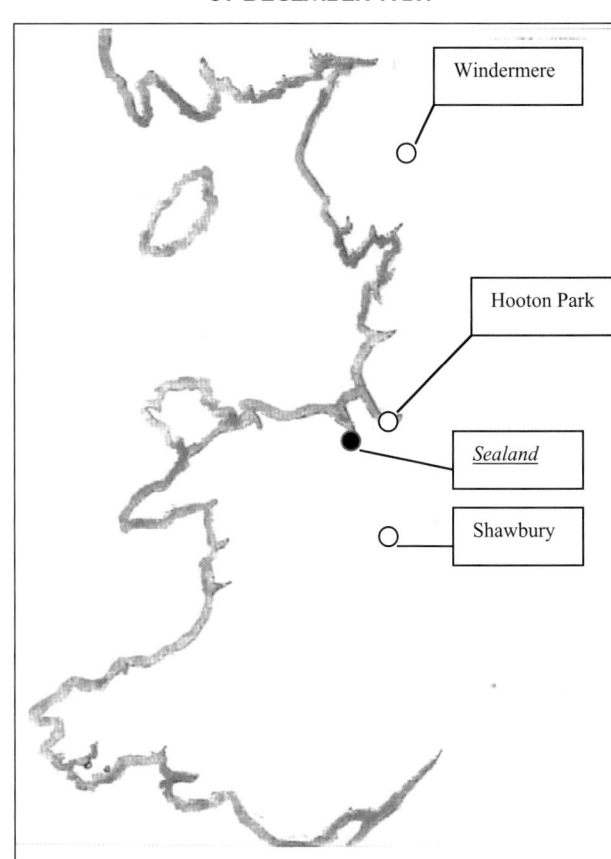

Windermere

Hooton Park

Sealand

Shawbury

Shawbury Salop, adjacent to Shawbury village
In 1917, to improve the chances of survival of pilots in combat, Shawbury was used by the RFC for pre-operational training, and No. 29 (Training) Wing formed on 1 September, but having too many different types of aircraft was not conducive to good training. Two of the squadrons involved combined to form 9 TDS on 1 March 1918, and training became more organized. When the war ended the airfield closed in May 1920. The hangars and most of the buildings were demolished and the site fell into disrepair.

Windermere 2 miles S of Ambleside
During the First World War Windermere was used by the RNAS to fly mails to the Isle of Man and so avoid loss caused by U-boat activity in the Irish Sea. The use of the lake for this purpose ended in 1918.

Airfields and Seaplane Bases in Scotland and Northern Ireland

Aldergrove Northern Ireland, 4 miles S of Antrim
Aldergrove was opened early in 1928 as No. 16 Aircraft Acceptance Park. The original intention was to test fly HP 1500s at the station that had been built at Harland and Wolff in Belfast, but teething troubles caused delays, which overran the war. Although Aldergrove was closed as a flying station in 1919, it had already been earmarked for future development and was retained by the RAF for reactivation during annual exercises. From June to September 1922 the station was used by No. 2 Squadron during the British withdrawal from the south of Ireland. In 1925 No. 502 Special Reserve Squadron was formed at Aldergrove on 15 May, equipped with Vimys. Further developments took place in the inter-war years, and it continues in active service to this day, although the site is shared with Belfast airport.

Acklington 3 miles NE of Felton
This was a First World War landing ground used by No. 77 Squadron and was closed post-war, not to be reopened until 1938.

Ayr (Racecourse) Just E of Strathclyde
Ayr (Racecourse) housed No. 1 School of Aerial Fighting in 1917, but on 10 May 1918 this became No. 1 School of Aerial Fighting and Gunnery, and it moved in July 1918, to be replaced by NW Area Flying Instructors' School, which moved to Redcar in 1919. No further service use was recorded.

Crail Fife, 1 mile NNE of Crail
The aerodrome opened in July 1918 to house No. 27 Training Depot Station. In August 1918 the Americans had a detachment of the 120th Aero Squadron. The only other use before closure in 1919 was to house No. 104

Squadron from 3 March 1919 until its disbandment on 30 June.

Cramlington Northumberland, 1 mile W of Cramlington
Cramlington opened in 1916. Most units that used the airfield during the First World War were transient, and its main use was as a night landing ground for HD squadrons until the end of the war. Close to the aerodrome there was also an airship station. The airfield closed in 1919.

Donibristle Fife, 2 miles E of Rosythe
Donibristle survived the First World War and remained open until 1959. Its first use in 1917 was, like Acklington, a landing ground for No. 77 Squadron, but it was later handed over to the RNAS as a naval air station accepting carrier-borne aircraft when the parent ship was in harbour and carrying out aircraft repairs. When the RNAS was absorbed into the RAF the station became a fleet repair depot. Torpedo trials were carried out here but in 1921 it was reduced to C & M. In 1925 it was reopened to accept disembarked carrier aircraft. On 1 October 1928 the Coastal Defence Torpedo Flight became No. 36 Squadron equipped with Horsley torpedo-bombers, and to the end of the decade Donibristle took part in exercises with naval aircraft from Rosythe.

Drem Lothian, 2 miles S of Dirleton
Drem began life as an HD landing ground for No. 77 Squadron in 1916/17, being known then as West Fenton. No. 2 TDS was formed on the airfield on 15 April 1918, flying Pups, Camels and SE5As. The American 41st Aero Squadron was also based at Drem from April to August 1918. When No. 2 TDS was disbanded in 1919 the airfield, renamed Gullane, remained unused until 1933.

Dundee (Stannergate) 2 miles E of Dundee
Opened originally as an RNAS seaplane station in 1914, by 1918 it had developed into a multi-squadron RAF seaplane base housing Nos 249 and 257 Squadrons, equipped with Short 184s, Felixstowe F2As, Curtiss H16s and Fairey Babies. The base also acted as an aircraft acceptance park for seaplanes in 1918. When the squadrons were disbanded the base closed down, probably in October 1919.

East Fortune Lothian, 3 miles NE of Haddington
Originally commissioned as an RNAS site on 23 August 1916, East Fortune's 504s carried out coastal patrols. It then became an airship station housing Coastal Class and North Sea Class blimps. East Fortune is perhaps best remembered as the departure point for the first E–W transatlantic crossing by the R34 in July 1919 to a point near New York, returning in August. The airfield was put up for disposal and closed on 5 February 1920.

AIRFIELDS AND SEAPLANE BASES OF SCOTLAND AND NORTHERN IRELAND ON 11 NOVEMBER 1918 AND 31 DECEMBER 1929.

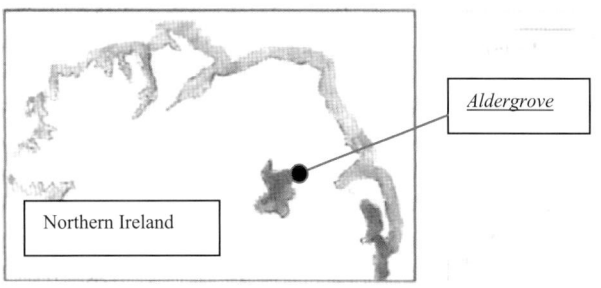

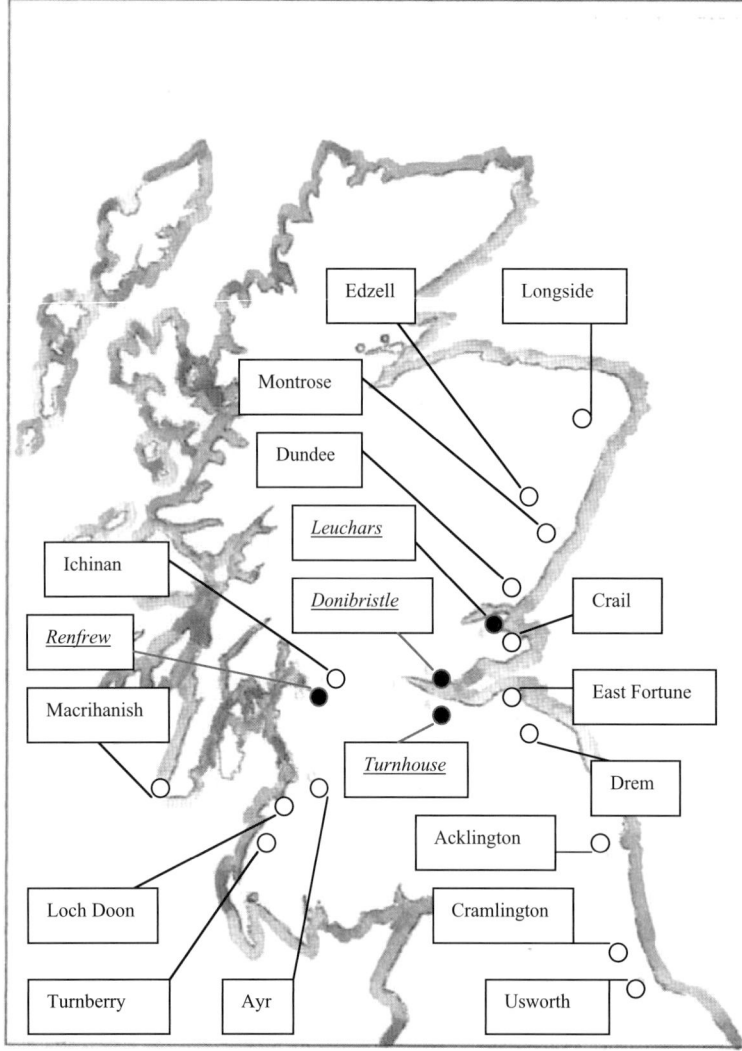

Edzell Tayside at Bridgend 2 miles NW of A94

Edzell opened in 1918 and housed No. 26 TDS, which formed on 15 July for single-seater fighter training, mainly using SE5As. In 1919 the unit disbanded and the station closed.

Leuchars Fife, 5 miles NW of St Andrews

This airfield has a very long history dating back to balloon experimentation by the Royal Engineers in 1911. It was established as an RAF airfield and remained in use after the First World War. No. 203 Squadron re-formed on 1 March 1920, with Nightjars, together with No. 205 Squadron, equipped with Parnall Panthers. It will be recalled that RAF squadrons numbered in the 200 series were ex-RNAS flights combined to make up squadron strength. There were, of course, still fleet fighter flights serving on aircraft-carriers, and Nos 403 and 404 Flights were formed at Leuchars in 1923. Following several changes in deployment, by September 1926 Nos 442 and 443 Flights were *in situ*. The fleet fighter units operated the Flycatcher, and the fleet reconnaissance units the Panther. Also at Leuchars at this time were three training flights: A Flight trained fighter pilots, B Flight trained spotter pilots and C Flight trained reconnaissance pilots. In 1927 these training flights were combined to become the Base Training Flight. Before the end of the decade Nos 445 and 446 Flights arrived with Fairey IIIFs.

Loch Doon on the shore of Loch Doon

In January 1917 the School of Aerial Gunnery was formed here, to be joined by the School of Aerial Fighting. On disbandment of both these units Loch Doon closed immediately after the First World war.

Longside 2 miles S of Longside

Longside was an airship patrol station from 1916 to 1918.

Macrihanish 3 miles W of Campbeltown

Macrihanish started life as a substation of the airship station at Luce Bay in August 1918, and was also the home station of No. 272 Squadron, equipped with DH6s, which flew coastal patrols over the River Clyde and the Hebrides. The station closed when the squadron disbanded in 1918.

Montrose   1 mile N of Montrose
This is Scotland's oldest military airfield, its connections with aviation dating back to 26 February 1913, when Montrose housed No. 2 Squadron RFC's Longhorns and BE2As. During the First World War it was a training station, and Nos 25, 80 and 83 Squadrons formed here. The American 41st Aero Squadron was on the station from March 1918 before moving to Gullane (Drem renamed). At the Armistice the airfield was abandoned, not to be reactivated until 1936, during the major RAF expansion.

Renfrew   Strathclyde
Renfrew was used from 1915 for testing aircraft such as the FE2B and DH9. It was also home to the Beardmore Flying School between 1915 and 1918. From 1918 Renfrew was home to No. 6 Aircraft Acceptance Park and No. 6 (Scottish) Aircraft Repair Depot. The airfield remained dormant after the First World War until 15 September 1925, when No. 602 Auxiliary Air Force Squadron was formed, and DH9s, Fairey Fawns and Westland Wapitis flew from Renfrew for the rest of the decade.

Turnberry   Strathclyde, 6 miles N of Girvan
Turnberry was first used in 1917 as the home of No. 2 (Auxiliary) School of Aerial Gunnery, renamed the No. 1 School of Aerial Fighting and Gunnery in May 1918. It was quite commonplace in the First World War for units to undergo frequent changes of title following reorganizations to meet operational needs, and the school was renamed No. 1 Fighting School later that month. The airfield closed after the war.

Turnhouse   Lothian, 5 miles W of Edinburgh
Opened in 1916 as the home of No. 26 Reserve Squadron, Turnhouse later housed A Flight of No. 77 HD Squadron. In July 1917 it was reduced to the status of a landing ground until No. 73 TS moved in from Thetford in September. It then became a fleet practice station and fleet aircraft repair depot. After the war Turnhouse came alive again as home to the newly formed No. 603 Auxiliary Squadron, dating from 14 October 1925, equipped with DH9As.

Usworth   Northumberland, 2 miles SW of Boldon
During the First World War the airfield was known as Hylton, and opened in October 1916 to house B Flight of No. 36 Squadron, then A Flight of the same unit up to the Armistice, when it also came to be called Usworth. Hylton/Usworth did not remain in service after the First World War, but in 1930 the airfield was selected to house No. 607 Auxiliary Air Force Squadron.

Airfields and Seaplane Bases Overseas

Abu Sueir   Egypt
Built on a site close to the Sweetwater Canal and the main Port Said railway, it was first chosen in 1917 and used as a training base in the First World War. It was selected for retention after the Armistice and became No. 4 FTS in April 1921, using Avro 504Ks for initial training and Bristol Fighters and DH9As for advanced courses. Vickers Vimys were also used, and in the late 1920s the Armstrong Whitworth Atlas. Between September 1919 and February 1920 the station had a bomber role and was home to No. 214 Squadron equipped with HP 0/400s.

Calafrana (Kalafrana)   Malta
With German submarines threatening British shipping in the Mediterranean during the First World War, it was deemed necessary to protect shipping routes between Gibraltar and the Aegean, and the Admiralty authorized work on a seaplane base to commence at the end of January 1916. By July that year it was possible to station five Curtiss H4 flying-boats at Calafrana to begin patrolling the approaches to Malta. They were effective in reporting enemy submarines to the convoys, even if they did not sink the U-boats. In March 1917 three Short 184s arrived from Dundee to replace the existing boats. More 184s were added, and two-seater FBA flying-boats were flown in. With the formation of the RAF in 1918, No. 268 Squadron was formed in the August and equipped with Short 184 and 320 floatplanes. After the Armistice No. 268 Squadron was disbanded, but No. 267 Squadron, which had formed in October 1918, had as its post-war role aerial support for the Mediterranean Fleet. At the same time as Calafrana became a self-accounting unit (i.e. not a satellite or lodger unit) in August 1923, No. 267 Squadron was reduced to flight status, being numbered No. 481 Flight and taking over the aircraft and personnel. And this was the only resident unit until 1 January 1929, when the flight reverted to being a squadron, this time No. 202, and equipped with Fairey IIID floatplanes. One other role that Calafrana performed during the 1920s was to receive carrier-borne aircraft from ships anchored in the Grand Harbour.

Drigh Road   India
An aircraft depot had been established in India in 1920 to undertake the assembly of aircraft shipped out from the United Kingdom and to undertake overhauls and engine repairs of aircraft on the inventory of squadrons. Moving from Lahore to Karachi (Drigh Road) in early 1921, the depot worked on DH9As, Bristol Fighters and later Wapitis.

Gibraltar
The earliest military flying from Gibraltar was in 1915, when the Admiralty realized the importance of

AIRFIELDS AND SEAPLANE BASES OVERSEAS ON 11 NOVEMBER 1918 AND 31 DECEMBER 1929.

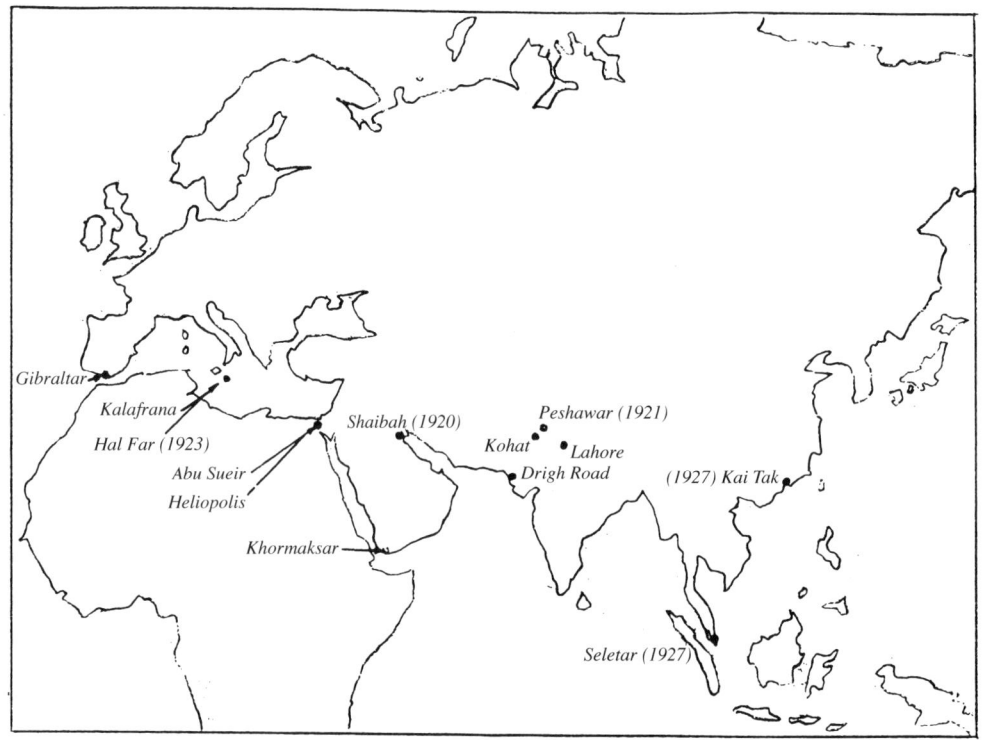

aircraft of the Fleet Air Arm.

Heliopolis Egypt

Heliopolis began life as an airfield in December 1915 with the arrival of No. 17 Squadron's BE2Cs. In 1916 the Australian Flying Corps arrived, and its unit was numbered 67 Squadron RFC. No. 14 Squadron also detached its BE2Cs to Heliopolis during 1916 from its base at Ismailia. By the end of 1916 these squadrons and detachments had left. What was to become No. 70 Squadron was then No. 58 Squadron, which came to Heliopolis on 2 May 1919 with HP 0/400s, which were replaced with Vickers Vimys. No. 58 Squadron was employed in supporting the convoy that was ploughing a furrow across the desert to mark out the route from Cairo to Baghdad in preparation for the weekly airmail service. During 1921 No. 1 Armoured-Car Company was formed at the station, and in January 1922 No. 58 Squadron, which had been renumbered No. 70 Squadron on 1 February 1920, left for Iraq.

In April 1925 No. 216 Squadron began a twenty-year stay. It was a bomber unit equipped with DH10s, later Vickers Vimys. In April 1927 No. 45 Squadron formed at the airfield with DH9As, and when that unit left in the October No. 208 Squadron with Bristol Fighters flew in. Chapter 4 records the squadron activities during this period. Heliopolis became an RAF station on 1 March 1928.

Kai Tak Hong Kong

The official opening of Kai Tak, for use mainly by aircraft of the Fleet Air Arm, took place on 10 March 1927. The airfield was located on the fringe of Kowloon on the Chinese mainland. Even though the station was opened, work was still going on to complete a sea wall and slipway for floatplanes and flying-boats. The resident unit was No. 442 Flight equipped with Fairey IIIFs. The Fairey IIIFs of No. 440 Flight and Fairey Flycatchers of No. 403 Flight also used the station. In November 1928 four Southampton flying-boats of the

maintaining an aerial watch over the Straits: after all, the German submarine U-21 was to sink two British battleships, so seaplane reconnaissance was vital. A mix of 184s, Curtiss H4s and some land-planes came to Gibraltar, and these early operations were hazardous, given the notorious wind turbulence round the Rock. When the RAF took over the existing RNAS Nos 265, 266 and 364 Flights, it formed them into No. 265 Squadron, which flew 184s and Felixstowe F3s on anti-submarine patrols until the unit's disbandment in 1919. During the inter-war years the only service aircraft to visit the Rock were those disembarking from ships.

Hal Far Malta

Hal Far was opened on 16 January 1923, and came under the control of Kalafrana. The latter, with its jetty and slipway, could receive disembarked floatplanes, but an airfield was necessary to receive wheeled aircraft, such as the Fairey Flycatcher that had disembarked from aircraft-carriers anchored in the Grand Harbour. Carrier operations in the Mediterranean began in 1924, and Hal Far was ready to receive aircraft from HMS *Eagle*'s four flights of Flycatchers, Darts, Blackburn Is and Seagull III amphibians taking part in exercises and trials. On 31 March 1929 Hal Far became an official RAF station under the command of Wing Commander C.W. Nutting. Fairey IIIFs equipped the station flight, and the airfield was regularly used by

Far East Flight from Singapore made a short stay at Kai Tak.

Kohat North-West Frontier of India
The use of Kohat as an airfield goes back to 1918, when BE2Cs of No. 31 Squadron called through with the mails. Between December 1921 and April 1923 the Bristol F2Bs of No. 28 Squadron took up residence and were employed on air-control operations. In 1925 the resident squadron was No. 60 equipped with DH9As. For an isolated North-West-Frontier base, the squadron personnel enjoyed the facilities of an indoor swimming pool, bungalows for married personnel, tennis courts and a golf course. The Kohat Range permitted local bombing training. In 1927 two Fairey IIIFs arrived at the station from Lahore for evaluation trials. Sadly one of them was lost in a fatal crash. Reorganization of the RAF in India in 1928 resulted in the formation of No. 1 (Indian) Wing at Kohat, and No. 27 Squadron joined No. 60 at the station. In the December the aircrews were issued with parachutes, even though some were reluctant. No. 1 Wing was involved in the Kabul rescue of December 1928, described in Chapter 3.

Khormaksar Aden
Khormaksar's career began in 1917 with the formation of the Aden Flight, tasked with reconnaissance since Turkish forces were threatening Aden and surrounding states. This involved aircraft of No. 31 Squadron detached from India, and these were later joined by aircraft from the Quetta-based No. 114 Squadron. But there was little to report and it was not until No. 8 Squadron arrived in the colony from Iraq early in 1927 that things hotted up. Operations were against the Zeidi forces, taking the form of demonstration flights, bombing and strafing attacks. From May 1928 these operations were carried out by Fairey IIIFs.

Lahore India
In September 1917, No. 114 Squadron was formed at Lahore to join No. 31 Squadron on frontier patrols. In March 1916 the aircraft park, which had accompanied No. 31 Squadron to India in 1915, had located at Risalpur. The aircraft park comprised an MT repair section, a small stores, aircraft and engine repair facilities and a test and dispatch section. When No. 97 Squadron arrived at Lahore in August 1919, it was tasked with supporting Army operations on the frontier. The considerable resources available in the park were used to form an aircraft depot at Karachi in February 1921, and this was ideally situated to erect aircraft that had arrived by ship from the United Kingdom. The aircraft park remained at Lahore as a stores distribution unit. The park was involved in the operations to quell riots at Amritsar in 1923, and in 1927 equipped the DH9As that were used for the inspection tour of India by Sir Samuel Hoare, the Secretary of State for Air. The park was required to erect and test a variety of aircraft, including the first Hawker Hart to arrive in India. In March 1929 the Heavy Transport Flight was formed at Lahore with two Handley Page Clives, and it was necessary to form a photographic section to process the survey work anticipated with the use of the Clives.

Peshawar India
Peshawar was only thirty miles from the Khyber Pass, and was first used by No. 31 Squadron's Bristol F2Bs in October 1921. No. 28 Squadron followed in April 1923, involved, as was 31 Squadron, in air-control operations. In January 1928 it was No. 20 Squadron that took over. All three squadrons were equipped with 'Brisfits'. Peshawar was involved in the Kabul rescue, but the Brisfits had not the range to reach Kabul. However, two Westland Wapitis were on wireless trials at the time, and so Peshawar could be kept up to date on the progress of the evacuation by wireless telegraphy.

Seletar Singapore
When the British government decided to build a naval base in Singapore, the necessity for an airfield and seaplane base was recognized. Seletar was selected following a photographic survey by a flight of Fairey IIIDs in January 1925, and work began in 1926. It was not an easy task to clear mangrove swamps, trees and vegetable gardens, and so by March the following year just enough land had been cleared for a landing strip. By the time the Far East Flight of four Southampton flying-boats arrived in February 1928, a concrete slipway had been constructed. When the commander of the Far East Flight, Group Captain Cave-Brown-Cave, returned to England, he left the senior pilot, Gerry Livock, as officer commanding the unit, which was to be renamed No. 205 (Flying-Boat) Squadron. In 1929 the airfield also accepted civilian aircraft, since the island lacked a civil airport.

Shaibah Iraq
Shaibah's first operational squadron was No. 84, which spent twenty years at the base from September 1920. This unit had DH9As, which carried out air control operations against dissident tribesmen. In 1923 the tribes began a revolt in the Samawa area of the Euphrates valley. In 1924 No. 84 Squadron helped to quell another uprising in the Lake Hammar area. Another important task was to carry out photographic surveys in preparation for remapping southern Iraq. In January 1928 the squadron contributed aircraft to AKFORCE during operations against the Akhwans. Finally the Squadron re-equipped with Wapitis at the end of the decade.

Chapter 8
Support Services, Technical and Supply

Technical training reorganization post-war – Technical training of airmen and apprentices – Technical duties on RAF squadrons - Supply organization – Supply depots – Administration of supply between supply depots, stations and HM ships

On the formation of the RAF in 1918, a body of technical airmen was inherited from the RFC and RNAS, but on the cessation of hostilities many of these wanted to return as quickly as possible to civilian life. In any event such men had marketable skills, so that the peacetime RAF was going to find it difficult to retain sufficient men to maintain the few squadrons left by 1921/2. Trenchard had already made it clear, in his 1919 Memorandum, that he intended to recruit boys and train them in technical subjects to take their place in the ranks of the service once they had reached adulthood, and that these men would form the nucleus for future expansion should that become necessary. But it would be a few years before his Aircraft Apprentices would enter service, and in the immediate post-war period technical airmen had to be retained and adult recruits trained to fill the posts on stations, squadrons and repair depots. Trenchard had also recognized the importance of sound technical training to ensure the serviceability of aircraft to prevent accidents.

When it came to the supervision of technical work, there was no Engineering or Technical Branch in Trenchard's 'pilots' air force'. If an officer was required to oversee technical work he was supposed to be a pilot first and technical officer second. Those undertaking the more detailed technical supervision in repair depots or on squadrons would go through a course at the Home Aircraft Depot at Henlow, and they would then earn the 'e' notation. Other specializations included photography, armament, signals and navigation, and again the officer concerned would carry the appropriate letter suffix after his name in the Air Force List. Thus Trenchard was producing the 'general-duties' officer in his officer corps, and even though in today's RAF there are specialist technical, administrative and supply branches, the term general-duties officer has persisted. From the very beginning at Cranwell in the early 1920s, the future permanently commissioned officers would be trained in technical, administrative and supply subjects. Technical specialization was to come later. Indeed, this matter was referred to during the debate in the House of Commons on the 1926 Air Estimates, when Sir Samuel Hoare, the Secretary of State for Air, said that he disagreed with the idea of an officers' engineering branch. He preferred the ideal, even if it was difficult to attain, of spreading engineering knowledge through the whole service and trying to make all airmen to some extent engineers.

Technical training prior to and during the First World War Prior to the outbreak of the First World War, the technical training of men was carried out at the Central Flying School, Netheravon. With the growing demand for technical schools, a number of additional schools were established. While the CFS took 200 trainees, No. 1 School of Instruction at Reading held 1,000, and from 27 October 1916 a converted jam factory at nearby Coley Park held 2,000. A further 300 men were also being trained in a former factory in Edinburgh. There was no basic engineering course for semi-skilled recruits, and 400 men were therefore sent to the polytechnics for training. This kind of improvization could not provide the men the RFC needed, and rationalization of the training machine became an urgent need.

Attention turned to the Rothschild estate at Halton Park, near Wendover in Buckinghamshire, which was first used by the Army for summer manoeuvres in September 1913. The Army was joined at Halton by No. 3 Squadron, RFC, under the command of Major Henry Brooke-Popham, with fewer than a dozen assorted aircraft, including Blériot monoplanes and Henri Farman biplanes. With the outbreak of hostilities, Alfred Rothschild offered to the Army the use of his estate, and his brother Nathaniel offered the use of the adjoining estate at Aston Clinton, and by September 1914 there were some 12,000 men of the Yorkshire Division camped on what is now the airfield. During the winter of 1914/15 a large number of wooden hutments were constructed on three sites. When the Yorkshire Division went off to war in the trenches they were succeeded by the East Anglians, and soon more than 200 acres were in use by the Army. At the end of 1916 the Halton estate was no longer home to Army divisions, and it was then used as a recruit training centre and home to RFC units. The RFC urgently needed technical tradesmen to service and repair its fast-growing number of squadrons and training units, and the Deputy Director-General of Military Aeronautics, General Sefton Brancker, submitted proposals to centralize the technical training of men, women and boys in a new school to be located at Halton. In July 1917 the sum of £100,000 was allocated for the construction of permanent workshops to house the RFC's many trade specialities. By that time only the RFC was in residence, and the fitters' and riggers' training was moved to Halton from Reading. On 20 August the School of Technical Training (Men) was formed, coming directly under the War Office and under the command of Lieutenant-Colonel Ian Bonham-Carter.

Halton's population was huge, the camp having grown to house 6,000 airmen mechanics, 2,000 boys at the Boys' Training Depot, West Camp, and 1,700 instructors and other staff. A further 2,000 women were also under training in a variety of aircraft trades, not to mention an Australian Flying Corps undergoing training and a supply depot that took up residence in East Camp in September 1917 as a lodger unit. At first the training facilities were poor, but by November the foundations of the huge new workshops had been laid and construction progressed rapidly, being carried by a large labour force, including a number of German prisoners of war. The workshop block, which can still be seen today, covered 300,000 sq. ft, each consisting of twelve bays 50 ft wide and 500 ft long. Designed to take a different trade specialization in each bay, the workshop bays were taken over, one at a time, as they were completed, so urgent was the requirement for trained technical men at the Front. In 1917 alone it was thus possible to turn out 14,000 mechanics.

Having sunk such a huge amount of capital into the Halton estate reminded the War Office that the Army did not own it. Halton had been loaned by the Rothschild family for the duration of hostilities, and under the terms of the agreement the estate would have to be handed back the way the Army found it. The cost of rehabilitation would be enormous, and so the Air Board drew up plans to purchase the Halton estate. Apart from technical training the Board also had in mind the siting of another permanent unit, which might be a recruit depot, staff college or cadet college. The War Office was none the less cautious in its approach to the Treasury, seeking approval in December 1917 to purchase just 1,340 acres of the estate at a maximum sum of £50,000. This bid was rejected, and on 31 January 1918 Alfred Rothschild died. Negotiations therefore continued with Major Nathan de Rothschild, and Treasury approval was finally given to purchase all 3,014 acres of the estate, which in 1919 included the mansion, which became the officers' mess.

Peacetime Reorganization The boys' training establishments were retained at both Halton and Cranwell for use by the peacetime RAF, and on 9 September 1919 the School of Technical Training (Boys) was formed at Halton. In March 1920 the title was changed to No. 1 School of Technical Training (Boys), and the Boys' Training Wing at Cranwell was renamed No. 2 School of Technical Training (Boys). The plan was that as soon as accommodation was built at Halton the boys from Cranwell could join their brothers-in-arms. In October 1919 the School of Technical Training (Men) moved from Halton to Manston, and training courses commenced there in May 1920. This left Halton as a boys' training station, and it soon became famous for its apprentices. By 1926 all but the electrical and wireless trades were trained at the station. Boys in the electrical and wireless trades went to Flowerdown, while Eastchurch provided training in armament and gunnery

RAF Apprentice Training

The Apprentice Scheme
Trenchard knew that he could not compete with civilian firms in the demand for technical tradesmen, so he planned to train the RAF's own tradesmen as boys, and when they became men to feed them into the service with the added bonus of a step up the promotion ladder, not to mention the top apprentices in each entry being granted a commission and training at the RAF Cadet College. The Apprentice Scheme was promulgated to local education authorities in October 1919, and selection examinations were held in London and at fourteen provincial centres. The first 235 boys were accepted for a three-year apprenticeship. They had to begin their training at Cranwell because permanent accommodation was still being built at Halton. The move to Halton coincided with the adoption of the rank of aircraft apprentice for boys rather than the earlier title of boy mechanic. In May 1922 the scheme of appointing apprentices to NCO ranks was introduced. Meanwhile apprentice training continued at Cranwell, with 981 boys still under training there in 1924, long after Halton had opened. But as has already been explained, the move to Halton was complete by 1926, except for those at Flowerdown.

At the heart of Trenchard's vision was the recruitment of well-educated boys because he saw ex-apprentices going on to form almost 40 per cent of the RAF's groundcrews and more than 60 per cent of its skilled tradesmen. It was thought that the selected boys, because of their resourcefulness and intelligence, could rapidly absorb the necessary technical training, and thereby complete their apprenticeship in three years rather than the normal five years in civilian trades, with a considerable saving in cost. The planned intake was about 1,000 a year.

Arrival at Halton
On arrival at RAF Halton the boys were medically examined and then 'signed on' for twelve years' service from the age of 18 years. After attestation the new apprentices were then allocated to one of the principal trades of fitter, carpenter, sheet-metal worker or electrical. The principal trades were further subdivided into particular specializations, such as fitter aero engines or fitter armourer. By the end of the 1920s the trade of rigger (metal) had been introduced to prepare apprentices for work on the new all-metal aeroplanes then under development. The majority of apprentices began their training at Halton, with those destined for

the electrical trades going to Flowerdown, near Winchester. Having been allocated to a trade and kitted out, apprentices were allotted to a section (later to become an apprentice wing), which served to subdivide into more manageable elements the huge organization that had grown out of the former Rothschild estate.

Apprentice dress at Halton The coloured headband was for long the key distinguishing feature of the Halton apprentice, with the 'Wheel' worn on the sleeve of the tunic. This badge stemmed from 1918, when it was considered that the boys needed something to distinguish them from the men. It thus made it easier to check for smoking and boys foregathering with the men. The design of the badge, which comprised a four-bladed propeller within a circlet, was authorized by Air Ministry Order 500, dated 17 April 1919, having been adopted the previous December. It was manufactured in brass so that it could be polished daily, and was worn on the sleeve of the left arm. The coloured headband was worn with service head-dress, and as the population of Halton grew it became necessary to identify quickly and with ease to which wing an apprentice belonged (or sections, as the first wings were called). The request was addressed to the Air Ministry by Air Commodore Scarlett CB, DSO, the Commandant of Halton, and the wearing of head-bands was approved in September 1920. In later years matching coloured discs were worn behind the badges of berets and behind the wheeled badge on the sleeve. The distinctive uniform was as distinctive as the term 'brat' by which the apprentices were affectionately known. There are a number of tales about the origin of this term, some more charitable than others. Perhaps the most plausible explanation is that, as Trenchard's protégés began to filter out into the RAF at large, many of the existing tradesmen saw them almost as troublesome children, perhaps even upstarts, given their accelerated promotion prospects, but as time passed and ex-apprentices began to prove their worth, the name 'brat' soon became a term of which to be proud.

Training programme and examinations Having started his training the newly arrived apprentice quickly found his life falling into a well-ordered pattern. Of the working week, twenty hours were devoted to technical training in the workshops, nine to physical training, drill and games, and eight to education. The remaining time was filled with barrack duties, inspections and preparation for technical or education subjects. Recreational facilities were available in abundance, including a debating society and model aircraft club in addition to a wide variety of sporting facilities.

At the end of the first year's work there was an immediate examination in educational subjects, followed by the final examinations at the end of the eighth term. Final examinations in skill of hand and trade knowledge were carried out in the final term. The marks obtained in the examinations would be used to determine the graduation rank and pay of the apprentice, while those who were highest in the Order of Merit would also be considered for cadetships to the Cadet College at Cranwell; Trenchard expected that ex-apprentices would provide up to 20 per cent of the cadets in each Cranwell entry. Technical training in the workshops came under the control of the Senior Technical Officer, and the technical staff included officers, NCO instructors and civilian instructors, a traditional mixture that continued to the end of the apprentice scheme. The workshops were divided into two main departments, the Fitters' Shop and the Carpenters' Shop. Aircraft apprentices were allocated to ten various trades, depending upon the vacancies available, while the preference of individuals and the results of the qualifying examinations were also taken into account. The trade of Wireless Operator was seen as the most important, and the top forty of each apprentice entry were sent to Flowerdown, near Winchester, for this training.

The first year of technical training on the course was given up almost entirely to basic training, such as the use of hand-tools and skill of hand, while those apprentices destined to be carpenter riggers spent most of their first year training in basic carpentry. Following basic training, the apprentices took up their specialist trades for advanced training, and within the overall fitter trades, the trade of fitter aero engine was assessed as the most important, followed by fitter driver petrol and fitter armourer. However, it was found that by the end of basic training, some of the apprentices did not meet the standards of knowledge and skill required for their selected trade, and from October 1924 the allocation to trades was not made until the end of basic training.

The first graduations of Halton apprentices

As the first entry of Halton apprentices reached the end of its training, it was fitting that Trenchard should review the Graduation Parade on 17 December 1922. There were 399 apprentices of No. 1 Entry. Squadron Leader A.J. Akehurst RAF Retd recalls that day when he passed out as one of eight fitter armourers. He was one of the original 'plumbers', as the RAF used to like calling their technical personnel. As Trenchard passed along the ranks of apprentices, resplendent in their parade uniforms, he stopped to talk to Akehurst. 'So you are now an AC1, eh?', but he was then deflated when Trenchard added, 'Well, I suppose that is some sort of start.' The CAS was not happy, for he wanted at least 80 per cent of each intake to pass out as LACs (leading aircraftmen). He believed that the efficiency of the RAF depended on the quality of the product of Halton and

Air Marshal Trenchard inspects the pass-out
of No. I Entry.

Cranwell. His pride in the apprentice scheme was again shaken with the pass-out of No. 3 Entry in December 1924. This time *The Times* gave the parade full coverage, and Trenchard was photographed taking the salute. He had been furnished with a report entitled 'RAF Training Centre – Developments at RAF Halton', and the results were below expectation. Only fifteen LACs and 121 AC1s had passed out from a total of, again, 399 apprentices. The 191 AC2s and sixty-seven failures would have their time at Halton extended for a further six months to see if they could then pass out, by which time he hoped that all or most of them would pass out as LACs. In the event only fourteen of those held back passed out as LACs. On the plus side there were two with cadetships at Cranwell, and eight proceeded to a Corporals' course. *The Times* did, however, pay the RAF the compliment of not hiding the failures in its striving for quality. After all, Halton was trying to achieve in three years what it took industry five years to complete. The results did in fact improve. The early teething troubles with the scheme stemmed partly from the lack of accommodation to provide an adequate supply of trained technical personnel to squadron or station service. There was accommodation at this time for 2,000 apprentices, but that number was to be doubled to take 4,000. At the time of Trenchard's inspection there were 1,889 boys at Halton, and it was this lack of accommodation that prevented the move of the Cranwell-based apprentices. It was emphasized that the

scheme could settle down once the move from Cranwell had taken place. On 22 October 1925 the move was made to form wings out of the previously named sections, and Wing Commander H.I. Hammer became the Officer Commanding No. 1 Wing at Henderson Barracks, Halton. He was assisted by seven junior officers, four sergeant-majors and eighteen corporals. No. 2 Section became No. 2 Apprentice Wing under the command of Wing Commander D. Harries AFC. Once the wings were in place, the boys, after attestation, were kitted out, with the Wireless and Instrument groups going to Flowerdown and Cranwell, the remainder being distributed between Nos 1 and 2 Wings. This was later changed, so that a complete Entry would be allocated to one wing, each of the two wings ending up with a Senior and a Junior Entry. Within the wings there were squadrons lettered A, B or C, and the apprentices were assigned to these squadrons according to their rating as average, above average or below average.

The Boys' Wing, Cranwell

Air Commodore Borton was Commandant of RAF Cranwell from August 1921 until 1926, when he was replaced by Air Vice-Marshal F.C. Halahan CMG, CBE, DSO, MVO, who remained as the AOC until 1929. The enhanced rank of AVM was due to Cranwell being accorded Command status. In September 1923 Air Commodore Sir Frank Whittle, the inventor of the jet engine, began his training as an apprentice rigger. Having almost failed his medical at Halton in 1922, his career was almost over before it began. The problem was his lack of height, and he successfully applied again for entry after a period of physical training, obviously including stretching exercises!

At Cranwell the school subjects were divided into two groups, namely English literature and history, and the second group included mathematics, physics and the theory of flight. On the practical side, workshop training covered repair and maintenance, but although more broadly based was not so thorough. Cranwell continued to train the overflow of fitters and riggers, as they were then called, from 1923 until 1926, by which time the barracks workshops and school that made up the training centre at Halton had been completed. The Cranwell apprentices who transferred to Halton to continue their airframe and engine training moved into No. 4 Wing in August 1926. With the Cranwell apprentices the Pipe Band came to Halton with their double-three drum roll instead of the usual five-roll beat. The 600 members of No. 8 Entry (Whittle's entry) were the last to complete their three-year training period at Cranwell. Cranwell Entries Nos 9 to 14 that arrived at Halton not only provided the receiving unit with a logistical problem, but it complicated the Entry numbering system. For example, the 12th Cranwell Entry called itself the 6th/12th Halton Entry.

The Flowerdown Apprentices

Flowerdown was the first RAF Electrical and Wireless School, and in 1927 the school was transferred to Cranwell, where it remained until 1952, when it went to RAF Locking, in Somerset as No. 1 Radio School. Apprentices were trained there from 1922, and one ex-boy of the 9th Entry, later Group Captain W.T.H. Nichols, recalls the tough living conditions on the station, which, he said, prepared him for his survival as a Japanese prisoner of war. The results were better than at Halton, and in December 1925 Sir Philip Sassoon inspected the school's pass-out parade. Of the 290 apprentices under training, forty were passing out that day. There was not one failure, and nine passed out as LACs, twenty as AC1s and eleven as AC2s. Four of these stayed at Flowerdown to complete an advanced course leading to promotion to corporal, and one had volunteered for pilot training. Of the 745 apprentices to pass through Flowerdown no fewer than 65 per cent were commissioned. A total of 100 reached the rank of wing commander or higher, and one ex-Flowerdown boy reached Air rank.

The RAF Halton debate in the House of Commons

When the Air Estimates were discussed in the House of Commons early in 1926 there were a number of interventions in debate by back-benchers, some of whom had been invited to Halton by Air Vice-Marshal Lambe. Sir Frank Nelson wanted to know why fatigue duties in dormitories and kitchens were being carried out by the 737 airmen of the administrative staff when there were 1,781 apprentices who could be rostered to undertake these duties by extending their training time at Halton by one month. He did concede that the apprentices were being given the finest possible technical education in just three years but wondered if the costs of their training could be reduced. He cited , as examples, the provision of tea for 7,000 parents at a Halton Parents' Day and the retention of fifteen aircraft on Halton airfield. The members of the permanent staff who were aircrew could do their annual refresher flying at a nearby airfield and there would not then be a justification for fifteen aircraft and a large airfield at Halton just to train ground staff. Sir Frank calculated that the cost to the country of training one apprentice was £230 per annum, which was greater than the cost to a parent sending his child to a public school, where the ratio of administrative staff to pupils was five to one, and not two to one, as at Halton. The cost for Sir Frank's son at Winchester was only £65 per term. He also questioned the apprentices' pocket money of one shilling a day. When the number of apprentices at Halton reached 3,000, pocket money costs would rise by £55,000. Since most of this money was spent in the canteen, half the amount, i.e. six old pence, would be adequate for their digestion. On Friday pay day the evening meal in the apprentice dining hall was not required because of the amount of money they had to spend in the canteen.

The Under-Secretary of State for Air, Sir Philip Sassoon, rose to reply. With regard to the exemption of apprentices in carrying out fatigue duties at Halton, he said that they would do less time on training if they were otherwise employed. If they were not given adequate pocket money then the RAF would have to provide them with railway warrants when they went on leave. He went on to justify the aerodrome and aeroplanes at Halton since apprentices had to learn to swing propellers and handle aircraft on the ground, as they would do on squadrons. He justified the amount spent annually on apprentice training by saying that at the end of the First World War it took eighty-four men to keep one aircraft in the air. That figure had been reduced to fifty men.

Brigadier-General Charteris was the next to raise a question. He wanted to know why Halton cost more to administer than the whole of Aldershot Command. Mr Charleton, another private member and a mechanical engineer, said that he had been delighted with what he saw at Halton. There were no square pegs in round holes, and if a boy was not fitted to one trade he was transferred to another. Another MP who had visited the station commented that if the technical work being carried out at Halton was being done on his railway, it would be done by machinery. Sir Philip retorted that in the Sahara Desert or the Plains of Iraq there was no machinery and technical tasks had to be performed by hand. Brigadier-General Warner was very impressed by what he saw at Halton and said that apprentices could form a fine basis for pilots.

The situation from 1927 to 1929

On 11 January Trenchard inspected the 576 apprentices of the 4th Entry, renumbered the 10th Entry, to incorporate the Cranwell entries. Forty-three apprentices had passed out as LACs but seventy-two had failed the course. There were three Cranwell cadetships, and twelve boys had been selected for advanced training to reach the rank of corporal. This scheme for rapid promotion to corporal was not well liked in the RAF, particularly among those adult entrants who were pushed back in the promotion queue, and it had to be discontinued. A significant achievement by the ninety-five carpenter riggers was to construct three Grebe fighter aircraft using metal fittings taken from crashed aircraft. After the parade Trenchard addressed the boys in the large gymnasium, and he congratulated them on their turnout and bearing, expressing the hope that one day an ex-apprentice might occupy his position as CAS. This in fact happened in October 1982, when Air Chief Marshal Sir Keith Williamson was appointed Chief of the Air Staff.

At the beginning of 1927, according to recruiting announcements, 3,500 apprentices had already joined the RAF, and by 1928 this figure had reached 5,000. There was then a new grouping within the apprentice wings whereby an entire Entry was attached to one specific wing. No. 1 Wing therefore comprised the January 1925 11th (Halton) Entry and the September 1926 14th Entry, No. 2 Wing housed the September 1925 12th (Halton) Entry and the January 1927 15th Entry, while No. 4 Wing comprised the September 1924 10th (Cranwell) Entry and the January 1926 13th (Halton) Entry.

The 6th/12th Entries of the January 1925 intake passed out in December 1925 with frozen thick snow on the ground, which prevented the usual ceremony and march past. Once again Trenchard was there and heard the 2,434 apprentices from the three wings being addressed by Air Vice-Marshal C.L. Lambe, who referred to the complete redrafting of the advanced training syllabus and the reorganization of the Entries that had taken place in January that year. He said that the drill had not reached the required standard because the drill instructors were 10 per cent below the barely adequate establishment. During his tour of the workshops Trenchard had been shown the *Mayfly* biplane that had been entirely designed and constructed at Halton and for which a Certificate of Airworthiness had been issued that June. The following year this aircraft was converted into a successful monoplane. In his address to the apprentices of this 6th Entry, Trenchard told them that their passing out would bring the total number of apprentices trained at RAF Stations Cranwell and Halton to 4,000, and he hoped that they were beginning to make their weight felt in the service. He was not so concerned about the standard of drill, but he *was* concerned about the calibre of the final product of the apprentice scheme. He wanted them to use their intelligence, and he saw no difference between technical and educational training since it all came under the heading of 'educational'. He quoted figures showing that the standard had improved over the years, but said that there should be at least 25 per cent of an Entry passing out as LACs and virtually no failures at graduation. One of the four apprentices to be awarded a Cranwell cadetship that year was later to be Air Chief Marshal Sir Alfred Earle, and Trenchard presented him with a trophy and a Wakefield Scholarship.

In May 1927 the Chief Scout, Sir Robert Baden-Powell, visited Halton and was very impressed with what he saw. When he asked to meet any apprentices who had been Boy Scouts he was very pleased to find 400 boys paraded before him. Later that year another distinguished visitor was HRH Princess Mary, who came to open the new hospital with its 204 beds, operating theatre and X-Ray department.

At RAF Cranwell from 1926 to 1929 there were no apprentices under training until the Electrical and Wireless boys moved from Flowerdown when that station closed. The new training unit was called No. 2 Electrical and Wireless School. According to the 1929 Estimates, aircraft apprentices and apprentice clerks who entered at about the age of 16 for training, to fill the technical and clerical trades respectively, would continue to be recruited for twelve years' active list service, counting from the age of 18, with no Reserve liability. Details of the apprentice entries during the 1920s are as follows:

Entry No.	Highest and Lowest Service Numbers		Arrival Date	Annual Totals
1	335282	335521	Feb 1920)	541
2	335582	335882	Sep 1920)	
3	361606	361779	Feb 1921)	579
4	361820	362224	Sep 1921)	
5	362249	362739	Feb 1922)	1,034
6	362790	363332	Sep 1922)	
7	363338	363790	Feb 1923)	1,113
8	363793	364452	Sep 1923)	
9	364462	365117	Jan 1924)	1,222
10	365127	365692	Sep 1924)	
11	365625	365988	Jan 1925)	848
12	366003	366486	Sep 1925)	
13	560001	560501	Jan 1926)	1,008
14	560504	561010	Sep 1926	
15	556101	561429	Jan 1927)	963
16	556143	561976	Sep 1927)	
17	561997	562392	Jan 1928)	986
18	562395	562964	Sep 1928)	
19	562967	563424	Jan 1929)	1,076
20	563425	564042	Sep 1929)	

TECHNICAL WORK ON STATIONS AT HOME AND OVERSEAS

A Day in the Life of Technical Personnel on a UK Station in the 1920s

After breakfast and the usual barrack-room cleaning, the men were paraded for inspection. The padre would then say prayers, but not before the Jews and Roman Catholics had been invited to fall out from parade. Thereupon the affected personnel would march to the edge of the parade ground and halt facing outwards. This is yet another of those delightful idiosyncrasies that are part of service life and was designed presumably, to ensure that the RCs and Jews would not have to hear anything which they might find unacceptable to their faiths. The author, being a conventional C of E, never had to march off the parade square, but has lived dangerously ever since, by marrying a Roman Catholic.

The men were then marched off to their squadron lines or other places of work. There they changed into blue overalls and consulted the flying programme to see which aircraft were required for the day, and these were given a daily inspection. The Form 535 would then be signed by the technical airman carrying out the checks and countersigned by an NCO of an aircraft trade. The huge corrugated doors of the hangar would then be pushed back against their stops, a task which would take several men to accomplish. The aircraft selected for flight that day were then lifted by the tail so that the skid could

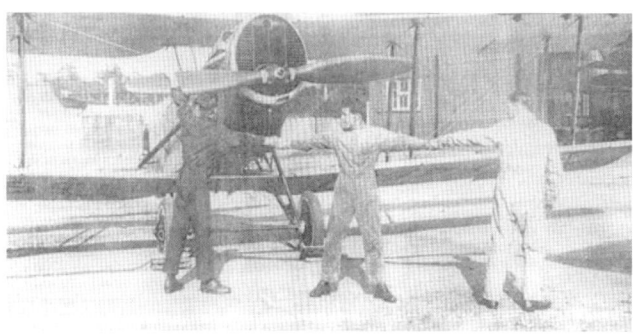

Two ways of swinging the propeller – the hard way and the easy way!

be lowered into a box on a steerable trolley. They were then wheeled out onto either the grass or the tarmac in front of the Flight Commander's office.

Munitions, known in service parlance as 'warlike stores', if required for an exercise, would include practice bombs and ammunition, together with cameras and W/T sets. When these were fitted the propeller would be 'swung', the engines having been doped with the ki-gas pump. Swinging the propeller was not an easy task against high cylinder compression. Three airmen would form a chain to provide the necessary muscle power, but they still pulled on one set of fingers. A stout bag could be used instead, placed over the propeller blade, and a pulling rope placed over the bag.

Of course there had to be a better way of starting an aircraft engine, and the Hucks starter was devised to start a number of aircraft types. A horizontal shaft was mounted on a Model T Ford chassis, the shaft being driven by a chain and clutch from the car engine. At the front end of the shaft was a dog clutch that engaged with a similar dog on the propeller boss. The shaft was then rotated by the vehicle engine until the aircraft engine fired, when the dogs disengaged.

The fitters on each aircraft then throttled up the engines until they were warm. On the arrival of the pilot, who replaced the fitter in the cockpit, the rigger helped to secure the parachute and seat straps. The oxygen and W/T lines were then attached and the pilot signalled the ground crew to move, one on each side of the tail and backs to the slipstream. With the tail thus weighted down, the pilot opened up the engine to check each magneto for a drop in revolutions, and then gave a brief burst to maximum revs. When the engine was throttled back, the ground crew moved round to the wheel chocks, which were removed as the pilot signalled by crossing his hands in front of his face. Thereupon the wheel chocks were pulled away and the men moved round to the wing tips. Then with helpful bursts of engine power to assist movements by the rudder, together with the airmen on the wing tips, the aircraft was manoeuvred into a position whereby the pilot could then taxi unassisted. The pilot then signalled that he was clear to taxi, and this was generally acknowledged by a salute from one of the airmen.

Once the aircraft had departed the men could get back to work in the hangar, which then became a scene of organized bustle as each man went about his task. Since the aircraft were all covered in fabric one could soon smell the scent of dope and fabric, mixed with smells of oil and grease. If all work was complete and it was a fine day, an airmen might have the luxury of lying on the grass outside the hangar until the aircraft returned. Back inside the hangar the aircraft that had been inspected and serviced had an aluminium black-painted folding board hung around the propeller boss that read P-O-W, meaning petrol,

Just in case the worst happened! Fire tender being given the spit and polish in the 1920s.

oil and water. This indicated that the aircraft was ready for flight. If the aircraft was unserviceable it would have the letters U/S in red, and this was painted on the reverse side of the board. Inside the board was the Form 535 for that aircraft. This was ruled off in columns to show the amounts of fuel, oil and water and columns for the signature of the airmen carrying out the work and one for the supervising NCO. Just like a car, the servicing could be minor or major, and there was a space to record inspections for both. It was important to record the hours flown, again just like a car, where the miles driven are recorded on a servicing document by a garage. The hours flown were important because airframes and engines have 'lives'. The hours flown were timed from 'chocks away' to replacing them at the end of the flight. The book where these times were recorded was held in the watch office that overlooked the airfield. The general servicing cycle for aircraft and engines was 120 hours, which was extended as aircraft became more reliable. Those who have served in the RAF in more recent years will be familiar with the Form 700 that replaced the Form 535, the latter becoming inadequate as aircraft became more complex.

A buzz of engines heralded the return of the aircraft, and the technical airmen left the hangar to be ready with the aircraft chocks as soon as they had been taxied in. The airmen on the wing tips were particularly important in the days when some aircraft did not have brakes, which is why the airmen wore hobnailed boots, the risk of sparks apparently being ignored. By the time all aircraft had arrived back there would be a concentration of wing tips, whirling propellers, and hot engines, all in a small space, and great care had to be taken to avoid collisions. Individual aircraft would be taken to the refuelling point. Work and flying continued until 12.00 hrs, when the main party was marched back to the domestic area to be dismissed for lunch before a return

to afternoon work. A few men might be left behind to deal with any late arrivals that would need marshalling and refuelling. On some stations there might be a duty crew or a duty flight if a large number of aircraft were involved.

For those technical personnel employed in station workshops there was a different routine. This would involve work not directly connected with aircraft and engines, although there might be a section of station workshops devoted to aircraft or engine repair beyond the capability of flights. Work would be on such equipment as welding gear and forges and the servicing of wireless equipment, weapons and electrical apparatus. MT drivers were nearly always on call, and there would be a duty driver available outside normal working hours. Many stations employed civilian drivers, for, as is explained in Chapter 9, it was difficult for the RAF to recruit in this trade.

Life for Technical Personnel Abroad

This section aims only to give a snapshot of RAF working life abroad in the 1920s. There were no hostilities in the United Kingdom at this time, and most, if not all, squadrons overseas were employed on operational duties. Probably the worst aspect of working in places like Aden, Iraq or India in the summer was the heat and flies. The men were not only thousands of miles away from their loved ones, but they were also that distance away from the supply of spares and new aircraft, although the Iraqi and Indian theatres did have an aircraft park.

Iraq   In Iraq the day would begin with bearers bringing a cup of 'gunfire', thick and strong, to the airmen at 05.00 hrs. No breakfast was taken before work started, for the men had to get to the hangars to take advantage of the relatively cool and dense air. Sorties were flown until 07.30 hrs, when the airmen stood down for breakfast. By the time the men got back to work, flying was taking place in rapidly rising temperatures, and dust clouds were stirred up by aircraft slipstreams. If aircraft had to stay out of doors for any length of time in the fierce heat special care had to be taken during inspections because of wood shrinkage. By the time the men were marched back to their bungalows and 'tiffin', the mid-day meal, the temperature could be up to 120 deg F. The pith helmet, or 'Bombay bowler' as it was known, was worn together with spine pads. The afternoon was taken up with 'siesta', and sports were played during the cool of the evening. A flickering film might also be shown for entertainment.

Engine changes   What made the working day of a technical *erk* serving overseas different in terms of work undertaken was in replacing engines in aircraft that had force-landed. The preceding section on apprentice training made clear that trainees were required to learn to do technical work without sophisticated workshop support in just the situation that technical tradesmen could find themselves in the outposts of the Empire. When the engine fitters arrived at the site of a downed aircraft there would not be a crane to lift out an engine that could not be repaired in the aircraft. Sheerlegs would have to be erected over the airframe to permit the lifting of the engine using ropes and pulleys. Motor vehicles from the base airfield might have to make a long hazardous journey with a spare engine, tentage, food and cooking equipment for the servicing crew, who could be away for some time. On occasion the transport might be of the four-legged variety.

The 'Smith saga' In his excellent book, *From the Ground Up*, J.W. Adkin describes a long flight from Hinaidi to India that involved technical airmen in what he calls the 'Smith Saga'. A Victoria that took two months flying escort to the Air Minister Sir Samuel Hoare was crewed by pilots Flight Lieutenant King and Flying Officer Stewart. Corporal Clarke was the wireless operator, AC Davidson the fitter and Smith the rigger. The Victoria left Hinaidi on 1 January 1927 and returned on 1 March, having flown via Shaibah, Bushire, Banda Abbas, Singah, Jask, Charbah, Karachi, Hyderabad (Sind), Jodhpur, Delhi, Ambala, Lahore, Peshawar, Kohat, Multan and Khanpur to Karachi and back to Hinaidi. This trip was memorable to Smith for several reasons. He had to assist with an engine change in the Sind Desert, he met Stack and Leete, two ex-RAF officers who were flying in a DH6 (Moth) from England to Australia and received assistance from Davidson, and he was introduced to the AOC India, Sir Geoffrey Salmond.

On leaving Karachi the starboard engine started to lose water and it was necessary to land on Hyderabad Racecourse. After topping up their water drums they took off again, but after only forty-five minutes there was a forced landing at Raragi . It was decided to try and top up the water tank in the air, and all available tubing was collected and connected to make a hose. With this the Victoria took off, and at a few hundred feet Flight Lieutenant King stood on his seat, reached up to the water-tank filler and inserted the hose. The ground crew then passed up a large kettle so that King could pour water down the hose. The water level was observed through a sight glass, but it was noticed that the water level still went down after the first filling, so he abandoned the idea, made a forced landing and decided that a new engine was needed. A telescopic aerial had to be erected so that Corporal Clarke could radio Hinaidi. The replacement engine and a set of sheerlegs were accompanied by an LAC Jackson travelling by train to Basra, by ship to Karachi, then a train to the nearest rail point, and by bullock cart to the stranded aeroplane. After the engine change Jackson had to return to Karachi with

the sheerlegs and damaged engine. This was an example of airmen using their initiative, just what Trenchard had in mind when devising apprentice training.

While waiting for the engine to arrive, the crews tried to move the Victoria with the help of local natives, and the port engine was started, but the idea was abandoned when the pulling power of the port engine was greater than that of the natives pulling on the starboard wing. They dropped the rope and ran. The fitter repaired the water leak and the ground crew removed the propeller, slackened the bearer bolts and loosened all connections. To remove the engine only two of the three sheerlegs were used as the engine was lifted from the bearings towards the legs. A rope was tied from the top of the legs to a screw picket set into the ground about thirty yards away and the engine was hoisted off the bearers by slackening the rear rope and tightening the other. Once clear of the aircraft the engine was lowered onto bits of wood. The new engine was installed by reversing the procedure. The crew were on the ground for some nine days before taking off for Jodhpur. The next day they picked up Sir Sefton Brancker, who slept nearly all the way to Delhi. As a postscript to the episode it was the opinion of Smith that the Victoria was easy to maintain since the aircraft had bell cranks fitted to the control runs at all turning points instead of pulleys. Changing control wires was hardly known, but Smith did have to exchange a broken swage rod with a spliced cable in the engine bay, working through the night to finish the job. Burst tyres were frequent, and because of the weight of the Victoria changing a wheel was a major task. These problems created interest and a challenge to technical personnel and contributed to high morale, which is why Smith enjoyed his time on No. 70 Squadron.

India In India the technical tradesmen of the early 1920s not only had to contend with the heat, sand and flies. The rundown of the RAF in India brought Air Vice-Marshal John Salmond out from the United Kingdom to investigate the situation and report to the Government of India. He found the aircraft almost unsafe to fly. There were no spare tyres, and some aircraft on operational missions had to take off and land on the wheel rims. Airmen had to go into the local bazaars to buy canvas to repair the aircraft fabric. The troubles with the DH10s of No. 60 Squadron were particularly noteworthy and are described in Chapter 4. The lack of spare parts was particularly galling at a time when these were being sold off to private buyers in the United Kingdom as war-surplus stock. The engines were often obsolete, being fitted with single-ignition harnesses. Add to these problems extremes of weather, since hurricanes could uproot Bessoneau hangars, damaging aircraft that could not then be repaired. In some cases it was necessary to transfer wheels and propellers from unserviceable aircraft to others to make them operational.

The Armoured Car Companies

One way that technical airmen could be employed directly on operational duties was through service on one of the armoured car companies (ACCs). Chapter 2 told of the process of air substitution whereby Army battalions and other support units were progressively replaced throughout the 1920s by RAF armoured car companies and locally raised Levy forces. Perhaps partly out of pique, the Army would not supply the mobile units that would complement the speed of aircraft and cooperate closely with them, so the RAF formed their own. They were manned by RAF officers and technical airmen, both gunner armourers and MT drivers. The units were equipped with Rolls-Royce armoured cars that mounted a water-cooled Vickers machine-gun, and initially these cars had solid tyres. The ACCs performed valuable service in protecting convoys and were constantly on patrol. When the RAF Regiment was formed in 1942, these ACCs were eventually absorbed into the corps.

The engine of the cars was a modified 1913 Silver Ghost 50 hp with six cylinders mounted on a 1925 chassis. The engine had coil and magneto ignition so that if one system failed the crew ran the other. This was an early fail-safe idea. Water-cooling was modified by the inclusion of a steam collector, which condensed the steam and returned it to the cooling system, proving most economical. Each car carried twelve gallons of water in felt containers, one on each side of the car . There were also six 'charguls'(one-gallon water bags tied with string at the top and used for drinking), three to each side of the vehicle. Rather in the same way as aircrews might secure water containers to the wing tips of their aircraft to provide cool water in the event of a forced landing, so the armoured-car crews might keep their charguls cool by securing them to the sides of the vehicles. Equipment for desert conditions included:

RAF armoured cars on patrol.

2 Spare wheels
2 Sand mats
  Steel towing cable
1 Pick and shovel
  Signal racks
  Enamel utensils
  Cutlery
1 Tool kit, complete

Each car had a medium, water-cooled Vickers 0.303 in. machine-gun and a Lewis gun, just like the DH9A and Bristol Fighter. There were several thousand rounds of 0.303 in. ammunition, a bag of Mills hand-grenades and a Very pistol with its cartridges fastened in clips to the inside of the door. Each member of the crew carried a .45 Webley and a Lee Enfield rifle, the latter being stored in a rack. The armament was the responsibility of the gunner, and the ammunition was checked regularly, since the loss of rounds could result in court martial action if there was not a good explanation.

RAF SUPPLY IN THE 1920S

The greatest change in the supply of material and equipment since the 1920s has undoubtedly been the computerization of supply records, inventories and vouchering. It is still the case that RAF supplies are made under contract, then by the Air Ministry and now by the MoD, for delivery to Maintenance Units (MUs), or Stores Depots in the 1920s, where equipment is and was held for delivery to RAF units on demand. Then, as now, some items and services are supplied locally where economies can be achieved by so doing or when urgency precludes going to an MU. What did surprise the author while researching the supply organization of the 1920s was that the administration of supply had

The Rolls-Royce Armoured Car.

changed so little between then and the 1950s. Having served for two years in the Equipment Branch of the RAF before transfer to the RAF Regiment, the author speaks with some experience in equipment accounting. The same forms were still being used, for example the Form 600 for equipment demanded by the station from an MU, the Form 674 for equipment demanded by a flight or squadron on the station from the station stores, and the Form 22, which recorded items of furniture held in a barrack room. He recalls one Guest Night on his station where the senior technical officer was being dined out on posting. In his after-dinner speech he could not resist a dig at the station equipment officer when he trotted out the rhyme:

'You can grovel on the floor with your 674,
  But you won't get your bins, ash, removable.'

In the days before computerization all voucher work was done with multiple copies of forms, and items held in stock were recorded in huge ledgers. Before moving on to describe how the system worked, the author will tell one story against himself as an illustration of the tedious paperwork that used to be involved. In the 1920s, as in the 1950s, equipment demanded by units on a station was classified under three headings:

Class A Stores This class consists of those articles that remain on charge and cannot be replaced except on their return to store and that, when defective and beyond the capacity or authority of the unit to repair, must be returned to the stores depot.

Class B Stores This class consists of those articles that remain on charge and cannot be replaced except on their return to store, but may be conditioned by the CO of the station on the recommendation of a local board of survey.

Class C Stores This class consists of all items that are totally consumed in use.

As the officer in charge of the Equipment Provisioning and Accounting Section (EPAS) at RAF Debden in 1956, the author had to make an assessment of quantities of equipment required in the following six months based upon the quantities demanded over the past year. It took many hours to go through a stock ledger, and where a fresh stock demand was justified he placed a paperclip in the top of the sheet so that the airman clerk could place an order for these items on a Form 600, which went to the appropriate MU. Virtually all the airmen in those days were national servicemen and were not experienced stores clerks. They just did as they were told. One day the process began by assessing how many sweeping brooms, mops and buckets might be required by the station based upon the previous year's

consumption. After a couple of hours of turning over page after page, the author was no longer paying attention to the items being demanded and was simply assessing the quantities required, but by then it was not brooms and buckets, but vehicles, engines and complete aircraft. At the maintenance units there were also national servicemen who doubtless were just doing as they were asked, and they sent a complete Ford engine to Debden as if it was an item that was just going to be kept on the shelf until required, but to their credit the MU did query Debden's demand for a complete Chipmunk aircraft. When the Ford engine arrived at the Receipts and Dispatch Section of Station Stores, the senior equipment officer, Flight Lieutenant Ralph Mansfield, very quickly learned of its totally unexpected arrival, and minutes later he stormed, red faced, into the author's office to demand who was the blankety-blank idiot whose stock demanded a complete engine. What follows is the complete unvarnished truth, for at that moment in came the station MT (Motor Transport) officer, who sagged down into a vacant chair in the office to declare that the station ambulance would have to come off the road until a replacement engine could be obtained. Whereupon Flight Lieutenant Mansfield replied triumphantly, 'You name it and this equipment section has got it!' This, then, gives the reader some idea, if not entirely representative, of RAF stores administration in the days before computers.

RAF Equipment Policy in the 1920s

The statement of policy with regard to the administration and accounting of RAF supplies in August 1925 was as follows:

The increasing importance of material in the evolution of the fighting services renders those services more and more expensive and it is only by the strictest economy and the elimination of all waste that it is possible to provide an efficient fighting force with the available funds. In these circumstances it is of the first importance that COs should give personal attention to their stores' organization to prevent waste of material and to ensure economy and efficiency in use. Further, the changing and developing nature of the RAF demands this in order that administrative methods may be adapted without delay to changing needs. For the same purpose it is essential that all responsible officers of a unit should have a good working knowledge of the main principles of the stores system so that they can fulfil their part in it intelligently.

The supply and maintenance of equipment came under two headings. Firstly, all factors arising prior to an article of equipment being received into service, and secondly, the receipt by the service and use of articles while on charge.

Supply Organization

Sources: RAF Stores Regulations, Volume 1, August 1925, and the RAF List for March 1926

RAF equipment, for the most part, was produced by civilian firms under contract to the Air Ministry. One major exception was the production of some aircraft for the RAF that were turned out by the Royal Aircraft Factory Farnborough, particularly during the First World War, although later the role of Farnborough was reduced to research and development of aircraft and associated equipment. Some equipment and services were provided locally and were bought on local purchase orders where this was the most economical method of obtaining such equipment or services or when the demand was urgent. Items of equipment produced by civilian firms were delivered to stores depots, where they were held until demanded by RAF stations or headquarters units. Some items, such as complete aircraft or engines, required special authorization before they could be demanded and supplied. This rule would apply to most Class A stores, whereas Class C stores were often demanded routinely and without prior authorization. The list of supply depots for the middle of the decade is shown as an example, and is taken from the RAF List for March 1926:

No. 1 Stores Depot	Kidbrooke, Inland Area No. 1 Group
	Group Captain A. Fletcher CMG, CBE, MC
No. 2 Stores (Ammunition Depot)	Broadheath, Altrincham, Inland Area No. 3 Group
	Squadron Leader J. Waddington OBE
No. 3 Stores Depot	Milton, Inland Area No. 1 Group Wing Command J. Sayer MC
No. 4 Stores Depot	Ickenham, Inland Area No. 1 Group
	Squadron Leader B.W.M. Williams
The Packing Depot	Ascot, Inland Area No. 1 Group Squadron Leader E.W. Havers
MT Repair Depot	Harlescott, Shrewsbury, Inland Area
	Wing Commander R.J. Mounsey OBE

Overseas Depots

Central Supply Depot	Hinaidi, Iraq Command
Iraq Command	Squadron Leader A. Burtenehaw OBE, MC
Stores Depot Iraq	Basrah, Iraq Command
	Squadron Leader W.J.B. Curtis OBE
Base Supply Depot	Basra, Iraq Command
	Flight Lieutenant F.S. Moore
Supply Depot Iraq	Iraq Command
	Flight Lieutenant R.V. Robinson OBE
Supply Depot Palestine	Sarafand, Palestine Command
	Flight Lieutenant H.S.F.T. Jerrard

There were depots in India at this time, notably at Lahore, but they do not appear in the RAF List.

Purposes served by Stores Accounting

The publication lists the four purposes, as follows:

1. The recording of stores transactions as they occur.
2. Detection of weakness in the organization and in the administration of the unit.
3. Estimating expenditure and future requirements.
4. The fixing of responsibility for the appropriation of material to specific work and for the custody of articles of equipment in use.

Chapter 2 of the source publication deals with the principles of stores accounting. Equipment administration is to be effected by means of vouchers for demand, return or transfer of equipment and for holding equipment on charge there. Ledgers (RAF Form 823)and tally cards in the stores and inventories (RAF Form 670) held by squadrons, flights or sections on a station. Accounts must not be permitted to fall into arrears and all ledger binders are to be kept locked when not in use and in the custody of the accounting officer. All entries are to be in ink with no erasures. Tally cards list equipment available in the storehouse and obviate the need for storehouse personnel to have access to the ledgers. The tally cards are used by stores officers in framing provisioning demands. 'Dues in' record the demands that cannot be met from stock and are recorded as 'Dues out' on the tally cards.

Provision and receipt of stocks by stores depots The Air Ministry places contracts for equipment and sends the appropriate stores depot four copies of each contract placed. The depots will be assigned maximum and minimum limits in respect of each item of stock held, i.e. stores depots must make periodical demands on the Air Ministry. Urgent and supplementary demands may be made on a Form 602. There is a distinction between recurring and non-recurring expenditure, e.g. non-recurring expenditure might be made on initial issues of permanent stores to units or establishments, gifts, or issues to other government departments. Recurring expenditure comprises all issues which it is anticipated will be periodically repeated.

Receipt of stocks under Air Ministry contracts and local purchase orders Deliveries may be of either aeronautical or non-aeronautical equipment. The Air Ministry is under no obligation to accept and pay for any quantity of equipment in excess of that ordered in the contract. However, officers commanding stores depots may accept and certify for payment excess deliveries without reference to the Air Ministry if:

The cost of excess deliveries is not more than 5 per cent of the cost of the quantity ordered under the contract or £25, whichever is less, if charged at contract prices. Or

If a higher cost of excess than above but where the equipment involved is of advantage to the public in which case Air Ministry approval must be sought.

Supplies may also be obtained by local purchase order (LPO) placed by local officers. Such purchases may be made wherever the articles can be obtained on the most advantageous terms, having regard to the nature and the urgency of the requirement. Such purchases may only be made by the stores depots, but do not apply to purchases made by the Works and Buildings Department and the experimental stations (such as Martlesham Heath, Felixstowe or Farnborough). Depots may resort to LPOs for stores up to a value of £25 for any single purchase, i.e. where the value is so small that no advantage would be gained by a purchase through the Air Ministry or when equipment is so urgently required that it cannot be obtained on time through the Air Ministry or no regular supply is held in any stores depot. Orders for any single purchase of equipment of the value of £5 or above is to be made the subject of a tender. Normally the lowest bid is accepted, but COs are to justify accepting higher bids.

Abroad   Demands made by the Stores Depot Egypt and by the Stores or Aircraft Depot Iraq for equipment are to be rendered in duplicate, half yearly. Supplementary demands may be made for equipment urgently required. When the Home Stores Depot receives a demand from an overseas depot, the CO is immediately to report to the Air Ministry the particulars of any equipment that requires hastening from the contractors. Perishable goods may be dispatched in equal monthly consignments.

The transfer of equipment to HM ships   With the RAF manning flights of the Fleet Air Arm aboard aircraft carriers in the inter-war years, it was necessary to lay down the arrangements to cover this unusual situation because the Navy had their own stores accounting procedures, which could, in certain circumstances, clash with those of the RAF, such as the holding of petrol, oils and lubricants (POL). Furthermore, with ships at sea away from an RAF stores depot or RAF station for considerable periods of time, the RAF units aboard had to have their own stores officers (see Chapter 6). Consequently the following were the instructions given:

RAF units, known as Fleet Air Arm Units permanently accommodated in aircraft-carriers, are accounting units and issues of equipment to them are to be made in the same manner as issues to accounting units on shore except as provided for in Section II of this chapter. The RAF Stores Officer on board will work with the RN Engineer Officer for the intake of quantities received, checking of receipts and stocks held. The RAF Stores Officer is to issue equipment to satisfy the internal demands of the RAF unit on board and he will do all the stores accounting, but he will not hold POL stocks except supplies for immediate use. When the ship is not a carrier, e.g. a cruiser, the RAF Officer or airman in charge of the RAF party on board is to be responsible for all RAF property and is to account for it. RAF personnel on board are subject to the Naval Discipline Act but that does not absolve them for the responsibility of the care of RAF equipment and that is to be held in a storeroom set aside for that purpose. If the Officer i/c of the Party is a pilot who might fly away from the ship for periods of time he is to nominate another officer or airman to deputise for him in being responsible for RAF equipment. When the Air Force party returns to land the balance of RAF equipment held is to be transferred to the RAF Unit nearest to the port of disembarkation or as may be ordered by the AOC Coastal Area.

Obtaining current supplies from outside sources (all units)   Particulars of standing contracts under which units may obtain supplies locally will be published in Weekly Orders. The unit requiring supplies is to demand on the contractor on a Local Order form. Group Commanders will be responsible for the issue of the necessary instructions to the units under their command to ensure that the demands drawn on standing contracts are made in accordance with service requirements.

Casual purchases   To meet exceptional requirements, e.g. when a breakdown occurs and some spare parts might have to be issued on the spot, the Commanding Officer may authorise expenditure up to a value of £5 per month.

Issues of equipment between the RAF and other 'Air Services'   Chapter 8 of the publication provides for the issue of equipment by an RAF unit to (i) the Civil Aviation service, (ii) the Aeronautical Inspection Department or certain experimental establishments and (iii) the Works and Buildings Department when vote adjustments are to be made. (This provides for the fact that each service receives a vote of money from the Treasury, and in this case the RAF vote will have to be credited with the sums involved in the equipment issue and set against the vote in the receiving department, e.g.

from an RAF stores depot to RAE Farnborough or the Royal Airship Works at Cardington.)

Issues of equipment out of the RAF (home procedure) All issues out of the RAF exclusive of short loans by units other than stores depots are to be made by the stores depot dealing with the class of equipment affected. In the event of an order being made for the issue of equipment from a unit other than a stores depot, the stores depot is to take all action to effect financial adjustment. Where machines or engines are issued on loan they are to be vouched to the appropriate stores depot.

Internal issues and receipts – general procedure No issue of equipment is to be made to RAF personnel whether free, on loan or on repayment except under general or specific authority of the Air Ministry. This order is intended to cover such items as uniform, protective clothing, aircrew watches, tools or the issue of clothing that has been rendered unfit for use other than fair wear or tear.

Airmen, for example, received a free issue of clothing on entry to the service and would be entitled to periodic changes of uniform when items had worn out, hence the expression 'fair wear and tear'. But if an airman was to alter his uniform, as described in Chapter 9, he would have to be issued with a replacement item on repayment. Items required for work such as flying clothing, aircrew watches or tools could be loaned to an officer or airman. The order goes on to say that with the exception of tools and appliances required for the work of the flight or section; flights or sections are not to hold equipment in bulk but are to demand items from the stores only as and when required for specific work actually in hand. Class A, B and C equipment referred to at the beginning of this section will clarify this point.

Furniture and barrack room equipment – messes, married quarters and other buildings Articles of furniture and barrack room equipment are to be issued in accordance with the authorized scale for rooms, married quarters, etc. The CO has to give authority for a room or premises to be furnished and a Form 22 displayed in the room or premises will show what furniture has been authorized. For married quarters an inventory will be held.

The scale of barrack equipment for officers' and airmen's married quarters varied with the rank. That occupied by an Air officer would be quite substantial. In the 1920s marriage of officers under the age of 30 years was discouraged, and most lived in the officers' mess. The photograph on the next page is that of the married quarter of the Second in Command of the Central Flying School at RAF Wittering. An airman's married quarter would be a modest semi-detached house with a small

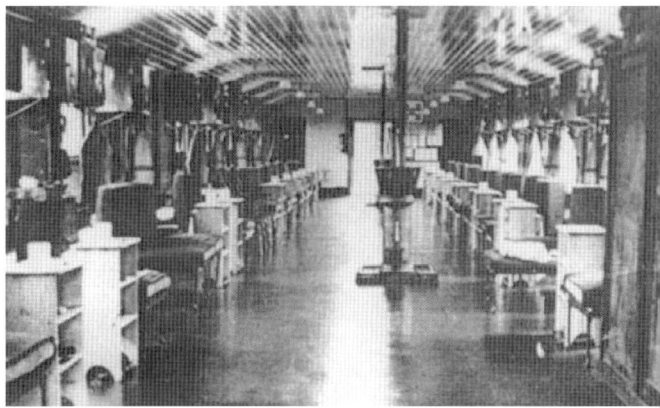

A typical barrack room of the period, which would be furnished to an authorized scale.

garden. Personnel in messes and married quarters were scaled with so much crockery and glassware. It was accepted that, in the best-run mess or married quarter there would be breakages, and so personnel were given a crockery and glass allowance. This is shown on page 266.

One of those delightful snobberies of life in the service used to apply to chamber pots. The lower ranks simply got Pots, Chamber, Airmen, whereas officers got Pots, Chamber, crested. Air officers on the other hand got Pots, Chamber, gilded and crested. I am sure that if a senior officer was ever caught short in the middle of the night he would be comforted in knowing that his chamber pot was suitably inscribed as befitted his rank.

Bedding It was particularly important in a closed community, such as airmen's barrack accommodation, that bedding was maintained in as clean a condition as possible to prevent the spread of infections, the more so in RAF hospitals. The orders in Chapter 32 stipulate that 'the stores officer is responsible that the bedding in the

A typical officer's married quarter of the period.

CROCKERY AND GLASSWARE EXPENSE ACCOUNT.   SPECIMEN QUARTERLY ACCOUNT.

Date.	Voucher No.	Receipts in Flight.	Returns to Store.	Loss or Breakage.	Value of Stock in use.	Breakage Allowance one-eightieth per month of Stock in use.	Value of Losses or Breakages Chargeable.	Charges paid by Individuals.	Remainder to be dealt with as a Collective Charge.	No. of Men Last Day of the Account.	Charge per Man.	Collective Charge paid.
1	2	3	4	5	6	7	8	9	10	11	12	13
		£ s. d.	£ s. d.	£ s. d.	£ s. d.	£ s. d.	£ s. d.	£ s. d.	£ s. d.		£ s. d.	£ s. d.
Jan. 1st	Stock	—	—	—	80 10 0	3 0 4¼	—	—	—	—	—	—
5th	27	4 2 8	—	—	—	—	—	—	—	—	—	—
12th	49	—	1 10 0	—	—	—	—	—	—	—	—	—
17th	53	—	—	4 6	—	—	—	4 6	—	—	—	—
20th	60	10 0	—	—	—	—	—	—	—	—	—	—
31st	61	—	—	2 6	—	—	—	2 6	—	—	—	—
Feb. 1st	63	3 5 0	—	—	—	—	—	—	—	—	—	—
14th	78	—	18 0	—	—	—	—	—	—	—	—	—
24th	84	—	—	13 0	—	—	—	4 0	—	—	—	—
Mar. 1st	91	—	5 6	—	—	—	—	—	—	—	—	—
15th	99	2 3 6	—	—	—	—	—	—	—	—	—	—
31st	102	—	—	(a) 5 10 0	—	—	—	15 0	—	—	—	—
		10 1 0	2 13 6	6 10 0	80 10 0	3 0 4¼	(b) 3 9 7¼	1 6 0	(c) 2 3 7¼	42	1 1	2 5 6
					(d) 17 6							
April 1st	Stock	—	—	—	81 7 6	(e) 3 1 0¼	—	—	—	—	—	—
						(f) 1 10½						

(a) Revealed by quarterly check of inventory.   (b) Column 5, less column 7.   (c) Column 8 less column 9.   (d) Balance of columns 3, 4 and 5 added (or deducted).   (e) Breakage allowance on new stock value.   (f) Excess charge previous quarter brought forward, i.e., excess of column 13 over column 10.

This would be the station C & G expense account. Where individuals had exceeded their allowance they would be charged.

stores is kept in a proper state of cleanliness and repair, and fit for immediate use. He is to ensure that all articles of bedding, especially sheets, are kept perfectly dry; he is also to ensure that bedding in bales is not unpacked until required for use, and that such bales are kept off the floor in a dry part of the storehouse. All articles of hospital bedding are to be kept separate and distinct from other bedding.' This applied especially to items of linen used by patients suffering from venereal disease. Bedding for use with patients suffering from infectious diseases was set to one side and marked with the letter 'I'. Articles of bedding were to be unfolded and shaken twice a year, or more often if necessary, as a protection against moths. It was acknowledged that items of bedding might have to be washed more often in hot climates, but the frequency should take economy into account. Personnel who stained their mattresses or who made them otherwise unfit for reissue could be required to pay for them. Finally it was permitted for an airman, his wife and child on the married roll proceeding on board vessels bound to and from ports in Great Britain, Ireland and the Channel Islands to be issued with a blanket.

Accounting for accessories in use with 'machines' The term machine could apply to aircraft, seaplanes or flying-boats, MT vehicles and marine craft. Such machines incorporated all manner of items of equipment that were detachable and of value in themselves, such as vehicle batteries, aircraft instruments, spare wheels, lifting jacks, etc. In demanding from stores, transferring between units or returning to stores a complete aircraft or vehicle, it was only necessary to put the aircraft serial number or vehicle registration on any vouchers, and not list all the separate items that were carried. Accordingly each aircraft, motor vehicle or marine craft would have its own inventory of equipment. On receipt it would be the responsibility of the receiving officer or NCO to check the inventory.

Torpedoes and torpedo stores accounting procedure Responsibility for the storage and issue of torpedoes and torpedo stores was divided between the RAF and the Royal Navy. To begin with they could be supplied from stocks that were the property of the RAF but held on deposit by the Admiralty or issues from Admiralty stocks. Those supplied from Admiralty stocks for use by the RAF would have to be paid for by the RAF, and regardless of ownership the freight and handling charges would be the responsibility of the RAF. RAF units requiring torpedoes in the UK or the Mediterranean could be issued with these weapons from RAF Gosport or RAF Base Malta respectively. Torpedoes and non-explosive items were held at RN torpedo depots, whereas warheads and other explosive items were held in RN armament depots.

Chapter 9
Personnel

The extracts from source materials chosen for this chapter are intended to provide a picture of the 1920s in the various aspects of personnel matters. This begins with the careers of a number of Air officers and a senior officer. It should not be forgotten that all senior officers and NCOs of the early 1920s had come from the Army and Navy. It was to be the 1930s before the first Cranwell cadets reached senior rank, such as Sir Thomas Pike, who was a flight cadet at Cranwell in 1924. He achieved the rank of squadron leader in 1937 and wing commander in 1940. The early 1920s were characterized by a massive rundown in personnel, but there was also recruitment at this time. However, one branch to which there was to be no recruitment was the Women's Royal Air Force, which was disbanded in its entirety in 1920, not to be resurrected until the late 1930s. The contribution of women during the period 1918–20 was enormous, and it is difficult to imagine the RAF of the 1920s being one that was virtually an entirely male service.

Air Officers' Careers

An Air officer is one who holds the rank of Air Commodore and above. Appendix N gives details of the career paths of the first four officers to be appointed Chief of the Air Staff, namely Sir Hugh Trenchard, Sir Frederick Sykes, Sir John Salmond and Sir Edward Ellington.

One thing is common to all four officers: they came from the Army. Trenchard had been a Fusilier and had risen to the rank of lieutenant-colonel in the Southern Nigerian Regiment before coming to aviation. Sykes had been a Hussar and had served in India and South Africa before taking up flying. Salmond started life as a subaltern with the Royal Lancaster Regiment and Ellington had come from an artillery background. They all started life as second lieutenants and would have been instructed in 'all arms' as officer cadets before taking up their specialization in the infantry, cavalry or artillery. They brought to the air arm their experience in Army tactics, training and administration. Sykes seemed to have gone on every course available, but this only served to make him a more proficient and knowledgeable Army officer. As long as air operations were in direct support of the land battle, this experience would be valuable, but when it came to using airpower strategically these leaders of the infant service were crossing new frontiers.

It was an obvious plus if the RAF's most senior commanders could pilot an aeroplane. Sykes qualified in 1911, and the remainder in 1912. If nothing else, they knew how an aeroplane flew, its obvious qualities as a new weapon system as well as its limitations, but did these officers then pursue an active flying career? Granted they hadn't much time, since only six years elapsed between the time they became pilots and the time they would be transferred from the Army to take over the running of the RAF. Sykes did help Sir David Henderson to set up the RFC and was briefly the air adviser during the Dardanelles campaign in 1915, but thereafter he returned to Army staff duties not related to flying. Yet he still emerged as the first Chief of the Air Staff (CAS), if one discounts the few days in 1918 when Trenchard held the post. Trenchard would not have been fit for flying duties in today's air force. Having been injured in the chest during the Boer War he had only one functioning lung. Nevertheless, he qualified as a pilot. He was an expert horseman but rated only as an indifferent pilot. However, he became a flying instructor at the Central Flying School and rose to Assistant Commandant. Ellington did not pursue an active flying career at any time. Only John Salmond was so involved: he commanded an operational squadron and wing in France, personally flew and tested new aircraft types and set a solo British altitude record of 13,140 feet.

Clearly, then, flying ability and experience was not a determining factor in the careers of any of these four men, neither was command of an operational formation in the field. Sykes did so as a junior officer and was second in command of the RFC, but then returned to purely Army staff duties until his appointment as CAS. John Salmond was actively involved, as has been shown. Trenchard was commander of a wing (of the RFC) in France and finally the commander of the Independent Bombing Force in France in 1918. It is Ellington's career that is most unusual. His only time spent with an operational unit was as a subaltern following his commissioning in 1897. Once he had attended the War College in 1908 he spent the next fourteen years as a staff officer. His first operational command was as AOC Middle East in 1922 in the rank of Air Vice-Marshal. Clearly it was his staff skills and his interest in aviation that propelled him to the top.

What must be appreciated is that only six years were to pass between 1912 when the military aeroplane was to be come part of the arsenal of war and 1918 when the

Sir Frederick Sykes, Chief of the Air Staff, 1918–19.

Sir Hugh Trenchard, Chief of the Air Staff, 1919–30.

Sir John Salmond, Chief of the Air Staff, 1930–33.

Sir Edward Ellington, Chief of the Air Staff, 1933–37.

RAF was formed. Those six years saw huge advances in aircraft design and armament that only the needs of war could bring about. The number of aircraft held by the RFC went from a mere handful to 22,000 plus, from flimsy Blériot types to four-engined bombers that could bomb Berlin from bases in Britain. The British Army and the Royal Navy are to be commended for putting together a huge training, supply and repair organization to fight the war. Then came the Smuts Report, which amalgamated the RNAS and the RFC into the RAF. The four officers mentioned, together with hundreds of senior and middle-rank officers, had to be trained to fly and put in command and staff positions in the service. In later years a future CAS would follow a typical career path from Cranwell cadet: flight, squadron and wing commander on a flying squadron, probably a spell as a flying instructor, staff college, station commander, then AOC Group and Command before becoming CAS. But such a career path was not in place in the period 1912–18. The rise to the most senior positions in the RAF by these four men may seem unorthodox by today's standards, particularly Ellington's, but they all met the needs of the moment. The qualities and qualifications of these

officers may be summarized as the ability to fly an aeroplane, an appreciation of the potential of airpower and the enthusiasm, drive and leadership that would be needed if the RAF was to survive the cuts of the early 1920s.

Senior Officers' Careers

A senior officer is one who holds the rank of squadron leader, wing commander or group captain. During the years 1918–29, the period covered by this volume, senior officers were to command squadrons, wings and stations and other formations, and to act in a staff capacity. Just like the Air officers, senior officers were to come from the Army or Royal Navy. One career has been chosen to illustrate the career path of an officer from First World War pilot to a senior staff officer, and this is Harold Whistler. Since Trenchard was determined to put in place the appropriate training institutions, RAF officers of First World War vintage were able to follow a career path very similar to that followed by the first graduates from Cranwell. Having served as Chief of Staff in India in the late 1930s in the rank of acting air commodore, Whistler might well have reached the top had it not been for a tragic accident when the Hannibal aircraft in which he was flying home to the UK to take up a new appointment was lost with all on board over the Persian Gulf.

Harold Whistler

Harold Whistler was commissioned into the Dorsetshire Regiment from Sandhurst in July 1916, and later seconded to the RFC, arriving in France in October of that year. In a short time he had been awarded the DSO and the DFC and bar, as well as Mentions in Dispatches, claiming twenty-three victories as well as flying many Army support and ground-attack sorties. Official dispatches spoke of him as 'a very courageous and enterprising patrol leader and a gallant officer of fine judgement and power of leadership'. In recognition of these qualities he was granted a permanent commission as flight lieutenant in the post-war Royal Air Force, and was appointed Adjutant at the Royal Air Force College, Cranwell.

Harold Whistler's career was very much in keeping with family traditions, which stretched back in direct line to the thirteenth century, providing soldiers, doctors, parsons (his father had been a naval chaplain) and some artistic talent in the nation's service. He was an ideal choice for the Cranwell post, as his leadership qualities and wartime record acted as an inspiration to the young cadets joining the service. He always attached great importance to the building up of 'esprit de corps' through a wide range of activities, sporting as well as social. There was a pack of beagles with a large following, and Whistler enjoyed tennis and hockey.

A large part of Whistler's career was to be devoted to the training of pilots, many of whom distinguished

Harold Whistler as a squadron leader in ceremonial dress. White gloves and sword have continued to be part of the ceremonial dress of officers today, but sadly, in the author's humble opinion, the head-dress based upon the old flying helmet did not survive the inter-war years.

themselves in the Battle of Britain. He later became Chief Flying Instructor, first at No. 5 FTS, Sealand, and then at the CFS, Wittering. He found time to take part in the King's Cup air race, a prestigious flying event of the inter-war years, for which he was lent a Moth.

Promoted to squadron leader in 1927, he spent some time in command of No. 55 Squadron in Iraq (refer to Chapter 4 for 55 Squadron operations records). Here he saw action against Nejd Bedouin tribesmen, narrowly escaping capture when his DH9A had to make a forced landing in the desert owing to engine failure. Fortunately Whistler managed to effect repairs before galloping tribesmen reached him.

The preparation for higher command involved staff training, and Squadron Leader Whistler went, first to the Staff College, Andover, in 1932, and later the Imperial Defence College in 1936 as a wing commander, and for two years he was Senior Intelligence Officer at Fighter Command. In 1937 he was posted to India as RAF Instructor at the Army Staff College. He then became

Chief of Staff in India in the rank of acting air commodore, and was returning home in March 1940 when he lost his life over the Persian Gulf.

Note: Please note that there will be references to establishments and strengths. A unit establishment, whether in peace or war, is the number of personnel that the Air Ministry deems necessary for such a unit to carry out its wartime or peacetime role. The unit strength is the actual number of men so employed, which may be up to, above or below establishment.

Demobilization and Recruitment

The period from the end of the war in 1918 to 1920 witnessed a massive rundown, not only in aircraft but also in the personnel who flew, serviced and supplied parts for them, not to mention the huge administrative tail that accompanies forces into the field or mans staff positions at home. Many officer pilots had interrupted careers or family businesses to return to, and others wished to fly in a civilian capacity. The technicians had highly marketable engineering skills that would be in demand, while others simply wished to return to 'civvy street', worn out by four years of a most gruelling war. On the other hand there were always some who wanted to stay, either because they enjoyed the ' service life' or because there was no other job for which they were qualified. Being housed, fed and paid to learn a trade had obvious attractions, particularly in the economic depressions which followed the war, so it was not simply the case that all those who wanted to stay stayed. Numbers had to be cut from a wartime strength of 291,170 officers and men to 60,000 by 1 October 1919, exclusive of those serving in India. A big reduction of strength was to be effected by running down the Women's Royal Air Force (WRAF) and civilian subordinates. At the same time there was some recruitment during the phase of massive rundown, for in any armed service there is always a need to recruit fit, young and unattached people, and those career officers and NCOs who wished to stay on needed to know if they still had a career in the RAF. Let it not be forgotten that Cranwell was looking for cadets in 1920, and at about the same time the Halton apprentice scheme was getting under way, but these institutions would not bear fruit until the mid to late 1920s.

Authorized Manpower for the 1920s

Year	Officers Air	Officers	WOs	NCOs	Airmen
1920	19	3,040	324	2,900	19,760
1921	19	2,913	329	3,433	21,845
1922	40	3,045	300	3,800	22,195
1923	31	3,186	250	4,124	22,731

1924	35	3,325	309	4,881	23,410
1925	35	3,592	330	5,360	24,500
1926	35	3,512	345	4,780	22,900
1927	35	3,401	320	4,700	20,525
1928	35	3,395	318	5,000	20,000
1929	38	3,300	420	5,000	19,880

The figures for Air officers has doubled, whereas the number of airmen has risen from 19,760 in 1920 only to fall back to almost that figure by the end of the decade. This can be explained by the rank structure of a peacetime service. That is to say, a service that has formations commanded by Air officers that can be expanded at short notice. The influx to meet emergencies or service expansion would be at the recruit stage, and there must be the number of NCOs to train the new entrants.

Officers – Commissions and Career Development
Situation during the period 1919–23   This period was one of great volatility when it came to manning the new service. The Air Ministry had the daunting task of reducing it from 188 squadrons and five flights to twenty-nine squadrons in 1921. There were not only squadron pilots but group, wing and squadron commanders and staff officers in the ranks of colonel, lieutenant-colonel and major who had to be either demobilized, returned to the Army or Navy from where they had been seconded, some unwillingly, or offered a full-time or part-time career in the RAF. Once the shape of the peacetime air force was settled, the future intakes would come from Cranwell for full career officers, and officer training and flying training schools for those on short-service commissions. In the months following the end of the war establishments at home and overseas had still to be filled. There would be some permanent commissions offered to serving Army and RN officers, as well as those of the RFC who had become officers of the RAF on 1 April 1918, even if they still retained their old Army ranks until the new ones were promulgated on 27 August 1919. Because the future shape of the RAF had not then been decided, and since the disbandment of squadrons would continue into 1922, a number of officers on temporary appointments would be required. The extracts from AMWOs that follow need to be read in this context.

Reduction in officer strengths
Source: Air Ministry Weekly Order No. 866, 31 July 1919

AMWO 866 deals with the eligibility for demobilization of officers of the Flying, Technical and Administrative Branches. A number of officers were seconded from their parent arm, Royal Navy or Army, for duties with the RAF, and they were invited to re-second without

prejudice to their subsequent return to their parent service. The order went on to state that there would be a certain number of permanent commissions, which would be awarded approximately six months from the date of the order for those serving on temporary commissions. In dealing with the eligibility of 'flying-risk' pay , this was absorbed into the pay for the rank for flying officers. Reference to Chapter 4 will impress upon the reader the number of fatalities and injuries sustained by aircrews, not directly on operations, but in flying accidents. Those who were granted a permanent commission, excepting certain technical officers, would be required to qualify as a pilot within twelve months of 1 August 1919. With regard to stores officers, they were to join the new Quartermasters' Branch. All others accepting commissioned service would be required to learn to fly, subject to medical fitness. Reduction in officer strength would be achieved by demobilization followed by the appointment of a limited number of officers to permanent commissions and appointing others to temporary ones (see next paragraph).

Scheme for immediate temporary entry of officers into the RAF   Source: Air Ministry Weekly Order 781 dated 7 June 1919

The Air Staff needed to retain sufficient officers in each speciality and in the appropriate ranks to man establishments of units subject to disbandment, redeployment, merging, etc. Granting too many permanent commissions in 1919 to officers who in the event might not be able to look forward to a full-time career would not be good for morale. Having a number of officers on temporary commissions gave the manning staff the flexibility they needed to meet rapidly changing manning needs. Notice how open ended is AMWO/781, which states that there was an immediate requirement for 2,500 temporary officers in addition to those granted permanent commissions. Among the figure of 2,500 were a number of officers lent to the RAF from the Army or the Navy. As a general rule these temporary officers were not to be more than 25 years of age on application, and the period of service would be for three years. On completion of two years' service this could be extended to four. During the period on the active list these officers could be required to serve anywhere in the world, and promotion would be open to them subject to their being qualified. On or before completion of the period of active service, temporary officers would be permitted to serve on the Reserve of Officers at the discretion of the Air Ministry. Even in peacetime, when manning positions are more settled, the Air Ministry has, from time to time, resorted to various means to ensure that it has the right number of officers for the present and future appointments. This can never be an exact science, indeed the author can remember the 'golden bowler' scheme intended to encourage those on long-term engagements to retire early. In more recent times there has been the 'specialist aircrew' scheme designed to give officers a continued active flying career in exchange for accepting a limit to future promotion.

Permanent Commissions in the RAF for Flying, Technical and Administrative Officers now holding Temporary Commissions therein

Sources: AMWO 99, dated 17 January 1919
AMWO 866, dated 31 July 1919
AMWO 109, dated 9 February 1921

And so there was always the carrot dangled before temporary officers that a permanent commission could be granted. In order to become eligible for a permanent commission in the Royal Air Force an officer would be required to fulfil the following conditions:

officers who might be given permanent commissions among those serving in Russia. The order stated that the list of officers gazetted on 1 August 1919 was not final, for there were also officers serving with the Department of the Controller-General of Civil Aviation and the Department of the Director-General of Supply and Research. Finally, the matter of granting permanent commissions to officers serving on airships had not then been settled, and AMWOs 109 of 9 February 1921 and 40 of 19 January 1922 provided for officers serving on short-service commissions to be considered.

Officer strengths between 1919 and 1920 The effectiveness of the Air Ministry's efforts to bring the number of RAF officers in to line with peacetime requirements may be judged by the figures between February 1919, before demobilization had begun to take effect, and January 1920. The publication of officers' personal occurrences appears in the London Gazette,

Substantive Rank as shown in the Air Force List	Lower Limit of Age	Higher Limit of Age	Age for Compulsory Retirement
Subalterns	No limit	27	42
Captains	No limit unless applications are too numerous, in which case length of service in that rank will count, rather than age.	35	45
Majors	25	38	47
Lieutenant-Colonels	30	45	52
Colonels	35	48	57

Medically they were to be in good mental and bodily health and free from any physical defect likely to interfere with the efficient performance of the duties required of them. A selection board under the chairmanship of Brigadier-General T.I. Webb-Bowen CMG was formed to visit home and overseas stations to interview applicants. The latter were not bound to accept permanent commissions even if selected, nor did selection guarantee the award of a permanent commission, since it depended on the number of applicants selected and the number of established posts to be filled. AMWO 866 took account of the number of

hence the reference to 'gazetted' officers. These occurrences are then incorporated into the next updating of the Air Force List, the official publication giving the dates of commissioning and promotions, both of which affect an officer's seniority in his rank. Every officer from the Chief of the Air Staff downwards had to be granted a commission in the Royal Air Force, and from August 1919 they all adopted the new rank titles. Accordingly the tables below are juxtaposed so that the reader can see the equivalence of the Army and RAF ranks, although there is no strict equivalence to the Army rank of Brigadier-General.

February 1919		January 1920	
General Officers (Major-Generals)	11	Air Officers	20
Colonels	35)	Group Captains	24
Acting Brigadier-Generals	29)		
Lieutenant-Colonels	254	Wing Commanders	103
Majors	770	Squadron Leaders	320
Captains	3,568	Flight Lieutenants	1,212
Lieutenants	11,914	Flying & Observer Officers	3,252
Second Lieutenants	15,573	Pilot Officers	2,101
	32,154		7,032

To this figure for 1920 must be added those officers who still retained their Army rank. They had not been commissioned into the RAF since there was no job for them. It may be assumed that all these officers were awaiting demobilization, which should not disguise the fact that a number of the 7,032 officers shown above were also hoping to be demobilized but were holding posts from which they could not then be released. Junior medical officers and dentists appeared on a separate list. Only medical officers of the rank of wing commander and above are included in the totals in the right-hand column.

Colonels	1
Lieutenant Colonels	60
Majors	375
Captains	2,205
Lieutenants	8,835
Second Lieutenants	11,173
	22,649

New RAF Officers' Ranks
AMWO 973 dated 25 August 1919

The new RAF officers' ranks published in August 1919, with two exceptions, are the same today:

Air Officers
Marshal of the Air (later
  Marshal of the RAF)
Air Chief Marshal
Air Marshal
Air Vice-Marshal
Air Commodore

Senior Officers
Group Captain
Wing Commander
Squadron Leader

Junior Officers
Flight Lieutenant
Flying Officer or Observer Officer
  (now just Flying Officer)
Pilot Officer

Short-Service Commissions
AMWO 26 dated 18 January 1923
294 dated 17 May 1923

AMWO 26 permitted officers of the GD Branch, Stores and Medical Branches to complete four, five or six years on the active list. AMWO 294 of May 1923 then fixed short-service commissions at five years. Those officers serving on four-year engagements were invited to extend to five years. Those officers who had their commissions extended to five years would not be debarred from volunteering for extensions to six and seven years should such extensions be called for. Such extensions would not affect an officer's liability to serve for four years on the Reserve. A 1919 order that required

officers to be prepared to serve anywhere in the world had been amended by this latest order to the effect that officers must be prepared to serve on any type of aircraft in the world, whether ashore or afloat. These 1923 orders reflect the more settled manning position of the service when the RAF could give a commitment to officers to serve for an extra year on the active list, still retaining the flexibility to obtain an individual officer's service for extra years in case of need, together with the commitment to Reserve service. The reference above to 'service afloat' is a reminder that the RAF provided pilots for the Fleet Air Arm aboard aircraft-carriers. Indeed, an order of July 1924 called for RAF volunteers to serve with the fleet.

Constitution of the General-Duties Branch
AMWO 426 dated 21 June 1928

A major statement of policy with regard to commissioned service was made in June 1928. The reader may recall that, following the post-war rundown of the RAF, the government had approved a gradual expansion of the RAF at home to provide, at some future unspecified date, for a force of fifty-two fighter and bomber squadrons. It has already been shown that a fighting force must try to keep the requisite numbers of officers in the various ranks with the required specializations and in the appropriate age bands to ensure that it can meet all its manning needs for its operational, staff, administrative and training personnel. The situation that the RAF faced in 1928 was firstly, that there was a high percentage of posts in the rank of flying officer; secondly, that the specialist requirements in armament, photography, signals and navigation could not be met, even if every permanent officer was required to specialize, whether or not he wished to do so; thirdly, it appeared that the proportion of flight lieutenants to more senior positions was such that promotion to these posts, which permanent officers should expect from a full-time career, could not be realized before some officers reached the compulsory retirement age for the rank. What the Air Ministry wanted was a permanent officer's career that would see promotion at reasonably low ages, subject always to suitability. Thus every suitable flying officer should expect to be promoted to flight lieutenant and flight lieutenant to squadron leader. Thereafter the word 'majority' is used, so the majority of squadron leaders should expect to be promoted to wing commander, and wing commander to group captain. The Air Staff regarded the rank of group captain as being a reasonable aim for a career officer pursuing a lifetime career. The number of officers reaching Air rank would, of course, be quite small, and so there would be a number of group captains simply serving their time until they reached the compulsory age of retirement for that rank. Thus wing commanders waiting for group captain posts would be frustrated. Accordingly group captains who had held one or more appointments in the rank and who were not selected for promotion to Air rank would be placed on half pay with a view to retirement. A number of group captain posts were to be gradually increased over the following years to accommodate those officers who would otherwise be forced to retire prematurely.

The retirement age for flight lieutenants and squadron leaders was to be 45 years, but the service could enforce retirement at 40 years. For wing commanders the age would be 48, group captains 53 and air commodores 57. With the tapering of posts to that of Chief of the Air Staff, the rule that applied to group captains had necessarily to be applied to Air officers. With this prospect of officers retiring in later life, the transition to civil life could be difficult, and a gratuity of £1,000 was to be granted to officers who were transferred to the Reserve after ten years' active service.

The success of the Airman Pilot Scheme meant that a number of junior officer posts could be filled by sergeants, who were normally promoted at the age of 22 years. This would alleviate the problem mentioned earlier of having too many officers in the rank of flying officer. The flying posts created by the Home Defence Expansion plan to fifty-two squadrons could be filled by airman pilots to reduce the officer requirement from approximately 3,650 to 3,150.

With regard to specialization, a number of aircrew officers had hitherto been required to specialize in either navigation, armament, signals or photography, for which the appropriate training was given. This was to ensure that each squadron had officers who could oversee work in those areas by other officers and the tradesmen of the unit. With regard to the navigation specialization, this was the day of the pilot navigator flying with a map on his knee. It was to be later, when navigating an aircraft required such skills and use of equipment and the undivided attention of one member of the crew, that a separate aircrew category of navigator was introduced. Technical officers, on the other hand, were those who undertook the more detailed work of repair of aircraft and ground equipment. But remember that in Trenchard's air force all permanent officers were expected to fly. This AMWO makes quite clear the Air Ministry requirement for technical officers to be experienced in flying duties so that they should not get out of touch with those who had to fly and fight. Their technical duties should therefore be interspersed with periods of general employment, making them eligible for promotion to the highest ranks of the service.

To summarize, the policy enunciated in AMWO 426 would provide a career for permanent officers. It recognized that in addition to the requirement for officers to fill command, staff and administrative posts there was a requirement for technical officers and personnel to fill junior flying posts. So the RAF's career officers should be able to fly, be versed in either photography, armament, signals or navigation, undertake detailed technical work and have the opportunity of rising to command and staff positions. Only one description fits this state of affairs, and that is a General-Duties Branch.

Conditions of Service of Medium-Service Officers
AMWO 427 dated 21 June 1928
The Air Ministry Weekly Order that constitutes the General-Duties Branch is immediately followed by Order No. 427, which establishes the Medium-Service Officer (MS) engagement. The Air Staff felt that there was a need for officers who would serve a term on the active list between, on the one hand, the Short-Service Commissioned Officer (SSC) and on the other the Permanently Commissioned officer (PC). The MS officers were to be selected from those serving on SSCs to serve a further five years on the active list, that is ten years in all. This they would do on completion of their first five years on an SSC. MS officers would normally be employed on flying duties appropriate to their rank and attend courses appropriate to their duties, but would not be eligible for specialist staff or language training.

The Cranwell Course
This is an appropriate point at which to consider how the new entrant to the service was trained for a full-time life career in the RAF. This was the flight cadet at Cranwell. By the end of the decade the training regime had had a chance to settle down, and the author felt he could do no better than to use the description of life at the RAF College in 1928 experienced by Douglas Bader, who was to achieve fame in the Second World War by flying in combat with artificial legs. It should be remembered that Trenchard's choice of Cranwell was partly influenced by its location far from the flesh pots of London. Cadets enjoying a night on the tiles could hardly expect much from down-town Grantham or Sleaford (the RAF College was affectionately known as 'Sleaford Tech').

Bader describes how flight cadets at Cranwell had only £4 per month pocket money and that they were allowed out, only after duty for the day, until 23.59 hrs at night. The time '23.59 hrs' is that lovely service euphemism for midnight, for by making it a minute to midnight the RAF could ensure that it was not mistaken for midnight the following night.

The flying began almost as soon as the cadet arrived at Cranwell, and this was on the Avro 504N for first-year cadets and the Armstrong Whitworth Atlas (Army Cooperation aircraft) for second years. For those cadets nominated for fighter squadrons, further training was carried out on either Fairey Foxes or Siskins. The NCO instructors bore the brunt of turning the cadets into officers, and drill, as ever, was the chosen way to ensure instant obedience to orders. Cadets were called on parade by a bugle, and on each Saturday morning there was a Colour-Hoisting Parade. This is a parade where the RAF Ensign is hoisted on the flagstaff beside the station parade ground. 'Fourth termers' had to command the cadet wing on parade as they would do when they became officers, and some senior cadets were promoted to under-officer, as was Bader on A Squadron.

The first year syllabus included mathematics, science, English and history. Science included aeronautical science, and history was about Imperial history (Britain still had an Empire) and military geography. There was workshop practice, including elementary engineering, concentrating on aero engines and the construction and rigging of airframes. From the second term onwards purely service subjects were taught and purely academic ones dropped. Service subjects included navigation, armament, RAF organization, basic accountancy, RAF stores procedures, structure and administration of the RAF discipline code. A breadth of interest was expected of cadets. Debating and drama were encouraged, and research was carried out to produce two theses. There was a minor topic at the end of the first year chosen from a list of great military encounters, and at the end of Year 2 cadets were required to produce a major work dealing with an aeronautical topic of the cadet's choice.

Bader had his first flight on 13 September 1928, and after only 11 hours 15 minutes of dual instruction he went solo. The ground-school element concentrated on the more practical aspects of navigation, aeronautical engineering, stores administration and RAF law. In the air there was a heavy programme of cross-country flights, with bad-weather flying thrown in for good measure. Pupils had to fly the 504s for ten hours on instruments only, with a hood mounted over the cockpit, because cadets had to learn to distrust their senses and rely upon their instruments.

Bader was beaten into second place for the Sword of Honour, and his course report described him as plucky, capable and headstrong. Sadly it was at RAF Kenley, where he was posted on to No. 23 Squadron, that this headstrong aspect of his character was to be his downfall, for he took unacceptable risks while flying aerobatics, and in spite of being warned about this by his flight commander, he crashed his aircraft when performing a roll over an airfield at low level, and in doing so he lost one leg and most of the other. For a man so keen on sport this was heartbreaking, but his determination to overcome his disability and eventually return to military flying is another story.

Airmen's Careers

Demobilization of airmen In common with the officers, the majority of airmen had had their fill of the death and privation of wartime, and could not wait to get out into civilian life. Demobilization involved millions of men and a few women (see next paragraph), and to handle this huge undertaking some of those currently under training were diverted to clerical duties to work at former recruiting depots such as Blandford and Crystal Palace. No wonder that with six forms to be filled out for each man or woman there was a lot of paperwork. The task confronting Trenchard was then to rebuild the RAF for peacetime service, not simply to provide the needs of a drastically reduced force, but also to prepare a foundation for rapid expansion should the need arise in the future, which it did in the 1930s. Trenchard's avowed intention was to have the finest tradesmen, who would be the envy of the world, but it would be the mid to late 1920s before his apprentices would make their presence felt in units. In spite of the huge numbers leaving the RAF, 1919 actually witnessed modest recruitment.

Reduction in WRAF and civilian subordinates' strengths Air Ministry Weekly Order No. 972, dated 25 August 1919, puts the total requirement for WRAF and civilian subordinates at 3,298 and 6,702 respectively, the greatest numbers being employed at stores depots. The order dealt next with the reduction in the numbers of other ranks, many of whom were on 'duration-of-war' engagements. If they had not volunteered for service with the forces of occupation in Germany and had attained the age of 31 years, they were considered as eligible for demobilization, their release to be carried out as soon as possible, and certainly no later than 15 September 1919. Even if not released by that date they could not be held simply because it was deemed that their services were indispensable. Since the WRAF was to continue for a few months longer, female personnel were to be allowed to stay on, bearing in mind the availability of female accommodation, trade qualifications, etc. The priority for discharge was for female civilian subordinates to be permitted to go first, followed by their male counterparts, immobile then mobile WRAF personnel, all releases to be completed by 30 September 1919.

Adult Entry

Enlistment/re-enlistment The diversity of trades open to recruits joining the RAF in 1919 says a lot about the state of aero engineering at the end of the First World War: trades that are now only past memories, such as blacksmith and coppersmith, riggers and fabric workers, motor-boat coxswains and airship riggers, and not forgetting 'drivers, steam'. The full list is as follows:

Technical

Acetylene welder	Armourer	Blacksmith
Boat builder	Camera repairer	Carpenter
Coppersmith	Draughtsman	Driver, motor boat
Driver, petrol	Driver, steam	Electrician
Fitter, aero engine	Fitter, general	Fitter, MT
Instrument repairer	Kite balloon telephonist	Millwright
Machinist	Magneto repairer	Moulder
Motor body builder	Motor-boat coxswain	Pattern maker
Rigger, aeroplane	Packer	Painter
Photographer	Propeller maker	Vulcaniser
Rigger, airship	Tinsmith and sheet metal worker	Upholsterer
Turner	Hydrogen worker	
Winch driver and fitter	Wireless operator	
Fitter, jig and tool maker	Wireless mechanic	

Non-technical

Assistant Armourer	Blacksmith's striker	Butcher
Caterer	Cook	Coppersmith's mate
Deckhand	Fabric worker	Hospital orderly
Labourer	Motor cyclist	Packer's mate
Seaplane wader	Shoemaker	Tailor
Telephone operator		

Clerks, Storemen and Administrative

Batman	Clerk, general	Clerk, pay
Clerk, shorthand typist	Clerk, stores	

Note: Before moving on, the reader is reminded that the flying-boat and the floatplane played a large part in the work of the RAF right up until after the Second World War. Trades connected with seaplane operations have since disappeared, together with the RAF Marine Branch.

There were still men serving in Germany with the Occupation Force in 1919, as well as those stationed in the outposts of the Empire, such as India, Egypt and Mesopotamia. Any airman who re-enlisted would receive a bounty on a sliding scale according to his term of engagement:

For 2 years – £20 payable in three increments of £6 13s 4d (£6.67)

For 3 years – £40 payable in four sums of £10

For 4 years – £50 payable in five sums of £10 at approximately yearly intervals

An airman who re-enlisted would also receive an extra leave entitlement in addition to a bonus if serving with the Occupation Forces. Only 1,106 men enlisted in the first two months of 1919, and only a quarter of these were technical tradesmen. Some trades were almost devoid of recruits, and it became necessary to hire civilian drivers to drive RAF vehicles, and the maintenance and repair of Rolls-Royce aero engines had to be contracted back to the parent company. The periods of service for which men then engaged were:

4 years' regular service + 8 on the Reserve
6 years' regular service + 6 on the Reserve
8 years' regular service + 4 on the Reserve

Potential recruits went to Halton for a medical examination and trade tests. If successful they would be attested (signed up for service). If they passed the medical but failed the Selection Board for a technical trade they could try for a non-technical or administrative trade or be sent home. If they did receive attestation they would remain at Halton for training. The non-technical tradesmen were posted to their various units.

The economic situation in Britain in 1919 was not brilliant, on top of which the nation had to absorb millions of demobilized men back into work. At least Britain did not suffer the fate of Germany, where the thousands of demobilized men joined the *Freikorps* that fought the Communists in the streets of Berlin, took part in two right-wing attempts to overthrow the government of Germany and was to provide many of the men for Hitler's Brownshirt Army, the *SturmAbteilung* (*SA*). Among the many demobilized servicemen in Britain there would always be those who would be attracted by the offer of a job where training, board and lodgings and working clothes were free.

One aircraftman who joined the RAF in 1921, for example, had suffered unemployment in the boat-building trade in Portsmouth. He faced an oral test, followed by the writing of a short essay and a mathematics test. By this time recruitment was at Uxbridge, for Halton had become the new Apprentice School. This particular man went to Manston, to where the School of Technical Training had moved from Halton. Training schools such as Manston were to provide the technical training for direct-entry adult recruits during these inter-war years. The syllabus at Manston allowed one day per week at school, the rest being spent on workshop practice, which included geometry, development of the triangulation method, radial line and parallel line. The men made pots and pans, square and round funnels, brazed joints and copper pipework. A petrol tank was made with filler cap, sump, drain cock and baffles. There were other technical training schools for adult entry, such as Flowerdown for the electrical and wireless trades and Eastchurch for armament and gunnery. The electrical fitter's course for boys was held at Flowerdown supervised by 350 NCOs and ten civilian instructors.

From among the non-technical trades came the clerks, who, given Parkinson's Law, were vital to deal with the ever-growing amount of paperwork. Entrance was by examination that was as difficult as that for technical tradesmen. The mathematics paper included Euclid, algebra, trigonometry, and calculations of areas and volumes. All entrants attended a general clerk's course at the RAF Record Office, Ruislip. Those who gained good marks could go for further training in stores and pay accounting. If they displayed particular aptitude, trainees might attend an advanced course, taking them up to the rank of corporal. Other non-technical trade training was carried out at such stations as Uxbridge, where drill and physical-training instructor courses were carried out.

Some Career Experiences of Airmen in the 1920s

A newly qualified fitter driver, petrol, having qualified at RAF Cranwell, was posted to the MOT Repair Depot in 1922. Here vehicles were repaired and overhauled for the RAF in the United Kingdom. The station also acted as a stores depot for vehicles held for overseas use. The work was hard but well organized. The vehicles were stripped and assembled on a flowline system, the components, such as gearboxes, being serviced in separate departments. Carpenter coach builders and coach painters restored the bodywork. Because of the small size of the RAF, promotion was exceedingly slow. A fitter driver, petrol might have to wait for eight to ten years between promotion to LAC and corporal, and for a cook this might be between ten and twelve years. Of course a man could remuster, that is to say change his trade group. If he could pass the trade test and providing there was an establishment, he could get better pay by going from a Group 3 to a Group 1 trade. But even then he might have to wait, for having remustered there

might not be an immediate vacancy. Such a man would know that ex-apprentices got preferred promotion. This could result in ex-apprentice LACs receiving instruction from more experienced direct-entry AC1s. Inevitably there were 'dead men's shoes' that held up promotion of eager young entrants, and this could discourage airmen from long-term engagements.

Technical airmen could attend an air gunner's course, which, apart from sergeant pilots, was the only way airmen could become aircrew in the 1920s. At flying training schools airmen could get airborne with trainee pilots. One such man was a rigger aero who spent a tour with the Fleet Air Arm, the Central Flying School and an Army Cooperation Squadron. In 1923 he had a lucky escape from an aircraft flown by a pupil pilot. When the aircraft span to the ground from 300 feet the pilot was killed, but this man's harness broke, and instead of being trapped inside the fuselage he was thrown out onto the starboard wing. He received thirty days' sick leave after leaving hospital. He went on to be discharged from the RAF in 1928, when he was transferred to Class E Reserve. In 1935 he re-enlisted in the Regular RAF, signing on for a four-year term.

An aircraftman posted to the Aircraft Repair Section (ARS) Henlow was employed on intensive repair of Avro 504s, Bristol Fighters. DH9s, DH9As and Sopwith Snipes. Since he, as an AC, was required to instruct newly arrived ex-apprentice LACs, it did not make for happy working relationships, and this was not, perhaps, anticipated by Trenchard when the Apprentice Scheme was introduced. This man felt that it killed any ambition he might have had, particularly in a shrinking air force with diminishing promotion prospects. This was a pity, because although the ex-apprentice might have received a better technical training he was not necessarily more intelligent and ambitious.

This did not make the Apprentice Scheme one that was ill conceived, for the problem lay in the circumstances peculiar to the immediate post-war period. Once there was some expansion, the situation for adult entry airmen improved.

The introduction of all-metal aircraft gave rise to proposals put forward in January 1923 by WO Tatum at RAF Halton, who instructed coppersmiths, sheet-metal Workers, tinsmiths and acetylene welders. WO Tatum proposed a new trade of aircraft metal worker, to service all-metal aircraft. This man had considerable experience in civilian life, the Royal Navy, RNAS and RAF, and his ideas of combining the aforementioned crafts into the one new one carried considerable weight. Although they reached Trenchard himself, the proposals were eventually turned down since it was felt that the proposed metal workers, in 'working' the metal, might interfere with or change the tensile strengths of the metals, which in turn might add stresses to the aircraft's structure. But all was not in vain, for with the gradual change from wood to metal construction, the trade of carpenter rigger was superseded by metal rigger, not fitter.

The above is an illustration of the encouragement that the RAF gave to airmen who had good ideas that would be of value to the service. That continues to this day, and station magazines and publications such as *Air Clues* will have 'Well Done' articles about airmen whose vigilance has saved an aircraft from a serious accident, or who have worked out a better way of performing technical and administrative tasks.

The Apprentice Scheme

The Aircraft Apprentice Scheme has been fully described in Chapter 8. There is no doubt as to its value to the RAF in the lead-up to the Second World War in providing a very highly skilled technical workforce. Altogether 155 Entries passed through Halton before the final one, which passed out on 24 June 1993. That truly marked the end of an era.

PAY AND ALLOWANCES

This section deals with the pay of officers and airmen and allowances. The latter included marriage, fuel and light, heating and other categories. The figures are in the old, pre-decimal currency, i.e. pounds, shillings and pence, and the daily and weekly sums must seem tiny in today's money; but then, the £ sterling has inflated somewhat over the years. Pay was awarded to cover the hazards of flying as well as for service, seniority, specialization and rank. Allowances were discriminatory in that they were paid only if certain conditions were met. For example, the marriage allowance only went to married personnel, senior officers received entertainment allowances, and personnel who used their private motor vehicles for duty purposes were paid mileage allowances. This section does not pretend to be all-inclusive, but extracts from AMWOs provide snapshots of pay and allowances during the 1920s. Readers will see a period of price deflation in the early 1920s, and there are no prizes for calculating the inflation rate prevailing over the entire decade.

Pay

Officers' pay In September 1919 officers' pay rates are given for four ranks:

Air Chief Marshal	£7 0s 0d per day
Wing Commander	£2 0s 0d
Flying Officer	£1 3s 0d
Cadet	5s 0d

Pay differed according to the number of years spent in the rank.

The following figures for 1924 give the rates payable on promotion to that rank, but note that the rates changed on 1 July that year:

	Standard Rate	Rate from 1 July 1924
Air Chief Marshal	£7 0s 0d	£6 12s 4d
Wing Commander	£2 1s 0d	£1 18s 8d
Flying Officer	19s 0d	18s 0d
Pilot Officer	15s 0d	14s 3d

This reduction of pay all round comes not long after the 'Geddes Axe', requiring economies from government departments. The rates for 1928 were back to where they were at the beginning of the decade, except for a flying officer:

Air Chief Marshal	£7 0s 0d
Wing Commander	£2 1s 0d
Flying Officer	£1 0s 0d
Pilot Officer	16s 0d

The examples of daily pay for officers of specialist branches are shown below for the year 1922:

Wing Commander – Stores and Accounts	£1 15s 0d
Flying Officer – Stores and Accounts	19s 0d
Pilot Officer – Stores and Accounts	15s 0d
Wing Commander – Medical	£2 6s 0d
Flying Officer – Medical	£1 4s 0d
Chaplains (after 30 years' service)	£2 10s 0d
" (on entry)	£1 0s 0d

Airmen's pay The rates of pay for airmen in 1919 are given for Technical Trade Groups. Group I included such trades as blacksmith, copper smith, draughtsman, instrument maker, etc., Group II included acetylene welders, electricians, pilot and wireless operator, and Group III comprised cooks, drivers, storekeepers and motor-boat crewmen, etc. These were the technical, and generally most highly paid, trades. Trade Groups IV and V were the administrative and non-technical groups, which attracted correspondingly lower rates of daily pay. Like the officers, four ranks have been selected to illustrate daily pay rates during the 1920s:

	Technical Group I	Technical Group II	Technical Group III
Sergeant-Major Class I	13s 0d	12s 6d	11s
Corporal	7s 9d	6s 8d	5s 10d
Aircraftman 2nd Class	4s 0d	3s 9d	3s 6d
Boy	1s 6d	1s 6d	1s 6d

The figures for February 1921 had not changed, except for the sergeant-major in Group I, whose daily pay rate went up from 13s 0d to 14s 0d. The table below gives the daily rates for 1921 on promotion to the rank for airmen of Administrative Group IV, which included general, pay, medical, stores and quartermaster services clerks. Those for the Non-technical Group V included physical training and gunnery instructors and visual signalling instructors:

	Administrative Group IV	Non-technical Group V
Sergeant-Major Class I	11s 0d	10s 0d
Corporal	5s 10d	5s 0d
Aircraftman 2nd Class	3s 6d	3s 0d
Boy	1s 6d	1s 6d

Allowances
There were a variety of allowances, which could be targeted at various groups and varied according to marital situation, rank, length of time in rank, etc.

Marriage allowance   AMWO 109 dated 9 February 1921 gives the allowance for married personnel as follows. For comparison the figures in brackets are as stated in AMWO 94 dated 5 February 1925. The rates are weekly:

Wife	9s 6d (7s 0d)
Wife + 1 Child	19s 0d (13s 6d)
Wife + 2 Children	26s 6d (18s 0d)
Wife + 3 Children	32s 0d (20s 0d)

For each additional child above three in 1921 the weekly sum was 3s 0d. In 1925 the figure of 1s 0d was payable to additional children above seven. Since these allowances were based on the cost-of-living index, the years 1921–5 were characterized by deflation.

Ration allowances   Rations were provided in part from service ration stores and in part from the NAAFI (Navy, Army and Air Force Institute). AMWO 531 of 1926 provides for 'Rations at Home'. The fixed ration from 1t October of that year for bacon, jam, marmalade, syrup, cheese and margarine was priced at a stipulated minimum quantity. For example, bacon was to be purchased in quarter sides at 133s 5d a cwt. Purchase of jam was ideally to be purchased in equal amounts of single and mixed fruit. For a 7 lb jar, plum jam cost 3s $2^1/2$d, while blackberry and apple cost 2s 11d.

Where rations could not be issued in kind a cash equivalent was admissible. The allowance was made up as follows:

Bacon	1.7868d
Cheese	0.6141d
Jam	0.5156d
Margarine	0.3850d
	3.3015d

The allowance per individual was at the rate of 3.3d. The contract prices for three staple items are given below for 1926. The figure for 1928 appears in brackets:

Bacon	1s 11d a lb (11d a lb)
Cheese	10d a lb (1s $0^1/2$d a lb)
Margarine	$6^1/4$d a lb ($5^1/4$d a lb)

AMWO 813 of 1928 reminds commanding officers of the desirability of purchasing produce of British origin when spending the commuted ration allowance with the NAAFI. The purchase of British goods was intended to benefit British trade at no extra cost to the unit, and in accordance with the policy of HMG as expressed by the Empire Marketing Board.

Fuel and light allowances   Source: AMWO 307–22 of 1926) Light allowances were admissible for all commissioned ranks at home and for all married personnel in Malta. Single personnel down to the rank of flight sergeant in Malta also received this allowance. From March 1926 onwards rates are given below for a representative sample of ranks:

	HOME			
	Married		Single	
	Winter	Summer	Winter	Summer
Air Chief Marshal	2s 5d	1s $2^1/2$d	1s $9^1/2$d	$10^1/2$d
Wing Commander	1s 0d	$6^1/2$d	$7^1/2$d	4d
Pilot Officer	$4^1/2$d	3d	$2^1/2$d	$1^1/2$d

	MALTA			
	Married		Single	
	Winter	Summer	Winter	Summer
Air Marshal	2s 4d	1s 2d	1s 9d	$10^1/2$d
Wing Commander	1s $1^1/2$d	$6^1/2$d	$8^1/2$d	$4^1/2$d
Pilot Officer	5d	3d	$2^1/2$d	$1^1/2$d
Sergeant	2d	$1^1/2$d		
AC2	2d	$1^1/2$d		

The order for fuel allowances appears in the same Weekly Order, and includes rates for home stations, Iraq, Palestine, Transjordan, Egypt, Aden and Malta. An Air Chief Marshal received 8s 8d against an AC2, who received 7d.

Motor mileage allowances   RAF personnel could be authorized to use and claim for duty journeys made on service business in their private motor vehicles in circumstances where either service transport (MT in service jargon) was not available or its use was inappropriate. The mileage allowances for August 1928 can be found in AMWO 530, dated the 9th of that month:

Vehicle	per mile
Motor- and pedal-assisted scooter	2d
Motor bikes without side cars	$2^1/_2$d
Motor bikes with side cars	$3^1/_2$d
Tri-cars and light cars up to 8 hp	$4^1/_4$d
Four-wheeled cars, 8 hp to 12 hp	$5^1/_4$d
Four-wheeled cars over 12 hp	$6^1/_4$d

AMWO 377 of June 1929 dealt with the insurance of privately owned vehicles and motor cycles that were used on official business. This had to include the insurance risks of a civilian chauffeur if employed.

Entertainment allowances The importance the services attached to hosting and entertaining visitors to air headquarters and stations is reflected in AMWO 241, dated 30 March 1922. Entertainment allowances were paid only to officers of Air rank and group captains, the latter often commanding RAF stations. The rates per day were:

Air Marshal	20s
Air Vice-Marshal	15s
Air Commodore	11s
Group Captain	7s 6d

THE WOMEN'S ROYAL AIR FORCE

Today women are fully integrated into the armed forces. Gone are the different rank titles for female personnel. Gone are the WRAF (Women's Royal Air Force), the WRAC (Women's Royal Army Corps) and the WRNS (Women's Royal Naval Service). So integrated have the forces become that a recent copy of the *RAF News* featured a 29-year-old female flight lieutenant who is not only a Tornado pilot but an instructor and instrument ratings examiner. There are servicewomen aboard HM ships at sea, and the latest debate is whether or not women should be combat soldiers. It is therefore perhaps difficult to comprehend a service, formed on 1 April 1918, that embraced women into its ranks yet dispensed with their services two short years later. The WRAF was disbanded on 1 April 1920. Not until 1938, with war looming on the horizon, did the RAF again accept women back into its ranks in the form of the WAAF (Women's Auxiliary Air Force). Since this volume is concerned only with the 1920s, only the very early history of the WRAF is considered. From 1920 onwards, with the exception of the Princess Mary's RAF Nursing Service, the RAF became a men-only service.

On 1 August 1918 there were 15,433 WRAF personnel on strength, 10,000 of these having been transferred from the Army and the Royal Navy and 5,000 directly recruited. The original intention was to create a force of about 90,000 airwomen, but at its maximum strength the force never exceeded 25,000 in any one month. In order to facilitate the replacement of men to release them for combat duties the WRAF took in women who served from their homes and were paid 14 shillings a week towards living expenses. They were called 'immobiles', and knew that they could not be called upon to serve away from home. The 'mobiles' could and did! So the men accused the women with the cry, 'There's a lot of widows you'll be responsible for!'

The situation in 1918 In 1918 women were recruited into more than forty trades, rising to more than fifty in the following two years. But this did not mean that WRAF entrants necessarily had a wide choice. New recruits or transferees were allocated to trades in a fairly arbitrary fashion, having more to do with vacancies in the various trades than their personal preferences. It was seen that the obvious jobs were either in the clerical or domestic field, and it is perhaps surprising, therefore, that women were involved in work on aircraft and engines, wireless and armaments, given the limited education many of them had received, particularly in the sciences. On entry to the service in 1918 there were four basic trade categories open to women:

Clerks and storewomen
Household workers
Technical workers
Non-technical workers

Category A – Clerks and Storewomen Maintaining pay ledgers and stores inventories, together with filing work in registries, gave employment to some 11,000 women. The shorthand typists were the élite, being able to type over 100 words a minute, and they were the most highly paid, receiving between 29 and 31 shillings a week. On the stores side women were employed in such places as No. 3 Stores Depot, Milton, where 1,150 WRAF storekeepers could be found. The work could be dirty and involved heavy lifting of aircraft, engine and other parts.

Category B – Household Approximately 9,000 women were employed in this category, and were the poorest paid, receiving only 10s a week (50p) for often unsocial hours. Many were employed in messes, the scale of cooks to personnel being 2:20, 3:75 and so on up to 13:600. Sometimes they worked with up-to-date equipment, sometimes they did not. Then there were pantry maids, mess orderlies, housemaids and general domestics working in female and male messes. Those who gave personal service to officers were called batwomen. An amused American officer with whom the author served a number of years ago could not get used to RAF officers' messes, and when asked where the batman had got to would reply, 'I should ask Robin'.

Category C – Technical Pay for WRAF personnel engaged in technical work varied according to the demand and technical knowledge. For example, dopers and painters only got 11s a week, while photographers got 26s. Women could be found working with cameras, armament, wireless equipment and flying instruments. In the aircraft repair shops crashed planes were rebuilt. Some women were employed as coppersmiths, tin smiths, sheet-metal workers and turners. At one station the electricity supply was maintained by a WRAF-maintained power station. Driving a variety of vehicles, including crash tenders and heavy lorries, was also carried out by women.

Category D – Non-technical Non-technical work attracted lower pay. Motor cyclists could earn 24s a week and telephonists 21s, whereas general labourers got as little as 10s. There were also tailoresses, packers, armament assistants, those who worked in sailmakers' shops and fabric workers who worked on airships and Kite balloons. Girls on motor cycles gave women a 'new image' in a day when only a few men could drive. Funnily enough, motor car drivers were Category C, while motor cyclists were only Category D.

New trades Over time new trades were opened up to WRAF personnel. Pigeon keepers and nurses appeared. Soon it was possible to replace Army nurses in RAF hospitals. In June 1918 trained nurses were enrolled into the RAF Nursing Service, later to become the Princess Mary's RAF Nursing Service, or PMs for short. This service survives to this day, indeed the author is married to a former PM under whose TLC he came too many years ago. WRAF personnel also helped maintain discipline, and manned patrols with their red-on-blue armbands, which indicated that they had received training before being sent out to stations. The women chosen had to be over 23 years old and of exceptional character and personality. Armed only with a lanyard and a whistle, they worked in pairs around their units. Finally, there were those who worked in the meteorological service.

WRAF officers So far the account has concentrated on the non-commissioned ranks. WRAF officers were commissioned with a much narrower choice of responsibilities. All officers had to be 'mobiles', and the RAF's need in 1918 was not for specialists but administrators. In the RAF after the Second World War only one WRAF officer on a station was deemed necessary to look after the needs of airwomen as women. She was the WRAF G officer, nick-named the 'Queen Bee', but in 1918 having a large female population suddenly implanted into a previously all-male service meant having administrators of the female element. A few were instructors and there were some female medical officers. Female officers' salaries were calculated annually, and with keep the lowest rank had 46 shillings a week. The Director had £500 flat rate without allowances.

Command of the WRAF

Finding someone to command the new women's service in 1918 proved to be something of a problem. Few women in public life had the experience to fit them to oversee a workforce of 15,000 officers and airwomen. The word 'oversee' rather than command is used, since the officers and airwomen at their various places of work were under the normal male chain of command. As was made clear in the last paragraph, what was required of female officers at this time was the care of airwomen. In the event there were three changes of Commandant in the first six months of the RAF.

The first was Lady Gertrude Crawford, daughter of the Earl of Sefton, who had been in charge of munitions workers in a northern factory. She soon found that all that was required of her was to be a figurehead, only able to lead through the guidance of senior male officers in the Directorate of Manning. She was not allowed to inspect WRAF units, except the one at Regent's Park, unless requested to do so. She was expected to work through a liaison officer in dealing with other Air Ministry departments. All in all she was not well pleased. Sir Godfrey Paine, the Master-General of Personnel who had nominated Lady Gertrude, heard of her dissatisfaction, and on 4 April called for her resignation.

Sir Godfrey had then to look, rather hastily, for a replacement. Names were suggested to him and he eventually settled on Miss Violet Douglas-Pennant, who had served with the London County Council Education Committee, hospital units, girls' youth clubs, and helped with the formation of the Women's Auxiliary Army Corps. Her last post had been in the National Health Insurance Commission as Commissioner for Wales. All of this added up to a considerable involvement in public affairs and made her eminently suitable. If she was to accept the post of Commandant, however, it would mean her taking a drop in salary of £500 p.a. The post was offered on 13 May 1918, to take effect exactly one

Lady Commandant, The Hon. Violet Blanche Douglas-Pennant.

month later, but on 11 June, having looked around to see what was expected of her, as well as her relationship with superiors and subordinates alike, together with the organization within which she would have to work, Miss Violet Douglas-Pennant declined. It seems that those with whom she would have to work had not even been consulted, and were not prepared to accept her authority, and she was blocked at every turn. But having lost one Commandant, Sir Godfrey was not prepared to lose a second, so he prevailed upon her to change her mind, offering her the title of Lady Commandant, with the equivalent rank of brigadier and to be responsible to himself. He would publish a reprint of the regulations governing her position. However, the publication did not occur until six months later, by which time she had been dismissed. There was an almost total lack of organization that would allow her to do her job. There was no filing system, letters were not being received and the promised WRAF uniforms did not materialize. She had a large number of airwomen for whom she was responsible, with too few female officers to care for them, and so inevitably complaints about the behaviour of airwomen increased. When she tried to organize a fast-track training course for officers at Berridge House, West Hampstead, the necessary furnishings were not provided, such was the degree of departmental obstruction. But Miss Violet was determined, and she secured the use of Southwood Hostels, Eltham, which enabled her to pass out 300 officers during her time in office. She also set up two new depots for airwomen.

Other difficulties were placed in her way, chiefly because of the attitude of many with whom she had to work, as well as the station commanders, under whose command the airwomen came. Therefore, through no fault of her own, complaints about her airwomen and her own performance increased in number. The situation was becoming intolerable. Airwomen at a Berkshire station staged a stoppage over a lack of bonus pay and proper uniforms, but since the trained WRAF officers, who might have nipped trouble in the bud, were not reaching RAF stations in sufficient numbers to deal with matters such as these, complaints continued to pour in, and the Commandant was blamed. When she again offered to resign, Sir Godfrey retorted that she was doing a good job. Nevertheless, the Air Minister, Lord Weir, was bound to act, and in late August she was dismissed. It was asserted that although she was very efficient she was highly unpopular with those with whom she had to work. One account of the period suggests that the manner of her going was illegal, since it breached the terms of her engagement. Miss Violet could not be summarily dismissed except for misconduct or a breach of her conditions, neither of which had occurred, and the one month's notice by the Air Council had not been given to her. Had she been furnished with an adverse report she could have rebutted the charges against her.

The publication of the reprint of the regulations pertaining to her service had been delayed, and so technically the RAF could claim not to be bound by regulations not officially in force.

The third attempt to secure the services of a Commandant centred on Dame Helen Charlotte Isabella Gwynne-Vaughan. She had been married to Professor Gwynne-Vaughan, a fellow scientist who sadly died in 1915. Dame Helen had taken up work with the Red Cross and the VADs. Her husband's illness and premature death left her childless, and while still grieving at the loss of her husband, voluntary work occupied her, and she was pleased to be thrown into war work. She was loaned by the War Office from her university for an indefinite period, and posted in March 1917 as Chief Controller (France) of the new Women's Army Auxiliary Corps. Yet again the RAF tried to secure the services of an unwilling nominee. She enjoyed her work with the WAAC, so much so that when she was summoned to the War Office on 1 September 1918 to be told that she was being offered the Head of the WRAF, she declined. Yet again the nominee was prevailed upon to change her mind, this time by the new Master-General of Personnel, Major-General Brancker. She did so, and this time the RAF would make sure that obstacles were not put in her way. Dame Helen was to receive all the support she needed to carry out her task.

In her first half-year she was to proceed at a brisk pace. She had the powers of an air commodore and was responsible to Brancker, with whom she had a good working relationship. Who is to say that Dame Violet would not have been equally successful with the right support? Berridge House, which she had tried to get up and running, was then properly equipped, allowing Dame Helen to organize a proper officers' training course. The officers' blue and airwomen's khaki uniforms began to appear, and Dame Helen was able, by the end of the month, to inspect the Officers' Training Unit. She was a good public speaker and could imbue her subordinates with her enthusiasm. Helped by her sister, whom she appointed as her deputy, and some of her former clerks, she was able to organize a programme of inspections of all units where there were WRAF personnel, and keep regular reports of all the visits. Further help was

Commandant Dame
Helen Charlotte Isabella
Gwynne-Vaughan.

provided by the appointment of Area Superintendents, and by the end of the year Sir Sefton Brancker felt able to claim that the WRAF was the best-disciplined and best-turned-out women's organization in the country. In 1919 she consolidated her achievements, and airwomen were serving in France and in Germany as part of the force of occupation following the Armistice. In June of that year she was made Dame Commander of the British Empire, only to be called upon to run down the service prior to its disbandment. She handed over her own office on 4 December 1919 after only fifteen months as Director. The WRAF was disbanded on 1 April 1920.

DISCIPLINE

Before the maintenance of service discipline during the 1920s is considered the methods used are described. Discipline is achieved in a variety of ways, but all three armed forces have found that drill on the parade square is the best way of teaching recruits to respond to verbal orders promptly and without question, to work together as team players and to take a pride in one's appearance. Without discipline members of the armed forces would simply be an aggregation of individuals. Servicemen have traditionally been subject to two sets of law – the criminal law and military law. A host of minor offences are punishable under military law and are dealt with by officers of the accused's unit in an orderly room. More serious cases go before a court martial. The orderly room may be equated to the civilian magistrates' court, the court martial to the Crown court.

At unit level minor offences under Air Force Law were dealt with in an orderly room by the subordinate commander, generally a junior officer. There would be a charge sheet stating the offence, and witnesses gave evidence to substantiate the charge. The accused could call witnesses in his defence, and if the case was unproved the charges would be dismissed. If guilty, the officer awarded the appropriate punishment within his powers to punish, but first he would ask the accused if he would accept the officer's punishment or wished to be tried by court martial. This is akin to the situation in the magistrates' court, where the accused is asked if he will accept the punishment of the court or elect to be tried by a jury in a Crown court. In both cases the accused risks a greater punishment if found guilty, and will probably opt to be punished by the lower court. Service punishment in the 1920s took the form of the deprivation of freedom and the carrying out of tedious chores, and was known in service jargon as 'jankers'. More serious charges at unit level could dealt with by the Commanding Officer, who could award corporal punishment (see 'Floggings at Halton'), but even his powers were limited, and if the offence merited punishment that was beyond the powers of the Commanding Officer the latter could order the taking of a Summary of Evidence, as a prelude to a possible court martial. If the evidence was such that the accused clearly had a case to answer, the matter was referred to the headquarters of the group to which the station belonged, and the Air Officer Commanding would have to decide whether or not a court martial was to be convened.

A court martial is one in which the officers of the court act as both judge and jury, and they are assisted by a member of the Judge Advocate General's department. If the accused is found guilty, punishments include long periods at a service detention centre, or in extreme cases, dismissal from the service. Officers who appear before such a court may be reprimanded or cashiered, resulting in the loss of the Sovereign's commission. The officers have no legal training, but the system works.

Experience of the 1920s

Adults Punishment of airmen mostly took the form of confinement to barracks (later to be called confinement to camp), the 'jankers' referred to above, and the man being punished was a defaulter. For the number of days that a defaulter had been awarded punishment he was not permitted to leave the camp or station, and to create the greatest inconvenience in his life, he was required to report to the main guardroom several times a day in walking-out dress and carrying his full pack. He had then to return to his room to change into working dress before reporting back to the guardroom to be given fatigues. This would probably include work in the highly polished guardroom, or cookhouse chores. As has been explained, more serious offences would be dealt with by a court martial, but this was rare, for the vast majority of cases were of a minor nature. The RAF, perhaps more than the Army, relied less on regimented discipline. RAF airmen, particularly technical ones, worked in small groups on aircraft, engines, electrical or armament equipment, etc., and they had to be relied upon to exercise judgement and self discipline in completing a job upon which the lives of pilots, observers and air gunners depended. Such men knew what was required of them.

Boys Boys were understandably treated differently from adults. They were given restrictions that included absolute silence during the working day except for ten minutes after meals, and they had to be seated two yards apart. Only instructional books were allowed when they were taken into a special reading and writing room, where, under supervision, they had also to write home twice weekly. A court martial was considered to be an inappropriate way to deal with serious offences committed by boys, who were dealt with in the civil courts, and persistent offenders could be dismissed the service. In March 1920 King's Regulations were amended to reflect the RAF's attitude to the disciplining of boys, who 'should be treated with tact and sympathy'. It was recognized that while discipline had to be maintained, it should not be based only on fear of punishment. Instead, officers and NCOs were encouraged to interest themselves in the boys as individuals and endeavour to win their confidence. A more positive approach should include the organization of amusements and occupations for all leisure hours.

Floggings at Halton   Between October 1925 and 1938 there were about ten instances of public floggings at Halton. In this the RAF was following the practice at most public and grammar schools of caning boys who misbehaved. Public flogging at Halton was carried out mostly for offences involving theft, and then only after the permission of the parents had been obtained. A hollow square was formed by officers, NCOs and apprentices, and the punishment was carried out in the presence of the Commanding Officer and Adjutant. The guilty apprentice was clad in gym shorts and was marched onto the parade ground to be spread-eagled over a vaulting horse by four police NCOs. A medical officer and orderlies were in attendance, and twelve strokes were administered by a police NCO, with the medical officer inspecting the boy's face and shorts between each stroke. It is evident that, from 1939, no more caning took place at Halton.

SOCIAL LIFE IN THE RAF

The following accounts of social life in the 1920s include recruit training at Uxbridge, as seen through the eyes of Lawrence of Arabia, or Aircraftman Ross, adult airmen, boy apprentices, the WRAF and officers.

A Day Book of the RAF – Extracts from 'The Mint'

This account of life at the RAF Depot, Uxbridge, between August and December 1922 and afterwards at RAF Cranwell is that of Colonel T.E. Lawrence. He was otherwise known as Lawrence of Arabia, where he had earned notoriety following his exploits with Arab forces fighting the Turks during the First World War. On his return home he sought anonymity and enlisted as a ranker, firstly in the RAF, until his true identity was discovered, followed by a short spell in the Army, which he disliked, then again in the RAF, where he served until his untimely death in 1935 as the result of a motorcycle accident. In the RAF he was No. 352087 Aircraftman Ross (later Shaw). He has recorded for posterity a very personal account of life at the depot in a book called *The Mint*. The occupants of Lawrence's hut are described as a fair microcosm of unemployed England, not of unemployable England, for the strict standards refuse the last levels of the social structure even though recruits earn but $1^1/_2$d an hour. They are kitted in khaki for training, not RAF blue, with puttees during working hours. This dress is like a prison garb to the men, for no one is allowed out in it and it could take up to a fortnight before the blue uniform is ready at the tailor's shop. The

optimists send their civilian clothes home, where they can wear them on leave.

Air Force duty craves food, not drink, but RAF food was not particularly appetising. Lawrence describes the dining hall as the mess deck, and the last two comers to a table have to go to the kitchen for the food. Meat comes in one tin, vegetables in the second, and often pudding in the third. The Officer of the Day comes to inspect the food and asks the men if they have any complaints, but there never are any. At Friday teatime biscuits replace bread, but since Friday is pay day one can always supplement the meagre ration with food from the canteen. The barrack room or hut has no armchairs so the airmen can only relax on their beds. 'Shake together fifty odd fellows, strangers of every class in a close room for twenty days, subject them to a new and arbitrary discipline and weary them with dirty, senseless uncalled for, yet arduous fatigues', said Lawrence. Yet in spite of this there is never a sharp word between any two of them. In charge of their hut is their immediate superior, Corporal Abner, whose job it is to harden the recruits. He is an ex-Army man, very much a man, if a little sad and quiet, and for this Lawrence is grateful because Abner does not bark like an imitation sergeant-major. There are no drying fires, and when the men's spare clothes get wet after heavy rain they must fold them for inspection, wet or dry. It might take a week of night airing to get them right. This is particularly important if the recruit is to escape censure at the hut inspection, which is carried out by a squadron leader, who is the first officer with whom the men have had any contact. On seeing a book in Danish in Lawrence's locker the squadron leader wishes to know what a learned man is doing in the ranks of the RAF. Lawrence can only reply that he had had a mental breakdown, whereupon the squadron leader instructs the sergeant-major to take his, Lawrence's, name. This can only mean one thing to the sergeant-major: Lawrence must be on a charge when airmen are punished for a variety of minor offences during what is called the 'Orderly Room'. When Lawrence appeared before him the squadron leader laughed, exclaiming that he only wanted his name in case he needed an intelligent man for a job.

It was usual for NCOs and not the officers to rule the lives of recruits. Indeed, this was the author's experience on joining the RAF in 1953, some thirty years later. The officers were totally eclipsed by the NCOs. Lawrence recounts that they are supposed to have a flight lieutenant in charge, but neither the sergeant nor the corporal knew of his name or face. Probationary officers under training suddenly appear on the parade ground immediately prior to Church Parade on Sunday. The officers gave the wrong orders and the corporal whispers the right ones, so that men can carry out the correct drill movements. In spite of needing to know the men under their command no single officer has spoken voluntarily to any of the recruits. Be that as it may, anyone in authority is to be humoured, jokes laughed at and orders instantly obeyed.

Drill and fatigues dominated the recruit's existence at the RAF depot in the early 1920s, but there was some time for periods in the classroom. Lawrence believed that no man left the depot without a hatred of drill that would last for seven years, so that service life held no terror for the man who had undergone the 'full Depot'. The daily timetable was as follows:

06.45 hrs	PT
07.45 hrs	Breakfast
08.10 hrs	First Drill Period
09.25 hrs	Loo Break
09.35 hrs	Second Drill Period
11.00 hrs	School
12.00 hrs	Return to Depot

The afternoon was much the same, with drill and PT followed by tea. School was just that, with a civilian schoolmaster (there being no education officer branch at the time) who wanted recruits to do things for themselves, whereas the depot instructors wanted the men to wait for and obey orders. For a man who had a degree in history leading to a research fellowship in political theory, Lawrence must have found it hard to be patient with the slow pace needed for the others. He recalls that semaphore was taught, even though the RAF no longer used it. The other recruits asked him why he did not apply for a commission, to which he replied, rather strangely, that the men must look after themselves, knowing the feebleness of power. It is as if life in the RAF goes on in spite of the officers. The structure is in place and each man knows his place in it. Each man gets on with his life, suffering what he has to suffer and grasping, whenever possible, moments of happiness and enjoyment.

Lawrence recalled that there were no signs at the depot of the proper business of the RAF, if one excepts the solitary Bristol Fighter that lay mouldering behind bars in the transport yard. Whether keen or not to fly, the RAF was moulding men to fit the character of the new service to make it distinct from the Army and the Navy. The men describe themselves as 'ack-emmas', the air mechanics of the First World War. The term 'urk' or 'erk' corresponds to the 'mallow' or 'swaddy', the men's own name for their serving conditions. There are 400 recruits, sixty officers and 100 sergeants at the depot, and the distinction between airmen and soldiers is drummed into all who come.

From the Depot, Lawrence was posted to the RAF college at Cranwell, where he joined B Flight. He travelled by rail in mid-August dressed in tunic, breeches and overcoat and carrying a set of complete equipment, which included his bayonet. His equipment was so thickly layered that at any moment its brown powder rained like pollen onto his clothes or those of his neighbours. The puttees covered the lower leg from the breeches down to the top of the boot and were wound round the leg like a bandage. Where the puttee met the breeches, the point where the puttee crossed over itself, had to be in line with the seam of the breeches. The author first learned of this requirement on meeting a Flight Lieutenant Summers in Bahrain in 1961. Summers had been a recruit at Uxbridge in those early days, and had come to the guardroom at the main gate, where there was a mirror for men to check their dress before leaving camp. Three times Summers had been sent back to his barrack room to adjust his dress, and it transpired that the fold of his puttees was $1/4$ in. out of line with the seam of his breeches. No doubt the police NCOs regarded this as great sport, but then, when it comes to the old 'hairies' and their dealings with new young 'sprogs', 'twas ever thus!

Conditions at Cranwell for the permanent staff were more relaxed than at the depot. Corporals did not have to be addressed by their rank nor was there a requirement to stand to attention when doing so, and beds did not have to be 'made up'. The food was not much better than depot food, but that just meant that the station canteen flourished. It was holiday time for the cadets at Cranwell when Lawrence arrived on the station, so the aircraft were valeted lazily to kill time in the working day. The hangars take fourteen aircraft, both Bristol Fighters and DH9As, and these are cared for by Flight Commander 'Tim' and his technical NCOs, with whom he gets on. Eight out of ten of the NCOs are ex-Army/Navy, but eventually the RAF will breed its own NCOs with their tools and their discipline, and it is they who will put the officers into the air. Without them no one will fly! Lawrence describes this new breed of technical NCO who understands the 'soul' of engines. The best of these will be promoted to sergeant and some will become sergeant pilots. Such men will come fresh from school, glib in theory and capable of writing essays, whereas the old hands have learned their trade 'hands on' and some could barely write. These men will not be cowed and owned body and soul as his contemporaries have been. Rather they will be the service, maintaining it and their rights within it, at one with the officers.

Before leaving this description of the social life of airmen recruits in the early days of the decade, it is worth remembering that Lawrence had been an officer and a field commander on active operations before joining the RAF. He could see things from both sides and is articulate and educated, which makes his impressions something of value. Such is the notoriety of the man who had been Lawrence of Arabia that, unlike any ordinary 'erk', he can correspond with Trenchard himself. Of course the Chief of the Air Staff will find accounts of life at the RAF Depot from one with inside experience of value in those formative years. For his part Lawrence recognised the greatness of his chief and would not hear a word against him. He shared the view of others who know Trenchard that it is not what the CAS actually says that instils confidence in the men of the RAF but what he is. He may be so inarticulate that one cannot follow his line of argument and his handwriting may be appalling, but his knowledge is like the Pole Star.

Social Life – Adult Airmen

Posting to a station   The popular RAF stations were those near London, such as Hornchurch, Kenley, North Weald, Northolt and Martlesham. Mountbatten was situated near the beauty spots of Devon, but would hardly excite a Scotsman, and Wick was so far from anywhere that it would please no one to be stationed there. In spite of this, most servicemen have always shown resilience and made the best of a 'bad job' when it came to a posting. The foregoing extracts from *The Mint* show that an airman travelled in best uniform, wearing boots and overcoat and carrying full service kit. On arrival at his new station he might well find the cookhouse closed. He would then be shown to his bed space for the first night. The older and wiser 'squaddie' would not unpack completely since he guessed that, on reporting to the Station Warrant Officer (SWO) the next day, he would be allocated his permanent bed space. The newcomer would then go to the canteen for a meal and a drink, and before long he would fall into conversation and the talk would be flowing. Those who have never served in the armed forces may find it difficult to comprehend how one can feel at home no matter where one is posted. In the RAF the layout of stations and the design of buildings such as messes and station headquarters could be virtually identical, particularly those built during the 'expansion period' of the 1930s. One could breakfast in the mess, travel 100 miles to another station and have lunch in a dining room that was identical to the one in which breakfast had been taken, and drink in a bar that was almost identical to the one left behind. It was not difficult to get the feeling that one belonged to a very large family.

Daily routine   The SWO was responsible directly to the Station Commander for discipline, parades and guard duties. Once an arriving airman had reported to the SWO he would then go to meet his flight or section disciplinary NCO, to be shown his place of work and meet work colleagues. His first full day would begin with Reveille at 06.30 hrs, followed by breakfast between 07.00 and 07.30 hrs. This would be followed by the cleaning and tidying of hut and bed spaces before reporting for work. There would be a break for lunch, afternoon work and tea. Some airmen would have been detailed for guard duties, but their more fortunate colleagues could then think about how to fill their leisure

hours. Given the more remote and rural location of many RAF stations, a motor cycle or small car was essential if a man was to get off station for the evening. Stations like Bircham Newton, for example, were at least twenty miles from everywhere! Motor cycles were cheaper than a car, but airmen might share a 'banger', which could set them back £5. There was always the gym or the sports field for the more athletic, or a man might simply laze on his bed. In the NAAFI there was no television in the early 1920s, but wireless sets with large horns, which produced a rather harsh sound, were just coming in. The 'sing-song' around the piano was quite popular if a pianist could be found.

Guard duties   For those on guard duty release from work was permitted to allow men to take an early tea. Then it was back to the hut to prepare personal kit, which would include 'best blue' with pantaloons, boots, puttees, skeleton web equipment and bayonet, together with a rifle. The guard duty was usually from 18.00 hrs to 06.00 hrs, and in groups of six, men would work two hours on patrol or point sentry duty, followed by four hours resting in the guardhouse. This made them immediatly available should the occasion demand. Ammunition was rarely issued in the United Kingdom, but Chapter 2 describes situations such as those in Ireland, where the threat of IRA attack was real. In winter the guardhouse could be very cold, and the off-duty men had to make sure that the coke fire did not go out. When the guard stood down at 06.00 hrs, the only concession that a man got was not to have to report for day duty until 10.00 hrs. If this was on a Wednesday a man had only to work until 12.30 hrs before lunch and sports afternoon, and an airman who had just come off guard duty might have some excuse to 'duck' an afternoon on the sports field.

Sport   Sport was, in the early 1920s, and still is, a very important element in the life of a serviceman. One has only to look at any issue of the *RAF News* to see that this is so. It is important for two reasons, firstly because a fighting service needs fit men, and secondly, because it helps to cement relationships in a service community. Inter-service and inter-station team events became part of the annual calendar. For the supporters, often on low pay, a match against a local team or nearby RAF station meant a trip off station in service transport with the prospect of an evening's entertainment in a local town. During their short time in the service, the members of the WRAF also took an active part in sporting activities, and in the 1919 Inter-Services Athletics Meeting at Stamford Bridge the relay race was won by the girls with a time of 55.5 seconds.

Married servicemen   Marriage in the RAF was not officially recognized until an airman reached the age of 26: that is to say, the age at which he would receive pay and other allowances. Married personnel lived on the 'married patch' on a station, and in the early 1920s these were occupied mostly by NCOs and older airmen, particularly those with larger families. This often meant that the younger married airmen had to seek accommodation in a nearby town or village. Before a man could marry he had to seek the permission of his Commanding Officer, when a check on the man's age could be made before permission was granted (see the note below). Both living-in and living-out married airmen went to the ration store to draw 'dry rations' comprising tea, meat, sugar and bread. On pay day an airman would draw the consolidated ration allowance (CRA) for himself and his family. For an Aircraftman 1st Class this would have been 3s (15p) at the daily rate. Altogether the dry rations and the CRA would be just enough to see him through the week. Only when a man attained SNCO rank could he feel comfortably well off.

Note: This is interesting in the light of a recent case of the 'partner' of an SAS man who was killed in the line of duty and she claimed a widow's pension. Since this was later granted, it shows the considerable shifts there have been in social attitudes that have affected the personal lives of members of the armed forces over the past eighty years.

Pay day Payment to airmen was a weekly ritual. A table draped with a blanket would be positioned in a hangar or gymnasium and the men to be paid were lined up waiting for the arrival of the paying officer and clerk. The poor unfortunates whose surnames began with Y or Z had to wait until last, and those with W were only marginally better off! When the paying officer arrived with his police escort, the money would be laid out on the table. When all was ready the clerk would call out the airman's name and the latter would reply in a loud voice, 'Sir 249',which would be the last three digits of his official service number, and he would then advance upon the table to collect his money, salute and retire. Waiting in the wings for him was the eagle-eyed SWO or his representative, as this was an excellent opportunity to pick men up for scruffy uniforms or haircuts.

Leave of absence Leave of absence could take one of three forms. Annual leave was granted to airmen subject to service contingencies. That is to say that operational needs would come first and a man could not expect to be away from his post during the annual AOC's Inspection.

There were also 'grants', which were really extended public holidays such as Christmas or Easter. Finally, there was the period between the end of a day's work and bed time. For this purpose living-in airmen received a permanent pass that entitled them to be out of barracks until 23.59 hrs. This was presumably to ensure that they did not loosely interpret it to mean midnight the following night!

Entertainment and romance Airmen in the 1920s often lived a life devoid of female company for long periods of time, particularly on overseas stations. Airmen's entertainment committees were formed on stations, and efforts were made to invite local people to station dances and concerts. It was at these occasions that airmen often met their future wives. The locals would reciprocate by inviting the 'erks' to one of their village hops, but because of low pay and the distance from towns the airmen would often make their own entertainment, as can be seen in the photograph below at RAF Upavon in 1926. If it was not beer and girls that was at the centre of any disputes, there was always the risk of carrying venereal disease. This is not to say that the girls who lived near RAF stations were 'unclean', but rather that the consequences of airmen concealing this disease were dire, and warnings and lectures on the matter were frequently given. Casual sex was therefore discouraged, and on 28s (£1.40) a week an 'erk' would find keeping a romance going quite expensive. So one way and another a man's love life was not exactly smooth, and although airmen inevitably boasted to their friends, 'womanizing' was much less than in civilian life.

Social Life – Boys
Immediate post-war period Conditions at Halton in the immediate post-war period were primitive. Poor food and accommodation caused an eruption in the East Camp, which housed the original boy's section, in November 1919. The boys from the West Camp were ordered to report, with their rifles and bayonets, to put down disturbances in the East Camp cookhouse and stores building, which had been set on fire. But this was before work had begun to rebuild the station to accommodate the future aircraft apprentices. On 9 October that year Halton had become No. 1 School of Technical Training (Boys). Halton was an open and scattered camp, and remains so to this day, which meant that the boys could easily leave and go into the local town of Wendover or venture into Aylesbury, but the authorities felt that the boys should not be let out of camp unsupervised without their parents' permission. They further believed that during the first six months drill, discipline and education should be in the forefront.

Halton during 1922 The conditions at Halton during 1922 were little improved. The wooden accommodation huts had no toilet facilities, and night urinal tubs had to be provided. Working dress and drill was the same as at the RAF Depot, Uxbridge, i.e. khaki uniform, puttees, boots and lots of 'square bashing'. Since the very small boys could not keep up with the marching pace, a temporary expedient was to form a 'small boys' squad', which would keep up by marching at twice the pace. One can only imagine their legs being worn down to the stumps in an effort to keep up! The weekly routine of an apprentice consisted of twenty hours of technical training in workshops, nine hours of physical training, drill and games and eight hours in education. Then there were barrack duties, inspections and preparation for technical or education subjects. Add to this a wide variety of sporting activities, a debating society and a model aircraft club.

The Halton Aeroplane Club One of the absorbing interests of a number of apprentices was the Halton Aeroplane Club. This was founded in 1925 by Flight Lieutenant N. Comper. An education officer at Halton, Captain C.H. Latimer Needham, was organizing secretary and treasurer. The aim was to involve the apprentices in the design and construction of a light aeroplane and to enter it in the *Daily Mail* and Air Ministry light aeroplane trials. The features of the aircraft that had been entered for the 1923/4 trials were analysed, and the best of these had been incorporated into the design of the Halton aircraft. Design work was completed by the end of 1925, when the club was founded, and the apprentices and instructional staff began work in February 1926 on the aircraft. It was named HAC-1 'Mayfly', powered by a 32 hp Bristol Cherub engine. Unfortunately it was not completed in time for the 1926 trials at Lympne in August. After being successfully test flown at Bicester on 31 January 1927, it was registered as G-EBOO and was prepared for air racing. Other aircraft followed, but eventually the Halton Aeroplane Club was transformed into the Halton branch of the Royal Aeronautical Society.

Social Life in the WRAF

It is interesting to contrast and compare the life of women in the lower ranks in 1919 and 1920 with the preceding account given by Lawrence. It is only possible to do this for the immediate post-war period, for the WRAF had gone by the end of 1920 and the only women remaining in RAF ranks until the late 1930s were the nurses of the Princess Mary's RAF Nursing Service. There was one important difference between the male and female servicemen at this time, apart from their sex, that is, and that was that the women were either 'mobile' or 'immobile'. 'Mobiles' would be posted to wherever their services were required by the RAF, whereas the 'immobiles' lived at home and commuted into work.

Accommodation WRAF accommodation was not very different from that provided for the men except that it was located well away from the men's quarters, surrounded by a wire fence and patrolled to keep out prying eyes. Except when the airwomen were at work, going off camp to organized functions or playing sport, it was in their quarters that the girls spent their off-duty time. Dormitory huts usually contained several rooms, with eight girls to a room. The total living accommodation usually comprised sleeping, dining and recreation huts, cookhouse, stores, medical isolation hut and officers' quarters. Where the dining accommodation was some distance from the living quarters, the girls would be marched to meals. The breakfast fare might well include porridge, bacon, fried bread and perhaps an egg, followed by bread and plum jam. During hostilities such things as bread, meat and sugar might be rationed.

Commuting and Routine Arrival at work, for the mobiles accommodated on camp, was achieved by marching. Tenders brought in those 'mobiles' who lived in hostels or lodgings, and the naval air station at Felixstowe could be reached by ferry from Harwich. Once on camp there was a roll-call and reading of the Orders of the Day. 'Get fell in' seems to have been the favourite order before the girls were marched off to their places of work, but there might be fatigues beforehand, which would include cleaning or collecting coal. Of course the daily routine differed from camp to camp. It was at 09.00 hrs that the 'immobiles' generally joined the others. The drill sergeant took over and the Lady Administrator would inspect the girls. The only jewellery allowed was a wedding ring, and the hair had be to pushed up under the cap. If it was long hair it had to be made into a bun and the latter pushed up under the hat out of sight, and shoes and buttons had to be shining. Some WRAF timetables provided for morning and afternoon drill and PT. The male drill sergeant was forbidden to swear at the airwomen, but swearing or not, they proved to be as good on the drill square as the men. Saluting was encouraged by the female officers, although some male officers found it unladylike. With orders like 'Get fell in', 'Jump to it' and 'March easy', the airwomen soon became a disciplined section of a disciplined service.

One ex-airwoman recalls meal times for both 'mobiles' and 'immobiles', when they sat on backless benches at long bare tables. The 'immobiles' brought in their own food, crockery and cutlery. A free-standing iron range was used to heat the dishes of meagre rations. There was no hot water or basin for washing up, only a stone sink with dish towels made from sailmakers' off-cuts. Another remembers being issued with large brick-hard biscuits that needed a hammer to break. She was therefore appreciative of cakes and cooked vegetables that a kind lady, who lived in a small cottage near Headquarters, gave to them.

When the 'immobiles' left for home, the others were able to retire to the rest room. What could have been a cold cheerless hut had received the woman's touch with cushions, curtains, flowers and pictures on the walls. There would be hot drinks and a piano or gramophone for entertainment. The rest room was therefore a popular place, and the only time it might be deserted was when the cinema was showing a 'silent' movie, when there was a dance in one of the messes or in the local town, or when the dramatic society was presenting a play. The girls would sit under the gas lights talking, sewing, cleaning their buttons or darning their black stockings until it was bed time. Only the officers were still up after the 10 p.m. 'lights out', completing administrative tasks.

On some camps there might be few recreational facilities, and the girls would borrow a bike to see the local countryside. Where facilities were available, tennis, hockey and athletics were popular. The WRAF Commandant obtained permission for the airwomen to fly in service aircraft on duty, but some managed to scrounge flights. One ex-WRAF girl recalls being flown in a DH9 by her CO, which was greatly enjoyed. On another occasion what might have been a pleasurable occasion was turned into a nightmare when some girls cadged a flight in a balloon. An aircraft from No. 9 Aircraft Acceptance Park, Newcastle-upon-Tyne, caught the wire holding the balloon, and the aircraft crashed, killing both pilots. The wire was nearly severed, and by rights, the girls should have jumped to safety, but the balloon was too close to the sea and the wind too strong for a safe parachute descent. Eventually another station provided the machinery to clasp the wire above the break and draw the balloon down.

Social Life – Officers

The focal point of social life of officers on an RAF station in the 1920s was, and remains, the officers' mess. The idea of a mess, or officers' home, originated with the British Army in Spain in 1700, when officers found it more convenient to club together to hire servants to cook and bulk-buy food. Previously they might have quartered in inns or local houses, turning up for duty as required. This system of communal living developed to the point where permanent buildings were erected to provide homes for the officers, particularly at permanent stations, and comprised sleeping accommodation, dining room, bar and lounge called, in RAF parlance, an ante-room.

When Trenchard modelled the RAF in the early 1920s, he had to decide whether to adopt the Army practice of maintaining the social division between the commissioned and non-commissioned ranks, i.e. between officers' messes on the one hand and warrant officer/sergeants' messes and airmen's barrack blocks on the other. T.E. Lawrence's description of the life of airmen at Uxbridge and Cranwell in this chapter, for

example, show that social life was centred on the barrack block, where men would sleep and relax. To eat or go for a drink meant going to other buildings, providing centralized eating or drinking of alcohol. The officers' mess provided all these facilities and could be described as 'gentlemen's clubs', for all officers on a station, married and unmarried, from the Commanding Officer to the lowliest pilot officer. Trenchard decided to maintain the social division.

Married officers on a station, accompanied by their wives and families, and living in married quarters, were equal members of the mess with the single or unaccompanied officers. The major difference between the RAF messes and their Army counterparts was that there were relatively more RAF officers in a station mess than Army officers in a battalion mess. A flying squadron had officer pilots specialized in armament, photography, signals or navigation. Trenchard's view was that if a man was good enough to be an officer he was good enough to be a pilot. Then there would be the chaplain, stores, dental, medical and accounting officers.

The eighteenth-century practice of hiring servants to attend the officers developed into the established service practice of providing batmen to look after officers in married quarters and the mess. They would have their beds made, their uniforms and suits pressed and their rooms cleaned. There were barmen at the bar and mess waiters to serve at table. Dinner in the mess was a relaxed affair after the day's work, and on certain occasions attendance at dinner, both for officers from married quarters and for 'living-in' officers, would be a parade. All officers had to attend to meet for a drink before dinner dressed in mess kit, which comprised a short 'shell' jacket with overalls and boots, stiff white shirt and bow tie. Pictures of both the home and tropical version of this dress is to be found in the Uniform section of this chapter and in Appendix P. After dinner there would be a loyal toast to the King, and there might well be speeches after the port had been passed around the table, port being a gentleman's drink that is sipped slowly to slow down the onset of drunkenness.

Speaking of gentlemen reminds us that many of the permanent officers were recruited from the public schools, where Officer Training Corps were established to assist in the grooming of future officer intakes. MRAF Sir John Slessor, in his book *The Central Blue*, tells of officers who would play golf, cricket or rugby football or, like Slessor himself, go hunting, Squadron Leader James, the OC No. 60 Squadron at Kohat, took three months' leave to go big-game hunting. For Slessor the three years 1925–8 were a happy time for him, with an interesting job, sport, ample leave and plenty of flying, but then the RAF had been described as the ' best flying club in the world'.

The mess buildings sometimes included sleeping accommodation. In the 1930s during the expansion period, which will feature in Volume II, the architect, Sir Edwin Lutyens, was tasked with designing a complete building, rather like a hotel, to comprise sleeping accommodation, dining rooms, lounge, bar, kitchens, games rooms and mess offices. These messes were built to a standard design across the UK, mainly in Lincolnshire, Yorkshire and East Anglia, at such stations as Swinderby, Catterick, Honington and Waddington, but the older stations, such as Netheravon and Manston, were not built to a standard pattern, and like Old Sarum and Netheravon had separate sleeping accommodation in bungalows.

The quality of social life for officers overseas was affected by several factors, including climate, mess facilities and frequent operational detachments, if employed on air-control duties. The hot Indian summer was punishing and temperatures could exceed 100 deg F, and so it was an annual event for both officers and men to retire to a hill station, where, apart from taking part in sporting and other recreational activities in the cooler temperatures, some limited training, including drill and musketry and lectures on the RAF constitution and discipline, could be carried out. Lower Barian was one such station, situated at a height of 6,000 ft, and a squadron leader would be made officer i/c the camp to ensure its smooth running. But it must not be imagined that life on the operational station on the North-West Frontier was sheer torture owing to the insufferable heat and sand. Kohat may have been one of the outposts of Empire, but it boasted tennis courts, a golf course, an indoor swimming pool and bungalows for married personnel. Where RAF squadrons worked closely with the Army, social life was often shared with officers from nearby regiments. No. 60 Squadron's history describes how the NCOs and other ranks lived on the RAF station about a mile south of Kohat, but the officers were part of the close-knit society of the Kohat Cantonment, which bordered on the south-east corner of the small native town. The RAF officers played cricket, rugby and soccer with such regiments as Probyn's Horse and the Garwhalis. There was a Gymkhana Club used by all European officers, their wives and families, and the officers' messes surrounded Richmond Park, a wide area of grass bordered by trees. The single officer, however, knew that there was the usual shortage of unattached girls in the rather limited expatriate society, as Wilfred Freeman found out during his tour in Palestine. It was not, however, always happy and serene, for it was in the April of 1923 that a major's wife was killed by outlaws and his daughter kidnapped from their married bungalow in the Kohat cantonment.

The conditions on detachment were not so comfortable. During Christmas 1922, for example, one of the squadron's DH10s flew to Dardoni with Christmas fare for Nos 27 and 60 Squadron detachments where they lived in freezing conditions relieved only by the

heat of braziers. The above picture shows another occasion when a squadron aircraft acted as Santa's sleigh. This was a DH9A of No. 47 Squadron at Helwan in Egypt in December 1926. Then there was the Christmas celebrated by units on the North-West Frontier during Christmas 1924. Christmas came, and with it the traditional Proclamation Day fly-past on 1 January 1925. From the point of view of the young officers this was one of the worst institutions with which the RAF in India had to contend. It meant that each year the best of the season's parties, seeing the New Year in at one or the other of the Cantonment clubs, was followed by a gruelling parade and formation flying, which made the morning after the night before more than normally unwelcome.

Without a doubt sport played an important part in an officer's and airman's social life. Sport was and still is encouraged in the RAF, and time off is generously given to those who participate in station, Group or Command team events. At RAF Martlesham in the 1920s, there were sporting teams playing rugger, hockey and football that participated in local leagues, entertaining and playing away, and usually well placed in their respective spheres. In the early days Flight Lieutenant Sidney Webster was the captain of Ipswich Town Football Club, which played in the Southern League. Wednesday

Member of Martlesham Concert Party.

afternoons have traditionally been sports afternoons in the RAF, and with the nearness of the River Deben to Martlesham, boating and swimming were both popular pastimes. The station was also proud of its Concert Party, which gave regular performances both at home and away. In 1926 the manager was Flying Officer R. Vaughan-Fowler, and on Thursday 14 October that year at 8 p.m., the Concert Party put on a performance in aid of the Royal Air Force Memorial Fund. It was billed as the 'Hush-Hush' Party and Jazz Band. Flying Officer Vaughan

No. 99 Squadron's Cricket Club.

was assisted by a Flight Sergeant F.W. Harris as his producer, Leading Aircraftmen King, Bishop and Rous as property manager, lighting and general assistant respectively, with Corporal Markham on the piano and Corporal Munro as bandmaster. With many stations situated in remoter rural areas, organizing entertainment on a station was an important part of a serviceman's social life.

UNIFORM
Sources: Dress Regulations for Officers of the Royal Air Force, Air Ministry Publication, May 1929
Customs and Traditions of the RAF
See also Appendix P for a complete list and illustrations of officers' uniforms

This section will show the changes that were made to the uniforms of officers and airmen during the 1920s. When the RAF was formed on 1 April 1918, all ranks wore khaki or naval uniforms and held Army or naval ranks, but Air Force Memorandum No. 2 of March 1918 prescribed uniform for the RAF. All ranks were to continue to wear khaki/navy blue for the remainder of the war, but then uniforms of the same patterns but in blue would be worn. As an option officers could wear a light blue mess kit before the war ended. The colour was originally to be light blue, later to be changed to the now familiar darker RAF blue. One rumour has it that a huge quantity of light or sky-blue cloth had been ordered from Britain to make uniforms for the Russian cavalry, but following the October 1917 Bolshevik Revolution this order was cancelled, leaving the supplier with a great deal of unwanted material. The RAF could therefore have sky-blue uniforms with gold-lace rings round the cuffs and flying and other badges of gold embroidery. This uniform was to be introduced in October 1919.

As it was a flying service, uniform in the air had to be considered. On the other hand, the wearing of swords was deemed inappropriate to men seated in flying machines, and although attempts were made to introduce swords as part of the normal dress of RAF officers, the expense of purchase by junior officers was felt to be unjustified, and thereafter swords were held on RAF charge, to be issued only for ceremonial occasions and service weddings. In this the RAF did not follow Army custom.

Trenchard was determined that his officers and men should meet their opposite numbers in the other services with a full range of uniforms to suit the occasion. This would mean introducing patterns for the following uniforms:

1. Ceremonial dress
2. Service dress, which became known as 'best blue' or No. 1 Dress
3. Mess dress
4. Working dress
5. Flying clothing
6. The tropical equivalents of the above.

Uniforms would adhere to a 'sealed pattern' approved by the Air Ministry, for these would be made by a variety of service and civilian tailors, and it was imperative that all concerned should stick rigidly to the approved pattern. At the outset the style of dress was naturally going to be dictated by the existing uniforms and items of flying clothing, and so breeches were carried through to the early 1920s, as was the wearing of puttees. The RFC officers wore the distinctive Sam Browne (see illustration) belt over their wrap-over tunics, but the RAF decided not to continue this practice, and discarded the belt for a cloth one of the same material as the tunic,

RFC uniforms – note the forage caps,
puttees and breeches.

fastened by a buckle. The airmen's working dress would be overalls, and this followed RFC practice.

Other decisions had to be made before the RAF could settle on its own distinctive range of uniforms in 1919. NCOs and aircraftmen would copy the Army practice and wear chevrons, but should officers wear 'pips' to denote rank like the Army, or rank braid like the Navy? The latter was decided upon. Then there was footwear, boots or shoes, the wearing of greatcoats in cold weather, the colour of shirt and tie for officers (as airmen wore tunics buttoned to the neck), and flying and other badges. The change-over from light or sky-blue to RAF blue-grey was the subject of Air Ministry Order 1049/19, dated 15 September 1919, and the new dress regulations came into effect on 1 October that year. Succeeding paragraphs will show how the original patterns and authorized items of dress were changed over the 1920s as they continue to change to this day.

Officers' Dress

Ceremonial dress The wearing of ceremonial dress with its distinctive helmet, or busby, which was based upon the flying helmet with ear flaps to keep out the cold, did not survive the inter-war years. Air Ministry Weekly Order 332 of 1920 introduced this dress in April of that year. It was to be made of blue Venetian cloth. The stand-up collar was to be laced in gold, with the ranks being denoted by acorns and oak leaves in different styles for Air officers, senior and junior officers. Originally the tunic was worn with trousers like those worn as mess dress, with ankle boots, but this was changed in 1928 to overalls and Wellington boots. The busby helmet replaced the normal service dress peaked

cap in June 1921. In the event this proved to be a very costly uniform, particularly for junior officers, and it was uncomfortable to wear. In any event its use was restricted to attendance at levees or other similar State occasions, when forming a Royal escort, guard duties at Royal residences, guards-of-honour and weddings. Since most junior officers could not afford to purchase the ceremonial dress, they might hire it, but if they did not they were permitted to wear service dress instead. King George VI let it be known that if this dress was to survive the Second World War, the busby would have to go. In the event, the wearing of both the helmet and the dress was discontinued. Squadron Leader Whistler is pictured in this uniform at the beginning of this chapter.

Service dress This has changed little over the years if one excepts the wearing of boots and puttees. The tunic with its patch pockets and blue belt remain to this day. (There was a short period after the Second World War when an optional service dress without the patch pockets was introduced, but it was unpopular and was discontinued in 1951.) When first introduced, the service dress comprised a tunic with either trousers, for working, or breeches and puttees. Officers of the rank of squadron leader and above had the option to wear field boots, but in March 1920 the wearing of field boots was made optional for all officers. Originally the shirt was to be blue or silver-grey, but this was changed to white with soft or stiff collars. If worn, trousers could have turn-ups if desired, and this conformed with the fashion in civilian wear. The wearing of swords on parade has

RAF Officers' service
dress with field boots.

Officers wearing puttees and white shirts with walking sticks.

A parade in 1922.

A parade in 1924.

already been mentioned, but officers on other occasions might carry a walking stick. Also in 1920 a greatcoat was authorized, and the rank braid was carried on shoulder straps. All of these variations are shown in the accompanying photographs.

In the parade photograph taken in 1922, both officers and airmen are wearing puttees, with the two senior officers wearing boots. The rifles are held 'at the shoulder', as was the practice in rifle regiments of the British Army of the day. In the parade photograph taken in 1924, both officers and airmen are again pictured. The

greatcoats worn by the airmen are buttoned to the neck. The officer is seen in a white shirt and wearing puttees.

Medal ribbons and flying badges were worn above the left-hand breast pocket, and the appropriate rank braid was worn on the sleeve, as pictured in the preface to this book. The wearing of breeches, puttees and field boots continued up to the outbreak of the Second World War, but was discontinued thereafter.

Mess dress This was worn mainly on dining-in or guest nights when dinner was served in the officers' mess, accompanied by certain rituals that made the occasions something of a parade. It was first authorized by AMWO No. 291, dated 25 March 1920, for both home and overseas wear. The mess jacket was made in Venetian cloth

Home mess kit.

with gold wire miniature flying badges and the rank braid was in gold lace. The white shirt had a stiff front and wing collar, and blue slacks were worn until 1928, when AMWO 535 replaced the trousers with overalls and Wellington boots. The Order did permit officers to continue to wear the trousers until they needed replacement. From the rank of flight lieutenant up to group captain, a gold wire lace stripe ran down the outer seams of the trousers, together with palladine silk stripe in pale blue. The stripes on the overalls of Air officers were simply wider. The tropical version of mess kit was first introduced for officers serving in India, and comprised a white duck jacket with roll collar of the same general style as the Army version. The overalls were also in white over Wellington boots. As an alternative to a white waistcoat, an Air Force blue cummerbund could be worn. The rank braids were mounted on white shoulder straps, which permitted their removal when the jacket was laundered. A stand-up collar to the jacket replaced the roll collar in October 1920, and this was fastened at the neck with a loop of white cord. Detachable blue shoulder straps with gold rank braid replaced the white ones, and the cummerbund was replaced by a white waistcoat of the same pattern as that worn at home. In June 1924 the roll collar returned, and overalls with Wellington boots were made optional. Obviously the 'powers that be' seemed undecided about the tropical mess kit in the 1920s because AMWO 629, dated 22 September 1927, discarded the white waistcoat and brought back a cummerbund of blue silk.

Tropical Mess Kit.

Working dress Photographs of pilots scrambling for their Hurricanes and Spitfires during the Battle of Britain in 1940 show them with Mae Wests over

the service dress with its patch pockets. In the cramped conditions of the cockpit the jackets soon became crumpled and baggy. It was not long before the battledress, copied from the Army version, replaced the service dress as standard working dress for officers. So the service dress was working dress during the inter-war years.

Dress Common to All Ranks

The pith helmet The pith helmet was worn by all ranks in tropical climates and was designed to shade the eyes and keep the sun off the nape of the neck. Somehow service personnel who have served in post-war years in hot climates have managed without the pith helmet, but there we are!

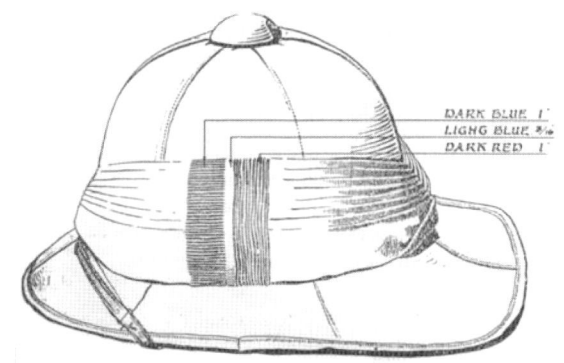

DARK BLUE 1"
LIGHT BLUE 3/4"
DARK RED 1"

The pith helmet.

Flying clothing Remembering that flying in the 1920s was carried out in open cockpits, aircrews needed garments that would keep out the wind and provide some warmth. At normal service ceilings the flying helmet, gloves and overalls were sufficient, but even as early as during the First World War experiments were being conducted in heated flying suits for higher altitudes and flights of long duration, such as night-bombing sorties. When extra warmth was essential, boots and overalls with fur collars would be worn The white flying overalls were popular and were worn by some pilots as late as the Battle of Britain, but as has been stated, aircrews in 1940 often flew in just service dress

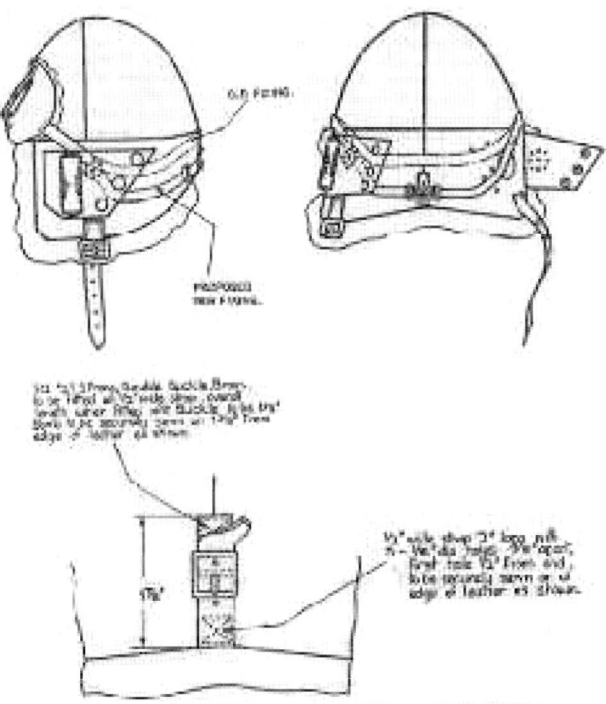

AMWO 567/1925 gave instructions for an alteration to the fur-lined cap and cork aviation helmet to prevent the loss of goggles during flight.

The pilot of an Armstrong Whitworth Siskin fighter in a heated flying suit.

and Mae West. The photograph on page 293 shows flying clothing worn in the late 1920s. In this case it is the CO's machine, a Fairey IIIF of the Cape–Cairo training flight. Behind the crewman is the RAF ensign and the squadron commander's pennant. The extract from AMWOs of 1925 and the photograph that follows are self-explanatory.

The photograph, bottom, left shows an airman adjusting the fuse mechanism of a British Aircraft Factory 520 lb bomb beneath a Vickers Virginia in 1928, when the RAF was engaged in air raid manoeuvres over London. The Virginia was a heavy bomber, with all members of the crew exposed to the elements in open cockpits. The Mk III Virginias of No. 9 Squadron had 'fighting tops', that is gun positions positioned in nacelles in the trailing edge of the upper wings. Warm flying clothing was essential in this situation. On the other hand, if a crewman was to operate equipment it meant removing a glove, as can be seen in the photograph. In the air this would severely restrict a man's ability to operate weapons. Until the introduction of enclosed cockpits and enclosed power-operated turrets this would remain a problem at high altitudes.

Airmen's dress The photograph on page 295 shows how ill fitting and uncomfortable the uniform could be, certainly by modern standards, with collars fastened up to the neck and made from serge, which made them even more uncomfortable. The man in the centre has breeches, puttees and webbing, the other two have belts that are buttoned, not fitted with a buckle, and they have turn-ups to the trousers. The uniforms at this time would still have some vestiges of the older services. In 1919 an airman would be issued with two grey Army shirts, grey

Three post war recruits at Halton North Camp.

socks, long woollen underpants, woollen vests, a khaki cardigan, two pairs of 'Ammo' boots, a pair of canvas shoes, a khaki 'dog collar' tunic and a pair of slacks. Some airmen were issued with three cap badges, one RNAS, one RFC and one RAF. The photograph shows

the men with RNAS badges. When a man was issued with a blue uniform the buttons were originally in black and the jacket was accompanied by pantaloons, or breeches, which were laced at the knees before the puttees were wound upwards from the boots to meet the breeches. If they were too tight it did not help the circulation. Some men tried to smarten the appearance of these breeches by tailoring them to give them a 'winged' appearance, but since all uniforms were, and still are, made to a sealed Air Ministry pattern, the alterations could be spotted during a parade inspection, whereupon the man could be required to buy replacement breeches or he would be placed on a charge for the illegal alterations. The two photographs bottom left show how the uniform changed over the decade, how ill fitting was the one on the left and how there was a slight improvement by the end of the decade, as worn by Lawrence of Arabia, then posing as Aircraftman Shaw, on the right. Notice that the uniform then had brass buttons and the dreaded breeches and puttees had gone. Keeping a neat crease in the trousers was a work of art, and it was not unknown for a man to sew a crease in his trousers. Lawrence does describe the uniforms going to the tailor's shop for fitting, but if these photographs are anything to go by the tailor does not seem to have worked any magic. Perhaps he faced an impossible task before he even attempted any alterations.

When it came to working dress, the airmen worked in their peaked caps and wore overalls. Even then some would work in their ordinary uniforms, as seen in the photographs on this page and page 296, where in one instance the men are servicing a Napier Lion engine, and in the second a Siskin fighter. In the former the man on the left seems to think it wiser not to damage the carefully nurtured shine on his boots by wearing his canvas shoes, whereas in the latter the men's boots can be seen to be shiny even though they are undertaking dirty work. The airman on the right who is servicing the Napier Lion engine has the rank of leading aircraftman,

or LAC. This was the next step up from aircraftman, and this rank would be given to a technical airman leaving Halton. So slow was the promotion in those early days when the RAF was not expanding that a man might end his term of engagement still in the rank of LAC. But at least he left the service with some highly marketable skills.

Tropical dress The pith helmet and tropical mess kit has already been mentioned. Common to both commissioned and non-commissioned ranks were shorts and shirts with either shoes or boots and puttees. Officers might wear breeches with field boots. Indeed, the history of No. 60 Squadron recalls the AOC's Inspection in 1921 when it was the practice for senior officers to be so attired. On this occasion two officers were flying to Risalpur as part of the inspection team, but had force-landed a few miles from the station and walked in, with the result that one of them had to have his boots cut off. After that officers wore their breeches with puttees or shorts with socks. The 60 Squadron scribe did concede that this may have been a temporary change of formal

dress, as the photograph, bottom left, taken on 30 April 1925, bears out. Air Vice-Marshal Swanne and his entourage are seen carrying out an inspection at Abu Sueir, where the officers have breeches and field boots, but those being inspected are wearing shorts and socks or working overalls. The universal pith helmet is well in evidence. Temperatures in Iraq and on the North-West Frontier could be punishing in the summer months, and in the Persian Gulf there was great humidity. It was part of life in the Raj that personnel and families of the Army and RAF would retire to a hill station at a cooler altitude during the months when the temperatures exceeded 100 deg F.

The airmen's kit layout The kit layout that was designed to permit officers and NCOs to check the service kit possessed by an airman for cleanliness and serviceability, and to ensure that no items are missing. The Form 1250 that appears as Item No. 15 in the illustration below is the serviceman's identity card.

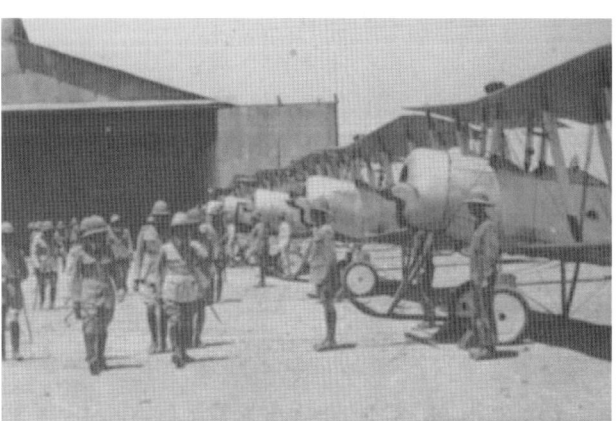

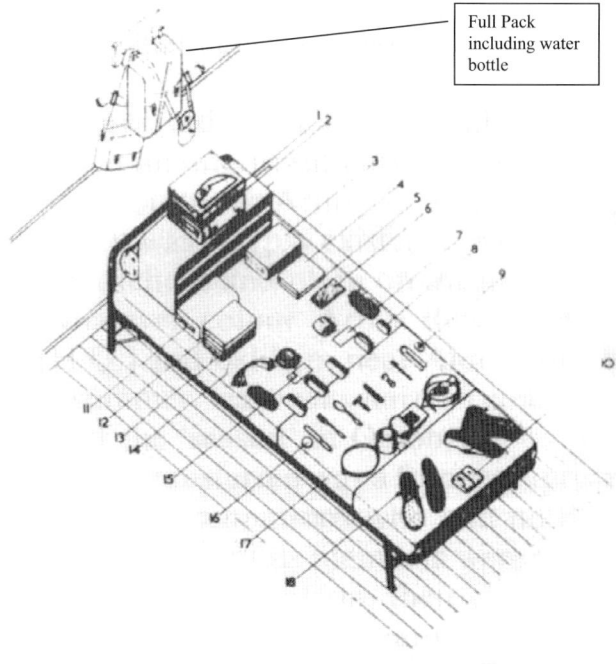

Full Pack including water bottle

Kit Layout on an Airman's Bed

1.	Best Blue tunic	2.	Best Blue trousers	3.	Kitbag
4.	Gym vest	5.	Gym shorts	6.	Cap comforter
7.	Laundry list	8.	Brushes (L – R) boot, clothes, hair, button and blacking		
9.	Soap	10.	Field dressing	11.	Groundsheet
12.	Towels	13.	Shirts	14.	Vest
15.	Form 1250	16.	Blacking	17.	Towel
18.	Laces				

Air Chief Marshal Sir Hugh Trenchard and Aircaftman Shaw (Lawrence of Arabia)

This chapter on personnel ends with an account of the relationship between Trenchard and Aircaftman Shaw. If Shaw had been simply just another airman, their ongoing correspondence would be inexplicable, but Shaw was famous and known nationally as Lawrence of Arabia. A description of his life at Uxbridge and Cranwell appeared in the section on social life in this chapter. Having served with distinction in Arabia leading Arab irregular forces against the Turks during the First World War, Lawrence left the Army, seeking anonymity and escape from the legend that he had become. He met Trenchard at the Cairo Conference in 1921 and expressed a desire to join the RAF. Trenchard naturally hoped that he would accept a commission, but Lawrence was determined to join as a ranker, and he enlisted as Aircraftman Ross, serving at the RAF Depot, Uxbridge, and then at the photographic unit at Farnborough. He told a friend that he would not leave the RAF for any other job, but when his true identity was discovered, the *Daily Express* made it a front-line story. He had falsified his identity and was discharged, and so he wrote to Trenchard in the hope of re-enlisting. He wanted to serve on a remote station where the press would be unlikely to discover his whereabouts, but the decision to discharge Lawrence was made by Hoare personally. Apparently the officers at Farnborough suspected, quite wrongly, that Lawrence had been planted on the station to spy on them. Again Trenchard offered a commission and again it was turned down.

At this point Lawrence sought help from friends at the War Office to enlist in the Army, and he became Private Shaw in the Royal Tank Corps, serving at Bovingdon, Dorset. But he disliked the Army as much as he enjoyed life in the RAF. When he tried yet again to get back into the RAF, his renewed application got to Hoare's attention and it was turned down. Lawrence then, perhaps dramatically, threatened to take his own life if he could not enlist. Another of Lawrence's acquaintances, the playwright George Bernard Shaw, got to hear of Lawrence's threat, and involved the Prime Minister, advising Baldwin that he should take a decision if a scandal was to be avoided. The episode coincided with the publication of the book by Lowell Thomas entitled *With Lawrence in Arabia*. This was a hero-worshipping account by the American journalist, and Lawrence's suicide would be the last thing that the government wanted. Baldwin overruled Hoare, and Lawrence found himself posted to the RAF Cadet College as Aircraftman Shaw.

Lawrence was grateful to Trenchard for tolerating his eccentric and wayward behaviour, for the latter would have been quite justified in objecting to his presence in the lowest ranks of the service. When he corresponded with Trenchard the latter replied. In November 1926 he told the CAS that he had got everything he wanted, but he still feared resentment if his true identity was again discovered, and so he got himself posted to India, hoping for a return to the United Kingdom once his name had hopefully faded from the public's memory. Geoffrey Salmond, then AOC India, was able to write to Trenchard to say that he had seen him at the Depot, Karachi, that he was a good influence and that the men were devoted to him.

The degree of trust that Trenchard had in Lawrence's discretion was remarkable, and in a letter to him, dated 10 April 1928, Trenchard unburdened himself over the military situation in the Middle East. A quarrel had broken out between Faisal and Ibn Saud, King of Hejaz and Nedj, later known as Saudi Arabia. The RAF had the task of stopping raids by both sides on each other's territory. Trenchard wrote:

I do not want to kill either side, and I am not doing much in it, but people who live by raiding almost all their lives do not understand our feelings on the subject, and they dislike it when we try to stop them and think our methods are more brutal than theirs. Equally, the poor unfortunate officers and men who are in the desert trying to stop the raiding do not like it – it is unpleasant, and they always, I expect, feel the faults are half on each side, like I do.

However, I hope for the best through patience and the Air, if I can only get the Ibn Saud fanatics to believe in it and go up in it. If I can bring this about, I feel I may yet make peace between Ibn Saud and Faisal. Perhaps you may say this is impossible. Could you do it?

So many people get alarmed about these raids. There are rumours of 30,000 men moving, and rumours of all sorts of dangers – yells for reinforcements by political officers – some working one way and others another. It is hard to keep a firm hand on it all, and I am getting tired with having been ten years in this office, and am beginning to wonder a little if I have done any good. Sometimes I feel I have done a lot, and at other times I wonder if I have done anything that will not collapse . . . Yesterday the last-joined told me how badly I had made the RAF, and if he is right then I have failed but I am beginning to feel that it was beyond my powers to do what I tried.

Trenchard has been described as an inarticulate man, and this is borne out in the letter, with its awkward phraseology and punctuation.

Lawrence's account of life at Uxbridge and Cranwell was published in *The Mint*, and features in earlier pages of this chapter. In the context of the Trenchard–Lawrence relationship the publication of the book made the CAS sad, for he had already had the book described to him as 'a worm's-eye view of the RAF – a scrappy uncomfortable thing', and in his letter of 10 April he continued:

I feel rather that what you have written is what is quite comprehensible to you and to me as we both understand the position, but it would be seized upon immediately by the Press *if they got hold of it*, and they would say what a hopeless Air Force it was – how badly it was run – what hopeless officers we had, etc., when I know that is not what you mean at all, though *I have not seen* what you have written. I am certain you will believe that this is the sort of thing the Press will do *if what* you have written is ever published.

And the Air Force is still young. It cannot go on continually abused by everybody, and I have enough of it as it is regarding accidents and one thing and another.

I do not feel a bit annoyed with you. I feel I always thought you would do it, though I hoped you would not. Anyhow I am going to see Garnett [the publisher] when I can, and I hope he will not publish it or let it be published, though when I have read it maybe I shall like it?

Lawrence reassured the CAS that he had the copyright and that *The Mint* would not be published without his permission. He told another friend that no part of *The Mint* was to appear before 1950 or 1970 if Trenchard preferred it. In his reply to the CAS he wrote:

The RAF is 30,000 strong, too huge for you to have personal contact with many of us: but there is hardly a barrack room in which your trumpet does not regularly sound: and these thousands of your champions find no opponents. We grouse and grumble at everything and everybody, except you: and all but that one per cent of ignorant airmen know you as our exemplar and creator, and try (does it frighten you? It would me) to be better copies.

Trenchard replied on 6 July, after he had finally read *The Mint*, which he had 'several times started to and always stopped',

I know I shall not hurt your feelings; it is what I had expected to read. I feel I understand everything you put down at the time and your feelings, but I feel it would be unfair to let this loose on a world that likes to blind itself to the ordinary facts that go on day after day. Everything you have written – I can see it happening – the way you have written it as if it was happening, but the majority of people will only say 'There are many things you have written which I do feel we know go on and we know should not go on', though what you have written does not hurt me one bit – far from it, and yet, if I saw it in print, if I saw it being published and misunderstood by the public, I should hate it, and I should feel my particular work of trying to make this force would be irretrievably damaged and that through my own fault . . . But as the Air Force gets more and more of the spirit I want it to get, so a lot of what you have written will automatically leave the Air Force without there seemingly being any alteration in the eyes of the public …

Last time I wrote to you I was sad, I am still a little sad and tired. I sometimes think people do not realise that I do not want to use the Air Force for killing only: the fact of an Air Force being about should in time ensure that we may not continually go on the warpath with as many casualties as we did in the past.

Trenchard wanted to impress upon Lawrence that he was trying very hard to improve RAF careers of both officers and men, but that he had been constrained through lack of money. He had got some funds from the Treasury but warned that his scheme for improvement would not bear fruit for at least ten to fourteen years, notwithstanding that the RAF might be disbanded in the meantime. In the same letter Trenchard informed Lawrence of his intention to resign, and asked him when he was coming home. Far from coming home, Lawrence had applied to Geoffrey Salmond for a posting to an even more remote location, to Fort Miranshah, Waziristan. There he was one of twenty-six airmen and five officers, together with 700 Indian Scouts, in a brick and earth fort with searchlights and machine-guns facing Afghanistan only ten miles distant.

On his return to the United Kingdom, Lawrence was stationed at Calshot, working on motor launches during the Schneider Trophy races. Shortly afterwards Trenchard retired, and Lawrence was to die in a motor cycle accident in May 1935, thus marking the end of this extraordinary relationship.

Chapter 10
Air Doctrine, The Air Ministry and Command of the Air

Development of air doctrine, 1919 to 1929 – The organization of the Air Ministry – Air Ministry developments and business – Air commanders and the quality of command

This chapter explores both the development of air doctrine and the quality of command during the 1920s. This necessarily involves a close look at the senior commanders of the RAF, both in the Air Ministry and in operational commands. The problem for Trenchard and his subordinates in developing air doctrine from 1919 onwards was that in creating an independent service they were breaking free from their own past experience and stepping into the unknown.

In developing strategic air doctrine alone, the Air Staff had precious little to go on. Trenchard himself had commanded the Independent Bomber Force for only a few months in 1918, to be converted from a tactical air commander to an exponent of strategic bombing. Even General Smuts, in making the case in his 1917 Report, which resulted in the formation of the RAF the following April, looked at the capacity of the Germans to bomb London and not the RAF's bombing of industrial and military targets in Germany. What followed in the early 1920s was a doctrine based more on speculation than experience. For all Trenchard insisted on a policy of offensive defence, not one squadron of four-engined HP V/1500 bombers survived the First World War. And when the time came to introduce the first postwar bomber into RAF service, it was the single-engined Aldershot. The *four-engined* successors to the HP V/1500 were the Sterling and Lancaster of the Second World War, and so an air force committed to carrying a future war to an enemy's homeland to destroy his industrial and military targets was obliged to conduct air exercises in the late 1920s with single-engined biplane bombers carrying a crew of two and bombs slung beneath the wings.

Operational experience during the inter-war years was of little help in developing doctrine for an air force which could find itself pitted against the forces of a developed nation using the latest designs of military aircraft. Instead, the commanders of the RAF in the Second World War were reared on punitive operations against primitive tribesmen in Iraq and India, the Sudan and Palestine. Since there was no threat from enemy fighters, the RAF's fighter squadrons remained at home. Since no strategic bombing operations were carried out nothing was learned here. All the RAF needed was a general-purpose aircraft, and the left-overs of the First World War, the DH9A and 10 and the Bristol Fighter, were adequate for the task of air control.

By 1919 the RAF was just one year old, it was fighting for survival and it had only four years' experience of military aviation to draw upon in the field of tactical battlefield support and cooperation, air defence of the home base and maritime reconnaissance and strike, but less than one year of strategic bombing operations. The earlier chapters of this book have forgiven Trenchard for overstating the case for the strategic employment of airpower. In Appendix Q appears correspondence between the Secretary to the Committee of Imperial Defence and the CAS, in which Hankey attempts gently to tone down some of the more extravagant claims that Trenchard was making for the efficacy of the strategic bombing offensive. But then, he was bound to make a case for a force that alone could conduct military air operations if the RAF was to survive as an independent service. Be that as it may, it was hardly fertile soil in which to plant the seeds of a reasoned and carefully thought-out air doctrine.

The Beginnings of Air Doctrine
Even before the commencement of hostilities in 1914, Frederick Sykes, the future Chief of the Air Staff, came to the conclusion that the classical principles of war did not apply to airpower. Could, he asked, aircraft win command of the air by a defeat of the enemy forces in being? Aircraft would never be able to obtain and maintain control of the air space as naval forces could obtain command of the sea, or land forces capture and hold ground. Since the air was a three-dimensional battle arena, finding aircraft, let alone bringing them to battle, meant that the 'big battle' could not be fought unless both sides sought to meet. In the days before radar it would be extremely difficult to be sure of intercepting an aircraft before it reached its target. This did not mean that pilots should not engage in combat if they met enemy aircraft, but when the First World War started aircraft were not equipped with guns save the side-arms of pilots or observers, and the military men saw them as auxiliaries helping Army commanders in the field or fleet commanders in the Navy, but there were some who saw a wider role for aircraft, given their speed and range. It was argued that aircraft should not be risked in a fight if they could proceed to some other, perhaps more important, objective. In 1916 Zeppelin airships, then Gotha bombers in 1917, could carry the war to the enemy, so aircraft would be needed for defence, which in turn would mean deciding on the proportion of aircraft and airships that should be committed to defence and offence.

The builder of the first British petrol car, F.W. Lanchester, joined the ranks of those with a view on the role of the military aircraft. He believed that while some components of the air force should fight the tactical war in direct support of the land forces, other aircraft should be free of the indecisive fighting on the Western Front and have the sole task of destroying all the enemy's aircraft and so be invulnerable to challenge. While accepting that some aircraft might be detached to attack targets remote from the battlefield, the maintenance of an air umbrella over the battlefield was the primary task, and in that sense aircraft might be the Army's fourth arm, co-equal with the artillery, cavalry and infantry. Domination of the sky could only be local and temporary. Only the troops on the ground could hold ground or ships hold a sea area. Supporters of the tactical employment of airpower said that aircraft could not achieve command of the air nor hold ground, therefore the application of airpower could never be decisive in war. The defeat of the enemy's armed forces remained the leading principle of war, to which airpower could only contribute. Ground battles and campaigns could be decisive, but Sykes disagreed. Because aircraft could detach themselves from the deadlock of the Western Front and fight independently they *could* prove decisive. When Germans used Zeppelins, and then Gothas, on bombing raids against Britain, Field Marshal Haig was bound to detach aircraft from the Allied war effort on the Western Front to defend London.

Where did this leave Sykes and Trenchard, the two leading players? Sykes believed that an independent bombing force should not suffer the fate of the land armies that had been locked in an indecisive struggle across 'no man's land', where thousands of lives had been sacrificed for little gain in territory. A large air space could be exploited to avoid an attritional campaign, and strategic air units would avoid enemy contact to attack economic and industrial targets remote from the battlefield, and in so doing, break down the enemy's morale. Sykes's aim was to follow a policy of strategic interception, that is to say maintaining a tactical presence while reserving units to prosecute the war independently of the land war. But the commander of the Independent Bombing Force, Hugh Trenchard, had found that it was essential to come to grips with the enemy air force. Of the 543 tons of bombs dropped by his force, 220 tons had been aimed at enemy aerodromes. Air fighting was essential if local air superiority was to be obtained, and then it would only be temporary unless contact with the enemy was maintained. Trenchard, having had the day-to-day responsibility to prosecute the air war in Western Europe, saw his force as contributing to the success of Haig's armies. Sykes, on the other hand, could perhaps afford to take a more detached view. He did not believe that, should the Allied

armies be successful in ending the stalemate of the trenches to break out into open country, the whole of the British air effort should immediately be thrown into the land battle.

At what point did the pursuit of a policy of strategic interception become the pursuit of strategic independence that would produce an independent air force with its own strategy? The dilemma would not go away by simply creating the RAF. The CAS and his staff at the Air Ministry would still have to decide what proportion of the air effort should be devoted to tactical air operations and what proportion to strategic bombing operations. There again it is ironic that the Smuts Report of 1917, which brought the RAF into being the following April, was directed at the disjointed attempts by the two services to defend London against bombing attacks by German Gotha aircraft, and it was again the air defence of the United Kingdom in 1940 that was the first major air battle of the Second World War. The Smuts Report was saying that the air war can be most successfully prosecuted, and waste through duplication of effort avoided, by a unified air service. However, when Trenchard assumed command of the RAF in 1919 he was to become the outspoken advocate of offensive defence, of carrying the war to the enemy, and for that there must be an independent air force. It was now left to him and his subordinates at the Air Ministry to formulate post-war air doctrine. The following paragraph itemises the factors that had to be taken into consideration, and these may be found useful in exploring the development of air doctrine.

Factors Affecting the Formulation of Air Doctrine during the early 1920s

The anticipated enemy or benchmark State Previous chapters have shown that France was the anticipated enemy. Or was the French Air Force simply being used as a benchmark, i.e. was France simply the country with the largest air force within striking distance of the shores of Great Britain? If so, the strength of the French Air Force and the qualities of its military aircraft had to be the benchmark.

The 'Ten-Year Rule' and disarmament For military planning purposes the government promptly declared the 'Ten-Year Rule', in that no major war affecting Great Britain could conceivably be fought for at least ten years. That figure was to be reviewed each year and carried forward or altered if circumstances changed. This was to be coupled with the creation of the League of Nations, when members of the League would pursue a policy of peace and disarmament.

Experience of the strategic employment of airpower during the First World War The German Air Force had used Zeppelins and Gotha bombers against the United

Kingdom, and the RAF's Independent Bombing Force had made forays against enemy targets behind the lines and against communications and economic and industrial targets The largest bombers used by the RAF were the twin-engined HP 0/100 and 0/400 aircraft. No experience was gained using the HP V/1500 against targets in Germany from bases in the United Kingdom. In other words there was not a wealth of experience in this field.

The indivisibility of the air   This meant that airpower was exercised in one element, i.e. the air, whether the forces were being employed in strategic or tactical attack, air defence, reconnaissance or on maritime operations. The exercise of airpower was therefore a matter for an air force.

The concept of offensive defence   While thought must be given to the proper air defence of the home base, the best way of ensuring the safety of the British Isles was to carry the war directly to the enemy and so incapacitate him, break his morale and get him to sue for peace.

RAF support to the Army and the Navy   The appropriate air units should be made available to give direct support to the land forces and to naval forces afloat. Land-based maritime forces would also assist the Navy within shore range. Agreement was to be reached between the RAF and the Army and Navy as to what were the appropriate force levels and the type of aircraft to be used and the manning of such aircraft. This matter was to give rise to considerable dispute between the RAF and its sister services.

The aims of strategic bombing   This was another area where there was a great deal of argument, particularly between the three service heads, always involving the government of the day. Would it be the aim for the RAF to win the war without the help of the other two services, and if not what degree of collaboration, joint planning and joint decision-making was thought to be necessary? Was the aim to break enemy morale to win and if a knockout blow was not to be inflicted on the enemy was the nation prepared and equipped to fight a long war of attrition? In any case what constituted winning a war?

Acceptable attrition rates   If the RAF was to be forced into a future war of attrition it would need to calculate what aircraft losses it could sustain and what would be the capacity of the aircraft industry to replace those losses. The only way of answering that question was through air exercises, imprecise as the answers might be. Coupled with this would be the capacity of the RAF to replace losses in personnel, which is why a well-trained Reserve was so important. These points will be considered further in exploring the development of RAF air doctrine, but the reader may already be finding that

the debate can get bogged down in jargon, something the author has been anxious to avoid, and so to make it easier to follow the ongoing debate a few terms are defined as follows:

Counter-Force Operations   These refer to air operations against an enemy's aircraft in the air and his airfields, aircraft-carriers or warships.

Strategic Air Operations   These are air operations completely divorced from the battlefield area, being aimed at the enemy's communications and economic and industrial targets.

Tactical Air Operations   These are air operations confined to the immediate battlefield and rear areas, i.e. enemy supply and reserves behind the front line.

Strategic Interception   These are air operations that comprise both counter-force and purely strategic air operations.

Air Superiority   This occurs when an air force has a clear superiority in air fighting capability that enables that air force to undertake operational sorties with little prospect of enemy interference. Air superiority in this sense is probably local and may be temporary.

Air Supremacy   This occurs when all enemy air opposition has been eliminated, so that there is no prospect of enemy air interference. As a matter of interest, this is exactly what the RAF and US air and naval air forces were seeking to achieve in the elimination of all Taliban air forces in Afghanistan.

Command of the Air   This is General Douhet's air theory about winning the air war, but there is some doubt as to whether this simply means achieving air supremacy or includes the complete destruction of an enemy's capacity to produce any more aircraft or air weapons.

Air Doctrine in the Immediate Post-war Years
In his book *British Air Strategy between the Wars*, Malcolm Smith joins most other commentators on Trenchard's ability to define in writing what he meant. He had been described as a being like a 'Pole star' in his knowledge, but was so inarticulate as to need younger, able staff officers to assist him to put his thoughts into words, people, that is, like Arthur Harris and John Slessor. The thoughts of the great man in 1919 seemed to have hardened and, some may think, narrowed, to an adoption of a doctrine based upon offensive defence. The question is – did Trenchard insist upon the strategic offensive as the most important role for the RAF simply because it was the one role that could only be carried out by an independent air force?

Having spoken of the indivisibility of the air, Trenchard was not prepared to divorce the tactical use from the strategic use of airpower. Slessor spoke in much more flexible terms. The whole point about the employment of airpower was its flexibility and mobility. Aircraft should be used wherever and whenever circumstances dictated they could be used to the greatest effect in furtherance of war aims. If he did try to separate the tactical from the strategic, Trenchard risked the Army and the Navy reclaiming their own air components. The problem with the 'indivisibility' approach, however, was that it left a great deal of leeway to planners and commanders in the field to interpret the situation in whatever way they pleased.

The morale effect of strategic bombing   Returning to the strategic use of airpower, we find Trenchard saying that it was far better to bomb the enemy in his homeland than to intercept his bombers coming in. On the other hand he seems, at times, to put the morale effects of bombing before the material effects, and he was much criticized for overstating the case for the former (see Appendix Q). Malcolm Smith argues that Trenchard was fond of using the unfounded statistic by placing the morale effect against the material effect of bombing at a ratio of 10:1. Were civilians so prone to panic as the Jews of the East End were reputed to be during the 1917 Gotha attacks on London, or would the French 'crack' before we British did? Some military writers went so far as to suggest that paramilitary discipline should be instilled into the civilian population to ensure that there was not a breakdown of the national will to resist. Experience in war is a far better guide than speculation. When Gotha bombs rained down on Folkestone in 1917, there was public alarm and questions were asked in the House of Commons, but it was not the end of civilization as we know it. The East Enders in London during the 1940 German air blitz endured the bombing with remarkable fortitude and sometimes humour, many taking to the London Underground stations during air raids, but in the heady days of 1919/20 who could tell? It was always a useful, if spurious, claim to make in justifying an air force. But one could go too far and be accused of terror bombing, an idea which Trenchard was anxious to dispel. But if the RAF was to bomb an enemy to the point where he would sue for peace it must be assumed that either he could not any longer sustain the material damage to his country, which seemed to have caused Slobodan Molosevic to call a halt to British and American bombing during the recent Kosovo conflict, or the civilian population was frightened to death. And so we see Trenchard trying to escape the accusation of advocating brutality by likening bombing to naval gunfire at a shoreline, when there might well be civilian casualties.

Douhet's air theory   The Italian General Giulio Douhet was a major air theorist of the period. His notable contribution to the development of airpower theory was his ideas about the 'command of the air'. Douhet believed that an independent air force had two separate functions: firstly, to win command of the air, and then, having won it, to exploit it. And such an air force must be trained and equipped to achieve it. What is not clear is whether command of the air was to be achieved by air fighting or by destroying the aircraft production and allied factories. Douhet was adapting the classical Clausewitzian theory, that the object in war is to defeat the armed forces of the enemy, to the war aims of an air force. The air commanders on the Western front had aimed at air superiority, whereas Douhet's air force would aim to secure 'the ability to fly against the enemy while the latter had been deprived of the ability to do so'. Douhet rejected what Trenchard had felt to be necessary in the First World War, that a counter-force policy was essential. Douhet could therefore take issue with Trenchard in not making his counter-force operations decisive, i.e. to obtain command of the air; but Sykes could criticize him for devoting too much effort to those operations, preferring that he should devote more effort to strategic interception.

Air Staff Theory, 1923   In the early 1920s the Air Staff still held to a counter-force policy. Air ascendancy was imperative and meant attacking the enemy air forces both in the air and on the ground. Winning command of the air was explicitly rejected. Instead there would be a struggle for air supremacy, but there was concern that the strength of the strike force could be frittered away fighting an indecisive campaign. The enemy could replace aircraft lost during such a campaign and air space cannot be physically occupied, so it was necessary for aircraft to keep returning to attack enemy reinforcements. To prevent the enemy from reinforcing its own air units it would be necessary to attack vital centres, and this was no less risky than attacking the enemy air force. The unstated implication of the Air Staff policy in 1923 was that a counter-force policy alone would be a wasteful diversion from the main offensive. The evidence from the First World War was that a considerable amount of effort was directed against German air assets with inconclusive results. The RAF wanted to avoid an attritional war like that in the trenches, and this meant avoiding contact with the enemy. There would need to be close defence of the most vital targets, and the bombers would need some defence, but the priority for the British air effort should be to paralyse the enemy's centres of production and lines of communication. Whereas both Trenchard and Douhet had held that command of the air was separate from the main offensive against strategic targets, the view of the

Air Staff in 1923 was that the gaining of air superiority was indistinguishable from the main offensive, i.e. only by attacking the enemy's productive capacity could the continued reinforcement of the enemy's air forces be prevented.

What this debate amounted to was that the air theorists of the day were trying to fit the new form of warfare into pre-existing classic theories that had already been adapted to encompass a navy's part in winning a war, and then an air force. Only an army could actually occupy an enemy's territory, but a navy and an air force could assist in achieving final victory. On the other hand, it could be argued that a navy alone could achieve final victory through blockading an enemy's ports, and an air force, single handed, by bombing an enemy into submission. At this juncture the ability of the RAF to achieve its war aims may be considered with the forces at its disposal.

RAF Inventory of Aircraft, 1924

The air doctrine prevailing in 1923 has been explained. The inventory of RAF fighter and bomber aircraft in the following year will show how well equipped the RAF was to carry out the roles and tasks decreed by the doctrine.

THE FIGHTERS

Snipe

Max. speed: 121 mph at 10,000 ft
Service ceiling: 19,500 ft

Snipe Mk IAs had been used as bomber escorts with the IBF in France and had been used as ground attack aircraft.

Snipe (eight squadrons).

Siskin

Max. speed: 134 mph at 6,500 ft
128 mph at 15,000 ft
Service ceiling: 20,500 ft

In 1924 the Siskin was just coming into service to replace the Nighthawks and Snipes.

Siskin (one squadron).

Nighthawk (one squadron)

Max. speed: 140 mph at 6,500 ft
138 mph at 10,000 ft
Service ceiling: 24,500 ft

Problem with the engine and vibration problems causing mechanical failure.

Nighthawk (one squadron).

The above ten squadrons comprised the RAF's fighter strength in mid-1924. The Snipe was of First World War vintage, and it and the Nighthawk were about to be replaced by the Siskin and Grebe. All these squadrons were based in the United Kingdom, since there was no prospect of air opposition during operations in the Middle East and India. If the fighters were employed purely in the defence of the United Kingdom the bases such as Northolt, Duxford, Hawkinge and Henlow would be adequate to cover the Home Counties and East Midlands, for they had a service ceiling that exceeded the bombers of the day and possessed the necessary endurance to permit them to intercept incoming aircraft, though not to provide close fighter support to the bomber streams leaving UK bases to bomb continental targets. The standard armament of all 1920s aircraft was the Vickers 0.303 in. forward-firing machine-gun. All of these fighters were faster than the British bombers of the day, and successful interception of potential enemy bombers could be expected. The ten squadrons of the front-line force would total some 120 aircraft.

In the foregoing discussion of doctrine, counter-force operations were considered. If enemy fighters were to be suppressed by bomber operations, that might be achieved by bombers operating from UK bases attempting to destroy enemy fighter aircraft on the ground. But airborne enemy fighters, fighting to defend continental targets, would need to be brought down by RAF fighters, which would have a very limited arc of operations from bases in South-East England or East Anglia. Counter-force operations involving the suppression of continental fighter forces would therefore mean RAF fighters operating from forward bases. If strategic RAF bombing aimed to avoid contact with the enemy, they would be unlikely to do so by having a service ceiling less than enemy fighters or the speed to outrun them, aircraft like the Fairey Fox being the exception. RAF bombers that were avoiding contact with the enemy would, none the less, expect to be intercepted as they approached their targets. In this case, without close fighter support, the RAF bombers would have to rely on trainable guns for the bombing aircraft, which would have to fly straight and level over the target area. In other words the bombers could not use fixed forward-firing guns unless, by sheer chance, an enemy fighter came into a bomber's sights. The RAF fighters and bombers of operational squadrons in 1924 are shown, together with their 'potential' French enemies.

THE LIGHT BOMBERS

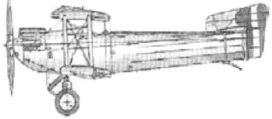

Fawn (three squadrons)

Range: 650 miles
Max. speed: 114 mph at sea level
Bomb load: 460 lb
Service ceiling: 13,850 ft

Fawn (three squadrons).

Conceived as an Army Cooperation aircraft, it replaced the DH9A in squadron service.

DH9A (two squadrons)
Range: 322 miles
Max. speed: 123 mph
Bomb load: 660 lb
Service ceiling: 16,750 ft

DH9A (two squadrons).

The DH9A was of First World War vintage and was being replaced by the Fawn, which had a smaller bomb load and lower service ceiling.

The home-based light-bomber force of mid-1924 comprised five squadrons. On the assumption that there would be twelve aircraft per squadron, one Fawn light-bomber squadron could deliver a maximum of 5,520 lb of bombs on a target, provided there was no fighter opposition, excellent weather, 100 per cent serviceability and detonation of all bombs. A DH9A squadron could deliver 7,920 lb of bombs at a greater speed than a Fawn squadron, with a greater service ceiling. The probability, given the inclement weather over northern Europe, the chances of being intercepted and the serviceability record of the DH9A, was that the tonnage of bombs dropped would be significantly less.

From the home stations of Spittlegate, Netheravon and Andover the Fawn's maximum range would take them to Berlin in the east and Milan to the south, but this would be the extreme of range and would not be accomplished under severe weather conditions or the necessity to take evasive action. The two DH9A squadrons at Spittlegate and Eastchuch could just reach Paris and the low countries. To penetrate deep into Europe both squadrons would require forward bases on the continent. The speed and service ceilings of both aircraft meant that they would be unlikely to outrun enemy fighters, and could not outclimb them. If intercepted the Fawn had two trainable guns, the DH9A just one. Would these five squadrons be used against strategic or tactical targets? If the British Army was not engaged on the continent, then all sixty aircraft of the light-bomber force would have to operate from UK bases, and could be used on counter-force operations or attacks on lines of communications. Over industrial targets they would almost certainly meet defensive fighters and anti-aircraft fire.

The Fawns that replaced the DH9As on light-bomber squadrons were themselves replaced by Horsleys and Foxes after only two years' service, and the latter would enhance the force considerably. The DH9As were more at home in India and the Middle East, where they were employed as general-purpose aircraft.

THE HEAVY-BOMBER FORCE
Range: 300 miles
Max. speed: 110 mph at sea level
Bomb load: 2,200 lb
Service ceiling: 14,500 ft

Aldershot (one squadr

Range: 900 miles
Max. speed: 100 mph at 6,500 ft
Bomb load: 2,476 lb
Service ceiling: 14,000 ft but with a full bomb load only 7,000 ft

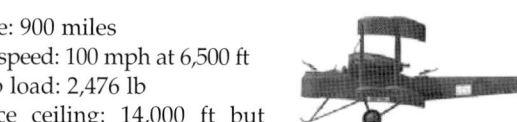

Vimy (two squadrons

Range: 985 miles
Max. speed: 98 mph at sea level
Bomb load: 3,000 lb
Service ceiling: 9,400 ft

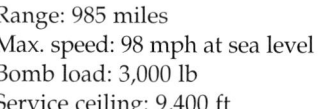

Virginia (one squadror

French Fighters
Max. speed: 146 mph
Service ceiling: 27,885 ft

Nieuport-Delage NI-D2

Max. speed: 143 mph
Service ceiling: 29,530 ft
This particular aircraft is one of a batch exported to Turkey.

Bleriot SPAD S.51-4.

French Bomber
Range: 248 miles
Max. speed: 99 mph
Bomb load: Not given
Service ceiling:13,125 ft
This civilian passenger aircraft was produced in a bomber version, F.60, delivered in 1922.

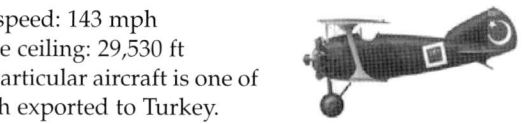

Farman Goliath.

According to the Air Staff doctrine of 1923, the RAF should avoid an attritional counter-force war and attempt to paralyse the enemy's centres of production and lines of communication as a matter of priority. Only by destroying the enemy's war-production capability could aircraft reinforcement be prevented. To achieve this in 1924 the RAF had four squadrons of heavy bombers. The planned Home Defence Force was going to comprise fifty-two squadrons, of which thirty-five would be bomber squadrons. Clearly this force of four squadrons was inadequate for the task outlined in the Air Staff Memorandum of 19 July 1923 sent by Trenchard to the Air Officers Commanding Central and Inland Areas, namely to paralyse an enemy's production centres and lines of communication and to break an enemy's morale. Any discussion about the RAF's planned ability to accomplish these aims must proceed on the basis of thirty-five, and not four, squadrons. Clearly the inability to meet the war aims of the RAF in 1924 does not invalidate the doctrine, but if, given the appropriate numerical strength plus adequate reserves of the latest design, the war aims still cannot be realized, then it does call into question the doctrine itself if, in all circumstances, it would be unachievable.

The Aldershot entered service in 1924, only served on one squadron and was withdrawn after only eighteen months. It was single-engined, and if force-landed would almost certainly have had to be dismantled to effect recovery. The Virginia and Vimy were two-engined bombers. The Aldershot had two trainable guns and a range of approximately 300 miles, and the other two each had three trainable guns and a range of close on 1,000 miles. Assuming a total of twelve aircraft per squadron, the combined bomb load of an Aldershot bomber squadron would be approximately 26,400 lb, a Vimy squadron 29,000 lb and a Virginia squadron 36,000 lb. These figures are absolute maxima, and ignore adverse weather conditions, fighter and anti-aircraft defence over the target, aircraft unserviceability and aircraft not reaching the target. All three aircraft had top speeds between 92 and 110 mph. The service ceilings of the Aldershot and Vimy bombers were below 15,000 ft, and that of the Virginia, even in the most advanced Mark, was below 10,000 ft. So none of these three bombers could outrun or outclimb any French fighters of the day: indeed, the latter had a service ceiling and speed superior to the British fighters of the day.

The development of bombs and bomb aiming   And so there are a number of factors that affect a bomber squadron's ability to accomplish its tactical or strategic objective. The above figures tell us nothing about the destructive force of a given bomb load, the quality of navigation, the tactics to be employed over the target, the effects of flying in formation, the hitting power and positioning of defensive armament and the armouring of aircraft, not to mention the target area defences, such as barrage balloons and anti-aircraft guns, as well as the fighter threat. Did the Air Staff in the early 1920s address these problems or did they proceed from the premise that the bomber will always get through? Little, if anything, appears to have been done in the inter-war years either to test the destructive power of bombs or to develop them in any way. The bomb loads of various aircraft are given, both in this chapter and in Appendix A, but it tells the reader nothing about the charge to weight ratio of bombs held in RAF bomb dumps in the early 1920s, which were mostly left-overs from the First World War. This situation prevailed right up to the outbreak of the Second World War, when, as John Terraine points out, British bombs were, generally speaking, awful. Often they failed to explode, and when they did they produced negligible

results. This view is confirmed by H.R. Allen, who put the figure at 20 per cent of those bombs dropped. With a charge to bomb weight ratio of 1:4, actual bomb loads begin to look less impressive, but Trenchard had stressed the morale effect of bombing, and it seems therefore not to have mattered how destructive British bombs were as long as they made a loud noise and frightened the civilians. With regard to bomb-release and bomb-aiming equipment, it is clear that again little, if anything, was done to learn from the lessons of the First World War. In the 1920s there was no dedicated member of the crew who would release the bombs, as was the case during the Second World War; indeed, one of the reasons why the Air Specifications called for bombers with minimal manning was that it reduced the problems of communication between crew members in flight. Bombs could either be dropped from high level, low level or using dive-bombing techniques. Bombing at low altitude meant that the bombers ran the gauntlet of fighters, barrage balloons and light anti-aircraft fire. Bombing from high altitude might have reduced these risks, but great accuracy could, because of wind and weather, be extremely difficult to achieve. Lack of advanced navigational equipment meant that the bombers would be likely to fly only in good weather where the target could be seen from the air and where navigation could be by reference to landmarks. There was no bombing development unit during the inter-war years, so that by the time Edgar Ludlow Hewitt took over Bomber Command in the period 1937–40, his Readiness Reports disclosed the Command's inability to reach even the general vicinity of a target, let alone hit it with any degree of accuracy. One explanation for this sorry state of affairs was that the adequacy of bombs and bomb-aiming equipment was sufficient for air-control operations, but not a European war.

Aircraft design   Chapter 5 deals, in considerable detail, with the wood versus metal debate that continued unabated during the 1920s. With the very limited funds available for aircraft research and development and the availability of a huge war surplus of wooden-built aircraft of First World War design, the situation facing the Air Staff militated against ordering or buying aircraft of a more advanced design. It has been told how the Air Staff kept the aircraft manufacturing firms alive with orders for prototypes, so it would be a brave firm that would ignore the Air Ministry Specifications for the different aircraft types. De Havilland and Short Brothers were less prone to design and build aircraft that slavishly followed RAF requirements, since they produced aircraft ordered by the airlines, who wanted speed with economy. The Silver Streak all-metal aircraft from Short is an example. On the other hand de Havilland produced aircraft of wooden construction that were in advance of aircraft being ordered by the Air

Ministry. All-metal construction meant added expense and delay, but in 1925 the Air Staff was working on three all-metal bombers, four fighters and one Army Cooperation aircraft, though in the event the future of all-metal aircraft was sacrificed in the name of expediency. The definition of all-metal underwent a subtle change, to mean a metal airframe covered by fabric. Moreover, the bombers and fighters remained biplanes with open cockpits. Metal armour might be fitted to protect crew positions, but every pound of metal added meant a sacrifice of speed or bomb load unless there was a compensating increase in engine power.

Defensive armament In the context of offensive bomber operations, the bomber that was going to get through in spite of all things would be the one that had the speed and manoeuvrability to avoid interception and destruction. If the capabilities of French fighters of 1924 are a guide, evading interception would be problematical, which made the alternative, to sacrifice speed and bomb load by fitting more defensive armament, a better proposition. To meet the fighter threat, what was needed was not simply fixed forward-firing machine-guns and one or two trainable Lewis guns, but guns in some or all of the other positions, which included the ventral, dorsal, nose, tail and beam gun positions. The HP V/1500 went a long way towards providing the RAF with a well-defended, long-range heavy bomber, but it was not retained in the peacetime RAF. The Air Staff's answer was the Aldershot, the first peacetime long-range bomber built to Air Ministry Specification 2/20 . This had one fixed forward-firing machine-gun and one Lewis gun in the mid-upper position, with the possibility of fitting another gun in the ventral position. A bomber is not like a fighter where the aircraft is manoeuvred into a position where the fixed forward-firing gun can be fired at an enemy aircraft, as the bomber must be kept straight and level over the target for the bombs to be aimed. And so the Aldershot crew would be hard put to fight off a fighter attack from a beam position or a head-on attack from above or below, and for the Aldershot to shake off fighters it had a maximum speed of only 110 mph at sea level and a cruising speed of 92 mph, with a service ceiling of 14,500 ft. In defence of the Air Staff's position, these were the days before radar. When RFC and RNAS fighters sought to defend London against Gotha attacks in 1917, there was no early warning from radar stations, and the chances of intercepting the German bombers were not good. Only if continuous air patrols were maintained could the chances of interception be improved, and that would require a large number of fighter squadrons, possibly round the clock, to give adequate protection to the capital. Flights of fighter squadrons were dispersed to a number of airfields around London, but the density

of cover required could only be achieved by withdrawing units from the Western Front.

The hitting power of the gun itself was also a matter that could have received Air Staff attention, but the 0.303 in. Vickers and 0.303 in. Lewis gun remained the standard armament of RAF aircraft throughout the 1920s. The 0.50 in. machine-gun had the hitting power but suffered from developmental problems. It could not sustain the rate of fire consistent with Air Staff requirements and was markedly heavier than the Vickers and Lewis guns, which meant that the maintenance of status quo was favoured. In particular the 0.50 in. machine-gun could not achieve the lethal density required, though this might have been achieved with a lower volume of fire. Experiments with cannon went little beyond the conceptual stage, and the COW gun also did not meet with Air Staff favour (see Chapter 5).

Bomber tactics on the approach to and over the target To ensure that the bomber would stand the best chance of reaching and successfully bombing the target, three possibilities could be considered and tested:

1. For the bomber to have the speed and manoeuvrability to evade detection and interception.
2. For the bomber formation to be provided with a long-range fighter escort.
3. For bombers to fly in formation so that the guns of each aircraft would provide an interlocking network of fire.

The Air Staff could adopt the attitude that the bomber would always get through and simply rely on speed and manoeuvrability to evade detection and interception, but even without radar that was decidedly risky, and Trenchard had ruled out long-range fighters with their high development costs. The vulnerability of bombing aircraft to fire from fighter aircraft was discussed in the preceding paragraph, and so a possible answer lay in formation flying, but how big a formation and what about the problems associated with control of the bomber formation and the direction of the fire of air gunners? A smaller formation would be better if effective control by the formation leader was to be maintained at night and in bad weather with poor visibility or where manoeuvrability was important in the face of fighter opposition. A larger formation could put up a greater volume of defensive fire but would lose the advantages of the smaller formation. What methods were to be employed to ensure that the formation leader could alert aircraft captains of the approach of enemy aircraft and vice versa, and how would the latter direct the fire of individual gunners onto attacking enemy fighters both by day and by night? These questions were not being asked or put to the test in the 1920s, and it was not until 1938 that Bomber Command's Senior Air Staff Officer,

Air Vice-Marshal D.S. Evill, put such questions to the Air Fighting Development Establishment. It is therefore of interest to reflect that the US Army Air Force was developing its 'Flying Fortress' in the late 1930s, and the defence of the bomber formation was meant to lie in the volume of interlocking fire of aircraft in close formation. But in the event unsustainable losses to the German Fw190s could only be prevented by the provision of close fighter escort from the Lightnings, Thunderbolts and Mustangs.

1927 Air Exercises

Since no attempt had been made to provide detailed answers to the above questions, the Air Staff in 1924 could not know whether the prevailing doctrine was valid. It was not until 1927 and 1928 that national air exercises were carried out, and these were then followed in 1929 by a restatement of the doctrine. The air exercises were described in Chapter 3, and in those of 1927 a formula was used that gave fighters only a 1 in 2 chance of making a successful interception, while the bombers were arbitrarily given twice the hitting power of a fighter. The accuracy of the bombing was assessed by using a camera to record the aircraft position at the moment of bomb release, but since no live bombs were used the umpires could only guess at the amount of damage sustained in the target areas. The forces pitted against each other were those of *Eastland*, comprising eight day- and night-bomber squadrons of the Wessex Bombing Area and eleven squadrons of the Fighting Area defending London known as *Westland*. The aim of the exercise was to see if the fighters could defend all the targets being attacked, some of which were outside London. Four years had elapsed since the declaration of the Air Staff theory in 1923, and it may be seen how far aircraft design and development had come since then. These were the opposing forces:

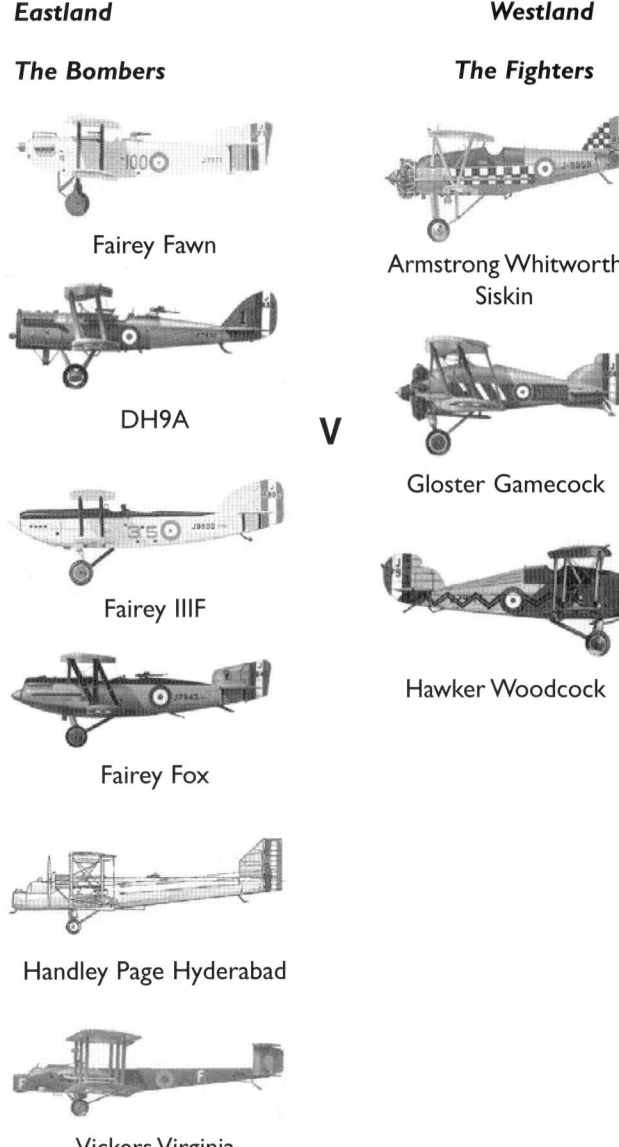

Eastland   *Westland*

The Bombers   *The Fighters*

Fairey Fawn   Armstrong Whitworth Siskin

DH9A   V   Gloster Gamecock

Fairey IIIF   Hawker Woodcock

Fairey Fox

Handley Page Hyderabad

Vickers Virginia

Remarks

There is little to choose between the light bombers and the fighters in appearance. The bombers are all a little slower than the fighters with the exception of the Fairey Fox which was marginally faster than the Gamecock and over 10mph faster than the Siskin. There is no improvement in the defensive armament of the bombers since 1923 except for the Hyderabad which had nose, midship and ventral gun positions but then the top speed of the Hyderabad was less than the Aldershot and carried only half the bomb load. The light bombers bombed by day and the heavy bombers by night. Radial engines were favoured for the fighters since their external cylinder pots made for easier maintenance but their unstreamlined shape gave them only a slight advantage in speed over the light bombers.

The results of the 1928 air exercises were much the same as those of 1927. There was held to be an improvement of the fighter's ability to intercept the bombers, but there had also been an improvement in the air pilotage of bomber crews. Clouds and strong winds were held to favour the bomber by day and the fighter by night, but since the heavy bombers were attacking by night it was these that the RAF was relying upon to break an enemy's morale and will to fight on. If the Hyderabad is a guide, the improvement in defensive armour was at the expense of bomb load. This was also the last bomber to be made out of wood.

Conclusion

There was only a little improvement in speed and armament of heavy bombers over the decade from the HP V/1500 to the Hyderabad. There was no improvement in the firepower of aircraft guns, and little or no attempts had been made to improve the destructive power of the bombs. There was a presumption that the enemy would adopt the same strategy as Britain, known as 'mirror imaging', i.e. they too would concentrate resources on bombers and so reduce the fighter threat to RAF bombers. If the enemy did not the RAF's faith in the ability of the bomber to get through was misplaced. But Trenchard was not to be moved on this central theme, and there follows a discussion of the air doctrine prevailing in 1929.

It is easy with hindsight to be critical of Trenchard and his staff in the 1920s. They did not know then that an even more destructive world war, ending with the nuclear bomb, was only a decade away. As far as they could see into the future the only operational work for the RAF was in controlling the activities of tribesmen overseas. The 'Ten-Year Rule', the Locarno Treaty, the Kellogg–Briand Pact, pacifist Labour governments and the pursuit of disarmament created an atmosphere of calm. The RAF's arsenal may not have been much improved over the decade, but at least the service was 'the best flying club' in the world. So what was the hurry?

Air Doctrine in 1929

Following the presentation of the Air Estimates to the House of Commons in March 1929, the Air Minister, Sir Samuel Hoare, praised the achievements of the RAF at home and abroad since its formation eleven years earlier. Now that the RAF was firmly established, Admiral Sir Herbert Richmond, Commandant of the Imperial Defence College, had recommended that it was time the 'principles of war' should appear in the Service Manual of all three services in identical terms. Trenchard suggested that this proposal had been prompted by the Army's and Navy's unwillingness to accept the Air Staff view that in future wars air attacks would most certainly be carried out against the vital centres of communication

and the manufacture of munitions of every sort, no matter where these centres were situated. Whatever the other two services believed were the main objectives of the RAF in war, Trenchard was determined to lay down a 'marker', and he clearly felt that this was a good time to state RAF doctrine explicitly. The resulting paper was titled 'The War Object of an Air Force', and in its essentials it was to form the basis of Air Staff strategic thinking until the Second World War.

The Defeat of an enemy nation   Trenchard believed that the object of all three services was to defeat the enemy nation, not just his armies in the field or its naval forces, nor the attainment of air superiority over an enemy's air force. The enemy nation meant its homeland, with its communications, industries, ports and cities. Having said that this should be the object of all three services, he was well aware that the RAF was uniquely placed to carry the war to the enemy homeland over the heads of Royal Naval ships and the British Army. For an army to achieve this objective, he reasoned, it must first defeat the enemy's army, and this was a barrier to overcome before the enemy nation could be defeated. But the RAF did not need to defeat an enemy's armed forces in order to defeat an enemy nation. To do this it would penetrate the enemy's air defences to attack the centres of production, transportation and communication. Destruction of these centres would mean that the armies in the field and naval forces at sea would eventually be deprived of supplies of munitions, spares, replacement aircraft, ships and tanks, etc., and thus be forced to retreat or surrender. He further believed that it would not be necessary for there to be a series of air battles where one side gained air superiority before proceeding to attack the enemy homeland. While conceding that there would be air battles of some intensity and that enemy air bases would have to be attacked, such attacks would not be the main operation. Thus the gaining of air superiority would be incidental to the main direct offensive on the enemy's homeland even if carried out simultaneously with it.

The air offensive and international law   Trenchard also addressed the question of the legality of aerial bombing under international law. The problem was that if the bombing of military, industrial, transport and communications were legitimate acts of war such targets might be close to or within centres of civilian populations. Trenchard answered this by likening aerial bombardment of coastal towns by naval guns when civilians might be caught up in it. The main thing was to do everything possible to limit the destruction of civilian life and property. What he did regard as illegitimate was the indiscriminate bombing of the civilian population for the sole purpose of terrorizing the people. This may have been the doctrine that the Air Staff took into the Second

World War, but things turned out very differently in the heat of battle. Of course we have the benefit of hindsight. Whether we are talking about the destruction of Coventry and the London blitz in 1940 or the sustained US/RAF bomber offensive involving the destruction of cities like Cologne, Hamburg or Dresden, such attacks hit civilian populations. Whether or not the purpose or the effect was to terrorize civilian populations is, of course, debatable. In the inter-war years there was a basic Air Staff assumption that sustained bombing would result in an enemy suing for peace. Again, whether or not that could be achieved by simply waging war against military and industrial targets is also debatable.

Finishing a war   Trenchard was careful not to assert that the RAF could finish a war alone. Airpower could be used in conjunction with naval forces to blockade, and with armies in the field to defeat enemy armies This would be materially to assist in keeping up the pressure on the enemy, but he returned to his main theme, the attacks on the enemy homeland, which would bring about the destruction of the enemy's means of resistance and the lowering of his determination to fight. He stressed the inevitability of aerial bombardment in a future war, something that, incidentally, the other service staffs did not deny. Where they differed from the Air Staff was in the claims made for the power of the Air. He then asserted that, in a vital struggle, all available weapons had been used in war and would continue to be used. He felt that there was not the slightest doubt that in the next war both sides would send their aircraft without scruples to bomb those objectives that they considered the most suitable. That was to suggest that an enemy might attack Britain by setting out to terrorize the British people. If an enemy fought 'with its gloves off', would Britain fight with them on or might this country be forced to do likewise? Was there a distinction between defeating an enemy nation and finishing a war? Was it not only an army that could occupy an enemy territory and disarm its forces, and was it not only the use of naval vessels that could ensure that all enemy vessels had been rounded up or sunk? Until that happened would the war be finished? These are questions that were not answered in the Memorandum.

Reactions to the Memorandum

It was inevitable that the Naval and Army Staffs would find the tone of Trenchard's paper condescending. The RAF would be the service to deliver the lethal blow, but the other two services could play their part in keeping up the pressure on the enemy. Predictably , Sir George Milne, the Chief of the Imperial General Staff, opposed Trenchard's Memorandum when it was circulated to the Chiefs of Staff Committee. He objected on three grounds.

Firstly, he felt that the RAF was proposing that it could fight a war independently of the Royal Navy and the Army. Secondly, he felt that the paper amounted to a declaration of 'unrestricted warfare' against the civil population of an enemy nation. And thirdly, the General Staff believed that the most probable conflict involving the British Empire would be against Russia in Central Asia. Milne conceded that Trenchard's air offensive might work against France, the least likely of enemies, but he could not see the RAF paralysing production centres in such a vast continent as Asia. And in a war against Japan carrier-borne air forces would be needed to attempt to achieve the Chief of the Air Staff's war object. Of course, heavy bombers could not take off from aircraft-carriers, and in 1929 it would have been difficult to imagine light bombers like the DH9A, the Fox and the Fawn, used in the 1927/28 air exercises, flying long distances over enemy territory with a pilot, a gunner and bombs slung beneath the wings. Another problem for Trenchard was the paucity of war experience upon which to base a doctrine. Nothing that happened in the First World War pointed to the certainty that Britain could paralyse an enemy through the use of airpower alone. The Independent Bombing Force came into existence only in the last year of the war. For the most part airpower had been used to support naval forces at sea and the armies in the field. The Zeppelin and the Gotha raids on Britain did involve civilian populations in war in a way never experienced before, but neither the life of London nor Britain's production centres were paralysed. And when the Central Powers (Germany, Austria-Hungary, Bulgaria and Turkey) did seek an armistice in late 1918, their economies were not in a state of near-collapse. Even supposing the war had continued into 1919 with aircraft like the HP V/1500 four-engined bombers attacking Berlin, evidence of sustained attacks on enemy targets showed that such attacks only hardened the will and strengthened the resolve to resist. Be that as it may, it was believable that sustained aerial bombardment would be a frightening prospect in the public's imagination. Who could tell for sure? In the event, Sir Maurice Hankey, the Secretary to the Chiefs of Staff Committee, considered that Trenchard tended to exaggerate 'both the actual power of the air and its morale effect', and he advised the CAS to recast his memorandum to recognize that the aerial offensive, although important in winning a war, was by no means the sole means. Indeed, Hankey brought to bear all his experience of the First World War in government meetings, in conversations with other authorities on air matters and in his own observations on the front line. The full texts of his letters to Trenchard and Trenchard's reply are to be found in Appendix Q. He went so far as to give his opinion that Trenchard's claims for the power of the Air were an 'abuse' of language. Hankey's criticisms were so hard hitting that he had to ask the Air

Marshal not to be cross, and to accept that the war object of the RAF was to contribute, with the Army and Navy, towards the breaking down of the enemy's means of resistance. And there for the time being the matter rested. The Chiefs of Staff failed to agree on a common definition of the war object of the three services for inclusion in a joint service manual.

Conclusion

The controversial nature of Trenchard's paper meant that it was hardly likely to meet with the approval of the other two services. He was on the point of retirement as CAS and he was understandably proud of what had been achieved under his stewardship in just ten short years. Given the sustained attack on his service by Admiral Beatty and General Wilson in the immediate post-war years, Trenchard may be forgiven for coming up with a 'big idea' that portrayed the RAF as the prominent service, with the Royal Navy and Army playing a supporting role. Some might say that his paper was impudent, and it is not surprising that it did not gain acceptance. When the war did come in 1939, the RAF did put light-bomber forces into the field, but in support of the land war, and in that it failed. It is one of those rich ironies that the RAF's first major battle since the statement of air doctrine in 1929 was a defensive fight for survival in the skies over Kent and the Home Counties in the late summer of 1940.

THE ORGANIZATION AND BUSINESS OF THE AIR MINISTRY

Organization of the Air Ministry from 1921 to 1929

The organization of the Air Ministry at the beginning and the end of the decade that is the subject of this volume may be found on the next two pages. This shows the considerable changes that had taken place in the Air Ministry's internal departmental structure. One example is the appearance of an Accidents Branch following the spate of accidents in the 1920s that gave rise to questions in the House of Commons. It shows a considerable narrowing of the sub-departments that came directly under the Chief of the Air Staff. Equipment, personnel, training and medical services all moved out to other departments. Throughout the period civil aviation came directly under the Secretary of State for Air. Works and buildings remained directly under Trenchard, an

indication of his determination to build up the RAF's real estate in these formative years. The RAF Cadet College at Cranwell is a particular case in point.

The Air Ministry in 1919

During the last few months of the First World War the RAF was administering a force of some 188 squadrons, 30,000 officers and 300,000 men. The HQ was in the Hotel Cecil in the Strand, and branches spread into several buildings in Kingsway. The Kingsway branches mostly housed those staff officers dealing with the delivery of contracts and supplies of raw materials to the contractors who were building aircraft and aero-engines.

Organization of the Air Ministry, 1921

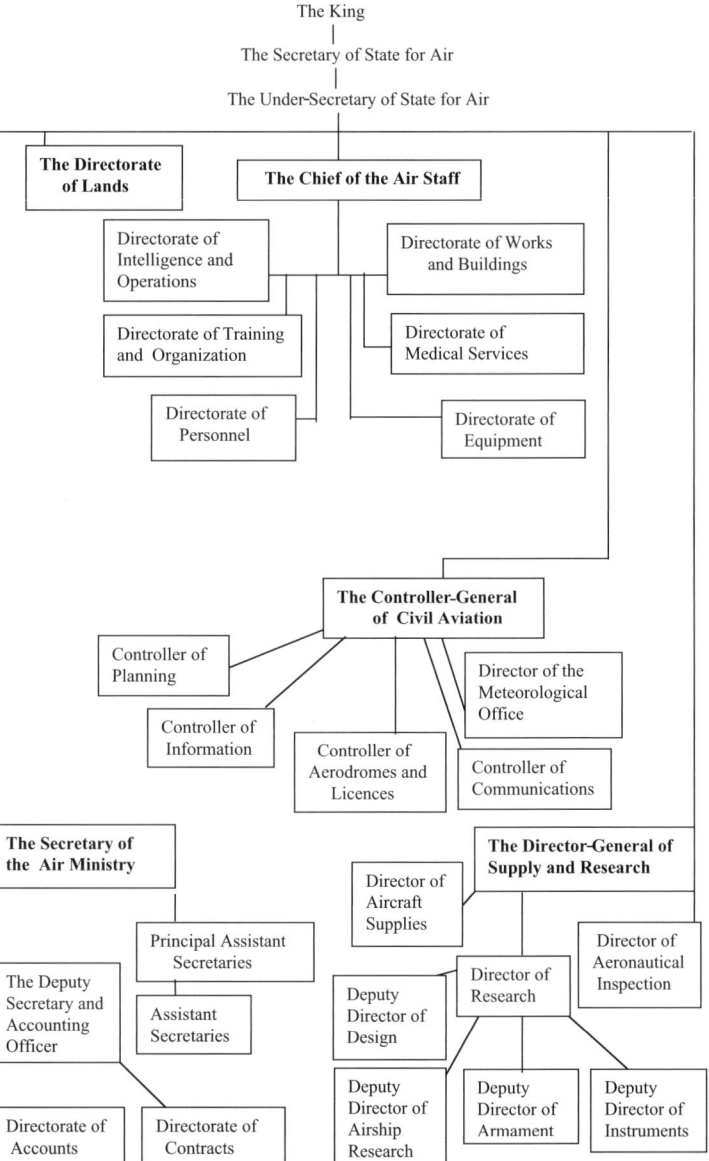

Their work also covered scientific research. Once hostilities ceased many of these offices on the west side of Kingsway and the Hotel Cecil were deserted, and the staff officers, known as the 'Kingsway Captains', got back into their plain clothes and returned to civilian life. It was at this point that the Air Staff sought a new home, and obtained premises on the east side of the south end of Kingsway. This became known as Air House, and was conveniently near to the War Office and the Admiralty.

Reference to the charts on pages 310 & 311 will show that the King headed the RAF, but since every RAF officer carried his commission this was unsurprising. Under him was the Air Council, headed by its political master, the Secretary of State for Air, and as a general rule, each member of the Air Council headed one of the departments into which the Air Ministry was divided. The Department of the Chief of the Air Staff was run by the RAF's most senior officer, Hugh Trenchard, who had a seat on the Council.

The Air Ministry in the 1920s

The Secretariat Much of the Ministry was run by civil servants who represented the Treasury when it came to spending money. It was the Secretariat of the Air Ministry that approved the price at which supplies were bought and refused payment if the goods were not up to specification. The first civil servant to head this department was Mr W.A. Robinson, followed by Mr W.F. Nicholson, who was appointed in April 1920 and remained for the rest of the decade. In these early days there were one or two interesting departments. One was earmarked for legal work, another was engaged in writing the Air History of the War for the Committee of Imperial Defence. Yet another was Secretary to the Commission of Awards to Inventors. Then there were the statisticians and accountants with a Directorate of Accounts and of Contracts. There were constant disputes with suppliers of all sorts in respect of raw materials, component parts, accessories, complete aircraft and engines, etc.

The Directorate of Lands The Directorate of Lands, known affectionately as 'Bricks and Buildings', had the responsibility to buy or commandeer land for aerodromes and to demolish old buildings. In those early days, however, the directorate was more concerned with selling off unwanted land or auctioning buildings and contents. Reference to the organization diagram for 1930 shows that the

directorate is absent. By that time the airfield situation at home had stabilized, and the unwanted airfields, seaplane bases and landing grounds had all been disposed of.

The Department of the Chief of the Air Staff This was the purely service department of the Air Ministry, which actually made war. The Chief of the Air Staff was in effect the Commander-in-Chief, and had overall operational control of the service, although the Cabinet and the Committee of Imperial Defence might have some input into operational decisions. The Directorate of

Organization of the Air Ministry, 1930

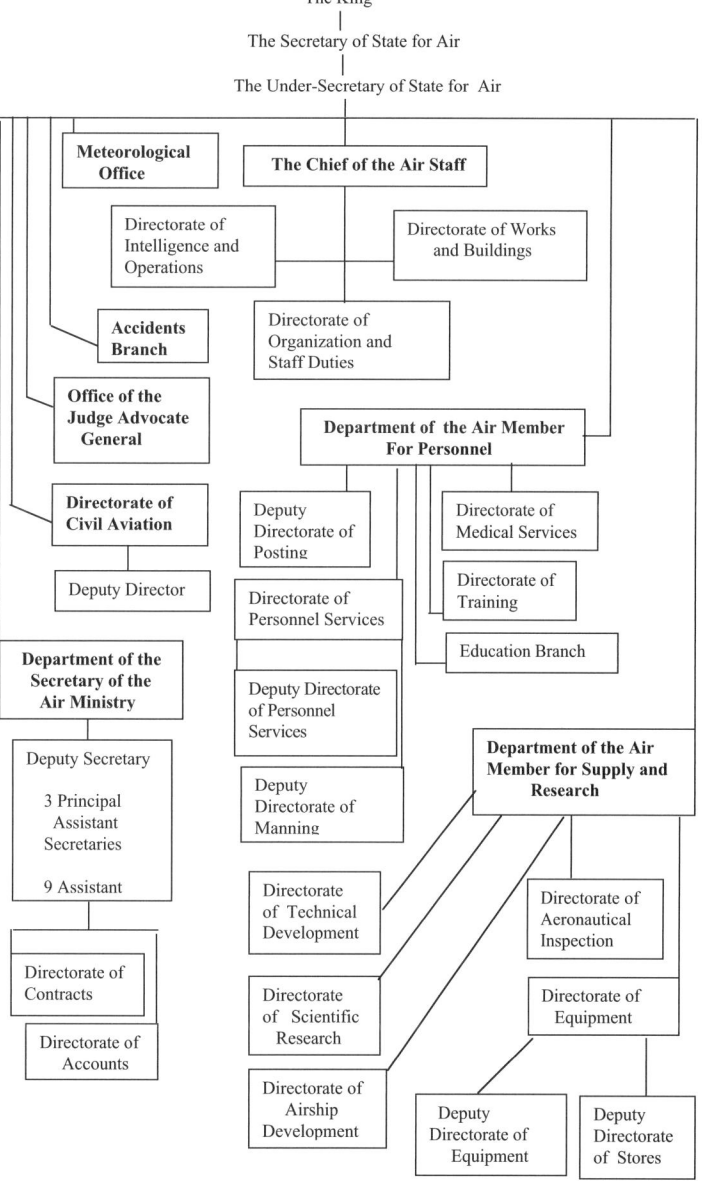

Operations and Intelligence dealt with plans for all operations being undertaken and for intelligence. This would include collecting, collating, filing and tabulating all sorts of apparently innocent bits of information. Pictures out of foreign newspapers, photographs of foreign celebrities and articles from newspapers could give away valuable information. An article written in all innocence could contain, quite unknown to the writer, information that could be of use to an enemy or potential enemy. Under this department came the Liaison Officers who worked with the British Dominions, and the Air Attachés who were accredited to foreign governments and were attached to British Embassies and Legations. Then there was Training and Organization. At the beginning of the decade personnel matters came under this directorate, but there was later a department devoted to personnel matters. Another directorate which came under the CAS in the early days was that for equipment, which covered the design of aircraft and aero-engines and the materials from which they were constructed.

The reason for placing the Director of Medical Services under the CAS in the early 1920s was that, apart from the need to have doctors treating war casualties in the field, they were also responsible for seeing that officers and men were fit to go to war if need be. That sub-department, too, was moved, later, to the Personnel Department. Works and Buildings came firmly under Trenchard's control, as has been explained, and the work involved the location of airfields and the design and construction of buildings in which men were housed. These all directly affected the readiness of the RAF to go to war.

The Controller-General of Civil Aviation   One of the first things that the Air Ministry did after the First World War was to impose a system of supervision over all civil aircraft and their pilots. Before anyone was allowed to fly outside an airfield at which he was a pupil, he had to qualify for an Aviator's Certificate. There were two classes of certificate for civil aviators – one the 'A' licence for a private pilot, and the other the 'B' licence for the commercial pilot. Those who had applied for both 'A' and 'B' licences had to submit to a medical examination by the same panel of doctors who examined RAF pilots. As it happened, the medical for the Class 'A' pilots was not as strict as that for RAF pilots, the doctors mainly wishing to ensure that the applicants would not faint in the air and had good eyesight. Before an aircraft was allowed to fly outside the airfield at which it was put together for flying, a Certificate of Airworthiness had to be obtained from the Department of Civil Aviation. The officials were members of the department of Supply and Research who examined the civil machines, and they had to consider whether the designs of aircraft were such that they could stand the stresses of flying. These

calculations were based on the known strength of the materials used for both civil and military aircraft.

A Controller of Communications worked on developing systems of signalling, radio-telephony and wireless telegraphy. This benefited military as well as civil aviation, and the Controller was served by two senior assistants, six junior assistants and four officers attached from the RAF, together with two officers detached from the map section of the War Office.

A further sub-department was that dealing with aerodromes and licences. Anyone who owned land who wanted to turn it into a public aerodrome had to get the approval of the Air Ministry. The two main criteria of fitness were, firstly, that the surface of the airfield was such that it would not break any normal aircraft on landing, and secondly, that the approaches to the airfield in all directions, particularly that of the prevailing wind, were such that a pilot of average ability could get down safely.

Finally there was the Meteorological Office (Met. Office for short), headed by a Director and served by three assistant directors and ten superintendents. The Met. Office was formed out of the Royal Meteorological Society, which itself was a complicated organization. Although placed under the Air Ministry, the Met. Office dealt with a vast number of other industries and organizations. Its forecasts were used, among others, by the Army, Navy and agriculture. It used to be said that before issuing a forecast the Met. Office would ring up sundry farmers and fishermen for their opinion. This may be a 'tall' story, but it reminds us that forecasting was not the more exact science it is today. Weather maps that might have become commonplace were not published during the Second World War in case they might be of use to the enemy. The table below serves as an illustration of the scope of Met. Office responsibilities of the various assistant directors and superintendents:

Observatories
Contributive Stations (with rain gauges and wind-
   measuring equipment)
Forecasts
Information to and from ships
Met. Research at Benson
The British Rainfall Organization

Supply and Research
Supply meant seeing that active service members of the RAF got the aircraft, aero-engines, spark plugs, bombs and cartridges they required in the quantities they required. Research meant that that equipment was of the highest quality given the latest state of technology. The first director-general of Supply and Research was Air Vice-Marshal Sir Edward Ellington, who worked alongside Trenchard in the early formative years. Sub-

departments dealt with aircraft, aero-engines, airship research, armament and instruments. The latter were in their infancy, for a pilot of the day would have just an altimeter to give him his height, an engine revolution counter, a compass and possibly an airspeed indicator.

The Air Force List for October 1921 showed that the Directorate of Research was manned almost entirely by serving officers with experience of the First World War who appreciated what needed to be done. On the other hand the Directorate of Aircraft Supplies was manned almost entirely by civilians. This may be explained by the need for heads of sub-departments to have experience in their dealings with people in the aircraft industry on the purely commercial and production side.

Aeronautical Inspection   This directorate was founded by Captain J.D.B. Fulton RA, one of the first Army officers to fly before the First World War. He was succeeded by General Bagnall-Wilde, who steadily improved the department's relationship with the aircraft industry, as did his successor, Colonel H.W.S. Outram. Not only aircraft and aero-engines had to be inspected, but so did every component part, including washers, nuts and bolts. Woods and metal being used for aircraft construction had also to be inspected. When the war ended many inspectors were demobilized, and the main problem was to retain sufficient numbers of inspectors of the right quality. As the reputation of the department increased, the aircraft industry could shelter behind the AID, knowing that if their products had got past the hands of the inspectors it must be of a good quality. Eventually the AID instituted a scheme of 'approved firms' that would take direct responsibility for the quality of their products, subject, of course, to periodic check inspections by the local AID inspectors.

Air Ministry Committees
The following committees give an indication of the wide scope of responsibilities of the Air Ministry:

The Aerodromes Committee   considered the suitability of aerodromes for their jobs and for commandeering the land for new aerodromes.

The Advisory Committee on Civil Aviation   had as its chairman Lord Weir, the former Air Minister. During the early 1920s civil aviation was going through a bad time. Mr George Holt-Thomas's Aircraft Travel and Transport Ltd had collapsed, and other airlines were struggling, but although a number of airlines did go out of business the network of airlines was spreading all over the world at the outbreak of the Second World War.

The Awards to Inventors and Patentees Committee   was kept busy recommending awards for things that were invented during the First World War and afterwards.

The Committee on the Future of Experimental Establishments   was a purely domestic affair of the Air Ministry studying the problems of the Department of Research in conjunction with financial problems.

The Contract Coordinating Committee   was a matter between the finance people at the Treasury, the Air Ministry and the aircraft industry. It brought in representatives of the Admiralty and the War Office to see that firms that were supplying all three fighting services were even-handed in their dealings with each.

The Committee on Cross-Channel Services (Subsidies) dealt with the problems facing four separate airlines trying to 'scratch' a living running services to the continent.

The Royal Air Force Committee   responded to the hazards facing the operators of aircraft that owned highly inflammable aircraft and gasoline. The committee brought in people from the Ministry of Transport, electrical engineers, personnel from Works and Buildings, the Metropolitan Police and others.

The Medical Advisory Board   coordinated the work of the RAF Medical Service with that of the other services and also civil practice.

The Meteorological Committee   brought in people from the War Office and the Colonial Office, the Board of Trade and the Royal Society, the Ministry of Agriculture, Fisheries and Food, the Scottish Office and the Royal Society of Edinburgh.

The Permanent Buildings Committee   was particularly concerned with giving RAF personnel decent accommodation after living in wooden huts that were built in a hurry during the First World War.

The Whitley Council   was set up in all government departments and in all industries to try to bring about better industrial relations. Its work covered men in the services, including the lower grades of civil servants.

The Industrial Whitley Council   dealt with manual labourers, and not office workers.

Other Committees   The Air Ministry also had representatives on a lot of inter-departmental committees, such as the Imperial Education Committee; the NAAFI; the Air Survey Committee; the Standing Committee of Representatives of the Government of Ex-Service Organizations; the Ordnance Committee, which dealt with armament, much of which was common to all three services; the Radio Research Board; the Advisory Council to the Committee for Scientific and Industrial Research; the Shell-shock committee, which dealt with cases of fighting men suffering this in battle; the United Services Trust; and the Wireless Telegraphy Board.

THE AIR COMMANDERS

Appendix R lists the names of members of the Air Council and commanders of RAF formations during the 1920s.

The paragraphs that follow will firstly provide a thumbnail sketch of those officers who held the highest command positions in the postwar years, followed by a representative sample of some officers in lower positions. Many very senior officers who commanded RAF brigades, wings and areas in a service of 188 squadrons during the First World War could not survive the peace with only a skeleton organization at home and a few squadrons overseas. Those few senior officers who survived filled the few command and staff posts in the early 1920s. The opening paragraphs of Chapter 9 briefly considered the careers of four of the most senior RAF commanders, and this chapter looks closely at the contribution they and subordinate commanders made to RAF operations, organization and administration.

Hugh Trenchard

Hugh Trenchard was born in Taunton in 1873 and was commissioned into the Royal Scots Fusiliers at the age of 20. He served in India before being sent to South Africa to fight in the Boer War. By this time he was an acknowledged good horseman at both polo and racing. When he was shot through the lung he went to convalesce in Switzerland, where he won the freshman's and beginner's Cresta Run, and largely cured his paralysis in the process. On his return to South Africa his skill as a horseman was put to the test when Lord Kitchener sent him to organize three mounted infantry battalions, and also to organize an expedition to capture the Boer Government, though Trenchard was unsuccessful in this.

When he returned to England in 1912 Trenchard was a 39-year-old major, with only one good lung and therefore limited career prospects. The newly formed RFC did provide an opportunity to advance himself, and he learned to fly in just thirteen days, whereupon he was sent to the Central Flying School at Upavon. Though an indifferent flyer, he had military experience and was soon made deputy to the first Commandant, Captain Godfrey Paine. From there he went to command the Military Wing at Farnborough on the outbreak of war in 1914, and in November of that year he was posted to France to command No. 1 Wing RFC. It took just nine months for him to succeed General Henderson as GOC Royal Flying Corps, with responsibility for all British air operations on the Western Front. These were difficult times owing to the success of the German Fokker aircraft, and their effectiveness against British aircraft

became known during this period as the 'Fokker scourge'. In spite of this Trenchard refused to let his pilots wear parachutes. Some might regard this as a rather callous stance, while others would suggest that it showed his determination that his pilots should at all times be more concerned with pressing home their attacks.

The Air Ministry that would oversee the new RAF was set up in December 1917, and having led the RFC in France with distinction, he was the obvious choice to become Chief of the Air Staff, and he accepted this post on 18 January 1918, only to resign in March over differences of policy with the Air Minister, Lord Rothermere. He was succeeded by Major-General Sykes. Trenchard was then prevailed upon to accept a post in France in command of the Independent Bombing Force. This was his opportunity to demonstrate the strategic employment of airpower, and targets in Germany, west of the Rhine, were attacked, but the war ended before Berlin could be bombed. Since there was no need for a strategic air force of the size of the 8th Brigade, with its five squadrons of 83rd Wing, equipped with HP 0/400 bombers, and with HP V/1500s coming on line, Trenchard was again without a job. But there had been a change at the top, and the new Minister for War and the Air was Winston Churchill, who was persuaded by Lord Weir that Trenchard was the man who would best lead the RAF during a period of economic stringency. So it was that Sykes was moved to civil aviation. In the event Weir was proved right, and Trenchard remained as Chief of the Air Staff until his retirement in 1929.

Frederick Sykes

Frederick Sykes was born in 1877, and on the outbreak of the Boer War, enlisted as a trooper. He was later commissioned into Lord Roberts's Bodyguard and was seriously wounded, but on his recovery he was granted a regular commission in the 15th Hussars. Apart from a brief spell in West Africa, he served mainly in India, where he attended the staff college at Quetta in 1908. His interest in aviation began as early as 1904, when he attended a course with the balloon section of the Royal Engineers. A soon as he could he undertook a flying course at Brooklands, where he went solo and gained his licence on a Bristol Boxkite in 1911. By that time he was a staff officer in the War Office and had become a firm believer in the importance of aerial reconnaissance in war. He was therefore the natural choice to join the Sub-Committee of the Committee of Imperial Defence to consider the way forward in military aviation. In 1912 that committee recommended the formation of the Royal Flying Corps, and he was selected to recruit, train and command the Military Wing at Farnborough. Sykes later wrote that this was the happiest and busiest period of his life. There was an added urgency to his work as war loomed larger. Treading entirely new ground, he had to acquire aircraft, construct a programme of flying training, find men to instruct trainee pilots and other men who had the technical skill to service and repair aircraft, test aircraft and carry our military manoeuvres with aircraft. This would be a daunting task for any man.

The flying units that went to war in 1914 were, therefore, largely his creation. However, Sykes did not have the seniority to command the RFC in France, and so General Sir David Henderson was placed in command, with Sykes as Chief of Staff. For the next nine months he either worked for Henderson or stood in for him. It was inevitable, given his position in the scheme of things, that he would get caught in the crossfire over the position of the RFC wings in relation to RFC HQ France. Trenchard, by then a commander of one of the RFC wings, felt that the wings should report directly to the corps or divisional commanders in whose sectors they operated. Others felt that all RFC wings should report direct to RFC HQ. These strains led to Sykes being transferred to Gallipoli in May 1915. There his services were required giving advice to the RNAS in its operations in support of Allied troops in the Dardanelles. The troops could not make any headway on the beaches held by Turkish forces, and required air support. He was therefore loaned to the Admiralty to command the air forces in the Eastern Mediterranean, and he directed these forces, in cooperation with the fleet, with success. He returned to the United Kingdom in 1916 to undertake several tasks: firstly, to organize the Machine-Gun Corps, then to work on manpower planning in the War Office, to be followed by service with the British section of the Anglo-French Supreme War Council in Versailles under General Wilson.

Having spent two years without any direct involvement with flying, it came as a surprise to find himself appointed to the post of Chief of Air Staff in the rank of major-general, vice Trenchard, who had resigned over his differences with Lord Rothermere. Sykes's immediate task was to integrate the RFC and RNAS into the new service organization. The RFC squadrons simply became RAF squadrons, but the RNAS flights were not reorganized into RAF squadrons until August of 1918. He was a staunch believer in the need for a separate Air Force and the setting up of an independent bomber force, which was needed to break the impasse of trench warfare.

Before he could turn round, the war had ended and he found himself leader of the British Air Section at the Versailles Peace Conference. He had to consider enemy disarmament and an international air code, and he pressed, unsuccessfully, for an 'open skies' policy, but it was his thoughts about the future size and role of the RAF that resulted in his replacement by Trenchard in March 1919. Sykes envisaged a series of permanent bases throughout the Empire from which an Imperial Air Force could be deployed. And so, only one month after

the war's end, he was proposing sixty-two service and ninety-two cadre squadrons, plus a further thirty-seven cadre squadrons in the Dominions. These proposals were far sighted, but they were completely out of tune with the thinking of politicians, where defence expenditure on the scale proposed was furthest from their minds.

The handover to Trenchard as CAS was described in the last section, but it left the government with a problem of what to do with a man at the peak of his profession and still only 41 years old. In what must seem a turbulent career, Sykes was moved after only one year as CAS to the post of Controller-General of Civil Aviation. With this high-sounding title went a seat on the Air Council. This would undoubtedly have been a sop to a man who was moving from head of a service that he had devoted so much time and effort in establishing to a department of the Air Ministry that attracted only a fraction of the funds allocated to the RAF. Although there was an enormous amount of work to be done for civil aviation in those early post-war years, such as producing new flying regulations, planning Empire air routes, establishing the International Commission of Aerial Navigation, etc., he resigned in 1922. It was because there was so much to be done and so little money with which to do it. He felt that the government was ignoring the needs of a growth industry, and he left to enter the House of Commons.

Edward Ellington

Edward Ellington was commissioned into the Royal Artillery in 1887, aged 20. Ten years later he graduated from Staff College and went to the War Office. While serving there he obtained his pilot's licence in 1912. He then went to General Henderson's RFC Planning Committee as secretary and afterwards headed the Air Policy and Administrative Section of the newly formed Military Aeronautics Directorate. From there he moved to Upavon, where he qualified as a military pilot in December 1913.

Having acquired these aeronautical skills Ellington was rather inexplicably moved to staff and regimental duties with the Artillery, where he spent most of the First World War, and it was not to be until November 1917 that he returned to military aviation, not flying, but again on staff duties, this time under John Salmond, where he was Deputy Director-General of Military Aeronautics. Two months later, when Salmond returned to France, Ellington succeeded him in the post, and in August 1918 he joined the recently formed Air Council as Controller-General of Equipment, later designated Supply and Research. In that post he was able to work alongside Trenchard to establish the structure of the RAF and solve its day-to-day problems. On 1 March 1922 he became AOC Middle East for a year before leaving to become AOC India on Guy Fawkes' Day 1923. Three years later he was AOC Iraq, where he remained until his return to the United Kingdom in January 1929 to become AOC-in-C Air Defence of Great Britain. Thereafter he was Air Member for Personnel before being promoted to Air Chief Marshal and taking up the post of CAS on 1 January 1933.

John Salmond

John Salmond joined the Army in 1900 at the age of 19. After graduating from Sandhurst he first served in South Africa and then went on to the South-West Frontier Force. Back home in 1907, he became seriously interested in the military possibilities of powered flight, having flown as a passenger from Hendon. His appetite whetted, he qualified as a pilot in 1912. Like Trenchard and Ellington, so too did Salmond attend the course at Upavon, where he qualified as a military pilot. He then became an instructor, and before the First World War had even started he had flown a BE biplane to 13,140 feet, a solo British altitude record.

When war broke out he was placed in command of No. 3 Squadron, which was engaged mainly on reconnaissance duties in France. In April 1915 he returned briefly to command the RFC Training Wing at Farnborough, but was soon back in France commanding No. 2 Wing under Trenchard. This was the time of mounting pilot losses in action, and so back to England went Salmond to reorganize the whole training system, since it was clear that RFC pilots arriving in France were quite unprepared for air action against German pilots. During the period Salmond did much flying himself, and tested new types.

In October 1917, still only 36 years old, John Salmond replaced Henderson on the Army Council as Director-General of Military Aeronautics. When Trenchard came home to take over as CAS, Salmond succeeded him as Commander of the RFC, with sixty-three squadrons under command to meet the German offensive of early 1918, and to take part in the counter-offensive that followed. This made Salmond the leading field commander of the RFC as the war came to an end.

Clearly Salmond was a very valuable member of Trenchard's post-war team, and he was placed in command of Inland Area, with its HQ at Uxbridge. In 1922 he was sent to India to report on the state of the RAF squadrons on the North-West Frontier, then in October 1922 he became the first-ever RAF officer to be placed in overall command of Army and RAF formations in an operational theatre. This was as AOC Iraq. He returned home in 1924, initially to Trenchard's staff at the Air Ministry, and then as AOC-in-C Air Defence of Great Britain. This kept Salmond busy, but he still had time to visit Australia and New Zealand in 1928 to advise on the development of their air forces. In January 1929 he became Air Member for Personnel, but

he held the post for only one year, since he succeeded Trenchard as the Chief of Air Staff at the end of the year.

Cyril Newall

Cyril Newall was born in India in 1886, and after a Sandhurst training, he was commissioned into the Royal Warwickshire Regiment in 1905 and served on the North-West Frontier. While he was home on leave in 1911 he learned to fly a Bristol biplane at Larkhill, and went on to Upavon to get his RFC 'wings' in 1913. He was then posted to the Central Flying School at Sitapur as an instructor.

When the First World War commenced, he returned home to join No. 1 Squadron as a flight commander. He was then made OC No. 12 Squadron in March 1915 as a temporary major, and went to France, taking part in the Battle of Loos, bombing railways and carrying out reconnaissance. He earned the Albert Medal by leading a party of airmen to put out a fire in a bomb store and thereby prevented what could have been a catastrophic explosion. He then went on to command both Nos 6 and 9 Wings as a temporary lieutenant-colonel. It was as OC No. 9 Wing under Trenchard's command that Newall's seven squadrons provided the RAF's long-range bombing and reconnaissance force in France. When No. 41 Wing was formed, Newall was the obvious choice to command, and in February 1918 No. 41 Wing became the VIIIth Brigade, whose task it was to bomb strategic targets. Under Newall's command the squadrons of the VIIIth Brigade carried out 142 raids, of which fifty-seven were against Germany. When the brigade became the Independent Bombing Force under Trenchard's command, Newall was his deputy.

When the war ended, Newall spent three years in the Air Ministry as Deputy Director of Personnel before proceeding to Halton in 1922 as deputy to the Commandant of No. 1 School of Technical Training. Between 1926 and 1931 he served in the Air Ministry as AOC of the Special Reserve and Auxiliary Air Force, as a member of the League of Nations Disarmament Committee, as Director of Operations and Intelligence and as Deputy Chief of Air Staff. This enormously diverse and rich experience, including wartime command and staff duties, prepared Newall for the ultimate command post in the RAF, that of CAS, to which he was appointed on 1 September 1937.

Charles Portal

Charles Portal, or Peter as he was known to his friends, was born in Hungerford in 1893 and was educated at Winchester and Christchurch, Oxford, but the war cut short his studies when he had intended to qualify as a barrister. He enlisted in the Royal Engineers as a dispatch rider and was sent to France. Given his background, he was soon commissioned, and without any previous training he found himself seconded to the

RFC, where he flew operationally with No. 3 Squadron as an observer. He then learned to fly, and in May 1916 returned to France to fly with No. 60 Squadron on artillery and spotting duties, moving later to No. 3 Squadron as a flight commander, and on 16 June 1917 he was posted to command No. 16 Squadron. He then earned an MC and two DSOs, and on 26 June 1918 he was made a temporary lieutenant-colonel to command No. 24 Wing, in which post he remained for the remainder of the war.

On his return to the England Portal was placed in command of No. 24 (Training) Wing at Grantham, and most of the time he was chief flying instructor at the newly opened RAF College, Cranwell. After attendance at the RAF Staff College at Andover, he joined the Operations and Intelligence staff at the Air Ministry. Obviously his wartime experience was of particular value in working out operational requirements, and he came to be highly regarded by Trenchard. Having attended the Senior Officers' War Course at Greenwich, he was posted in March 1927 to be OC No. 7 Squadron at Bircham Newton, and in 1929 he attended the Imperial Defence College. By the end of the decade he had acquired operational, training and staff experience necessary to equip him for higher command, and he was appointed Chief of the Air Staff in October 1940.

Arthur Harris

Arthur Harris was born in Cheltenham in 1892, and at the age of 16 he went looking for adventure in Rhodesia, taking on a variety of jobs until the outbreak of war in 1914, when he joined the 1st Rhodesia Regiment as a bugler. Although he served briefly in German South-West Africa, he wanted to be closer to the action, and returned to the United Kingdom, where he was accepted for training with the RFC. Having completed his pilot training in January 1916, he was posted to No. 39 Squadron, with which he flew against Zeppelins. After a period on day-fighters in France, he returned to England to train a new night-fighter squadron at Marham, then back to France to take command of No. 44 Squadron.

It was not until the end of the First World War that Harris was granted a permanent commission in the RAF. The years 1919 and 1920 were depressing for him, since he spent much of this time closing down units, and a posting to No. 31 Squadron in India saw him contemplating resignation when he found the RAF in India in such an appalling state. In July 1922 matters improved when he was posted to Iraq, first to the HQ in Basra, then to command No. 45 Squadron on air-control duties. Here Harris was able to use some imagination, employing the squadron's Vernons both as troop carriers and bombers. Three years later, in 1925, he returned to the UK to command No. 58 Squadron with Vickers Virginias at Worthy Down. In July 1927 he was promoted to the rank of wing commander, and attended the Army

Staff College at Camberley before proceeding to the Middle East as Senior Air Staff Officer (SASO). Apart from a spell as OC No. 210 Flying-Boat Squadron, Harris would spend the rest of his career in staff and senior command positions. He did not become CAS, but his place in history is secure following his position as AOC-in-C Bomber Command during the Second World War.

Other Air Commanders

Other senior officers played an important part in the early development of the RAF. They were those officers who already held senior positions in the RFC, and these names crop up frequently in accounts of those early days – names such as Scarlett, Brooke-Popham, Game, Vyvyan, Lambe, Bonham-Carter, Higgins and Ludlow Hewitt. Some, like Longmore, had come from the RNAS. There were those who were to reach the giddy heights and become Chief of the Air Staff, like Tedder and Dickson, but they did not get involved in staff work until the late 1920s. Then there were the first of the purely RAF types who would later become CAS and who joined as flight cadets at Cranwell, as did Dermot Boyle in 1922 and Pike in 1924. This chapter is concerned for the most past with the participation of senior commanders in the early, most formative years.

Quality of Command

Before considering the contribution that the most senior RAF officers made to the early development of the service, the reader is asked to cast aside the benefits of hindsight. This and the succeeding volume is a history of the inter-war years, but in the year 1919 and those that followed there were no inter-war years. Try to visualize a staff officer going in to work at the Air Ministry in late 1919. A war to end all wars had just finished. There was a 'Ten-Year Rule' that had been instituted by the government, which meant that Britain could not be expected to be involved in a major war during that period. Some 160 RAF squadrons were in the process of being disbanded. Thousands of men were being demobilized and surplus aircraft were being scrapped or sold off as war surplus. The nation was war weary, the Air Estimates for the year had just come down from over £56 million to under £20 million and the Army and Navy wanted the RAF dismembered and handed back to their former owners. There were a handful of squadrons left in the outposts of the Empire by the end of the First World War, tens of thousands of aircraft per year were leaving the aircraft factories, only to be burnt on arrival at the aircraft parks, and one was entitled to ask if the country any longer had a use for an air force. Mussolini had not then gained power in Italy, and Hitler had only just left the Army to dabble in minor politics in Munich. As far as one could see, stretching away endlessly into the future, was peace, the League of Nations and disarmament.

The first future CAS trained and recruited entirely by the RAF was not due to report to the RAF College Cranwell until 1922. All Trenchard's men came from the RFC and the RNAS. During the battles between the Army and the RAF over the latter's independence, the War Minister, Lord Derby, had asserted that the RAF did not have sufficient staff officers capable of filling all the staff appointments at the Air Ministry, and as if to rub salt into the wound, offered to lend some on secondment to Trenchard. The experience of most RAF senior commanders and staff officers in 1919 was mostly Army, and many of those who had worked in staff positions in the RFC at home and abroad had confined their attentions to air matters. It was alleged that they did not see the 'big picture', acting more as air advisers at various Army command levels, and even in their special field, the air, none of them would have been trained as a military pilot until just before or during the First World War. Reference to the preceding accounts of the careers of senior officers show that they were moved with almost breathtaking speed from one post to another, out to France and back again, then out again to command at flight, squadron and wing levels. No sooner had they become pilots than they were instructors. No sooner had they commanded a squadron than they were training a squadron. The RFC strength had gone from four squadrons at the outbreak of war to 188 squadrons. The pace of expansion meant that officers who had reached senior positions in the RAF were still young.

Chapter 6 explains how some naval officers regarded service with the RNAS as an unwelcome deviation from their chosen career path. Similarly the Army officer who saw himself as a future CIGS or corps or divisional commander might see service with the RFC as a diversion. Those who held senior positions in the RAF in 1919 had gone out of their way to fly. The preceding paragraph shows that there would not have been any difficulty in promoting officer pilots quickly to fill posts in a fast-expanding service, as well as to replace battle casualties. As fast as pilots could be trained, they were needed for squadrons and for flying training schools both at home and overseas. They were also needed at Farnborough and Upavon and to fill staff posts at the War Office and the various formations.

Parameters for planning   Trenchard's memorandum of 1919 laid down the foundations of an independent air force. New rank titles did more than anything to remind officers and men that they belonged to a new service. Flights, squadrons and wings were retained, but brigades went, to be replaced by groups and areas. Air units were to be allocated to the Army and Navy for work with those services, but the rest of the RAF would be divided between fighting and bombing squadrons, which was pure air force business. Experience in the air defence of London and with the IBF in France provided

at least a basis of experience from which to move forward. Then came air control, and for the next twenty years the RAF had an operational *raison d'être*. Trenchard knew that he needed an RAF staff college, a cadet college and an apprentice school to cultivate his 'air force spirit'.

Trenchard's post-war team

There can be no denying Trenchard's vision, and his immediate subordinates could see where they fitted into the scheme of things. They had the necessary mix of experience. Salmond had the operational command experience, but Ellington might almost have been a civil servant working in the Air Ministry who also had an interest in aeroplanes. He had never gone into action in the air, let alone commanded a flying unit. Unlike many of his colleagues, he had no DFCs or Military Crosses, but he could see the 'big picture' and had been involved with the use of aeroplanes in war from the very beginning. Newall and Portal had the necessary combat and command experience to make a valuable input into operational plans. Perhaps the biggest loss to the RAF was Sykes. He had enormous organizational ability and had worked with military aircraft from the very beginning, but he always seemed to be in the wrong place at the time, and had to be moved by his superiors through conflict of interest or outlook. Although we have said that he was a loss, he would not have fitted easily into Trenchard's post-war team.

Air Staff planning   One thing in which all the senior RAF commanders believed was offensive defence. Salmond, in particular, believed that one could not, through air defence alone, provide complete protection against air attack, and that it was necessary to strike hard at the enemy's military and industrial targets from the outset. It is therefore hard to understand how operational requirements for the first post-war bomber should result in the Avro Aldershot discussed earlier in this chapter. The RAF had to tread carefully. Retaining, say, just two squadrons of four-engined HP V/1500s in 1919 with the capability to bomb Berlin neither fitted with the reduced budget nor sent the right signals in a period of disarmament. The Air Staff might talk about offensive defence, but the diminutive DH9A looked far less menacing. A couple of squadrons of Vimys and DH10s could be paraded in the guise of Imperial policing, and then air control. In this context, therefore, the equipping of the RAF with Avro Aldershots and Fairey Foxes in the 1920s can be understood. It is clear that the Air Staff allowed its ideas about the bomber to become entrenched dogma before it had considered them in a serious analytical fashion. Eventually the Air Staff began to believe its own rhetoric. Specifications for aircraft throughout the 1920s, when compared with advances in civil aviation, lagged behind. Those specifications resulted in the introduction of aircraft with performance levels not greatly surpassing those of some of the aircraft that saw service in the First World War. A study of Appendix A will show this to be the case. Compare, for example, the Gamecock with the Bristol M1C in speed and service ceiling, or the Virginia with the HP V/1500 in terms of service ceiling and defensive armament. It has already been made clear that firms not held back by the constraints of Air Ministry specifications produced aircraft with a more exciting performance.

The Staff College, Andover The quality of the future operational commanders and staff officers would be determined largely by the RAF having its own staff college, which was part of Trenchard's philosophy, that flying was an art to be mastered and the use of aircraft in war was a matter for an independent air force. As staff officers began to emerge from the Staff College, they would have been schooled in the thinking of the day. Wilfred Freeman was appointed senior instructor at the Staff College on 14 October 1921 before the college opened. The first Commandant was Brooke-Popham, and among the first intake were the future senior commanders of the RAF, including Sholto Douglas, Keith Park of Battle of Britain fame and Charles Portal. The courses surveyed the principles of war, imperial strategy, the tactics and organization of air, ground and naval forces, intelligence, supply and communications, domestic and foreign policy and the relationship of economics, commerce and science to RAF affairs. Basic staff duties had to be mastered, which included letter

The RAF Staff College Course of 1922 Wilfred Freemen is second from the left in the front row. Other famous names are Brooke-Popham (front row 4th from left), Park (2nd from the right), Sholto Douglas (middle row 4th from Right), Portal (back row 2nd from Left) and Pierce (back row 3rd from left).

and report writing, and students were taught how to organize formal receptions, for Brook-Popham set high standards on social occasions. The courses lasted a year, during which time students had to maintain flying practice, surveyed sites for airfields and had to consider a wide range of non-RAF matters. They visited the Navy, the London Docks and a railway terminus, and there were exchange visits to the Navy and Army Staff Colleges. With the Navy, for example, students considered the defence of Singapore, an exercise which was to become reality nineteen years later for the Commandant, Brooke-Popham.

Notable Contributions made by Individual Commanders

Edward Ellington

From March 1922 there followed seven years abroad, firstly as Air Officer Commanding in the Middle East, then in India and finally in Iraq, before returning home. He flew a fair amount during his tours abroad, but as a passenger. These tours gave him extensive experience of operational command, the first that he had personally experienced. It is, to say the least, most unusual and almost unique for a commander in any of the three services to start the operational part of his career in one of the highest ranks of his service. He was an AOC when his squadrons were regularly engaged in peace-keeping operations, but that did not prepare him for his eventual rise to the post of Chief of the Air Staff in 1933, planning for a European war. Of course Ellington was not alone in this respect, for most senior air commanders of the 1930s had only air-control experience to add to that gained in the First World War, and he, like the others, was wedded to the belief in offensive defence. How effective a commander Ellington would have been in a fighting war against an enemy that put up resistance in the air we shall never know. He stepped down from active service just before the Battle of Britain. Maurice Dean, Ellington's private secretary, spoke of him in his relations with Ministers. At times, says Dean, it was the Ministers rather than Ellington who led the way, since he had little personal knowledge of aviation, which sounds unbelievable in an Air Marshal. On the other hand he had an acute mind and was quick to embrace new ideas. He was, as CAS, in his element. He had always been, and continued to be, a superb staff officer, and it was during his tenure of that post that the specifications were issued for the Spitfire and Hurricane.

John Salmond

John Salmond was the natural successor to Trenchard when the latter retired at the end of 1929. His contribution was vital, having first-hand command experience in action and being a very able pilot. He was the natural choice to be AOC in Iraq in October 1922, and he was not afraid to take hard decisions, particularly in his handling of Turkish incursions into northern Iraq. He took over at a bad moment. The Turks were threatening the northern province of Mosul, and a Kurdish rebellion led by Sheik Mahmud was under way. Salmond received no firm political direction from the United Kingdom, and there were those, especially critics in the Army, who were watching closely to see how well he handled the situation, no one more so than the CIGS, Sir Henry Wilson, who refused to allocate the necessary armoured-car units to Salmond. But he did not protest at this unfriendly act, and simply formed his own RAF armoured-car units. The judicious use of bombing and moving his ground troops quickly forward by air meant that he was able to use his limited resources effectively. It was Salmond's masterly handling of the situation that demonstrated the effectiveness of air control. His report on the state of the RAF in India was also a most valuable exercise, resulting in a gradual improvement of the quality of aircraft maintenance and supply during the 1920s. In the late 1920s he was in command of the air defence of Great Britain. He had scarce resources and still outdated aircraft with which to conduct the first annual air exercises in the UK, where, as Chapter 3 makes clear, he was wedded to the then current air doctrine of offensive defence, and the odds were stacked in favour of the bomber. When he did finally succeed to the post of CAS, he was not able to achieve very much, for it was the height of the great economic depression, when resources were scarce, and the Geneva Disarmament Conference, which began in 1932, meant that Salmond faced calls for air and other disarmament.

John Slessor

John Slessor's own account of his contribution to the work of the Air Ministry from his book *The Central Blue* is illuminating. He had never taken the view that staff appointments are a fate to be avoided if humanly possible, and believed that one should get a fair ration of both command and staff duties. He recalled that his first posting to a staff position was in 1923, but at rather too early an age. He thought that RAF officers should remain on flying duties for at least the first ten years of the service, and he knew of some potentially first-class officers being spoiled by being condemned too early to an office stool. Having lost the sharpness of constant flying practice, it was sometimes difficult to get it back. (In fairness to the service, provision was made for those in office jobs at the Air Ministry to fly as regularly as possible at Hendon.) Worse still was that if a staff officer was particularly good he might be rotated around the various positions until, in Slessor's words, he became 'a

sort of goldfish swimming round in a bowl without ever getting out into the open sea'. Such officers might then be denied the top command posts in the service, which was manifestly unfair. In arriving at really important judgements, Slessor felt that any amount of theoretical knowledge and the deepest study of military history cannot compensate for lack of experience of having to take responsibility for decisions oneself in contact with the enemy, which, of course, makes Ellington's case so unusual.

Brooke-Popham

Brooke-Popham was one of the founding fathers of the RFC and the RAF. He was an Air Vice-Marshal as Commandant of the RAF Staff College, a very able administrator and utterly devoted to the Service until his death in 1953. Under his leadership the Staff College got the first course under way, commencing in 1922. Slessor recalls that the students had to feel their way towards a doctrine of air warfare, for there was little experience to guide them. The air service having been an auxiliary to the Army and Navy in the First World War, it was up to Trenchard and his officers to have the faith and vision to evolve a theory of air warfare based on the supremacy of the offensive. The faith in the offensive may seem to have been premature in the 1920s, but Brooke-Popham played a vital role in ensuring that new arts were being learned by his students. He went on to command Fighting Area in the late 1920s, and his units took part in the 1927 and 1928 air exercises. When the Second World War started in 1939, most of his ex-students held important command and staff positions in the RAF.

Hugh Dowding

Hugh Dowding is probably best known as head of Fighter Command during the Battle of Britain in 1940. He did not, however, succeed to the post of CAS, being retired in 1942. As it happens, he had already been told that he was due for retirement, even before the war started. This is to say that Dowding's progress to senior rank was not always smooth. Even as the First World War ended, Dowding had to wait to see if he was to be awarded a permanent RAF commission, and be able to join the new team to fashion the post-war service. He had already had differences of opinion with Trenchard when in command of the 9th Headquarters Wing in France during the Battle of the Somme, and he was sent back home for the rest of the war to command the Southern Training Brigade at Salisbury. He did secure a command post as a staff officer in HQ No. 1 Group, and had responsibility for organizing the first Hendon Air Pageants, and then as Chief Staff Officer, first at HQ Inland Area, then at HQ Iraq. He came into his own in 1926 when he was appointed Director of Training, and he was then able to influence policy. His previously strained relations with Trenchard improved. At the end of the decade he was appointed AOC Transjordan at a time of growing hostility between Jew and Arab.

Wilfred Freeman

Surprisingly, Freeman did not like instructing at the Staff College. He said it made him feel like a schoolmaster, and he seriously considered leaving the RAF. This is not to understate, however, the importance that staff training had and still has for future air commanders. He was promoted to group captain in January 1923, and headed the directing staff for the third course to pass through the college. He was then posted to the Central Flying School at Upavon, tasked with preparing to move the school to Wittering in 1925. The CFS, built on Smith-Barry's pioneering system of flying training, achieved a worldwide reputation for flying instruction on its eleven-week courses. In the interval between courses the instructors would visit other flying schools to monitor standards. A notable contribution that Freeman made to aerobatic flying was to persuade the Air Ministry to purchase six 'Genet' Moths and prepare a number of his instructors to form a team for the 1927 Hendon Air Display. The DH 60G Moths with the light Genet radial engines had been lent to the CFS to teach Greek pupils, who were used to the aircraft, and Freeman found them a delight to fly. The members of the team, led by D'Arcy Greig, included Atcherley, Waghorn and Stainforth, all future members of the RAF High-Speed Flight. Freeman was remembered by his CFS staff as a brilliant officer. He was quiet and reserved but had a sense of humour. On the other hand he could be intolerant and incapable of suffering fools gladly. He corrected the rather lax regime of 'Topsy' Holt, who encouraged his instructors to carry out all sorts of stunts, sometimes damaging aircraft in the process.

On 27 February 1927 he left CFS for the Air Ministry, to become Deputy Director of Operations and Intelligence, spending almost two years working closely with Trenchard. But Freeman suffered from migraines,

and after working in London for eighteen months he became frequently more ill, and suffered from intermittent fever. Trenchard took pity and had him posted to command the RAF station Leuchars, which was out of doors and to his liking. He ended the decade as SASO of the UK Inland Area.

Wing Commander R.C.M. Pink

There can be no doubt that Wing Commander Pink was one of the outstanding commanders of the inter-war years. He showed initiative in organizing long-distance flights that would not only 'show the flag' but would practise his pilots in navigation and working a long way from their home base. The operations during March to May 1925 against the Abdur Rahman Khel tribe have become known as 'Pink's War', and when he briefed his men for these operations he so impressed them that he reportedly got a round of applause. Everyone who speaks of Pink tells of his qualities of leadership, and he often flew with his pilots, accepting the risks that they took. It is thus all the more sad that cancer claimed his life in 1932, bringing short what would have undoubtedly been a career that would have taken him to the top.

Squadron Leader Harris – bombing and night flying

Earlier in this chapter it was mentioned that the RAF did not have a bombing development unit until the later 1930s. The Air Staff simply worked on the premise that the bomber would get through, and that, in any case, the morale effect of bombing was more important than the destructive effect. And so nothing was done to improve bombing techniques and the quality of bombs. When Squadron Leader Harris assumed command of No. 45 Squadron in Iraq, he had a squadron of troop transports. One of his flight commanders, Flight Lieutenant Ralph Cochrane, stated that, 'We literally took the beer up to the troops and brought back the casualties. But that wasn't at all in accord with Bert Harris's idea of what he wanted to do.' Not one to let the grass grow under his feet, Harris set out to investigate improved methods of bombing in various conditions. He calculated that it was theoretically possible for a single Vernon aircraft to carry a bomb load equivalent to the load-carrying capacity of an entire squadron of DH9As (Ninaks), the standard bombing aircraft of the RAF. In carrying out experiments, Harris was, in effect, undertaking operational research, something the Air Staff should have been doing.

Turning the troop-carrying Vernons into bombers required adaptation, and this is what Harris undertook. The standard method of aiming and dropping bombs from a DH9A at this time was for the pilot to look through a sight on the side of the fuselage, and the air gunner in the rear cockpit dropped the bombs on a signal from the pilot. Harris sought to improve upon this

The 'Genet' Moths of CFS.

method by developing a line-of-flight sighting mechanism. A hole was cut in the floor of the aircraft's nose so that the bomb-aimer could lie prone, looking down through the sight and with the ability also to release the bombs at just the right moment. This left the pilot free to concentrate on keeping the aircraft straight and level on the run-up to the target with the bomb-aimer calling out corrections to the pilot as necessary. This was to be the method used by RAF Bomber Command throughout the Second World War.

Another innovation was to design an air current indicator. In hot climates the lift of aircraft is much reduced, and a fully loaded Vernon might not be able to get above 100 feet. Such an instrument would indicate to the pilot when he could take advantage of air currents to reach a greater altitude. Once Harris had designed the equipment, he needed to practise his squadron using dummy bombs. Hours were spent flying upwind of the target at between 1,000 and 2,000 feet, and the crews got their bombs to within ten or fifteen yards. With a ground speed of not much more than 40 mph – the maximum airspeed of a Vernon being 80 mph – achieving accuracy was not too difficult. But Harris's aircraft were not encountering bad weather or enemy fighter and anti-aircraft fire. He nevertheless took his ideas to his AOC, John Salmond, proposing a competition between his squadron and the squadrons of DH9As and Bristol Fighters currently engaged in operations on the front. Salmond agreed, and the improvement in bombing accuracy by the Vernon crews resulted in No. 45 Squadron taking over the bombing role.

A further development undertaken by Harris was in night flying. What was needed for effective bombing at night was pathfinding and target marking. Little had been achieved during the First World War to overcome the problems associated with bombing at night, and until Harris carried out his experiments, nothing had been done in the early post-war years. Since Harris believed that night bombing could be extremely effective, he knew that good navigation was the key to success. And so he practised his squadron in night flying to the point where they could be relied upon to arrive near the target at the right time. What was then needed was to mark the target for the benefit of all crews in the formation. To do this Harris devised a target marker using a Very light attached to a standard bomb. He had to admit that the conditions under which he was operating were ideal, clear skies and low level, something that would hardly pertain in a European war against sophisticated airpower in poor weather. The point in this context is that Harris was illustrating in a very practical way the problems that had to be overcome, and in the event, they were not to be overcome until well into the Second World War. This was a classic example of the Air Staff making claims for the potential of airpower that had no basis in practical experience.

William Dickson

William Dickson's name has been included in a consideration of the contribution made by commanders to the work of the RAF in its early years because he was one of the few to come over from the RNAS. Trained to fly seaplanes, first on Lake Windermere and then at Calshot, he flew anti-submarine patrols and also flew against the Gotha bombers. He was then posted to HMS *Furious*, where he learned of the difficulties facing a navy pilot trying to put down on the sea. He then went on to help pioneer deck landings and later took part in the first carrier-based bombing raid against a Zeppelin base at Tondern. By August 1919 he was Fleet Aviation Officer on HMS *Queen Elizabeth*, but he was somewhat disheartened by the Navy's attitude towards aircraft, and he was persuaded of the need for an independent air force. By then the RNAS had been absorbed into the RAF, and he had the option of remaining a naval officer, albeit with an equivalent RAF rank, or becoming a RAF officer proper. He was granted a permanent RAF commission, and his expertise and background made him a valuable addition to the staff, the more so because Trenchard knew little about naval aviation. After a motor cycle accident that cut short his work as a test pilot at Farnborough, he found himself as the sole flight lieutenant on the staff at the Air Ministry, where he doubled up as Personal Assistant to Sir John Steele, the DCAS. This came at a time when Trenchard was having to fight off attempts by the Navy to regain its own integral air arm, and Dickson's knowledge was valuable. It certainly established his reputation as a clever staff officer, and after a distinguished career he rose to become CAS in 1953.

Conclusion

The individual and collective contribution to the development of the RAF and to the study and development of air theory of other officers may not appear in the paragraphs above, not because they do not merit recognition, but simply that they more or less mirror the experiences of those whose contributions are described. These would include such names as Geoffrey Salmond, Edgar Ludlow-Hewitt, John Steele, Sholto Douglas, Bonham-Carter *et al*. The conclusions that may be drawn from their collective experience are as follows. Firstly, that Trenchard provided the leadership, the vision and the determination to lay the foundations of the RAF of the future, built in peace but prepared to expand to meet the needs of a major war. Secondly, that his immediate subordinates and the Air Ministry staff shared his vision and determination to succeed. Trenchard had the necessary mix of experience and skills with which to move forward, and although some of his staff officers might not, initially, have had the experience that fitted them to see the wider picture, from 1922 the RAF Staff College course at Andover would rectify this deficiency. Thirdly, the Air Staff may have been slow to develop modern types of aircraft throughout the decade of the 1920s, but one could say, in its defence, that since no major war for ten years was the rule there were more important jobs to be done from meagre funds, such as buildings at Cranwell and Halton, the development of Imperial air routes and air policing overseas, for which duties the DH9A and Bristol Fighter aircraft were adequate. Finally, many of the senior officers of the period were relatively young and therefore likely to be vital. This was an accident of history, that so many men who happened to show an interest in flying and entered service with the RFC and the RNAS found themselves receiving early promotion to meet the demands of rapidly expanding air arms. Those, like John Salmond, could not have expected to succeed to Air rank at such a young age in a peacetime or an established air force. One

could argue that most of those mentioned above were fortunate to have been in the right place at the right time.

This chapter could not be concluded without mention of the junior officers, NCOs and airmen whose qualities and achievements brought credit to the new service. Their names would be too numerous to include in this chapter, but they do appear in the squadron diary accounts in Chapter 4. There were those who showed great initiative in developing equipments for aircraft to suit certain operational requirements, including such things as parachutes for supply dropping, the Gosport tube, unauthorized additions to the kit that festooned the DH9As, getting downed aircraft back to base in one or several pieces and developing engineering techniques that permitted aircraft to be maintained in primitive surroundings. There was never going to be a shortage of talent upon which Trenchard could draw.

Chapter 11

The Royal Air Force and Government

Governments of the 1920s – Air Estimates, 1919 – The Liberal government – The first Labour government – The Conservative governments of the mid to late 1920s

This final chapter describes the relationship between the various governments of the 1920s and the RAF. Of course most interaction was between the politicians and members of the Air Council. Chapters 1 to 3 showed that the attitude of members of the Cabinet towards the fledgling RAF was mixed. It was to be expected that successive War Ministers and First Lords of the Admiralty would adopt a hostile and negative stance, but Trenchard did have his friends and supporters. Airpower offered politicians a new way of waging war, and one that would certainly avoid a repetition of years of static trench warfare. Aeronautics was still in its infancy, and one could not help but be attracted by the excitement of flying. A few politicians took an active interest in flying and some were themselves pilots. Typical of the new breed of politician/air enthusiast was Major-General Seely, the Parliamentary Under-Secretary for Air in 1919, who on one occasion alighted on the River Thames in a seaplane by the House of Commons Terrace, having flown under Tower Bridge, and was rebuked by the Lord Mayor.

Be that as it may, whether hostile or supportive, Trenchard and his brother officers knew that in the immediate post-war years funds would be tight. The Air Estimates represent the Air Force's needs for public funds for a financial year and must be approved by Parliament. Those for the financial year 1919/20 are shown at Appendix S, the year when the strength of the RAF would fall from 150,000 to 35,000, excluding the RAF in India, which was funded by the Government of India. These should be consulted because they show the various heads of vote to which the moneys were allocated, e.g. Pay, Technical and Warlike Stores, Land and Buildings, etc. From a total of £54 million in that year the sum would drop to around £15 million in succeeding years.

The 1920s are an interesting time politically because these years witnessed the first-ever Labour government of 1923, the Geddes Axe of that period, the General Strike of 1926, the Locarno Treaty and the Kellogg–Briand Pact. No one could be sure how the new Labour government would react to demands for defence expenditure. In the ranks of the Labour party there were pacifists deeply committed to disarmament who could be expected to wish to cut the armed forces to the bone. In the event it was to be economic circumstances and not deeply held political beliefs that were to result in government calls for cut-backs in defence expenditure, and the RAF had to accept its share.

The Air Estimates

The RAF's share of the overall defence budget is shown in the following table for the 1920s, and it seems that the new service was the poor relation. The sum for the RAF for 1922 would not buy one Tornado in today's money, which is a sobering thought, even allowing for inflation over the years.

	Navy £	Army £	RAF £
1920	90,872,300	125,000,000	22,992,230
1921	83,444,000	93,714,000	18,411,000
1922	64,883,700	62,300,000	10,895,000
1923	58,000,000	52,000,000	12,011,000
1924	55,800,000	45,000,000	14,861,000
1925	66,500,100	44,500,000	15,513,000
1926	58,100,000	42,500,000	16,000,000
1927	58,000,000	41,565,000	15,550,000
1928	57,300,000	41,050,000	16,250,000
1929	55,865,000	40,545,000	16,960,000

The presentation to Parliament of the Annual Air Estimates was the occasion for the successive Air Ministers to justify the sums required and to give Parliament an update on air matters. Then the members of the Houses of Commons and the Lords would be called upon to vote the sums required. The overall sum was broken down under the following heads:

Effective Services
1. Pay, etc. of the RAF
2. Quartering, stores (except technical; supplies animals and transport)
3. Technical and warlike stores
4. Works, buildings and lands
5. Air Ministry
6. Miscellaneous effective services

Non-effective Services
7. Half pay, pensions and other non-effective services

The air estimates will be referred to again as they crop up in the discussion of the 1920s. As a matter of interest, the various governments under which succeeding Air Ministries had to work are shown on the facing page. The Chief of the Air Staff throughout the entire period was Hugh Trenchard. Within each Cabinet there was the man holding the purse strings, namely the Chancellor of the Exchequer, as well as the Prime Minster and Cabinet, who had to be convinced of the need for spending money. The official policy expressed by the Cabinet on 15 August 1919 was one of economy and disarmament, and that, in forming their estimates for the year, the three services were to assume that the British Empire would not be engaged in any great war in the following ten years and that no expeditionary force was required for that purpose. Thus the famous 'Ten-Year Rule' came into existence, and the period of ten years, originally intended to take Britain up to the year 1930, was extended several times until 1928, when the then Chancellor of the Exchequer, Winston Churchill, suggested that each year the Estimates for the Fighting Services be framed annually on the basis that from any given date the period was ten years unless the Committee of Imperial Defence felt otherwise. This would simplify matters for the three service ministries in making their plans for equipment, manning, training and deployments. It would not, however, prevent the three service chiefs from attempting to increase the overall budget or their share of it. This book has already described the bitter battles between the Navy and the Army on the one hand and the RAF on the other. The reader has also been appraised of the employment of air control in Britain's overseas territories as an economical way of keeping the peace.

GOVERNMENTS AND SECRETARIES OF STATE IN THE 1920S

	Government & Prime Minister	Secretary of State for Air	Parliamentary Under Secretary
1918		Lord Rothermere 3/1/18 – 27/4/18 Lord Weir 27/4/18 – 14/1/19	Major J L Baird MP 3/1/18 – 10/1/19
1919	Lloyd George Coalition until 19th October 1922	Mr Winston Churchill 14/1/19 - 5/4/21	Maj. General J E B Seely 10/1/19 – 23/12/19 MP
1920			Major G C Tryon 23/12/19 – 2/4/20 Marquis of Londonderry 2/4/20 – 18/7/21
1921		Captain F. E. Guest MP 5/4/21 – 2/11/22	Lord Gorell 18/7/21 – 2/11/22
1922			
1923	Conservative – Bonar Law 19/10/22 – 21/5/23	Sir Samuel Hoare Bt. MP 2/11/22 – 23/1/24	Duke of Sutherland 2/11/22 – 23/1/24
1924	Conservative - Baldwin 21/5/23 – 12/23 Labour/Liberal Coalition Ramsay Mac Donald 12/23 – 9/10/24 Conservative - Baldwin 6/11/24 – 10/5/29	Lord Thomson 23/1/24 – 7/11/24	Mr W Leach MP 23/1/24 – 12/11/24
1925		Sir Samuel Hoare 7/11/24 – 8/6/29	Sir Philip Sassoon Bt. MP 12/11/24 – 11/6/29
1926			
1927			
1928			
1929	Labour/Liberal Coalition Ramsay Mac Donald 31/5/29 – 24/8/31	Lord Thomson 8/6/29 – 18/10/30	Mr. F Montague MP 11/6/29 – 3/9/31
1930			

1919–21

The Chancellor of the Exchequer in Lloyd George's post-war coalition was Austen Chamberlain. He wrote to Winston Churchill, at that time Minister for War and the Air, on 2 September 1919 to say that things seemed to be moving in a vicious circle, since Trenchard was asking what money he could spend and the government was asking what air forces were felt to be needed in the post-war situation. Trenchard, as we have seen, was determined to create a real air service, and not one of airborne chauffeurs, which is what the Army wanted. Three schemes were put forward, but the one finally adopted was described in detail in Chapter 2, namely the Trenchard Memorandum. This was to be the blueprint for the development of the RAF in the 1920s.

Major-General Seely as US of S for Air

Major-General Seeley was appointed to the post of Under-Secretary of State for Air in January 1919, and it was the Prime Minister's intention that Seely should preside over the Air Council, but according to Statute this could only be done by the Minister for War and the Air, Winston Churchill. Seely found that his position was untenable, since he was supposed to be in charge of the Air Department of the War Office but felt that he wasn't. What was needed was a separate Ministry with its own Air Minister, and it seemed strange that Churchill, who had done so much to create an independent air force, should not push hard for a separate Air Ministry. This may be understood if it is true that Winston was grooming himself to be the new Minister of Defence and head of a unified government department. Seely therefore tried to resolve matters through an intermediary, namely the newspaper proprietor, Lord Riddell, who was a close friend of Lloyd George. Lord Riddell let the PM know that Seely found his position impossible and wished to resign. But Lloyd George had no intention of creating a new government department at this time, for this would have added unacceptably to public expenditure. Thereupon Seely promptly resigned, much to Trenchard's regret, never to hold political office again, although he

Major-General J.E.B. Seely MP, Under-Secretary of State for Air from 10 January to 22 December 1919.

did continue to support the RAF from the back benches as a Liberal MP until his defeat in the 1924 General Election.

Lord Londonderry as US of S for Air

Churchill wanted Seely to be replaced by Lord Londonderry as the new Under-Secretary of State for Air, for he had been answering questions on air matters in the House of Lords and was the finance member of the Air Council. But there was opposition to his appointment from within the Conservative party, and he was passed over for Major G.L. Tryon, who only remained in post for a few months before being moved to another department in a government reshuffle. By this time opposition to Londonderry's appointment had subsided, and he took up the post on 3 April 1920. He was soon

Lord Londonderry (left) with Winston Churchill.

actively engaged on air matters, and on 11 May 1920 he introduced the Air Navigation Bill into Parliament, which would form the basis of an international law of the air. Londonderry did his best to promote Britain's leadership in the air, and he appreciated the potential of airpower, but it was mostly in a social capacity that he was an asset to Trenchard.

Some members of the Board of the Admiralty, the War Office and others looked down their noses at the new Air Ministry, but Churchill did not. Socially the Ministry needed a big name, and it seems that they had found one in the new Under-Secretary of State, who was an aristocrat and a landowner, and had a wife who was a prominent hostess in London. Trenchard understood the importance of making contacts and influencing the right people on the golf course or at social functions. Lord Londonderry could fulfil that role, and the men became good friends.

Major-General Sykes as Controller-General of Civil Aviation

In 1919 there was no separate government department to cover civil aviation, and Major-General Sykes was appointed Controller-General of Civil Aviation, thus relieving Trenchard of responsibility for civil air matters. Indeed, there was no reference to them in his 1919 Memorandum. The Air Ministry, however, was the umbrella under which Sykes operated his department.

THE ROYAL AIR FORCE AND GOVERNMENT **327**

Major-General Sykes.

This was responsible for planning, communications, meteorological services, licences, inspections and information. From February 1919 the Air Ministry would be responsible for the issuing of public weather forecasts, and for many years to come references would be made to the temperature, humidity and wind speed on the Air Ministry roof. These services had to be provided from very limited financial resources, and it seemed unfair that Sykes should have to provide a service that served the whole country. He had much greater need for money for research into blind flying, landing at night and flying-boats that would be needed for the Imperial air routes, but three-quarters of the £2 million allocated to research went to military flying, i.e. he had to manage on £500,000 a year. The government's view was that if extra money was wanted for civil aviation then Parliament should have to vote for it. But this raised the question that was to crop up time and again during these formative years. The very essence of commercial flying was that it was supposed to be run by private enterprise and subject to market forces. To provide public moneys might be regarded as the granting of a subsidy to firms in competition, although this never seemed to worry the French, who at that time were Britain's most serious competitors on the cross-Channel routes. What Sykes needed was something spectacular to boost civil aviation. Crossing the Channel could be lucrative, but ever the Imperialist, Sykes was thinking of the routes to Egypt and the Far East and to Canada and the USA. The Vimy flights by Alcock and Brown from Newfoundland to Britain, and Ross Smith's from Hounslow to Port Darwin, provided much-needed publicity to show what was possible in the future. What Sykes may have lacked in government support was in part compensated for by the leading newspapers, notable the *Daily Mail*, which would sponsor major aeronautical events. Sykes had been very positive in his first departmental progress report of 1 November 1919, and the Weir Committee had looked at ways of developing British civil aviation (see Chapter 2), but in the context of government–RAF relations it is evident that Sykes had been given a post that did not make sufficient demands upon his organizing ability and experience. His more grandiose plans for an Imperial air force were not what the government was looking for at a time of financial stringency, and Trenchard was, in this respect, the much safer bet. Having been Chief of the Air Staff and the

leading service member of the Air Council, as Controller-General of Civil Aviation he did not warrant a seat on the Council, in spite of his impressive title, and so it could be seen as a demotion. This, together with the paucity of funding, had clearly reduced the status of his department, and Sykes resigned on 1 April 1922.

1921 Air Estimates
Churchill introduced the Air Estimates for the financial year 1921/2 to the House of Commons on 1 March 1921. Only £800.000 had been appropriated for civil aviation from a total of £18,410,000, and it was this that led to Sykes's resignation a year later. *The Times* was particularly critical, alleging the neglect of civil aviation by the government. Lloyd George's response was to separate War and Air into two separate departments, presumably on the grounds that an Air Minister could devote more time to both civil and military aviation without the distraction of Army matters. In the government reshuffle that followed, Churchill was moved to the Colonial Office. As it happened, Churchill was thus able to keep very close links with the RAF and give the service a real peacetime raison d'être, for it was at the Cairo Conference of 1922 that, with Churchill's backing, air control was accepted as a new way of maintaining internal security in the outposts of Empire.

The new Ministers for War and the Air
The Conservative, Sir Laming Worthington-Evans, became the new Minister for War, and the Liberal, Captain the Hon. F.E. (Freddie) Guest, became the new Air Minister, but without a seat in the Cabinet. For the coming battles with the Navy and the Army the RAF would not be able to defend itself in the Cabinet, but on a more positive note Guest was very popular at Westminster. He was an active sportsman, a big-game hunter, and he held a pilot's licence. He had been a Liberal MP since 1911 and had been made Patronage Secretary to the Treasury. Both he and his brother, Lord Wimborne, were related to Winston Churchill. When Captain Guest took part in the debates on the 1921 Estimates it was remarked that he knew very little about aviation but that, to his credit, he did not pretend to know. He had stated that the First

Captain the Hon. F.E. Guest DSO, CBE.

World War had advanced the science of aviation one hundred years, which was a cheerful and positive note upon which to start his term of office as Air Minister. *The Times* of 5 April took a contrary view: 'Military ideas had been supreme at the Air Ministry during Churchill's time in office, including such things as the introduction of high-sounding titles and the building of elaborate aerodromes, whereas the science of flying had been neglected, there had been little progress made in the design of engines and civil aviation had been left in the cold.' Be that as it may, Trenchard would be able to report to a minister whose undivided attention would be on Air matters, so vital in his battles with the War Office and the Admiralty. Not that Churchill, as Minister for War and the Air, had done a bad job. On the contrary, it was he who had supported Trenchard when the latter submitted his 1919 Memorandum, which laid the foundations for the permanent organization of the peacetime air force, and he insisted on the new rank titles, which emphasized the separate identity of the RAF. Even when he went to the Colonial Office he was in an excellent position to help the RAF establish air control in Iraq in 1922.

Awareness of the importance of airpower

If the RAF was to remain an independent service it was essential for succeeding governments to be persuaded of the RAF's case. The Lord President of the Council, Mr Balfour, had submitted his report on the threefold relationship between the RAF and its sister services. Balfour's committee had appreciated the importance of not relegating the RAF to an inferior position, and there was a recommendation that during the conduct of air-defence operations the Navy and the Army should play a secondary role. The Smuts Report of 1917 had pointed to the vital necessity of coordinating single-service attempts to defend the capital against bombardment at a time when the first priority of the Admiralty was protection of the fleet in home waters. On the other hand, the committee recommended that during the conduct of military operations on land or naval operations at sea the RAF should play a subordinate role. Where military operations were not clearly in any one sphere it was concluded that relations between the services should be a matter of cooperation rather than strict subordination. Unfortunately the other two service chiefs did not see things in that light, and did not therefore regard the findings of the Balfour Committee as the last word on the matter. Sir Henry Wilson, Chief of the Imperial General Staff, questioned Balfour's judgement, and to his oft repeated calls for the RAF's abolition he added a demand for an investigation into the RAF's finances. Initially Trenchard was taken aback, but then said that he would accept such an investigation provided it was also applied to the other two services. As it happens, the government had just set up a committee to do precisely that.

The Geddes Committee

In May 1921 the Treasury had sent a circular to all government departments to the effect that there must be heavy cuts in expenditure. This would affect not only the armed forces but also the departments dealing with education, health, war and old-age pensions, labour and unemployment. The Estimates for the year 1922/3 were to be reduced from £603,000,000 to £490,000,000, but then the government decided that a further £62,000,000 should be saved, which brought about the formation of the Geddes Committee. Sir Eric Geddes was Minister for Transport, and a close friend of the Prime Minister, and he was joined on the committee, to investigate national expenditure, by Sir Guy Granet, Lord Faringdon and Sir Joseph Maclay. Predictably Sir Henry Wilson pressed for the abolition of the RAF to effect some of the required savings. The least the other two services would settle for was the return of the Fleet Air Arm and Army Cooperation units to the Navy and Army respectively. Perhaps Trenchard's attempts to 'educate' the chairman bore fruit, because the committee felt that the RAF came out well following its investigations. The members were persuaded that a division of the RAF in this way would lead to duplication, which in turn would lead to extravagance, and this was to echo the 1917 Smuts Report. The committee, in submitting its report to the Chancellor of the Exchequer in December 1921, also remained unconvinced that the RAF was less well administered than the other two services. There was, nevertheless, a recommendation that the RAF's budget be cut from £18.5 million to £13 million, including the cost of the RAF in the Middle East. Excluding the costs of the latter, the Cabinet approved the sum of £10.75 million.

The exclusion from the Estimates of the costs of maintaining RAF squadrons in the Middle East could be justified on the grounds of operational necessity in the three theatres of operations, Palestine, Iraq and Egypt. Thus, in contradiction to the Geddes recommendation that the RAF strength of five squadrons in Egypt and Palestine could be reduced, to effect a saving of £2.5 million, Winston Churchill had raised the strength to eight squadrons. In a statement to Parliament on 9 March 1922 he stressed the success achieved in substituting air for ground forces. These eight squadrons represented one-third of the entire squadron strength of the RAF, and were concentrated around Baghdad to provide 'the principal agency by which the local Levy forces all over the country are supported'.

Trenchard still had his RAF, but at a price, and it seemed that he had a stark choice. He could cut back on the front-line strength, already reduced to a mere twenty-nine squadrons, or cut back on spending on training establishments, without which he could not create the foundations of a well-trained and efficient air force. In the event Trenchard decided to reintroduce the wartime scheme of training NCOs to become pilots. Additionally the rehousing of officers and men at home stations was postponed, and the staffs of overseas commands were reduced. Chapter 5 explains how the lack of funds prevented Trenchard from modernizing the RAF's aircraft inventory but how he helped keep the struggling aircraft industry alive by issuing orders for a succession of prototypes. This at least permitted the various firms to keep a basic design and construction staff in employment.

1922–1924

Reassessment of the Air Threat to the UK

In April 1922 the Standing Defence Sub-Committee of the CID, with Balfour in the Chair, rendered a report on the dangers to which the UK was exposed in the event of air attack. The two salient points were firstly, that the continental air threat demanded a greater degree of preparedness than then existed, and secondly, if somewhat bizarrely, that France constituted an air menace. The Chiefs of Staff did not attach much importance to any threat from France, but the politicians took a contrary view. The French had the largest air force in Europe, with 596 combat aircraft, and in the politicians' view this might lead them to be prepared to take risks in diplomacy. Consequently Britain needed a force that could both defend the British Isles and retaliate against France. The matter had further received consideration by the Standing Defence Sub-Committee, and Balfour and Trenchard had submitted notes with a view to obtaining a policy decision either from a full meeting of the CID or the Cabinet.

On 29 May 1922 Balfour went further in a note to Trenchard. He considered Britain's position to be one of extreme peril. Expansion of the RAF was necessary, but Trenchard, in reply, opined that to attain and maintain air parity with France would require conscription. The last thing Trenchard wanted was a too sudden expansion before his Cranwell and Halton schemes had had a chance to bed in and provide the permanent cadre of officers and men upon which to build up an enlarged air force; i.e. he had not then built 'the foundations of a cottage on which to build a castle'. Instead the Air Staff proposed a small mixed force of regular and auxiliary squadrons that could be expanded on the outbreak of a war. Once the nucleus was established a larger nucleus could be planned, taking the force to fifty squadrons on the outbreak of war. But since the French had the capacity to increase their strength to more than 1,000 aircraft, the RAF would still be numerically inferior, and superior enterprise and efficiency would be necessary to restore some balance. Trenchard and the Air Staff felt that a force of twenty-three squadrons would be a powerful deterrent to French aggression, and on 3 August 1922 the Cabinet approved. The government was in fact approving a force of five hundred machines at an increased cost of £2 million per annum, £900,000 of which would be found by making economies in the following year's Air Estimates.

Change of Government – Sir Samuel Hoare becomes Air Minister

At this time Lloyd George was still Prime Minister, but in October 1922 the Coalition fell. Out went Austen Chamberlain, Worthington-Evans and Freddie Guest. And the inquiry that was set up to look into the system of air and naval cooperation, and intended to reconcile the differences between the two services, was never completed. With Bonar Law back as Prime Minister, the post of Air Minister was offered to Lord Londonderry, who refused, since he was heavily committed in Northern Ireland as Education Minister, and so Sir Samuel Hoare was offered it, although he had not previously held public office. Hoare was a back-bencher who had played a significant part in bringing down the Coalition government and he was advised by Bonar Law that, in accepting the post, he might only hold it for a few weeks, for the Prime Minister had it in mind to divide the RAF between the Army and the Navy, in which case the post would no longer exist. The advice that the RAF and Air Ministry were too expensive a luxury came from Sykes, Bonar Law's son-in-law. Not only was the future of the RAF in jeopardy, but Bonar Law believed that Britain should move out of Iraq, where Sir John Salmond had recently taken over command. Finally Hoare was advised that the post would not be in the Cabinet.

It is difficult to imagine anyone accepting such a position on these terms, but Hoare was ambitious. He was a member of an old banking family, was a second baronet, 42 years of age, fluent in Russian and had other intellectual interests, but knew little about air matters. Perhaps for a man who expected to be Air Minister for only a few weeks this did not matter: after all, his only flying experience had been to fly in an airship over Rome during a British military mission to Italy. In spite of the Prime Minister's declared intention to disband the RAF, Hoare was determined to lose no time in learning everything he could about military and civil air matters, and except for ten months in 1924 when there was a Labour government in power, he was destined to be Secretary of State of Air until the end of the decade.

On meeting Trenchard, Hoare made no mention of Bonar Law's intentions

Sir Samuel Hoare Bt MP.

regarding the future of the RAF, and it took some time for mutual trust and confidence to be built up between the two men. Trenchard, for his part, appreciated Hoare's affability and intelligence, but felt that he needed to be 'educated' in air force matters. He expressed his sentiments in a letter to Salmond in India, telling him that Hoare wanted to know about the dispute between the Army and the Navy and was keen to get into the Cabinet, where he could better put the RAF's case. The more Hoare got to know about Trenchard, the more he understood the latter's single-mindedness and determination to develop an 'air force spirit', an air force with its own strategy and tactics. He saw Trenchard as a prophet and his role as political interpreter.

Hoare v. Earl of Derby and L.S. Amery

Hoare was appointed Secretary of State for Air on 2 November 1922. His Principal Private Secretary was Christopher Bullock, an exceptionally able civil servant who had served as Churchill's Private Secretary and was an ex-RFC man. Following the formation of the new government, Hoare found himself opposite the Earl of Derby at the War Office and L.S. Amery at the Admiralty. Since he did not like the office he had been given in Adastral House, home of the Air Ministry, he moved to Gwydyr House in Whitehall, close to the other two service chiefs, both of whom were ready to carry on the fight to regain their air components and close down the RAF. Derby's plan was for the liquidation of the RAF, and as a sop to Hoare, to offer the latter a post of Vice-President of the Army Council, with special responsibility for Army aviation. Amery wanted Hoare to surrender all military aviation, leaving his department the responsibility only for civil air matters, so that the creation of Empire air routes could receive its undivided attention. Behind the scenes Beatty was busy lobbying Parliament, and at a Lord Mayor's Banquet in the

Admiral, the Earl Beatty.

London Guildhall he gave a thirty-five-minute speech during which he made an unconcealed attack on the RAF. By then Hoare was clear where he stood, and was prepared to fight to save his department.

In February 1923 Hoare brought matters to a head and put the argument for an independent air force to the Prime Minister. He made it clear that the strategic employment of airpower was only possible with a centralized force, although he saw no reason why such a force could not have military and naval wings. The alternative was two separate air forces, which would not be capable of operating strategically, that is outside the theatre of land or sea operations, since both forces would be trained and equipped to work closely with their respective arms. Hoare prevailed upon the Prime Minister to delay a decision one way or the other on the grounds that any sudden change in the status of the RAF on the scale envisaged could cripple it. What followed is dealt with in Chapters 2 and 6.

Hoare and Sefton Brancker

Sir Sefton Brancker had succeeded Sykes in the retitled post of Director of Civil Aviation, but unlike Sykes he did not have a seat on the Air Council, yet both he and his small department was answerable to the Council and not to the Secretary of State. But to sit in Air Council meetings, where military air matters would have predominated, would have meant that civil aviation would have been overshadowed, and Sefton Brancker was not prepared for the inevitable disagreements, particularly when it came to spending priorities. He was prepared to get on with the job on his own, working to the best of his ability. He was a good organizer and soon established a national air service. He was short in stature, dapper, monocled, charming and high spirited. He displayed energy and shrewdness in his pursuit of a mission to increase the number of flights and route miles flown. For his part, Hoare admired the work of QANTAS in Australia, which united the scattered communities of that continent in the way he hoped that Brancker's efforts would unite the scattered outposts of Empire. To permit the airlines to develop to take on the task of providing long-range air travel, the Hambling Committee made its recommendations (see Chapter 2), and this led to the formation of Imperial Airways, a single monopoly company formed from six constituent airlines.

Presentation of the Air Estimates for 1923/24

On 14 March 1923 Hoare presented the Air Estimates for the financial year 1923/4. In his speech he compared the output of 300 civil and military machines in Britain during 1922 with the 3,300 machines built in France during the same period, of which 300 alone were civil machines. Some sources put the figure for Britain as low as 200 machines overall, but this only emphasizes the

Sir Sefton-Brancker, Director of Civil Aviation.

Stanley Baldwin.

inequality in numbers. From a total of £11,880,000 in the Estimates, only £287,000 was earmarked for civil aviation. An alternative means of funding civil aviation was to grant subsidies, but this could only be at the expense of military flying. In this sense Trenchard and Brancker were competitors for limited funds, and the demands of both men were ultimately Hoare's responsibility. Hoare compared the Naval Estimates of £58 million and the Army Estimates of £52 million with the £12 million granted to the RAF. If a 'one-power' standard was to be applied to the Air there would either have to be reductions in the Navy and Army Estimates to release the necessary funds for an increase in air strength, or an immediate increase of £5 million, rising eventually to £17 million, if Britain was to keep pace with the other Great Powers. He impressed upon the House that, with little more than double the present cost, the RAF could experience a fourfold increase in numbers. In the meantime the RAF had quality, if not quantity. Fifteen squadrons were being formed for home defence, to be in place by April 1925, with three squadrons for the Navy, and there would be a new Auxiliary Air Force and a Reserve.

In the ensuing debate Lord Hugh Cecil, the MP for Oxford University, found it difficult to understand a policy that made preparation for defence that was sufficiently large to be costly but not sufficiently large to be efficient, a view shared by RAF officers. Captain Wedgwood Benn wanted an assurance that the Navy now regarded the RAF as an independent service, and he reminded the House that, during the First World War, the Admirals displayed little interest in the Air yet desired their own Naval Air Arm. Sykes, by then an MP, warned that if the Navy and the Army obtained separate tactical units there might be pressure to dispense with the development of long-range bombing when this should be the subject of particular attention, a point made by Hoare to the Prime Minister.

Bonar Law's Resignation – Baldwin becomes Prime Minister

Bonar Law's illness was catching up with him, and in May 1923 he had to step down. His place as Prime Minister was taken by the Chancellor of the Exchequer, Mr Stanley Baldwin. Hoare was asked to stay on as the Secretary of State for Air, and Baldwin offered him a seat in the Cabinet. He appreciated the offer, not only for what

he could do for the RAF, but for giving civil aviation a voice, through him, in Cabinet. Notwithstanding the advantages, Hoare still faced public ignorance on Air matters, so he decided to take to the air on official journeys to help publicize flying. The *Morning Post* condemned Hoare for wasting money by not using conventional, less costly, means of transport, describing his flights as 'dangerous and objectionable stunts'. Hoare naturally took the opposite view, and wanted to make flying an everyday unsensational occurrence. In August he flew to the International Aeronautical Exhibition at Gothenburg with his wife and Sefton Brancker in a DH34 airliner of Daimler Airways. He worked hard to establish Imperial Airways, but with so little money available for civil aviation research, long-distance aircraft were not available to cover the vast distances in reaching Egypt, India, Australia and New Zealand economically and in reasonable time, which is why airships were such an attractive alternative to fixed-wing aircraft. Later, at an Imperial Economic Conference in London, Hoare outlined the financial difficulties in establishing Imperial air routes, and announced that money had been put to one side for the construction of an experimental aircraft capable of long-distance flights. This was followed by a demonstration at Hendon of between fifty and sixty military and civil aircraft to emphasize how aeronautically determined was the Air Ministry.

The First Labour Government

Parliament reassembled in the autumn of 1923 against a background of rising unemployment. Baldwin had still retained most of Bonar Law's ministerial team, and felt bound by the latter's pre-election promises not to impose tariffs nor to extend Imperial preference by duties on food. Restricting the flow of imports would give the home market to domestic firms and thus stimulate employment. Baldwin was therefore keen to call an election to bolster his own position and to permit him to form his own ministerial team. So he confided in

Ramsay MacDonald, Britain's first Labour Prime Minister.

Lord Thomson with his Principal Private Secretary, Christopher Bullock.

Hoare, the Cabinet newcomer, that he planned to ask the King for a dissolution of Parliament. Hoare was not keen. Having at last got a Cabinet post and having worked out his long-term programme for his department, he did not want to risk losing office, which is precisely what happened. In the General Election the Conservatives lost ninety seats in the House of Commons, and in came Ramsay MacDonald at the head of the first-ever Labour government, with the Liberals in coalition.

This might have been the moment for Trenchard to go with Hoare, but in a letter to a colleague he wrote, 'The more I stay on as CAS the more difficult it is to go. Now I try to make the excuse that the change of government precludes my going. After the Labour government comes in (if it does come in) I think we shall have more friends than ever before.' Friends or not, Trenchard would have to 'educate' yet another Air Minister, for the new incumbent lacked departmental knowledge like his predecessors. Brigadier-General C.B. Thomson had been appointed as Secretary of State for Air, but he had failed three times to secure a seat in the House of Commons after joining the Labour party in 1919. The Prime Minster had therefore to elevate Thomson to the peerage in order to secure his services as Air Minister, and William Leach MP was appointed as Under-Secretary of State to speak for the Air Ministry in the House of Commons.

Reaction to the new government was awaited with interest. To begin with, the new Labour MPs were largely free from the prejudice in favour of the Army and Navy. Trenchard was astute in working with men in government whose social background was very different from those with whom he had dealings in the past. He had paid the trade union leaders the compliment of seeking their advice before instituting the Halton apprentice scheme, and now he faced a former clerk as Prime Minster, an engine driver in the Colonial Office, a foundry labourer in the Home Office and a millhand as Lord Privy Seal. Thomson would have to face Lord Chelmsford at the Admiralty and Mr Stephen Walsh at the War Office. It being a coalition government, MacDonald offered government posts to his Liberal partners. Lord Haldane, who was appointed Lord Chancellor, was the man who had remodelled the British Army and now found himself chairman of the CID, in which he had previously served and which had given him experience of inter-service rivalries. Given the pacifist tendencies of a number of Labour MPs, including the Chancellor of the Exchequer, Mr Philip Snowden, the three Service ministers and their Service chiefs might have feared the worst, but it was Haldane who prevailed upon the Chancellor to pass the Service Estimates from the point of view of the Treasury.

Debate on the Air Estimates for 1924

No sooner had the government taken office than Hoare was prodding the Under-Secretary of State into a declaration of policy. In the Commons on 19 February 1924, Hoare moved: 'That this House, whilst earnestly desiring further limitation of armaments so far as is consistent with the safety and integrity of the Empire, affirms the principle laid down by the late Government and accepted by the Imperial Conference, that Great Britain must maintain a Home Defence Air Force of sufficient strength to give adequate protection against air attack by the strongest air force within striking distance of her shores.' He informed the House that in October 1922, the time of the Chanak crisis, there were only twenty first-line aircraft available for home defence, but thanks to a Conservative government there were about eight fighters and twenty Army Cooperation aircraft. He then cited a member of the French Chamber of Deputies and First World War pilot, M. René Fonck, who had calculated that a force of 500 aircraft could, in the space of a single night, obliterate a city the size of Paris. By comparison France had 1,000 front-line aircraft, 600 of which belonged to the French Independent Striking Force and 400 were Army Cooperation aircraft. The

Expansion Plan described in Chapter 2 would take Britain's Home Defence Force to 600 aircraft. Hoare finished by assuring the House that he did not wish this force to herald an arms race, nor was hostility towards Britain's neighbours implied. Clearly Hoare and Trenchard were prone to overstate the case for offensive defence. The RAF would have needed a fleet of four-engined heavy bombers to create havoc on the scale envisaged.

Mr Leach replied for the government to the effect that he was not alarmed by the disparity between the British and French force levels, but he affirmed that there would not be any change in policy. With regard to aircraft to equip the expanded force, there was a sufficient number to equip squadrons formed during 1924. Until sufficient aircraft were available, some squadrons would have to make do with training aircraft. He said that the further development of airships was being considered and would be encouraged, and that civil aviation would be similarly fostered. With regard to the disparity between Britain and France, Mr Leach's opinion was that even if Britain was circled with defensive fighters giving a ratio of 50:1 in Britain's favour, there would still be those who would say that that was not enough. The only impregnable defence that he could see was a changed international atmosphere, and he added, 'If we continue to put fear at the helm and folly at the prow we should steer straight for the next war.' But at least Trenchard could content himself that the Expansion Plan would pass the Commons, and in the Lords it was left to Lord Londonderry to confront Lord Thomson, who was to make his first statement on Air policy. He confirmed what Leach had said: Britain would confer with other nations to try to find a method of all-round disarmament. His speech created a favourable impression in which he expressed the view that, for the Labour government, 'the flower of idealism is rooted in common sense'.

The Air Estimates were published on 7 March. Trenchard got the £2,840,000 he needed to equip eight new Home Defence squadrons, while the Navy was to experience a £2 million cut and the Army one of £7 million; but even then there was a huge disparity between the RAF and the other two services. The Estimates, which had been prepared by the former Conservative government, were introduced by Lord Thomson, and contained two fresh votes for educational and medical services. The largest individual increase was for technical equipment and research. There would be some reconditioning of existing aircraft and engines, but the new squadrons, including those to be employed on naval cooperation, would receive new aircraft, which meant no relaxation in experiment and research. The Estimates did not provide for airship development, but this was being actively considered, and a decision would be communicated to Parliament in due course, any extra

spending being the subject of a Supplementary Estimate. On 25 May Mr Leach had more to say on airships. He regarded the preceding few years of aerial endeavour as moribund and the development of airships as disappointing. He said:

> After the war, when the general slump began, plant, airships and material were offered free to anybody who would have gone on with the scheme of airship development. Not an offer was forthcoming. Efforts were also made to enlist the interest of the Dominions, but these came to nought. So for three or four years nothing has been done except that the Research Department has been accumulating knowledge. However, throughout these years Commander Burney, the Member for Uxbridge, has displayed considerable faith in lighter-than-air travel and kept alive the flame that would otherwise have been extinguished.

This ignored the work done by Vickers, and it did not stop the government rejecting the Burney Airship Scheme for six airships to be built over a number of years by private enterprise. The government took the view that military considerations should be kept in view at all times. Accordingly the State would build one at Cardington, which could be used for commercial flights, but in time of war could be used for naval reconnaissance. This was to be the R101, and in parallel private enterprise would build R100 with State help. In addition the State would recondition two existing airships, the R33 and R36. This gave Hoare the opportunity to denounce the government, and he retorted:

> Today the Hon. Gentleman has come before us, not only as a full blooded Imperialist, but as a full blooded militarist as well. The scheme of our late Government was a commercial scheme. The sole original contribution of the present Government to the development of British aviation is the building by direct labour of a military airship that the late militarist Conservative Government would never have dreamed of proposing. The Under-Secretary has made a travesty of the late Government's scheme, for we proposed a loan, without interest, of £400,000 a year, repayable from profits, and at the end we expected six large airships operating a commercial service between England and India. The present Government's scheme is likely to be much more expensive, for it has no ultimate object in view, and at the end of three years would be little further forward. There are few Air Ministry officials who know anything about airships, so a great airship department must be created, and a big government organization set up for a single airship – and, what appears no less

dangerous, a new construction organization at Cardington. What does the Government intend once the experimental period is over?

Mr Leach replied:

As to where we are going, what the nature of our policy, what is visualised years ahead – I could not tell yet. The Government is looking at a more or less dead industry which we want to put on its feet if possible. The airship industry has a chequered past; there is no certainty about its future security. The six airships of the Burney Scheme would have taken seven years to provide, whereas the three under the Government scheme – one new and two reconditioned – should be provided inside three years.

It is a sad irony that by the time the R101 was ready for its maiden flight to India, Lord Thomson would again be the Secretary of State for Air and would die, along with Sefton Brancker, when the R101 crashed in flames near Beauvais in France in October 1930.

The Auxiliary Air Force Knowing of Haldane's Army reforms, which included the institution of the Territorial Army, Trenchard would flatter Haldane by proposing a similar RAF force of 'weekenders'. Not only would this bring Haldane 'on side', but it would also appeal to the cost-conscious Snowden. The idea of 'winged Terriers' was thus approved by the Cabinet. (Terriers was the name given to members of the Territorial Army.) To be fair, Trenchard had already spoken of the need for a Reserve in Paragraph 4 of his 1919 Memorandum, so this was not a new idea. He had tried it on Churchill when he was the Minister for War and the Air, but Winston did not support the idea of training part-timers as pilots.

The Fall of the Labour–Liberal Coalition

The Labour–Liberal coalition government was not in power long enough to have any appreciable impact on air policy, and it did little more than confirm the previous Conservative government's Expansion Plan and put the airship-building plan into operation. They were concerned with discussions over the defence of Singapore, and during their period of office the Fleet Air Arm was formed, albeit with RAF crews. With regard to the policy of air control, pacifist elements in the Labour Party would ask why the RAF was bombing women and children. Trenchard wrote to Air Vice-Marshal Higgins in July 1924 that he believed that, although there were repeated calls to halt air-control operations, the Ministers understood. Lord Thomson wrote the following words in a Command Paper of air-control operations in Iraq: 'Air action can be taken swiftly at the focus of trouble and before disturbances against which it is directed have time to permeate to a larger area. It

has the immense advantage that, compared with the slow movements of ground forces over unfamiliar country, it offers to the tribesmen no chance of loot or retaliation by ambush or concentration against small ground forces.'

Ramsay MacDonald, it must be remembered, headed a coalition government that included Liberals. He had therefore to keep them 'on board' if his government was to survive. Only seven years had elapsed since the Bolshevik revolution in Russia, and in 1920 the Communist Party of Great Britain (CPGB) was formed. When one remembers that the Spartacists (Communists) had staged an uprising in Berlin in 1919 there was always the risk that the CPGB would attempt to follow suit and provoke a workers' uprising to overthrow Britain's democratically elected government. Lenin had tried to alleviate the economic plight of his people with his New Economic Plan, but the situation had been aggravated by years of civil war between the Bolsheviks and the White Russians, when the RAF had assisted the White Russian forces. Given these circumstances and Ramsay MacDonald's sympathy for Russia, with his proposed 'Bolshevist loan', as *The Times* called it, there was growing concern that the government might be playing into the hands of the Communists and their sympathizers. For example, the government had withdrawn a prosecution against Mr J.R. Campbell, acting editor of the *Workers' Weekly*. Mr Campbell had been arrested under the Incitement to Mutiny Act of 1797 for an article urging soldiers not to fire on fellow workers. The Conservatives tabled a Motion of Censure and the Liberals demanded a Select Committee of Inquiry. The matter was debated on 8 October 1924, when the Attorney-General, Sir Patrick Hastings, said that the decision not to prosecute Mr Campbell was his, but that the Prime Minister and Home Secretary had been consulted. With hindsight the Prime Minister might have been rash in making the winning of the votes on both the Resolution and the Amendment a condition for Labour remaining in office. The vote was 364 to 198 against the government, and so the Prime Minister went to the King to ask for a dissolution of Parliament, paving the way for a General Election on 29 October.

Suspicion was further aroused that the Labour party was playing into the hands of the CPGB with the publication of the famous 'Zinoviev' letter by *The Times* four days before the election. The authenticity of this letter is in doubt, but the effect of its publication, authentic or not, was to lose Labour the election. Mr Zinoviev was President of the Communist International in Moscow, and the mission of this body was to spread the Marxist/Leninist creed in the hope of bringing about Soviet-style governments around the world. This letter was addressed to the Central Committee of the CPGB, urging the proletariat to rise up in insurrection. A protest from the Foreign Office to the Russian Chargé d'Affaires in London only added substance to the argument that the letter was authentic. That the CPGB would have been unsuccessful in any attempt to get the British workers to overthrow the government by force there can be little doubt. The very reason for the formation of the Labour party in 1900 was the determination of the trade unions to gain power through the ballot box, and in this they had succeeded in twenty-three short years. Had Ramsay MacDonald been faced with even a limited attempt at insurrection he might have had to order troops to fire on rioters. But 1924 was also the year of Lenin's death, and Stalin, who assumed power in the Soviet Union after a brief power struggle, was determined to consolidate Socialism in the USSR before exporting it to the rest of the world. In this he fell out with Trotsky, who was eventually forced to leave Russia and obtain exile in Mexico, until Stalin's 'hatchet' men went after him and ended his life. Be that as it may, it ended the term of the first Labour-led government. Labour lost forty seats and the Conservatives were returned with 419 seats, gaining 161. The Liberals dropped to third place, where they have remained ever since, losing 116 seats, which left them with only forty Members of Parliament . From now on Labour would be His Majesty's main Opposition.

1925-1926

The New Conservative Government

It was not until May 1929 that Labour returned to power, again in coalition with the Liberals. Until then there would be a Conservative government, which for Trenchard would mean stability for the remainder of the decade and up to his retirement. He would have Mr Baldwin as Prime Minster, with Sir Samuel Hoare as Secretary of State and Sir Philip Sassoon as Under-Secretary. Baldwin formed his government on 7 November 1924, and reappointed most of his previous Cabinet. Austen Chamberlain became Foreign Secretary, Neville Chamberlain the Minister of Health; Joynson-Hicks the Home Secretary and Winston Churchill the Chancellor of the Exchequer. Hoare lost no time in getting back to work on air business. Having firmly expressed his view on airships when in opposition, he had to make clear what the new government's policy would be. On 18 November he went to Cardington with Sassoon and Air Vice-Marshal Sir Geoffrey Salmond. Group Captain Peregrine Fellowes, Major Colmore, Colonel Richmond and Major Scott made up the party. Airships had captured the interest of Parliament, and by making his visit to Cardington he was wearing his 'civilian' hat. In spite of the intense use made of airships in the First World War, Trenchard had virtually written them out of his 1919 Memorandum, but then he was 'strapped for cash', and a small research team at Howden was all that was provided for. This indicated an open mind on the matter, but the military use of airships was limited, given their slow speed and lack of manoeuvrability. The Labour government, on the other hand, had committed public funds to the building of the R101 and the refurbishment of airships R33 and R36. The R33 was being equipped as a test vehicle so that air pressures and stresses could be measured during violent manoeuvres. The R36 was having its nose strengthened prior to an experimental trip to India to test the feasibility of regular air services. With his military hat, Hoare explained government policy at the Lord Mayor's Banquet. He reported that eighteen of the fifty-two planned Home Defence squadrons would be formed by the end of the financial year, and he praised Lord Thomson for his continuity of policy. He then went on to state the defence benefit of reduced journey times by airship, since better air communications would help solve, economically, many urgent questions in the Near East. Sefton Brancker was meanwhile promoting the idea of Empire air communications by taking a stage-by-stage flight in the second prototype DH50, with Alan Cobham as pilot, to attend a conference with the Indian government in January concerning the big airship scheme.

Air Estimates 1925/6

The Estimates for 1925/6 were introduced by Hoare on 12 March 1925. There would be an increase in the Gross Estimate of £1½ million over Labour's Estimates of the previous year, taking the total to £21,319,200. The increase would provide for seven new squadrons for home defence. There were fifty-four squadrons already in existence, forty-three squadrons and two flights organized as such, eight squadrons in Iraq, six squadrons in India, four squadrons and one flight in Palestine and Egypt and eighteen Home Defence squadrons. Then there were twenty-one flights for the FAA, and for the first time the Navy made a grant to the RAF of £400,000 in respect of equipment for the FAA. During 1925/6 the number of squadrons to be formed would be two Regular, one Special Reserve and four Auxiliary Air Force. From First World War days Farnborough had produced service aircraft, but the importance of experiment and research was underlined by reserving Farnborough for this purpose. Finally Hoare said that the total provision for airships would be £500,000, and an initial payment had been made to the Burney Airship Guarantee Company.

The Auxiliary Air Force squadrons did prove to be a conspicuous success, in spite of Churchill's earlier objections, for Winston did not believe that 'weekend fliers' would be of much use in war. These squadrons had the advantage of keeping their personnel, whereas the regular squadrons experienced a constant turnover. John James makes this point quite clear in his book *The Paladins*, saying that the RAF had the choice to keep their pilots with squadrons and perhaps wings, like officers of Army regiments who served their careers with their regiments, but chose instead to post aircrews to squadrons for a tour of duty, sometimes never to return to that squadron. All ranks of auxiliary squadrons therefore got to know each other very well. In the same year university air squadrons were formed to introduce undergraduates to flying and the RAF, in the hope of recruiting brains into the service.

Problems with the Expansion Plan

By the summer of 1925 progress on the Expansion Plan saw twenty-five of the planned fifty-two Home Defence squadrons formed, but with the impending conclusion of the Treaty of Locarno (see the opening paragraph of Chapter 3), the Cabinet began to wonder whether the rate of progress should not be slowed down. The favourable international situation, together with the need to be seen to be honouring the spirit of international disarmament, could not be ignored. The French Army had been withdrawn from the Rhineland, Germany had been admitted to the League of Nations and the projected expansion of the French Air Force had not materialized. Economy in defence expenditure seemed a reasonable aim in this atmosphere, and Churchill wrote privately to Trenchard on 11 October 1925:

> I have not at all altered my views as to the desirability of a separate Air Force so far as efficiency and leadership in the air are concerned. The expense is another matter, and I am not convinced that large savings would not result from the less satisfactory solution of division. Everything now turns on finance, and I am sure that if the Air Force is going to continue to swell our expenditure upon armaments from year to year it will draw upon itself a volume of criticism which will bring the question of division into the forefront of defence problems.
>
> The Navy reproach me bitterly for only criticising and attacking their expenditure while the Air Force they say is favoured and the Army let alone. You have only to read the papers to see how cruel is the pressure to which I am subjected. We are at present heading for large increases in expenditure next year with consequent reimposition of taxation. I am sure the Cabinet will recoil from this prospect when they are confronted with it and that desperate efforts will be made to cut down.
>
> I do hope that you will be able to help the Treasury in this task. You have many friends there who have confidence in your own frugality of administering and see the usefulness of your intervention against the extravagance both of the Navy and of the Army. I am sure that the present relations not only justify but demand a complete reconsideration of the rate of the expansion scheme, and I should be bound to resist by every means in my power any attempt to carry the total of Air Votes in the coming year beyond the figure under all heads for this.

> W.S. Churchill

This was certainly a 'shot across the bows', with yet another threat that the RAF would be divided up between the Army and the Navy, and this time from one of Trenchard's supporters and one-time Minister for the Air. But in 1925 Winston was the Chancellor of the Exchequer, charged with the task of keeping public expenditure under control. When a Cabinet committee was set up under Lord Birkenhead to consider the Expansion Plan for home defence, Trenchard wrote to Ellington, then AOC India, in a letter dated 25 November 1925, expressing the opinion that the committee realized the importance of having a proper scheme of defence and that substantial savings could not be effected by stopping or delaying the plan, but on 27 November the committee recommended that the rate of expansion be slowed down:

> The present world position would not justify us in cutting down our forces below the limits of safety. In addition to political security, some measure of practical security is required. We are therefore of the opinion that the scheme of Air Force expansion announced in 1923 should remain the goal at which we aim and we do not believe that the Cabinet in remitting this question for our consideration had any other thought in their minds.

The recommendation to the Cabinet was that the completion of the Expansion Plan should be delayed until 1935/6. On 3 December the Cabinet agreed. This was two days after the signing of the Locarno Treaty in the Foreign Office, and the decision was announced to the Commons by Hoare on 25 February 1926, when he introduced the Air Estimates for 1926/7. There was a £450,000 drop from the previous year, and he explained to the House the government's decision to relax the efforts to complete the plan on time in view of the international and financial position. Only two extra regular squadrons were to be provided that year, with a third that had become available from overseas. Finally, he stressed that there was no change in the total strength to be attained, only a slow-down in the rate of expansion.

The Colwyn Committee

The government had therefore considered Britain's good relations with France and the general improvement of the international situation following the signing of the Locarno Treaty. Britain could not be seen to be rearming when disarmament should assume greater importance in the scheme of things, but the government could present the Expansion Plan as purely defensive. Be that as it may there had been a steady rise in the Service Estimates since 1922, and so the government set up a 'Special Services Economy Committee' on 13 August 1925. This was to be a Treasury committee under the chairmanship of Lord Colwyn, a businessman who had served on similar bodies in the past. His committee would have no service representatives on it and he was to be assisted by Lord Chalmers and Lord Bradbury, two ex-Permanent Secretaries to the Treasury.

Since the spotlight was on all three services in an attempt to cut defence expenditure, the Navy seized the opportunity to resurrect the old dispute with the RAF over the FAA. The Navy's case was that it would be more economical if the Navy ran its own air arm. In spite of the Trenchard–Keyes agreement, which laid down the ground rules for the operation of RAF Coastal Area and RAF involvement in naval operations afloat, and was working well enough, the Admiralty could not resist the opportunity presented by the Colwyn Committee investigations. But with Admiral Beatty off sick at this time, the Admiralty's case was not presented as well as it might have been. The claim was made that the Trenchard–Keyes agreement was not in fact working well at all, and sure enough the Army then leapt in with its claim for a return of air units working with the Army.

This was well-trodden ground, but Trenchard had, yet again, to trot out the usual defence of his position. It seemed he was back to Square One. Again he repudiated the idea that his agreement with Admiral Keyes was not working. There was an absence of duplication in aircraft procurement, aircrew training and research and development, etc. What he particularly objected to was that whenever the question of economies were raised the Army and the Navy would renew their attacks upon his service. He said that the amount of time which the air service had to devote year after year to defending its existence was incalculable. It was bad for the whole service, it was bad for the development of the country's defences and it was bad for the economy itself.

The Colwyn Committee reported to the Prime Minister on 23 December 1925, having collected a considerable amount of evidence, both oral and written. The committee found that the figures for the Service Estimates were inconsistent with the 'Ten-Year Rule'. The total of £127,000,000 could not be justified, given the signing of the Locarno Treaty, the assessment of a lack of threat to the country and the proposals for international disarmament. This was put down to a lack of coordination between the service departments in framing defence policy and controlling expenditure. The CID, it seemed, had not been able to exercise the necessary control, yet the committee did not believe that a combined Service Department or Ministry of Defence

was the solution, any more than the abolition of the Air Ministry. Instead, the committee reaffirmed the view that an Air Ministry administering a unified service carrying out all the air work for all three services would achieve the greatest economy, particularly if air substitution was extended. With regard to the FAA, the committee found that substantial additional reductions in both Navy and Air Votes would accrue if the Air Ministry's control over the FAA was strengthened. It was felt that having naval officers as observers made sense because the man who was observing a situation afloat should be a man who understood naval matters, the speed and course of ships either sailing or closing for action, tides and all other things to do with naval deployments. But when it came to pilots no reason could be found by the committee for the employment of naval officers beyond the 30 per cent of officer personnel normally embarked as pilots on carriers and other warships. The committee did accept that this 30 per cent should be eligible for senior appointments in Air Force units connected with the training and maintenance of the FAA. The remaining 70 per cent should remain RAF officers, including a suitable proportion of officers on short-service commissions, so as to provide an adequate reserve on an economical basis. The committee also found that naval ratings should be substituted for RAF other ranks in the carriers if a definite reduction in numbers would thus be effected.

The Colwyn Committee then recommended reductions in the Service Estimates, £7$\frac{1}{2}$ million for the Navy and £2 million each for the Army and RAF. The Navy was criticized on administrative grounds for 'being completely out of touch with up-to-date civilian experience, particularly in respect of dockyard organization where economies might be effected'. The Army was found to be efficient and prudent, while the Air Ministry was censured for not giving full value for taxpayers' money. This was, however, put down to the relative lack of experience of staff in the Air Ministry, to frequent changes in government policy and the perpetual inter-departmental warfare. The committee concluded that only radical revision of the existing standards of defence would effect large and lasting economies, but this was not in their remit.

The Navy predictably opposed the committee's proposals. The Admiralty had lost £7,500,000 and the battle to regain control of the FAA. It was then reported that the Admiralty would accept the financial cuts but would ignore those clauses that related to the 70–30 per cent officer manning of the FAA. It thus appeared that the Navy had left itself the option of a fresh attack on the RAF at some time in the future, so Trenchard sent a 'private and personal' letter to Churchill. He wanted a 'once and for all' assurance that the Colwyn Committee's findings would be endorsed, inasmuch as the RAF would then be left alone to get on with its job.

Churchill was sympathetic, and sent Trenchard's letter to the Prime Minister, the latter being happy to publicly endorse the relevant passages in the Colwyn Report. He went further in response to a question in the House of Commons in affirming that the government had no intention of reopening the question of a separate air arm and Air Ministry. Imperial defence would henceforth be organized on the existing basis of three co-equal services, and Baldwin urged that controversy on this subject should cease.

Continuing Controversy between the Air Ministry and the Admiralty

But the controversy was set to continue. Heretofore the RAF had raised and trained units of the FAA, but once these units went to sea in carriers and warships they were subject to naval discipline and control. But the RAF shore-based units that were employed on maritime operations, such as coastal reconnaissance and the escorting of convoys proceeding up the English Channel, were under the command and operational control of RAF Coastal Area. The Admiralty was entitled to argue that maritime air operations were the business of the Navy, whether the units involved were shore or ship based. Increased use of naval officers as pilots in the FAA could be justified on the grounds that naval officers better understood naval warfare, but evidence presented to the Colwyn Committee showed that the cost of a 70 per cent manning of the FAA by naval pilots was £400,000 more expensive than an 80 per cent manning by RAF officers. This did not stop the Admiralty laying claim to the complete control of the shore-based aircraft known as Coastal Reconnaissance Flights and airships. Furthermore they wished to have naval officers trained in flying so that they could replace RAF officers in technical posts. At that time there were only two coastal reconnaissance flights in existence, but more were planned, for both home and overseas, and they were manned and administered by the Air Ministry.

A war of words continued, with a brief truce being observed during the 1926 General Strike, when it was 'all hands to the pump' to keep essential supplies flowing and to preserve law and order. After the strike had been settled, both the First Lord of the Admiralty and the Air Minister wrote to the Prime Minister, asking for a final and rapid settlement of their claim. On 2 July 1926 Baldwin replied to both men but satisfied neither. He endorsed the principle of an independent Air Ministry, and the arbitration was expressed under four heads:

1. The Air Ministry must continue to be responsible for raising, training and maintaining the FAA subject to the adjustments made in the Balfour Report and the Trenchard–Keyes agreement. This provided that there must be a 70 per cent naval and Royal Marine manning of FAA units. Those naval and Royal Marine officers carried dual RAF/naval rank and were eligible for advancement in the RAF.
2. Baldwin was not prepared to reverse the recommendations of the Balfour Committee, which provided that at least 30 per cent of RAF officers, whether regular or short service, should serve on aircraft-carriers.
3. The 70/30 ratio in favour of the Navy should apply only to FAA units, i.e. not shore-based units employed on maritime duties.
4. The question of the coastal reconnaissance flights or naval-cooperation flights, as the Navy called them, should be a matter of cooperation between the two services, as suggested by Austen Chamberlain in his House of Commons statement of 16 March 1922, rather than one of strict subordination. This matter was therefore to be dealt with by the Chiefs of Staff Committee.

The Prime Minister did not deal with the matter of airships. It will be remembered that the R101 was nicknamed the 'Socialist' airship, to be built with public money at Cardington, and the R33 and R36 airships were to be refurbished, all in the name of commercial aviation. But there was some justification for the expenditure of public money on the R101 in that it could be used for reconnaissance in a time of national emergency. This would inevitably mean maritime reconnaissance, since airships were no match for aircraft over land, and this, in turn, would mean the Navy laying claim to its manning and operation. The operation of the R101 would therefore only lead to another squabble, which was something the government was keen to avoid.

Baldwin then proceeded to 'bang heads together'. He felt it was time for the two services to stop the constant bickering, and he told them to enter into a new spirit of cooperation. Both service heads then wrote to each other, giving an assurance of whole-hearted cooperation, and Trenchard backed this up with a letter to all his Air Vice-Marshals, explaining the Prime Minister's ruling. One tangible result was the agreement that the programme of training and exercises in peacetime should be arranged to secure the maximum amount of cooperation between shore-based units and the Navy. To this end Trenchard worked with the Deputy Chief of Naval Air Staff, Vice-Admiral Sir Frederick Field, representing Beatty, who was still absent from duty owing to sickness.

There was one more hiccup between the two services before the year was out, and that was caused by the inability to attract sufficient naval officer volunteers to fill the 70 per cent quota for the FAA. The Admiralty had proposed training ratings and marines in the same way as the RAF trained airman pilots. The Air Ministry disagreed with this proposal on two grounds. Firstly, the object of providing a core of naval officers with air experience who would eventually be promoted to the higher ranks of the service would be defeated. Secondly, the posts that the Navy could not fill should go to airman pilots, since the latter were experienced at working with aircraft in a flying environment, and they had served a three-year apprenticeship covering various aspects of aircraft maintenance; this was something that naval ratings or marine recruits would lack. The Navy's response was that it would not reduce its quota, and the First Lord went on to propose the appointment of non-commissioned pilots. The Air Ministry then claimed that this was a new proposal that had not been included in those matters that were the subject of the Prime Minister's arbitration of July 1926. But Baldwin had other things on his mind and was not going to be deflected by this latest difference between the two services.

1927–1928

Presentation of the Air Estimates, 1927/8

On 5 March 1927 the Air Estimates for 1927/8 were published. Parliament was being asked to vote £15,550,000, which was a reduction of £450,000 on the previous year, savings having been made on personnel, works and buildings. There was some compensation in that the spending on technical equipment would increase by £635,000, including new types of aircraft. In Hoare's words, 'The policy of replacing aeroplanes and engines of wartime design by modern types is making steady progress and it is the intention that, in future, no more aircraft or engines of wartime designs should be bought.' A subsidy of £137,000 was to go to Imperial Airways for its European services, and £93,600 for the Cairo–Karachi route. £8,000 was to go to meteorological services, £10,000 for a new wireless telegraphy station and £110,000 for alterations to Croydon Airport, which were scheduled to be completed by 1928.

The Debate on the Estimates took place on 11 March. *The Times*, in reporting the debate, said, 'Sir Samuel Hoare has all the scrupulous precision which he proudly ascribed to British aeroplane engines, and, like them on his great Imperial flight last year, he went through the long journey of his Estimates purring like a kitten.' This did not impress either Conservative or Labour MPs, who felt that too little progress had been made. Among these was Lieutenant-Colonel Moore-Brabazon, who felt that Sir Samuel Hoare's triumphant speech was cynical, given the rate of progress since the First World War. He recalled how change from one design to another took a matter of months during the war, and referred to the Italians' ability to prepare their team for the Schneider Trophy races in six months at a time when British technical experts believed that two years would be necessary. Perhaps they had not appreciated that war provides an enormous incentive to make rapid strides, involving expenditure that would

never be accepted in peacetime. Indeed, it was the lack of funds in the early 1920s that prevented Trenchard from ordering and the aircraft industry from developing new aircraft types. With 10,000 war-surplus aircraft dumped on the market in 1919, it is hardly surprising that reconditioned DH9As and Bristol Fighters were much more economical, and it cannot be denied that these two gave sterling service in India, Palestine and Iraq during the 1920s.

The debate was characterized by vociferous contributions from those who thought that the RAF vote from a total Service Estimate of £115,000,000 was disproportionately small, and the 'disarmers' who thought otherwise. But it was RAF air accidents that excited the greatest interest of Members. The Prime Minister put these accidents down to pilot error, given the adventurous spirit, nerve and temperament of RAF pilots. It was in their nature to take risks, and accidents in training, he felt, were unavoidable. C.G. Grey, the editor of the *Aeroplane*, took issue with the Prime Minister, and believed that Baldwin had taken considerable trouble to investigate air accidents, yet had based his findings on entirely false premises. Accidents could be prevented, said Grey, if Air Ministry technical experts could be forced to work with greater speed and greater intelligence to equip the Air Force with apparatus that would prevent a large proportion of such accidents.

Bridgeman v. Hoare

On 19 February 1927 William Bridgeman, the First Lord of the Admiralty, wrote to Hoare saying that he had noted the Air Minister's views on the inability of the Admiralty to man its 70 per cent quota of naval officer pilots in the FAA, and insisted on the Navy's right to determine for itself who should and who should not fill the pilot vacancies. Again the two Ministers took their dispute to the Prime Minister for arbitration, but Baldwin was preoccupied with his visit to Canada with the Prince of Wales, and no decision was taken in 1927. In January 1928 he was still preoccupied, this time with government business of the new session of Parliament, and so he asked the Lord Privy Seal, Lord Salisbury, to arbitrate on his behalf. But it seems that the Admiralty had grown impatient, and on 10 February issued a Fleet Order altering the period of attachment for naval pilots to the FAA, notwithstanding the Air Ministry's disagreement and the fact that the whole matter was *sub judice*. There followed an angry exchange of letters, with Hoare ceasing to address his opposite number in official correspondence with his usual 'My Dear Willie', and substituting the formal 'Dear First Lord'. Bridgeman responded in similar fashion.

On 15 March Salisbury sent his recommendations to the CID. To begin with, it was conceded that the FAA was an integral part of the fleet. This was not the difficult part of the arbitration, since even the Air Ministry could hardly claim to know best how to deploy aircraft from a carrier during fleet operations perhaps thousands of miles from British shores. Salisbury held the view that the FAA hardly differed from any other arm of the service, such as the submarine service and the Royal Marines. Gradually the Air Ministry would have to concede that it was no longer constitutionally nor permanently part of the RAF. Indeed, Trenchard had anticipated as much in his 1919 Memorandum (see Appendix C, page 421, para. 1). But 1928 was not the year to make the break. Naval aviation needed time to develop before it could stand on its own. In the light of the Ten-Year Rule there was no urgency to make a precipitate move.

With regard to the specific matters for which the two services required arbitration, Salisbury's recommendations were as follows:

1. The source from which naval pilots were to be recruited was the ranks of naval *officers*.
2. The period of attachment to the RAF of all naval pilots was to be prescribed by the Admiralty, with the concurrence of the Air Ministry, such concurrence 'not to be unreasonably withheld'.
3. If there remained any point that could not be adjusted between the two services by themselves, an appeal should be made to the Chiefs of Staff Committee presided over by the chairman of the CID.

And there the matter rested. The two service chiefs had been asked, yet again, to enter into a spirit of cooperation. What can be said in defence of the view taken by Hoare and Trenchard is that, given the number of occasions when the independence of the RAF had come under attack, what might be seen as an over-reaction can perhaps be understood. During the period of rapid expansion of the RAF in the late 1930s, when the separate existence of the RAF was no longer in dispute, the Air Ministry was prepared to set the FAA free.

Schneider Trophy and Pilotless Bombers With the slow-down of the Expansion Plan, Trenchard and the Air Ministry looked for other avenues where progress could be made. British success in the Schneider Trophy races was evidence of progress in experimental aircraft design, the Supermarine S5 and S6 being the forerunners of the world-famous Spitfire fighter aircraft. But in the field of air weaponry experiment and research had to be abandoned owing to the economies required in service expenditure. For example, an early type of flying bomb had been undergoing development since the early 1920s, and was successfully tested in 1927. It looked like a conventional aircraft, and when one crashed into the English Channel during tests, and the wreckage was retrieved by a French warship, her captain expressed his

regret that no trace had been found of a body. This caused the trials to be transferred to the deserts of southern Iraq, where leaks of intelligence would be less likely. Trenchard appealed through the CID for the funds to develop this weapon. He argued that stockpiles of these missiles could be used in war to supplement manned bombers, particularly in bad weather. He also warned that other nations might take such a project forward and Britain would lose its lead. But the extra expenditure, estimated to be less than £1 million, was not authorized by the Treasury or the Cabinet. This was partly because of opposition from within the CID and the two service chiefs, Field Marshal Sir George Milne, the CIGS, and Sir Charles Madden, who had succeeded Beatty as the First Sea Lord. For the time being the matter rested, but it was taken up again by Trenchard's successor, Sir John Salmond.

The Larynx pilotless bomber

Engine: Armstrong Siddeley Lynx 160 hp
Range: 200 miles
Speed: 300 mph
Bomb load: 250 lb
Cost: £450 per bomber

This bomber could be guided by an automatic pilot to within five miles of its target at a range of 200 miles. It was first catapulted from the deck of a destroyer. Additions to stockpile estimated to be 50 missiles per week.

Air Intelligence Trenchard's attempts to secure the funds to develop the Larynx missile was evidence that the CAS wanted to be ahead of other countries in scientific developments that had military applications. But this begged the question as to why Britain should not attempt to learn of scientific developments in other countries. The idea in 1921 was that Germany might have developed a 'death ray', powerful electromagnetic rays capable of killing personnel and detonating explosives. The Air Ministry went so far as to offer £1,000 to anyone who could demonstrate the use of such a ray, but to no avail. Military intelligence did not disclose any serious threats to this country in the 1920s resulting from scientific discovery or development.

The RAF's tenth birthday On 1 April 1928 the RAF was ten years old, and Lord Weir, who was largely involved in its wartime conception, sent Trenchard a cable: 'I regard it as incomparably the most efficient Air Force in existence, creditable alike to British organization and British character. It is welcome portent to the Empire that this new fighting service affords opportunity not only to the British qualities of courage, determination and enterprise, but also to the spirit of true scientific progress.' A closer inspection, however, showed that it was in the field of engine design, and not aircraft, that the greatest strides had been made.

1929

The Air Estimates 1929/30

The Estimates showed a decrease of £50,000 compared with the previous year, and Parliament was asked to vote £16,200,000 net. Seven RAF squadrons were to be added to the seventy-five in existence. With regard to manpower to fill these new squadrons, it was emphasized that permanently commissioned officers would be provided to fill these posts only where career officers were essential to ensure a nucleus for future expansion in the event of war. The remainder of the officer manning would come from short-service commissioned pilots. The latter would be provided with educational support to enable them to find civilian employment on completion of their engagements. For technical and warlike equipment there was an increased vote of £615,000. Nineteen squadrons, including two in India and several training units, would be equipped with aircraft of the latest design (which still meant biplanes). There was an increase of £102,500 for research and development, of which £40,000 was for a new variable-density wind tunnel. £450,000 was to go to civil aviation, of which £349,000 was for Imperial Airways and £16,000 to subsidize thirteen light aeroplane clubs. Finally, £3,000 was added for National Flying Services to establish twenty aerodromes and eighty landing grounds within three years.

The Debate on the Estimates began on 7 March, and Hoare announced the construction of the Short Sarafand, as a larger flying-boat than any yet built in Britain, and the Blackburn monoplane/biplane, without divulging the names of the manufacturers. He emphasized the change-over from wood to metal construction, and spoke of the efforts being made to prevent air accidents. There was a recognition that structural as well as human failure was to blame, and he mentioned the work being done at Farnborough and Martlesham to investigate 'wing flutter', and the introduction of the slotted wing. The slow-down in the rate of expansion of the plan to produce fifty-two Home Defence squadrons had resulted in only thirty-one squadrons being complete, but Hoare countered by saying that those squadrons were more efficient than any other squadrons in the world, and he applauded the quality of the auxiliary and Special Reserve squadrons.

The General Election

The Parliamentary session ended on 10 May, and Baldwin decided to go to the country. The Prime Minister could point to the Kellogg–Briand Pact, which had improved the atmosphere in international relations, but he had to face a situation of a steady increase in unemployment, which then totalled 1,200,000, not including those who were not in the insurance scheme. The Liberals pledged themselves to conquer unemployment and the Labour party claimed that they would do it better. Baldwin countered by saying that trade was recovering and the gravity of unemployment was exaggerated. He promised more technical education, slum clearance and a better welfare scheme for mothers.

Light aircraft were used in the campaign, with Moths in the ascendant. Moths were used by Squadron Leader the Hon. 'Freddie' Guest, the Member for Bristol North, Captain Harold Balfour, the Thanet MP, the Marquess of Douglas and Clydesdale for the Govan District of Glasgow, and H.R. Murray Philipson for Peeblestone. The Conservative candidate for Chertsey, Sir Philip Richardson, used his own DH50, and the Unionist candidate for West Belfast commuted between Baldonnel, Dublin and Aldergrove in a friend's Gypsy Moth.

Women over the age of 21 were allowed to vote for the first time in the 1929 Election, adding 29 million to the

The Labour Cabinet of 1929.

electorate. In spite of this, there was initial apathy and an indecisive result on 30 May. The Labour party had 287 seats, the Conservatives 260 and the Liberals 50. Together the Conservatives and the Liberals could outvote a Labour government, but Baldwin chose resignation. He advised the King to send for Ramsay MacDonald, and on 4 June MacDonald was invited to form a government. Snowden became Chancellor of the Exchequer and Arthur Henderson the Foreign Secretary, and Trenchard and John Salmond, his successor as CAS, would experience the return of Lord Thomson as Secretary of State for Air. Given Labour's pacifist outlook, would Thomson maintain the rate of expansion of the Home Defence squadrons or would the desire for international disarmament bring a demand for cuts, not expansion? Hitler and Mussolini were shortly to change the international political landscape.

Trenchard's Swan Song

Since Trenchard retired at the end of 1929, he had only brief dealings with Lord Thomson. During the summer of that year serious inter-communal conflict broke out in Palestine between Jew and Arab, and this showed up the limitation in the use of airpower in restoring order. The success of air-control operations in Iraq and India could not be repeated in Palestine, where inter-communal rioting, looting and murder was mainly confined to built-up areas. Neither the employment of the RAF nor the Army was appropriate in these circumstances. What was needed were police and gendarmerie forces of adequate size and quality, properly trained in the use of small-arms and well supplied with mechanical transport. What the RAF could usefully provide was aerial reconnaissance.

In November 1929, a few weeks before his retirement, Trenchard addressed a paper to Lord Thomson entitled 'The Fuller Employment of Air Power in Imperial Defence', afterwards known in staff circles as his 'swan song'. In it he emphasized that the Air Staff had never contended that air action was appropriate in internal security situations such as the one in Palestine. While thus admitting the limitations of the employment of the RAF in internal security operations, he nevertheless went on to argue that the time had arrived for the further substitution of air control for land and naval forces. He did not wish to imply that in such situations the requirement for land and naval forces would be eliminated, rather that every scheme of air control required the cooperation of some land and naval forces or both. His specific proposals for the extension of air control to operational theatres included the North-West Frontier, the Sudan, British East and West Africa, the substitution of air for naval forces for routine patrol

duties, such as those associated with the slave trade in the Persian Gulf and the Red Sea, and the replacement of coastal guns by RAF bombers at home and overseas. Trenchard expected close inspection and searching criticism of these proposals, which he said he welcomed.

Trenchard himself called this his 'last will and testament', and Thomson prevailed upon the Prime Minister to circulate it as a Cabinet paper. The CIGS, the First Sea Lord and Hankey all objected to Thomson's endorsement of Trenchard's proposals, saying that it was a departure from the normal rules of procedure. 'I do not at this stage ask my colleagues to reach any definite conclusion on the details of Sir Hugh's proposals', wrote Thomson. 'In view, however, of the urgent need for economy in any one of the very few directions in which early reductions in expenditure can be effected, I ask that these proposals should be seriously considered as the fruits of his unique and wide experience.' Trenchard has also suggested that an authoritative committee should be appointed without delay by the Cabinet to review the whole matter.

Trenchard's departure Towards the end of 1928 Trenchard had told Hoare that he wished to resign as CAS. Although he had served for ten years, he believed that his successors should serve no longer than five years, for a young service needed people with young ideas. When he became CAS, the average age of an air officer was $40^1/_2$ years, and none of the existing air marshals and air vice-marshals were over 43 years of age. If another appointment was made in 1935, eleven of the existing air vice-marshals would be over 55 years. The choice of the new CAS was not agreed until the last minute. Sir John Salmond was the Air Member for Personnel and a member of the Air Council. John, his brother Geoffrey and Edward Ellington, who had just returned from two years as AOC Iraq, were considered. Christopher Bullock, in speaking of the Salmond brothers described John as having broader and more determined, if less fertile, ideas than Geoffrey. Liddell Hart, the military expert, opined that Ellington, if not selected, could afford to wait for another four years, as he was only 50 years of age. In fact Ellington was 52, four years older than John Salmond. In the event John Salmond was appointed as CAS and was succeeded by his brother Geoffrey, who sadly died shortly after his appointment, and John had to return as CAS until Ellington could take over. A peerage was conferred on Hugh Trenchard in the New Year's Honours List, and from his seat in the House of Lords he would continue to press his views on air policy and the development of the RAF, which was so dear to his heart.

Epilogue

This volume has been about Trenchard's air force and his insistence upon the primacy of the bomber in offensive defence. It is as well, therefore, to reflect upon the outcome of the Second World War, the first major conflict in which his air force went to war. The complete destruction of the Japanese cities of Hiroshima and Nagasaki in August 1945 by one atomic bomb dropped on each city by just one aeroplane must surely prove beyond all doubt that the offensive use of the bomber aircraft can bring a country to its knees and force its government to sue for peace, or, in this case, unconditional surrender. But then, these weapons were used, not to wage war, but to end a war in which all three services had taken part. Strategic bombing had been only part of the overall employment of military forces, including the use of submarines, which it may be claimed could have bought Britain to its knees. Secondly, only one power had the atomic weapon at the time, but now several countries have them. To attempt to end a war with nuclear weapons alone may not defeat an enemy nation nor finish a war, but results in the mutually assured destruction of both aggressor and the country or alliance of countries seeking to counter the aggression. After the start of the Cold War, NATO had very soon to adopt a policy of flexible response in the hope of avoiding nuclear confrontation, in which there would be no winners. Finally, and this is probably the salt that is rubbed in Trenchard's wounds, it is the Royal Navy and not the RAF that is today tasked with delivering the strategic nuclear weapon, using the Trident missile.

It is clear that the extravagant claims made for the offensive use of bombers in a war were made by a man who had to exaggerate his case or risk seeing his force dismembered and shared out to the Army and the Royal Navy. For this he can be forgiven, not only because he was the proud father of the new service, but because he was right to have insisted upon a professional airmen's service. One can only speculate what would have happened if Lord Gort had taken the BEF to France in 1939 with its own air corps. This would doubtless have been fed with flying squadrons in a vain attempt to win the ground war. Where else would the War Office have used its aeroplanes, and would not the defence of the home base have been a primary consideration only after Dunkirk? By this time there might not have been anything left with which to fight an air war. As it was, Air Marshal Dowding refused to fulfil Churchill's promise to the French Premier to send more fighter squadrons to France. Lastly one may speculate as to what sort of an air force it would have been in 1939, schooled in the arts of supporting a ground war and not in air combat.

It may be concluded that Trenchard was wrong in insisting upon the air doctrine adopted by the RAF in the 1920s, but that with hindsight he was absolutely right in his insistence that military pilots should be more than the Army's taxi drivers.

Appendices

A. Aircraft Technical Specifications

B. Squadron Locations and Aircraft, 1918 to 1939

C. The Trenchard Memorandum

D. Flying Operations Carried Out by No. 11 (Irish) Wing, April 1921

E Extract of Report on Iraq Administration by the High Commissioner
  April 1922 – March 1923

F. RAF Squadron Disbandments 1918 – 1923

G. Strategic Air Doctrine 1921

H. Military and Civil Aircraft Tested at Martlesham Heath. 1919 – 1929

J. Administrative Arrangements for RAF Personnel to see the 1929 Schneider Trophy Contest

K. Orders Issued for Joint Operations by Nos.1 and 2 (Indian) Wings on 5th and 6th June 1927 against Mohmand
  tribesmen.

L. Arrangements for Naval Officer Volunteers for Service with the Fleet Air Arm (A.M.W.O. No.551)

M. Pilots on the strength of Fighter, Fleet Spotter and Reconnaissance
  Flights of the Fleet Air Arm.

N. The Career Paths of Hugh Trenchard, John Salmond, Frederick Sykes and Edward Ellington

P. The Various Home and Tropical Officers' uniforms – 1925

Q. Correspondence Relating to the Cabinet Memorandum – 'The War Object of an Air Force'

R. Members of the Air Council and Commanders of RAF Formations in the 1920s.

S. The Air Estimates – Financial Year 1919 – 1920.

Appendix A

AIRCRAFT TECHNICAL SPECIFICATIONS

PART I – AIRCRAFT IN OPERATIONAL SQUADRON SERVICE BETWEEN 11 NOVEMBER 1918 AND 31 DECEMBER 1929

PART II – NON-SQUADRON TRAINING AIRCRAFT, HIGH-ALTITUDE, HIGH-SPEED AND LONG-DISTANCE AIRCRAFT

Notes:
1. The information shown relates to a representative mark/version of the type.
2. Details of test flying and development are to be found in Chapter 5.
3. Aircraft by squadrons are shown in Appendix B.

PART I
AIRCRAFT IN OPERATIONAL SQUADRON SERVICE BETWEEN 11 NOVEMBER 1918 AND 31 DECEMBER 1929

1. Avro Aldershot
2. Armstrong Whitworth Atlas
3. Avro 504K
4. Armstrong Whitworth FK8
5. Sopwith Baby
6. Royal A/C Factory BE2E
7. Royal A/C Factory BE12A
8. Bristol F2B
9. Bristol M1C
10. Bristol Bulldog
11. Sopwith Camel
12. Fairey Campania
13. Sopwith Cuckoo
14. Curtiss H.12
15. Curtiss H.16
16. Airco DH4
17. Airco DH6
18. Airco DH9
19. Airco DH9A
20. Airco DH10
21. Sopwith Dolphin
22. Fairey IIID Land-Plane
23. Fairey IIID Floatplane
24. Fairey IIIF Land/Float Plane
25. Fairey Fawn
26. Felixstowe F2A
27. Felixstowe F3
28. Felixstowe F5
29. Royal A/C Factory FE2B/C/D
30. Fairey Fox
31. Gloster Gamecock
32. Gloster Grebe II
33. Handley Page Hinaidi
34. Hawker Horsley
35. Handley Page 0/400
36. Handley Page V/1500
37. Handley Page Hyderabad
38. Blackburn Kangaroo
39. Martinsyde G100/102
40. Nieuport 17, 23, 24
41. Nieuport Nightjar
42. Nieuport Nighthawk
43. Parnall Panther
44. Royal Aircraft Factory RE8
45. Sopwith Salamander
46. Royal Aircraft Factory SE5A
47. Short 184
48. Short 320
49. Boulton Paul Sidestrand
50. Armstrong Whitworth Siskin IIIA
51. Sopwith Snipe
52. Supermarine Southampton II
53. SPAD VII
54. Vickers Vernon
55. Vickers Victoria
56. Vickers Vimy
57. Vickers Virginia
58. Westland Walrus
59. Westland Wapiti
60. Wight Converted
61. Hawker Woodcock

Aircraft Specification Sheet (1): AVRO ALDERSHOT

Span: 68 ft
Length: 45 ft
Wing area: 1,064 sq. ft
Weights: Empty, 6,310 lb
Loaded, 10,950 lb
Power plant: One 650 hp
Rolls-Royce Condor III
Armament/Bomb load:
One fixed Vickers forward-firing machine-gun, one trainable gun in mid-upper position and provision for one Lewis gun in ventral position; bomb load, 2,200 lb

Performance
Max. speed: 110 mph at sea level
Cruising speed: 92 mph
Endurance: 6 hr
Service ceiling: 14,500 ft

Air Ministry Specifications:
2/20, which called for a long-range bomber

History
The first prototype, J6852, made its maiden flight at Hamble, flown by Bert Hinkler in October 1921. The aircraft was in competition for RAF acceptance against a de Havilland Derby. The aircraft had a large four-bladed propeller and double undercarriage. The fuselage was metal-tube framed with wooden wings, fin and tail. The prototype was flown in the presence of Sir Geoffrey Salmond and Air Ministry officials. Hinkler took off in just 300 yards and reported that it was nice on the controls and easy to manage. The Aldershot was then delivered to RAE Farnborough, whose staff found it stable in flight, making it suitable for night flying. The Aldershot made a public appearance at the 1922 Hendon Air Pageant, flown by Flying Officer C.E. Horrex. Only fifteen were built, Serials J6942 to 6956, and it entered service as the Aldershot III (from J6945 onwards) in August 1924 with 99 Squadron at Bircham Newton, but remained in service only until the end of 1925, since it was by then Air Ministry policy not to employ any more single-engined heavy bombers. Given its weight, if one force-landed in a field it would have to be dismantled, whereas a two-engined bomber would be much less likely to suffer total engine failure. It was replaced by the twin-engined Hyderabad, which served with 99 Squadron for six years.

Aircraft Specification Sheet (2): ARMSTRONG WHITWORTH ATLAS

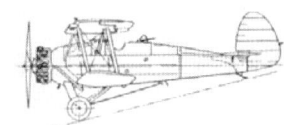

Span: 39 ft 6.5 in.
Length: 28 ft 6.5 in.
Wing area: 391 sq. ft
Weights: Empty, 2,550 lb
Loaded, 4,020 lb
Power plant: One 450 hp
Armstrong
Siddeley Jaguar IVC
Armament/Bomb load:
One fixed forward-firing
Vickers machine-gun; one

trainable Lewis gun on Scarff ring; four 112 lb bombs below wings

Performance
Max. speed: 142.5 mph at sea level
124 mph at 15,000 ft
Climb rate: 5.5 min to 5,000 ft
28 min to 15,000 ft
Endurance: 3 hr 15 min
Range: 480 miles
Service ceiling: 16,800 ft

Air Ministry Specifications:
Design Specification – 33/26 Prototype J8675
Production Contract – 11/28 Production prototype J9951
Dual-Control Trainer – 12/28 Prototype J8792
Army Co-operation Dual Control – 9/31 Prototype K2514

History
The prototype Atlas J8675 made its first flight on 10 May 1925, and continued in production until 1933. Of a total of 446 aircraft built, 175 were dual-control trainers. The Atlas was the first to enter RAF service specifically designed as an Army Co-operation aircraft. The Trenchard Memorandum, setting out the shape of the peacetime RAF, provided for squadrons that would be earmarked for work with the Army in support of land operations. Hot-weather trials were conducted with No. 5 Squadron at Peshawar in 1927, since it was planned to use the aircraft to work with the Indian Army. These trials, described in Chapter 4, showed that the supercharged engine was unsuitable for use in hot climates. Both at home and overseas the Atlas proved to be a rugged and reliable aircraft. Work entailed spotting for the artillery, signalling results by radio, photographic reconnaissance, supply dropping, ground attack with bombs and machine-guns and message retrieval using a retractable hook pivoted on the undercarriage spreader bar. The first squadron to be equipped was No. 26 Squadron at Catterick in October 1927. They then replaced Bristol Fighters on No. 208 Squadron in Egypt in 1930. They were also used as station communications aircraft and with the School of Photography. Eventually the Atlas was replaced in service by the Hawker Audax.

Aircraft Specification Sheet (3): AVRO 504K

Span: 36 ft 0 in.
Length: 29 ft 5 in.
Wing area: 330.0 sq. ft
Weights: With Le Rhône engine
Empty, 1,231 lb
Loaded, 1,829 lb
Power plant: One 130 hp Clerget 9B rotary, 110 hp Le Rhône or 100 hp Monosoupape
Armament/Bomb load:
Lewis gun mounted on the top wing

Performance:
Max. speed: approx. 105 mph at 6,500 ft
Endurance: 2 hr 45 min
Service ceiling: 19,000 ft

History

When Alliot Verdon Roe designed the 504 in 1913, he thought he would be lucky if he got an order for six machines. In the event over 10,000 were built, and some were still in service at the outbreak of the Second World War. Although used operationally in the First World War, it was as an *ab initio* trainer that this aircraft would be best remembered. The prototype flew at Brooklands in July 1913 and it then went for trials at the Royal Aircraft Factory, where the aircraft achieved a top speed of 80.9 mph and an altitude of 14,420 ft, a British record at the time. The RFC used the 504 for reconnaissance and home defence, but the RNAS employed it in the bombing role, carrying 16 or 20 lb bombs. The most celebrated raid was that on the Zeppelin sheds on 21 November 1914. The 504 variants ranged from A to L. The A and B variants were issued to the RFC and the RNAS respectively. The C and D variants were used for home defence, having an upward-firing Lewis gun to fire at the underside of Zeppelins. Scarff rings were also mounted to the rear cockpit for defensive armament. The best-known variants are the J and K versions. The J version was brought out in 1916 specifically for flying training, in which role it was exceptional. The K version had an engine mounting that could be adapted to accept a variety of engines –the 80 hp Le Rhône, the 80 hp Gnome, *150 hp Bentley BR1* and the 100 hp Monosoupape. This allowed the continued use of 504 beyond the date when it was officially declared obsolete in 1921. The final wartime model was the L version, which had twin landing floats and a tail float.

Aircraft Specification Sheet (4): ARMSTRONG WHITWORTH FK8

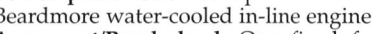

Span: 43 ft 6 in.
Length: 31 ft 0 in.
Wing area: 540.0 sq. ft
Weights: Take-off, 2,811 lb
Power plant: One 160 hp Beardmore water-cooled in-line engine
Armament/Bomb load: One fixed forward-firing Vickers gun; one trainable Lewis gun on Scarff ring; bomb load 160 lb

Performance

Max. speed: 93 mph at 8,000 ft
Endurance: 3 hr 0 min
Service ceiling: 13,000 ft

History

The AW FK8 (FK = Frederick Koolhoven) was a scaled-up version of the FK3, which started life as a simplified version of the BE2C for reconnaissance and bombing duties. The maiden flight was in May 1916. The aircraft was a contemporary of the RE8. The early version had a 120 hp Beardmore engine, but this was replaced by a 160 hp version. Armed with a Vickers and a Lewis gun on a Scarff mounting in the rear cockpit. It could carry a 160 lb bomb and was employed on reconnaissance, day and night

bombing and ground attack. The aircraft was built by Armstrong Whitworth and Angus Sanderson and Co., and production ended in July 1918. At the Armistice there were 694 of these aircraft on RAF charge. By that time 40 per cent of AW FK8s were in store and fewer than two hundred were on front-line service in France. This aircraft did not long survive the First World War.

Aircraft Specification Sheet (5): SOPWITH BABY BATCHES ALSO MADE BY FAIREY, BLACKBURN AND PARNALL

Span: 25 ft 8 in.
Length: 23 ft 0 in.
Wing area: 240.0 sq. ft
Weights: Take-off, 1,715 lb
Power plant: One 130 hp Clerget 9B rotary
Armament/Bomb load: One fixed forward-firing Lewis gun (But the Blackburn batch carried Ranken darts or Le Prieur rockets for anti-Zeppelin attacks instead.)

Performance

Max. speed: 98 mph at sea level
Endurance: 2 hr 0 min
Service ceiling: approx. 7,600 ft

History

The Sopwith Baby was developed from the Schneider floatplane built for the RNAS. The Baby had a rotary engine enclosed in a horseshoe cowling. The original versions had a Monosoupape engine, but the remaining ninety-five, built by Sopwith, were fitted with the 110 hp Le Clerget, which also powered sixty-one Babies built by Blackburns, twenty by Faireys and thirty by Parnall. The 130 hp Le Clerget was also fitted to the Baby aircraft by these companies, bringing the total Baby production to 457. The Sopwith aircraft were fitted with a Lewis gun that fired forward and upwards through a small cut in the top wing. The other manufacturers fitted a forward-firing Lewis gun in the front of the cockpit, except in forty of the Blackburn machines, which were fitted with Ranken darts or Le Prieur rockets for attacking Zeppelins. The 'Hamble' Babies, so called because they were built at the Hamble works, had thicker wings with full-span trailing-edge flaps and an angular fin plus improved floats. The Baby served for most of 1917–18 on maritime duties around the British coasts (see deployment map on page 12 in Chapter 1) and aboard eleven seaplane-carriers on North Sea and Mediterranean patrols, whereas in Egypt, Italy, Palestine and the Aegean they were employed mainly for bombing. Withdrawal of the Babies began before the Armistice, and they were declared obsolete in November 1918. On 31 October 1918 there were eighty Babies on charge to the RAF of one kind or another.

Aircraft Specification Sheet (6): ROYAL AIRCRAFT FACTORY BE2E

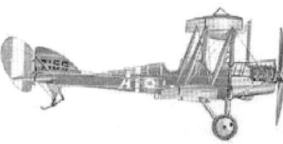

Span: 40 ft 9 in.
Length: 27 ft 3 in.
Wing area: 360.0 sq. ft
Weights: Max. take-off, 2,100 lb

Power plant: One 90 hp RAF 1A air-cooled V type
Armament/Bomb load: Original versions were not armed, the observer using personal firearms. Later versions were fitted with a trainable gun

Performance
Max. speed: 82 mph at 6,500 ft
Endurance: 4 hr 0 min
Service ceiling: 10,000 ft

History
The BE2E was the final production model of the BE2 series, and was slightly lighter on the controls and faster than its predecessors. There was a reversion to the out-moded back-to-front seating, and it climbed more slowly than the BE2C. Structurally it differed considerably from previous models. The tailplane and elevator tips were also raked back and a larger more curved vertical fin was fitted. There was a pronounced difference in span between the upper and lower wings. The BE2Es were first delivered to the RFC in July 1916, and flew in Macedonia, India, Mesopotamia, Palestine and on the Western Front. They arrived in France on 15 July 1916 with No. 34 Squadron, and for over a year they were used for artillery observation until replaced by the RE8s and FK8s. About ninety-five BE2E aircraft were transferred from the RFC to the RNAS for training duties. Even the US Navy bought them for this purpose. The building programme for the BE2E was very widespread. In addition to the Royal Aircraft Factory, at least twenty-two other UK manufacturers participated. Upwards of 1,800 were built, about half this number being employed on training, and the BE2E remained in RAF service until April 1920 with No. 114 Squadron, Ambala, India.

Aircraft Specification Sheet (7): ROYAL AIRCRAFT FACTORY BE12A

Span: 37 ft 0 in.
Length: 27 ft 3 in.
Wing area: 371.0 sq. ft
Weights: Max. take-off, 2,352 lb
Power plant: One 150 hp RAF4A air-cooled V type

Armament/Bomb load: Early versions had a Lewis gun on either side of the cockpit on a Strange-type mounting. Later versions were equipped with a trainable gun

Performance
Max. speed: 102 mph at sea level
Endurance: 3 hr 0 min
Service ceiling: 12,500 ft

History
The BE12A was a development of the BE12. The latter failed miserably as a fighter and had to be withdrawn from fighting duties in September 1916 on Trenchard's advice. Even though they had been used as bombers before their withdrawal, in both roles their losses were heavy. The BE12A was a single-seater scout powered by an RAF (Royal Aircraft Factory) 4A engine, and had the same wing arrangement as the BE2E. During the flight trials probable overbalance of the top-wing ailerons almost killed the pilot, Captain L.R. Tait-Cox, and so the aircraft was fitted with the wings of a BE2E, which had ailerons on both the upper and lower wing surfaces. The BE12A also had the enlarged fin and BE2E tailplane with raked tips. Following Trenchard's condemnation of the BE12, only one unit under his command had the 12A, a special-duty flight of the 9th (HQ) Wing. A few went to Palestine but were relinquished in February 1918. On home-defence duties both the 12 and 12A were used with some degree of success, and a 37 Squadron BE12 claimed Zeppelin L48, which was shot down in the early hours of 17 June 1917. The BE12A survived the war by only one month on No. 150 Squadron in the Aegean before that squadron was disbanded in September 1919.

Aircraft Specification Sheet (8): BRISTOL F2B

Span: 39 ft 3 in.
Length: 25 ft 10 in.
Wing area: 405.6 sq. ft
Weights: Take-off weight, 2,848 lb
Power plant: One 275 hp

Rolls-Royce Falcon III water-cooled V type
Armament/Bomb load: Two or three 0.303 in. machine-guns (one fixed and one trainable) and up to twelve 20 lb bombs

Performance
Max. speed: 123 mph at 5,000 ft
Endurance: 3 hr 0 min
Service ceiling: 18,000 ft

History
Of all F.S. Barnwell's designs the Bristol Fighter was the most successful. The aircraft originated as the R2A, which had a centrally mounted forward-firing Vickers gun and a single Lewis gun mounted on a Scarff ring in the rear cockpit. Deliveries began in December 1916 with No. 48 Squadron in France. They were operated as previous two-seaters, with the observer's Lewis gun being the primary weapon, but losses were heavy. Once the aircraft was flown as a front-gun fighter, the Bristol Fighter was an immediate success. With many hundreds more Bristol Fighters on order, the F2B version had wider-span tailplanes, modified lower centre-sections and an even better view from the front cockpit. It was this version that went on to serve with such distinction, not only during the First World War, but on air policing duties throughout the Empire during the 1920s. By the spring of 1918 the 'Brisfit', as it had been nicknamed, had established a formidable reputation, and enemy fighters could be relied upon not to attack more than two Brisfits at a time. Under wartime contracts more than 5,250 Bristol Fighters were ordered, and 3,101 are known to have been accepted by the RFC/RAF units by November 1918. The Americans also bought this design, but fitted unsuitable 400 hp Liberty 12 engines, which made their aircraft a failure. The British version had the very successful Falcon engines but the supply of these could not keep up with the demand, and other engines had to be considered, of which the Sunbeam Arab was the most widely used. They served in all wartime theatres, with squadrons on the Western Front, in

Palestine and Italy, and No. 111 Squadron used them to transport Colonel T.E. Lawrence between General Allenby's headquarters and the Arab guerrilla forces. The Bristol Fighter remained in post-war service until 1932, but in the air policing role it did not meet air opposition, and together with its stable-mate, the DH9A, it can be more accurately described as a general-purpose aircraft.

Aircraft Specification Sheet (9): BRISTOL M1C

Span: 30 ft 9 in.
Length: 20 ft 5.5 in.
Wing area: 145.0 sq. ft
Weights: Take-off, 1,348 lb
Power plant: One 110 hp Le Rhône 9J rotary
Armament/Bomb load: One Vickers machine-gun

Performance
Max. speed: 130 mph at sea level
Endurance: 1 hr 45 min
Service ceiling: 20,000 ft

History
F.S. Barnwell believed that a monoplane could perform better than biplanes. When RFC monoplane crashes prompted the setting up of a committee in 1912 to investigate these losses, monoplanes were not condemned, but there was a prejudice against them. Barnwell's M1A prototype, Serial A5138, reached 132 mph during trials with a 110 hp Clerget 9Z rotary engine, but these aircraft also had a 110 hp Le Rhône engine, with cut-outs in both wings and a centrally mounted machine-gun. The M1Bs had an uprated engine and were used for service trials. Two M1Bs went to the Middle East in June 1917, where they were used operationally, but the War Office felt that the landing speed of 49 mph was too high for small French airfields, and only 125 M1Cs were ordered. Probably fewer than twenty saw operational service, none of them on the Western Front. In Mesopotamia and Macedonia there was a need for a good escort fighter, but the M1C lacked the range. The remaining aircraft were allocated to training units in Egypt and the UK. By the end of the First World War the RAF had only forty-seven Bristol M1Cs on charge, of which thirty were based in the UK.

Aircraft Specification Sheet (10): BRISTOL BULLDOG II/IIA

Span: 33 ft 11 in.
Length: 25 ft 2 in.
Wing area: 306.6 sq. ft
Weights: Empty, 2,412 lb
Take-off, 3,503 lb
Power plant: One 490 hp Bristol Jupiter VIIF radial piston engine
Armament/Bomb load:
Two 0.303 in. fixed machine-guns

Performance
Max. speed: 174 mph at 10,000 ft
Climb rate: 14 min 30 sec to 20,000 ft
Range: 275 miles
Service ceiling: 27,000 ft

History
The Bulldog was built to AM Specification F9/26, and the prototype flew on 17 May 1927, to be followed by the prototype MkII, J.9480, on 21 January 1928. The Bulldog was chosen to replace the Siskin on RAF fighter squadrons after an Air Ministry competition involving the Hawfinch, Starling, Goldfinch and Partridge. Bulldogs entered service with No. 3 Squadron at Upavon in May 1929, and appeared in the Hendon Air Display that summer. By 1932 nine squadrons were equipped with this aircraft, and in 1936 No. 3 Squadron's Bulldogs were sent to the Sudan during the Abyssinian crisis. In spite of it being a spectacular aerobatic aircraft, it was not as fast as the RAF's light bombers of the early 1930s, and having comprised 70 per cent of the RAF's fighter strength during the inter-war years it was replaced by the Gladiator in 1937, on being declared obsolete. A total of 312 Bulldogs were supplied to the RAF, being MkII and IIA. The IIA had certain refinements, including a redesigned oil system, a tailwheel to replace the skid, Bendix wheel brakes and a modified fin.

Aircraft Specification Sheet (11): SOPWITH CAMEL

Span: 28 ft 0 in.
Length: 18 ft 9 in.
Wing area: 231.0 sq. ft
Weights: Take-off, 1,482 lb
Power plant: One 130 hp Clerget 9B rotary (but see text below)
Armament/Bomb load: Twin Vickers guns in front of cockpit

Performance
Max. speed: 104.5 mph at 10,000 ft
Endurance: 2 hr 30 min
Service ceiling: 18,000 ft

History
The prototype was flown in December 1916, powered by a 110 hp Clerget 9Z. Production Camels were based on the prototype powered with a 130 hp Clerget. Clerget 9Bs and Bentley 150 hp engines were also used, and deliveries to the service began in May 1917. The first Camels actually went to the RNAS. RFC orders for the aircraft specified either Clerget 9Bs or 110 hp Le Rhône 9Js. Clerget Camels were on the whole faster, but Le Rhône Camels had a faster climb. By the end of 1917 1,325 Camels had been delivered. They were used mostly in the ground-attack role, using 20 lb Cooper bombs in the Battles for Cambrai and Ypres. When heavy losses were experienced among the ground-attack versions, an armour-plated TF.1 (Trench Fighter 1) appeared. The 100 hp Monosoupape Camels were used for training, and from August 1917 the Le Rhône Camels were used for home-defence duties.

Discounting prototypes and cancelled contracts, 5,490 Camels were ordered. At the Armistice the RAF had 2,548 Camel F1s on charge, more than half of them having Clerget engines. The shipboard version, the 2F1, numbered 129.

The Camel did not remain in service long after the First World War, as it was replaced by the Snipe, but it left military service with a credited record of having shot down more enemy aircraft than any other Allied type. It was designed by Herbert Smith to replace the Sopwith Pup, but was not a docile aircraft, and it had to be mastered before it could be flown successfully. The torque from the rotary engine meant that it could out-turn any German fighter except possibly the Fokker Dr.I. Its name was unofficial, the camel's-hump appearance resulting from the fairing over the breeches of its twin Vickers guns.

Aircraft Specification Sheet (12): FAIREY CAMPANIA

Span: 61 ft 7 in.
Length: 43 ft 4 in.
Wing area:
Weights: loaded, 5,530 lb
Power plant: Carrier-borne, Rolls-Royce Eagles; Land-based, Sunbeam Maori engines
Armament/Bomb load: Single Lewis gun in rear cockpit and light bomb load on external racks

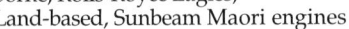
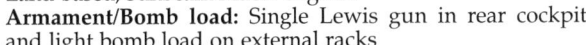

Performance
Max. speed: 85 mph at sea level
Service ceiling: 6,000 ft

History
The Campania was only the second type to be built by the Fairey Aviation Company, and the aircraft took its name from the carrier vessel for which it was designed, the former Cunard passenger liner of the same name, which was purchased by the Admiralty in 1914. The dimensions of the hatchways and the storage capacity for ten seaplanes in HMS *Campania* determined the aircraft's dimensions. The prototype Campania, N1000, was powered by a 275 hp Rolls-Royce MkI engine (later the Eagle), but such was the demand for Rolls-Royce engines at the time that the Sunbeam Maori was substituted in production aircraft from N1006 onwards. Production contracts were signed for 100 Campanias, and this work was shared by sub-contractors. The aircraft was designed for flying off the carrier only, and was placed on a form of trolley, the wheels being discarded after take-off. This was deemed essential, since attempts to fly seaplanes off the sea cost much in broken floats and sunken aircraft. The first take-off from HMS *Campania* was on 6 August 1915 by Flight Lieutenant W.L. Welsh, flying a Sopwith Schneider while the ship steamed at 17 knots into the wind. This flight proved that there would be insufficient take-off length for the Campanias, and the flying deck was lengthened to approximately 200 feet. The Campania was to be a patrol seaplane, and the first of these aircraft made a flight from the Isle of Grain to Scapa Flow in the Orkneys, which was a considerable achievement for the time. The aircraft was fitted with two main and wing-tip floats and a tail float. At the Armistice forty-two Campanias were serving at coastal air stations and on seaplane-carriers. In 1919 five Campanias embarked on the carrier *Nairana* for Archangel, and operated with the White Russian forces against the Bolsheviks. The Campania did not feature in the post-war RAF order of battle thereafter.

Aircraft Specification Sheet (13): SOPWITH CUCKOO

Span: 46 ft 9 in.
Length: 28 ft 6 in.
Wing area: 566.0 sq. ft
Weights: Take-off, 3,572 lb
Power plant: One 200 hp Hispano-Suiza water-cooled V type
Armament/Bomb load: One 1,000 lb torpedo

Performance
Max. speed: 103.5 mph at 6,500 ft
Endurance: 3 hr 45 min
Service ceiling: 15,600 ft

History
A requirement for a land-plane torpedo-bomber resulted in the first prototype Cuckoo B.1496, and the official trials began in July 1917. This was the Admiralty's first attempt to replace seaplane torpedo-carriers with a land-plane. In 1916 Captain Murray F. Sueter officially approached Sopwiths with a view to their producing an aircraft capable of carrying one or two 1,000 lb torpedoes and with an endurance of four hours. Orders went out in August 1917 for 100 Cuckoos, with an order for a further 50 in November. The 200 hp Hispano-Suiza engine originally used to power the Cuckoo was needed for the SE5A fighters, and the 200 hp Sunbeam Arab engine replaced it. Fairfield, Pegler and Blackburn also assisted in production when only the latter had former experience of building aircraft, and their product was not delivered until the autumn of 1918, to No. 185 Squadron at East Fortune in Scotland, which also served as the Torpedo Aeroplane School preparing pilots for the Cuckoos. They embarked on HMS *Argus* on 19 October 1918, but were too late in service to see combat. At the Armistice just over ninety Cuckoos had been delivered and contracts for 350 aircraft had been placed. Many of these were cancelled, but limited production continued throughout 1919 of a MkII version powered by a Wolseley Viper engine. Cuckoos served for a number of years on aircraft-carriers and with shore-based torpedo squadrons, but were finally withdrawn when No. 210 Squadron disbanded at Gosport in April 1923.

Aircraft Specification Sheet (14): CURTISS H 12

Span: 92 ft 8.5 in.
Length: 46 ft 6 in.
Wing area: 1,216.0 sq. ft
Weights: Empty, 7,293 lb Loaded, 10,650 lb
Power plant: Two 275 hp Rolls-Royce Eagle Is, then two 345 hp Eagle VIIs or 375 hp Eagle VIIIs
Armament/Bomb load: Up to four Lewis guns on flexible mountings and four 100 lb or two 230 lb bombs below the wings

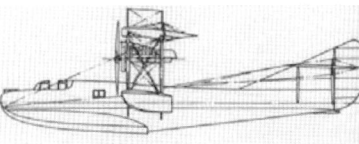

Performance
Max. speed: 85 mph at 2,000 ft
Climb rate: 3.3 min to 2,000 ft, 29.8 min to 10,000 ft
Endurance: 6 hr
Service ceiling: 10,800 ft

History

The Curtiss H12 was also called the 'Large America', and was a development of the H4 'Small America', being larger and more powerful. Although it had a distinguished operational record it did suffer from a hull planing bottom weakness, so that take-offs in all but calm seas could be hazardous. Rolls-Royce engines replaced the Curtiss power plants since the latter proved inadequate. A total of seventy-one aircraft reached the RNAS/RAF in two batches, i.e. Nos 8650 to 8699 and N4330 to 4350. These flying-boats were based at Great Yarmouth and Felixstowe. The H12 was used both as an anti-Zeppelin and anti-submarine aircraft; indeed, the first Zeppelin to be shot down by a seaplane was L22 on 14 May 1917 by F/Lt Galpin from Great Yarmouth, but a month later, on 14 June, another Zeppelin, L43, was shot down by an H12 from Felixstowe flown by F/Sub Lt Hobbs. Successes against U-boats were in May 1917 (UC-36), July 1917 (UB-20) and September 1917 (UC-6). Some of the H12s were later modified, becoming very similar in appearance to the Felixstowe F2As, and were known as the 'Converted Large Americas', At the cessation of hostilities there were eighteen H.12 flying-boats still on charge to the RAF.

Aircraft Specification Sheet (15): CURTISS H 16

Span: 95 ft 0 in.
Length: 46 ft 1.5 in.
Wing area: 1,000 sq. ft
Weights: Empty, 7,363 lb
        Loaded, 10,670 lb
Power plant: Two 375 hp Rolls-Royce Eagle VIIIs
Armament/Bomb load: Twin Lewis machine-guns on ring mountings in bows and midships. Provision for two further Lewis guns to fire through side of hull and for bombs mounted on under-wing racks

Performance
Max. speed: 98 mph at 2,000 ft; 95 mph at 6,500 ft; 92 mph at 10,000 ft
Initial climb rate: 512 ft/min
Climb: 3.7 min to 2,000 ft; 14.6 min to 6,500 ft; 28 min to 10,000 ft
Endurance: 6 hr
Service ceiling: 12,500 ft

History

The Curtiss H16 was a larger and updated version of the H12. Of most importance was the stronger and more seaworthy Porte-type hull, which brought the US boats into line with their British counterparts, the Felixstowe boats. Initially the Admiralty placed an order for fifteen boats, Serials N4060 to 4074, which were fitted with the 250 hp Rolls-Royce Eagle engines. A second contract for 110 aircraft, featuring the 375 hp Eagle engines, was placed (Serial Nos N4890 to 4999), but the last fifty were cancelled

when the war ended. This flying-boat had a crew of four, was of wooden construction and had wood and fabric covering.

Although they were as good as the Felixstowe boats, the H16s did not achieve any notable successes in the war against the U-boats. Thirty H16s were in service at the end of the First World War, and thirty-nine were in storage or with contractors. The US Navy was also operating approximately fifty of these boats around the shores of Britain. The US Navy versions were fitted with the 330 hp Liberty engines and were based at Killingholme. There is a story that one US Navy pilot actually looped an H16 while at Killingholme. The British H16s served with No. 228 Squadron at Great Yarmouth and Killingholme, No. 230 Squadron at Felixstowe, No. 238 Squadron at Cattewater (Mount Batten Plymouth) and No. 257 squadron at Dundee.

Aircraft Specification Sheet (16): AIRCO DH4

Span: 42 ft 4⅝ in.
Length: 30 ft 8 in.
Wing area: 434.0 sq. ft
Weights: Take-off, 3,313 lb
Power plant: One 250 hp Rolls-Royce Eagle III water-cooled V type
Armament/Bomb load: One fixed forward-firing 0.303 in. Vickers machine-gun and one 0.303 in. Lewis gun in rear cockpit. External pylons with provision for 460 lb of bombs

Performance
Max. speed: 117 mph at 6,500 ft
Endurance: 3 hr 45 min
Service ceiling: 17,400 ft

History

The DH4 was the first British aircraft to be designed for day-bombing duties. The power unit was to have been the 160 hp Beardmore, but then Sir William Beardmore, F.B. Halford and T.C. Pullinger (B-H-P) got together to produce the 230 hp BHP engine, and the first of these engines was running in June 1916. After bench testing it was fitted to the prototype DH4, but difficulties were experienced in producing these engines in quantity, and the first production BHPs did not appear until mid-1917. In the meantime the 250 hp Rolls-Royce Eagles were fitted. Tests with both engines were successful, and when Rolls-Royce progressed to the 375 hp Eagle VIII the DH4 performed better than most fighters of the day. It was made almost entirely of wood, with fabric covering. More powerful engines meant longer propellers, and so undercarriages with longer legs had to be fitted. The modifications carried out to the BHP engine meant that it would not then fit into the airframe, and the latter had to be returned to the shops for modification. Other DH4 engines included the 200 hp RAF 3a, the 260 hp Fiat and the 250 hp Siddeley Puma. In the air the DH4 handled well for a two-seater, was very light on the controls, comfortable to fly and easy to land, and its speed and ceiling meant that it could, on occasion, out-run pursuing enemy fighters. One snag in flight was the distance separating the pilot from the observer. The petrol tank was in that space, which meant that in combat when close cooperation between the two men was vital, the speaking tube was all but useless. The observer could, if need be, fly the aircraft from his cockpit. The DH4s first went to France with No. 55 Squadron on 6 March 1917, and from then until the Armistice this machine served the RFC, RNAS and RAF as a day-bomber, fighter and photographic reconnaissance and anti-Zeppelin/anti-submarine aircraft. Two DH4s were fitted with the Coventry Ordnance Works (COW) 1.5 lb quick-firing gun to attack Zeppelins, which meant strengthening the airframes to absorb the recoil. DH4s also served in the Aegean and the Italian peninsula, where flights of over 400 miles over water were made to attack enemy submarine bases. After the Armistice DH4s served in Russia in support of the White anti-Bolshevik forces.

Aircraft Specification Sheet (17): AIRCO DH 6

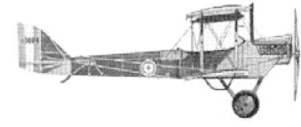

Span: 35 ft $11^1/_8$ in.
Length: 27 ft 3.5 in.
Wing area: 436.3 sq. ft
Weights: Take-off, 2,027 lb
Power plant: One 90 hp RAF 1A air-cooled V type
Armament/Bomb load: up to 100lb bombs for AS operations

Performance
Max. speed: 66 mph at 6,500 ft
Range: approx. 195 miles
Service ceiling: 10,000 ft

History
Chapter 7 on airfields records the activity of the DH6 from most of the coastal airfields around Britain during the latter part of the First World War. It gained the reputation as a submarine hunter. Its other role was as a trainer. It was designed for safety in the air and ease of production and was very angular in appearance, unlike the elegant shape of other de Havilland designs. When flown in the anti-submarine role its inherent safety was an asset, since the lone crewman was too intent on searching for the tell-tale signs of U-boat activity to worry about the control of his aircraft. It was when the Avro 504K began to replace the DH6 in the training role that it turned to coastal reconnaissance, when it was flown as a single-seater with a 100 lb bomb on board. It served with both British and US Navy coastal units until the Armistice, when there were 1,050 DH6s on strength to the RAF. Some production aircraft had 90 hp Curtiss OX-5 or 80 hp Renault engines.

Aircraft Specification Sheet (18): AIRCO DH9

Span: 42 ft $4^5/_8$ in.
Length: 30 ft 9.5 in.
Wing area: 434.0 sq. ft
Weights: Empty, 2,544 lb
Loaded, 3,667 lb

Power plant: 430 hp Napier Lion
Armament/Bomb load: One fixed forward-firing Vickers machine-gun + either a single- or double-yoked Lewis gun mounted on a Scarff ring; bomb load consisted of two 230 lb/four 112 lb bombs or an equivalent load of smaller bombs

Performance
Max. speed: 144 mph at ground level; 138 mph at 10,000 ft
Climb: 1 min 12 sec to 2,000 ft; 7 min 10 sec to 10,000 ft
Endurance: 3.5 hr
Service ceiling: 23,000 ft

History
The DH9 began life as an extensively modified version of the DH4, and the prototype DH9, Serial No. A7559, was flying in July 1917. The Gotha daylight raids on London showed the General Staff how potent a bomber could be as a weapon of offence, and the DH9 was substituted for the DH4 in all running contracts for the latter. The War Office had decided to increase the number of service squadrons from 108 to 200, the majority of the new squadrons being bomber. Since the 230 hp BHP engine had been selected for large-scale production, it was decided to install it in the DH9, but trouble with the cylinder blocks meant that the engines had to be derated. The required service ceiling and bomb load of the DH9 was thus unobtainable, and a decision was made to restrict its issue to no more than fifteen squadrons, and the pilots of these units just had to make the best of it. The DH9 was thus a good aeroplane spoiled by a bad engine. It had been expected to lift a heavier load than the DH4, but its lack of ceiling and performance meant that it fell foul of enemy scouts. Trenchard prophesied that it would be obsolete and outclassed by June 1918, and this was borne out in operations, for it needed fighter protection, which limited its effectiveness, and to the end of the war DH9s were hampered by engine trouble. They were more successful on other fronts, however, where the opposition was not as great, in Macedonia, Palestine and the Aegean. At home they replaced DH6s on anti-submarine patrols. Later the DH9s were fitted with Fiat and Napier Lion engines (photographed above), and after the war these aircraft saw service in Russia in support of the White armies against Bolshevism. It soldiered on until replaced by the DH9A, and surplus DH9s were sold at a low price to foreign countries by the Aircraft Disposal Company.

Aircraft Specification Sheet (19): AIRCO DH9A

Span: 45 ft 11 in.
Length: 30 ft 3 in.
Wing area: 487.0 sq. ft
Weights: Empty, 2,800 lb
Max. take-off, 4,645 lb
Power plant: One 420 hp Packard Liberty 12V 12-piston
Armament/Bomb load: One fixed forward-firing 0.303 in. Vickers machine-gun, and one or two 0.303 in. Lewis guns on Scarff ring in rear cockpit; external pylons with provision for 660 lb of bombs

Performance
Max. speed: 123 mph
Endurance: 5 hr 15 min
Service ceiling: 16,750 ft

History
The DH9A, or Ninak, as it was fondly called, was the workhorse of the inter-war years in India and the Middle East in the air policing role. While classified as a general-purpose aircraft in the 1920s overseas, the Ninak started life as a bomber during the First World War, and continued as such in light bomber squadrons at home. It was a refined version of the DH9 fitted with a 400 hp American Liberty engine, 3,000 of these having been ordered from the USA in 1917. Although only 1,050 engines reached the UK, there was a sufficient number to power the Ninaks constructed during the war. The larger engine meant bigger wings than those of the DH9. The fuselage was redesigned and a large frontal radiator fitted. By the time of the Armistice four squadrons in France had these aircraft, but since two of these squadrons received their Ninaks in November 1918 the aircraft saw little operational service. After the war the Ninak remained in service, nearly 2,500 being built by a dozen British manufacturers, but predominantly Westland and de Havilland. This aircraft began to be replaced in the late 1920s by the Wapiti, and it continued only in the training role until 1931.

Aircraft Specification Sheet (20): AIRCO DH 10/10A

Span: 65 ft 6 in.
Length: 39 ft 7 in.
Wing area: 837.0 sq. ft
Weights: Empty. 5,585 lb Max. take-off, 9,000 lb
Power plant: One 400 hp Packard Liberty
Armament/Bomb load: Single or twin 0.303 in. Lewis guns on Scarff ring mounting in nose and midship cockpits; external pylons with provision for a maximum bomb load of 900 lb

Performance
Max. speed: 112 mph
Endurance: 1 hr 45 min
Service ceiling: 16,500 ft

History
The initial contract for the DH10 was for four prototypes. The first of these had 230 hp BHP

pusher engines, two auxiliary wheels under the nose and cut-outs in the trailing edges of the wing to clear the arcs of the propellers. This aircraft first flew on 4 March 1918 with an all-up weight of 6,950 lb, but this would not have allowed for a very large bomb load, so although the performance was acceptable, the second prototype, C8659, was fitted with the 360 hp Rolls-Royce Eagle VIII. The third prototype, named Amiens III, had Liberty 12 tractor engines, which performed well and were used in the production aircraft, which had a modified nose from which the auxiliary wheels were absent. The first three contracts, for a total of 450 aircraft, were placed on 10 March, only six days after the flight of the first prototype, but by 31 October

only eight of these bombers had reached the Independent Bomber Force in France. There seems little doubt that, had the war continued, the DH10 would have been an effective addition to the Force, having a useful bomb load, good performance and defensive armament. The DH10 did, however, suffer from a problem not uncommon at that time in other types, that is with the use of windmill-driven fuel pumps. At speeds lower than 70 mph, the pumps were not effective enough to ensure adequate fuel to both engines, and one could fail on take-off, the worst possible moment! (Refer to the history of No. 60 Squadron in Chapter 4.) In the DH10A or Amiens IIIA this problem was eventually overcome, and at the same time the engines were lowered to sit on the lower wings instead of standing free supported by pylons. This resulted in a cleaner appearance and improved performance. Although the DH10As did not take an active part in the war, they were used experimentally afterwards. They also carried the mails from Hawkinge to Cologne for the British Army of Occupation as part of No. 120 Squadron, and some saw service on the North-West Frontier of India.

Aircraft Specification Sheet (21): SOPWITH DOLPHIN

Span: 32 ft 6 in.
Length: 22 ft 3 in.
Wing area: 263.25 sq. ft
Weights: Max. take-off, 2,003 lb
Power plant: One 200/220 hp Hispano-Suiza 8E water-cooled V type
Armament/Bomb load: Twin forward-firing Vickers guns enclosed under engine decking + twin 0.303 in. Lewis guns mounted on top-wing attachment

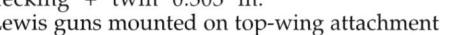

Performance
Max. speed: 128 mph at 10,000 ft
Endurance: 1 hr 45 min
Service ceiling: 21,000 ft

History
The Dolphin followed the Camel into service from the Sopwith stable, passing out from the experimental department on 23 May 1917. It was powered with a 200 hp Hispano-Suiza engine and had an upper wing set low on top of the fuselage to give the pilot the best possible view both up and down. But this unusual position in relation to the fuselage meant that the wings had to have a negative stagger to ensure the correct relationship between lift and the centre of gravity. The first official test report on the Dolphin was in June 1917, and probably relates to the prototype. The first Dolphin to go to France for operational trials left on the 13th of that month. Several modifications were put into effect before the Dolphin went into production, including a tapered engine cowling to replace the unstreamlined frontal radiator. This exposed some of the barrel of the Vickers guns and improved the pilot's view forward. There were also modifications to the fin and rudder, and two extra Lewis guns were fitted to fire upwards at an angle of 45 degrees. Knowing of the tendency for the DH5, which had negative wing stagger, to nose over following a bad landing, Dolphin pilots feared decapitation if it happened to them, sitting high as they did. Pylons made of steel tube were therefore fitted to the upper wings to protect the head in a somersault (see photograph). A total of

121 Dolphins were delivered by the end of 1917, including a night-flying version. In the event it did not prove dangerous and was pleasant to fly, but like the SE5a it suffered from engine trouble with the Hispano-Suiza engines. The Dolphins of Nos 19 and 79 squadrons participated in operations to counter the German offensive of March 1918, being employed on ground-attack duties. Like the SE5As they received battlefield modifications to suit the needs of individual pilots. The Lewis guns were rarely carried in combat, however, since the gun butts could swing and strike the pilot's face. On No. 87 Squadron the Lewis guns were fitted on the lower wings to fire outside the propeller arc. Dolphins saw brief service on home defence, but with a water-cooled engine, like the SE5A, take-off was delayed while the engines warmed up. They acquitted themselves well on the Western Front, but did not survive the squadron disbandments of 1919.

Aircraft Specification Sheet (22): FAIREY IIID LAND-PLANE

Span: 46 ft 1.25 in.
Length: 36 ft 0 in.
Wing area: 500.0 sq. ft
Weights: Empty, 3,430 lb
Loaded, 5050 lb
Power plant: One 450 hp Napier Lion II, V or VA
Armament/Bomb load: One Vickers gun forward + one Lewis gun aft. Light bomb load

Performance
Max. speed: 120 mph at sea level
Climb: 12.5 min to 10,000 ft
Range: 475 miles (normal); 550 miles max.
Service ceiling: 17,000 ft

History
The Fairey IIID was directly descended from the IIIC, which was first delivered to the RAF in November 1918 and some saw action with the RAF contingent fighting in support of the White Forces in Northern Russia in 1919. The IIID, being a floatplane and land-plane, could operate as a bomber, as a reconnaissance and artillery-spotting aircraft and for maritime reconnaissance. The floats and oleo legs could be changed to make the conversion. The original version flew in August 1920 powered by a 375 hp Rolls-Royce Eagle VIII engine, and the land-plane had a pneumatic oleo leg (undercarriage). Air Ministry Specification 38/22 was for the production contract, and N9451 was the first of 207 IIIDs to be produced, ending in 1925 with Serial No. S1108. The Eagle VIII engine was used in the earlier aircraft, the Napier Lion in the later ones. The Serial N9451 shows that the aircraft was destined for use with the Fleet Air Arm of the RAF; indeed, most twin-float IIIDs were so used, but it was a land-plane that made the history books. At Northolt in November 1925 was formed the first of the Cape Flights equipped with IIIDs. Led by Wing Commander C.W.H. Pulford, the Cape Flight left Heliopolis on 1 March 1926 bound for Cape Town. On the return journey, which went via Greece, Italy and France, the oleo legs were changed to floats at Aboukir for the final legs home. The flight arrived at Lee-on-Solent on 21 June 1926. The distance covered was 13,901 miles, and no mechanical failures were recorded. In the Far East the floatplanes operated from Singapore. No. 202 Squadron in Kalafrana, Malta, was the last to have IIIDs,

and they were replaced by Fairey IIIFs in July 1930, although the last IIID, S1107, did not leave Malta until March 1932.

Aircraft Specification Sheet (23): FAIREY IIID FLOATPLANE

Span: 46 ft 1.25 in.
Length: 37ft 0 in.
Wing area: 500.0 sq. ft
Weights: with Lion engine:
Empty, 3,990 lb
Max. take-off, 5,050 lb
Power plant: One 375 hp Rolls-Royce Eagle VII or Napier Lion IIB, V or VA
Armament/Bomb load: One fixed and one trainable machine-gun

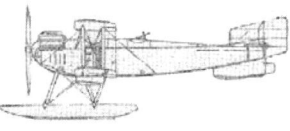

Performance
Max. speed: 106 mph at optimum altitude with Eagle engine
Climb: 6 min 40 sec to 5,000 ft
Range: 550 miles
Service ceiling: 16,500 ft

History
See No. 22

Aircraft Specification Sheet (24): FAIREY IIIF LAND-PLANE

Span: 45 ft 9 in.
Length: 36 ft 8⁵/₈ in.
Wing area: 438.5 sq. ft
Weights: Empty, 3,890 lb; Loaded, 6,041 lb
Power plant: One 455 hp Napier Lion XIA
Armament/Bomb load: One Vickers one Lewis gun; bomb load, 500 lb

Performance

Max. speed: 120 mph at 10,000 ft
Climb: 6 min to 5,000 ft
Range: 400 miles with 80 gal, 1,520 miles with 237 gal and no bombs

History

The prototype Fairey IIIF (N198) flew on 19 March 1926, and was built to Air Ministry Spec. 19/24. Like the IIID, it was both a floatplane and land-plane, but had a much more streamlined appearance. Chapter 4 discloses its first operational use with No. 47 Squadron in the Sudan, and then No. 8 Squadron in Aden and No. 14 Squadron in Palestine, in which case, as with the DH9A, the Bristol Fighter and the Wapiti, the term 'general-purpose' was applied to the land-plane. A three-seater reconnaissance version was built for the Fleet Air Arm. Production ended in 1932, with 560 having been built, of which 215 were of the MkIV variety in use with the RAF. Air Commodore C.R. Samson led four Fairey IIIFs from Cairo to the Cape in March 1927 (Serial Nos 1141–4). These flights continued in 1928 and 1929, and in the early 1930s IIIFs flew to West Africa and took part in a joint reinforcement exercise with the South African Air Force, when over 9,000 route miles were flown by five of these aircraft. The Fairey IIIF floatplanes equipped No. 202 Squadron, Kalafrana, Malta when they replaced the IIIDs, and remained there until the Scapa flying-boats came into service. In the United Kingdom the IIIF was used as both a bomber and a communications aircraft. In December 1927 No. 207 Squadron, Eastchurch, received IIIFs in place of the ageing DH9As. Eventually they were replaced by the Fairey Gordon, a derivative of the IIIF. Two Fairey IIIFs, Serial Nos J9061 and K1115, were part of the No. 24 Squadron at Hendon used for VIP communications when time was of the essence. HRH the Prince of Wales flew in one during the 1930 air-defence exercises, and was intercepted by Siskins. On another occasion Lord Londonderry flew to the 1932 Disarmament Conference in Geneva in one of these aircraft, which has been described as bad judgement, given that it was a military plane.

Aircraft Specification Sheet (25): FAIREY FAWN

Span: 49 ft 11 in.
Length: 32 ft 1in
Wing area: 550.0 sq. ft
Weights: Empty, 3,481 lb
Max take-off, 5,834 lb
Power plant: One 470 hp Napier Lion II in-line piston

Armament/Bomb load: One fixed and two trainable 0.303in machine-guns and up to 460 lb of bombs

Performance

Max. speed: 114 mph at sea level
Climb: to 10,000 ft in 17 min 30 sec
Range: 650 miles
Service ceiling: 13,850 ft

History

This rather unattractive aircraft was built to Air Ministry Specification 5/21, which called for a light day-bomber. At a time when most RAF squadrons were still flying aircraft of First World War vintage, the Fawn was the first light bomber built in peacetime to reach squadron service. It was conceived as an Army-cooperation aircraft, and the first prototype flew in March 1923. This had a short fuselage like the Pintail amphibian from which it had been developed, but longitudinal stability was improved by lengthening the fuselage in the second and third prototypes, J6908 and 6909, and this feature appeared in all production aircraft built to Air Ministry Specification 20/23. The Fawn MkIII built to Specification 1/25 was given a more powerful 468 hp Lion V engine. Production of the Fawns ended in 1926 when the Fawn was replaced by the Horsley. It therefore had a very short service life, entering service in April 1924 with the small home-based bomber force to replace the DH9As, and equipped Nos 11, 12 and 100 Squadrons. The Fawn ended its days with the Auxiliaries from 1926 to 1929, equipping Nos 503 and 602 Squadrons.

Aircraft Specification Sheet (26): FELIXSTOWE F2A

Span: 95 ft 7.5 in.
Length: 46 ft 3 in.
Wing area: 1,133 sq. ft
Weights: Empty, 7,549 lb
Loaded, 10,978 lb
Power plant: Two 345 hp Rolls-Royce Eagle VIIIs

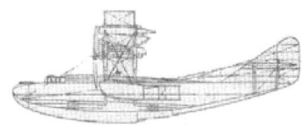

Armament/Bomb load: From four to seven free-mounted Lewis machine-guns – in bow, waist positions, rear cockpit and above pilot's cockpit + two 230 lb bombs in racks beneath wings.

Performance

Max. speed 95.5 mph at 2,000 ft; 80.5 mph at 10,000 ft
Climb: 3 min 50 sec to 2,000 ft; 39 min 30 sec to 10,000 ft
Endurance: (Normal) 6 hours
Service ceiling: 9,600 ft

History

Of critical importance to the performance of a flying-boat is the shape and seaworthiness of its hull. Following his success with the F1, Squadron Commander Porte was developing larger hulls to combine seaworthiness of a Porte hull with the flying surfaces of the 'Large America' Curtiss H12 flying-boats (See No. 14). The result was to be the Felixstowe F2A. The method of construction was such that firms without any previous knowledge of boat-building could undertake the work, an asset in wartime. The first F2As were delivered in late 1917, and by March the following year 160 were on order. The numbers built would have been greater had contracts not been issued for the F3, which some regarded as inferior to the F2A. Although intended originally for operation in sheltered harbours, the F2A proved seaworthy, but there were problems with the fuel system, from blocked fuel lines and the windmill-driven fuel pumps. The boats were operated differently from base to base. At some the crews carried extra fuel to extend the endurance, up to nine and a half hours in some cases. At others the cabin was removed to provide an open cockpit for improved speed and observation, and to aid recovery in the event of ditching the aircraft were painted in bright diagonal and zig-zag patterns. In tracking U-boats the 'spider's web' patrol system was devised from April 1917, centred on the North Hinder light vessel, when one flying-boat could cover a quarter of the whole web in about three hours. But this remarkable aircraft was not only successful against U-boats: one successfully attacked Zeppelin L62 over Heligoland, and on 4 June 1918 a formation of F2As won a 'dog fight' over the enemy coast against a formation of fourteen enemy seaplanes. Their range could be further extended by towing them on lighters nearer the scene of action in the fashion of the Short 320 attack from Otranto (See No. 48). The F2A remained in service right up to the time of the Armistice, but did not survive the disbandment of the parent squadrons in 1919.

Aircraft Specification Sheet (27): FELIXSTOWE F3

Span: 102 ft 0 in.
Length: 49 ft 2 in.
Wing area: 1,432 sq. ft
Weights: Empty, 7,958 lb
Loaded, 12,235 lb
Power plant: Two 375 hp Rolls-Royce Eagle VIIIs
Armament/Bomb load:
Four Lewis guns on free-mountings and four 230 lb bombs in racks beneath the wings

Performance
Max. speed: 91 mph at 2,000 ft; 86 mph at 6,500 ft
Climb: 5.25 min to 2,000 ft; 24 min to 6,500 ft
Endurance: 6 hr
Service ceiling: 8,000 ft

History
Opinion has it that the F3 was inferior to the F2A. Admittedly it could carry twice as many bombs, but it was slower and less manoeuvrable, and could not, as the F2A had done, take on enemy seaplane fighters in combat. One compensating factor was its longer range, and it was useful on anti-submarine patrol work both at home and overseas. The F2A served only at home, but the F3s were to be found in the Mediterranean, and in October 1918 they accompanied a naval attack on Durazzo in Albania. So extensive was the use of this aircraft that they were manufactured in the naval dockyards in Malta. The prototype F3 (N64) differed from production aircraft in having twin 320 hp Sunbeam Cossack engines instead of the Rolls-Royce Eagles. Its maiden flight was made in February 1917, and by March 1918 production contracts had reached 263 in number. When the First World War ended, only about one hundred had been completed in the UK and eighteen had been built in the Maltese dockyards. Some F3s were completed as F5s and were delivered after the war.

Aircraft Specification Sheet (28): FELIXSTOWE F5

Span: 103 ft 8 in.
Length: 49 ft 3 in.
Wing area: 1,409.0 sq. ft
Weights: Empty, 9,100 lb
Loaded, 12,682 lb
Power plant: Two 375 hp Rolls-Royce Eagle VIIIs

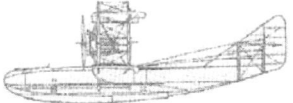

Armament/Bomb load:
One Lewis gun in bow + three midships; bomb load, 920 lb

Performance
Max. speed: 88 mph at 2,000 ft
Climb: 30 min to 6,500 ft
Endurance: 7 hr
Service ceiling: 6,800 ft

History
The Felixstowe F5 was the standard flying-boat in service with the RAF in the immediate post-war years, and was too late for combat service during the First World War. The prototype N90 passed through its acceptance tests in May 1918, was 10 mph faster than the F3 and had a wing structure of greater span. Other improvements included a new type of wing section and rectangular horn-balanced ailerons on the upper wings. In production the F5 was modified to accept many F3 components, which increased its loaded weight and thus impaired its performance, to make it inferior to the F3. The prototype was built at Felixstowe, where Lieutenant-Commander John Porte, the designer, had done so much work to improve the design of operational flying-boats during the First World War. The production of F5s was contracted out to Short Brothers on the Medway, the Phoenix Dynamo Company of Bradford, Boulton and Paul at Norwich, which just built the hulls, the Aircraft Manufacturing Company of Hendon and S.E. Saunders of the Isle of Wight. Based at Felixstowe, then Calshot, the F5s' tasks were naval cooperation with the Portsmouth Submarine Flotilla at Portland and exercises with the Atlantic Fleet. In July 1919 an F5, Serial No. N4044, made a tour of Scandinavia, a flight of 2,450 miles, in 27 days. In December 1924 an F5, N177, was turned out from Short Brothers with a metal hull, the first military flying-boat to depart from the practice of building hulls in wood. By then the F5 had been retired from RAF service.

Aircraft Specification Sheet (29): ROYAL AIRCRAFT FACTORY FE2B/C/D

Span: 47 ft 9 in.
Length: 32 ft 3 in.
Wing area: 494.0 sq. ft
Weights: Empty, 1,993 lb
Loaded, 2,967 lb

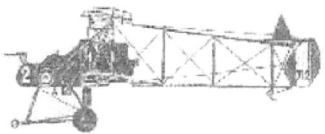

Power plant: One 120 hp Beardmore water-cooled in-line
Armament/Bomb load: A single Lewis gun mounted on a bracket on front of observer's cockpit

Performance
Max. speed: 80.5 mph at sea level
Endurance: 2 hr 30 min
Service ceiling: 9,000 ft

History
The FE2D was a development of the proved FE series built by the Royal Aircraft Factory. The FE2B powered with the 120 hp and 160 hp Beardmore engines gave excellent service, but the 160 hp engines had not proved as reliable as the 120 hp ones, and many forced landings had resulted. The FE series proved also to be excellent aircraft for night flying, and the FE2C was modified by the Royal Aircraft Factory for this purpose. But there was a need for increased performance in the air, and a 250 hp Rolls-Royce engine was fitted to the basic airframe to become the FE2D. On the prototype FE2D the exhausts ran forward and upwards in the time-honoured fashion of R A/C Factory aircraft. On the production models these exhaust stacks were removed and a smaller radiator fitted (see lower photograph). The first FE2D to go to France was flown by a pilot who lost his way in poor visibility and landed, by accident, on a German aerodrome at Lille on 30 June 1916. No. 20 Squadron RFC was the first unit to receive FE2Ds, to be followed by Nos 25 and 57 Squadrons, but of course the element of surprise was lost, since the enemy knew of the new aircraft's capabilities. With the additional power of its 250 hp engine, the FE2D could carry extra guns, including a fixed forward-firing Lewis gun to be fired by the pilot. Flown by aggressive crews, these aircraft gave a good account of themselves in battle and on home-defence squadrons. They did not long survive the First World War. As a matter of interest, the cost to the taxpayer of an FE2D was: airframe £1,540 0s 0d; the engine £1,430 0s 0d.

Aircraft Specification Sheet (30): FAIREY FOX

Span: 37 ft 8 in.
Length: 28 ft 3 in.
Wing area: 324.5 sq. ft
Weights: Empty, 2,609 lb
Loaded, 4170 lb
Power plant: One 240 hp
Curtiss D-12 Felix
Armament/Bomb load:
One Vickers gun forward
+ one Lewis gun aft;
bomb load: 460 lb

Performance
Max. speed: 156.6 mph at sea level; 150 mph at 10,000 ft
Climb: 1.8 min to 2,000 ft, 39.75 min to 19,000 ft
Range: 500 miles at 130 mph
Service ceiling: 19,3000 ft

History
The original Fox prototype flew on 3 January 1925, and in August that year a demonstration in front of Air Chief Marshal Trenchard so impressed the Chief of the Air Staff that he promptly ordered a squadron of Foxes. This was to be No. 12 Squadron, which received the aircraft to replace its Fawns. But in spite of this aircraft's superb performance, financial economies meant that only twenty-eight were built for the RAF. The Fox was 50 mph faster than the Fawns and could outpace the fighters of the day. In the Air Defence Exercises of 1928 the Fox evaded all fighter defences. The secret of the aircraft's success was its clean aerodynamic shape. With the radiators being mounted in the wings, the bulky front end of aircraft like the Fawn and DH9A was replaced by a streamlined nose, and the Scarff ring was replaced by a high-speed mounting to reduce drag. With the Curtiss D12 engine to power the Fox, a top speed of 156 mph was achievable. When the Rolls-Royce Kestrel IIA replaced the Curtiss engine the aircraft was designated IA. The first production Fox flew on 10 December 1925, built to Air Ministry Specification 21/25, and the Fox IA to Specification 1/27. The MkII was entered for the competition for a new light bomber to Specification 12/26, but Fairey lost to Hawker with that company's new Hart light bomber. Although the Fox had a short life on only one squadron, Fairey showed that a streamlined appearance could be achieved with a water-cooled engine, and much impetus was given to British designers of the period.

Aircraft Specification Sheet (31): GLOSTER GAMECOCK

Span: 29 ft 5 in.
Length: 19 ft 8 in.
Wing area: 264.0 sq. ft
Weights: Empty, 1,930 lb
Loaded, 2,863 lb
Power plant: One 645 hp
Bristol Mercury VIS 2
Armament/Bomb load:
Two synchronized Vickers
on sides of fuselage

Performance
Max. speed: 155 mph at 5,000 ft; 145 mph at 10,000 ft
Climb rate: 7.6 min to 10,000 ft; 27 min to 20,000 ft
Service ceiling: 22,000 ft

History
The first prototype Gamecock, J7497, flew in February 1925 and was built to Air Ministry Specification 37/23. It was to be the last biplane fighter built of wood, and was the sister aircraft to the Gloster Grebe, very alike in appearance but powered by a Jupiter IV engine. The rounded fuselage had blast channels for the side-mounted guns and it had new ailerons. Ninety Gamecock Is were built for the RAF to Air Ministry Specification 18/25. In 1926 the Gamecock entered squadron service with No. 43 Squadron at Henlow, giving the squadron its nickname 'Fighting Cocks', which later appeared as a device on the squadron's badge. No. 23 Squadron also received these aircraft, which it kept until 1931, when they were replaced by Bulldogs. In spite of its aerobatic qualities the Gamecock, like the Grebe, suffered from wing-flutter and had to be fitted with Vee struts outboard of the interplane struts. Pilots were warned not to attempt right-hand spins, even though the fighter did survive a 275 mph dive as well as twenty-two spins. During the 1931 RAF Display at Hendon, Flight Lieutenant M.M. Day and Flying Officer D.S. Bader gave a display of individual aerobatics. The Gamecock was declared obsolete in March 1933.

Aircraft Specification Sheet (32): GLOSTER GREBE II

Span: 29 ft 4 in.
Length: 20 ft 3 in.
Wing area: 254 sq. ft
Weights: Empty, 1,720 lb
Loaded, 2,624 lb
Power plant: One 400 hp
Armstrong Siddeley Jaguar IV
Armament/Bomb load: Twin synchronized Vickers on nose decking

Performance
Max. speed: 152 mph at sea level; 145 mph at 10,000 ft
Climb rate: 23 min to 20,000 ft
Endurance: 2 hr 45 min
Service ceiling: 23,000 ft

History
Three Grebe prototypes were built, and one, J6969, was displayed at the Hendon RAF Display in June 1923, powered by a 325 hp Jaguar III engine, and production went ahead in August when Gloster's chief test pilot, Larry Carter, flew J7283, the first production Grebe II. The high-lift upper wing and medium-lift lower wing had been tested on the Grouse I and II aircraft, and the production models were fitted with Jaguar IV engines. One hundred and nine of the MkII Grebes were built for the RAF, together with twenty-one two-seater trainers, which were delivered in 1925. A number of the latter, named the Grebe IIIDC, was used by No. 25 Squadron to hone the skills of its pilots in formation aerobatics. Grebe IIIDC Serial No. J7520 won the 1929 King's Cup Air Race, flown by Flight Lieutenant R.L.R. Atcherley. The Grebe fighter and the Siskin were the first postwar fighters to equip squadrons after the First World War, and No. 25 Squadron was the first to be equipped with Grebes. At the Hendon Display the squadron performed demonstrations of air drill and formation aerobatics, and Squadron Leader A.H. Peck used W/T to lead the performance. The Grebe, like the Gamecock, suffered from wing-flutter, which resulted in a number of fatal accidents. The Vee struts, like those fitted to the Gamecock, can be seen in the photograph. Experiments carried out with the Grebe included the launching of J7385 and J7400 from Airship R33 at 2,000 feet in 1926. Then a terminal dive of 240 mph was survived. In May 1929 No. 25 Squadron's Grebes were replaced by Siskins.

Aircraft Specification Sheet (33): HANDLEY PAGE HINAIDI

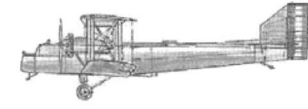

Span: 75 ft 0 in.
Length: 59 ft 2 in.
Wing area: 1,471.0 sq. ft
Weights: Empty, 5,040 lb
Loaded 14,500 lb
Power plant: Two 450 hp Bristol Jupiter VIIIs
Armament/Bomb load: Three Lewis guns in nose, midships and ventral positions; bomb load: 1,568 lb

Performance
Max. speed: 122.5 mph at sea level; 115 mph at 10,000 ft
Cruising Speed: 75 mph
Initial climb rate: 495 ft/min; 16 min to 6,560 ft with 1,448 lb bombs
Range: 850 miles
Service ceiling: 14,900 ft

History
The Handley Page Hinaidi was a heavy night-bomber derived from the Hyderabad, the two aircraft showing great resemblance; indeed, the prototype Hinaidi, J7745, was a converted Hyderabad and made its maiden flight on 26 March 1927. Even the first eleven MkI Hinaidis were Hyderabad conversions. The two features that distinguished the two aircraft were that the Bristol Jupiter radials replaced the Lion engines and the Hinaidi was built from metal, not wood. Thus, with better performance the Hinaidi could carry a greater bomb load. Only one new-build MkI was produced by Handley Page, and this featured a $2^1/2$ per cent sweep-back of the outer wing panels. It was not until two years later that the first all-metal MkII prototype was flown, on 8 February 1929, and this had a more pronounced wing sweep-back to counter a tendency to nose heaviness. In October 1929 No. 99 Squadron at Upper Heyford received the first Hinaidis, and these remained in service for four years until replaced by the Heyford, but the former continued to fly with the Special Reserve until 1935. In February 1928 Air Ministry Specification C20/27 called for a troop-carrier, and Handley Page responded with the Chitral, later to be named the Clive (both names have Indian connotations). The Clive was a Hinaidi development and could carry twenty-three troops. Built in wood, then in metal, the Clive served in India with the Heavy Transport Flight based at Lahore.

Aircraft Specification Sheet: (34): HAWKER HORSLEY

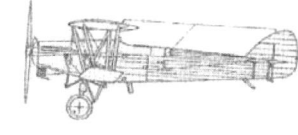

Span: 56 ft 5.75 in.
Length: 38 ft 10 in.
Wing area: 693.0 sq. ft
Weights: Empty, 4,760 lb
Take-off, 7,800 lb
Power plant: One 665 hp Rolls-Royce Condor IIIA in-line piston
Armament/Bomb load: Two 0.303in. machine-guns, one fixed and one trainable, and up to 1,500 lb of bombs or one 18 in. torpedo

Performance
Max. speed: 125 mph at 6,000 ft
Climb: to 15,000 ft in 23 min
Endurance: 10 hr 0 min
Service ceiling: 14,000 ft

History
The Hawker Horsley day-bomber was designed to Air Ministry Specification 26/23. The prototype J7511 flew in 1925 and was named after T.O.M. Sopwith's residence at East Horsley, Surrey. Production began in July 1926 and ended in November 1931, during which time 133 were built for the RAF. The MkI and MkII versions were day-bombers,

and a torpedo-bomber version was built to Air Ministry Specification 24/25, first flown in May 1927. Forty-eight torpedo-bombers in all were built. Early production models were built in wood, then wood/metal and finally all-metal. In the day-bombing role the Horsley replaced the Fawns of No. 100 Squadron in August 1926, followed by No. 11 Squadron in January 1927. The torpedo-bomber version went to the newly re-formed No. 36 Squadron at Donibristle, Scotland in October 1928, and in 1930 the squadron, with its all-metal Horsleys, became the first land-based torpedo squadron to be based overseas when it moved to Singapore. The Horsley is also remembered for a long-haul flight when Flight Lieutenant C.R. Carr, with Flight Lieutenant L.E.M. Gillman as his navigator, left Cranwell in Serial No. J.8607 for a non-stop flight to India, only to be forced down in the Persian Gulf after completing 3,420 miles in 34$\frac{1}{2}$ hours Another attempt made by Flight Lieutenant Carr is referred to in the section dealing with Martlesham Heath in Chapter 3, when, accompanied by Flight Lieutenant P.H. Hackworth in Horsley II Serial J8608, the flight had to be aborted because of an oil leak, and Carr had to land at Martlesham with 1,000 gallons of fuel on board. The Horsley ceased to be employed as a bomber in March 1930 when Hawker Harts replaced it on No. 33 Squadron, Eastchurch. The torpedo-bombers of Nos 100 and 36 Squadrons were phased out in 1932 and 1935 respectively. No. 504 (County of Nottingham) Special Reserve Squadron at Hucknall retained its Horsleys until March 1934, and they saw out their days as target-towing aircraft at Kai Tak, Hong Kong, until February 1937.

Aircraft Specification Sheet (35): HP 0/400

Span: 100 ft 0 in.
Length: 62 ft 10.25 in.
Wing area: 1,648.0 sq. ft
Weights: Take-off 13,360 lb
Power plant: Two 360 hp Rolls-Royce Eagle VIII water-cooled, V types
Armament/Bomb load: Twin 0.303 in. Lewis guns on flexible mount in nose cockpit; one Lewis gun on flexible mount in ventral and dorsal positions; bomb load in the internal bomb bay either eight 250 lb bombs or sixteen 112 lb bombs

Performance
Max. speed:97.5 mph at sea level
Endurance: 8 hr
Service ceiling: 8,500 ft

History
The prototype HP 0/400 (Serial 3138) was a converted 0/100 airframe, for the 0/400 was a development of the latter.

The main difference was that the fuel tanks of the 0/400 were transferred from the engine nacelles to the fuselage,

giving the aircraft much shorter nacelles. Successively Eagle IV, VII and VIII engines, with greater power, were fitted, and some 0/400s had 260 hp Fiat or 275 hp Sunbeam Maori engines. Nearly 800 were ordered during the First World War, of which about 550 were built in the UK and 107 were assembled from components built in the USA, these being powered by Liberty engines. In April 1917 the HP 0/100s were transferred to night operations, and the 0/400 became operational initially as a day-bomber in France, until it too was employed on night operations. These aircraft figured prominently in the operations of the strategic Independent Bomber Force, which struck industrial and military targets removed from the battlefield. At the end of hostilities 258 HP 0/400s were on charge to the RAF, by which time they were carrying 1,650 lb bombs. In the spring of 1918 two of these aircraft were converted as passenger carriers and conveyed pilots to and from France. The 0/400 remained in service until 1920 as a transport and communications aircraft, and officials going to and from the Paris Peace Conference in 1919 were conveyed in them. The aircraft pictured (with wings folded) belonged to No. 1(Communications) Squadron at Hendon in 1919, and was used for this purpose.

Aircraft Specification Sheet (36): HP V/1500

Span: 126 ft 0 in.
Length: 62 ft 10.25 in.
Wing area: 3,000 sq. ft
Weights: Take-off 30,000 lb
Power plant: Four 375 hp Rolls-Royce Eagle VIII, water-cooled, V types
Armament/Bomb load: Single or twin-yoked Lewis guns in nose, midships and tail; bomb load, 7,500 lb

Performance
Max. speed: 90.5 mph at 6,000 ft
Endurance: 6 hr
Service ceiling: 11,000 ft

History
Since the First World War was expected to drag on into 1919, the War Office wanted a bomber that could help bring about a decisive outcome by permitting the bombing of Berlin from UK bases. The first contract for a long-range four-engined bomber with the necessary range and load-carrying capacity was for twenty HP V/1500s dated 27 January 1918, the aircraft being ordered off the drawing board. The first prototype was flown from Cricklewood in May 1918 by Captain Busby, who found that the control responses were not satisfactory. After some modifications to the ailerons and rudder, directional control was still unsatisfactory and the fin area was increased. Ultimately a drastically revised tail unit was fitted and modifications were made to the engines and radiators. Sadly Captain Busby and all but one of those aboard the prototype, which crashed in June, were killed when the aircraft burned out. This delayed the introduction of the V/1500 into service, and a second machine was not ready until October. Although virtually the entire Independent Bomber Force, under Major-General Trenchard's command, was based in France, No. 27 Group, which was forming in September 1918, was to be based at Bircham Newton. The first unit to be mobilized was No. 166

Squadron, manned by pilots and observers from night-bombing FE2B squadrons, but of a total of 255 aircraft that had been ordered only three V/1500s were ready for operations by the time of the Armistice. By late 1918 the RAF had a 3,300 lb bomb for use with this aircraft, but there was no place for the V/1500 in the vastly scaled-down peacetime air force, so one can only guess how successful a bomber it might have been. One V/1500 was used after the war to attack Kabul when the Afghan war broke out, but its use as an airliner was ruled out owing to the expense of operating it. This is a pity given its success in several notable long-distance flights.

Aircraft Specification Sheet (37): HANDLEY PAGE HYDERABAD

Span: 75 ft 0 in.
Length: 59 ft 2 in.
Wing area: 1,471.0 sq. ft
Weights: Empty, 8,910 lb
Loaded, 13,590 lb
Power plant: Two 450 hp Napier Lion IIs or 500 hp Lion Vs
Armament/Bomb load: Three Lewis guns in nose, midships and ventral positions; bomb load, 1,100 lb

Performance
Max. speed: 109 mph at sea level
Initial climb rate: 495 ft/min climb to 6,500 ft in 16 min
Range: 500 miles
Service ceiling: 14,000 ft

History
The Handley Page Hyderabad was built as a heavy night-bomber and developed from the W8 commercial airliner. The prototype J6994 made its first flight in October 1923, built to Air Ministry Specification 31/22. The first production model, J7738, was flown in December 1925, and was the last heavy bomber of the RAF to be built of wood. Only one Hyderabad, J8813, was built to incorporate the HP leading-edge wing-slats. The first of these aircraft went to No. 99 Squadron at Bircham Newton in December 1925 to replace the single-engined Avro Aldershots, which had been in service for only a year. Air Ministry policy had changed to the effect that heavy bombers should not in future have to rely on a single engine. If a forced landing was made, a single-engined bomber would probably have to be dismantled unless a very long take-off run was possible. No. 10 Squadron at Upper Heyford was next to receive Hyderabads, but not until January 1928. Two cadre squadrons of the Special Reserve were selected in 1929 for re-equipment with these aircraft. These were No. 503 Squadron at Waddington, which had Fairey Fawns, and No. 502 Squadron at Aldergrove, Northern Ireland, which had Vickers Vimys. In all, forty-four Hyderabads were built for the RAF.

Aircraft Specification Sheet (38): BLACKBURN KANGAROO

Span: 74 ft 10? in.
Length: 46 ft 0 in.
Wing area: 880.0 sq. ft
Weights: Take-off, 8,017 lb

Power plant: Two 255 hp Rolls-Royce Falcon II water-cooled, V types
Armament/Bomb load: Two Lewis guns, one at the front and one at the rear; bomb load, four 230 lb bombs or smaller bombs of an equivalent weight

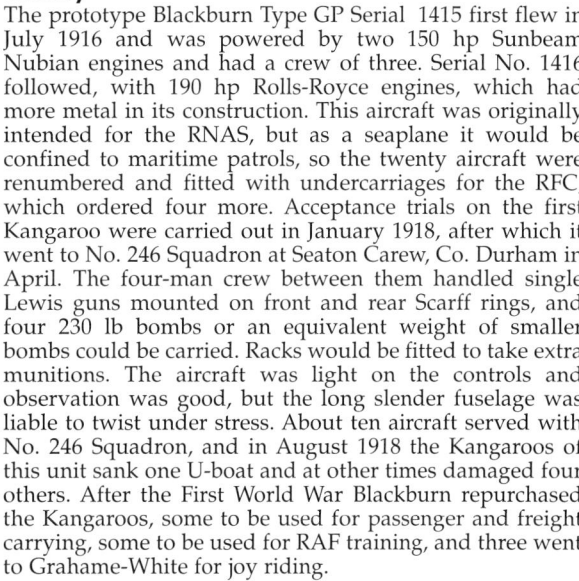

Performance
Max. speed: 100 mph at sea level
Endurance: 8hr 0 min
Service ceiling: 10,500 ft

History
The prototype Blackburn Type GP Serial 1415 first flew in July 1916 and was powered by two 150 hp Sunbeam Nubian engines and had a crew of three. Serial No. 1416 followed, with 190 hp Rolls-Royce engines, which had more metal in its construction. This aircraft was originally intended for the RNAS, but as a seaplane it would be confined to maritime patrols, so the twenty aircraft were renumbered and fitted with undercarriages for the RFC, which ordered four more. Acceptance trials on the first Kangaroo were carried out in January 1918, after which it went to No. 246 Squadron at Seaton Carew, Co. Durham in April. The four-man crew between them handled single Lewis guns mounted on front and rear Scarff rings, and four 230 lb bombs or an equivalent weight of smaller bombs could be carried. Racks would be fitted to take extra munitions. The aircraft was light on the controls and observation was good, but the long slender fuselage was liable to twist under stress. About ten aircraft served with No. 246 Squadron, and in August 1918 the Kangaroos of this unit sank one U-boat and at other times damaged four others. After the First World War Blackburn repurchased the Kangaroos, some to be used for passenger and freight carrying, some to be used for RAF training, and three went to Grahame-White for joy riding.

Aircraft Specification Sheet (39): MARTINSYDE G100

Span: 38 ft 0 in.
Length: 26 ft
Wing area: 410.0 sq. ft
Weights: Take off, 2,424 lb
Power plant: One 120 hp Beardmore, water-cooled in-line
Armament/Bomb load: One Lewis gun mounted on top of the wing to fire forward and one to the left and behind the pilot. When used in the ground-attack role it could carry one 230 lb or two 112 lb bombs

Performance
Max. speed: 95 mph at 6,500 ft
Endurance: 5 hr 30 min
Service ceiling: 14,000 ft

History

The Martinsyde G100, also known as the Elephant, for it was a large single-seater, was designed by A.A. Fletcher in mid-1915. The prototype, Serial No. 4735, was powered by a 120 hp Austro-Daimler engine. When the aircraft was fitted with a Beardmore engine in the late autumn of 1915, a less bulky cowling was possible. Delivery to the RFC began in 1916 to serve as escorts for reconnaissance aircraft in France, Palestine and Mesopotamia. Only No. 27 Squadron in France was equipped solely with Elephants. The main armament was a Lewis gun mounted on the top of the wing to fire at an angle over the propeller, but a second Lewis gun could be mounted on a bracket behind the pilot's left shoulder, but this was very difficult for the pilot to use and was usually omitted. It was not a good fighter, being too heavy and unresponsive, but as a bomber and ground-attack aircraft it was well suited, for it had good lift in its broad wings and it was stable in the air. The G100 could carry one 230 lb bomb or two 112 lb bombs This capacity was slightly increased in the G102, which had a 160 hp Beardmore engine. One hundred G100s and 170 G102s were built to equip both operational and training units.

Aircraft Specification Sheet (40): NIEUPORT 17,23 & 24

Span: 26 ft 11$^5/_8$ in.
Length: 18 ft 10 in.
Wing area: 158.8 sq. ft
Weights: Take-off, 1,246 lb
Power plant: One 110 hp Le Rhône 9 J rotary
Armament/Bomb load: See below

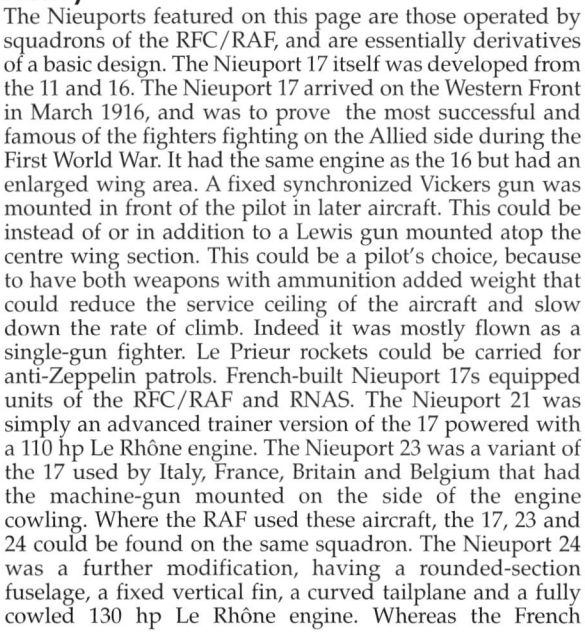

Performance

Max. speed: 110 mph at 6,562 ft
Endurance: 2 hr
Service ceiling: 17,388 ft

History

The Nieuports featured on this page are those operated by squadrons of the RFC/RAF, and are essentially derivatives of a basic design. The Nieuport 17 itself was developed from the 11 and 16. The Nieuport 17 arrived on the Western Front in March 1916, and was to prove the most successful and famous of the fighters fighting on the Allied side during the First World War. It had the same engine as the 16 but had an enlarged wing area. A fixed synchronized Vickers gun was mounted in front of the pilot in later aircraft. This could be instead of or in addition to a Lewis gun mounted atop the centre wing section. This could be a pilot's choice, because to have both weapons with ammunition added weight that could reduce the service ceiling of the aircraft and slow down the rate of climb. Indeed it was mostly flown as a single-gun fighter. Le Prieur rockets could be carried for anti-Zeppelin patrols. French-built Nieuport 17s equipped units of the RFC/RAF and RNAS. The Nieuport 21 was simply an advanced trainer version of the 17 powered with a 110 hp Le Rhône engine. The Nieuport 23 was a variant of the 17 used by Italy, France, Britain and Belgium that had the machine-gun mounted on the side of the engine cowling. Where the RAF used these aircraft, the 17, 23 and 24 could be found on the same squadron. The Nieuport 24 was a further modification, having a rounded-section fuselage, a fixed vertical fin, a curved tailplane and a fully cowled 130 hp Le Rhône engine. Whereas the French

preferred a fixed, synchronized, Vickers gun, British pilots seemed to prefer a non-synchronized Lewis gun mounted atop the wing centre section. These aircraft were bought by America, seventy-five being delivered to the American Expeditionary Force, and they were built by Macchi of Italy under licence.

Aircraft Specification Sheet (41): NIEUPORT NIGHTJAR

Span: 28 ft 0 in.
Length: 19 ft 2 in.
Wing area: 270.0 sq. ft
Weights: Loaded, 2,165 lb
Power plant: One 230 hp Bentley BR2
Armament/Bomb load: Two fixed synchronized Vickers machine-guns

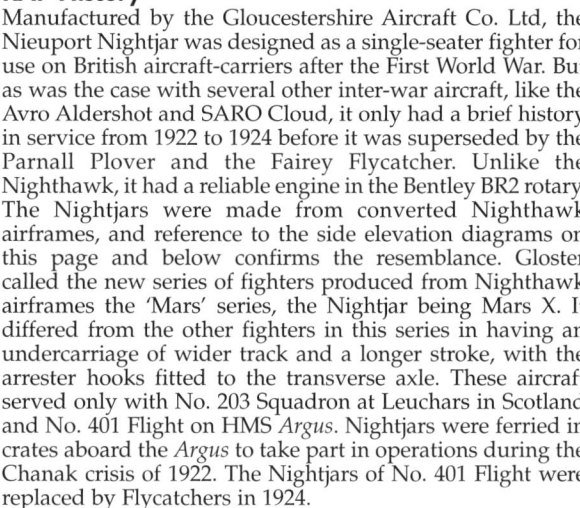

Performance

Max. speed: 120 mph at sea level; 110 mph at 15,000 ft
Endurance: 2 hours at 3,000 ft
Service ceiling: 15,000 ft

RAF History

Manufactured by the Gloucestershire Aircraft Co. Ltd, the Nieuport Nightjar was designed as a single-seater fighter for use on British aircraft-carriers after the First World War. But as was the case with several other inter-war aircraft, like the Avro Aldershot and SARO Cloud, it only had a brief history in service from 1922 to 1924 before it was superseded by the Parnall Plover and the Fairey Flycatcher. Unlike the Nighthawk, it had a reliable engine in the Bentley BR2 rotary. The Nightjars were made from converted Nighthawk airframes, and reference to the side elevation diagrams on this page and below confirms the resemblance. Gloster called the new series of fighters produced from Nighthawk airframes the 'Mars' series, the Nightjar being Mars X. It differed from the other fighters in this series in having an undercarriage of wider track and a longer stroke, with the arrester hooks fitted to the transverse axle. These aircraft served only with No. 203 Squadron at Leuchars in Scotland and No. 401 Flight on HMS *Argus*. Nightjars were ferried in crates aboard the *Argus* to take part in operations during the Chanak crisis of 1922. The Nightjars of No. 401 Flight were replaced by Flycatchers in 1924.

Aircraft Specification Sheet (42): NIEUPORT NIGHTHAWK

Span: 28 ft 0 in.
Length: 18 ft 6 in.
Wing area: 276.0 sq. ft
Weight: Empty, 1,500 lb; Loaded, 2,218 lb
Power plant: 320 hp Dragonfly I
Armament/Bomb load: Two fixed forward-firing Vickers machine-guns

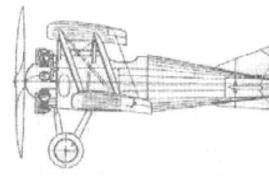

Performance

Max. speed: 140 mph at 6,500 ft; 138.5 mph at 10,000 ft

Climb: 3 min to 5,000 ft; 7 min 10 sec to 10,000 ft
Endurance: 3 hr
Service ceiling: 24,500 ft

History

In order to speed up production the Nighthawk incorporated parts from the SE5A fighter. It was highly manoeuvrable, and given its speed and climb, it would have been a good fighter had it not been for the unreliability of its Dragonfly engine. The Air Board had been persuaded to use this engine instead of the Bentley BR2, which had been ordered in quantity. The engine designer claimed that the Dragonfly would deliver 340 hp for a weight little over 600 lb. And since the designer's previous Wasp engine had been successful he pressed his new design. In this he was successful, and 11,050 Dragonflies were ordered from thirteen contractors, the programme aiming to supply 4,135 of these engines by the end of June 1919. In the event it proved to be heavier and gave less power than expected. But more seriously it suffered from considerable vibration, resulting in mechanical failure in a matter of hours. The problem was described as synchronous torsional vibration and dynamic imbalance. The failure of the ABC Dragonfly programme brought about the collapse of the Nighthawk production programme, and the Armistice intervened before the engine could be taken into service. For the few Nighthawks that survived the war the Bristol Jupiter engine could be used to replace the Dragonfly. The aircraft did see service in India, and No. 1 Squadron had them in addition to its Snipes before they were declared obsolete and withdrawn in the spring 1923. There were airframes in store to be converted into Nightjars (see No. 41), and the Gloucestershire Aircraft Co., which took over the Nieuport designs in 1920, converted several Nighthawk airframes into various Gloster 'Mars' types.

Aircraft Specification Sheet (43): PARNALL PANTHER

Span: 29 ft 6 in.
Length: 24 ft 11 in.
Wing area: 336.0 sq. ft
Weights: Empty, 1,328 lb
Loaded, 2,595 lb
Power plant: One 230 hp Bentley BR2

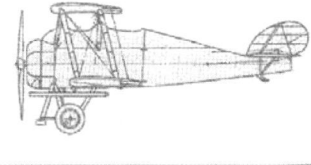

Armament/Bomb load: One trainable Lewis gun in rear cockpit and one fixed forward-firing Vickers gun mounted on port side

Performance

Max. speed: 108.5 mph at 6,500 ft; 103 mph at 10,000 ft
Climb: 2 min 20 sec to 2,000 ft; 9 min 20 sec to 6,500 ft; 17 min 5 sec to 10,000 ft
Endurance: 4.25 hr at 10,000 ft
Service ceiling: 14,500 ft
Admiralty Specifications: N2A

History

The Parnall Panther was the brainchild of Mr Harold Bolas, who had been released from the Air department of the Admiralty to become chief designer of Parnall & Sons. The specification called for a two-seater, deck-landing reconnaissance aircraft. The first prototype, N91, flew in 1917,

to be followed by five more, N92 to N96. The fuselage folded sideways aft of the cockpits to conserve space on board the carrier. The high cockpits gave the pilot an excellent forward view even if he did have to reach his seat via a hole in the upper wing (see photo above). The aircraft also carried flotation bags beneath the bottom wings and a hydrovane to prevent the aircraft nosing-over if it came down in the sea. The Armistice saw a reduction in orders from 300 to 150, and it equipped Fleet Spotter Reconnaissance Flights aboard HMS *Hermes* and HMS *Argus*. The owners of the Parnall Company, W. & T. Avery Ltd of Smethwick, would not agree to the post-war reduction in orders, so the contract for the remaining 150 aircraft went to the British and Colonial Aeroplane Company. The deck arrester gear used with the Panther was unsatisfactory, and during 1924 on the *Argus* only five out of six deck landings escaped mishap, but in the air the Panther handled well and remained in service until superseded by the Fairey IIID.

Aircraft Specification Sheet (44): ROYAL AIRCRAFT FACTORY RE8

Span: 42 ft 7 in.
Length: 27 ft 10.5 in.
Wing area: 377 sq. ft
Weights: Take-off, 2,678 lb
Power plant: One 150 hp RAF 4a air-cooled V type
Armament/Bomb load: Vickers synchronized gun mounted under port-side engine panels + Lewis gun aft

Performance

Max. speed: 102 mph at 6,500 ft
Endurance: 4 hr 15 min
Service ceiling: 13,500 ft

History

The RE8 was the most widely used British two-seater on the Western Front, and was nicknamed in Cockney rhyming slang the 'Harry Tate'. It was designed to meet an RFC requirement for a two-seater reconnaissance/ artillery spotting aircraft, and was to provide the RAF with a better-defended replacement for the BE2 series. But the Royal Aircraft Factory persisted in producing aircraft that were inherently stable, and this meant that their nimbler German opponents could outmanoeuvre them. The RE8s had wings resembling those of the BE2s, with marked stagger and dihedral. Production began in August 1916, with deliveries commencing in the December being issued firstly to No. 56 Squadron. It was found that the fin area was too small, resulting in accidents until the tail was redesigned.

Duties included observation, reconnaissance and ground-support patrols, ground attack and night bombing, for which 65 lb and 112 lb bombs were used. Gun armament consisted of a ring-mounted Lewis gun in the rear cockpit and a Vickers fixed forward-firing machine-gun mounted under the port-side panels.

Aircraft Specification Sheet (45): SOPWITH SALAMANDER

Span: 30 ft 1.5 in.
Length: 19 ft 6 in.
Wing area: 266.5 sq. ft

Weights: Take-off weight, 2,510 lb
Power plant: One 230 hp Bentley BR2 rotary
Armament/Bomb load: Twin synchronized Vickers guns; four 25 lb Cooper bombs under fuselage

Performance
Max. speed: 125 mph at 500 ft
Endurance: approx. 1 hr 45 min
Service ceiling: 14,000 ft

History
The first of three prototype Salamanders flew on 27 April 1918 and went to France for evaluation. It was powered by a Bentley BR2 rotary engine. It was armed with two synchronized Vickers guns, each with 1,000 rounds. The pilot's position and the fuel tanks were encased in armour, which added 650 lb to the aircraft's weight. Four 25 lb bombs could also be carried beneath the fuselage. Five hundred of these ground-attack aircraft were ordered from Sopwith, plus 600 more from five other manufacturers. But these planes came too late in the war. Although units in the UK were formed to receive this aircraft, only thirty-seven were on charge on 31 October 1918, with only two arriving in France. Sopwith continued production into 1919, and more than 150 were constructed.

Aircraft Specification Sheet (46): ROYAL AIRCRAFT FACTORY SE5A

Span: 26 ft 7³/₈ in.
Length: 20 ft 11 in.
Wing area: 245.8 sq. ft
Weights: Take-off, 1,988 lb
Power plant: One 200 hp Wolseley W4A Viper water-cooled V type
Armament/Bomb load: One synchronized Vickers gun + one drum-fed Lewis gun on Foster mounting above the centre section

Performance
Max. speed: 120 mph at 15,000 ft
Endurance: 3 hr
Service ceiling: 19,500 ft

History
One could fill pages with the exploits of the SE5A flown, as it was, by fighter aces of the First World War, such as Captain Albert Ball VC. In common with all Royal Aircraft Factory aircraft, the SE5s were stable, for, given the demand for pilots in wartime, the War Office wanted aircraft that could be flown by pilots who would not always be experienced. Sometimes over emphasis on stability put this characteristic before manoeuvrability, but the SE5s were exceptional fighting aircraft. Indeed, Major 'Mick' Mannock VC, DSO, MC scored fifty of his seventy-three victories while flying SE5As. During 1917 the SE5A became available in increasing numbers, although there was some trouble with

the engines and the Constantinesco interrupter gear that allowed the gun to be fired through the arc of the propeller. In squadron service the SE5A underwent various modifications to suit the needs of individual pilots. Another ace, McCudden, took personal charge of the servicing of his aircraft, and he could reach 20,000 ft with his SE5A where the service ceiling was 19,500 ft. While some SE5s had Hispano-Suiza engines, others were fitted with the Wolseley W4A Viper, but this engine resulted in a less streamlined appearance. Others were fitted with the W4B Adder engines, which had a reduction gear to the airscrew shaft. Apart from active service on the Western Front, SE5As were also used for home defence to intercept enemy bombers. They were fine once airborne but when scrambled for action their engines took longer to warm up than the rotary-engined Camels, which replaced them in this role. They were also difficult to land on emergency landing grounds at night. SE5As also saw action in Macedonia, Palestine and Mesopotamia. Some remained in service after the war, but the type was soon withdrawn.

Aircraft Specification Sheet (47): SHORT 184

Span: 63 ft 6.25 in.
Length: 40 ft 7.5 in.
Wing area: 688.0 sq. ft
Weights: Empty, 3,703 lb; Max. take-off, 5,363 lb
Power plant: One 260 hp Sunbeam Maori in-line piston
Armament/Bomb load: One trainable 0.303 in. machine-gun + 14 in. torpedo, or up to 520 lb of bombs, increased to 585 lb if the type was flown as a single seater

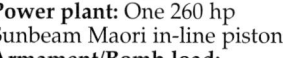

Performance
Max. speed: 88 mph at 2,000 ft
Initial climb rate: 8 min 35 sec to 2,000 ft
Endurance: 2 hr 45 min
Service ceiling: 9,000 ft

History
The Short 184 has its place in history, being the first aircraft in the world to sink an enemy ship at sea by means of a torpedo attack, and it was also the only aircraft to play a part in the Battle of Jutland. But the early success in the summer of 1915 in the Dardanelles campaign, when Flight Commander C.H.K. Edmonds sank a Turkish merchantman on 12 August, was not to be repeated. The head of the Air department of the Admiralty, Commander Murray Sueter, had expressed an interest in the torpedo as an RNAS weapon, and Short Brothers was approached to build a torpedo-carrying aircraft. The result was the Short 184, but armed with a torpedo slung between the twin floats it was difficult to fly and could not take off from any but the calmest sea. The aircraft handled well enough when employed in maritime reconnaissance, bombing and anti-submarine patrols, and it was in these other roles that the 184 was employed. From the flight of the first prototype in early 1915 until the Armistice the 184 did important if often humdrum work in virtually every operational theatre. The designation 184 was derived from the Admiralty practice at the time of using the serial number of the first aircraft, but

later the Admiralty based the designation on the horsepower of the engine, e.g. Short 320. On that basis the 184 should have been the Short 225. In February 1916 five 184s went to Mesopotamia to operate from the River Tigris, and during the siege of Kut these aircraft dropped food supplies. In home waters 184s did a vast amount of routine anti-submarine patrolling, flying from coastal bases or seaplane-carriers. The engines were uprated Sunbeam or Renault makes. The late-production 184s were powered by a 260 hp Sunbeam known as the Dover type, and had a car-type radiator behind the airscrew. Total production exceeded 650 machines, of which 300 were still in RAF service by the Armistice. For a short time after the First World War 184s were employed on mine-detection patrols.

Aircraft Specification Sheet (48): SHORT 320

Span: 75 ft 0 in.
Length: 45 ft 9 in.
Wing area: 810.0 sq. ft
Weights: (with torpedo)
Empty, 4,933 lb
Loaded, 7,014 lb
Power plant: One 310 hp or 320 hp Sunbeam Cossack
Armament/Bomb load: One free-mounted Lewis gun above front cockpit level with the wing; one 18 in. torpedo or two 230 lb bombs below fuselage

Performance
Max. speed: (with torpedo) 72.5 mph at 1,200 ft
Climb: 12 min to 2,000 ft
Endurance: (with Sunbeam engine) 3 hr
Service ceiling: (with Sunbeam engine) 3,500 ft

History
The prototypes Nos 8317 and 8318 made their first flights in 1916, and a contract for twenty-five production aircraft followed in June 1917. The aircraft's name was derived from the horsepower of the engine, the Sunbeam Cossack. The Admiralty requirement was for an aircraft to combine long range with sufficient load-carrying capacity to carry the new MkIX 18 in. 1,000 lb torpedo. Their range/payload capacity was to be important in the Italian theatre, ranging out from the Italian peninsula as part of the Otranto barrage. Sadly, the first time the 320 was used offensively in this theatre the operation was aborted. Gales and heavy seas on 3 September 1917 prevented six 320s from attacking enemy submarines lying off Cattaro, for motor launches were to have towed them nearer the target, enabling them to take off from that point. By 31 March 1918 the RNAS had 110 Short 320s, and of the fifty remaining in service at the Armistice thirty were in the Mediterranean. In the post-war RAF carrier-borne land-planes were to be used for torpedo attack, and the 320s were no longer needed. The last surviving 320s were those of No. 268 Squadron and the Torpedo School in Malta, and this unit was disbanded in October 1919.

Aircraft Specification Sheet (49): BOULTON PAUL SIDESTRAND

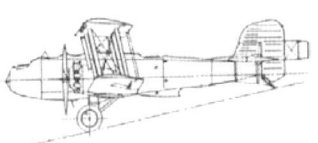

Span: 71 ft 11 in.
Length: 46 ft 0 in.
Wing area: 979.5 sq. ft
Weights: Empty, 6,010 lb
Loaded, 10,200 lb
Power plant: Two 460 hp Bristol Jupiter VIIIFs
Armament/Bomb load: Three 0.303 in. Lewis guns in nose, midships, dorsal and ventral positions; max. bomb load, 1,050 lb

Performance
Max. speed: 140 mph at 10,000 ft
Climb: 19 min to 15,000 ft
Range: 500 miles
Service ceiling: 24,000 ft

History
The Sidestrand I prototype, J7938, built to Air Ministry Specification 9/24, made its maiden flight in 1926. It was descended from two twin-engined bombers, the Bourges and Bugle. The RAF equipped only No. 101 Squadron with this aircraft, designated a medium bomber. This was the first twin-engined bomber since the retirement of the DH10 from service. From their base at Bircham Newton the Sidestrands used the Catfoss ranges for bombing practice. The results were extremely good, for this bomber provided a stable gunnery and bombing platform, which made it an outstanding bomber. The Sidestrand was extremely manoeuvrable, so it had the agility of a light bomber yet the range and bomb load of a night-bomber. During the 1929, 1932 and 1933 Hendon Displays they had mock battles with fighters. There were eighteen production Sidestrands, both MkII and MkIII. In the MkIIIs the ungeared Jupiter VI engines were replaced with the geared Jupiter VIIIFs built to Air Ministry Specification 10/29. In January 1935 the Sidestrands of No. 101 Squadron were replaced by a very similar bomber, the Overstrand.

Aircraft Specification Sheet (50): ARMSTRONG WHITWORTH *SISKIN IIIA*

Span: 33 ft 1in.
Length: 23 ft 0 in.
Wing area: 296.0 sq. ft
Weights: Empty, 1,830 lb; Loaded, 2,735 lb
Power plant: One 325 hp Armstrong Siddeley Jaguar III
Armament/Bomb load: Twin fixed synchronized Vickers guns

Performance
Max. speed: 134 mph at 6,500 ft; 128 mph at 15,000 ft
Climb: 5 min to 6,500 ft; 8.5 min to 10,000 ft; 16.5 min to 15,000 ft
Service ceiling: 20,500 ft

History

Together with the Gloster Grebe, the Armstrong Whitworth Siskin was the first of the post-war fighters to reach squadron service as a replacement for the Sopwith Snipes of First World War vintage. There had been earlier versions of the AW Siskin, such as the Siddeley Siskin of 1919, but it was the Siskin III and IIIA that equipped RAF squadrons. The prototype Siskin III, J.6853, flew on 7 May 1923. It was all-metal and the first to have 'V' interplane struts. The first production aircraft, J.6981, which flew on 24 March 1924, followed the placing of contracts by the Air Ministry in 1923. From a total of sixty-two aircraft built for the RAF, thirty-two were built as two-seater trainers. No. 41 Squadron at Northolt received its Siskin IIIs in May 1924, and No. 11 Squadron at Duxford in the following June, to be replaced by IIIAs in 1927. These were the only two squadrons to be equipped with the IIIs, which could be identified by greater dihedral on the upper wing and the extension of the fin below the fuselage. What really distinguished the IIIA was its superior performance at altitude, having a supercharged Jaguar IVS engine, and the prototype flew for the first time on 21 October 1925. Besides Armstrong Whitworth, the Blackburn, Bristol, Gloster and Vickers companies produced the IIIAs, bringing the total to 343 to equip eleven squadrons. No. 56 Squadron was the last to operate the Siskin, until October 1932.

Aircraft Specification Sheet (51): SOPWITH SNIPE

Span: 30 ft 1in
Length: 19 ft 9 in.
Wing area: 270.0 sq. ft
Weights: Empty, 1,312 lb
Loaded, 2,020 lb
Power plant: One 230 hp
Bentley BR2 rotary
Armament/Bomb load:
Twin synchronized
Vickers and one 112 lb
or four 25 lb bombs for
ground attack

Performance

Max. speed: 121 mph at 10,000 ft
Initial climb rate: 970 ft/min
Service ceiling: 19,500 ft

History

The Snipe came into service to replace the Camel, and had improved performance and view from the cockpit. With six prototypes on order in 1917, tests showed that the 230 hp Bentley BR2, and not a 150 hp BR1, would give the desired performance, and several modifications were made after fitting the more powerful engine. The Snipe went into production in the spring of 1918. Experiments were carried out by adding a Lewis gun to the twin Vickers, the former being mounted on the top wing, but like the Dolphin, this proved to be a nuisance, and it impaired the aircraft's performance. Contracts were placed for 1,700 Snipes with Sopwith and six other manufacturers. The Snipe became operational in September with No. 43 Squadron, and by the end of that month 161 Snipe MkIs had been issued, with long-range Mk1As issued to the Independent Bomber Force in France to provide fighter protection. In addition to this escort work, the Snipe could be used for ground attack, as it could carry four 20 lb Cooper bombs beneath the fuselage. Snipes were also used for home-defence duties, and it was

also seen as a potential night-fighter in 1919. Altogether contracts went out for 4,515 Snipes, but this was scaled back following the Armistice. Snipes went on to serve with peacetime squadrons both at home and overseas, and these aircraft were part of the occupation force in Germany in 1919. Some were converted to two-seater trainers, and in 1924 it was replaced by the Gloster Grebe.

Aircraft Specification Sheet (52): SUPERMARINE SOUTHAMPTON II

Span: 75 ft 0 in.
Length: 51 ft 1in
Wing area: 1,449.0 sq. ft
Weights: Empty, 9,000 lb
Loaded, 15,200 lb
Power plant: Two 502 hp
Napier Lion VAs
Armament/Bomb load:
Three Lewis guns in bow
and midships; bomb load,
1,100 lb

Performance

Max. speed: 108 mph at sea level
Cruising speed: 83 mph
Initial climb rate: 610 ft/min
Range: (normal) 770 miles (maximum) 930 miles
Service ceiling: 14,000 ft

History

The Felixstowe flying-boats were the mainstay of the Naval Air Service in the First World War, with the F2A and F3 boats. The Felixstowe F5 that followed remained in squadron service until the Southampton boats replaced them. The prototype Southampton N218 was derived from the civil Swan and was built to Air Ministry Specification R18/24. The MkIs had wings with straight leading edges and wooden hulls. The first, of an order of six, made its maiden flight on 10[h] March 1925. Then followed an order for eighteen MkIs and forty-two MkIIs, the latter having duralumin hulls and uprated Lion V engines. Southamptons built from 1927 onwards featured sweep-back in the outer-wing panels. By the end of 1933, when production ceased, the RAF had received sixty-six of these aircraft. All boats that had been built with wooden hulls were reassembled with all-metal ones. Southamptons first went into service with No. 480 (Coastal Reconnaissance) Flight at Calshot. During their service with the RAF some memorable long-distance flights were made. These included a 10,000-mile cruise around the British Isles in 1925, a 7,000-mile return flight to Egypt from Plymouth in 1926, a 19,500-mile return flight by No. 205 Squadron from Singapore to Nicobar and the Andaman Islands in 1929, and the 27,000-mile cruise by the Far East Flight (later titled No. 205 Squadron) from Felixstowe, leaving on 14 October 1927, for Singapore and Hong Kong. The latter was led by Group Captain Henry Cave-Brown-Cave. In December 1936 the last Southampton boats in service were with No. 201 Squadron at Calshot, where they were replaced by London flying-boats.

Aircraft Specification Sheet (53): SPAD VII

Span: 25 ft 7.75 in.
Length: 20 ft 2$\frac{1}{8}$ in.
Wing area: 193.8 sq. ft

Weights: Empty, 1,124 lb
Max. take-off, 1,632 lb
Power plant: One 150 hp
Hispano-Suiza 8Aa water-
cooled, V type
Armament/Bomb load:
One synchronized Vickers
machine-gun

Performance
Max. speed: 119 mph at
6,562 ft
Endurance: 2 hr 15 min
Service ceiling: 17,500 ft

History
The prototype SPAD VII flew for the first time in April 1916.
It was powered by a 140 hp Hispano-Suiza engine and
armed with a single fixed forward-firing Vickers gun
mounted in front of the pilot. Deliveries to squadrons began
in September 1916, and 495 had been built by August the
following year. Engine upratings went up to 150 hp, and
then 175 hp. In addition to the SPAD VIIs bought for the
RFC, two hundred were constructed under licence in the
United Kingdom. One hundred of these were earmarked for
the RNAS, but were urgently required by the RFC, and the
naval service had to be content with Sopwith triplanes. The
SPAD VII was popular with pilots and was the choice of two
French air aces, Rene Fonck and Georges Guynemer. It was
less manoeuvrable than the Nieuport fighter but it was
faster and stronger. All told, about 6,000 of the 175 hp
Hispano 8Ac-engined variants were built. Foreign sales
included 189 to the USA, fifteen to Belgium and 214 to Italy,
with others going to Brazil, Greece, Peru, Portugal,
Rumania, Siam, Russia and Yugoslavia.

Aircraft Specification Sheet (54):VICKERS VERNON II

Span: 68 ft 1in
Length: 43 ft 8 in.
Wing area: 1,330.0 sq. ft
Weights: Empty, 7,890 lb
Loaded, 12,500 lb
Power plant: Two 450 hp
Napier Lion IIs
**Armament/Bomb
load:** Nil – troop
transport

Performance
Max. speed: 118 mph
Cruising speed: 80 mph
Climb: 13.5 min to 6,000 ft
Range: 320 miles

History
The RAF's first purpose-built troop-carrying aircraft was
the Vickers Vernon, which entered service in 1922.
Production of the aircraft began in 1921, and the MkI, J6864,
was the first to be delivered. This had Rolls-Royce Eagle VIII
engines mounted midway between the wings. The MkIs
were intended for immediate operational use in the hot
climates of the Middle East. It was then found that the Eagle
engines did not have sufficient power in rarefied
atmospheres, so all Vernons from J.6884 onwards were fitted
with the Napier Lion II engines, becoming MkII Vernons.
Initially these engines were faired into the lower wings but
were later uncowled. The first squadron to receive the

Vernon was No. 45 Squadron at Hinaidi in March 1922, and
in November of that year No. 70 Squadron received their
MkII Vernons. Both these squadrons used their aircraft for
the famed Cairo–Baghdad mail run. From September 1923
to September 1924 No. 70 Squadron operated the mail run,
but once No. 45 Squadron received its MkIIs it took over the
service until February 1926, in conjunction with the Vimys
of No. 216 Squadron. To add colour to the mail run, names
were given to the Vernons, such as 'Venus' and 'Valkyrie'.
Another role fulfilled by the Vernons in the 1920s was as an
air ambulance. Chapter 2 describes the evacuation of
soldiers suffering from dysentery from Northern Iraq to
hospital in Baghdad in a matter of hours. The Vernon was
superseded by the Victoria in 1927.

Aircraft Specification Sheet (55): VICKERS VICTORIA *MKV*

Span: 87 ft 4 in.
Length: 59 ft 6 in.
Wing area: 2,179.0 sq. ft
Weights: Empty, 10,030 lb
Loaded, 17,760 lb
Power plant: Two 570
hp Napier Lions
Armament/Bomb load:
Nil – troop transport

Performance
Max. speed: 110 mph at
sea level
Climb: 11 min to 4,920 ft
Range: 770 miles
Service ceiling: 16,200 ft

History
The Victoria was designed to Air Ministry Specification 5/20
as a replacement for the Vernon. On 22 August 1922 the first
prototype, J6860, was flown, followed by a second, J6861.
These prototypes, MksI & II, had dihedral only on the
bottom wing, with the engines mounted on the lower wing,
whereas the production MkIIIs did not. It was not until 1926
that the first MkIII was built, and forty-six had been
produced by March 1928. By fitting HP slats and substituting
metal outer wings to thirteen MkIIIs they became MkIVs.
One newly built MkIV, J9250, had Jupiter radials fitted in
1927. This aircraft served on No. 70 Squadron and was later
fitted with Pegasus engines. In common with other types
produced during the 1920s there was a transition to all-metal
construction, and Air Ministry Specifications 7/29 and 6/31
resulted in the all-metal Victoria MkV. Thirty-seven MkVs
were built and were delivered to the RAF between
September 1929 and September 1933. These featured all-
moving fins and rudders, and Lion XIBs replaced Lion II
engines. The final Mark was the VI, which differed from the
later Valentia by the inclusion of a tail skid in place of a tail
wheel. The Victoria entered service in February 1926 with
No. 70 Squadron in Iraq, followed by No. 216 Squadron in
the July. Both squadrons changed their Victorias for
Valentias in 1935. Victorias participated in the Kabul rescue
of December 1928 described in Chapter 3, this operation
being the first major airlift in history. These aircraft also
engaged in long-distance training flights and were used for
troop reinforcement during outbreaks of trouble, such as
occurred in Cyprus in 1932. Only a handful of Victorias flew
in the United Kingdom. One notable example was the use by
the Central Flying School for training pilots in blind-flying
techniques.

Aircraft Specification Sheet (56): VICKERS VIMY IV

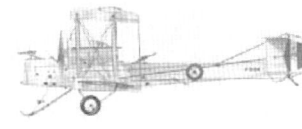

Span: 68 ft 0 in.
Length: 43 ft 6.5 in.
Wing area: 1,330.0 sq. ft
Weights:
Power plant: Two 360 hp
Rolls-Royce Eagle VIII,
water-cooled, V types
Armament/Bomb load:
One Lewis gun in nose
and two midships;
bomb load, 2,476 lb

Performance
Max. speed: 100 mph at
6,500 ft
96 mph at 10,000 ft
Initial climb rate: 360 ft/min; 25.9 min to 10,000 ft
Range: 900 miles approx.
Service ceiling: (normal load) 14,000 ft (Max load) 7,000 ft

History
The RAF chose the Vimy to be its heavy bomber into the peace years, six years in front-line service, and until 1933 in a variety of training roles. The prototype B9952 made its maiden flight on 30 November 1917, and was powered by two 207 hp Hispano-Suiza engines, whereas the MkII had the 280 hp Sunbeam Maoris. The upratings continued, the MkIII having the 310 hp Fiat engines and the MkIV the Rolls-Royce Eagle VIIIs. With the signing of the Armistice the plan to build 1,500 of these aircraft was shelved. As it was, aircraft were being delivered directly into storage, since 200 Vimys had already been completed on wartime contracts, giving the RAF eighty-eight Vimys on strength in 1921. Post-war contracts between 1923 and 1925 produced only thirty more of these bombers, and it was the MkIV that became the standard version for the RAF, entering full-time service in July 1919, when the Vimys replaced the HP 0/400s of No. 58 Squadron in Egypt (renumbered No. 70 Squadron in 1920). No. 216 Squadron received its Vimys in June 1922, and they were used on the Cairo–Baghdad mail run until 1926. In the United Kingdom only D Flight of No. 100 Squadron at Spittlegate had Vimys. Then in June 1923 No. 7 Squadron was re-formed at Bircham Newton, and for a while was the only home-based heavy-bomber unit until joined by Nos 9, 58 and 99 Squadrons. No. 58 Squadron had, by this time, been re-formed, the old number plate becoming No. 70. During the years 1924 and 1925 the Vimys were progressively replaced by Virginias on first-line squadrons, but they remained in service with No. 502 Special Reserve Squadron until July 1928. Thereafter they served at flying training schools and with the parachute training school at Henlow. They were modified for dual control and had either Jupiter or Jaguar radials, and were finally retired from No. 4 FTS Egypt in 1933. The famous transatlantic flight in a Vimy by Alcock and Brown is described in Chapter 2.

Aircraft Specification Sheet (57): VICKERS VIRGINIA X

Span: 87 ft 8 in.
Length: 62 ft 2.75 in.
Wing area: 2,178.0 sq. ft
Weights: Empty, 9,650 lb;
Loaded, 17,600 lb
Power plant: Two 580 hp
Napier Lion VBs

Armament/Bomb load: One Lewis gun in nose, twin Lewis guns in tail; bomb load, 3,000 lb, usually comprising nine 112 lb bombs internally and a combination of 550, 250, 112 and 20 lb bombs carried externally

Performance
Max. speed: 98
mph at sea level
108 mph at 5,000 ft
Climb: 14 min to
5,000 ft
Range: 985 miles
Service ceiling: 9,400 ft

History
The Vickers Virginia took over the role of RAF heavy bomber from the Vimy during 1924/5 and remained in service until 1937. During that time ten Marks were introduced to incorporate a number of modifications. The MkI was built to Air Ministry Specification 1/21, and the prototype, J6856, flew at Brooklands on 24 November 1922. On 6 June 1924 a Virginia MkIII prototype, J6992, was delivered to No. 7 Squadron at Bircham Newton. Thereafter issues were made to Nos 7, 9 and 58 Squadrons between 1924 and 1928 through the various Marks up to MkX, and can be seen by reference to the appropriate squadron numbers in Appendix B. The prototype had Napier Lion engines in rectangular nacelles mounted on the lower wings, but production Virginias had oval nacelles raised above the lower wings. Raising the engines above the lower wing also occurred on the Vernon and Victoria. The MksIII to V maintained the feature of the prototype in having dihedral on the lower wings only. From MkVI onwards the nose was redesigned and lengthened, and there was sweep-back of the wings. MkIX and X both had gun positions in the tail, but perhaps the most interesting features, shown in the photograph above, are the 'fighting tops' on the MkVIII, J6856, of No. 9 Squadron. Enclosed power-operated turrets were still to come, but this was intended to provide defensive fire from attack from above and behind. Finally the MkX was of all-metal construction with fabric covering. By the time production ended in December 1932, the RAF had received 124 Virginias. Of these, fifty were new-build MkXs. No. 7 Squadron was the first to receive Virginias with automatic pilots, which helped the squadron to win the Lawrence Minot bombing trophy eight times. The Virginias of No. 51 Squadron were still in Bomber Command's order of battle in February 1938, the month they left the service.

Aircraft Specification Sheet (58): WESTLAND WALRUS

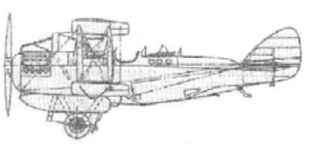

Span: 45 ft 0 in.
Length: 30 ft 0 in.
Wing area: 496.0 sq. ft
Weights: Loaded, 4,994 lb
Power plant: One 450 hp
Napier Lion II
**Armament/Bomb
load:** One Vickers
gun forwards and
one Lewis gun aft
on Scarff ring

Performance
Max. speed: 124 mph

Climb: 10 min to 9,840 ft
Endurance: 3.5 hours
Service ceiling: 20,000 ft.

History

The Westland Walrus was a modified version of the DH9A. Westland was the prime contractor for the Airco DH9A, and it was its practice to use components in later aircraft, as it did with DH9A parts in the Wapiti. The Walrus was issued to No. 3 Squadron at Leuchars in January 1922. No. 3 Squadron, which had been disbanded in India, was re-formed at this Scottish airfield from a flight of No. 205 Squadron. On 8 November 1922 No. 3 Squadron's Walruses moved to Gosport. On 1 April the following year the squadron was broken down into Nos 420, 421 and 422 Flights, and in the November No. 423 Flight was also equipped with this aircraft. This can be explained by the policy of the newly formed RAF in 1918 of forming the RNAS flights of naval aircraft into RAF squadrons, which happened in August of that year, numbered in the 200 series. With the controversy between the RAF and the Royal Navy over the future of the naval air arm, it was decided that the RAF would man and service maritime aircraft on both land and at sea, those units that were land based remaining as squadrons numbered in the 200 series. Those units that would serve at sea, mostly on aircraft-carriers, would again be flights to serve in the Fleet Air Arm. The break-up of No. 3 Squadron was in readiness for its aircraft to operate with the fleet. This meant that No. 3 Squadron RAF had to be re-formed a second time, on 1 April 1924 at Manston.

Aircraft Specification Sheet (59): WESTLAND WAPITI IIA

Span: 46 ft 5 in.
Length: 31 ft 8 in.
Wing area: 488.0 sq. ft
Weights: Empty, 3,810 lb Loaded, 5,400 lb
Power plant: One 550 hp Bristol Jupiter VIII or VIIIF
Armament/Bomb load: One fixed forward-firing Vickers gun + one Lewis gun aft; bomb load, 580 lb

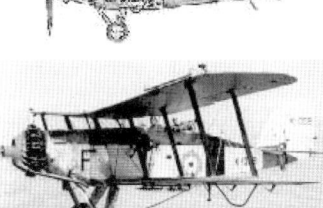

Performance

Max. speed: 135 mph at 5,000 ft
Cruising speed: 110 mph
Initial climb rate: 1,140 ft/min 9.5 min to 10,000 ft
Range: 360 miles
Service ceiling: 18,800 ft

History

The Wapiti was the workhorse of the RAF in India and Iraq during the inter-war years. In 1928 the RAF began to re-equip squadrons that had for years used another workhorse, the DH9A, and No. 84 Squadron at Shaibah was the first to receive the MkIs in June of that year. A number of the components from the DH9A were used for the Wapiti. The prototype J8495 first flew on 7 March 1927, and the MkI had a 420 hp Jupiter VI engine. By 1933 twenty squadrons had been equipped with this aircraft, eleven regular and nine

auxiliary and special reserve. No. 55 Squadron, Iraq, flew Wapitis until 1937, while on the North-West Frontier the Wapiti equipped eight squadrons that had previously used DH9As and Bristol Fighters. During the 1930s the Wapitis were progressively replaced with Harts and Audaxes, but No. 5 Squadron soldiered on with its Wapiti until June 1940 before getting Harts. These aircraft were just as busy training or with the auxiliary and reserve units. Again they replaced DH9As on the auxiliary day-bomber squadrons, except No. 602 Squadron at Renfrew, where they replaced Fairey Fawns. It was not until 1937 that the Auxiliary Air Force gave up its Wapitis, but not before these aircraft belonging to Nos 600, 601, 604 and 605 Squadrons gave impressive formation-flying demonstrations at the annual RAF Hendon Display. Four hundred and sixty Wapitis in all were delivered to the RAF. The MkII was of composite construction, and the IIA was the first all-metal version with an uprated Jupiter VIII engine. The Wapiti V was designed for Army-cooperation work and the VI was a dual-control trainer with a Jupiter XIF engine. It was these aircraft that mostly went to the reserve and auxiliary units. Finally there were the Wapiti IAs, J9095 and 9096 of No. 24 Squadron at Northolt in 1928. They were used by HRH the Prince of Wales, Prince Edward, when flying on official visits.

Aircraft Specification Sheet (60): WIGHT CONVERTED

Span: 65 ft 6 in.
Length: 44 ft 8.5 in.
Wing area: 715 sq. ft
Weights: Empty, 3,758 lb with Eagle engine and 3,957 lb with Maori engine Loaded, 5,556 lb with Eagle engine and 5,394 lb with Maori engine
Power plant: One 322 hp Rolls-Royce VI or 265 hp Sunbeam Maori

Armament/Bomb load: One Lewis gun on Scarff mounting aft, and provision for 100 lb or 112 lb bombs below wings

Performance

Eagle engine
Max. speed: 84.5 mph at 2,000 ft
82.5 mph at 6,500 ft
Climb rate: 4 min 20 sec to 2,000 ft; 42.5 min to 10,000 ft
Endurance: 3.5 hr
Service ceiling: 9,600 ft

History

The Wight 'Converted' seaplane, so called because it was descended from a Wight land-plane bomber (N501), was the third type of seaplane to be used by the RNAS. Early batches of this aircraft had the Rolls-Royce engines, but later the Maoris were fitted. This aircraft, although very small in number compared with the other seaplane types used during the First World War, put in a great deal of work on maritime patrols. It is alleged that the Wight Converted was the first RAF aircraft to sink a U-boat by direct air attack. On 22 September 1917 the Wight hit the submarine with its first 100 lb bomb. This aircraft was piloted by Flight Sub-Lieutenant C.S. Mossop operating out of Cherbourg. Only two squadrons were equipped with this aircraft, namely No. 241 Squadron based at Portland and No. 243 Squadron based at Cherbourg. A total of fifty Wight seaplanes had been ordered by the Admiralty, but only thirty-seven were built, since it was decided to standardize production on the Short 184 seaplane.

The Serial Numbers allocated were 9841 to 9860, N1280 to 1289 and N2180 to 2199. Only seven of this type were listed as on strength at the Armistice, and these were based at the two locations given above.

Aircraft Specification Sheet (61): HAWKER WOODCOCK II

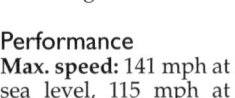

Span: 32 ft 6 in.
Length: 26 ft 2 in.
Wing area: 346.0 sq. ft
Power plant: One 420 hp Bristol Jupiter IV
Armament/Bomb load: Twin synchronized Vickers guns on sides of fuselage

Performance
Max. speed: 141 mph at sea level, 115 mph at 10,000 ft
Climb rate: 8.8 min to 10,000 ft; 16.2 min to 15,000 ft; 30.9 min to 20,000 ft
Endurance: 3.5 hr
Service ceiling: 20,000 ft

History
The Woodcock was a fighter built by the then recently formed Hawker Engineering Co. Ltd, formerly Sopwith.

The first prototype J6987, powered by an Armstrong Siddeley Jaguar radial made its maiden flight in March 1923 and was built to Air Ministry Specification 25/22. This aircraft had two-bay wings, whereas the second prototype, J6988, was a single-bay arrangement, the same as the production aircraft, and the Jaguar engine was replaced by a Bristol Jupiter radial. It was this second prototype that was ordered for the RAF and was the Woodcock II. It had a very wide undercarriage, which was particularly useful with the Fleet Air Arm variant, the Hawker Hedgehog. The other interesting feature was the enclosure of the projecting cylinder pots inside 'helmets' to improve streamlining. The production Woodcocks were built to Air Ministry Specification 3/24, a start being made in 1925. Sixty-three of these fighters had been delivered to the RAF by April 1927, the first going to No. 3 Squadron at Upavon in May 1925. These replaced the Snipes, the last surviving fighter of First World War vintage. No. 17 Squadron at Hawkinge was the only other unit to be equipped with Woodcocks, which happened in March 1926. It therefore made sense to move the two squadrons together for both operational and supply points of view, and No. 17 Squadron joined No. 3 at Upavon, where they became night-fighting squadrons. Both units had the Woodcocks replaced in 1928 by Gamecocks. From such a very short operational life this aircraft can perhaps best be remembered by the demonstration of night flying at the Birmingham Torchlight Tattoo of May 1926, when each aircraft of No. 3 Squadron carried lights on racks below the wings. No. 17 Squadron did much the same thing at the Aldershot Torchlight Tattoo in 1927.

PART II
NON-SQUADRON TRAINING AIRCRAFT, HIGH-ALTITUDE, HIGH-SPEED AND LONG-DISTANCE AIRCRAFT IN SERVICE BETWEEN 11 NOVEMBER 1918 AND 31 DECEMBER 1929

62. Avro 504N
63. Fairey Postal
64. Supermarine S5
65. Supermarine S6–6B

Aircraft Specification Sheet (62): AVRO 504N

Span: 36 ft
Length: 28 ft 6 in.
Wing area: 320 sq. ft
Weights: Empty, 1,584 lb Loaded, 2,240 lb
Power plant: One 180 hp Armstrong Siddeley Lynx IV or 215 hp Lynx IVC

Performance
Max. speed: 100 mph
Cruising Speed: 85 mph at 2,000 ft
Initial Climb rate: 770 ft/min
Range: 250 miles
Endurance 3 hr
Service ceiling: 14,600 ft

History
The Avro 504N was designed as a replacement for the wartime Avro 504K, and was known as the Lynx Avro. It became the first RAF trainer to be adopted after the end of the First World War and was used at Cranwell, the flying training schools and university air squadrons. It was to remain in service as a trainer until 1932, when it was replaced by the Avro Tutor. There were 590 Avro 504Ns built, and production continued until 1933. In addition to its use as a trainer with No. 1 FTS (Netheravon), No. 2 FTS (Digby), No. 3 FTS (Grantham), No. 4 FTS (Abu Sueir) and No. 5 FTS (Sealand), the 504N was used as a communications aircraft with No. 24 (Communications) Squadron and by the auxiliary squadrons. At the CFS Wittering the six 504Ns of E Flight were used to pioneer instrument flying, being fitted with blind-flying hoods and Reid and Sigrist turn indicators. They had less dihedral than standard to reduce inherent instability. Finally they featured in the RAF Displays, Hendon, from 1930 until 1933, where they gave exhibitions of 'crazy flying' (see Chapter 3).

Aircraft Specification Sheet (63): FAIREY POSTAL

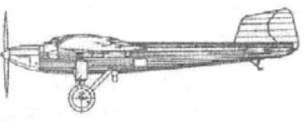

Span: 82 ft
Length: 48 ft 6 in.
Wing area: 900 sq. ft
Weights: 15,500 lb
Power plant: One 570 hp Napier Lion XIA

Performance
Cruising Speed: 110 mph
Range: over 5,000 miles
Take-off run for record flight, 1,600 yd

History

Following the failure of the Hawker Horsley in 1927 to gain the world long-distance record for Britain, the Air Ministry made the decision to purchase an aircraft for this purpose. The Fairey Postal was chosen, having long-span cantilever wings and a large fuel capacity of over 1,000 gallons, which gave the aircraft a range of more than 5,000 miles. Two of these aircraft were constructed, and the first, J9479, made its initial flight at Northolt in November 1928. In April 1929 Squadron Leader A.G. Jones-Williams, with Flight Lieutenant N.H. Jenkins, made the first non-stop flight from England to India. The aircraft left Cranwell on 24 April and landed at Karachi on 26 April, after a flight of 4,130 miles, with a flying time of 50 hr 37 min. Strong headwinds prevented the two men from reaching the intended destination of Bangalore. As it was, only eight gallons of fuel remained on landing at Karachi, and the distance record remained unbroken. A second attempt was made to South Africa, but J.9479 crashed in Tunisia, killing both occupants.

Aircraft Specification Sheet (64): SUPERMARINE S5

Span: 26 ft 9 in.
Length: 24 ft
Wing area: 115 sq. ft
Weights: Loaded (direct-drive engine) 3,100 lb; (geared engine) 3,250 lb
Power plant: One 900 hp Napier Lion VIIA

Performance

Max. speed: 319.57 mph at sea level in 1928
Alighting speed: 85 mph

History

The RAF entered a team in the Schneider Trophy contest for the first time in 1927, and three high-speed seaplanes were ordered from Supermarine. R.J. Mitchell designed the S5, developed from the S4 Cantilever mid-wing monoplane that gained the world speed record by flying at 226.6 mph on 13 September 1925. The S5 differed from the S4 in having a low wire-braced wing. The pilot's cockpit was moved forward and the wooden floats and fuselage were replaced with ones made of duralumin. The three S5s were numbered N219, 220 and 221. The aircraft chosen for the contest, which took in Venice in 1927, were N219 and N220. A description of the contest is to be found in Chapter 3. The S5/21(N219) version had the direct-drive engine, the S5/25(N220) version the geared engine. Flight Lieutenant O.E. Worsley flew N219 and Flight Lieutenant Webster N220. The aircraft were conveyed to Venice aboard the carrier HMS *Eagle*, and Webster won the competition with an average speed of 281.65 mph, Worsley coming second at an average speed of 273.07 mph. During the 1927 contest Flight Lieutenant Webster set up a new world record over 100 km at 283.66 mph. In 1928 Flight Lieutenant D'Arcy Greig set up a new British record in an S5 with a speed of 319.57 mph.

Aircraft Specification Sheet (65): SUPERMARINE S6–6B

Span: 30 ft
Length: 28 ft 10 in.
Wing area: 145 sq. ft
Weights: Empty, 4,560 lb
Loaded, 6,066 lb
Power plant: One 1,900 hp Rolls Royce 'R' in the S6 and the 2,300 hp in the S6B

Performance

Max. speed: 407 mph in 1931
Alighting speed: 95 mph

History

The RAF High-Speed Flight was formed at Felixstowe in April 1929 in readiness for the 1929 Schneider Trophy contest. The S6s were destined for this contest, the S6Bs for the one held in 1931. The first of the S6s were delivered five weeks before the race. Two Gloster VI seaplanes (N249 and N250) were also delivered to the flight, but were withdrawn from the race owing to problems with the engines, and were used as training aircraft. The notable development was the replacement of the Napier Lion engines with the Rolls-Royce engines, which were specially developed for racing. The S6 had a 1,900 hp engine, the S6B one of 2,300 hp. The water-cooling radiators of the S6B occupied almost the entire wing surfaces, and the upper parts of the floats and oil-cooling ducts lined the fuselage. Britain, having won the 1927 Schneider Trophy contest, was the venue for the one in 1929, and since Britain also won the 1929 contest the 1931 event was also held in the UK. (There were no contests in 1928 and 1930.) Since, therefore, Britain won the contest on three consecutive occasions, the rules of the competition meant that this country held the trophy in perpetuity. N247 was flown by Flying Officer Waghorn in the 1929 contest, and he was declared the winner with an average speed of 328 mph. Flying Officer Atcherley gained the world speed record in N248, flying at 332 and 331 mph over the 50 km and 100 km courses respectively. On 12 September Squadron Leader Orlebar AFC raised the world speed record to 357.7 mph in N247. When these two S6 seaplanes were fitted with larger floats they were designated S6A. The economic situation in Britain was such that the government was not prepared to fund the 1931 contest at Spithead, but through the generosity of Lady Houston the funds were found, and S6B Nos S1595 and S1596 with larger floats and the 2,300 hp engines were the two team aircraft. Flight Lieutenant J.N. Boothman in S1595 won the contest, averaging 340.08 mph. On 29 September Flight Lieutenant G.H. Stainforth achieved a world speed record with a speed of 407.5 mph. This made the Supermarine S6B the first aircraft in the world to fly at a speed in excess of 400 mph.

Appendix B

SQUADRON LOCATIONS AND AIRCRAFT, 1918–39
NO. 1 SQUADRON TO NO. 616 SQUADRON
(Note: Only those squadrons are listed that were in existence and service on 11 November 1918 or were formed or re-formed on or before 3 September 1939 and were still in service on the latter date.

F   = Formed
RF   = Re-formed
DB   = Disbanded
Det/Dets = Detachment/s
(1/23) = Indicates month and year when aircraft ceased to be operational with that unit.

No. 1 SQUADRON   MOTTO: In omnibus princeps (First in all things)

Date	Location	Aircraft Type	Remarks
11/11/18	Bouvincourt	SE5A(2/19)	from 26/10/18
18/11/18	to Le Hameau	"	
3/3/19	to London (Colney)	"	as cadre
19/9/19	to Uxbridge	"	as cadre
21/1/20	Re-established at Risalpur	Snipe (11/26)	
1/4/20			Redesignated No. 1 Sqn
11/5/20	to Bangalore	"	
20/4/21	to Hinaidi	"	Det Sulaimania
4/23		Nighthawk (9/23)	
1/11/26	DB		
1/2/27	RF Tangmere		
2/27		Siskin IIIA (2/32)	
2/32		Fury I (11/38)	
2/37		Gladiator I (3/37)	
10/38		Hurricane I (4/41)	

No. 2 SQUADRON   MOTTO: Hereward

Date	Location	Aircraft Type	Remarks
11/11/18	Genech	AW FK8(2/19)	
14/2/19	to Bicester		as cadre
9/19	to Weston-on-Green		
20/1/20	DB		
1/2/20	Re-formed at Oranmore		
2/20		Bristol F2B(1/30)	Det Castlebar, Fermoy, No. 105 Sqn renumbered
7/20	to Fermoy		Det Oranmore
13/2/22	to Digby		
2/6/22	to Aldergrove		
29/9/22	to Farnborough		Det Aldergrove
17/9/23	to Andover		
31/3/24	to Manston		
20/4/27	*en route* to China		via HMS *Hermes*
31/5/27	to Shanghai Racecourse		
13/9/27	*en route* to UK		via HMS *Hermes*
27/10/27	to Manston		
12/29		Atlas (6/33)	
5/33		Audax (11/37)	
30/11/35	to Hawkinge		
11/37		Hector (9/38)	
7/38		Lysander I (2/40)	

No. 3 SQUADRON   MOTTO: Tertius primus erit (The third shall be first)

Date	Location	Aircraft Type	Remarks
11/11/18	Inchy	Camel (2/19)	
15/2/19	to Wye		as cadre

Date	Location	Aircraft Type	Remarks
2/5/19	to Swingate Down		
15/10/19	to Croydon		
27/10/19	to Uxbridge DB		
21/1/20	Re-established at Ambala		initially identified as A Sqn
22/3/20	to Bangalore		
1/4/20			A Sqn redesignated No. 3 Sqn
6/20		Snipe (3/21)	
1/4/21	to Ambala		
30/9/21	DB		
1/10/21	RF Leuchars		
10/21		DH9A (3-seater) (10/22)	
1/22		Walrus (4/23)	
8/11/22	to Gosport		
1/4/23	DB		
1/4/24	RF Manston		
4/24		Snipe (8/25)	
30/4/24	to Upavon		
5/25		Woodcock II (8/28)	
8/28		Gamecock I (6/29)	
6/29		Bulldog II/IIA (7/37)	
10/5/34	to Kenley		
18/10/35	to Port Sudan		
22/10/35	to Khartoum		
22/1/36	to Port Sudan		
28/8/36	to Kenley		
3/37		Gladiator I (3/38)	
3/38		Hurricane I (7/38)	
7/38		Gladiator I (7/39)	
1/5/39	to Biggin Hill		
5/39		Hurricane I (4/41)	
2/9/39	to Croydon		

No. 4 SQUADRON   MOTTO: In futurum videre (To see into the future)

Date	Location	Aircraft Type	Remarks
11/11/18	Linselles	RE8 (2/19)	
16/11/18	to Ascq		
3/12/18	to Linselles		
13/2/19	to Northolt		as cadre
20/9/19	to Uxbridge		
30/4/20	to Farnborough		re-established Dets Stonehenge, Aldergrove and Baldonnel
4/20		Bristol F2B (10/29)	
26/9/22	*en route* to Turkey		via HMS *Ark Royal* and HMS *Argus*
11/10/22	to Kilya Bay		
11/12/22	to Kilid el Bahr		
5/9/23	*en route* to UK		
18/9/23	to Farnborough		
10/29		Atlas (2/32)	
12/31		Audax (7/37)	
16/2/37	to Odiham		
5/37		Hector (1/39)	
12/38		Lysander II (9/40)	

No. 5 SQUADRON   MOTTO: Frangas non flectas (Thou mayst break but shall not bend me)

Date	Location	Aircraft Type	Remarks
11/11/18	Aulnoy	RE8 (9/19)	
27/11/18	to Cognelée		
7/12/18	to Elsenborn		
21/12/18	to Hangelar		
3/19		Bristol F2B (10/19)	
19/9/19	to Bicester		
9/10/19			Reduced to cadre
20/1/20	DB		
1/4/20	RF Quetta		No. 48 Sqn renumbered Det Loralai

		Bristol F2B (5/31)	
4/20			
26/10/22	to Ambala		Det Saugor
10/3/24	to Dardoni		
22/1/25	to Kohat		Dets Tank, Miranshah and Jhelum
15/10/25	to Risalpur		Dets Quetta, Miranshah Hassani Abdel and Jhelum
15/12/28	to Quetta		Dets Risalpur and Drigh Road
16/5/30	to Kohat		Det Miranshah
15/5/31	to Quetta		Dets Secunderabad, Poona, Jubbulpore, Ford Sandeman
5/31		Wapiti (6/40)	
9/6/35	to Drigh Road		as cadre
31/7/35			Re-established
1/8/35	to Risalpur		
15/10/35	to Chaklala		Dets Julalpore, Lahore, Risalpur, Kohat and Miranshah
6/3/37	to Miranshah		
20/4/37	to Risalpur		Dets Miranshah and Chaklala
8/11/37	to Chaklala		Dets Miranshah
23/4/38	to Risalpur		Dets Arawali,Kohat,Miranshah Ford Sandeman, Hakimpet and Sialkot

No. 6 SQUADRON   MOTTO: Oculi exercitus (The eyes of the army)

Date	Location	Aircraft Type	Remarks
11/11/18	Gondecourt	RE8 (7/20)	
16/11/18	to Pecq		
6/12/18	to Gerpinnes		
2/19		Bristol F2B (4/19)	
19/3/19	to Sart		
14/4/19	*en route* to Middle East via Marseilles		
16/7/19	to Basra		
6/9/19	to Baghdad West		Dets Bushire, Abu Kemal and Annah
7/20		Bristol F2B (6/32)	Dets Samawah,Hillah. Kirkuk Mosul and Sulaimania
9/10/22	to Hinaidi		
19/5/24	to Mosul		
20/10/26	to Hinaidi		
28/10/29	to Ismailia		Dets Semakh, Ramleh, Haifa & Qasaba
6/31		Gordon (10/35)	
9/35		Hart (1/38)	
10/35		Demon (11/36)	
29/5/36	to Ramleh		Det Semakh
19/11/36	to Ismaila		
22/11/37	to Ramleh		
1/38		Hardy (4/40)	
8/39		Gauntlet I & II (4/40)	
9/39		Lysander I (12/39)	

NO. 7 SQUADRON   MOTTO: Per diem, per noctem (By day and by night)

Date	Location	Aircraft Type	Remarks
11/11/18	Menin	RE8 (10/19)	
15/11/18	to Stacegham		
25/11/18	to Peronnes		
26/11/18	to Fort Cognelée		
6/12/18	to Elsenborn		
15/12/18	to Bickendorf		
20/12/18	to Spich		
11/5/19	to Bucheim		
7/8/19	to Heumar		
21/9/19	to Old Sarum		
9/10/19			Reduced to cadre
27/10/19	to Eastleigh		

19/11/19	to Farnborough		
31/12/19	DB		
1/6/23	RF Bircham Newton		from D Flt 100 Sqn
6/23		Vimy(4/27)	
5/24		Virginia III (5/25)	
9/24		Virginia II (2/27)	
9/24		Virginia IV (6/25)	
1/25		Virginia V (5/26)	
6/25		Virginia VI (8/26)	
3/27		Virginia VII (1/33)	
7/4/27	to Worthy Down		
9/27		Virginia IX (8/33)	
11/28		Virginia X (4/38)	
4/35		Heyford II (4/38)	
4/36		Heyford III (4/38)	
3/9/36	to Finningley		
4/37		Wellesley (4/38)	
3/38		Whitley II (12/38)	
11/38		Whitley III (5/39)	
4/39		Hampden (4/40)	
1/9/39	to Doncaster		

No. 8 SQUADRON   MOTTO: Upsiam et passim (Everywhere unbounded)

Date	Location	Aircraft Type	Remarks
11/11/18	Malincourt	AW FK8 (12/18)	
16/11/18	to La Bellevue		
12/18		Bristol F2B (7/19	
11/5/19	to Sart		
28/7/19	to Duxford		
20/1/20	DB		
18/10/20	RF Helwan		
10/20		DH9A (Jun 28)	
11/12/20	to Suez		
23/2/21	to Basra		
4/3/21	to Baghdad West		
29/12/21	to Hinaidi		
27/2/27	to Khormaksar		
1/28		Fairey IIIF (3/35)	
2/35		Vincent (11/40)	
10/35		Demon	Oct 35 – 1 flight only
			Det Burao
4/39		Blenheim (10/41)	Dets Riyan, Berbera & Sheikh Othman

No. 9 SQUADRON   MOTTO: Per noctem volamus (Through the night we fly)

Date	Location	Aircraft Type	Remarks
11/11/18	Tarcienne	RE8 (5/19)	
11/12/18	to Fort Cognelée		
19/12/18	to Clavier		
3/1/19	to Ludendorf		
2/19		Bristol F2B (7/19)	
30/7/19	to Castle Bromwich		
31/12/19	DB		
4/24		Vimy (10/25)	
30/4/24	to Manston		
9/24		Virginia IV (3/27)	
1/25		Virginia V (5/26)	
6/25		Virginia VI (4/27)	
7/26		Virginia VII (6/30)	
1/27		Virginia VIII (3/27)	
7/27		Virginia IX (2/32)	
1/29		Virginia X (4/36)	
26/11/30	to Boscombe Down		
15/10/35	to Andover		

15/1/36	to Aldergrove		
3/36		Heyford III (5/39)	
1/10/36	to Scampton		
10/3/38	to Stradishall		
1/39		Wellington I (12/39)	
15/7/39	to Honington		
9/39		Wellington I (9/40)	Det Lossiemouth

No. 10 SQUADRON   MOTTO: Rem acu tangere (To hit the mark)

Date	Location	Aircraft Type	Remarks
11/11/18	Stacegham	AW FK8 (2/19)	
15/11/18	to Menin		
1/12/18	to Reckem		
17/2/19	to Ford Junction		as cadre
15/10/19	to Croydon		
31/12/19	DB		
3/1/28	RF Upper Heyford		
1/28		Hyderabad (11/31)	
12/30		Hinaidi (9/32)	
1/4/31	to Boscombe Down		
9/32		Virginia X (1/35)	
8/34		Heyford IA (1/36)	
11/35		Heyford III (6/37)	
25/1/37	to Dishforth		
3/37		Whitley I (6/39)	
5/39		Whitley IV (5/40)	Dets Villeneuve & Kinloss

No. 11 SQUADRON   MOTTO: Ociores acrierosque aquilis (Swifter and keener than eagles)

Date	Location	Aircraft Type	Remarks
11/11/18	Béthencourt	Bristol F2B (10/19)	
18/11/18	to Aulnoy		
19/12/18	to Nivelles		
20/5/19	to Spich		
3/9/19	to Scopwick		
9/10/19			Reduced to cadre
31/12/19	DB		
15/1/23	RF Andover		
1/23		DH9A (4/24)	
16/9/23	to Bircham Newton		
4/24		Fawn (5/27)	
31/5/24	to Netheravon		
11/26		Horsley (11/28)	
10/28		Wapiti (8/32)	
29/12/28	*en route* to India		
22/1/29	to Risalpur		Det Miranshah
2/32		Hart (7/39)	Dets Gilgit, Arawali & Miranshah
7/39		Blenheim I (1/41)	
7/8/39	to Tengah		

No. 12 SQUADRON   MOTTO: Leads the field

Date	Location	Aircraft Type	Remarks
11/11/18	Estourmel	RE8 (7/19)	
		Bristol F2B (7/22)	
29/11/18	to Clavier		
19/12/18	to Duren		
5/5/19	to Heumar		
17/11/20	to Bickendorf		
27/7/22	DB		
1/4/23	RF Northolt		
4/23		DH9A (3/24)	
24/3/24	to Andover		
3/24		Fawn (12/26)	
6/26		Fox (1/31)	
1/31		Hart (10/36)	
4/10/35	*en route* to Aden		
20/10/35	to Khormaksar		

Date	Location	Aircraft Type	Remarks
18/5/36	to Robat		
28/7/36	to Khormaksar		
11/8/36	*en route* to UK		
29/8/36	to Andover		
10/36		Hind (2/38)	
2/38		Battle (11/40)	
9/5/39	to Bicester		
2/9/39	to Berry-au-Bac		

No. 13 SQUADRON   MOTTO: Ajuvamus tuendo (We assist by watching)

Date	Location	Aircraft Type	Remarks
11/11/18	Carnières	RE 8 (3/19)	
1/12/18	to Vert Galand		
19/1/19	to St Omer		
27/3/19	to Sedgeford		as cadre
31/12/19	DB		
30/5/24	RF Kenley		
4/24		Bristol F2B (1/38)	
30/5/24	to Andover		
8/27		Atlas (7/32)	
23/9/29	to Netheravon		
5/32		Audax (5/37)	
3/5/35	to Old Sarum		
5/37		Hector (2/39)	
1/39		Lysander II (1/41)	

No. 14 SQUADRON   MOTTO: I spread my wings and keep my promise

Date	Location	Aircraft Type	Remarks
11/11/18	Mikra Bay	RE8 (11/18)	
9/12/18	*en route* to UK		
1/1/19	to Tangmere		as cadre
2/2/19	DB		
1/2/20	RF Ramleh		No. 111 Sqn renumbered
2/20		Bristol F2B (2/36)	Dets Amman, Damascus, Aleppo, Mafraq & Beersheba
6/24		DH9A (3/30)	
15/2/26	to Amman		
11/29		Fairy IIIF (9/32)	
7/32		Gordon (4/38)	
3/38		Wellesley (12/40)	
24/8/39	to Ismailia		

No. 15 SQUADRON   MOTTO: Aim sure

Date	Location	Aircraft Type	Remarks
11/11/18	Selvigny (Ferme Guilleman)	RE8 (2/19)	
2/12/19	to Fowlmere		as cadre
31/12/19	DB		
20/3/24	RF Martlesham Heath		as A & AE Trials Unit
3/24		DH9A (10/26)	
10/26		Horsley (5/34)	
31/5/34	DB		Equipment was largely notional, and would have been that operated in the event of mobilization.
1/6/34	RF Abingdon		
6/34		Hart (6/36)	
3/36		Hind (7/38)	
6/38		Battle (12/39	
2/9/38	to Betheniville		

No. 16 SQUADRON   MOTTO: Operta aperta (Hidden things are revealed)

Date	Location	Aircraft Type	Remarks
11/11/18	Auchy	RE8 (219)	
14/2/19	to Fowlmere		as cadre

Date	Location	Aircraft Type	Remarks
31/12/19	DB		
1/4/24	RF Old Sarum		Co-op Sqn of School of Army Co-operation redesignated
4/24		Bristol F2B (3/31)	
1/31		Atlas (1/34)	
12/33		Audax (10/38)	
5/38		Lysander I (4/39)	
4/39		Lysander II (11/40)	

No. 17 SQUADRON   MOTTO: Excellere contende (Strive to excel)

Date	Location	Aircraft Type	Remarks
11/11/18	Amberkoj	DH9 (11/19)	Flts at Philippopolis, Mustapha Pasha, Mikra Bay & Batum
12/18		Camel (11/19)	
28/1/19	to San Stephano		Dets Kars & Tiflis
14/11/19	DB		
1/4/24	RF Hawkinge		
4/24		Snipe (3/26)	
3/26		Woodcock II (1/28)	
14/10/26	to Upavon		
1/28		Gamecock I (9/28)	
9/28		Siskin IIIA (10/29)	
10/29		Bulldog II/IIA (8/36)	
23/5/39	to North Weald		
6/39		Hurricane I (2/41)	
2/9/39	to Croydon		

No. 18 SQUADRON   MOTTO: Animo et fide (With courage and faith)

Date	Location	Aircraft Type	Remarks
11/11/18	La Brayelle	DH9A (8/19)	
28/11/18	to Maubeuge		
24/1/19	to Bickendorf		
1/5/19	to Merheim		
9/9/19	to Weston-on- the-Green		as cadre
31/12/19	DB		
20/10/31	RF Upper Heyford		
10/31		Hart (5/39)	
7/1/36	to Bircham Newton		
4/36		Hind (5/39)	
7/9/36	to Upper Heyford		
5/39		Blenheim (5/40)	

No. 19 SQUADRON   MOTTO: Possunt quia posse videntur (They can because they think they can)

Date	Location	Aircraft Type	Remarks
11/11/18	Abscon	Dolphin (1/19)	
9/2/19	to Genech		
18/2/19	to Ternhill		as cadre
31/12/19	DB		
1/4/23	RF Duxford		One flight only, attached to No. 2 FTS
4/23		Snipe (12/24)	
1/6/24			Brought up to strength
12/24		Grebe II (4/28)	
3/28		Siskin IIIA (9/31)	
9/31		Bulldog IIA (1/35)	
1/35		Gauntlet I (3/39)	
9/36		Gauntlet II (2/39)	
8/38		Spitfire I (12/40)	

No. 20 SQUADRON   MOTTO Facta non verba (Deeds not words)

Date	Location	Aircraft Type	Remarks
11/11/18	Iris Farm	Bristol F2B (5/19)	
3/12/18	to Ossogne		
30/4/19	*en route* to India		
16/6/19	to Risalpur		

7/19		Bristol F2B (3/32)	Dets Tank & Sorarogha
21/7/19	to Parachinar		Dets Risalpur & Bannu
2/9/19	to Bannu		Det Tank
18/7/20	to Parachinar		Det Tank
5/11/20	to Tank		
20/4/21	to Parachinar		
17/10/21	to Ambala		
24/10/22	to Quetta		Det Loralai
5/1/25	to Peshawar		Det Miranshah
22/5/25	to Kohat		Dets Miranshah
12/10/25	to Peshawar		Dets Miranshah, Quetta & Manzai
1/32		Wapiti (12/35)	Dets Miranshah, Hassani Abdel, Jhelum & Quetta
12/35		Audax (12/41)	
2/12/36	to Peshawar		Dets Risalpur, Hassani Abdel & Arawali
7/1/37	to Miranshah		
14/8/37	to Peshawar		Det Miranshah
13/5/38	to Miranshah		
20/5/39	to Peshahwar		Dets Miranshah, Kohat & Prarachinar
29/8/39	to Miranshah		Dets Manzai & Peshawar

No. 21 SQUADRON   MOTTO: Viribus vincimus (By strength we conquer)

Date	Location	Aircraft Type	Remarks
11/11/18	Froidmont	RE8 (2/19)	
16/11/18	to Sweveghem		
18/12/18	to Coucou		
14/2/19	to Fowlmere		as cadre
1/10/19	DB		
3/12/35	RF Bircham Newton		Nucleus from 82 Sqn
12/35		Hind (8/38)	
25/7/36	to Abbotsinch		
3/11/36	to Lympne		
15/8/38	to Eastchurch		
8/38		Blenheim I (9/39)	
2/3/39	to Watton		
9/39		Blenheim IV (3/42)	Dets Bassingbourne, Horsham St Faith & Bodney

No. 22 SQUADRON   MOTTO: Preux et audacieux (Valiant and brave)

Date	Location	Aircraft Type	Remarks
11/11/18	Aniche	Bristol F2B (8/19)	
17/11/18	to Aulnoye		
22/11/18	to Wiheries		
20/12/18	to Nivelles		
21/5/19	to Spich		
31/8/19	to Ford Junction		as cadre
31/12/19	DB		
24/7/23	RF Martlesham		as A & AE Trials Unit Heath
7/23		DH9A (10/26)	
10/26		Horsley (5/34)	
1/5/34	DB		Equipment was largely notional and would have been that operated in the event of mobilization.
1/5/34	RF Donibristle		
5/34		Vildebeest I (10/35)	
5/35		Vildebeest III (2/40)	
10/10/35	to Hal Far		
29/8/36	to Donibristle		
10/3/38	to Thorney Island		
3/38		Vildebeest IV (2/40)	
9/39		Vildebeest I (11/39)	

No. 23 SQUADRON   MOTTO: Semper aggressus (Always having attacked)

Date	Location	Aircraft Type	Remarks
11/11/18	Bertry East	Dolphin (3/19)	

3/12/18	to Clermont		
15/3/19	to Waddington		as cadre
31/12/19	DB		
1/7/25	RF Henlow		
7/25		Snipe (4/26)	
4/26		Gamecock I (9/31)	
6/2/27	to Kenley		
7/31		Bulldog IIA (4/33)	
7/31		Hart Fighter (7/32)	
7/32		Demon (12/38)	
17/9/32	to Biggin Hill		
21/12/36	to Northolt		
16/5/38	to Wittering		
12/38		Blenheim IF (4/41)	

No. 24 SQUADRON   MOTTO: In omnia parati (Ready in all things)

Date	Location	Aircraft Type	Remarks
11/11/18	to Bisseghem	SE5A (1/19)	
16/11/18	to Ennetières		
12/2/19	to London Colney		as cadre
19/9/19	to Uxbridge		
1/2/20			Re-established at Kenley from the Air Council Inspection Squadron
2/20		Bristol F2B (7/30)	
7/20		DH9A (6/27)	
15/1/27	to Northolt		
1/27		Avro 504N	
1/27		Moth (7/33)	
6/28		Wapiti (/30)	
7/28		Fairey IIIF (/33)	
7/30		Tomtit (/33)	
11/31		Tutor (10/32)	
1/33		Hart C (7/41)	
6/33		Tiger Moth (6/38)	
10/7/33	to Hendon		
7/33		Audax (2/38)	
3/35		Dragon Rapide /Dominie (10/44)	
7/37		Nighthawk (9/38)	
10/37		DH86 Express (3/43)	
6/38		Magister I (/40)	
6/38		Anson I (6/38)	
10/38		Mentor (8/44)	
11/38		Vega Gull (10/42)	
9/39		Leopard Moth (4/40)	

No. 25 SQUADRON   MOTTO: Feriens tego (Striking I defend)

Date	Location	Aircraft Type	Remarks
11/11/18	La Brayelle	DH9A (10/19)	
29/11/18	to Maubeuge		
26/5/19	to Bickendorf		
7/7/19	to Merheim		
6/9/19	to South Carlton		
9/10/19			Reduced to cadre
3/12/19	to Scopwick		
31/1/20	DB		
26/4/20	RF Hawkinge		
4/20		Snipe (10/24)	
28/9/22	*en route* to Turkey		
11/10/22	to San Stephano		
22/9/23	*en route* to UK		
3/10/23	to Hawkinge		
10/24		Grebe II (7/29)	
5/29		Siskin IIIA (3/32)	
2/32		Fury I (/37)	
11/36		Fury II (10/37)	
10/37		Demon (6/38)	
6/38		Gladiator I (2/39)	

Date	Location		Aircraft Type	Remarks
26/9/38	to Northolt			
12/10/38	to Hawkinge			
12/38			Blenheim IF (1/41)	
22/8/39	to Northolt			

No. 26 SQUADRON   **MOTTO: 'N Wagter in die Lug (A guard in the sky)**

Date	Location	Aircraft Type	Remarks
11/10/27	RF Catterick		
10/27		Atlas (9/33)	
7/33		Audax (9/37)	
8/37		Hector (5/39)	
2/29		Lysander III (11/40)	

No. 27 SQUADRON   **MOTTO: Quam celerrime ad astra (With all speed to the stars)**

Date	Location	Aircraft Type	Remarks
11/11/18	Villers-les-Cagnicour	DH9 (3/19)	
28/11/18	to Bavay		
18/3/19	to Scopwick		as cadre
22/1/20	DB		
1/4/20	RF Mianwali		No. 99 Sqn renumbered
4/20		DH9A	(5/30)
14/4/20	to Risalpur		Dets Tank & Dardoni
14/12/22	to Dardoni		
20/4/23	to Rislapur		Dets Dardoni, Miranshah & Arawali
26/5/25	to Peshawar		
12/10/25	to Risalpur		Det Miranshah
17/12/28	to Kohat		
4/30		Wapiti (11/40)	Dets Manzai, Miranshah, Juhu, Arawali,Gilgit & St Thomas Mount

No. 28 SQUADRON   **MOTTO: Quicquid agas age (Whatsoever you may do, do)**

Date	Location	Aircraft Type	Remarks
11/11/18	Sarcedo	Camel (2/19)	
10/3/19	to Yatesbury		as cadre
29/3/19	to Leighterton		
20/10/19	to Eastleigh		
20/1/20	DB		
1/4/20	RF Ambala		No. 114 Sqn renumbered
4/20		Bristol F2B (9/31)	
15/10/21	to Kohat		Dets Dardoni & Tank
15/4/22	to Parachinar		
10/10/22	to Kohat		
12/12/22	to Dardoni		
17/3/23	to Tank		
19/4/23	to Peshawar		Dets Dardoni, Hassani, Abdel & Tank
5/1/25	to Quetta		Det Poona
15/12/26	to Ambala		Dets Poona, Bangalore, Deolali, Secunderabad, Jubbulpore, Saugor & Miranshah
13/8/30	to Risalpur		
1/12/30	to Ambala		
9/31		Wapiti (7/36)	Dets Jhelum, Delhi, Peshawar, Mhow & Jullundur
6/36		Audax (12/41)	Det Delhi)
23/4/37	to Manzai		Det Miranshah
6/7/37	to Ambala		Dets Delhi, Juhu & Miranshah
3/3/39	to Kohat		Dets Miranshah,Peshawar, Arawali Manzai, Risalpur, Quetta, Drigh Rd, Dum Dum, Fort Sandeman, Jhelum, Jullundur & Sialkot

No. 29 SQUADRON   **MOTTO: Impiger at acer (Energetic and keen)**

Date	Location	Aircraft Type	Remarks
11/11/18	Marcke	SE5A (8/19)	
26/11/18	to Nivelles		
19/12/18	to Bickendorf		

Date	Location		Remarks
11/8/19	to Spittlegate		as cadre
31/12/19	DB		
1/4/23	RF Duxford		
4/23		Snipe (1/25)	
1/25		Grebe II (3/28)	
3/28		Siskin IIIA (6/32)	
1/4/28	to North Weald		
6/32		Bulldog IIA (4/35)	
3/35		Demon (3/36)	
31/10/35	to Amiriya		
3/36		Gordon (8/36)	
20/7/36	to Helwan		
6/8/36	to Aboukir		
12/9/36	to North Weald		
10/36		Demon (Turret) 12/38	
22/11/37	to Debden		
12/38		Blenheim IF (2/41)	Det Martlesham Heath

No. 30 SQUADRON   MOTTO: Ventre a terre (All out)

Date	Location	Aircraft Type	Remarks
11/11/18	Kifri	Martinsyde G100 (2/19)	Flt at Baquba dets Hamadan and Zinjan
23/11/18	to Baquba		Flts at Kifri, Kazvin, Baghdad & Bushire
1/19		SE5A (2/19)	
2/4/19	to Baghdad		
9/4/19			Reduced to cadre
1/2/20			Re-established at Baghdad West from No. 63 Sqn
2/20		RE8 (1/21)	Dets Mosul, Kazvin, Bushire, Ramadi & Samawah
1/21		DH9A (9/29)	
3/12/22	to Hinaidi		Det Kirkuk
11/4/27	to Kirkuk		Dets Hinaidi & Sulaimania
27/10/27	to Hinaidi		
4/29		Wapiti (8/35)	
23/10/29	to Mosul		
4/35		Hardy (4/38)	
19/10/36	to Dhibban		
1/38		Blenheim I (3/41)	
25/8/39	to Ismailia		Det El Daba

No. 31 SQUADRON   MOTTO: In caelum indicum primus (First into Indian skies)

Date	Location	Aircraft Type	Remarks
11/11/18	Risalpur	BE2E (2/20)	Dets Bannu, Tank, Khanpur, Dera Ismail Khan, Dera Ghazi Khan & Lahore
6/19		Bristol F2B (4/31)	Dets Bannu, Tank & Kohat
15/4/20	to Mhow		
26/11/20	to Cawnpore		
31/10/21	to Peshawar		Dets Tank & Dardoni
17/4/23	to Dardoni		
13/3/24	to Ambala		Dets Quetta
15/12/26	to Quetta		Dets Jubbulpore, Mhow, Fort Dandeman & Loralai
2/31		Wapiti (8/39)	Dets Fort Sandeman, Secunderabad, Hakimpet & Mhow
8/6/35	to Drigh Road		as cadre
1/8/35			Re-established. Dets Quetta, Hakimpet, Jubbulpore, Fort Sandeman, Poona & Risalpur
27/10/38	to Lahore		Dets Fort Sandeman, Jubbulpore, Ambala & Risalpur
4/39		Valentia (8/41)	

No. 32 SQUADRON   MOTTO: Adeste comites (Rally round comrades)

Date	Location	Aircraft Type	Remarks
11/11/18	La Brayelle	SE5A (3/19)	
16/1/18	to Le Hameau		
18/1/19	to Serny		
5/3/19	to Tangmere		as cadre

Date	Location	Aircraft Type	Remarks
8/10/19	to Croydon		
31/12/19	DB		
1/4/23	RF Kenley		
4/23		Snipe (12/24)	
11/24		Grebe II (1/27)	
9/26		Gamecock I (4/28)	
4/28		Siskin III (1/31	
1/31		Bulldog IIA (7/36)	
21/9/32	to Biggin Hill		
7/36		Gauntlet II (10/38)	
10/38		Hurricane I (7/41)	

No. 33 SQUADRON   MOTTO: Loyalty

Date	Location	Aircraft Type	Remarks
11/11/18	Kirton-in-Lindsey	Avro 504K (6/19)	Dets Scampton & Elsham
2/6/19	to Harpswell		
13/6/19	DB		
1/3/29	RF Netheravon		
3/29		Horsley (3/30)	
14/9/29	to Eastchurch		
2/30		Hart (2/38)	
5/11/30	to Bicester		
27/11/34	to Upper Heyford		
4/11/35	*en route* to Egypt		
25/10/35	to Mersa Matruh		Det Ramleh
13/7/36	to Amman		Det Ramleh
10/8/36	to Gaza		
14/11/36	to Ismailia		
2/38		Gladiator I (6/40)	Det Ramleh
29/9/38	to Heliopolis		Det Ramleh
3/10/38	to Ismailia		
21/10/38	to Ramleh		Dets Lydda & Amman
24/4/39	to Helwan		
25/5/39	to Ismailia		Dets El Daba & Qasaba
5/8/39	to Qasaba		
1/9/39	to Mersah Matruh		

No. 34 SQUADRON   MOTTO: Lupus vult, lupus volat (The wolf wishes, the wolf flies)

Date	Location	Aircraft Type	Remarks
11/11/18	San Luca	Bristol F2B (7/18)	
16/11/18	to Villaverla		
28/2/19	to Caldiero		
3/5/19	to Old Sarum		as cadre
15/10/19	DB		
3/12/35	RF Bircham Newton		Nucleus from No. 18 Sqn
1/36		Hind (7/38)	
30/7/36	to Abbotsinch		
3/11/36	to Lympne		
12/7/38	to Upper Heyford		
7/38		Blenheim I (11/41)	
2/3/39	to Watton		
12/8/39	*en route* to Far East		
	to Tengah		

No. 35 SQUADRON   MOTTO: Uno animo agimus (We act with one accord)

Date	Location	Aircraft Type	Remarks
11/11/18	to Grand Fayt	Bristol F2B (1/19)	
13/11/18	to Elincourt		
29/11/18	to La Bellevue		
19/1/19	to Ste-Maries-Vappel		as cadre
3/3/19	to Netheravon		
26/6/19	DB		
1/3/29	RF Bircham Newton		
3/29		DH9A (1/30)	
11/29		Fairey IIIF (9/32)	

7/32		Gordon (8/36)	
4/10/35	*en route* to Middle East		
18/10/35	to Ed Damer		
7/4/36	to Gebeit		
14/8/36	*en route* to UK		
26/8/36	to Worthy Down		
11/36		Gordon (9/37)	
7/37		Wellesley (5/38)	
4/38		Battle (2/40)	
20/4/38	to Cottesmore		
7/39		Anson I (4/40)	
25/8/39	to Cranfield		

No. 36 SQUADRON   MOTTO: Rajawali raja langit (Eagle king of the sky)

Date	Location	Aircraft Type	Remarks
11/11/18	Hylton/Usworth	Bristol F2B	Dets Seaton Carew & Ashington
13/6/19	DB		
9/10/28	RF Donibristle		Coastal-defence torpedo flight redesignated
10/28		Horsley (7/35)	
14/10/30	to Far East by sea		via Leuchars
14/11/30	to Seletar		
7/35		Vildebeest III (3/42)	Dets Kota, Bahru, Gong Kedak & Kuantan

No. 37 SQUADRON   MOTTO: Wise without eyes

Date	Location	Aircraft Type	Remarks
11/11/18	Stow Maries	Camel (7/19)	Det Goldhanger
17/3//19	to Biggin Hill	Snipe (7/19)	
1/7/19	DB		Renumbered as No. 39 Sqn
26/4/37	RF Feltwell		from B Flt, No. 214 Sqn
4/37		Harrow (6/39)	
5/39		Wellington I (11/39)	

No. 38 SQUADRON   MOTTO: Anter lucem (Before the dawn)

Date	Location	Aircraft Type	Remarks
11/11/18	Harlebeck	FE2B (1/19)	
16/12/18	to Serny		
14/2/19	to Hawkinge		as cadre
4/7/19	DB		
16/9/35	RF Mildenhall		Nucleus from B Flt, No. 99 Sqn
9/35		Heyford III (6/37)	
11/36		Hendon II (1/39)	
5/5/37	to Marham		
11/38		Wellington I (4/40)	
9/39		Wellington IA (6/40)	

No. 39 SQUADRON   MOTTO: Die noctuque (By day and night)

Date	Location	Aircraft Type	Remarks
11/11/18	North Weald	Bristol F2B (11/18)	
16/11/18	DB		Deployment to Bavichore abandoned before completion
1/7/19	RF Biggin Hill		No. 37 Sqn renumbered
7/19		Snipe (10/19)	
14/10/19			Reduced to cadre
20/12/19	to Uxbridge		
12/4/20	to Kenley		
12/3/21	to Spittlegate		Re-established
4/21		DH9A (11/28)	
12/1/28	to Bircham Newton		
29/12/28	*en route* to India		
22/1/29	to Risalpur		
3/29		Wapiti (12/31)	Dets Miranshah, Gilgit & Peshawar
11/31		Hart (7/39)	Dets Jhelum, Delhi, Gilgit & Miranshah
6/39		Blenheim I (1/41)	
12/8/39	to Tengah		

No. 40 SQUADRON   **MOTTO: Hostem coelo expellere (To drive the enemy from the sky)**

Date	Location	Aircraft Type	Remarks
11/11/18	Aniche	SE5A (2/19)	
29/12/18	to Orcq		
13/2/19	to Tangmere		as cadre
4/7/19	DB		
1/4/31	RF Upper Heyford		
4/31		Gordon (11/35)	
8/10/32	to Abingdon		
11/35		Hart (Special) (3/36)	
3/36		Hind (8/38)	
7/38		Battle (12/29)	
2/9/39	to Béthenville		

No. 41 SQUADRON   **MOTTO: Seek and destroy**

Date	Location	Aircraft Type	Remarks
11/11/18	Halluin	SE5A (2/19)	
10/2/19	to Tangmere		as cadre
8/10/19	to Croydon		
31/12/19	DB		
1/4/23	RF Northolt		
4/23		Snipe (5/24)	
5/24		Siskin III (3/27)	
3/27		Siskin IIIA (11/31)	
10/31		Bulldog IIA (8/34)	
7/34		Demon (10/37)	
4/10/35	*en route* to Aden		
20/10/35	to Khormaksar		
18/3/36	to Sheikh Othman		
11/8/36	*en route* to the UK		
25/9/36	to Catterick		
10/37		Fury II (1/39)	
1/39		Spitfire I (11/40)	

No. 42 SQUADRON   **MOTTO: Fortiter in re (Bravely in action)**

Date	Location	Aircraft Type	Remarks
11/11/18	Ascq	RE8 (2/19)	
14/11/18	to Marquain		
26/11/18	to Aulnoy		
11/12/18	to Saultain		
30/12/18	to Abscon		
18/2/19	to Netheravon		as cadre
26/6/19	DB		
14/12/36	RF Donibristle		from B Flt, No. 22 Sqn
12/36		Vildebeest III (12/37)	
1/37		Vildebeest I (3/37)	
3/37		Vildebeest IV (4/40)	
11/3/38	to Thorney Island		Dets Eastleigh, Lee-on-Solent, Tangmere & Gosport
28/9/38	to Thornaby		
11/10/38	to Thorney Island		
18/8/39	to Bircham Newton		
9/39		Vildebeest III (4/40)	

No. 43 SQUADRON   **MOTTO: Gloria finis (Glory in the end)**

Date	Location	Aircraft Type	Remarks
11/11/18	Bouvincourt	Snipe (9/19)	
15/11/18	to Bisseghem		
26/11/18	to Fort Cognelée		
19/12/18	to Bickendorf		
12/8/19	to Eil		
25/8/19	to Spittlegate		
28/9/19			Reduced to cadre
31/12/19	DB		
1/7/25	RF Henlow		

7/25		Snipe (5/26)	
4/26		Gamecock I (6/28)	
12/12/26	to Tangmere		
6/28		Siskin IIIA (5/31)	
5/31		Fury I (1/39)	
12/38		Hurricane I (4/41)	

No. 44 SQUADRON   MOTTO: Fulmina regis justa (The King's thunderbolts are righteous)

Date	Location	Aircraft Type	Remarks
11/11/18	Hainault Farm	Camel (6/19)	
1/7/19	to North Weald		as cadre
	Basset		
31/12/19	DB		
8/3/37	RF Wyton		
3/37		Hind (12/37)	
18/3/37	to Andover		
16/6/37	to Waddington		
12/37		Blenheim I (2/39)	
2/39		Anson I (6/39)	
2/39		Hampden (12/41)	Det Lossiemouth

No. 45 SQUADRON   MOTTO: Per ardua surgo (Through difficulties I arise)

Date	Location	Aircraft Type	Remarks
11/11/18	Bettoncourt	Camel (1/19)	
10/18		Snipe (1/19)	
21/11/18	to Izel-le-Hameau		
19/1/19	to Liettres		
17/2/19	to Rendcombe		as cadre
15/10/19	to Eastleigh		
31/12/19	DB		
1/4/21	RF Helwan		
4/21		DH9A (7/21)	
11/7/21	to Almaza		
7/21		Vimy (2/22)	
2/22		Vernon (1/27)	
14/3/22	to Basra		
14/4/22	to Baghdad West		
16/5/22	to Hinaidi		
17/1/27	to Helwan		as cadre
25/4/27			Re-established at Heliopolis
4/27		DH9A (9/29)	
21/10/27	to Helwan		Det Ramleh
8/29		Fairey IIIF	Dets Amman, Gaza, Ismailia, Hinaidi, Mosul, Shaibah & Eastleigh
9/35		Hart (1/36)	
11/35		Vincent (12/37)	
1/36		Gordon (12/36)	Eastleigh det of the squadron became nucleus of 223 Sqn
11/37		Wellesley (6/39)	
3/1/39	to Ismailia		
6/39		Blenheim I (2/41)	
4/8/39	to Fuka		

No. 46 SQUADRON   MOTTO: We rise to conquer

Date	Location	Aircraft Type	Remarks
11/11/18	Busigny	Camel (2/19)	
16/11/18	to Baizieux		
10/2/19	to Rendcomb		as cadre
31/12/19	DB		
3/9/36	RF Kenley		from B Flt, No. 17 Sqn
9/36		Gauntlet II (3/39)	
15/11/37	to Digby		
3/39		Hurricane I (5/41)	

No. 47 SQUADRON   MOTTO: Nili nomen roboris omen (The name of the Nile is an omen of our strength)

Date	Location	Aircraft Type	Remarks
11/11/18	Yanesh	AW FK8 (1/19)	Flts at Mikra Bay, Kukush, Snevche
		DH9 (10/19)	Hadzi, Junas, Kirec, Kalabac, Hajdarli, Amberkoj, dets Thasos, Florina, Mudros, Gmuldjina & Dedeagatch
14/2/19	to Amberkoj		
24/4/19	to Novorossisk		
4/6/19	to Ekaterinodar		Flts at Velikoknyajaskaya, Zimovniki, Kotelnikovo, Gniloaksaiskaya & Beketovka
8/19		DH9A (10/19)	
9/19		Camel (10/19)	
7/10/19	to Beketovka		
20/10/19	DB		Redesignated as Nos 11, 12 & 13 Sqns, Russian 7th Division
1/2/20	RF Helwan		No. 206 Sqn renumbered
2/20		DH9 (9/20)	Det Khartoum
6/20		DH9A (6/28)	
21/10/27	to Khartoum		
12/27		Fairey IIIF (1/33)	
1/33		Gordon (12/39)	
7/36		Vincent (8/40)	
6/39		Wellesley (3/43)	Det Kapoeta

No. 48 SQUADRON   MOTTO: Forte et fidele (Bravely and faithfully)

Date	Location	Aircraft Type	Remarks
11/11/18	Reckem	Bristol F2B (5/19)	
17/11/18	to Nivelles		
19/12/18	to Bickendorf		
26/5/19	en route to India		
27/6/19	to Quetta		
8/19		Bristol F2B (4/20)	Det Loralai
1/4/20	DB		Renumbered as No. 5 Sqn
25/11/35	RF Bicester	from C Flt, No. 101 Sqn	
16/12/35	to Manston		
1/36		Clouds (6/36)	B Flt Seaplane Training Squadron attached from Calshot 17/1–6/36
6/1/36			X Flt, School of Air Navigation attached until 1/9/38
3/36		Anson I (12/41)	
1/9/38	to Eastchurch		
28/9/38	to Thorney Island		
10/10/38	to Eastchurch		
4/8/39	to Manston		
13/8/39	to Eastchurch		
25/8/39	to Thorney Island		Dets Bircham Newton, Detling, Guernsey & Carew Cheriton

No. 49 SQUADRON   MOTTO: Cave canem (Beware of the dog)

Date	Location	Aircraft Type	Remarks
11/11/18	Villers-lès-Cagnicourt	DH9 (7/19)	
24/11/18	to Bavai		
29/5/19	to Bickendorf		
18/7/19	DB		
10/2/36	RF Bircham Newton		from C Flt. No. 18 Sqn
2/36		Hind (12/38)	
8/8/36	to Worthy Down		
14/3/38	to Scampton		
9/38		Hampden (4/42)	Det Kinloss

No. 50 SQUADRON   MOTTO: From defence to attack

Date	Location	Aircraft Type	Remarks
11/11/18	Bekesbourne	Camel (6/19)	
13/6/19	DB		
3/5/37	RF Waddington		

5/37		Hind (1/39)	
12/38		Hampden (4/42)	Dets Lossiemouth, Wick & Kinloss

No. 51 SQUADRON   MOTTO: Swift and sure

Date	Location	Aircraft Type	Remarks
11/11/18	Marham	Camel (6/19)	Dets Mattishal & Tydd St Mary
14/5/19	to Suttons Farm		
13/6/19	DB		
15/3/37	RF Driffield		from B Flt, No. 58 Sqn
3/37		Virginia X (2/38)	
24/3/37	to Boscombe Down		
3/37		Anson I (2/38)	
2/38		Whitley II (12/39)	
20/4/38	to Linton-on-Ouse		
8/38		Whitley III (3/40)	

No. 52 SQUADRON   MOTTO: Sudore quam sanguine (By sweat other than through blood)

Date	Location	Aircraft Type	Remarks
11/11/18	Aulnoy	RE8 (2/19)	
16/11/19	to Linselles		
23/11/18	to Aulnoy		
18/2/19	to Netheravon		as cadre
28/6/19	to Lopcombe Corner		
23/10/19	DB		
18/1/37	RF Abingdon		from B Flt, No. 15 Sqn
1/37		Hind (12/37)	
1/3/37	to Upwood		
11/37		Battle (4/40)	
2/39		Anson I (4/40)	Det Alconbury

No. 53 SQUADRON   MOTTO: United in effort

Date	Location	Aircraft Type	Remarks
11/11/18	Sweveghem	RE8 (4/19)	
16/11/18	to Seclin		
28/11/18	to Laneffe		
15/3/19	to Old Sarum		as cadre
25/10/19	DB		
28/6/37	RF Farnborough		
6/37		Hector (3/39)	
8/4/38	to Odiham		
1/39		Blenheim IV (8/41)	

No. 54 SQUADRON   MOTTO: Audax omnia perpeti (Boldness to endure anything)

Date	Location	Aircraft Type	Remarks
11/11/18	Merchin	Camel (2/19)	
17/2/19	to Yatesbury		as cadre
25/10/19	DB		
15/1/30	RF Hornchurch		
1/30		Siskin IIIA (12/30)	
4/30		Bulldog IIA (9/36)	
8/36		Gauntlet II (5/37)	
4/37		Gladiator (4/39)	
3/39		Spitfire I (2/41)	

No. 55 SQUADRON   MOTTO: Nil nos tremefacit (Nothing shakes us)

Date	Location	Aircraft Type	Remarks
11/11/18	Azelot	DH4 (1/19)	
16/11/18	to Le Planty		
2/12/18	to André-aux-Bois		
1/2/19	to Renfrew		as cadre
1/1/20	to Shotwick		
22/1/20	DB		
1/2/20	RF Suez		No. 142 Sqn renumbered

Date	Location	Aircraft Type	Remarks
2/20		DH9 (9/20)	Det Ramleh
6/20		DH9A (2/30)	
8/7/20	*en route* to Turkey		
12/7/20	to Maltepe		
3/9/20	*en route* to Basra		via HMS *Ark Royal*
23/9/20	to Basra		
30/9/20	to Baghdad West		Dets Bushire & Mosul
20/3/21	to Mosul		
19/5/24	to Hinaidi		
2/30		Wapiti (3/37)	
2/37		Vincent (5/39)	
14/9/37	to Dhibban/Habbaniyah		
3/39		Blenheim I (12/40)	
25/8/39	to Ismailia		

No. 56 SQUADRON   MOTTO: Quid si coelum ruat (What if heaven falls)

Date	Location	Aircraft Type	Remarks
11/11/18	La Targette	SE5A (2/19)	
22/11/18	to Béthencourt		
14/2/19	to Narborough		as cadre
30/12/19	to Bircham Newton		
22/1/20	DB		
1/2/20	RF Aboukir		No. 80 Sqn renumbered
2/20		Snipe (9/22)	Det San Stephano (Remained until 8/23)
23/9/22	DB		
1/11/22	RF Hawkinge		
11/22		Snipe (11/24)	
7/5/23	to Biggin Hill		
9/24		Grebe II (9/27)	
9/27		Siskin IIIA (10/32)	
12/10/27	to North Weald		
10/32		Bulldog IIA (5/36)	
5/36		Gauntlet II (7/37)	
7/37		Gladiator I (5/38)	
4/38		Hurricane I (2/41)	

No. 57 SQUADRON   MOTTO: Corpus non animum muto (I change my body not my spirit)

Date	Location	Aircraft Type	Remarks
11/11/18	Beauvois	DH4 (5/19)	
22/11/18	to Vert Galand		
24/11/18	to Le Casteau		Det Spa
12/12/18	to Spa		Dets La Louveterie & Franc Waret
7/1/19	to Morville		
2/19		DH9A (7/19)	Dets Sart, Maisoncelle, Nivelles & Marquise
4/8/19	to South Carlton		as cadre
31/12/19	DB		
20/10/31	RF Netheravon		
11/31		Hart (5/36)	
5/9/32	to Upper Heyford		
5/36		Hind (5/38)	
3/38		Blenheim I (5/40)	

No. 58 SQUADRON   MOTTO: Alis nocturnis (On the wings of the night)

Date	Location	Aircraft Type	Remarks
11/11/18	Provin	HP 0/400 (1/20)	
12/4/19	*en route* to Egypt		via Marseilles
2/5/19	to Heliopolis		
7/19		Vimy (1/20)	
1/2/20	DB		Renumbered as No. 70 Sqn
1/4/24	RF Worthy Down		
4/24		Vimy (5/25)	
12/24		Virginia V (11/26)	
3/25		Virginia III (4/26)	
7/25		Virginia VI (5/27)	
8/26		Virginia VII (12/30)	
4/27		Virginia IX (4/34)	

1/28		Virginia X (1/38)	
13/1/36	to Upper Heyford		
3/9/36	to Driffield		
2/37		Anson I (11/37)	
24/3/37	to Boscombe Down		
10/37		Whitley I (4/38)	
10/37		Whitley II (7/39)	
20/4/38	to Linton-on-Ouse		
4/39		Heyford III (5/39)	
5/39		Whitley III (4/40)	Dets Reims & Boscombe Down

No. 59 SQUADRON   MOTTO: Ab uno disce omnes (From one learn all)

Date	Location	Aircraft Type	Remarks
11/11/18	Caudry	Bristol F2B (8/19)	
29/11/18	to Gerpinnes		
14/3/19	to Bickendorf		
3/5/19	to Duren		
4/8/19	DB		
28/6/37	RF Old Sarum		
6/37		Hector (9/39)	
5/39		Blenheim IV (8/41)	
11/5/39	to Andover		

No. 60 SQUADRON   MOTTO: Per ardua ad aethera tendo (I strive through difficulties to the sky)

Date	Location	Aircraft Type	Remarks
11/11/18	Quiévy	SE5A (1/19)	
23/11/18	to Inchy		
17/2/19	to Narborough		as cadre
1/1/20	to Bircham Newton		
22/1/20	DB		
1/4/20	RF Risalpur		No. 97 Sqn renumbered
4/20		DH10/10A (4/23)	Dets Mianwali, Rajkot, Juhu, Tank, Karachi and Dardoni
3/23		DH9A (5/30)	Dets Hassani Abdel, Dardoni, Quetta, Arawali, Delhi & Miranshah
29/5/25	to Peshawar		Dets Quetta & Drigh Road
15/10/25	to Kohat		Dets Risalpur, Drigh Road, Quetta, Arawali & Miranshah
3/30		Wapiti (7/39)	Dets Miranshah, Delhi, Seletar, Drigh Road, Arawali, Manzai, Gilgit, Kanpur & Dum Dum
3/3/39	to Ambala		
3/39		Blenheim I (2/42)	Dets Dum Dum, St Thomas Mount, Juhu, Drigh Road, Sharjah & Peshawar

No. 61 SQUADRON   MOTTO: Per purum tonantes (Thundering through the clear sky)

Date	Location	Aircraft Type	Remarks
11/11/18	Rochford	Camel (6/19)	
13/6/19	DB		
8/3/37	RF Hemswell		
3/37		Audax (4/37)	
3/37		Anson I (2/38)	
1/38		Blenheim I (3/39)	Det Wick

No. 62 SQUADRON   MOTTO: Insperato (Unexpectedly)

Date	Location	Aircraft Type	Remarks
11/11/18	Villers-lès-Cagnicourt	Bristol F2B (7/19)	
18/11/18	to Aulnoye		
14/12/18	to Bouge		
20/12/18	to Nivelles		
2/5/19	to Spich		
31/7/19	DB		
3/5/37	RF Abingdon		From B Flt, No. 40 Sqn
5/37		Hind (3/38)	
12/7/37	to Cranfield		

Date	Location	Aircraft Type	Remarks
2/38		Blenheim I (1/42)	
12/8/39	*en route* to the Far East		to Tengah

No. 63 SQUADRON   MOTTO: Pone nos ad hostem (Follow us to find the enemy)

Date	Location	Aircraft Type	Remarks
11/11/18	Tikrit	Martinsyde G102 (8/19)	
12/11/18	to Samara		Dets Mosul & Ramadi
17/2/19	to Baghdad		Dets Ramadi, Kazvin, Bushire, Kermanshah, Mosul & Kirkuk
2/19		SE5A (4/19)	
5/19		Camel (9/19)	
29/2/20	DB		Used to re-establish No. 30 Sqn
15/2/37	RF Andover		from B Flt, No. 12 Sqn
2/37		Hind (4/37)	
3/3/37	to Upwood		
3/37		Audax (8/37)	
5/37		Battle (4/40)	
3/39		Anson I (4/40)	

No. 64 SQUADRON   MOTTO: Tenax propositi (Firmness of purpose)

Date	Location	Aircraft Type	Remarks
11/11/18	Aniche	SE5A (2/19)	
22/11/18	to Saultain		
4/12/18	to Froidmont		
14/2/19	to Narborough		as cadre
31/12/19	DB		
1/3/36	RF Heliopolis		Nucleus from Nos 6 & 208 Sqns via No. 29 Sqn
3/36		Demon (12/38)	
9/4/36	to Ismailia		
1/8/36	to Aboukir		
16/8/36	*en route* to the UK		
12/9/36	to Martlesham Heath		
18/5/38	to Church Fenton		
12/38		Blenheim IF (4/40)	
7/8/39	to Duxford		
12/8/39	to Sutton Bridge		
24/8/39	to Church Fenton		Dets Leconfield, Catterick & Evanton

No. 65 SQUADRON   MOTTO: Vi et armis (By force of arms)

Date	Location	Aircraft Type	Remarks
11/11/18	Bisseghem	Camel (2/19)	
12/2/19	to Yatesbury		as cadre
25/10/19	DB		
1/8/34	RF Hornchurch		
8/34		Demon (7/36)	
7/36		Gauntlet II (6/37)	
6/37		Gladiator I (4/39)	
3/39		Spitfire I (4/41)	

No. 66 SQUADRON   MOTTO: Cavete praemonui (Beware, I have given a warning)

Date	Location	Aircraft Type	Remarks
11/11/18	San Pietro-in-Gu	Camel (3/19)	
10/3/19	to Yatesbury		as cadre
29/3/19	to Leighterton		
25/10/19	DB		
20/7/36	RF Duxford		from C Flt, No. 19 Sqn
7/36		Gauntlet II (12/38)	
10/38		Spitfire I (11/40)	

No. 70 SQUADRON   MOTTO: Usquam (Anywhere)

Date	Location	Aircraft Type	Remarks
11/11/18	Menin	Camel (3/19)	
25/11/18	to Fort Cognelée		

Date	Location	Aircraft Type	Remarks
7/12/18	to Elsenborn		
18/12/18	to Bickendorf		
1/19		Snipe (9/19)	
27/8/19	to Spittlegate		
28/9/19			Reduced to cadre
22/1/20	DB		
1/2/20	RF Heliopolis		No. 58 Sqn renumbered
2/20		HP 0/400 (4/20)	
2/20		Vimy (11/22)	
16/1/22	to Baghdad West		
11/22		Vernon (12/26)	
31/5/22	to Hinaidi		
1/24		Victoria I (3/26)	
2/26		Victoria III (6/34)	
11/28		Victoria IV (5/34)	
4/30		Victoria V (8/35)	
7/31		Victoria VI (11/35)	
11/35		Valentia (10/40)	
16/10/37	to Dhibban/ Habbaniya		
30/8/39	to Helwan		Det Habbaniyah

No. 72 SQUADRON MOTTO: Swift

Date	Location	Aircraft Type	Remarks
11/11/18	Baghdad	Bristol M1 C (2/19)	Flts at Mirjana, Samarra, dets
		SE5A (2/19)	Hamadan, Tikrit, Baku, Kazvin & Zinjan
		SPAD VII (1/19)	
		Martinsyde G.100 (11/18)	
25/11/18			Squadron reunited at Baghdad
1/2/19			Reduced to cadre
22/9/19	DB		
22/2/37	RF Tangmere		Nucleus from No. 1 Sqn
3/37		Gladiator I (5/39)	
1/6/37	to Church Fenton		
4/39		Spitfire I (4/41)	

No. 73 SQUADRON MOTTO: Tutor et ultor (Protector and avenger)

Date	Location	Aircraft Type	Remarks
11/11/18	Malincourt	Camel (2/19)	
15/11/18	to Baizieux		
10/2/19	to Yatesbury		as cadre
2/7/19	DB		
15/3/37	RF Mildenhall		
3/37		Fury II (7/37)	
12/6/37	to Debden		
6/37		Gladiator I (7/38)	
9/11/37	to Digby		
7/38		Hurricane I (1/42)	

No. 74 SQUADRON MOTTO: I fear no man

Date	Location	Aircraft Type	Remarks
11/11/18	Cuerne	SE5A (2/19)	
17/11/18	to Froidmont		
30/11/18	to Halluin		
10/2/19	to Lopcombe Corner		as cadre
3/7/19	DB		
1/9/35	RF Hornchurch		Initially referred to as 'the Demon Flights'
3/9/35			Established on board HMT *Neuralia*
			en route to Malta
9/35		Demon (4/37)	
11/9/35	to Hal Far		
21/9/36	to Hornchurch		
3/37		Gauntlet II (2/39)	
2/39		Spitfire I (9/40)	

No. 75 SQUADRON   MOTTO: Ake ake kia kaka (Maori – For ever and ever be strong)

Date	Location	Aircraft Type	Remarks
11/11/18	Elmswell	Avro 504K (NF) (6/19)	Dets Harling Road & Hadleigh
22/5/19	to North Weald Basset		
13/6/19	DB		
15/3/37	RF Driffield		from B Flt, No. 215 Sqn
3/37		Virginia X (9/37)	
3/37		Anson I (11/37)	
9/37		Harrow (7/39)	
11/7/38	to Honington		
3/39		Anson I (10/39)	
7/39		Wellington I (4/40)	
13/7/39	to Stradishall		

No. 76 SQUADRON   MOTTO: Resolute

Date	Location	Aircraft Type	Remarks
11/11/18	Ripon	Avro 504K (NF) (5/19)	Dets Copmanthorpe, Helperby & Catterick
18/3/19	to Helperby		Dets Copmanthorpe and Catterick
30/5/19	to Tadcaster		as cadre
13/6/19	DB		
12/4/37	RF Finningley		from B Flt, No. 7 Sqn
4/37		Wellesley (4/39)	
3/39		Hampden (4/40)	
5/39		Anson I (4/40)	

No. 77 SQUADRON   MOTTO: Esse potius quam videri (To be rather than seen)

Date	Location	Aircraft Type	Remarks
11/11/18	Penstone	Avro 504K (NF) (6/19)	Det Whiteburn
13/6/19	DB		
14/6/37	RF Finnningley		from B Flt, No. 102 Sqn
6/37		Audax (11/37)	
7/7/37	to Honington		
11/37		Wellesley (11/38)	
25/7/38	to Driffield		
11/38		Whitley III (10/39)	
9/39		Whitley V (10/42)	Dets Villeneuve & Kinloss

No. 78 SQUADRON   MOTTO: Nemo non paratus (Nobody unprepared)

Date	Location	Aircraft Type	Remarks
11/11/18	Suttons Farm	Camel (7/19)	Det Biggin Hill
		Snipe 7/19)	
1/7/19			Reduced to cadre
31/12/19	DB		
1/11/36	RF Boscombe Down		from B Flt, No. 10 Sqn
11/36		Heyford III (10/37)	
1/2/37	to Dishforth		
7/37		Whitley I (12/39)	
6/39		Whitley IVA (6/40)	Det Ternhill
8/39		Whitley V (3/42)	Det Linton-on-Ouse

No. 79 SQUADRON   MOTTO: Nil nobis obstare potest (Nothing can stop us)

Date	Location	Aircraft Type	Remarks
11/11/18	Reckem	Dolphin (7/19)	
26/11/18	to Nivelles		
20/12/18	to Bickendorf		
15/7/19	DB		
22/3/37	RF Biggin Hill		From B Flt, No. 32 Sqn
3/37		Gauntlet II (11/38)	
11/38		Hurricane I (7/41)	

No. 80 SQUADRON   MOTTO: Strike true

Date	Location	Aircraft Type	Remarks
11/11/18	Flaumont	Camel (12/18)	
12/11/18	to Grand Fayt		
3/12/18	to Strée A		
12/18		Snipe (2/20)	
3/19	to Clermont		
26/5/19	*en route* to Egypt		via Marseilles
10/6/19	to Aboukir		
1/2/20	DB		Renumbered as No. 56 Sqn
8/3/37	RF Kenley		from B Flt, No. 17 Sqn
3/37		Gauntlet II (5/37)	
15/3/37	to Henlow		
5/37		Gladiator I (11/40)	
9/6/37	to Debden		
30/4/38	*en route* to Egypt		
10/5/38	to Ismailia	Det Ramleh	
24/9/38	to Amiriya		
9/10/38	to Ismailia		
16/1/39	to Helwan		
21/4/39	to Amiriya		
19/5/39	to Helwan		Det Amiriya
15/7/39	to Amiriya		

No. 81 SQUADRON   MOTTO: Non solum nobis (Not for us alone)

Date	Location	Aircraft Type	Remarks
25/11/18	RF Upper Heyford		Also designated as No. 1 Sqn
			Canadian Air Force
11/18		Dolphin (4/19)	
2/5/19	to Shoreham		
5/19		SE5A (1/20)	
28/1/20	DB		

No. 82 Squadron MOTTO: Super omnia ubique (Over all things everywhere)

Date	Location	Aircraft Type	Remarks
11/11/18	Menin	AW FK8 (2/19)	
19/11/18	to Bertangles		
15/2/19	to Shoreham		as cadre
5/19	to Tangmere		
4/7/19	DB		
14/6/37	RF Andover		from B Flt, No. 142 Sqn
6/37		Hind (3/38)	
8/7/37	to Cranfield		
3/38		Blenheim I (9/39)	
22/8/39	to Watton		
8/39		Blenheim IV (3/42)	Dets Odiham, Lossiemouth, Tangmere & Luqa

No. 83 SQUADRON   MOTTO: Strike to defend

Date	Location	Aircraft Type	Remarks
11/11/18	Estrées-en-Chausée	FE2B (2/19)	
13/12/18	to Serny		
14/2/19	to Hawkinge		as cadre
9/19	to Lympne		
15/10/19	to Croydon		
31/12/19	DB		
4/8/36	RF Turnhouse		
8/36		Hind (12/38)	
14/3/38	to Scampton		
11/38		Hampden (1/42)	Det Lossiemouth

No. 84 SQUADRON   MOTTO: Scipiones pungunt (Scorpions sting)

Date	Location	Aircraft Type	Remarks
11/11/18	Bertry West	SE5A (8/19)	
3/12/18	to Thuilles		

Date	Location	Aircraft Type	Remarks
13/5/19	to Bickendorf		
6/7/19	to Eil		
12/8/19	to Tangmere		as cadre
8/10/19	to Croydon		
1/20	to Kenley		
30/1/20	DB		
13/8/20	RF Baghdad West		
8/20		DH9A (1/29)	
20/9/20	to Shaibah		Dets Baghdad West, Nasiriyah & Bushire
6/28		Wapiti (1/35)	
12/34		Vincent (6/39)	
2/39		Blenheim I (4/41)	Det Sharjah

No. 85 SQUADRON   MOTTO: Noctu diuque venamur (We hunt by day and night)

Date	Location	Aircraft Type	Remarks
11/11/18	Phallempin	SE5A (2/29)	
7/12/18	to Ascq		
19/2/19	to Lopcombe Corner		as cadre
3/7/19	DB		
1/6/38	RF Debden		from A Flt, No. 87 Sqn
6/38		Gladiator(4/41)	
9/38		Hurricane (4/41)	
18/10/38	to Aldergrove		
4/11/38	to Debden		

No. 87 SQUADRON   MOTTO: Maximus me metuit (The most powerful fear me)

Date	Location	Aircraft Type	Remarks
11/11/18	Boussières	Dolphin (2/19)	
9/2/19	to Ternhill		as cadre
24/6/19	DB		
15/3/37	RF Tangmere		Nucleus from No. 54 Sqn
3/37		Fury II (6/37)	
7/6/37	to Debden		
6/37		Gladiator I (8/38)	
7/38		Hurricane I (9/42)	

No. 88 SQUADRON   MOTTO: En garde (Be on your guard)

Date	Location	Aircraft Type	Remarks
11/11/18	Bersée	Bristol F2B (8/19)	
18/11/18	to Aulnoy		
13/12/18	to Dour		
14/12/18	to Franc Waret		
18/12/18	to Nivelles		
10/8/19	DB		
7/6/37	RF Waddington		Nucleus from No. 110 Sqn
6/37		Hind(12/37)	
17/7/37	to Boscombe Down		
12/37		Battle (4/41)	

No. 90 SQUADRON   MOTTO: Celer (Swift)

Date	Location	Aircraft Type	Remarks
11/11/18	Buckminster	Avro 504K (NF) (6/19)	Dets Stamford & Leadenham
13/6/19	DB		
15/3/37	RF Bicester		from A Flt, No. 101 Sqn
3/37		Hind (6/37)	
5/37		Blenheim I (4/39)	
3/39		Blenheim IV (4/40)	
10/5/39	to West Raynham		
13/8/39	to Penrhos		
27/8/39	to West Raynham		
3/9/39	to Bircham Newton		

No. 91 SQUADRON   MOTTO: We seek alone

Date	Location	Aircraft Type	Remarks
11/11/18	Kenley	Dolphin 7/19	
7/3/19	to Lopcombe Corner		
3/7/19	DB		

No. 92 SQUADRON   MOTTO: Aut pugna aut morere (Either fight or die)

Date	Location	Aircraft Type	Remarks
11/11/18	Bertry East	SE5A (8/19)	
3/12/18	to Thuilles		
14/6/19	to Eil		
7/8/19)	DB		

No. 93 SQUADRON   MOTTO: Ad arma parati (Ready for battle)

Date	Location	Aircraft Type	Remarks
11/11/18	Port Meadow	Dolphin (11/18)	
21/11/18	DB		

No. 94 SQUADRON   MOTTO: Avenge

Date	Location	Aircraft Type	Remarks
11/11/18	Senlis-le-Sec	SE5A (1/19)	
19/11/18	to Izel-le-Hameau		
17/1/19			Reduced to cadre
30/6/19	DB		
26/3/39	RF Khormaksar		
3/39		Gladiator I (4/40)	
3/39		Gladiator II (6/41)	
2/5/39	to Sheikh Othman		Dets Berebera, Laferug & Little Aden

No. 95 SQUADRON   MOTTO: Trans mare exivi (I went out over the sea)

Date	Location	Aircraft Type	Remarks
11/11/18	Kenley	(for Buzzard)	Nucleus from Nos 21, 28, 30 and 51 TDS
20/11/18	DB		

No. 96 SQUADRON   MOTTO: Nocturni obambulamus (We prowl by night)

Date	Location	Aircraft Type	Remarks
11/11/18	Wyton	Salamander (12/18)	Nucleus from Nos 2, 32, 38 & 46 TDS
9/12/18	DB		

No. 97 SQUADRON   MOTTO: Achieve your aim

Date	Location	Aircraft Type	Remarks
11/11/18	Xaffévillers	HP 0/400 (3/19)	
17/11/18	to St-Inglevert		
4/3/19	to Ford Junction		
4/19		DH10 (3/20)	
19/7/19	*en route* to India		
23/8/19	to Allahabad		Dets Lahore, Risalpur & Mianwali
15/11/19	to Lahore		Dets Mianwali, Karachi, Juhu & Rajkot
28/3/20	to Risalpur		
1/4/20			Renumbered No. 60 Sqn
16/9/35	RF Catfoss		from B Flt, No. 10 Sqn
9/35		Heyford IA (1/36)	
26/9/35	to Boscombe Down		
11/35		Heyford III (2/39)	
7/1/37	to Leconfield		
2/39		Anson I (4/40)	
2/39		Whitley II (4/40)	
2/39		Whitley III (4/40)	

No. 98 SQUADRON   **MOTTO: Never failing**

Date	Location	Aircraft Type	Remarks
11/11/18	Abscon	DH9 (3/19)	
27/12/18	to Marquain		
19/1/19	to Alquines		
28/3/19	to Shotwick		as cadre
24/6/19	DB		
17/2/36	RF Abingdon		from C Flt, No. 15 Sqn
2/36		Hind (6/38)	
21/8/36	to Hucknall		
6/38		Battle (7/41)	Dets Weston Zoyland, Upwood & Bassingbourne

No. 99 SQUADRON   **MOTTO: Quisque tenax (Each tenacious)**

Date	Location	Aircraft Type	Remarks
11/11/18	Azelot	DH9 (11/18)	
9/18		DH9A (3/20)	
16/11/18	to Auxi-le-Chateau		
29/11/18	to St-André-aux-Bois		
12/12/18	to Aulnoy		
14/5/19	*en route* to India		via Marseilles
15/6/19	to Ambala		
26/9/19	to Mianwali		Det Ambala
1/4/20	DB		Renumbered as No. 27 Sqn
1/4/24	RF Netheravon		
4/24		Vimy (12/24)	
31/5/24	to Bircham Newton		
8/24		Aldershot (12/25)	
12/25		Hyderabad (1/31)	
5/1/28	to Upper Heyford		
10/29		Hinaidi (12/33)	
12/33		Heyford (11/38)	
15/11/34	to Mildenhall		
10/38		Wellington I (12/39)	
1/9/39	to Newmarket		
9/39		Wellington IA (4/40)	

No. 100 SQUADRON   **MOTTO: Sarang tebuan jangan dijolok (Malay – Never stir up a hornet's nest)**

Date	Location	Aircraft Type	Remarks
11/11/18	Xaffévillers	HP 0/400 (9/19)	
25/11/18	to Ligescourt		Dets St-Inglevert & Quilen
16/6/19	to St-Inglevert		
12/9/19	to Baldonnel		as cadre
1/2/20			Re-established (Absorbed cadre of No. 141 Sqn)
2/20		DH9A (6/21)	
2/20		Bristol F2B (3/22)	Dets Castlbar & Oranmore
4/2/22	to Spittlegate		
2/22		DH9A (5/24)	
2/22		Avro 504K (5/24)	
2/22		Vimy (5/24)	
5/24	to Eastchurch		
5/24		Fawn (12/26)	
7/24	to Spittlegate		
8/26		Horsley (4/33)	
10/1/28	to Bicester		
3/11/30	to Donibristle		
11/32		Vildebeest I (9/33)	
8/33		Vildebeest II (1/41)	
7/12/33	*en route* to the Far East		
6/1/34	to Seletar		
12/37		Vildebeest III (2/42)	

No. 101 SQUADRON   **MOTTO: Mens agitat (Mind over matter)**

Date	Location	Aircraft Type	Remarks
11/11/18	Hancourt	FE2B (3/19)	
12/11/18	to Catillon		

Date	Location	Aircraft Type	Remarks
29/11/18	to Strée		
13/12118	to Morville		
12/3/19	to Laneffe		as cadre
18/3/19	to Filton		
11/10/19	to Eastleigh		
31/12/19	DB		
21/3/28	RF Bircham Newton		
4/28		Sidestrand (7/36)	
12/10/29	to Andover		
1/12/34	to Bicester		
1/35		Overstrand (8/38)	
6/38		Blenheim I (4/39)	
4/39		Blenheim IV (7/41)	
9/5/39	to West Raynham		Dets Manston & Brize Norton

No. 102 SQUADRON   MOTTO: Tentate et perficite (Attempt and accomplish)

Date	Location	Aircraft Type	Remarks
11/11/18	Bevillers	FE2B (3/19)	
14/12/18	to Serny		
26/3/19	to Lympne		as cadre
3/7/19	DB		
1/10/35	RF Worthy Down		from B Flt, No. 7 Sqn
10/35		Heyford II & III (11/38)	
3/9/36	to Finningley		
7/7/37	to Honington		
11/7/38	to Driffield		
10/38		Whitley III (1/40)	Det Villeneuve

No. 103 SQUADRON   MOTTO: Nili me tangere (Touch me not)

Date	Location	Aircraft Type	Remarks
11/11/18	Ronchin	DH9 (3/19)	
26/1/19	to Maisoncelle		
28/3/19	to Shotwick		as cadre
1/10/19	DB		
10/8/36	RF Andover		
8/36		Hind (8/38)	
26/2/37	to Usworth		
7/38		Battle (10/40)	
2/9/38	to Abingdon		
1/4/39	to Benson		
2/9/39	to Challerange		

No. 104 SQUADRON   MOTTO: Strike hard

Date	Location	Aircraft Type	Remarks
11/11/18	Azelot	DH9 (2/19)	
20/11/18	to Maisoncelle		
11/18		DH10 (2/19)	
1/2/19	to Turnhouse		
3/3/19	to Crail		as cadre
30/6/19	DB		
7/1/36	RF Abingdon		from C Flt, No. 40 Sqn
7/36		Hind (5/38)	
21/8/36	to Hucknall		
2/5/38	to Bassingbourne		
5/38		Blenheim I (4/40)	
5/39		Anson I (4/40)	

No. 105 SQUADRON   MOTTO: Fortis in proeliis (Valiant in battles)

Date	Location	Aircraft Type	Remarks
11/11/18`	Omagh	RE8 (12/19)	Dets Oranmore & Castlebar
12/18		Bristol F2B (2/20)	
28/1/19	to Oranmore		Dets Castlebar, the Curragh, Tallaght & Fermoy
1/2/20	DB		Renumbered as No. 2 Sqn
12/4/37	RF Upper Heyford		from B Flt, No. 18 Sqn

26/4/37	to Harwell		
4/37		Audax (10/37)	
8/37		Battle (5/40)	
2/9/39	to Reims		

No. 106 SQUADRON   MOTTO: Pro libertate (For liberty)

Date	Location	Aircraft Type	Remarks
11/11/18	Fermoy	RE8 (1/19)	
1/19		Bristol F2B (10/19)	Dets Birr & Oranmore
8/10/19	DB		
1/6/38	RF Abingdon		from A Flt, No. 15 Sqn
6/38		Hind (7/38)	
7/38		Battle (5/39)	
1/9/38	to Thornaby		
26/9/38	to Grantham		
14/10/38	to Thornaby		
5/39		Anson I (9/39)	
5/39		Hampden (3/42)	Det Evanton
1/9/39	to Cottesmore		

No. 107 SQUADRON   MOTTO: Nous y serons (We shall be there)

Date	Location	Aircraft Type	Remarks
11/11/18	Moislains	DH9 (3/19)	
18/11/18	to Bavay		
13/12/18	to Franc Waret		
20/12/18	to Nivelles		
4/1/19	to Maubeuge		
18/3/19	to Hounslow		as cadre
13/8/19	DB		
10/8/36	RF Andover		
9/36		Hind (9/38)	
16/2/37	to Old Sarum		
15/6/37	to Harwell		
8/38		Blenheim I (6/39)	
3/5/39	to Wattisham		
5/39		Blenheim IV (2/42)	Dets Lossiemouth, Newmarket, Ipswich, Swanton Morley, Hunsdon & Horsham St Faith

No. 108 SQUADRON   MOTTO: Viribus contractis (With gathering strength)

Date	Location	Aircraft Type	Remarks
11/11/18	Bisseghem	DH9 (2/19)	
16/11/18	to Gondecourt		
16/2/19	to Lympne		as cadre
3/7/19	DB		
4////1/37	RF Upper Heyford		from B Flt, No. 57 Sqn
1/37		Hind (6/38)	
18//2/37	to Farnborough		
7/7/37	to Cranfield		
2/5/38	to Bassingbourn		
6/38		Blenheim I (4/40)	
5/39		Anson I (4/40)	

No. 110 SQUADRON   MOTTO: Nec timeo nec sperno (I neither fear nor despise)

Date	Location	Aircraft Type	Remarks
11/11/18	Bettoncourt	DH9A (8/19)	
20/11/18	to Auxi-le-Chateau		
30/11/18	to Maisoncelle		
3/7/19	to Marquise		
27/8/19	DB		

18/5/37	RF Waddington		
5/37		Hind (1/38)	
1/38		Blenheim I (9/39)	
11/5/39	to Wattisham		
6/39		Blenheim IV (6/42)	Dets Lossiemouth, Horsham St Faith, Manston, Lindholme, Ipswich, Luqa, Martlesham Heath, Brize Norton & Swanton Morley

No. 111 SQUADRON MOTTO: Adstantes (Standing by)

Date	Location	Aircraft Type	Remarks
11/11/18	Qantara		
1/19		Bristol F2B (2/20)	
6/2/19	to Ramleh		Dets Damascus & Aleppo
1/2/20	DB		Renumbered as No. 14 Sqn
1/10/23	RF Duxford		
10/23		Grebe II (1/25)	
4/24		Snipe (1/25)	
6/24		Siskin II (11/26)	
9/26		Siskin IIIA (2/31)	
1/31		Bulldog IIA (6/36)	
12/7/34	to Northolt		
6/36		Gauntlet I & II (1/38)	
12/37		Hurricane I (4/41)	

No. 112 SQUADRON MOTTO: Swift in destruction

Date	Location	Aircraft Type	Remarks
11/11/18	Throwley	Camel (6/19)	
/19		Snipe (6/19)	
13/6/19	DB		
16/5/39	RF on board HMS *Argus*		
26/5/39	to Helwan		
6/39		Gladiator I & II (6/41)	Dets Port Sudan, Summit & Erkowit

No. 113 SQUADRON MOTTO: Velox et vindex (Swift to vengeance)

Date	Location	Aircraft Type	Remarks
11/11/18	Sarona	RE8 (2/20)	Dets El Affule & Haifa
18/11/18	to Qantara		
16/2/19	to Ismailia		
2/19		BE2E (12/19)	
1/2/20	DB		Renumbered as No. 208 Sqn
18/5/37	RF Upper Heyford		
5/37		Hind (6/39)	
31/8/37	to Grantham		
30/4/38	*en route* to Egypt		
11/5/38	to Heliopolis		
29/9/38	to Mersah Matruh		
11/10/38	to Heliopolis		
21/4/39	to El Daba		
21/5/39	to Heliopolis		
6/39		Blenheim I (4/40)	

No. 114 SQUADRON MOTTO: With speed I strike

Date	Location	Aircraft Type	Remarks
11/11/18	Lahore	BE2C (10/19)	Det Jubbulpore
		BE2E (4/20)	
26/3/19	to Quetta		Dets Lahore & Cawnpore
20/5/19	to Lahore		Dets Quetta, Cawnpore & Kohat

16/6/19	to Quetta		Dets Bannu & Loralai
2/10/19	to Ambala		
10/19		Bristol F2B (4/20)	Det Agra
1/4/20	DB		Renumbered as No. 28 Sqn
1/12/36	RF Wyton		
12/36		Hind (3/37)	
3/37		Audax (4/37)	
3/37		Blenheim I (5/39)	
5/39		Blenheim IV (9/42)	

No. 115 SQUADRON   MOTTO: Despite the elements

Date	Location	Aircraft Type	Remarks
11/11/18	St-Inglevert	HP 0/400 (3/19)	
4/3/19	to Ford Junction		as cadre
18/10/19	DB		
15/6/37	RF Marham		from B Flt, No. 38 Sqn
6/37		Hendon II (8/37)	
6/37		Harrow (6/39)	
3/39		Wellington I (10/39)	
9/39		Wellington IA (8/40)	Det Kinloss

No. 116 SQUADRON   MOTTO: Precision in defence

Date	Location	Aircraft Type	Remarks
11/11/18	Feltham	HP 0/400 (11/18)	
20/11/18	DB		

No. 117 SQUADRON   MOTTO: It shall be done

Date	Location	Aircraft Type	Remarks
11/11/18	Norwich	DH9 (10/19)	
30/11/18	to Wyton		
23/3/19	to Tallaght		
24/4/19	to Gormanston		
6/10/19	DB		Absorbed by No. 141 Sqn

No. 119 SQUADRON   MOTTO: By night by day

Date	Location	Aircraft Type	Remarks
11/11/18	Wyton	Various aircraft	
9/18		DH9 (12/18)	
6/12/18	DB		

No.120 SQUADRON   MOTTO: Endurance

Date	Location	Aircraft Type	Remarks
1/11/18	Bracebridge Heath	Various aircraft	
23/11/18	to Wyton		
11/18		DH9 (10/19)	
20/2/19	to Hawkinge		
17/7/19	to Lympne		
21/10/19	DB		

No. 122 SQUADRON   MOTTO: Victuri volamus (We fly to conquer)

Date	Location	Aircraft Type	Remarks
11/11/18	Upper Heyford	DH10	
20/11/18	DB		

No. 123 SQUADRON

Date	Location	Aircraft Type	Remarks
20/11/18	RF Upper Heyford		Also designated No. 2 Sqn Canadian Air Force
11/18		DH9A (2/20)	
31/3/19	to Shoreham		
5/2/20	DB		

No. 132 SQUADRON   MOTTO: Cave leopardum (Beware the leopard)

Date	Location	Aircraft Type	Remarks
11/11/18	Castle Bromwich	Various aircraft	
23/12/18	DB		

No. 138 SQUADRON   MOTTO: For freedom

Date	Location	Aircraft Type	Remarks
11/11/18	Chingford	Bristol F2B (2/19)	
1/2/19	DB		

No. 139 SQUADRON   MOTTO: Si placet necamus (We destroy at will)

Date	Location	Aircraft Type	Remarks
11/11/18	Arcade	Bristol F2B (2/19)	
14/11/18	to Grossa		
30/1/19	to Caldiero		
25/2/19	to Blandford		as cadre
7/3/19	DB		
3/9/36	RF Wyton		
9/36		Hind (7/37)	
7/37		Blenheim I (9/39)	
7/39		Blenheim IV (12/41)	

No. 141 SQUADRON   MOTTO: Caedimus noctu (We slay by night)

Date	Location	Aircraft Type	Remarks
11/11/18	Biggin Hill	Bristol F2B (2/20)	
1/3/19	to Tallaght		Dets the Curragh & Birr
14/12/19	to Baldonnel		Dets Gormanston & Birr
1/2/20	DB		Absorbed into No. 100 Sqn

No. 142 SQUADRON   MOTTO: Determination

Date	Location	Aircraft Type	Remarks
11/11/18	Ramleh		Dets Damascus & Haifa
25/11/18	to Qantara		
1/19		DH9 (2/20)	
16/2/19	to Suez		
1/2/20	DB		Renumbered as No. 55 Sqn
1/6/34	RF Netheravon		
6/34		Hart (11/36)	
3/1/35	to Andover		
3/10/35	*en route* to the Middle East		
13/10/35	to Aboukir		
26/10/35	to Mersa Matruh		Det Helwan
3/8/36	to Ismailia		
5/11/36	to Aboukir		
20/11/36	*en route* to the UK		
3/12/36	to Andover		
1/37		Hind (4/38)	
3/38		Battle (11/40)	

9/5/39	to Bicester		
2/9/39	to Barry-au-Bac		

No. 143 SQUADRON   MOTTO: Vincere et vivere (To conquer is to live)

Date	Location	Aircraft Type	Remarks
11/11/18	Detling	Camel (10/19)	
6/19		Snipe (10/19)	
31/10/19	DB		

No. 144 SQUADRON   MOTTO: Who shall stop us

Date	Location	Aircraft Type	Remarks
11/11/18	Mikra Bay	DH9 (12/18)	Dets Mudros & Amberkoj
4/12/18	*en route* to the UK		
16/12/18	to Ford Junction		as cadre
4/2/19	DB		
11/1/37	RF Bicester		from B Flt, No. 101 Sqn
1/37		Overstrand (2/37)	
2/37		Anson I (9/37)	
9/2/37	to Hemswell		
3/37		Audax (9/37)	
8/37		Blenheim I (4/39)	
3/39		Hampden (3/43)	

No.145 SQUADRON   MOTTO: Diu noctuque pugnamus (We fight by day and night)

Date	Location	Aircraft Type	Remarks
11/11/18	Qantara	SE5A (2/19)	
8/2/19			Reduced to cadre
16/2/19	to Suez		
6/9/19	DB		

No. 148 SQUADRON   MOTTO: Trusty

Date	Location	Aircraft Type	Remarks
11/11/18	Erre	FE2B (2/19)	
9/12/18	to Serny		
17/2/19	to Tangmere		as cadre
4/7/19	DB		
7/6/37	RF Scampton		Nucleus from No. 9 Sqn
6/37		Audax (7/37)	
6/37		Wellesley (11/38)	
10/3/38	to Stradishall		
11/38		Heyford III (3/39)	
3/39		Wellington I (4/40)	
4/39		Anson I (4/40)	

No. 149 SQUADRON   MOTTO: Fortis nocte (Bold at night)

Date	Location	Aircraft Type	Remarks
11/11/18	Ste-Marguerite	FE2B (8/19)	
26/11/18	to Fort Cognelée		
24/12/18	to Bickendorf		
26/3/19	to Tallaght		as cadre
1/8/19	DB		
12/4/37	RF Mildenhall		from B Flt, No. 99 Sqn
4/37		Heyford III ((5/37)	
5/37		Heyford IA (3/39)	
1/39		Wellington I (12/39)	
9/39		Wellington IA (6/40)	

No. 150 SQUADRON   MOTTO: Always ahead (Greek script)

Date	Location	Aircraft Type	Remarks
11/11/18	Mikra Bay	Bristol M1C (1/19)	Dets Kiree, Gumuljina & Dedeagatch
		SE5A (2/19)	
		Camel (2/19)	
		BE12A (12/18)	
		BE2E (1/19)	
12/18		AW FK8 (1/19)	
15/3/19			Reduced to cadre
11/6/19	to San Stephano		
18/9/19	DB		
8/8/38	RF Boscombe Down		
8/38		Battle (9/40)	
3/4/39	to Benson		
2/9/39	to Chellerange		

No. 151 SQUADRON   MOTTO: Foy pour devoir (Fidelity unto duty)

Date	Location	Aircraft Type	Remarks
11/11/18	Bancourt	Camel 2/19	
5/12/18	to Liettres		
21/2/19	to Gullane		as cadre
10/9/19	DB		
4/8/36	RF North Weald		from B Flt, No. 56 Sqn
8/36		Gauntlet II (3/39)	
12/38		Hurricane I (6/41)	Dets Martlesham Heath

No. 152 SQUADRON   MOTTO: Faithful ally

Date	Location	Aircraft Type	Remarks
11/11/18	Carvin	Camel (2/19)	
29/11/18	to Liettres		
21/2/19	to Gullane		as cadre
30/6/19	DB		

No. 153 SQUADRON   MOTTO: Noctividus (Seeing by night)

Date	Location	Aircraft Type	Remarks
11/11/18	Hainault Farm	Camel (6/19)	
13/6/19	DB		

No. 155 SQUADRON   MOTTO: Eternal vigilance

Date	Location	Aircraft Type	Remarks
11/11/18	Chingford	DH9A (12/18)	
7/12/18	DB		

No. 156 SQUADRON   MOTTO: We light the way

Date	Location	Aircraft Type	Remarks
11/11/18	Wyton	DH9A (11/18)	
9/12/18	DB		

No. 157 SQUADRON   MOTTO: Our cannon speak our thoughts

Date	Location	Aircraft Type	Remarks
11/11/18	Upper Heyford	Salamander (2/19)	
1/2/19	DB		

No. 158 SQUADRON　　　MOTTO: Strength in unity

Date	Location	Aircraft Type	Remarks
11/11/18	Upper Heyford	Salamander	
20/11/18	DB		

No. 166 SQUADRON　　　MOTTO: Tenacity

Date	Location	Aircraft Type	Remarks
11/11/18	Bircham Newton	HP V/1500 (5/19)	
31/5/19	DB		
1/11/36	RF Boscombe Down		from B Flt, No. 97 Sqn
11/36		Heyford III (9/39)	
20/1/37	to Leconfield		
6/39		Whitley I (2/40)	Dets Benson & Boscombe Down

No. 167 SQUADRON　　　MOTTO: Ubique sine mora (Everywhere without delay)

Date	Location	Aircraft Type	Remarks
11/11/18	Bircham Newton	HP V/1500 (5/19)	
21/5/19	DB		

No. 185 SQUADRON　　　MOTTO: Ara fejn hu (Maltese – Look where it is)

Date	Location	Aircraft Type	Remarks
11/11/18	East Fortune	Cuckoo (4/19)	
9/4/19			Reduced to a cadre
14/4/19	DB		Listed as a cadre until 6/11/19, when it was DB retrospectively.
1/3/38	RF Abingdon		from B Flt, No. 40 Sqn
3/38		Hind (7/38)	
6/38		Battle (6/39)	Det Thornaby
1/9/38	to Thornaby		
27/9/38	to Grantham		
15/10/38	to Thornaby		
6/39		Hampden (4/40)	
8/39		Hereford (4/40)	
8/39		Anson I (4/40)	
24/8/39	to Cottesmore		

No.186 SQUADRON　　　MOTTO: Nil

Date	Location	Aircraft Type	Remarks
31/12/18	Formed on board HMS *Argus*		
17/2/19	to Gosport		
6/19		Cuckoo (2/20)	
1/2/20	DB		Renumbered as No. 210 Sqn

No. 201 SQUADRON　　　MOTTO: Hic et ubique (Here and everywhere)

Date	Location	Aircraft Type	Remarks
11/11/18	La Targette	Camel (1/19)	
22/11/18	to Béthencourt		
5/2/19			Reduced to cadre
17/2/19	to Lake Down		
2/9/19	to Eastleigh		
31/12/19	DB		
1/1/29	RF Calshot		No. 490 Flt renumbered
1/29		Southampton II (12/36)	
4/36		London I (6/38)	
1/38		London II (4/40)	
29/9/38	to Invergordon		

7/10/38	to Calshot		
9/8/39	to Sullom Voe		

No. 202 SQUADRON   MOTTO: Semper vigilate (Be always vigilant)

Date	Location	Aircraft Type	Remarks
11/11/18	Bergues	DH4 (3/19)	
25/11/18	to Varssenaere		
27/3/19	to Driffield		as cadre
12/19	to Spittlegate		
22/1/20	DB		
9/4/20	RF Alexandria		from A Flt, No. 267 Sqn
4/20		Short 184 (5/21)	
16/5/21	DB		
1/1/29	RF Kalafrana		No. 481 Flt renumbered
1/29		Fairey IIID (9/30)	
7/30		Fairey IIIF (8/35)	
5/35		Scapa (11/37)	
9/37		London II (6/41)	

No. 203 SQUADRON   MOTTO: Occidens oriensque (West and East)

Date	Location	Aircraft Type	Remarks
11/11/18	Bruille	Camel (3/19)	
24/11/18	to Auberchicourt		
22/12/18	to Orcq		
18/1/19	to Boisdinghem		
27/3/19	to Waddington		as cadre
12/19	to Scopwick		
21/1/20	DB		
1/3/20	RF Leuchars		
3/20		Camel (8/22)	
8/22		Nightjar (4/23)	
18/9/22	*en route* to Turkey		via HMS *Argus*
27/9/22	to Kilya Bay		
19/12/22	*en route* to UK		via HMS *Argus*
4/1/23	to Leuchars		
1/4/23	DB		Split into Nos 401 & 402 Flts
1/1/29	RF Mount Batten		No. 482 Flt renumbered
1/29		Southampton II (4/31)	
28/2/29	*en route* to Persian Gulf		
14/3/29	to Basra		
3/29		Fairey IIIF (4/29)	
3/31			Det Felixstowe for
		Rangoon (9/35)	
8/35			Det Pembroke Dock for
		Singapore III (3/40)	
26/9/35	to Isthmus		
24/8/36	to Basra		
2/9/39	to Isthmus		

No. 204 SQUADRON   MOTTO: Praedam mari quaero (I seek my prey in the sea)

Date	Location	Aircraft Type	Remarks
11/11/18	Heule	Camel (2/19)	
11/2/19	to Waddington		as cadre
31/12/19	DB		
1/2/29	RF Mount Batten		
2/29		Southampton II (10/35)	
8/35		Scapa (1/37)	
27/9/35	to Aboukir		
22/10/35	to Alexandria		
5/8/36	to Mount Batten		
10/36		London I & II (7/39)	
6/39		Sunderland I (9/43)	

No. 205 SQUADRON   MOTTO: Pertama di - Malaya (First in Malaya)

Date	Location	Aircraft Type	Remarks
11/11/18	Moislains	DH9A (3/19)	
27/11/18	to Maubeuge		
12/1/19	to La Louveterie		
21/3/19	to Hucknall		as cadre
12/19	to Scopwick		
22/1/20	DB		
15/4/20	RF Leuchars		
4/20		Panther (4/23)	
11/11/18	DB		Became Nos 440, 441 & 442 Flts
8/1/29	RF Seletar		from Far East Flight
1/29		Southampton II (2/36)	
4/35		Singapore III (10/41)	

No. 206 SQUADRON   MOTTO: Nihil nos effugit (Naught escapes us)

Date	Location	Aircraft Type	Remarks
11/11/18	Linselles	DH9 (1/20)	
26/11/18	to Nivelles		
20/12/18	to Bickendorf		
27/5/19	to Maubeuge		
7/6/19	*en route* to Egypt		via Marseilles
19/6/19	to Heliopolis		
27/6/19	to Helwan		
1/2/20	DB		Renumbered as No. 47 Sqn
15/6/36	RF Manston		from C Flt, No. 48 Sqn
6/36		Anson I (6/40)	
1/8/36	to Bircham Newton		

No. 207 SQUADRON   MOTTO: Semper paratus (Always prepared)

Date	Location	Aircraft Type	Remarks
11/11/18	Estrées-en-Chaussée	HP 0/400 (8/19)	
1/12/18	to Carvin		
1/1/19	to Merheim		
10/5/19	to Hangelar		
22/8/19	to Tangmere		as cadre
8/10/19	to Croydon		
10/1/20	to Kenley		
16/1/20	to Uxbridge		
20/1/20	DB		
1/2/20	RF Bircham Newton		Nucleus from No. 274 Sqn
4/21		DH9A (1/28)	
29/9/22	*en route* to Turkey		
11/10/22	to San Stephano		
22/9/23	*en route* to the UK		
3/10/23	to Eastchurch		
12/27		Fairey IIIF (9/32)	
9/11/29	to Bircham Newton		
8/32		Gordon (4/36)	
28/10/36	to Ed Damer		
6/4/36	to Gebeit		
4/36		Vincent (7/36)	
29/8/36	to Worthy Down		
8/36		Gordon (11/37)	
9/37		Wellesley (4/38)	
20/4/38	to Cottesmore		
4/38		Battle (4/40)	
7/39		Anson I (4/40)	
24/8/39	to Cranfield		

No. 208 SQUADRON   MOTTO: Vigilant

Date	Location	Aircraft Type	Remarks
11/11/18	Maretz	Camel (11/18)	
11/18		Snipe (11/19)	
3/12/18	to Strée B		
23/5/19	to Heumar		
7/8/19	to Eil		
9/9/19	to Netheravon		
7/11/19	DB		
1/2/20	RF Ismailia		No. 113 Sqn renumbered
2/20		RE8(11/20)	Det Ramleh
10/20		Bristol F2B (5/30)	
28/9/22	to San Stephano		
26/9/23	to Ismailia		
27/10/27	to Heliopolis		Det Ramleh
5/30		Atlas (8/35)	
4/34		Audax (1/39)	
9/35		Demon (3/36)	D Flt only dets Mersah Matruh & Amiriya
24/1/36	to Mersah Matruh		
18/4/36	to Heliopolis		Dets Ramleh, Fayid, Helwan, Burrumbul, Mersah Matruh & Aboukir
28/9/38	to Mersah Matruh		
13/10/38	to Heliopolis		
1/39		Lysander I & II (5/42)	
26/2/39	to Mersah Matruh		
16/3/39	to Heliopolis		
7/8/39	to Mersah Matruh		
1/9/39	to Qasaba		

No. 209 SQUADRON   MOTTO: Might and main

Date	Location	Aircraft Type	Remarks
11/11/18	Bruille	Camel 2/19	
22/11/18	to Saultain		
11/12/18	to Froidmont		
14/2/19	to Scopwick		as cadre
24/6/19	DB		
15/1/30	RF Mount Batten		
2/30		Iris III (12/32)	
2/32		Saro A7(7/32)	
6/32		Iris V (6/34)	
8/32		Singapore II (11/32)	
2/33		Southampton II (6/34)	
1/34		Perth (12/34)	
10/34		Southampton II (11/34)	
10/34		London I (11/34)	
1/35		Southampton II (2/35)	
1/35		London I (2/36)	
2/35		Stranraer (9/35)	
4/35		Short R.24/31 (9/35)	
1/5/35	to Felixstowe		
7/35		Perth (5/36)	
1/36		Southampton II (7/36)	
2/36		Singapore III (3/39)	
22/9/37	to Kalafrana		
31/9/37	to Arzeu		
17/12/37	to Felixstowe		
29/9/38	to Invergordon		
8/10/38	to Felixstowe		
12/38		Stranraer (4/40)	
22/5/39	to Stranraer		
17/6/39	to Felixstowe		
12/8/39	to Invergordon		
22/8/39	to Felixstowe		
30/8/39	to Invergordon		Det Falmouth

No. 210 SQUADRON   MOTTO:Yn y nwyfre yn hedfan (Hovering in the heavens)

Date	Location	Aircraft Type	Remarks
11/11/18	Boussières	Camel (2/19)	
17/2/19	to Scopwick		as cadre
24/6/19	DB		
1/2/20	RF Gosport		No. 186 Sqn renumbered
2/20		Cuckoo (4/23)	
1/4/23	DB		Renumbered as Nos 460 & 461 Flts
1/3/31	RF Felixstowe		
5/31		Southampton II (8/35)	
15/6/31	to Pembroke Dock		
11/34		Singapore III (4/35)	Ferried to No. 205 Sqn
7/35		Singapore III (8/35)	Ferried to No. 203 Sqn
8/35		Rangoon (9/36)	from No. 203 Sqn
28/9/35	to Gibraltar		
10/35		London II (11/35)	
10/35		Stranraer (11/35)	
7/8/36	to Pembroke Dock		
8/36		Singapore III (11/38)	
22/9/37	to Arzeu		
18/12/37	to Pembroke Dock		
6/38		Sunderland I (4/41)	
29/9/38	to Tayport		
8/10/38	to Pembroke Dock		

No. 211 SQUADRON   MOTTO:Toujours a propos (Always at the right moment)

Date	Location	Aircraft Type	Remarks
11/11/18	Iris Farm	DH9 (3/19)	
3/12/18	to Thuilles		
15/3/19	to Wyton		as cadre
24/6/19	DB		
24/6/37	RF Mildenhall		
7/37		Audax (10/37)	
8/37		Hind (5/39)	
2/9/37	to Grantham		
12/5/38	to Helwan		
18/7/38	to Ramleh		Det Semakh
29/9/38	to Helwan		
31/1/39	to Ismailia		
4/39		Blenheim I (11/41)	Det El Daba
10/8/39	to El Daba		Det Qotafiyah

No. 212 SQUADRON   MOTTO:A mari ad astra (From the sea to the stars)

Date	Location	Aircraft Type	Remarks
11/11/18	Great Yarmouth	DH4 (1/19)	
		DH9A (2/20)	
		DH9 (2/20)	
		Camel (1/19)	
7/3/19	to Swingate Down		
9/2/20	DB		

No. 213 SQUADRON   MOTTO: Irritatus lacessit crabro (The hornet attacks when roused)

Date	Location	Aircraft Type	Remarks
11/11/18	Bergues	Camel (3/19)	
27/11/18	to Stalhille		
19/3/19	to Scopwick		as cadre
31/12/19	DB		
8/3/37	RF Northolt		from A Flt, No. 111 Sqn
3/37		Gauntlet II (3/39)	
1/7/37	to Church Fenton		
18/5/38	to Wittering		
1/39		Hurricane I (3/42)	

No. 214 SQUADRON   MOTTO: Ultra in umbris (Avenging in the shadows)

Date	Location	Aircraft Type	Remarks
11/11/18	Chemy	HP 0/400 (2/20)	
4/7/19	to Abu Sueir		
1/2/20	DB		Absorbed into No. 216 Squadron
16/9/35	RF Boscombe Down		from B Flt, No. 9 Sqn
9/35		Virginia X (4/37)	
15/10/35	to Andover		Det Aldergrove
1/10/36	to Scampton		
1/37		Harrow (6/39)	
19/4/37	to Feltwell		
5/39		Wellington I (5/40)	
3/9/39	to Methwold		
9/39		Wellington IA (9/40)	

No. 215 SQUADRON   MOTTO: Surgite nox adeste (Arise, night is at hand)

Date	Location	Aircraft Type	Remarks
11/11/18	Xaffévillers	HP 0/400 (2/19)	
21/11/18	to Alquines		
2/2/19	to Ford Junction		as cadre
18/10/19	DB		
1/10/35	RF Worthy Down		from C Flt, No. 58 Sqn
10/35		Virginia X (9/37)	
14/1/36	to Upper Heyford		
3/9/36	to Driffield		
2/37		Anson I (11/37)	
8/37		Harrow (12/39)	
25/7/38	to Honington		
7/39		Wellington I (4/40)	

No. 216 SQUADRON   MOTTO: CCXVI dona ferens (216 bearing gifts)

Date	Location	Aircraft Type	Remarks
11/11/18	Rovilles-aux-Chenes	HP 0/400 (10/21)	
17/11/18	to Quilen		
14/12/18	to Marquise		
3/7/19	to Qantara		
7/20	to Abu Sueir		
8/20		DH10 (6/22)	
15/4/21	to Heliopolis		
6/22		Vimy (1/26)	
12/25		Victoria II (10/26)	
7/26		Victoria III (4/35)	
2/29		Victoria V (8/34)	
4/29		Victoria IV (4/31)	
4/33		Victoria VI (11/35)	
2/35		Valentia (9/41)	Det Eastleigh

No. 217 SQUADRON   MOTTO: Woe to the enemy

Date	Location	Aircraft Type	Remarks
11/11/18	Crochte	DH4 (3/19)	
25/11/18	to Varssenaere		
29/3/19	to Driffield		as cadre
19/10/19	DB		
15/3/37	RF Boscombe Down		
3/37		Anson I (12/40)	
7/37	to Tangmere		
16/8/37	to Bicester		
13/9/37	to Tangmere		
28/9/38	to Warmwell		
10/10/38	to Tangmere		
25/8/39	to Warmwell		

No.218 SQUADRON   **MOTTO: In time**

Date	Location	Aircraft Type	Remarks
11/11/18	Reumont	DH9 (2/19)	
16/11/18	to Vert Galand		
11/2/19	to Hucknall		as cadre
24/6/19	DB		
16/3/36	RF Upper Heyford		from C Flt, No. 57 Sqn
3/36		Hart (3/38)	
1/38		Battle (5/40)	
22/4/38	to Boscombe Down		
2/9/39	to Auberives-sur-Suippes		

No. 219 SQUADRON   **MOTTO: From dusk till dawn**

Date	Location	Aircraft Type	Remarks
11/11/18	Westgate/Manston	DH9 (6/19)	Seaplanes Nos 406 & 442 Flights
		Camel (6/19)	at Westgate. Land-planes Nos 470,
		Short 184 (2/20)	555 & 556 Flts at Manston
		Fairey IIIB (2/20)	
7/2/20	DB		

No. 220 SQUADRON   **MOTTO: We observe unseen (Greek script)**

Date	Location	Aircraft Type	Remarks
11/11/18	Imbros	DH4 (1/19)	
		DH9 (1/19)	
		Camel (1/19)	
2/19	to Mudros		as cadre
21/5/19	DB		
17/8/36	RF Bircham Newton		Nucleus from No. 206 Sqn
8/36		Anson I (12/39)	
21/8/39	to Thornaby		
9/39		Hudson I, III & VI (6/42)	Dets St Eval & Wick

No. 221 SQUADRON   **MOTTO: From sea to sea**

Date	Location	Aircraft Type	Remarks
11/11/18	Mudros	DH9 (9/19)	Assets absorbed by No. 222 Sqn
12/18			Re-established
29/12/18	*en route* to South Russia		via HMS *Riviera* & HMS *Empress*
5/1/19	to Batum		
10/1/19	to Baku		
15/1/19	to Petrovsk Kaskar		Dets Chechen & Lagan
4/19		DH9A (9/19)	
18/8/19			Began evacuation
1/9/19	DB		

No. 222 SQUADRON   **MOTTO: Pambili Bo (Zulu)**

Date	Location	Aircraft Type	Remarks
11/11/18	Mudros	DH9 (2/19)	Dets Amberkoj & Dedeagatch
		DH4 (2/19)	
		Camel (2/19)	
15/11/18	to San Stephano		
23/11/18	to Mudros		
27/2/19	DB		

No. 223 SQUADRON   **MOTTO: Alae defendunt Africam (Wings defend Africa)**

Date	Location	Aircraft Type	Remarks
11/11/18	Mudros	DH4 (5/19)	
		DH9 (5/19)	

Date	Location	Aircraft Type	Remarks
16/5/19	DB		
15/12/36	RF Nairobi		from flt of No. 45 Sqn
12/36		Gordon (2/37)	
2/37		Vincent (7/38)	
6/38		Wellesley (4/41)	Det Summit

No. 224 SQUADRON   MOTTO: Fedele all' amico (Italian – Faithful to a friend)

Date	Location	Aircraft Type	Remarks
11/11/18	Pizzone	DH4 (4/19)	
		DH9 (4/19)	
15/4/19	DB		
1/2/37	RF Manston		from C Flt, No. 48 Sqn
2/37		Anson I (7/39)	
15/2/37	to Boscombe Down		
9/7/37	to Thornaby		
17/1/38	to Eastleigh		Dets Montrose & Gosport
26/3/38	to Thornaby		
1/9/38	to Leuchars		
5/39		Hudson I (5/41)	Det Aldergrove

No. 225 SQUADRON   MOTTO: We guide the sword

Date	Location	Aircraft Type	Remarks
11/11/18	Pizzone	Camel (12/18)	
18/12/18	DB		

No. 226 SQUADRON   MOTTO: Non sibi sed patriae (For country not for self)

Date	Location	Aircraft Type	Remarks
11/11/18	to Taranto	DH4 (11/18)	
		DH9 (11/18)	
		Camel (11/18)	
18/12/18	DB		
15/3/37	RF Upper Heyford		from B Flt, No. 57 Sqn
3/37		Audax (11/37)	
16/4/37	to Harwell		
10/37		Battle (5/41)	
2/9/39	to Reims		Dets Perpignan/La Salanque

No. 227 SQUADRON

Date	Location	Aircraft Type	Remarks
11/11/18	Pizzone	DH4 (12/18)	
		DH9 (12/18)	
9/12/18	DB		Without ever having become fully established

No. 228 SQUADRON   MOTTO: Auxilium a caelo (Help from the sky)

Date	Location	Aircraft Type	Remarks
11/11/18	Great Yarmouth	Felixstowe F.2A (3/19)	
		Curtiss H12/16 (/19)	
30/4/19	to Brough		as cadre
5/6/19	to Killinghome		
30/6/19	DB		
15/12/36	RF Pembroke Dock		
2/37		Scapa (8/38)	
2/37		London I (9/38)	
4/37		Stranraer (4/39)	
4/37		Singapore III (9/37)	
29/9/38	to Invergordon		
11/38		Sunderland I (8/41)	
5/6/39	to Alexandria		

No. 229 SQUADRON   **MOTTO: Be bold**

Date	Location	Aircraft Type	Remarks
11/11/18	Great Yarmouth	Short 184 (3/19) Short 320 (3/19) Fairey IIIC (3/19)	
3/3/19	to Killinghome		as cadre
31/12/19	DB		

No. 230 SQUADRON   **MOTTO: Kita chari jauh (Malay – We seek far)**

Date	Location	Aircraft Type	Remarks
11/11/18	Felixstowe	Felixstowe F.2A (3/19) Curtiss H16 (3/19) Camel (12/18) Felixstowe F.3 (3/19) Short 184 (3/19) Fairey IIIB/C (3/19)	Det Butley
13/3/19			Reduced to cadre
31/12/19			Re-established from No 4 (Communications) Sqn
1/20		Felixstowe F.3 (9/21)	
1/20		Fairey IIIC (6/21)	
1/20		Felixstowe F.2A (4/23)	
1/20		Felixstowe F.5 (4/23)	
7/5/22	to Calshot		Renumbered as No. 480 Flt
1/4/23	DB		
1/12/34	RF Pembroke Dock		
4/35		Singapore III (12/38)	
23/9/35	*en route* for Egypt		
24/10/35	to Alexandria		
24/11/35	to Lake Timsah		
1/12/35	to Alexandria		
30/7/36	*en route* to the UK		
3/8/36	to Pembroke Dock		
14/10/36	*en route* to Far East		
8/1/37	to Seletar		
6/38		Sunderland I (1/43)	Dets Trincomalee, Colombo, Penang & Koggala

No. 231 SQUADRON

Date	Location	Aircraft Type	Remarks
11/11/18	Felixstowe	Felixstowe F.2A (3/19) Felixstowe F.3 (3/19) Felixstowe F.5 (3/19)	
13/3/19			Reduced to a cadre
7/7/19	DB		

No. 232 SQUADRON   **MOTTO: Strike**

Date	Location	Aircraft Type	Remarks
11/11/18	Felixstowe	Felixstowe F.2A (1/19) Felixstowe F.3 (1/19)	
5/1/19	DB		Redesignated as No.4 (Communicatioms) Sqn

No. 233 SQUADRON   **MOTTO: Fortis et fidelis (Strong and Faithful)**

Date	Location	Aircraft Type	Remarks
11/11/18	Dover Harbour & Guston Road	DH9 (3/19) Camel (11/18) Short 184 (5/19)	Det Walmer
1/19		DH4 (5/19)	
15/5/19	DB		
18/5/37	RF Upper Heyford		

5/37		Anson I (12/39)	
9/7/37	to Thornaby		
1/9/38	to Leuchars		
28/9/38	to Montrose		
10/10/38	to Leuchars		
8/39		Hudson I (6/41)	

No. 234 SQUADRON   MOTTO: Ignem mortemque despuimus (We spit fire and death)

Date	Location	Aircraft Type	Remarks
11/11/18	Trescoe	Curtiss H.12 (5/19)	
		Short 184 (5/19)	
		Felixstowe F.3 (5/19)	
15/5/19	DB		

No. 235 SQUADRON   MOTTO: Jaculamur humi (We strike them to the ground)

Date	Location	Aircraft Type	Remarks
11/11/18	Newlyn	Short 184 (2/19)	
22/2/19	DB		

No. 236 SQUADRON   MOTTO: Speculati nuntiate (Having watched, bring word)

Date	Location	Aircraft Type	Remarks
11/11/18	Mullion	DH6 (3/19)	
		DH9 (5/19)	
31/5/19	DB		

No. 237 SQUADRON   MOTTO: Primum agmen in caelo (The vanguard is in the sky)

Date	Location	Aircraft Type	Remarks
11/11/18	Cattewater	Short 184 (5/19)	
15/5/19	DB		

No. 238 SQUADRON   MOTTO: Ad finem (To the end)

Date	Location	Aircraft Type	Remarks
11/11/18	Cattewater	Curtiss H.16 (/19)	
		Short 184 (5/19)	
		Felixstowe F.2A (5/19)	
		Felixstowe F.3 (5/19)	Dets Holy Island, Killinghome & Calshot
15/5/19			Reduced to cadre
20/3/22	DB		

No. 239 SQUADRON   MOTTO: Exploramus (We seek out)

Date	Location	Aircraft Type	Remarks
11/11/18	Torquay	Short 184 (5/19)	
31/5/19	DB		

No. 240 SQUADRON   MOTTO: Sjo-Vordur Lopt-Vordur (Guardian of the sea, guardian of the sky)

Date	Location	Aircraft Type	Remarks
11/11/18	Calshot	Short 320 (5/19)	
		Felixstowe F.2A (5/19)	
		Campania (5/19)	
		Short 184 (5/19)	
		Curtiss H.12 (/19)	
15/5/19	DB		
30/3/37	RF Calshot		Ex-C Flt, Seaplane Training Squadron
3/37		Scapa (1/39)	
11/38		Singapore III (7/39)	

7/39		Lerwick I (9/39)	
7/39		London II (7/40)	
12/8/39	to Invergordon		Det Falmouth

No. 241 SQUADRON   **MOTTO: Find and Forewarn**

Date	Location	Aircraft Type	Remarks
11/11/18	Portland	DH6 (1/19)	
		Short 184 (6/19)	
		Campania (6/19)	
		Wight Converted (6/19)	Det Chickerall
18/6/19	DB		

No. 242 SQUADRON   **MOTTO: Toujours pret (Always ready)**

Date	Location	Aircraft Type	Remarks
11/11/18	Newhaven	Short 184 (5/19)	
		DH6 (1/19)	
		Campania (11/18)	Det Telscombe Cliffs
15/5/19	DB		

No. 243 SQUADRON   **MOTTO: Swift in pursuit**

Date	Location	Aircraft Type	Remarks
11/11/18	Cherbourg	Short 184 (5/19)	
		Wight Converted	
15/3/19	DB		

No. 244 SQUADRON

Date	Location	Aircraft Type	Remarks
11/11/18	Bangor	DH6 (1/19)	Dets Tallaght, Llangefni & Luce Bay
22/1/19	DB		

No. 245 SQUADRON   **MOTTO: Fugo non fugio (I put to flight, I do not flee)**

Date	Location	Aircraft Type	Remarks
11/11/18	Fishguard	Short 184 (5/19)	
10/5/19	DB		

No. 246 SQUADRON

Date	Location	Aircraft Type	Remarks
11/11/18	Seaton Carew	Kangaroo (11/18)	
		Short 184 (3/19)	
15/3/19	DB		

No. 247 SQUADRON   **MOTTO: Rise from the East**

Date	Location	Aircraft Type	Remarks
11/11/18	Felixstowe	Felixstowe F.2A (1/19)	
		Felixstowe F.3 (1/19)	
22/1/19	DB		

No. 248 SQUADRON   **MOTTO: Il faut en finir (It is necessary to make an end of it)**

Date	Location	Aircraft Type	Remarks
11/11/18	Hornsea	Sopwith Baby (11/18)	
		Short 184 (3/19)	
		Short 320 (3/20)	Det North Coates
10/3/19	DB		

No. 249 SQUADRON   **MOTTO: Pugnis et cacibus (With fists and heels)**

Date	Location	Aircraft Type	Remarks
11/11/18	Dundee	Sopwith Baby (11/18) Hamble Baby (11/18)	
3/3/19	to Killinghome	Short 184 (3/19)	as cadre
8/10/19	DB		

No. 250 SQUADRON   **MOTTO: Close to the sun**

Date	Location	Aircraft Type	Remarks
11/11/18	Padstow	DH6 (5/19) DH9 (1/19)	Det Westward Ho
31/5/19	DB		

No. 251 SQUADRON   **MOTTO: However wind blows**

Date	Location	Aircraft Type	Remarks
11/11/18	Hornsea	DH6 (5/19) DH9 (1/19)	Dets Atwick, Greenland Top, West Ayton Owthorpe,Seaton Carew & Redcar
31/1/19	to Killinghome		as cadre
30/6/19	DB		

No. 252 SQUADRON   **MOTTO: With or on**

Date	Location	Aircraft Type	Remarks
11/11/18	Tynemouth	DH6 (1/19)	Dets Cramlington, Seaton Carew & Redcar
31/1/19	to Killinghome		as cadre
30/6/19	DB		

No. 253 SQUADRON   **MOTTO: Come one, come all**

Date	Location	Aircraft Type	Remarks
11/11/18	Bembridge	Hamble Baby (5/19) Short 184 (5/19) Campania (5/19) DH6 (1/19)	Dets Barding & Chickerall
31/5/19	DB		

No. 254 SQUADRON   **MOTTO: Fljuga vakta ok ljosta (Norse – To fly, to watch and to strike)**

Date	Location	Aircraft Type	Remarks
11/11/18	Prawle Point	DH6 (2/19) DH9 (2/19)	Det Mullion
22/2/19	DB		

No. 255 SQUADRON   **MOTTO: Ad auroram (To the break of dawn)**

Date	Location	Aircraft Type	Remarks
11/11/8	Pembroke	DH6 (1/19)	Dets Llangefni & Luce Bay
14/1/19	DB		

No. 256 SQUADRON   **MOTTO: Addimus vim viribus (Strength to strength)**

Date	Location	Aircraft Type	Remarks
11/11/18	Seahouses	DH6 (1/19)	Dets New Haggerston, Rennington Cairncross & Ashington
11/18		Kangaroo (1/19)	
31/1/19	to Killinghome		as cadre
30/6/19	DB		

No. 257 SQUADRON   MOTTO: Thay myay gvee shin shwe hti (Burmese – Death or glory)

Date	Location	Aircraft Type	Remarks
11/11/18	Dundee	Felixstowe F.2A (4/19)	
		Curtiss H.16 (/18)	
4/19			Reduced to cadre
30/6/19	DB		

No. 258 SQUADRON   MOTTO: In medias re (Into the middle of things)

Date	Location	Aircraft Type	Remarks
11/11/18	Luce Bay	DH6 (3/19)	
		Fairey IIIA (3/19)	
5/3/19	DB		

No. 260 SQUADRON   MOTTO: Celer et fortis (Swift and strong)

Date	Location	Aircraft Type	Remarks
11/11/18	Westward Ho	DH6 (2/19)	
		DH9 (2/19)	
22/2/19	DB		

No. 263 SQUADRON   MOTTO: Ex ungue leonem (From his claws one knows the lion)

Date	Location	Aircraft Type	Remarks
11/11/18	Otranto	Sopwith Baby (5/19)	Det Santa Maria di Leucca
		Hamble Baby (5/19)	
		Short 184 (5/19)	
		Short 320 (5/19)	
		Felixstowe F.3 (5/19)	
11/18	to Taranto		
16/5/19	DB		

No. 264 SQUADRON   MOTTO: We defy

Date	Location	Aircraft Type	Remarks
11/11/18	Suda Bay	Short 184 (12/18)	Det Siros
12/18			Reduced to cadre, personnel withdrawn to Malta
1/3/19	DB		

No. 266 SQUADRON   MOTTO: Hlabezulu (The stabber of the sky)

Date	Location	Aircraft Type	Remarks
11/11/18	Mudros	Short 184 (3/19)	Det Skyros
		Short 320 (3/19)	
10/3/19	to Petrovsk Port		Det Chechen
1/9/19	DB		

No. 267 SQUADRON   MOTTO: Sine mora (Without delay)

Date	Location	Aircraft Type	Remarks
11/11/18	Kalafrana	Short 184 (10/21)	Det Alexandria
		Felixstowe F.2A (2/23)	
		Felixstowe F.3 (6/21)	
12/20		Fairey IIID (8/23)	Dets HMS *Ark Royal* & Kilya Bay
1/8/23	DB		Redesignated as 481 Flt

No. 268 SQUADRON   **MOTTO: Adjidaumo (Chippeway Indian – Tail in the air)**

Date	Location	Aircraft Type	Remarks
11/11/18	Kalafrana	Short 184 (10/19)	
		Short 320 (10/19)	
11/10/19	DB		

No. 269 SQUADRON   **MOTTO: Omnia videmus (We see all things)**

Date	Location	Aircraft Type	Remarks
11/11/18	Port Said	BE2E (3/19)	
		Short 184 (11/19)	
12/18		DH9 (3/19)	
15/9/19	to Alexandria		
15/11/19	DB		Absorbed by No. 267 Sqn
7/12/36	RF Bircham Newton		from C Flt, No. 220 Sqn
12/36		Anson I (6/40)	
30/12/36	to Abbotsinch		
17/1/38	to Eastleigh		
24/3/38	to Abbotsinch		
29/9/38	to Thornaby		
6/10/38	to Abbotsinch		
25/8/39	to Montrose		

No. 270 SQUADRON

Date	Location	Aircraft Type	Remarks
11/11/18	Alexandria	Short 184 (9/19)	
		Sopwith Baby (4/19)	
		Felixstowe F.3 (9/19)	
		DH9 (/19)	
15/9/19	DB		Merged into No. 269 Sqn

No. 271 SQUADRON   **MOTTO: Death and life**

Date	Location	Aircraft Type	Remarks
11/11/18	Taranto	Short 184 (12/18)	Det Otranto
		Felixstowe F.3 (12/18)	
9/12/18	DB		

No. 272 SQUADRON   **MOTTO: On, on!**

Date	Location	Aircraft Type	Remarks
11/11/18	Macrihanish	DH6 (3/19)	
		Fairey IIIA (3/19)	
5/3/19	DB		

No. 273 SQUADRON

Date	Location	Aircraft Type	Remarks
11/11/18	Burgh Castle	DH4 (3/19)	Dets Covehithe, Westgate & Manston
		DH9 (3/19)	
		Camel (3/19)	
14/3/19			Reduced to cadre
6/19	to Great Yarmouth		
5/7/19	DB		
1/8/39	RF China Bay		
8/39		Seal (3/42)	
		Vildebeest III (3/42)	Det Ratmalana

No. 274 SQUADRON   MOTTO: Supero (I overcome)

Date	Location	Aircraft Type	Remarks
15/6/19	F Bircham Newton		Nucleus from No. 5 (Communications) Sqn
6/19		HP V/1500 (1/20)	
20/1/20	DB		

No. 500 SQUADRON County of Kent   MOTTO: Quo fata vocent (Whither the fates may call)

Date	Location	Aircraft Type	Remarks
16/3/31	F Manston		as a Special Reserve Squadron
3/31		Virginia X (1/36)	
1/36		Hart (5/37)	
25/5/36			Transferred to AAF
2/37		Hind (3/39)	
28/9/38	to Detling		
3/39		Anson I (4/4I)	
30/7/39	to Warmwell		
13/8/39	to Detling		

No. 501 SQUADRON City of Bristol 1930–6 County of Gloucester 1936–57   MOTTO: Nil time (Fear nothing)

Date	Location	Aircraft Type	Remarks
14/6/29	F Filton		as a Special Reserve Squadron
3/30		DH9A (11/30)	
9/30		Wapiti (3/33)	
1/33		Wallace (7/36)	
1/5/36			Transferred to AAF
7/36		Hart (3/38)	
3/38		Hind (3/39)	
3/39		Hurricane I (5/41)	

No. 502 SQUADRON Ulster   MOTTO: Nihil timeo (I fear nothing)

Date	Location	Aircraft Type	Remarks
15/5/25	F Aldergove		as a Special Reserve Squadron
6/25		Vimy (7/28)	
7/28		Hyderabad (2/32)	
12/31		Virginia X (10/35)	
10/35		Wallace (4/37)	
4/37		Hind (4/39)	
1/7/37			Transferred to AAF
1/39		Anson I (10/40)	Det Hooton Park

No. 503 SQUADRON County of Lincoln

Date	Location	Aircraft Type	Remarks
5/10/26	F Waddington		as a Special Reserve Squadron
10/26		Fawn (6/29)	
2/29		Hyderabad (1/34)	
10/33		Hinaidi (11/35)	
8/35		Wallace (7/36)	
1/5/36			Transferred to AAF
6/36		Hart (11/38)	
6/38		Hind (11/38)	
1/11/38	DB		Moved to Doncaster and renumbered 616 Sqn

No. 504 SQUADRON County of Nottingham   MOTTO: Vindicat in ventis (It avenges in the wind)

Date	Location	Aircraft Type	Remarks
26/3/28	F Hucknall		as a Special Reserve Squadron
10/29		Horsley (3/34)	
3/34		Wallace I (5/37)	

Date	Location		Remarks
3/36		Wallace II (5/37)	
18/5/36			Transferred to AAF
5/37		Hind (11/38)	
11/38		Gauntlet II (8/39)	
5/39		Hurricane I (7/41)	
27/8/39	to Digby		

No. 600 SQUADRON City of London   MOTTO: Praeter sescentos (More than 600)

Date	Location	Aircraft Type	Remarks
14/10/25	F Northolt		
10/25		DH9A (10/29)	
18/1/27	to Hendon		
8/29		Wapiti (1/35)	
1/35		Hart (5/37)	
2/37		Demon (4/39)	
1/10/38	to Kenley		
4/10/38	to Hendon		
1/39		Blenheim IF (10/41)	
25/8/39	to Northolt		

No. 601 SQUADRON County of London

Date	Location	Aircraft Type	Remarks
14/10/25	F Northolt		
6/26		DH9A (10/30)	
18/1/27	to Hendon		
11/29		Wapiti (6/33)	
2/33		Hart (8/37)	
8/37		Demon (12/38)	
12/38		Gauntlet II (3/39)	
1/39		Blenheim IF (2/40)	
2/9/39	to Biggin Hill		

No. 602 SQUADRON City of Glasgow   MOTTO: Cave leonem cruciatum (Beware the tormented lion)

Date	Location	Aircraft Type	Remarks
12/9/25	F Renfrew		
10/25		DH9A (1/28)	
9/27		Fawn (10/29)	
7/29		Wapiti (4/34)	
20/1/33	to Abbotsinch		
2/34		Hart (6/36)	
6/36		Hind (11/38)	
11/38		Hector (1/39)	
1/39		Gauntlet II (5/39)	
5/39		Spitfire I (6/41)	

No. 603 SQUADRON City of Edinburgh   MOTTO: Gin ye daur (If you dare)

Date	Location	Aircraft Type	Remarks
14/10/25	F Turnhouse		
10/25		DH9A (5/30)	
3/30		Wapiti (3/34)	
2/34		Hart (2/38)	
2/38		Hind (3/39)	
3/39		Gladiator II (10/39)	
9/39		Spitfire I (11/40)	

No. 604 SQUADRON County of Middlesex   MOTTO: Si vis pacem, para bellum (If you want peace, prepare for war)

Date	Location	Aircraft Type	Remarks
17/3/30	F Hendon		
4/30		DH9A (10/30)	
9/30		Wapiti IIA (/34)	
9/34		Hart (6/35)	
6/35		Demon (1/39)	
1/39		Blenheim I (5/41)	
2/9/39	to North Weald		Det Martlesham Heath

No. 605 SQUADRON County of Warwick   MOTTO: Nunquam dormio (I never sleep)

Date	Location	Aircraft Type	Remarks
5/10/26	F Castle Bromwich		
10/26		DH9A (7/30)	
4/30		Wapiti IIA (11/34)	
2/34		Hart (9/36)	
8/36		Hind (1/39)	
4/39		Gladiator I (11/39)	
6/39		Hurricane I (12/40)	
27/8/39	to Tangmere		

No. 607 SQUADRON County of Durham

Date	Location	Aircraft Type	Remarks
17/3/30	F Usworth		
12/32		Wapiti IIA (1/37)	
9/36		Demon (8/39)	
12/38		Gladiator I (5/40)	

No. 608 SQUADRON County of York – North Riding (North Riding from May 1937)   MOTTO: Omnibus ungulis (With all talons)

Date	Location	Aircraft Type	Remarks
17/3/30	F Thornaby		
6/30		Wapiti IIA (1/37)	
1/37		Demon (3/39)	
3/39		Anson I (5/41)	

No. 609 SQUADRON West Riding   MOTTO: Tally Ho

Date	Location	Aircraft Type	Remarks
10/2/36	F Yeadon		
5/36		Hart (1/38)	
1/38		Hind (8/39)	
8/39		Spitfire I (5/41)	
27/8/39	to Catterick		

No. 610 SQUADRON County of Chester   MOTTO: Alifero tollitur axe Ceres (Ceres rising in a winged car)

Date	Location	Aircraft Type	Remarks
10/2/36	F Hendon		
16/4/36	to Hooton Park		
5/36		Hart (5/38)	
5/38		Hind (9/39)	
9/39		Hurricane I (9/39)	
9/39		Spitfire I (2/41)	

No. 611 SQUADRON West Lancashire   MOTTO: Beware, beware

Date	Location	Aircraft Type	Remarks
10/2/36	F Hendon		
1/4/36	to Liverpool		
6/5/36	to Speke		
6/36		Hart (4/38)	
4/38		Hind (5/39)	
5/39		Spitfire (9/40)	
13/8/39	to Duxford		

No. 612 SQUADRON County of Aberdeen   MOTTO: Vigilando custodimus (We stand guard by vigilance)

Date	Location	Aircraft Type	Remarks
1/6/37	F Dyce		
12/37		Hector (11/39)	
6/39		Anson I (1/41)	Dets Stornaway & Wick

No. 613 SQUADRON City of Manchester   MOTTO: Semper parati (Always ready)

Date	Location	Aircraft Type	Remarks
1/3/39	F Ringway		
4/39		Hind (4/40)	

No. 614 SQUADRON County of Glamorgan   MOTTO: Codaf I geislo (Welsh – I rise and search)

Date	Location	Aircraft Type	Remarks
1/6/37	F Pengam Moors		
6/37		Hind (1/38)	
4/38		Hector (2/40)	
7/39		Lysander II (7/41)	

No. 615 SQUADRON County of Surrey   MOTTO: Conjunctis viribus (By our united force)

Date	Location	Aircraft Type	Remarks
1/6/37	F Kenley		
11/37		Audax (3/38)	
11/37		Hector (2/39)	
12/38		Gauntlet II (9/39)	
6/39		Gladiator I (10/39)	
2/9/39	to Croydon		

No. 616 SQUADRON South Yorkshire   MOTTO: Nulla rosa sine spina (No rose without a thorn)

Date	Location	Aircraft Type	Remarks
1/11/38	F Doncaster		from No. 503 Sqn
11/38		Hind I (1/39)	
1/39		Gauntlet II (12/39)	
5/39		Battle (11/39)	

Appendix C
The Trenchard Memorandum

AN OUTLINE OF THE SCHEME FOR THE PERMANENT ORGANIZATION OF THE ROYAL AIR FORCE

Note: The presentation of the memorandum is precisely as the original document, which may be found in AIR 1/17 in the National Archives.

NOTE BY THE SECRETARY OF STATE FOR AIR

The scheme outlined in the following memorandum on the permanent organization of the Royal Air Force has been prepared during the course of the present year under my direction by the Chief of the Air Staff, and has in principle received the approval of the Cabinet.

The many complications of the Air Service and its intricate technical organization are not perhaps fully appreciated, even by those who take a general interest in the subject. It therefore appears desirable to lay this memorandum in both Houses of Parliament, in order that they may understand the character and the problem and the complications that are being faced.

It should be added that the financial provision which the Cabinet have approved as governing the scale of the Royal Air Force during the next few years is approximately 15 million pounds per annum. It is upon this basis that this scheme has been prepared, and it is upon this basis that it is hoped the Estimates of next year will, apart from any extraordinary expenditure which the military situation may render necessary, be framed.

WINSTON S. CHURCHILL

11th December, 1919.

MEMORANDUM BY THE CHIEF OF THE AIR STAFF

1. *The problem confronting us.* – The problem of forming the Royal Air Force on a peace basis differs in many essentials from that which confronts the older services. The Royal Air Force was formed by the amalgamation of the Royal Flying Corps and the Royal Naval Air Service, and one may say, broadly speaking, that the whole Service was practically a war time creation on a temporary basis, without any possibility of taking into account that it was going to remain on a permanent basis. The personnel, with few exceptions was enlisted for the duration of the war, and put through an intensive but necessarily hurried course of training. Material was created in vast quantities, but rapid development often rendered it obsolete even before it reached the stage of bulk production. The accommodation provided had perforce to be of an entirely temporary character. The force may in fact be compared to the prophet Jonah's gourd. The necessities of war created it in a night, but the economies of peace have to a large extent caused it to wither in a day, and we are now faced with the necessity of replacing it with a plant of deeper root. As in nature, however, decay fosters growth, and the new plant has a fruitful soil from which to spring.

   The principle to be kept in mind in forming the framework of the Air Service is that in the future the main portion of it will consist of an Independent Force, together with the Service personnel required in carry out Aeronautical Research.

   In addition there will be a small part of it trained for work with the Navy, and a small part specially trained for work with the Army, these two small portions probably becoming, in the future, an arm of the older services.

   It may be that the main portion, the Independent Air Force, will grow larger and larger, and become more and more the predominating factor in all types of warfare.

2. *Governing principles.* – In planning the formation of the peace Royal Air Force it has been assumed that no need will arise for some years at least for anything in the nature of general mobilisation. It has been possible therefore to concentrate on providing for the needs of the moment as far as they can be foreseen and on laying the foundations of a highly-trained and efficient force which, though not capable of expansion in its present form, can be made to do so without any drastic alteration should the necessity arise in the years to come. Broadly speaking, the principle has been to reduce service squadrons to a minimum considered essential for our garrisons overseas with a very small number in the United Kingdom as a reserve and to concentrate the whole of the remainder of our resources on perfecting the training of officers and men.

   It is intended to preserve the numbers of some of the great squadrons who have made names for themselves during the war, in permanent service units with definite identity, which will be the homes of the officers belonging to them, and will have the traditions of the war to look back on.

   There will be found in the Appendix a statement showing detailed particulars of squadrons, stations, schools, depots &c., which it is hoped to provide in the next three years at home and abroad. It will be understood that this programme is to be regarded as provisional only.

3. *Service units.* – It is proposed to provide 8 squadrons for India and 3 for Mesopotamia with the necessary facilities for repair. As regards India this is in accordance with the proposal put forward from India and now under consideration by the Government of India. The cost of the units in India will fall on the Government of India on exactly the same basis as in the case of the military garrison. Recent events have shown the value of aircraft in dealing with frontier troubles and it is not perhaps too much to hope that before long it may prove possible to regard the Royal Air Force units not as an addition to the military garrison but as a substitute for part of it. One great advantage of aircraft in this class of warfare approximating to police work is their power of acting at once. Aircraft can visit the scene of incipient unrest within a comparatively few hours of the receipt of news. To organize a military expedition even on a small scale takes time, and delay may result in the trouble spreading. The cost is also much greater , and very many more lives are involved.

   In Egypt it is proposed to station 7 service squadrons. Under existing conditions in that country aircraft are a most valuable means of communication. Distances are long and ground communication confined to a few main routes. On the other hand the country and the climate are ideal for flying. From a wider aspect Egypt is the Clapham Junction of the air between east and west, and is situated within comparatively easy reach of the most probable centres of unrest, and this added to its natural advantages for aviation, makes it the obvious locality for a small Royal Air Force reserve.

As regards our Naval bases and important coaling stations overseas, future developments will almost certainly lead to the necessity of providing aircraft as part of their garrisons, but in the majority of cases the need of this is not urgent under existing conditions, and for the present it is only proposed to station a small seaplane unit in Malta, and a similar unit in the Eastern Mediterranean, probably at Alexandria.

The Service squadrons quartered in the United Kingdom apart from those for co-operation with the Army and Navy will eventually number four, but not more than two of these squadrons will be formed in the next financial year. These squadrons will be employed on communications and similar duties in peace and will form a small reserve in case of need. For co-operation with the Army it is proposed to provide eventually squadrons on the basis of a flight per division for work with the troops at all stages of their training, and in addition one or more squadrons for co-operation with the artillery both during their winter training and their annual gun practice. During the next financial year it is proposed to form two squadrons in all, one at Farnborough for co-operation with the troops at Aldershot and Salisbury, and the second at Stonehenge for work with the artillery. Small units will, if necessary, be provided in addition for co-operation with the Garrison Artillery School at Golden Hill, and the Anti-aircraft School when formed.

There remain the Service squadrons for co-operation with the Fleet. It is proposed eventually to provide at home three Aeroplane squadrons and two Seaplane squadrons. To secure economy and to give the units a corporate existence and ample facilities for practice it has been decided that aeroplanes will no longer be carried normally in capital ships as was done during the war, but will only be embarked when required to take part in Fleet exercises. The Aeroplane squadrons will consist of one reconnaissance and spotting squadron, and one squadron of fighter machines and one of torpedo-carrying machines. The two former will be based on the Firth of Forth where ample facilities exist for practice and the embarkation and disembarkation of machines, a most important point. The torpedo-carrying squadron will be located at Gosport, the most suitable station for torpedo work, and it is proposed to provide a small experimental unit at the same station in order to develop fully this form of co-operation with the Navy, which is of primary importance. Of these three squadrons it is proposed to provide only one, the reconnaissance squadron, at full strength in the ensuing financial year. This is necessary in order to study and perfect the system of observation of artillery fire which from various causes was not so highly developed on the naval side as on the land side during the war. The torpedo squadron will be maintained at sufficient strength to carry on the essential research work while the fighting squadron will be formed in the first instance at a strength of one flight only. In addition, the Admiralty propose to keep two aircraft carriers in commission. One of these will be equipped with seaplanes for service abroad, while the other will remain at home and be used primarily for training and experimental purposes and ready if necessary to embark a flight of torpedo or other machines.

The provision of these two carriers is of the first importance since we must look forward to the time, as suitable machines develop when fleets will so to speak take their aerodromes with them in the shape of a carrier, and the carriage of aircraft on capital ships with its attendant disadvantages and dangers will be a thing of the past.

Of the two seaplane squadrons, it is only proposed at present to form one flight only. The seaplane has obvious advantages over the aeroplane for long distance work over water, and a time may probably come when all work in co-operation with the Navy will be done by this class of machine. For this reason, if for no other, it is essential to have a few such units.

The lighter-than-air service is a difficult problem. The cost of providing such a service on a large scale in peace is prohibitive, and the use of airships in war may be said to be still in the experimental stage. It is proposed therefore to keep one airship station only at Howden, where sufficient accommodation exists for two rigid and a few smaller ships, and to retain as a commencement one rigid and two non-rigids only. This will allow research work and development to continue, and the use of airships in peace and war to be further studied.

4. *Reserves.* – Although mobilisation on a large scale is not taken into account, it is very necessary to provide a small reserve to meet any sudden call in the case of a small war anywhere in the Empire. For the next year or two there will, doubtless, be no difficulty in enrolling as many ex-officers and men as are likely to be required, and all that will be necessary to provide facilities for their training and practice flying.

It is intended, however, if possible, in addition to lay the foundation of a future Air Force on a territorial basis. No detailed scheme has yet been worked out, but it is probable that the eventual organization will provide for training both on a unit and an individual basis. It is hoped that the manufacturing and commercial firms will assist by forming units of their employees. In addition there will doubtless be many individuals who will be glad to train themselves voluntarily with a certain amount of state assistance, and to undertake to serve, either overseas or at home, if called upon to do so. It is not intended to embark on the formation of any units during the next financial year, but it is proposed to commence with the training of individuals in the populous centres. This training will be carried out at the flying training wings whose functions will be described below.

5. *Extreme importance of training.* – We now come to that on which the whole future of the Royal Air Force depends, namely, the training of its officers and men. The present need is not, under existing conditions, the creation of the full number of squadrons we may eventually require to meet strategical needs, but it is first and foremost the making of a sound framework on which to build a service, which while giving us now the few essential service squadrons, adequately trained and equipped, will be capable of producing whatever time may show to be necessary in the future.

Before explaining our proposals in detail it is necessary to lay down certain postulates.

Firstly, to make an Air Force worthy of the name, we must create an Air Force spirit, or rather foster this spirit which undoubtedly existed in a high degree during the war, by every means in our power. Suggestions have been made that we should rely on the older services to train our cadets and Staff officers. To do so would make the creation of an Air Force spirit an impossibility apart from the practical objection, among others, that the existing naval and military cadet and staff colleges are not provided with aerodromes or situated in localities in any way suited for flying training.

Secondly, we must use every endeavour to eliminate flying accidents, both during training and subsequently. This end can only be secured by ensuring that the training of our mechanics in the multiplicity of trades necessitated by a highly technical service, is as thorough as it can be made. The best way to do this is to enlist the bulk of our skilled ranks as boys and train them ourselves. This has the added advantage that it will undoubtedly foster the Air Force spirit on which so much depends.

Thirdly, it is not sufficient to make the Air Force officer a chauffeur and nothing more.

Technical experts are required for the development of the science of aeronautics, still in its infancy. Navigation, meteorology, photography and wireless are primary necessities if the Air Force is to be more than a means of conveyance, and the first two are requisite for safety, even on the chauffeur basis.

6. *Training of Officers.* – It is now necessary to sketch very briefly the training proposed both for officers and men. Owing to the necessity of a large number of officers in the junior ranks, and to the comparative paucity of higher appointments, it is not possible to offer a career to all. Consequently some 50 per cent only of the officers have been granted permanent commissions, the remainder being obtained on short service commissions or by the seconding of officers from the Army and Navy. Great importance attaches to the last class since an interchange of officers is bound to make for closer and more intelligent co-operation between the services.

The channels of entry for permanently commissioned officers will be through the Cadet College, from the Universities and from the ranks. The cadet college will be the main channel. The course will last two years, during which the cadets will be given a thorough grounding in the theoretical and practical sides of their profession, and will in addition learn to fly the approved training machine, at present the Avro. The college is to open at Cranwell in Lincolnshire early next year, an ideal place for the purpose with a large and excellent aerodrome and perfect flying surroundings. It will be necessary to accommodate the college temporarily in huts erected during the war, but every endeavour has been made to render these as suitable as possible, and it is proposed to erect a permanent college in the near future. On leaving the college, cadets will be commissioned and will undergo a short course in air pilotage and practical cross-country flying at Andover. This school will probably not be required before early in 1921. As soon as the cadets have passed this course they will be posted to a service squadron, as it is most important that they should join a unit which they can regard as their home, as the sailor does his ship or the soldier his regiment, as early as possible. Subsequently they will undergo a course in gunnery, without which no flying officer can be regarded as a service pilot. The gunnery school will be established at Eastchurch, but as the bulk of our present pilots have war experience, will not be required in the next financial year. After 5 years' service officers will be required to select the particular technical subject they will make their special study during their subsequent career, e.g. navigation, engines, wireless. Short and long courses will be provided in these subjects to cater both for the officer who wishes to continue primarily as a flying officer with a working knowledge of one or more of the technical subjects, and for those who wish to become really expert in a particular branch. Technical knowledge will, *inter alia*, qualify an officer for selection for high command.

The career of officers commissioned from the Universities or from the ranks – except in the case of boy mechanics receiving commissions, whose case can be dealt with later – will be identical with that of those from the cadet college, except that they will be taught to fly at flying training wings before joining their squadrons. Short service and seconded officers will be taught to fly at flying training wings and will attend a course of aerial gunnery and probably one of air pilotage. In view of their short service, it is not proposed, save in special cases, to send them through the advanced technical courses. These officers will be eligible for promotion during their service in exactly the same way as the permanent officers. The technical schools required at once are those dealing with navigation, wireless, photography and engineering. Aerial navigation is practically a new science. An attempt has been made during the current year to work out the theoretical principles in practice at Andover, and considerable progress has been made, but is obvious that the chief need of aerial navigation will arise when flying over the sea, where the map is of no service, and it is consequently proposed to reopen this school at Calshot in the spring of next year.

Schools of wireless and photography are now in existence at Flowerdown, near Winchester, and at Farnborough respectively, while it is proposed to commence an engineering course, at a suitable station, shortly after Christmas.

For the training of University candidates, short service and seconded officers and officers of the reserve or Territorial Force, it is estimated that seven training wings would eventually be required.

In view, however, of the fact that the short service list has been filled by officers who have already been trained as pilots during the war, it is only proposed to form two of these on a reduced basis during the next financial year to deal with the training of University candidates, a small number of reserve officers and of certain officers granted permanent commissions, with the proviso that they must learn to fly within 12 months. In view of the exceptional facilities for training in Egypt, it is proposed to locate, at least, one of the training wings, together with branch schools of gunnery and air pilotage in that country, but whether it will be convenient to do so next year cannot yet be definitely foreseen.

One other important school in connection with the training of the officer is essential, and it will probably be necessary to start it on a small scale in1920. This is a school for flying instructors. The first school of its kind was started during the war at Gosport, and it is hardly too much to say that it revolutionised the art of flying. The science of flight was carefully analysed and the analysis practically applied to the problem of tuition with remarkable results. It is essential in future that all instructors in training wings and all officers of or above the rank of flight commander in service squadrons should have passed through this course. A liberal amount of dual control with a qualified instructor is one of the chief safeguards against the faulty flying which is the cause of the majority of accidents.

Although it is not proposed to open it during the next financial year, an Air Force Staff College must be formed as soon as possible. It is intended to establish this at Halton in the house of the late Mr Alfred Rothschild, purchased by the Government at his death with the whole estate. The house and its surroundings are eminently suited for the purpose, and there is an aerodrome within a quarter of a mile.

7. *Training of men.* – The most difficult problem of all in the formation of this force is the training of the men. Demobilization has removed most of our best mechanics, and the efficiency of the squadrons to be formed depends on the most thorough instruction of those who are to take their place. It has, therefore, been decided to enlist the bulk of those belonging to long apprenticeship trades as boys, who will undergo a course of three years' training before being passed into the ranks. With a preliminary training of the nature contemplated and the practice of their subsequent service, it is confidently anticipated that these mechanics on passing to civil life will have no difficulty in securing recognition as skilled

tradesmen. This is an important consideration since any tendency for the Air Force to be regarded as a blind alley occupation would be fatal. The training of all these boys will eventually be carried out at Halton Park, where ample and well equipped technical shops are already in existence. Pending the erection of permanent barracks to replace wooden war-time huts, use will be made of Cranwell, in Lincolnshire. It has been necessary to speed up the training of some 5,000 boys enlisted during, and shortly after, the war, and the residue of these, some 3,000, will complete their training, at Halton. A scheme has been drawn out for the future enlistment of boys by means of competitive examination, and the local education authorities have been circularized with a view to their nominating suitable boys to sit for the examination. By this means it is hoped to secure a really high standard. The first entry under this scheme will take place early in 1920, and the boys will commence their training at Cranwell and will be moved to Halton as soon as the permanent accommodation is ready.

The boys, on successfully passing their final examination, will be graded as leading aircraftmen, and a certain number will be specially selected for a further course of training, at the end of which they will either be granted commissions, or promoted to corporal. Those granted commissions will join the cadet college.

It is intended to enlist the remainder of the mechanics of whom more than half will belong to short apprenticeship trades as men, and these will undergo 12 months training at Cranwell as soon as the boys have moved to Halton. Pending the move, it is proposed to carry out the training of these men at Eastchurch, which, as has already been said, will not be required in its eventual capacity as a gunnery school for another 12 months at least.

Non-technical men will be given a short course of recruit training at the depot at Uxbridge.

8. *Higher organization at home.* – As regards higher organization in the United Kingdom, all units working with the Navy have lately been formed into one command known as the Coastal Area Royal Air Force. The two remaining commands, now known as the Southern and Northern Areas, will, early in 1920, be amalgamated into one command to be known as the Inland Area. This cannot be done earlier owing to the very large amount of work entailed in closing up surplus stations, demobilizing surplus personnel and generally clearing up after the effects of the war.

9. *Depots.* – Each of the two Areas in the United Kingdom will have its repair depot, at Henlow for the Inland Area, and at Donnisbristle, near Rosythe, for the Coastal Area. During the next financial year it will be necessary to retain three of the existing stores depots, but it may prove possible at a later date to reduce the number to two, though this is by no means certain. It is hoped that eventually arrangements will be made for all Royal Air Force mechanical transport to be repaired at Slough, but in view of the arrears of work it will be necessary to retain for the present our repair depot at Shrewsbury. Each overseas theatre will have a combined repair and store depot of a size suitable to the number of squadrons based upon it.

10. *Necessity for large capital outlay on accommodation.* – From the above outline of our proposals it will be seen that every endeavour is being made to reduce expenditure on personnel during 1920–1921 to the minimum absolutely essential to create the framework of our future Air Force. This is necessary if, for no other reason, owing to the peculiar position in which the Royal Air Force is placed as regards permanent accommodation. Though some wartime buildings can be made to serve for a year or two in their present state, the Air Force does not possess one single permanent barracks, and a large capital outlay on the provision of new buildings and the adaptation of the most suitable of the temporary buildings is inevitable during the first few years. This will be balanced to a certain extent during the next two years by the small requirements in technical equipments due to the large stock remaining over from the war. The principle followed has therefore been to exercise rigid economy at the outset over personnel and technical equipment in order to free a large a part as possible of the total sum provided towards the provision of barracks. As time goes on, the building services will absorb less, while the cost of technical equipment, and, to a lesser extent, of personnel, will increase, until eventually the works vote will be little in excess of the cost of maintenance.

It must be recognized, however, that the total cost of building will be large. The boys' barracks at Halton, for instance, with the necessary accessory buildings and the cadet college will no doubt be a heavy item. These are undoubtedly the two most expensive services, but the accommodation for personnel at the majority of our stations will have to be rebuilt or adapted at considerable cost. The outlay must, however, be faced, and it is undoubtedly wise to undertake the bulk of the work in the first few years, while the expense of the other services can be kept down.

11. *Research.* – One matter of supreme importance has not yet been mentioned, namely, the provision to be made for research. The departments of Supply and Research are now being transferred from the Ministry of Munitions to the Air Ministry, and a portion of the experimental establishments are a charge on the Air Force votes. Steady and uninterrupted progress in research is vital to the efficiency of the Air Force, and to the development of aviation generally, and on it depends both the elimination of accidents and the retention of the leading position we have established at such heavy cost during the war. The existing establishments must therefore be retained during the ensuing financial year at a sufficient strength to ensure that urgent work shall continue. Some of the work which was urgent under war conditions can, however, now be postponed until progress with the building programme liberates more money for other purposes. The principal aeroplane research establishments are at Farnborough, Biggin Hill, Martlesham Heath, and Grain, while airships' research will be undertaken at Cardington and Howden.

12. *Civil Aviation.* – No allusion has been made to civil aviation in this paper, which has been confined to the Service aspect of the question.

H.M. TRENCHARD,
Chief of the Air Staff

AIR MINISTRY
25th November, 1919.

Appendix D
Flying Operations Carried Out By No. 11 (IRISH) Wing, April 1922
(Extracts)

1st April

Reconnaissance of roads Ardmore–Ringville–Dungarvan was carried out by 2 Sqn. Picked up six cars with troops going to Whitechurch. Two trenches were located on road 3 miles west of Ringville. Dropped message at Dungarvan. Mails were delivered to Tipperary–Cahir–Fethard and Clonmel. No. 2 Sqn made a reconnaissance of roads Ardmore–Dungarvan. Picked up 5 cars with troops going towards Dungarvan. Trenches located in road 4 miles south of Dungarvan. Dropped message asking troops if 'OK'. Answer 'Yes'. Informed them of trenches in road. Mails were delivered to Buttevant, Castletown and later to Ballincollig. Machine delivering mail to Buttevant force landed at Kanturk. This machine located from the air, dismantled and taken to Fermoy by rail. Mails were delivered to Limerick. In Dublin area a road patrol of the Naas–Dublin road was carried out by 100 Sqn as an ambush was suspected. Nothing seen.

2nd April

2 Sqn escorted troop train from Fermoy to Kanturk. Mails delivered to Tipperary, Fethard, Cahir, Clonmel, Clogheen and Dungarvan. Co-operate with 17th Infantry Brigade in round-up of area. Picked up 15 vehicles with Auxiliaries and troops at Donoughmore. Landed at Ballincollig and reported progress. Thoroughly reconnoitred and kept in touch with troops by means of Klaxon horn and ground signals. Landed by troops on completion of operations. On way back to aerodrome patrolled roads. Reported bridges destroyed and trenches in roads at various points. Mails delivered to Ballincollig, Buttevant and Castletown. No. 100 Squadron sent up a machine to patrol the railways and roads in the Tullamore–Clara–Athlone–Banagher area to report nature of an ambush that had occurred. Patrols were sent up to meet the Bristol Fighters flying from Shotwick in connection with re-armament of 100 Squadron.

3rd April

2 Sqn reconnoitred roads Ballyhooley, Kildorrery, Michelstown, Glanworth. 16th Infantry Brigade informed all roads clear with the exception of two second class roads south-west of Glanworth. Special duty to Buttevant. Machine landed at Buttevant and took Brigade Major of Kerry Brigade to visit detachment at Bere island thence to Ballincollig and Fermoy. Visiting this detachment by air saved a journey of three days by rail and boat. Landing grounds at Bere Island not very good. Difficulty in taking off owing to confined space. Mails delivered to Limerick. Mails were delivered by 100 Sqn to Fermoy, Curragh, Athlone and Aldergrove and a reconnaissance was made of the Kilmashogue District for illegal drilling and rifle practice. The report of this reconnaissance was dropped at Dublin Castle.

4th April

In the 6th Divisional Area railway Fermoy–Ballyduff reconnoitred. Found line torn up one mile west of Ballyduff, this was being repaired. Train standing at Ballyduff station. Roads all clear. Informed 16th Infantry Brigade. Mails were delivered to Clogheen, Clonmel, Dungarvan, Waterford and Kilkenny. Conveyed District Inspector of RIC [Royal Irish Constabulary] Fermoy to Curragh. Mails dropped at Buttevant and Kanturk. Patrolled area west of Buttevant. Found all roads between Buttevant and Kanturk blocked. Landed at Buttevant and reported state of roads. This information prevented convoy proceeding as state of roads was not known when machine landed. Two aerial reconnaissances were carried out in the Galway Brigade area by D Flight of 100 Squadron for any unusual activity. Nothing unusual to report.

Appendix E

Extract from Report on Iraq Administration by the High Commissioner, April 1922 to March 1923

The progress of the Royal Air Force Scheme of Control in Iraq from 1 October 1922 to 31 March 1923
Source: Appendix II to Air Staff Memorandum No. 48 S.29711

The Royal Air Force took control of British Forces in Iraq from 1 October 1922 when (then) Air Vice-Marshal Sir John Salmond KCB, CMG, CVO, DSO assumed command.

Throughout the period under review, Iraq was faced with serious external menace from Turkey, there were considerable concentrations at Jazirah-ibn 'Umar, while other centres had been gradually affected. This situation on the Northern Frontier, has, as has been stated, its reactions on the internal affairs in Iraq. It served to foment restlessness and to give moral support to intriguers and ill-disposed persons wherever their propaganda could obtain a foothold, to delay the development of a normal state of security in the country; and in general to confuse the original problem of maintaining internal security under Air Command.

As an instance, the Turkish irregulars operating south-eastwards from Rowanduz were enabled, because of the moral support which the external Turkish menace gave them, to achieve results among the turbulent Kurds of this area which never could have been achieved had it not been felt by the tribesmen that the regular forces of Turkey were behind them.

This Turkish menace which had not been calculated for at the time when the scheme of RAF Control was decided upon, necessitated the continued maintenance of ground troops far beyond the scheme. Reductions in this respect were not begun during the period covered by this report.

The details of this menace and the measures taken to meet it are not for consideration in this report, but its existence and effect as a factor aggravating the various minor problems of internal lawlessness with which the Air Force scheme was called upon to deal must be borne in mind.

In tracing the progress made during this first six months towards a normal condition of internal order and security, it is convenient to consider Iraq proper separately from Kurdistan in Iraq.

During the six months under review various minor air operations were carried out in Iraq proper.

Thus, in October, in the Nasiriyah area, air action became necessary in consequence of the attitude of defiance to Government adopted by a group of five Sheikhs. Offensive action was taken against the ringleader and demonstration flights were made over the remaining four. As a result three of the confederates submitted to Government, while the ringleader's own tribesmen, together with those of his one remaining supporter, deserted him. He remained, however, at the head of some 200 malcontents and fugitives from justice, with whom he proceeded to hold up caravans on the roads and to terrorise the district.

Air action was continued against him and in a very short space he made unconditional surrender. At the same time another local Sheikh in this district thought that an opportune moment had now arrived to defy the Government. An ultimatum dropped on him from the air, however, immediately secured a satisfactory change in his views.

At the end of October, in the Diwaniyah division, in an area so intricately intersected by irrigation channels that any operations by ground troops are very slow and inconvenient, armed defiance of the police called for air action. As a result the police were enabled to effect the arrest of the offending Sheikhs.

In December certain Sheikhs of the turbulent tribes situated on the banks of the Adhaim River refused to come in to Government. An aerial demonstration was made and leaflets were dropped warning them to report under the threat of air action. As a result the Sheikhs submitted without air action becoming necessary.

At the end of January, near Diwaniyah, a car containing the Divisional Adviser was fired on, and the Adviser wounded, by some brigands on the road. These brigands, it transpired later, were at the time lying in wait for a Sheikh whom, at the instigation of a Sheikh of a neighbouring tribe, they intended to murder.

The Sheikh concerned was ordered to hand them over and to come into Government for an inquiry to be made into an outbreak involving several neighbouring inter-tribes in tribal fighting. An air demonstration, however, persuaded the disputants to submit their claims to Government decision, and stabilised the situation.

These were principal occasions on which aircraft were engaged in operations in Iraq proper during the period now under review.

In every instance air action was only necessary on a surprisingly limited scale. Had it been necessary to exact obedience by the employment of ground troops, the cost in time and money, if not also in lives, would have been immensely greater. A further consideration which is very pronounced in dealing with lawlessness, particularly amongst the Euphrates tribes, is the presence of ground troops in these districts serves as a focus for concentrating rebellious action by the tribes, while any small success on the part of the latter may magnify a minor disturbance into a serious rising. Further, the despatch of ground reinforcements to any particular spot is liable to give birth to wild rumours among the surrounding tribes to the effect that a rising is about to take place, and thus to produce an atmosphere of excitement and unrest in places that were previously tranquil. These dangers are altogether avoided by the use of air action.

In Kurdistan in Iraq the situation at the end of September, 1922, was far from satisfactory.

As has been described elsewhere, a Turkish garrison had been holding Rowanduz for the previous two years and from this base a campaign of propaganda had been carried on south-eastwards through Kurdistan, as far even as to Halabja. This campaign, under the able and energetic control of Euz Demir, had been backed by lavish promises of Turkish regular support, by gifts of ammunition to the tribes, and by the establishment of posts of Turkish irregular troops at the various points of tactical or tribal importance along the main routes towards Arbil and Rania.

Various small Levy columns which had from time to time been sent into Kurdistan, had not succeeded in stabilising this situation in our favour, and in September 1922, i.e. one month before the assumption of control by the RAF, a mixed column of Imperial and Levy troops, which had been sent to Rania to restore the unsatisfactory situation which had arisen there as a result of Euz Demir's activities, met with a reverse. It was with difficulty extricated, with some loss both in men and material, including parts of two guns.

In consequence of this reverse it had been considered advisable to abandon our hold on Sulaimania also.

The prestige of the Turkish irregulars had been very greatly enhanced and their activities redoubled as a result of this twofold success, and it had been possible by the middle of September for Euz Demir to establish Turkish posts at Keui Sanjaq and at one of the crossings of the Lesser Zab, within 40 miles of Kirkuk.

The situation thus prevailing at the end of September called for immediate and drastic action if the whole of Kurdistan were not to move out of the influence of Iraq altogether and to lapse into disorder, which must spread rapidly to the more settled districts of Arbil and Kirkuk.

Extensive air action was accordingly taken. By 5th October the Turkish post at Keui had been forced to leave and a political officer with a political escort had been enabled to re-enter the town without firing a shot and to re-establish there a Government control which has been maintained ever since.

Throughout October the Turkish posts in Kurdistan were attacked by air wherever located and were forced to withdraw from the Rania district.

During the next four months air action, and, where tactically suitable, combined action by aircraft and small Levy detachments and tribal lashkars, was maintained against such of these Turkish irregular detachments as took up positions from which they could have a prejudicial effect upon the law and order of the districts which were under our settled and effective Government administration.

Although the weather at this time of the year is unfavourable for air action amongst the Kurdish mountains, and in spite of the fact that the RAF units were being distracted by the Turkish menace north of Mosul, air action definitely checked the further infiltration of Turkish irregular troops and the extension of the area under the direct influence of Euz Demir, and was the first actual set-back given to the Turkish activities in this region.

Sheikh Mahmud, however, who had been reinstated by us after the evacuation of Sulaimania, soon began to intrigue with the Turks actively against us, and it was known early in the New Year that he had formed a plan to attack Kirkuk in March. Meantime the fortunate capture by the police of Euz Demir's despatches to GOC, Jezirah (Turkish) front, disclosed plans for the recapture of Keui Sanjaq and for an attack upon Arbil and Kirkuk by Turkish forces.

A situation had arisen in southern Kurdistan, the seriousness of which was in no small measure due to the Turkish menace. If it had developed into an air attack, an aggressively hostile southern Kurdistan on the right rear flank of the troops concentrated at Mosul would have proved a serious embarrassment. It was necessary, therefore, to deal with this situation promptly and decisively.

Air action alone in such difficult country might have taken too long to achieve its object but information as to the progress of events at Angora at this time showed that it would be possible to use the troops at Mosul for this purpose, and still have time, if the external menace became imminent, to bring them back to the threatened front. It was accordingly decided to clear up the whole Kurdistan situation in as short a time as possible by a combined ground and air operation for the capture of Rowanduz.

The employment of ground troops on an extensive scale in southern Kurdistan had been considered a hazardous and unsound undertaking by previous GOCs, and this opinion was probably a very wise one.

However, the introduction of air control gave full value to the air factor, and the AOC, with his particular knowledge of this new factor, was able to judge such an operation as suitable. The operations themselves do not properly belong to this report for they were not only carried out after the end of March 1923, but were also necessitated by external influences. Their success, however, proves the soundness of the original decision to undertake them, which decision would not have been arrived at by a Commander who did not possess an intimate knowledge of the air arm and the inestimable value of air power.

The progress achieved during these first six months of air control may be summarised as follows:

An ordinary outbreak of lawlessness of defiance of Government could be rapidly, effectively and economically dealt with by air action. An outbreak on a large scale is less likely to occur owing to the rapidity and simplicity of checking it in its incipient state by air action, while the non-committal nature and unattractive barrenness in profit to the rebel of such action undoubtedly had its damping effect. It is a fair corollary that the absence of detachments which the great mobility of air action admits, and the unprofitable task of 'beating the air', may prove a sure deterrent to any outbreak developing on a large scale.

The above deals with the aspect of punitive action, but the effectiveness of air control would only be partially considered if mention was omitted of its value as a threat and as a means to close co-ordination and co-operation of administrative effort over an immense area not provided with other means of communication. An aeroplane or formation of aeroplanes either employed for the purpose or on some administrative duty can be seen in the air by a widely spread population and that provides a tactful but effective reminder to many of the existence and power of Government.

Without air transport the niceties of administrative and military touch are impossible with other existing means of travel in Iraq, and perhaps the greatest achievement of air control in Iraq, during the six months under review, has been the introduction of this inestimable asset. By its means it has been possible to achieve a highly centralised yet widely understanding intelligence, which is the essence of wise and economical control.

Appendix F
RAF Squadron Disbandments, 1918–23

Date	Squadron No.	Location	Date	Squadron No.	Location
1918			**1919**		
20/11	116	Feltham	30/6	94	Tadcaster
21/11	93	Port Meadow	30/6	104	Crail
6/12	119	Wyton	30/6	152	Gullane
7/12	155	Chingford	30/6	228	Killinghome
9/12	96	Wyton	30/6	251	Killinghome
9/12	156	Wyton	30/6	252	Killinghome
9/12	271	Taranto	30/6	256	Killinghome
18/12	225	Pizzone	30/6	257	Dundee
23/12	132	Castle Bromwich	1/7	37	Biggin Hill
			2/7	73	Yatesbury
1919			3/7	74	Lopcombe Corner
			3/7	85	Lopcombe Corner
14/1	255	Pembroke	3/7	91	Lopcombe Corner
22/1	244	Bangor	3/7	102	Lympne
22/1	247	Felixstowe	3/7	108	Lympne
1/2	138	Chingford	4/7	38	Hawkinge
1/2	157	Upper Heyford	4/7	40	Tangmere
2/2	14	Tangmere	4/7	82	Tangmere
4/2	144	Ford Junction	5/7	273	Great Yarmouth
22/2	235	Newlyn	15/7	79	Bickendorf
22/2	254	Prawle Point	18/7	49	Bickendorf
27/2	222	Mudros	27/7	12	Bickendorf
5/3	272	Macrihanish	31/7	62	Spich
10/3	248	Hornsea	1/8	149	Tallaght
15/3	243	Cherbourg	4/8	59	Duren
15/3	246	Seaton Carew	7/8	92	Eil
15/4	224	Pizzone	10/8	88	Nivelles
10/5	245	Fishguard	13/8	107	Hounslow
15/5	233	Dover/Guston Road	27/8	110	Marquise
15/5	234	Trescoe	1/9	221	Petrovsk Kasker
15/5	240	Calshot	6/9	145	Suez
15/5	242	Newhaven	15/9	270 (merged)	Alexandria
16/5	223	Mudros	18/9	150	San Stephano
16/5	263	Taranto	22/9	72	Baghdad
21/5	167	Bircham Newton	1/10	21	Fowlmere
21/5	220	Mudros	1/10	103	Shotwick
31/5	166	Bircham Newton	1/10	120	Lympne
31/5	236	Mullion	8/10	106	Fermoy
31/5	239	Torquay	8/10	249	Killinghome
31/5	250	Padstowe	11/10	268	Kalafrana
31/5	253	Bembridge	18/10	115	Ford Junction
13/6	33	Harpswell	18/10	215	Ford Junction
13/6	36	Hylton/Usworh	19/10	217	Driffield
13/6	50	Bekesbourne	20/10	47	Beketouka
13/6	51	Suttons Farm	23/10	52	Lopcombe Corner
13/6	61	Rochford	25/10	34	Old Sarum
13/6	75	North Weald	25/10	53	Old Sarum
13/6	76	Tadcaster	25/10	54	Yatesbury
13/6	77	Penstone	25/10	65	Yatesbury
13/6	90	Buckminster	25/10	66	Leighterton
13/6	153	Hainault Farm	31/10	143	Detling
18/6	241	Portland	7/11	208	Netheravon
24/6	87	Ternhill	14/11	17	San Stephano
24/6	209	Scopwick	15/11	269 (absorbed)	Alexandria
24/6	210	Scopwick	16/11	39	North Weald
24/6	211	Wyton	20/11	158	Upper Heyford
24/6	218	Hucknal	31/12	7	Farnborough
26/6	35	Netheravon	31/12	9	Castle Bromwich
26/6	42	Netheravon	31/12	10	Croydon

31/12	11	Scopwick	22/1	202	Spittlegate
31/12	14	Sedgeford	22/1	205	Scopwick
31/12	15	Fowlmere	30/1	34	Kenley
31/12	16	Fowlmere	31/1	25	Scopwick
31/12	18	Weston-on-the-Green	1/2	58	Heliopolis
31/12	19	Ternhill	1/2	80 (renumbered)	Aboukir
31/12	22	Ford Junction	1/2	111	Ramleh
31/12	23	Waddington	1/2	113	Ismailia
31/12	29	Spittlegate	1/2	141 (absorbed)	Baldonnel
31/12	32	Croydon	1/2	186 (renumbered)	Gosport
31/12	41	Croydon	1/2	206 (renumbered)	Helwan
31/12	43	Spittlegate	1/2	214 (absorbed)	Abu Sueir
31/12	44	North Weald	2/2	63	Baghdad
31/12	45	Eastleigh	5/2	123	Shoreham
31/12	46	Rendcombe	7/2	219	Manston/Westgate
31/12	57	South Carlton	9/2	212	Swingate
31/12	64	Narborough	1/4	48	Quetta
31/12	78	Suttons Farm	1/4	97 (renumbered)	Risalpur
31/12	83	Croydon	1/4	99	Mianwali
31/12	101	Eastleigh	1/4	114 (renumbered)	Ambala
31/12	204	Waddington			
31/12	213	Scopwick	**1921**		
			16/5	202	Alexandria
1920					
			1922		
20/1	8	Duxford			
20/1	207	Uxbridge	20/3	238	Cattewater
20/1	274	Bircham Newton			
21/1	203	Scopwick	**1923**		
22/1	27	Shotwick			
22/1	55	Shotwick	1/4	203	Leuchars
22/1	56	Bircham Newton	1/4	230 (renumbered)	Calshot
22/1	60	Bekesbourne	1/8	267 (redesignated)	Kalafrana
22/1	70	Spittlegate			

The renumbering of squadrons took place after Air Marshal Trenchard had decided which squadron numberplates were to survive the rundown after the First World War. Many of these numberplates were to be resurrected in the early to late 1930s, and some after the outbreak of the Second World War.

Appendix G

Strategic Air Doctrine, 1921

I. AIR STAFF PAPER – THE ROLE OF THE AIR FORCE IN THE SYSTEM OF IMPERIAL DEFENCE

The claims put forward for the RAF were as follows:

(a) The primary function of the Air Force in the future would be the defence of the British Isles from invasion by air from the continent of Europe. This defence would largely take the form of a counter-offensive from the air, assisted by a ground organization coordinated by the Air Ministry.

(b) Certain responsibilities assigned to the Navy and the Army could be more economically and just as adequately carried out by air units, notably the maintenance of order in certain areas of unrest in the Middle East, the protection of the British Isles from overseas invasion, coastal defence and the protection of merchant shipping in certain areas.

(c) Under present conditions the strength of the RAF at home was absorbed by its functions as an auxiliary to the Navy and Army, and while the proper discharge of these functions was of vital importance, there should be more use made of the Air Force as an independent arm used, not as an auxiliary, but as a substitute for naval and military forces.

The Balfour Report, speaking for the government and dated 26 July 1921, made the following points:

1. The Air Force must be autonomous in matters of administration and education.
2. In case of defence against air raids the Army and Navy must play a secondary role.
3. In case of military operations by land or naval operations by sea, the Air Force must be in strict subordination to the General or Admiral in supreme command.
4. In other cases, such as the protection of commerce or attack on enemy harbours or inland towns, the relations between the Air Force and the other services must be regarded more as a matter of cooperation than that of strict subordination necessary when aeroplanes were acting merely as auxiliaries.

Appendix H

Military and Civil Aircraft Tested at Martlesham Heath, 1919–29

Note 1. Aircraft are listed by manufacturers in alphabetical order. 2. Civil aircraft can be distinguished by their serial letters/numbers, e.g. Military: F.3492 (N denotes naval aircraft) or Civil: G-EAOX

Aircraft	Serial No.	Month	Remarks
1919			
Alliance P2 Seabird	G-EAOX	Oct	C of A (Certificate of Airworthiness) trials
Avro 533 Manchester MkII	F.3492	Jan	Bomber and motor trials
Avro Manchester 533 MkI	F.3493	Oct	Modified airframe trials
Austin Greyhound	H.4317	May	Airframe and motor trials
Austin Whippet	K.158/G-EAGS	Aug	Lightplane C of A trials
Armstrong Whitworth Ara	F.4971	–	Prototype fighter trials
	F.4972	–	2nd prototype fighter trials
BE2E	C.6980	Aug	Metal wing trials aircraft
Blackburn Kangaroo	G-EADG	Sep	C of A performance trials
Boulton & Paul 1A	F.2903	Aug	ABC Dragonfly motor trials
Boulton & Paul Bourges 1B		Oct	Gull-wing trials aircraft Atlantic
Bristol Badger F.2.C.MkII	F.3496	Sep	Airframe and motor evaluation
Bristol Fighter F.2.B	E.2400	Feb	300 hp Hispano motor trials
	C.9883	Aug	Sunbeam Arab motor trials
	D.7968	Aug	Sunbeam Arab motor trials
	E.2306	Aug	Sunbeam Arab motor trials
Bristol Braemar MkII	C.4297	Jul	Performance trials. Later crashed
British Air Transport FK.25	F.2907	–	2nd prototype aircraft trials
Basilisk	F.2908	–	1st prototype aircraft trials
Central Centaur IV	K.108/G-EABI	–	C of A performance trials
de Havilland (Airco) 4	A.7446	Aug	Rolls-Royce (RR) Eagle VII tests
de Havilland (Airco) 9	C.6078	Jan	Prototype Napier Lion motor tests
	D.5792	Jul	Silencer trials with Puma motor
	C.2207	Aug	Trials with H.C. Puma motor
	D.5625	May	Engine trials and tests
	D.3010	Jul	Engine trials and tests
de Havilland 16	K.130	–	C of A performance trials
Grahame-White E.IV Ganymede	C.3481	Sep	Bomber trial and tests
Later . . .	G-EAMW		
Handley Page V/1500		Jun	Trial aircraft
Martinsyde Buzzard		May	Evaluation and trials aircraft
Nieuport Nighthawk	F.2910	Jun	Airframe and engine trials
SE5A	C.8735	Jun	Standard aircraft. Engine tests
	C.9117	Aug	Standard aircraft. Fuel tests
	F.5696	Jun	Parachute development aircraft
Short Shirl	N.112	–	Further prototype trials
Siddeley R.T.1	B6630	Mar	Motor and radiator trials
Siddeley Deasy SR 2 Siskin	C.4541	Jul	Fighter and motor trials
Sopwith Bulldog	C.4543	Aug	3rd prototype for evaluation
Sopwith Camel	F.6394	Aug	180 hp Clerget motor trials
Sopwith Buffalo	H.5893	Feb	2nd prototype for evaluation
Sopwith Cobham MkII	H.671	Aug	Bomber and bombing trials
Sopwith Dragon	E.7990	Feb	Trials aircraft
	F.7017	Aug	Modified airframe for test
Sopwith Snapper RAF Type 1	F.7031	Sep	Airframe and armament trials
Sopwith Snark	F.4068	Nov	Type test and engine trials
	F.4070	Nov	3rd prototype for evaluation
Sopwith Snipe	E.8089	–	Revised tail surfaces trials aircraft
Westland Limousine I	G-EAFO	–	C of A performance trials
Westland Limousine II	G-EAJL	–	Revised tail unit for test
Westland Weasel	F.2912	Apr	Airframe and Dragonfly motor tests
	F.2914	Nov	Airframe and Jaguar motor tests

1920

Austin Greyhound	H.4137	Apr	Engine and airframe trials
	H.4318	Apr	Service trials
	H.4319	Aug	Performance trials
Austin Kestrel	G-EATR	Mar	Air Ministry Competition trials aircraft
Avro 504K	H.2431	Mar	Fuel consumption tests
	D.6308	Mar	100 hp Mono motor. Metal wings
	H.2041	Mar	Propeller trials
Avro 547A	G-EAUJ	Aug	Air Ministry Competition aircraft
Beardmore W.B.X	G-EAQJ	Aug	Air Ministry Competition aircraft
Boulton & Paul P.7 Bourges	F.2903	Jan	Propeller trials
Bristol F.2B. MkII	J.6790	Sep	Undercarriage trials – Existed as G-ACCG until 1939
	F.4864	Oct	Fuel consumption trials
Bristol Badger	F.3495	Jan	Rudder modifications
	F.3497	Apr	Engine change. New rudder
Bristol Braemar II	C.4297	Jan	Full-load performance trials 4 Libertys fitted 2.20
Bristol Pullman	C4298	Sep	C of A performance trials G-EASP
Bristol Air Transport FK.23 Bantam	F.1661	May	Civil performance trials
Central Centaur IIA	G-EAPC	Jun	Air Ministry Competition aircraft
de Havilland (Airco) 4A	F.5764	Jun	C of A trials. Later G-EAWH
de Havilland (Airco) 9	E8903	Feb	Altitude control tests
de Havilland (Airco) 9A	E.753	Apr	Napier Lion engine trials. Later G-EAOH
	F979	Jun	RR Eagle engine tests
	E.9697	Jun	RR Eagle engine trials
de Havilland II Oxford	H.8591	Sep	Performance and engine trials
de Havilland 15 Gazelle	J.1937	May	Performance and engine trials
de Havilland 18	G-EARI	Mar	Civil performance trials
	G-EAWX	–	Civil performance trials
Fairey IIIC	N.2246	Jul	Performance trials
Handley Page V/1500	J.6573	Jun	High altitude 28,000 ft trials
Martinsyde F.4 Buzzard	H.7716	Jul	Calibration tests
Martinsyde F.4 Buzzard	H.7781	Oct	Fuel consumption trials
Martinsyde Semiquaver	G-EAPX	Mar	Speed record aircraft – 161.43 mph
Nieuport & General Aircraft Goshawk	G-EASK	June	Speed record aircraft – 166.5 mph
Nieuport & General Aircraft London MkI	H.1740	Jun	Bomber performance trials
Nieuport & General Aircraft Nighthawk	H.8533	Dec	Badly damaged on arrival, never flew
	J.2403	Feb	Unreliable Dragonfly engine. Scrapped after 43 hours' flying
Parnall Panther	N.7516	Jul	Performance trials for RNAS
SE5A	E.5923	Apr	Experimental tail unit
	F.9097	Dec	Consumption trials
	D.7018	Jun	Trials aircraft
SE5B	A.8947	Jun	Comparison with D.7018
Siddeley Siskin SR.2	C.4541	Jan	Engine and performance trials
	C.4542	Jan	Engine trials. Burnt out
	C.4543	Mar	Performance trials
Sopwith Cuckoo T.1	N.8005	Jun	Parachute development aircraft
Sopwith Cobham MkI	H.672	May	2nd prototype. Performance trials
	H.671	Jul	Fitted with Puma motors. Trials
Sopwith Grasshopper	G-EAIN	May	C of A performance trials
Sopwith Scooter	G-EACZ	Jul	Civil evaluation trials
Sopwith Snark	F.4068	Mar	Dragonfly re-engined trials
	F.4069	Apr	Performance trials
	F.4070	Oct	Performance trials and tests
Vickers Vimy	F.3175	Jan	Armament performance trials
	H.5081	Jan	Fitted with 67 mm COW Gun. Trials
Westland Walrus	N.9500	May	Trials for Fleet Air Arm
	N.9523	Apr	Performance trials
	N.9515	Aug	Modified wing trials
Westland Weasel	F.2913	Sep	3rd prototype for performance tests
	J.6577	Jul	Jaguar engined prototype for trials
	F.2914	Nov	Stability tests. Crashed

Also during the year were all the civil aircraft taking part in the Air Ministry Civil Aeroplane Competition.

1921

Air Navigation & Engineering Ltd (ANEC) 1A	J.7056	May	Ex-G-EBIL. Evaluation trials
Armstrong Whitworth Siskin I	C.4541	Aug	Re-engined prototype for trials
	C.4541	Jun	Jupiter-engined trials aircraft
Armstrong Whitworth Siskin II	J.6583	Mar	First all-metal airframe
Avro 504K	H.2401	Nov	Propeller trials
BE2E	C.6980	Jan	Metal-winged aircraft for evaluation
Blackburn Dart	N.140	Oct	Fleet Air Arm performance trials
Blackburn Swift MkI (G-EAVN)	N.139	Dec	Fleet Air Arm performance trials
Boulton & Paul Bourges MkII	F.2905	Mar	Performance trials with full load
Bristol Badger II	J.6492	Jun	4th prototype
Bristol F2B Fighter	F.4819	Jun	Metal propeller tests
	H.1436	Jun	Parachute development aircraft
	H.1559	Mar	Dual-control aircraft. Parachute work
Mk.II	J.6586	Jan	Full performance trials
	J.6753	Jul	Radiator performance trials
Bristol Ten-seater	G-EAWY	Jul	Performance trials
British Air Transport FK.23 Bantam	J.6579	Feb	Wasp engine trials
de Havilland 9A	H.3629	May	Fuel system trials
	J.597	Jan	Last Norwich-built aircraft for test
de Havilland 10	E.6041	May	Fuel system trials
de Havilland 10A	F.8423	Feb	Performance trials. Wrecked March 1921
de Havilland 14 Okapi	J.1938	Mar	Performance engine trials
	J.1939	Aug	Armament performance trials
de Havilland 18B	G-EAWW	Aug	Civil evaluation trials
'City of Brussels'	G.EAWX	Nov	3-bladed airscrew trials
de Havilland 29 Doncaster	J.6849	Sep	Aerodynamic research trials
Fairey IIID	–	Mar	Performance and armament tests
Gloucestershire Aircraft Co. Mars I Bamel	G-EAXZ	Dec	Speed record aircraft, 196.4 mph
Gloucestershire Aircraft Co. Mars VI	H.8534	May	Performance and motor trials
Handley Page 0/100	G-EAKG	–	Civil performance trials
Handley Page 0/400	Several aircraft	–	Weighing procedures for C of A
Junkers J.1A	G/3 BDE/31	Apr	German aircraft on trial. Destroyed in hangar fire
Martinsyde F.4. Buzzard 1A	H.6542	Jun	Long-range experimental aircraft tests
Nieuport & General Aircraft Co. London	H.1471	Jan	Full performance trials
Nieuport & General Aircraft Nighthawk	H.8534	May	First Jaguar-engined aircraft tests
	J.2405	Jun	Modified ABC Dragonfly engine
	J.2416	Jan	Parachute development aircraft
Nieuport & General Aircraft Co. Nightjar	H.8535	May	Full performance trials
Nieuport & General Aircraft Co. Sparrowhawk	JN.400	May	Trials for Japanese Navy
Parnall Possom	J.6862	Jul	Experimental mail plane trials
Sopwith Snark	F.4070	Feb	3rd prototype. Engine trials
Sopwith Snipe	E.8137	Jan	General performance trials
	E.7534	Mar	General performance trials
Vickers Vernon ex G-EAUY	J.6864	Aug	Performance trials as bomber
Vickers Vimy Ambulance (Vernon)	J.6855	Mar	Evaluation and performance
Westland Wagtail	C.4292	Jul	General performance trials
	J.6581	Jan	Dragonfly and Wasp motor trials
	J.6582	Feb	Dragonfly and Lynx motor trials
Westland Weasel	J.6577	Nov	Fitted with Jaguar AS.2 motor

1922

Armstrong Whitworth Siskin II	G-EBEU	Mar	C of A trials with 2-seater aircraft
Avro Aldershot Mk.I	J.6852	May	Full performance trials
Avro Bison	N.153	Aug	1st prototype. Performance trials
	N.154	Sep	2nd prototype. Performance trials

Avro 504K (later N)	E.9265	Jul	Trials with Lynx engine
	E.9261	Jul	Extended engine trials
	H.2202	Sep	Carburettor trials aircraft
Beardmore W.B.IIB	G-EARY	Apr	C of A performance trials
Blackburn Dart	N.141	Jan	Comparison trials
	N.142	Feb	Full performance trials
	N.9542	Aug	7th production aircraft trials
	N.9545	Nov	Production aircraft proving trials
Blackburn Blackburn	N.150	Aug	Handling trials. Performance tests
	N.151	Sep	Radiator and engine trials
	N.152	Sep	Full performance trials. Destroyed in hangar fire
Boulton & Paul P.15	J.6584	Oct	Full evaluation testing
Bristol Bullfinch Type 52	J.6901	May	Performance and engine trials
Bristol Type 62	G-EAWY	–	C of A performance trials
Bristol M.I.C	G-EASR	Sep	C of A trials of ex-service aircraft
Bristol F2B Fighter MkII	J.6790	Mar	Used for drop tests
	J.6800	Jan	Long-range trials aircraft
de Havilland (Airco) 9A	H.3657	Feb	Oleo undercarriage trials
de Havilland 18	G-EAWX	Jan	3-bladed airscrew tests
de Havilland 27 Derby	J.6894	Nov	Performance trials
de Havilland 29	G-EAYO	Sep	Civil Doncaster for C of A trials
de Havilland 34	G-EBBQ	Jul	C of A trials 9-seater aircraft
	G-EBBN	Jul	C of A trials 9-seater aircraft
'City of Glasgow'	G-EBBR	Apr	Performance trials
Fairey IIID	N.9451	Jul	RR Eagle-engined version trials
Gloucestershire Aircraft Co. Mars I Bamel	G-EAXZ	Nov	Modified aircraft for performance tests
Gloucestershire Aircraft Co. Mars IV Nighthawk	J.2405	Aug	Jupiter III engined version
	H.8534	Sep	Siddeley Jaguar IV AS 4 engine tests
Handley Page Hanley Mk.I HP 19	N.143	Apr	Modified aircraft for trials – 3 visits
Handley Page Hanley Mk.III HP 10	N.145	Apr	Developed aircraft. Performance trials
Handley Page W8B HP 18	G-EBBG	Apr	C of A performance trials
Handley Page W18/G 'Bombay' Later 'Princess Mary'	–	–	Revised airframe for C of A trials
Hawker Duiker	J.6918	–	Evaluation trials
Nieuport Nightjar Mars X	H.8535	May	Prototype aircraft for test – damaged
Parnall Pixie	G-EBKM	Jun	C of A trials. Single-seater light plane
Parnall Plover	N.160	Apr	Fleet aircraft performance trials
	N.162	Jul	3rd prototype. Structural failure
Vickers Vernon	J.6884	Feb	1st production aircraft. Range trials
	J.6879	Mar	Undercarriage trials
Vickers Viking V	N.156	Aug	Land trials of amphibian MAEE
Vickers Virginia Type 57	J.6856	Dec	Full-load trials with propeller tests
Vickers Vulcan Type 61	G-EBBL	Oct	C of A performance trials
	G-EBEJ	Nov	Further civil trials
	G-EBEC	Nov	Engine trials for C of A
	G-EBEK	Dec	Freight version for Air Ministry. Underpowered
Westland Wagtail	J.6582	Oct	Revised airframe tests. Lynx motor
Westland Weasel	J.6577	Mar	Performance trials with Jaguar motor

1923

Armstrong Whitworth Awana	J.6897	Oct	Troop carrier performance trials
Armstrong Whitworth Wolf AW18	G-EBHI	Feb	Civil version of RAF trainer. Tests
Armstrong Whitworth Siskin III	J.6921	Mar	Trials and performance aircraft
	J.6583	Jun	First steel aircraft. Performance trials
	J.6982	Dec	Aerobatic strength trials
Avro Aldershot MkIII	J.6952	Jan	Trials with lengthened fuselage
	J.6953	Jan	Tailplane modification trials
Avro Bison	N.154	Sep	Double-bay wings and Lion motor. Tests.
	N.155	Jun	Single-bay wings. Propeller tests
Avro 504K	–	Apr	Fitted with Lucifer radial motor
Avro 504N	E.9261	Jun	Trials aircraft
	J.733	Aug	Developed K with Lucifer motor
	J.750	Oct	Developed K with Lynx motor
	G-EADA	Jun	Flying test-bed for Bristol motor

Blackburn Blackburn MkI	N.9581	Apr	Torpedo and armament trials
Boulton & Paul Bodmin	J.6910	–	Bomber performance trials
Boulton & Paul Bugle MkI P25	J.6984	Sep	Type tests. Heavy controls
Bristol Bullfinch Type 51	J.6903	Apr	Lower wing fitted to mono aircraft
Bristol Jupiter Fighter	G-EBEF	–	Civil demonstrator for export
Bristol Taxiplane Type 73	G-EBEW	Apr	C of A evaluation
Bristol Trainer	G-EBFZ	Jul	2-seater trainer for C of A trials
	G-EBGE	Jul	2-seater trainer for C of A trials
de Havilland (Airco) 9A	J.6957	Apr	Lion-engined aircraft for trials
de Havilland Doncaster	J.6849	Sep	Full load and vibration tests
	G-EAVO	Jun	Civil version. Little flown
de Havilland Dormourse	J.7005	Nov	Type trials. Jaguar motor trials. Trials with engine bearers
de Havilland 37	G-EBDO	Jul	C of A trials. Performance tests
Dornier Komet I	J.7276	Apr	German aircraft purchased for trials
English Electric Wren	J.6973	Jul	Ultra-light plane for evaluation
Fairey Fawn II	J.6908	Mar	Revised production-aircraft trials
	J.7198	Apr	Production trials
Fairey Fawn MkIII	J.6907	Jun	Developed MkII for trials
Goucestershire Aircraft Co. Nighthawk. Grebe prototype	J.6969	Jun	Fighter performance trials
	J.6970	Jul	Fighter performance trials
Gloucestershire Aircraft Co. Grebe II	J.7283	Oct	1st production-aircraft trials
Gloucestershire Aircraft Co. Mars X Nightjar	J.6941	May	Trials aircraft.To RAF Leuchars
Gloster Bamel I	J.7234	Dec	High-speed aircraft trials
Handley Page HP 19 Hanley 11	N.144	Sep	Fleet aircraft performance trials
Handley Page HP 21	–	Jun	Fleet fighter for US Navy. Crashed
Handley Page Hyderabad HP 24	J.6994	Oct	Heavy bomber trials. Armament tests
Hawker Duiker	J.6918	Dec	Army Co-operation trials aircraft. Little flown
Hawker Woodcock. MkI	J.6987	Aug	Wing flutter trials. Performance
Junkers J.10	–	Jun	All-metal German aircraft for trials
Nieuport Nighthawk	J.6925	Feb	Experimental metal aircraft trials
	J.6941	Apr	Bentley B.R.2 motor trials
Parnall Pixie I	–	Jun	S/Set ultra-light plane trials
Parnall Pixie II	–	Aug	S/Set ultra-light plane. Increased motor power
Parnall Plover	N.162	May	Jaguar-engined aircraft for trials
	N.160	Dec	Jupiter-engined aircraft for trials
Parnall Possum	J.6862	–	Experimental postal aircraft
Short Springbok MkI S.3	J.6974	Apr	Performance trials. Crashed
	J.6975	May	Trials with new wings
Short Springbok MkII S.3A	J.7295	Jul	Trials with lighter wing
	J.7296	Jul	Performance trials
	J.7297	Aug	Modified tailplane trials
Supermarine Seagull II	N.158	Jan	Revised MkI for performance trials
Vickers Vanguard Type 62	J.6924	Apr	Troop-carrier trials
	G-EBCP	Jun	Civil performance trials
Vickers Vernon II	J.6976	May	1st production aircraft. Fuel tests
Vickers Victoria II Type 56	J.6861	Feb	Troop carrier performance trials
		Sep	Fuel and endurance trials
Vickers Viking IV Type 60	G-EBED	Jul	Civil amphibian performance trials
Vickers Virginia	J.6856	Apr	Armament trials
	J.6857	Jul	Modified nacelle trials. Later MkVII
Vickers Vimy	F.9176	Oct	Trials on rebuilt aircraft
	F.9158	Jun	Undercarriage and brake tests
Vickers Vixen I Type 71	None	Mar	Private venture aircraft. Trials
Vickers Vulcan	G-EBEC	Mar	C of A performance trials
	G-EBFC	Apr	Further C of A trials

1924

ANEC1	J.7506	Aug	Lightplane performance trials
Armstrong Whitworth Siskin III	J.6981	Jun	1st metal aircraft. Performance trials
	J.8148	Apr	Comparison motor trials. Crashed
	G-EBIS	Apr	Civil aircraft. Increased tankage
Armstrong Whitworth Awana	J.6898	Feb	2nd prototype for evaluation
Armstrong Whitworth Wolf	J.6921	Apr	Performance trials

Avro 560	J.7322	Apr	Evaluated as light trainer aircraft
Avro 561 Andover	J.7261	Aug	Ambulance duties performance
Avro 555A Bison	N.154	Aug	Fleet Air Arm trials
Bison MkII	N.9844	Oct	Production trials
Beardmore Wee Bee WB XXIV	G-EBJJ	Jul	2-seater light plane trials
Blackburn Cubaroo	N.166	–	Performance and motor trials
Boulton & Paul P.25 Bugle MkI	J.7235	Jul	Re-engined and modified aircraft
Bristol Bloodhound Type 84	G-EBGG	Jan	Evaluation trials
Bristol Brownie	G-EBJL	Nov	Evaluated for light plane use
	G-EBJK	Dec	Larger-span wooden wings
	G-EBCE	–	Return visit. Load trials
Bristol taxiplane	G-EBEY	Jan	Tested as 3 seater. Failed
Bristol Type 75	–	May	C of A performance trials
Cranwell C.L.A.2	G-EBKC	May	Performance trials. Crashed
de Havilland 18B	G-EAWW	May	Used for flotation trials
de Havilland Dingo 1. DH42A	J.7006	Jun	General-purpose trials. Crashed
de Havilland Dormouse DH.42	J.7005	May	Performance trials
DH42B Dingo II	J.7007	Jul	Steel tubular fuselage trials
Fairey Fawn II	J.7184	Nov	Production aircraft trials
Gloucestershire Aircraft Co. Grebe III	J.7519	Jul	Tested as a 2-seater
Gnosspelius Gull	No.19	–	Ultra-light plane. Performance
Handley Page W.8F Hamilton	–	–	C of A trials. 3-engined aircraft
Handley Page Hendon HP.25	N9724	–	Rebuild of Hanley. FAA trials
Hawker Hedgehog	N.187	Sep	FAA evaluation. Cancelled
Hawker Woodcock II	J.6988	Aug	Night-fighter trials
Martinsyde F.4	–	May	Jaguar-engined civil aircraft trials
Parnall Pixie III	–	May	Light plane performance trials
Parnall Plover	N.9608	Jul	Trials aircraft
Raynham Monoplane	J.7518	Aug	Performance trials. Light plane
Supermarine Seagull II	N.158	Jun	Amphibian for land trials
Vickers Venture Type 94	J.7277	Jun	Revised Vixen II. Performance
Vickers Virginia I	J.6856	Apr	Condor-engined aircraft for trials
Vickers Vixen Type 87	G-EBEC	May	General-purpose aircraft trials
Vickers Vixen III	G-EBIP	May	Cleaned-up MkII. Performance
Westland Pterodactyl MkI	J.8067	–	Tailless monoplane for trial
Westland Widgeon MkI	–	–	2-seater club plane for trials

1925

Airdisco Avro	–	Mar	504K fitted with RAF motor
Airdisco Martinsyde	–	Jun	F.4 Buzzard fitted with Jaguar motor
Avro Ava Mk.I Type 557	N.171	May	Large bomber performance trials
Avro Avis	–	Jun	2-seater ultra-light plane
Avro Andover Type 563	G-EBKW	Apr	Civil Andover for Imperial Airway
Armstrong Whitworth Atlas	G-EBLK	Nov	Prototype Army Co-operation Aircraft. Trials.
	J.8777	Jul	2nd prototype performance
Armstrong Whitworth Siskin III	J.7552	May	2-seater trainer performance tests
Siskin IIIDC	J.7000	Jun	Performance trials
Siskin II	G-EBHY	Jun	Civil demonstrator. Trials
Armstrong Whitworth Ajax	G-EBLM	May	Army Co-operation aircraft for evaluation. Later J.9128
Beardmore W.B.26	None	Jan	2-seater fighter for Latvia
Boulton & Paul Bugle MkII	J.7266	–	Modified MkI. Armament trials
Blackburn Blackburn MkII	N.150	May	Modified MkI. Raised tailplane
	N.9589	–	Trainer version for trials
Blackburn Cubaroo	N.167	Jul	2nd aircraft for service trials
Breguet 19	J.7507	Jan	French aircraft for extended trials. Written-off during trials
Bristol Berkeley Type 90	J.7403	Mar	Comparison trials aircraft
Bristol Bloodhound Type 84	J.7248	Mar	Trials aircraft
	J.7236	Jun	Performance trials
	G-EBGG	Jun	C of A trials. Civil version
Bristol Boarhound Type 93	G-EBLG	Aug	Comparison trials aircraft
Bristol Brandon Type 79	J.6997	Apr	Performance trials as transport
Bristol Fighter F2B MkIII	J.8251	Jun	Army Co-operation trials aircraft
de Havilland 53 Humming Bird	J.7268	May	Lightplane for service trials
	J.7325	Oct	Special aircraft for airship trapeze use

de Havilland 60A	G-EBKT	May	2-seater light club trainer C of A
	J.8030	Jun	Service trials. Slotted-wing tests.
de Havilland Moth 60X	J.8820	Sep	Genet-I-engined version. Trials
	J.8816	Sep	Service trials aircraft
Fairey Fawn MkIII	J.7768	May	Napier engine trials (Lion)
Fairey Ferret MkI	N.190	Oct	First Fairey all-metal aircraft.Trials
Fairey Fox	J.7941	Jun	2-seater bomber evaluation trials
Gloucestershire Aircraft Co.	J.7497	May	Prototype fighter evaluation
Grebe II. Later Gamecock	J.7756	Jun	2nd aircraft with Jupiter motor
Grebe II. Later Gamecock MkI	J.7757	Sep	3rd aircraft for armament trials
	G-EBNT	Oct	Civil demonstrator
Hawker Cygnet I	G-EBMB	–	Ultra-light plane for C of A
Hawker Cygnet II	G-EBJH	–	Ultra-light plane for C of A
Handley Page HP.22/23	J.7265	–	Light plane for service trials
Handley Page W.9 Hampstead	–	–	Civil C of A performance trials
Handley Page Handcross HP.28	J.7498	Sep	Light bomber service trials
	J.7500	Dec	All-metal for trials
Hawker Hedgehog	N.187	Feb	Drooping aileron trials
Hawker Horsley	J.7511	Feb	Day-bomber service trials
	J.7721	May	2nd prototype for trials
Hawker Woodcock MkII	J.7512	Jun	Trials aircraft. Extended tests
	J.7513		
	J.7514		
	J.7515		
	J.7516		
	J.7517		
	J.7594	Aug	Night-flying trials
Parnall Pixie III	G-EGJG	Sep	Tested with detachable upper wing
Raynham monoplane	J.7518	May	Further service evaluation
Short Springbok II.S.3A	J.7295	Apr	Further service trials
Vickers Vernon MkII	J.7548	Mar	Armament trials
Vickers Vespa MkI Type 113	None	Jun	General-purpose evaluation
Vickers Venture II	J.7282	All year	Used as station 'hack'
Vickers Virginia VIII	J.6856	Mar	Armament trials. Gun positions on trailing edge of upper wing
	J.6993	Apr	Full trials as MkVII
Westland Westbury	J.7766	Feb	Trials with COW Guns
Westland Widgeon MkII	–	May	Light civil aircraft for trials
Westland Yeovil MkI	J.7508	Aug	Day-bomber evaluation trials

During this year comparison trials were held at the A&AEE with the following aircraft participating:

Air Ministry Specification	Bristol Berkeley	
	No. 26/23	Handley Page Handcross
	Hawker Horsley – this aircraft gained the production contract	
	Westland Yeovil	
Air Ministry Specification	Bristol Bloodhound	
No.8/24	Armstrong Whitworth Atlas – this aircraft gained the production contract	
	de Havilland Hyena	
	Vickers Vespa	
Air Ministry Specification for light single-seater aircraft for training	De Havilland Avro 560 Parnall Pixie III	Humming Bird – this aircraft gained the production contract

1926

Avro Ava Mk.I	N.172	Jun	Metal version for performance trials
Avro Avenger Type 566	G-EBND	Aug	Fighter for evaluation trials
Avro Avian	G-EBOV	May	C of A evaluation for club aircraft
Avro Buffalo Type 571	G-EBNW	Aug	Fleet Air Arm trials aircraft
Armstrong Whitworth Argosy	G-EBLF	Jun	Large airliner for C of A trials
Armstrong Whitworth Atlas	G-EBLK	Jun	Prototype for further tests
	G-EBNI	Feb	C of A for civil version . Demonstrator
Armstrong Whitworth Siskin IIIB	J.8627	Apr	Modified aircraft for evaluation
IIIA	J.7001	Jan	Prototype aircraft. Further trials
IIIA	J.8428	Feb	Further trials aircraft
V	None	Jun	Export aircraft for trials. Rumania

Blackburn Airedale	N.189	Jun	Deck-landing trials for FAA
Blackburn Blackburn MkI	S.1056	Oct	Performance trials
Blackburn Ripon MkI T.5	N.203	Aug	Evaluation as a torpedo-bomber
Blackburn Spratt TR.I	N.207	May	Advanced trainer for evaluation
Boulton & Paul P.29 Sidestrand	J.7938	Mar	Prototype 3-seater bomber trials
	J.7939	Jun	2nd prototype for trials
Bristol F2B MkIV	F.4587	May	Developed aircraft with HP slots
Bristol Boarhound	G-EBLG	Jul	Revised prototype. Load tests
Bristol Brownie	G-EBJK	Aug	Rebuilt light plane with metal wings
Cranwell C.L.A.4	G-EBPB	Jun	2-seater light plane for trials
de Havilland 9A	J.6957	May	Re-engined Lion trials aircraft
de Havilland 9AJ Stag	J.7028	May	Jupiter-engined DH9 for GP use
de Havilland 9J	G-AARS	Apr	Jaguar-engined 9A with short fuselage. Evaluation trials
de Havilland 54 Highclere	G-EBKI	Jun	C of A trials for 14-seater airliner
de Havilland 56 Hyena	J.7780	Jul	Performance trials with Jaguar III
	J.7781	Aug	Performance trials with Jaguar IV
de Havilland 66 Hercules	G-EBMW	May	Airliner C of A performance trials
Fairey IIIF Mk.IV.M	J.9053	Sep	RAF version of IIIF GP aircraft
	N.198	May	Prototype for load trials
	N.225	Aug	2nd prototype for type trials
GP	J.9164	Oct	Long-range trials aircraft
Fairey Fawn III	J.7978	Jul	1st aircraft of last production batch
Fairey Ferret II	N.191	Feb	Fleet performance trials
	N.192	Mar	2-seater aircraft for GP trials
Fairey Firefly I	–	Jun	PV fighter for performance trials
Fairey Fox	J.8427	May	Further performance trials
Fokker F.VIIA/3m	J.7986	May	Dutch aircraft for cantilever wing test
Gloucestershire Aircraft Co. Gamecock Mk.I	J.7891	Aug	1st production aircraft for performance test
Handley Page W.10	G-EBMM	Apr	C of A for civil airliner
Handley Page Hamlet HP 32	G-EBNS	May	Experimental high-wing monoplane
Handley Page Harrow HP.31	N.205	Oct	Fleet performance trials
Hawker Cygnet	G-EBJH	Jun	Ultra-light plane for trials
Hawker Heron. Later G-EBYC	J.6989	May	Load tests of steel fuselage
Hawker Hornbill	J.7782	Jul	Single-seater fighter for performance tests
Hawker Horsley MkI	J.8006	Aug	Components trials
	J.8007	Aug	Tyre burst investigations
Parnall Perch	N.217	Jan	Fleet evaluation trials
Parnall Pixie III	G-EBJG	Feb	Return visit further performance trials
Vickers Vendace MkI	N.208	Aug	Advanced trainer for evaluation
Vickers Vespa Type 113 MkI	G-EBLD	Sep	Armed aircraft for trials
Vickers Virginia MkVI	J.7558	Feb	Performance trials with Lion motors. Later built as MkIX
	J.7717	Oct	Performance trials with Lion motors. Later built as MkX
Vickers Vivid Type 146	G-EBPY	Jul	GP aircraft for evaluation
Vickers Vixen Type 148	G-EBIP	Mar	Modified aircraft for performance trials
Westland Wizard MkII	J.9252	Jun	Fighter monoplane for performance trials

During the year the following Contract Competitions were held:

Air Ministry Specification 7/24
  Avro Avenger
  Gloster Gorcock
  Hawker Hornbill

None of the aircraft was accepted.

Air Ministry Specification 21/23
  Avro Buffalo
  Blackburn Ripon
  Handley Page Harrow

The Blackburn Ripon gained the contract.

Air Ministry Specification 5A/24
  Blackburn Spratt
  Vickers Vendace
  Parnall Perch

No contract was placed, as the requirement was not fulfilled.

The de Havilland 66 Hercules tested during this year was so named after a competition had been run in the June 1926 *Meccano Magazine* to find a name for this three-engined airliner for Imperial Airways.

1927

Armstrong Whitworth Atlas			
ex-G-EBLK	J.8675	Nov	Tests with new wings
Armstrong Whitworth Siskin	J.7180	May	Dual-control trainer aircraft for test
Armstrong Whitworth Starling L.	J.8027	Jun	Prototype fighter for evaluation
Boulton & Paul P.31 Bittern	J.7936	Mar	Armament and performance trials
Bristol Beaver Type 93A	G-EBQF	Apr	Redesigned Boarhound for trials
Bristol Badminton Type 99A	G-EBMK	Jul	C of A trials for rebuilt Type 99
Bristol Bulldog I	None	Jun	Single-seater evaluation trials
Cranwell C.L.A.4A	G-EBPB	Apr	C of A performance trials
de Havilland 65A Hound	G-EBNJ	Apr	GP trials. Wooden structure. Rejected
de Havilland 71 Tiger Moth	G-EBQU	Jul	C of A performance trials
Fairey IIIF MkIV CM	–	Mar	Special evaluation aircraft
Fairey Fox MkIA	J.9026	Jun	Re-engined aircraft for trials
Gloster Gamecock MkI	J.7910	May	Flutter trials and aileron tests
	J.8075	Jul	Mercury IIa motor trials
Gloster Goldfinch G.23	J.7940	May	Single-seater fighter evaluation. Lion IV motor
	–	Aug	Extended fin trials. Metal aircraft
Gloster Goral G.22	J.8673	Jun	GP biplane for evaluation
Gloster Gorcock G.16/16A	J.7501	May	Single-seater fighter evaluation. Lion IV motor
	J.7502	Jun	Tests with Napier Lion VIII motor
Halton H.A.C.I Mayfly	G-EBOO	Jun	Aeroclub built for performance trials
Handley Page HP.32 Hamlet	G-EBNS	Feb	Re-engined aircraft for further trials
Handley Page Hendon	N.9729	Aug	Service trials aircraft
Handley Page HP.33 Hinaidi I	J.7745	May	Rebuild of Hyderabad for trials
Hawker Harrier MkI	J.8325	Dec	Performance trials and load tests
Hawker Hawfinch	J.8776	Jul	Single-seater fighter for evaluation
Hawker Horsley MkII	J.8932	May	Standard aircraft for performance trials
Hawker Horsley MkII	J.8612	May	Standard aircraft for performance trials
Parnall Imp	–	Mar	Revised aircraft for tests
Short Chamois S.3B	J.7295	Apr	Converted Springbok II for performance tests
Vickers Type 131 Valiant	No.11	Jun	GP aircraft for evaluation trials
Vickers Virginia MkX	J.7439	Aug	1st aircraft with metal wings. Trials
	J.7424	Feb	Auto-pilot trials
MkVII	J.7432	Apr	Slotted-wing trials
MkVII to X	J.7434	Apr	Auto-pilot trials
Vickers Vixen VI	G-EBEC	Sep	GP evaluation trials

The Gloucestershire Aircraft Company changed its name on 11 November 1926 to the Gloster Aircraft Company, thus making a change in aircraft designations.

Contract Competitions held in 1927:

Air Ministry Specification	Bristol Bullpup Type 108A
F.20/27 (Revised F9/26)	Hawker Hawfinch
	Boulton & Paul Partridge
	Armstrong Whitworth XVI
	Westland F.20/27
	Gloster Goldfinch
	Gloster SS.19
	Bristol Bulldog (awarded the contract)

1928

Armstrong Whitworth Atlas	J.8675	Feb	Further trials with metal wings
	J.8792	May	Dual-control trainer trials
Armstrong Whitworth Ajax	J.8802	Sep	Army Co-operation evaluation aircraft
Avro 583 Antelope	J.9183	Sep	2-seater day-bomber evaluation
Beardmore Inflexible	J.7557	–	Feb Large research aircraft. Assembled at Martlesham Heath

Boulton & Paul P.31 Bittern	J.7937	Apr	Modified prototype for trials
Boulton & Paul P.33 Partridge	J.8459	Jun	Evaluation and comparison tests
Boulton & Paul P.29 Sidestrand III	J.9176	Feb	1st production aircraft for testing
Blackburn F.2 Lincock MkI	G-EBVO	Jul	Single seater fighter evaluation
Blackburn Turcock	G-EBVP	Feb	Export fighter. Crashed at Martlesham
Bristol Bulldog MkII	J.9480	Aug	Developed MkI for performance trials
Bristol Type 101	G-EBOW	Jul	C of A trials
de Havilland 60.G Gipsy Moth	J.9922	May	Trainer performance trials
60.M	K.1227	Aug	Service trials
de Havilland Type 65 Hound	J.9127	Sep	Rebuilt aircraft. Not tested
de Havilland Type 65 Hound II	-	Dec	Revaluation for Australian government
Fairey Ferret III	N.192	Mar	Cleaned-up Ferret II for armament trials
Fairey Flycatcher II	N.216	Aug	Redesigned MkI for evaluation
Fairey Fox IIM	J.9834	Jun	Evaluation aircraft
Fairey Long-Range Monoplane I	J.9479	Mar	Experimental aircraft trials
Gloster Gamecock MkI	J.8047	Feb	Aircraft for spinning trials
	J.8804	Jul	Modified aircraft with Jupiter VI motor.
Gloster Gorcock	J.7503	Sep	3rd prototype performance trials
Gloster Goring G.25	J.8674	Mar	Performance trials as day-bomber
Handley Page HP 42	G-AAGX	–	C of A for large 4-engined airliner
Handley Page HP 35 Clive III	J.9126	May	Troop-carrier performance trials
Handley Page HP 34 Hare	J.8622	Jun	Performance trials as day-bomber
Hawker F.20/27	J.9123	May	Propeller trials
Hawker Harrier MkI	J.8325	Jul	Further load trials
Hawker Hart	J.9052	All year	Performance and extended trials
Hawker Hoopee	N.237	May	Naval fighter for evaluation
Hawker Horsley MkII	J.8606	May	Handling trials
	J.8604		
	J.8610		
	J.8619		
	J.8620	Feb	Metal aircraft for evaluation
	J.8612	Jul	Standard aircraft for performance trials
Hawker Tomtit	J.9772	All year	2-seater trainer performance trials
Parnall Imp	G-EBTE	–	Civil C of A trials with Genet II
Saro Windhover	G-ABJP	Jun	3-engined amphibian for C of A
Simmonds Spartan	G-EBYU	Apr	2-seater biplane for C of A performance trials
Vickers Type 141	None	Oct	Converted Type 123. Performance tests
Vickers Vellore MkI Type 134	G-EBYX	Oct	Transport C of A performance trials
Vickers Vendace MkII Type 133	G-EBPX	Nov	2-seater GP biplane performance trials
Vickers Victoria MkIII	-	Mar	Test vehicle for Virginia tail unit
Vickers Victoria MkIV	J.9250	Oct	Performance trials. Known as Jupiter Victoria
Vickers Vildebeest Type 132	N.230	Sep	Torpedo-bomber evaluation trials
Vickers Vireo	N.211	May	Metal fleet fighter for performance tests
Vickers Virginia MkIX	J.8236	Sep	Fitted with French Gnome Rhone Jupiters
MkX	J.7717	Nov	Armament testing
MkIX	J.7715	May	Upgraded aircraft for trials
Vickers Vixen Type 124 MkVI	G-EBEC	May	Further performance trials. Re-engined
Westland Wapiti MkI	J.8495	Jun	2-seater GP biplane evaluation
Westland Widgeon MkIII	–	–	Civil monoplane C of A trials
Westland Wapiti MkII	J.8492	Aug	Re-engined with Jupiter VIII tests
	J.9238	Dec	Comparison trials
Westland Witch MkI	J.8596	Apr	Bomber monoplane evaluation trials
Wibault (Vickers) Type 122c2	J.9029	Jun	2-seater French-built aircraft for test

No. 15 Squadron had the following Hawker Horsley Mk.IIs for bombing trials: J.8604, J.8606, J.8610, J.8619

1929

Armstrong Whitworth Argosy Mk.II	–	Jun	23-seater development of the Mk.I C of A
Armstrong Whitworth Siskin III DC	J.9236	Jun	Trials for Royal Canadian Air Force
Armstrong Whitworth Starling MkI	J.8027	Aug	Single-seater interceptor evaluation trials
MkII	J.8028	Dec	As above with alternative wings
Avro 621 Trainer	G-AAKT	Dec	2-seater trainer for service trials
Avro 616 Avian IVa	G-AACV	Mar	Metal version of MkIII. Trials

	J.9783	Jul	Comparison trials with Tomtit
Avro Avian 594B MkIII	J.9182	May	2-seater trainer for standard testing
Avro Avocet Type 584	N.209	Apr	Fleet fighter for trials
	N.210	Jul	2nd aircraft for further trials
Avro Gosport 504R Ex-G-EBUY	J.9175	Apr	Evaluation trials
Blackburn Beagle	N.236	Jul	Evaluation and comparison trials
Blackburn Bluebird IV	–	Mar	Development of earlier aircraft C of A
Blackburn Nautilus 2F1	N.234	Mar	Evaluation for fleet aircraft
Bristol Bullpup	J.9051	May	Developed with Bulldog. Performance trials
Clarke Cheetah	G-AAJK	Aug	C of A trials of civil aircraft
Comper CLA Swift	–	Apr	Light plane C of A performance trials
de Havilland 71 Tiger Moth	–	Mar	Trials aircraft
de Havilland 80 Puss Moth	G-AAHZ	Jun	Civil aircraft for C of A testing
Desoutter IIIF	–	Mar	C of A certification trials
Fairey III MkIV M/A	J.9164	–	Further developed IIIF. Performance trials
	J.9150	Aug	Fitted with Jupiter VIII motor
Fairey IIIF Mk3M	S.1354	Sep	Fitted with experimental tail unit
Fairey Firefly MkIIM	–	May	Single-seater interceptor. Performance trials
Fairey Firefly MkIIIM	–	Aug	Naval version of above. Performance trials
Fairey Fleetwing	N.235	Jun	Evaluation of 2-seater fleet spotter
Gloster AS.31 Survey	G-AADO	Feb	Civil survey aircraft. C of A trials
	K.2602	May	Service version of above
Gloster SS.18	J.9125	Oct	Single-seater interceptor. Evaluation
Gloster SS.18A	J.9125	Dec	SS18 re-engined with Jupiter VIIF
Gloster SS35 Gnatsnapper	N.227	May	Single-seater fighter evaluation trials
Hawker Harrier I	J.8325	Jan	Further load trials as bomber
Hawker Hart	J.9052	Jan	Further extended trials
Hawker Hornet. Later Fury	J.9682	May	Single-seater interceptor for evaluation
Hawker Hoopee	N.237	Feb	Revised airframe for trials
Hawker Horsley	J.8932	Mar	All-metal airframe for testing
Hawker Tomtit	J.9773	Feb	Service evaluation aircraft
	K.1453	Apr	Production aircraft for testing
Hawker G.22/26 Naval Hart (Osprey)	J.9052	Mar	Original Hart with folding wings
Hendy Hobo	G-AAJG	–	Light monoplane C of A trials
Henderson-Glenny Gadfly	G-AAEY	–	Civil aircraft for C of A trials
Parnall Pippit	N.232	Feb	Fleet fighter evaluation. Crashed
Parnall Elf	–	Jul	Civil light plane for trials
SARO A.10 F.20/27	None	Apr	Single-seater interceptor evaluation
Short Gurnard II. S.10	N.229	May	2-seater fleet spotter. Evaluation
	N.228	Jun	As above with Jupiter motor
Southern Martlett	G-AAII	Aug	Light aircraft for club use. C of A
Vickers Vimy	F.9168	Mar	Fitted with Jupiter radials
Vickers Type 141	None	Jan	Rebuild of previous aircraft for Navy
Vickers Type 143	None	Jun	Single-seater scout for Brazilian Air Force
Vickers Victoria MkV	J.9766	Oct	Performance trials with slotted wings
Vickers Virginia MkIX	J.7562	Oct	Performance trials to Mk.X
	J.7715	Apr	Performance trials to Mk.X
Vickers Virginia MkIX MkX	J.7720	Jul	Cockpit canopy trials
	J.8238	Sep	Lion XI engine trials
Westland F.20/27	J.9124	May	Single-seater interceptor for performance trials
Westland IV (Later Wessex)	G-EBXK	Apr	Original aircraft re-engined with Genet Majors
Westland Wapiti MkII	–	Apr	Metal-structured version. Performance trials

Appendix J

Administrative Arrangements for RAF Personnel to see the 1929 Schneider Trophy Contest

Source: Air Ministry Weekly Order No. 425/1929 dated 6 July 1929

425.– Schneider Trophy Contest, 1929 (918354/29)

1. In connection with the Schneider Trophy Contest on 7th September next, the War Office has kindly placed part of Gilkicker Fort at the disposal of officers of the RAF and their friends. Gilkicker Fort is situated on the sea coast south of Gosport, and since the course to be flown passes over it, it affords an admirable view-point.

2. The accommodation allotted to the Royal Air Force is for 800 spectators. In order to meet the cost of certain essential work within the fort to adapt it for the purpose it will be necessary to make a charge of 1/- [5p] a head for admittance. Arrangements are also being made for the provision of buffet refreshments at a moderate price. There will be no further charge for admittance on succeeding days in the event of the contest being postponed.

3. The United Services Golf Club – whose grounds surround the Gilkicker Fort – are arranging for a car park in the immediate vicinity of the fort. The charge per car is not definitely fixed, but it will not exceed 10/- [50p] which will cover the cost of admission on any subsequent day should the contest be postponed. There will also be a free car park on the parade ground at the School of Electric Lighting, Fort Monckton Hutments, distant half a mile from Gilkicker Fort.

4. Seating accommodation in the fort will be limited, and spectators are therefore advised to bring car rugs, shooting sticks etc. Spectators arriving by train are advised to book to Portsmouth Harbour Station, crossing to Gosport by ferry. Those arriving by road are advised to travel via Fareham and Alverstoke.

5. It is hoped to arrange a portion of the foreshore in the vicinity of Gilkicker Fort to be reserved for the use of soldiers, sailors and airmen in uniform and their friends. Admittance will be free.

6. Since the number of officers and their friends who can be admitted to Gilkicker Fort is limited to 800, tickets of admission at 1/- each will be allocated, if required, to commands in the following proportion:

Inland Area	300
A.D.G.B (Air Defence of Great Britain)	200
Coastal Area	100
Cranwell	55
Halton	25
Staff College	18
Imperial Defence College	6
Cardington	3
Oxford University Air Squadron	24
Cambridge University Air Squadron	26
Air Ministry	33
Held in reserve for Dominion Officers and Special guests	10

No officer may bring more than one guest.

A.Os.C and C.Os will allot their quota of tickets to stations or units within their commands in proportion to establishments. There is no need for officers using the fort to be in uniform.

7. (ii) To facilitate the arrival of officers and airmen to view the contest arrangements are being made to accommodate service aircraft from all commands at Gosport aerodrome. 170 visiting aeroplanes can be accommodated and the allotment to commands is as follows:

Inland Area	70
A.D.G.B.	45
Coastal Area	20
Cranwell	13
Halton	7
Staff College	5
O.U.A.S.	5
C.U.A.S.	5

Visiting aircraft will arrive at Gosport not later than Thursday 5th September and will not leave before Sunday 8th September. To avoid congestion in the air, it may be necessary for a certain number of aeroplanes to arrive on Wednesday, 4th September, but further orders will be issued as to the time at which aircraft from different commands should endeavour to land.

(ii) All personnel travelling by air will be considered as being on duty but only those who are pilots or crew (including personnel travelling by air in accordance with para. 8 below) will be eligible for the issue of subsistence allowance if entitled under K.R [King's Regulations] and A.C.I [Air Council Instructions]. Personnel who travel by rail will receive warrants and subsistence allowance under normal rules only when ordered to perform specific duty in connection with the contest. During the stay at Gosport, subsistence allowance will not be issued when rations and accommodation are provided.

8. One airman for each two aircraft will be supplied by the commands concerned to assist in the maintenance of aircraft, to act as guards, etc. In addition the following will be provided:

3 N.C.Os. from Inland Area
3 N.C.Os. from A.D.G.B.
2 N.C.Os. from Coastal Area
1 N.C.O. from Cranwell
1 N.C.O. from Halton

The above airmen may travel either in the aircraft or by train to arrive at Gosport before their aircraft.

9. Sleeping and messing accommodation at the RAF base, Gosport, will be available for 330 officers. Priority will be given to officers arriving by air. After these have been provided for, any surplus accommodation will be available for other officers in proportion to the numbers given in para. 6. Officers need not bring mess dress. [This was the formal attire for guest nights and dining-in nights in officers' messes.]

10. The following airmen will be supplied by commands in connection with the accommodation of officers:

(i) 1 batman for every 6 officers, and also,
(ii) 1 cook from Inland Area
1 cook from ADGB
1 cook from Cranwell
1 cook from Halton

[A batman was an officer's personal servant, but since on this occasion the officers were away from their normal home station these special arrangements were deemed necessary.]

The above airmen will report at Gosport on Tuesday, 3rd September.

11. Sleeping and messing accommodation at the RAF Base, Gosport, will be available for 200 airmen. After the personnel enumerated in paras. 8 and 10 have been accommodated, the remaining accommodation will be allotted to commands in proportion to their establishments, but only the personnel enumerated in paras 8 & 10 will be supplied with travelling warrants at the public expense.

12. A.Os.C. and C.O.s will notify the Air Ministry by 1st August –

(i) the number of aeroplanes – by types – which will arrive at Gosport;
(ii) the number of officers and airmen arriving by air;
(iii) the number of airmen proceeding to Gosport other than by air, in accordance with paras 8 & 10;
(iv) the number of tickets required under the provisions of para. 6.

13. When the above information has been received, a Weekly Order will be published concerning:

(i) Charge for car park or golf course.
(ii) Arrangements for traffic control on the approaches to Gilkicker Fort.
(iii) Arrangements made on the foreshore for sailors, soldiers and airmen and their friends.

Appendix K

Operation Orders Issued by No. 1 (Indian) Wing and its Constituent Squadrons for Air Operations Against the Mohmand Tribes, June 1927

The details of these operation orders show how a wing went into action against hostile tribesmen on the North West Frontier in the late 1920s. They show the support equipment involved and armament of aircraft for specific parts of the operation. All of these extracts are taken from the Unit Diary of No. 20 Squadron. The first set of orders is from the OC No. 20 Squadron to those members of his unit who would be detached to provide support for the squadron's operations under the command of OC No. 5 Squadron.

1. Orders were issued by the Officer Commanding No. 20 Squadron for a detachment to proceed to Shabkadar, Map Reference 38N. The orders issued were as follows:

Intention

   (a) To Assist No. 5 (Army Co-operation) Squadron in operating from Shabkadar.
   (b) Pilot Officer D.R.J. Hylton will be in charge of the detachment.
   (c) The detachment will proceed to Shabkadar Fort and report to the Officer Commanding No. 5 Squadron on its arrival.
   (d) The following transport will be detached:

     Two heavy tenders to carry 160 gallons of aviation petrol, 10 gallons of Castrol Oil and 200 × 20 lb Cooper Bombs with detonators.
     One light tender to carry Officer i/c Party, three wireless operators and one WT Pack.

   (e) The duties of the wireless personnel are to erect the wireless set and to get in touch with Risalpur and Peshawar at the earliest possible moment.
   (f) The convoy will leave the aerodrome at 14.00 hrs and must reach Shabkadar by 15.30 hours.

2. The following was received at 11.55 hours on 5th June 1927 from Wing Commander A.A. Walser MC, DFC, commanding No. 1 (Indian) Wing, Peshawar.

   (a) Information has been received that a large party of Mohmands is moving down from the hills tonight and will probably be in the open between Hafiz Kot and Shabkadar tomorrow morning.
   (b) Squadron Leader Capel is carrying out a reconnaissance at dawn tomorrow and parties of enemy will be attacked upon receiving a WT report.
   (c) OC No. 20 Squadron will send as many aeroplanes, not less then four, to Shabkadar tomorrow morning to land there not later than 05.30 hours.
   (d) 20 lb bombs should be carried, not detonator fused, but if there is any difficulty in this, aeroplanes should leave a little earlier and bomb up at Shabkadar. If bombs are carried OC Shabkadar should be informed by telephone to have detonators ready.
   (e) Pilots are to proceed to Shabkadar so as to avoid Michni or any approach to the Mohmand border.
   (f) A tender or lorry with spare 20 lb bombs is to be sent to Shabkadar as early as possible.

3. *6th June 1926 – 01.20 hrs* The following extracts are quoted from No. 2 (Indian) Wing Order No. 11 Copy No. 6, date and time of origin as shown.

   (a) *Information* Air reconnaissance on the evening of the 5th inst. reports a gathering of approximately 200 just south of Shabkadar moving slowly north with one white banner. The Deputy Commissioner reports that Haji have moved over into the Pandiala valley, also that a Lashkar, which may number as many as 1,000, is moving down into Gandao Kewar to join the Paqir. It is expected that the whole Lashkar will move south tonight and may attack Michni, Shabkadar or Matta.
   (b) *Intention* To carry out reconnaissance to endeavour to locate this Lashkar or any movement towards Michni, Shabkadar or Matta or in the sangar or Ghalanai area, also to reconnoitre the Pandiala valley for any unusual gatherings.
   (c) *Reinforcement* Arrangements have been made for No. 5 Squadron to be reinforced by all available machines of No. 20 Squadron at Shabkadar.
   (d) *Detail* Machines doing reconnaissance will carry guns and ammunition but not bombs. They will fly at such a height as will enable them to carry out a thorough reconnaissance of the area according to the visibility at the time, but in no case should they descend lower than 2,000 ft above the ground except when they are reconnoitering the foothills, which may be done from 1,500 ft if necessary. No offensive action may be taken under any circumstances by reconnaissance machines. No. 20 Squadron machines at Shabkadar will carry an armament of eight 20 lb bombs, guns and ammunition. Subsequent orders will be issued verbally to OC No. 20 Squadron at Shabkadar.

4. *6th June 1927 – 03.15 hrs* The following orders were issued by OC No. 20 Squadron at the time stated. Orders for the movement of No. 20 Squadron detachment at Shabkadar:

(a) Flight Lieutenant N.S. Paynter will be OC Detachment aeroplanes and will proceed to Shabkadar landing ground, leaving the ground (taking off) at 04.45 hrs on the morning of 6th June 1927. On arrival at Shabkadar the detachment is to be prepared to carry out active operations against the Mohmands and will come under command OC No. 5 Squadron. The following pilots and air gunners will proceed by air forming the detached flight:

Machine No. 4908	Flight Lieutenant Paynter	Corporal Walstow
No. 1601	Flying Officer Spencer	LAC Barnes
No. 1428	Flying Officer Spittle	AC1 Atwell
No. 4693	Flying Officer Pilling	LAC Morris
No. 6621	Flying Officer Smith	LAC Clark

(b) Machines will be armed as under:

87×20 lb bombs and rear guns with a full complement of ammunition.

(c) The following route will be followed from Peshawar to Shabkadar (as given). The convoy to carry the ground party to operate the detached flight will proceed as under:

The light tender will leave at 04.45 hrs. Personnel and load: Armourers – 2; Fitters – 1; Riggers – 2. Spare detonators and rations.

(d) *Attack Orders* for Nos 1 and 2 Wings to attack the enemy force in the area. Squadrons will be combined for this raid as follows:

Nos 5 and 20 Squadrons under OC No. 5 Squadron. Nos 27 and 60 Squadrons under OC No. 27 Squadron. Bristol Fighters will be over Hafiz Kor at 18.20 hrs and bomb all enemy in the area. As above they will clear target by 18.55 hrs at the latest. If all bombs are dropped at that time green verey lights will be fired as soon as the target is cleared. The height of the bombing will be 4,000 ft above sea level. On completion of bombing two Bristol Fighters will break formation and reconnoitre for any enemy on the route Karappa to Kandao to Nahakki. No offensive action will be taken. These two Bristol Fighters will return to the target area at 19.40 hrs and will remain over the area as long as possible attacking with machine-guns any concentrations seen. The DH9As will rendezvous with Bristol Fighters over Hafiz Kor at 18.20 hrs at 1,500 ft above sea level and conform to their movements. They will bomb any (enemy) seen at 19.00 hrs or, alternatively, six minutes after the Bristol Fighters have cleared targets. Height of bombing is to be 5,000 ft above sea level. Target to be cleared by 19.35 hrs. All aeroplanes will be armed with 20 lb bombs. The two Bristol Fighters mentioned above will carry Lewis guns and ammunition. All circuits over the target area should be right hand. On no account are any villages to be attacked. On completion of raids squadrons will return to their own aerodromes. Squadrons will prepare for further raids which may commence at any time after 05.00 hrs tomorrow 7th June 1927. OC No. 5 Squadron will arrange for petrol and bombs to be available at Shabkadar for Nos 5 and 20 Squadrons. Officers commanding squadrons will report by telephone to Peshawar as soon as possible after landing.

Appendix L

Arrangements for Naval Officer Volunteers for Service with the Fleet Air Arm (AMWO No. 551)

551. – Fleet Air Arm – Admiralty Orders. (51392/24)

The following Admiralty Fleet Orders regarding the Fleet Air Arm are reproduced for information and guidance:-

1058 Naval Air Work – Volunteers for, other than, for Air Observation – REPORT
(C.W.3850/24 – 25.4.1924)

1. Volunteers are required for the Naval Air Work of the Fleet, under the arrangements made by H.M. Government, by which, to the extent of 70%, the Officer personnel of the Royal Air Force employed in the Fleet Air Arm may be provided from Naval Officers attached temporarily to the Royal Air Force for specific periods.
2. Officers volunteering must be of the rank or relative rank of Lieutenant or Sub Lieutenant, and must not be above the age of 28 on 1st July 1924. Sub Lieutenants must have obtained their watchkeeping certificates. In the main, Officers selected will be of the Executive Branch, but a small number of (E) Officers and Officers, Royal Marines, who satisfy the conditions as to relative rank and age, are also required. Officers before selection will be required to pass a medical examination.
3. Officers who apply are required to volunteer for service in the Fleet Air Arm, involving attachment to the Royal Air Force for certain periods, the duration of which will be decided by the Admiralty from time to time. Officers who volunteer will not be required to undertake a second or subsequent period of attachment, except with the consent of the Officer concerned. For the present, it is intended that the periods of attachment and General Naval Service shall be approximately as follows:-

   A. – 1st Period: Air – Four years, which will include a period of training
   B. – 2nd Period: General Naval Service – Two years
   C. – 3rd Period: Air – Two years for 50 per cent of the Officers who have completed A. (first period) The rest remain in General Naval Service
   D. – 4th Period: Air – Two years for 60 per cent of the Officers who have completed C. (3rd period) The rest remain in General Naval Service
   E. – 5th Period: General Naval Service, or For remainder, if any, of Lieutenant Commander's Air, as required time for all officers who have completed D. (fourth period)

4. Appointments of attached officers will be made by the Air Ministry on the nomination of the Admiralty.
5. Naval or Marine Officers attached to the Royal Air Force will be granted Air Force rank during attachment, the initial rank granted being that of Flying Officer, and will be eligible for advancement in the Royal Air Force irrespective of their rank in the Royal Navy. They will continue to wear the uniform of their Naval or Marine rank, but will wear also a distinguishing badge indicating that they are attached to the Royal Air Force for service in the Fleet Air Arm.
6. They will continue during the attachment to draw their Naval full pay and will receive in addition an allowance

of 6s a day. The allowance may be drawn in addition to the (E) pay or to G.T. or similar specialist allowance. It will be paid during attachment under the general conditions laid down for submarine allowance (Article 1372, clauses 2 & 3 K.R. (King's Regulations) and A.I. (Admiralty Instructions), KR 17/23) During the periods of Naval General Service, however, when the Officers cease to be attached to the Royal Air Force, the allowance for flying duties will not be payable.
7. When attached to RAF establishments on shore, they will either be accommodated and rationed, or will be eligible to receive in lieu, in addition to the Naval full pay and flying duties allowance, where applicable, lodging and provision allowance at the Naval rates.
8. When embarked during periods of attachment their flying duties will be considered as equivalent to specialist duties. They will therefore have the rank and status and authority of their Air Force rank when they are engaged in specialist air duties; at other times when they are engaged in General Naval duties, they will have their Naval or R.M. rank, status and authority. They will be available for ship duty in addition to flying duty, and in order to emphasise this, they will, when appointed to a carrier or other of HM ships, receive an appointment from the Admiralty as well as an appointment from the Air Ministry.
9. Attached Officers will, as stated in Paragraph 5, be eligible for advancement in the Royal Air Force under RAF Regulations, irrespective of rank in the Royal Navy or Royal Marines, and such advancement will be determined by the Air Ministry, in consultation with the Admiralty.
10. The promotion in the Royal Navy or Royal Marines of R.N. and R.M. Officers serving in the Fleet Air Arm will be governed by Naval or Marine Regulations, and this service will be considered to be as good service towards promotion as if they had served in any other specialist branches. Naval and Marine Officers who have had six or eight years air experience will be favourably considered for employment in the higher posts in the Fleet Air Arm both ashore and afloat.

    Consequently, an appreciable proportion of such Officers who receive promotion to Commander and above in the Royal Navy, or equivalent rank in the Royal Marines will be required for attachment to the Royal Air Force in higher ranks.

    In addition, there can be little doubt that, with the continued development of Naval air work, air questions must enter more and more largely into Naval staff work, and a knowledge of such questions, must become a very valuable asset for a War Staff Officer, even if it does not become a necessity.
11. Commanding Officers are to bring this Fleet Order to the notice of all Officers concerned and, in doing so, they should draw their special attention to the following points:-

    (a) Officers will not, during any of the periods of attachment, lose their association with the Royal Navy. They will, as stated in paragraph 5, continue to wear Naval and Marine uniform, and, except for the initial period of training, they will normally be employed on Fleet air work. It has been arranged that no Naval of Marine Officer attached to the Royal Air Force shall be appointed to a non-Naval unit without the express consent of the Admiralty, and such consent should only be given in exceptional cases, and then only if the Officer himself is willing.

(b) Attached Officers, when appointed to carriers or to one of HM Ships will, as indicated in Paragraph 8, be employed as far as practicable, on ship duties as well as Naval air duties, and they will therefore be in a position to keep up their knowledge of other Naval duties. Time in such an appointment to a sea-going ship will count as time at sea for the purpose of qualifying for promotion.

(c) All reports, confidential or otherwise, on attached Officers, serving in units of the Fleet Air Arm will be signed by the Captain of the ship and forwarded through Naval and Air Force channels to the Admiralty and Air Ministry. In the event of attached Officers not being borne on the books of one of HM Ships, the reports will be forwarded to the Admiralty through Air Force channels.

The good service of an attached Officer will therefore come as much under the notice of the Admiralty as if the Officer was serving entirely under Admiralty authority.

(d) Officers at present serving as observers and other specialist Officers (G), (T), (N) etc., are not debarred from volunteering under this scheme, and will be considered subject to their services being spared.

Author's Note 1: Observers who did not apply for pilot training were specifically excluded from the above provisions. Naval observer posts were never to be manned by RAF officers, and Naval observers remained always under normal Navy Command and under the Admiralty's authority.

Author's Note 2: The purpose of these Admiralty Orders, apart from bringing RAF attachments to the notice of Naval and Marine Officers, was to emphasize the attractiveness of such attachments in career terms.

1924 – Fleet Air Arm – Attached Officers to receive Air Force Commissions
(C.W. 6376/24. – 25.7.1924)

With reference to the first sentence of paragraph 5 of A.F.O. 1058/24 (see above) which reads 'Naval…Navy.' it has been decided that in order to ensure the status and authority of attached Naval Officers under Air Force law while under training or at such times during their attachment when they may have to command RAF personnel not under the Naval Discipline Act, they will be given temporary R.A.F. commissions while attached. Such commissions will be given for the above purposes only and will not in any way whatsoever affect their Naval or R.M. status or authority. Attached Naval Officers will invariably be addressed by their Naval titles and if their Naval rank is relatively higher than their Air Force rank they will take precedence (but not command) among Air Force Officers in accordance with their Naval rank.

Appendix M

Pilots on the Strength of Fighter, Fleet Spotter and Reconnaissance Flights of the Fleet Air Arm

The following is the Order of Battle for January 1924

No. 401 Flight, Coastal Area

Flight Lieutenant	H. Slatter OBE, DSC
Flying Officers	W. Jones
	J. Medcalf
	J. Lynch
	J. Murray
Pilot Officers	J. Wilson
	G. Reeves

No. 402 Flight, Coastal Area

Flight Lieutenant	C. Foster
Flying Officers	G. Lugg
	C. Wincott
	J. Burd MC
	A. Bateman
	M. Wiblin
Pilot Officer	L. Barnes

No. 403 Flight, Coastal Area

Flight Lieutenant	A. Fletcher DFC, AFC.
Flying Officer	T. Brewin
	J. Comerford
	E. Cummins DFC
	S. Trower
	L. Young
	G. Dean

No. 404 Flight, Coastal Area

Flying Officer C. Horsfield

No. 421 Flight, Coastal Area

Flight Lieutenants	E. Openshaw
	L. Chandler MBE.
Flying Officers	L. Hilton DFC
	F. Van Blommestein
	A. Revington
	P. Hume-Wright
Pilot Officers	S. Connolly
	R. Carter

Attached from the RN:

Lieutenants	M. Deane
	M. Farquhar
	A. Rodger
	I. White DSC
	L. Mackintosh
	H. Smith

No. 422 Flight, Coastal Area

Flight Lieutenant	R. Munday DSC
Flying or Observer Officers	
	G. Russell DFC
	E. Kingston
	W. Thompson
	C. Hancock
	C. McL. Reid
	M. Garnons-Williams
Pilot Officer	W. Venmore

Attached from the RN:

Lieutenant Commander	P. Butter
Lieutenants	R. de H. Burton
	G. Langley
	J. Hawkins
	E. Knocker
	A. Dodington

No. 423 Flight, Coastal Area

Flight Lieutenant	J. Grigson DSO, DFC
Flying Officers	T. Williams MC, DFC
	H. le V. Noel DFC
	W. Payne
	A. Scroggs
	C. Brill
	L. Hirsh
Pilot Officer	J. Newall

No. 440 Flight, Coastal Area

Flight Lieutenants	W. Walker DSC, AFC.
	L. Maxton
Flying Officers	S. Harker
	W. Watson
	G. Burge
	C. Dagg AFC.
	G. Hicks DFC
	S. Tipper
	A. Ball
	R. Rose
	N. D'Aeth
Pilot Officers	F. Cator
	G. Nicholets

No. 441 Flight, Coastal Area

Flight Lieutenants	E. Hopcraft DSC.
	C. Boumphrey DFC
	G. Johnston
Flying Officers	W. Swann
	J. Mehigan
	W. Bradford
	F. Foster DFC, DSM
	A. Chipper
	G. Dalley
	A. Drysdale
Pilot Officer	C. Guppy

No. 442 Flight, Coastal Area

Flight Lieutenants	B Harrison AFC
	K. Tilman
Flying Officers	W Umpleby
	B. Caswell
	G. Holmes
	G. Lansdowne DSC
	S. Kirsten
	H. Waterfield
Pilot Officers	G. Worthington
	R. Lewes
	G. Randle

No. 460 Flight, Coastal Area

Flight Lieutenants	W. Mackensie AFC.
	C. Riddle
	E.Bryant
Flying Officers	C. Gifford (Hon. Flt Lt)
	G. Brown

No. 461 Flight, Coastal Area No. 10 Group

Flight Lieutenants	R. Gardner DSC
	S. Watkins AFC
Flying Officers	A. Paull
	W. Gardner DFC

No. 481 Flight, Mediterranean

Flight Lieutenants	H. Stewart
	M. Simpson
	A. Durston
	J. Sadler
	V. Scriven AFC
	F. Norton
	D. Carnegie AFC
	E. Ades

Flying Officers	E. Moulton-Barrett
	V. Simons
	E. Waring
	J. Sugars
	I. Hodgson
	H. Hackney
	K. Mackenzie
	A. Adams DFC
	H. White
	R. Mollard
	V. Clift

By comparison, the change in fleet titles is revealed in the Order of Battle for February 1928

Note 1. The names of pilots who featured in the previous order of battle *
   2. The increase in the number of RN pilots bearing RAF ranks

No. 401 (Fleet Fighter) Flight, HMS *Tamar*, China Station
Aircraft – FLYCATCHER

Flight Lieutenant	B. Caswell*
Flying Officers	H. Day (Capt Royal Marines)
	T. Bulteel (Lt RN)
	T. Villiers (Lt RN)
	K. Hunt (Lt RM)
	N. Young
	J. Wallis (a)

No. 402 (Fleet Fighter) Flight, HMS *Eagle*, RAF Base Malta
Aircraft – FLYCATCHER

Flight Lieutenants	R. St A. Malleson (Lt-Cdr RN)
	C. Wincott
Flying Officers	J. Ainger (Lt RN)
	R. Langton (Lt RN)
	C. Keighley-Peach (Lt RN)
	J. Ryde (a)

No. 403 (Fleet Fighter) Flight, HMS *Hermes*, China Station
Aircraft – FLYCATCHER

Flight Lieutenant	E. Abel-Smith (Lt RN)
Flying Officers	M. Wiblin
	I. Grant (Lt RN)
	R. Aldridge (Lt RN)

G. Renwick (Lt RN)
J. Robertson (Lt RN)
A. Pilling (Lt RN)

No. 404A (Fleet Fighter) Flight, Coastal Area
Aircraft – FLYCATCHER

Flying Officers	C. Tidd (Lt RN)
	O. Jones (Lt RN)
	G. Willoughby (Lt RN)
	R. Giles (Lt RM)
	C. Campbell (Lt RN)

No. 404B (Fleet Fighter) Flight, HMS *Argus*, China Station
Aircraft – FLYCATCHER

Flight Lieutenant	C. Atkinson (Lt RN)
Flying Officers	W. Baxter
	J. Keary

No. 405 (Fleet Fighter) Flight, HMS *Furious*
Aircraft – FLYCATCHER

Flight Lieutenant	F. Bond
Flying Officers	M. Ward
	J. Burroughs (Lt RN)
	L. Sharman (Lt-Cdr RN)
	R. Allen (Lt RN)

C. Byas (Lt RN) (see p. 199 as pilot on M2 submarine)
R. Barrett (Lt RN)
E. Thompson

No. 406 (Fleet Fighter) Flight (Merged temporarily in No. 401 Flight)

Flying Officer	E. Carnduff (Lt RN)

No. 407 (Fleet Fighter) Flight, Donibristle, Coastal Area
Aircraft – FLYCATCHER

Flight Lieutenant	L. Briggs
Flying Officer	H. Ditton (Lt RN)
	A. Rundle (Lt RN)
	G. Birley (Lt RN)
	J. Franks (a)
	S. Long (Lt RN)
	R. Kilroy (Lt RN)

No. 420 (Fleet Spotter) Flight, HMS *Furious*
Aircraft – BLACKBURN

Flight Lieutenant	E. Knocker (Lt RN)
Flying Officers	M. Slattery (Lt RN)
	J. Pocock
	E. Lane (Lt RN)
	G. Cooper (Lt RN)
	A. Brock (Lt RN)
	J. Bowles

No. 421A (Fleet Spotter) Flight (see 443 Composite Flight)

No. 421B (Fleet Spotter) Flight, HMS *Eagle*, Mediterranean
Aircraft – BISON

Flying Officers	L. Robertson (Lt RN)
	W. Gordon (Capt RN)
	E. Burt (Lt RN)

No. 422 (Fleet Spotter) Flight, HMS *Argus*, China Station

Flight Lieutenant	L. Hope AFC
Flying Officers	E. Ellison (Capt RM)
	R. Peyton (Lt RN)
	A. Murray (Lt RN)
	N. Bassett (Lt RN)

No. 423 (Fleet Spotter) Flight, HMS *Eagle*, Mediterranean
Aircraft – BISON

Flight Lieutenant	M. Williams MC, DFC
Flying Officers	D. Cummings DFC (a)
	W. Knowles (Lt RM)
	T. Morgan (Lt RN)
	N. Grey (Lt RN)
	S. Lea (Lt RN)

No. 440 (Fleet Spotter Reconnaissance) Flight, HMS *Hermes*, China Station
Aircraft – FAIREY IIIF

Flight Lieutenant	R. Brookman (a)
Flying Officers	G. Warren (Lt RM)
	C. John (Lt RN)
	A. Watson (Lt RN)
	F. May
	A. Hale

No. 441 (Fleet Reconnaissance) Flight, HMS *Argus*, China Station
Aircraft – FAIREY IIID

Flight Lieutenant	G. Wildman-Lushington (Capt RM)
Flying Officers	F. Oliphant (Lt RN)
	E. Price (Lt RN)
	C. Lentaigne (Lt RN)
	R. Cecil (Lt RN)
	J. St C. Arthbuthnott
	D. Mackendrick (Lt RN)

No. 442 (Fleet Reconnaissance) Flight, HMS *Tamar*, China Station
Aicraft – FAIREY IIID

Flight Lieutenant	W. Gardner DFC*
Flying Officers	G. Randle*
	J. Healing (Lt RN)
	A. Keene (Lt RN)
	J. Hawkins (Lt RN)
	J. Hale (Lt RN)

No. 443 (Composite) Flight, HMS *Furious*
Aircraft – FAIREY IIIF

Flight Lieutenant	J. McFarlane MC
Flying Officers	J. Heath (Lt RN)
	S. Woolley (Lt RM)
	F. Stephenson (Lt RN)
	R. Barlow
	R. Garnett (Lt RN)
	J. Fenton (Lt RN)
	H. Smallwood (Lt RN)

Appendix N

The Career Paths of Hugh Trenchard, John Salmond, Frederick Sykes and Edward Ellington

Marshal of the Royal Air Force the Viscount Trenchard GCB, OM, GCVO, DSO, DCL, LLD

Promotions		Appointments
9/9/93	Second Lieutenant	Royal Scots Fusiliers
12/8/96	Lieutenant	
28/2/00	Captain	
22/8/02	Brevet Major	
24/10/03	Temporary Lieutenant-Colonel	Southern Nigerian Regiment
4/11/10		2nd Battalion, Royal Scots Fusiliers
17/8/12		Central Flying School – Course
1/10/12		Central Flying School – Instructor
23/9/13		Assistant Commandant, Central Flying School
7/8/14		Officer Commanding, Military Wing, South Farnborough
18/11/14		Officer Commanding, HQ No. 1 Wing, France
18/1/15	Brevet Lieutenant-Colonel	
3/6/15	Brevet Colonel	
25/8/15	Temporary Brigadier-General	Officer Commanding, Royal Flying Corps, France
34/3/16	Temporary Major-General	General Officer Commanding, Royal Flying Corps, France
1/1/17	Major-General	
3/1/18	Temporary Major-General, RAF	
18/1/18		Chief of the Air Staff
12/4/18		Resigned
15/5/18		Special Duty, Headquarters RAF, France
15/6/18		General Officer Commanding, Independent Force, France
26/10/18		Commander-in-Chief, Inter-Allied Air Force
20/11/18		Air Ministry
31/3/19		Chief of the Air Staff
1/8/19	Air Vice-Marshal	
11/8/19	Air Marshal	
1/4/22	Air Chief Marshal	
1/1/27	Marshal of the Royal Air Force	
1/1/30		Appointment relinquished

Marshal of the Royal Air Force Sir John Salmond GCB, CMG, CVO, DSO, DCL, LLD

8/1/01	Second Lieutenant	King's Own Royal Lancaster Regiment
5/4/04	Lieutenant	
26/6/10	Captain	
17/8/12		Central Flying School
12/11/12	Flight Commander, RFC	Instructor, Central Flying School
31/5/13	Squadron Commander, RFC	
30/4/14		Officer Commanding, No. 3 Squadron, Farnborough
12/8/14		Officer Commanding, No. 3 Squadron, France
13/4/15	Wing Commander, RFC	Advanced Wing Headquarters, Farnborough
19/8/15		Officer Commanding, No. 2 Wing, France
9/3/16	Temporary Brigadier-General	Officer Commanding, No. 6 Brigade
22/6/17	Temporary Major-General	Officer Commanding, Training Division
18/10/17		Director-General of Military Aeronautics, War Office
18/1/18		General Officer Commanding, Royal Flying Corps (in the Field)
1/4/18	Major-General, RAF	General Officer Commanding, Royal Air Force (in the Field)
7/5/19		Officer Commanding, Rhine Headquarters
1/8/19	Air Vice-Marshal	
19/8/19		Air Officer Commanding, South Area
1/4/20		Air Officer Commanding, Inland Area
1/10/22		Air Officer Commanding, Headquarters Iraq
2/6/23	Air Marshal	
1/1/25		Air Officer Commanding in Chief, Air Defence of Great Britain
1/1/29	Air Chief Marshal	Air Member for Personnel
1/1/30		Chief of the Air Staff

1/1/33	Marshal of the Royal Air Force	
1/4/33		Appointment relinquished

Major-General the Right Honourable Sir Frederick Sykes PC, GCSI, GCIE, GBE, KCB, CMG

1900		Imperial Yeomanry Scouts, South Africa
		Lord Roberts's Bodyguard, South Africa
2/10/01	Second Lieutenant	15th Hussars, India
		West African Regiment, Sierra Leone
1905	Captain	15th Hussars, India
1908		Staff College, Quetta
1909		South Africa
10/10	Major	Directorate of Operations, War Office
13/5/12	Lieutenant-Colonel RFC	Officer Commanding, Military Wing
		RFC Farnborough
13/8/14	Lieutenant-Colonel, RFC	Chief of Staff, Headquarters British Expeditionary Force
21/12/14	Temporary Colonel	Second-in-Command, Royal Flying Corps
26/5/15		Placed at the disposal of the Admiralty
24/7/15	Temporary Captain, RNAS	Officer Commanding Air Service Units, Dardanelles
14/3/16	Colonel	Returned to Army Service as AA & QMG,
		4th Mounted Division, Colchester
1916	Brigadier-General	Deputy General of Organization, War Office
11/17		Representative of AG and QMG on Supreme War Council
12/4/18	Major-General, RAF	Chief of the Air Staff
1/4/19		Retirement

Marshal of the Royal Air Force Sir Edward Ellington GCB, CMG, CBE

1/9/97	2nd Lieutenant	Royal Artillery
1/9/00	Lieutenant	
27/4/04	Captain	
1908		War College, Portsmouth
24/8/09		Staff Captain, War Office
9/8/10		GSO 3, War Office
8/5/13	Temporary Major	GSO 2, Directorate of Military Aeronautics, War Office
17/12/13	Squadron Commander, RFC	
5/10/14	Major, Royal Artillery	DQQMG, Headquarters British Expeditionary Force, France
6/3/15	Temporary Lieutenant-Colonel	AA & QMG, 2nd Cavalry Division, British Expeditionary Force
22/7/15	Temporary Colonel	GSO 1, 2nd Army, British Expeditionary Force
5/2/16	Temporary Colonel	GSO 1, War Office
14/1/17	Temporary Brigadier-General	General Staff, 8th Army Corps, France
20/11/17		Deputy Director-General of Military Aeronautics, War Office
18/1/18		Director-General of Military Aeronautics, War Office
10/4/18	Temporary Major-General, RAF	Acting Controller-General of Equipment, Air Ministry
22/8/18		Controller-General of Equipment/Director-General of Supply and Research, Air Ministry
1/8/19	Air Vice-Marshal	
1/3/22		Air Officer Commanding, Headquarters, Middle East
5/11/23		Air Officer Commanding, Headquarters, India
19/11/26		Air Officer Commanding, Headquarters, Iraq
1/1/29		Air Officer Commanding-in-Chief, Air Defence of Great Britain
1/7/29	Air Marshal	
26/9/31		Air Member for Personnel
1/1/33	Air Chief Marshal	
22/5/33		Chief of the Air Staff
1/1/37	Marshal of the Royal Air Force	
1/9/37		Inspector-General of the Royal Air Force
4/4/40		Appointment relinquished

Appendix P

The Various Home and Tropical Officers' Uniforms, 1925

Ceremonial Dress

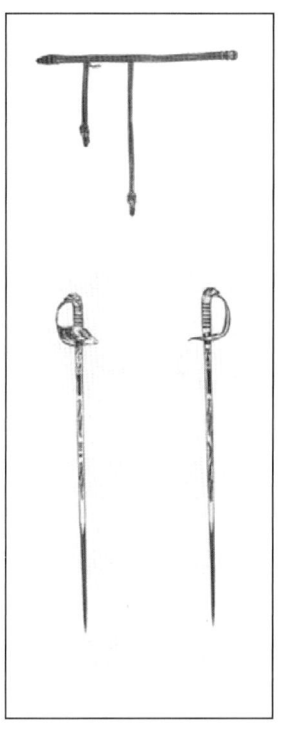

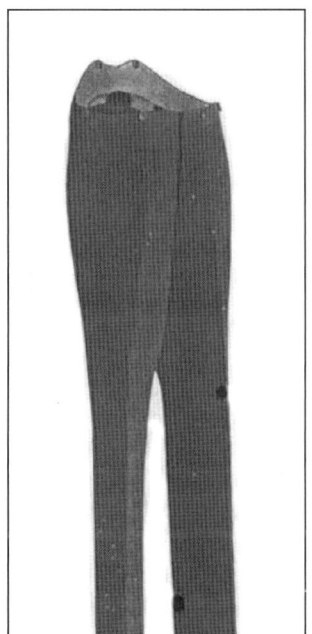

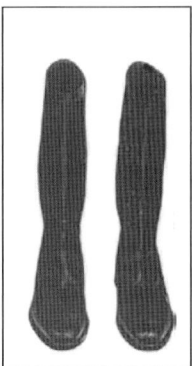

Service Dress

  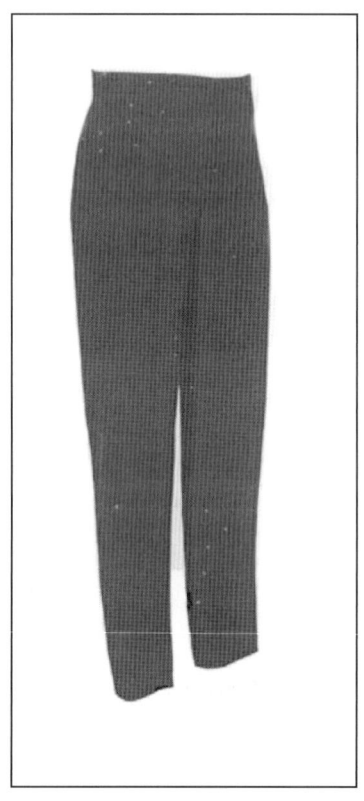

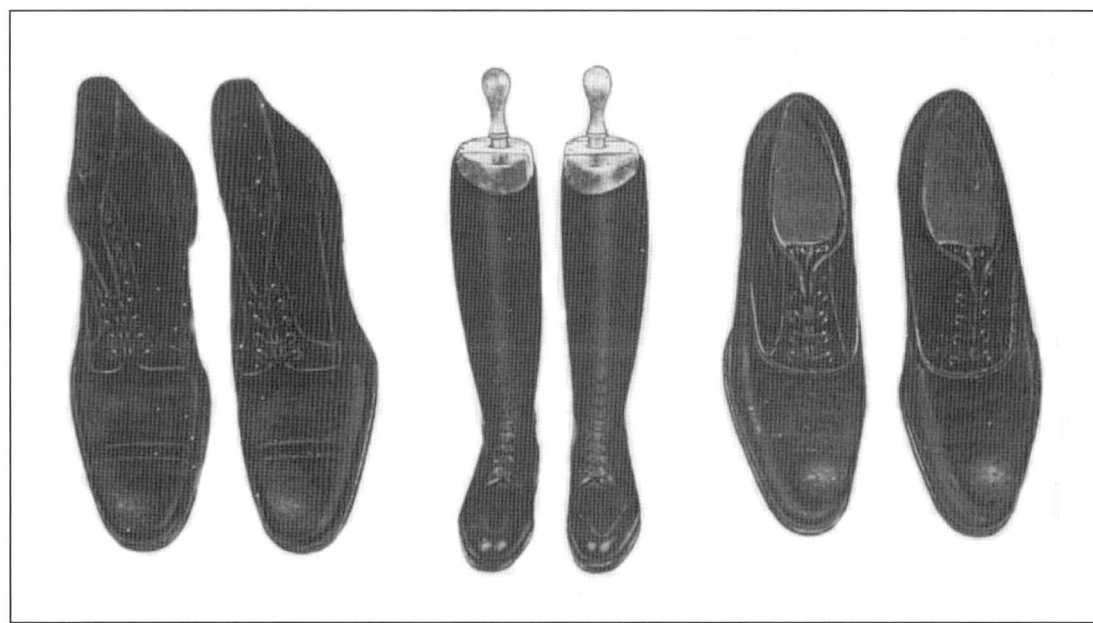

During the 1920s the service dress could be worn with either breeches or trousers, with or without turn-ups. The puttees were interchangeable with field boots, above, and boots were interchangeable with shoes when worn with trousers. When breeches were worn with puttees, boots would be worn.

Mess Dress (Home)

Mess Dress (Tropical)

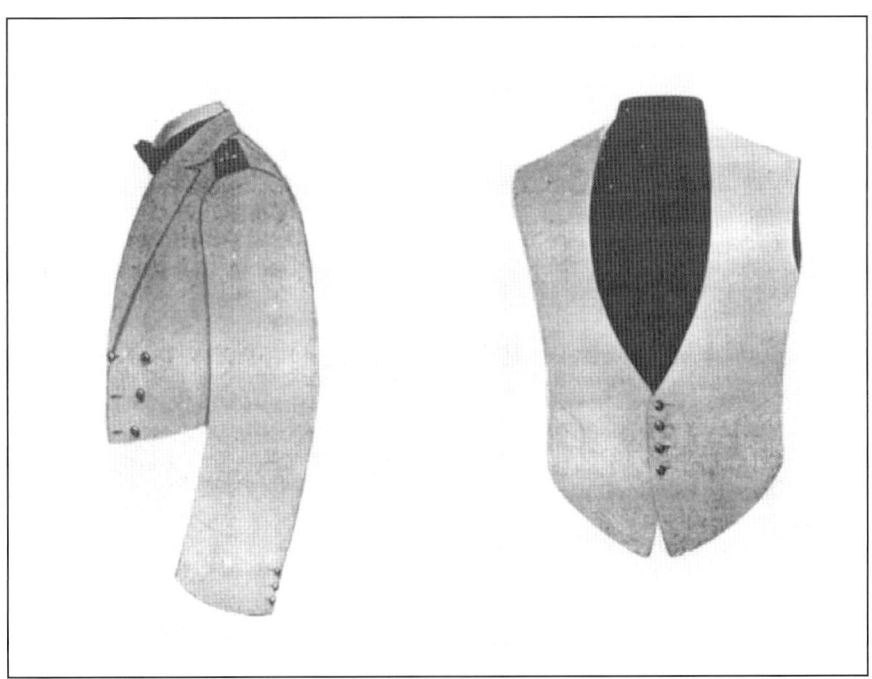

Service Raincoat and Greatcoat

Service Cap Peaks

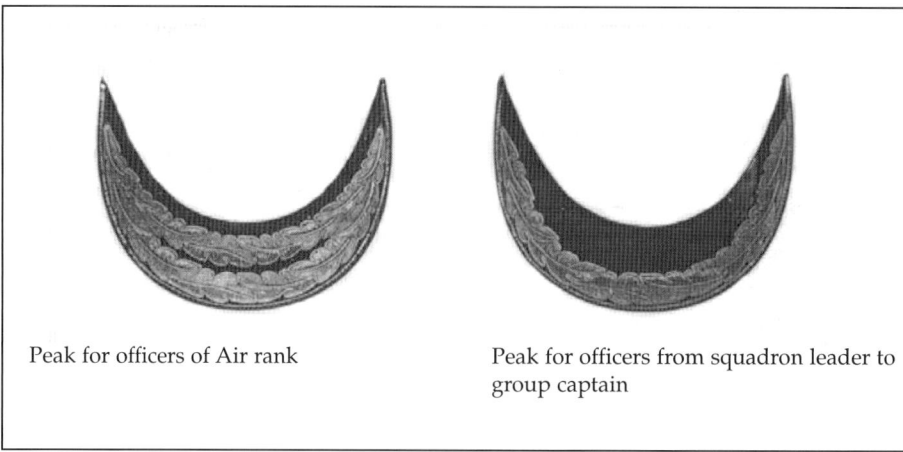

Peak for officers of Air rank

Peak for officers from squadron leader to group captain

Service Dress (Tropical)

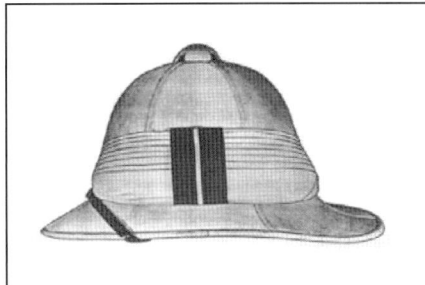

Cap Badges

Air Officers

Other Officers

Appendix Q

Correspondence Relating to the Cabinet Memorandum, 'The War Object of an Air Force'

Source: National Archives, CAB/21/314

The following copies of Cabinet papers between Sir Maurice Hankey and Air Marshal Trenchard in April/May 1928 relate to the latter's submission of a memorandum intended to state the prevailing Air Staff Doctrine. Hankey's response and Trenchard's reaction to that response are to be found in National Archives documents, and these have been reproduced below.

TEXT OF A LETTER FROM SIR MAURICE HANKEY, SECRETARY TO THE CHIEFS OF STAFF SUB-COMMITTEE TO AIR MARSHAL SIR HUGH TRENCHARD, CHIEF OF THE AIR STAFF, dated 28 April 1928, hereafter referred to as Letter No. 1

SECRET AND PERSONAL

My Dear Trenchard,

I am returning herewith your very interesting paper on the War Object of an Air Force.

In our conversation yesterday afternoon I undertook to deal with the question under two heads:-

(i) As Secretary to the Chiefs of Staff Sub-Committee I undertook to give you my views as to the best method of handling the business in bringing it before your colleagues.

(ii) As Hankey, I undertook to express privately my personal criticism of the Paper.

In this letter I am dealing only with the former point, the latter being dealt with in a separate letter Marked No. 2.

I think your best plan would be to circulate the Memorandum officially to the Chiefs of Staff Sub-Committee, covered by a Note recalling the genesis of the question and stating that before taking your final decisions on the doctrine which you lay down for the RAF War Manual you are anxious to discuss the matter at the Chiefs of Staff Sub-Committee, and that your memorandum is intended as a basis for discussion.

On the whole I prefer this method to circulating it privately. The proceedings of the Chiefs of Staff Committee can be very informal when they desire. I am inclined to think that in this case it might be well to have a preliminary discussion, without any Minutes, and it might be worth mentioning this in your covering Note. This is a procedure by no means unknown to Cabinet of CID Committees, or even, on occasions, the Cabinet itself, when rather controversial and difficult matters have to be discussed.

Do not try to settle this particular question in one Meeting. Let everyone express their views on the deal level, and you will probably exercise some effect on one another's opinion and get halfway to agreement. Then go away and think it over and at the next meeting you may quite likely reach an agreement. That is my advice.

Yours ever,

M.P.A. Hankey

p.s. The other letter will take longer but I hope to send it not later than Monday M.P.A.H.

LETTER No. 2, dated 28 April

SECRET AND PERSONAL

My Dear Trenchard,

In this letter I give my personal views on your memorandum, 'The War Object of an Air Force'. If in some respects they do not square with your own do not be angry. It is no use for me to write unless I speak freely.

I do not object to the terms in which provisionally you state the aim of the Air Force, though I do criticise some of the arguments you use to support it and I think that they carry you a good deal further than does the actual formula you propose.

You examine the matter under three heads, the first being, 'Does this doctrine violate any true principle of war?'

With this part of your argument I am in general agreement. Not only do I think that it violates no true principle of war, but I agree with you when you say, 'there is no new principle involved'. (Page E-4) The destruction of an enemy's base or source of supply or loss of communications has always been recognised as a legitimate objective of war from the earliest times. Scipio Africanae [*sic*] brought Hannibal to a standstill by capturing his base at Carthagena, Alexander the Great before invading Persia, destroyed the sea power of the Persians in the Mediterranean by occupying the coasts of Syria, Palestine and Egypt and so depriving the fleet of attacks on the coast roads and depots at both ends of the Pyrenees, thus supplementing the action of the Spanish guerrillas in hampering the communications of the French. In the late War we ruined the original German attack on commerce by depriving the enemy of his bases and his means of communications by cable and wireless.

Your own proposal to use the Air Arm in order to break down the enemy's means of resistance by attacking his bases of supply and his communications appear to me to be on all-fours with these instances (which no doubt could be multiplied indefinitely) of the use of naval and military force for attacks in supplies and essential communications.

The second question you raise is as to whether an air offensive of this kind is contrary to international law or to the dictates of humanity.

Here again, I find myself in general agreement with you. I think, however, that if your policy is carried out the tendency in the future will be to segregate war manufacture and supply as far as possible from the ordinary civil life of the nation. This, however, will be a very slow process and need not trouble us at this stage.

Your third question is as to whether your methods will lead to victory and in that respect therefore a correct employment of Air power. On this third head I think that you exaggerate both the actual power of the Air and its moral effect, and that you underrate the resisting power of a nation which is fighting for its existence or some cause which it rates equally highly.

First, as regards Air Power. At present I think it is admitted that the effective radius of action of aircraft is strictly limited. I do not know what the present limit is nor do I much care. It may be 200 miles or 250. Beyond that distance, however, the enemy's factories, supplies and communications will be immune from constant attack and only subject to occasional raids such as we had in the late War. Consequently it is only necessary for the enemy to develop his sources of supply and manufacture outside the effective range of your aircraft to defeat your ends. Beyond your effective radius your physical effect will be small, and your morale effect almost nil. London never cared a rap when Hull was bombed and vice versa. I have myself seen men scream with laughter at seeing a Turkish shell burst in a British ammunition ship! That is simply human psychology.

You may of course tell me that in time aircraft will be able to fly much further. No doubt this will be the case. But in order to fly further they will become larger and more expensive. The numbers which nations will be able to maintain in time of peace will become smaller. It will be exactly like the Capital Ship. Before the War I suppose we had fifty, now owing to their greater cost, only twenty. You will not have numbers at the onset of a war to cover the vast spaces of a country like France or Germany effectively. The munitions and supply works will be scattered and you will never be able to find anywhere to deal a decisive blow. Moreover, as you yourself indicate, there will be continued fighting in the air. Both sides will have to divert air energy (using the term in its widest sense) from bombers to fighters. The risks to your long-distance aircraft, which will be making long journeys over enemy territory and will be liable to be encountered and intercepted over vast distances, will be very great.

Up to now I have spoken of the areas outside your effective radius. Even inside your radius of action your centres of production and supply will be scattered. You yourself, in your Memorandum, say that an organized armed force, whether land sea or air, is very difficult to destroy and applying this to the Air Force, you point out how air bases can be camouflaged, and how personnel and material can be well protected against bomb attack, the layout arranged and speed to prevent a difficult target and so forth. You will get exactly the same thing in your national supply arrangements. They will be scattered, camouflaged, laid out with skill and as many of them as possible put beyond your range. Personally I do not think we are doing enough in this direction. We ought to do all we can to encourage every kind of manufacture of war material away from London. We are far too dependent upon Woolwich Arsenal and London resources, it will take years to escape this dependence, but in my opinion we ought to adopt a definite policy of doing so and I wish the Chiefs of Staff would take a lead in urging it.

Even with comparatively short distances of your aerodromes, I cannot but feel the gravest doubt as to whether you do not exaggerate the power of the Air Force. Just about ten and a half years ago Lloyd George and the War Cabinet were considering whether they should stop the Battle of Flanders. Haig was extraordinarily anxious to continue I asked him privately why? He replied that he wanted to capture some ridge from which he could bombard the Roulers–Thooroet Railway only a few miles behind the Front, which was used for maintaining the enemy's coast section. I asked him privately why he did not use his air forces, of which he had enormous numbers in the Flanders area. He replied that for this kind of purpose the air forces were perfectly useless. Or take the case of Zeebrugge not so many miles from our aerodromes in the coast region. In

order to put to sea the German destroyers and submarines at Bruges had to traverse several miles of canal, an obligatory defile where one would think, in theory, they must be intercepted. One would say that all that was needed was for a scouting aeroplane to see the destroyers and submarines coming out of Bruges, to wireless the moves across our lines whence a force of aircraft would descend on these vessels, sink them and block the canal for a month. Yet there is not a single instance, so far as I know, in the whole War of such an interruption. I could multiply these things indefinitely. The Germans never prevented us from using Dunkirk. They never interfered in the smallest degree with our traffic in the Thames though they were constantly flying over our ships and I have myself counted several hundred merchant ships lying in the Downs. They tried once or twice to attack merchant ships but nearly always missed their target. I remember well some bridge in the Lille region, which our soldiers wanted to have bombed. It was attacked again and again but traffic was never interrupted across it. Every time I crossed the big railway bridge on the way to Paris after leaving Abbeville I used to see more and more shell holes on the river bank. I believe the bridge was never hit.

Even admitting an advance has been made since the war in the accuracy of shooting, the power of your bombs, and so forth, I have seen no evidence of anything which would justify us in discarding the experience of the War in this respect. Even if your highly trained professional airmen can make better shooting than in the past, in time of war they will soon disappear and their places taken, as in the late War, by hordes of gallant but half-trained pilots of the type who, as I have was so often told by an intimate friend in the Flying Corps during the war, simply loosed off their bombs without using their aiming apparatus at all.

As regards morale, I have always thought in my heart, that you over-rate the morale effect of air attacks on a population. I was at the centre of the War the whole time, and although Cabinet Ministers sometimes got in a fret about air raids, it was only because Parliament made itself unpleasant. The result was that a certain amount of force had to be diverted to air defence. I have lately re-read my war diary and I cannot find a single occasion on which I did not brush aside the time spent at the War Cabinet or War Committee on air raids as a sheer waste of time. Although I several times visited the attacked quarters and saw the destruction after the event, and although I and my family were within a short distance of one of the most destructive attacks made I never regarded the morale effect very seriously. Of course it has increased but I think that, to describe it as 'overwhelming' as you do on Page 7, is an abuse of language. You yourself admit that the rifleman or the sailor will stand the fire because he is disciplined. The only reason we never tried it in the late War was that we never really had the need. You will of course get particular areas where temporarily you will have panic, just as you can cause panic amongst the best disciplined troops. But you will never drive a determined nation to universal panic. Hull will always jeer at London and vice versa. One saw in France peasants and villagers living for years within the most dangerous zones. I remember well, as late as 1918, being taken with the utmost precautions up a slag heap, at the foot was a half-ruined cottage; the children were playing at the door and the peasant was ploughing his land at the foot of the slag heap. They had been there the whole War. Civilians do not differ essentially from soldiers and are not going to be beaten by sheer bluff, if their hearts are in the war.

To summarise, then, I do not dispute the main conclusion you reach, which seems to me both moderately and modestly worded. I do not see how it can be claimed that you violate any principles of war. I do not think that you necessarily violate the laws of war or the dictates of humanity though you may easily be led by inaccurate intelligence to cross the borderline of humanity. I do not think though that when you talk of securing victory by Air Defence you pitch your case too high. In a word I support your theory but I regard the Air Force merely as one of many means of exercising pressure on an enemy e.g., sea power and blockade, the defeat of his armies and Air power. It is not by any one, but by a combination of the three that we must seek to overcome a really determined enemy. I believe you would really strengthen your case if you would recognize this principle and recast your Memorandum so as to make clear that it is rarely, if ever, a sole means of winning a war, though it is an important contribution.

What we really want is an Imperial Defence Manual into which the other three would be fitted.

Yours ever,
Signed *P.A. Hankey*

P.S. Please don't be cross with this note. It is exclusively my own and I have consulted no one in writing it.

TRENCHARD'S REPLY

2nd May 1928

My Dear Hankey,
Your letter No. 2 of April 28th on the subject of my Memorandum, also your letter No. 1

Thank you so much for letting me have all these points. I have re-read my paper in the light of them, and perhaps it does give the impression I did not mean it to, namely, that the Air was going to win a European war without the help of the Army and Navy and Blockade etc., and I must make certain that this side does not mislead others.

I am not a bit annoyed with your frank statement, though you will probably realise I don't agree with some of it, and some of it shows me how important it is for me to still further explain what it is we claim to be able to do. All the cases you mention of the Great War are not quite appropriate to what I am advocating, but I will have to talk with you again on the subject, and in sending my paper, I will try to correct the impression that I expect to win the war without the Army and Navy.

At the same time, you must remember I am writing this paper on the Air Force objectives, where in certain wars, such as the one just on – the Imam – we have definitely done what you rather say we cannot do, but I take it your letter really applied to the big organized European nations and not to a semi-civilised little countries like that of the Imam's.

Yours ever,
H.M. Trenchard

Appendix R

Members of the Air Council and Commanders of RAF Formations in the 1920s

Air Council 3 January 1918

The Secretary of State for the Air Force	The Rt Hon. Lord Rothermere
Parliamentary Under-Secretary of State	Major J.L. Baird CMG, DSO, MP
Additional Member and Vice-President	Lieutenant-General Sir David Henderson KCB
Chief of the Air Staff	Major-General Sir Hugh Trenchard KCB
Deputy Chief Air Staff	Rear Admiral Mark Kerr CB
Master-General of Personnel	Commodore Godfrey M. Paine CB
Controller-General of Equipment	Major-General W.S. Brancker
Director-General of Aircraft Production	Sir William Weir
Administrator of Works and Buildings	Sir John Hunter KBE
Secretary	Mr W.A. Robinson CB, CBE

Air Council 11 November 1918

The Secretary of State for the Air Force	The Rt Hon. Lord Weir of Eastwood PC
Parliamentary Under-Secretary of State	Major J.L. Baird CMG, DSO, MP
Chief of the Air Staff	Major-General F.H. Sykes CMG
Inspector-General of the RAF	Major-General Sir Godfrey M. Paine KCB, MVO
Master-General of Personnel	Major-General W.S. Brancker
Controller-General of Equipment	Major-General E.L. Ellington
Director-General of Aircraft Production	Sir Arthur Duckham KCB
Administrator of Works and Buildings	Sir John Hunter KBE
Secretary	Mr W.A. Robinson CB, CBE

Air Council 31 March 1919

The Secretary of State for Air	The Rt Hon. W.S. Churchill MP
Parliamentary Under-Secretary of State	Major-General J.E.B. Seely CB, CMG, DSO, MP
Finance Member of the Council	The Most Hon., the Marquess of Londonderry MVO
Chief of the Air Staff	Major-General Sir Hugh Trenchard KCB, DSO
Controller-General of Civil Aviation	Major-General Sir F.H. Sykes KCB, CMG
Director-General of Supply and Research	Major-General E.L. Ellington CB, CMG
Administrator of Works and Buildings	Sir John Hunter KBE
Additional Member	Brig.General W. Alexander CMG, DSO
Additional Member	Sir James Stevenson Bt
Additional Member	Sir Arthur Duckham KCB
Secretary	Sir W.A. Robinson KCB, CBE

Air Council 31 March 1920

The Secretary of State for Air	The Rt Hon. W.S. Churchill MP
Parliamentary Under-Secretary of State	The Most Hon., the Marquess of Londonderry KG, MVO
Chief of the Air Staff	Air Marshal Sir Hugh Trenchard KCB, DSO
Controller-General of Civil Aviation	Major-General Sir F.H. Sykes GBE, KCB, CMG
Director-General of Supply and Research	Air Vice-Marshal E.L. Ellington CB, CMG, CBE
Additional Member	Wing Commander Sir W. Alexander KBE,CBE, CMG, DSO, TD
Additional Member	Sir James Stevenson Bt
Secretary	Mr W.F. Nicholson

Air Council 31 March 1921

The Secretary of State for Air	The Rt Hon. W.S. Churchill MP
Parliamentary Under-Secretary of State	The Most Hon., the Marquess of Londonderry KG, MVO
Chief of the Air Staff	Air Marshal Sir Hugh Trenchard Bt, KCB, DSO, ADC
Controller-General of Civil Aviation	Major-General F.H. Sykes GBE, KCB, CMG
Director-General of Supply and Research	Air Vice-Marshal Sir E.L. Ellington KCB, CMG, CBE, p.s.c.
Additional Member	Rear-Admiral Sir C.F. Lambert KCB
Additional Member	Sir James Stevenson Bt
Secretary	Mr W.F. Nicholson CB

Air Council 31 March 1922

The Secretary of State for Air	Captain the Rt Hon. and Hon. F.E. Guest CBE, DSO, MP
Parliamentary Under-Secretary of State	The Rt Hon. Lord Gorell CBE, MC
Chief of the Air Staff	Air Marshal Sir Hugh Trenchard Bt, KCB, DSO, ADC
Controller-General of Civil Aviation	Major-General F.H. Sykes GBE, KCB, CMG
Director-General of Supply and Research	Air Vice-Marshal Sir W.G.H. Salmond KCMG, CB, DSO, p.s.c.
Secretary	Mr W.F. Nicholson CB

Air Council 31 March 1923

The Secretary of State for Air	Lieutenant-Colonel the Rt Hon. Sir Samuel Hoare Bt, CMG, MP
Parliamentary Under-Secretary of State	His Grace the Duke of Sutherland ACM
Chief of the Air Staff	Air Chief Marshal Sir Hugh Trenchard Bt, KCB, DSO, ADC
Air Member for Personnel	Air Vice-Marshal O. Swann CB
Air Member for Supply and Research	Air Vice-Marshal Sir W.G.H. Salmond KCMG, CB, DSO, p.s.c.
Secretary	Sir W.F. Nicholson KCB

Air Council 31 March 1924

The Secretary of State for Air	Brigadier-General the Rt Hon. the Lord Thomson PC, CBE, DSO, p.s.c.
Parliamentary Under-Secretary of State	William Leach Esq., MP
Chief of the Air Staff	Air Chief Marshal Sir Hugh Trenchard Bt, KCB, DSO, ADC
Air Member for Personnel	Air Vice-Marshal P.W. Game CB, DSO, p.s.c.
Air Member for Supply and Research	Air Vice-Marshal Sir W.G.H. Salmond KCMG, CB, DSO, p.s.c.
Deputy Chief of Air Staff	Air Commodore J.M. Steel, CB, CMG, CBE
Secretary	Sir W.F. Nicholson KCB

Air Council 31 March 1925 and 1926

The Secretary of State for Air	Lieutenant-Colonel the Rt Hon. Sir Samuel Hoare Bt, CMG, MP
Parliamentary Under-Secretary of State	Major Sir Philip Sassoon Bt, GBE, CMG, MP
Chief of the Air Staff	Air Chief Marshal Sir Hugh Trenchard Bt, KCB, DSO
Air Member for Personnel	Air Vice-Marshal Sir P.W. Game KCB, DSO, p.s.c.
Air Member for Supply and Research	Air Vice-Marshal Sir W.G.H. Salmond KCMG, CB, DSO, p.s.c.
Deputy Chief of Air Staff	Air Vice-Marshal J.M. Steel CB, CMG, CBE
Secretary	Sir W.F. Nicholson KCB

Air Council 31 March 1927 and 1928

The Secretary of State for Air	Lieutenant-Colonel the Rt Hon. Sir Samuel Hoare Bt, CMG, MP
Parliamentary Under-Secretary of State	Major Sir Philip Sassoon Bt, GBE, CMG, MP
Chief of the Air Staff	Marshal of the RAF Sir Hugh Trenchard Bt, GCB, DSO
Air Member for Personnel	Air Vice-Marshal Sir P.W. Game KCB, DSO, p.s.c.
Air Member for Supply and Research	Air Vice-Marshal Sir John F.A. Higgins KBE, CB, DSO, AFC
Secretary	Sir W.F. Nicholson KCB

Air Council 31 March 1929

The Secretary of State for Air	Lieutenant-Colonel the Rt Hon. Sir Samuel Hoare Bt, GBE, CMG, MP
Parliamentary Under-Secretary of State	Major Sir Philip Sassoon Bt, GBE, CMG, MP
Chief of the Air Staff	Marshal of the RAF Sir Hugh Trenchard Bt, GCB, DSO, DCL. LL.D
Air Member for Personnel	Air Chief Marshal Sir John M. Salmond KCB, CMG, CVO, DSO, ADC
Air Member for Supply and Research	Air Vice-Marshal Sir John F.A. Higgins KCB, KBE, DSO, AFC
Secretary	Sir W.F. Nicholson KCB

RAF COMMANDS, 1918 to 1929

August 1918

South-Eastern Area	Major General F.C. Heath Caldwell CB, p.s.c.
South-Western Area	Major General M.E.F. Kerr CB, MVO
Midland Area	Major General J.F.A. Higgins DSO
North-Eastern Area	Major General the Hon. Sir F. Gordon KCB, DSO, p.s.c.
North-Western Area	Major General G.C. Cayley CB

31 March 1919

South-Eastern Area	Colonel (Acting Major-General) T.I. Webb-Bowen CMG
South-Western Area	Colonel (Acting Major-General) C.A.H. Longcroft CMG, DSO, AFC
Midland Area	Colonel (Acting Major-General) C.L. Lambe CMG, DSO
North-Western Area	Major-General G.C. Cayley CB

March 1920

Northern Area	Air Vice-Marshal J.F.A. Higgins CB, DSO, AFC
Southern Area	Air Vice-Marshal Sir J.M. Salmond KCB, CMG, CVO, DSO
No. 11 (Irish) Group	Group Captain I.M. Bonham-Carter OBE
Coastal Area	Air Vice-Marshal A.V. Vyvyan CB, DSO
RAF HQ Cranwell	Air Commodore C.A.H. Longcroft CMG, DSO, AFC
RAF HQ Halton	Air Commodore F.R. Scarlett CB, DSO
Middle East	Air Commodore W.G.H. Salmond DSO
India	Air Commodore T.I. Webb-Bowen CB, CMG
Mediterranean District	Air Commodore O. Swann CB, CBE

April 1920

Inland Area	Air Vice-Marshal Sir J.M. Salmond KCB, CMG, CVO, DSO
No. 11 (Irish) Group	Group Captain I.M. Bonham-Carter OBE
Coastal Area	Air Vice-Marshal A.V. Vyvyan CB, DSO
Middle East	Air Vice-Marshal Sir W.G.H. Salmond KCMG, CB, DSO
Indian Group	Air Commodore T.I. Webb-Bowen CB, CMG
Mediterranean Group	Air Commodore O. Swann CB, CBE
RAF HQ Cranwell	Air Commodore C.A.H. Longcroft CMG, DSO, AFC
RAF HQ Halton	Air Commodore F.R. Scarlett CB, DSO

31 March 1921

Inland Area	Air Vice-Marshal Sir J.M. Salmond KCB, CMG, CVO, DSO
No. 11 (Irish) Group	Group Captain I.M. Bonham-Carter OBE
Coastal Area	Air Vice-Marshal A.V. Vyvyan CB, DSO
RAF HQ Cranwell	Air Commodore C.A.H. Longcroft CMG, DSO, AFC
RAF HQ Halton	Air Commodore F.R. Scarlett CB, DSO
Middle East Area	Air Vice-Marshal Sir W.G.H. Salmond KCMG, CB, DSO
Indian Group	Air Commodore T.I. Webb-Bowen CB, CMG
Mediterranean Group	Group Captain E.L. Gerrard CMG, DSO

31 March 1922

Inland Area	Air Vice-Marshal Sir J.M. Salmond KCB, CMG, CVO, DSO
Coastal Area	Air Vice-Marshal A.V. Vyvyan CB, DSO
RAF HQ Cranwell	Air Commodore C.A.H. Longcroft CMG, DSO, AFC
RAF HQ Halton	Air Commodore F.R. Scarlett CB, DSO
RAF Middle East	Air Vice-Marshal Sir E.L.Ellington KCB, CMG, CBE, p.s.c.
RAF Iraq	Group Captain A.F. Borton CB, CMG, DSO, DFC
RAF India	Air Commodore T.I. Webb-Bowen CB, CMG
Mediterranean Group	Air Commodore C.R. Samson CMG, DSO, AFC
RAF Ireland	Group Captain I.M. Bonham-Carter OBE

31 March 1923

Inland Area	Air Vice-Marshal J.F.A. Higgins CB, DSO, AFC
Coastal Area	Air Vice-Marshal A.V. Vyvyan CB, DSO
RAF HQ Cranwell	Air Commodore C.A.H. Longcroft CMG, DSO, AFC
RAF HQ Halton	Air Commodore F.R. Scarlett CB, DSO
RAF Middle East	Air Vice-Marshal Sir E.L. Ellington KCB, CMG, CBE, p.s.c.
Iraq Command	Air Vice-Marshal Sir J.M. Salmond KCB, CMG, CVO, DSO
RAF India	Air Vice-Marshal P.W. Game CB, DSO, p.s.c.
RAF Mediterranean	Group Captain A.W. Bigsworth CMG, DSO, AFC
Palestine Command	Major-General (temporary Air Vice-Marshal) Sir H.H. Tudor KCB, CMG

31 March 1924

Inland Area	Air Commodore T.I. Webb-Bowen CB, CMG
Coastal Area	Air Vice-Marshal Sir Vyell Vyvyan KCB, DSO
RAF HQ Cranwell	Air Commodore A.F. Borton CB, CMG, DSO, DFC

RAF HQ Halton	Air Commodore C.L. Lambe CB, CMG, DSO
RAF Middle East	Air Vice-Marshal Sir Oliver Swann KCB, CBE.
Iraq Command	Air Marshal Sir J.M. Salmond KCB, CMG, CVO, DSO
RAF India	Air Vice-Marshal Sir E.L. Ellington KCB, CMG, CBE, p.s.c.
RAF Mediterranean	Group Captain A.W. Bigsworth CMG, DSO, AFC
Palestine Command	Air Commodore E.L. Gerrard CMG, DSO

31 March 1925

Air Defences of Great Britain	Air Marshal Sir J.M. Salmond KCB, CMG, CVO, DSO, ADC
Inland Area	Air Commodore T.I. Webb-Bowen CB, CMG
Coastal Area	Air Vice-Marshal F.R. Scarlett CB, DSO
RAF HQ Cranwell	Air Commodore A.F. Borton CB, CMG, DSO, DFC
RAF HQ Halton	Air Commodore C.L. Lambe CB, CMG, DSO
RAF Middle East	Air Vice-Marshal Sir Oliver Swann KCB, CBE.
Iraq Command	Air Vice-Marshal J.F.A. Higgins CB, DSO, AFC
RAF India	Air Vice-Marshal Sir E.L. Ellington KCB, CMG, CBE, p.s.c.
Palestine Command	Air Commodore E.L. Gerrard CMG, DSO

31 March 1926

Air Defences of Great Britain	Air Marshal Sir J.M. Salmond KCB, CMG, CVO, DSO, ADC
Inland Area	Air Vice-Marshal T.I. Webb-Bowen CB, CMG
Coastal Area	Air Vice-Marshal F.R. Scarlett CB, DSO
RAF HQ Cranwell	Air Commodore A.F. Borton CB, CMG, DSO, DFC
RAF HQ Halton	Air Commodore C.L. Lambe CB, CMG, DSO
Special Reserve & Auxiliary Air Force	Air Commodore J.G. Hearson CB, CBE, DSO
RAF Middle East	Air Vice-Marshal Sir Oliver Swann KCB, CBE.
Iraq Command	Air Vice-Marshal J.F.A. Higgins CB, DSO, AFC
RAF India	Air Vice-Marshal Sir E.L. Ellington KCB, CMG, CBE, p.s.c.
RAF Mediterranean	Air Commodore R.H. Clark Hall CMG, DSO, p.s.a
Palestine Command	Air Commodore E.L. Gerrard CMG, DSO

31 March 1927

Air Defences of Great Britain	Air Marshal Sir J.M. Salmond KCB, CMG, CVO, DSO, ADC
Inland Area	Air Vice-Marshal C.A.H. Longcroft CB, CMG, DSO
Coastal Area	Air Vice-Marshal F.R. Scarlett CB, DSO
RAF HQ Cranwell	Air Commodore F.C. Halahan CMG, CBE, DSO, MVO
RAF HQ Halton	Air Commodore C.L. Lambe CB, CMG, DSO
RAF Middle East	Air Vice-Marshal T.I. Webb-Bowen CB, CMG
Iraq Command	Air Vice-Marshal Sir E.L. Ellington KCB, CMG, CBE, p.s.c.
RAF India	Air Vice-Marshal Sir Geoffrey H. Salmond KCB, KCMG, DSO, p.s.c.
RAF Mediterranean	Air Commodore R.H. Clark Hall CMG, DSO, p.s.a

31 March 1928

Air Defences of Great Britain	Air Marshal Sir J.M. Salmond KCB, CMG, CVO, DSO, ADC
Inland Area	Air Vice-Marshal C.A.H. Longcroft CB, CMG, DSO
Coastal Area	Air Vice-Marshal F.R. Scarlett CB, DSO
RAF HQ Cranwell	Air Commodore F.C. Halahan CMG, CBE, DSO, MVO
RAF HQ Halton	Air Commodore C.L. Lambe CB, CMG, DSO
RAF Middle East	Air Vice-Marshal T.I. Webb-Bowen CB, CMG
Iraq Command	Air Vice-Marshal Sir E.L. Ellington KCB, CMG, CBE, p.s.c.
RAF India	Air Vice-Marshal Sir Geoffrey H. Salmond KCB, KCMG, DSO, p.s.c.
RAF Mediterranean	Air Commodore R.H. Clark Hall CMG, DSO, p.s.a
Aden Command	Group Captain W.G.S. Mitchell CBE, DSO, MC, AFC
RAF China	Group Captain E.D.M. Robertson DFC

31 March 1929

Air Defences of Great Britain	Air Vice-Marshal Sir E.L. Ellington KCB, CMG, CBE, p.s.c.
Inland Area	Air Vice-Marshal C.A.H. Longcroft CB, CMG, DSO
Coastal Area	Air Vice-Marshal C.L. Lambe CB,CMG, DSO
RAF HQ Cranwell	Air Vice-Marshal F.C. Halahan CMG, CBE, DSO, MVO
RAF HQ Halton	Air Commodore I.M. Bonham-Carter CB, OBE
RAF Middle East	Air Vice-Marshal T.I. Webb-Bowen CB, CMG
Iraq Command	Air Vice-Marshal Sir Robert Brooke-Popham KCB, CMG, DSO, AFC
RAF India	Air Vice-Marshal Sir Geoffrey H. Salmond KCB, KCMG, DSO, p.s.c.
RAF Mediterranean	Air Commodore J.L. Forbes OBE
Aden Command	Group Captain W.G.S. Mitchell CBE, DSO, MC, AFC

Appendix S
The Air Estimates, Financial Year 1919–20

AIR ESTIMATES.

STATEMENT

BY THE

SECRETARY OF STATE FOR AIR

RELATING TO THE

AIR ESTIMATES FOR THE YEAR 1919-20.

Presented to Parliament by Command of His Majesty.

LONDON:
PUBLISHED BY HIS MAJESTY'S STATIONERY OFFICE.

To be purchased through any Bookseller or directly from
H.M. STATIONERY OFFICE at the following addresses:
Imperial House, Kingsway, London, W.C. 2, and 28, Abingdon Street, London, S.W. 1;
37, Peter Street, Manchester; 1, St. Andrew's Crescent, Cardiff;
23, Forth Street, Edinburgh;
or from E. PONSONBY, Ltd., 116, Grafton Street, Dublin.

1919.

Price 1d. Net.

[Cmd. 483.]

ABSTRACT OF AIR ESTIMATES, 1919 – 1920

> I - NUMBERS

VOTES

Pages 3	Nos. A	TOTAL NUMBER OF OFFICERS AND MEN ON THE ESTABLISHMENT OF THE ROYAL AIR FORE, EXCLUSIVE OF THOSE SERVING IN INDIA	TOTAL NUMBERS (a) 150,000

		II – EFFECTIVE SERVICES	Gross Estimate	Approp- riations In Aid	Net Estimate
			£	£	£
5	1	Pay &c of the Air Force	21,501,000	450,000	21,051,000
8	2	Quartering, Stores (Except technical) supplies, animals and transport	6,712,000	609,000	6,103,000
10	3	Technical and warlike stores	19,867,850	545,000	6,103,000
12	4	Works, buildings and Lands	6,801,000	399,000	6,402,000
15	5	Air Ministry	692,100	100	692,000
22	6	Miscellaneous effective services	204,000	1,000	203,000
		TOTAL EFFECTIVE SERVICES	55,777,950	2,004,100	53,773,850
		III – NON-EFFECTIVE SERVICES			
24	7	Half pay, pensions and other non-effective services	258,000	1,000	257,000
		TOTAL EFFECTIVE AND NON-EFFECTIVE SERVICES	56,035,950	2,005,100	54,030,850

(a)   Number voted by the House of Commons on the 14th March 1919 See Page 3

WINSTON S. CHURCHILL
LONDONDERRY

H.M.TRENCHARD, C.A.S.
F.H.SYKES, C.G.C.A.
E.L.ELLINGTON, D.G.S.R.
J. STEVENSON
Wm. ALEXANDER.

W.A.ROBINSON,
Secretary.

Air Ministry,
10th December, 1919

NUMBER OF OFFICERS, WARRANT OFFICERS, NON-COMMISSIONED OFFICERS AND MEN ON THE ESTABLISHMENT OF THE ROYAL AIR FORCE, EXCLUSIVE OF THOSE SERVING IN INDIA

The House of Commons agreed on the 14th March 1919:-

"That a number of Air Forces, not exceeding 150,000 all ranks, be maintained for the Service of the United Kingdom of Great Britain and Ireland at Home and Abroad, excluding His Majesty's Indian Possessions, during the year ending on the 31st March 1920."

The Maximum Number of Officers and Men on the Establishment of the Royal Air Force at Home and Abroad, exclusive of those serving in India is:-

150,000

This number will be reduced by 31st March 1920 to:-

35,000

STATEMENT showing the Allocation to Air Votes of the sums of £45,000,000 (Vote on Account) and £9,030,850 (Balance of Final Estimate)

Votes	Total Net Estimate	Allocated From Vote On Account	Balance
I – EFFECTIVE SERVICES			
1. Pay &c. of the Air Force	21,051,000	17,533,000	3,518,000
2. Quartering, Stores (except Technical), Supplies, Animals and Transport	6,103,000	5,083,000	1,020,000
3. Technical and Warlike Stores	19,322,850	16,093,000	3,229,850
4. Works, Buildings and Lands	6,402,000	5,332,000	1,070,000
5. Air Ministry	692,000	576,000	116,000
6. Miscellaneous Effective Services	203,000	169,000	34,000
Total Effective Services	53,773,850	44,786,000	8,987,850
II – NON-EFFECTIVE SERVICES			
7. Half-Pay, Pensions, and other Non-effective Services	257,000	214,000	43,000
TOTAL EFFECTIVE AND OTHER NON-EFFECTIVE SERVICES	54,030,850	45,000,000	9,030,850

VOTE 1.

I. ESTIMATE of the Sum which will be required in the Year ending 31st March 1920 to defray the Expense of the Pay, &c of the Air Force.

Twenty-One Million and Fifty-One Thousand Pounds (£21,051,000)

II. Subheads under which this Vote will be accounted for.

	1919-20

		£
A.-	PAY AND PERSONAL ALLOWANCES OF OFFICERS - - - - - - - -	4,600.000
B-	PAY AND PERSONAL ALLOWANCES OF MEN - - - - - - - - - - -	6,400,000
C-	SEPARATION ALLOWANCE - - - - - - - - - - - - - - - - - - -	2,250,000
D-	MISCELLANEOUS ALLOWANCES - - - - - - - - - - - - - - - -	500,000
E-	WOMEN'S ROYAL AIR FORCE - - - - - - - - - - - - - - - - -	900,000
F.	CIVIL EMPLOYEES -	1,601,000
G.	SERVICE GRATUITIES TO OFFICERS , AND TO MEN ON DISCHARGE, &c -	5,100,000
H.	AIR FORCE RESERVE -	30,000
J.	RECRUITING STAFF AND EXPENSES - - - - - - - - - - - - - -	120,000

GROSS TOTAL 21,501,000

Deduct,-

K. APPROPRIATIONS IN AID - 450,000

NET TOTAL - - - - - - £21,051,000

A- PAY AND PERSONAL ALLOWANCES OF OFFICERS:

	1919 – 1920 £

Average Number Throughout the Year 1919 – 1920		1919 – 1920 £
	1. Staff (excluding Air Ministry -)	
	2. Flying Branch (including grants for Air Pilot's Certificates))	
8,830	3. Technical and Administrative Branches (including Physical)	– 4,110,000
	Training Branch, Chaplains, Officiating Clergy and any)	
	Other officers, &c., not otherwise classified) - - - - - - - -)	
	4. Medical (includes Nurses, Civil Medical Practitioners, pay)	
	of V.A.D. and Dental Treatment and Services) - - - - - - - -)	
	5. Allowances (includes all personal Allowances drawn in cash and commuted ration allowance.) - - - - - - - - - - - - -	450,000
	Charges in respect of Pay and Allowances, during the financial Year 1918-19, of officers loaned by Canada to the Air Force -	40,000

	4,600,000

B – PAY AND PERSONAL ALLOWANCES OF MEN

Average Number throughout the year 1919-1920		1919 – 1920 £
59,600	Pay and personal Allowances, including commuted ration allowance and cadets' messing allowance - - - - - - - - - - - - -	6,260,000
	Allowances in lieu of plain clothes on demobilisation - - - - -	140,000
		6,400,000

C – SEPARATION ALLOWANCE -

	2,250,000

D – MISCELLANEOUS ALLOWANCES :

1.   Outfit allowances:-
Payments in respect of compensation for sums expended on outfits by Flight Cadets, Cadets and Colonial Cadets who, owing to the cessation of hostilities, have not been commissioned, or who will be commissioned and repatriated to their country - **470,000**
Probable charges in respect of new commissions during 1919 – 1920 - - **5,000**

2.   Other allowances:-
Charges in respect of Funeral Expenses, Contingent Allowances for men and WRAF and grants in aid of formations of officers' and sergeants' messes, &c., - **25,000**

E – WOMEN'S ROYAL AIR FORCE

	500,000

Average Number throughout the year 1919 – 1920		1919 – 1920 £
9,450	Pay and personal Allowances of officers and members of W.R.A.F. and payments in respect of demobilisation benefits –	900,000

F – CIVIL EMPLOYEES

		1919 – 20
Average Number throughout the Year 1919 –20		£
8,500	Pay and personal Allowances of all Civil Employees, male and female, and Police	1,601,000

G – SERVICE GRATUITIES TO OFFICERS, AND TO MEN ON DISCHARGE:

Payments in respect of Service and War Gratuities to officers and men:-

(i)	Officers -	3,000,000
(ii)	N.C.O.'s and men -	2,100,000
		5,100,000

H – AIR FORCE RESERVE:

To meet probable charges in respect of a certain number of men entitled to enter the Air Force Reserve during the year on expiration of their Colour Service - 30,000

J – RECRUITING STAFF EXPENSES

Number 1919-20		
	Pay, &c., of Recruiting Staff -	21,000
109	Recruiting Advertisements and Contingent Expenses of Recruiting -	15,000
	Recruiting Rewards, fees, &c on enlistment of recruits for Royal Air Force -	4,000
	Bounties on re-engagement or extension of service - - - - - - - - -	80,000
		120,000

K – APPROPRIATIONS IN AID

Miscellaneous receipts - 450,000

Vote 2

QUARTERING, STORES (EXCEPT TECHNICAL), SUPPLIES, ANIMALS, AND TRANSPORT

I   AN ESTIMATE of the Sum which will be required in the Year ending 31st March, 1920, to defray the Expense of QUARTERING, STORES (except TECHNICAL), SUPPLIES, ANIMALS, AND TRANSPORT.

Six Million One Hundred and Three Thousand Pounds (£6,103,000)

II   SUBHEADS under which the Vote will be accounted for.

	1919 – 20 £
A – HIRE OF BUILDINGS -	190,000
B - BILLETING -	10,000
C - BARRACK SERVICES -	46,000
D - FUEL AND LIGHT -	400,000
E - GENERAL STORES -	720,000
F - CLOTHING -	2,195,000
G - PROVISIONS AND FORAGE - - - - - - - - - - - - - - - - - - -	1,755,000
H - HORSES -	1,000
J - MEDICAL SERVICES -	195,000
K - TRANSPORT -	1,200,000
Deduct:- GROSS TOTAL	6,712,000
L - APPROPRIATIONS IN AID -	**609,000**
NET TOTAL	6,103,000

III   DETAILS of the foregoing

	1919 – 20
	£
A – HIRE OF BUILDINGS: Probable charges in respect of Hire of Buildings, including compensatory payments made for buildings taken under the Defence of the Realm Regulations , and compensation for damage -	190,000
B- BILLETING: Payments made for billets, provided under the Air Force Act, i.e., through police agency as therein laid down -	10,000
C - BARRACK SERVICES: 1. Water -	20,000
2. Scavenging, sanitary services, window cleaning, sweeping chimneys, cleaning allowances, and washing charges - - - - - - - - - - - - - - - - - -	26,000
	46,000
D - FUEL AND LIGHT: Fuel and light for general use, including rent of, and fees for testing, electric light and gas meters and charges for electric current, gas, coal, candles etc.,	400,000
E – GENERAL STORES: 1. Equipment and miscellaneous stores (i.e., for equipment of personnel or horses and all general stores not included in (2) - - - - - - - - - - - - - - -	230,000
2. Accommodation stores (i.e., furniture, barrack equipment &c.), including Washing and repairing of Camp bedding by the Army Ordnance Dept. - -	490,000
	720,000
F – CLOTHING: Cost of clothing, including payments for repair of clothing and boots at Unit's Stations: 1. Royal Air Force -	2,150,000
2. Women's Royal Air Force -	45,000
	2,195,000
G – PROVISIONS AND FORAGE: 1. Provisions, including cost of diets in Royal Air Force hospitals - - - - - - -	1,750,000
2. Forage, including cost of paillasse -	5,000
	1,755,000
H – HORSES: Purchase and upkeep of horses, including cost of veterinary medicines and Appliances; also horse hire -	1,000
J - MEDICAL SERVICES : 1. Medical stores and Supplies, including cost of medicines, surgical instruments and requisites -	45,000
2. Hospital Charges in respect of Army and Civil Hospitals - - - - - - - - - -	150,000
	195,000
K - TRANSPORT: 1. Charges for movement of Personnel by land and sea, and compensation for damage arising from Mechanical Transport, movement of troops &c.,	900,000
2. Charges for carriage of Stores, Supplies, Animals, &c., by land and sea.	300,000
	1,200,000
L – APPROPRIATIONS IN AID: Miscellaneous Receipts allocated to the various Subheads as follows: 1. Subheads A – D -	2,000
2. Subheads E & F -	545,000
3. Subheads G to J -	60,000
4. Subhead K -	2,000
	609,000

Vote 3.

TECHNICAL AND WARLIKE STORES

I – AN ESTIMATE of the Sum which will be required in the Year ending 31st March 1920, to defray the Expense of TECHNICAL AND WARLIKE STORES.

Nineteen Million, Three Hundred and Twenty-two Thousand, Eight Hundred and Fifty Pounds (£19,322,850)

II -   SUBHEADS under which this Vote will be accounted for.

	1919 – 1920
	£
A – AEROPLANES , SEAPLANES, ENGINES AND SPARES - - - - - - - - - - - - -	1,413,000
A(A) – AIRSHIPS, AIRSHIP ENGINES AND SPARES - - - - - - - - - - - - - - - - -	144,000
B - BALLOONS, WINCHES AND SPARES -	72,300
C - AIRCRAFT TECHNICAL AND WARLIKE STORES - - - - - - - - - - - - - - -	158,550
D - ARMAMENT AND AMMUNITION -	168,200
E - ELECTRICAL AND ENGINEERING STORES - - - - - - - - - - - - - - - - - - -	169,700
F - HANGARS -	64,500
G - MECHANICAL AND OTHER TRANSPORT -	23,000
H - MARINE CRAFT AND EQUIPMENT -	7,500
J - PETROL AND OIL -	1,522,100
K - REWARDS TO INVENTORS -	25,000
L – AIRCRAFT SUPPLIES DELIVERED UNDER WAR CONTRACTS - - - - - -	16,100,000
M – AIRCRAFT INSPECTION DEPARTMENTS , SALARIES AND WAGES - -	———
N - R.A.E. FARNBOROUGH, SALARIES AND WAGES - - - - - - - - - - - - - - -	———
GROSS TOTAL Deduct:-	19,867,850
O - APPROPRIATIONS IN AID -	545,000
NET TOTAL	19,322,850

III - Details of Technical and Warlike Stores	1919 – 20 £
A – AEROPLANES, SEAPLANES, ENGINES AND SPARES - - - - - - - - - - - - -	1,413,000
A (A) – AIRSHIPS, AIRSHIP ENGINES AND SPARES - - - - - - - - - - - - - - -	144,000
B – BALLOONS, WINCHES AND SPARES -	72,300
C – AIRCRAFT, TECHNICAL, AND WARLIKE STORES :	
1. Instruments -	65,800
2. Photographic Equipment -	10,750
3. Miscellaneous -	82,000
	158.550
D – ARMAMENT AND AMMUNITION:	
1. Armament -	152,700
2. Ammunition -	15,500
	168,200
E – ELECTRICAL AND ENGINEERING STORES:	
1. Wireless -	54,400
2. Electrical Equipment -	37,800
3. Telephone and Telegraphic Stores - - - - - - - - - - - - - - - - - -	500
4. Machine Tools -	65,500
5. Miscellaneous -	11,500
	169,700
F – HANGARS -	64,500
G – MECHANICAL AND OTHER TRANSPORT - - - - - - - - - - - - - - - - - -	23,000
H – MARINE CRAFT AND EQUIPMENT -	7,500
J - PETROL AND OIL :	
1. Petrol -	1,294,100
2. Lubricants -	228,000
	1,522,100
K - REWARDS FOR INVENTORS -	25,000
L - AIRCRAFT SUPPLIES DELIVERED UNDER WAR CONTRACTS - - - - -	16,100,000
M - AIRCRAFT INSPECTION DEPARTMENT – SALARIES AND WAGES - -	———
N - ROYAL AIRCRAFT ESTABLISHMENT, FARNBOROUGH, SALARIES AND WAGES	———
O - APPROPRIATIONS IN AID -	545,000

Vote 4

WORKS AND BUILDINGS

I   ESTIMATE of the Sum which will be required in the Year ending 31st March
1920, to defray the Expense of Works, Buildings, Repairs, and Lands,
including Civilian Staff and other Charges connected forthwith.

Six Million Four Hundred and Two Thousand Pounds.
(£6,402,000)

II   SUBHEADS under which this Vote will be accounted for.

		1919 – 20
		£
A. -	STAFF FOR WORKS SERVICES	155,000
	Part I	
B.-	NEW WORKS, ADDITIONS, ALTERATIONS, AND SPECIAL REPAIRS AMOUNTING TO £2,000 EACH AND UPWARDS	5,072,000
	Part II	
C.-	MINOR NEW WORKS, ADDITIONS, AND ALTERATIONS UNDER £2,000 EACH	135,000
	Part III	
D.-	ORDINARY REPAIRS AND MAINTENANCE	921,000
E.-	GRANTS-IN-AID OF WORKS	5,000
F.-	PURCHASES OF LANDS AND BUILDINGS	217,000
G.-	RENTS, COMPENSATIONS, AND REINSTATEMENTS	248,000
H.-	INCIDENTAL EXPENSES OF AIR MINISTRY ESTATES	2,000
J.-	PROVISION OF TELEGRAPH AND TELEPHONE SERVICES	10,000
K.-	MISCELLANEOUS WORKS SERVICES	30,000
L.-	PURCHASES OF STORES AND PLANT FOR WORKS (NET)	6,000
	Gross Total	6,801,000
	Deduct:-	
M.-	APPROPRIATIONS IN AID	399.000
	Net Total - - -£	6,402,000

Vote 4. WORKS, BUILDINGS AND LANDS – continued

	1919-20
A.- STAFF FOR WORKS SERVICES - - - - - - - - - - - - -	£155,000

B.- PART I – NEW WORKS, ADDITIONS, ALTERATIONS, AND SPECIAL REPAIRS AMOUNTING TO £2,000 AND UPWARDS.

(i) Reconstruction works:-

STATION	DESCRIPTION OF WORK	Total Estimate for the	To be voted in 1919-20	Further amount required for completing the work
		£	£	£
Cattewater	1. Sea wall -	2,500	2,500	-
Cranwell	1. Alterations to huts, and mess deck for cadets' Accommodation -	18,000	18,000	-
Halton Park	1. Additional work to put camp in sanitary condition -	40,000	40,000	-
	2. Isolation Hospital; structural alterations for Southern Area -	4,000	4,000	-
	3. Boys' Training Establishment - - - - - - - - - - - -	1,290,000	20,000	1,270,000
Old Sarum	1. Alterations and additions to Group Clearing Station -	4,350	4,350	-
Biggin Hill	1. Electric lighting, battery room and earthing System -	6,400	6,400	-
Bircham Newton	1. Electric lighting and battery room - - - - - - - - -	3,700	3,700	-
Henlow	1. Electric lighting and battery room - - - - - - - - -	7,400	7,400	-
Martlesham Heath	1. Electric lighting and battery room - - - - - - - - -	2,050	2,050	-
Netheravon	1. Completion of large flight shed, electric lighting, battery room, and sewage disposal	22,500	12,500	10,000
Shrewsbury	1. Electric lighting, power mains and battery room	7,700	7,700	-
Uxbridge	1. Electric lighting -	2,000	2,000	-
Hawkinge	1. Completion of two flight sheds, electric Lighting and battery room - - - - - - - - - - - -	18,000	18,000	-
Stonehenge	Electric lighting and battery room - - - - - - - - -	2,050	2,050	-
Calshot	1. Electric lighting -	7,000	7,000	-
Felixstowe	1. Electric lighting -	4,550	4,550	
Grain	1. Completion of flying boat shed and pavings &c., - - - - - - - - - -	7,000	6,000	1,000
	2. Additional electric lighting and power for Station -	9,300	9,300	-
Uxbridge	1. Accommodation for records - - - - - - - - - - - -	3,500	3,500	-
Donibristle	1. Repairs to breakwater and locomotive shed - - -	5,000	5,000	-
	Total item (1) (Carried forward) £ --		186,000	

Vote 5.

I ESTIMATE of the sum which will be required in the Year ending 31st March 1920,
To defray the Expense of the AIR MINISTRY

Six Hundred and Ninety- two Thousand Pounds (£692,000.)

II SUBHEADS under which this Vote will be accounted for.

	1919 – 20
	£
A.- SALARIES AND ALLOWANCES OF THE AIR MINISTRY - - - - - - - -	613,323
B.- PAY OF MESSENGERS AND PORTERS - - - - - - - - - - - - - - - - -	76,777
C.- CONTINGENT EXPENSES -	2,000
GROSS TOTAL - - - - -	692,100
Deduct:- D.- APPROPRIATIONS IN AID -	100
NET TOTAL - - - - - - -	692,000

ABSTRACT OF SUBHEAD A.- Salaries and Allowances

	ESTIMATE 1919 – 20
	£
AIR COUNCIL -	15,998
DEPARTMENT OF THE SECRETARY -	68,198
FINANCE DEPARTMENT -	84,703
DEPARTMENT OF THE CHIEF OF AIR STAFF- - - - - - - - - - - - - - - -	186,721
DIRECTORATE OF MEDICAL SERVICES - - - - - - - - - - - - - -	11,264
DIRECTORATE OF WORKS AND BUILDINGS- - - - - - - - - - - - -	110,747
AIR INVENTIONS BRANCH -	2,244
DEPARTMENT OF THE CONTROLLER-GENERAL OF CIVIL AVIATION	38,523
DEPARTMENT OF THE DIRECTOR GENERAL OF SUPPLY AND RESEARCH- -	-
AIR DIVISION , ADMIRALTY -	3,239
HEADQUARTERS OF THE WOMEN'S ROYAL AIR FORCE - - - - - - - -	5,407
TYPING SECTION -	30,906
WAR BONUS -	48,000
OVERTIME -	7,373
TOTAL - - - - - - - - - - - - £	613,323

A, - SALARIES AND ALLOWANCES OF THE AIR MINISTRY - continued

Numbers 1919-20		Minimum £	Increment £	Maximum £	ESTIMATE 1919-20 £
	Brought forward - - - - - -				187,906
	DEPARTMENT OF THE CHIEF OF AIR STAFF - continued				
	DIRECTORATE OF TRAINING AND ORGANIZAION				
1	Director of Training and (Prior to 1/8/19 - - - - - - - - -	1,500	-	1,500 }	1,833
	Organization (From 1/8/19 - - - - - - - - - - -	2,000	-	2,000 }	
2	Directors (for one month) - - - - - - - - - - - - - - - - -	(c.) 1,200	-	1,200	200
2	Deputy Directors (for one month) - - - - - - - - - - - - -	(c) 950	-	950	158
4	Staff Officers, 1st Class (for one month) - - - - - - - - - -	(c) 800	-	800	267
14	Staff Officers, 2nd Class (for one month) - - - - - - - - - -	(c) 650	-	650	759
12	Staff Officers, 3rd Class (for one month) - - - - - - - - - -	(c) 500	-	500	500
2	Staff Officers, 4th Class (for one month) - - - - - - - - - -	(c) 400	-	400	67
1	Staff Officer, 2nd Class (for three months) - - - - - - - - -	(c) 650	-	650	163
1	Staff Officer, 3rd Class (for three months) - - - - - - - - -	(c) 500	-	500	125
2	Deputy Directors (for 11 {prior to 1/8/19 - - - - - - - - - -	1,000	-	1,000 }	2,500
	Months) - - - - - - - - - { From 1/8/19 - - - - - - -	1,500	-	1,500 }	
4	Staff Officers, 1st Class (for 11 months) - - - - - - - - - -	(c) 800	-	800	2,934
7	Staff Officers, 2nd Class (for 11 months) - - - - - - - - - -	(c) 650	-	650	4,171
11	Staff Officers, 3rd Class (for 11 months) - - - - - - - - - -	(c) 500	-	500	5,042
1	Staff Officer, 4th Class (for 11 months) - - - - - - - - - -	(c) 400	-	400	367
-	Attached Officers (g) -	RAF Pay and Allowances			
-	Army of Occupation Bonus to Officers - - - - - - - - - - -	-	-	-	1,902
29	Temporary Employees -	-	-		4,698
-	National Health Insurance Contributions - - - - - - - - - -	-	-		18
	DIRECTORATE OF PERSONNEL				
1	Director of Personnel - - -{Prior to 1/8/19 - - - - - - - - -	1,500	-	1,500 }	1,833
	(From 1/1/19 - - - - - - - - - -	2,000	-	2,000 }	
1	Director (for three months) - - - - - - - - - - - - - - - - -	(c) 1,200	-	1.200	300
7	Staff Officers, 1st Class for one month) - - - - - - - - - -	(c) 800	-	800	467
19	Staff Officers, 2nd Class for one month) - - - - - - - - - -	(c) 650	-	650	1,029
13	Staff Officers, 3rd Class(for one month) - - - - - - - - - -	(c) 500	-	500	542
1	Director (for three months) - - - - - - - - - - - - - - - - -	(c) 1,200	-	1,200	300
1	Deputy Director (for 11 months) { prior to 1/8/19 - - - - -	1,000	-	1,000 }	1,250
	{from 1/8/19 - - - - - -	1,500	-	1,500 }	
4	Staff Officers, 1st Class(for 11 months) - - - - - - - - - -	(c) 800	-	800	2,934
10	Staff Officers, 2nd Class (for 11 months) - - - - - - - - - -	(c) 650	-	650	5,959
7	Staff Officers, 3rd Class (for 11 months) - - - - - - - - - -	(c) 500	-	500	3,209
2	Staff Officers, 4th Class (for 11 months) - - - - - - - - - -	(c) 400	-	400	734
1	Chaplain-in-Chief -	(c)1,000	-	1,000	1,000
-	Attached Officers (g) -	RAF Pay and Allowances			
-	Army of Occupation Bonus to Officers - - - - - - - - - - -	-	-	-	2,119
3	Ex-Soldier Clerks, Class "A" - - - - - - - - - - - - - - - -	49s	3s	70s	453
1	Ex- Soldier Clerk, Class "B" - - - - - - - - - - - - - - - -	31s 6d	1s 6d	42s	90
210	Temporary Employees -	-	-	-	33,041
-	National Health Insurance Contributions - - - - - - - - - -	-	-	-	120
	DIRECTORATE OF EQUIPMENT				
1	Director of Equipment { Prior to 1/8/19 - - - - - - - - - -	1,500	-	1,500 }	1,833
	{From 1/8/19 - - - - - - - - -	2,000	-	2,000 }	
2	Directors (for one month) - - - - - - - - - - - - - - - - - -	(c)1,200	-	1,200	200
3	Deputy Directors (for one month) - - - - - - - - - - - - - -	(c) 950	-	950	158
9	Staff Officer, 1st Class (for one month) - - - - - - - - - -	(c) 800	-	800	600
26	Staff Officers, 2nd Class (for one month) - - - - - - - - - -	(c) 650	-	650	1,408
25	Staff Officers, 3rd Class (for one month) - - - - - - - - - -	(c) 500	-	500	1,042
8	Staff Officers, 4th Class (for one month) - - - - - - - - - -	(c) 400	-	400	267
1	Deputy Director (for 11 months) {Prior to 1/8/19 - - - - -	1,000	-	1,000 }	1,250
	{From 1/8/19 - - - - - -	1,500	-	1,500 }	
1	Deputy Director (for 11 months) {Prior to 1/8/19 - - - - -	1,000	-	1,000 }	1,050
	{From 1/8/19 - - - - - -	1,200	-	1,200 }	
11	Staff Officers, 1st Class (for 11 months) - - - - - - - - - -	(c) 800	-	800	8,067
20	Staff Officers, 2nd Class (for 11 months) - - - - - - - - - -	(c) 650	-	650	11,917
	Carried Forward - - - - - - - - - - - - - - - - - - -	-		-	296.782

A, - SALARIES AND ALLOWANCES OF THE AIR MINISTRY - continued

Numbers 1919-20		SALARY			ESTIMATE 1919 – 20
		Minimum	Increment	Maximum	
		£	£	£	£
	Brought forward - - - - - -	- - - - - -	- - - - - -	- - - - - -	296,782
	DEPARTMENT OF THE CHIEF OF AIR STAFF - continued				
	DIRECTORATE OF EQUIPMENT – continued.				
33	Staff Officers, 3rd Class (for 11 months) - - - - - - - - - - -	(c) 500	-	500	15,125
9	Staff Officers, 4th Class (for 11 months) - - - - - - - - - -	(c.) 400	-	400	200
-	Attached Officers (g) =	RAF Pay and Allowances			
-	Army of Occupation Bonus to Officers - - - - - - - - - - -	-	-	-	5,969
1	Ex-Soldier Clerk, Class "B" - - - - - - - - - - - - - - - - -	31s 6d	1s 6d	42s	87
150	Temporary Employees -	-	-	-	22,658
-	National Health Insurance Contributions - - - - - - - - - - -	-	-	-	98
	DIRECTORATE OF DEMOBILISATION				
1	Director of Demobilisation (for six months) - - - - - - - - -	(c) 1,200	-	1,200	600
1	Deputy Director (for one month) - - - - - - - - - - - - - - - - -	(c) 950	-	950	79
3	Staff Officers, 1st Class (for six months) - - - - - - - - - - - -	(c) 800	-	800	1,200
9	Staff Officers, 2nd Class (for six months) - - - - - - - - - - -	(c) 650	-	650	2,925
12	Staff Officers, 3rd Class(for six months) - - - - - - - - - - -	(c) 500	-	500	3,000
-	Attached Officers (g) -	RAF Pay and Allowances			
-	Army of Occupation Bonus to Officers - - - - - - - - - - -	-	-	-	1,051
36	Temporary Employees -	-	-	-	2,732
-	National Health Insurance Contributions - - - - - - - - - - -	-	-	-	14
	DIRECTORATE OF MEDICAL SERVICES				
1	Director (for 11 months) { prior to 1/8/19 - - - - - - - - - - -	1,500	-	1,500	)
	{from 1/8/19 - - - - - - -	2,000	-	2,000	) 1,833
1	Deputy Director (for 11 months) { prior to 1/8/19 - - - - -	900	-	900	}
	{from 1/8/19 - - - - - -	1,200	-	1,200	} 1,100
4	Staff Officers, 1st Class (for five months) - - - - - - - - - - -	(c) 800	-	800	1,333
1	Staff Officer, 2nd Class (for five months) - - - - - - - - - - -	(c) 650	-	650	271
1	Staff Officer, 1st Class (for seven months) - - - - - - - - -	-	-	-	467
2	Staff Officers, 2nd Class (for seven months) - - - - - - - - -	-	-	-	758
-	Army of Occupation Bonus to Officers - - - - - - - - - - -	-	-	-	346
1	Woman Medical Officer -	(c) 700	-	700	700
1	Principal Matron -	300	15	350	300
26	Temporary Employees -	-	-	-	3,706
-	National Health Insurance Contributions - - - - - - - - - - -	-	-	-	15
	ALLOWANCES				
-	To two Acting Staff Clerks lent from the Admiralty	-	-	-	235
-	To Officer on loan from National Medical Research Committee	-	-	-	200
	DIRECTORATE OF WORKS AND BUILDINGS				
1	Director (for nine months) -	1,500	-	1,500	1,125
	Established staff:-				
1	Acting Director of Marine Works - - - - - - - - - - - - - -	1,000	-	1,000	1,000
1	Acting Assistant Director of Marine Works - - - - - - - -	800	-	800	800
1	Acting Superintending Civil Engineer - - - - - - - - - - - -	650	-	650	650
1	Civil Engineer -	400	20	625	426
1	Acting Civil Engineer -	400	-	400	400
1	Assistant Civil Engineer -	200	15	400	320
1	Chief Surveyor -	600	25	800	625
2	Surveyors -	400	20	600	1,270
1	Staff Clerk -	350	15	450	365
2	Minor Staff Clerks -	200	10	300	434
3	First Class Draughtsmen - - - - - - - - - - - - - - - - - - -	320	15	400	800
	Carried Forward - - - - - - - - - - - - - - - - - - -				375,099

A, - SALARIES AND ALLOWANCES OF THE AIR MINISTRY - continued

Numbers 1919-20		SALARY			ESTIMATE 1919 – 20
		Minimum	Increment	Maximum	
		£	£	£	£
	Brought forward - - - - - -	- -			375,099
	DIRECTORATE OF WORKS AND BUILDINGS continued				
	Quasi-Permanent				
2	Civil Engineers -3	400	-	600	1,020
	Assistant Civil Engineers -	200	-	400	930
1	Acting Minor Staff Clerk - - - - - - - - - - - - - - - - - 19	200	10	300	210
	Draughtsmen -3	130	10	300	4,396
	Accountant Clerks,2ⁿᵈ Class- - - - - - - - - - - - - - - - -	6s 6d a day.	-	13s a day	554
1	Ex-Soldier Clerk, Class A -	49s	3s	70s	166
3	Ex-Soldier Clerk, Class B - - - - - - - - - - - - - - - - - - - 1	31s 6d	1s 6d	42s	293
	Surveyors Clerk -	35s	-	87s 6d	182
	Temporary Staff:-				
310	Staff Officers, Technical , Administrative, and Clerical Staff -	-	-	-	85,769
	Army of Occupation Bonus -	-	-	-	8,935
	National Health Insurance Contributions - - - - - - - - - -	-	-	-	77
	AIR INVENTIONS BRANCH				
1	Vice-Chairman (for six months) - - - - - - - - - - - - - - - -	-	-	-	255
1	Assistant Principal (for six months) - - - - - - - - - - - - -	600	25	800	300
		(400	20	600 }	
2	Examiners (for six months) - - - - - - - - - - - - - - - - - -	(350	15	500 }	575
5	Temporary Employees -	-	-	-	1,067
-	National Health Insurance Contributions - - - - - - - - - - -	-	-	-	2
	ALLOWANCE				
-	To Chief Examiner lent from Patent Office - - - - - - - - - -	-	-	-	45
	DEPARTMENT OF THE CONTROLLER- GENERAL OF CIVIL AVIATION				
2	Controllers (for 11 months) - - - - - - - - - - - - - - - - - -	1,800	-	1,800	3,300
1	Controller -	1,500	-	1,500	1,500
4	Deputy Controllers (for five months) - - - - - - - - - - - -	1,500	-	1,500	2,500
2	Senior Assistants (for six months) - - - - - - - - - - - - -	800	-	800	800
8	Senior Assistants (for 11 months) - - - - - - - - - - - - - -	800	-	800	5,900
25	Junior Assistants (for 11 months) - - - - - - - - - - - - - -	300	-	700	12,600
2	Staff Clerks -	350	15	450	800
2	Minor Staff Clerks -	200	10	300	500
14	Assistant Clerks -	50	5	85 }	
			71. 10s	130 }	980
63			10	200 }	
37	Temporary Employees - - - -				9,000
-	National Health Insurance Contributions - - - - - - - - - - -	-	-	-	43
	Allowances ;-				
-	To two Senior Assistants (for six months) - - - - - - - - -	200	-	200	200
-	To four Junior Assistants and Senior Assistants for flying duties - - -	100	-	100	400
	Carried Forward - - - - - - - - - - - - - - - - - - -				518,398

A, - SALARIES AND ALLOWANCES OF THE AIR MINISTRY - continued

Numbers
1919-20

	Minimum	Increment	Maximum	ESTIMATE 1919 – 20
	SALARY			
	£	£	£	£
Brought forward - - - - - -				518,398
DEPARTMENT OF THE DIRECTOR-GENERAL OF SUPPLY AND RESEARCH. (h)				
AIR DIVISION ADMIRALTY				
1. Director (for six months) - - - - - - - - - - - - - -	(c) 1,500	-	1,500	750
1 Staff Officer, 1st Class (for six months) - - - - -	(c) 800	-	800	400
3 Staff Officers, 2nd Class (for six months) - - - -	(c) 650	-	650	975
3 Staff Officers, 3rd Class (for six months) - - - -	(c) 500	-	500	750
Army of Occupation Bonus - - - - - - - - - - -	-	-	-	364
TYPING SECTION	135	5	150	138
1 Controller of Typing Staff - - - - - - - - - - - - -	135	5	150	414
3 Acting Chief Superintendents - - - - - - - - - - -	50s	-	50s	130
1 Superintendent - - - - - - - - - - - - - - - - - -	-	-	-	30,012
230 Temporary Employees - - - - - - - - - - - - - - -	-	-	-	150
- National Health Insurance Contributions - - -				
ALLOWANCE				
To Controller -	-	-	-	62
HEADQUARTERS STAFF OF WOMEN'S ROYAL AIR FORCE				
Salaries of Officers and Members - - - - - - - -	-	-	-	5,407
MISCELLANEOUS				
War Bonus -	-	-	-	48,000
Overtime -	-	-	-	3,373
TOTAL SUBHEAD A. - - -£				613,323
B.- PAY OF MESSENGERS, PORTERS, CLEANERS, &c				
- Temporary Male Messengers - - - - - - - - - - -	-	-	-	23,700
- Cleaners and Lavatory Attendants - - - - - - -	-	-	-	13,750
- National Health Insurance Contributions - - -	-	-	-	327
- War Bonus -	-	-	-	36,000
- Overtime -	-	-	-	3,000
TOTAL SUBHEAD B- - - -£				76,777
C.- CONTINGENT EXPENSES OF AIR MINISTRY				
- Constables on duty at the Air Ministry - - - - -	-	-	-	1,600
- Newspapers, press cuttings, &c - - - - - - - - - -	-	-	-	100
- Washing of Towels, dusters &c - - - - - - - - - -	-	-	-	200
- Miscellaneous -	-	-	-	100
TOTAL SUB HEAD, C - £				2,000
D.- APPROPRIATIONS IN AID				
- Miscellaneous receipts - - - - - - - - - - - - - - -	-	-	- £	100

Vote 6.

MISCELLANEOUS EFFECTIVE SERVICES

I   AN ESTIMATE of the Sum which will be required in the Year ending 31st March 1920, to defray the Expense of MISCELLANEOUS EFFECTIVE SERVICES.

II   SUBHEADS under which this Vote will be accounted for.

		1919-20 £
A.-	FIELD INTELLIGENCE -	1,000
B.-	COMPENSATION FOR LOSSES , &c., - - - - - - - - - - - - - - - - - - - -	26,000
C.-	LOSSES BY EXCHANGE, &c., -	20,000
D.-	MEDALS -	52,000
E.-	POSTAL, TELEGRAPHIC AND TELEPHONE CHARGES - - - - - - -	20,000
F.-	ADVERTISEMENTS -	3,000
G.-	MISCELLANEOUS -	53,000
G. (G) -	GRANT FOR METEOROLOGICAL OFFICE - - - - - - - - - - - - - - - -	12,000
H. (E) -	EXTRA REGULATION EXPENDITURE - - - - - - - - - - - - - - - - - - -	1,000
H. (P)	PRISONERS OF WAR -	1,000
H. (H)	DEMOBILISATION EDUCATION SCHEME - - - - - - - - - - - - - - - -	15,000
	GROSS TOTAL - -	204,000
J.	*Deduct* APPROPRIATIONS IN AID -	1,000
	NET TOTAL - - - - -	203,000

III   DETAILS of the foregoing.

	1919-20
A.- FIELD INTELLIGENCE	1,000
B.- COMPENSATION FOR LOSSES:-	
1. Compensation to officers and men	1,000
2. Compensation to civilians for personal injuries, and gratuities to Widows &c., of civilians accidentally killed	15,000
3. Compensation to others for losses, damage to property by Aeroplanes, and incidental expenses relating thereto	10,000
	26,000
C.- LOSSES BY EXCHANGE &c.:	
Discounts and losses by Exchange; Commission to local banks for Supply of Specie &c.,	20,000
D.- MEDALS	
Cost of medals and incidental expenses in connection with the supply of medals and decorations	52,000
E.- POSTAL, TELEGRAPHIC AND TELEPHONE CHARGES:	
Expenditure on Postage, Foreign Telegraphic Communications, and for rental &c., of Telephone lines installed other than at the Air Ministry	20,000
F.- ADVERTISEMENTS:	
Advertisements in Newspapers	3,000
G.- MISCELLANEOUS:	
Awards for apprehension of Deserters; legal expenses, Charitable Grants in Aid or Institutions. &c., Charge for Death Certificates; Haircutting; Motor Licences, &c.,	53,000
G (G).- GRANT FOR METEOROLOGICAL OFFICE:	
Grant towards the expenses of the Meteorological Office, to supplement the grant of £47,000 from Civil Service Estimates, Class 4, Vote 8, Subhead B	12,000
H.(E) - EXTRA REGULATION EXPENDITURE:	
To meet charges against the amount placed at the disposal of the Secretary of State for the expenditure of small sums for air purposes not covered by regulation without reference to the Treasury.	1,000
H (P).- PRISONERS OF WAR:	
To meet charges in respect of Prisoners of War	1,000
H (H).- DEMOBILISATION EDUCATION SCHEME:	
Pay of Civilian Staff, Grants to Local Education Authorities, cost of Text Books, Apparatus, &c., and other incidental Expenses in connection with The Education Scheme	15,000
J.- APPROPRIATIONS IN AID:	
Miscellaneous receipts, including amounts received to replace lost Medals and gains by Exchange, &c.,	1,000

NON-EFFECTIVE SERVICES

Vote 7.

HALF PAY, PENSIONS, AND OTHER NON-EFFECTIVE SERVICES

I   AN ESTIMATE of the Sum which will be required in the Year ending 31st March 1920 to defray the Expense of Rewards; Half Pay; Retired Pay; Widows' Pensions; and other Non-Effective Services

Two Hundred and Fifty-seven Thousand Pounds (£257,000)

II   Subheads under which this Vote will be accounted for.

	1919-20
	£
A.- REWARDS TO OFFICERS, WARRANT OFFICERS, NON-COMMISSIONED OFFICERS AND MEN - - - - - - - - - - - - - - - - - - -	300
B.- HALF PAY OF OFFICERS -	1,400
C.- RETIRED PAY OF OFFICERS -	10,800
D.- PENSIONS AND GRATUITIES TO WOUNDED OFFICERS - - - - - - - - - -	233,000
E.- SERVICES PENSIONS (MEN) -	3,000
F,- PENSIONS AND COMPASSIONATE ALLOWANCES TO WIDOWS AND CHILDREN -	500
G.- GRANTS UNDER THE SUPERANNUATION ACTS - - - - - - - - - - - - - - -	2,000
H.- PAYMENTS UNDER THE WORKMEN'S COMPENSATION ACTS - - - - -	7,000
Gross Total	£258,000
Deduct,--	
J.- APPROPRIATIONS IN AID -	1,000
Net Total	£257,000

Bibliography

The remarks below are those of the author, who wishes to explain the value of the source books in compiling the encyclopedia.

Publications

Hyde, Montgomery, *British Air Policy between the Wars*, London, Heinemann
Very good on relations between governments and the RAF, Air Estimates, the unfolding international scenario from 1919 and inter-service rivalry.
Bowyer, Chas, *RAF Operations 1918 to 1939*, London, William Kimber
Factual accounts of operations. Places squadrons and personnel in context.
Hayes, Karl E., *History of the Royal Air Force and US Naval Air Service in Ireland 1913–1923*, in association with Irish Air Letter
Indispensable for anyone who wishes to study this probably least well-known aspect of RAF operations between the wars.
James, John, *The Paladins, a social history of the RAF up to the outbreak of World War II*, Macdonald & Co. Ltd
The inspiration for the compilation of this encyclopedia.
Taylor, John W.R., *Pictorial History of the RAF, Volume I, 1918–1939*, Ian Allan
A wealth of photographs, each of which tells a story.
Various, 'Action Stations' series, Various publishers
This series of publications covers RAF airfields and miscellaneous establishments in the entire United Kingdom and a selection of bases overseas. Chapter 7 of this encyclopedia was based almost exclusively on these works.
Jefford, Wing Commander C.G., MBE, *RAF Squadrons*, Airlife Publishing Ltd
This book was invaluable in compiling Appendix B.
Penrose, Harald, *British Aviation – the adventuring years 1920 to 1929*, Putnam Press
——, *British Aviation – widening horizons 1930 to 1934*, HMSO
——, *British Aviation – ominous skies 1935 to 1939*, HMSO
All three works are excellent, not only in charting the development of aircraft and the aircraft industry, but in weaving in political, international and economic events that served as a backdrop to the period.
Slessor, MRAF Sir John, *The Central Blue*, Cassell and Company Ltd
Good on the contribution of senior RAF officers to the development of British airpower.
Armitage, Michael, *The Royal Air Force, an illustrated history*, Arms and Armour Press
Some useful photographs.
Thetford, Owen, *Aircraft of the Royal Air Force since 1918*, Putnam Press
Invaluable for compiling Appendix A.
Kinsey, Gordon, *Martlesham Heath*, Terence Dalton, Lavenham, Suffolk
This was invaluable in compiling the data for Appendix H.
Bowyer, Chas, *RAF Operations 1918 to 1939*, London, William Kimber Press
A 'no-nonsense' account of RAF operations in the outposts of Empire.

Together with source material from the National Archives, Kew, and the RAF Museum Hendon. All sources are quoted in the text to which they refer.

Index